Visit us at

www.syngress.com

Syngress is committed to publishing high-quality books for IT Professionals and delivering those books in media and formats that fit the demands of our customers. We are also committed to extending the utility of the book you purchase via-additional materials available from our Web site.

SOLUTIONS WEB SITE
To register your book, visit www.syngress.com/solutions. Once registered, you can access-our solutions@syngress.com Web pages. There you may find an assortment of valueadded features such as free e-books related to the topic of this book, URLs of related Web sites, FAQs from the book, corrections, and any updates from the author(s).

ULTIMATE CDs
Our Ultimate CD product line offers our readers budget-conscious compilations of some of our best-selling backlist titles in Adobe PDF form. These CDs are the perfect way to extend your reference library on key topics pertaining to your area of expertise, including Cisco Engineering, Microsoft Windows System Administration, CyberCrime Investigation, Open Source Security, and Firewall Configuration, to name a few.

DOWNLOADABLE E-BOOKS
For readers who can't wait for hard copy, we offer most of our titles in downloadable Adobe PDF form. These e-books are often available weeks before hard copies, and are priced affordably.

SYNGRESS OUTLET
Our outlet store at syngress.com features overstocked, out-of-print, or slightly hurt books at significant savings.

SITE LICENSING
Syngress has a well-established program for site licensing our e-books onto servers in corporations, educational institutions, and large organizations. Contact us at sales@syngress.com for more information.

CUSTOM PUBLISHING
Many organizations welcome the ability to combine parts of multiple Syngress books, as well as their own content, into a single volume for internal use. Contact us at sales@syngress.com for more information.

D1580644

214 960

S®

The Best Damn IT Security Management Book Period

Bryan Cunningham
Ted Dykstra
Ed Fuller
Chris Gatford
André Gold
Matthew Paul Hoagberg
Amanda Hubbard
Chuck Little

Steve Manzuik
Greg Miles
C. Forrest Morgan
Ken Pfeil
Russ Rogers
Travis Schack
Susan Snedaker

KEY	SERIAL NUMBER
001	HJIRTCV764
002	PO9873D5FG
003	829KM8NJH2
004	BAL923457U
005	CVPLQ6WQ23
006	VBP965T5T5
007	HJJJ863WD3E
008	2987GVTWMK
009	629MP5SDJT
010	IMWQ295T6T

PUBLISHED BY
Syngress Publishing, Inc.
Elsevier, Inc.
30 Corporate Drive
Burlington, MA 01803

The Best Damn IT Security Management Book Period

Printed in the United States of America
1 2 3 4 5 6 7 8 9 0

ISBN: 978-1-59749-227-0

Publisher: Amorette Pedersen
Cover Designer: Michael Kavish
Copy Editor: Adrienne Rebello

For information on rights, translations, and bulk sales, contact Matt Pedersen, Commercial Sales Director and Rights, at Syngress Publishing; email m.pedersen@elsevier.com.

About the Authors

Bryan Cunningham (JD, Certified in NSA IAM, Top Secret security clearance) has extensive experience in information security, intelligence, and homeland security matters, both in senior U.S. Government posts and the private sector. Cunningham, now a corporate information and homeland security consultant and Principal at the Denver law firm of Morgan & Cunningham LLC, most recently served as Deputy Legal Adviser to National Security Advisor Condoleezza Rice. At the White House, Cunningham drafted key portions of the Homeland Security Act, and was deeply involved in the formation of the National Strategy to Secure Cyberspace, as well as numerous Presidential Directives and regulations relating to cybersecurity. He is a former senior CIA Officer, federal prosecutor, and founding co-chair of the ABA CyberSecurity Privacy Task Force, and, in January 2005, was awarded the National Intelligence Medal of Achievement for his work on information issues. Cunningham has been named to the National Academy of Science Committee on Biodefense Analysis and Countermeasures, and is a Senior Counselor at APCO Worldwide Consulting, as well as a member of the Markle Foundation Task Force on National Security in the Information Age. Cunningham counsels corporations on information security programs and other homeland security-related issues and, working with information security consultants, guides and supervises information security assessments and evaluations.

Ted Dykstra (CISSP, CISA, CCNP, MCSE, IAM/IEM) is a Security Consultant for Security Horizon, Inc., a Colorado-based professional security services and training provider. Ted is a key contributor in the technical security efforts and service offerings for Security Horizon, and an instructor for the National Security Agency (NSA) Information Assurance Methodology (IAM). Ted's background is in both commercial and government support efforts, focusing on secure architecture development and deployment, INFOSEC assessments and audits, as well as attack and penetration testing. His areas of specialty are Cisco networking products, Check Point and Symantec Enterprise Security Products, Sun Solaris, Microsoft, and Linux systems. Ted is a regular contributor to *The Security Journal*, as well as a member of the Information System Security Association (ISSA) and Information Systems Audit and Control Association (ISACA).

Ed Fuller (CISSP, GIAC GSEC) is the Chief Operating Officer and Principle Security Consultant with Security Horizon, Inc., a Colorado-based professional security services and training provider. He currently is the lead instructor for the NSA IAM and IEM courses and leads assessments and evaluations as well leading the IA-CMM appraisals. His specialties include implementation of the NSA IAM and IEM into commercial environments and the IA-CMM. Ed's background includes positions as a senior consultant for Titan Systems, and JAWZ, Inc, and Averstar, Inc.

Ed is a retired United States Navy Chief Petty Officer and later participated on the development of System Security Engineering Capability Maturity Model (SSE-CMM). Ed has also been involved in the development of the Information Assurance Capability Maturity Model (IA-CMM). Ed is a frequent contributor to *The Security Journal* and co-author of *Security Assessment: Case Studies for Implementing the NSA IAM*. Ed holds a Bachelor of Science in Information Management from the University of Maryland. He lives in Colorado with his family Patience and Leila.

Chris Gatford works for Pure Hacking Ltd. in Sydney, Australia as a Senior Security Consultant performing penetration tests for organizations all around the world. Chris has reviewed countless IT environments and has directed and been responsible for numerous security assessments for a variety of corporations and government departments.

Chris is an instructor for the Pure Hacking OPST course and in his previous role at Ernst & Young he was the lead instructor for eXtreme Hacking course. In both these roles Chris has taught the art of professional hacking to hundreds of students from global organizations.

Chris is a frequent speaker at many security related conferences (most recently presenting at AusCERT 2006). He is a member of several security professional organizations and is a Certified Information Systems

Security Professional. More details and contact information is available from his homepage, www.penetrationtester.com and his current employer http://www.purehacking.com.

André Gold is currently the Director of Information Security at Continental Airlines, one of the world's largest and most successful commercial and freight transportation providers. André was appointed to this position by the company's former CIO, making him the first person to hold this post in the company's 50-year history. As the Director of Information Security, André has established a risk-based information security program based in part on increasing the security IQ of over 42,000 employees and protecting the over $2.5 billion continental.com property.

As an identified security practitioner, André has been featured in SC, Information Security, and CSO Magazine. André also presents at or participates in industry-related events. In 2006 André was named an Information Security 7 award winner in the retail sector, for his security contributions in the start-up and air transportation markets.

Before assuming his current role, André served as Technical Director of Internet and Network Services. In this role, he built and was responsible for Continental's infrastructure and continental.com property; a property which accounts for close to 25% of the company's revenue.

In his spare time, André is pursuing his MBA at Colorado State and has a BBA in Computer Information Systems from the University of Houston-Downtown. André was also a commissioned officer in the Army, receiving his commission from Wentworth Military Academy.

In addition to his position at Continental, André server on the Microsoft Chief Security Officer Council, the Skyteam Data Privacy and Security Subcommittee, Goldman Sachs' Security Council, as well as eEye Digital Security's and ConSentry Networks' Executive Advisory Councils.

Matthew Paul Hoagberg is an information technology and security professional with diverse experience in IT, personnel management, technology training, and business development support with Security Horizon, Inc., a Colorado-based professional security services and training provider. Matthew contributes to the security training, assessments, and evaluation that Security Horizon offers.

He currently serves as a Security Consultant, along with guidance from the Department of the Interior (DOI) and National Institute of Standards and Technology (NIST), to enhance the Bureau of Reclamation's (BOR) IT security management processes with a goal of improving the BOR's compliance with the Federal Information Security Management Act (FISMA) requirements. Review gap analysis performed by BOR identifying FISMA weaknesses. Work to establish a mechanism for identifying the minimum products necessary to ensure the target Departmental FISMA reporting grade.

Matthew holds a bachelor's degree from Northwester College and is a member of the Information Systems Security Association (ISSA), and co-author of *Security Assessment: Case Studies for Implementing the NSA IAM* (Syngress Publishing, ISBN 1-932266-96-8). Matthew currently resides in Monument, Colorado with his family.

Amanda Hubbard [JD] is a Trial Attorney assigned to the Computer Crime and Intellectual Property Section of the U.S. Department of Justice working on national security and computer intrusion issues. Prior to this assignment, Ms. Hubbard worked as an attorney for the Intelligence Community and the military on issues of computer forensics, electronic evidence, encryption, network security, vulnerability assessments, criminal law, and information sharing. She also serves as an Adjunct Professor for the Columbus School of Law at Catholic University where she co-teaches the seminar "National Security Law in Cyberspace," and a guest lecturer at: the Naval Postgraduate School Information Warfare Workshops; the Air Force Judge Advocate General School Information Warfare Course; the U.S. Secret Service; Federal Bureau of Investigation, and the United States Department of Justice National Advocacy Center. Ms. Hubbard regularly speaks to international audiences on cybersecurity and cybercrime. Prior works include portions of the 2002 ABA Committee on Cyberspace publication, "Patriot 'Games' No Longer: The Business Community's Role in Cybersecurity", and submissions to the International Telecommunications Union and the United Nations. She has been named as a 2005–06 Fulbright Scholar to the Norwegian Research Center for Computers and Law at the University of Oslo to research and write on transnational cybercrime issues.

Chuck Little (CCSA, NSA IAM, NSA IEM) is a Senior Security Consultant for Security Horizon Inc. Security Horizon is a small veteran-owned business focused on INFOSEC, headquartered in Colorado Springs, Colorado. His specialties include Checkpoint FW-1, NetScreen Firewall/IDS/IPS, Perl coding, Linux, Solaris, Mac OS X, compliance auditing, network security architecture and design, and snowboarding.

Chuck is a veteran of the US Army, having spent over seven years on active duty. Chuck holds a bachelor's degree in Applied Computer Science from Illinois State University, with a minor in Philosophy. He is an occasional contributor to the MIND Project, a research venture into cognitive sciences, at Illinois State University. Chuck currently resides in Denver, Colorado; with winter weekends spent at Loveland Ski Area.

Steve Manzuik currently holds the position of Senior Manager, Security Research at Juniper Networks. He has more than 14 years of experience in the information technology and security industry, with a particular emphasis on operating systems and network devices. Prior to joining Juniper Networks, Steve was the Research Manager at eEye Digital Security and in 2001, he founded and was the technical lead for Entrench Technologies. Prior to Entrench, Steve was a manager in Ernst & Young's Security & Technology Solutions practice, where he was the solution line leader for the Canadian Penetration Testing Practice. Before joining Ernst & Young, he was a security analyst for a world wide group of white hat hackers and security researchers on BindView RAZOR Team.

Steve has co-authored *Hack Proofing Your Network, Second Edition*. In addition, he has spoken at Defcon, Black Hat, Pacsec, and CERT conferences around the world and has been quoted in industry publications including CNET, CNN, InfoSecurity Magazine, Linux Security Magazine, Windows IT Pro and Windows Magazine.

Greg Miles, (Ph.D., CISSP#24431, CISM#0300338, IAM, IEM) co-author of *Security Assessment: Case Studies for implementing the NSA IAM* (Syngress Publishing, ISBN 1-932266-96-8) is a Co-Founder, President, and Chief Financial Officer of Security Horizon, Inc. Security Horizon is a global veteran-owned small business headquartered in Colorado Springs, Colorado. Security Horizon provides global information security professional service, training, and publishes *The Security Journal*. Greg is an U.S. Air Force Veteran and has been supporting the technology and security community for the last 18 years. Greg's background includes work with NSA, NASA, and DISA. Greg has supported efforts covering security assessments, evaluations, policy, penetration testing, incident response, and computer forensics.

Greg holds a Ph.D. in Engineering Management from Kennedy Western University, a master's degree in Management Administration from Central Michigan University, and a bachelor's degree in Electrical Engineering from the University of Cincinnati. Greg is a member of the Information System Security Association (ISSA) and the Information System Audit and Control Association (ISACA). He is also a co-founder of the Global Security Syndicate and teaches network security for the University of Advancing Technology.

C. Forrest Morgan (JD (1987), Trained in NSA IAM) has extensive experience in corporate practice and structure including contracting, corporate formation, and operations. Mr. Morgan advises information security consultants on drafting and negotiating contracts with their customers to best protect them against potential legal liability. Mr. Morgan's practice also has emphasized commercial contract drafting and reorganization, and corporate litigation, providing in-depth understanding of the business and legal environment. He has represented both national corporations and regional firms in state and federal courts and administrative agencies in matters of litigation, creditors' rights, bankruptcy, administrative law and employment issues. Mr. Morgan served as the Regional Editor of the Colorado Bankruptcy Court Reporter from 1989 to 1992, and he co-authored the Bankruptcy section of the Annual Survey of Colorado from 1991 to 1997. As a Principal of the Denver law firm of Morgan & Cunningham, LLC, Mr. Morgan's practice also includes corporate information and security consulting. He counsels corporations on information security programs, including development of corporate policies and procedures to minimize business risks and litigation exposure.

Ken Pfeil's IT and security experience spans over two decades with companies such as Microsoft, Dell, Avaya, Identix, BarnesandNoble.com, Merrill Lynch, Capital IQ, and Miradiant Global Network. While at Microsoft Ken coauthored Microsoft's "Best Practices for Enterprise Security" white paper series. Ken has contributed to many books including *Hack Proofing Your Network, Second Edition* (Syngress, 1928994709) and *Stealing the Network: How to Own the Box* (Syngress, 1931836876).

Russ Rogers (CISSP, CISM, IAM, IEM, HonScD), author of the popular *Hacking a Terror Network* (Syngress Publishing, ISBN 1-928994-98-9), co-author on multiple other books including the best selling *Stealing the Network: How to Own a Continent* (Syngress Publishing, ISBN 1-931836-05-1), and Editor in Chief of *The Security Journal;* is Co-Founder, Chief Executive Officer, and Chief Technology Officer of Security Horizon; a veteran-owned small business based in Colorado Springs, Colorado. Russ has been involved in information technology since 1980 and has spent the last 15 years working professionally as both an IT and INFOSEC consultant. Russ has worked with the United States Air Force (USAF), National Security Agency (NSA), and the Defense Information Systems Agency (DISA). Mr. Rogers is a globally renowned security expert, speaker, and author who has presented at conferences around the world including Amsterdam, Tokyo, Singapore, Sao Paulo, and cities all around the United States.

Mr. Rogers has an Honorary Doctorate of Science in Information Technology from the University of Advancing Technology, a Masters Degree in Computer Systems Management from the University of Maryland, a Bachelor of Science in Computer Information Systems from the University of Maryland, and an Associate Degree in Applied Communications Technology from the Community College of the Air Force. He is a member of both ISSA and ISACA and Co-Founded the Global Security Syndicate (gssyndicate.org), the Security Tribe (securitytribe.com), and acts in the role of Professor of Network Security for the University of Advancing Technology (uat.edu).

Travis Schack (CISSP) is the founder and CEO of Vitalisec Inc., a Denver-based information security research and services company. Prior to founding Vitalisec, Travis worked in the network communications and financial industries, where he has performed numerous security application reviews as well as network attack and penetration tests against Unix, Linux, Windows, network, and communication systems. He has extensive knowledge in attack methodologies, intrusion detection, wireless networking, VoIP, security tools, physical security, fraud detection and investigation, incident response, and computer security standards. He maintains his own test laboratory for researching the latest system vulnerabilities, attack methods/trends, and how to defend against them.

Travis has been published in multiple publications and has been a featured speaker at numerous security events around the world. He is an adjunct instructor for Denver University, teaching a technical hands-on Security Testing course for DU's Master program in Information Security. In his spare time, he organizes DC303, contributes to the Open Source Vulnerability Database (OSVDB) and Voice over IP Security Alliance (VOIPSA), and is a co-founder of the Global Security Syndicate (GSS).

Travis currently resides in Arvada, Colorado with his wife Kendra and 5 children, Kelsea, Austin, Gavin, Olivia, and Vivienne.

Susan Snedaker, Principal Consultant and founder of Virtual Team Consulting, LLC has over 20 years experience working in IT in both technical and executive positions including with Microsoft, Honeywell, and Logical Solutions. Her experience in executive roles at both Keane and Apta Software provided extensive strategic and operational experience in managing hardware, software and other IT projects involving both small and large teams. As a consultant, she and her team work with companies of all sizes to improve operations, which often entails auditing IT functions and building stronger project management skills, both in the IT department and company-wide. She has developed customized project management training for a number of clients and has taught project management in a variety of settings. Susan holds a Masters degree in Business Administration (MBA) and a Bachelors degree in Management. She is a Microsoft Certified Systems Engineer (MCSE), a Microsoft Certified Trainer (MCT), and has a certificate in Advanced Project Management from Stanford University. She recently completed an Executive program in International Management at Thunderbird University's Garvin School of International Management.

Contents

## Part 1

From Vulnerability to Patch

## Chapter 1

Windows of Vulnerability

Solutions in this chapter:

- What Are Vulnerabilities?
- Understanding the Risks Posed by Vulnerabilities

☑ Summary

Introduction

This chapter will address vulnerabilities and why they are important. It also discusses a concept known as Windows of Vulnerability, and shows how to determine the risk a given vulnerability poses to your environment.

What Are Vulnerabilities?

So, what are vulnerabilities? In the past, many people considered a vulnerability to be a software or hardware bug that a malicious individual could exploit. Over the years, however, the definition of *vulnerability* has evolved into a software or hardware bug or *misconfiguration* that a malicious individual can exploit. Patch management, configuration management, and security management all evolved from single disciplines, often competing with each other, into one IT problem known today as vulnerability management.

NOTE

Throughout this book, we will reference vulnerabilities by their CVE numbers. CVE stands for Common Vulnerabilities and Exposures, and a list of CVE numbers was created several years ago to help standardize vulnerability naming. Before this list was compiled, vendors called vulnerabilities by whatever names they came up with, making vulnerability tracking difficult and confusing. The CVE created a list of all vulnerabilities and assigned each one a CVE ID in the format *CVE-year-number*. Vendors have been encouraged to use CVE numbers when referencing vulnerabilities, a practice which has removed most of the confusion. More information on CVE numbers is available at http://cve.mitre.org.

On the surface, vulnerability management appears to be a simple task. Unfortunately, in most corporate networks, vulnerability management is difficult and complicated. A typical organization has custom applications, mobile users, and critical servers, all of which have diverse needs that cannot be simply secured and forgotten. Software vendors are still releasing insecure code, hardware vendors do not build security into their products, and systems administrators are left to clean up the mess. Add to this compliance regulations that make executives nervous, and you have a high-stress situation which is conducive to costly mistakes.

The complications surrounding vulnerability management create what is known as a Window of Vulnerability. Although this may sound like a clever play on words to draw attention to the most commonly run operating system, it is actually used in reference to the length of time a system is vulnerable to a given security flaw, configuration issue, or some other factor that reduces its overall security. There are two types of Windows of Vulnerability:

- **Unknown Window of Vulnerability**   The time from when a vulnerability is discovered to when the system is patched.

- **Known Window of Vulnerability**   The time from when a vendor releases a patch to when the system is patched.

Most organizations pay attention to the second type, Known Window of Vulnerability, but as you will see in later chapters, calculating the Unknown Window of Vulnerability is valuable when planning mitigation strategies.

NOTE

Many organizations offer, as a paid service, information on discovered vulnerabilities before vendor patches are available. Many larger enterprises see a value in such a service. If your organization is considering such a service, be sure to research the quality and quantity of vulnerabilities the service typically discovers, as such services are generally expensive.

Usually administrators use a table, such as the one shown in Table 1.1, to track when a vulnerability is reported and when the vendor patches it. You can use this table to calculate Unknown Windows of Vulnerability versus Known Windows of Vulnerability.

Table 1.1 Calculating Windows of Vulnerability

Vulnerability Name	Approximate Date Reported to Vendor	Date Vendor Released Patch	Time Delta	Date Patch Installed/ Risk Mitigated
IE create text range Vulnerability (CVE-2006-1359)	2006-02-10	2006-04-11	60 days	
Sendmail Race Condition (CVE-2006-0058)	2006-01-01	2006-03-22	80 days	
WMF Vulnerability (CVE-2005-4560)	2005-12-27	2006-01-05	9 days	
QuickTime QTS Overflow (CVE-2005-4092)	2005-11-17	2006-01-10	54 days	
MediaPlayer BMP Overflow (CVE-2006-0006)	2005-10-17	2006-02-14	120 days	

Recently, a trend has emerged that adds another metric to be tracked. That metric is third-party vendors releasing unofficial patches, as shown in Table 1.2.

Table 1.2 Tracking Unofficial Third-Party Patches

Vulnerability Name	Approximate Date Reported to Vendor	Date Vendor Released Patch	Date Third-Party Time Delta	Patch Released	Time Delta	Date Patch Installed/ Risk Mitigated
IE create textrange Vulnerability (CVE-2006-1359)	2006-02-10	2006-04-11	60 days	2006-03-24	42 days	
WMF Vulnerability (CVE-2005-4560)	2005-12-27	2006-01-05	9 days	2005-12-31	4 days	

In this case, the second time delta is the time between the approximate date of report to the vendor (or public disclosure) and the release of the third-party patch. At the time of this writing (April 2006), there have been only two cases of a third-party patch being released. In both cases, the patch was well received by general users, so it is safe to assume that this trend will continue.

> **NOTE**
>
> Although some people welcome third-party patches, these patches have some limitations that organizations should consider. For instance, third-party patches are never superior to vendor-supplied patches. In addition, you should be able to easily remove any third-party patch you use once the vendor addresses an issue. Furthermore, third-party patches may not receive as much regression testing as vendor-supplied patches and could cause unwanted side effects. Organizations considering using a third-party patch should weigh these risks, consider the source, and take into account the true exposure a vulnerability presents to them.

The last metric in Table 1.2—Date Patch Installed/Risk Mitigated—will vary from organization to organization. You can use this final metric to calculate a third time delta based on either the notification to the vendor or the release of the public patch. The key here is to ensure that this final delta is as short as possible to minimize the total amount of time systems are vulnerable to flaws. As you read this book, you will see how implementing a proper vulnerability management plan can help you keep your overall risk to a minimum.

Before we get to implementing such a plan, yet another statistic is important to understand when planning a vulnerability management strategy. That statistic is the delta between either the time a vulnerability is reported to the vendor or the time the patch is released, and the time it takes for a working exploit to be released to the public. This statistic is important because the risk a vulnerability represents to an organization increases exponentially when working exploit code is available to the general public.

The timelines in Figure 1.1 represent some of the more serious vulnerabilities as well as all of the important data points concerning them.

Figure 1.1 Timeline of Serious Vulnerabilities

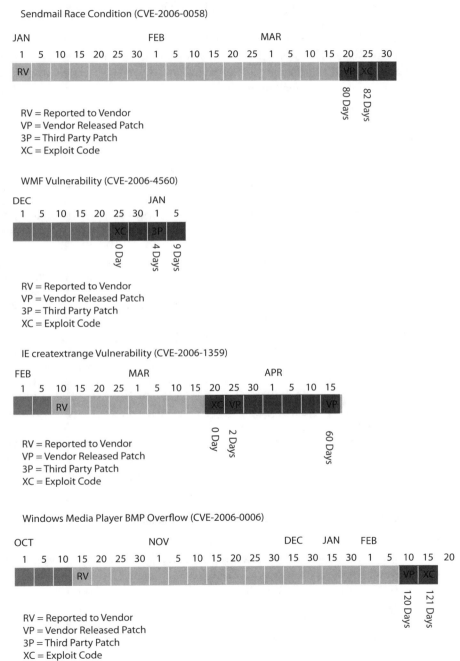

So, what does Figure 1.1 actually mean? As you can see, it illustrates the time between when a vendor became aware of an issue to when an issue was patched. Other data points are the date that the exploit code was released and the date a third-party patch was released. The figure helps show how long an organization can be vulnerable to an issue before it is even made aware of that issue. Once an organization becomes aware of an issue, its vulnerability to that issue extends until it can either patch the issue or mitigate it.

Most corporations are left at the mercy of the vendor and, in some cases, the person/organization that discovered the issue to make them aware that it exists. You can use a number of resources to remain up-to-date on security issues and their patches. For instance, most vendors offer patch and security issue mailing lists; also, multiple public mailing lists post issues. Table 1.3 is a list of security mailing lists and their relative usefulness.

Table 1.3 Security Mailing Lists

List Name	Web Site	Comments
Bugtraq	www.securityfocus.com/ archive/1/description	This is one of the original security mailing lists. Traffic is high, but if an issue exists, it is almost always posted to this list.
VulnWatch	www.vulnwatch.org	This is comparable to Bugtraq, with the exception of the high volume of traffic, as it is not a general discussion list but a security issue announcement list only.
Full-Disclosure	https://lists.grok.org.uk/ mailman/listinfo/ full-disclosure	This is an unmoderated list. Traffic is extremely high and the list frequently goes off topic. You must have thick skin and a lot of time to filter e-mail.
Microsoft Security Bulletins	www.microsoft.com/ technet/security/bulletin/ notify.mspx	This is the Microsoft Security Bulletin list where you can be notified of issues concerning Microsoft products.
Apple Security Alerts	http://lists.apple.com/ mailman/listinfo/ security-announce	This is the Apple Computer Security Bulletin list.

Vendors become aware of vulnerabilities in many different ways. In an ideal world, the vendors themselves would find and fix all security issues before they ship their products, but the complexity of code combined with aggressive development cycles is conducive to development mistakes in the area of security. Usually an independent or commercial security researcher notifies vendors of vulnerabilities, and in some cases, vendors become aware of vulnerabilities at the same time the general public does, when they are disclosed without any prenotification.

Understanding the Risks Posed by Vulnerabilities

Regardless of how a vulnerability becomes public, the vulnerability poses a risk to an organization. The amount of risk the vulnerability presents depends on a number of factors:

- Vendor risk rating
- Number of affected systems within an organization
- Criticality of affected systems within an organization
- Exposure affected systems present to the organization

An organization can calculate risk in a number of ways. One of the more logical ways, at least at a higher level, is by using the following formula:

Risk = Vulnerability × Attacks × Threat × Exposure

where:

V = Vulnerability   A measure of issues that are considered vulnerabilities. This measure is usually a function of a vulnerability assessment—for example, an audit conducted with Tenable Network Security's Nessus or eEye Digital Security's Retina.

A = Attacks   A measure of actual attacks and dangers, which is typically a function of a host- or network-based intrusion detection/prevention tool—for example, eEye Digital Security's Blink or the open source network intrusion detection system, Snort. Organizations that do not have these tools in place can use public attack tracking services.

T = Threat   A measure of lurking or impending danger. This is known as the threat climate, which comprises such factors as availability and ease of exploit.

E = Exposure   An accounting of an organization's vulnerability to an attack, or how much periphery must be protected and how poorly it is being protected.

As you can see, two terms do not appear in this list: criticality and vendor risk rating. *Criticality* is a measure of how valuable an affected asset is to the organization if it is compromised. Some schools of thought place a lot of importance in this metric, perhaps too much importance, because if you consider a typical network, every system is interconnected to foster communication of various protocols. A system that is considered highly critical, by its very nature, is able to communicate with those that are not critical.

Penetration testers and even malicious attackers will typically attempt to compromise the lowest-hanging fruit first. These are the systems that are easy to compromise because an organization does not consider them critical enough to patch quickly. These systems then become staging points for further attacks on the internal infrastructure and the more critical systems. So, for example, if an organization's accounting systems are of the highest criticality, how do you rate all of the workstations that connect to these systems? If they are not equally critical, they could be left vulnerable and used as an attack vector against the truly critical accounting systems.

When dealing with patch management methodologies, which we will explain in depth later in this book, criticality becomes more of an issue, and it is definitely recommended to patch critical systems before noncritical ones, but in the case of calculating a risk rating, it is not as important as the other factors.

NOTE

A large banking institution has taken measures to place all financial audit systems on its own network and behind its own independent firewalls. Although segregating important systems is a good strategy, it does not take into account the fact that a large number of employees need to access this data. So, what you essentially have is a firewall acting as an expensive logging device, allowing a set of client machines through. Sure, the firewall protects against some threats, but if the threat is coming over an allowed communications channel, the firewall is not going to be of help. The real solution here is to put the entire department on its own segregated network and not allow any outside access to this network.

Vendor risk rating is typically an arbitrary rating assigned by the vendor with the vulnerable software. Although you should consider this measure, it is not as important as the preceding factors, which are environment specific.

NOTE

At the time of this writing, there was a lot of media attention surrounding what vendors were truly patching with patches. A presentation at the Black Hat Briefings Europe (www.blackhat.com) by one of this book's authors, Steve Manzuik, and a co-worker, Andre Protas, titled "Skeletons in Microsoft's Closet," highlighted a practice by all vendors, not just Microsoft, of silently fixing internally found vulnerabilities when releasing patches for publicly found vulnerabilities. In addition, various posts by other researchers on the technical mailing list Dailydave (www.immunitysec.com/mailman/listinfo/dailydave) highlighted other issues and their potential impact. Consider the impact this practice has on your internal threat assessment of a vulnerability. Can an organization know the true threat of a vulnerability if the vendor is not disclosing all potential issues?

Let's get back to our formula for measuring risk, and expand on it by looking at it in a different way. Those who have been in the information security industry for even the briefest amount of time probably recognize the classic analogy of a castle when referring to various protection mechanisms. Keeping with this analogy, let's use a castle that needs defending to better illustrate risk calculation.

You can view a computing asset—for example, a server—as a castle. Castle walls protect an inner sanctum containing gold. Armies are attempting to breach the castle walls and enter the inner sanctum to get the gold or disrupt the castle.

With this analogy, the following applies:

- **Exposure** How exposed the castle is to attack.

- **Periphery** A measure of the extent of the castle walls and the openings that can be attacked.

- **Lack of protection** A measure of how poorly this castle periphery is protected (by moats, guards, gates, etc.).

- **Threat** A measure of the enemy armies lurking on the hills surrounding the castle, who are priming for attack.

- **Attacks** A measure of the actual arrows and bombs and breach attempts on the walls and inner sanctum.

- **Vulnerabilities** A measure of how easy it is for the inner sanctum to be breached and used to gain access to the gold.

- **Asset value/criticality** A measure of how valuable and important the castle and inner sanctum are in terms of value (gold) and importance to the empire.

If each measure is given a binary number that is scaled between 1 and 5—1 being low and 5 being high—this method of risk calculation is very straightforward and simple. The higher the number, the higher the risk is to which the organization is exposed.

As an example, we'll discuss a fictional server environment in a popular Web hosting company consisting of systems vulnerable to the Sendmail Race Condition (CVE-2006-0058). In this case, Vulnerability would receive a score of 5 because of its impact on affected systems.

At the time of this writing, Attacks would receive a 2 based on the nature of the attack required to exploit this vulnerability and public reports of attacks exploiting this vulnerability. In addition, working exploit code is not available to the public.

Threat would receive a 4 based on the popularity of the company and the frequency with which it comes under attack.

Exposure in this case would receive a 5 because the service affected, Sendmail, is exposed to the Internet and is not easily protected.

Remember:

Risk = Vulnerability × Attacks × Threat × Exposure

So in this case:

Risk = 5 × 2 × 4 × 5

Risk = 200

The maximum risk will always be 625 and the minimum will always be 1. To further clarify this calculation let's look at the same environment but perform the calculation using the Windows Metafile (WMF) vulnerability (CVE-2005-4560).

As with the Sendmail vulnerability, Vulnerability in this case would receive a high score of 5 because it allows for remote code to be executed on affected systems.

At the time of this writing, Attacks would also receive a 5 because use of this vulnerability has been reported to be widespread and working exploit code is easily found on the Internet.

Threat for this vulnerability against this specific environment would actually receive the lowest score of 1 because this is a server environment running Sendmail. This vulnerability relies on users surfing to malicious Web sites to be effective, something that is not typically done from a server environment running Sendmail.

Exposure for this specific environment would also receive a 1. As stated earlier, Web browsing is not typically done from this environment.

Therefore:

Risk = 5 × 5 × 1 × 1

Risk = 25

If you take this same vulnerability but perform the calculation for an end-user environment that is constantly surfing the Internet, the calculation would look something like this:

Risk = 5 × 5 × 5 × 3

Risk = 375

We went to the trouble of explaining this based on two separate vulnerabilities multiple times to ensure that you understand that the risk score is completely dependant on the environment at risk. This also helps to illustrate how something such as a vendor risk rating does not really matter a heck of a lot to most organizations.

NOTE

Readers should check out the Common Vulnerability Scoring System (CVSS) for an alternate, vendor-agnostic, open standard of scoring vulnerabilities. CVSS is an attempt to solve the problem of multiple vendors having their own scoring system, which can cause confusion for IT security professionals trying to understand multiple systems.

Summary

This chapter covered the basic concepts of what a vulnerability is and how it can affect your environment. We talked about the different ways your network can be attacked and the different levels of exposure an organization has while waiting for patches. We looked briefly at some recent cases of third-party patches and some of the reasons to be wary of such things. We discussed the various free places to get security information but avoided talking about some of the pay vulnerability services, as we address those later in the book. Finally, we covered in great detail one way to calculate risk and determine an actual risk rating, as well as things to consider when securing systems, such as which systems communicate with each other. We also covered an alternate way to calculate risk, known as CVSS.

## Chapter 2

Vulnerability Assessment 101

Solutions in this chapter:

- **What Is a Vulnerability Assessment?**
- **Seeking Out Vulnerabilities**
- **Detecting Vulnerabilities via Security Technologies**
- **The Importance of Seeking Out Vulnerabilities**

☑ **Summary**

Introduction

Vulnerabilities exist; they always have and always will. Just think of the potential impact to the economy if vulnerabilities weren't present, at least in commercial-grade products. Would major organizations still invest in a security program? What sort of work would we be doing, if not security? As security practitioners and business leaders, we must realize that vulnerabilities are a part of life; a part of our consumption of technology. As such, we must practice due diligence in ensuring that vulnerabilities don't represent an undo liability to our organization, creating an unacceptable level of risk. This chapter focuses on what a vulnerability assessment is; traditional and alternative methods for discovering vulnerabilities; and the importance of seeking out vulnerabilities.

What Is a Vulnerability Assessment?

One might equate a vulnerability assessment (or VA) to a reconnaissance mission within the military. The purpose of the recon exercise is to go forth, into foreign territory, and ascertain weakness; vulnerabilities within the opposition. Upon completion of the exercise, military commanders should have greater insight and intelligence regarding their target(s); knowing its strengths as well as its weaknesses. Like reconnaissance missions, vulnerability assessments are security exercises that aid business leaders, security professionals, and hackers in identifying security liabilities within networks, applications, and systems.

In this section, we'll discuss the steps involved in conducting a vulnerability assessment: information gathering/discovery, enumeration, and detection. This section will provide an introductory view to vulnerability assessment. The next chapter will dive into the how-to and technical details associated with vulnerability assessments.

Step 1: Information Gathering/Discovery

Information gathering and discovery is the process an individual or group performs to ascertain the breath/scope of an assessment. The purpose of this step is to identify and determine the total number of systems and applications that will be assessed. Output of this step typically consists of host names, Internet Protocol (IP) addresses, available port information, and possibly target contact information.

You can divide the information-gathering process into two components: nonintrusive and semi-intrusive efforts. *Nonintrusive efforts* reflect the public gathering of information regarding the target; the target is unaware of these activities. This includes *whois* queries to identify all of the domain names the target owns, as well as possible targets and IP address lookups via sites such as www.arin.net to identify IP address ranges associated with the target. Figure 2.1 shows a *whois* query against one of the IP addresses that hosts www.microsoft.com.

Figure 2.1 A whois Query

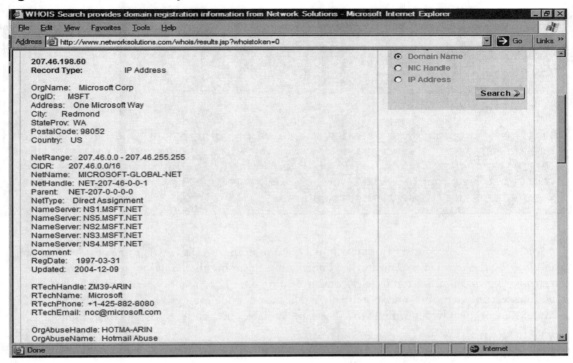

In Figure 2.1, we went to www.networksolutions.com/whois and conducted a *whois* query for 207.46.198.60, a Microsoft Web server. We determined the IP address by performing a domain name system (DNS) lookup, a process used to resolve an IP address to a domain name, against www.microsoft.com; another noninvasive information gathering technique.

By performing a *whois* query against the IP address, we were able to gather the following information:

- The company's physical address
- Contact information
- The IP address range used by the company
- DNS servers responsible for the domain

Having a better idea of the target footprint, we can proceed to discovering what systems and possible applications reside on the target network.

Tools & Traps

Who What?

whois is a program that provides people with registered information regarding domain names and their registrants: for instance, the administrative contact, name servers, domain expiration, and so on. InterNIC maintains the *whois* database. Users can either leverage the *whois* tool on their local machine, if available, or visit www.internic.net to query for information.

Semi-intrusive efforts consist of nondisruptive communications calls between the attacker and target in an effort by the attacker to gain further information regarding the target's systems; the target can detect this. This communication usually consists of ping sweeps, to identify active hosts, and port scans, to ascertain what ports and, potentially, applications, reside on a given system. Utilizing Nmap software, we can quickly determine what hosts are available on a network, as shown in Figure 2.2.

Figure 2.2 An Nmap Ping Sweep

```
Command Prompt
C:\>nmap -v -sP 10.192.82.243/24

Starting Nmap 4.03 ( http://www.insecure.org/nmap ) at 2006-05-11 11:23 Central
Daylight Time
Initiating ARP Ping Scan against 243 hosts [1 port/host] at 11:23
The ARP Ping Scan took 2.31s to scan 243 total hosts.
DNS resolution of 103 IPs took 8.09s. Mode: Async [#: 3, OK: 81, NX: 22, DR: 0,
SF: 0, TR: 137, CN: 0]
Host 10.192.82.0 appears to be down.
Host 10.192.82.1 appears to be up.
MAC Address: 00:00:0C:07:AC:01 (Cisco Systems)
Host 10.192.82.2 appears to be down.
Host 10.192.82.3 appears to be up.
MAC Address: 00:D0:02:6D:4C:00 (Ditech)
Host 10.192.82.4 appears to be up.
MAC Address: 00:04:28:B0:B8:00 (Cisco Systems)
Host hqs47e4006_1.nam.coair.com (10.192.82.5) appears to be up.
MAC Address: 00:03:E3:59:23:FF (Cisco Systems)
Host 10.192.82.6 appears to be up.
MAC Address: 00:01:96:A8:86:40 (Cisco Systems)
Host 10.192.82.7 appears to be up.
MAC Address: 00:10:83:5A:B6:00 (Hewlett-packard Company)
Host 10.192.82.8 appears to be up.
MAC Address: 00:30:C1:54:ED:2F (Hewlett-packard)
```

Using the *–sP* (ping scan) switch within Nmap, we can conduct a ping sweep of the target network. This will help us determine what hosts are active and available. Once we've determined this, the information-gathering/discovery step is complete. It's now time to proceed to step 2, enumeration, and determine what operating systems and applications the target possesses.

Step 2: Enumeration

Enumeration is the process used to determine the target operating system—a process called *OS fingerprinting*—and the applications that reside on it. Upon determining the operating system, the next step is to substantiate the applications that reside on the host. Ports 0 through 1023 are considered *well-known ports*, or port numbers reserved for assignment by the Internet Corporation for Assigned Names and Numbers (ICANN).[1] Ports within this range are reserved for specific applications; for example, http is assigned port 80 and https (secure http) is assigned port 443. Though ports 0 through 1023 are reserved for specific applications, this does not preclude other applications from utilizing them.

Keeping with Nmap, we use its *–sV* (service/version info) switch to determine what applications are residing on what ports (see Figure 2.3).

Figure 2.3 Nmap Service Detection

```
C:\>nmap -sV 10.192.82.0/24

Starting Nmap 4.03 ( http://www.insecure.org/nmap ) at 2006-05-11 12:56 Central
Daylight Time
Interesting ports on hqs4747c01(10.192.82.6 ):
(The 1668 ports scanned but not shown below are in state: closed)
PORT      STATE SERVICE       VERSION
135/tcp   open  msrpc?
139/tcp   open  netbios-ssn
443/tcp   open  smtp          Microsoft ESMTP 6.0.3790.1830
445/tcp   open  microsoft-ds  Microsoft Windows XP microsoft-ds
3000/tcp  open  ppp?
3389/tcp  open  ms-term-serv?
8081/tcp  open  http          Network Associates ePolicy Orchestrator (Computerna
me: HQS4747C01)
MAC Address: 00:14:C2:E6:99:A4 (Hewlett Packard)
Service Info: OS: Windows

Interesting ports on 10.192.82.7:
(The 1671 ports scanned but not shown below are in state: closed)
PORT      STATE SERVICE VERSION
23/tcp open  telnet  Cisco router
79/tcp open  finger  Cisco fingerd
```

Notice anything interesting in Figure 2.3? Take a look at what service is running on tcp 443; it's Microsoft's Simple Mail Transfer Protocol (SMTP) service rather than a secure Web server, the reserved application for tcp 443.

Port enumeration plays a pivotal role in vulnerability assessment because it ensures that we map vulnerabilities to respective applications. Given Figure 2.3, if we were to assume the host in question was running a secure Web server rather than an e-mail server on port 443, it would have been highly unlikely that we would have been able to determine the host's vulnerabilities, negating future penetration possibilities. With the grunt work of information gathering and enumeration complete, it's now time to detect vulnerabilities on the target systems.

Step 3: Detection

Detection is the method used to determine whether a system or application is susceptible to attack (i.e., vulnerable). This step doesn't confirm that vulnerabilities exist; penetration tests do that. The detection process only reports the likelihood that vulnerabilities are present.

[1] http://searchsmb.techtarget.com/sDefinition/0,,sid44_gci514078,00.html

To detect vulnerabilities we'll need to utilize a vulnerability assessment tool such as Tenable Network Security's Nessus or eEye Digital Security's Retina. Neither tool is free, so we'll need to evaluate the cost or pursue open source alternatives prior to conducting this step.

Once we have procured a VA tool, we can continue the assessment, targeting the systems we've evaluated in steps 1 and 2 to determine whether they have any vulnerabilities. VA tools detect vulnerabilities by probing remote systems and comparing the systems' response to a set of good (expected) and bad (vulnerable) responses. If the VA tool receives what it considers a bad response it assumes the host is vulnerable.

Tools & Traps

Assessment Complete?

In today's information age, vulnerability assessments are a must, but they are not the be-all and end-all. VAs need to be supported by an enterprise remediation strategy, and assessments should target not only Windows, UNIX, and Linux systems, but also all IP-connected devices and applications within your infrastructure.

Notes from the Underground

Intrusive or Not Intrusive?

Vulnerability assessments, unlike good reconnaissance, can be intrusive. I recall walking into the office one morning, firing up e-mail, printing off an attachment, and walking over to the printer, only to hear, "You can print?" Unbeknownst to me, the vulnerability assessment I had launched the night before knocked out all the company's Hewlett-Packard direct cards and, ultimately, the printers. I was able to print because I was printing to the printer's Line Printer Remote (LPR) interface. After a little investigating, we found out that the firmware on the jet directs hadn't been upgraded in more than three years and simply port-pinging the jet directs rendered them unavailable. Who knew? Technically the printers weren't vulnerable, but their inability to handle port pings and our failure to include them in the company's remediation strategy caused some disruption.

Seeking Out Vulnerabilities

Identifying vulnerabilities across an enterprise is a major endeavor. We can't simply install a vulnerability scanner in selected locations and press Go. It doesn't work that way. It doesn't because today's enterprises consist of thousands of servers and tens of thousands of hosts connected via hundreds of network circuits with varying speeds. We simply can't get the required coverage within the desired timeframe. So what do we do? Do we stop conducting enterprise-level assessments knowing that 95 percent of all security breaches occur due to misconfigurations of systems or known vulnerabilities that have not been remediated?[2] The answer, of course, is *no*. Enterprise-level assessments are still required. Instead of simply dropping scanners onto our networks, as done in years past, we should leverage our company's existing vulnerability management investment—its investment in security, patch, and configuration management technologies—and develop a hybrid approach to vulnerability assessment that takes advantage of the strength of each respective technology.

Detecting Vulnerabilities via Security Technologies

Traditionally when we wanted to ascertain system- or application-level vulnerabilities, we installed vulnerability assessment scanners throughout our enterprise. These scanners were responsible for detecting network hosts (information gathering), discovering available applications (enumeration), and ascertaining vulnerabilities (detection). VA scanners were typically network appliances running VA software or VA software running on a company-owned asset. Figures 2.4 and 2.5 represent a typical organization's VA infrastructure.

Figure 2.4 A Typical VA Scanner

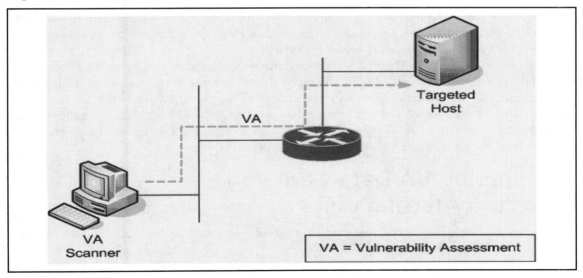

---

[2] CERT, 2003.

Figure 2.5 An Enterprise VA Deployment

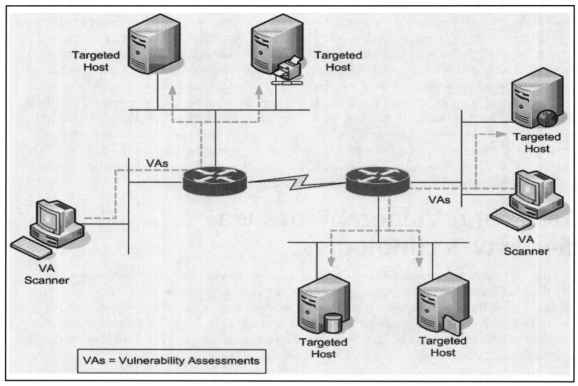

As you can see in Figures 2.3 and 2.4, in smaller networks, a single VA scanner may be sufficient for conducting the organization's vulnerability assessments. However, larger enterprises will require multiple VA scanners to support their assessment needs.

As you can imagine from Figure 2.5, traditional methods of gathering vulnerability assessment data could pose many challenges for large enterprises. Not only must an organization be concerned with managing the remediation infrastructure to address the discovered vulnerabilities, but it must also concern itself with the VA infrastructure used to ascertain these liabilities. Though traditional VA methodologies may pose some manageability and scalability challenges, they are often the only sure way to validate vulnerabilities exposed to a remote entity.

Deciphering VA Data Gathered by Security Technologies

Vulnerability assessment reports provide a lot of insightful information, as listed here and depicted in Figure 2.6:

- Duration of the assessment
- Number of machines scanned

- Vulnerabilities by severity
- List of all identified vulnerabilities
- Vulnerabilities per host

Figure 2.6 Vulnerability Analysis Results Using Retina

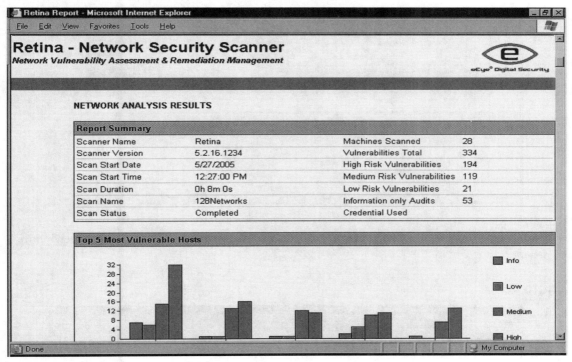

As a security analyst, manager, or business unit leader, you can quickly gauge your organization's susceptibility to known security vulnerabilities. In Figure 2.6, 334 vulnerabilities are present across 28 machines, 194 of which are considered high risk. In Figure 2.7, vulnerabilities are further broken down by risk, percentages, and average number of vulnerabilities by risk category per host.

Figure 2.7 Vulnerability Breakout

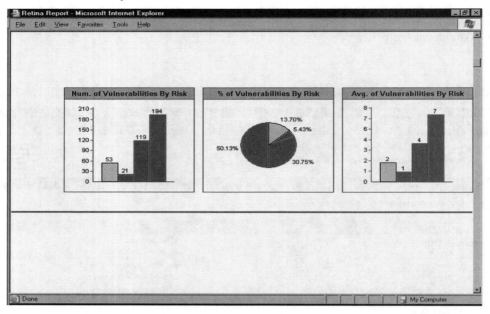

Analyzing the VA report further, we're able to discern what our most prominent vulnerabilities are, as reflected in Figure 2.8.

Figure 2.8

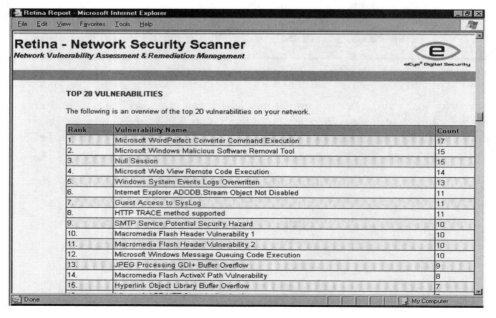

Figure 2.8 Top Vulnerabilities To a security practitioner and business professional, the chart in Figure 2.8 provides insightful and more reflective information regarding the true security posture of the organization. Figure 2.7 illustrated that more than 50 percent (194 out of 334) of the discovered vulnerabilities were of high risk. Figure 2.8 lists the top 20 vulnerabilities within the environment. Using these two figures, we can make risk determinations regarding the true security risk to the organization. By evaluating each vulnerability listed against its applicability to our organization, we can discern whether the vulnerabilities reported represent a benign (false) or malignant (real) threat to our organization. We can then decide whether our organization is operating at an elevated level of risk. How many vulnerabilities in Figure 2.8 would represent a benign (or questionable) threat to your organization? Table 2.1 shows 74 questionable vulnerabilities.

Table 2.1 Questionable Vulnerabilities

Vulnerability Description	Count
Microsoft Windows Malicious Software Removal Tool	15
Null Session Exposures	15
Windows System Events Logs Overwritten	13
Guest Access to Sys Instances	11
Macromedia Flash Header Vulnerability 1	10
Macromedia Flash Header Vulnerability 2	10
Total	**74**

These vulnerabilities are questionable or benign because they may not represent vulnerabilities within our organization. This means we have compensating controls to address the risk, or that as an organization, we've decided to accept the risk presented by the identified vulnerabilities.

Table 2.1 highlights the need for security and business professionals to know what represents a liability to an organization. Vulnerabilities are often deemed high or critical by software manufacturers, but that may not be accurate in terms of our own environments. Manufacturers and research companies are at the mercy of classifying vulnerability risk based on the lowest common denominator; the ultimate impact to an asset given no security or compensating controls.

Notes from the Underground

Detect This

Vulnerability scanners are great at detecting known vulnerabilities and are pretty good at detecting configuration errors that represent vulnerabilities, but they, as well as most technologies, are inept at detecting 0 day (zero day) vulnerabilities, or vulnerabilities that haven't been released to the general public.

Accessing Vulnerabilities via Remediation (Patch) Technologies

Today all companies have remediation strategies and supported processes, and if they don't, they should. Most strategies outline how and when applications and systems are remediated. Prior to the past decade, these processes and supporting technologies focused on providing application stability—addressing things such as memory leaks—and application enrichment, adding new levels of functionality. The phrase, "if it ain't broke, don't fix it," was certainly the motto during this era.

Over the past 10 years, the remediation landscape has changed. Remediation efforts have gone from manual to automated processes, creating a new product industry. In addition, the primary objective and purpose of a remediation strategy is no longer to support application stability and enrichment, but to address application- and system-level vulnerabilities. In identifying this, remediation technology providers and patch management companies have added new interfaces within their products, allowing for a new and nontraditional way to identify vulnerabilities.

As we mentioned earlier, traditionally a company would have to roll out vulnerability assessment sensors to gather VA data. What if we haven't invested in VA technology or simply can't afford it? What should we do? Considering that most patching technologies keep a history of the systems and applications they've patched, we can simply leverage our remediation repository to help us assess the security state of our environment.

Extracting VA Data from Remediation Repositories

Many capable remediation solutions are available today. However, prior to selecting one, we should be cognizant of the scope of our remediation efforts. Are we simply concerned with Windows systems? Maybe we need to address UNIX, Linux, and possibly a mainframe environment, too. Whatever the solution, our selected technology should be able to provide us with VA information similar to what's presented in the following example.

The following two figures reflect VA reports that were generated via Microsoft's Systems Management Server (SMS). SMS refers to these figures as compliance reports, but we can also use the same information to infer vulnerability information. If we go to the SMS reporting home page, the screen in Figure 2.9 appears.

Figure 2.9 SMS Reporting Home Page

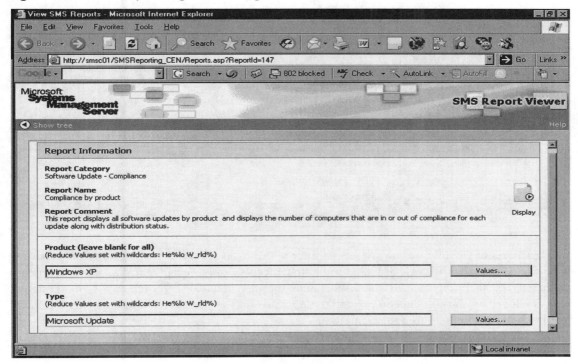

Upon accessing SMS' home page, we can generate compliance reports for operating systems, products, security bulletins, and so on. In Figure 2.9, we wanted to generate a compliance report for all Microsoft security updates on Windows XP hosts within our environment. The output of the report should reflect security patches and respective quantities that have been applied within our environment. Though SMS references Figure 2.10 as a compliance report, we also can use this report to determine vulnerabilities.

Figure 2.10 SMS Compliance Report

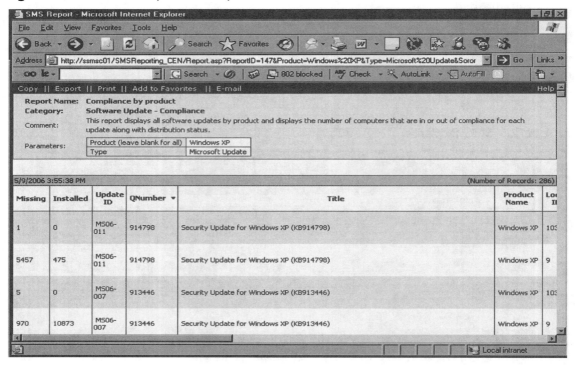

Regardless of whether we use SMS or another remediation solution, the purpose of the preceding illustration was not to showcase SMS, but to illustrate how we can leverage remediation environments to extract VA data. In Figure 2.10, 5,457 systems are missing MS06-011, QNumber 914798. If malware were developed against this bulletin, we could use reports such as that depicted in Figure 2.10 to help determine the level of risk to our organization.

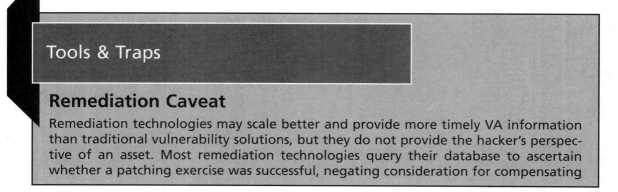

Tools & Traps

Remediation Caveat

Remediation technologies may scale better and provide more timely VA information than traditional vulnerability solutions, but they do not provide the hacker's perspective of an asset. Most remediation technologies query their database to ascertain whether a patching exercise was successful, negating consideration for compensating controls that may exist that would prevent the vulnerability from being exploited. Some also don't take into consideration whether a system has rebooted since it was last patched. A machine that has failed to reboot may still be vulnerable.

Leveraging Configuration Tools to Assess Vulnerabilities

Many corporations have invested in management/configuration tools. They often use these tools for fairly routine tasks, but we can extend them to extract vulnerability data from within our environments. Take, for example, Symantec's (formerly BindView's) bv-Control and bv-Admin products. Using both products, an organization could handle most of its daily Windows Active Directory operations. Conversely, we can also use these products to discover vulnerabilities within our organizations. To understand this better, let's take a look at a BindView deployment.

BindView's infrastructure has two key components (see Figure 2.11):

- **The BindView Information Server (BVIS)**   The brain of the BindView technology.
- **The Query Engine**   Handles query fulfillment and acquisition of requested data.

Figure 2.11 BindView Infrastructure

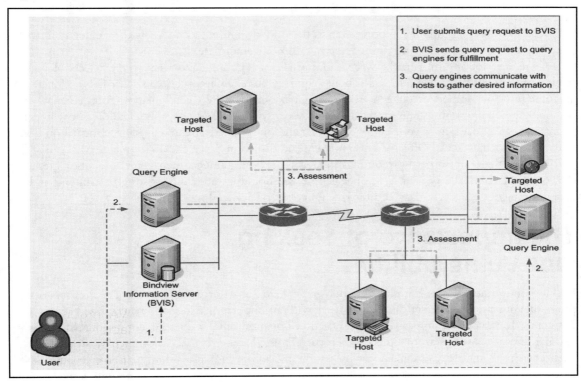

Leveraging our configuration management investment, we could (1) submit a query to the BVIS seeking to gather information regarding system patch levels. The BVIS would then (2) forward that request to the appropriate query engines and the query engines in turn would (3) gather the requested information. Figure 2.12 shows output of such an exercise.

Figure 2.12 BindView Output

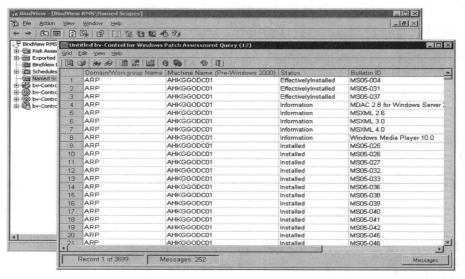

We can leverage BindView reports such as the one in Figure 2.12 to assess the vulnerability risk posed by a single host or a collection of hosts within our enterprise.

There are a lot of similarities between traditional VA and configuration management technologies. Both require infrastructure and they go about acquiring vulnerability data in a similar fashion. There are some subtle, yet important, differences, though. Unlike traditional VA, configuration management technologies require administrative rights to fully assess a system. In addition, configuration management technologies are unaware of your entire enterprise and must be fed or extract system information from a repository such as Active Directory or a Network Information Service (NIS) domain.

Though there are some shortcomings in leveraging configuration management technologies as the source of vulnerability data, as businesspeople we should leverage our existing investments and take advantage of the secondary and tertiary functions of our tools.

The Importance of Seeking Out Vulnerabilities

Seeking out vulnerabilities is important and is a vital part of an organization's information security program. Vulnerabilities present malicious users with an opportunity to gain unauthorized access to a system. Most everyone agrees with this. Whether organizations are due diligent in addressing this is another question. Many corporations do their part. Those that aren't may no longer have an option regarding this. Regulatory compliance, which we'll discuss later, as well as third parties, your business partners, are now mandating that companies conduct vulnerability assessments along with a plethora of other security requirements. Failure to seek out vulnerabilities and substantiate this to your business partner or a regulated body could spell a breach of contract and qualify as a termination of said contract.

Seeking out vulnerabilities is part of "Common Sense Security 101." Common Sense Security 101 refers to conducting security measures that make common sense; doing the things your customers and business partners would expect of you. It only makes sense to seek out vulnerabilities and integrate this process into your organization's information security program, given that more than 22,800 vulnerabilities have been released since 2003.[3]

Looking Closer at the Numbers

The number of vulnerabilities that have been discovered and publicly disclosed has steadily increased since 2000. CERT, a federally funded research and development center operated by Carnegie Mellon University, has been maintaining reported vulnerability statistics since 1995. For the purpose of our efforts, we'll focus on reported vulnerability data since 2000. Vulnerability data prior to 2000 does not indicate the number of vulnerabilities that existed in commercial software. Furthermore, there wasn't as much emphasis on vulnerability research before 2000 as there is today. To illustrate this let's take a look at reported vulnerabilities from 1995 to 1999 (Table 2.2) and 2000 to 2005 (Table 2.3).

Table 2.2 Vulnerabilities Reported from 1995 to 1999

Year	Vulnerabilities Reported
1995	171
1996	345
1997	311
1998	262
1999	417
Total	**1506**

Numbers provided by CERT[2]

Table 2.3 Vulnerabilities Reported Since 2000

Year	Vulnerabilities Reported
2000	1,090
2001	2,437
2002	4,129
2003	3,784
2004	3,780
2005	5,990
Total	**21,210**

Numbers provided by CERT[2]

---

[3] CERT

From 1995 to 1999, only 1,506 vulnerabilities were publicly reported. In 2000 alone, 1,090 vulnerabilities were reported. Using 2000 as the base year, the period from which relative levels are measured, 2005 represents a more than 500 percent increase in the number of vulnerabilities reported annually. Figure 2.13 graphically displays this point.

Figure 2.13 Vulnerabilities Since 2000

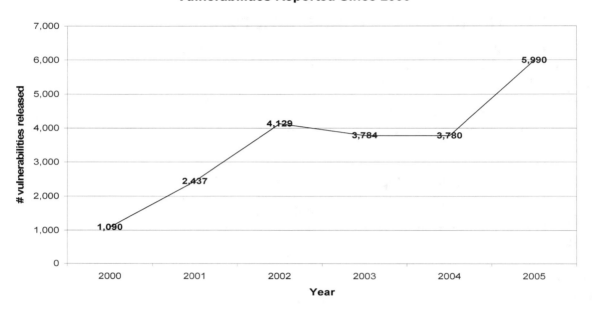

Having plotted the reported data since 2000, we can now use statistics to compare the number of expected vulnerabilities to the number of actual (reported) vulnerabilities between 2000 and 2005. To help us with that we'll use liner regression and we'll add a *best fit line* to Figure 2.14. The best fit line will plot an expected average of the reported vulnerabilities that we should have witnessed from 2000 to 2005 and will allow us to estimate reported vulnerabilities in future years.

Tools & Traps

Best Fit Lines

Best fit line is a statistical term in regression analysis that describes minimizing the sum of the squares of the vertical distance between the actual Y values—reported vulnerabilities in our case—and the predicted values of Y, or estimated vulnerabilities. Confused? Me, too. No worries. Excel can handle the calculations for us. Simply input your data, graph it, and add a trend line, or best fit line, via the Chart menu.

Figure 2.14 Vulnerabilities with Best Fit Line

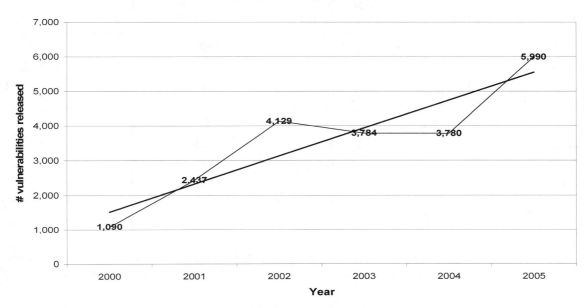

Vulnerabilities Reported Since 2000

From Figure 2.14, we can infer that reported vulnerabilities will continue their upward trend, as they have since 2000. As we can see, the best fit line isn't an absolute measure of the number of vulnerabilities that is or will be reported, but it does help us estimate future reported vulnerabilities. How many reported vulnerabilities should we expect in 2006 and 2007? To help us to determine this we'll need the best fit line equation associated with Figure 2.14; the equation is generated via Excel (see Table 2.4).

Table 2.4 Best Fit Line Equation

Equation $y = 805.26x + 716.6$

Values	Description
y	Estimated Number of Vulnerabilities for a Given Year
x	Time Period Estimating (e.g., 2000 = 1, 2001 = 2, 2006 = 7)
805.26	Slope
716.6	y-intercept

Now let's compare the actual number of reported vulnerabilities from 2000 to 2005 to the estimated number of vulnerabilities for that same period and estimate the number of reported vulnerabilities for 2006 and 2007. To do this we'll replace x in the best fit line equation with the year and time period and compute the equation. Table 2.5 shows the results.

Table 2.5 Estimated Reported Vulnerabilities for 2006 and 2007

Year	Period	Reported Vulnerabilities	Estimated Vulnerabilities	Difference*
2000	1	1,090	1521.86	(432)
2001	2	2,437	2327.12	110
2002	3	4,129	3132.38	997
2003	4	3,784	3937.64	(154)
2004	5	3,780	4742.9	(963)
2005	6	5,990	5548.16	442
2006	7	?	6353.42	
2007	8	?	7158.68	

* Reported Vulnerabilities minus Estimated Vulnerabilities.

Given the estimated reported vulnerabilities for 2006 and 2007—6,353 and 7,158, respectively—security practitioners, remediation teams, and business leaders alike should be busy drafting plans to address these future liabilities.

Though Microsoft recently bore the brunt of vulnerability news, independent of what operating systems and applications we run within our organizations all systems and applications are subject to vulnerabilities and will undoubtedly possess vulnerabilities throughout their life cycle. Figure 2.15 highlights the number of software vulnerabilities respective to their underlying operating system.[4]

Figure 2.15 Software Vulnerabilities in 2005

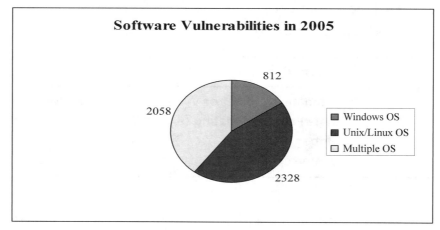

[4] www.us-cert.gov/cas/bulletins/SB2005.html

Vulnerabilities are a part of technology. Even if we're wrong on our 2006 and 2007 reported vulnerability estimates, vulnerabilities will continue to be present and will still require management. With the creation of new technologies such as Web services, as well as service-oriented architectures, new vulnerabilities and conduits of attack are bound to arise. Managing those vulnerabilities is not simply a technical challenge, but more important, is a business challenge, especially for organizations with limited resources.

Summary

As discussed in the previous chapter, single disciplines such as patch management, configuration management, and security management have evolved to support a function known as vulnerability management. Patch and configuration management technologies have traditionally supported nonsecurity-related initiatives, but nowadays they are primarily leveraged to detect and remediate security liabilities.

If we were conducting a vulnerability assessment five years ago, we would have installed VA software on a machine and conducted the exercise. Today we may query our system for a specific file and version number via our patching infrastructure or utilize remote configuration technologies to discern risk.

Are traditional VA methods antiquated? Of course not; traditional methods of vulnerability assessment still provide the most accurate level of vulnerability information, because VA doesn't require administrative rights, is capable of detecting all hosts residing within our network, and most important, provides us with the hacker perspective of our devices. In today's environment, though, a hybrid approach to vulnerability assessment that leverages security, patch, and configuration technologies will provide the greatest gains with optimal efficiency.

Chapter 3

Vulnerability Assessment Tools

Solutions in this chapter:

- **Features of a Good Vulnerability Assessment Tool**
- **Using a Vulnerability Assessment Tool**

☑ **Summary**

Introduction

In the first few chapters of this book, we outlined the higher-level concepts of vulnerability management and vulnerability assessment. Chapter 2 in particular outlined the various methods for performing vulnerability assessments as well as the pros and cons of each method. In this chapter, we will explain and demonstrate the different tools available for performing vulnerability assessments. Our goal is not to recommend a specific tool, but rather to provide examples from the most common, industry-leading tools on the market today.

So how exactly do vulnerability assessment tools function? On a high level, a vulnerability assessment tool will probe a system for a specific condition that represents a vulnerability. In Chapter 1, we defined a vulnerability as a software or hardware bug or misconfiguration that a malicious individual can exploit, thereby impacting a system's confidentiality and/or integrity. It is the assessment tool's job to identify these bugs and misconfigurations.

Some tools operate by using an *agent*, which is a piece of software that must run on every system to be scanned; other tools operate without the use of agents, and some use a combination of the two configurations. The architecture of the scanning engines, agents, and systems will vary from product to product, but it is this architecture that affects overall scanning performance.

Features of a Good Vulnerability Assessment Tool

Before we get into specific tools and what they can and cannot do, let's discuss what makes a good vulnerability assessment tool. Regardless of the type of tool you are using, at a minimum a good tool should have the following features:

- Low rate of false positives   One of the challenges that many vulnerability assessment tool developers face is that of false positives. A false positive occurs when the tool identifies an issue that does not actually exist, or wrongly identifies an existing issue as something else. Although it is debatable whether tools can completely avoid false positives, a high rate of false positives should be considered unacceptable. Later in this chapter, we will discuss in more detail why this can cause a problem on larger enterprise networks.

- **Zero false negatives**   Probably the worse thing that a vulnerability assessment tool can do is not detect a vulnerability. This is typically referred to as a *false negative*. Not detecting a vulnerability not only leaves a system vulnerable, but also leaves the user of the vulnerability assessment tool with a false sense of security.

- **A concise and complete checks database**   This is the one area of vulnerability assessment where vendors play what we refer to as a numbers game. One of the problems in the area of vulnerability assessment is the lack of standard naming conventions for vulnerabilities. This allows vendors to name and count issues however they want. For example, say vendor A claims its tool can scan for 1,400 issues and vendor B claims its tool can scan for 2,000 issues.

Does this mean that vendor B's tool is actually checking for more issues, or is it simply counting issues in a different way? The Common Vulnerabilities and Exposures (CVE) database, created by Mitre Corp., has gone a long way toward solving this problem, but many vendors simply add the CVE references to their checks and continue to count them in their own way.

- For example, MS06-001–Vulnerability in Graphics Engine Could Allow Remote Code Execution (CVE-2005-4560) was a single vulnerability that was assigned a single CVE reference, CVE-2005-4560. But if you read the vendor advisory on the issue (www.microsoft.com/technet/security/Bulletin/MS06-001.mspx), you can see that the vulnerability affects seven different operating systems. So if you are a vulnerability scanning vendor, do you count this as one vulnerability check or seven? Obviously, there is a clear marketing reason to count this as seven vulnerability checks rather than one, which is what many vendors do. The best advice we can offer is to compare every tool being considered based on Mitre's CVE database (http://cve.mitre.org).

- **Credentialed checks**   In the early days of vulnerability assessment tools, the concept of scanning a system with credentials was not really considered. Vendors marketed early tools as being capable of giving the outside "attackers' view" of a system. The reality is that threats to systems have always existed from both the outside and the inside, so having credentials on the system when scanning it helps detect these vulnerabilities. Furthermore, having credentials on a system allows for more accurate scan results, as you can more reliably check many issues by looking at the actual system settings or at such things as Registry keys and file versions. All of these types of checks require credentials.

- **Noncredentialed checks**   Although credentialed checks are important for accuracy, noncredentialed checks are equally important to help show true remote threats. When performing a risk assessment on systems, it is important to take into account how the system can be compromised. Checks that return data without the use of credentials truly show what an attacker, who also would not have credentials, would be able to see. These checks are considerably more difficult for vulnerability assessment tool vendors to create, so this is a great metric to use when judging what software vendor to go with.

- **Low network traffic impact**   Anyone who has been in the vulnerability assessment market for a long time has grown accustomed to running scans late at night, when network traffic is low, because of the impact that older vulnerability assessment tools had on network bandwidth. Over the years, most tools improved in efficiency and reliability, removing the requirement of scanning after hours. A good scanning tool will require bandwidth that is low enough to allow for scanning at any time on most networks. Typically environments with slow links will still want to wait until nonpeak times, to minimize network impact.

- **Minimal system impact**   No matter what tool you use to perform your assessment, your scans may cause unexpected results on the systems being scanned. For example, printers with out-of-date firmware, out-of-date routers, and even certain older operating systems do not react well to being scanned.

- **Intuitive and customizable reporting engine**   Vulnerability assessment is all about the data produced, meaning that the reporting capabilities of a vulnerability assessment product should be considered to be very important. A tool that has all of the preceding features implemented perfectly becomes less valuable if you cannot gather the data in an easily readable and presentable fashion.

- **Customizable checks**   One complaint that we have always had and probably share with most IT professionals who perform a lot of vulnerability assessments is how many vulnerability assessment products leave the user at the mercy of the vendor in regard to what to check for. The ideal vulnerability assessment tool allows users to customize or even create new checks for issues that matter to their specific enterprise.

- Enterprise scalability All of the preceding features become useless quickly if the vulnerability assessment tool does not handle large enterprise networks well. Some of the best tools and some of the best ideas for tools are invalidated by the simple fact that the tool does not function well in an environment comprising multiple computers. So what does enterprise scalability mean exactly? This is more than just a marketing buzzword. To be truly scalable a VA tool must encompass all of the preceding features but also perform each of them in a way that takes into account the large amount of data that an enterprise network will return to the scanner. Typically, this is a lot easier said than done for most tools on the market today.

Although some vulnerability assessment tools will include additional features, any tool you consider using should have at least the features covered in the preceding list.

Now that you know some of the features to look for when deciding on a vulnerability assessment tool, let's take a look at how to use two of the more popular tools on the market.

Using a Vulnerability Assessment Tool

If you were to pick up your favorite IT industry magazine, you would easily find a handful of reviews of vulnerability assessment tools, all given good marks based on that magazine's criteria. Years ago, one of this book's authors even wrote such reviews for popular print and online publications. However, should you place all of your trust in magazine reviews when deciding which vulnerability assessment tool to use? One of the flaws in doing so is that you never really know what the full test criteria were. Did the reviewer scan a network of 10 systems or 100 systems? What if your network has 1,000 systems, or more? What if your network looks like the one in Figure 3.1? Would it be easy to get an accurate assessment of security threats in such a network?

Figure 3.1 A Large Network

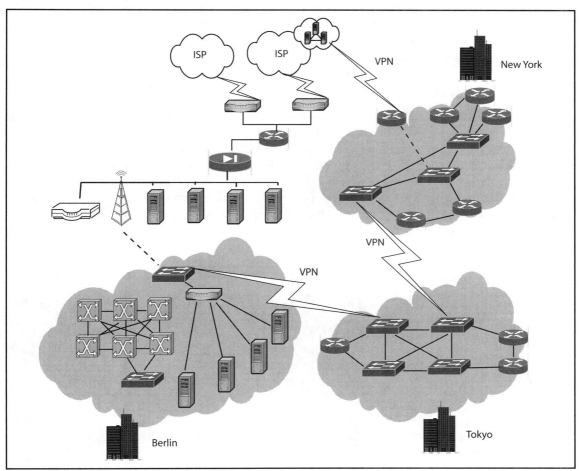

As you can see in Figure 3.1, vulnerability assessment is not as simple a process as loading the VA tool onto a system and feeding it a list of Internet Protocol (IP) addresses. To get a better feel for the process, in this section we will discuss how two popular vulnerability assessment tools work: the commercially available Retina from eEye Digital Security and the open source Nessus from Tenable Network Security.

NOTE

Although this section focuses on two of the more popular vulnerability assessment tools available today, a simple Google search for "Vulnerability Assessment Tool" yields millions of results.

Selecting a tool to use in your organization will not be an easy task, so hopefully this chapter will assist you in at least creating a short list of products to look at. There are many of Vulnerability Assessment Tools available today and each of them has their strengths and weaknesses. So let's get started with using the tools we selected for this book. Chapter 2 outlined a vulnerability assessment method; here we will attempt to match that method.

Step 1: Identify the Hosts on Your Network

As you may remember from Chapter 2, you cannot accurately judge how vulnerable your network is if you do not know about every device on your network. You can determine this information by performing what is usually called a *ping sweep* or *discovery scan*. Most tools will simply send an Internet Control Message Protocol (ICMP) ECHO (ping) packet to identify hosts on the network. If a system responds, it is alive; if a system does not respond, it is considered dead. Many tools will take things a step further and attempt to identify the remote operating system. Better tools, such as the examples we're using in this book, do more than a simple ICMP ECHO and give the user options. Figure 3.2 shows the options that Retina users have.

Figure 3.2 Retina Discovery Scan

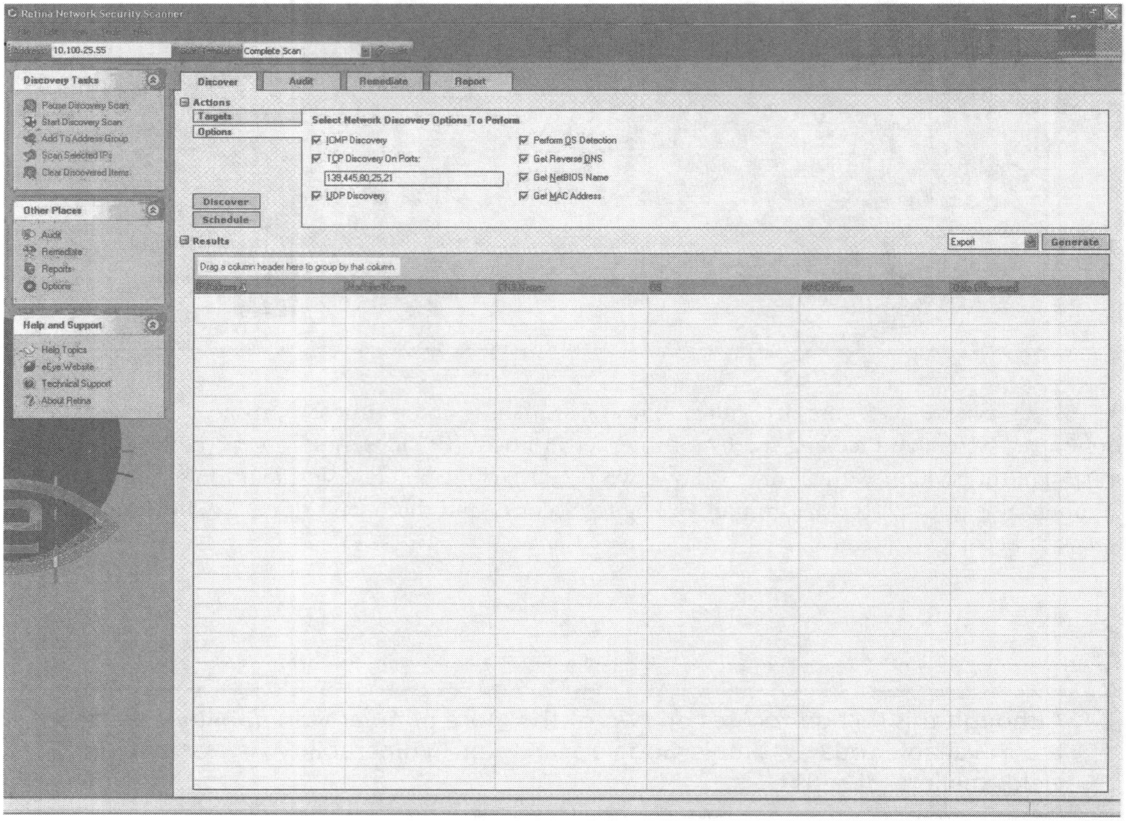

As you can see, Retina presents users with seven different check boxes that they can select, but only three of them relate to identifying live hosts on a network. It is important to know the difference between these options, how they work, and their potential impact on your network:

> **NOTE**
>
> Network Mapper (Nmap; http://insecure.org/nmap/index.html) is a great lightweight tool for quickly mapping a network. It is an open source tool that has been trusted and used since 1997, when the tool was first discussed in the Phrack Magazine article located at http://insecure.org/nmap/p51-11.txt.

- **ICMP Discovery**   This is the simplest method of identifying systems on a network. An ICMP packet is also known as a ping packet. Although ICMP discovery is the most reliable way of identifying hosts, many IT professionals are taught to disable a system's (or switch's) ability to respond to ICMP as mitigation from unauthorized scans. Of course, although they're protecting against unauthorized ICMP scans, they have also effectively hidden their systems from legitimate scans as well.

- **TCP Discovery on Ports**   This is a good way to identify hosts when ICMP might be disabled. Simply put, the Transmission Control Protocol (TCP) discovery method will attempt to connect to every IP address in the scan range on a specific port. If that port is open and listening for connections, the host will be considered alive. If none of the selected ports is alive and listening, the host will be considered dead.

- **UDP Discovery**   This type of scan works a little differently. Although a TCP port scan looks for a response on an open port, a User Datagram Protocol (UDP) scan will actually look for closed ports. When a UDP scan hits a port that is closed, a specific error will be returned which proves that there is, in fact, a live system at that IP address.

You can use the preceding methods to detect that a host is alive. Once the host is detected as being alive, most vulnerability assessment tools will take things a step further by offering the following options:

- **Perform OS Detection**   This is not a scan to identify hosts on a network, but rather an option that tells the tool to attempt to identify the remote operating system of the systems found to be alive. Different tools perform this step in multiple ways, each with their own degree of accuracy.

Are You Owned?

Operating Sytem Detection

Operating system detection tools can be, and have been, fooled in some cases. You can find a great, Nmap-specific paper on this subject at http://insecure.org/nmap/misc/defeat-nmap-osdetect.html. Essentially, the way to get past any operating system detection tool is to ensure that your operating systems report incorrect data back to the scanner. Although some see this as somewhat of a defensive measure, it does affect the reliability of your vulnerability assessment and you are best to not do this if you want accurate results from your scanners.

- **Get Reverse DNS**   This option should be self-explanatory. It will simply match the IP address of live hosts to their domain name system (DNS) name. For example, the system at 155.212.56.73 has the DNS name of host73.155.212.56.conversant.net, which also happens to be the system hosting the Syngress Web site.

- **Get Netbios Name**   This option should also be self-explanatory. It will cause the tool to map the NetBIOS names of each system being scanned to the IP address.

- **Get MAC Address**   This option will map the network Media Access Control (MAC) address of each live system to the rest of the data collected.

Figure 3.3 shows the output of a Retina discovery scan performed on a smaller network, with sensitive information blacked out.

Figure 3.3 Retina Discovery Scan Results

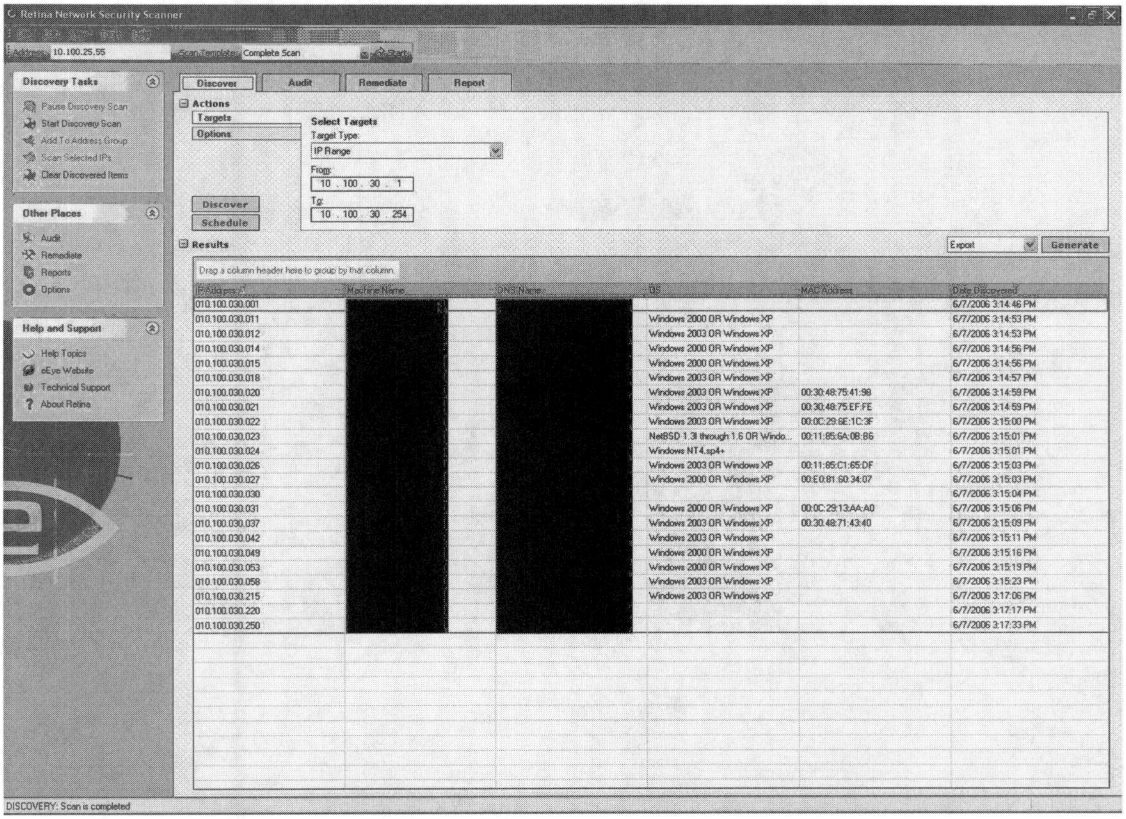

Step 2: Classify the Hosts into Asset Groups

We covered this step of the vulnerability assessment process in Chapter 2, but we'll review it here as well. By creating logical groups of hosts based on department or even physical location, you can more effectively approach scanning larger networks by section instead of trying to scan and deal with data from a mass scan. Take care to exclude any systems that you do not have permission to scan. Figure 3.4 shows the options you have for adding a group of hosts using Retina.

Figure 3.4 Adding to an Address Group in Retina

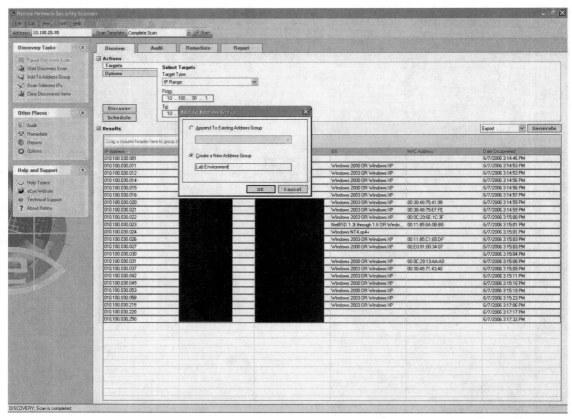

Step 3: Create an Audit Policy

For the most part, we recommend that all audits be used for initial scans. In some cases, you may not want to run certain audits, so you will want to exclude those audits. In Nessus, audits are called plug-ins (see Figure 3.5).

Figure 3.5 Nessus Plug-in Setup

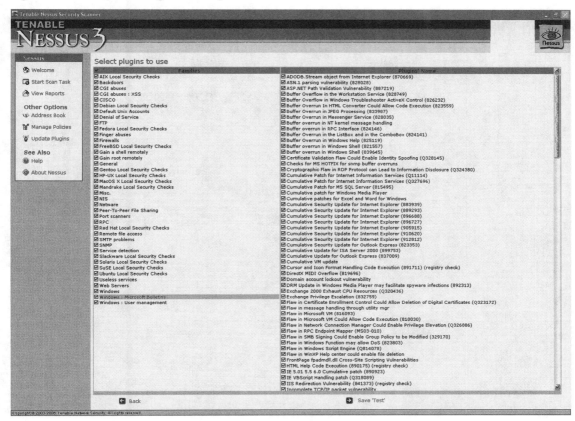

Retina, on the other hand, calls them audits, but the way you select them is similar to the approach you'd use in Nessus (see Figure 3.6).

Figure 3.6 Retina Audit Groups

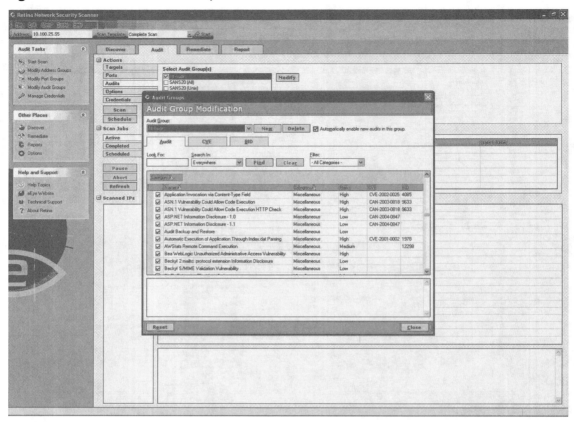

Step 4: Launch the Scan

This step is quite simple: Launch the scan and wait for your results (see Figure 3.7 and Figure 3.8).

Figure 3.7 Launching a Nessus Scan

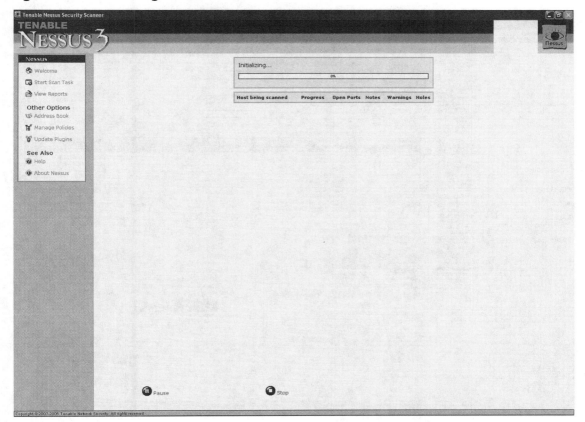

Figure 3.8 Launching a Retina Scan

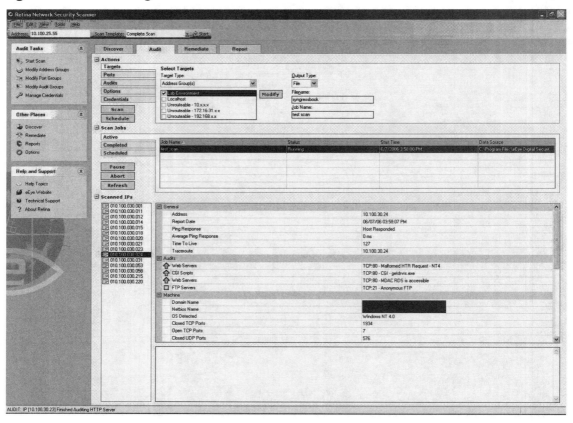

Of course, scanning an enterprise network is not as easy; otherwise, you wouldn't need this book! In fact, you must consider and configure multiple additional options using these tools. One that we hinted at in the beginning of this chapter is whether to use credentials. Although the preceding examples do not use any credentials, entering various credentials for systems being scanned, especially at the domain level, can greatly improve the results the tools return. A number of other options are available, depending on the tool you use, but they are beyond the scope of this book, so we will leave them up to you, the reader, to explore.

Step 5: Analyze the Reports

In a perfect world, these tools would produce a report that is completely perfect and accurate. In the real world, most vulnerability assessment tools make their reporting customizable because no two users will want the same type of report. Luckily most tools simply create a standard report in Hypertext Markup Language (HTML) format, making customization very easy (see Figure 3.9).

Figure 3.9 A Standard Report in Nessus

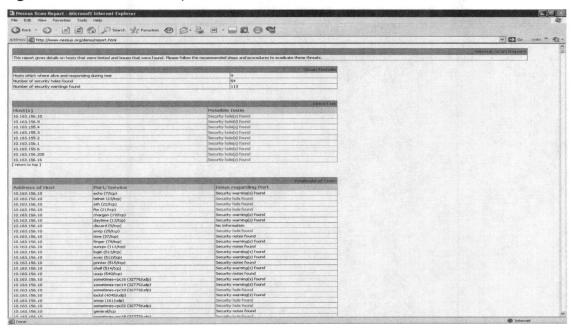

Step 6: Remediate Where Necessary

This step does not fit into this chapter of the book, but we thought we would include it here to simply give some hints as to what you will read in future chapters. The entire point of a vulnerability assessment tool is to identify vulnerabilities so that they can be remediated. Most vulnerability assessment tools will offer remediation advice, and although the tools discussed in this book have proven to be accurate, your mileage may vary. Therefore, we recommend that you carefully research all remediation plans before taking any action.

Summary

In this chapter, we discussed how two popular vulnerability assessment tools work. The real goal of this chapter was to give readers who may be new at performing vulnerability assessments an idea of what to expect, and more important, enough knowledge to successfully evaluate and select a tool that meets your organization's needs.

## Chapter 4

Vulnerability Assessment: Step One

Solutions in this chapter:

- **Know Your Network**
- **Classifying Your Assets**
- **I Thought This Was a Vulnerability Assessment Chapter**

☑ **Summary**

Introduction

This chapter will begin our discussion of developing a vulnerability assessment (VA) methodology, by outlining the first steps to performing a proper vulnerability assessment. A vulnerability assessment is different from a penetration test in that typically you perform a VA with broad knowledge of the environment you are testing; as you will learn in an upcoming chapter, a pen test is typically more in-depth and focused. The purpose of a vulnerability assessment, as we previously discussed, is to take a broad snapshot of an environment that shows exposures to known vulnerabilities and configuration issues. Note the wording in that last sentence: *known vulnerabilities and configuration issues*. If your goal is to find new vulnerabilities, a VA tool will not help you.

The first two chapters of this book demonstrated the importance of vulnerability management, what vulnerabilities are, and what they mean to an organization. In Chapter 2, we discussed at a high level the basics of vulnerability assessment. In this chapter, we will provide examples of how to perform a vulnerability assessment. Whether your network is small or large, the basic VA framework is the same, but in some cases, the tools you can use differ. We will point out variances that may occur depending on the size of your network, as well the different tools you can use.

Performing a vulnerability assessment is only one step in developing a vulnerability management framework, but it is a very important step. You can perform a vulnerability assessment either internally or externally. In Chapter 2, we discussed how to identify external network hosts, using various tools on the Internet as well as Nmap. In this chapter, we will go into more detail regarding use of Nmap and commercial tools to scan systems once you have identified the network range you are assessing.

We will assume that you are performing your vulnerability assessment under optimal conditions: in other words, that you have actual knowledge of the network you are assessing. By *knowledge* I am referring only to the Internet Protocol (IP) range(s) that your network is configured to use.

Know Your Network

You cannot perform an effective vulnerability assessment if you do not know exactly what is on your network. I have lost count of the number of times I have been brought in to perform an assessment based on a network diagram that the IT manager thought was correct, yet I ended up identifying multiple systems on the network that he either forgot about or didn't know existed. The simplest way to address this is to scan your entire network to identify hosts. As we discussed in Chapter 3, you can accomplish this in a number of different ways; we will review the steps here.

For a smaller network, it is very easy to perform an Nmap scan of your address space. Nmap is an extremely efficient tool. Figure 4.1 shows Nmap for Windows running.

Figure 4.1 Nmap for Windows

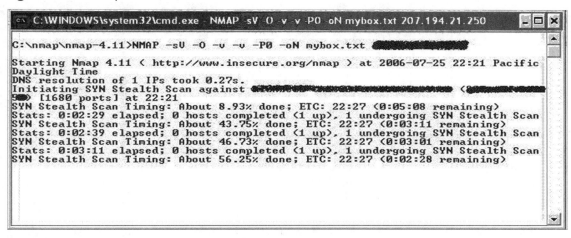

As you can see in Figure 4.1, I used the following Nmap syntax to scan my systems:

```
#NMAP -sV -O -v -v -P0 -oN network.txt <network address range>
```

This is a rather generic example, and I highly recommend that you review the Nmap documentation for alternate, more efficient ways to scan for hosts on a network. The key here, however, is that you scan across your entire network range, not just the systems that you know exist.

> **NOTE**
>
> Over the years, we have seen various devices, operating systems, and services crash when hit with Nmap or other scans. Typically, you will find that IT managers exclude these things from scan ranges to prevent them from crashing. What these IT managers are doing, however, is excluding systems that are so out-of-date that they are probably the most attractive target to an attacker. In today's environments, there is no good reason for a system to crash when it receives network traffic from a scanner. Systems that do should be replaced with something more robust, as the system's crashing is, in fact, a denial of service (DoS). Ignoring the problem will not make it go away, nor will it increase your overall security posture.

In the preceding line of code, –s V tells Nmap to probe open ports and write back listening service version information. You can also control how Nmap performs this with the following:

- **--version-intensity <level>** Set from 0 (light) to 9 (try all probes).
- **--version-light** Limit to most likely probes (intensity 2).

- ■ **--version-all**   Try every single probe (intensity 9).

- ■ **--version-trace**   Show detailed version scan activity (for debugging).

–O tells Nmap to perform operating system detection on each host. You can customize how aggressive Nmap performs this with the following:

- ■ **--osscan-limit**   Limit operating system detection to promising targets.

- ■ **--osscan-guess**   Guess operating system more aggressively.

–v sets the verbosity level of the Nmap output. Using it twice sets it to maximum verbosity.

–P0 tells Nmap to skip the host discovery and assume that all hosts are online and attempt a port scan. This is important to identify hosts that do not respond to ping packets.

–oN network.txt tells Nmap to output all the results into a text file named network.txt. You can also have Nmap output the scan in XML format, which can be helpful if you are trying to use this tool on a larger network.

<network address range> is the IP address range of your network. Again, I cannot stress enough that you need to make sure you are including the entire IP range you are using, even if you are sure that sections of it are empty. Sometimes you will find systems you forgot about, or worse, that you never knew about.

> **NOTE**
>
> Documentation, more information, and the latest versions of Nmap are available at www.insecure.org/nmap.

As I alluded to earlier, Nmap is a great tool if your network is small enough that you can manage the data or if your IT guys have the time and ability to parse through all of the data it returns. An important part of vulnerability management is asset classification, which is difficult to do by hand, and therefore, makes Nmap not the greatest option for larger organizations. In fact, I would argue that if you have more than 50 systems to assess, Nmap is not your best option.

If you are attempting to perform a large assessment, simply using Nmap will not scale, so this is where commercial tools come in. These tools will allow you to create asset groups of hosts which will help you perform a better risk assessment. For example, some people find it helpful to organize systems by physical location or even by organizational department.

In the preceding chapter, we talked about two commercial tools: Tenable Network Security's Nessus and eEye Digital Security's Retina. Both of these tools perform the same function as Nmap, but they represent the data in a way that allows for easier asset classification. Both vendors offer enterprise management consoles that can take asset classification one step further for more complex networks. As a quick review from Chapter 3, Figure 4.2 shows what the discovery scan looks like in Retina.

Figure 4.2 A Discovery Scan in eEye Digital Security's Retina

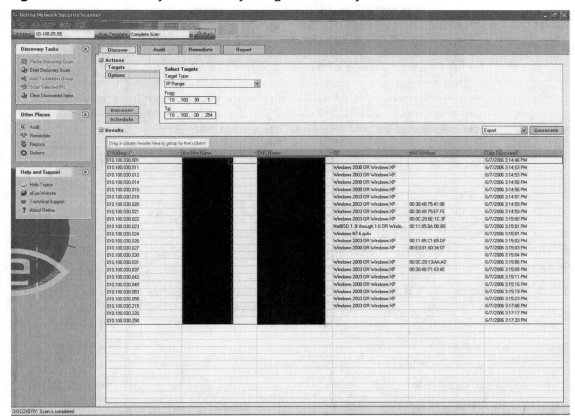

In this case, the tool is scanning an entire network range for systems that are alive—in other words, the system either is responding to a ping, or an Internet Control Message Protocol (ICMP) packet, or has services listening for connections. As you may know, many administrators will typically disable a system's ability to respond to a ping packet, as this used to be a good way to thwart basic port scanning software. Of course, port scanning software and vulnerability assessment software have both advanced to the point where disabling ICMP responses does not effectively hide a system, although it does dramatically slow down the scanning software.

Once your scan is complete, you should have a list of the systems on the network, their corresponding IP addresses, the names of the system, and hopefully the operating systems they are running. Depending on your software, you may even have the Media Access Control (MAC) address of the systems, which some people like to keep track of. This data may be helpful later for other things, including forensics, systems management, and system tracking.

It is a good idea to track down systems for which you don't have operating system data, and fill in that information. Most vulnerability assessment tools should be able to detect most mainstream operating systems, but nondefault system configuration, customized applications, and nonstandard operating systems may present problems.

NOTE

If you find that Nmap does not identify some of your systems, you should consider sending the fingerprint to the Nmap development team for them to integrate into their fingerprint database. The plus side of doing this is that most commercial products use portions of Nmap in their technologies, which means you are indirectly helping vendors keep their tools up-to-date as well. You can submit fingerprint information at www.insecure.org/cgi-bin/nmap-submit.cgi.

Once you have a complete list of systems on your network, it is a good idea to go through the time-consuming task of verifying the data the tool found. In a perfect world, you would be able to skip this step, but when it comes to vulnerability assessment you are better off being safe than sorry. Missing one machine can mean the difference between keeping a hacker out of your network and letting one in. Ensure that you have the following data for each machine:

- **IP address**   This seems pretty obvious at first, but note that some systems may have multiple IP addresses. Be sure to identify which systems are *multihomed* and have multiple IP addresses. In some cases, these systems may even communicate on multiple networks.

- **MAC address**   As eluded to earlier, this isn't essential to your vulnerability assessment, but it is nice to have data points on all systems for various reasons.

- **Operating system**   This one is obvious. Because so much of vulnerability management is centered on patch and configuration management, you need to track the operating systems of all of your machines. You should include printers, routers, and other network devices.

- **Operating system patch level**   Every vulnerability assessment tool should be able to give you this data point.

- **Services (Web, database, mail, etc.)**   Having a list of what services each system is supposed to be offering to users is essential when considering a secure configuration. You should review all systems and turn off any services that are not required.

- **Software installed**   This should comprise a complete list of all authorized software installed on the system. You can use a tool such as Microsoft's Systems Management Server (SMS) to inventory the complete system and then cross-reference that inventory with a list of what is authorized. The concept of authorized software is not just a licensing concern, but also a security concern, as the patch level and overall security of an unauthorized package would be relative unknowns to IT.

The last bullet item is one that I find a lot of people seem to overlook. With all the attention on operating systems—particularly Microsoft operating systems—over the years, everyone seems to have forgotten about applications. Recently this has become more apparent, as we have seen a major increase in application-level vulnerabilities. So while corporations have concentrated on their operating systems, they have left themselves open to application attacks. Luckily, most good vulnerability assessment tools have kept up on application as well as operating system vulnerabilities.

NOTE

There is a distinct difference between a vulnerability assessment and an application audit. The typical vulnerability assessment will check common applications for patch levels and misconfigurations, and an application audit is typically more in-depth and includes testing for issues for which most vulnerability assessment tools cannot test.

Once you have a list of all systems on your network, you are ready to start organizing your assets into logical groups for easier management. This is the first step of an asset classification exercise that will, in the long run, make managing your systems much easier. If I were to perform a vulnerability assessment on my employer's network, I would organize my assets into the following generic groups:

- North America
    - Operations
    - Sales
    - Marketing
    - Engineering
- Europe
    - Operations
    - Sales
    - Marketing
    - Engineering
- Global Outsourced

Figure 4.3 Creating Asset Groups in Retina

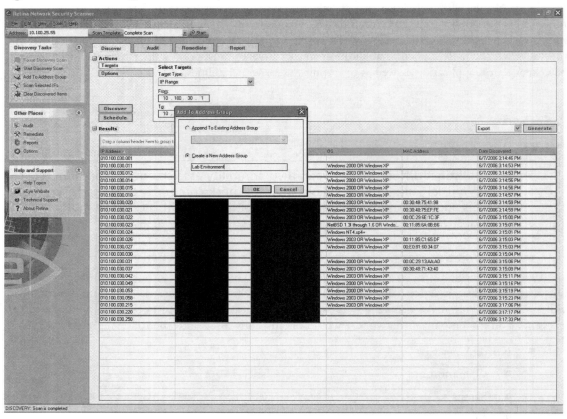

You can structure your own groups in whatever way is easiest for you. Just remember that for larger networks, organizing your groups will facilitate asset classification.

By performing asset classification, you are assigning a value to an asset in order to organize it according to its sensitivity to loss or disclosure. Once you do this, you can better target your information security efforts to protect more sensitive systems on the network. Of course, you do all of this in the context of your network architecture and existing security controls.

One thing many organizations still seem to overlook, especially when doing asset classification, is the network architecture and which systems can "talk" on the network to other systems. For example, you may have a group of systems that is perceived as low risk but may connect directly to higher-risk systems. Therefore, lax security on the low-risk systems may, in fact, expose an attack vector on the higher-risk systems.

Classifying Your Assets

In Chapter 1, we discussed the concept of risk ratings and how organizations calculate the risk they are exposed to. In doing so, we presented the following formula:

Risk = Vulnerability * Attacks * Threat * Exposure

While this is a good way to calculate the risk an asset is exposed to, it is not a good way to calculate the value or the classification of an asset itself.

ISO 17799 states:

> "The organization should be in a position to understand what information assets it holds, and to manage their security appropriately.
>
> This section contains the following sub-sections:
>
> 5.1 Accountability for assets - an inventory of information assets (IT hardware, software, data, system documentation, storage media and ICT services) should be maintained. The inventory should record ownership and location of the assets.All [information] assets should be accounted for and have a nominated owner. An inventory of information assets (IT hardware, software, data, system documentation, storage media and ICT services) should be maintained. The inventory should record ownership and location of the assets, and owners should identify acceptable uses.
>
> 5.2 Information classification - information should be classified and labeled accordingly."

While the preceding statement is about as vague and helpful as Section 404 of the Sarbanes–Oxley Act of 2002, we will attempt to give you some actual ideas and direction regarding what it takes to perform the boring and often long task of truly classifying your assets. As we said earlier, asset classification is the art of assigning a value to an asset so that you can organize it according to its sensitivity to loss or disclosure. How exactly do you determine this? For small organizations this step is typically quite easy. For larger organizations this task can be very time consuming.

The major steps required for asset classification and control are as follows:

- **Identifying the assets**   For this step, you need to identify what assets are critical to your business. The easy way to do this is to think about what systems, data, and software are essential for the business to function. In addition, you should consider any assets that contain critical or confidential information.

    - You can classify assets into four categories: information assets, software assets, physical assets, and services. *Information assets* include every piece of information inside your organization. This can include databases, customer information, data files, operations and support procedures, archived information, and continuity plans. Identifying all of the information assets in your organization is typically the hardest and most time-consuming step, as this is difficult to automate with tools.

    - *Software assets* comprise system and application software that your organization has purchased or in some cases developed in-house. Take care in this step to identify which software assets are custom developed or are no longer available for purchase.

    - *Physical assets* comprise the computing hardware, storage media, and even printers in your organization. You can use Nmap to classify these assets, as long as all the devices are using Transmission Control Protocol/Internet Protocol (TCP/IP).

■ *Services* are sometimes overlooked, but this category should include anything that your organization has outsourced or is provided by a third party, such as data centers and phone systems.

Are You owned?

Printers Are Threats

Despite the various research projects presented in public forums on the ways to use devices such as printers as an attack platform, many organizations fail to include these in their vulnerability management strategy. Most network-aware printers allow for File Transfer Protocol (FTP), Hypertext Transfer Protocol (HTTP), and in some cases, Telnet communications, which can allow an attacker the ability to leverage the printer and the limited storage on the printer in an attack.

■ **Identifying who is accountable for the assets**   It would be impossible for any IT employee or manager to be able to identify the criticality of an asset, especially when the IT resources do not work with all of computing assets on a daily basis. What is critical to IT may not necessarily be critical to the business. This is why every asset needs to have an asset owner. The asset owner needs to be intimately familiar with the asset he is assigned to. The folks in the IT department are ultimately the ones who manage most of the assets, but they should not be the owners of those assets.

■ **Preparing a schema for information classification**   When preparing a schema for asset classification, the criteria you use could include the following:

■ **Confidentiality**   Can the information be freely distributed, or do we need to restrict it to certain identified individuals?

■ **Value**   What is the asset's value? Is it a high-value item and, therefore, costly to replace, or is it a low-value item?

■ **Time**   Is the information time sensitive? Will its confidentiality status change after some time?

■ **Access rights**   Who will have access to the asset?

■ **Destruction**   How long will the information be stored? How can it be destroyed, if necessary?

You need to evaluate each asset against the preceding criteria and classify it for easy identification. For instance, you can define confidentiality in terms of the following:

- **Confidential**   The access is restricted to a specific list of people. These could be company plans, secret manufacturing processes, formulas, and so on.

- **Internal only**   The access is restricted to internal employees only. These could be customer databases, manufacturing procedures, and so on.

- **Shared**   The resources are shared within groups or with people outside of the organization. This could be operational information and contact information, such as the organization's internal telephone book, to be shared with business partners and agents.

- **Unclassified**   The resources are publicly accessible. This could include the company sales brochure and other publicity material.

Similarly, you can define value based on whether the asset is of high, medium, or low value. In such cases, you should prepare a detailed explanation, giving your reasons for this classification. For instance, a critical component costing a few rupees may be a very high-value item, as it is not easily available and could stop the production of a high-cost item.

You should define access rights for individuals as well as groups. Who is cleared to access confidential information in the organization? And who decides on the access rights? Logically, the asset owner will decide on access rights.

Destruction should be a scheduled and controlled activity. The information the company no longer needs but which could still be useful to competitors should be destroyed as per a predetermined schedule and method—depending on the confidentiality classification. For information recorded on hard disk, mere deletion of files does not obliterate them. A more stringent procedure such as multiple overwriting may be needed.

Classification schema should lead to a structure that you can implement. It should be simple to understand and identify.

I Thought This Was a Vulnerability Assessment Chapter

Asset classification is a necessary evil that all information security managers need to perform as part of their jobs. And performing asset classification as well as vulnerability assessment all boils down to one thing: Knowing Your Network.

So let's jump back to the beginning of this chapter, where we talked about creating asset groups. While some organizations find it easier to simply group assets by physical or even logical location, when you are dealing with a large-scale vulnerability management process it is far more efficient to break the generic asset groupings into smaller subsets so that you can complete more focused vulnerability assessments. To use my network example earlier in this chapter, we started with the following:

- North America
  - Operations
  - Sales
  - Marketing
  - Engineering

- Europe
  - Operations
  - Sales
  - Marketing
  - Engineering
- Global Outsourced

After conducting an asset classification exercise, my generic groups would expand into the following:

- North America
  - Operations Confidential
  - Sales Confidential
  - Marketing Confidential
  - Engineering Confidential
  - Operations Internal Only
  - Sales Internal Only
  - Marketing Internal Only
  - Engineering Internal Only
  - Operations
  - Sales
  - Marketing
  - Engineering
- Europe
  - Operations Confidential
  - Sales Confidential
  - Marketing Confidential
  - Engineering Confidential
  - Operations Internal Only
  - Sales Internal Only
  - Marketing Internal Only
  - Engineering Internal Only
  - Operations
  - Sales

- Marketing
- Engineering
- Global Outsourced

As you can see, anything below the Internal Only Classification is grouped together. You will also notice that I prefer to keep a separate asset group for any asset that is outsourced, because typically there are contractual requirements regarding outsource agreements when it comes to vulnerability assessment and pen testing. In some cases, you may even want to add a "special cases" group comprising an asset group of systems that have special requirements that need to be met before, during, or after a vulnerability assessment is performed on them. Before doing this, however, you should review my note earlier in this chapter about excluding certain systems from your tests.

By grouping your assets in this way, you gain multiple advantages when it comes to security. First, you can schedule your tests based on the criticality of the assets. For example, I know of multiple organizations that schedule internal vulnerability assessments at regular time intervals. In fact, I recommend that you schedule scanning of confidential and internal assets more often than other assets.

Leaving the geographic groupings in place also allows you to accommodate potential bandwidth limitations of scanning remote systems. For example, one financial organization I worked with during my consulting days had a number of branch offices in remote locations connected with slow links. By grouping their assets geographically, I was able to easily schedule the scans of these remote offices to take place during nonbusiness hours to limit the impact on the network. In addition, larger organizations find it very helpful to deploy distributed scanners that report back to a single reporting host.

This is why I recommend you use Nmap to identify assets only if you are running a small network. Commercial tools really shine when it comes to performing this task, and although some manual intervention is still necessary, having a tool that allows you to enter and track each group is essential.

Summary

In this chapter, we discussed how to identify assets on a network using both Nmap and commercial tools. We discussed ISO 17799 and asset classification and explained why they are important to vulnerability management. At this point, you should have a good idea of what you have on your network, what it does, and how important it is to your business. The next chapter will take us into the really fun stuff: actually scanning systems and identifying vulnerabilities.

## Chapter 5

Vulnerability Assessment: Step Two

Solutions in this chapter:

- An Effective Scanning Program
- Scanning Your Network
- When to Scan

☑ **Summary**

Introduction

In the preceding chapter, we talked about the boring but necessary first steps of conducting a vulnerability assessment. This chapter will expand on that and move into the more enjoyable steps of actually identifying and confirming vulnerable systems. This is a appropriate topic, because now is the perfect time to demonstrate why a good VA program is required: as we were putting together this chapter, the information technology (IT) world was scrambling to deal with a new form of malware that was exploiting an issue with the Microsoft Windows Server Service. Although some organizations were on high alert and their IT staff were being worked to death dealing with this threat, other organizations were calm and in a business-as-usual mindset because they had a proper vulnerability assessment (VA) methodology in place.

In this case—and really in any case where a new threat is exploited in the wild—just by following the steps outlined in the preceding chapter an organization would already have a list of systems that it needs to check for the existence of a threat, as well as a list of systems which it should not waste time checking. This chapter will take you through the steps of scanning not only for specific threats, but also for every known vulnerability in existence.

One thing to remember when performing any vulnerability assessment, or even a penetration test, for that matter, is that you are conducting a point-in-time assessment. To borrow from a famous Bruce Schneier quote: Vulnerability management is a journey, not a destination. This means that you cannot perform a vulnerability assessment only once and forget about it. You must check your networks constantly.

An Effective Scanning Program

So, how often should you be scanning your networks? Unfortunately, that question is not easy to answer, and the answer depends on your organization. We will, however, attempt to provide you with some general guidelines based on our experiences with various organizations.

There are essentially three different reasons you would want to perform a vulnerability assessment:

1. A new threat becomes evident and you want to verify that your systems are not vulnerable or identify systems that are vulnerable.

2. A vendor releases a patch or a number of patches and you want to verify that your systems are patched and are not vulnerable, or some other event causes wide-scale changes to your environment.

3. You want a point-in-time assessment of your current security posture and a list of vulnerabilities affecting your organization.

NOTE

A few years ago, a large financial institution solicited consulting organizations to provide bids on performing a quarterly vulnerability assessment on its entire network. The vendors attempting to win the bid did not know that the organization was selecting not one vendor for the work, but four different vendors. The organization's idea was to use two different vendors every quarter, and then correlate and compare their results. This would ensure not only that each vendor was performing a thorough job, but also that the organization requesting the work would receive a complete picture from two different perspectives. This institution still has this practice in place today, and it works well. This may or may not be the correct way for your organization to handle this task, but it might be worth investigating.

The first reason in the preceding list—a new threat becomes evident and you want to verify that your systems are not vulnerable or identify systems that are vulnerable—has become very necessary recently. As stated earlier, at the time of this writing, many IT departments were battling a new form of malware that was leveraging a known and patched vulnerability. In addition, we have seen multiple vulnerabilities released without vendor patches. This, of course, leads to the question, "How can a mostly reactive VA tool help with 0 day vulnerabilities?" A good VA tool can, in fact, help you with this, but not in the easy and direct way that many vendors may want you to believe. As you may remember from Chapter 3, one feature of a good VA tool is its capability to report back (sometimes referred to as *write-back*) the software versions of key operating system components. So, in the case of an Internet Explorer 0 day vulnerability, although you won't be able to detect the specific vulnerability, you will be able to detect what version of Internet Explorer your systems are running and cross-reference that to what versions are vulnerable to the specific 0 day vulnerability.

The second reason you may want to run a vulnerability assessment is to either double-check that all systems have been patched for a vulnerability, or obtain a list of systems that require a patch. This is a great way to verify that your patch management software actually did its job and rolled out the patches. So, for example, if a vendor such as Microsoft releases patches on the second Tuesday of every month and your patch management methodology states that all patches will be rolled out by the following Tuesday, on Wednesday it would be a great idea to run a vulnerability scan to identify any systems that were missed. In addition, if some other event, such as a software roll-out project or a new hardware implementation, causes a major change to your environment, you will want to verify that all systems are up-to-date and are not vulnerable.

The last and probably most common use of a VA tool is to take point-in-time snapshots of your overall network security posture. A good tool will also baseline each snapshot and provide you with a differential report, allowing for clear and concise trending of how well your organization is handling vulnerabilities. A typical organization will implement a program to use a VA tool in this fashion at a set interval.

At this point, you may be wondering what scanning program is best for your organization. Every organization is different and has its own policies, so we can't tell you in this book exactly what you should do, but hopefully the information we present will give you enough insight to determine your organization's needs.

Scanning Your Network

In the preceding chapter, we talked about identifying hosts on your network as well as classifying those hosts. Now we move on to the fun stuff and actually start scanning systems and identifying vulnerabilities. Regardless of what tool you are using, by now you should have a list of every system on your network that is communicating using the Transmission Control Protocol/Internet Protocol (TCP/IP). If you followed the advice we gave in the preceding chapter, you have also organized these systems in a logical way as well as given each group, or subset of groups, a classification. You did this based on the assumption that you would want to more consistently scan resources containing higher-risk data.

If you remember, we created the following groups:

- North America
    - Operations Confidential
    - Sales Confidential
    - Marketing Confidential
    - Engineering Confidential
    - Operations Internal Only
    - Sales Internal Only
    - Marketing Internal Only
    - Engineering Internal Only
    - Operations
    - Sales
    - Marketing
    - Engineering
- Europe
    - Operations Confidential
    - Sales Confidential
    - Marketing Confidential
    - Engineering Confidential
    - Operations Internal Only
    - Sales Internal Only
    - Marketing Internal Only
    - Engineering Internal Only
    - Operations
    - Sales
    - Marketing
    - Engineering
- Global Outsourced

For the sake of not boring you, we will concentrate on only one asset group, North America, when explaining the following steps. Obviously, you will want to repeat each step for every asset group. One nice feature of almost all VA products is the fact that they have built-in scheduling features that allow you to automate redundant tasks. We will address this a bit more, later in the book. For the following examples, we used eEye Digital Security's Retina, simply because one of the authors was recently employed at the company and we had a license handy, but the same concepts exist, or at least should exist, for all VA tools. Figure 5.1 shows the creation of specific asset groups. We had to black out the host names and domain name system names because we collected all of this data from a live network.

Figure 5.1 Creating Asset Groups

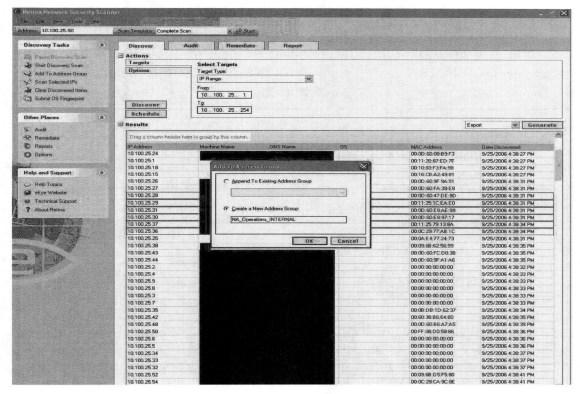

Table 5.1 lists the asset groups we created which fall in line with our original asset classification.

Table 5.1 Asset Group Names and Descriptions

Group Name	Description
NA_Operations_CONFIDENTIAL	North America Operations–Confidential Data Systems
NA_Operations_INTERNAL	North America Operations–Internal Data Systems
NA_Operations	North America Operations–Other Systems
NA_Sales_CONFIDENTIAL	North America Sales–Confidential Data Systems
NA_Sales_INTERNAL	North America Sales–Internal Data Systems

Continued

Table 5.1 Continued

Group Name	Description
NA_Sales	North America Sales–Other Systems
NA_Marketing_CONFIDENTIAL	North America Marketing–Confidential Systems
NA_Marketing_INTERNAL	North America Marketing–Internal Data Systems
NA_Marketing	North America Marketing–Other Systems
NA_Engineering_CONFIDENTIAL	North America Engineering–Confidential Data Systems
NA_Engineering_INTERNAL	North America Engineering–Internal Data Systems
NA_Engineering	North America Engineering–Other Systems

The group names we created are self-explanatory. As your network grows, you will find that the more self-explanatory your group names are, the easier it will be to recall which systems are in which groups. Clearly, if we had listed every asset group in Table 5.1, the table would be much larger, but hopefully the more abbreviated version we provided gets the point across.

The next step is to actually run scans against hosts. Obviously, as part of your vulnerability management strategy, you would schedule scans to run in set intervals. We discussed this a little bit in Chapter 4 as well. At a minimum, your organization should scan all hosts, concentrating on the Confidential and Internal Only hosts first, after every patching cycle. As you will learn while you read this book, there is a definite connection between patch management and vulnerability assessment.

When you are performing your scans, you may choose to scan either by asset classification (i.e., all confidential asset groups first, all internal asset groups next, etc.), or by operational area (i.e., all Operations groups first, all Sales groups next, etc.). We recommend that you concentrate on the higher-risk systems—the Confidential and Internal Only groups—from each organizational group, because despite improvements by vendors to increase the performance of their scanner engines, scanning large networks still takes time, and the longer it takes to identify and deal with vulnerable systems, the larger the window of vulnerability will be.

In Figure 5.2, we are scanning all confidential asset groups first. One step we did not address here (but which we will get to) is what to scan for. For this initial step, we are assuming that you have not performed a vulnerability assessment in the past, so to create a baseline you will need to scan for every possible vulnerability. Chapter 11 of this book will tie everything together and offer a complete plan that not only covers this step, but also takes into account every other aspect, including patch management and vulnerability remediation.

Figure 5.2 Scanning All Confidential Asset Groups First

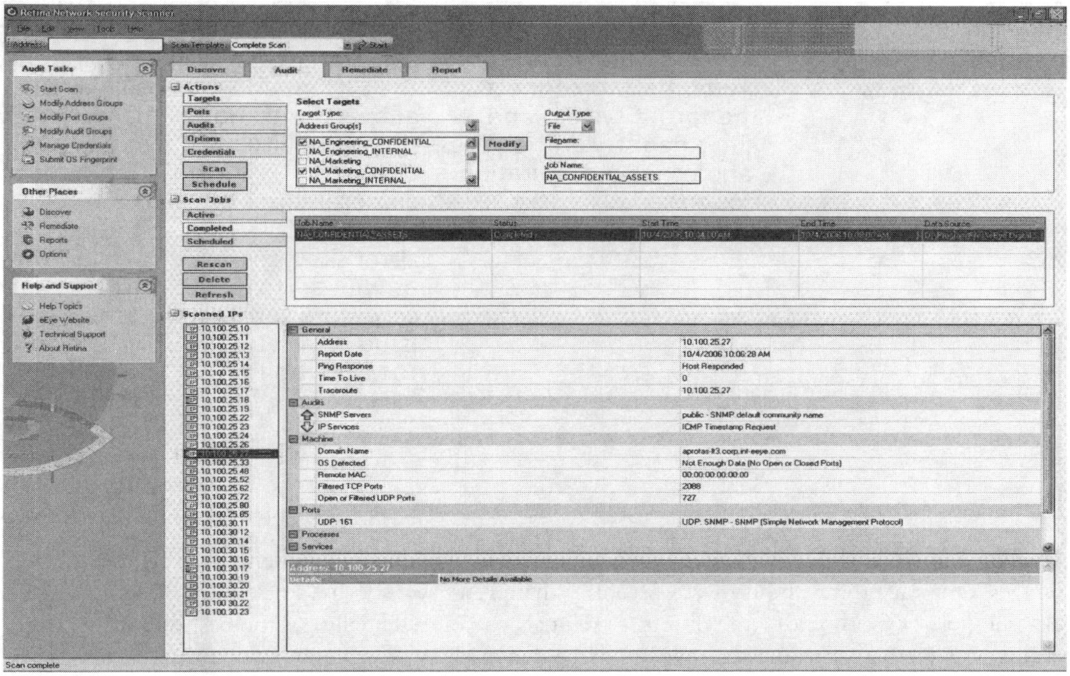

It is also important to note that in Figure 5.2, we are not supplying user credentials to the scanner product because we are scanning a production network. As we discussed earlier in the book, you will see different scan results based on whether you supply credentials; Table 5.2 provides a quick review of that earlier discussion.

Table 5.2 Scanning with and without Credentials

Option	What It Does	Benefits	Problems
Scan without credentials	The scanner will attempt to audit the target system without authenticating to that system with any user rights.	This gives you the "hacker's" view of a system, as the typical attacker would not have credentials.	Scanning in this manner will not identify the patch level of the system or vulnerabilities that a user with credentials could leverage.

Continued

Table 5.2 Continued

Option	What It Does	Benefits	Problems
Scan with credentials	The scanner will use administrator-level credentials to connect to the target system and audit Registry entries, files, and other configuration options.	This gives a more complete scan of the system and allows the scanner the capability to check for vulnerabilities in things such as client-side software as well as configuration issues that equate to vulnerabilities.	Some feel that this does not give a true hacker's view of a system. Although this is a true statement, getting the true hacker's view of a system and actually securing a system are two different things.

As you can see in Table 5.2, there is a definite advantage to using credentials over not using credentials. One nice thing about most VA tools is that even if you do use credentials, the noncredentialed checks will (or at least should) run without credentials, so you essentially get the best of both worlds.

Now that we have run the scan we are presented with an overview of what the scanner found to be vulnerable, along with a list of the vulnerabilities (see Figure 5.3). As you will remember from Chapter 3, a good VA tool offers a wide range of reporting options.

Figure 5.3 Network Analysis Results

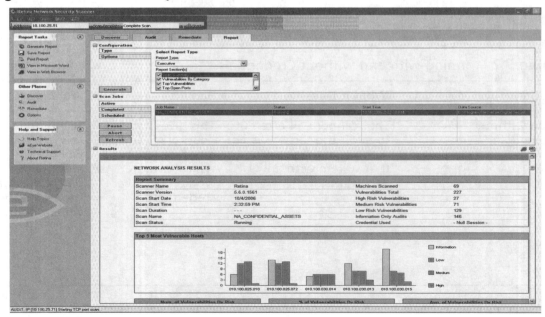

In addition, some products offer an enterprise console for managing large amounts of vulnerability information across an enterprise. Figure 5.4 shows an example.

Figure 5.4 Security Management Console for Managing Large Amounts of Vulnerability Information

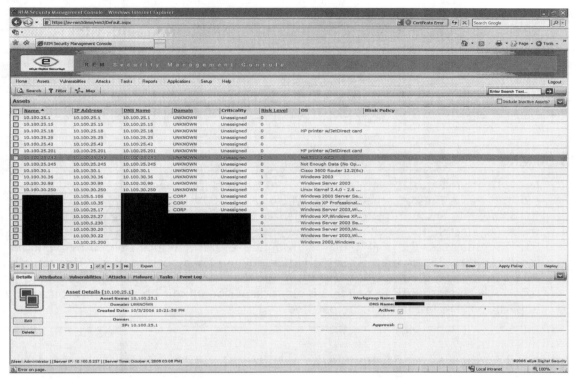

When to Scan

By now, it should be obvious how easy it is to scan a network for vulnerabilities. But it might not be obvious when or how often you should conduct a scan. In this section, we will discuss how to determine optimal timing of your vulnerability scanning program.

Earlier in this chapter we discussed the three different scenarios that should be considered triggers for the need to run a vulnerability assessment. As a reminder, we will repeat them here:

- A new threat becomes evident and you want to verify that your systems are not vulnerable or identify systems that are vulnerable.

- A vendor releases a patch or a number of patches and you want to verify that your systems are patched and are not vulnerable, or some other event causes wide-scale changes to your environment.

- You want a point-in-time assessment of your current security posture and a list of vulnerabilities affecting your organization.

This list should not only give you an idea of why you would want to scan your systems, but also allow you to infer when to scan, and even how to do it. When we showed an example of how to run a simple scan in this chapter, we simply left all audits enabled. This meant that our scanner checked our network for every potential vulnerability, which also meant that our scan took longer to complete.

One of the battles every VA vendor fights on a constant basis when developing products is scan performance versus scan completeness. The more you are auditing for, the longer your scans will take. The typical goal of most vendors is to get as much coverage with audits as possible, while still allowing scans to run in a relatively quick manner. That being said, to scan a Class B network for all possible vulnerabilities can take multiple days, regardless of what product you are using.

Because of the amount of time it takes to conduct a complete scan, and because of how frequently one of the three triggers that should cause a scan occurs, it is impractical to try to scan for every vulnerability every time you run a scan. With that in mind, we suggest the scan schedule shown in Table 5.3.

Warning

Many IT organizations, even large ones, get trapped into reacting constantly to the monthly Patch Tuesday schedule that Microsoft uses. Although it makes perfect sense to release patches monthly on a set schedule, one unintentional side effect is that those responsible for patching and systems security become so focused on Microsoft's Patch Tuesday that they fail to plan and sometimes fail to notice when other vendors, most of which do not follow a set schedule, release an important patch. This actually assists in shifting the attack surface from one that has been operating system (and core application) specific to one that is more client side specific because other third-party applications are less likely to be patched.

Table 5.3 Suggested Scan Schedule

Trigger	When to Scan	What to Scan For
A new threat becomes evident and you want to verify that your systems are not vulnerable or identify systems that are vulnerable.	This is a reactive scan issue that you need to deal with when you are made aware of the threat.	
In this case, you will want to assess which assets on your network are most exposed to the threat and begin scanning those first, moving down the list to systems less at risk.	Performance and accuracy are important in this type of scan. You will want to scan for only a specific threat in order to create a comprehensive list of systems that you should reconfigure or patch to defend against the issue.	

Table 5.3 Continued

Trigger	When to Scan	What to Scan For
Note that in some cases, this will be a 0 day threat, so you may be able to scan for only specific operating systems or software versions and not the actual vulnerability itself. But this is purely product dependant and something to consider when choosing what VA tool to use.		
A vendor releases a patch or a number of patches and you want to verify that your systems are patched and are not vulnerable.		
Some other event causes wide-scale changes to your environment.	As you will learn when you get to the chapters on vulnerability remediation and patch management, it is very difficult for an organization, especially a large one, to test and roll out a patch quickly. So for this scan event trigger you will need to coordinate with your patching process for the exact timing.	
It makes sense to schedule your vulnerability assessment for the evening after all patches have been rolled out. This will help you get a list of all systems that, for whatever reason, were not patched.	Usually a good VA vendor will have released audits for new issues the same day it releases a patch.	
Scan for just these vulnerabilities, starting with your highest-risk asset group. Note that in some cases, you can scan for both the presence of the patch (a credentialed scan) and the remote exploitability of the issue (a noncredentialed scan). When possible, it is a good idea to do both, because sometimes a patch can fail during installation in a way that fools the VA tool.		

Continued

Table 5.3 Continued

Trigger	When to Scan	What to Scan For
You want a point-in-time assessment of your current security posture and a list of vulnerabilities affecting your organization.	This scan trigger is the most predictable and easiest to plan for. Scheduling this depends solely on how often your environment changes.	
Most organizations will do an enterprisewide vulnerability scan once per quarter, and sometimes more often, such as once every two months, in order to detect changes.	In this case, you will want to scan for every potential vulnerability that your scanning tool can detect. This will allow you to find systems that, for whatever reason, are not up to patch or secure configuration levels.	
This full scan will also allow you to track the progress being made by those who are responsible for securing machines. For example, if a group of systems is vulnerable to something the first time you run a scan, by the second time the issues should have been fixed.		
This is also the time to generate a baseline to report against each scan cycle in order to prove that your vulnerability management program is in fact working.		

Summary

In this chapter, we covered the actual scanning of systems for vulnerabilities and discussed the reasons why you would want to perform a scan. We outlined each reason in detail, and although there may be others that we did not list, we did cover the most common ones. We looked at one scanning tool in particular—eEye Digital Security's Retina—and discussed how it works as well as what types of reports you can create with it. Finally, we provided a sample scanning schedule that should have given you some clear guidelines as to when you should be scanning your network and what you should be scanning for.

This chapter should have provided you with the basic framework to plan your own VA schedule which will dramatically help you to improve your organization's security posture.

## Chapter 6

Going Further

Solutions in this chapter:

- **Types of Penetration Tests**

- **Scenario: An Internal Network Attack**

- **Penetration Testing**

- **Vulnerability Assessment versus a Penetration Test**

- **Internal versus External**

☑ **Summary**

Introduction

Vulnerability assessment (VA) represents a key element of an organization's information security program. A VA highlights an organization's security liabilities and helps asset owners, security managers, and business leaders determine information security risk. VAs only report vulnerabilities, though. They don't substantiate that vulnerabilities actually exist; penetration tests do that.

The past few chapters discussed the tools, methodologies, and concepts that go into VA. This chapter assimilates that information and continues with penetration testing. We'll discuss the two types of penetration (pen) tests, walk through a pen test, cover the differences between VAs and pen tests, and discuss the pros and cons of conducting penetration tests from within versus externally to our corporate network.

Types of Penetration Tests

Penetration testing is the process of evaluating the security posture of a computer system, network, or application (assets). The process involves analyzing assets for any weaknesses, configuration flaws, or vulnerabilities. The analysis is carried out from the perspective of a potential attacker and leverages exploitation of known and possibly unknown security vulnerabilities.

There are two types of penetration tests: black box and white box tests. Black box testing assumes no prior knowledge of the environment to be tested and the testers must first determine the location and extent of the assets before commencing their analysis. At the other end of the spectrum, white box testing provides the testers with complete knowledge of the environment to be tested; often including network diagrams, source code and Internet Protocol (IP) addressing information. As one might assume, there are many shades of gray too.

Black box testing is what we often associate with penetrating testing. Black box testing is usually carried out by a malicious attacker, sometimes a trusted third party, seeking to gain unauthorized access to an asset. To accomplish this a black box tester may leverage known and unknown, 0 day, security vulnerabilities to penetrate a host. The purpose and intent of a black box tester vary. If a nefarious attacker is conducting the exercise, the attacker could seek unauthorized access for:

- **Staging**   Staging future attacks. Attackers often like to exploit assets via intermediary sources. This aids in concealing their identity.

- **Information disclosure**   Unearthing sensitive data on a system. Data could include password files, credit card numbers, company propriety information, and so on.

- **Bots**   Attackers could seek to convert an exploited asset into a bot. The attackers could then use the exploited system to carry out programmatic requests such as spamming or denial of service (DoS) attacks on their behalf.

Notes from the Underground…

Bots

Bots, also called *zombies*, are compromised computers that are used to create DoS or spam attacks, among other things. These computers are typically compromised via a vulnerability or malicious piece of software and wait for commands from the person in control of the bot.

There are no rules of engagement or restrictions for black box testing, unless a third party is conducting the attack. Everything from cross-site scripting, SQL injection, and even DoS attacks is fair game. Some exploits can render a system unavailable. To the malicious attacker this is a moot point.

There are rules of engagement for white box testing. We might expect this, considering the fact that white box testers are usually organizations and contracted third parties. For an organization, discovering and validating vulnerabilities is important, but maintaining an asset's availability during a penetration test is vital too. Because of this, organizations tend to place the following restrictions on penetration tests:

- **Scheduled** Tests need to be scheduled and coordinated during off-peak hours to minimize the impact to the business.

- **Authorized** Tests need to be approved by the security team as well as the asset/business owner.

- **Limited** Exploits that render the system unavailable are typically excluded. Unknown, 0 day, vulnerabilities are not tested either; organizations typically don't have access to this information and corresponding exploits.

Like vulnerability assessments, penetration tests are a key element of an organization's information security program. Penetration tests not only determine an asset's security liability to the organization, but they also:

- **Validate information security programs** Independent, third-party assessments of an organization's environment can validate the strengths and weaknesses of a company's information security program.

- **Substantiate product liability** Pen tests conducted against technologies an organization consumes enable a company to determine the security liability of the technology prior to procurement.

- **Confirm security controls**   Most organizations practice *defense in-depth strategies*, or the layering of security technologies to protect an asset. Pen tests can aid in identifying weak spots within this strategy.

- **Support Internet Audits (IAs)**   Due to an onset of new federal and industry regulations, IA departments are under pressure to substantiate their organization's information security programs. IA departments are exercising their resolve in ensuring that their organizations are practicing due diligence in protecting their corporate assets. For all organizations, penetration tests are part of this due diligence equation.

Scenario: An Internal Network Attack

We've conducted a vulnerability assessment and believe an asset is vulnerable, but what's the true liability of that asset to our organization? Depending on how we've discovered the vulnerability—via security, remediation, or configuration technologies—the asset may or may not pose a liability to our organization. To determine the asset's true risk to the organization we'll expand upon our VA efforts and conduct a pen test.

Penetration tests can be sourced externally or internally to a company's network. External pen tests provide the outsider's perspective of an asset, and internal pen tests illustrate the asset's susceptibility to insider attacks. We'll further discuss the differences between external and internal tests later in this chapter. For now, we'll focus on internal penetration testing.

To aid our pen test discussion we'll walk through an internal penetration test against a front-end Web server and a supporting database server. The Web server in our example supports the company's e-commerce initiatives, and the database houses customer records. The purpose of the pen test is to determine whether we can gain unauthorized access to the customer data that's housed within the database. To do this we'll conduct a direct attack against the database server. If we're unsuccessful in penetrating the database server, we'll attempt to compromise the Web server and see whether we can use it as a conduit to the database server and, ultimately, the customer records. Table 6.1 and Figure 6.1 depict the landscape of the internal network.

Client Network

Following is the list of assets that comprised the client's network.

- 1 Internet facing router
- 2 Internal routers
- 1 Intrusion Prevention System (IPS)
- 2 Web servers
- 1 Database server
- 1 Application server

Table 6.1 Target Systems

#	Host	IP Address	Operating System	Open Ports
1	Web	10.192.144.54	?	?
2	Database	10.192.146.34	?	?

Figure 6.1 Client Network Diagram

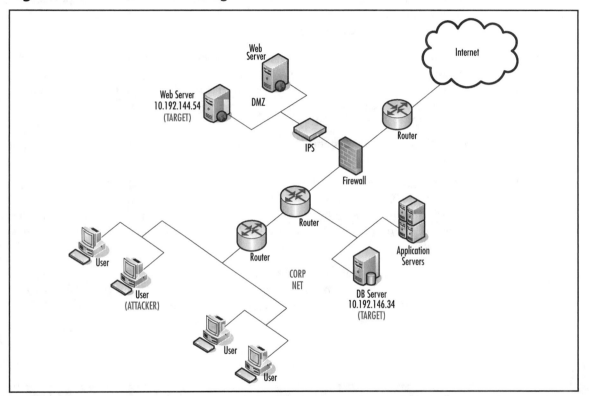

Whether we're conducting an internal or an external penetration test the process is the same. We must:

1. **Gather information**   Determine the available hosts, their underlying operating system, and running services.

2. **Detect vulnerabilities**   Assess the systems for vulnerabilities.

3. **Attack and penetrate**   Leverage the vulnerabilities we've discovered in the previous step to attack and penetrate the host(s); gain unauthorized access.

To assist us with our penetration test we'll use:

- Nmap 4.03 from www.insecure.org/nmap for information gathering
- Retina 5.0 from eEye Digital Security for vulnerability assessment
- Core Impact 5.1 from Core Security for attack and penetration

Step 1: Information Gathering

First things first: We must get a lay of the land. We need to obtain as much information as possible about the assets in question: the database server and Web server. We already know their IP addresses, but we need additional information regarding the hosts. We need to know:

- **Operating systems**   Determining the underlying operating systems will aid us in assessing the assets for vulnerabilities. Some applications run on only certain operating systems—for example, Microsoft SQL does not run on UNIX. Based on this it would be pointless to assess a UNIX host for Microsoft SQL vulnerabilities knowing that UNIX is not a Microsoft SQL-supported platform.

- **Open ports**   Discover open (listening) ports on the hosts. Open ports will provide insight into the services running on the systems.

- **Running applications/services**   Enumerate the applications/services running on the hosts. In our scenario, we'll be attacking a Web server and a database server, but what other applications are running on these hosts? The Web and database services may be secure, but other applications could possess vulnerabilities that we could leverage to gain unauthorized access to the systems.

Since this attack is being sourced from within the client's network, we'll begin our assessment by actively fingerprinting the systems, seeking to discover their operating systems, and then determine open (listening) ports on the Web and database servers. Upon determining the open ports, we'll attempt to identify the services/applications running on each system.

Note

OS Fingerprinting

OS fingerprinting, also called TCP/IP stack fingerprinting, is the process of determining the identity of a remote operating system by analyzing packets received from that host. There are two types of OS fingerprinting: active and passive. Passive OS fingerprinting identifies the remote operating system by *sniffing* (capturing) packets exchanged between the source and remote systems. Active OS fingerprinting is the process of sending packets to a host and interpreting the response or lack thereof from that host.

Operating System Detection

In order to determine the operating system, or to conduct a pen test, for that matter, we must be able to establish IP connectivity to the Web and database servers. Simply pinging the hosts could validate connectivity. Ping tends to be blocked by most corporate firewalls, so we'll need a utility that's not solely predicated on ICMP to validate connectivity and ultimately determine the underlying operating systems. For this, we'll utilize Nmap; specifically, Nmap version 4.03.

Nmap is a great freeware utility that can aid us in gathering information. It will help us determine the availability of our targets and the ports the systems expose, and enumerate the applications/ services running on the systems.

To determine the Web and database servers' availability we'll use Nmap's −sP (ping scan) switch. This command will help us identify whether we have IP connectivity to the target hosts from our position within the internal network. Upon executing the command (see Figure 6.2), we can see that connectivity does indeed exist between us and the target systems, and that the corporate firewall isn't blocking ICMP after all. If the firewall was blocking ICMP, we could have leveraged the −P0 (treat all hosts as online) switch to determine connectivity. This command attempts to make a Transmission Control Protocol (TCP) connection, a socket connection, to well-known ports on the systems to establish connectivity.

Figure 6.2 Nmap Ping Scan Command

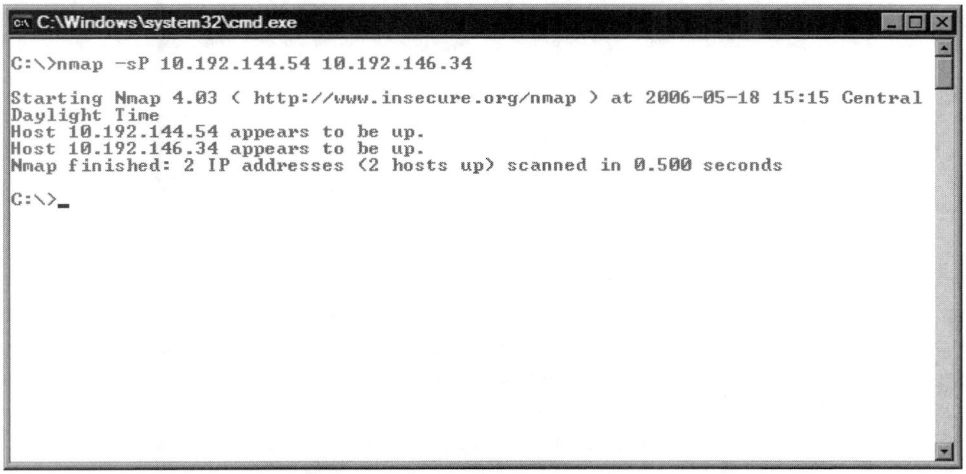

```
C:\Windows\system32\cmd.exe

C:\>nmap -sP 10.192.144.54 10.192.146.34

Starting Nmap 4.03 ( http://www.insecure.org/nmap ) at 2006-05-18 15:15 Central
Daylight Time
Host 10.192.144.54 appears to be up.
Host 10.192.146.34 appears to be up.
Nmap finished: 2 IP addresses (2 hosts up) scanned in 0.500 seconds

C:\>_
```

Upon determining IP connectivity to our targets, our next step is to determine their underlying operating systems. For this, we'll utilize Nmap's −O (enable operating system detection) switch. Figure 6.3 illustrates the output of that command. The actual command is *namp −O 10.192.144.54 10.192.146.34. TCP/IP fingerprint was removed from Figure 6.3.*

Figure 6.3 Nmap Operating System Detection Command

```
Starting Nmap 4.03 ( http://www.insecure.org/nmap ) at 2006-05-18 16:01
Central Daylight Time
Interesting ports on 10.192.144.54:
(The 1664 ports scanned but not shown below are in state: closed)
PORT       STATE SERVICE
135/tcp    open  msrpc
139/tcp    open  netbios-ssn
443/tcp    open  https
445/tcp    open  microsoft-ds
1043/tcp   open  boinc-client
2105/tcp   open  eklogin
2301/tcp   open  compaqdiag
3372/tcp   open  msdtc
3389/tcp   open  ms-term-serv
49400/tcp  open  compaqdiag
No exact OS matches for host (If you know what OS is running on it, see
http://www.insecure.org/cgi-bin/nmap-submit.cgi).

Interesting ports on 10.192.146.34:
(The 1665 ports scanned but not shown below are in state: closed)
PORT       STATE SERVICE
111/tcp    open  rpcbind
135/tcp    open  msrpc
139/tcp    open  netbios-ssn
445/tcp    open  microsoft-ds
1433/tcp   open  ms-sql-s
3389/tcp   open  ms-term-serv
4125/tcp   open  rww
4987/tcp   open  maybeveritas
5555/tcp   open  freeciv
No exact OS matches for host (If you know what OS is running on it, see
http://www.insecure.org/cgi-bin/nmap-submit.cgi).

Nmap finished: 2 IP addresses (2 hosts up) scanned in 13.038 seconds
```

Leveraging the −O switch within Nmap we were unable to ascertain the operating system of the Web and database servers. Referring back to Figure 6.3 Nmap reported "No exact OS matches for the host". We could infer the operating system based upon the ports Nmap discovered. In Figure 6.3, Nmap detected that *tcp 139*, *netbios-ssn*, *tcp 445*, and *microsoft-ds* were open on the Web and database servers. Considering that *netbios-ssn* and *microsoft-ds* are specific to the Windows operating systems we could deduce that both the Web and database servers are running a version of Windows.

Discovering Open Ports and Enumerating

In the preceding section, we leveraged Nmap to validate connectivity and accessibility to the Web and database servers (targets). Upon discovering that we had IP connectivity, we then inferred the underlying operating system of each system based on the output that Nmap provided. Having garnered these two pieces of information, it's now time to discover the available (open) ports on each host and the applications or services running on each system. Remember, enumerating an asset will allow us to accurately assess it for vulnerabilities.

The Nmap −O switch gave us insight into the available services on each host. Though the intent of the switch is to determine the operating system, it also provided available port and service information. The command didn't provide us with the version number of each identified service, though. Considering that different versions of a respective application may contain different vulnerabilities, we'll leverage Nmap's −sV (server detection) switch to provide the version number or description of each enumerated service. Figure 6.4 recants the open port information from Figure 6.3 and displays the version or description of each running service. Take a look at the *Service Info:* attribute of each host too.

Figure 6.4 Nmap Service Detection Command

Via the −sV switch, we're able to determine the version number or description of each listening service. The −sV switch also provided further insight into each system's underlying operating system. Recall that when we attempted to detect the operating system via the −O switch, Nmap reported "No exact OS matches for host". We still don't have an exact operating system match, but we're able to now validate that the targets are running a version of the Windows operating system. When using the −O switch Nmap leveraged Transmission Control Protocol/Internet Protocol (TCP/IP) stack fingerprinting to deduce the underlying operating system. This command doesn't take into account the running services, like the $-sV$ command does. By utilizing the $-sV$ command, we can better determine the operating system based on the running applications on the targets.

For operating system detection and enumeration, we utilized multiple Nmap commands. We did this for illustration purposes only and to aid in the discussion of information gathering. To garner the same level of information we could have leveraged Nmap's $-A$ (enable operating system and version detection) switch. Figure 6.5 illustrates the output of this command; *the TCP/IP fingerprints were removed from Figure 6.5.*

Figure 6.5 Nmap Operating System and Version Detection

```
Starting Nmap 4.03 ( http://www.insecure.org/nmap ) at 2006-05-19 00:03
Central Daylight Time
Interesting ports on 10.192.144.54:
(The 1664 ports scanned but not shown below are in state: closed)
PORT       STATE SERVICE        VERSION
135/tcp    open  mstask         Microsoft mstask (task server -
c:\winnt\system32\Mstask.exe)
139/tcp    open  netbios-ssn
443/tcp    open  https?
445/tcp    open  microsoft-ds   Microsoft Windows 2000 microsoft-ds
1043/tcp   open  msrpc          Microsoft Windows RPC
2105/tcp   open  msrpc          Microsoft Windows RPC
2301/tcp   open  http           Compaq Diagnostis httpd (CompaqHTTPServer 5.7)
3372/tcp   open  msdtc          Microsoft Distributed Transaction Coordinator
3389/tcp   open  microsoft-rdp  Microsoft Terminal Service
49400/tcp  open  http           Compaq Diagnostis httpd (CompaqHTTPServer 5.7)
No exact OS matches for host (If you know what OS is running on it, see
http://www.insecure.org/cgi-  bin/nmap-submit.cgi).

Service Info: OS: Windows

Interesting ports on 10.192.146.34:
(The 1665 ports scanned but not shown below are in state: closed)
PORT       STATE SERVICE        VERSION
111/tcp    open  rpcbind         2 (rpc #100000)
135/tcp    open  mstask         Microsoft mstask (task server -
c:\winnt\system32\Mstask.exe)
139/tcp    open  netbios-ssn
445/tcp    open  microsoft-ds   Microsoft Windows 2000 microsoft-ds
1433/tcp   open  ms-sql-s?
3389/tcp   open  microsoft-rdp  Microsoft Terminal Service
4125/tcp   open  msrpc          Microsoft Windows RPC
4987/tcp   open  maybeveritas?
5555/tcp   open  omniback       HP OpenView Omniback

Service Info: OS: Windows

Nmap finished: 2 IP addresses (2 hosts up) scanned in 116.968 seconds
```

As reflected in Figure 6.5, the $-A$ command provides the same level of information we collected via the $-O$ and $-sV$ switches. In streamlining the information-gathering process, we could have combined the operating system detection and application enumeration processes by running Nmap with the −*A* switch.

Having determined the underlying operating systems and running services on each host, we've successfully completed step 1 of the penetration test, information gathering. It's now time to proceed to step 2, vulnerability detection. In step 2, we'll seek to identify any application or system-level vulnerabilities that we can later leverage in step 3, attack and penetration, to exploit the Web and database servers. Before we continue, let's organize the data we gathered via Nmap and update our System Information Table. Table 6.2 represents the updated System Information Table.

Table 6.2 Updated System Information with Nmap Results

#	Host	IP Address	Operating System	Open Ports		
1	Web	10.192.144.54	Windows	135/tcp	open	mstask
				139/tcp	open	netbios-ssn
				443/tcp	open	https?
				445/tcp	open	microsoft-ds
				1043/tcp	open	msrpc
				2105/tcp	open	msrpc
				2301/tcp	open	http
				3372/tcp	open	msdtc
				3389/tcp	open	microsoft-rdp
				49400/tcp	open	http
2	Database	10.192.146.34	Windows	111/tcp	open	rpcbind
				135/tcp	open	mstask
				139/tcp	open	netbios-ssn
				445/tcp	open	microsoft-ds
				1433/tcp	open	ms-sql-s?
				3389/tcp	open	microsoft-rdp
				4125/tcp	open	msrpc
				4987/tcp	open	maybeveritas?
				5555/tcp	open	omniback

Step 2: Determine Vulnerabilities

Having complete step 1, information gathering, we now need to assess the Web and database servers for vulnerabilities. To do this we'll need to switch tools. Nmap aided in the information-gathering process, but it's not a vulnerability assessment tool; its strengths reside in the information-gathering arena. To detect vulnerabilities we need a vulnerability assessment utility. Several VA tools are on the market, but for our purposes, we'll utilize Retina 5.0 from eEye Digital Security. Table 6.3 includes a partial list of the vulnerability scanners on the market today.

Table 6.3 List of VA Scanners

Company	Product	URL
eEye Digital Security	Retina	www.eeye.com
Tenable Network Security	Nessus	www.nessus.org
Internet Security Systems (ISS)	Internet Scanner	www.iss.net

Setting Up the VA

Within Retina, we need to create a scan job. The scan job will define the parameters of our vulnerability assessment. As per the Retina User Guide, these parameters include:

- **Hosts**   Hosts to be assessed
- **Ports**   TCP and User Datagram Protocol (UDP) ports that are included in the assessment
- **Audits**   Vulnerabilities the hosts are evaluated against
- **Options**   Attributes such as operating system detection, reverse domain name system (DNS) query, and so on
- **Credentials**   Account information, if any, used to remotely connect to a system

The following steps will guide us through setting up a scan job within retina.

1. Upon launching Retina, select the **Audit** tab from the **Retina** interface. Figure 6.6 shows the Audit interface.

Figure 6.6 Retina Audit Interface

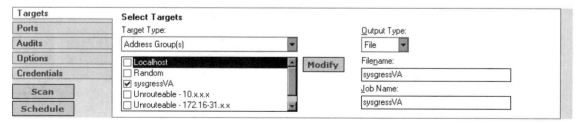

2. Next, select the **Targets** tab and create an Address Group associated with the Web and database servers by selecting the **Modify** button on the Targets tab.
3. After creating the Address Group, supply a Filename and Job Name to the scan and select the **Ports** tab. The **Filename** and **Job Name** parameters are simply descriptors for the scan. Selecting the Ports tab displays Figure 6.7.

Figure 6.7 Retina Ports Interface

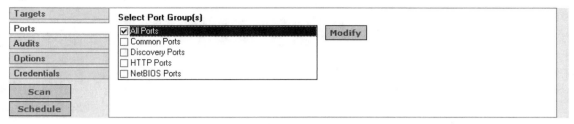

For our purposes, select **All Ports**. We're doing this to ensure that we don't miss any applications or services that could be running on an uncommon or frequently used port. If we were conducting a vulnerability assessment against our enterprise, we would need to reduce the number of ports evaluated to improve the audit speed and performance. Accessing every host against more than 65,000 ports could prove to be quite time consuming. Since we're evaluating only two hosts, this isn't an issue for use. Following are descriptions for the various Port Group options:

- **All Ports**   Scans on all ports

- **Common Ports**   Scans common application ports such as TCP port80 for web servers and TCP port 25 for email servers

- **Discovery Ports**   Scans those ports used in Discover.

- **HTTP Ports**   Scans ports 80 and 443

- **NetBIOS Ports**   Scans ports 135, 139, and 445

4. After selecting All Ports, continue to the **Audits** tab and check **All Audits**. Figure 6.8 displays Retina's default audit selection. Recall that audits determine which known vulnerabilities our hosts will be evaluated against.

Figure 6.8 Retina Audit Groups

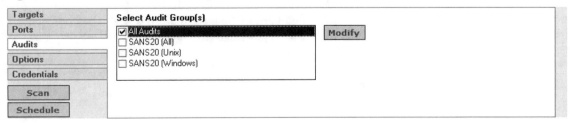

We've decided to evaluate the Web and database servers against all the vulnerabilities within the Retina database. Once again, if this were an enterprise assessment, we'd want to scope this. Since we're evaluating only two hosts, we'll select **All Audits** to unearth all possible system and application-level vulnerabilities.

5.   Next we'll define the options of the scan by selecting the **Options** tab. These options include:

- Perform OS Detection

- Get Reverse DNS

- Get NetBIOS Name

- Get MAC Address

- Perform Traceroute

- Enable Connect Scan Connect to the target port and complete a full three-way handshake (SYN, SYN/ACK, and ACK).

- Enable Force Scan

- Perform the Various NetBIOS Enumerations

For our scan, we select **Perform OS Detection**, **Enable Connect Scan Mode**, and **Perform the Various NetBIOS Enumerations**. Notice that we're repeating some of the same efforts we conducted in the information-gathering phase. Unfortunately, Retina can't utilize the information gathered via Nmap. Because of this, we'll need to repeat these exercises to accurately detect the vulnerabilities present on the Web and database servers. We could have leveraged Retina to begin with. We instead utilized Nmap for its robust operating system detection and enumeration options.

6.   Having finalized our options, and because we're not leveraging credentials within this scan, we select the **Scan** button shown on the left-hand side in Figure 6.8 to initiate the vulnerability assessment.

Interpreting the VA Results

Once the vulnerability assessment is complete, we analyze the results to see whether any vulnerabilities were discovered on the Web and database servers. Remember that the goal of the penetration test is to see whether we can gain unauthorized access to customer records housed on the database. Ideally we'd like to discover a vulnerability on the database server and use it as an avenue into the system. If a vulnerability isn't present on the database server, we'll look to exploit the Web server in an attempt to gain access to the customer records. Figure 6.9 contains the output of our vulnerability assessment. Table 6.4 is our System Information Table, updated to include the Retina data.

Figure 6.9 Retina Vulnerability Output

```
eEye Digital Security

Retina Network Security Scanner
Network Vulnerability Assessment & Remediation Management

Summary Report

10.192.146.34

_____

General        10.192.146.34 (Machine Information - DB Server)

_____

Machine Name: N/A
NetBIOS Domain: N/A
DNS Name:
IP Address:   10.192.146.34
MAC Address: N/A
Traceroute:
Time to Live: 125
Ping:  Host Responded
Open TCP Ports:     N/A
Open UDP Ports:     N/A
Operating System:   Windows 2000

_____

Audits 10.192.146.34        (Vulnerability Detail)

_____

Limited Null Session

Risk Level:   Low
BugtraqID:    494
CVE:    CVE-2000-1200

DCOM Enabled

Risk Level:   Medium
BugtraqID:    N/A
CVE:    CAN-1999-0658
No Remote Registry Access Available
```

Continued

Figure 6.9 Continued

```
Risk Level:   Information
BugtraqID:    N/A
CVE:   N/A


TCP:3389 - Terminal Services enabled

Risk Level:   Low
BugtraqID:    N/A
CVE:   N/A


Microsoft Windows Non-Default User Service

Risk Level:   Information
BugtraqID:    N/A
CVE:   N/A


ICMP Timestamp Request

Risk Level:   Low
BugtraqID:    N/A
CVE:   CVE-1999-0524
_____


Ports  10.192.146.34        (Open Ports)
_____


111   :    TCP   :    Open   :    SUNRPC - SUN Remote Procedure Call
135   :    TCP   :    Open   :    RPC-LOCATOR - RPC (Remote Procedure
                                  Call) Location Service
139   :    TCP   :    Open   :    NETBIOS-SSN - NETBIOS Session
                                  Service
445   :    TCP   :    Open   :    MICROSOFT-DS - Microsoft-DS
1433  :    TCP   :    Open   :    MS-SQL-S - Microsoft-SQL-Server
3389  :    TCP   :    Open   :    MS RDP (Remote Desktop Protocol) /
                                  Terminal Services
4987  :    TCP   :    Open   :    Unknown Port
5250  :    TCP   :    Open   :    Unknown Port
5555  :    TCP   :    Open   :    ServeMe
10204 :    TCP   :    Open   :    CA License Client/Server
_____


10.192.144.54
_____


General     10.192.144.54 (Machine information - Web Server)
_____
```

Figure 6.9 Continued

```
Machine Name: N/A
NetBIOS Domain:       N/A
DNS Name:
IP Address:  10.192.144.54
MAC Address: N/A
Traceroute:
Time to Live:125
Ping:  Host Responded
Open TCP Ports:     N/A
Open UDP Ports:     N/A
Operating System:  N/A
_____

Audits 10.192.144.54        (Vulnerability Detail)
_____


TCP:2301 - JetPhoto Server "Name" And "Page" Variables Cross Site Scripting

Risk Level:  Low
BugtraqID:   N/A
CVE:   N/A


DCOM Enabled

Risk Level:  Medium
BugtraqID:   N/A
CVE:   CAN-1999-0658


Microsoft MSDTC and COM+ Buffer Overflow (902400) - Remote

Risk Level:  High
BugtraqID:   15056,15057
CVE:   CAN-2005-1979,CAN-2005-2119,CAN-2005-1978


TCP:3389 - Terminal Services enabled

Risk Level:  Low
BugtraqID:   N/A
CVE:   N/A


TCP:2967 - Norton AntiVirus Corporate Edition (managed service) detected

Risk Level:  Information
BugtraqID:   N/A
CVE:   N/A


ICMP Timestamp Request

Risk Level:  Low
BugtraqID:   N/A
CVE:   CVE-1999-0524


No Remote Registry Access Available
```

Continued

Figure 6.9 Continued

```
Risk Level:    Information
BugtraqID:     N/A
CVE:   N/A


_____


Ports  10.192.144.54          (Open Ports)

_____


135    :      TCP    :      Open   :      RPC-LOCATOR - RPC (Remote Procedure
                                          Call) Location Service
139    :      TCP    :      Open   :      NETBIOS-SSN - NETBIOS Session
                                          Service
443    :      TCP    :      Open   :      HTTPS - HTTPS (Hyper Text Transfer
                                          Protocol Secure) - SSL (Secure Socket Layer)
445    :      TCP    :      Open   :      MICROSOFT-DS - Microsoft-DS
1065   :      TCP    :      Open   :      HP OpenView
2103   :      TCP    :      Open   :      ZEPHYR-CLT - Zephyr Serv-HM
                                          Conncetion
2105   :      TCP    :      Open   :      EKLOGIN - Kerberos (v4) Encrypted
                                          RLogin
2301   :      TCP    :      Open   :      CIM - Compaq Insight Manager
3389   :      TCP    :      Open   :      MS RDP (Remote Desktop Protocol) /
                                          Terminal Services
```

Table 6.4 Summary of Retina Output

#	Host	IP Address	Operating System	Open Ports	Vulnerabilities/ Severity
1	Web	10.192.144.54	Windows 2000	135/tcp	
				139/tcp	
				443/tcp	
				445/tcp	
				1043/tcp	
				2105/tcp	
				2301/tcp	
				3372/tcp	
				3389/tcp	
				49400/tcp	JetPhoto (Low)
					DCOM (Medium)
					MSDTC (High)
					TS (Low)

Table 6.4 Continued

#	Host	IP Address	Operating System	Open Ports	Vulnerabilities/ Severity
					Norton (Low)
					ICMP(Low)
2	Database	10.192.146.34	Windows 2000	111/tcp	
				135/tcp	
				139/tcp	
				445/tcp	
				1433/tcp	
				3389/tcp	
				4125/tcp	
				4987/tcp	
				5555/tcp	Null Session (Low)
					DCOM (Medium)
					TS (Low)
					ICMP (Low)

Referring to Table 6.4 we notice that the database doesn't contain a high-level vulnerability that we can exploit to gain unauthorized access to it. The highest-level vulnerability it possesses is associated with Microsoft Distributed Component Object Model (DCOM) being enabled, which really doesn't represent a vulnerability. The Web server, on the other hand, does possess a high-level vulnerability. It's susceptible to a Microsoft Distributed Transaction Coordinator (MSDTC) and Component Object Model (COM)+ buffer overflow. In an effort to gain access to the customer records, we'll need to first exploit the Web server. If we're successful, we'll attempt to leverage the Web server to gain access to the database.

Penetration Testing

Penetration tests utilize the vulnerabilities discovered during a VA to *exploit*, or gain unauthorized access to, targeted systems. Whereas a vulnerability assessment identifies security holes within a system or application, a penetration test takes advantage of these weaknesses to gain unauthorized system-level access.

Having reported and detected the vulnerabilities present on the Web and database servers, it's now time to exploit, attack, and penetrate these weaknesses. To aid us we'll leverage Core Impact 5.1 from Core Security. Additional penetration tools include Dave Aitel's Canvas and Metasploit. You can also find free vulnerability exploits at www.packetstormsecurity.org and www.securityfocus.com/bid.

Step 3: Attack and Penetrate

In our scenario, we discovered a high-level vulnerability on the Web server. We will now attempt to exploit this vulnerability to gain unauthorized access to the system. To do this we'll:

1. Upload the data we obtained during steps 1 and 2, information gathering and vulnerability assessment, into Core Impact (Impact).

2. Execute Impact's Attack and Penetration Module to attack and exploit the Web server.

3. Leverage the Web server to gain access to the database.

Uploading Our Data

Upon launching and configuring a workspace within Impact, we're presented with the window shown in Figure 6.10. This is the interface we'll leverage to conduct our attack.

Figure 6.10 Impact Interface

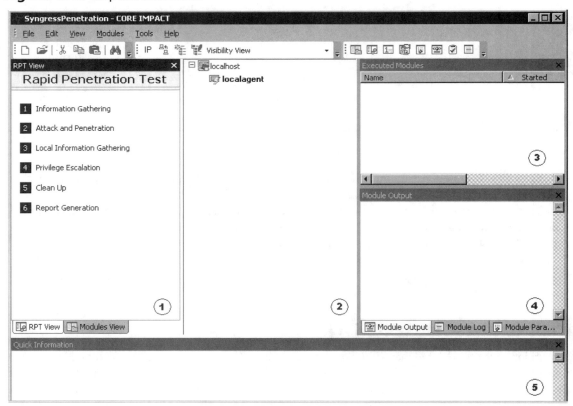

Here's an explanation of the different parts of the Impact user interface, as explained in the Core Impact User Guide

1. **The Modules panel**   Provides access to Impact modules. Modules are the actions, such as information gathering, attacking, sniffing, and so on, that we can perform on the network or against a host.

2. **The Entity View panel**   Displays information about our targets. This panel initially contains only an entry for the local host (the machine on which Impact is running). As we attack and exploit systems, they, too, are added to the Entity View panel.

3. **The Executed Modules panel**   Displays information about each module or action that was performed during the penetration test.

4. **The Executed Module Info panel**   Displays information about the currently selected module or action in the Executed Modules panel.

5. **The Quick Information panel**   Displays information about the currently selected item in the console. For example, if we select a module, the panel displays module documentation. If we select a host, the panel displays information about that host.

To upload our data into Impact we select the **Modules View** tab within the **Modules** panel. We then expand the **Import–Export** module. Figure 6.11 shows the available import–export options for Impact.

Figure 6.11 Impact Import-Export Module

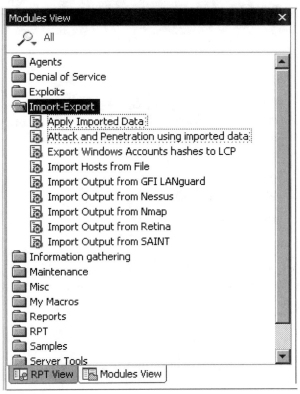

As shown in Figure 6.11, Impact has import modules for Nmap and Retina; the two tools we utilized during steps 1 and 2 of our penetration test. To streamline our penetration efforts we'll upload the data we previously collected. To upload the data we simply click on the corresponding module and follow the instructions. Figure 6.12 depicts the Nmap interface.

Figure 6.12 Impact Nmap Import Interface

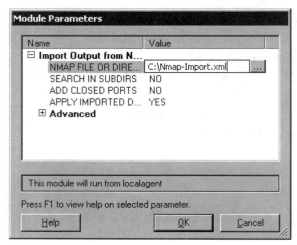

We generate the Nmap file value referenced in Figure 6.12 by appending the $-oX$ (*<filename>*) tag to the Nmap commands we executed earlier during the information-gathering phase. When we append these arguments, Nmap will output the results to an XML file.

Upon uploading the Nmap and Retina data into Impact, our Entity View panel is updated with the following:

- The IP addresses of the Web and database servers
- Open ports on both systems
- Vulnerabilities discovered during the VA

Once we have both of these systems defined within the entity view, we can proceed to the attack and penetration phase of our test. Figure 6.13 reflects the updated entity view.

Figure 6.13 Updated Entity View

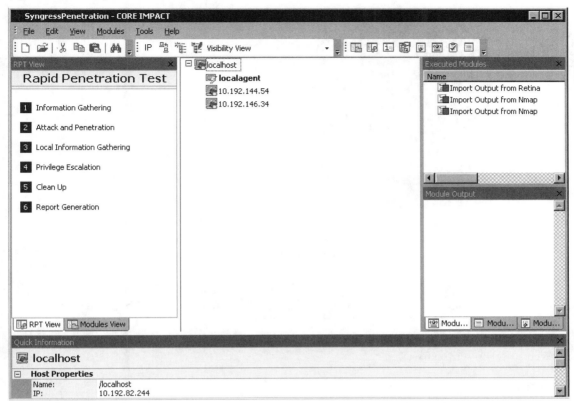

Attack and Penetrate

Based on the vulnerabilities previously discovered, we know we must first exploit, or penetrate, the Web server if we hope to gain access to the customer records. We need to do this because there were no identified vulnerabilities on the database server.

To exploit the Web server we could either selectively, or manually, run Impact exploits against the Web server, or we could leverage Impact's Attack and Penetration Wizard to exploit the host. The Attack and Penetration Wizard will compare the Web server's vulnerabilities and open ports against exploit modules within Impact and attempt to automatically exploit the system.

To invoke the Attack and Penetration Wizard click on the **RPT View** tab within the **Modules** panel and select **Attack and Penetration**. Upon doing so, Figure 6.14 appears.

Figure 6.14 Attack and Penetration Wizard

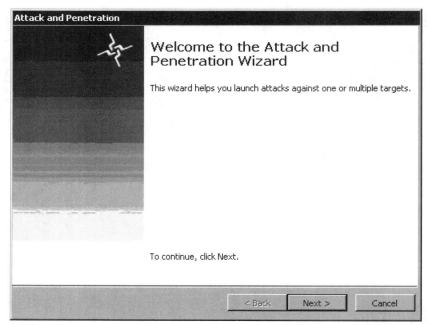

Click **Next**, and the screen in Figure 6.15 appears. Here we define the system we want to attack; the Web server in our scenario.

Figure 6.15 Target Selection

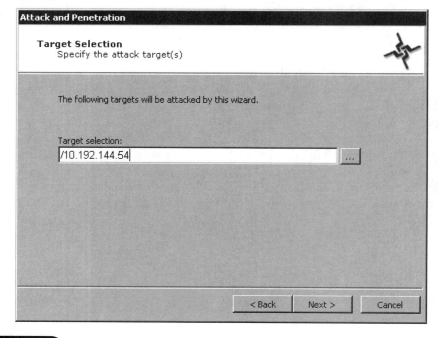

In an effort to maintain system stability, we will not run any exploits that might render the system unavailable (see Figure 6.16).

Figure 6.16 Exploit Selection

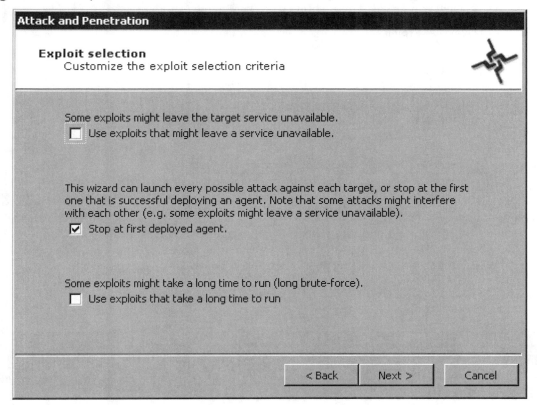

After clicking **Next**, we assume the remaining default settings and allow Impact to begin its attack on the Web server. We can follow the status of the attack by viewing the attack modules within the Executed Modules panel. Following the attack, we see that Impact is able to penetrate the Web server via the MSRPC UMPNPMGR exploit (see Figure 6.17), and loads a level 0 agent on the system. If we had our speakers on during the attack, we would have heard Impact announce "New Agent Deployed."

Figure 6.17 Module Output

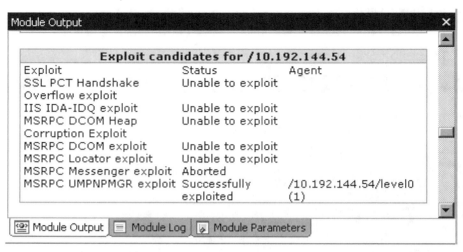

Notice that Impact exploited the remote Web server via the MSRPC UMPNPMGR vulnerability and not via a DCOM-related one. This is because we configured Impact to stop its attack upon successfully deploying its first agent. Although we provided Impact with VA data, Impact attacked, or ran exploits against, the system based upon the Web server's open ports and vulnerabilities.

Note

Agent Levels

Within Impact, a level 0 agent provides basic shell access to the remote system supporting a finite number of commands. A level 1 agent is an administrator or root equivalent agent that has the ability to do anything and everything on the remote system. Communication calls between the Impact operator and the level 1 agent are also secure, but they are not with a level 0 agent.

Having gained unauthorized access to the Web server, we now need to determine the context, or identity, under which we're operating. By connecting to the level 0 agent and launching a mini-shell, we execute the *whoami* command to determine the identity we've assumed. Figure 6.18 highlights the output of the *whoami* command.

Figure 6.18 whoami command

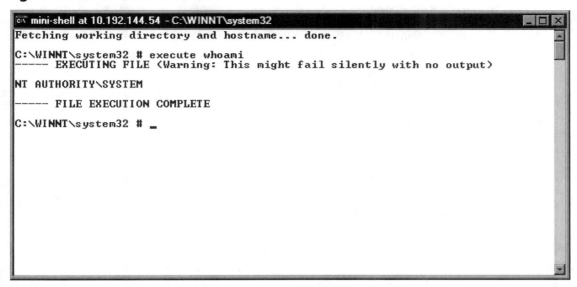

The *whoami* command displays the identity of the logged-in user. In Figure 6.18, we've determined we're operating under the context of Authority\System; a Windows built-in administrative equivalent account. Via Impact, we've gained unauthorized administrative access to the Web server. We'll now upgrade to a level 1 agent. Upgrading to a level 1 agent will provide us with a rich mini-shell and allow us to execute command-line arguments as though we are at the Web server's console. Figure 6.19 reflects an updated entity module containing the level 1 agent.

Figure 6.19 Entity Module: Level 1 Agent

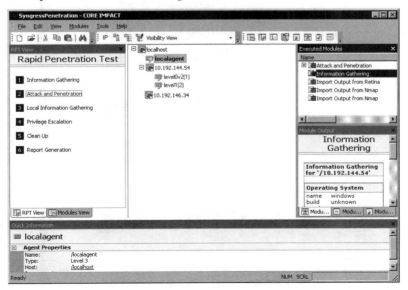

Having established a level 1 agent on the Web server, we now have several options regarding attacking the database server and ultimately gaining access to the customer records. We could:

- **Source attacks from the Web server**   Since the database supports the Web server, the firewall between the two systems may contain a more liberal set of firewall rules. If this were the case, we could repeat steps 1 and 2, information gathering and VA, sourcing these efforts from the Web server. Doing so may provide insight into vulnerabilities that were undetectable from our position within the network.

- **Install software on the Web server**   We could install a packet driver, remote control software, and so on. Doing so may allow us to discover credentials that are leveraged by the Web server to access the database.

- **Search the Web server for information**   We could search the Web server for information. Such a search may disclose proprietary company data or other sensitive data housed on the system, or enable us to access credentials to other resources.

Searching the Web Server for Information

Of the aforementioned options, searching the Web server for information is the easiest to conduct and the hardest to detect. If we installed a remote piece of software on the Web server, its antivirus program may detect and quarantine that software, and sound an alarm concerning this. Sourcing our penetration efforts from the Web server is a viable option, but it requires that we restart our penetration efforts from scratch. Looking back at our System Information Table will provide further insight as to why this is the best option (see Table 6.5).

Table 6.5 System Information Table

#	Host	IP Address	Operating System	Open Ports	Vulnerabilities/Severity
1	Web	10.192.144.54	Windows 2000	135/tcp	
				139/tcp	
				443/tcp	
				445/tcp	
				1043/tcp	
				2105/tcp	
				2301/tcp	
				3372/tcp	
				3389/tcp	
				49400/tcp	JetPhoto (Low)
					DCOM (Medium)

Table 6.5 Continued

#	Host	IP Address	Operating System	Open Ports	Vulnerabilities/Severity
					MSDTC (High)
					TS (Low)
					Norton (Low)
					ICMP (Low)
2	Data base	10.192.146.34	Windows 2000	111/tcp	
				135/tcp	
				139/tcp	
				445/tcp	
				1433/tcp	
				3389/tcp	
				4125/tcp	
				4987/tcp	
				5555/tcp	Null Session (Low)
					DCOM (Medium)
					TS (Low)
					ICMP (Low)

In Table 6.5, we've highlighted two key attributes. On the Web server, we've highlighted the operating system and on the database we've highlighted the open port, TCP 1433. This tells us two things:

1. The Web server is more than likely running Microsoft Internet Information Server (IIS) 5.0. IIS 5.0 runs only on Windows 2000.
2. If we're able to detect database credentials on the Web server, we can use our position from within the network to connect to the database server for TCP 1433, the Microsoft SQL default port.

Discovering Web Services

Until now, we've discovered no information to validate that the Web server is indeed a Web server. Looking at Table 6.5, you can see that TCP port 80 is not referenced as an open port. This could be due to a variety of reasons. Considering that this is the client's e-commerce Web server, it's highly unlikely that the client changed the system's default port; doing so would require the client to inform its customers as to what the new port is, and this simply doesn't scale. More than likely the client has filtered the port, via its firewall, from its internal clients. To determine this we'll leverage our Impact mini-shell and dump all of the TCP port 80 connections to the Web server (see Figure 6.20), to ascertain whether the server is indeed accepting Web connections. We'll use the *netstat* command for this purpose; *netstat* is used to display protocol statistics and current TCP/IP connections. From Figure 6.20, we can confirm that the Web server is indeed accepting TCP connections on port 80.

Figure 6.20 Web Server Detection

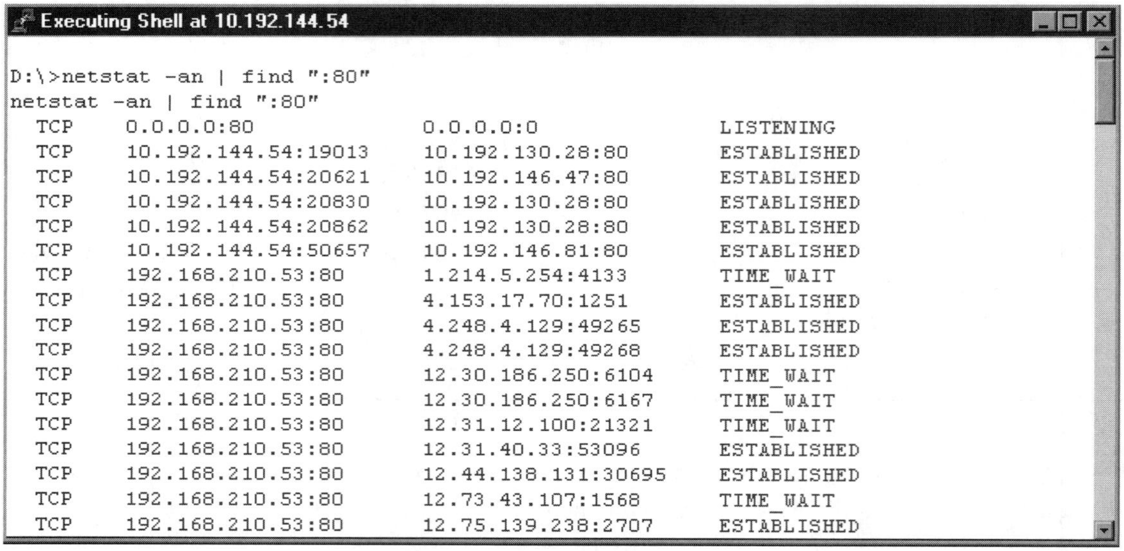

```
 Executing Shell at 10.192.144.54                                         _ □ ×

D:\>netstat -an | find ":80"
netstat -an | find ":80"
  TCP    0.0.0.0:80                0.0.0.0:0                LISTENING
  TCP    10.192.144.54:19013       10.192.130.28:80         ESTABLISHED
  TCP    10.192.144.54:20621       10.192.146.47:80         ESTABLISHED
  TCP    10.192.144.54:20830       10.192.130.28:80         ESTABLISHED
  TCP    10.192.144.54:20862       10.192.130.28:80         ESTABLISHED
  TCP    10.192.144.54:50657       10.192.146.81:80         ESTABLISHED
  TCP    192.168.210.53:80         1.214.5.254:4133         TIME_WAIT
  TCP    192.168.210.53:80         4.153.17.70:1251         ESTABLISHED
  TCP    192.168.210.53:80         4.248.4.129:49265        ESTABLISHED
  TCP    192.168.210.53:80         4.248.4.129:49268        ESTABLISHED
  TCP    192.168.210.53:80         12.30.186.250:6104       TIME_WAIT
  TCP    192.168.210.53:80         12.30.186.250:6167       TIME_WAIT
  TCP    192.168.210.53:80         12.31.12.100:21321       TIME_WAIT
  TCP    192.168.210.53:80         12.31.40.33:53096        ESTABLISHED
  TCP    192.168.210.53:80         12.44.138.131:30695      ESTABLISHED
  TCP    192.168.210.53:80         12.73.43.107:1568        TIME_WAIT
  TCP    192.168.210.53:80         12.75.139.238:2707       ESTABLISHED
```

We then confirm that the client is running IIS via the *iisreset /status* command (see Figure 6.21), which is unique to IIS.

Figure 6.21 iisreset /status Command

```
Executing Shell at 10.192.144.54                                    _ □ ×

D:\>iisreset /status
iisreset /status

Status for World Wide Web Publishing Service ( W3SVC ) : Running

D:\>
```

Having validated the existence of a Web server, it's now time to unearth access credentials to the database. To do this we consider:

- Both the Web and the database servers are running Windows 2000.

- The Web server supports the client's e-commerce initiatives.

- Active Server Pages (ASP) is the primary method to support dynamic Web content on Windows 2000 and IIS.

- Active data objects (ADO) and Object Linking and Embedding Data Base (OLE DB) are the predominant application program interfaces (APIs) used to connect to a database from a Web server.

Maintaining access to our mini-shell we search the Web server for all .asp files that contain "sqloledb." These files contain access credentials to databases. Hopefully we'll find at least one file that references the customer database. Figure 6.22 contains the output of our search.

Figure 6.22 findstr Output

```
 Executing Shell at 10.192.144.54                                    _ □ ✕
D:\>findstr /i /s "sqloledb" *.asp
findstr /i /s "sqloledb" *.asp
WebServ\wwwroot\companyabc.com\Company\investor\news.asp:          'adoCON.Open "Pr
ovider=SQLOLEDB.1;Password=LFAPP;User ID=Factor_APP;Initial Catalog=Intranet
;Data Source=10.192.146.34
WebServ\wwwroot\companyabc.com\Company\investor\news.asp:          'adoCON.Open "Pr
ovider=SQLOLEDB.1;Password=LFAPP;User ID=Factor_APP;Initial Catalog=Intranet
;Data Source=10.192.146.34
WebServ\wwwroot\companyabc.com\Company\investor\news.asp:          'adoCON.Open "Pr
ovider=SQLOLEDB.1;Password=LFAPP;User ID=Factor_APP;Initial Catalog=Intranet
;Data Source=10.192.146.34
WebServ\wwwroot\companyabc.com\Company\investor\news.asp:           adoCON.Open "Pro
vider=SQLOLEDB.1;Password=LFAPP;User ID=Factor_APP;Initial Catalog=Intranet;
Data Source=10.192.146.34
WebServ\wwwroot\companyabc.com\Search.asp:                                       m
objECD.ConnectionString = "Data Source=10.192.146.34;Initial Catalog=customer ;
User ID=Engine; Password=bkeng10; Provider=SQLOLEDB;"
WebServ\wwwroot\companyabc.com\fSearch.asp:
mobjECD.ConnectionString = "Data Source=10.192.146.34 itial Catalog=ECDTest; Use
```

Well, well, well. Look at what we've found. Leveraging the *findstr* command within Windows we're able to uncover a connection string and credentials to the customer database. Figure 6.23 highlights the output from Figure 6.22 that references the customer database.

Figure 6.23 SQL Credentials

```
WebServ\wwwroot\companyabc.com\Search.asp:                                       m
objECD.ConnectionString = "Data Source=10.192.146.34;Initial Catalog=customer ;
User ID=Engine; Password=bkeng10; Provider=SQLOLEDB;"
```

At this point, there's no need to continue our attack from the Web server. Having garnered user credentials to the database and with the database, TCP 1433, being available to us from our attack position, we can simply connect to the database from our local machine. To connect to the database we'll use Microsoft's SQL Query Analyzer and the credentials from Figure 6.23. Upon connecting, we're presented with the screen shown in Figure 6.24.

Figure 6.24 Query Analyzer Connection

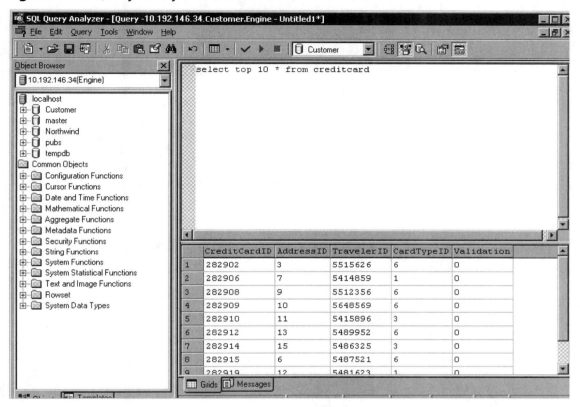

As we can see by viewing the available databases within Figure 6.24, the customer database represents the only user-created database; the rest of the databases are installed by default with Microsoft SQL. Expanding **Customer** we locate a table titled "creditcard." Upon querying the creditcard table, selecting its 10 top records, we uncover customer data. Now it's only a matter of joining the fields within the creditcard table and the rest of the tables within the customer database to assemble the complete customer record. At this point, we have accomplished our objective. We have accessed customer records. The penetration test is over.

Vulnerability Assessment versus a Penetration Test

After walking through a vulnerability assessment and a penetration test, we might think penetration tests are the way to go. Penetration tests do substantiate the vulnerabilities unearthed during an assessment. In some situations, penetration tests are necessary. In others, they simply aren't reasonable or practical.

Penetration tests are great for a small or targeted collection of assets; for example, network perimeters, third-party peering points, and internal financial or human resources systems. Unfortunately, penetration tests do not scale when we get into the hundreds, thousands, tens of thousands, and hundreds of thousands of systems which comprise major enterprise environments. Comparatively speaking, vulnerability assessments do scale. Not only do they scale, but also they are cheaper in terms of both time and resources, and they give us a more exhaustive view of security liabilities across our enterprise.

Tips for Deciding between Conducting a VA or a Penetration Test

If you are undecided as to whether to conduct a vulnerability assessment or a penetration test, here are some tips to help facilitate your decision.

You should conduct a vulnerability assessment when:

- **Time is a constraint**   Penetration tests can be very time consuming, depending on the number of assets we are evaluating and the number of vulnerabilities that are present on any given host. Imagine how long a penetration test would take against 100 or perhaps 1,000 hosts. On most occasions, we're not interested in whether a vulnerability can be exploited, for we may have compensating controls to mitigate the exploitation, but we would still like to know whether the vulnerability appears to exist. Though a vulnerability may not be exploitable today, this may not hold true for tomorrow. Many times vulnerabilities are re-released with new attack vectors allowing for new conduits of exploitation. Think we've seen the last re-release of a Microsoft Remote Procedure Call (RPC) vulnerability?

- **Cost is an issue**   Not only do penetration tests require substantially more time, but they also cost more to conduct. In many instances, companies have to contract out penetration work, for they simply do not have the expertise on staff. Most organizations today, though, are fairly adept at conducting vulnerability assessments; especially given the number of VA products on the market.

- **Validating**   Want to know the success of that latest service pack push? Run a VA against the hosts in question. Systems often remain vulnerable after patches have been deployed, simply because the machines haven't been rebooted. VAs are great at identifying this. Let's compare our VA reports against the remediation team's reports. We may find ourselves asking, "So, fellows, are we sure those machines were patched?"

- **Trending**   How have we done at managing vulnerabilities across our enterprise today as compared to yesterday, last month, or perhaps last year? Sure, the number of vulnerabilities is increasing and the window between disclosure and exploit is shrinking, but trending vulnerabilities across our enterprise can provide valuable insight into our organization's remediation and change control processes.

You should conduct a penetration test when:

- **You have a limited number of assets**   Penetration tests are very practical against a small number of hosts—for example, the company's financial or accounting systems. Where a vulnerability assessment attempts to identify all weaknesses, a penetration test simply seeks to exploit any one of the N number of vulnerabilities on a given system. Attempting to exploit all vulnerabilities is usually pointless. It doesn't matter whether the front door or back window of our house is unlocked; a thief can effectively use either of these avenues as an entry point into our home.

- **Confirmation is needed**   We conduct a VA and find five high-level vulnerabilities on a system. Is that system truly vulnerable? Can an unauthorized entity compromise that system? The only true way to substantiate this is to conduct a penetration test. If we can leverage one of the identified vulnerabilities to gain access to the system, someone else can too.

- **You are fiscally flexible**   Penetration tests are typically outsourced to a company's information technology (IT) provider, an external auditor, or a third party. Outsourcing the work validates the organization's security posture, supports the company's security program, and is required by most regulations. Outsourcing application development and support services may have their cost benefits, but outsourcing penetration testing can be quite expensive.

- **Time is not of the essence**   What takes longer, hacking five systems or conducting a vulnerability assessment against those same five systems? Who said there was no such thing as a stupid question? Penetration tests depend on vulnerability information, so naturally, they take longer to conduct. If we want to confirm that the identified vulnerabilities exist and time is on our side, penetration tests are the way to go.

Internal versus External

We can conduct vulnerability and penetration assessments either from within our network or external to it. An internal assessment will expose vulnerabilities that employees, contractors, third parties, or anyone else that has access to our internal network can exploit. An external assessment gives us a view of our security liabilities as seen by customers, competitors, business partners, and hackers.

To further distinguish internal and external assessments and the value proposition of each, let's look at a typical network, as shown in Figure 6.25.

Figure 6.25 A Typical Network

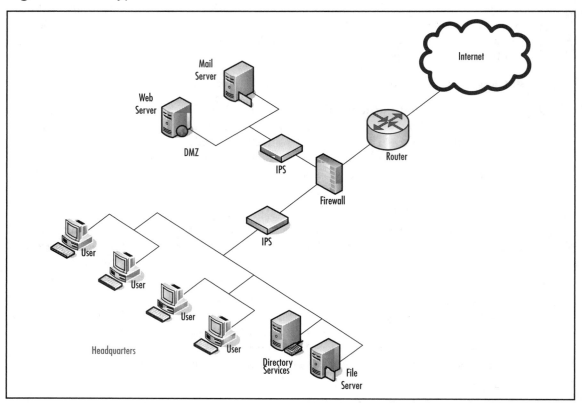

In Figure 6.25, as in most organizations, a firewall represents the first line of defense against outside threats. Some organizations also enable firewall capabilities on their edge, Internet router. Behind the firewall and before the corporate network resides the company's *DMZ*; a hardened and semitrusted portion of the company's network used to host Web, e-mail, and other Internet services. Behind the DMZ, separated by yet another firewall, resides the corporate network where end users and enterprise services live.

Given Figure 6.25, if we were to conduct an internal assessment—say, against the Directory Services server—we would, in essence, be evaluating the security posture of that respective host and the applications that reside on it. If that server possessed vulnerabilities, any one of the four illustrated users could attempt to exploit, penetrate, and gain unauthorized access to the system without transversing any security infrastructure. Though many organizations have implemented firewalls, IPSes, and other types of security infrastructure within their corporate network, these devices do not protect the vast majority of internal systems. Because of this, an organization should develop a comprehensive vulnerability assessment process that identifies all vulnerabilities on all network-connected devices.

Conversely, if we were external to the network depicted in Figure 6.25 and conducted an assessment—say, against the company's Web or e-mail server—our assessment would transverse multiple layers of security; a firewall followed by an intrusion prevention device. In this scenario, exploitation of a vulnerability is more difficult, for we have to successfully pass through both the company's firewall and IPS devices.

Organizations should routinely conduct both internal and external assessments. External assessments are great at testing and measuring a company's defense-in-depth strategy and provide valuable insight into what an entity, foreign to the company's network, may be able to gain access to. Internal assessments aid organizations in identifying process, change control, configuration, and remediation weaknesses for assets, when evaluated from this perspective, typically are not protected by security infrastructure. Even if they are, it's usually not to the same extent to which DMZ assets are protected.

Internal assessments are also good at identifying vulnerabilities that internal users can exploit. Remember that the internal threat is just as great, if not greater than, the external threat. We never know when an employee or contractor may attempt to sabotage or break into an internal system, while it's pretty safe to assume that this activity is constantly occurring from sources outside our organization's network.

Summary

As mentioned at the beginning of this chapter, vulnerability assessments and penetration tests are valuable components of a company's information security program. However, before conducting either test, we should identify what we're trying to accomplish. Are we attempting to validate that a vulnerability exists? Perhaps we would like to know whether an outsider can gain unprivileged access to our system. Still yet, we may simply want to know the success of our last remediation push.

Vulnerability assessments and penetration tests can provide answers to these questions. Both have their strengths, as well as relative weaknesses, depending on our ultimate objective. A wise man once said, proper prior planning prevents piss-poor performance. We should heed that advice when deciding whether to conduct a pen test when all we need is VA data. There's nothing like attempting to exploit a thousand machines when all we want to know is whether they are vulnerable.

## Chapter 7

Vulnerability Management

Solutions in this chapter:

- **The Vulnerability Management Plan**
- **The Six Stages of Vulnerability Management**
- **Governance (What the Auditors Want to Know)**
- **Measuring the Performance of a Vulnerability Management Program**
- **Common Problems with Vulnerability Management**

☑ **Summary**

Introduction

Back in the good old days, the typical approach to vulnerability management was to have the security group identify threats and then "toss" them to information technology (IT) administrators for remediation. As the number of security threats mounted over the years, this casual approach was no longer viable. In previous chapters, we discussed vulnerability discovery through the use of vulnerability assessment (VA) scanners, patch management, and configuration management tools. However, vulnerability management requires more than just the use of one of these previously mentioned tools.

Vulnerability management is best defined as the overall process of managing the risk presented to an enterprise due to vulnerabilities, whether they are software or hardware related. Vulnerability management ties directly into vulnerability discovery and vulnerability assessment in many ways, and depends greatly on the patch management process as well.

Vulnerability management also includes the grouping of security practices and processes which assist in managing security liabilities, allowing you to integrate vulnerability management into existing information security and IT workflows.

This chapter outlines the building blocks of a vulnerability management program and discusses what's necessary to maintain an effective program.

NOTE

Don't assume that large enterprises solve the vulnerability management problem simply by throwing people at it. Regardless of an organization's size, you can't address vulnerability management by adding more people to the team. For example, one large international corporation created a team of more than fifty people dedicated to vulnerability management and patch deployment. Despite having labs dedicated to testing patches and fixes, the company still couldn't keep up with the tide of work, primarily because of poor and undocumented processes.

The Vulnerability Management Plan

As with any plan, unless it's documented, receives appropriate sponsorship, and is effectively communicated, it's probably not very attainable. The same holds true for a vulnerability management plan. You must document the plan's goals, objectives, and success criteria. To help the plan along, you also must receive executive buy-in and sponsorship if you hope for the plan to be effective. Without senior management support, the ability to enforce vulnerability management policies, processes, and practices is forever hampered.

NOTE

Historically, vulnerability assessment has been viewed as a technology or IT problem, and not an organizational or risk management problem.

In an effort to garner senior management buy-in, your vulnerability management plan must be measurable and mapped to organizational risk as well as IT risk. By doing this, you can change senior management's predisposition regarding vulnerability management and get them to understand that this is a business issue and not solely an IT matter.

Planning a vulnerability management program is no different from planning for any other project or program. As mentioned earlier, the plan should clearly articulate its intent and relevance to the business. If you have not established a vulnerability management program, the following five steps can help you in this endeavor:

1. Gain an understanding of your organization's tolerance and appetite for risk.

2. Define acceptable levels of risk and timeframes in which elevated levels of risk are to be remediated.

3. Establish asset and vulnerability classifications. Understanding which assets are important to the business and coming up with a vulnerability classification system will increase the effectiveness and efficiency of your vulnerability management program.

4. Assign roles and responsibilities. Identify and document asset owners, custodians, and the entity responsible for an asset's remediation.

5. Finally, develop a method for measuring the program's success. If you can't measure it, you can't attest that the organization is operating within or at an acceptable level of risk.

A well-thought-out and vetted vulnerability management plan will receive input from various business units and all levels of management from within the company. This is especially true when developing a vulnerability management plan for the first time, as information about security is shared across multiple layers of the organization in an attempt to map information security to business risk.

The Six Stages of Vulnerability Management

Establishing a vulnerability management plan is pretty straightforward, but the devil is in the details of your environment. As mentioned earlier, vulnerability management comprises the identification, assessment, remediation, and monitoring of software and hardware vulnerabilities. In total, a vulnerability management plan consists of six stages, as shown in Figure 7.1.

Figure 7.1 Stages of a Vulnerability Management Plan

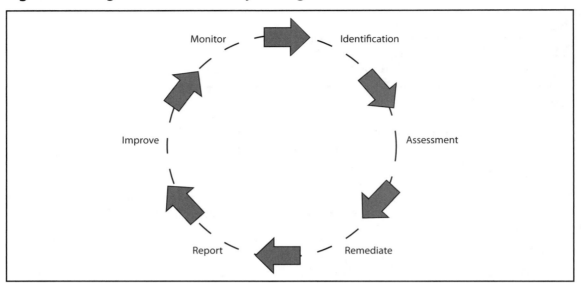

Stage One: Identify

The critical first step in vulnerability management is to identify, check, and track all the information assets attached to your network. Establishing an asset inventory is the first port of call for understanding the "vulnerability terrain." Maintaining an accurate asset database often is unattainable for many companies; however, without an accurate asset inventory, a vulnerability management plan will be severely hampered and possibly doomed to failure. The accuracy of your inventory impacts your ability to know which security alerts are applicable to your environment.

NOTE

Inevitably, you'll forget about some of the technologies in place at your organization, only to stumble across them years later, littering the dark corners of your data centers and closets. Typically, such technologies include machines in development labs, nomadic home/work machines, machines hidden behind a network address translator device, vendor-maintained devices, fax machines, printers, and many other rogue and network-aware devices.

Other, more obscure examples include production machinery (factory robots), supervisory control and data acquisition devices, and medical equipment.
These devices are just as susceptible to vulnerabilities as mainstream technologies are (sometimes they're even more susceptible). Don't discount them!

The types of technologies that you have implemented within your organization map directly back to the types of vulnerabilities present in your environment. Leveraging an accurate asset inventory will help you to ensure that only applicable vulnerability information is processed or considered within your environment.

If you don't already possess an up-to-date asset database, you should leverage the following best practices before creating one:

- Establish a single point of authority for the inventory.

- Identify and document the assets' owners and custodians.

- Establish a process to update the asset management system via inputs and outputs from the change management process.

- Use an asset numbering scheme and consistent abbreviations and notations when entering data.

- Validate the inventory at least annually to ensure its accuracy.

- Ensure that the classification of each asset is recorded (refer to Chapter 1 for asset classification guidance).

- Ensure that the inventory database is extensible, because you might add additional information to the asset record down the road (for example, the last day and time that the asset was assessed for vulnerabilities).

Stage Two: Assess

Having established the list of assets to be assessed, you can now turn your attention to assessing your corporate assets for vulnerabilities. As part of the assessment, you must classify as well as identify the level of criticality each discovered vulnerability represents. Categorizing a vulnerability as having a high, medium, or low level of severity will help you to prioritize your remediation efforts later.

Vulnerability identification is the cornerstone of the vulnerability management process, and we covered it in more detail in Chapter 2. As noted in that chapter, you should make scanning and remediation a priority. You should first assess your highly sensitive, mission-critical systems and line-of-business systems, followed by the rest of the assets within your organization. How you prioritize the remaining assets is subjective, and each company does it differently. You may choose to scan the testing and development environments first, for they represent the organization's next generation of corporate assets, or you could elect to scan all employee desktops. Once again, this is up to you, but you should make sure that whatever process you choose reflects which assets are most important to your organization.

- Before performing your vulnerability assessment, keep these best practices in mind:

- Begin your assessment with the output from your asset inventory system.

- Ensure that you have the authorization to conduct an assessment, and follow appropriate company protocol during the assessment.

- Test new scanners and new vulnerability checks in a lab to identify any false positives, false negatives, and potential service disruptions prior to the assessment.

- Document the assessment methodology. This ensures that the assessment process is consistent and repeatable across the organization.

Stage Three: Remediate

Remediation is a key part of every vulnerability management program. We will cover remediation in more detail in Chapter 9, but it's important to highlight some of the key aspects of it here because it's so integral to your vulnerability management plan.

In the remediation stage, you develop your strategy for remediating the vulnerabilities you've discovered within your environment. This course of action reflects of a combination of technologies, processes, policies, and training. Because vulnerabilities impact the entire organization, this step will typically include multiple business groups. Depending on the breadth of exposure and presented risk, all business units within an organization may hold a level of remediation responsibility and accountability.

To ensure that your remediation efforts are repeatable and sustainable, you should formalize your remediation process. As part of formalizing these efforts, you should also ensure that the organization's most critical assets receive priority. By doing this, you can establish a systematic method by which vulnerabilities are remediated within the organization.

Before remediating any vulnerabilities, you should keep these best practices in mind:

- Consider utilizing a tool or suite of tools that can notify asset owners and custodians of vulnerabilities present on their systems. Otherwise, your teams will have to spend time sending out notification e-mails to users.

- Specific remediation goals may vary based on the criticality of the system. Focus on the highest-risk vulnerabilities present on your most critical assets. For example, some organizations may rely heavily on Web presence as a source of revenue (for instance, an online auction site, an online retail site, etc.). For such organizations, their Internet infrastructure (Web server, applications, back-end systems, and network devices) may have the highest priority.

- Track and measure remediation efforts. You can break out this process by individual, team, or division, depending on whom within your organization is responsible for remediation. Tracking remediation efforts in this manner allows you to analyze efforts, measure them for effectiveness, and track them against agreed-upon goals.

- Work with business units in advance to determine acceptable levels of risks. Get the business units to agree on remediation time frames and have them acknowledge the risks of not remediating vulnerabilities in a timely manner. Having business units sign off on risk helps champion the seriousness of vulnerability management.

Stage Four: Report

As with anything, especially anything within the realm of security, you must be able to attest to the level of effort you've put forth. Vulnerability management reporting provides you with this level of attestation for your vulnerability management program. It also helps you to communicate the importance of vulnerability management throughout the organization. Without such reports, it would be hard to assess the organization's security posture and associated level of risk. Reporting also provides that gap analysis between what is fixed and what needs to be fixed, and you can use it as the tangible asset given to management to measure the success and failure rates of your vulnerability management program.

You can perform the reporting step before the remediation step, but performing it after the remediation step allows you to report on the quick wins. You can use this to demonstrate to management that actions are being taken to mitigate organizational liabilities.

There is a challenge, however, of in balancing vulnerability management reporting against remediation efforts. Without the proper information at the beginning of your program (quantifiably fiscal information and vulnerability statistics), it is difficult to bring vulnerability management full circle. Many organizations, especially those with little or no documentation, will also have problems connecting the right people with the correct vulnerability management reports. When people and assets are aligned, reporting helps you to hold business units and departments accountable for patching and fixing vulnerable hosts; provided you don't have a centralized remediation team.

When you are ready to create your reports, keep these best practices in mind:

- Determine which reports are relevant to your organization's respective lines of business.

- Determine which reports indicate the risk present within the environment.

- Focus your reports on the highest risk vulnerabilities associated with the most critical assets first.

Stage Five: Improve

Whether you've just established your vulnerability management program or have had one for some time, your program probably can stand a little improvement. As part of improving and enhancing your vulnerability management program, you should review the wealth of data collected from each preceding stage and look for opportunities to modify your organization's security policies, practices, or procedures to improve your program's effectiveness and, more important, reduce organizational risk.

Common areas to improve include:

- **Asset management process.**   As mentioned previously, most organizations struggle to maintain an up-to-date asset inventory database. However, maintaining such a database is critical to any vulnerability management program and organizations should strive to accomplish this. In populating your database, you need to decide which assets belong in it and which ones don't. Does an asset you own, but outsource from a monitoring and management perspective, belong in the database? Some companies incorporate these assets into their asset management systems. If you follow this practice, and the asset does become a corporate-managed asset, you need to ensure that its information is input into your corporate database.

- **Configuration management process.**   From time to time, organizations change the tools they use to manage their environments. When such a change occurs in your organization, you need to ensure that your previous tool set is removed from all supported systems and that the system documentation referencing the tools is updated. Doing this has a twofold effect: you reduce your attack surface on your assets because you're removing a tool you no longer need that may possess existing or future vulnerabilities, and you potentially ensure the integrity of your asset management system if you are leveraging your management tool to populate your asset database.

■ **Assessment process.**   Tools used to discover vulnerabilities have changed over the years (accelerated by recent acquisitions and mergers within the security space), and may become less effective and require replacement over time. Because of this, you should pay attention to the process and technology you use to discover vulnerabilities within your environment. As mentioned in Chapter 2, you can leverage configuration, remediation, and security technologies to aid in assessing systems and applications for vulnerabilities. Over time, you may need to rethink and adjust how you leverage these tools for assessment purposes, though.

Stage Six: Monitor

This step involves ascertaining applicable vulnerabilities against your organization's assets. To be effective, monitoring efforts should be proactive. As a regular course of business, security staff should track vulnerabilities through security advisories and vulnerability information sources.

Monitoring consists of more than simply checking security newswires for the latest vulnerabilities and exploits, though. It also entails evaluating security information to determine its applicability within your organization based upon your technology usage and any underlying compensating controls. Evaluating adequate protection and compensating controls, as they relate to the applicability of a vulnerability, is a very time-consuming and potentially arduous task, but it's a vital part of any vulnerability management program.

In Chapter 1, we identified resources of vulnerability information. All vendors of commercial vulnerability management tools embed this information within their products and frequently update their products via functions included within the technology, but reliance on this or any one source for this information is not a sound practice. Often we focus solely on security data pertaining only to the technology our organization consumes, but it's also important to have a general level of understanding for the vulnerabilities present in other platforms or applications because one day, we may be asked to weigh in on the security liabilities of a technology not currently present within our environment.

NOTE

Not every post to a vulnerability disclosure list should cause you to panic and set off the corporate alarms. Eight vulnerabilities, on average, are discovered daily (as of August 2006). Trying to assess each newly announced vulnerability is a waste of time and resources, because only a fraction of new vulnerabilities will actually apply to most organizations.

Monitoring vulnerability data can be challenging due to the sea of information available and the disparate methods by which it is shared. Most organizations find it difficult to manage the breadth of new security information and use it effectively.

However, it can be done. In essence, monitoring is composed of two key steps: collating the new vulnerability information, and communicating the filtered information to the appropriate recipients. In-house or external sources can be responsible for gathering the VA data; internal members generally gather the information from locations such as vendor notices, vulnerability disclosure groups, security groups, and National CERTS (Computer Emergency Response Teams). You then can catalog applicable vulnerabilities according to the systems they affected; you should be able to leverage your current inventory data to draw this correlation. Once you know what systems are subject to each vulnerability, you can communicate this information to the asset owner or custodian. This enables faster and more effective resolution.

Here are some best practices to assist in vulnerability monitoring:

- Centralize the acquisition of vulnerability data/information.

- Disseminate vulnerability data to impacted parties.

- Utilize tools to assist in prioritizing and alerting the organization of vulnerability data.

- Have a process in place to ensure that urgent alerts are sent in a timely manner.

- In situations where patches have not yet been released but vulnerabilities are publicly known, consider the use of other defenses, such as intrusion prevention systems.

- Have security teams and lines of business discuss new vulnerabilities, virus activity, malicious activity, and other important security issues frequently.

Governance (What the Auditors Want to Know)

In light of recent corporate scandals and the security liabilities that are present in our highly connected, highly technology-based world, corporate governance based on IT controls and attestation to such controls is on the radar of every C-level executive these days. If information security wasn't important to organizations in the past, government legislation and industry regulations such as the Sarbanes-Oxley Act, the Gramm-Leach-Bliley Act, the Health Insurance Portability and Accountability Act, and the Payment Card Industry Data Security Standard have brought information security to the forefront.

In response, many organizations have had to reevaluate their approach to IT governance. This review has led to an understanding that information security is not just a technical issue that the CIO's office can address, but rather an issue that the organization's CEO must sponsor and champion throughout the heart of the business and across all lines of business.

When the auditors come knocking, and you know they will, they will be very interested in your vulnerability management program because this program is key to reducing an organization's level of IT risk and protecting the organization's assets. To prepare for the auditors you should ensure the following:

- Appropriate sponsorship and buy-in have been established for the vulnerability management program and associated processes.

- Members from the business, IT, and security groups represent and participate in the program.

- Key stakeholders have been identified and appointed.

- The scope of assets has been appropriately defined.

- Information security policies, standards, and guidelines exist, are documented, and are accessible.

- Risk-based determination and classification of risks exist.

- Roles and responsibilities have been defined, documented, and communicated.

- Effective communication and escalation processes have been documented and communicated.

- The capability to track remediation of vulnerabilities exists.

- A method of quickly identifying new vulnerabilities is available.

- Monitoring controls have been integrated to minimize the impact of vulnerabilities.

- Measurement of the effectiveness of the program has been established.

- Reports are routinely created and distributed to key stakeholders and interested parties.

Measuring the Performance of a Vulnerability Management Program

Measuring the performance of a vulnerability management program is a complicated affair, because there is no definitive process to follow. For example, first measuring the statistics of the vulnerabilities identified during the assessment stage and then measuring the number of vulnerabilities remediated is one form of measurement. Unfortunately, it's not the best form. Nor is measuring the time between when a vulnerability was released to the public and when it was remediated within your organization.

This is because as your vulnerability management program matures, the number of new vulnerabilities capable of impacting your organization should diminish because you have established process and compensating controls to mitigate vulnerabilities, as well as a more mature method of assessing vulnerability risk. Coupled with this, studies show that the number of vulnerabilities released in the coming years is only going to increase. As such, the number of vulnerabilities remediated within your environment is not a meaningful unit of measurement. With the increasing number of vulnerabilities released each year, you should naturally remedy more this year than last, and so on.

Measuring the maturity of a vulnerability management program is a more effective method of determining the current state of your program. Table 7.1 represents a scorecard that you can use to measure the maturity of your vulnerability management program.

Instructions

Score yourself by ticking off the tasks/processes your organization operates and performs. Your score for that section is then the level in which your organization managed to achieve all bullet points. As an example in the first row we have scored our organization at Level 1 despite having an item in Level 2 ticked and have a score of 1.

Table 7.1 Vulnerability Management Program Scorecard

Level 0 (Ad Hoc)	Level 1 (Reactive)	Level 2 (Proactive)	Level 3 (Continuous/ Validated)	Score
IDENTIFICATION AND ASSESSMENT MATURITY				
No process is in place to identify vulnerabilities.	Vulnerabilities are assessed when a vendor releases an announcement. Scanning may occur to determine the extent of the vulnerability.	Mailing lists are monitored for applicable vulnerabilities. Proactive network scanning for vulnerabilities is in place. Loose integration with asset management and infrastructure administration processes exists.	Participate in a National CISRT. Alert service and profiling software are utilized. Proactive network and host vulnerability detection capabilities for critical assets are in place. Medium to tight integration with asset management and infrastructure administration processes are in place.	1
MANAGEMENT MATURITY				
No process is in place to manage the assignment of responsibilities.	High-level policies define the risk model. Little or no documented processes (e.g., call lists) are in place.	Manual processes, review and assess responsibilities Some process documentation exists. Risk classification criteria are predefined.	Vulnerabilities are reviewed and assessed on a periodic basis based on predefined criteria that are tied to business criticality (risk/ asset criticality). Response mechanisms are predefined and automated where appropriate (e.g., alert notifications, etc.).	

Continuted

Table 7.1 Continued

Level 0 (Ad Hoc)	Level 1 (Reactive)	Level 2 (Proactive)	Level 3 (Continuous/ Validated)	Score
APPLICATION MATURITY				
No process is in place for risk the mitigation defined.	Some procedures are defined for some business areas and platforms. Informal linkages to change management exist. Informal reporting on results and metrics is in place. Informal linkages with administration and change management exist.	Formal linkages with change management exist. Application/ deployment target windows are linked to risk classification. Formal reporting on results and metrics exists. Applicability for managed devices exists. Semi-formal linkages to administration and change management exist.	Medium to tight integration with software management processes is in place. Policies for both managed and unmanaged devices are in place. Predefined and automatic (where appropriate) deployment mechanisms are in place. Formal linkages to administration and change management are in place.	
COMPLIANCE MATURITY				
No process is in place to check compliance.	Manual and informal reporting exist. Limited metrics are available.	Formal reporting exists. Technology is used to validate application of patches/fixes; usually through deployment software.	Independent validation on the mitigation of vulnerabilities is performed.	

Table 7.1 Continued

Level 0 (Ad Hoc)	Level 1 (Reactive)	Level 2 (Proactive)	Level 3 (Continuous/ Validated)	Score
MAINTENANCE MATURITY				
No process is in place for updating baselines, standards, and configurations.	Manual, informal, or inconsistent updating of baselines, standards, and configurations exists. Usually based on discovery after deployment.	Update of baselines, standards, and configurations after remediation of vulnerabilities has performed.	Update of baselines, standards, and configurations prior to or in parallel with remediation of vulnerability is performed.	
GOVERNANCE MATURITY				
No policy is in place to address vulnerability management. No executive insight into vulnerability management processes exists.	Executive management has approved vulnerability management policies and processes. Executive management insight into vulnerability management processes is in place.	Exceptions are detected and executives are required to formally sign off on associated risks. Responsibilities are clearly assigned and enforced. Enterprise wide consistency in results of the VM program exists.	Vulnerability management program is benchmarked against others. Tight linkages between objectives of vulnerability management and overall infrastructure administration (e.g., availability, etc.) exist.	

TOTAL

Score total from all six sections.

A score of 12 or more indicates a well-established and practiced vulnerability management program. Anything less than 12 reflects a vulnerability management program that is a little rough around the edges. In such cases, you must tweak your program to align it with what are considered industry best practices.

Common Problems with Vulnerability Management

The term *vulnerability management* has always been misunderstood, because it was never conceived to be a collection of security practices and procedures, all working together. However, after reading this chapter, you should have a better understanding of vulnerability management, its dependencies (e.g., patch management, an accurate asset database, etc.), and how they are interrelated. Vulnerability management poses several challenges and has numerous dependencies, so it should be of no surprise to hear that effective vulnerability management isn't an easy thing for organizations to attain.

Here are some of the problems organizations typically encounter:

- **Problem: Vulnerabilities are not being remediated.** The first and most abundant problem in many organizations is the discovery of vulnerabilities. Assessing assets for vulnerabilities across an enterprise can be a daunting task. Nothing is worse than going through this exercise to discover that the asset owners or the remediation team responsible for remedying the vulnerability hasn't patched the vulnerability or instituted a compensating control.

- **Solution:** Ensure that the entity responsible for remediation is held accountable for the vulnerability. This party must be informally as well as formally responsible for remediation.

- **Problem: Patching is perceived as the vulnerability management panacea.** Patching a vulnerability is not the same as vulnerability management!

- **Solution:** You cannot effectively mitigate many vulnerabilities simply via patching. In some instances, you need to modify policies, processes, and perhaps system configurations to ensure that vulnerabilities are expunged from your environment. Changing the policies and processes that introduced the vulnerability may be the appropriate solution to ensuring the longer-term removal of the vulnerability from your environment. This is a much better solution than the "Patch Tuesday" process of fire fighting.

- **Problem: Failure to prioritize vulnerability information and assets.** Organizations tend to focus on the small and quick remediation wins instead of remediating more critical company assets or focusing on more task-intensive vulnerability management efforts.

- **Solution:** It's important to remediate all unacceptable vulnerabilities within your environment. Instead of focusing only on the test machine at your desk, you should develop a remediation matrix, disseminate it to the appropriate parties, and highlight company assets that need to be remediated in order of importance.

NOTE

It's quite common to hear an end user or asset owner defending the presence of a vulnerability after being audited. "Oh, that's a test machine," or "We are replacing that next week" are typical comments you'll hear from users attempting to justify the existence of a vulnerability. Unfortunately, these are just excuses, because often such vulnerabilities will remain for months, if you allow them to.

Summary

In this chapter, we discussed the elements and aspects of an effective vulnerability management program. We talked about setting goals for the program and the need to get buy-in from senior management. We also highlighted the importance of communication and the inclusion of all parties (lines of business, IT, and security) to the success of a program

As you now know, vulnerability management is composed of six stages: identification, assessment, remediation, reporting, improving, and monitoring. We explained the intricacies of each stage and suggested best practices for each. We also briefly mentioned governance and its impact on a vulnerability management program, as well as the roles which regulations have played in elevating IT governance within corporate America. We gave pointers as to what to expect when the auditors come knocking.

In addition, we detailed how to measure a vulnerability management program and gave examples of how to do this. We also discussed the more effective method of measuring the maturity of a vulnerability management program, and a method for determining the current state of a program. We mentioned that the term *vulnerability management* has always been misunderstood, and that as a result, some common problems often surface. We also provided solutions to these problems.

Vulnerability management is a tough job, and no snake oil will help. Proper vulnerability management requires that you roll up your sleeves and get a little dirty, but once you do, you'll see that establishing or enhancing your organization's vulnerability management program and associated strategy will be well worth the effort.

## Chapter 8

Vulnerability Management Tools

Solutions in this chapter:

- **The Perfect Tool in a Perfect World**
- **Evaluating Vulnerability Management Tools**
- **Commercial Vulnerability Management Tools**
- **Open Source and Free Vulnerability Management Tools**
- **Managed Vulnerability Services**

☑ **Summary**

Introduction

Numerous tools are available to assist with vulnerability management. However, determining which tool(s) to leverage is not easy, because no one product can address all of the aspects of vulnerability management, as we discussed in Chapter 7. Therefore, when deciding which vulnerability management tool(s) to use, it's important that you understand each tool's capabilities, and how the available tools work with each other. In this chapter, we will discuss what to look for when evaluating vulnerability management tools, as well as discuss some of more popular commercial and open source tools available today.

The Perfect Tool in a Perfect World

To determine what to look for in a vulnerability management tool it helps to think about what the perfect tool would offer. The perfect vulnerability management tool would include capabilities for asset management, vulnerability assessment, configuration management, patch management, remediation, reporting, and monitoring, all working well together, and it would integrate well with third-party technologies.

Ideally, the tool's asset management, vulnerability management, and patch management capabilities would work particularly well together, for three reasons. First, asset management represents the foundation of a vulnerability management program. Without a complete and up-to-date asset inventory, your vulnerability management program will be only marginally effective. Therefore, it's critical that your tools leverage this repository for the list of assets represented within your environment.

Second, you're developing a vulnerability management program, so it would be nice if your vulnerability management tools and auxiliary tools could communicate with one another. A primary example is in your vulnerability assessment (VA) scanner leveraging the asset database to obtain the list of devices that are present within your environment. From that list, the VA scanner knows which assets to assess for security liabilities. VA tools are also helpful in developing system configuration baselines within your environment. You can use these baselines later to identify possible weaknesses and points of exposure within your infrastructure.

And third, patching and configuration management are key elements of the remediation process and, more important, of your vulnerability management plan. Understanding which systems are patched, along with their respective configurations, is one thing; but having this information populated within your asset database and being able to extract this data and use it to make informed security decisions is a capability which all security practitioners wish they had.

Notes from the Underground...

Useful Sites: INFOSEC Mailing Lists, Tools, and Information

Here are some rather useful sites for security tools and security mailing lists:

- Tools and mailing lists: www.securityfocus.com
- Tools: packetstormsecurity.nl

- Mailing list: lists.apple.com/mailman/listinfo/security-announce
- Mailing list archives: seclists.org
- Tools and security advisories: www.frsirt.com/english/index.php
- Tools and security advisories: www.microsoft.com/technet/security/

Evaluating Vulnerability Management Tools

Vendors typically market their tools as the panacea for everything; vulnerability management vendors are no exception. Although some products address multiple areas of the vulnerability management life cycle, others attempt to bridge the gap between vulnerability management tools in an effort to provide synergy among products—for example, integrating patch management tools with vulnerability scanners. In the end, no one vendor or solution provides all of the components necessary to support a vulnerability management program.

Prior to deciding upon a tool, you must understand its capabilities as well as its shortcomings. To aid you in this you should consider the following points when evaluating vulnerability management technologies:

- **Asset management.** Does the technology provide an asset inventory database? If so, can you extend the database schema to support additional fields, such as asset classification? If not, can the technology integrate with other asset management repositories?

- **Coverage.** What's the breadth and platform coverage of the technology? Many technologies can perform operations against the Windows family of products, but you'll need technologies that can operate in a heterogeneous environment and can support a variety of platforms, applications, and infrastructure devices.

- **Aggregation of vulnerability data.** Does the product interoperate with other security technologies? Can the product aggregate data from security technologies such as Internet Security Systems' IIS Scanner, Microsoft's MBSA, Tenable Network Security's Nessus, McAfee's Foundstone, eEye's Retina, and Symantec's BindView bvControl? The ability to aggregate data from multiple and disparate sources is key.

- **Third-party vulnerability references.** Is the product Common Vulnerabilities and Exposures (CVE) compliant? Does it identify the source from which it received its information?

- **Prioritization.** Can the tool prioritize remediation efforts?

- **Remediation policy enforcement.** Does the product provide the capability to designate the selected remediation at varying enforcement levels, from mandatory (required) to forbidden (acceptable risk), via a centralized policy-driven interface?

- **Remediation group management.** Does the tool allow for the grouping of systems to manage remediation and control access to devices?

- **Remediation.**   Can you use the product to address vulnerabilities induced by a system misconfiguration as well as vulnerabilities represented by not having the appropriate patch? For example:

    - Patch management, or deploying patches to the operating system or applications

    - Configuration management, or deploying changes to the operating system or application, such as disabling and removing accounts (i.e., accounts with no password, no password expiration, etc.), disabling and removing unnecessary services, and so on

    - The ability to harden services for NetBIOS, anonymous FTP, hosts.equiv, and so on

- **Patch management.**   Does the product include or integrate with existing patch management tools?

- **Distributed patch repository.**   Does the product provide the capability to load balance and distribute the bandwidth associated for patch distribution to repositories installed in various strategic locations?

- **Patch uninstallation support.**   Can the tool report whether a patch was unsuccessful and whether it needs to be reapplied?

- **Workflow.**   Does the product have a workflow system that allows you to assign and track issues? Can it auto-assign tickets based on rule sets defined (i.e., vulnerability, owner, asset classification, etc.)? Can it interface with common corporate workflow products such as BMC Software's Remedy and the Hewlett-Packard HP Service Desk?

- **Usability.**   Can the tool participate in network services with minimal impact to business operations? Is the user interface intuitive?

- **Reporting.**   Does the tool provide reports to determine remediation success rates? Can you use the tool for trending remediation efforts? Is the reporting detailed and customizable?

- **Appliances.**   Is the tool software based or appliance based? Appliances often offer performance and reliability advantages. However, software solutions are more affordable and may be able to run on existing hardware, helping to reduce upfront capital expenditures.

- **Agents.**   Does the application require agents? Is the application capable of leveraging existing agents on the system? If agents are necessary, can you deploy agents to groups of assets simultaneously, to facilitate ease of deployment? Agents generally provide more information on a particular system, but also increase the system's complexity. An ideal application would allow for the collection of system information with or without the use of agents.

- **Configuration standards.**   Does the technology possess predefined security configuration templates that you can use to assess the system? Some products have defined operating system standards and are able to perform reporting based on defined templates to support some regulatory requirements (e.g., Sarbanes-Oxley, HIPAA, and the ISO/IEC 27000 series).

- **Vulnerability research.**   Does the vendor have its own vulnerability research team? Does the vendor actively participate in the security community through the identification and release of security vulnerabilities? Does the vendor practice responsible disclosure? Does the vendor release checks for vulnerabilities it has discovered prior to the OEM remediating the vulnerability? How has the vendor responded to vulnerabilities in its own products?

- **Vulnerability updates.**   How frequently does the vendor release updates? How are the updates distributed? Does the distribution mechanism leverage industry-recognized security communications protocols?

- **Interoperability.**   Can the application integrate into existing patch management, configuration management, and/or monitoring tools and services?

Note that the items in the preceding list aren't applicable to all vulnerability technologies. We presented a germane list of points that apply to the collection of tools which support a vulnerability management program.

Commercial Vulnerability Management Tools

The vulnerability management space is changing frequently due to mergers, acquisitions, and new partnerships. In the remainder of this section, we will discuss some of the vendors that offer solutions in this space.

eEye Digital Security

www.eEye.com

eEye Digital Security is a leader in vulnerability research. It also develops a suite a tools that can assist you in vulnerability management. The suite consists of the Retina Network Security Scanner (a vulnerability assessment tool), Blink Professional (a host-based security technology), and the REM Security Management Console. The management console provides the centralized management interface for the company's other products. It also handles vulnerability management workflow, asset classification, and threat-level reporting, and it can integrate with CA's UniCenter, IBM's Tivoli, and HP's OpenView.

Symantec (BindView)

www.bindview.com

BindView's Compliance Manager is a software-based solution which allows organizations to evaluate their assets against corporate standards or industry best practices, without the need for agents in most cases. Assets are evaluated against standards and practices based on a pass/fail notion; either an asset is compliant or it's not. Data is then aggregated and assembled to produce reports that the remtediation team can leverage to support their efforts, or the internal audit group can use for compliance issues. You also can use the reports generated to support other initiatives.

As mentioned, you can evaluate assets against internal standards or to industry best practices. The industry standards included are CIS Level 1 and Level 2 Benchmarks for Windows, Red Hat Linux, BindView's Security Essentials for Sun Solaris, and NetWare. In addition to these standards, the Compliance Manager also provides Report Views for the following regulations and frameworks: ISO 17799, Sarbanes-Oxley based on COBIT, FISMA based on NIST SP 800-53, HIPAA, Basel II, and GLBA.

The Compliance Manager does not include its own workflow capability, but it does provide an interface that allows users to open incidents in Remedy and HP Service Desk. In addition, leveraging its bvControl technology, BindView is capable of delivering patch and configuration management to Windows hosts.

Attachmate (NetIQ)

www.netiq.com

NetIQ's Compliance suite, a combination of NetIQ's Security Manager and Vulnerability Manager tools, brings together vulnerability scanning, patch management, configuration remediation, and reporting. The NetIQ Vulnerability Manager enables users to define and maintain configuration policy templates, vulnerability bulletins, and automated checks via AutoSync technology. It also has the capability to evaluate systems against those policies. Predefined templates are available for Sarbanes-Oxley, HIPAA, and ISO/IEC 27000. These allow you to report and score your information systems against these standards.

The Compliance suite also supports a classification system that allows you to adjust risk scores based upon the asset's classification. The NetIQ suite also looks for common signs of system compromise, such as modified Registry keys and known malicious files, and it has an OEM relationship with Shavlik to provide integrated patch management.

StillSecure

www.stillsecure.com

StillSecure is the manufacturer of VAM, an integrated suite of security products that perform vulnerability management, endpoint compliance monitoring, and intrusion prevention and detection. It also includes a built-in workflow solution (Extensible Vulnerability Repair Workflow) which automatically performs assignment of repairs, scheduling, life cycle tracking, and repair verification, all while maintaining detailed device histories.

VAM interoperates with other third-party scanners too, taking input from Nessus, the ISS Internet Scanner, Harris STAT, and others. Enterprises may want to be wary regarding VAM, because its reporting module is not as well refined as the other vendors' and it relies on third-party information and integration for asset management, patch management, and vulnerability resolution.

McAfee

www.mcafee.com

McAfee's Foundstone Enterprise is an agentless solution that offers asset discovery, inventory, and vulnerability prioritization with threat intelligence, correlation, remediation tracking, and reporting. It integrates with McAfee's IntruSheild network-based intrusion prevention system (IPS), McAfee's Preventsys Compliance Auditor, and other vulnerability and trouble-ticket management systems. One of its more appealing features is its SSH credentialed scans for Red Hat Enterprise, Solaris, AIX, Microsoft Windows, and to the surprise of many, Cisco IOS!

Compliance templates for Sarbanes-Oxley, FISMA, HIPAA, BS7799/ISO17799, and the Payment Card Industry (PCI) standard are included, expediting the preparation of audits. Foundstone Enterprise can also auto-assign tickets, streamlining and simplifying the remediation process.

Open Source and Free Vulnerability Management Tools

The open source community has created some great security tools over the years. However, none of them represents a complete vulnerability management solution. In some cases, though, the open source tools integrate well together, forming a formable foe to the commercial offerings.

In the following sections, we cover open source tools that you can use to support your vulnerability management program.

Asset Management, Workflow, and Knowledgebase

One tool we recommend in this space is Information Resource Manager (IRM), available at http://irm.stackworks.net. IRM is a powerful Web-based asset tracking and trouble-ticket system built for information technology (IT) departments and help desks. All elements are interwoven into a seamless Web application, with a MySQL engine at the back end doing the heavy lifting.

Host Discovery

For host discovery, NMAP (www.insecure.org) is a free, open source utility for network exploration or security auditing. It was designed to rapidly scan large networks, although it works fine against single hosts. NMAP uses raw Internet Protocol (IP) packets in novel ways to determine what hosts are available on the network, what services (application name and version) those hosts are offering, what operating systems (and versions) they are running, what type of packet filters/firewalls are in use, along with dozens of other characteristics. NMAP runs on most types of computers and both command-line and graphical versions are available.

Vulnerability Scanning and Configuration Scanning

Nessus, from Tenable Network Security (www.tennable.com), is a tool for vulnerability scanning and configuration scanning. The Nessus Project was started by Renaud Deraison in 1998 to provide the Internet community with a free, powerful, up-to-date, and easy-to-use remote security scanner. Nessus is the best free network vulnerability scanner available, and the best to run on UNIX at any price. It is constantly updated (more than 11,000 plug-ins are available for as a free feed), but registration and EULA acceptance are required. Key features include remote and local (authenticated) security checks, client/server architecture with a GTK graphical interface, and an embedded scripting language for writing your own plug-ins or understanding the existing ones.

Nessus 3 is now closed source, but it is still free unless you want the very newest plug-ins. If you decide to rely on only Nessus for vulnerability scanning, consider also choosing a product that can manage and schedule scans, such as Tenable Security's Security Center product (www.tenablesecurity.com).

Configuration and Patch Scanning

Microsoft's Baseline Security Analyzer (MBSA) is an easy-to-use tool designed for the IT professional that helps small and medium-size businesses determine their security state in accordance with Microsoft security recommendations, as well as offers specific remediation guidance. Built on the Windows Update Agent and Microsoft Update infrastructure, MBSA ensures consistency with other Microsoft management products including Microsoft Update (MU), Windows Server Update Services (WSUS), Systems Management Server (SMS), and Microsoft Operations Manager (MOM). MBSA on average scans more than 3 million computers each week! For more information, visit www.microsoft.com.

Vulnerability Notification

Advchk (Advisory Check), available at http://advchk.unixgu.ru, reads security advisories so that you don't have to. Advchk gathers security advisories using RSS feeds, compares them to a list of known services, and alerts you if you are vulnerable. Because adding hosts and services by hand would be a boring task, Advchk leverages NMAP for automatic service and version discovery.

Also available in this space is SIGVI (http://sigvi.sourceforge.net). This product is a recent release but could be a promising solution if maintained and developed further. SIGVI downloads vulnerabilities from defined sources, stores them to a database, and then compares them to the products currently installed on the assets (as previously defined in the main application).

The application is flexible in the way that it lets you define your own sources. By default, the application supports the NVD (National Vulnerability Database at http://nvd.nist.gov) format. Periodically, the application will contact the sources, download the vulnerabilities, and store them into the SIGVI database. Those vulnerabilities are then available through the pages of the SIGVI main window.

Security Information Management

Ossim (www.ossim.org) stands for Open Source Security Information Management. Innately a SIM, OSSIM does incorporate several aspects of vulnerability management and over time should become a more comprehensive and complete vulnerability management tool. OSSIM's goal is to provide a comprehensive compilation of tools which, when working together, grant a network/security administrator a detailed view of the network and devices.

Besides getting the best out of open source tools, some of which are described in the following list, OSSIM provides a strong correlation engine, detailed reporting, and incident management tools. Here is a list of open source tools that integrate with OSSIM:

- **Arpwatch.**   Used for Media Access Control (MAC) address anomaly detection.
- **P0f.**   Used for passive operating system detection and operating system change analysis.
- **Pads.**   Used for service anomaly detection.

- **Nessus.**   Used for vulnerability assessment and cross-correlation (IDS versus Security Scanner).

- **Snort.**   An IDS, used for cross-correlation with Nessus.

- **Spade.** A statistical packet anomaly detection engine, used to gain knowledge about attacks without a signature.

- **Tcptrack.**   Used to gather session data information that can provide useful information for attack correlation.

- **Ntop.**   A network usage tool that builds an impressive network database from which you can derive aberrant and anomalous behavior.

- **Nagios.**   Monitors host and service availability information.

- **Osiris.**   A great host-based intrusion detection system (HIDS).

Managed Vulnerability Services

Many organizations have elected to outsource the challenging task of vulnerability management; if not in total, certainly in parts. Outsourcing a vulnerability management program can help you to reduce head count, administrative overhead, and equipment and personnel expenses. However, before you get too excited about the advantages of outsourcing vulnerability management, you need to keep in mind that an effective outsourced solution is going to be based in part on how well you've defined your requirements.

Tired and weary veterans of outsourcing know that clear and concise service-level agreements (SLAs), which have been drafted in conjunction with legal counsel, represent the foundation of all outsourcing relationships and aid in remedying issues that arise during the term of a contract.

NOTE

One mistake people often make is to believe that business risk is transferred when you outsource a portion of your security program, such as vulnerability management. However, risk is not transferable. Organizations remain responsible, even when their operations are completely outsourced, although they may shift the financial liability to the third party. With that said, it's critical to assess a provider's financial stability when considering outsourcing.

When leveraging a third party to support all or part of your vulnerability management program you should consider the following:

- **Escalation procedures.**   Ensure that escalation procedures exist and communication processes are defined. Also ensure that ownership is well documented and agreed upon in writing by both parties.

- **Data access.**   Ensure that you have access to the data that the outsourcer is collecting. Many times an outsourcer will collect data from your assets, but won't provide you with access to the data. You could use this data to better ascertain risk within your environment, and it could help you to make appropriate risk-based decisions. If the outsourcer doesn't allow you access to your data, you should think twice before signing the contract. Also, it is important that you understand how the outsourcer shares your data within its ownorganization. Is your data privy to everyone who works for the outsourcer?

- **The toolset.**   Before selecting a vendor, you should confirm which products the vendor uses, and why. There may be a conflict between the vendor's tools and yours, or the vendor may simply be using inferior technology to support your operations.

- **Metrics.**   How will the provider be evaluated/measured? It is important that you ensure that these metrics are clearly defined. Depending on the level of service the outsourcer is providing, the metrics used to evaluate the outsourcer may be different; for example, if the provider is providing path management, how long does the provider have before it must patch all of the assets it manages? You should define, understand, and clearly agree upon these metrics up front.

Summary

In Chapter 7, we discussed the methodology behind vulnerability management. In this chapter, we discussed what an ideal vulnerability tool features, although we know and understand why such a tool doesn't exist. However, as we discussed, some vendors are getting close to delivering complete solutions in this comparatively new discipline in information security.

We briefly discussed some of the players, but gave no suggestions regarding the pros and cons of the tools because there is no one tool that fits all the requirements of an organization. Although the open source community has a wealth of great tools available, there isn't one tool that supports all of the facets of vulnerability management; rather, there are bits and pieces scattered among many authors.

To close out the chapter, we discussed some of the pros and cons of leveraging an outsourcer to manage parts of a vulnerability management program. It's conceivable, and many organizations do it, but it's imperative to put in place some serious guidelines and detailed service-level agreements beforehand to ensure that no one becomes disappointed with the delivery of the service.

## Chapter 9

Vulnerability and Configuration Management

Solutions in this chapter:

- **Patch Management**
- **Building a Patch Test Lab**
- **Patch Distribution and Deployment**
- **Configuration Management**
- **Change Control**

☑ **Summary**

Introduction

Dealing effectively with vulnerabilities in today's networks includes not only managing and dealing with the vulnerability process itself, but also integrating the previous approach toward vulnerability assessment (leveraging scanners to discovery vulnerabilities) into the correlative frameworks and processes of patch management, configuration management, and change control. This chapter focuses on these frameworks and processes. Understanding what these processes are, their similarities and differences, and how they integrate with the vulnerability life cycle is essential to pulling an effective vulnerability management program together.

Patch Management

Why patch a system? This question can seem rather remedial in nature, but it is certainly a valid question. Far too often our answer is, "Because the vendor said to." You should never patch a system unless it is absolutely necessary; otherwise, causing system instability is well within the realm of possibility. Patching a system is as much an art as it is a science. There are numerous reasons why you may want to patch a system, but patches are generally applied to do the following:

- Enable new functionality
- Mitigate discovered vulnerabilities or security risks
- Fix stability issues

Patches can be software or hardware related, and the results of one patch can often affect the operation of both the primary and secondary functions of another patch. One common example that is often overlooked is the upgrade of a system's BIOS. Functions or features enabled (or re-enabled) in the system BIOS can have widespread consequences from the operating system perspective. Let's look at the release notes for a common BIOS upgrade available from Dell, remembering that each BIOS upgrade is a "roll-up" of previous fixes and changes. So if you are going from A07 BIOS revision to A09, all of the fixes/changes introduced in A08 will also be present.

```
BIOS Release Notes

Systems: OptiPlex GX110
Version: A09
Release Date: 01-22-2003


The following changes have been made to BIOS rev A08 to create A09:


1. Fix LPT code for HP All-in-one printers

BIOS Release Notes

Systems: OptiPlex GX110
Version: A08
Release Date: 08-30-2001
```

The following changes have been made to BIOS rev A07 to create A08:

1. ESCD is cleared when asset tag PASS:xx/xx changes.

2. Added ability to turn the USB controller on and off in setup.

3. Updated selectable boot capability. When a device is removed its place in the boot list is saved in case it is ever readded.

4. Updated some CPU microcodes.

5. Added BBS calling interface to SMBIOS.

6. During NVRAM updates the reset and power buttons are now disabled.

7. Added support for 48-bit LBA disk drives.

8. System now beeps when CTRL-ALT-F10, or F12 is pressed

9. Fixed a few potential Plug & Play configuration errors.

10. Added a fix to allow certain cards (PERC/3) to work properly.

11. IRQ 12 is now reserved.

From the release notes listed here, several of these changes could potentially impact our system from the operating system perspective—most notably, number 2: "Added ability to turn the USB controller on and off in setup." This particular addition to the BIOS can also play an important role in the mitigation process if a patch for a related vulnerability is not available. Figure 9.1 shows the typical life cycle of a patch. Patches are issued, tested, deployed, and superseded, and eventually reach an end-of-life. When an operating system reaches end-of-life, patches typically stop being issued by an OEM, although it is often possible to obtain them for a substantial fee.

Figure 9.1 The Life Cycle of a Patch

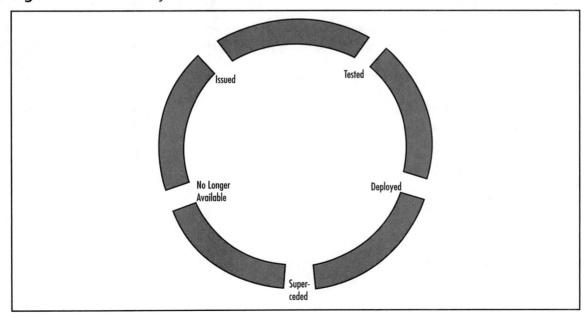

Perhaps one of the most crucial components of a vulnerability management framework lies in the establishment of a patch management program. Figure 9.2 shows a rudimentary patch management process. This much-simplified, scaled-down process consists of steps involving system classification, system inventory, and the Patch Management Tracking System (PMTS), which all interoperate with the change control and testing and deployment mechanisms.

For smaller organizations and companies just starting to implement a comprehensive vulnerability management program, this simplified approach can often yield fairly satisfactory results with a low margin of error, and it directly compliments the more in-depth approach we'll cover later in this chapter.

Figure 9.2 A Rudimentary Patch Management Program

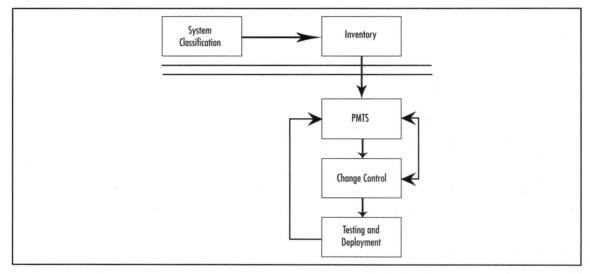

A more common patch management process (shown in Figure 9.3) typically has many moving parts to it. As you can see, there are many components to an effective patch management framework. This is the preferred framework for enterprise use, and in this chapter we'll cover each component in detail.

A patch management framework consists of the following:

- System inventories
- System classification
- System baselines
- Notification
- Mitigation
- Policy
- Prioritization
- Research and testing
- Distribution and deployment
- Logging and reporting

Figure 9.3 A More Common Patch Management Process

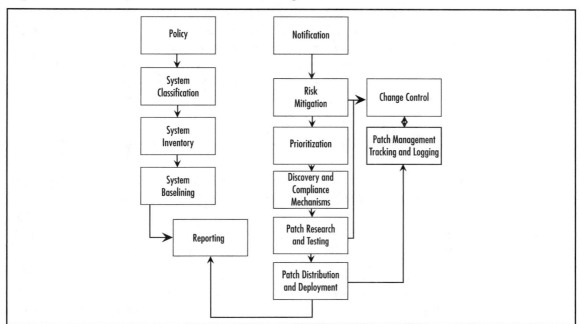

System Inventories

A *system inventory* is a process used to garner as much available information about a system as possible. Remember Y2K? This was probably the last time that many organizations conducted a full system inventory. Your vulnerability discovery process will no doubt assist in garnering a plethora of information about your systems, but additional information is essential to successfully integrating this into your patch management framework. You often can collect a wealth of information, but it's entirely possible in some cases that you can collect *too much* information. As is the general rule with log information, you should never collect more information than you can possibly hope to use or interpret. That having been said, the following elements are typically collected in a system inventory:

- **The system name and physical location.**   This is a "no-brainer." The primary reason you need this information is that different patch standards could exist due to language packs and other local settings that may not be evident at first glance.

- **The operating systems and applications, including versions.**

- **Existing patch levels.**   In order to be effective in the following steps, it is imperative that you understand what patch level (if any) the system state is currently in. Some vendors require some patches to be applied in a certain order; deviating from that order can result in an inoperable system.

- **System owner and contact information.**   You often can obtain this information by enumerating the user accounts on the system, the system's NetBIOS name, or the user profiles stored on the system.

- **Services running and open ports.**

- **Proximity in relation to other systems.**   The primary reason you need this information is so that you can derive a more accurate picture as to relative risks to the environment. If the system is contained or isolated by network segmentation, the risk factor and weight can be lower. In Chapter 8, we covered several tools that can assist in this regard. Another tool that is free (but unfortunately is no longer being maintained) is Cheops, available at www.marko.net/cheops.

- **Open shares.**   Open shares create an avenue for worm propagation.

- **BIOS revision.**   As stated previously, your system BIOS revision can have a significant impact on your overall risk.

- **Processor type.**   In the case of patches that have stringent hardware requirements, this is a must-have. There are also patches that are processor dependent—for example, RISC versus x86.

- **Network information.**   This includes Internet Protocol (IP) and Media Access Control (MAC) addresses, single or dual homed, manufacturer name, and adjustable properties.

As we've discussed here, a full system inventory should consist not only of existing patches, but also of all installed applications, dependencies, and correlations to other programs. The GDI+ vulnerability in Microsoft products and most MSDE vulnerabilities are prime examples of why you need this data.

For your first baseline you shouldn't worry so much about getting everything, as this will expand and the amount of detail and accuracy will improve over time. You should break down these inventories into independent categories within the individual system role inventory for easier management. Common examples of this include "Productivity Application" (such as Microsoft Office or Open Office), "BIOS/Firmware," "Operating System," "Network Application" (such as DNS and NTP), "Web Application," "Database," and so on.

System Classification

System classification is defined as the classification of systems based upon their particular function in the enterprise. As you can see in Figure 9.4, you can divide systems into three major categories: devices, servers, and desktops. You can get as granular with these classifications as you want, but for a first pass at classification it is suggested that you keep it simple and add one classification at a time. The key to setting an effective classification for a system is to find the common denominator with them. Within your classifications, you should also assign roles that these systems play within their given classification. In this example, we have assigned the roles of "Web," "Database," and "Application" within the Server classification. Given our environment we could easily classify "Infrastructure" as another classification for domain controllers, domain name system (DNS), print servers, and so on.

Figure 9.4 Classification of Systems

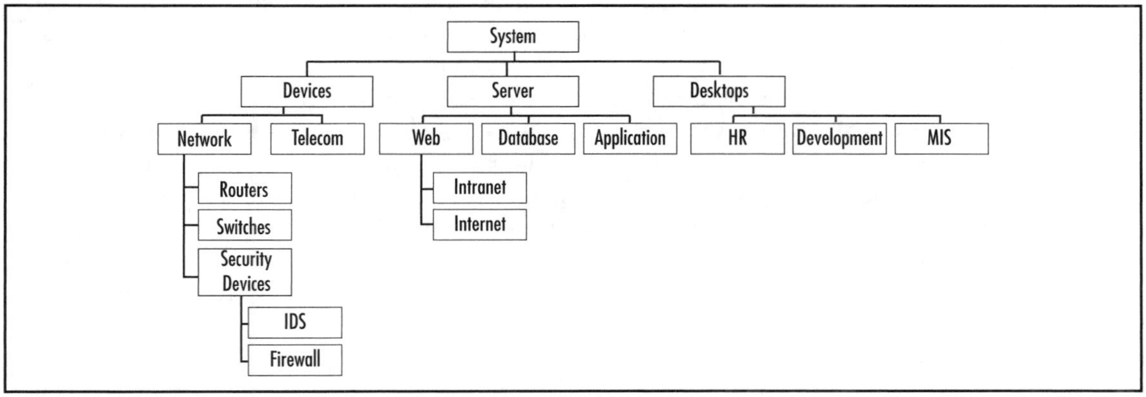

You may be asking, "What is the importance of classifying systems and assigning roles?" The answer to this question is fairly simple. You assign classifications and roles to systems for some of the following reasons:

- **It makes it easier to assign risk weight.** Not all vulnerabilities will have the same weight (or priority) assigned to them. Some influences on vulnerability weighting include your overall risk classification scheme, the timeline for testing and deployment, and your particular business model. For instance, if your company is an application service provider, those systems supporting your application service provider's services would more likely have a higher weight and priority assigned to them than systems which are used only internally.

- **Different risks are associated with different system types.** A Microsoft Word vulnerability may not impact your SQL servers, for instance, but if the patch happens to be a core operating systems patch, it may come up flagged as "missing." Knowing what risk is acceptable for what given length of time will assist you immensely in your patch research, testing, and deployment cycles.

- **It assists in identifying and assigning priority based in part upon system roles.** System roles are a key part of the classification process and you should not overlook them. You have to define the system's role in order to fully understand its operational impact on your organization, as well as the potential impact on the systems around it. A GPO locking vulnerability would be applicable to the classification mentioned previously as "Infrastructure" and to the role of Domain Controller.

System Baselines

What is *patch management baselining*? In a nutshell, patch management baselining is the common fundamental frame of tested and deployed patches for a given device which meet established levels of acceptable security risk. In other words, this is the minimum acceptable patch level of any given system or device. Baselining enacts a forward-moving starting point for patch testing, deployment, and maintenance. If you have never performed a patch baseline you can start either from scratch with a bare operating system, or "as is" with an existing system. You should bear in mind that an existing system will prove to be more time consuming and complex in the way of system inventory and risk classification. A bare-bones system will allow you more flexibility in documenting the system fully, and allow you to test the functional impact of patches as you move forward.

Why establish baselines? In order to have an effective patch management strategy for your enterprise, it is important that you have a way to measure progress and implement changes that *minimally* impact the operation of systems across the enterprise. Every patch in existence alters the system or device in some fashion, even though the results may not be readily apparent to the naked eye. A baseline helps with a "roll back" as well as a "move forward." Just because a patch was released, it doesn't necessarily mean that it is needed and *must* be deployed. Mitigation should *always* precede patching as a first line of defense, but patching is a necessary "evil" for a healthy security posture.

Creating a Baseline

Now that we've defined what a baseline is and laid out some key areas contained within the process, let's put this all together in a quick, step-by-step formation of a simple baseline on a base operating system installation, briefly explaining each step:

1. **Assign system roles.**   You should assign system roles to each system in your environment so that you can make an "apples to apples" comparison of specific baselines. This comparison can help you identify where deficiencies lie in regard to existing patch management policy and where patches can be deployed in a more expeditious manner the next time the same conditions exist. The system roles probably will not change, but exposure and priority may. A role is generally assigned to a system based on its particular function in the enterprise, and its relationship to the systems around it. A simple network diagram will often tell you the number and type of roles that already exist in your environment.

2. **Inventory individual systems.**   Inventory and document all of the packages and applications installed on a system or device. You should store these results in a spreadsheet or database for easier correlation and comparison to the same system roles later. From this you can derive your inventory matrix of approved applications. Inventory the systems for current patch levels compared to what is currently available from the vendor. Plenty of patch management tools and vulnerability assessment (VA) scanners are available to help you collect this information; we covered many of them in Chapter 8.

3. **Evaluate vulnerability/patch applicability.**   Decide whether the patch or vulnerability is applicable to the system at this point in time, and consider the consequences of someone (or something) being able to change the state of the system that would affect applicability. One example of this would be the vulnerability listed in Microsoft Security Bulletin MS02-028, "Heap Overrun in HTR Chunked Encoding Could Enable Web Server Compromise (Q321599)." If you do not have *.htr* mapped on your Web server, you will not be immediately affected, and you could consider the patch to be "not applicable." However, if someone were to enable *.htr* mapping on that particular Web server, the system would be placed in a vulnerable state.

4. **Evaluate level of exposure.**   Based on factors such as system placement and available access to untrusted or semitrusted systems and users, you can get a good idea of a system's exposure level to a given vulnerability for which a patch has been released:

a. **Internal.**   Internally accessible systems generally have a lower risk value in relation to border or external systems due to internal users being granted a certain degree of trust to participate on the network in the first place.

b. **External.**   External systems are border area systems accessible to any extent to anyone outside your network. Web, e-mail and DNS servers and firewalls are all examples of external systems.

c. **Bridged.**   are systems or devices that can connect to any external resources. If your users have Internet access via browser, instant messaging, FTP, and so on, this is a prime example of bridged access. Remote/virtual private network (VPN) users and proxy servers are other examples. Bridged is typically the highest risk of the three exposure classifications outlined here.

5. **Timing.**

a. **Exploit or virus available that uses vulnerability/required patch.**   If a virus, or exploit code, has been released to the general public using an existing vulnerability, this will often change patch applicability and affect your baseline.

b. **time to complete deployment of patch.**   If the system is going to remain vulnerable for a period outside what is considered acceptable for the exposure level, this will obviously affect your future baseline. You should flag this patch and document it as a follow-up item, as well as add it to the baseline once you can test it properly. An example of this would be a patch that you can apply, but that you cannot enable until you reboot the system at a later date.

6. **Risk weight/priority.**   you have evaluated the preceding factors, you can assign a weight/priority to each patch to add to your baseline. Some organizations prefer to use a numeric rating system (e.g., 1–5), and others prefer to keep with Microsoft's ratings of "Low," "Moderate," "Important," and "Critical."

Baseline Example

Having a better understanding of the components and interdependencies of a patch management framework, you can now look back at Figure 9.2 with a greater appreciation and understanding. Say, for instance, that the first patch you look at for addition to your base operating system configuration happens to be an Internet Explorer vulnerability for which Microsoft released a patch labeled "Critical." What should you do? Based on what we've covered thus far, you should leverage the following steps to understand the overall risk the vulnerability presents:

1. After researching the impact, you determine that for this vulnerability to work, it requires user intervention and administrative rights on the applicable system. Looking at Figure 9.2 you determine that the systems that have Internet Explorer installed and are used most frequently with elevated rights are the MIS systems and possibly some developer systems. Although other systems have Internet Explorer installed by default, your policy and practices prohibit the use of Internet Explorer on the other systems (Web, DB, Application, Infrastructure, etc.). You assign a risk weight of "2".

2. Comparing this to your recent system inventory and scan reports, you determine that all desktops do not already have this patch applied. A few MIS folks updated some of the

systems via automatic updates, but most of the systems do not have this patch. You do not assign a weight to this item.

3.   All systems are internally placed, but have external Internet access via Internet Explorer. No other Web browser is used on these systems, so the vulnerability is applicable. You assign a risk weight of "3".

4.   You look at your exposure classifications, and see that all desktops can be classified as "bridged". This raises the risk factor. You assign a risk weight of "3".

5.   Exploit code is currently available. However, antivirus and content management can help mitigate the overall risk. Patch installation requires reboot, which is not an issue with desktop systems. You assign a risk weight of "4".

6.   The total risk weight assigned based on the preceding factors is 12 out of 20. Your patch management policy states that any patch with an applicable risk weight or priority score of 14 or better should be added to the patch baseline. This one falls a bit short.

7.   Lather, rinse, and repeat for each patch that is not in your baseline.

8.   When you think you've reached the end of the available list of patches (and this will take a lot of research initially), you now have your baseline.

The Common Vulnerability Scoring System

The Common Vulnerability Scoring System (CVSS; www.first.org/cvss) is a joint initiative started by CERT/CC, Cisco, DHS/MITRE, eBay, Internet Security Systems, Microsoft, Qualys, and Symantec to assign universal numeric risk ratings on reported vulnerabilities. It uses a fairly flexible approach toward classification and numeric risk weight assignment, and it works well within the patch management framework discussed here. Figure 9.5 shows an example. Here you can see three vulnerabilities and their relative scores of severity, as calculated by the CVSS scoring methods. CVSS scoring is based on a number of metrics explained fully at www.first.org/cvss/cvss-guide.html.

Figure 9.5 Vulnerability Scoring Worksheet

Common Vulnerability Scoring System (CVSS) Version 0.2

Vulnerability	Microsoft Outlook Express Scripting vulnerability	Microsoft LSASS vulnerability	BGP potential DOS
CVE number	CAN-2004-0380	CAN-2004-0533	CAN-2004-0569
URL			

Base Metrics	Access Vector	REMOTE	REMOTE	REMOTE
	Access Complexity	HIGH	LOW	HIGH
	Authentication	NOT-REQUIRED	NOT-REQUIRED	NOT-REQUIRED
	Confidentiality Impact	COMPLETE	COMPLETE	NONE
	Integrity Impact	COMPLETE	COMPLETE	NONE
	Availability Impact	COMPLETE	COMPLETE	COMPLETE
	Impact Bias	NORMAL	NORMAL	AVAILABILITY
	BASE SCORE	**8.0**	**10.0**	**4.0**
Temporal Metrics	Exploitability	FUNCTIONAL	FUNCTIONAL	UNPROVEN
	Remediation Level	OFFICIAL-FIX	OFFICIAL-FIX	UNAVAILABLE
	Report Confidence	CONFIRMED	CONFIRMED	CONFIRMED
	TEMPORAL SCORE	**6.6**	**8.3**	**3.4**

Collateral Damage Potential	NONE	NONE	NONE
Target Distribution	HIGH	HIGH	HIGH
ENVIRONMENTAL SCORE	**6.6**	**8.3**	**3.4**

Creating a baseline is not a complicated process, but it does require attention to detail, process methodology, accountability, planning, and hindsight. It is important that you continually evaluate additions to your baseline to keep your systems on an even keel. It's not as important *what* tools you use to assist you in establishing your baseline, but it *is* important that you understand the process methodology, and the variables that drive the processes.

Building a Patch Test Lab
Establish a Patch Test Lab with "Sacrificial Systems"

Ideally, your Patch Test Lab will have one copy of every mission-critical system in a similar isolated networked environment. Obviously, this could get quite expensive from a hardware perspective, and it is often not within the realm of possibility, with today's technology and security budgets being as lean as they are. The average security budget in the mid-market sector, for example, is roughly 2% to 5% of the overall technology budget. In order to meet your goals, therefore, you must often improvise and use the solutions that are available, being creative at times. As a result, one of the best strategies for your test lab can be the use of simulation. The two key concepts we'll cover here briefly include:

- Using virtualization
- Using environmental simulation programs

Another way that you can accomplish this is to take a sampling of actual live systems on your network to use for testing. Some organizations are large enough to have systems or users that can be interrupted on an occasional basis, and although this isn't the best way to do things in a world of tight budget constraints for both cash and time, it is sometimes the only choice.

Let's jump back to the better way to do things and talk about how, if you had the time and budget, you could really do things right.

Virtualization

We've all heard of VMware, and even Microsoft has jumped on the virtualization bandwagon with Microsoft Virtual PC. Disk space and memory are relatively cheap these days, so setting up a lab with virtual systems may be just what the doctor ordered for fast, easy, and cheap testing of patch management scenarios.

Figure 9.6 shows a screenshot of the VMware Server Console. The VMware Server is available for download at www.vmware.com/download/server. It is completely free and it allows you to take a snapshot of a system so that you can roll back to any previous image at any time. You can create a virtual network of interconnected devices, test the results of your patching, and then roll back to either your baseline image or any deviation. Backing up theses images is as easy as including the VMware image directories in your backup plan.

In the example shown in Figure 9.6, you can see Checkpoint's Secure Platform version R60, a Windows XP Professional system, a BEA Weblogic 8.1 SP4 server, and an IBM DB2 server running SUSE. All of these images and a number of others (except Windows XP) are available for download free of charge on VMware's Virtual Appliance page, located at www.vmware.com/vmtn/appliances. Figure 9.7 illustrates VMWorkstation 5.0's Snapshot Manager, where you can manage your rollbacks.

Figure 9.6 VMware Server Console

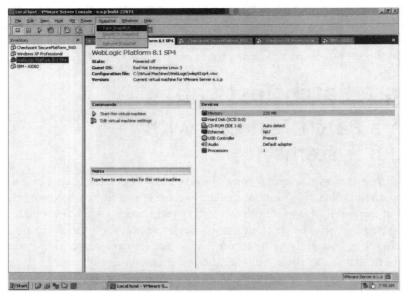

Figure 9.7 VMware Snapshot Manager

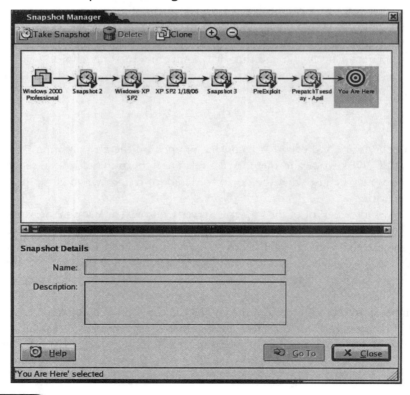

Environmental Simulation

Environmental simulation programs such as Karalon's Traffic IQ Pro and RedSeal's Security Risk Manager (SRM) can also be extremely helpful in your lab environment for inspecting traffic conditions that may be induced by system changes in real time, and you can use them to replay certain exploits in order to test that vulnerabilities are fully remediated. One of the really cool things about these products is that you don't necessarily need to have the actual routing and networking devices in the environment, just the configuration files. When used with the virtualization technique just described, you can simulate nearly any condition that could present itself in a production environment. Figures 9.8 and 9.9 show RedSeal's SRM solution.

Figure 9.8 RedSeal's Threat Graph

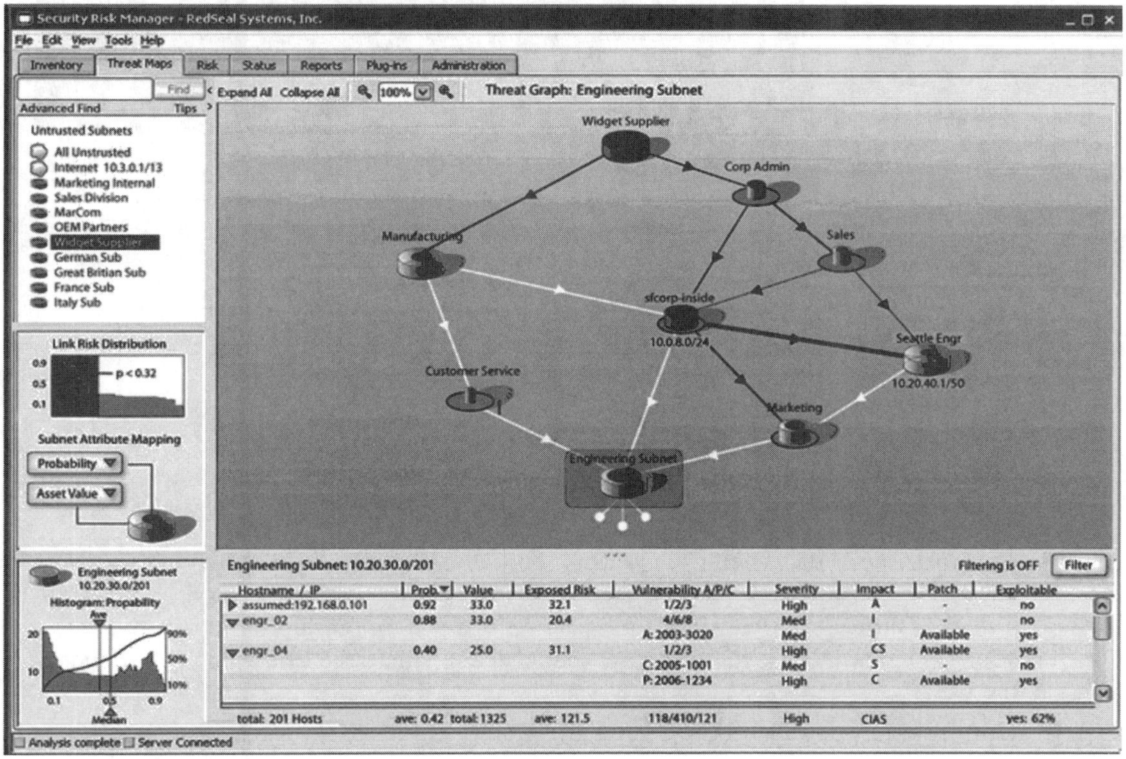

Figure 9.9 RedSeal's Risk Trend Virtualization

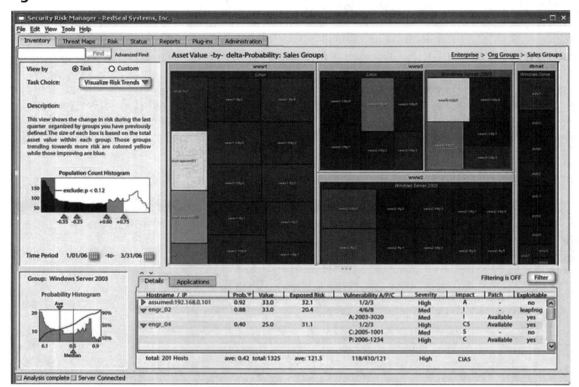

Your fundamental concern and priority with your patch deployment lab should be to determine how a given patch will affect the system's operation, or the operation of the environment into which it is placed. Some root-cause issues that will help you to make these vital determinations include:

- **Reboot.**   Does the system(s) require a reboot or a service to be restarted in order to work effectively after the patch has been applied? This will no doubt affect the operation of the system or device from the service perspective, as well as in relation to the environment into which it is placed. Can your other servers handle the increased load while you round-robin the patch?

- **Rollup patch.**   If the patch is a "rollup," it will most likely supersede many previous patches, not only affecting the patch baseline that you previously established, but also perhaps requiring additional reboots and frequent system snapshots.

- **How deep the patch goes into the system.**   A patch can have far-reaching consequences to system operation, affecting not only network performance but also operations to other functions that you would not typically associate with its current classification or role. If your system will be "recycled" for use in the future to include operations outside of its current scope, you should plan for this in advance. An Internet Explorer or MSXML patch, for example, could affect not only the application itself, but also the operating system.

- **Integration issues with third-party applications.** You should test critical services and applications first, in order of priority to the system's classification and role. For example, a Dynamic Host Configuration Protocol (DHCP) server's capability to perform lease reservations and BOOTP operations would be of paramount concern for that role.

So, what other scenarios do you need to consider when testing a patch or configuration change? How about failures? In some cases, a patch can fail due to a variety of reasons. Some scenarios to test to see how your patches react are:

- Loss of network connectivity during package delivery

- System shutting down, rebooting, or losing power during the installation

- Normal and higher-than-normal system use during the patch install

- Other scenarios that can cause an interruption of the install or delivery process

The whole point of creating an in-depth plan and testing this plan is to minimize surprises. You need to account for every possible scenario, not just application incompatibilities.

Patch Distribution and Deployment

Patch distribution and deployment are much more complicated than simply pushing a patch to a system or having someone click a button and update a system. You need to consider numerous factors, only some of which include the following:

- The location of the system from a protocol perspective

- The bandwidth needed and the tools (if any) used

- Personnel (plan on something going not quite right)

You can deploy patches in a number of ways, each with their own benefits and drawbacks. They are:

- **Push technology.** Tools such as Microsoft SMS use what is called *push technology*, in which a centralized console must have a copy of the patch, sometimes called a *package*, and then pushes that patch to each system specified. The biggest drawback of this method is reliability of delivery. You have no real way to ensure that a system is online and will remain online long enough to receive the package. It also requires more administration overhead, especially in cases where you have to create your own custom package.

- **Pull technology.** Tools such as the built-in Microsoft Windows Update and even Red Hat's RHN are considered *pull technology* because each client will, on its own, contact the update server and pull the patches down and then install them. Note that you can set up your own patch repositories internally; instead of having all your systems access the Internet, you can have them access an internal system instead. The drawback to this technology is that it typically offers less control to administrators and in some cases can have a higher impact on network utilization.

- **Sneakernet.** Although some of you may chuckle when you read this, the unfortunate reality of some organizations is that some systems are not as easily accessible via the network as others are. This means that important upgrades and patches need to be delivered and installed manually, usually via CD or USB device. The drawbacks to this method are very obvious, as this is the most time-consuming way to patch systems.

Logging and Reporting

So, after you have deployed all of your patches, how do you know for sure that they have installed correctly and that your systems are no longer vulnerable? Most patch deployment tools offer some sort of logging capability—some centralized and some stored on the individual systems. In addition, it is highly recommended that you rerun the vulnerability scans that identified that the systems needed patching in the first place. This will ensure, especially if you are using a quality scanning product that actually tests against the vulnerability, that the patch was not only successfully installed, but also properly fixes the issue.

Configuration Management

One area we have not talked about very much in this chapter is configuration management. The principles behind configuration management are very similar to those of patch management. The rule of document, test, deploy, and test again are as true here as they are with patch management.

There are two main reasons for having to worry about patch management. The first is enterprisewide system configuration change and the second is vulnerability mitigation. Over the past few years, the concept of secure desktop and secure server configuration has become increasingly popular because it is a viable option to prevent certain attack vectors from being successful. The initial problem with this practice is that it has always been a struggle for information technology (IT) departments to roll out and then change system configurations once systems are in production. A multitude of configuration management vendors have stepped up to the plate to solve this issue, and as suspected, this aligns closely with patch management.

So, we have a choice here. We can retype this entire chapter, replacing the words *patch management* with *configuration management*, or you the reader can simply understand that the concepts presented here apply to any change to your systems, be they patch installations or configuration changes.

For some ideas on secure configuration options for your organization, look at the NIST Security Configuration Checklists (http://checklists.nist.gov/repository/1014.html) and adapt them to your organization.

Change Control

No matter what you are doing on your network, be it a simple patch installation or a configuration change, you have to do it in a controlled and logical manner. All of the concepts discussed in this chapter should fit into your organization's existing change control procedures.

If computing asset change is not planned properly, it will fail, and ultimately your security initiatives will fail along with it. You need to plan, test, track, and retest all changes to all systems. This will ensure that any bad changes will be caught before they affect the overall user base, and possibly more important, it will ensure that you completely understand and plan for any security impact these changes may have.

When creating your change and patch management process you need to ensure that you cover the following steps:

1. Create a test group that is a sampling of all assets on your network.
2. Document the proposed change in detail.
3. Document a "roll-back" plan to undo the change.
4. Obtain sign-off from asset owners on the planned change.
5. Implement the change on your test group.
6. Monitor for adverse effects.
7. Roll out the change enterprisewide if the test group is successful.
8. Undo the change if the test group is not successful.

Although this appears to be a lengthy list of steps that could be time consuming and not conducive to quickly addressing vulnerabilities, with the right tools and the proper organizational buy-in, this process can move fairly quickly and even account for emergency changes. The key is proper documentation and testing; this will save you a lot of work when things go badly.

Tools & Traps...

Types of Documents That Require Tracking

This sidebar presents samples of documents you can use to perform and track the progress of your security assessment. Specific naming of documents is organizationally dependent, so this list may not include all the names you may encounter. All documents should be logged on a simple document-tracking sheet.

Policy Documents:

- Acceptable-Use/Internet Usage Policy
- Business Strategy
- Corporate Mission
- Employee Code of Conduct
- Information Security Policy
- Information Systems Security Policy
- Internet Usage Policy
- IT Strategy

Continued

- Mission Statement
- Organization Chart
- Organizational Description
- Organizational Security Policy/Procedures
- Personnel Security Policy
- Physical Security Policy
- Security Policy
- Security Strategy
- Strategy Document

Guideline/Requirements Documents:

- Administrative Security Requirements (Marking, Labeling, Storage, Transport of Documentation and Removable Media)
- Business Continuity/DRP
- Communications Security (COMSEC) and COMSEC Key Management Procedures
- Concept of Operations (CONOPs)
- HR Procedures (Hiring, Transfer, Retirement, Termination)
- List and Description of HW, SW, FW, OS, DB, GOTS, COTS, DOI/NBC Unique Applications
- Maintenance Standards/Change Control
- Mission Needs Statement (MNS)
- Network Connection Rules (External)/ External Connection MOU/MOA
- Operational Requirements Document (ORD)
- Security Concept of Operations (SECCONOPS)
- Security Department/Committee Mandates
- Security Programming/Testing Standards
- Technical Standards/Guidelines

System Security Plan Documents:

- Contingency Plan/Continuity of Operations Plan (COOP)
- Configuration Management Plan
- Network Diagrams/Architecture with Narrative
- Network Diagram (High and Low Level) *Required*
- Personnel Security Plan
- Physical Security Plan

- Prior Assessment (Threat/Risk/Security)
- Prior Audits (Internal or External)
- System Security Authorization Agreement (SSAA)
- Security Test Plans

User Documents:

- Account Management and Data Transfer Procedures in Hiring, Transfer, Retirement, Termination
- Audit Procedures
- Data Backup Procedures
- Desktop Support Security Procedures
- Desktop Support End-User Security Awareness
- Identification and Authentication Procedures
- Incident Response Plan
- Maintenance Plan/Procedures
- Password Management Procedures
- Personnel Security Procedures
- Physical Security Procedures
- Rules of Behavior
- Security Administrator Procedures
- Security Administrator's Manual
- Security Education Awareness Training Plan
- Security Features User's Guide
- Server/OS Administration Procedures
- Standard Operating Procedures (SOPs)
- Systems Admin Professional Development
- Systems Admin Security Procedures
- User's Guide
- Vendor Documentation
- Virus/Malicious Code Protection

Summary

This chapter covered the process of remediating vulnerabilities. In reality, an entire book could be written on this subject, as this is probably the most difficult and time-consuming part of the vulnerability management process. That being said, this chapter gave you the tools you need to properly build a test environment, to test patches and configuration changes, to document those changes, and to ultimately increase the overall security of your organization.

## Chapter 10

Regulatory Compliance

Solutions in this chapter:

- **Regulating Assessments and Pen Tests**
- **Drafting an Information Security Program**

☑ **Summary**

Introduction

Vulnerability assessments (VAs) and penetration tests (pen tests) have long been major components of information security programs. In fact, security managers have historically defined when and how they would conduct these exercises, as well as the scope of such exercises. Nevertheless, a missed assessment or pen test traditionally wasn't a big deal. Considering the resource constraints of most information security departments, missing an assessment period, or even two, was quasi-acceptable.

But that is no longer the case. Today businesses and industries are being besieged by compliance statutes. As security professionals and business leaders, we are no longer left to our own accord regarding how we create and implement our information security programs. In this chapter, we'll discuss the impact that regulatory agencies have had on vulnerability assessment and pen testing, as well as how to draft an information security program to meet an ever-changing business environment.

Regulating Assessments and Pen Tests

Unless we're operating a family diner, have an insignificant number of patrons, don't offer a healthcare plan to our employees, and run our entire business on cash, our organization is probably subject to at least one government/industry regulation. In fact, most organizations today are feeling the compliance burden and are subject to not one, but many compliance statutes. For instance, hospitals and healthcare providers are being besieged by the Health Insurance Portability and Accountability Act of 1996 (HIPAA), and many companies are still grappling with the Sarbanes-Oxley Act (SOX). Merchants and credit card processors now face the Payment Card Industry (PCI) standard, and government agencies must endure the Federal Information Security Management Act (FISMA). Financial institutions, probably the most regulated, are subject to the Gramm-Leach-Bliley Act (GLBA), Basel II, and a slew of other compliance regulations.

To complicate this, very few organizations are subject to only one regulatory statute. Take, for example, a Fortune 500 company that has an online storefront and outsources its healthcare program, but subsidizes its employees' healthcare costs. This company must comply with at least SOX, PCI, and HIPAA. In this section, we'll provide a high-level overview of each regulation and discuss their impact on vulnerability assessment and penetration testing.

The Payment Card Industry (PCI) Standard

Credit card theft has been with us ever since there have been credit cards. In the past, though, before the advent of the Internet and electronic commerce, a thief's accessibility to credit card data was relatively limited. Sure, a thief could compromise our credit card number and maybe the credit card number of 10, 20, or perhaps 100 other people, but it was relatively unlikely, with the exception of organized crime, for a criminal to have access to hundreds of thousands or even tens of thousands of credit card numbers. The advent of the Internet, coupled with the adoption of electronic commerce and online storefronts, has changed this. Now, upon exploiting a repository that supports an online storefront, a thief can easily gain access to hundreds of thousands, if not millions, of customer records and credit card numbers.

In an effort to address the liabilities associated with credit card theft, credit card companies, beginning with Visa in 2001 with its Cardholder Information Security Program (CISP), began enacting data protection standards governing the processing, transmission, and storage of credit card data. Other credit card companies soon followed suit and developed and enacted their own credit card legislation.

As a merchant or service provider, complying with the credit card data protection standards initially could be quite cumbersome and exhaustive, because no credit card vendor acknowledged and honored the other's credit card program. After three years of credit card mayhem, Visa and MasterCard collaborated and sponsored the PCI data protection standard. PCI doesn't usurp the data protection standards of the respective credit card companies, but Visa, MasterCard, Discover, American Express, Diners Club, and the Japan Credit Bureau (JCB) all endorse it.

Having garnered credit card unification and support, and with a rise in credit card theft, by the end of 2004 credit card companies began mandating that all merchants and service providers comply with either PCI or the data protection standard for the credit cards they accept or process. In Visa's case, organizations that do not comply with PCI must submit a report on compliance (ROC) and a remediation plan to Visa. The ROC is intended to identify an organization's level of compliance to the PCI standard and the remediation plan is intended to detail what an organization is doing to become compliant.

Part of securing the processing, transmission, and storage of credit card data is identifying vulnerabilities within the supporting infrastructure: servers, switches, routers, and applications used to support the credit card process. In an attempt to ensure that vulnerabilities do not exist or are identified and remediated within the credit card process, PCI requires vulnerability assessments and a penetration test of the merchant or service provider's cardholder environment. Table 10.1 lists PCI's VA and pen testing requirements.

Table 10.1 PCI VA Requirements*

Requirement #	Requirement Description
11	Regularly test security systems and processes.
11.2	Run internal and external network vulnerability scans at least quarterly and after any significant change in the network (e.g., new system component installations, changes in network topology, firewall rule modifications, product upgrades).
Note that external vulnerability scans must be performed by a scan vendor qualified by the PCI.	
11.3	Perform penetration testing on network infrastructure and applications at least once a year, and after any significant infrastructure or application upgrade or modification occurs (e.g., operating system upgraded, subnetwork added to environment, Web server added to environment).

*http://usa.visa.com/download/business/accepting_visa/ops_risk_management/cisp_PCI_Data_Security_Standard.pdf.

As noted in Table 10.1, external vulnerability scans must be performed by an approved PCI vendor. Table 10.2 reflects a partial list of approved PCI VA vendors. For a complete list, go to https://sdp.mastercardintl.com/vendors/vendor_list.shtml. For further information regarding PCI, visit http://usa.visa.com/business/accepting_visa/ops_risk_management/cisp.html.

Table 10.2 Approved PCI VA Vendors

Vendor Name	Product Name	Locations Served
403 Labs, LLC	PCI Compliance Testing	Global
Accume Partners	SDP Compliance Assessment	Global
Accuvant	Accuvant Compliance Scan	North America
Akibia, Inc.	Credit Card Security Compliance Services	Global
AlertSite	AlertSite Security Vulnerability Scan	Global
Alexander Open Systems, Inc.	Alexander Open Systems, Inc.	North America
Ambersail Ltd.	Ambersail Assured	UK and Europe
AmbironTrustWave	TrustKeeper	Global
Ascure nv	Ascure SDP Assessment Services	Global
Avanteg Bilgi ve lletisim Hizmetleri Ticaret A.S.	Avanteg Preventive Solutions–SDP Compliance Testing	Global

TIP

PCI focuses heavily on protecting a credit card number throughout its life cycle. It does not address protecting the customer's personal data associated with that credit card number—for example, street address, customer name, and so on. As we evaluate credit card exposure within our environment, we should also assess the customer data we possess and create a strategy that mitigates the security liabilities associated with the unauthorized disclosure of both.

The Health Insurance Portability and Accountability Act of 1996 (HIPAA)

When visiting a physician's office these days we're frequently presented with a document detailing our rights as a patient. Not only are we presented with our rights, but we're also given our physician's process for ensuring the security, confidentiality, and integrity of our health data. Securing patient health data hasn't always been a major concern; it wasn't prior to the last decade. A lot has changed since then, and this has become a focal point, thanks in large part to the Health Insurance Portability and Accountability Act of 1996 (HIPAA).

Congress passed HIPAA in August 1996. The intent of the legislation was to make healthcare delivery more efficient by:

- Simplifying the administrative process
- Defining the underwriting process for medical coverage
- Standardizing the electronic transmission of billing and claims information

By standardizing the transmission of billing and claims data, the potential for theft and abuse of patient health information (PHI) increased. To lessen this threat Congress expanded HIPAA and included safeguards to protect the confidentiality and security of patient data. These safeguards dictate that only authorized individuals have access to patient information and only to the information necessary to support a given task. HIPAA was also expanded to regulate not only PHI such as printouts, but also electronic PHI (ePHI) such as voice mails and e-mails.

HIPAA went into effect April 14, 2001, but organizations were given until April 2003 to become compliant. After April 13, 2003, organizations could be penalized for noncompliance.

Hospitals, as we might expect, are subject to HIPAA, but they aren't the only ones. Following is a list of entities that must be HIPAA compliant as of today (see NIST Special Publication 800-66):

- **Covered healthcare providers** Any provider of medical or other health services, or supplies, who transmits any health information in electronic form in connection with a transaction for which the Department of Health and Human Services (HHS) has adopted a standard.

- **Health plans** Any individual or group plan that provides, or pays the cost of, medical care, including certain specifically listed government programs (e.g., a health insurance issuer and the Medicare and Medicaid programs).

- **Healthcare clearinghouses** A public or private entity that processes another entity's healthcare transactions from a standard format to a nonstandard format, or vice versa.

- **Medicare prescription drug card sponsors** A nongovernmental entity that offers an endorsed discount drug program under the Medicare Modernization Act. This fourth category of "covered entity" will remain in effect until the drug card program ends in 2006.

Logically we would expect healthcare providers, clearinghouses, and drug card sponsors to be subject to HIPAA. Many health plans have been caught off guard by this legislation, though. Recall that a health plan is any individual or group plan that provides or pays for the cost of medical care. Because of this definition many companies are subject to HIPAA, for they provide employee assistance programs and subsidize their employees' healthcare costs.

Entities subject to HIPAA must appoint a security official. This official is responsible for conducting and filing a HIPAA risk assessment, usually with the entity's fiduciary. The main purpose/intent of the assessment is to ensure that PHI and ePHI are protected with appropriate controls and measures; the ePHI that a covered entity creates, receives, maintains, or transmits must be protected against reasonably anticipated threats, hazards, and impermissible uses and/or disclosures. Table 10.3 (from NIST Special Publication 800-66) outlines HIPAA's vulnerability assessment requirements. For a detailed listing of the HIPAA security requirements, visit www.hhs.gov/ocr/hipaa/.

Table 10.3 HIPAA VA Requirements

Standard	Section	Implementation Specifications
Security awareness and training	Protection from malicious software	Determine the health plan's level of vulnerability to the threat of malicious software.
Security awareness and training	Protection from malicious software	Review adequacy of current safeguards for guarding against, detecting, and reporting malicious software.
Security awareness and training	Protection from malicious software	Develop a policy and procedure for protection from malicious software.
Security awareness and training	Log-in monitoring	Determine the health plan's level of vulnerability to the threat of unauthorized access to ePHI or the health plan's information system by internal or external individuals inappropriately using a workforce member's log-in information.

NOTE

HIPAA, unlike other compliance statutes, doesn't require us to submit our risk assessment to an external party; not to HHS or any other independent agency. Although HHS has received more than 19,000 HIPAA-related complaints, it has yet to levy a fine. HHS has the authority to impose fines for civil violations ranging from $100 to $25,000, and officials can refer possible criminal violations to the Department of Justice (www.kaisernetwork.org/daily_reports/rep_index.cfm?DR_ID=37687).

The Sarbanes-Oxley Act of 2002 (SOX)

The early part of the twenty-first century was marred by corporate financial scandals and collapses. At Enron, WorldCom, Adelphia Communications, and more, many corporate executives were manipulating investors and stakeholders alike by inflating the profits of their respective companies via unethical accounting practices. As a result, many of these once admired and idolized companies imploded; filing bankruptcy, laying off thousands of employees, and staving off the myriad retaliatory lawsuits brought by shareholders. In response to this and in an effort to restore the integrity of financial reporting, the Sarbanes-Oxley Act of 2002 (SOX) was enacted.

In 15 years, Enron grew from nowhere to become America's seventh largest company. But the firm's success turned out to be an elaborate scam. Enron lied about its profits and stands accused of a range of shady dealings, including concealing debts so that they didn't show up in the company's accounts (for more, visit http://news.bbc.co.uk/1/hi/business/1780075.stm). After more than four years of criminal inquiry, Enron's former CEO, CFO, and other corporate executives were found guilty and some have been imprisoned for their corporate wrongdoings. Prior to facing sentencing Ken Lay, Enron's former CEO, died on July 5, 2006 after suffering a massive heart attack in his Aspen, Colorado vacation home. The irony is that by dying, Lay achieved something he could not do when he was alive. He cleared his name and wiped a conviction that it took the US Government more than four years to win. This is for when a defendant who pleads not guilty dies before being sentenced, the conviction is wiped out on the grounds that the defendant did not have the opportunity to appeal (for more, visit http://www.theage.com.au/news/business/in-death-as-in-life-lay-cheats-his-detractors/2006/07/07/1152240489467.html).

The Sarbanes–Oxley Act has fundamentally changed the business, regulatory, and information technology (IT) environments (the entire document can be viewed at http://www.isaca.org/Content/ContentGroups/Research1/Deliverables/IT_Control_Objectives_for_Sarbanes-Oxley_7july04.pdf). By holding corporate executives, chief executives, and financial officers explicitly responsible for establishing, evaluating, and monitoring the effectiveness of internal control over financial reporting, SOX strengthens internal checks and balances, corporate accountability, and ultimately, corporate financial reporting.

Unlike with HIPAA and PCI, many feel that the compliance requirements articulated within SOX are somewhat vague and disconcerting; especially section 404. Within section 404, organizations must attest to their financial and general IT controls. Financial controls measure and verify our accounting practices and general IT controls assess the accessibility and safeguards we have governing our technology, our financial systems, and our supporting infrastructure.

As a part of measuring, testing, and attesting to our general IT controls, we must identify the risks related to our IT systems and design and implement safeguards or compensating controls to mitigate these risks. Part of identifying and assessing this risk is conducting vulnerability assessments and pen tests against our IT systems. Though SOX doesn't specifically define a frequency for these activities, all publicly traded companies, for the most part, must annually undergo a SOX audit, and such an organization needs to annually conduct at least one vulnerability assessment and pen test. In seeking due diligence, many internal audit departments are asking that these exercises be conducted more frequently and by a recognized third party. Note that the recognized third party cannot be the same independent auditor that's used to substantiate the company's financial reporting process.

Compliance Recap

As noted in the previous section, regulatory statutes are beginning to exert force upon and shape our VA and pen test processes; ultimately impacting our information security programs. Figure 10.1 represents a partial list of the regulatory landscape.

Figure 10.1 Partial Regulatory Landscape

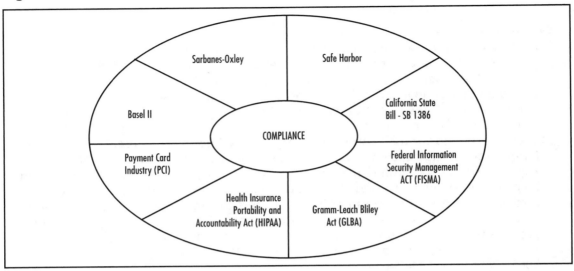

Table 10.4 lists the primary industry each form of legislation impacts and provides a brief summary of each statute.

Table 10.4 Compliance Summary

Regulation/Standard	Sector Affected	Summary	Effective Date
PCI	Cross-sector	Data protection standard governing the processing, storage, and transmission of cardholder data.	2004
HIPAA	Healthcare	Regulation governing the privacy, security, availability, and confidentiality of patient health data.	2003
GLBA	Financial	Privacy requirements for customers' financial data. Mandates the publication of privacy standards used by financial institutions and restricts the use and transfer of data between organizations.	2004
FISMA	Government	Act requiring government agencies to secure the information and systems supporting their operations and assets.	2002

Table 10.4 Continued

Regulation/Standard	Sector Affected	Summary	Effective Date
California State Bill–SB 1386	Cross-sector	Requires individuals and organizations to properly notify California residents if their personal identifiable information (PII) is disclosed as part of a security breach or any other exposure.	2004
Safe Harbor	Cross-sector	U.S. complement to the European Union's (EU's) Directive on Data Protection, which prohibits the transfer of personal data to entities that do not meet the EU's "adequacy" standard for privacy protection.	2000
SOX	Cross-sector	Created to restore investor confidence in corporate financial reporting through good corporate governance, ethical business practices, and sound financial and IT auditing and controls.	2003
Basel II Accord	Financial	Regulation to introduce a more risk-sensitive capital framework in international financial institutions.	2006

Drafting an Information Security Program

Coupled with the fact that we live in a very litigious society, as security practitioners and business leaders we also now live in a highly regulated business environment. Because of this, drafting policies and standards and delivering an information security program that meets all of the compliance statutes, as well as an organization's needs, can be quite daunting.

Smaller or siloed business may be able to structure an information security program around the major regulatory statute they're subject to, but this simply doesn't scale for large enterprises because, as illustrated earlier, most organizations are subject to many statutes. Complicating this, many organizations partner with others that operate outside their primary industry and have other regulatory compliance obligations. Therefore, you often see security addendums attached to contracts to protect the compliance requirements of each partner. Figure 10.2 is an excerpt from of a standard security addendum.

Figure 10.2 Security Addendum Excerpt

> 1. **Governance.** VENDOR will maintain Information Security Policies and Procedures that meet the standards of its respective industry and privacy regulations applicable it.
>
> 2. **Audits**
>
>   2.1 **Security Audits**
>
>   a. VENDOR and its contractors (to the extent that such contractors have access to the COMPANY's information) must have a comprehensive risk management program for its systems that contain the COMPANY's data. This should include a process for identifying newly released information about security patches for any such systems.
>
>   b. If VENDOR has not already had a security audit performed by a mutually agreed upon third party, VENDOR will have such audit conducted within a timeframe agreeable to both parties. This initial audit will determine the state of security and readiness within VENDOR's environment. Prior to VENDOR accessing, gathering, storing, or processing COMPANY data, VENDOR will resolve any issues identified through the initial security audit as mutually agreed upon by the parties.
>
>   c. If VENDOR has had a security audit performed by an industry recognized third party as mutually agreed upon by the parties, then the requirements of Section 2.b above will be waived and the following obligations will apply:
>
>   i. Prior to VENDOR accessing, gathering, storing, or processing COMPANY data, VENDOR will provide COMPANY with the scope and summary of the most recent security audit performed by that third party. The scope of this audit must include the proposed COMPANY-related environment.

So what are we to do? Do we draft policies around HIPAA, SOX, or perhaps PCI? Prior to making this decision, we must remember that the most effective information security programs are tailored around an organization's people, process, and technology. Figure 10.3 shows the relationship among these three elements.

Figure 10.3 Relationship Among People, Process, and Technology

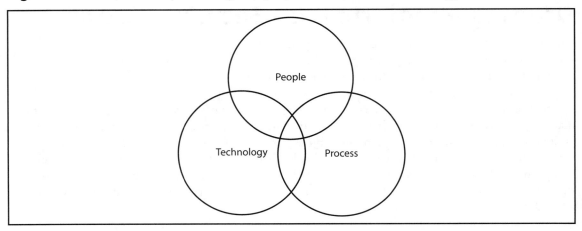

Information security isn't all about technology. If we were to align people, process, and technology in order of importance, our output would look similar to Figure 10.4, with people representing the foundation of our information security program, followed by process and technology. A lot of the time, we can get by with inferior technology if we have well-defined and functioning processes being executed by individuals with an elevated security IQ.

Figure 10.4 Order of Importance of People, Process, and Technology

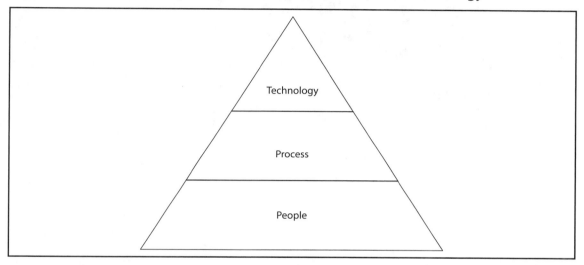

Because of today's regulatory environment, drafting and executing an information security program is somewhat of a challenge. In the past, many of us have adopted the International Organization for Standardization (ISO) standard, ISO 17799, and our internal audit departments have leveraged the Committee of Sponsoring Organizations (COSO) or Control Objectives for Information and related Technology (COBIT) to evaluate our information security programs. ISO is a good and well-established framework, but it lacks defining elements. ISO articulates that statements such as auditing should be enabled, and many of the regulations we're subjected to dictate the level of auditing and the frequency with which it should be reviewed. Independent of whether we're using ISO or another security framework, we should develop and tailor our programs with risk mitigation in mind. Figure 10.5 is an example of META Security Group's Risk-Management-Based Policy Framework.

NOTE

COBIT is a set of best practices (a framework) for IT management created in 1992 by the Information Systems Audit and Control Association (ISACA) and the IT Governance Institute (ITGI). COBIT provides managers, auditors, and IT users with a set of generally accepted measures, indicators, processes, and best practices to assist them in maximizing the benefits derived through the use of IT and developing appropriate IT governance and control in a company.

Figure 10.5 META Security Group's Risk-Management-Based Policy Framework

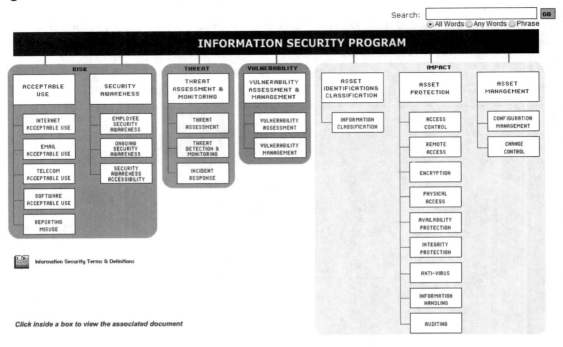

Leveraging a framework such as that shown in Figure 10.5 or organizing our existing framework in the same fashion will allow us to:

- Organize our information security programs into digestible modules that our employee groups can easily understand

- Adapt to changing threats, environments, and regulations

- Focus on the people and process elements of information security

Upon organizing our program in this fashion, we can then develop a compliance matrix associated with the various regulations we're subject to. Figure 10.6 is an example of such a matrix. To accomplish this we don't necessarily have to modularize our information security program into high level policy statements with supporting standards, as illustrated in Figure 10.5, but as chief information security officers or security/compliance leaders we are typically responsible for the program's policies and standards and by modularizing our program we can:

- Communicate changes to the program in an easy and concise manner. We simply have to communicate the policy or standard that has changed and not the entire program.

- Easily make changes to the program to support new threats or other security/business concerns

- Potentially make modifications to the program without requiring executive signoff. While senior management needs to signoff on the program, executive sponsorship usually isn't required when modifying standards or supporting procedures.

Figure 10.6 Compliance Matrix (www.actgov.org/actiac/documents/
051018FedRegComplianceMatrix.pdf)

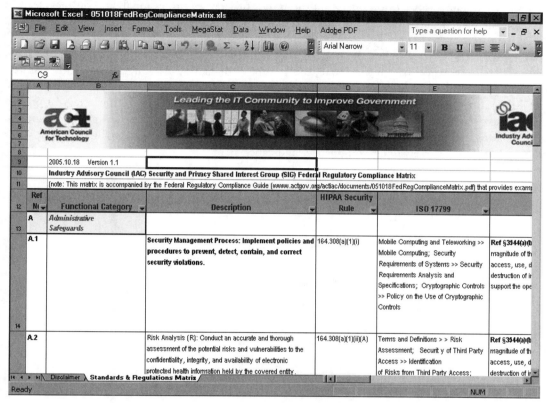

Over the past several years, technologies such as Symantec's Bindview Policy Manager have come to market. Policy Manager maps created policy to best-practice frameworks, such as ISO 17799, and multiple regulations, like HIPPA, and supplies proof of compliance to policy through integration with Symantec and third-party infrastructure assessment software (for more, visit http://www.symantec.com/Products/enterprise?c=prodinfo&refId=1261&cid=1004). For CISOs and Compliance Officers the beauty of Policy Manger and similar technologies is that it:

- negates the need for compliance matrixes like Figure 10.6 for we no longer have to physically map regulatory controls to our company's policy statements

- aids us in drafting information security programs in alignment with the regulatory environment we are subject to

- allows organizations to automatically, via technology, attest to their level of compliance

Drafting an information security program in this day and age is somewhat of a chore, but if we take a holistic view of the challenge and tailor it toward risk mitigation, drafting policies and standards to meet today's evolving and regulated environment, while minimizing the security liabilities faced by our organizations, is certainly attainable.

Summary

Protecting corporate assets has long been on the minds of security professionals and business leaders. Protecting the data which resides on those assets is now even more important, given the regulatory environment in which we operate.

PCI, HIPAA, and SOX reflect the first wave of compliance statutes that our organizations are subject to. The next wave may include state, and possibly federal, notification and disclosure statutes governing our organization's responsibility to publicly disclose security breaches to our constituents.

The regulatory landscape is fairly new, so we should expect the expected—more regulations—and the unexpected—changes to existing regulations. Drafting an information security program that is modular, flexible, and focused on risk mitigation and common-sense security will go a long way toward tackling the ever-evolving compliance landscape.

## Chapter 11

Tying It All Together

Solutions in this chapter:

- A Vulnerability Management Methodology
- Step One: Know Your Assets
- Step Two: Categorize Your Assets
- Step Three: Create a Baseline Scan of Assets
- Step Four: Perform a Penetration Test on Certain Assets
- Step Five: Remediate Vulnerabilities and Risk
- Step Six: Create a Vulnerability Assessment Schedule
- Step Seven: Create a Patch and Change Management Process
- Step Eight: Monitor for New Risks to Assets

Introduction

This chapter should tie vulnerability management procedures together nicely and give you a concise guide. Concepts, examples, and product screen shots aside, we want readers to literally tear this chapter from the book and keep it handy on their desks as a comprehensive methodology checklist for vulnerability management.

A Vulnerability Management Methodology

If you have ever had the pleasure of writing a book, or even online content, you are aware that it can drive even the best of authors into a 12-step program to recovery. So, in honor of such programs, we offer the following eight essential steps for vulnerability management. Perform the following steps for a year and you won't get a token or a certificate, but you will find yourself having successfully created a vulnerability management program that becomes easier to administer day by day:

- Step one: know your assets.
- Step two: categorize your assets.
- Step three: create a baseline scan of all of your assets.
- Step four: perform a penetration test on certain assets.
- Step five: remediate vulnerabilities and risk.
- Step six: create a vulnerability assessment (VA) schedule.
- Step seven: create a patch and change management process.
- Step eight: monitor for new risks to assets.
- Wash, rinse, and repeat.

We discuss each step in the sections that follow. Within those sections, we provide the following information:

- What you need to do
- Why you need to do it
- How to do it
- What tools exist to help you do it

Step One: Know Your Assets

What You Need to Do

You should document every asset on your network that "speaks" the Transmission Control Protocol/ Internet Protocol (TCP/IP) language—at both a logical and a physical level. As simple as this may sound, you should read it over and over again in order to truly understand that when we say *every asset* we *mean* every asset. This can include obvious things, such as workstations and servers, but it can also mean equipment such as printers, copy machines, routers, switches, Internet Protocol (IP) phones, and network attached storage, and even items such as game consoles, toasters, and fridges (yes, some kitchen appliances actually speak TCP/IP; go to www.lge.com).

Even if your VA tool does not support the scanning of more obscure devices, you still need to know they exist.

NOTE

Are you running IPv6? Even if you are not officially running it, you might want to perform network scans for both IPv4 and IPv6 devices, because it's not uncommon for organizations to find unsupported networks in their environments. Be sure to check that your chosen tools support IPv6 as well. What about other protocols, you ask? Although you cannot scan them, you should always be aware of what is in your environment.

Why You Need to Do It

Although on the surface, this appears to be a simple inventory task, it is actually a very important security step. We know of organizations that have identified devices that should not exist on their networks. This is also an important part of the compliance puzzle; the last thing an information technology (IT) administrator wants is an auditor finding systems that are not only unknown, but also do not comply with specific regulatory issues. In addition, multiple presentations have been given at various conferences, showing how you can use various devices such as game consoles to allow unauthorized access to corporate networks. So consider this step as something that should become a constant task which you schedule along with your vulnerability scans.

How to Do It

You can use a number of tools to document assets on your network. There are a few different ways to accomplish this task, as well:

- **ICMP discovery.** This is the simplest method of identifying systems on a network. An Internet Control Message Protocol (ICMP) packet is also known as a *ping packet*. Although it is the most reliable way to identify hosts, many IT professionals are taught to disable a system's (or switch's) capability to respond to ICMP as a form of mitigation from unauthorized scans. Of course, while you have protected your network against unauthorized ICMP scans, you have also effectively hidden your systems from legitimate scans as well.

- **TCP port discovery scan.** This is a good way to identify hosts when ICMP might be disabled. Simply put, this method will attempt to connect to every IP address in the scan range on a specific port. If that port is open and is listening for connections, the host will be considered alive. If none of the selected ports is alive and listening, the host will be considered dead.

- **UDP discovery scan.** This type of scan works a little differently. Whereas a TCP port scan looks for a response on an open port, a User Datagram Protocol (UDP) scan will actually look for closed ports. When a UDP scan hits a port that is closed, a specific error will be returned which proves that there is, in fact, a live system at that IP address.

When identifying assets you should document some key things. Table 11.1 summarizes what you should document, and why.

Table 11.1 Things to Document When Identifying Assets

What to Document	Why to Document It
IP address of the asset	Even if your organization is using dynamically assigned IP addresses (DHCP), you cannot scan a system unless you know the IP address. In addition, keeping track of the IP address that a system is assigned leaves a good audit trail in the event that an incident needs to be investigated.
MAC address of the asset	As we discussed before, this is the physical address of the system. This is a static 12-character value—for example, *00-0E-35-E9-98-A6*—that will allow you to map physical systems to the IP address assigned.
DNS/NetBIOS name of the asset	This is the name of the system; typically the domain name system (DNS) name and the NetBIOS name will be the same. This is one more way to map the system to the IP address and the Media Access Control (MAC) address.
Operating system of the asset	Although obvious, this is important to the patch management process. If you don't know what your systems are running, it is difficult if not impossible to know what vulnerabilities to monitor for, and to plan the patching stages.
Listening services on the asset	ne of the oldest concepts in information security is the one of least privilege. Systems should not have services listening on them that are not being used. Documenting what is listening on each system and what is needed on each system is a critical step.
Physical location of the asset	This is the physical location and department of the asset. This is an obvious thing to document, because from time to time, IT resources may have to physically access the system.

Table 11.1 Continued

What to Document	Why to Document It
Owner of the asset	There are two data points for this category. You should know both who the typical user of the system is, as well as whom in the organization is ultimately responsible for that asset on both an IT and a management level.
Classification of the asset	This is the classification of the asset and the data contained on that asset. As we discussed, this is an important step in the entire vulnerability management process.

What Tools Exist to Help You Do It

One of the unfortunate realities that has constantly plagued IT and security administrators is the fact that no one tool does everything perfectly. This has forced many administrators to use multiple tools and to piece together the data the tools provide.

For commercial tools, we talked about many that can collect this data. Although it would be easy to simply recommend a tool, it is far better for an organization to test each product and judge for itself which one meets its minimum criteria. In Chapter 3, we talked about what a good VA tool should do for you. By using this chapter as a guide, you should be able to select the tool that is best for your organization.

If you were using the free and open source tool, NMAP, to perform these tasks, you would do the following, logged in as *root* on a *nix system or as *Administrator* on a Windows system:

```
#NMAP -sV -O -p1-65535 <ip address range> -oN <scanname.txt>
```

This would perform a scan of the specified IP range and log the host, the operating system of that host, and the services, including the version number listening on that host. The *-p* option tells NMAP to scan all TCP ports, meaning that your scans may take a long time. More information on NMAP and the various options you can use to make this first step easy to perform is available in the online documentation, and is included in the NMAP help file, which you can download from www.insecure.org. We also covered the various NMAP options in Chapter 4.

As for commercial tools, in this book we used the two leading products in our examples: Tenable Network Security's Nessus and eEye Digital Security's Retina. Here is a more complete list of commercial products that, in our opinion as practitioners, are worth taking a look at to see whether they fit into your organization:

- Retina (eEye Digital Security, www.eeye.com)

- Nessus (Tenable Network Security, www.tenablesecurity.com)

- QualysGuard (Qualys, www.qualys.com)

- Network Security Inspector (Sunbelt, www.sunbelt.com)

- IP360 (nCircle, www.ncircle.com)

- ISS Scanner (Internet Security Systems, www.iss.net)

- Foundstone (McAfee, www.mcafee.com)

- BindView bvControl (Symantec, www.bindview.com)

Step Two: Categorize Your Assets

What You Need to Do

As we discussed in Chapter 4, ISO17799 states:

> The organization should be in a position to understand what information assets it holds, and to manage their security appropriately.

Asset classification is the art of assigning a value to an asset in order to organize it according to its sensitivity to loss or disclosure. The major steps required for asset classification and controls are:

- Identification of assets

- Accountability of assets

- Classification of assets

Although it is great to simply repeat the high-level information provided by the various standards, this doesn't really specify exactly what you need to do to classify your assets. Basically, you need to organize every asset in a way that best suits your organization. The example we used in Chapter 4 was based on the following criteria:

- Physical location

- Organizational location

- Asset classification

Physical location is quite obvious because this is the actual place the asset is located. You can use a city or even an office name, which is a good idea if you have multiple locations in one city.

NOTE

An issue that many organizations have struggled with is remote workers. If you have employees who work offsite or from home you should be sure to add them to a group or create a separate group for them. Imagine the impact to your organization and your career if the home workstation of a developer who telecommutes is compromised and is used to attack the corporate network because you failed to account for it in your vulnerability management program.

Organizational location is valuable because it helps determine who the asset owner or owners may be in your organization. For smaller organizations this isn't a big deal, but larger corporations can have multiple departments or even multiple suborganizations, each with their own IT functions.

Finally, asset classification is the stage in which you determine the value of the asset and assign it a classification, such as *unclassified*, *internal only*, or *confidential*. Base this classification on the impact the asset or the data on that asset would have your organization if it was lost or stolen.

Why You Need to Do It

Although asset classification, and probably asset identification, is typically considered to be very boring and time consuming, it is important, especially for large organizations where it can be difficult to perform a full network assessment in a timely manner. As corporations grow, their networks grow, meaning that it takes a longer time to scan these networks. Many organizations battle this by deploying distributed scanners, all reporting to a central reporting server, but deploying enough scanners can quickly become cost prohibitive, and the reports they generate can become a new bottleneck. So, the solution is to scan parts of your network in stages, starting with the more-critical assets and finishing with the less-critical ones. In addition, critical assets or critical locations are typically scanned more often as well.

It's also good to perform this step in case an attacker compromises your network. Without knowing every detail of your network, along with their value to the organization, you cannot possibly determine what the lapse in security cost the organization.

How to Do It

To perform this step you must have completed the preceding step, because the data from the first step is essential. For an organization that has never undergone this sort of task, this will be difficult and time consuming to accomplish.

During this stage, you must sort every system that was detected in step one, into categories based on location and importance. It can be helpful to sort each group in the following way:

- Geographic location 1/Confidential
- Geographic location 2/Confidential
- Geographic location 3/Confidential
- Geographic location 1/Internal Only
- Geographic location 2/Internal Only
- Geographic location 3/Internal Only
- Geographic location 1/Unclassified
- Geographic location 2/Unclassified
- Geographic location 3/Unclassified

Obviously your organization may have more or fewer geographic locations, and in some cases more or fewer asset classifications.

What Tools Exist to Help You Do It

This is an area on which vendors have not focused in terms of providing great solutions. Data classification tools are available, but none of them supports the rest of the process, and VA tools do not completely support the asset classification process.

Some tools try to fill this gap, but in our opinion (and please email us if you think otherwise), none of them completely helps with this step. In all honesty, we have found that what works best is to create a spreadsheet with your favorite spreadsheet application and then import that data into your VA tool, or manually create your groups if your tool doesn't support importing.

Step Three: Create a Baseline Scan of Assets

What You Need to Do

After you have documented and classified your assets, you can move on to the more fun and interesting step of actually performing a baseline vulnerability assessment. In Chapter 5, we addressed the issue of credentialed scans versus noncredentialed scans. Table 11.2 provides a summary.

Table 11.2 Credentialed Scans versus Noncredentialed Scans

Option	What It Does	Benefits	Problems
Scan without credentials	The scanner will attempt to audit the target systems without authenticating to those systems with any user rights.	This gives you the "hacker's" view of a system, as the typical attacker would not have credentials.	Scanning in this manner will not identify the patch level of the system, or vulnerabilities that a user with credentials could leverage
Scan with credentials	The scanner will use administrator-level credentials to connect to the target system and audit Registry entries, files, and other configuration options.	This gives a more complete scan of the system and allows the scanner the capability to check for vulnerabilities in things such as client-side software, as well as configuration issues that equate to vulnerabilities.	Some feel that this does not give a true hacker's view of a system. Although this is a true statement, getting the true hacker's view of a system and actually securing a system are two different things.

Based on the benefits and drawbacks listed in Table 11.2, it is clear that if your goal is to improve security through vulnerability management, you will want to run your scans with credentials because that will give you the most coverage. There is also the question of internal versus external scans. For this step you will want to concentrate on running your scans internally. If you are responsible for a large organization, these scans may take some time to complete. It is important that you scan all assets in this step, because you are creating a baseline of your current security posture.

Why You Need to Do It

This step is pretty obvious, because it is the most important step of a vulnerability management program: detecting vulnerabilities. This step is your first initial scan which will create a baseline of your current security posture and give you a point of reference to track improvements.

How to Do It

In this step, you will leverage the work you put into the preceding two steps. Smaller organizations (those with networks that have fewer than 500 hosts) will not need to go to as much trouble as larger organizations, so if you are lucky enough to have fewer than 500 hosts to manage, you can skip scanning by asset group and simply follow the directions we provide here for every asset on your network.

If you are scanning a larger network, you unfortunately will not have the luxury of simply entering your network addresses and scanning, because the time required to perform large scans, regardless of what tool you use, is dramatically high when running an in-depth scan such as that which we need to do to create an initial baseline scan.

As noted earlier, this is where the asset groups you created in step two can be very helpful. As we discussed in Chapter 5, you will want to start with the most-critical assets and work your way down to the less-critical ones. When you conduct your scans be sure to check your tool's settings to ensure that you are

- enabling a full port scan for both TCP and UDP ports
- enabling operating system detection
- enabling all vulnerability checks

If any of the VA tool vendors were to read the preceding list, they would immediately object because the options we suggested will cause your scans to take a considerable amount of time to complete. In this case, this is a good thing because you want your baseline to be as complete as possible, which means you have to scan for everything. To get around the time issues such scans create you should consider running your scanners in a distributed model, which means having multiple scanning engines scanning different asset groups and reporting the results to a central console or reporting server.

Enabling a full port scan on both TCP and UDP ports will allow you to identify every potential service running on the system—both legitimate and illegitimate. Remember, a lot of Trojans and other malware use high ports to communicate, so this is also a great way to detect any systems that are compromised.

Operating system detection will help you fill out the list of assets and what is running on them. As we have said multiple times, this is an important step when it comes to monitoring for both new vulnerabilities and patches.

Enabling all vulnerability checks, while adding to the scan time, is the only way you will get a complete list of all vulnerabilities, configurations, and policy issues with your systems. On the positive side, you won't have to always scan for all ports and all vulnerabilities, as you will see in upcoming steps.

What Tools Exist to Help You Do It

In this book, we used the two leading products in our examples: Tenable Network Security's Nessus and eEye Digital Security's Retina. Here is a more complete list of commercial products that, in our opinion, are worth investigating to see whether they fit into your organization:

- Retina (eEye Digital Security, www.eeye.com)
- Nessus (Tenable Network Security, www.tenablesecurity.com)
- QualysGuard (Qualys, www.qualys.com)
- Network Security Inspector (Sunbelt, www.sunbelt.com)
- IP360 (nCircle, www.ncircle.com)
- ISS Scanner (Internet Security Systems, www.iss.net)
- Foundstone (McAfee, www.mcafee.com)
- BindView bvControl (Symantec, www.bindview.com)

Remember to judge these tools based on the criteria presented in Chapter 3, as well as additional criteria that are specific for your organization.

Step Four: Perform a Penetration Test on Certain Assets

What You Need to Do

Those of you who have experienced vulnerability assessment and management before are probably asking "Why haven't they covered penetration testing?" Although pen testing is arguably a waste of time and money for most organizations (see sidebar, "Wasted Security Budget?"), it does still have its place in the vulnerability management life cycle.

NOTE

We are sure the comment in this chapter about pen testing being somewhat of a waste of time and money will raise some eyebrows, so hopefully we can explain here exactly what we meant by that comment. Most organizations will hire a third-party firm to perform a pen test before doing any of their own work to build an infrastructure. This almost guarantees that the pen test team will successfully compromise your hosts. Does it not make more sense to build an infrastructure first, and then to test it via a pen test?

The argument that a pen test is needed to show that the infrastructure, or better yet, the budget for the infrastructure, is needed is no longer valid. Today, every executive understands the need for an effective information security program.

Now that you have a plan in place, it is time to perform a pen test. Because you can do this only if you have a plan in place, you need to make sure that you have already set aside time and, more important, money for steps five through eight before performing this step. Otherwise, consider this stage completely optional and, in times of budget cuts, the first budget item to be cut.

That being said, there is great value in performing a pen test on assets that are accessible externally to your organization.

Why You Need to Do It

Although the value of a pen test is up for debate, when such tests are conducted at the right time and on the right assets, they can be very helpful. This is truly the only way you can get a real attacker's view of your network, as we explained in previous chapters of this book.

How to Do It

You have a number of options when performing a pen test. You can do it yourself or you can contract the work out to a third party. When performing this step yourself you will have the advantage of having a more accurate view of your network versus if an outside third party conducted the test.

You will want to concentrate on only the assets that are accessible from the outside world. If yours is one of the unlucky organizations that have multiple assets exposed to the world, you will want to approach the pen test in the same manner that you approach the baseline vulnerability assessment. Start with the highest-risk assets and work down to the lower-risk ones.

Remember, depending on your network configuration, each asset will have, or should have, been scanned during step three, but from the inside of your corporate network. So this is also a good time to compare the results of the pen test with those of the vulnerability scan from the internal interface. In addition, note that most pen tests include some level of application security testing that a typical vulnerability scanner cannot perform. So to perform your pen test you will want to be sure to cover the following steps:

- Profile external systems
- Profile external applications
- Identify potential architectural weaknesses
- Identify potential exploitable vulnerabilities
- Exploit weaknesses and vulnerabilities
- Report

In your profile of external systems you will document everything that is publicly available about your externally facing network. This includes open ports, DNS records, and domain name records.

You also should document externally facing applications, including what the application is running, what types of user input it accepts, and what type of data is saved on the application servers. Externally, it should be possible to get an idea of the general architecture and layout of your applications.

Once you have created the initial profile it should be easy to identify both potential architectural weaknesses that can expose systems to unnecessary risk, as well as potential vulnerabilities that could be exploited. After you've validated each weakness, you should create a report that shows what was found and what was exploited. It is important to also document potential issues because the failure of your pen testing team to exploit something does not equal system security, and these weaknesses should still be manually addressed.

What Tools Exist to Help You Do It

What tools you use for your pen test will depend on whether you are doing the work yourself or are outsourcing the project to a third party. In terms of free open source tools, you have a lot of choices. The following two tools are among the more popular today:

- Framework (Metasploit, www.metasploit.org)
- NMAP (Insecure.org, www.insecure.org)

On the application side of the house, we recommend using the resources and tools available at the Open Web Application Security Project (OWASP), located at www.owasp.org.

Multiple options also are available in the commercial tools arena. Probably the best and most advanced pen testing tool is Core Impact; the following list includes another one you may want to check out:

- Core Impact (Core Security Technologies, www.coresecurity.com)
- Immunity CANVAS (Immunity Inc., www.immunitysec.com)

In the application security arena these commercial tools are useful:

- AppDetective (Application Security Inc., www.appsecinc.com)
- AppScan (Watchfire Corp., www.watchfire.com)

Step Five: Remediate Vulnerabilities and Risk

What You Need to Do

Each of the four preceding steps should have generated a lot of reports, each with their own level of detail. Once you have progressed to this step, you should have a list of every asset on your network and what vulnerabilities and risks those assets face.

This is the step where you actually go out and fix the vulnerabilities present in your systems. When you get to this step, remember our definition of a vulnerability from Chapter 1:

> **A vulnerability is a software or hardware bug or misconfiguration that a malicious individual can exploit.**

We remind you of this because many people fail to realize that issues such as configuration management also apply when dealing with vulnerabilities, because a misconfigured system that is completely patched can still be vulnerable to a number of issues that can lead to system compromise.

Why You Need to Do It

The reason to remediate at this stage should be obvious. You have a long list of vulnerable systems from your baseline scans, so now you must bring these systems up to a secure state before moving forward with your vulnerability management plans.

This step isn't meant to replace step seven, but it is meant to set the framework and make step seven a lot easier to accomplish.

How to Do It

The larger your organization is, the harder this step will be to complete. We suggest that you approach this in much the same way that we have recommended you approach large-scale vulnerability assessments. Start with higher-risk assets and finish with lower-risk ones.

There are two different types of issues that you will have to remediate. The first, of course, is vulnerabilities, and the second is configuration issues. To add a level of confusion to your remediation plans, some vulnerabilities may not have patches and may need to be addressed via configuration changes.

Unfortunately, it isn't a safe bet to simply apply patches and configuration changes, so the first step of remediation is to take a sample of your systems and make those your test case. These are the systems that you will use to test patches and configuration changes, so be sure to get a true sampling of your network. When choosing systems think about what custom applications and third-party software may react adversely to patch or configuration changes. These are the systems you want in your test group.

Once you have tested each configuration change and patch on your test systems, you will be ready to roll out your changes to the entire network. Again, you will want to start with the higher-risk systems and move to the lower-risk ones when applying the changes and patches.

> **NOTE**
>
> One concept that can be difficult to grasp for new security practitioners is that of accepting risk. There will be systems on your network which, for whatever reason, you will not be able to patch or reconfigure. Although this goes against building a secure infrastructure, it is a reality in most corporate environments. Typically in such cases, the asset owner will sign a document that lists the security risks and the reasons for not making the necessary changes to the system. As a security professional, you will become very familiar with the phrase *cover your ass*. Although this document will do that, you also should try to place such systems on their own network that have mitigating controls to prevent attacks.

One of the mistakes that many IT and security administrators make is that once they have rolled out their configuration changes, they fail to validate that the changes took place and that the systems are actually secure. That's why it's important to repeat step three after you have patched. You might be surprised to see that some systems, for various reasons, were not actually patched or reconfigured. With that in mind, these are the steps we recommend you follow during this stage:

1. Create an accurate sampling of your assets.

2. Test all patches and configuration issues on your sampling.

3. Document results and document accepted risk for sign-off.

4. Roll out patches and configuration changes.

5. Repeat step three to validate roll-out.

What Tools Exist to Help You Do It

This is not an area where you will find a lot of open source tools that can help you, so you will be forced to look at a commercial solution. One such solution that we recommend is ECM, from Configuresoft, but do not take our word for what tools to use, because your organization may have different requirements. Do, however, review Chapter 8 and, as we recommend when picking any tool, create a list of your requirements and evaluate each tool and how it meets your requirements. Here are some tools to look at:

■   ECM (Configuresoft, www.configuresoft.com)

■   PatchLink Update (PatchLink Corp., www.patchlink.com)

■   Microsoft Systems Update Services (Microsoft, www.microsoft.com)

■   bvControl (Symantec, www.symantec.com)

■   UpdateEXPERT (St. Bernard Software, www.stbernard.com)

Step Six: Create a Vulnerability Assessment Schedule

What You Need to Do

By now, you should have a pretty good idea of how long it will take to not only scan your entire network, but also remediate any issues found. So, now is the time to create a schedule to continue your vulnerability assessments.

Why You Need to Do It

As we said in previous chapters, and even in this one, a vulnerability management program is a perpetual activity which, although time consuming, does get easier over time. This is the step which, if you approach it logically, can make the entire process easy to deal with.

How to Do It

By now, you should have noticed a theme of starting with critical assets and working down to less-critical ones. This step is no different, and although your schedule will depend entirely on how paranoid your organization is, there are some basic guidelines to follow concerning when to perform assessments.

Like we said in Chapter 5, there are three specific triggers that should cause you to initiate a scan of your network:

1. A new threat becomes evident and you want to verify that your systems are not vulnerable or identify systems that are vulnerable.

2. A vendor releases a patch or a number of patches and you want to verify that your systems are patched and are not vulnerable, or some other event causes wide-scale changes to your environment.

3. You want a point-in-time assessment of your current security posture and a list of vulnerabilities affecting your organization.

How can you schedule around these three triggers so that your vulnerability management plans are more proactive than reactive? Luckily, many vendors that are serious about supporting their enterprise customers publish specific patch dates. If your vendor doesn't follow a specific schedule, you can create your own which, although hard to pin down, will at least let you plan scan and patch events more clearly. Table 11.3 provides a sample schedule we recommend for implementing vulnerability assessments.

Table 11.3 A Sample Schedule for Implementing Vulnerability Assessments

Scan Trigger	What to Scan	When to Scan	What to Scan For
Point-in-time assessment	Confidential Asset Groups	The last Monday of every month	All vulnerabilities and configuration issues.
Point-in-time assessment	Internal Only Asset Groups	The last Friday of every month	All vulnerabilities and configuration issues.
Point-in-time assessment	Unclassified Asset Groups	The second-to-last Monday of every quarter (three-month schedule)	All vulnerabilities and configuration issues.
Vendor releases a patch, or some other event causes wide-scale changes	Confidential Asset Groups	Immediately after the trigger event, and again after remediation is completed	Scan for the vendor-released patches or issues that the patch addresses. If a wide-scale change is the trigger, scan for all vulnerabilities related to the change.

Continued

www.syngress.com

Table 11.3 Continued

Scan Trigger	What to Scan	When to Scan	What to Scan For
Vendor releases a patch, or some other event causes wide-scale changes	Internal Only Asset Groups	Immediately after Confidential Asset Group scans are complete, and again after remediation is completed	Scan for the vendor-released patches or issues that the patch addresses. If a wide-scale change is the trigger, scan for all vulnerabilities related to the change.
Vendor releases a patch, or some other event causes wide-scale changes	Unclassified Asset Groups	Immediately after Internal Only Asset Group scans are complete, and again after remediation is completed	Scan for the vendor-released patches or issues that the patch addresses. If a wide-scale change is the trigger, scan for all vulnerabilities related to the change.
A new threat becomes evident	Confidential Asset Groups	Immediately after the trigger event, and again after remediation is completed	Scan for operating systems, applications, or configurations that are related to the new threat.
A new threat becomes evident	Internal Only Asset Groups	Immediately after Confidential Asset Group scans are complete, and again after remediation is completed	Scan for operating systems, applications, or configurations that are related to the new threat.
A new threat becomes evident	Unclassified Asset Groups	Immediately after Internal Only Asset Group scans are complete, and again after remediation is completed	Scan for operating systems, applications, or configurations that are related to the new threat.

As you can see, only one of the three trigger events is something you can actually plan for: you can partially plan for the patch release trigger if your vendor has a set schedule or if you are able to create your own schedule. By breaking the scans into groups, you decrease the amount of work required at each stage, and therefore, decrease the length of time from vulnerability to patch.

Step Seven: Create a Patch and Change Management Process

What You Need to Do

We listed this as a separate step, but in reality, you should do this the same time you create your VA schedule (step six), because each of these steps relies on the other. Any organization that allows change to its computing assets without some sort of logical testing and planning is doomed to experience long system downtime and will never achieve a successful vulnerability management program.

To prevent this from happening you need to create a process that covers all potential problems that patching or reconfiguration can cause. In our experience, this process will never be perfect, and it should be open to evolving with an organization and account for potential shortcomings. Change, when managed properly, can be a good thing, but even the process for handling change needs to be adaptable.

Why You Need to Do It

As we mentioned earlier, if computing asset changes are not planned for properly, the changes will fail, and ultimately, your security initiatives will fail along with them. You need to plan, test, track, and then retest all system changes. This will ensure that any bad changes will be caught before they affect the overall user base, and it will ensure that the organization understands and plans for any impact to its security that these changes will create.

How to Do It

When creating your change and patch management process, you need to ensure that you follow these steps:

1. Create a test group that is a sampling of all assets on your network.
2. Document the proposed change in detail.
3. Document a "roll-back" plan to undo the change.
4. Obtain sign-off from asset owners on the planned change.
5. Implement the change on your test group.
6. Monitor for adverse effects.
7. Roll out the change enterprisewide if the test group is successful.
8. Undo the change if the test group is not successful.
9. Initiate step 6.

Although this appears to be a lengthy list of steps that could be time consuming and not conducive to quickly addressing vulnerabilities, with the right tools and the proper organizational buy-in, this process can move fairly quickly and even account for emergency changes. The key is proper documentation and testing; this will save you a lot of work when things go badly.

What Tools Exist to Help You Do It

Unfortunately, some of the best, and even the worst, change management tools we have had the pleasure to work with over the years have been custom-built systems. That being said, there are a lot of commercial products that can help you, and some of them even integrate with some of the more popular VA tools. Here's a list of tools we like:

- Tivoli (IBM, www.ibm.com)

- netViz Change Management (netViz, www.netviz.com)

- BMC Remedy (BMC Software, www.bmc.com)

Step Eight: Monitor for New Risks to Assets
What You Need to Do

This is the final step of our eight-step program to vulnerability management, and it's probably the one that can be the most frustrating for IT security engineers. Once you have completed the preceding seven steps you may feel like you are almost done, but unfortunately, now the hard work begins. After all of the work you put into creating a baseline and a plan for changes, you now have to sit back and wait for events that you have no control over but will create hard work for your team.

This is the reality of the security practitioner: just when your systems are secure, you have to remain vigilant and wait for the coming storm.

Why You Need to Do It

Although it would be easy to bury your head in the sand and pretend that after performing steps one through seven, you are done with this process and your organization is secure, as any attacker would gladly prove to you this is not the best strategy, because eventually something outside of your control will impact the security of your network.

So, the only thing you can do is constantly monitor for new events that have an impact on your security and deal with them in a timely manner. Think about the first chapter in this book, where we discussed windows of vulnerability. This is the key point to vulnerability management: reducing the length of time those windows are open.

How to Do It

Now that we have made you a little more paranoid than you already are, we will try to help you deal with that paranoid feeling that everyone is out to get you and your organization's network, because the reality is that everyone *is* out to get you and your organization's network.

Before you can monitor for new threats, you need to know what the threats could be. The following is a list of things you need to keep your IT security staff aware of on a constant basis. We are sure you will notice that all of these were trigger events for a vulnerability assessment:

- Vendor-released patches
- Configuration weaknesses
- 0 day vulnerability releases
- Large-scale attacks

Each issue in the preceding list can have an impact on your organization's security, so you need to come up with an easy way to say "in the know" when it comes to emerging issues. Unfortunately, this requires a lot of work.

What Tools Exist to Help You Do It

One of the ways you can track vendor-released patches is to subscribe to vendor patch release mailing lists. Table 11.4 provides a list of popular vendors and where you can find information on their release processes. You also should create a list of vendors you use in your environment (do not forget application vendors).

Table 11.4 Vendor Patch Release Mailing Lists

Vendor	Patch Release Information
Microsoft	www.microsoft.com/technet/security/default.mspx
Apple	www.apple.com/support/security/
Citrix	www.citrix.com/site/jumpPage.asp?pageID=22214
Sun Microsystems	http://sunsolve.sun.com/pub-cgi/show.pl?target=patchpage
Oracle	www.oracle.com/technology/deploy/security/alerts.htm
Red Hat Linux	www.redhat.com/security/updates/
Hewlett-Packard	www1.itrc.hp.com/service/index.do
Mozilla	www.mozilla.org/security/#Security_Alerts
IBM	www-306.ibm.com/software/sw-bycategory/
Cisco	www.cisco.com/iam/unified/ipcc1/Cisco_Product_Security_Overview.htm
Juniper	www.juniper.net/support/security/security_notices.html
Nortel Networks	www130.nortelnetworks.com/go/main.jsp

Configuration weaknesses, security advisories, 0 day releases, and even large-scale attacks are typically reported via various mailing lists. A great resource for getting a complete list of every information security mailing list comes from our friends at Neohapsis, http://archives.neohapsis.com.

Table 11.5 provides a short list of good mailing list resources that you can use to monitor for various security issues.

Table 11.5 Mailing List Resources

List Name	URL
VulnWatch	www.vulnwatch.org
VulnDiscuss	www.vulnwatch.org
BugTraq	www.securityfocus.com/archive/1/description
Full-Disclosure (warning: unmoderated)	https://lists.grok.org.uk/mailman/listinfo/full-disclosure
North America Network Operators Group (NANOG)	www.nanog.org/mailinglist.html
Patch Management	www.patchmanagement.org/
Incidents Mailing List	www.securityfocus.com/archive/75/description

The typical network is a diverse environment, so manually monitoring all of these resources can be time consuming. As such, some organizations go so far as to hire security analysts whose job is to do nothing but monitor for new threats. Luckily, some vendors have stepped up to the plate and created solutions that are designed to help you battle the massive amounts of information this work generates, and concentrate only on the issues that matter to your organization. As with any software tool, we highly recommend that you test each solution based on your own criteria before committing to a specific one. There are a lot of players in this market, some with a lot of experience and others who are quite new to it, so be cautious with your decisions:

- Symantec DeepSight (www.symantec.com/Products/enterprise?c=prodcat&refId=1017)
- Computer Associates eTrust (www3.ca.com/services/subpractice.aspx?ID=5012)
- FrSIRT Alerting Service (www.frsirt.com/english/services/)
- Telus Assurent (www.assurent.com/)
- CyberTrust (www.cybertrust.com/solutions/managed_security_services/)
- Secunia (http://corporate.secunia.com/products/9/vulnerability_management_products_enterprise)

## Part 2

Network Security Evaluation

## Chapter 12

Introducing the INFOSEC Evaluation Methodology

Solutions in this chapter:

- **What Is the IEM?**
- **What the IEM Is Not**
- **Standards and Regulations**

☑ **Summary**

Introduction

Security providers around the world have been trying for years to engineer an effective means for conducting technical evaluations that is meaningful to the customer. For too long, we've seen fly-by-night consulting companies walk into a customer organization, run a security vulnerability scanner, print out the default application report (after replacing the logo), and present that to the customer as the final deliverable. Although the initial paper factor of this type of work might be impressive to the uneducated customer, once they start digging into the actual contents of the report and trying to understand how it applies to their organization, they normally discover that this level of service is lacking.

Until recently, the use of a repeatable, structured, and flexible methodology to provide these services was on a per-company basis. Customers could never really be sure what to expect when they asked for a security evaluation. Would it be a penetration test? A full Red Team? Would it even be comprehensive, or did the consultants see the work as a game? It all really came down to *who* was doing the work. The majority of final reports the customer dealt with lacked even enough basic similarity to allow the customer to compare results from year to year.

The INFOSEC Evaluation Methodology (IEM) presents a viable solution to this problem. It's offered by the National Security Agency (NSA) as a baseline set of criteria for conducting technical evaluations for any organization. The deliverables of this methodology are intended to have meaning for all customers. And although the format and core components of the final deliverables remain the same across evaluations, no two final reports will be the same. A number of variables at each customer organization directly impact the manner in which the evaluation, and the assessment, must be conducted. For instance, assuming we have two similar banking customers that require technical evaluations of their network infrastructure, they will still have differences. These include the network architecture and layout; the organization's management and vision; software and applications that are utilized; and the policies and procedures put into place by the organization's management. When each of these banks receives its final report, it should look familiar, be interpretable, and apply specifically to the organization. That means that even through the reports look similar, the results of one cannot be applied to the other.

Admitting we have a problem is the first step in the healing process, and there's no doubt that the majority of experienced INFOSEC professionals in the industry have found themselves looking for a solution. The NSA IEM is one of the solutions that is finding widespread acceptance in the community. In this chapter, we'll present the reader with the basic layout of the IEM. By the time you finish this chapter, you will understand what the IEM is intended to address, why this type of work is requested, where it could potentially be applied, and the phases into which the IEM is organized. We also include a discussion on how the NSA INFOSEC Assessment Methodology (IAM) and IEM relate to one another, helping to achieve a comprehensive and meaningful security assessment/evaluation solution for our customers.

What Is the IEM?

The IEM is a follow-on methodology to the NSA IAM. It provides the technical evaluation processes that were intentionally missing from the IAM. The IEM is a hands-on methodology, meaning you'll be actively interacting with the customer's technical environment. As such, the NSA intended for the

IAM and IEM processes to work hand in hand. The IEM can be placed directly atop the IAM, much like two Lego blocks.

But in contrast to the origins of the IAM, which was originally developed for use within the federal and military arenas, the IEM was developed over a period of three years and included input from government and commercial entities. With the resounding success of the IAM in the commercial world, it was decided that the IEM should be applicable to a wide range of organizations and industries. Input and feedback were solicited from commercial firms, contracting companies, and a variety of government agencies. The IEM is the final result of all the hard work put in by all these organizations and individuals.

Whereas the IAM provides us with an understanding of organizational security as it relates to policies and procedures, the IEM offers a comprehensive look into the actual technical security at the organization. Together, these two processes allow us to more accurately determine the information security posture of our customers. The ratings of our findings are based on the customer's view of their information's criticality, industry-accepted ratings for each of the findings, and the expertise of the evaluation team.

Consider for a minute what we learned from the IAM. The core of the IAM was customer input. Our customer defined their organizational mission and told us what information types were critical for achieving their mission goals. With your guidance, they also went so far as to create impact definitions that help gauge the actual impact on their organization should they lose the confidentiality, integrity, or availability of those pieces of information. These customer-defined components are taken into account as we step through the 18 areas of the IAM and perform our analysis.

This concept is key because, as a security professional, you must admit that you understand security, not widgets. If the customer has been creating widgets for 45 years, they likely have a greater understanding concerning what is required to make quality widgets and retain a competitive advantage in the widget marketplace. *Your* role is to provide guidance and recommendations on information security. If we utilize both the customer expertise and your expertise, the final deliverables from any security assessment or evaluation will have greater value and impact.

Tying the Methodologies Together

As we begin engaging the customer and working to determine their objectives, we're simultaneously setting the scope of the security work. The IEM is no different. The process begins with the basic coordination processes, which can be conducted concurrently with the IAM pre-assessment phase. In the IEM we call this the *IEM pre-evaluation*. You'll notice as you look at the names of the phases in the IEM that they match almost exactly the names we use in the IAM. This is intentional and aids in coordinating the performance of both the IAM and IEM concurrently.

In Figure 12.1, you see a depiction of the IAM phases. Notice that we have three phases, beginning with the pre-assessment and ending with the post-assessment. As you'll find out in later chapters, the activities in the IAM pre-assessment are required before moving to the follow-on IAM activities or beginning the IEM.

Figure 12.1 The Phases of the IAM

Pre-Assessment Phase	On-Site Phase	Post Assessment Phase
* Identify Information Criticality * Identify System Configuration * Set Scope of the Assessment * Documentation Request * Documentation Review * Team Assignment * Pre-Analysis * Site Visit Coordination	* On-Site In-Brief * Interview Site Personnel * System Demonstrations * Documentation Review * On-Site Out Brief	* Additional Documentation Review * Finalize Analysis * Consult Additional Expertise * Generate Recommendations * Final Report Coordination

The IEM also contains three phases. Figure 12.2 provides a general overview of the activities in the three IEM phases. Notice how similar these are to the IAM. Although the IEM is much more technically focused, we'll use a lot of the same type of information that we used in the IAM. The distinction between the two is the organizational nature of the IAM versus the technical nature of the IEM. The devil is in the details, and we'll be moving from the higher-level activities we focused on in the IAM to a much more granular approach in the IEM.

If you compare Figures 12.1 and 12.2, you'll see that the on-site phase in each one is where the rubber meets the road. In the IAM, this is where we delve into the policies, procedures, and regulations to determine the customer's security posture from an organization viewpoint. In the IEM, however, it's where we actually check the technical proficiency of the target networks, servers, hosts, and high-assurance components, such as routers, firewalls, or switches.

Figure 12.2 The Phases of the IEM

Pre-Evaluation Phase	On-Site Evaluation Phase	Post Evaluation Phase
* Identify Systems and Boundaries * Determine System Architecture * Legal Coordination * Create Rules of Engagement * Determine Evaluation Scope * Develop Evaluation Plan * On-Site Visit Coordination	* On-Site In-Brief * Evaluation Testing - 10 Baseline Activities * On-Site Out Brief	* Conduct Final Analysis * Consult Additional Expertise * Generate Final Report * Create Security Road Map * Deliver Final Report * Follow Up with Customer

NOTE

The IEM is not just a network evaluation methodology. Although we do run scanning tools and look for network accessible services or applications, the IEM delves much deeper into the customer's technical presence. This includes testing the configuration on all servers, hosts, routers, firewalls, and other high-assurance components.

We'll also be testing password strength and analyzing the architecture of the customer network from a security perspective. The IEM is a comprehensive evaluation methodology, and therefore, we must address the entirety of the customer's technical exposure.

Figure 12.3 shows these two methodologies together as a cohesive unit, allowing you to better visualize how the processes of each methodology can work together. The image tries to convey the fact that many of the activities we're already performing for the IAM require very little modification or addition to be useful to the IEM. For example, the final analysis and report-generation activities can all be performed at the same time without too many problems. We're already working on detailing the findings for the customer and laying out appropriate recommendations to improve their organizational security. It doesn't require a huge stretch of one's imagination to see that we can easily integrate the technical findings and recommendations into this phase as well.

Looking at Figure 12.3, you get an idea of how the entire security assessment and evaluation process is intended to operate. In the pre-analysis phase, we're performing all our up-front work. This entails finding out what the customer is expecting, laying out our acceptable rules of engagement, protecting the customer and ourselves by utilizing the appropriate legal documentation, and working with the customer to define the critical information within the organization.

WARNING

Never underestimate the importance of the pre-analysis phase. This area is often neglected and can result in unsatisfied customers, poor results, findings that lack true value, or even legal liability on the part of you or your organization. As mentioned before, the customer understands widgets, but not necessarily the evaluation process. In many cases, the customer has had a different understanding of the evaluation process than the evaluation team intended. If this is the case, your deliverables may not meet customer expectations. Bear in mind that word of mouth spreads quickly when the news is negative.

The other negative side effect most often associated with poor performance of the pre-analysis phase is a lack of total understanding on the part of the evaluation team. The customer has requested A and your team provides B. By the time you realize the disconnect, you're already behind schedule and over your intended budget for the work. Now your team has to go back and fix the work to meet the actual customer expectations.

Figure 12.3 Combined Assessment and Evaluation Activities

Pre-Analysis	Analysis	Final Analysis

Pre-Analysis
* Define the Mission
* Information Criticality
* Impact Definitions
* System Definitions
* Information Flow
* Scoping
* Coordination
* Rules of Engagement

Analysis

Assessment
* Infrastructure
* Policies
* Procedures
* Regulations
* Organizational
* Management

Evaluation
* Technical Implementation
* Server/Host Security
* High Assurance Devices
* Network Security
* Application Security
* Entry Points
* Configurations

Final Analysis
* Vulnerability Analysis
* Recommend Solutions
* Draft Final Report
* Enable Prioritization
* Security Roadmap
* Relate to Customer Impact

In the analysis phase, we've combined all the activities from the IAM and IEM. Because the methodologies differ so dramatically in this area, it can be difficult to visualize how a single team could accomplish all the critical points. But you do have options.

Using two teams that work simultaneously is not unheard of and often works quite well. I've seen many large consulting or contracting companies operate in this fashion, especially internally. For instance, a single team might have the primary responsibility to perform IAM-like functions on the organization. They might gauge organizational compliance with federal regulations, industry security guidelines, or regulations and policies based on the organization's mission. Another independent team might be responsible solely for the technical security within the organization. They're the ones that come in twice a year and run all the nifty tools on the network to ensure that the organization understands its actual security exposure.

Another option that works quite well is one that we've used in the past: Members of a single team with both organizational and technical experience work together on both methodologies at the same time. So let's say we have a team of four individuals that goes into a large hospital to conduct the IAM and IEM. Many of the onsite activities for the IEM can be completed while the interviews or documentation review is being done for the IAM. Not all evaluation tools require active participation by the security professional. With that said, we try not to leave while the tools are running in case they cause some accidental downtime. Still, this process works very well. We prefer to have a larger office with multiple network connections, allowing us to maintain our technical work while we're conducting interviews of documentation review for the IAM.

One thing that every team lead should understand is that the qualifications and skills required for the IEM are vastly different, in most instances, from those required in the IAM. For instance, whereas the IAM is focused around the organizational layer of information security, the IEM is decidedly more technical in nature. For this reason, the individuals on an evaluation team will need tounderstand the details of how the network, operating systems, and applications operate. The members of an IAM team will need to understand information criticality; regulations, policies and procedures; and how to communicate with a cross-section of employees at most organizations, from management to the cleaning crew. These skill sets are not, however, mutually exclusive, and at times you'll be lucky enough to have an individual on your team who can operate fluently within both arenas.

In the final analysis phase, we combine our efforts to create a cohesive final product for the customer. This is where we ensure that all our findings are correct for the customer and that our recommendations are useful to the customer environment. We're not just dumping the report from a commercial product and changing the logo. In fact, the IEM is so intent on providing value and presenting our findings to the customer in an understandable way that we create a security road map, which you'll read more about in later chapters. If the customer doesn't understand or can't use the information we give them, their money and time went to waste. NSA addresses this issue in this final stage of the methodologies.

NOTE

Although we stress the importance of utilizing both the IAM and the IEM, they do not have to be conducted concurrently. At times it simply is not feasible for the customer organization to undertake both activities at the same time. These occasions could include financial, time, or resource restrictions. However, it's important to note that in instances where the IAM has been conducted six months or more prior to the evaluation activities, it might be beneficial to revisit the original IAM pre-assessment process to verify that the customer information is still relevant. As with all things in life, information ages as time progresses. But in contrast with some things in life, information does not always improve with age. Corporate vision and priorities often change as the organization's leadership and infrastructure change. The IEM depends on an accurate representation of these items to provide the customer with a final product of the highest relevance and quality.

What the IEM Is Not

The IEM is just one part of the overall picture of information security presented by the NSA. Three levels of security analysis must occur, according to the NSA (see Figure 12.4). The level 1 process is the INFOSEC assessment, on which the IAM is based. This is a cooperative methodology with heavy customer involvement. It's the start of the information security triad and measures organizational security at a policy and procedural level. The IAM is a hands-off process. This means that we're not actually going to sit at a customer computer or run security tools against their technology.

The level 2 process consists of the INFOSEC evaluations, on which the IEM is based. For this level, we actively test the technical security of the organization. This is a hands-on process. We use state-of-the-art software and methods to detail misconfiguration weaknesses, system exposures, and potential vulnerabilities.

Although the customer is still involved in the IEM, it's not as profound as we saw in the IAM. We want to gain a comprehensive look at all the potential problem areas we can in the amount of time we have available. The objective is not to "break in" or "get root." This is not a penetration test, nor is it adversarial. Activities are performed internally and externally, where appropriate.

Level 3 is where the process becomes adversarial. There is currently no NSA sponsored methodology for conducting Red Team activities, so there is no officially endorsed training course or process. But the NSA defines these Red Team activities as the Red Team Methodology, or RTM. Simulating the appropriate adversary, the Red Team tests every possible security scenario until it manages to break into the customer network. Red Team activities are *not* comprehensive. We're trying to find a way to the customer's information, through any path possible. In most real-world cases, this means that we sit outside the customer network and organization, trying to find a way in that hasn't been locked down.

To best understand the difference between the IEM and a Red Team, let's look at what happens in a Red Teaming situation. Most teams of this nature start out *in the dark*, meaning they are given very little information from which to start the testing. This information could be limited to as little as a domain name on the Internet. The testing team is then left to its own devices to discover information that would further its attempts to break into the customer network. This is often referred to as a *black box assessment*.

As the team members start out, they look specifically for the easiest potential targets on the customer network—those that could provide the easiest path into the network. As they progress, only vulnerabilities along that path are analyzed, leaving potential vulnerabilities on other paths untested, unaltered, and intact. At the end of the process, the customer receives a report detailing how the intrusion occurred and what vulnerabilities were taken advantage of, but all other potential vulnerabilities remain hidden away on the network.

The IEM is *not* a Red Team activity. The IEM is comprehensive in that we want to find every possible security finding we can so that the customer can lock it down. The Red Team simply tries to get to the information using any means possible. The IEM is cooperative with the customer; the Red Team is adversarial based on the industry in question. If we're looking at a military customer, maybe we're simulating a terror organization. If the customer is a research and development firm, maybe we're simulating a competitor and trying to get at the organization's "crown jewels." The IEM aims to find the vulnerabilities without exploiting or compromising the customer network. The primary goal of a Red Team *is* to compromise the network, especially by exploitation.

Figure 12.4 The NSA INFOSEC Triad

> **NOTE**
>
> All three phases of the NSA information security triad have their value, but we need to remain cognizant of the timing of each one. For example, if we conduct the IEM prior to performing the IAM, our findings cannot be related back to the customer organization. What value do the findings hold if we can't relate them back to the impact they have on the organization? In this same manner, it's considered unwise to conduct an *attack and penetration test,* or *pen test,* before the customer has had the luxury of a full evaluation. Breaking into a customer when they haven't had the opportunity to see the full representation of their security posture or the chance to lock down their information is a waste of time and money.
>
> For the purposes of this book, we'll work from the premise that the information security life cycle will be conducted with the IAM occurring just before or concurrently with the IEM, followed sometime after by a Red Team activity. Conduct the IAM and IEM, give the customer a chance to put up their defenses, and then test those defenses through Red Team activities.

The IEM Is *Not* an Audit or Inspection

As with most things in life, people don't typically react favorably to being put under a microscope and analyzed. No one likes feeling as though someone is peering over his shoulder, trying to find mistakes he's made. These are connotations often associated with internal audits or inspections. When you discuss the evaluation methodology with the customer, ensure that you avoid these terms. We need their help if we want them to have a real understanding of their security posture. For example, say that an evaluation team comes in, conducts interviews, reviews documentation, tests processes, and associates shortfalls with particular areas or individuals. People in situations like this tend to withhold information, be less than helpful, and shy away from dangerous situations.

When we consider evaluations in the context of the NSA IEM, we want to ensure that every person we interact with understands the nonattribution characteristics of the NSA methodologies. We associate no blame to particular individuals; we're only interested in the truth. In many instances, it's useful to let the end users or administrators know that we're trying to find all the holes in the system so they can be fixed before the organization is audited or inspected. This view makes our job easier, makes the employee more comfortable, and allows the findings to better reflect reality.

What does this do for the security professional who is going to work in these potentially hostile environments? It means that you, as the consultant, will need to act as both a security professional *and* a human psychologist. You need to understand how your actions may be interpreted by the various human minds that exist and work within the target organization. This requires a certain finesse and ability to communicate. The evaluation team lead is normally responsible for mediating customer perception, but each team member should have training in how to communicate with the customer.

You'll also want to know how to *sell* the process to each person you run into. I'm not talking about being one of those over-the-top sales folks who push the product down the customer's throat, but you want to understand the aspects of the work you'll be performing that appeal to the person you're speaking with. Explain how your work will benefit them and they're more likely to help make the process successful.

Every good security consultant understands that even though he or she is there to help secure the customer, they'll also need to manage the individuals within the organization. You're never *just* a security professional. Forgetting these key aspects of human interaction could result in a painful evaluation experience.

The IEM Is Not a Risk Assessment

Let's get this straight right now: The IAM and IEM are *not* risk assessment or risk management methodologies. It's true that many of the activities associated with the NSA methodologies are similar to the requirements for a risk assessment, but no one is pretending that they meet al*l* the requirements. The IAM and IEM are vulnerability assessment methodologies. The intent is to identify as many vulnerabilities as possible, allowing the customer to fix or mitigate those findings to improve their security posture. Although we do address threat and risk from a cursory level within the IAM and IEM, the NSA methodologies don't go into the detail needed for actual risk assessments or risk management.

If we look at modern definitions of risk, we see that risk is a combination of the value of the asset (or impact of the loss), the associated threats, and the existing potential vulnerabilities. Taking these three things into account, we notice that the vulnerabilities are the only area in which the customers can effect dramatic change.

> **NOTE**
>
> I've seen countless articles written by individuals who don't truly understand the goals of the IAM and IEM. These have resulted in some confusion for readers and practitioners of the NSA methodologies. The primary goal of the NSA processes is to identify vulnerabilities. It make no attempt to become a risk assessment methodology. We are aware that using the IAM and IEM will get you *closer* to a risk assessment, but readers should not mistakenly associate the two as one and the same.

Standards and Regulations

Nations around the world are implementing a number of information security-related regulations with the intention of protecting consumers and organizations. The United States has led the way in this arena by creating a massive number of regulations based on varying industries, from the federal government and military to healthcare, education, and utilities.

At first glance, it's almost intimidating. How is an organization supposed to understand all these differing pieces of legislation? Even companies in other countries that do work within the United States are starting to pay attention. For instance, companies around the world with a U.S. presence are starting to work on becoming Sarbanes-Oxley compliant. Fortunately, the inherent flexibility that NSA built into the IAM and IEM allow security firms to address necessary security regulations.

Take a real-world example: We utilize parts of the NSA processes to address the certification and accreditation (C&A) requirements of the federal government. The IEM lends itself nicely to performing the requisite security testing and evaluation (ST&E). We've used the entire process on organizations from high-level universities to healthcare offices.

Most security regulations are fairly general, preferring to give vague allusions to what is intended versus laying out the law directly. The term most used for meeting these general requirements is *best practices*. Best practices are simply what are commonly thought to be the best course of action regarding security. But an organization that makes widgets probably hasn't got a clue as to where to begin. This is where *your* expertise and experience come into play.

Lack of Expertise

The NSA methodologies have the ability to be used in nearly every industry in existence. The key component that the IAM and IEM cannot give you is experience. If I sat you down in the NSA courses and taught you, one on one, the methodologies and how they work, I still couldn't teach you what experience will show you. We could expand the course to two weeks and still not meet our goal.

Performing the IAM and IEM is simple. You follow some basic guidelines consistently to create a final product. We teach these methodologies to college students at the University of Advancing Technology. They have a project requirement associated with each course to perform the methodologies on the university. But when they begin the courses, they have little to no experience in performing these types of activities. They have lots of questions and many things they need to learn.

We've had individuals like this in our courses, and it's important to note that simply understanding the methods and following the steps will not provide the customer with the required value in the final deliverables. The value is derived from your ability to interpret the results of the assessment and evaluation and associate those back to the customer. Ask yourself these questions:

- Does this vulnerability apply?

- How does this finding affect the information the customer told me was critical to their mission?

- How does the finding impact the customer from a regulatory or privacy perspective?

- How will the organization be changed by implementing the recommendations provided for each finding?

- Are there any limitations on the types of security controls that can be introduced into the organization's environment?

My point here is that understanding the methodologies is not enough, in and of itself, to provide value to the customer. There are steps in experience level that begin with being a team member in training and eventually lead to being the team leader. Failure to adhere to these basic facts concerning information security experience results in so many customers being dissatisfied with the results of their final reports. It's easiest to think of it along the lines of the blacksmith's apprentice: There are basic things you need to know before you go out and do this work on your own. Try to work under an experienced and reputable mentor before performing this work for your own customers.

Certification Does Not Give You Expertise

I've seen more and more requests for proposal (RFPs) and bid items requiring any number of certifications from the individuals who will be performing the work. These could include anything from the standard Certified Information Systems Security Professional (CISSP) certification that ISC(2) maintains to even the NSA IAM and IEM certifications. What customers don't understand is that these methodologies mean that certified individuals understand core concepts about information security. They don't indicate those individuals' ability to provide value on the customer's findings.

As with any other certification, the NSA IAM and IEM certifications only state that you understand what we taught you in class; you understand how to perform the methodologies based on what we've taught you. The piece we will not certify is that you can perform these tasks in such a way as to provide the necessary value to the customer. Learning these methodologies is only the first step.

Summary

This chapter is intended solely to act as your introduction to the IEM process. Although the IEM is extremely effective as a standalone methodology, it is intended to work in conjunction with the organizational focus provided by the IAM. Whereas the IAM focuses on the critical information, identifying critical systems, and looking for vulnerabilities related to processes, procedures, documentation, and operations, the IEM delves into much deeper detail, looking for vulnerabilities within the technical infrastructure and providing recommendations for customers on how to eliminate or mitigate those findings.

The IEM is a vulnerability evaluation methodology, nothing more. Although we must have a solid understanding of threat and risk, the IEM does not attempt, nor does it pretend, to become a full risk assessment or threat management methodology. It is also much more comprehensive than a penetration test or a Red Team activity. Instead of focusing our effort solely on finding a pathway into the network, we look at all possible avenues. By doing so, we can locate the greatest number of vulnerabilities and exposure, allowing the customer to better protect their informational assets.

Finally, you should also understand from this chapter that simply knowing how to work within the methodologies presented by the National Security Agency does not make you a security expert. The value derived from the methodologies depends heavily on your own expertise and knowledge, which only come with time, effort, and working within the field. The NSA methodologies for performing assessments and evaluations are simply tools to be added to your tools kit and used as appropriate to aid you in helping create positive change in your customer's information security posture.

## Chapter 13

Before the Evaluation Starts

Solutions in this chapter:

- **The Evaluation Request**
- **Validating the Evaluation Request**
- **The Formal Engagement Agreement**
- **Customer and Evaluation Team Approval**

☑ **Summary**

Introduction

Some actions are necessary precursors to the actual evaluation. To effectively conduct the evaluation, you must first obtain a subset of information about the customer and its network for you to determine that an evaluation is really desired. This chapter focuses on those activities that occur prior to the start of the evaluation. This chapter includes discussion on how and why the evaluation may be requested, the process of validating the evaluation request, and the formal evaluation agreement. These are all actions that occur primarily before the IEM pre-evaluation phase. These are also business process areas that NSA does not cover in the IEM.

The Evaluation Request

The evaluation request plays a critical role in understanding the scope of the evaluation effort. It provides an opportunity to understand the requesting organization's market position, industry, and internal desires. This process also provides an opportunity to educate the customer on the difference among assessments, evaluations, and penetration testing.

Why Are Evaluations Requested?

Evaluations are requested for many different purposes. They are related to the organization's needs, the industry in which it works, and its internal policies, procedures, and goals. Some of the primary reasons are related to legal and regulatory compliance requirements, response to suspicious activities, third-party reviews, and the knowledge that it is the right thing to do for the organization. For the evaluation to be effective, we do need to understand the answers to these questions so that we can effectively implement the evaluation process.

Compliance With Laws and Regulations

Laws and regulations are a driving force for determining the proper INFOEC posture for an organization. Without this knowledge, the security implementation will be flawed. The following sections discuss a few of the U.S. laws and regulations that can affect an organization's security posture requirements.

The Sarbanes-Oxley Act

The Sarbanes-Oxley Act, also called SarbOx or SOX, was established in 2002 to address public company financial accountability in the wake of the Enron and MCI accounting scandals. SOX holds public companies and their officers directly accountable for accurate reporting of their companies' fiscal condition. SOX also contains provisions to assure the protection of sensitive information and the accuracy of accounting statements.

Federal Information Security Management Act

The Federal Information Security Management Act (FISMA) is focused on a requirement for each federal agency to develop, document, and implement an agencywide program to provide information security for the information and information systems that support the operations and assets of the agency, including those provided or managed by another agency, contractor, or other source (FISMA Implementation Project, http://csrc.nist.gov/sec-cert/).

Health Insurance Portability and Accountability Act of 1996

Health Insurance Portability and Accountability Act of 1996 (HIPAA) legislation covers two primary considerations:

- **Health insurance reform**   This provision covers protecting health insurance coverage for workers and their families. It does not have an information security-related provision.

- **Administrative simplification**   This provision establishes standard code sets and identifiers for providers, health plans, and employers. It also has an information security and privacy area for protecting health information. HIPAA's goal is to establish standards that will improve the efficiency and effectiveness of the health care system by encouraging the use of electronic data interchange (EDI) in health care (see Centers for Medicare & Medicaid Services, www.cms.hhs.gov/hipaa/).

The Gramm-Leach-Bliley Act

The Gramm-Leach-Bliley Act (GLBA), also known as the Financial Services Modernization Act of 1999, provides limited privacy protections against the sale of your private financial information. GLBA also established protections against the practice of obtaining personal information through false pretenses.

The Family Educational Rights and Privacy Act

The Family Educational Rights and Privacy Act (FERPA) is focused on protecting the privacy of student educational records. This law applies to any school that receives funds from the U.S. Department of Education (see www.ed.gov/policy/gen/guid/fpco/ferpa/index.html).

The DoD Information Technology Security Certification and Accreditation Process

The DoD Information Technology Security Certification and Accreditation Process (DITSCAP) is applicable to Department of Defense (DoD) only. Also known as DoD Instruction 5200.40, DITSCAP provides the certification and accreditation (C&A) guidance on establishing whether systems/networks can operate in the DoD environment. Approval to operate is required for the organizational Designated Approval Authority (DAA). This process includes system documentation and formal security test and evaluation (ST&E).

The National Information Assurance Certification and Accreditation Process

Virtually identical to the DITSCAP, the National Information Assurance Certification and Accreditation Process (NIACAP) is focused on the U.S. federal civilian departments, agencies, contractors, and consultants.

Defense Information Assurance Certification and Accreditation Process

The Defense Information Assurance Certification and Accreditation Process (DIACAP) will eventually replace DITSCAP as a more robust process that will not only standardize the C&A process, C&A documentation, and the requirements traceability process but will also standardize the requirements definition process.

ISO 17799

An international standard that provides relatively comprehensive guidance on establishing a set of controls that comprise security best practices, ISO 17799 covers the following key security areas:

- Security policy
- Organizational security
- Asset classification and control
- Personnel security
- Physical and environmental security
- Communications and operations management
- Access control
- Systems development and maintenance
- Business continuity management
- Compliance

The North American Electric Reliability Council

The mission of the North American Electric Reliability Council (NERC) is to ensure that the bulk electric system in North America is reliable, adequate, and secure. At the time of writing, NERC has a set of draft cyber-security Critical Infrastructure Protection (CIP) standards that address the cross-section of security concerns. The current Web site for NERC is www.nerc.com. These standards are organized as follows:

- CIP-002-1 Critical Cyber Assets
- CIP-003-1 Security Management Controls
- CIP-004-1 Personnel & Training
- CIP-005-1 Electronic Security
- CIP-006-1 Physical Security
- CIP-007-1 System Security Management
- CIP-008-1 Incident Reporting and Response Planning
- CIP-009-1 Recovery Plans

Response to Suspicious Activities

One of the primary reasons an evaluation is requested is as a result of recent or ongoing suspicious activity. This suspicious activity is often a "wake-up call" to an organization that they need to further examine their INFOSEC posture. Why does it take this kind of action for an organization to start addressing INFOSEC? Primarily it's because of the fear of the security problems directly or indirectly affecting the customer, the fear of bad press, and/or the fear that the cost of implementing information security will damage the financial bottom line.

Recent Successful Penetration

Organizations often ask for a security evaluation because of a recent successful penetration. The purpose of this type of request has three objectives:

- Identify the method and source of the attack.

- Assure the penetration recovery is complete.

- Ensure that there are no other vulnerabilities that can be exploited to attack the systems/networks.

Suspected Possible Penetration

In other incidents, a customer may request an evaluation because they are concerned that they have been penetrated, but they do not know for sure. In this case, the evaluation is requested for four reasons:

- Identify whether a penetration has occurred.

- Ensure that if a penetration has occurred, steps are taken to recover from the penetration.

- Identify the method and source of the attack.

- Ensure that there are no other vulnerabilities that can be exploited to attack the systems/networks.

Unsuccessful Penetration Attempt

Why would an organization want to conduct an evaluation after an unsuccessful penetration attempt? Primarily it is part of the organization's due-diligence process. They have obviously been a target. Just because the attacker was unsuccessful the first time, that does not mean the attacker will not keep trying and may find exploitable vulnerabilities. For the unsuccessful penetration, we really want to accomplish the following in our evaluation:

- Identify the method and source of the attack.

- Review system/network security to ensure that the attack truly was not successful.

- Ensure that there are no other vulnerabilities that can be exploited to attack the systems/networks.

"I Don't Know If Our Organization Has Been Penetrated"

Unfortunately, many organizations do not know the current security posture of their systems/networks. Without this knowledge, they are not meeting basic due-diligence requirements and certainly are not meeting any legal or regulatory requirements. Organizations that claim not to know their security posture put themselves at risk of both being attacked and encountering legal issues. In this case, the evaluation does the following:

- Baselines the current security posture of the organization
- Establishes a road map to improve the overall security posture of the organization

Third-Party Independent Reviews of Security Posture

In many cases, independent reviews are required, perhaps because of an organization's customers, service-level agreements (SLAs), and/or insurance provider requirements. The independent review provides a powerful and valuable mechanism for verifying and improving security posture. One form of independent review you might have heard of is the *independent verification and validation* (IV&V). This activity was very prevalent in addressing the year 2000 software issues and was used to basically verify that software functioned appropriately. Such a review was handled by an independent third party to avoid a conflict of interest and help to address the problem of being so close to the programs that important issues were missed.

At times an organization may develop "blinders" and miss important security considerations. The independent security review should provide an unbiased review of the organization's security posture and should catch areas that may have been missed by the internal security reviews.

Customer-Required Reviews

In our security practice, we have seen a third-party review requested by an organization to satisfy one of their customers' contractual requirements. Customers want to have a sense of confidence that the organizations they deal with have addressed important areas such as data protection and sensitive customer information. In some cases, we have seen where the concerns of many customers have driven the need for an organization's security. This has been prevalent in the banking and credit card industries. Identity theft is a very high-profile issue, and individual customers would like some level of confidence that their information is protected.

Insurance-Required Reviews

Insurance companies have begun to require companies in some industries to conduct independent security reviews before they issue insurance or initiate reduced rates on insurance. The insurance industry has recognized the importance of information security from a business and liability perspective. The insured must prove a level of due diligence to reduce the threat of liability concerns.

Notes from the Underground…

Security for Insurance

Several insurance companies have resorted to a security questionnaire to be answered by the potential insured party to determine the level of security within an organization. For example, our team did some support for a company that was insured by AIG Insurance. A 14-page questionnaire had to be filled out, and if the company got an 80 or better on the questionnaire, they were eligible for up to $100,000 in insurance premium adjustments. Results may vary; check with your insurance provider first.

SLA-Required Reviews

SLAs often drive how people do business. When you think of the SLA, you generally think in terms of uptime, availability, response time, and the like. From an information security perspective, the SLA can require a minimum level of security on the provider's systems or some required duration between security reviews to include both internal reviews and third-party reviews. The SLA plays an important role in how much a provider is paid for the services provided. If they default on the SLA, the business is damaged as a result.

It's The Right Thing To Do

What motivates an organization to do the right thing? Sometimes it is truly a desire to protect its information for the sake of protecting its information. But in reality, an organization is most likely driven by one or more of the other factors we've discussed. Whether it is protect the organization's image, customers, or bottom line, when it comes to information security, it generally comes down to some business purpose being the motivator. Most organizations will only spend the minimum amount necessary on security. In reality, they need to determine the value of the information to determine the appropriate level of security implementation.

How Are Evaluations Requested?

The evaluation request can possibly come from any source available to a customer. In our practice, we have received requests via the typical e-mails and phone calls. But we have also received requests in uncommon locations, including on an airplane and while sitting in an audience at a technology event. The most common methods of receiving requests are:

- **Referrals**   Probably the most important way we get ongoing business is by doing a quality job for our customers. Word-of-mouth advertising should never be slighted. Providing a quality service to a customer at a reasonable rate is a great way to spread the word about your services.

- **Statements of work (SOWs)/requests for proposals (RFPs)**   These are very common mechanisms for receiving requests for an evaluation. The intent of these documents is to detail the customer's requirements for the evaluation. Depending on who develops the SOW/RFP, the packages can include a wide range of detail. These documents can be very short in length (one page) or very long and detailed with a great deal of legal jargon, or somewhere in between. At times, you could have the opportunity to assist in writing an SOW or RFP for a potential work effort. Doing so can help you gain a greater understanding of requirements for the work.

- **Conference/meeting presentations**   Often, we receive requests for information about the evaluation process as a follow-up to presentations we make on the IEM throughout the country at various conferences or meetings.

- **Informal discussions**   These are discussions that can occur at the airport, in an airplane, on a train, or in a hallway. These informal discussions often start with the "What do you do?" question. The answers can lead to IEM opportunities.

- **Warm contacts**   These are people who might have heard of us through conferences or advertising and may call for information on having an IEM conducted on their organization.

- **Cold contacts**   These are people who contact us by finding us in the phone book or through an Internet search.

Validating the Evaluation Request

Once the evaluation request is received, it is important to evaluate the request to ensure that there is a common understanding of the customer's desires. There also must be a common understanding of the definitions of the various types of requests that may be received.

NOTE

Assessment   A security review that is focused on the security of the organizational aspects within a customer's environment. This includes policies, procedures, information flow, and architecture.

Evaluation   A security review that is focused on the technical security aspects of systems, networks, and high-assurance components.

Penetration test   A security review that takes the perspective of the adversary to determine the avenues of attack that could be used to gain access to systems and networks.

Red team   A security review that takes the perspective of the adversary to determine the avenues of attack. This can include systems and networks and may also involve social engineering, dumpster diving, and other technical and physical security violations.

Sources of Information for Validation

You must approach the validation process from a logical perspective and determine what information is available to help with this process. The two primary areas where this information comes from are the customers themselves and publicly available information. Figure 13.1 gives a basic flow of how the engagement process may occur and who has responsibility or must take action within that process.

Figure 13.1 Engagement Process Flow

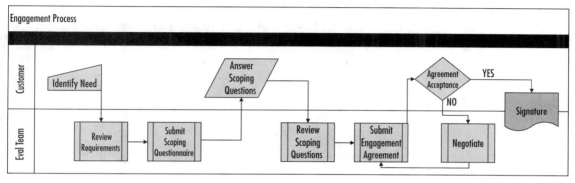

Validating with the Customer

The source of the greatest amount of information, and hopefully the most accurate, is customers themselves. The process of validation should be approached as a learning opportunity for the customer. Frequently used buzzwords, such as *penetration test* and *red team*, may throw the customer off from their true objective. The time you spend with the customer validating information is crucial to a successful effort. Without this time, the likelihood of a miscommunication of need will occur.

There are two primary recommended means of validation with the customer:

- The engagement scoping questionnaire
- Customer discussions and information confirmation

The Engagement Scoping Questionnaire

The scoping questionnaire is identified as part of the pre-evaluation phase of the IEM. The information, however, serves a key role in the contracting process. The scoping questionnaire is necessary to determine the level of effort for the evaluation, which ultimately drives the cost of the evaluation process. The scoping questionnaire is discussed in detail in Chapter 15. You will want to consider utilizing the scoping questionnaire or a subset of the scoping questionnaire in the process of putting the formal engagement documents in place.

Customer Discussions and Information Confirmation

Once information is collected from the customer about the actual work to be conducted, you'll need to confirm the validity of the information with the customer to ensure that the appropriate actions take place.

Publicly Available Information

Public sources of information can be used to validate some of the information the customer provides and can also be used to identify where the customer may have missed a critical area that should be evaluated. You can use multiple sources of public information to obtain this information:

- **Customer Web site**   This source is generally useful to verify the customer's mission, industry, and business/product focus.

- **Customer marketing material**   This information provides valuable information on the customer's business/product focus.

- **10 K/10 Q**   These publicly available reports are required for publicly held companies on a quarterly basis. Key information such as number of employees and number of physical work locations can be useful in determining whether a key customer area was missed.

- **Blogging sites**   You can use forums, such as Raging Bull, to gather some information about an organization.

- **Arin.net**   Publicly available information can be found out about a URL or an IP address based on the registration through Arin.net. This information can be used to validate IP range ownership and/or point of contact within the organization being evaluated.

WARNING

Information collected from sites like Raging Bull should not be taken as absolute. In many cases, people post to such sites just to vent and might not have an appropriate or true view of the actual workings of the organization.

Understanding the Level of Effort

A good understanding of what the customer is asking for is essential. As we said before, to ultimately set the boundaries for the evaluation, you might have to spend some time educating the customer on the details of an IEM evaluation. Expectations will be different for each customer you work with. Here are some things to consider:

- Identify the level of detail the customer requires for recommendations. This assists in determining the level of effort required to develop and document the recommendations that are created as part of the evaluation. Level of detail includes the amount of technical detail put into each recommendation and determining whether saying something as simple as "Upgrade the server operating system to Windows 2000 or higher" is enough of a recommendation or whether step-by-step "how-to" will be required.

- Knowledge of any regulations or legislation with which the customer will have to be compliant at the end of the evaluation. This information is used to determine some of the organization's security objectives and directly affects the recommendations that are made to the customer.

- Knowledge of any evaluations that were conducted in the past is useful to show the level of detail in previous evaluations as well as to provide a good indicator of whether the customer will implement your recommendations.

The Formal Engagement Agreement

The formal engagement agreement will be in the form of a contract, a memorandum of understanding (MOU), or a memorandum of agreement (MOA). MOUs and MOAs are primarily used for evaluations of organizations by an internal entity. Contracts are more formal and contain more protective clauses for both the customer and the evaluation team. The purpose of this section is not to provide you with a cut-and-paste contract suitable for all occasions but to give you a reference guide to the items that should be included. Chapter 16 will give you additional understanding of the legal aspects related to the evaluation process.

WARNING

It is highly recommended that you address your evaluation contracts with your contracting specialists and your legal counsel. Each organization has varying levels of contracting requirements that should be addressed for the engagement.

Nondisclosure Agreements

Executing a nondisclosure agreement between the customer and the evaluation team is essential to maintain the customer's comfort level. Portions of the customer's most critical and sensitive assets will be exposed to the evaluation team. The nondisclosure agreement puts a legal requirement for protection of sensitive information in place to avoid any misunderstanding about the use of the customer's sensitive information.

Engagement Agreement Composition

Every organization has its own contracting format, proposal methodology, and bidding process. The information in the following sections is not intended to replace those elements but is included to assist you in ensuring that your review include a minimum set of information. In all cases, consult with your contracting department and/or legal counsel on appropriate and acceptable contents of the contract. In today's business market, contracting is a combination of multiple skills, including project management, negotiation, financial analysis, risk management, and intellectual property management.

Minimum Engagement Agreement Contents

The following items should be included in some form in all contracts for evaluations. Evaluation companies may want to consider these elements in proposals and SOWs. Many times, these documents are rolled directly into a contract or agreement:

- **Purpose**   This section describes in simple terms the purpose of the evaluation, how it relates to the customer, and the benefits the organization will receive from the evaluation process. It is essential that you use common terminology relevant to the organization to ensure that this material is understood.

- **Methodology**   This section describes the methodology that will be used to conduct the evaluation. This is a good place to emphasize the IEM as a standard methodology to conduct technical INFOSEC evaluations, developed and approved by the National Security Agency. This section includes the phases, processes, and steps to be used during the evaluation.

- **Scope**   This section is a detailed demonstration of the level of effort, boundaries, and limitations of the evaluation. Appropriate assumptions are a critical part of the scoping process. The scope section provides a detailed listing of known assumptions affecting the evaluation. Assumptions are critical in demonstrating an understanding of the customer environment and detailing how that environment will affect the evaluation. The types of assumptions may include number of physical locations, number and type of systems, number and type of networks, relevant POC information, information about scheduling of the technical scans and conducting the 10 baseline IEM activities, and any associated constraints that can be listed as assumptions.

- **Roles and responsibilities of customer staff**   This section identifies the expectations of the customer's staff to support the evaluation effort. Activities can include introductions, scheduling, coordination, and communications. Utilize this space to ensure that the customer has an understanding of what they need to do to support the evaluation effort.

- **Roles and responsibilities of the evaluation team**   This section identifies the expectations and responsibilities of the evaluation team to support and communicate with the customer staff.

- **Deliverables**   An accurate list of deliverables with a brief description of each will assist in managing expectations. Often the customer's expectations of a deliverable will be different than what was planned by the evaluation team. Ensuring that you have given an accurate description of the deliverables in the signed agreement is important to the process.

- **Change control**   This section identifies the process for managing change within the terms of the contract to avoid "scope creep" and out-of-scope work. Change control should include a process whereby both the customer and the evaluation team will approve any changes to the scope of the effort as well as any related cost changes.

- **Letter or authorization requirement**   Due to the nature of the evaluation effort, a formal approval to conduct the evaluation must be given in writing to avoid issues with law enforcement and other security-monitoring agencies. A copy of this letter of authorization should be in the evaluator's possession any time they are conducting the evaluation effort.

- **Period of performance**   The necessary schedule for the evaluation can be extremely important. Gaining an understanding of customer availability and the consultant's availability is key to planning a successful evaluation. Depending on the schedule requirements, it might not be possible to list specific dates at this point. If this is the case, be sure to include the expectation of time for activities so the customer's staff can look at their calendars and begin planning when the evaluation makes sense.

- **Location of the work**   Work location figures directly into the cost of the evaluation. In this section, be sure to list where the onsite work is to be conducted, where offsite work is to be conducted, whether multiple locations will need to be visited, and where the analysis and reporting will be conducted. Be sure to take into account whether the evaluation team will be dealing with classified information and the potential necessity for additional security controls while conducting evaluation activities.

- **Service fees with any relevant quotation notes**   This is your pricing table for the effort. Be as detailed as possible to show the plan of action along with associated costs. The actual cost of your evaluation service depends entirely on your own organization's policy and will not be addressed.

- **Payment schedule**   Generally, net 30 days or net 45 days are common payment schedules. However, with some customers, you might have to work out a special agreement for payment. This is a business process specific to your organization and is not covered in detail in this book.

- **Deliverable acceptance/rejection process**   This section identifies the process for accepting or rejecting a deliverable and how to resolve issues. It is also important to establish timeframes for when draft deliverables become final deliverables, if the customer does not provide any comments on the deliverables.

- **Signatures**   The signature section of the contract addresses your organization's approved statement of terms and conditions. The acceptance section may include information on the length of the agreement, scheduling coordination requirements, termination terms and costs, any other related penalties for cancellation, and acceptance of the terms of the proposal/agreement.

- **Organizational qualifications**   This section describes and demonstrates how your organization is best qualified to execute the work the customer requires. This will likely be a detailed background of your organization, your organization's qualifications, qualifications of the proposed members of the team, and how those qualifications will assist the customer in meeting their goals.

Understanding the Pricing Options

Fixed price? Time and materials? When scoping, it is important to understand what the customer may consider reasonable in terms of evaluation costs. Can a customer endure three to four months of hourly billing at a standard hourly rate? You won't know how long the evaluation is going to take before you have completed the pre-evaluation process. These are all challenges that make the commercial contracting world different from the government contracting world.

Government Contracting

In federal government contracting, a great deal of the professional services work is accomplished using a time-and-materials (hourly) costing basis. There is a direct correlation between cost and the number of hours worked under the contract. Rates in government contracting are generally lower; however, there is generally more flexibility in terms of time to accomplish activities necessary to complete the evaluation. However, be cautious to ensure you are meeting the customer expectations from a scoping and time perspective.

The strategy with government contracting is to be involved as a prime contractor or as a subcontractor on various possible contract vehicles to include indefinite delivery, indefinite quantity (IDIQ) contracts, or Government Services Administration (GSA) schedule. Although these are common ways to gain government contracts for evaluations, they are not the only mechanism to get a government contract. Ultimately, it comes down to contacts, being at the right place at the right time. Keep in mind that, generally speaking, labor and other direct costs (travel, equipment, and so on) have to be billed under different "colors of money" with the government.

NOTE

A *prime contractor* is an organization that has a direct contract with the government to provide services or products. A *subcontractor* is an organization that has an agreement with a prime contractor to provide services in support of the prime's contract with the government.
Colors of money refers to how the funding is allocated in the budget. For example, there are different budgetary line items for labor, equipment, travel, and so on. Each of these is a type of "color of money."

Commercial Contracting

Commercial contracting often functions differently than government contracting. Corporations take multiple avenues to meet their contracting needs. These include basic purchase orders, signed proposals, and extensive contracts with page after page of stipulations and requirements. Be sure to include the minimum amount of specific project-related data that is needed to meet your needs; also have your contracting department and/or legal counsel review any information you might not be familiar with. It's always a good idea to include your legal counsel in the process, especially when something changes from standard templates. The actual contracting process is a specific business-related process for your organization and varies from company to company.

Fixed Price vs. Hourly Rate

So what's the best choice? Obviously we cannot tell you what is best for your organization, but Table 13.1 shows the pros and cons of each. There are other contract avenues not addressed here. Fixed price is popular with many of our customers, since they know what they are getting for the money. Open-ended and hourly rate contracts tend to be scary at a time when organizations are keeping a tight rein on their pocketbooks.

Table 13.1 Fixed Price vs. Hourly Rate

Advantages	Disadvantages
Fixed price	Flexibility with staffing
Flexibility with charge rates	
Incentive to keep down costs	All major and minor scope changes require a change order
Difficult to bill until the evaluation is complete, unless specific interim payments are authorized in the contract	Generally a higher risk and therefore higher cost for same level of effort compared with hourly rate
Hourly rate	Typically lower cost for same level of effort compared with fixed price
Flexibility with scope changes since any increase in effort will simply result in more hours burned (until the maximum hours run out)	More closely monitored in both labor hours and other direct costs
Loss of staffing flexibility since rates are based on labor categories and skill sets	

WARNING

The technical evaluation plan, which is developed in the pre-evaluation phase of the IEM, may change the level of effort thought to be needed for the evaluation. You should consider having a clause in the contract allowing for rescoping for significant changes once the pre-evaluation phase of the IEM is completed and accepted. Another approach would be to contract the pre-evaluation as a separate agreement from the remaining phases of the IEM evaluation. This allows the technical evaluation plan to be used as the scoping input for an onsite evaluation contract.

Additional Engagement Agreement Contents

As we discussed earlier, organizations will have to follow their own contracting processes when bidding and contracting work with customers. There are many more possible inclusions in a contract; the following is only a sampling of items you might find. Consult the appropriate legal and contractual expertise for purposes of creating contracts that will meet your organization's needs. Some of the additional items you might find in your contracts or required by the customer are as follows:

- **Insurance information**   Many organizations require specific levels of insurance, both general liability and professional liability, before they'll work with an organization. This information needs to be included in any final agreement.

- **Personnel qualifications**   Proof of qualifications for personnel proposed to work a contract may be required by the contracting organization. This proof can include certifications, year of experience, educational levels, and specific types of insurance.

- **Warranties**   Include any associated warranty information for products or services provided.

- **Representations**   Generally identifies that there are no other representations other than the written contract or agreement.

- **Independent contractor statement**   To avoid tax issues, many contracts include independent contractor statements and associated responsibilities for wages and benefits for each organization.

- **Assignment of rights**   This section normally does not allow for the contract rights to be assigned to another entity without the express written approval of the contracting organization.

- **Confidentiality statements**   This section focuses on protecting the confidential information of both the contracting and the contracted parties.

- **Document ownership statements**   For our purposes, this section specifically identifies that all documents belong to the customer.

- **Indemnification**   An indemnification statement might look like the following: "The Contractor and contractee agree that they shall indemnify and hold harmless the other and its respective officers and employees from any loss, cost, damage, expense, or liability of every kind and nature which they may incur, arising out of, or in connection with performance under this Agreement, occasioned in whole or in part, by the negligent actions or willful misconduct of other, or by its lower tier subcontractors." This is a legal protection mechanism to avoid huge lawsuits for normally acceptable problems that arise due to anything other than neglect or misconduct.

- **Survival of obligations**   This section focuses on the length of time that obligations within the contract will persist. This section also specifies that if one section of the contract is deemed unusable, the other sections still remain intact.

- **Waiver and severability**   This section states that any provision or portion thereof of the contract is held to be invalid under any applicable statute or rule of law, it shall be, to that extent, deemed omitted without invalidating the remaining portions of the contract.

- **Governing law**   This section addresses what federal and state laws shall government the legal aspects of the contract.

- **Force majeure**   This section addresses failure of a contract due to circumstances beyond the control of the contractor. Wording may look like the following: "Neither party to the Subcontract shall be considered to be in default of its obligations under this Subcontract to the extent that failure to perform any such obligation arises out of causes beyond the control and without the fault or negligence of the affected party. Examples of these causes are (1) acts of God or of the public enemy, (2) acts of the Government in either its sovereign or contractual capacity, (3) fires, (4) floods, (5) epidemics, (6) quarantine restrictions, (7) strikes, (8) freight embargoes, and (9) unusually severe weather. In each instance, the failure to perform must be beyond the control and without the fault or negligence of the affected party. *Default* includes failure to make progress in the work so as to endanger performance. However, Subcontractor shall not be excused for failure to perform any obligation under this Subcontract if such failure is caused by a subcontractor of the Subcontractor's at any tier and the cause of such failure was not beyond the control of both the Subcontractor and its lower-tiered subcontractor, and without the fault or negligence of either."

Dealing with Contract Pitfalls

An awareness of contracting pitfalls and how to deal with them is essential to the effective handling of the contracting process. Failure in the contracting process could result in lost time, lost money, and a great amount of frustration for both the customer and the evaluation team. Our goal is to make the customer happy, so avoiding the contract pitfalls is key to continuous management of customer expectations.

"Scope Creep" and Timelines

Unplanned and unbid scope changes in projects, often called "scope creep," occur when a project deviates from the written scope to a higher level of effort. Controlling scope creep effectively can assist in effectively managing the overall project. Scope creep not only has an impact on the financial aspects of the project—it also has an impact on project timelines and the ability for the evaluation team to complete the job on time.

Scope creep can be caused by poor planning, unknown areas of the organization that need to evaluated, or a customer's desire to further investigate a certain security area that is being analyzed by the evaluation team. Scope creep can also occur when a customer wants to get more out of the effort than they are paying for. The project manager, team lead, and customer representative should work closely together to avoid scope creep. Any agreed-on changes need to appropriately documented and, if necessary, recosted into the project. This doesn't mean that all scope changes have to be considered in a negative light or even that they require a cost increase. But it does recommend an evaluation of the change on a case-by-case basis to ensure that expectations are being met.

Notes from the Underground

Common Scope Creep

The most common example of scope creep occurs when more systems or more locations need evaluating than the customer originally identified. This is generally due to the lack of full communication by the customer with their technical staff or a communications

Continued

disconnect between the evaluation team and the customer. For this reason, it is extremely important to be detailed in the assumptions section of your contract. Another example of scope creep occurs with the discovery of additional systems that need to be reviewed as part of the evaluation that were not originally identified as part of the effort.

Uneducated Salespeople

Educate your security sales staff on the evaluation process before they are sent out to the field to sell an evaluation. They do not have to be experts on the entire process, but they need to understand what an evaluation is composed of, reasonable expectations from the process, the role of the customer in the process, and the impact of customer complexity on the process. Then, working in conjunction with the evaluation "experts," they can put together a quality sales presentation and proposal. Ensure that they understand not to make promises that they are not sure your organization can keep. This includes factors such as level of effort, cost, and unreasonable expectations regarding timeframes.

Evaluations 101

The purpose of an INFOSEC evaluation is to:

- Provide a technical security review of systems and networks
- Examine the customer's technical security from an internal and external perspective
- Analyze the network architecture
- Examine the security configuration of servers, workstations, and network devices for vulnerabilities and exposures
- Examine the security configuration of critical applications
- Identify vulnerabilities and exposures
- Recommend solutions to mitigate or eliminate those vulnerabilities

Notes from the Underground

Sold Up the River

The following comment is not intended as a general slam on salespeople; however, we have experienced several incidents where an uneducated salesperson sold a service without knowledge of what the effort entailed or how it could be accomplished. Package-pricing a security evaluation without knowledge of who the evaluation is for or how the evaluation will be conducted can result in serious mission and financial failure for your organization. Success is not only measured by how well you do your job but also whether the customer is satisfied with the service they were provided at the price they paid.

Bad Assumptions

Making poor assumptions can kill your contract. A great deal of effort needs to be put into developing and reviewing the assumptions that are made for each contract. Assumptions list the understood environment in which the evaluation will be conducted. They will also identify the expected involvement of the customer in the process—staff availability, scheduling requirements, and timeframes.

Assumption Topic Areas

The following are examples of information that need to be included in the assumptions section and that must be as accurate as possible to avoid confusion and poor scoping:

- Location in which the evaluation will be conducted
- Number of sites at which the evaluation will conducted
- Availability of customer personnel for the evaluation
- Scheduling of evaluation scanning
- Travel requirements
- Documentation availability
- Necessary support from the customer in managing the evaluation
- Technical and organizational points of contact for the evaluation
- The process for determining the systems, network devices, and applications to be evaluated
- Availability and currency of the network architecture diagrams
- Operating system types for servers and workstations
- Technical expertise of the customer

Poorly Written Contracts

Poorly written contracts are the basis for poor evaluations. Generally, poor contracts are based on bad information, bad assumptions, and lack of attention to detail. A boilerplate evaluation contract can be dangerous if not properly tailored to the current customer. Every organization has different expectations and requirements to meet. The worst kind of evaluation contract will not have any specific detail related to the customer being assessed.

Poor Scope Definition

Poor scope definition generally results from a poor understanding of the requirements and expectations associated with the project. From a provider perspective, poor scope definition could mean a loss in revenue and profits for an effort. Poor scoping can result in your consultants having to spend unplanned hours on the job and eventual cost overruns. Another major mistake in the scoping effort is not having the customer approve the scope with a signature. By having the customer sign for approval of the scope, you'll help avoid future issues such as the customer denying that they agreed to the scope or possibly forcing additional work for no additional money. Be sure to protect your company. Don't assume anything. Document the terms of the agreement in detail.

NOTE

Contracts are one area in which large companies generally have an advantage over smaller companies. Large companies normally have years of experience, a dedicated contracting staff, and strong legal counsel that support their needs in the contracting process.

Underbid or Overbid: The Art of Poor Cost Estimating

Pricing a proposal can be as critical as the quality of the information put into the proposal. Understanding the customer environment and limitations from a financial perspective will help you properly price the effort. This closely ties into the assumptions section of the project. The assumptions help determine the level of effort. It's always dangerous to price a project low to win the work. Bidding low cuts into the flexibility and profit margin the project may carry. Bidding high can price you out of contention for the project. True pricing has to come from actual expected effort and your experience as to what it will take to complete the effort.

Many outside influences can impact the costing efforts. As mentioned previously, a poor understanding of the requirements and expectations associated with the project are one influence. Another is salesperson influence on the process. If a salesperson tries to pressure the pricing process in an attempt to win a bid, the end result may be an improperly priced effort. Another pressure from the sales staff is along the lines of, "I said we could do this for $25,000, so we have to do the evaluation for $25,000."

Notes from the Underground

Contracting Differences

Don't assume that your experience with either government contracting or commercial contracting fully prepares you for all aspects of contracting for the other. Government contracts and commercial contracts are as unique in nature as the differences between government agencies or commercial industries. Be prepared to learn something new with the different entities you will be working with, and don't get frustrated when one entity does contracting differently than another.

Customer and Evaluation Team Approval

The final step before starting the actual evaluation is to finalize the formal approval of the engagement agreement. Both the customer and the evaluation team must be prepared for the time and possible negotiations required to reach a formal and mutual agreement. The goal is to develop an engagement agreement that meets the needs of both the customer and the evaluation team. This includes critical scoping information, legal statements, timelines, and pricing.

The Customer Approval Process

The customer is likely to have the more rigid approval process for the engagement agreement. Most customers will pass the agreement to their contracts and legal department for review and comment. Many times, the customer will request an additional provision or a wording change to clarify things. If the evaluation team has been writing evaluation engagement agreements for awhile, the changes will usually be minor. However, every organization is unique, and you could find that significant changes are needed. The end result may be a signed agreement or a purchase order (PO) that directly references the final agreement. This signed agreement or PO is the formal approval to proceed with the evaluation.

The Evaluation Team Approval Process

The evaluation team will likely be the entity that is writing up the agreement due to their experience with the process. The evaluation team will have to review any customer requests for changes to the agreement and determine the appropriateness of the request. If significant changes are requested, the evaluation team's legal counsel will likely have to be involved before final approval.

Summary

Before the actual formal evaluation begins, a series of activities must take place. Since NSA does not address business processes that occur prior to the start of the pre-evaluation process within their methodologies, we have attempted to address those needs in this chapter.

Evaluations are requested for many reasons to help organizations meet their security goals. This includes consideration for laws and regulations within the industry or industries in which the organization functions, concerns about being attacked, concerns about market position from a security perspective, or insurance requirements. The reason the evaluation is requested will drive some of the considerations and content of the engagement agreement and, ultimately, the final evaluation report. This understanding is essential to meeting the customer's expectations.

The engagement request validation process is critical to ensuring that you reach a common understanding with the customer and avoid missing some of the fine detail needed to properly scope the level of effort for the evaluation. The primary source of validation is through the customer, but you can also use publicly available information to further validate the information.

The formal engagement agreement is the contract between the evaluation team and the customer. It outlines the activities that will occur and identifies the estimated cost to conduct the evaluation. Since this activity is likely taking place before the technical evaluation plan is developed and as part of the pre-evaluation phase of the IEM, the engagement agreement must be flexible enough to address scope changes identified in the IEM pre-evaluation.

The final step before starting the actual evaluation is to finalize the approval of the engagement agreement through the processes of both the customer and evaluation team organizations. This will address the final contracting and legal means necessary to meet each organization's needs from both the engagement and a liability protections point of view.

## Chapter 14

Setting Expectations

Solutions in this chapter:

- **Objectives of the Pre-Evaluation Phase**
- **Understanding Concerns and Constraints**
- **Obtaining Management Buy-In**
- **Obtaining Technical Staff Buy-In**
- **Establishing Points of Contact**

☑ **Summary**

Introduction

In this chapter we delve into one of the most crucial preparation aspects of doing any evaluation: assessing customer expectations, the tangible and intangible factors, that will affect the outcome of the evaluation. If you fail to adequately address your customer's expectations, you can expect to waste your time and the customer's money. A good example is to show up for a technical evaluation and find out at the in-briefing that the customer is expecting a full risk assessment. Your team will be unprepared and probably missing some skill sets needed to accomplish the customer goals. From that point on everything that can go wrong will, and you will fail to achieve the prime goal of any provider of services to any customer: customer satisfaction. Setting expectations is more than just asking what the customer is concerned with or what they want. You and your customer need to come to an understanding of what is going to be done and what is *not* going to be done.

Objectives of the Pre-Evaluation Phase

As already covered in the previous chapters, you need to define the timeline for performing the evaluation. As you already know, the timeline is essential from the evaluator's perspective to define the resource requirements. It is also essential from the customer's perspective for resource scheduling. Will the evaluation be performed as a follow-on to the organizational assessment or will it be performed concurrently with the IAM? Both approaches are good and will work. But each provides only a picture of the security posture at any given point in time; it's a snapshot. As such, it is most effective to have the evaluation accomplished at the same time as the organizational assessment. From the customer's perspective doing the evaluation does provide an output of findings that need to be mitigated. But have you provided enough information to tie the findings back to what is critical to the mission of the organization? With out the organizational assessment your team will not have enough information to tie the findings to what is really important to the customer. If no organizational assessment has been accomplished within the last six months the odds are that your team will either not have any Organizational, or System, Information Criticality Matrix. These are essential to providing a quality output for the customer as you have to have both the matrixes and the impact definitions that accompany them. You can see in Figure 14.1 that conducting the organizational assessment and evaluation at the same time is easily accomplished. Most all customers, that understand the process, will want to have them done concurrently. This allows for that defined point in time definition of the security posture to be easily related to each other. This also prevents their internal arguments about what is/was/will be fixed from the organizational assessment to the organizational evaluation.

Figure 14.1 The NSA View of IAM and IEM Utilization

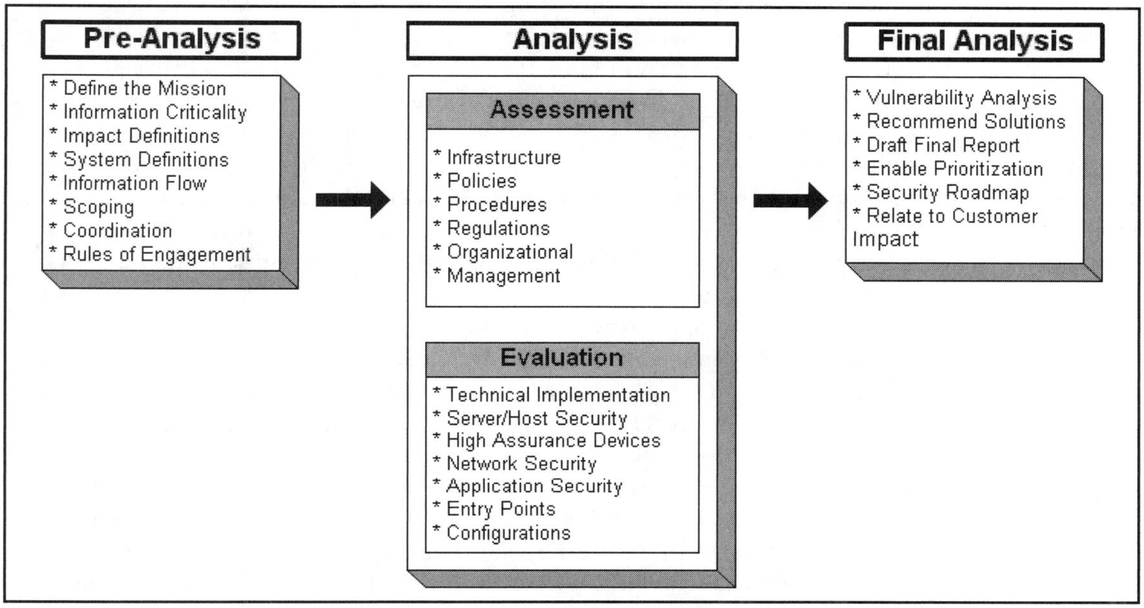

Pre-Analysis	Analysis	Final Analysis
* Define the Mission * Information Criticality * Impact Definitions * System Definitions * Information Flow * Scoping * Coordination * Rules of Engagement	**Assessment** * Infrastructure * Policies * Procedures * Regulations * Organizational * Management **Evaluation** * Technical Implementation * Server/Host Security * High Assurance Devices * Network Security * Application Security * Entry Points * Configurations	* Vulnerability Analysis * Recommend Solutions * Draft Final Report * Enable Prioritization * Security Roadmap * Relate to Customer Impact

Conducting the organizational assessment and evaluation concurrently provides for a complete analysis of your customer's security posture. One of the objectives when you have finished the work and delivered the final report is that the report tie the proposed security road map back to the defined impact definitions and, ultimately, to the mission impact. This is how you will provide the customer with sufficient information to do good risk management without you there holding their hand. This is a project-oriented approach in that both the assessment and evaluation have a starting point, which is the pre-analysis phase; an analysis phase; and a final analysis phase. The pre-analysis phase is designed to define the customer needs and expectations and is the focus of this chapter. This includes setting the evaluation's goals and objectives. The analysis phase is the validation of the actual security posture and will be covered in depth in future chapters. This is where your team will provide proof by showing the customer's actual exposures. The final analysis phase is the data-crunching and reporting phase and will also be covered in depth in future chapters. Remember, if you cannot tie the findings to the impact definitions, the customer will have insufficient information for good risk management after you are gone.

Understanding the customer requirements is both complicated and easy. It is complicated because each customer and its social/political environment are unique and require you and your team to understand the environment. It is easy because you and your team have the knowledge and experience to understand the currently implemented technical and operational controls. The first part involves simply gaining an understanding of the customer mission. When all is said and done and you have delivered the final report, how has what you've done affected the customer mission? Providing technological recommendations without understanding the reason for the way the current technology is used does a disservice to the customer. Improving an organization's security posture does not involve stopping business or providing solutions that do not fit the organization's goals. If you don't have the organizational assessment report, you will have to define these parts yourself. Asking the question "Why are you in business?" is one way to find out a firm's goals, but it might not provide the answers you are looking for. Every organization in the world has an underlying mission of making money. It does not matter what the organizations is. You could get the charter from a nonprofit or not-for-profit organization to see why they are in business and you'd still find that money is the bottom line. Even the U.S. federal government needs to make money. They get a bigger budget by spending their entire budget every year to allow them to ask for more money in their budget next year. We need to know the organization's mission and draw it in from the organizational assessment.

Understanding customers' needs or expectations is as simple as understanding why you were brought in to do the evaluation. You can identify these needs from your discussions with the customer about their expectations and by defining their concerns or constraints. Sometimes the customer will not tell you more that what is based on an RFP or an SOW. Sometimes their needs are based on unspoken issues such as a merger or acquisition where the customer is looking to identify unnecessary or excess areas that can be trimmed, making the organization more efficient and effective. But in today's world of legislative requirements, the real reason for doing most evaluations tends to be compliance. Don't get us wrong—there is nothing the matter with having compliance be the reason for the evaluation, but we have seen occasional customers who feel they are being forced to do an evaluation to meet a higher-authority requirement. When the only reason is to "get the check mark," there is usually little or no management support to implement mitigation or improve the security posture.

Customer expectations will be defined as part of the scoping of the evaluation. It is not unusual for the customer to refine their expectations as they become familiar with the evaluation process or better understand their compliance requirements in more detail. This process often results in the customer adding pieces to the evaluation. That can result in "scope creep," or the addition of work that your team is not prepared for, if the customer's input is not controlled or expectations are not readdressed during the onsite evaluation process instead of during the pre-evaluation phase.

Understanding Concerns and Constraints

Customers will always have specific reasons for asking for an evaluation. It is crucial that you and your team understand what the customer is concerned about and address those concerns throughout the evaluation. Understanding the concerns and addressing them are significant steps in creating positive customer satisfaction. In the organizational assessment, we addressed the concerns from the executive level, some of which could be:

- Legislative or regulatory requirements
- FISMA, Sarbanes-Oxley, Gramm-Leach-Bliley, and so on

What Are the Requirements?

Responding to public issues of identity theft and fraud, the U.S. government has passed legislation to enhance and strengthen previously existing legislation dealing with infrastructure security through bills that include Sarbanes-Oxley (SOX), the Health Insurance Portability and Accountability Act

(HIPAA), the U.S. Government Federal Information Security Management Act (FISMA), the Gramm-Leach-Bliley Act (GLBA), and the Children's Internet Protection Act (CIPA). What are these pieces of legislation, and why does management care? A more detailed description of these regulations and standards can be found in Chapter 12 of this book.

Other Significant Regulations

California has passed a law, known variously as Senate Bill (SB) 1386 or the California Database Protection Act, requiring companies doing business with customers in California to notify them if they suspect that any of their customers' personal information has been accessed by an unauthorized party. This law applies to any company that has California customers, even if the company has no physical presence in California.

And this is only the start. You can expect that more states will start adopting similar regulations to try to provide some measure of protection for their constituents. Personal privacy is always a hot topic, and with the rise in publicity that occurs when a company loses customers' personally identifiable information, more legislation will be forthcoming. Another example is the new law signed by the governor of Colorado. Consumers in Colorado will have the right to put a security freeze on their credit files, effective July 1, 2006. This is to prevent identity thieves from opening new credit accounts in their names. Colorado is the sixth state to provide some form of security freeze directly to consumers. Many other states around the country are considering such laws in the wake of a string of data security breach and identity theft scandals in 2004–2005.

Finally, the private sector has joined in, with Visa and MasterCard regulating both their merchants and service providers. Visa's initiative is called the Cardholder Information Security Program (CISP); MasterCard's is called the Site Data Protection (SDP) program. Both programs require that all merchants and service providers be assessed for key information security best practices and, depending on the size of the merchant, evaluate systems involved in the handling or processing of cardholder information for security vulnerabilities.

Visa USA has instituted the CISP, first mandated in June 2001. The program is intended to protect Visa cardholder data, no matter where it resides. The idea is to ensure that cardholders, merchants, and service providers maintain the highest information security standards. CISP compliance is required of all merchants and service providers that store, process, or transmit Visa cardholder data. The program applies to all payment channels, including retail (brick-and-mortar), mail/telephone order, and e-commerce.

The MasterCard SDP Program is a proactive, global solution offered by MasterCard through its acquiring members. The program provides acquiring members with the ability to deploy security compliance programs, assisting online merchants and Member Service Providers to better protect against hacker intrusions and account data compromises. The program takes a proactive approach to security by identifying common possible vulnerabilities in a merchant Web site and makes recommendations for short- and long-term security improvements. The solution addresses the security issues that online merchants and their acquiring banks face in the virtual world and concerns arising from these issues, such as Internet fraud, chargebacks, brand image damage, consumer information safety and privacy, and the cost of replacing stolen account numbers.

To achieve compliance, merchants and service providers must adhere to the Payment Card Industry (PCI) Data Security Standard (see Table 14.1), which offers a single approach to safeguarding sensitive data for all card brands. This standard is a result of the collaboration between Visa and

MasterCard and is designed to create common industry security requirements. Using the PCI Data Security Standard as the framework, the Visa and MasterCard security programs provide the tools and measurements needed to protect against cardholder data exposure and compromise. The PCI Data Security Standard, downloadable at http://usa.visa.com/download/business/accepting_visa/ops_risk_management/cisp_PCI_Data_Security_Standard.pdf?it=il|/business/accepting_visa/ops_risk_management/cisp.html|PCI%20Data%20Security%20Standard, consists of 12 basic requirements supported by more detailed subrequirements:

Table 14.1 PCI Data Security Standard

Goal	Execution
Build and maintain a secure network.	1. Install and maintain a firewall configuration to protect data.
	2. Do not use vendor-supplied defaults for system passwords or other security parameters.
Protect cardholder data.	3. Protect stored data.
	4. Encrypt transmission of cardholder data and sensitive information across public networks.
Maintain a vulnerability management program.	5. Use and regularly update antivirus software.
and applications.	6. Develop and maintain secure systems
Implement strong access control measures.	7. Restrict access to data by business "need to know."
	8. Assign a unique ID to each person with computer access.
	9. Restrict physical access to cardholder data.
Regularly monitor and test networks.	10. Track and monitor all access to network resources and cardholder data.
	11. Regularly test security systems and processes.
Maintain an information security policy.	12. Maintain a policy that addresses information security.

Budgetary Concerns

Security has been and will continue to be an overhead expense for all organizations, much like payroll and other administrative tasks that are required to keep an organization running. The question that seems to pop up every few months in the security industry is, what is the value of all the security work that takes place within an organization? Organizations want to see the current *and* expected return on investment (ROI) for the security budget.

When talking about IT security, ROI has historically focused on returning actual organizational payback where implementing tools, devices, or training, should be reducing operating costs. This is almost never the case. Since security acts as a version of insurance for your data or information, any return from required security should focus on this aspect.

There have been many endeavors over the years to find the ROI for security. All the studies have yet to be able to define the ROI calculation. There is by no means only one way to determine ROI for security; currently, several projects are under way that are still working to determine this calculation. You can find more information on this topic by doing a simple search on the Internet for *security ROI*.

For our purposes, we use a simplified formula that is based on annual loss expectancy. Simply put, how much do you expect to lose from a single security incident each year? So the annual loss expectancy of a single security breach that costs $1 million and that has a 35 percent probability of occurring can be reflected as:

Incident Cost × Probability = Annual Loss Expectancy

$1,000,000 × 0.35 = $350,000

Although this is good, it does not include the factor of mitigation into the equation, so we add this factor by multiplying the probability by the mitigation factor. Consider the impact that computer worms have had over the past few years, or even the various Sober virus variants. If you have installed up-to-date antivirus software, you can expect to have mitigated about 50 percent of the probability of loss. Or if you implemented strong user awareness training, you could mitigate about 80 percent of the probability of occurrence. (Can anybody say customer choices?) This makes the formula slightly different, as follows:

Incident Cost × (Probability × Mitigation) = Annual Loss Expectancy

$1,000,000 × (0.35 × 0.5) = $1,000,000 × 0.175 = $175,000
(Antivirus Software Mitigation)

$1,000,000 × (0.35 × 0.2) = $1,000,000 × 0.07 = $70,000
(User Awareness Training Mitigation)

So if the cost of implementation is known—antivirus $75,000, user awareness program $10,000—you can show a simple ROI by showing that the cost of mitigation is less than the cost of loss. Please note that this does not take all factors into account and is not meant as an introduction or tutorial on determining ROI.

Cyber-Insurance

Traditional insurance companies cover physical types of risks and exposures. They do not cover nonphysical types of risks and exposures that come from the Internet—such issues as cyber-terrorism, hacking, and electronic fraud and theft. That's where cyber-insurance comes in. Cyber-insurance can cover denial-of-service (DoS) attacks that bring down e-commerce sites, electronic theft of sensitive information, virus-related damage, losses associated with internal networks crippled by hackers or rogue employees, privacy-related suits, and legal issues associated with Web sites, such as copyright and trademark violations.

Like its real-world equivalents in a brick-and-mortar environment, a cyber-insurance company provides insurance and risk management services against various types of Internet risk. From a process point of view, the first thing that an insurance company does before quoting a policy to a customer is try to assess the customer by asking them to complete a short questionnaire. This self-assessment questionnaire is sent to the risk analysis department. After reviewing the questionnaire, the risk analysis department comes up with a solution that the insurance agent can then use for quoting a policy price based on the customer's existing security model. The simpler the solution that has to be implemented, the lower the cost of insurance premiums.

Cyber-insurance policies are already being issued by companies such as Lloyd's e-comprehensive, Chubb's cyber security, and AIG's Net Advantage Security. These policies can provide coverage for business interruption, electronic data damage, extortion, network security liability, (downstream) network liability, media liability, professional errors and omissions, coverage for financial loss resulting from data damage, destruction, corruption, and loss of income from network security apart from the coverage. Some insurers also offer risk management services, including online and onsite security assessment.

Brick-and-mortar insurance policies have evolved over several decades. Insurance and risk mitigation are backed by decades' worth of valuable data, speculations, statistical analysis, and projections. In contrast, Internet and cyber-policies such as insurance are relatively new concepts. Due to lack of quantifiable data on cyber-risk, cyber-insurance policies require high premiums and deductibles. Depending on the size of the company and the coverage, the required premiums can run into the hundreds of thousands of dollars. If an insurer's assessment does not find appropriate levels of computer network security, the policy may even be denied unless the applicant meets or exceeds the insurer's recommended security specifications. In the absence of decades' worth of information, some of the biggest challenges for an insurance firm in providing a cyber-insurance package are calculating the cost of investment for a particular policy and determining the cost of loss.

System Accreditation

FISMA

The Federal Information Security Management Act (FISMA) utilizes NIST Special Publication (SP) 800-37, *Guide for the Security Certification and Accreditation of Federal Information Systems,* as its compliance standard. NIST SP 800-37 provides guidelines for certifying and accrediting information systems supporting the executive agencies of the federal government. NIST SP 800-37 applies to all federal information systems other than those systems designated as national security systems, as defined in FISMA.

The certification and accreditation package consists of the following documents:

- System security plan (SSP)
- Security assessment report
- Plan of action and milestones (POAM)

The key document for the certification and accreditation process is the system security plan (SSP), detailed in NIST Special Publication 800-18, *Guide for Developing Security Plans for Information Technology Systems.* The purpose of the SSP is to:

- Provide an overview of the system's security requirements and describe the controls in place or planned for meeting those requirements

- Delineate responsibilities and expected behavior of all individuals who access the system

DoD Information Technology Security Certification and Accreditation Process

DoDI 5200.40 (DITSCAP) establishes a standard DoD-wide process, set of activities, general tasks, and a management structure to certify and accredit information systems (IS). Certification and accreditation (C&A) uses a single-document approach for all classified and unclassified systems in the DoD. All the information relevant to the C&A is collected into one document, the systems security authorization agreement (SSAA), which is then submitted to the Designated Approval Authority for approval.

National Information Assurance Certification and Accreditation Process

The National Security Telecommunications and Information System Security Instruction (NSTISSI) 1000 defines the National Information Assurance Certification and Accreditation Process (NIACAP). The NIACAP establishes a standard national process, set of activities, general tasks, and a management structure to certify and accredit systems that will maintain the information assurance (IA) and security posture of a system or site. NSTISSI 1000 provides an overview of the NIACAP process, roles of the people involved, and the documentation produced during the process. More detailed procedures will be included in the NIACAP implementation manual when it is released.

Defense Information Assurance Certification and Accreditation Process

The Defense Information Assurance Certification and Accreditation Process (DIACAP) (now in draft form) will supercede the DITSCAP (DoDI 5200.40). The DIACAP will establish the standard DoD process for identifying, implementing, and validating IA controls, for authorizing the operation of DoD information systems, and for managing IA posture across DoD information systems consistent with Title III of the E-Government Act, FISMA, and DoD Directive 8500.1. All DoD systems will be required to transition to DIACAP in the future.

The DIACAP is independent of the system life cycle, and its activities may be initiated at any system life-cycle stage—during acquisition, during operation, or at the inception of a major system modification. Generally, the earlier in the system life cycle the DIACAP is initiated, the less expensive and problematic is the implementation of IA capabilities and services.

Response to Suspected Threats or Intrusions

All of these concerns and possibly many others could be drawn from the organizational assessment. This is far from an extensive list of possible management concerns. You will have to understand customers and their motivations to identify the real management concerns. These could be the same reasons for requesting the evaluation, but there are usually more. Technical concerns should be addressed equally with the organizational concerns. Technical concerns usually come from senior technicians and are not normally expressed by management. Some of these could be:

- Blame for findings
- Impact to normal operations
- System downtime
- Loss of data

As you can see, these are concerns that will not normally come from the executive or senior management level of an organization. Middle management or senior technicians are usually the source of technical concerns. Technical concerns during an evaluation will be identified as the team begins working with the technical POCs and can be added as you proceed and discover the previously unknown quirks of the network operations.

Constraints are the factors that will limit or hinder the team in doing the evaluation. Every customer has constraints. The constraints can range from financial considerations, timeframes, resource limitations, and politics to third-party connectivity, legacy applications, and proposed environmental changes. If you fail to address and fully understand the customer constraints in the pre-evaluation, as you proceed with the evaluation you will fail to meet customer expectations. Some of the constraints will be drawn from the organizational assessment and can also be identified by asking common questions such as:

- What are the available times for evaluation activities?
- Are there any financial restrictions on mitigation?
- What personnel staffing issues will limit mitigation or evaluation activities?
- Are there any organizational politics to deal with?
- What third-party connections are there?

If you merge these questions with the technically focused questions to identify any, and hopefully all, of the technical constraints, your team should be able to address all the customer issues. Technical issues have to do with the daily operations and limitations to the evaluation caused by these issues. Some of the technical constraints that you should address include but are not limited to:

- Level of invasiveness
    - Will DOS testing be allowed?
    - How will password-compliance testing be handled?
- Level of detail for recommendations
- Periods of time that the evaluation cannot interfere with normal operations
    - Batch processing periods or expected surge activities
- Are there components that should be considered out of scope of the assessment?
- Are legacy applications or hardware running?

The sources of concerns and constraints can vary from formal discussions held during the scoping of the evaluation or even from informal discussions held during tours of the facility. Just sitting down in the break room with the system administrators will yield information that should be addressed in terms of how it will affect the evaluation. One of the best ways to identify constraints after the initial executive interviews is to do a tour of the facility to see exactly where the systems are maintained and operated. As you are doing the tour, your expertise and experience will lead you to ask questions that will usually bring to light any constraints that were not previously identified. Identifying and continuously managing your customer's concerns and constraints will greatly assist you in obtaining and maintaining management buy-in.

Figure 14.2 Management and Security

Alright, Russ. Tell me everything I need to know
to have good INFOSEC. You've got 10 minutes

Obtaining Management Buy-In

Why do you need management buy-in to the evaluation process? Without management buy-in, the process will have a significantly lower probability of success and usefulness to the customer. Furthermore, if management agrees with the purpose, goals, and concepts behind an evaluation, finding money for security becomes easier. The "worker bees" will quickly realize that this is important to management and will be more willing to open up and assist in completing the evaluation.

What is buy-in? Buy-in is the visible and tangible support given from the executive level down to ensure that the evaluation is completed fully and in a timely manner. This can be seen by something as simple as the sponsor saying a few words during the opening kick-off meeting or as complicated as having a daily reporting of accomplishments and status.

Understand that in terms of evaluations, management usually comes in two flavors. First is the most common management knuckling under to "forced compliance"; the second less likely to be seen as the "Make us better" type. Both will have hired your team to do the evaluation, but their reasons and motivations are different.

The forced compliance group is likely to want the least impact needed to meet regulatory compliance. They usually do not want to do any more than is strictly required to meet the regulatory compliance guidelines. If possible, they would like you to show that the evaluation isn't really necessary because they've already met all the requirements. These evaluations tend to be lowball ones in terms of pricing and to want everything done as quickly as possible so they can get back to business. The final report is viewed as the "check mark in the box" needed for compliance. Motivating this type of management involves more education and perseverance than anything else. Educating without making it seem like you are teaching will, hopefully, cause a leap of logic in their minds and convert them to the second type of management.

The "Make us better" management group is one that we all wish we had all the time. This is the management team that is truly concerned with improvement in organizational security posture. Due to constraints, they may not have had the opportunity to do an evaluation prior to your team being hired. Sometimes the management that is new and really wants to have a fresh set of eyes tell them the truth about their organization's security posture. Either way, positive management will need little if any motivation. "Make us better" management is already motivated to complete a through evaluation. The only help that they will need is usually in understanding new technical issues and the options for mitigation. Again, this will involve covert education of the management team.

Having ready access to the sponsor or senior management during the evaluation allows for timely response to issues or obstacles that cannot be addressed at lower levels. If management is willing and able to show their public support for the evaluation, workers will realize that the evaluation is important and be willing to cooperate. Workers who respect their management will see the value of the evaluation and in turn be advocates for the process.

Notes from the Underground

Overzealous Management

On occasion we have seen a case where the management has taken what could be construed as too great an interest in what is being accomplished during an assessment. This is the prime cause of what we call the 4-14 syndrome, since it usually is federal service GS-14s or DoD officer grade 04 or above that level who are "afflicted." This syndrome occurs when management wants to ensure that they get a positive report output from the evaluation. Senior management then ensures that the primary POC understands that their promotion or evaluation will be directly tied to the outcome of the evaluation report.

This "promise" causes the primary POC to try to become overly involved and try to steer the evaluation report. The primary POC spends an excessive amount of time trying to "over-the-shoulder watch" everything that occurs and take immediate action to mitigate any finding. Although this is a noble effort, the result involves continually asking the team to revalidate the findings as closed or mitigated, which will significantly increase the evaluation team resources need to complete the evaluation in a timely manner.

Figure 14.3 IT Staff and Security

The boss says that security is extremely important and top priority.
That is, unless it makes something inconvenient.

Obtaining Technical Staff Buy-In

Technical staff buy-in is different from management buy-in. We have seen three types of technical staff buy-in from our experience in doing evaluations. First there is the *IT zealot*. Second is the *IT status quo* personality. Third is the *Keep-it-running* personality. One thing to note here is that all three personality types usually exist within any IT staff.

The zealot is the one that we most prefer to work with. They are hungry to learn anything they can and see the evaluation as a way to learn. The zealot is anxious to find everything that could possibly be wrong because they see it as a significant method to improve the operations and security, which in turn makes them look good to management. These people are easily identified by management as the go-getters. They are ready to start the evaluation before your team is. They will usually come to the initial meeting with network diagrams in hand and try to anticipate anything your team will need. When doing console reviews or scans, they will normally be at your side asking questions and taking notes. They are most likely to try to fix any finding as soon as it is identified. Zealots don't take much motivation to get them involved or get their buy-in. Most of the work is in controlling them or slowing them down. They do not like having any findings on their systems. For a zealot, your team will have to explain that it is not possible to rescan or review every machine every time they fix something. They should understand that it is in their best interest to show how much they have already fixed when the final report is delivered.

The status quo person is the most common one that we find and work with. They are the balancers of requirements and user requests. They see their job as not to improve but to maintain operations, to keep users happy. These workers can be identified as the "always busy" IT staff. They will show up to the initial meeting with a notepad and wait to see what they have to do. These are the people who will be most involved with identifying when network scans or console reviews should *not* be done. They will be at your side to observe console reviews but usually disappear during scans. They want to evaluate any finding and the recommended mitigations. Status quo people are ready to fix any critical findings but are hesitant to fix any other finding until they evaluate the impact to operations. Status quo people need motivation to get their buy-in. Usually it can be done by showing them how implementing mitigations will improve the overall system operations.

The keep-it-running folks are the worst that we have to work with. They usually don't have any emphasis from management or drive to improve security. They usually take the stance, "If it's not broken, why fix it?" They are usually reluctant to give access and question everything that is done. They will argue that identified findings are not really as important as the team makes them out to be and will not want to implement changes that will make them spend time doing what is not already in their schedule. Keep-it-running people are not easy to work with and fortunately are not a very common type to find in an IT shop.

The easiest way to get these people to buy into the evaluation and be willing to assist in the evaluation is to show how this evaluation will benefit them. Part of this effort is ensuring that they understand that you are not part of an audit or inspection, unless of course you are. Set the technical staff at ease as much as possible right at the start by showing how the results are intended not to carry retribution. We normally ensure that all levels of participants understand that we will, as much as possible, assist them with real-time fixes. One point we like to make is that we would love to be able to have a final report with only positive findings.

Figure 14.4 IT Project Assignments

Greg, this is the perfect way to pick who is going to work this project.

Establishing Points of Contact

In learning how to implement the INFOSEC Assessment Methodology (IAM), you learned that there has to be a single senior management point of contact. This person has the responsibility to coordinate the administrative issues such as workspace and access for the evaluation team. This administrative POC is critical to completing the evaluation and will have all the same responsibilities. Your team may even choose to utilize the administrative POC during interviews and system demonstrations.

That's your call, but don't underestimate the importance of the administrative POC in crossing the political boundaries that exist in every organization. You need to identify the senior system administrator for each and every system that is included in this evaluation. Use the administrative POC to coordinate the assignment of the technical POCs.

In a perfect world, we would work with all the administrators of each system. Reality check: They have other work that they'll be required to finish even while you are doing the evaluation. Hopefully you will get to work with the most experienced administrators for each system, but don't be surprised if that is not always the case.

So how many is too many technical POCs? The answer is really up to you. From our perspective, we look to have the senior system administrator assigned to each system. This is an issue in many organizations because they may have organized the administrators by host or network operating systems. In this case, you should try to organize the evaluation time periods to consolidate the time requirements of the technical POCs assigned. This means that you might want to look at grouping particular operating system components such as Windows into one evaluation time period. This will allow for the customer to schedule any extra hours required without detriment to the technical POC. Remember, if you are the cause of an administrator being forced to work extra hours, that administrator is not likely to be very cooperative with you.

What is the job or role of these technical POCs? They are both your safety net and operational expertise for the organization. They are the people who will provide you with the root or administrator access for console reviews. Technical POCs will be able to show you how applications interface with the network and what the normal operating conditions are. When you are doing network vulnerability scans, technical POCs represent the body of knowledge for what is normal and what is abnormal. When you are doing network scans, it is entirely possible that some machines will freeze and require restarting. One single job or responsibility of the technical POCs is to validate that when you are complete with each evaluation scenario, the system is functioning normally. To do this, the technical POC checks each of the components to validate normal operation. You and your team want this to occur after each session to ensure that you did not introduce operational errors or unnecessary downtime.

Summary

In this chapter we covered the most significant aspect of doing an evaluation: the pre-assessment. The pre-assessment is crucial to the successful completion of the evaluation. In the pre-assessment, you will identify and obtain the required information that was gathered during the organizational assessment. This information is normally available in the INFOSEC assessment plan or in the final report, if the organizational assessment was accomplished prior to the evaluation. From experience we have found that it is easier and more comfortable for the customer to accomplish the assessment and evaluation at the same time, but there is no requirement to do so. As long as the information from the assessment is available, you can accomplish the evaluation. But without the information from the assessment, you cannot complete the evaluation. Some of the things that you will need include the mission statement, the organizational information criticality matrix and system information criticality matrix(es), customer concerns and constraints, and background requirements that have been identified. These are the absolute minimum pieces of information you'll need, and it is strongly recommended that you get the entire plan or report. If the assessment plan was not done or is not available, you and your team will have to create them to proceed with the evaluation. Without this information you will not be able to adequately map findings back to what the customer has determined is important or to the impact on the organizational mission.

Understanding the customer concerns and constraints is the next area covered in this chapter. This is where you as the evaluator need to understand why you were brought in to do the evaluation. This requires that you completely understand what the customer is concerned about. Most of the time the concerns are focused on compliance issues, and we did cover many of the common requirements, with brief descriptions, that drive executive management. We also include a brief and simplistic way to look at the ROI for security. Management is very concerned with the value of the work being accomplished, and though there is no industry standard for determining the ROI, you can provide some input to the customer on the value of the mitigation versus the probability of expected annual loss.

Next we covered an almost intangible topic: obtaining management buy-in. This is an area in which every evaluator must be knowledgeable. Without management buy-in, the evaluation will have a significantly lower probability of success. When there is management buy-in, the layers of the hierarchy below senior management will quickly realize that the evaluation is important, and this leads to significant improvement in cooperation. We discussed the two most common types of management support: forced compliance and "Make us better." In the forced compliance situation, the management is supporting this evaluation based on pressure from external sources, which tends to lead to minimal support to accomplish the evaluation and not much else. The second type is the preferred one—when management is sincere about improving the security posture, they tend to be more open and flexible to accomplishing the evaluation. When senior management is proactive, they will be accessible and interested in the project's progress. This normally leads to positive evaluations because everybody involved has a positive attitude toward the goal.

Obtaining technical staff buy-in is different. In our experience, you will normally have to deal with three different personalities: the *IT zealot, IT status quo,* and *keep-it-running.* You need to be aware that all three of these types of personality usually exist within any given organization. It has always been out preference to work with the zealot's as they are the most proactive and anxious to learn. Zealots tend to show up to meetings well prepared and ready to hit the ground running. Zealots ask a lot of questions and are almost always taking notes to improve their work habits. Although the zealots are our favorites, the most common type of worker is the status quo type. They are the ones that seem to be always busy. Status quo people are the IT staff personnel who try to maintain a constant balance between management requirements and user requests. They tend to be very observant during console reviews but tend to disappear during scanning activities. The worst to work with are the keep-it-running people. These are the folks who do not want to make changes. They tend to question every request and do not want to implement any changes or fixes without doing research first.

In the last section of the chapter, we talked about the establishing the POCs. As you know, you will always need the administrative or organizational POC. This POC is critical to completing the evaluation because they have the functions of coordinating interviews, demonstrations, technical POC accessibility, and reporting to management how the evaluation is going. The administrative POC is very important to your evaluation team because they are knowledgeable about your customer's political landscape and usually have the authority to be able to cross political boundaries. But how many technical POCs do you want? It is our desire to work with the senior administrator for each system. The role of the technical POC is to be your source of knowledge on how and why components are configured the way they are. Technical POCs should be used to validate that all components are functioning correctly when you are done with each evaluation step. They are also the individuals who will be responsible for implementing any recommendation that your team makes, and their understanding of the operational requirements will make your evaluation go more smoothly.

## Chapter 15

Scoping the Evaluation

Solutions in this chapter:

- **Focusing the Evaluation**
- **Identifying the Rules of Engagement**
- **Finding the Sources of Scoping Information**
- **Staffing Your Project**

☑ **Summary**

Introduction

Scoping a project to meet the customer's needs and the evaluation team's capabilities is probably the most challenging activity of the evaluation process. The quality of the evaluation scope is directly correlated to the quality of the evaluation itself. The adage "Measure twice, cut once" applies here. Just as in systems engineering, if you do a good job in the requirements and design phase, the rest of the project will go much more smoothly.

The scoping process identifies the agreed-on steps that will occur during the evaluation process. The scope will ultimately be documented and approved in the technical evaluation plan (TEP). Doing a poor job in the scoping process will result in wasted resources for both the customer and the evaluation team. This will cause extra hours on the job and over-expenditure of financial resources. Poor scope results from a poor understanding of the requirements and expectations of the customer, which may ultimately result in failure to meet customer expectations.

In this chapter, we discuss the components and activities of the scoping process that will give us the majority of the information needed to do an effective and efficient job during the evaluation process. We will look at the process of focusing the evaluation to meet customer expectations. We will talk about what can happen when, and if, the scoping process fails. We also address the areas that will be required to complete the TEP to include reporting level of detail, identifying the rules of engagement, ascertaining system boundaries, and staffing the project. We also look at sources of scoping information and the importance of the scoping questionnaire.

The bottom line is that without a quality scoping process, you will not have a quality evaluation. Doing a good job on the scoping process will give you the greatest opportunity for project success.

Focusing the Evaluation

The purpose of the evaluation scoping process is to ensure that the proper focus is placed on the customer's critical security interests. This focus must take into account customer expectations, deliverables, customer requirements beyond their expectations, and a critical understanding of what happens when scoping fails.

The true success of any project is driven by whether the customer is happy with the process and the end result of the project. This is especially true where the NSA IEM is concerned. The management of expectations starts from the initial customer contact and runs to the end of the project life cycle, during which the evaluation team will answer any remaining questions about the results. If at any point the customer appears not to be satisfied with the process, the evaluation team should make extra efforts to understand the dissatisfaction and come to some resolution.

The Power of Expectations

Expectations drive the customer's sense of satisfaction from the evaluation process and the resulting final deliverables. Well-managed expectations will result in a satisfied customer who feels they have gotten the greatest value for their money. Poorly managed expectations may result in a dissatisfied customer who feels their money and time have been wasted. The really damaging thing about poorly managed expectations, beyond the obvious, is that the customer is less likely to spend the funds necessary for security evaluations in the future, which could reduce their overall security posture. Managing customer expectations and ultimate satisfaction is critical to the success of the evaluation.

What Does the Customer Expect for Delivery?

Many evaluations start with the customer not understanding what they are truly looking for as a result of the evaluation process. Providing customer satisfaction can be difficult if you don't exert the appropriate effort during the scoping process to understand the customer needs. This requires an understanding of the level of detail for the recommendations, the boundaries desired for the evaluation, and a strong understanding of the desired use of the results.

   Understanding the desired use of the evaluation results will assist the evaluation team lead in determining how the final report can be focused to meet the customer needs. For example, if a department within a company requested the evaluation for the purpose of enlightening senior company management on issues they are not currently addressing, the evaluation results must address those areas of concern. Or the evaluation may be done as proof of due diligence for the organization's insurance company in the current liability insurance renewal process. Understanding what the customer expects for delivery will assist the evaluation team in properly focusing the evaluation effort.

Tools & Traps

Common Definitions

Approximately 50 percent of the evaluation, assessment, and/or penetration-testing engagements for which we are invited to submit a proposal do not use consistent terminology and definitions and therefore result in an initial misunderstanding of what the customer is looking for. Buzzwords are prevalent throughout the technology industry, including the information security arena. Many customers approach us with a request for a "penetration test." After discussing the project with the customer and understanding what results and deliverables they want out of the process, we find they are commonly looking for an evaluation or a combination assessment/evaluation.

Adjusting Customer Expectations

Expectations will change throughout the evaluation process. Over time, the customer will gain a greater understanding of the evaluation process and the added value of the evaluation to the organization. This normally results in "extras" added to the evaluation and a slightly expanded scope. This could include adding systems to the list of systems to be evaluated and increasing the number of sites or divisions to be included in the process. Changing expectations may also change some of the details of the final deliverable. The business process for changes will determine whether pricing or time lines will need to change as well. Ultimately, the deliverable will be a combination of the original expectations plus the customer's changing expectations or desires as the evaluation process moves forward.

When Scoping Fails

Common mistakes during the scoping process can derail the evaluation effort. Although we can't address every possible scenario, taking into consideration the concerns discussed here will help you avoid the common pitfalls associated with scoping the evaluation. A poorly implemented scoping process will result in an unhappy customer, poor word-of-mouth advertising about your firm, and a frustrating experience for all individuals involved. Changes in the scope of the effort are expected, but they need to be controlled. Otherwise we end up with "scope creep," lost revenue, and busted time lines.

"Scope Creep" and Time Lines

Unplanned and unbid scope changes in projects are often called *scope creep*. This occurs when a project deviates from the written scope at a higher scale. Controlling scope creep can help you effectively manage the overall project. Scope creep not only has an impact on the financial aspects of the project, it also has an impact on the project time lines and the evaluation team's ability to complete the job on time.

Scope creep can be caused by poor planning, unknown areas of the organization that need to be assessed, or a customer desire to further investigate a certain security area that is being analyzed by the evaluation team. Scope creep can also occur when a customer wants to get more out of the effort than they are paying for.

Tools & Traps

Scope Creep

The most common example of scope creep occurs when more systems or more locations need to be evaluated than were originally identified by the customer. This is generally due to the lack of full communication by the customer with their technical staff or a communications disconnect between the evaluation team and the customer. This is why it is extremely important to be detailed in the assumptions section of the evaluation agreement (the contract). Another example of scope creep occurs with the discovery of additional systems that need to be reviewed as part of the evaluation that were not originally part of the effort.

Restricting Scope Slippage in the Contract

The project manager, team lead, and customer representative should work closely together to avoid scope creep. Any agreed-on changes need to be appropriately documented and, if necessary, those costs should be added into the project. This doesn't mean that all scope changes have to be considered negative or even require a cost increase. However, we do recommend an evaluation of the changes on a case-by-case basis to ensure that expectations are being met.

There are legal ramifications within government contracts for things like scope slippage. To better understand government contracting, you need to go deeper into contracting than is possible this book. Entirely different sets of terminology are related to government contracting. Obtain the necessary expertise to create an appropriate contract for the situation.

Contracting Differences

Don't assume that your experience with either government contracting or commercial contracting fully prepares you for all aspects of contracting. Government contracts and commercial contracts are unique in nature, as are the differences between the government agencies or commercial industries. Be prepared to learn something new with the various entities you work with, and don't get frustrated when one entity does contracting differently than another.

You'll find many sources out there on government contracting. Try a Web search for the most current links, but some possibilities include:

- Business.Gov (www.business.gov/)
- The Small Business Administration (www.sba.gov/GC/)
- Federal Business Opportunities (www.fedbizopps.gov/)

Uneducated Salespeople

Educate your security sales staff on the evaluation process before they are sent into the field to sell an evaluation based on the IEM. They do not have to be experts on the entire process, but they do need to understand what an evaluation is composed of, reasonable expectations of the process, involvement of the customer in the process, and the impact of a complex customer environment on the process.

If you are using the IEM process for evaluations, consider sending the sales staff to an IEM training course. It is an excellent method of obtaining a better understanding of the process and will hopefully result in a better understanding of security overall for the sales staff. Working in conjunction with the evaluation "experts," sales staff can put together a quality sales presentation and proposal. Ensure that they understand not to make promises that they are not sure your organization can keep. This includes level of effort (which impacts cost) and unreasonable expectations on time frames.

Evaluations 101

Here is a simple, high-level overview of the various purposes of an INFOSEC evaluation:

- Reduce the likelihood of external and internal attacks on the network or system
- Identify exposed information through the identification and verification of customer information system assets
- Identify vulnerabilities to systems that process, store, or transmit critical information
- Identify network vulnerabilities
- Identify unintended network presence or services
- Link customer needs, regulatory requirements, and industry best practices to identify the proper INFOSEC posture for the customer

- Validate the technical INFOSEC posture for these systems

- Recommend solutions to mitigate or eliminate those vulnerabilities

- Implement security measures to assist with cost avoidance

Tools & Traps

Sold up the River

This is not intended as a general slam on salespeople, but we have experienced several incidents where an uneducated salesperson sold a service without knowledge of what the effort entailed or how it could be accomplished. Package pricing a security evaluation without knowledge of who the evaluation is for or how an evaluation is conducted can result in serious mission and financial failure for the evaluation team. Success is measured not only by how well you do your job but also by whether the customer is satisfied with the service they were provided at the price they paid.

Bad Assumptions

Making poor or inappropriate assumptions can have a serious negative impact on your evaluation. A great deal of effort needs to be put into developing and reviewing the assumptions that are made for each evaluation agreement. Assumptions detail the understood environment in which the evaluation will be conducted. They will also identify the expected involvement of the customer in the process in terms of staff availability, scheduling requirements, and time frames.

Why do we have assumptions to begin with? Assumptions are the anticipated conditions or actions that will occur in preparing for or conducting the evaluation process. The assumptions are listed in agreements to ensure that the customer understands what is anticipated of them to support the evaluation team or what they can expect from the evaluation team.

Assumption Topic Areas

The following are examples of information that needs to be included in the assumptions section and that must be as accurate as possible to avoid confusion and poor scoping:

- Location(s) at which the evaluation will be conducted

- Availability of customer personnel for the evaluation

- Scheduling of the evaluation activities to avoid customer impact

- Travel requirements (if any)

- Documentation availability

- Necessary support from the customer in managing the evaluation

- Availability and currency of the network diagrams
- Operating system types for servers and workstations
- Technical expertise of the customer for the detail of recommendations

Poorly Written Contracts

Poorly written contracts are the basis for poor evaluations. Generally speaking, poor contracts are based on bad information, bad assumptions, and lack of attention to detail. A boilerplate evaluation contract can be dangerous if not properly tailored to the current customer. Every organization has different expectations and requirements to meet; the worst kind of evaluation contract has no specific detail related to the customer being evaluated. Several factors can contribute to poorly written contracts: poor scope definition, underbidding, or overbidding of a contract.

Poor Scope Definition

Poor scope definition generally results from a poor understanding of the requirements and expectations associated with a project. From a provider perspective, poor scope definition could mean a loss in revenue and profits for an effort. Poor scoping can result in your consultants having to spend unplanned hours on the job as well as eventual cost overruns. Another major mistake in the scoping effort is *not* having the customer approve the agreed-on scope with a signature. By having the customer sign off on their approval of the scope, you help avoid future issues of the customer denying that they agreed with the scope or possibly forcing additional work for no additional money. Be sure to protect your company. Don't assume anything. Document the agreement in detail.

NOTE

Contracts are one area in which large companies generally have an advantage over smaller companies. They normally have years of experience, a dedicated contracting staff, and strong legal counsel that support their needs in the contracting process.

Underbid or Overbid: The Art of Poor Cost Estimating

Pricing of a bid can be as critical as the quality of the information put into the bid. Understanding the customer environment and limitations from a financial perspective will help you properly price the effort. This closely ties into the assumptions section of the project agreement and the TEP's rules of engagement. The assumptions help determine the level of effort you'll need to put into a project. It is always dangerous to bid a project low to win the bid. Bidding low cuts into your flexibility and profit margin. Bidding high can price you out of contention for the project. True pricing has to come from actual expected effort and your experience as to what it will take to complete it.

Many outside influences can impact the costing efforts. As mentioned, a poor understanding of the requirements and expectations associated with the project is one. Another is salesperson influence on the process — trying to force undue pressure on the process in an attempt to win the bid. This pressure may result in mistakes being made in the costing of the effort. Another pressure from the sales staff runs along the lines of "I said we could do the evaluation for $25,000, so we have to do it for $25,000."

Identifying the Rules of Engagement

The rules of engagement are the boundaries and limits that currently exist or are established to help control the execution of the evaluation. Rules of engagement will basically become a list of "do's" and "don'ts" for the evaluation. The primary concern of the rules of engagement is to ensure the understanding of the customer's and the evaluation team's expectations and limits while the evaluation is under way.

Customer Concerns

Generally a customer will have specific reasons for asking for an evaluation. It will be important to understand the specific concerns the customer wants to address as part of this process. This information contributes directly to the scoping process and helps meet customer expectations. Some of the reasons customers ask for an evaluation are:

- Legislative/regulatory requirements
- Insurance requirements
- Protection of critical infrastructure
- To provide the system owners a certain level of confidence that their information is protected
- As part of a good security engineering and management practice
- In response to suspected threats, security incidents, and Red Team activities
- For an independent review to validate internal reviews
- Because it's the right thing to do

Stating the Evaluation Purpose

Customer concerns have a direct tie to the purpose for the evaluation. We need to understand this purpose as part of the scoping process to better define and document the customer needs. This information will then be included in the TEP.

Customer Constraints

All customers have constraints of some kind, whether time, financial, human, political, or third-party involvement. Failure to discuss, recognize, and clarify constraints with the customer up front and throughout the evaluation process can result in failure of the evaluation project. Some common constraints that may be missed or ignored include:

- Ascertaining available time frames to execute the evaluation
- Financial constraints on the organization to conduct the evaluation
- Personnel resources to support the effort
- Organizational politics
- Third-party control of resources (boundaries)

Impact Resistance and Acceptable Levels of Invasiveness

The evaluation process is not meant to damage or change the customer's business operations or business practices. The intent of the evaluation is to *help* the customer. However, by their nature hands-on evaluations can be intrusive. Therefore, a good understanding of the customer's business processes will help you define factors such as scanning times, node exclusions, and tool limitations. Evaluations that include activities such as DoS testing, war dialing, and password-compliance testing add complexity and intrusiveness to the process. Be sure to address this up front with the customer because this issue will drive the level of effort the evaluation team needs to put into the project, which is a key part of the scoping process. Ultimately you are trying to limit the impact to the customer by not being overly intrusive.

Identifying Scanning Times

To avoid impact to the customer during peak operational and processing times, you need to reach an agreement on when the technical scans and technical testing will be conducted. Often our customers ask us to do scanning between 8:00 P.M. and 6:00 A.M. to avoid operational impact.

When considering this area, you may have four different possible allowable time frames for testing based on the type of testing that is occurring. Discuss with the customer the acceptable testing time frames for the following:

- Administrative network components and systems (noncritical)
- Sensitive information segments
- Mission-critical information segments
- Host evaluations (must be physically present at the system)

Off-Limit Nodes

There may be some systems the customer does not want you scan for vulnerabilities. Work with the customer to define these systems and gain an understanding about the purpose of the exclusion. Be sure to document this understanding in the TEP. The reasons for these off-limit systems will vary, but they could include:

- The system is owned by someone other than the customer.
- The system is so critical that they cannot afford even a remote chance that the system's operations might be impacted.
- The customer knows the system will crash and might not be brought back to operation.
- The customer knows the system will be replaced in the next few days or weeks.

Are You Owned?

Systems Too Critical to Evaluate

Some customers identify systems they do not want touched because they are too critical to operations to even risk a remote chance that the system might crash. This, of course, is the proverbial "Catch-22." If you don't test a system to know whether it's vulnerable, you cannot have some level of assurance that a malicious hacker or even an accidental hacker won't be able crash the system for you. It is better to crash a system in a controlled environment than to leave the system hanging out there with unknown vulnerabilities. This type of situation may also indicate issues with a customer's business continuity planning or disaster recovery planning processes and procedures, which could need to be identified and addressed on the organizational security side (the IAM).

Evaluation Tool Limitations

Some customers may have had previous negative experiences with some evaluation tools and will not want them run on their network. This should be documented in the TEP and understood by the evaluation team. There may also be an opportunity to further educate the customer on evaluation tools and be able to explain to the customer why they had issues with the tools. The customer could appreciate your candor and change their mind about that specific tool. Some customers also have policies against the use of freeware or shareware tools, which might need to be taken into account when planning the toolkit for the evaluation. This is especially true in some federal government and military locations.

Notification Procedures

Just as every company should have a tested disaster recovery plan, every evaluation should have established procedures in case something goes wrong during the evaluation process. The intent of the evaluation is to *not* break anything, but accidents do happen due to testing tool misconfiguration, misconfigured customer systems, and sometimes just plain old bad luck. Establish who you are going to call in case something seems to quit responding. Normally you'd call the technical POC for the department or group you are evaluating or their designate. Also identify who will be contacted in the event a critical security finding is identified and the evaluation team feels that the customer needs to address it immediately.

Evaluation Addressing

When you're conducting an evaluation, it is best for the evaluation team to utilize static IP addresses for both internal and external evaluation testing so there is no question of whether a potential security incident is a result of the evaluation or a real, malicious hacker. In doing external scanning, be sure to provide the customer with the IPs that the testing is coming from. Don't forget to have the evaluation team members keep a copy of the LOA with them at *all* times while the evaluation is under way, to avoid problems with the customer's internal incident response team or law enforcement. It's also helpful for the evaluators to maintain a constant log of their activities so that if problems or issues do crop up, you'll be better equipped to backtrack and locate the reason for the outage.

Some customers may prefer that you perform the external scanning from just outside the router or firewall instead of over the Internet. Discuss this with the customer to clarify their expectations from an external testing perspective.

Reporting Level of Detail

Working with the customer on identifying the level of detail required for the findings, discussion, and recommendations in the final report is an important process during scoping. The NSA identifies three specific levels of technical detail for the purposes of completing the final report. These are:

- **Low detail** This level of detail is reserved for the executive summary. Low detail is not overly technical and serves the purpose of providing executives with a view of the security posture without bogging them down in the technical detail.

- **Moderate detail** This is the standard level of detail for the main body of the final report. It is a level of detail that is very technical in nature but not a step-by-step "how-to." This level of detail generally addresses the needs of the supervisors or system/security administrators.

- **High detail** This level of detail is reserved for customers that do not have the technical depth to understand the detail at the moderate level. Developing the recommendations for findings with this level of detail will generally require a great deal more time. High detail will be very technical and will include step-by-step implementation procedures for the customer to follow.

When conducting the scoping process, it is important to address the level-of-detail expectations with the customer. This will drive the level of effort that needs to be estimated in the delivery of the final report. This level of effort clearly affects the resources and amount of time needed to prepare the final report. In other words, time is money.

Clear and Concise Writing

All writing, whether for the TEP or the final report, needs to be clear and concise to ensure proper understanding by the customer and to increase the chance that the customer will actually implement your recommendations. Your writing does not need to be verbose, but it should be easy to understand at the appropriate level to which it is written. Avoid slang and jargon that will potentially confuse the reader. Try to write around the industry you are addressing, using the appropriate terminology for the customer you are working with. We all have a tendency to speak in slang, but this should be avoided in the formal documentation.

Establishing the Evaluation Boundaries

One of the biggest challenges that any evaluation team will confront while trying to define the evaluation process will be locating known or perceived boundaries for the system. Boundaries provide a delineation of the system and limit the scope of each system. A system in the context of the evaluation activities is something that transmits, stores, or processes the critical information types within the customer organization as defined by our IAM pre-assessment process. A system can be a single server or include the workstations that communicate with the server and all media between the two. When we define boundaries, we define them based on the physical aspect of the boundary or the logical transfer of the information from one responsible hand to another.

Physical Boundaries

Physical boundaries are often the easiest for the customer and the evaluation team to understand. The physical boundary of a system may be as simple as the network jack on a wall, a port on a switch, or an interface on a perimeter firewall. In a more metropolitan-based system, the system could be delineated by the particular building within a city in which the system is used exclusively. On a more global basis, perhaps the system is defined by a particular set of replicated servers and workstations at each of 12 global sites that all share the same information database. Again, physical boundaries tend to be more tangible than logical boundaries because they can be "touched" in some physical manner. The following list gives common examples of some physical boundaries you'll see during evaluations:

- Switch port
- Firewall interface
- Perimeter router
- Subnet router interface
- Building entrances and exits

NOTE

Physical boundaries are defined by the locations (for instance, a room, a building, or a complex) of the system equipment and local procedures regarding the handling and processing of particular types of information.

Logical Boundaries

Logical boundaries are less tangible than physical boundaries and often more difficult for the customer to understand and define. These types of boundaries refer to where the critical information changes hands to another entity that then becomes the responsible party for controlling access to the data. A good example is where a bank transfers information on customer transactions to a partner bank. Once the information leaves the hands of the local bank and moves into the customer's own bank, the information then becomes the responsibility of the partner bank. Thus the security of that information passes to the partner bank as well.

These types of relationships are the best way to view logical boundaries. From an internal customer perspective, maybe we're dealing with multiple entities or branches within the organization that control the same information in different phases of its life cycle. Information may arrive in the system via a Web environment that is strictly controlled by the Web or IT teams and then passes from this network to the procurement department. When the information changes hands and the originating party loses control of and responsibility for the information, we've located a logical boundary for the system at hand. The easiest method for locating these logical boundaries is to create a data flow diagram with the customer. Data flow diagrams emulate the flow of critical information types within the network. This includes flows from primary servers to workstations or hosts that use the information. Network components, such as routers, switches, hubs, and cabling, are also considered during this process.

Logical boundaries are something that might not be easy for upper management and most middle management to understand and recognize. A logical boundary is the point at which the customer has lost their logical control over the information. Usually management does not recognize that this is an issue. The problem is that senior management often does not understand that they really don't have any control over all their information components. This is where you, as the evaluator, must educate them. The customer must understand how the logical boundaries will affect the evaluation scoping. Consider the issues of having the logical boundary set at the perimeter router. Who owns the router? In many organizations, the ISP or a parent organization owns the perimeter router. If the ISP is one of the major providers such as Sprint, MCI, or AT&T, they might not agree to allow any evaluation of the router. The service-level agreement could even forbid review of the rule sets used.

NOTE

Logical boundaries are defined by understanding where responsibility for or authority over the critical information changes hands.

Critical Path and Critical Components

The concepts of critical path and critical components play a key role in how information is handled across the network and how much protection is put into place on the customer's network. *Critical path* is the logical path of communications across the network in which critical information flows. If the path breaks at any point along the critical path, it hampers the organization's ability to perform its mission or serve its customers.

Critical components are those devices that process, transmit, and/or store the critical information. The compromise of critical components, or high-assurance devices, can also hamper the organization's ability to perform its mission or serve its customers.

As part of the scoping effort, the evaluation team needs to work with the customer to ensure that there is a mutual understanding of these key concepts. This is directly related to the processes of identifying critical information and critical systems within the customer's environment as defined by IAM pre-assessment process.

NOTE

Third-party connectivity also plays a key role in the definition of physical and logical boundaries. Typically a third-party connection ends up being both a physical and a logical boundary at the same time. This is due to the fact that control of the information is generally handed off at this point (logical) and there is normally some device or location (firewall, perimeter router, or the like). These are physical boundaries.

Finding the Sources of Scoping Information

Scoping information can come from multiple sources. One of the obvious sources for scoping information is the SOW or RFP that the customer issues to obtain the evaluation services. Generally this information is truncated and requires additional details to properly determine the scope. Additional sources of scoping information can include the customer representative assigned to the project. They will generally provide additional nonproprietary information that is specifically requested of them. If it is a competitive bid, they will generally be required to provide this information to all potential bidders.

Additionally, customer documentation is an excellent source of information about the organization and any related security programs, if the information is available. Useful documentation can include acceptable-use policies, security policies, network architecture diagrams, and results of previous evaluations or audits. Another excellent source of scoping information comes through asking the right questions on a scoping questionnaire.

Customer

The customer is the most critical source of information for the evaluation scope. The customer has some idea what they are looking for and a (normally) general idea of how the results will be used. The customer will provide technical information through the scoping questionnaire, the administrative staff, and the technical POCs.

The Scoping Questionnaire

Obtaining the information you need to properly scope an effort can be a challenge for the proposal team or evaluation team. More often than not, we find that customer SOWs or RFPs are poorly scoped when they are developed. They do not contain enough information or are boilerplate RFPs that contain erroneous information. Many times we have to go back to the customer to collect additional information to finalize any bidding or scoping process we are working on.

This is one instance in which a scoping questionnaire can be useful in obtaining the information needed. A scoping questionnaire provides customers with an easy-to-complete form that asks the relevant questions relating to information needed to properly scope the level of effort for a project. The questionnaire gives a good baseline of information and may lead to additional necessary questions to finalize the details. The scoping questionnaire answers many of the normal questions up front to provide the clarification needed on the project.

NOTE

You should create your own scoping questionnaire using your INFOSEC experience as the basis. This gives you the information you need to develop your contractual scope and make estimates of level of effort and pricing for the contract. Here we provide examples to help get you started.

Information Gained from the Questionnaire

The evaluation scoping questionnaire is the most valuable source of information for collecting the initial information about the customer and the type of work to be conducted. This questionnaire, combined with clarification from the customer, will result in a well understood, documented, and accomplishable evaluation. The critical types of information you are looking for include the following:

- Name of the customer (don't laugh, many forget to tell you)
- POC information for business activities (address, phone, e-mail)
- Administrative POC for the evaluation (address, phone, e-mail)
- Technical POC(s) for the evaluation (address, phone, e-mail)
- Customer mission/industry information
- Emergency situation POC(s) (address, phone, e-mail)
- Physical access coordination information for internal evaluation (site visit requirements and internal scanning information)
- Primary customer concerns for themselves and for their industry
- Applicable legislative, regulatory, or other industry security drivers
- Number of sites they have (including location)
- Number of sites involved with the evaluation (including location and reasons for exclusions)
- Number of internal IP addresses to be evaluated
- Number of external IP addresses to be evaluated
- Network protocols in use by the customer
- Number of workstations to be evaluated
- Number of servers to be evaluated
- Operating systems in use

- How many and type of web servers
- Primary services running on the servers
- Firewall information
- Intrusion detection/prevention information
- Remote access information
- Virtual private network (VPN) information
- Wireless network information
- Converged network information
- Identifiable physical and logical boundary information
- Security architecture that is currently implemented (layered security?)
- Implemented access controls (key cards, biometrics, passwords, single sign-on, and so on)
- Previous evaluation, assessment, audit information
- Security policy and procedure information
- Risk management information, including an understanding of what is being protected and why (IAM information and system criticality information)
- Security review policy (how often are internal and third-party reviews conducted?)
- Physical security policy and procedures
- Incident response policy and procedures
- Disaster recovery policy and procedures
- Personnel security policy and procedures
- Type of evaluation the customer is looking for (how comprehensive)
- IEM baseline activities inclusion and exclusion information
- Date the customer expects/must have the evaluation completed by
- Any limitations/restrictions on the evaluation team

Tools & Traps

Assumptions Will Hurt You Again and Again and Again

Do not assume anything about your customer. Verify even the most basic anticipated actions to be sure that the customer is on the same page in relation to the rules of engagement and expectations from the evaluation process. Ask questions even when you think you already know the answers. It is better to confirm an answer than be surprised. For example, when dealing with the network protocol used by the customer, you know that 95 percent of the world uses TCP/IP, but through our own painful experiences; we have found that some customers still use IPX as their primary networking protocol. Not many commercial tools will do scanning on IPX networks. This is a bit of critical information that would be helpful to understand prior to starting the evaluation effort.

Value of the Questionnaire

The scoping questionnaire clearly provides a tremendous amount of information for the evaluation team and the customer. The benefit of the scoping questionnaire is twofold:

- It provides critical information for the evaluation team to determine the scope of the effort to make a reasonable estimate of level of effort and, ultimately, the cost of the evaluation.

- It forces the customer to think in detail about what they are trying to accomplish and what they really want to be asking for and can expect from the evaluation process.

Example Responses on a Scoping Questionnaire

The following information shows an example of responses you could see on a scoping questionnaire.

Q: ORGANIZATION NAME

A: TOrganization for Critical Healthcare

Q: THow many physical sites do you have?

A: 3

Q: What is the address of the location(s)?

A: OUCH Headquarters

123 Main St.

Mt. Anywhere, US 11111

OUCH Pediatrics

125 Main St.

Mt. Anywhere, US 11111

OUCH Rehab

121 Main St.

Mt. Anywhere, US 11111

Q: Mission or Business Description

A: The Organized Union for Critical Healthcare (OUCH) has been contracted by Our Lady of Perpetual Pain, Memorial Hospital to handle their information processing.

The facility can house up to 5000 patients at a time. The day-to-day operations require automated information systems support for tracking and controlling information that includes admitting/releasing patients, administering medications, scheduling surgeries, feeding patients, tracking traffic to and from the hospital morgue, and various other information for doctors, nurses, and staff. OUCH has developed a single networked system that allows all the functions to be performed from terminals throughout the facility. The connectivity includes all databases and applications, so the information is readily available no matter where in the facility it is needed.

Q: Are there any regulations or legislation that governs your business operations from a security or privacy perspective? (Please list.)

A: Health Insurance Portability and Accountability Act (HIPAA), Joint Commission on Accreditation of Healthcare Organizations (JACHO)

Q: How many total active users are there?

A: 568

Q: How many internal server IP addresses are to be evaluated (by locations)?

A: HQ–5, Pediatrics–0, Rehab–0

Q: How many internal workstation IP addresses at each site to be evaluated?

A: HQ–427, Pediatrics–11, Rehab–5

Q: How many external server IP addresses are to be evaluated?

A: 5

Q: How many external workstation IP addresses are to be evaluated?

A: None

Q: What networking protocols are you running? (TCP/IP, IPX, etc.)

A: TCP/IP

Q: What operating systems are on the workstations?

A: 4 on 98, 4 on Windows XP, remainder on 2000

Q: What operating systems are on the servers?

A: Windows NT and Windows 2000

Q: What services are running on the servers? (Web, DNS, etc.)

A: WINS, DNS, Web

Q: Do you have a firewall(s)?

A: Yes, 2—Checkpoint NG running on Nokia

Q: Do you have an active network and/or host-based IDS?

A: No

Q: Will you require war dialing at any/all sites to detect rogue modems?

A: Yes, all sites, 65 numbers

Q: Do you require any tests on denial of service (DOS) vulnerabilities?

A: Yes, during nonpeak hours

Q: How many Web servers are active and accessible by the public?

A: Web servers hosted by external third party

Q: What type of Web servers (Apache, IIS)?

A: Apache over Slackware

Q: How many Web servers are active and for internal use only?

A: 1

Q: What type of Web servers (Apache, IIS)?

A: IIS on Windows 2000

Q: Do you currently utilize a RAS server for external access?

A: Yes, Cisco

Q: Do you currently utilize a remote VPN product for external access (i.e., Altiga VPN concentrator)?

A: Yes, Checkpoint VPN

Q: Who will be the primary point of contact (POC) at your organization?

A: Name: Bob Smith

Phone: 555-111-1111

Cell: 555-222-3333

E-mail: bsmith@ouch.me

Job title: IT Director

Q: Are you utilizing a domain architecture?

A: Yes

Q: Are you utilizing a Windows Active Directory-based architecture?

A: No

Q: Are you utilizing a Novell NDS–based architecture?

A: No

Q: Do you have wireless networking?

A: Yes

Q: Do you have mainframe environments?

A: Yes, RS6000

Q: Is there third-party connectivity?

A: Yes

Q: Are you using voice-over-IP (VOIP) or IP telephony?

A: No

Q: Are you using a converged network architecture?

A: No

Q: Do you have documented security policies?

A: Yes, but outdated

Q: Are there any known limitations we need to be aware of?

A: No

Q: Do you have a date on which the assessment/evaluation must be completed?

A: Yesterday

Evaluation Requestor

The individual or group requesting the evaluation will provide key evaluation information. The requestor may not be the primary person or even in the group inside the organization for which you will be doing the evaluation. Normally this occurs in some kind of formal services request such as SOW or RFP. These formal requests normally don't contain the level of detail necessary to fully scope out an effort. This identifies the importance of the scoping questionnaire and the interaction with other individuals.

Customer Senior Leadership

The customers' senior leadership will have a general idea of what they want to accomplish with the IEM process. They generally possess information about their customers, mission, and suppliers and what they need to accomplish from the evaluation process.

Administrative Customer Contact

The administrative customer contact will play multiple roles in the scoping process. One role is to be a central location for the collection of information as it is requested and provided. They will also be able to recommend people to talk to for collecting additional detailed information. They also arrange for evaluation team office space, phone access, and facility access. The administrative customer contact will likely be the person coordinating answers for the scoping questionnaire.

Technical Customer Contacts

The technical customer contacts (remember, there is likely to be more than one) will provide critical technical information in the scoping process. They will identify the appropriate IPs and subnets that will be scanned, along with the appropriate and acceptable time frames for each of the subnets being dealt with. The technical customer contacts will also know the critical nodes and the off-limit nodes within their environments. These individuals may be the emergency contacts for their area or department during the evaluation. You will want to have this information well documented.

Evaluation Team

The evaluation team is also a reasonable source of information for scoping information. They will spend time researching the customer and collecting information on their operations before you begin the evaluation effort. They will be able to speak to the validity of some of the information provided. The evaluation team is composed of the team lead and team members, each of whom may be able to provide good scoping information.

Evaluation Team Lead

The evaluation team lead plays a crucial role in the scoping process. The team lead will likely have spent time talking to the customer and gaining valuable information on evaluation objectives and goals. The team lead may have also been involved in previous engagements with the customer, such as assessments, evaluations, Red Teams, or other activities that would add value to the scoping process.

Evaluation Team Members

The evaluation team members also play a key role in the scoping process. They will likely have spoken with the technical members of the customer's staff and gained additional understanding of the customer's technical security needs. This can help bring forward scoping issues that might otherwise be overlooked by the customer's management.

Validating Scoping Information

After you complete the process of gathering scoping information, it is helpful to validate the information through multiple sources, as available. Always keep in mind that the customer will have likely missed something that should have been included. Once an error is discovered, discuss with the customer the options and implement the necessary changes with as little impact as possible.

Staffing Your Project

Deciding on the correct composition of the evaluation team is important in making the project a success. Having the wrong mix for the team can result in an unsatisfied customer and potentially the failure of the project. In this section, we look at how the team composition for each evaluation is important and some of the assurances needed when naming the evaluation lead and the evaluation team.

Job Requirements

The actual scope of the project determines the team composition for the evaluation. It is important for the team lead and the team members to be knowledgeable of the industry the customer is working in, the related regulations and guidance that govern the customer, and any legislative requirements that drive the customer's business. For example, if your team has been contracted to perform an evaluation on a medical institution, it would be most beneficial to have team members familiar with HIPAA. A close examination of the customer's environment will also determine the technical composition of the evaluation team.

TIP

The critical thing to remember is that the success of the evaluation process depends on the technical expertise and critical thinking of the evaluation team members. Almost anyone can run a scanning tool, but it takes specific expertise to understand and accurately interpret the results.

Networking and Operating Systems

Gaining an understanding of the technical operating environment is critical for selecting the best team members. A major failure in many evaluations is having the wrong technical expertise on the team. Having an individual with primarily strong UNIX skills evaluate Microsoft Windows systems would probably prove to be a bad decision, as would having a Cisco Networking expert evaluate UNIX systems. The technologies are not the same, and to garner respect and cooperation in the evaluation efforts, the evaluation team needs to speak the same language as the person or team being evaluated. This is not to say that you cannot have an individual on your team with strong skills in multiple technical areas. In fact, your evaluation team will most likely be more successful if you have technical team members with multiple applicable skills that can be utilized during the evaluation process.

Some of the most critical expertise to have involved on your team could include Windows Server and WorkStation Operating Systems (Win NT, Win 2000, Win 2003, Win XP), UNIX expertise (Sun Solaris, HPUX), Linux expertise (Red Hat, Slackware, Mandrake), Cisco IOS expertise, and possibly mainframe expertise (AS400, VAX, or VMS). Each customer has a different combination of technical networking and computer operating systems. Good sources of this information are the network architecture descriptions and current network diagrams.

Hardware Knowledge

Understanding the various types of hardware the customer uses is also helpful. These can include various types of firewalls, intrusion detection systems, server platforms, routers and switches, and phone systems. This information will also be useful in conducting the evaluation. If you have a customer that is purely a Cisco shop, you will want an individual who is versed in Cisco on the team. If they have a combination of hardware and software, consider having a very knowledgeable generalist on the team.

Picking the Right People

Final selection of the evaluation team is a process of matching the understood needs of the customer with the expertise of available team members. Finding the right match for the IEM pre-evaluation phase and ultimately the onsite phase is critical to team success.

Matching Consultants to Customers

Consultants are matched to each customer based on the industry the customer is working in and the specific technologies the customer utilizes in their operational environment.

- **Team lead characteristics**   The team lead is the single most critical member of the evaluation team and should be the team leader for both the pre-evaluation and onsite evaluation phases. This individual is responsible for constant communication and coordination with both the evaluation team and the customer. The team lead should have a minimum of three security evaluations supporting other team leaders to ensure that he or she understands the dynamics involved and has adequate experiences to fall back on and share with the customer. This individual must be an extremely dynamic person capable of facilitating discussion in multiple types of environments and multiple political situations. The team lead should be knowledgeable in the industry in which the customer is primarily working. The team leader does not necessarily have to be a technical expert, but understanding the terminology of the organization and industry is important. It is wise to assign a dynamic technical team member to back up the team lead in case of emergency or some other situation.

- **Technical team members**   Technical team members need to be experienced in a variety of technologies specifically related to the technical environment of the customer. Industry expertise would be a value-add, but technical expertise is more essential in this case. Technical team members need to be dynamic enough to communicate well with the customer team to obtain the information needed to fully evaluate the customer security environment.

Personality Issues

In any effort, there is the possibility of personality conflicts between team members or with members of the customer organization. The team lead needs to understand this possibility and attempt to avoid these situations or implement buffers to prevent the situation from being an issue. This is more of a political issue than anything. Customers will sense tension between team members, which can detract from the overall success of the evaluation. When a conflict does arise and the issues cannot be resolved in a less restrictive manner, team member reassignment may be necessary. Since the effort is about customer satisfaction, the team members need to attempt to adjust to the customer first before trying to force a change in the customer.

Summary

Effectively scoping your evaluation will save a great deal of time and headaches as the evaluation moves forward. This basic foundation sets the tone for the entire evaluation process, gives the evaluation team its first opportunity to gain detailed information about the customer, and gives the customer its first opportunity to communicate with the evaluation team. Creating a good environment throughout the scoping and contracting process generally leads to positive results throughout the entire evaluation process.

Once the customer is convinced that an evaluation is needed, they may begin working with you directly or may be required to go out for competitive bid through an RFP or some other proposal solicitation process. The RFP will contain important information necessary to write a proposal or a contract. The most critical challenge is establishing the scope of the effort and related assumptions to determine the level of effort and costing required for executing the project.

Another challenge is avoiding the normal pitfalls that can occur with any scoping process. The pitfalls come from lessons learned over years in the contracting process. Be sure to use recommendations from your legal staff and experienced team members in putting together your final scope and contract. Unfortunately, the pitfall information is made up of primarily "thou shall not" statements:

- Thou shall not miss addressing specific customer concerns in your scoping process.

- Thou shall not make bad scope assumptions.

- Thou shall not allow outside influences to affect the accuracy of the scoping process.

- Thou shall not let "scope creep" go unmanaged.

- Thou shall not write bad contracts that either underbid or overbid a project.

You must establish, early in the process, the customer's expectations as related to the level of detail of recommendations that must be included in the final reporting process. *High* level of detail will require additional resources during the reporting process and are not considered standard, whereas the standard *medium* level of detail will be easier to estimate. *Low* level of detail is reserved for the executive summary.

The rules of engagement encompass several activities that will determine certain actions and help you manage customer expectations. These activities help establish ground rules for executing the task. The areas that will be addressed in this process include:

- Determine acceptable levels of invasiveness for the evaluation.

- Determine time frames for the actual technical testing.

- Establish notification procedures during the evaluation process (emergency and nonemergency).

- Establish and report the IPs that will be used for the evaluation.

- Carry out legal reviews and a letter of authorization.

Critical to the success of the evaluation is understanding the physical and logical boundaries for the evaluation process. This can also include third-party relationships and network architecture limitations. The evaluation team and the customer want to avoid crossing these boundaries and creating problems within the customer organization.

There are several sources of scoping information to include regarding both the customer and the evaluation team. The most valuable source of initial detailed customer information is via the scoping questionnaire. The scoping questionnaire plays a vital role in information collection and will help to get the customer focused on thinking about the critical technical resources within their environment.

Selecting your project staff depends on the size of the customer organization being evaluated, the industry in which the customer works, and the technologies the customer employs. The number of people necessary to conduct the evaluation depends on similar factors and also must take into consideration the customer's desired time line and the geographic separation of the customer's organizational components. Technical drivers to consider include the types of hardware and software the customer is using as well as the operating systems in use on the servers, workstations, and network components. Experience will drive the process of matching the consultants to the customers. No technology or cookie-cutter template can replace the experience and critical thinking of the evaluation team.

Throughout the entire process of scoping and preparing for the evaluation, never lose sight of your number-one goal: meeting customer expectations. How do you do this? Through effective communication with the customer, communication with the evaluation team, customer education, working with customer time lines, and gaining a common understanding of the level of commitment required to complete the evaluation process.

## Chapter 16

Legal Principles for Information Security Evaluations[1]

Solutions in this chapter:

- **Uncle Sam Wants You: How Your Company's Information Security Can Affect U.S. National Security**

- **Legal Standards Relevant to Information Security**

- **Selected Federal Laws**

- **Do It Right or Bet the Company: Tools to Mitigate Legal Liability**

- **What to Cover in IEM Contracts[2]**

- **The First Thing We Do…? Why You *Want* Your Lawyers Involved From Start to Finish**

---

[1] This chapter was written jointly by: Bryan Cunningham, Principal at Morgan & Cunningham LLC, a Denver-based homeland security consulting and law firm, and formerly Deputy Legal Adviser to the U.S. National Security Council and Assistant General Counsel, Central Intelligence Agency; C. Forrest Morgan, Principal at Morgan & Cunningham LLC, and Amanda Hubbard, Trial Attorney, U.S. Department of Justice with extensive experience in the U.S. Intelligence Community. The authors also gratefully acknowledge the research and analysis assistance of Nir D. Yarden. The views expressed herein are solely those of the authors and do not necessarily represent the views of the publisher or the U.S. government.

[2] This section drew, in part, from portions of pages 7–11 of *Security Assessment: Case Studies for Implementing the NSA IAM*, used by permission of Syngress Publishing, Inc.

WARNING: THIS CHAPTER IS NOT LEGAL ADVICE

This chapter provides an overview of a number of legal issues faced by information security evaluation professionals and their customers. Hopefully, it will alert readers to the issues on which they should consult qualified legal counsel experienced in information security law. This chapter, however, does not provide any legal advice or counsel to its readers. Readers should not, under any circumstances, purport to rely on anything in this chapter as legal advice. Likewise, following any of the suggestions in this chapter does not create an "advice-of-counsel" device to regulatory or law enforcement action or to civil legal claims. Readers involved in information security are strongly urged to retain qualified, experienced legal counsel.

Introduction

You have watched the scene hundreds of times. The buttoned-down, by-the-book police lieutenant and the tough-as-nails, throw-out-the-rules-to-save-lives detective debate in front of the police chief. A child is kidnapped and the clock is ticking; a murder is about to be committed and the judge will not issue a warrant. The world-weary police chief has to make a split-second decision. Is there a way to live within the law but save the child? How does the police chief balance the duty to protect the people of the city with fealty to the rulebook? Is there a creative way to do both? On television, this scene usually happens in an aging, shabby, police headquarters office furnished with Styrofoam cups of stale coffee, full ashtrays, fading green walls, and rickety metal desks. Now, imagine this same drama being performed on an entirely different stage.

Uncle Sam Wants You: How Your Company's Information Security Can Affect U.S. National Security

It is September 2011. As the tenth anniversary of al-Qa'ida's devastating attacks on our nation approaches, the president is faced with increasingly clear intelligence that what's left of the infamous terrorist group has fulfilled its longstanding ambition to be able to launch a devastating attack on the U.S. through cyberspace. Perhaps they will disable our air traffic control or financial exchange network. Perhaps they will penetrate Supervisory Control and Data Acquisition (SCADA) systems to attack dams or other energy facilities. Perhaps they will shut down power to hundreds of hospitals where surgery is underway. Or maybe they will directly target our heavily information systems-dependent military forces. The targets and magnitude are far from clear.

As September 11, 2011 dawns, it becomes obvious that cyber-attacks are underway, even though the perpetrators are undetermined. What becomes increasingly clear is that the attacks are striking us directly from dozens, perhaps hundreds, of university and corporate servers right here in the U.S. The scene that follows plays out in the stately, wood-paneled, electronically sophisticated confines of the Situation Room in the West Wing of the White House. Our protagonists here are the secretary of defense, the Director of National Intelligence, the National and Homeland Security Advisors to the president, and the attorney general. And, of course, in this scene, the decision maker carrying the weight of the world is not a big city police chief, but rather the president of the United States.

In all likelihood, the president will receive conflicting advice from his senior advisors. Some will insist that U.S. law prohibits the government from disabling the servers within the U.S. from which the attacks are coming, or even trying to learn who is behind the attacks. These advisors urge caution, despite intelligence indicating that the attacks are actually coming from terrorists overseas, using the servers in the U.S. as "zombies" to carry out their plot. These advisors will further argue that the president has no option but to use the cumbersome and time-consuming criminal law process to combat these attacks. The attorney general's law enforcement officers must collect information, go to a federal judge, and get a warrant or, in this case, dozens or hundreds of warrants, to try to determine who is behind the attacks (unless emergency access without a warrant is authorized by law). Even in such emergencies, organizing and directing law enforcement control over hundreds or thousands of zombies is an overwhelming effort.

Other officials will advise the president that by the time any progress will be made going the law enforcement route, devastating damage to the critical infrastructure may already have occurred, and the overseas perpetrators disappeared, covering their tracks. These advisors will argue strenuously that the president has ample constitutional and legal authority to use any element of U.S. power (military, intelligence, or law enforcement) to defeat the attacks and defend the nation. They will argue that using the normal law enforcement route would not only be futile, but would amount to an abdication of the president's primary constitutional responsibility to protect our nation and its people from attack. Finally, they will respectfully remind the president of the sage advice of Vietnam War era U.S. Supreme Court Justice Arthur Goldberg that "While the constitution protects against invasions of individual rights, it is not a suicide pact."[3]

As a purely legal and constitutional matter, the president's more hawkish advisors will likely be correct.[4] However, in no way will it lessen the terrible moral, ethical, and political burden that will fall on the president: whether or not, in the absence of perfect information, to order counterattacks on information infrastructures inside the U.S.

While reasonable experts still disagree on the probability that such a scenario will arise in the next decade (and there are differences of opinion even among the authors of this chapter), most agree that

---

[3] *Kennedy v. Mendoza-Martinez*, 372 U.S. 144, 160 (1963).

[4] *See, e.g.,* the 1993 opinion of the U.S. Department of Justice Office of Legal Counsel: "The concept of 'enforcement' is a broad one, and a given statute may be 'enforced' by means other than criminal prosecutions brought directly under it." *Admissibility of Alien Amnesty Application Information in Prosecutions of Third Parties*, 17 Op. O.L.C. (1993); *see also* the 1898 opinion of Acting Attorney General John K. Richards:

> The preservation of our territorial integrity and the protection of our foreign interests is intrusted, in the first instance, to the President. … In the protection of these fundamental rights, which are based upon the Constitution and grow out of the jurisdiction of this nation over its own territory and its international rights and obligations as a distinct sovereignty, the President is not limited to the enforcement of specific acts of Congress. [The President] must preserve, protect, and defend those fundamental rights which flow from the Constitution itself and belong to the sovereignty it created.

Foreign Cables, 22 Op. Att'y Gen. 13, 25-26 (1898); *see also Cunningham v. Neagle,* 135 U.S. 1, 64 (1890).

the scenario is technically possible.[5] The U.S. National Strategy to Secure Cyberspace describes the following necessary conditions (which exist today) for "relative measures of damage to occur [to the United States] on a national level, affecting the networks and systems on which the Nation depends:

■ Potential adversaries have the intent;

■ Tools that support malicious activities are broadly available; and

■ Vulnerabilities of the Nation's systems are many and well known."[6]

Thus, even in an unclassified publication, the U.S. government has confirmed that our adversaries, whether terrorists, rogue states, or more traditional nation-state enemies, possess a classic combination for the existence of threat: intent + capability + opportunity. If September 11, 2001 taught us anything as a nation, it is that when these three are present, we had better be prepared.

More concretely, senior Federal Bureau of Investigation (FBI) officials and others have testified before congress that terrorist groups have demonstrated a clear interest in hackers and hacking skills; the FBI predicts that, "terrorist groups will either develop or hire hackers."[7] Material found in former al-Qa'ida strongholds in Afghanistan showed al-Qa'ida's interest in developing cyber-terror skills.[8] Former U.S. government "cyberczar" Richard Clarke, pointed out that a University of Idaho student, arrested by FBI agents on allegations of terror links, was seeking a PhD in cyber security. Clarke warns that, "similarly to the fact that some of the Sept. 11 hijackers had training in flight training, some of the people that we're seeing now related to [al-Qa'ida] had training in computer security."[9] Several experts, including cyber experts at Sandia National Laboratories and the U.S. Naval Postgraduate school, have bluntly asserted that adversaries could disrupt significant portions of the U.S. power grid, for time periods ranging from minutes, to days, and even longer.[10]

Cyber attacks have already been used to disrupt online elections in Canada, and attacks by terrorist groups have been launched to "crash" government computers during elections in Indonesia, Sri Lanka, and Mexico.[11] Finally, apart from terrorist groups and rogue states, a number of nations

---

[5] The idea of a crippling cyber attack against the U.S. by terrorist groups is far from universally accepted. *See, e.g.,* James A. Lewis, Assessing the Risks of Cyber Terrorism, Cyber War and Other Cyber Threats, Center for Strategic and International Studies, December 2002, at *http://www.csis.org/tech/0211_lewis.pdf.* For information security professionals and their customers, however, the prudent course—given the conjunction in our adversaries of capability, intent, and opportunity and the stated U.S. government policy of being prepared to respond to cyber attack—is to assume the possibility of such an attack.

[6] United States National Strategy to Secure Cyberspace, February 14, 2003 (hereinafter "National Strategy") at 10. The National Strategy is available at: *http://www.whitehouse.gov/pcipb/.*

[7] See *Testimony of Keith Lourdeau, Deputy Assistant Director, Cyber Division, FBI Before the Senate Judiciary Subcommittee on Terrorism, Technology, and Homeland Security,* February 24, 2004 ("The FBI assesses the cyberterrorism threat to the U.S. to be rapidly expanding, as the number of actors with the ability to utilize computers for illegal, harmful, and possibly devastating purposes is on the rise. Terrorist groups have shown a clear interest in developing basic hacking tools and the FBI predicts that terrorist groups will either develop or hire hackers, particularly for the purpose of complimenting large physical attacks with cyber attacks."); Robert Lenzner and Nathan Vardi, *Cyber-nightmare, http://protectia.co.uk/html/cybernightmare.html.*

[8] *Ibid.*

[9] *Frontline* interview conducted March 18, 2003, at *http://www.pbs.org/wgbh/pages/frontline/shows/cyberwar/interviews/clarke. html.*

[10] *http://www.pbs.org/wgbh/pages/frontline/shows/cyberwar/interviews/clarke.html.*

[11] *http://www.pbs.org/wgbh/pages/frontline/shows/cyberwar/interviews/clarke.html;* Hildreth, CRS Report for Congress, Cyberwarfare, Updated June 19, 2001, at 18, at http://www.fas.org/irp/crs/RL30735.pdf

potentially adversarial to the U.S. now openly include cyber warfare as part of their existing military doctrine, including China and Russia.[12]

This scene, then, is far too plausible,[13] except that we will be lucky if it takes until 2011 to play out.

Many international legal experts assert that, under internationally recognized laws of armed conflict, attacks by foreign nations or international terrorists using bits and bytes through cyberspace can be acts of war just as can the use of guns or bombs or fuel-laden airliners.[14] If a nation determines that a cyber attack is an act of war against it, that determination, in turn, triggers a number of rights on the part of those attacked to take defensive or responsive action against their attackers.[15] Recognizing the threat of a cyber attack and the potential need for more than a law enforcement response, President Bush in 2003 announced a new U.S. policy with regard to such attacks:

"When a nation, terrorist group, or other adversary attacks the United States through cyberspace, the United States response need not be limited to criminal prosecution. The United States reserves the right to respond in an appropriate manner. The United States will be prepaged for such contingencies."[16]

In a cyber attack (unlike in a conventional military attack), it may be difficult for decision makers to know against whom to take action to stop the attack and/or respond. Unlike a terrorist bombing, though, or even the heinous September 11, 2001 attacks, a cyber attack may continue for a long enough period of time that rapid defensive action may dramatically reduce the damage done to the critical infrastructure and economy, even where the perpetrator is still unknown.

Thus, a cyber attack in progress using "zombied" servers inside the U.S. will present decision makers with a uniquely vexing dilemma. If they do nothing in the initial minutes and hours after the attack is underway, they may allow far greater damage than if they take decisive action to stop the attack and disable the attacking machines. Taking such action, however, risks damage or destruction to the zombied servers themselves, perhaps without identifying the guilty parties. Further, doing so can destroy information that may be needed later to identify and apprehend the perpetrator(s).

Making the situation even more dangerous and complex is the fact that, "distinguishing between malicious activity originating from criminals, nation state actors, and terrorists in real time is difficult."[17] In many cases, affirmative attribution will be nearly impossible with today's technology. Thus, decision makers facing the agonizing choice of taking action to disable or destroy zombied servers inside the

---

[12] *Cyberwarfare.* at 2.

[13] The idea of a catastrophic cyber attack against the U.S. by terrorist groups is far from universally accepted. See, e.g., James A. Lewis, *Assessing the Risks of Cyber Terrorism, Cyber War and Other Cyber Threats*, Center for Strategic and International Studies, December 2002, at *http://www.csis.org/tech/0211_lewis.pdf*. Indeed, as noted above, one of the three authors of this chapter believes that, while technically possible, this threat is often overstated, at least as a near-term possibility. For information security professionals and their customers, however, the prudent course—given our adversaries' capability, intent, and opportunity and the stated U.S. Government policy of being prepared to respond to cyber attack—is to assume the possibility of such an attack. In addition, the plethora of known active threats to information security, including extortionists, identity thieves, gangs attempting to amass and cell financial and other valuable personal information, malicious hackers, and others, provide precisely the same incentive to secure information systems' as do would-be cyber-terrorists.

[14] *See, e.g., Law of Armed Conflict and Information Warfare—How Does the Rule Regarding Reprisals Apply to an Information Warfare, Attack?*, Major Daniel M. Vadnais, March 1997, at 25 ("To the extent that information warfare is manifested by traditionally understood damage to sovereign integrity, the law of armed conflict should apply, and proportional reprisals may be justified. On the other hand, to the extent that damage to a sovereign's integrity is not physical, there is a gap in the law."). *http://www.fas.org/irp/threat/cyber/97-0116.pdf*

[15] *Id.*

[16] National Strategy at p. 59 (A/R 5-4).

[17] National Strategy at p. 49 (Priority V: National Security and International Cyberspace Security Cooperation).

U.S. or risking greater damage to our nation if they wait, may not know in time to make a sound decision on whether a true attack is underway or whether what looks like the initial stages of an attack is instead other malicious activity.

What does this mean to information security evaluation professionals and their customers? First and foremost, it means that *you do not want the "zombied" servers used in a cyber attack to be yours*. When the U.S. (or another nation)[18] decides to mount an official response against the hijacked servers being used to launch an attack, it will be a very bad day for the entity whose servers are being used. Additionally, though prudent information security consultants will remain current on all potential threat vectors for purposes of protecting your customers' networks, the identity of any particular threat will be largely irrelevant, even if the origin could be determined. Custodians of sensitive information of any kind have myriad reasons to develop and maintain a reasonable information security posture: business operational needs; preventing economic loss and industrial espionage; mitigating potential litigation, regulatory, and prosecution risks; and maintaining a reputation for responsible security vis-à-vis others in the same business.

The risk of involuntarily becoming part of a cyber attack or defending against such an attack, adds another important incentive to do what most businesses and educational institutions already recognize as the right thing to do. Unlike other motivations for information security, however, avoiding involvement in a cyber attack is important even if an organization does not maintain any "sensitive" information. Unlike "traditional" hackers, criminals, and others who might exploit information security vulnerabilities, terrorists do not ignore companies simply because they are unable to find sensitive information. Instead, terrorist's care about what damage can be done using your servers as proxies. And governments (ours or others) also will not care what information you have or do not have, if it is determined that your servers are involved in an attack and must be neutralized (or worse).

Second, understanding the way governments see information security provides a context for understanding how policy statements contribute to the development of a legal "duty" for individuals and organizations to secure their portions of cyberspace (discussed in greater detail below). In a nutshell, the actual knowledge or constructive knowledge (i.e., information in the public domain) of public policy mandating private "owners" of cyberspace to secure their components, may create a legal "duty" to do so, which could be the subject of future litigation. Likewise, emerging federal policy on potential cyber attacks could well contribute to the movement, already gathering steam, to further regulate private information security at the federal level.

---

[18] Nearly as dangerous for our Nation as attacks from within the U.S. directed *at* us, would be if zombied servers were being used to launch an attack *against another nation*. Imagine the reaction of China or Iran if servers inside the U.S. were being used to damage their infrastructure or harm their people. First, they likely would not believe denials by our government that these acts of war were being carried out deliberately by our government. Second, even if they did believe such denials, they still might feel compelled to respond with force to disable or destroy the systems of, and/or punish, those they perceived to be their attackers.

Legal Standards Relevant to Information Security

Laws are made by politicians and politicians are driven by public and media reaction to specific incidents. Laws, therefore, are made piecemeal, at least until a critical mass is reached, which then leads lawmakers to conclude that an emerging patchwork of related, but often inconsistent, laws and regulations require an omnibus law to create consistency and greater predictability. In the absence of such a unifying federal law, particular industries or sectors are targeted for regulation as perceived problems in those industries become public. Laws and regulations covering targeted industries are gradually expanded through civil litigation and regulatory action that is limited only by the patience of judges and the imagination of plaintiffs' lawyers, prosecutors, and regulators.

This is the current situation in the law of information security. As discussed in "Selected Federal Laws" below, federal law regulates information security for, among other things, personally identifiable health care information, financial information of individuals, and, to an increasing degree, financial information in the hands of publicly traded companies. Though there is no "omnibus" federal statute governing all information security, the standards of care being created for these specific economic sectors are being "exported" to other business areas through civil litigation, including by regulators and state attorneys general.[19]

For information security practitioners, this is a good news/bad news story. Often, attempts at "comprehensive" regulation turn out to be a jumbled mess, particularly when multiple economic sectors with differing operational environments and needs are being regulated. Such regulation can be particularly ineffective (or worse) when promulgated before the private sector, which has developed solid, time-tested best practices and implements a workable solution. On the other hand, a patchwork of different federal, state, and international laws and regulations (as is the current state of information security law), can be confusing and puts a premium on careful, case-specific legal analysis and advice from qualified and experienced counsel.

Selected Federal Laws

To illustrate the array of laws that impact information security, the following provides a general survey of statutes, regulations, and other laws that may govern information security consultants and their customers. This list is not exhaustive, but may help identify issues in working with customers and in understanding which "best practices" have actually been adopted in law.

Gramm-Leach-Bliley Act

One of the earliest U.S. government forays into mandating information security standards was the Gramm-Leach-Bliley Act (GLBA).[20] Section 501(b) requires each covered "financial institution" to

---

[19] Particularly in the wake of the 2005 publicity surrounding security breaches at ChoicePoint, LexisNexis, MasterCard, major banks, other commercial entities and universities, a number of pieces of legislation requiring disclosure of information security breaches and/or enhanced information security measures were working their way through the U.S. congress, or were threatened in the near future. *See* Roy Mark, *Data Brokers Step Into Senate Panel's Fire,* e-Security Planet.com, http://66.102.7.104/search?q=cache:REXdffBCvEYJ:www.esecurityplanet.com/trends/article. php/3497591+specter+and+information+security+and+disclosure&hl=en.

[20] 15 U.S.C. §§ 6801, *et. seq.*

establish "appropriate safeguards" to: (1) ensure the security and confidentiality of customer records and information; (2) protect against anticipated threats or hazards to the security or integrity of those records; and (3) protect against unauthorized access to, or use of, such records or information which could result in substantial harm or inconvenience to any customer.[21] GLBA required standards to be set by regulation for safeguarding customer information.[22] This task was accomplished with the promulgation of the Interagency Guidelines Establishing Standards for Safeguarding Customer Information (the "Guidelines").[23]

The Guidelines apply to "Customer Information" maintained by covered "financial institutions," both terms of which are broadly defined under applicable law and regulations. The Guidelines require a written security program specifically tailored to the size and complexity of each individual covered financial institution, and to the nature and scope of its activities.[24]

Under the Guidelines, covered institutions must conduct risk assessments to customer information and implement policies, procedures, training, and testing appropriate to manage reasonably foreseeable internal and external threats.[25] Institutions must also ensure that their board of directors (or a committee thereof) oversees the institution's information security measures.[26] Further, institutions must exercise due diligence in selecting and overseeing, on an ongoing basis, "service providers" entities that maintain, process, or otherwise are permitted access to customer information through providing services to a covered institution).[27] Institutions also must ensure, by written agreement, that service providers maintain the appropriate security measures.[28]

Health Insurance Portability and Accountability Act

The Health Insurance Portability and Accountability Act of 1996 (HIPAA) became law on August 21, 1996. Section 1173(d) of HIPAA required the secretary of Health and Human Services (HHS) to adopt security standards for protection of all Electronic Protected Health Information (EPHI).[29] Development of these security standards was left to the HHS secretary, who promulgated the HIPAA Security Final Rule (the "Security Rule") on February 13, 2003.[30] All covered entities, with the exception of small health plans, must now comply with the Security Rule.[31]

Because HIPAA has, in some ways, the most elaborate and detailed guidance available in the realm of federal law and regulation with regard to information security, we focus more on the HIPAA Security Rule than any other single federal legal provision. In addition, many of the general

---

[21] 15 U.S.C. § 6801(b).

[22] 15 U.S.C. §§ 6804 – 6805.

[23] Available at *http://www.ffiec.gov/ffiecinfobase/resources/elect_bank/frb-12_cfr_225_appx_f_bank_holding_non-bank_affiliates.pdf.*

[24] *Guidelines.*

[25] *Id.*

[26] *Id.*

[27] *Id.*

[28] *Id.*

[29] EPHI is defined in the law as individually identifiable health information that is transmitted by, or maintained in, electronic media, except several narrow categories of educational, employment, and other records. 45 C.F.R. part 106.103. Note, however, that the separate HIPAA Privacy Rule also requires "appropriate security" for all PHI, even if it is not in electronic form.

[30] 45 C.F.R. part 164.

[31] Compliance with the Security Rule became mandatory for all but small health care plans in April 2005. "Small" health care plans have until April 2006 to comply.

principles articulated in the Security Rule are common to other legal regimes dealing with information security. As a general framework, the HIPAA Security Rule: (a) mandates specific outcomes; and (b) specifies process and procedural requirements, rather than specifically mandated technical standards. The mandated outcomes for covered entities are:

- Ensuring the confidentiality, integrity, and availability of EPHI created, received, maintained, or transmitted by a covered entity[32]

- Protecting against reasonably anticipated threats or hazards to the security or integrity of such information[33]

- Protecting against reasonably anticipated uses or disclosures of EPHI not permitted by the HIPAA Privacy Rule[34]

- Ensuring compliance with the Security Rule by its employees[35]

Beyond these general, mandated outcomes, the Security Rule contains process and procedural requirements broken into several general categories[36]:

- **Administrative Safeguards**[37]   Key required processes in this area include: conducting a comprehensive analysis of reasonably anticipated risks; matrixing identified risks against a covered entity's unique mix of information requiring safeguarding; employee training, awareness, testing and sanctions; individual accountability for information security; access authorization, management, and monitoring controls; contingency and disaster recovery planning; and ongoing technical and non-technical evaluation of Security Rule compliance.

- **Physical Safeguards**[38]   Physical security safeguard measures include: mandated facilities access controls; workstation use and workstation security requirements; device and media controls; restricting access to sensitive information; and maintaining offsite computer backups.

- **Technical Safeguards**[39]   Without specifying technological mechanisms, the HIPAA Security Rule mandates automated technical processes intended to protect information and control and record access to such information. Mandated processes include authentication controls for persons accessing EPHI, encryption/decryption requirements, audit controls, and mechanisms for ensuring data integrity.

---

[32] 45 C.F.R. part 164.

[33] *Id.* One reason it is crucial for information security professionals to retain, on an ongoing basis, qualified, experienced counsel is that "reasonably anticipated" is essentially a legal standard best understood and explained by legal counsel and because what is "reasonably anticipated" is constantly evolving as new threats are discovered and publicized, and information security programs must evolve with it in order to mitigate legal liability.

[34] *Id.*

[35] *Id.*

[36] It is worth remembering that a significant majority of the process and procedural requirements are not technical. This, among other considerations, counsels the use of multidisciplinary teams, of which technical experts are only one part, to conduct and document information security evaluations.

[37] 45 C.F.R. Part 164.308.

[38] 45 C.F.R. Part 164.310.

[39] 45 C.F.R. Part 164.312.

The Security Rule contains other requirements beyond these general categories, including: ensuring, by written agreement, that entities with whom a covered entity exchanges EPHI, maintain reasonable and appropriate security measures, and hold those entities to the agreed-upon standards; developing written procedures and policies to implement the Security Rule's requirements, disseminating such procedures, and reviewing and updating them periodically in response to changing threats, vulnerabilities, and operational circumstances.

Sarbanes–Oxley

The Sarbanes-Oxley Act of 2002 (SOX) creates legal liability for senior executives of publicly traded companies, potentially including stiff prison sentences and fines of up to $ 5,000,000 per violation, for willfully certifying financial statements that do not meet the requirements of the statute.[40] Section 404 of SOX requires senior management, pursuant to rules promulgated by the Securities and Exchange Commission (SEC), to attest to: "(1) the responsibility of management for establishing and maintaining an adequate internal control structure and procedures for financial reporting; and (2) …the effectiveness of the internal control structure and procedures of the issuer for financial reporting."[41] Pursuant to SEC regulations, Section 302, requires that officers signing company financial reports certify that they are "responsible for establishing and maintaining internal controls," and "have evaluated the effectiveness" of those controls and reported their conclusions as to the same.[42]

Federal Information Security and Management Act

The Federal Information Security and Management Act of 2002, as amended (FISMA) does not directly create liability for private sector information security professionals or their customers.[43] Information security professionals should be aware of this law, however, because the law:

- Legally mandates the process by which information security requirements for all federal government departments and agencies must be developed and implemented

- Directs the federal government to look at the private sector for applicable "best practices" and to provide assistance to the private sector (if requested) with regard to information security

- Contributes to the developing "standard of care" for information security by mandating a number of specific procedures and policies

FERPA and the TEACH Act

The Family Educational Right to Privacy Act (FERPA)[44] prohibits educational agencies and programs, at risk of losing federal funds, from having a policy or practice of "permitting the release of" specified educational records. FERPA does not state whether or not the prohibition places affirmative

---

[40] 18 U.S.C. § 1350.
[41] SOX § 302.
[42] SOX § 404.
[43] FISMA, Title III of the E-Government Act of 2002, Public Law No. 107-347.
[44] As enacted, the TEACH Act amended Section 110 of the Copyright Act. 17 U.S.C. §110.

requirements on educational institutions to protect against unauthorized access to these records through the use of information security measures. It is certainly possible that a court could conclude in the future that an educational institution, which fails to take reasonable information security measures to prevent unauthorized access to protected information, is liable under FERPA for "permitting the release" of such information. The 2002 Technology, Education and Copyright Harmonization Act (the "TEACH Act") explicitly requires educational institutions to take "technologically feasible" measures to prevent unauthorized sharing of copyrighted information beyond the students specifically requiring the information for their studies, and, thus, may create newly enforceable legal duties on educational institutions with regard to information security.[45]

Electronic Communications Privacy Act and Computer Fraud and Abuse Act

These two federal statutes, while not mandating information security procedures, create serious criminal penalties for any persons who gain unauthorized access to electronic records. Unlike laws such as HIPAA and GLB, these two statues broadly apply, regardless of the type of electronic records that are involved. The Electronic Communications Privacy Act (ECPA) makes it a federal felony to, without authorization, use or intercept the contents of electronic communications.[46] Likewise, the Computer Fraud and Abuse Act of 1984 (CFAA) makes the unauthorized access to a very wide range of computer systems (including financial institutions, the federal government, and any protected computer system used in interstate commerce) a federal felony.[47] As a result, information security professionals must take great care—and rely on qualified and experienced legal professionals—to ensure that the authorizations they receive from their customers are broad and specific enough to mitigate potential criminal liability under ECPA and CFAA.[48]

State Laws

In addition to federal statutes and regulations implicating information security, there are numerous state laws that, depending on an entity's location and the places in which it does business, can also create legal requirements related to the work of information security professionals.

Unauthorized Access

In Colorado (and in other states), it is a crime to access, use, or exceed authorized access to or use of, a computer, computer network, or any part of a computer system.[49] It is a crime to take action against a computer system to cause damage, to commit a theft, or for other nefarious purposes.

---

[45] Pub. L. No. 99–508, 100 Stat. 1848 (1986) codified in Title 18 of the U.S. Code.

[46] 18 U.S.C. § 2510, *et. seq.*

[47] 18 U.S.C. § 1030, *et. seq.*

[48] Other federal laws and regulations potentially relevant to the work of information security professionals and their customers include, but are not limited to, the Children's Online Privacy Protection Act of 1998, information security standards promulgated by the National Institute of Standards, Presidential Decision Directive 63 (May 22, 1998), and Homeland Security Presidential Directive 7 (December 17, 2003). In addition, numerous state laws, including provisions of the Uniform Commercial Code and Uniform Financial Transactions Act, as enacted in the various states, implicate information security requirements for specific economic sectors and/or types of transactions.

[49] Colorado Revised Statutes § 18-5.5-102.

However, it is particularly important for information security professionals to be aware that it is also a crime to knowingly access a computer system without authorization or to exceed authorized access. This is one reason it is critical for information security professionals, with the advice of qualified and experienced counsel, to negotiate a comprehensive, carefully worded, Letter of Authorization (LOA) with each and every customer (discussed in detail below).

Deceptive Trade Practices

Deceptive trade practices are unlawful and may potentially subject anyone committing them to civil penalties and damages.[50] In Colorado (as in many other states), "deceptive trade practices" include:

- "Knowingly mak[ing] a false representation as to the characteristics ... [or] benefits of goods, ... services, or property"[51]

- "Fail[ing] to disclose material information concerning goods, services, or property which information was known at the time of an advertisement or sale if such failure to disclose such information was intended to induce the consumer to enter into a transaction"[52]

Deceptive trade practices laws have been used by regulators to impose (through lawsuits) information security requirements on entities in industries not otherwise subject to statutory or regulatory standards.

These are only two of the many types of state laws potentially applicable to information security professionals and their customers. In addition, common law negligence doctrines in every state can create civil legal liability for information security professionals and their customers (discussed below in "Do it Right or Bet the Company: Tools to Mitigate Legal Liability")

Understanding the myriad state laws that apply to information security and to any particular entity, and how such laws overlap and interact with federal laws, is complex and constantly evolving. Information security professionals and their customers should consult qualified and experienced legal counsel to navigate this challenging legal environment.

Enforcement Actions

What constitutes the "reasonable standard of care" in information security, as in all areas of the law, will continue to evolve, and not only through new statutes and regulations. Prosecutors and regulators will not be content to wait for such formal, legal developments. In lawsuits, prosecutions, and enforcement actions against entities not directly covered by any specific federal or state law or regulation, prosecutors and regulators have demonstrated the clear intent to extend "reasonable" information security measures even to those entities not clearly covered by specific existing laws. This is being done through legal actions leading to settlements, often including consent decrees (agreements entered into to end litigation or regulatory action) wherein a company agrees to "voluntarily" allow regulators to monitor, (e.g., for 20 years) the company's information security program.[53]

---

[50] Colorado Revised Statutes § 6-1-105.
[51] Colorado Revised Statutes § 6-1-105(e).
[52] Colorado Revised Statutes § 6-1-105(u).
[53] Between 2001 and 2005 such actions included those against: Microsoft Corporation, Victoria's Secret, Eli Lilly, and Ziff Davis Media, Inc., among others. *See, e.g., http://www.ftc.gov/os/2002/08/microsoftagree.pdf; http://www.oag.state.ny.us/press/2002/aug/aug28a_02_attach.pdf.*

Since these agreements are publicly available, they are adding to the "standard of care" to which entities will be held, in addition to providing added impetus for similar enforcement actions in the future. Thus, customers of information security professionals should take scant comfort in the fact that there are not yet specific laws explicitly targeted at their companies or industries.

Three Fatal Fallacies

Conventional wisdom is a powerful and dangerous thing, as is a little knowledge. Unfortunately, many entities realizing they have legal and other requirements for information security have come to believe some specific fallacies that sometimes govern their information security decisions. More disturbingly, a significant number of information security providers, who should know better, also are falling victim to these fallacies. Herewith, then, let the debunking begin.

The "Single Law" Fallacy

Many information security professionals, both within commercial and educational entities, and among the burgeoning world of consultants, subscribe to the "single law" fallacy. That is, they identify a statute or set of regulations that clearly apply to a particular institution and assume that, by complying with that single standard, they have ended all legal risk. This assumption may be true, but in many cases is not. Making such an assumption could be a very expensive error, absent the advice of qualified and experienced legal counsel.

Take, for example, a mid-sized college or university. Information security professionals may conclude that, since FERPA clearly applies to educational records, including electronic records, following guidance tailored to colleges and universities based on what they conclude are the appropriate Department of Education standards, is sufficient to mitigate any potential legal liability. Worse yet, they may decide to gamble that, given current ambiguity about whether FERPA requires affirmative action to prevent unauthorized access to such records, they need not take any affirmative steps to try and prevent such access. This could be an expensive gamble, particularly if the educational institution does not ask itself the following questions:

- Does the school grant financial aid or extend other forms of credit? If so, it could be subject to GLBA.

- Does it operate hospitals, provide psychiatric counseling services, or run a student health service? If so, it could be subject to HIPAA.

- Does the school's Web site contain any representations about the security of the site and/or university-held information? If so, it could be subject to lawsuits under one or more (depending on whether it has campuses in multiple states) state deceptive trade practices laws.

The Private Entity Fallacy

Focusing on SOX and the resulting preoccupation with publicly traded companies, some companies take solace in being private and in the fact that, so the argument goes, they are not subject to SOX and/or that they can somehow "fly under the radar" of federal regulators and civil litigants. Again, a dangerous bet. First, the likelihood of comprehensive federal information security regulation reaching well beyond publicly traded companies grows daily. Second, anyone who believes that lawyers for future plaintiffs (students, faculty, victims of attack or identity theft) will be deterred by the literal terms of SOX is misguided. The argument (potentially a winning one) will be that the appropriate "standard of care" for information security was publicly available and well known. The fact that one particular statute may not apply, by its plain terms, does not relieve entities of awareness of the standard of care and duty not to be negligent. Third, and most importantly, a myopic focus on SOX (or any other single law or regulation) to the exclusion of the numerous other potential sources of liability, will not relieve entities of the responsibility to learn about, and follow, the dictates of all other sources of law, including, but not limited to, HIPAA, GLBA, state statutes, and common law theories and, depending on where an entity does business, international and foreign law, such as the complex and burdensome European Union Privacy Directive.[54]

The "Pen Test Only" Fallacy

Every information security professional has dealt with the "pen test only" customer, probably more than once. This customer is either certain that their information security posture is so good that they just need an outside party to try and "break in" (do a penetration test) to prove how good they are, or feels an internal bureaucratic need to prove to others in the company how insecure their systems are. Generally, the customer has a limited budget or simply does not want to spend much money and wants a "quick hit" by the information security professional to prove a bureaucratic point. One variation on this theme is the customer who wants the penetration test as a first step, before deciding how far down the Information Security Assessment/Evaluation road to walk.

There is no way to say this too strongly: *starting with a penetration test is a disaster*, particularly if there is no way to protect the results from disclosure (see "Attorney-client Privilege" below). The NSA methodology itself, as outlined herein and in *Security Assessment: Case Studies in Implementing the NSA IAM*, demonstrates this, with its sound reliance on a holistic and evolving set of assessments, rather than a one-shot test and report. At least as important are the horrendous legal consequences that can flow from starting with a penetration test without establishing a more comprehensive, longer-term relationship with qualified and experienced lawyers and, through them, information security technical consultants. Not only will the customer almost certainly "fail" the penetration test, particularly if done as the first step without proper assessment, evaluation, and mid-stream remediation, this failure will *be documented in a report not subject to any type of attorney-client privilege or other protection from disclosure*.[55]

In short, testing done at the worst possible time in the process in terms of exposing vulnerabilities will be wide open to discovery and disclosure by your customers' future adversaries. From the standpoint of the information security technical professional, this also could lead to your being required later to testify, publicly and under oath, as to the minutest of details of your work for the customer, your methodology and "trade secrets," and your work product.[56]

---

[54] Directive 95/46/EC of the European Parliament and of the Council of 24 October 1995 on the protection of individuals with regard to the processing of personal data and on the free movement of such data, Official Journal of the European Communities of 23 November 1995 No L. 281, 31, available at *http://www.cdt.org/privacy/eudirective/EU_Directive_.html*.

[55] *See, e.g.*, Transcript of Hearing Before U.S. District Judge Royce Lamberth in which an information security consultant is examined and cross-examined under oath, in public, for multiple days, concerning penetration test work done for the U.S. Bureau of Indian Affairs. http://66.102.7.104/search?q=cache:d30x73ieDSwJ:www.indiantrust.com/_pdfs/3am. pdf+lamberth+and+cobell+and+transcript+and+miles&hl=en

[56] *See, e.g.*, Transcript of Hearing Before U.S. District Judge Royce Lamberth in which an information security consultant is examined and cross-examined under oath, in public, for multiple days, concerning penetration test work done for the U.S. Bureau of Indian Affairs. http://66.102.7.104/search?q=cache:d30x73ieDSwJ:www.indiantrust.com/_pdfs/3am. pdf+lamberth+and+cobell+and+transcript+and+miles&hl=en

Do It Right or Bet the Company: Tools to Mitigate Legal Liability

In recent years, numerous articles have been written on how to protect your network from a technical perspective,[57] but, at least throughout mid-2005, the headlines swelled with examples of companies that have lost critical information due to inadequate security. Choice Point, DSW Shoes, several universities, financial institutions including Bank of America and Wachovia, MasterCard and other credit providers, and even the FBI have been named in recent news articles for having lost critical information. As one example, ChoicePoint was sued in 2005 in actions brought in states ranging from California to New York and in its home state of Georgia. Allegations in the lawsuits included that ChoicePoint failed to "secure and maintain confidential the personal, financial and other information entrusted to ChoicePoint by consumers"[58]; failed to maintain adequate procedures to avoid disclosing some private credit and financial information to unauthorized third parties; and acted "willfully, recklessly, and/or in conscious disregard" of its customers rights to privacy.[59] Legal theories used in future information security-related lawsuits will be limited only by the imagination of the attorney's filing the suits.

It is hardly a distant possibility that every major player in information security will be sued sooner or later, whether that suit is frivolous or not. It is a fact of business life. So, how can information security consultants help their customers reduce their litigation "target profile?"

We Did our Best; What is the Problem?

Many companies feel that their internal information technology and security staffs are putting forth their best efforts to maintain and secure their networks. They may even be getting periodic penetration tests and trying to make sense out of the hundreds of single-spaced pages of "vulnerabilities" identified in the resulting reports. So why isn't that good enough? The answer is that "doing one's best" to secure and maintain a network system will not be enough unless it is grounded in complying with external legal standards (discussed above). Penetration tests alone are likely not enough to demonstrate reasonable efforts at meeting the standard of care for information security. In ChoicePoint's case, at least based on what has been made public as of mid-2005, penetration tests would not have helped. ChoicePoint appears to have fallen victim to individuals who fraudulently posed as businessmen and conned people into giving them what may have been otherwise secure information.

Ameliorating any one particular potential point of failure will almost never be enough. Companies today must understand the potential sources of liability that apply to all commercial entities as well as those specific to their industry. Only through understanding the legal environment and adopting and implementing policies to assure a high level of compliance with prevailing legal requirements can a company minimize the risk of liability. Of course, this system approach is not static. It requires ongoing review and implementation to assure compliance in an ever-changing legal environment.

---

[57] For example, B. Grimes *The Right Ways to Protect Your Net* PC World Magazine, September 2001, offers tips for tightening your security and protecting your enterprise from backdoor hackers and thieves.

[58] *http://wsbradio.com/news/0223choicepointsuit.html.*

[59] *Harrington v. ChoicePoint Inc.*, C.D. Cal., No. CV 05-1294 (SJO) (JWJx), 2/22/05).

The Basis for Liability

A company's legal liability can arise as a result of: (a) standards and penalties imposed by federal, state, or local governments; (b) in the form of civil liability based upon breach of contractual agreements; or (c) as a result of other non-contractual civil wrongs (torts) ranging from fraud, invasion of privacy, and conversion to deceptive trade practices and negligence. Avoiding liability for criminal misconduct involves an understanding of the statutes and regulations applicable to your business and adhering to those requirements. Federal and state statutes may impose both criminal penalties as well as form the basis for private lawsuits. Examples of laws and the effect on private and public companies are discussed in more detail below.

Negligence and the "Standard of Care"

The combination of facts and events that can give rise to civil claims when information security is breached and the specific impact on business operations, are too numerous to discuss in detail. Understanding the basis for liability and conducting business in a manner designed to avoid liability is the best defense. In many cases, the claim of liability is based in a charge that the company and its officers and directors acted "negligently." In law, "negligence" arises when a party owes a legal duty to another, that duty is breached, and the breach causes damages to the injured party. Generally speaking, acting "reasonably" under the circumstances will prevent information security consultants or their customers from being found "negligent."[60] The rub is that what is "reasonable" both: (1) depends on the particular circumstances of individual situations; and (2) is constantly evolving as new laws and regulations are promulgated and new vulnerabilities, attack vectors, and available countermeasures become known.

Certainly, when a company maintains personal or confidential customer information, or has agreed to maintain as confidential the trade secret information of another business, its minimum duty is to use reasonable care in securing its computer systems to avoid theft or inadvertent disclosure of the information entrusted to it. Reasonable care may range from an extremely high standard when trust and confidence are reposed in a company to secure sensitive information, to a standard of care no more than that generally employed by others in the industry.

A reasonable "standard of care" is what the law defines as the minimum efforts a company must take not to have acted negligently (or, put another way, to have acted reasonably). A strong foundation to avoid liability for most civil claims begins with conducting the company's affairs up to the known standard of care that will avoid liability for negligence.

The appropriate, reasonable standard of care in any given industry and situation can arise from several sources, including statutes, regulations, common law duties, organizational policies, and contractual obligations. Courts look to the foreseeability of particular types of harm to help determine an industry standard of care. In other words, a business must exercise reasonable care to prevent an economic loss that should have been anticipated. As a result of ongoing public disclosure of new types of harm from breaches in information security, it is increasingly "foreseeable" that critical information may be lost through unauthorized access, and the policies and practices used to protect that information will take center stage in any negligence action.

---

[60] Generally speaking, a post-hoc calculation of "reasonability" will be based on balancing such factors as: (1) the probability of reasonably anticipated damage occurring; (2) the severity of the damage if it does occur; (3) reasonably available risk mitigation measures; and (4) the cost of implementing such measures.

What Can Be Done?

Fully understanding the risks as assessed by qualified and experienced counsel, is an essential first step. Taking action that either avoids liability or minimizes the consequences when things go wrong is the next stride. The following are some suggestions that will help in the journey.

Understand your Legal Environment

Mitigating legal liability begins with understanding the laws applicable to a company's business. (A variety of potentially applicable legal requirements are outlined in the "Legal Standards Relevant to Information Security" section above.) Ignorance of the law is no excuse, and failure to keep pace with statutory requirements is a first source of liability. Working with professionals, whether inside or outside of the company, to track changes in legislation and tailor your information security policies is the first line of defense. Careful compliance with laws not only helps reduce the potential for criminal liability or administrative fines, but also evidences a standard of care that may mitigate civil liability.

Comprehensive and Ongoing Security Assessments, Evaluations, and Implementation

Working with qualified and experienced legal counsel and technical consultants, a company must identify and prioritize the information it controls that may require protection, and catalogue the specific legal requirements applicable to such information and to the type of business the company is in. Next, policies must be developed to assure that the information is properly maintained and administered and that the company's personnel conduct themselves in accordance with those policies. Policy evaluations must include the applicable legal requirements, as well as reasonable procedures for testing and maintaining the security of information systems.

Critically, the cycle of using outside, neutral, third-party assessments/evaluations, implementation and improvement, and further assessment, must be ongoing. A static assessment/evaluation sitting on your shelf is worse than none at all. Almost equally bad is actually implementing the results of assessments/evaluations, but never reassessing or modifying them or insufficiently training employees on them, and evaluating those employees on their understanding and implementation of such results.

Use Contracts to Define Rights and Protect Information

Most businesses understand the process of entering into contracts and following the terms of those contracts to avoid claims of breach. What is not so easily identified is how contractual obligations impact the potential of civil liability based on how information is secured and managed within a particular business? Many areas within a company's business require contracts to be developed and tailored to avoid liability and preserve the integrity of the business. One example is the Uniform Trade Secrets Act (UTSA), adopted in nearly all states and intended to protect confidential information of value to a company's business. Under the UTSA, confidential information may include formulas, patterns, compilations, program devices, methods, techniques, or processes that derive independent economic value from not being generally known to the public and for which the company has made reasonable efforts to maintain confidentiality. Almost every company has trade secrets—from its customer lists to its business mythologies—that afford a competitive advantage. Any protection for these valuable assets will be lost if a company fails to make reasonable efforts to maintain the information as confidential.

At a minimum, contracts must be developed that commit employees not to disclose the trade secrets of the company, or any information legally mandated to be protected (e.g., individual health care or financial information). These agreements are often most effective if entered into at the time of, and as a condition to, employment. This is because most contracts require value to support enforceability and because a delay in requiring a non-disclosure agreement may allow sensitive information to be disclosed before the contract is in place.

Employment policies should reinforce the employee's obligation to maintain confidentiality. These policies should also provide clear guidance on procedures to use and maintain passwords and to responsibly use the information secured on the network. Regular interviews and employee training should be implemented to reinforce the notion that these requirements are mandatory and taken seriously by management. Vendors and service providers that may need to review confidential information should only be permitted access to such information under an agreement limiting the use of that information and agreeing to maintain its confidentiality. Hiring a consultant to perform a network security evaluation without a proper confidentiality agreement could later be found to be sufficient evidence that a company failed to take reasonable efforts to maintain information as confidential, with the result that the information is not longer a trade secret entitled to protection.

Use Qualified Third-party Professionals

Working with qualified information security professionals to implement proper hardware and software solutions to minimize a security breach is critical, but never enough. These functions need to be performed in conjunction with a system of evaluation testing and retesting that integrates legal considerations, and under the supervision and guidance of qualified and experienced legal counsel.

In addition, working with qualified and experienced outside counsel can substantially improve success in the event that claims of negligence are asserted (using attorneys and technical professionals trained to conduct comprehensive and ongoing systems assessments and evaluations of the reasonableness of the efforts to prevent the loss). Companies' internal staff may be equally competent to develop and implement the strategies of information security, but regulators, courts, and juries will look to whether or not a company retained qualified and experienced outside counsel and technical consultants before a problem arises. Working with these experts' increases the probability that best practices are being followed and independent review is the best way to mitigate against foreseeable loss of sensitive information.

As discussed in more detail below, retaining outside professionals in a way that creates an attorney-client privilege may offer protection (in the event of civil litigation, regulatory, or even criminal action) from disclosure of system vulnerabilities discovered in the information security assessment and evaluation processes. The privilege is not absolute, however, and may have different practical applications in the civil and criminal contexts and, in particular, when a customer elects to assert an "advice-of-counsel" defense.

A key requirement emerging as a critical part of the evolving information security standard of care is the requirement to get an external review by qualified, neutral parties.[61] These requirements

---

[61] *See, e.g., Assurance of Discontinuance, In the Matter of Ziff Davis Media Inc.*, at 7, available at *http://www.oag.state.ny.us/press/2002/aug/aug28a_02_attach.pdf.; Agreement Containing Consent Order, In the Matter of Microsoft Corporation*, at 5, available at *http://www.ftc.gov/os/2002/08/microsoftagree.pdf.*

are based on the sound theory that, no matter how qualified, expert, and well intentioned an entity's information technology and information security staff is, it is impossible for them to be truly objective. Moreover, the "fox in the hen house" problem arises, leaving senior management to wonder whether those charged with creating and maintaining information security can and will fairly and impartially assess the effectiveness of such security. Finally, qualified and experienced outside legal counsel and technical consultants bring perspective, breadth of experience, and currency with the latest technical and legal developments that in-house staff normally cannot provide cost-effectively.

Making Sure Your Standards-of-care Assessments Keep Up with Evolving Law

As suggested above, the legal definition of a "reasonable" standard of care is constantly evolving. Policymakers take seriously the threats and the substantial economic loss caused by these cyber-attacks. New laws are continually being enacted to punish attackers and to shift liability to companies that have failed to take reasonable information security measures. Contractual obligations can now be formed instantly and automatically simply by new customer's accessing your customer's Web sites and using their services, all over the Internet and, thus, all over the world. As new vulnerabilities, attacks, and countermeasures come to public attention, new duties emerge. In short, what was "reasonable" last month may not be reasonable this month.

Information security assessments and evaluations provide a tool to evaluate, and enhance compliance with, best practices in protecting critical information; however, they are, at best, only snapshots unless they are made regular, ongoing events. Best practices begin with understanding and complying with applicable laws, but can only be maintained through tracking and implementing evolving statutory requirements. Working with qualified and experienced counsel to follow new legal developments in this fast-moving area of the law and advise on the proper interpretation and implementation of legislative requirements is becoming essential to navigate through this ever-changing landscape.

Plan for the Worst

Despite all best efforts, nothing can completely immunize a company from liability. Failing to plan a crisis management and communications strategy in the event of lost or compromised information can invite lawsuits and create liability despite a track record showing your company exercised a reasonable standard of care in trying to protect information. Avoiding liability involves planning for problems. For example, one class action filed against ChoicePoint alleges that shareholders were misled when the company failed to disclose (for several months) the existence of its security breach and the true extent of the information that was compromised. Having policies in place to provide guidance to executives in communicating with customers and prospective shareholders may well have avoided these allegations. California currently has a Notice of Security Breach law that was enacted in 2002.[62] As of May 2005, Arkansas, Georgia, Indiana, Montana, North Dakota, and Washington have followed suit by enacting some form of legislation requiring disclosure relating to breaches of security, and bills have been introduced in not less than 34 other states to regulate in this area.[63] As of mid-2005, there was no similar federal regulation, although, several disclosure bills have been introduced in congress.

---

[62] California Civil Code Sections 1798.29 and 1798.82 accessible at *http://www.leginfo.ca.gov/calaw.html.*
[63] 2005 Breach of Information Legislation. http://www.ncsl.org/programs/lis/CIP/priv/breach.htm.

A strategic policy to deal with crisis management must take into account disclosure laws in all states in which a company operates. Making disclosures that comply with multiple laws and that minimize the adverse impact of information security breaches and disclosures of them must be planned far in advance of a crisis. Again, this is a constantly changing landscape, and these policies need to be reviewed and updated on a regular basis. It is critical that these policies and plans are developed and carried out with the assistance of qualified and experienced counsel.

Insurance

As more information security breaches occur and are disclosed, the cost to businesses and individuals will continue to rise. In 2002, the Federal Trade Commission (FTC) estimated that 10 million people were victims of identity theft. According to Gartner, Inc., 9.4 million online users in the U.S. were victimized between April 2003 and April 2004 with losses amounting to $11.7 billion.[64] Costs to business from these losses will likely grow to staggering levels in the coming years, and this trend is capturing the attention of some of the more sophisticated insurance companies. Some companies are developing products to provide coverage for losses resulting from breaches of information security. Companies should contact their carriers and do their own independent research to determine what coverage, if any, is or will become, available.

Customers of information security consultants, with the advice of qualified and experienced counsel, must take into account all of these issues in determining how best to mitigate their legal risk. A key component of mitigating that risk is the relationships established with information security consultants, including qualified and experienced counsel and skilled and respected technical consultants. Those relationships, of course, must be established and governed by written contracts (discussed in the next section).

What to Cover in IEM Contracts[65]

The contract is the single most important tool used to define and regulate the legal relationship between the information security consultant and the customer. It protects both parties from misunderstandings and should clearly allocate liability in case of unforeseen or unintended consequences, such as a system crash, access to protected, proprietary, or otherwise sensitive information thought secure, and damage to the network or information residing on the network. The contract also serves as a roadmap through the security evaluation cycle for both parties. A LOA (described in the next section) serves a different purpose from a contract and often augments the subject matter covered in a contract or deals with relationships with third parties not part of the original service contract. In most evaluations, both will be required.

The contract should spell out each and every action the customer wants the provider to perform. Information security consultants should have a standard contract of services or packages of services, but should be flexible enough for negotiation in order to meet the specific needs of the customer. What is, or is not, covered in the contract, and how the provisions should be worded, are decisions

---

[64] P. Britt, *Protecting Private Information* Information Today (Vo. 22 No. 5 May, 2005) *http://www.infotoday.com/it/may05/britt. shtml.*
[65] This section drew, in part, from portions of pages 7–11 of *Security Assessment: Case Studies for Implementing the NSA IAM*, used by permission of Syngress Publishing, Inc.

A special note to attorneys new to this field: While IEM contracts are highly technical legal documents, they should follow the general principles for drafting a reliable commercial contract. DO adapt the contracts to the specific needs of the client.
DO understand the needs and technical standards the contract should meet. If you don't understand what your client is trying to do, how could you explain it to a judge or jury?
DO NOT leave blanks or checkboxes for a client to fill in later.
DO NOT allow either party to insert technical slang that the average judge would not understand.
DO NOT include language that authorizes verbal modifications without written notice to both parties.

both parties must make only with the advice of qualified and experienced counsel familiar with this field. As with any other legal agreement between parties, both signatories should fully understand all the terms in the contract, or ask for clarification or re-drafting of ambiguous, vague, or overly technical language. Contract disputes often arise in situations where two parties can read the same language in different ways. Understand what you are signing.

What, Who, When, Where, How, and How Much

The following paragraphs provide an overview of what should be included in IEM contracts, though these principles are equally applicable to contracts for the Information Security Assurance Methodology (IAM) and many other types of information security service contracts. They include checklists of questions that the contract should answer for both parties; however, remember that each assessment is different because customer's needs and the facts of each evaluation process will differ. Make sure the contract you sign clearly covers each of the topics suggested here, but keep in mind that this is not an exhaustive list and cannot replace the specific advice of your own legal counsel for your specific circumstances.

What

The first general requirement for a contract for information security evaluation services is to address the basic services the consultant will perform. What are the expectations of both parties in performing the non-technical aspects of the business relationship, such as payment, reporting, and documentation? What services does the contract cover? What does the customer want? What can the information security consultant provide? A number of categories of information should appear in this first section.

Description of the Security Evaluation and Business Model

In the initial part of the contract, the information security consultant should describe the services to be provided and, generally, how its business is conducted. This information provides a background on the type of contract that is to be used by the parties (e.g., a contract for services or a contract for services followed by the purchase and installation of software to remediate any identified vulnerabilities). This initial section should also identify the customer and describe its business model. For example, is the customer a financial organization, a healthcare organization, an organization with multiple geographic locations under evaluation, or subject to specific legal requirements and/or industry regulations?

Definitions Used in the Contract

Each contract uses terms that will need further explanation so that the meaning is clear to both parties. Technical terms such as "vulnerability" and "penetration" should be spelled out. Executives sign contracts. Attorneys advise executives whether or not to sign the contracts. Both must understand what the contract means.

Description of the Project

The contract should provide a general statement of the scope of the project. If the project is a long-term endeavor or a continuing relationship between the two parties, this section should also include a description of how each part of the project or phase in the relationship should progress and what additional documents will cover each phase or part of the project. This section also clearly defines what the information security consultant will and will not do throughout the evaluation. Also, in the description of the project, the customer should clearly define the objectives it wants the information security consultant to accomplish. Are all the entity's networks included? What types of testing are required? This section should also include the types of vulnerabilities that the information security consultant is not likely to discover based on the types of testing, the networks tested, and the scope of the overall evaluation, as permitted by the customer.

Assumptions, Representations, and Warranties

In every assessment, the parties must provide or assume some basic information. These assumptions should appear in the contract. Assumptions are factual statements, not a description of conversations the parties have had (e.g., "The schedule in this contract is based on the assumption that all members of the evaluation team will work from 8:30 A.M. to 5:30 P.M. for five days per week for the full contract period."). With regard to the network assumptions, the customer should provide basic information on network topology upon which the assessment team can base assumptions for the types of vulnerabilities they will look for and testing methodologies that will successfully achieve the customer's objectives (e.g., "The evaluation methodology applied to the customer network under this contract relies on the assumption that the customer maintains servers in a single geographic location, physically secured, and logically segregated from other networks and from the Internet.")[66] The language in this section should also address responsive actions should the assumptions prove false: Under what circumstances, is the contract voided? What can make the price go up or down? In the event of unexpected security or integrity problems being created during an evaluation, when should the testing be stopped? Who decides? When should the customers' management be informed? At what levels?

IEM contracts should include "representations and warranties" by the customer spelling out certain critical information that the customer "warrants" to be true such as: descriptions of the customer's business operations and information they hold within their systems; what agreements the customer has with third-party vendors and/or holders of their information; what information systems external to those controlled by the customer, if any, could be impacted by the evaluation and testing to be done, and what measures the customer has taken to eliminate the possibilities of such impact;

---

[66] Assuming the NSA IAM is used, of course, much of this critical work will already have been documented prior to initiation of the IEM.

and the degree to which the customer exclusively owns and controls information and systems to be evaluated and/or tested or has secured written agreements explicitly authorizing evaluation and testing by others that do own or control such information and systems.[67]

Boundaries and Limitations

In addition to stating what the evaluation will cover, this initial section should also address what the assessment will not cover in terms of timing, location, data, and other variables. The general goal of the evaluation cycle is to provide a level of safety and security to the customer in the confidence, integrity, and availability of its networks. However, some areas of the network are more sensitive than others. Additionally, each customer will have varying levels of trust in the evaluation methodology and personnel. Not all evaluation and testing methodologies are appropriate for all areas of a network. The customer should give careful consideration to what is tested, when and how, as well as what the evaluators should do in the event of data contamination or disclosure.

If a customer runs a particular type of report on a specific date to meet payroll, accounting, regulatory, or other obligations, that date is not a very good time to engage in network testing. Even if the testing methodology is sound and the personnel perform at peak efficiency and responsibility levels, human nature will attribute any network glitch on that date to the testing team. Sensitive data requires an increased level of scrutiny for any measure taken that could damage or disclose the information, or make the use of the information impossible for some period of time. Such actions could result in administrative or regulatory penalties and expensive remediation efforts.

Data privacy standards vary by industry, state, country, and category of information. A single network infrastructure may encompass personnel records, internal audits or investigations, proprietary or trade secret information, financial information, and individual and corporate information records and databases. The network could also store data subject to attorney-client or other legal privilege. Additionally, customers should consider where and how their employees store data. Does the customer representative negotiating the scope of the project know where all the sensitive data in his/her enterprise are stored, and with what degree of certainty? Again, much of this information should have been developed during the IAM phase of a comprehensive information security assessment/evaluation. Does the customer have a contingency plan for data contamination or unauthorized access? How does the security evaluation account for the possibility that testing personnel will come in contact with sensitive data (see the Secrecy Non-Disclosure Agreements section below)? In this portion of the contract, the customer should specify any areas of the network where testing personnel may not conduct evaluations, either for a period of time or during specific phases.

Both parties should be sensitive to the fact that the customer may not own and control all areas of the network. A customer can only consent to testing those portions of the network it owns and controls.

---

[67] The issue of securing complete authorization for all types of information and systems (internal and external) that may be impacted by evaluation and testing, is intentionally covered in multiple parts of this section. It is absolutely critical to the legal well being of both the consultant and the customer to ensure clarity of responsibility for these, which is why this section provides multiple different avenues for addressing this problem. Equally critical is a clear understanding of the "division of liability" for any damage that, notwithstanding best efforts of both sides, may result to external systems. This should be taken care of through a combination of indemnification (described below), clear statements of responsibility in the contract, written agreements with third parties, and insurance.

NOTE

Evaluation of other portions of a larger corporate network or where the evaluation proceeds through the Internet, requires additional levels of authorization from third parties outside the contractual relationship, and should never be carried out without explicit agreements negotiated and reviewed by qualified and experienced counsel.

In some cases, the evaluation can continue through these larger networks, but will require additional documentation, such as a LOA (see "Where the Rubber Meets the Road: the Letter of Authorization as Liability Protection" below).

Identification of Deliverables

Without feedback to the customer presented in a usable format, evaluating and testing the network is a waste of resources. The contract should state with a high degree of specificity what deliverables the customer requires and for what level of audience. For example, a 300-page technical report presented to a board of directors is of little use. A ten-slide presentation for the officers of a customer company that focuses on prioritizing the vulnerabilities in terms of levels of risk is far more valuable. Conversely, showing those same ten slides to the network engineering team will not help them. The key in this section of the contract is to manage expectations for the various levels of review within the customer's structure.

Who

The second general requirement for a contract for security evaluation services is to spell out the parties to the agreement and specify the roles and responsibilities of each (including specific names and titles of responsible individuals) for successfully completing the evaluation. This identity and role information is critical for reducing the likelihood of contract disputes due to unmet expectations.

Statement of Parties to the Contractual Agreement

Each party should be clearly identified in the contract by name, location, and principal point of contact for subsequent communications. Often, the official of record for signature is not the same person who will be managing the contract or engaged in day-to-day liaison activities with the evaluation personnel. Additionally, this section should spell out the procedures for changing the personnel of record for each type of contact.

Authority of Signatories to the Contractual Agreement

Ideally, the level of signatory to the contract should be equal, and, in any event, the signing official must be high enough to bind the entities to all obligations arising out of the contractual relationship. It is often also helpful for the customer signatory to be a person empowered to make changes based on recommendations resulting from the evaluation.

Roles and Responsibilities of Each Party to the Contractual Agreement

Spelling out the levels of staffing, location of resources, who will provide those resources, and the precise nature of other logistical, personnel, and financial obligations is critical. It allows both sides to proceed through the evaluation cycle with a focus on the objectives, rather than a daily complication of negotiating who is responsible for additional unforeseen. Some common areas of inclusion in this section are:

- Who provides facilities and administrative support?

- Who is responsible for backing up critical data before the evaluation begins?

- Who is responsible for initiating communication for project status reports. Does the customer call for an update, or does the evaluation team provide regular reporting? Must status reports be written or can they be oral and memorialized only in the information security consultants' records?

- Who is responsible for approving deviations from the contract or evaluation plan and how will decisions about these be recorded?

- Who will perform each aspect of each phase of the evaluation (will the customer provide any technical personnel)?

- Who is responsible for mapping the network before evaluation begins (and will those maps be provided to the evaluation team, or kept in reserve for comparison after the evaluation ends)?

- Who is responsible for briefing senior officers in the customer organization?

- Who is responsible for reporting discrepancies from the agreed project plan to evaluation POCs and executives?

- Who is responsible for reporting violations of policies, regulations, or laws discovered during the evaluation?

- Who has the authority to terminate the evaluation should network irregularities arise?

- Who bears the risk for unforeseen consequences or circumstances that arise during the evaluation period?

Non-disclosure and Secrecy Agreements

Many documents and other information pertaining to information security evaluations contain critical information that could damage one or both parties if improperly disclosed. Both parties bear responsibility to protect tools, techniques, vulnerabilities, and information from disclosure beyond the terms specified by a written agreement. Non-disclosure agreements should be narrowly drawn to protect sensitive information, yet allow both parties to function effectively. Specific areas to consider including are: ownership and use of the evaluation reports and results; use of the testing methodology in customer documentation; disclosures required under law; and the time period of disclosure restrictions. It is often preferable to have non-disclosure/secrecy agreements be separate, stand-alone documents so that, if they must be litigated later in public, as few details as possible of the larger agreement must be publicly exposed.

Assessment Personnel

A security evaluation team is composed of a variety of expert personnel, whether from the customer organization or supplied by the contractor. The contract should spell out the personnel requirements to complete each phase of the assessment successfully and efficiently. Both parties should have a solid understanding of each team member's skills and background. Where possible, the contract should include information on the personnel conducting the assessment. Both parties should also consider who would fund and who would perform any background investigations necessary for personnel assigned to evaluate sensitive networks.

Crisis Management and Public Communications

Network security evaluations can be messy. No network is 100 percent secure. The assessment team will inevitably find flaws. The assessment team will usually stumble across unexpected dangers, or take actions that result in unanticipated results that could impact the network or the data residing on the network. Do not make the mistake of compounding a bad situation with a poor response to the crisis. Implementing notification procedures at the contract phase often saves the integrity of an evaluation should something go wrong. The parties also should clearly articulate who has the lead role in determining the timing, content, and delivery mechanism for providing information to the customer's employees, customers, shareholders, and so forth. This section should also spell out what role, if any, the customer wants the assessment team or leader to play in the public relations efforts. A procedure for managing crisis situations is also prudent. Qualified and experienced legal counsel must be involved in these processes.

Indemnification, Hold Harmless, and Duty to Defend

Even more so than in many other types of contracts for services, the security evaluation contract should include detailed provisions explicitly protecting the information security consultants from various types of contract dispute claims. In addition to standard contract language, these sections should specifically spell out the responsibilities and their limits of both the customer and the information security consultants to defend claims of damage to external systems or information and intellectual property or licensing infringement for software, if any, developed by the information security consultant for purposes of the evaluation.

Ownership and Control of Information

The information contained in the final report and executive level briefings can be extremely sensitive. Both parties must understand who owns and controls the disclosure and dissemination of the information, as well as what both parties may do with the information following the review process. Any proprietary information or processes, including trade secrets, should be marked as such, and covered by a separate section of the contract. Key topics to cover include: use of evaluation results in either party's marketing or sales brochures; release of results to management or regulatory bodies; and disclosure of statistics in industry surveys, among other uses. The customer should spell out any internal corporate controls for the information in this section. If the customer requires encryption of the evaluation data, this section should clearly spell out those requirements and who is responsible for creating or providing keys.

One important ownership area that must be specifically covered in information security evaluation contracts is how reports and other resulting documentation from the evaluation are to be handled. May the information security consultants keep copies of the documents, at least for a reasonable period of time following the conclusion of the evaluation (e.g., in case the customer takes legal action against the consultant)? Who is responsible for destroying any excess copies of such information? May the information security consultant use properly sanitized versions of the reports as samples of work product in the future?

Intellectual Property Concerns

Ownership and use of intellectual property is a complicated area of the law. However, clear guidance in the prior section on the ownership and use of evaluation information will help the parties avoid intellectual property disputes. The key to a smooth legal relationship between the parties is to clearly define expectations.

Licenses

The evaluation team must ensure that they have valid licenses for each piece of software used in the evaluation. The customer should verify valid licensing.

When

The third general requirement for a security evaluation services contract is to create a schedule for conducting the evaluation that includes all of the phases and contingency clauses to cover changes to that schedule. At a minimum, the contract should state a timeline for the overall evaluation and for each phase, including:

- A timeline for completing deliverables in draft and final formats
- Estimated dates of executive briefings, if requested
- A timeline for any follow-up work anticipated

Actions or Events that Affect Schedule

Inevitably, something will happen to affect the schedule. Personnel move, network topography changes; a variety of unforeseen factors can arise. While the contract team cannot control those factors, it can draft language in the contract to allow rapid adaptation of the schedule, depending on various factors. Brief interruptions in assessments can mean long-term impacts if the team is at a sensitive point in the assessment. At the contracting phase, both sides should consult with other elements in their companies to determine what events could affect the schedule. Failure to plan adequately for scheduling conflicts or disruptions could result in one party breaching the contract. Both parties should agree on a contingency plan if the evaluation must terminate prematurely. Contingency plans could include resuming the evaluation at a later time or adjusting the total amount of the contract cost based on the phases completed.

Where

The fourth general requirement for a contract for security evaluation services is to define the location(s), both geographic and logical, subject to the evaluation. Where, precisely, are you testing? To create boundaries for the evaluation and prevent significant misunderstandings on the scope of the assessment or evaluation, list each facility, the physical address and/or logical location, including the Internet Protocol (IP) address range. Make sure that each machine attached to that IP space is within the legal and physical control of the customer. If any of the locations are outside the U.S., seek the immediate advice of counsel on this specific point. While covering the rapid developments in overseas law of this field is beyond the scope of this section, understand that many countries are implementing computer crime laws and standing up both civil and criminal response mechanisms to combat computer crime. Various elements of a network security evaluation can look like unauthorized access to a protected computer. Both the evaluation provider and the customer need to take additional cautionary measures and implement greater notification procedures when considering an evaluation of a system located even partially abroad. Additionally, this section should cover the location the evaluation team will use as their base of operations. If the two locations are separate geographically, the parties must address the electronic access needed for the evaluation.

Exercise an extra level of caution if the evaluation traverses the Internet. Use of the Internet to conduct evaluations carries an additional level of risk and legal liability because neither party owns or controls all of the intermediate network structures.

WARNING

Do not act where your evaluation and testing must traverse the Internet without the advice of qualified and experienced counsel.

How

The fifth general requirement for a contract for security evaluation services is to map out a methodology for the completing the evaluation. This section should identify and describe each phase of the evaluation and/or the overall testing cycle if the contract will cover a business relationship that will span multiple assessments (e.g., IAM and IEM). The key is to prevent surprises for either party. Breaking complex assessments and/or evaluations up into phases in the contract allows the reviewing officials to understand what they are paying for and when they can expect results. State with precise language what the evaluator will be doing at each phase, the goals and objectives of each phase, each activity the evaluation team will complete during that phase, and the deliverables expected. Do not use technical slang. A separate background document on evaluation and testing methodology (i.e., NSA/IAM, IEM, ISO 17799, and so on) is often more useful than cluttering the contract with unnecessary technical detail. This section should also state and describe the standards the evaluation team will use for measuring the evaluation results. Testing should bear results on a measurement scale that allows for comparisons over time and between locations.

How Much

The sixth, and final, general requirement for a contract for security evaluation services is to spell out the costs of the evaluation and other associated payment terms. This section is similar to any other business service contract. At a minimum, it should include the following five elements.

Fees and Cost

The parties should discuss and agree to a fee structure that meets the needs of both parties, which in most cases will call for multiple payments based on phase completion. A helpful analogy is the construction of a house. At what phases will the homeowner pay the general contractor: excavation and clearing the lot; completion of the foundation; framing; walls and fixtures; or final walkthrough? Also, consider the level of customer management who must approve phase completion and payment. In most cases, the final payment on the contract will be tied in some way to the delivery of a final report. Both parties should also carefully discuss the costs for which the customer is responsible. If evaluation teams must travel to the customer's location, who pays for the travel, food, lodging, and other non-salary costs for those personnel, and what level of documentation will be needed to process payment? Do the costs include airfare, lodging, mileage, subsistence (meals and incidentals), and other expenses? Does the customer require that the expenses be "reasonable" or must a customer representative authorize the expenses in advance? To avoid disputes that detract the team's attention from the assessment, spell out the parties' expectations in the contract. The parties should also cover who pays for extraordinary unanticipated expenses such as equipment failure. In some circumstances, the best method for dealing with truly unexpected expenses is to state affirmatively in the contract that the parties will negotiate such costs as they arise.

Billing Methodology

In order for the customer's accounting mechanisms to adequately prepare for the obligations in the contract, the billing or invoicing requirements should be spelled out. If the customer requires a specific type of information to appear on the invoice, that information should be provided to the contractor in writing, preferably in the contract. The types of fees and costs that will appear on the invoice should also be discussed, and the customer should provide guidance on the level of detail they need while the contractor should explain the nature of their billing capabilities.

Payment Expectations and Schedule

The contract should clearly represent both parties' expectations for prompt payment. Will the contractor provide invoices at each phase or on a monthly cycle? Are invoices due upon receipt or on a specific day of the month? Where does the contractor send the invoice and to whom within the customer's structure? Does the contractor require electronic payment of invoices, and if so, to what account? What penalties will the contractor assess for late payments or returned checks? Again, the key factor is to address both parties' expectations to prevent surprises.

Rights and Procedures to Collect Payment

In the event of problems in the contractual relationship or changes in management that affect the contract, what are the parties' rights? As with other commercial contracts, articulating the rights and remedies is essential to minimize or avoid altogether the expense of disputes.

Insurance for Potential Damage During Evaluation

Which party, if either, will carry insurance against damage to the customer's systems and information as well as to those of third parties?

Murphy's Law (When Something Goes Wrong)

The final standard set of clauses for the contract deals with the potential for conflict between the parties or modifications to the contract.

Governing Law

Where both parties are in the same state, and the evaluation is limited to those facilities, this clause may not be necessary. However, in most cases, the activities will cross state borders. The parties should agree on which state's law applies to the contract and under which court's jurisdiction parties can file lawsuits. Determining venue for disputes before they arise can reduce legal costs.

Acts of God, Terror Attacks, and other Unforeseeable Even

Attorneys and network engineers share at least one common trait; neither can predict with any certainty when things will go wrong, but all agree that something will eventually happen that you did not expect. Natural disasters, system glitches, power interruptions, military coups, and a thousand other events can affect a project. Where the disruption is the fault of neither party, both sides should decide in advance on the appropriate course of action.

When Agreement is Breached and Remedies

When one party decides not to fulfill or becomes incapable in some way of performing the terms of the contract, or believes that the other party has not met it is contractual obligations, a party can claim a breach (breaking) of the agreement and demand a remedy from the opposing. Many types of remedies exist for breach of a contract. Either party can also take the matter to court, which can be very messy and extremely expensive. Anticipating situations such as these and inserting language in the contract to deal with potential breaches could save thousands of dollars in attorney fees and court costs. Both parties should discuss the following options with counsel before negotiating a contract for security evaluation services. First, are arbitration or mediation options appropriate or desirable? Second, should the matter proceed to court, one party will inevitably claim attorney's fees as part of the damages. Anticipate this claim and include language that specifies what fees are part of the remedy and whether the party who loses the dispute will reimburse attorney's fees, or whether both sides will be responsible for its own attorney's fees.

Liquidated Damages

Liquidated damages are an agreed, or "liquidated," amount that one party is required to pay the other in the event of a breach or early termination of a contract. Liquidated damages are valuable to bring certainty to a failed relationship but are not appropriate if used to create a windfall or punish a party for not completing their contractual obligations. Instead, to be legally enforceable, a liquidated damages clause must estimate the parties' reasonably anticipated damages in the event of a breach or early termination of the contract. Liquidated damages cannot be a penalty and are not appropriate if actual damages can be readily determined.[68] Courts in Colorado, for example, generally will enforce a liquidated damages clause in a contract if: (1) at the time contract was entered into, anticipated damages in case of breach were difficult to ascertain; (2) parties mutually intended to liquidate them in advance; and (3) the amount of liquidated damages, when viewed as of the time the contract was made, was a reasonable estimate of potential actual damages breach would cause.[69] If these factors apply to your transaction, liquidated damages should be considered to avoid protracted debates regarding the parties' harm when a breach occurs.

Limitation on Liability

Limitations on liability should always be considered and, if possible, incorporated in any contract for assessment services. Typical clauses might state that liability is limited to an amount equal to the total amount paid by the customer under the contract. Other limitations on damages may require the customer to waive incidental or consequential damages or preclude recovery arising from certain conduct by the information security consultant. Like liquidated damages, however, the ability to limit or waive damages may be restricted by both statute and court decisions. For example, in some states, contractual provisions that purport to limit liability for gross negligence or for willful or wanton conduct are not enforceable.[70] In most states, limitations of liability are acceptable and will be enforced if the agreement was properly executed and the parties dealt at arms length.[71] Accordingly, you should try to limit the customer's right to recover consequential damages, punitive damages, and lost profits. Working with qualified counsel will assist in determining what limitations are enforceable in each specific transaction.

Survival of Obligations

This section makes clear what happens to specific contractual obligations, such as duties of non–disclosure and payment of funds owed, following the expiration of the contract.

Waiver and Severability

This section of the contract describes what happens if either party wants to waive the application of a portion of the contract, and allows for each section of the contract to be severable from the contract as a whole, should a court rule that one clause or section is not enforceable. This section is also standard contract language and should be supplied by the attorney for the party drafting the contract.

Amendments to the Contract

For contracts that span significant periods of time, it is likely that one or both parties may require modifications to the contract. To avoid disputes, the original contract should spell out the format for any amendments. Amendments should be in writing and signed by authorized representatives of both

---

[68] *See, e.g., Management Recruiters, Inc. v. Miller*, 762 P.2d 763, 766 (Colo.App.1988).

[69] *Board of County Commissioners of Adams County v. City and County of Denver*, 40 P.3d 25 (Colo.App., 2001).

[70] *See, e.g., Butler Manufacturing Co. v. Americold Corp.*, 835 F.Supp. 1274 (D.Kan. 1993).

[71] *See, e.g., Elsken v. Network Multi-Family Sec. Corp.*, 838 P.2d 1007 (Okla.1992).

parties. The parties should also discuss the financial arrangements surrounding a change to the contract. Proposed amendments to the contract must be accepted by the receiving party.

Where the Rubber Meets the Road: The LOA as Liability Protection

The contract functions as the overall agreement between the organization performing the security assessment and the company or network that will be tested or assessed. A LOA should be used between any two parties, whether party to the same original evaluation contract or not, to document consent to specific activities and protect against different types of adverse liability. For example, Widgets-R-Us contracts with Secure-Test to test the security of a new online shipping management network linked to Widgets' warehouses. ISP-anywhere provides the bandwidth for Widgets' east coast warehouses. Widgets should provide a LOA to Secure-Test consenting to specific network traffic that could trigger ISP-anywhere guards or intrusion detection systems. A copy of the letter should be provided to ISP-anywhere, in advance of the testing, as notice of the activity and a record of Widgets' consent. Additionally, depending on the language of the service agreement between Widgets and ISP-anywhere, Widgets may need to ask ISP-anywhere to provide a LOA for any of Secure-Test's activities that could impact their network infrastructure or otherwise void the bandwidth service agreement. ISP-anywhere was not a party to the original information security evaluation contract and, therefore, Secure-Test needs this additional form of agreement for the activities.

It is an unusual case in which a customer is the sole user of a third-party network system. Accordingly, the network hosts information for businesses and individuals that may maintain confidential information or information not owned by the customer. Merely accessing this information without proper authorization can result in both criminal and civil penalties. In addition, agreements between the customer and the network host may prohibit such access to the system altogether. You, along with your counsel, must always review these relationships with your customer, comply with contractual limitations, and obtain appropriate authorizations.

In many cases, the LOA will turn out to be the single most important document you sign. In addition to the potential civil liability for any damage to your customer's or third parties' systems that occur during periods when you arguably exceed your authorized access, failing to obtain adequate authorization may result in the commission of a crime. As discussed in "Legal Standards Relevant to Information Security" above, the federal Computer Fraud and Abuse Act imposes criminal liability for unauthorized access to computer systems and for exceeding the scope of authorization for accessing certain computers. Every state has passed some form of law that prohibits access to computer systems without proper authority.[72] Working with qualified and experienced legal counsel is vital to assure that your work avoids violation of law and the potential for criminal liability.

Another typical use of a LOA is augmentation of a part of the evaluation or correction of unforeseen technical challenges during the course of the contract (e.g., Widgets-R-Us acquires a warehouse on the west coast after the security evaluation begins, and wants to add this warehouse to the list of facilities Secure-Test will review). Widgets-R-Us does not need a new contract, and most likely does not need to amend the current contract, so long as the both parties will accept a LOA to expand the scope

---

[72] National Conference of State Legislatures information page accessible at *http://www.ncsl.org/programs/lis/cip/hacklaw.htm.*

of the security assessment. Whether or not to allow LOA amendments to a standing contract should be a term written into the contract itself.

An important section of a LOA (similar to the overall contract itself) is a comprehensive and detailed statement of what a customer is not authorizing (i.e., certain systems or databases that are off limits, specific times that testing is not to be done, the tools the information security consultant will, and will not use, security measures that the customer will not permit the consultant to take, and so forth). This is equally important for the customer and the information security consultant.

LOAs should be signed by officials for each party with sufficient authority to agree to all specified terms. Importantly, LOAs between a customer and information security consultant should identify any and all types of information or specific systems for which the customer does not have the authority to authorize access. While LOA provisions can be part of the basic contract itself, as with non-disclosure agreements, it is often preferable to have the LOA be a separate, stand-alone agreement so that if the LOA must be litigated later in public, as few details as possible of the larger agreement must be publicly exposed.

Beyond You and Your Customer

Simply obtaining your customer's consent to access their computer systems is necessary but it is not always enough. Your customer has obligations to its customers, licensors, and other third parties. Honoring these commitments will avoid potential liability for both you and your client.

Software License Agreements

Typically, software used by the customer will be subject to a license agreement that governs the relationship between the customer and the software provider. It is not uncommon for software license agreements to prohibit decompilation, disassembly, or reverse engineering of the software code and to limit access to the software.

The use of tools to penetrate computer systems can constitute the use, access, and running of executable software using the computer's operating system and other programs in a manner that may violate the license agreement. To avoid civil liability, the consultant should have qualified and experienced legal counsel review applicable license agreements and, where appropriate, obtain authorization from the licensor prior to conducting tests of the customer's system.

Your Customer's Customer

To avoid creating liability for your customer, you need to understand your customer's customers and their expectations. Your customer should be able to identify their customers' confidential information and any specific contractual requirements. Understanding the source of third-party information (how it is stored and where appropriate or required), and obtaining consent to access their information is essential. To maintain the integrity of your work, you must respect the confidentiality of your customer and third party-information available to your customer. This is true even if no formal demand is made or no written agreement is entered into. You will be perceived as an agent of your customer; professionalism requires discretion and maintaining privacy.

Similarly, you need to recognize and honor intellectual property rights of the customer and its clients. In general, to protect your customer, you must also protect their customers with the high standards of respect for information privacy and security you provide to your customer.

The First Thing We Do...? Why You *Want* Your Lawyers Involved From Start to Finish

Few of Shakespeare's words have been more often quoted (and misquoted) than the immortal words of "Dick the Butcher": "The first thing we do, let's kill all the lawyers."[73] What generally is left out by modern lawyer bashers cheering Dick on in his quest is that Dick, and the band of rogues to which he belonged, were planning to overthrow the English government when this battle plan was suggested. The group followed up the lawyer killing idea shortly thereafter by hanging the town clerk of court.

The most reasonable reading of this passage is that Shakespeare intended to demonstrate that those who helped people interpret and litigate the law were, in fact, necessary to the orderly functioning of society. This interpretation is not without fierce challenge, however. In fact, a cottage industry emerges from time-to-time on the Internet debating whether Shakespeare was pro- or anti-lawyer. One prolific Internet lawyer-basher even suggests that the fact that lawyers use Shakespeare to justify our existence is conclusive evidence both of our ignorance and, to put it more charitably than the author, willingness to twist the facts to our own ends.[74]

Two things are certain. First, lots of people hate lawyers, some with very good reason. Second, the only thing worse than your own lawyer is the other guy's lawyer.

Having litigated numerous cases, and advised information security professionals inside and outside the federal government, we can assure information security professionals and their customers that, if and when you are sued by victims of attack or identify theft, or find yourselves in the sights of regulators or prosecutors, you will look to your lawyer as, if not a friend, at least a most necessary evil. And you will wish you had consulted that lawyer much, much sooner. Here's why.

It would seem obvious that, when the task is to determine how an entity may most effectively come into compliance with the numerous and complex legal requirements for information security, a qualified and experienced attorney should be involved. Surprisingly, this does not appear to be the case today with information security evaluations. Most assessments and evaluations are conducted by computer engineers, accounting, and consulting firms, to be sure that each of these professional competencies plays the necessary role in information security evaluations. However, since a key question is how to best comply with the current standards of care and, thus, mitigate potential legal liability, experienced and qualified counsel should be quarterbacking this team, much as a surgeon runs an operating room, even though nurses, anesthesiologists, and other competent professionals are crucial parts of the operating team.

! WARNING: DO NOT PRACTICE LAW WITHOUT A LICENSE

In virtually every U.S. state, individuals are legally prohibited from practicing law without a license. For example, in Colorado, "practicing law" is defined, by law, to include, "counseling, advising and assisting [another] in connection with" legal rights and duties.[75] Penalties for the unauthorized practice of law in Colorado can include

---

[73] *Henry VI*, Part 2, act iv, scene ii.
[74] *See, e.g.,* Seth Finkelstein, "The first thing we do, let's kill all the lawyers" – It's a Lawyer Joke, *The Ethical Spectator,* July 1997., available at: *http://www.sethf.com/essays/major/killlawyers.php.*
[75] *Koscove v. Bolte,* 30 P.3d 784 (Colo.App. 2001).

fines or imprisonment.[76] Information security consultants should not, under any circumstances, purport to advise customers as to the legal implications of statutes such as the HIPAA, Gramm-Leach-Bliley financial information privacy provisions, or other federal, state, or local laws or regulations. First, the consultants risk legal action against them by doing so. Second, they do their customers a grave disservice by leading them to believe that the customers can take any legal comfort from advice given them by non-lawyers.

Beyond this seemingly obvious reason for including the services and expertise of experienced and qualified legal counsel in conducting information security evaluations, a number of other factors also support doing so.

Attorney-client Privilege

The so-called attorney-client privilege is one of the oldest protections for confidential information known to the law, and it is quite powerful. In every state, though with varying degrees of ease in establishing the privilege and differing degrees of exception to it, communications of legal advice from legal counsel to a client are "privileged," that is, protected, from compelled disclosure, including in civil lawsuits.[77] Information given by the client to the lawyer for the purpose of seeking legal advice is similarly protected.[78] In many but not all jurisdictions, at least in civil litigation, once a court finds that the privilege applies, no amount of need for the privileged information claimed by a legal adversary cannot outweigh the protection created by the privilege.[79] This near-absolute protection is less certain, however, in at least some jurisdictions, in the criminal context.[80]

Further, courts in many states appear to apply a heightened level of scrutiny to corporate counsel or other "in-house" attorneys than they do to outside law firms retained by a corporation to perform particular legal services.[81] That is, courts force corporations to jump through more evidentiary "hoops" before allowing the attorney-client privilege for communications with in-house counsel than they do to communications with outside law firms.[82]

Importantly for information security consultants, courts have held (albeit in contexts analogous, but not identical, to information security, such as work with environmental consultants and accountants) that technical work performed by expert consultants can also enjoy attorney-client privilege protection.[83] Critically, though, this protection attaches to the consultant's work if and only if the client hires the attorney to perform a legal service (i.e., advising the client on how best to comply with HIPAA and/or other laws and then the attorney hires the consultant to provide the attorney with technical information needed to provide accurate legal advice).[84] And this chain of employment cannot be

---

[76] *See* Rule 238(c), Colorado Court Rules (2004).

[77] *See, e.g., Pacamor Bearings, Inc. v. Minebea Co., Ltd.*, 918 F.Supp. 491, 509–510 (D. N.H. 1996).

[78] *Id.*

[79] *See, e.g., Diversified Indus., Inc. v. Meredith*, 572 F.2d 596, 602 (8th Cir. 1978).

[80] *See, e.g., People v. Benney*, 757 P.2d 1078 (Colo.App. 1987).

[81] *See, e.g., Southern Bell Telephone & Telegraph Co. v. Deason*, 632 So. 2d 1377 (Fla. 1994); *McCaugherty v. Sifferman*, 132 F.R.D. 234 (N.D. Cal. 1990). *United States v. Davis* 132 F.R.D. 12 (S.D.N.Y. 1990).

[82] *See, e.g., United States v. Chevron*, No. C-94-1885 SBA, 1996 WL 264769 (N.D. Cal. Mar. 13, 1996).

[83] *See, e.g., Gerrits v. Brannen Banks of Florida* 138 F.R.D. 574, 577 (D. Colo. 1991).

[84] *See, e.g., id.*

a sham or mere pass-through used by the client to get the technical information but improperly cloak that data improperly with the privilege protection.[85]

The potential for the technical aspects of information security evaluations to enjoy enhanced protection from disclosure has obvious implications for information security evaluation results. If done honestly and correctly, the "chain of employment" (the hiring of a lawyer to provide legal advice which, in turn, requires assessment/evaluation work by technical experts) protects all of the work. The legal advice, as well as, for example, technical reports showing identified potential vulnerabilities in the client's information security may be protected under the attorney-client privilege.

It is important to recognize that, like information security measures, the attorney-client privilege is never "bullet proof." It is not absolute and there are, in every jurisdiction, well-recognized exceptions and ways to waive the protection (e.g., information provided to an attorney for the purpose of perpetrating a crime or fraud is not protected).[86] The protected nature of appropriately privileged information may disappear if the client or the attorney reveals that information to third parties outside the communication between the attorney (and consultants hired by the attorney) and certain company personnel (or in the presence of such third parties, even if the attorney is also present).[87] There are also times when it is appropriate to waive the privilege (e.g., a business or educational institution may choose to waive the privilege in order to assert an "advice-of-counsel" defense.) Also, the so-called Thompson Memorandum, issued by U.S Deputy Attorney General Larry Thompson in January 2003,[88] encourages companies to cooperate with the government in investigations by setting forth factors that are used to determine whether the government will pursue criminal prosecution. One important factor is whether the company is willing to waive the attorney-client and work-product privileges. Still, it is better to have these privileges to waive in an effort to encourage the government not to prosecute than not to have the privilege at all.

Courts have concluded that the societal benefit of not discouraging entities from conducting their own assessments of their compliance with applicable law outweighs any potential downside of the privilege, such as preventing all relevant information from coming out at trial.[89] This also makes good common sense. Entities will be far more likely to initiate their own compliance assessments/evaluations in information security, as in numerous other areas, if they are confident the results will be protected.[90]

Advice of Counsel Defense

Unfortunately, many information security consultants, auditors, and others attempt to advise customers about how to comply with laws and regulations they believe are applicable. This is problematic

---

[85] *See, e.g., Sneider v. Kimberly-Clark Corp.*, 91 F.R.D. 1, 5 (N.D. Ill. 1980)

[86] *See, e.g., In re Grand Jury Proceedings*, 857 F.2d 710, 712 (10th Cir. 1988).

[87] *See, e.g., Winchester Capital Management Co. vs. Manufacturers Hanover Trust Co.*, 144 F.R.D.170, 174 (D. Mass. 1992).

[88] U.S. Department of Justice, *Federal Prosecution of Business Organizations in Criminal Resource Manual* No. 162 (2003) available at *http://www.usdoj.gov/usao/eousa/foia_reading_room/usam/title9/crm00162.html* and amended and available at *http://www.usdoj. gov/dag/cftf/corporate_guidelines.html.*

[89] *See, e.g., Union Carbide Corp. v. Dow Chem. Co.*, 619 F. Supp. 1036, 1046 (D. Del. 1985).

[90] A related protection to that of the attorney-client privilege is the so-called "work product" doctrine. This protection for materials that might tend to show the strategies or other "mental impressions" of attorneys when such materials are prepared "in anticipation of litigation" would cover the work of information security consultants assisting attorneys in preparing materials for use at a trial or to deal with regulators or law enforcement officials. Work-product protection is significantly more susceptible to being held inapplicable by the court, upon a sufficiently high showing of need by your adversary, than is the attorney-client privilege.

for several important reasons. First, generally speaking, experienced and qualified attorneys will be better able than others to accurately interpret and advise concerning the law. Second, as noted several times already, non-attorneys may run afoul of state law by purporting to provide legal advice.

In addition to these reasons, following the advice of non-lawyers as to how to comply with the law does not provide the same level of legal defense in future lawsuits, regulatory proceedings, or prosecutions as following an attorney's advice. In general, a client who provides full and accurate information to an attorney in the course of seeking advice on how to comply with information security law, and makes a good faith effort to follow that advice, enjoys what is known as the "advice of counsel" defense.[91] This defense is a significant protection against legal liability. Following an attorney's advice on information security legal compliance protects the client, even if that advice turns out to have been in error.[92]

Establishment and Enforcement of Rigorous Assessment, Interview, and Report-writing Standards

Important components of information security evaluations and assessments are the interviews of key customer personnel and reviews of their documents. While this work can be, and often is, performed exclusively by engineers or other consultants, interviewing and document review are skills in which lawyers tend to be particularly proficient. These two tasks form major portions of the daily work of many lawyers. As important as actually conducting interviews and reviewing documents is making certain that the right people are interviewed and that all relevant documents are located and carefully reviewed. These tasks, in turn, require the evaluation team to be flexible and alert to new avenues of inquiry that arise during the course of an evaluation (as well as during preparation for, and follow up to, the evaluation). Again, these skills are ones that lawyers exercise virtually every day in their ordinary practices.

Regardless of how much information is collected, it is useless to the customer until it is put into a form that is clear, understandable, and placed in its appropriate context. Extraneous information must be removed. Simple, declarative language must be used. The implications of each piece of information included in the report must be clearly identified. Here again, clear, understandable writing is the stock in trade of good lawyers. Attorney involvement in the drafting, or at least reviewing and editing, of information security evaluation reports can add significantly to the benefit of the process and the final product to the customer.

Creating a Good Record for Future Litigation

Many qualified and experienced lawyers also know how to write for judges and juries. There is a flip side of the coin of attorney-client privilege to help protect confidential results of information security evaluations from compelled disclosure in court. That is, the benefit of managing the process so that the resulting reports will work well in court in the event that the privilege fails for some

---

[91] *See, e.g., United States v. Gonzales*, 58 F.3d 506, 512 (10th Cir. 1995).
[92] *Id.*

reason (inadvertent waiver of it by the customer, for example) and a report must be disclosed, *or* a report ends up being helpful in litigation and you *want* to disclose it. In such circumstances, two things will be important. First, the evaluation process and resulting report(s) must stand up under the evidentiary standards imposed by the civil litigation rules. For example, good records of interviews and document reviews should be kept in such a way as to prove a defensible "paper trail" that will convince the court that the information is reliable enough to be allowed into evidence in a trial. Second, reports should be written in a way to clearly describe threats and vulnerabilities, but not overstate them or speak of them in catastrophic terms when such verbiage is not warranted.

Lawyers, and especially experienced trial lawyers, tend to be skilled at both tasks.

Maximizing Ability to Defend Litigation

In a real sense, all of the benefits of involving qualified and experienced counsel previously discussed will help information security professionals and their customers defend against future litigation and, as important, deter would-be litigants from suing in the first place. There is an additional benefit for defense of potential litigation, often phrased as "in on the takeoff, in on the landing." Particularly in business areas with a significant inherent risk of litigation or enforcement action, having qualified and experienced trial lawyers involved early in the business process and throughout that process, will help maximize the ability of the work of information security consultants and their customers to stand up to future litigation.

Dealing with Regulators, Law Enforcement, Intelligence, and Homeland Security Officials

Your meeting with Uncle Sam could happen in at least two ways: you may call him, or he may call you. The first is preferable.

The first scenario may unfold in several ways. Your customer may believe it is a victim of an attack on its information systems, terrorism-related or otherwise, and either not be able to stop the attack as it unfolds, not be able to ascertain its origin after it is over, or not be able to determine whether the attackers left behind surprises for further attack at a later time. Or your customer may simply believe contacting the authorities is the right thing to do. In any event, those authorities likely will want to talk with you—and potentially subpoena you to testify in court—as part of their investigation. Alternatively, an attack may take place while you are working on the customer's systems, making you, in effect, the "first responder."

The second scenario, Uncle Sam reaching out affirmatively to you and/or your customers, also may unfold in multiple ways but two things are fairly constant. One, the government will be looking at your customer's systems well before they contact your customer. Two, when they come, they generally will get the information they need, even if a subpoena or warrant is necessary. As demonstrated by the National Strategy to Secure Cyberspace, and, particularly since 9/11, the existence of some type of "cyber unit" at many national law enforcement, intelligence, and homeland security organizations, Uncle Sam is keenly interested in any breaches of cyber security that could threaten our national security. This interest, and the government's aggressiveness in pursuing it, is likely only to increase.

In either scenario (voluntary or involuntary contact with the government [including state law enforcement agencies]), what you and/or your customers do in the first few hours may be critical to how intact their information systems and sensitive information are when the process is complete. Who has the authority to speak to government authorities? What can and cannot be said to them?

How much legal authority (request vs. search warrant vs. subpoena) will be required before allowing them in? Is there any information that they should not be allowed to review? What is the potential legal liability for sharing too much information? Too little? Obviously, your customers (and you, if you are involved) will want to cooperate with legitimate requests and, in fact, may have requested the government's help, but all businesses, educational institutions, and information security consultants must take care not to create civil or criminal liability for themselves by how they conduct their contacts with governmental authorities.

Here again, the keys are: (1) immediately gain the assistance of qualified legal counsel experienced both in information security law and in dealing with law enforcement, intelligence, and homeland security officers; and (2) have a plan in place beforehand for how such authorities will be dealt with, including having legal counsel retained and ready to go.

Notes from the Underground

What to Look For in Your Attorney's

There are a number of obvious characteristics one should seek in any attorney retained for any purpose. These include integrity, a good reputation in the legal community, and general competence. You also want to consider an attorney with a strong background in corporate and business transactions who is familiar with the contracting process. One useful tool for evaluating these qualities as you attempt to narrow your list of potential attorneys is to interview is a company called Martindale Hubbell (*www. martindale.com*). Look for lawyers with an "AV" rating (Martindale's highest).
(Note: Never hire any attorney without at least one face-to-face meeting to learn what your gut tells you about whether you could work with him or her.)

In the area of information security evaluation, you will want to look for attorneys with deep and broad expertise in the field. The best way to do so is to look for external, independently verifiable criteria demonstrating an attorney or law firm's tested credentials (e.g., is the lawyer you seek to retain listed on the National Security Agency Web site as including individuals certified as having been trained in NSA's Information Security Assurance Methodology (IAM)? If so, on the appropriate NSA Web page (e.g., *www.iatrp.com/indivu2.cfm#C*), you will find a listing similar to this:

Cunningham, Bryan   03/15/05   (303) 743-0003   bc@morgancunningham.net

Has an attorney you are considering authored any published works in the area of information security law? Has he or she held positions, in the government or elsewhere, related to information security? Finally, there's the gut check. How does your potential lawyer make you feel? Are you comfortable working with him or her? Does he communicate clearly and concisely? Does he or she seem more interested in covering their own backside than in providing you with legal counsel to protect your interests?

The Ethics of Information Security Evaluation[93]

The eighteenth century philosopher, Immanuel Kant, observed, "[i]n law a man is guilty when he violates the rights of others. In ethics he is guilty if he only thinks of doing so."[94] To think and act ethically requires more than just strict compliance with the law. It requires an understanding of your customer, their business environment, and the duties your customer owes to others under statutory requirements as well as private contracts. The reward is an increased likelihood of compliance with laws and establishing credibility in the community that will reduce the likelihood of disputes with customers and increase your marketability. Ethics relate to your conduct and not to the conduct of those with whom you are transacting business. Accordingly, it is not unethical to be alert to the possibility that others with whom you are dealing are themselves unethical. Do not be naive. Pursuit of an ethical practice does not replace the need to protect yourself through reliable processes, consistent methodologies, and properly drafted contracts that include defined work, limitations on liability, and indemnifications.

Do not think of violating the rights of others. Do not take short cuts. Do not assume that you can conduct your work without understanding the needs and rights of others and acting to protect those rights. Failing to understand the rights of customers you have been retained to help or of those involved with your customers is tantamount to thinking of violating their rights. Ethical business, therefore, requires that you understand the players and whose rights are at stake.

Finally, though it sounds intuitive, do your job well. Martin Van Buren counseled that "[i]t is easier to do a job right than to explain why you didn't." Customers often insist on short cuts and reject proposals that require time delays to document the relationship and obtain the appropriate consents before the work begins. Customers soon forget their front-end demands for cost savings and expedience in completing the project. Hold firm. Do the job right and avoid having to explain to an angry customer, a prosecutor, a judge, or a jury why you did not.

---

[93] Entire books could be written on this topic, and some have, at least on the broader topic of IT ethics. *See, e.g., IT Ethics Handbook: Right and Wrong for IT Professionals*, Syngress Publishing, Inc. A comprehensive discussion of Information Security Evaluation ethics is beyond the scope of this book. This discussion is simply to remind us all of some things we learned from our parents that translate into our business relationships.

[94] Available at *http://en.thinkexist.com/quotation/in_law_a_man_is_guilty_when_he_violates_the/7854.html*.

Chapter 17

Building the Technical Evaluation Plan

Solutions in this chapter:

- Purpose of the Technical Evaluation Plan
- Building the Technical Evaluation Plan
- Customizing and Modifying the Technical Evaluation Plan
- Getting the Signatures

☑ Summary

Introduction

The *technical evaluation plan* (TEP) plays a critical role in setting and meeting customer expectations. The TEP also establishes how the entire evaluation will be accomplished. In the previous chapters we went into great detail about the TEP's sections and the fact that the TEP should be considered the core product of the pre-evaluation process. The TEP combines any and all created or discovered the information into an easily understood summary of the organization about to be evaluated.

The purpose or goal of the TEP is to be an integral part of the IEM. In fact, the TEP *becomes* the IEM road map after the pre-evaluation is complete. Not only is the TEP a summary of the *understood* status of the target organization, it also discusses the major action items to be covered during the evaluation process as well as any fundamental concerns, constraints, or focal points the customer would like addressed. In this chapter we discuss the various aspects of the TEP and some of the things we want it to accomplish.

We also lay out the TEP in a detailed format for discussion. Each portion of the plan covers different topics in different levels of detail. Some of the topics share concerns, such as ease of use and level of detail. Both of these are factors to be determined between the customer and the evaluating teams, as we'll see later. And of course we review the topic-specific items and how they support the IEM process and the overall goal of improving the customer's total INFOSEC posture.

Lastly, we cover some of the options you can use to customize the TEP. As we detail the requirements, keep in mind that some pieces may be added or modified to fit the needs of individual scenarios. We don't cover all possible changes, but we do look at some of today's more common ones. Don't worry — the major components of the TEP that are considered vital by NSA standards are explained throughout the chapter. The goal is to create the most customer-centric management tool possible, without losing the key concepts that promote information security best practices.

Purpose of the Technical Evaluation Plan

The TEP is designed to tie together all aspects of an IEM between the customer and the evaluation team. It is the primary agreement used to maintain customer expectations, which is crucial to successful security evaluations. The TEP is meant to be the guide for the evaluation process as well as a tool the customer organization and the independent evaluation team use to maintain focus during the project. Expect the TEP to be a heavily used and discussed document. The TEP focuses on some of the most important, and often dynamic, aspects of a security evaluation:

- Dates and scheduling
- Personnel involvement
- Understood boundaries
- Deliverables
- Priority concerns
- Priority constraints
- Evaluation tools and tool limitations

This is only a brief list of items addressed in this chapter, but as you can see, they would be considered major management topics for just about any project or engagement. In simplified terms, the IEM TEP lays out those concerns with a focus on security practices and makes them clear and easily understood topics for all involved parties.

In both commercial and government environments, you can see that this tool is an excellent method for maintaining scope between the customer and the evaluation team. It can help prevent the misunderstandings that often occur in very large organizations such as government agencies or multinational corporations. From a consulting perspective, the TEP also manages to help protect payments, since it gives you approved documentation clearly stating the objectives, deliverables, and timeline of the project as agreed on by both parties. It also helps eliminate scope drift, which can be a real killer in any fixed-price engagement agreements.

The IEM TEP, like all other documentation you create or send the customer, should be considered a controlled document that would have security implications if released publicly. The information disclosed in the TEP alone should not be enough to cause a security incident, but it will discuss architectures, security measures, current concerns, and other issues that the organization most likely would not like to become public knowledge. There is no reason to make available *any* extra information to possible criminal threat sources. Here are some specifically dangerous topics that a TEP will include (but you're not limited to these):

- Detailed network diagrams
- Software brands and version levels
- Internal addressing schemes
- Descriptions of high-assurance components

The IEM TEP plays two roles in the IEM process. It serves as an agreement between the customer and the evaluation team. It also serves as a road map for the execution of the evaluation.

The IEM TEP as an Agreement

As an agreement, the TEP's focus is to assure that all the customer and evaluation team concerns and constraints are addressed to a mutual satisfaction. Just like any agreement or contract, it will contain legal terminology addressing the legal concerns of the evaluation, but it will also give a great deal of detail about what the customer expects before, during, and following the evaluation. After completing and reviewing the IEM TAP, both the customer and the evaluation organization should approve the document via signature. This helps ensure the understanding of both parties and works to keep everyone fully informed. It also provides direct evidence to the original agreement in regard to the deliverables expected and their timeframes.

The TEP is often compared to a statement of work (SOW) because it outlines and details actions and deliverables as well as the level of effort and objectives intended. It would not be unheard of to define this in any contracts or SOWs as the proper method for handling change control issues. Depending on your legal counsel's advice, it may be acceptable to simply create addendums to the TEP, approved by mutual signature, as the process for documenting and accepting any changes in scope within the original project. For independent firms, this is an excellent method for ensuring proper adherence to accepted responsibilities.

The TEP is a living document that can and probably will be modified during the execution of the evaluation process. Often, these changes occur following a meeting with the customer leadership, when the progress of the evaluation is being discussed and the customer realizes they desire additional activities to occur. In such a situation, a simple change-order process can be utilized. It doesn't always require a change in cost, but it certainly does require documenting the change and having both parties sign off on it. Since the TEP is a road map to conducting the evaluation, changes may impact the customer and require additional resources or time to accomplish the evaluation. Ultimately, the final TEP will become part of the final report.

WARNING
_____

Don't make the mistake of using the same TEP content for every customer. This TEP is a customized document that helps define the IEM process for that specific customer only. The outline for the TEP is good, but the content is customized on a customer-by-customer basis.

The TEP as Road Map

As a road map, the TEP functions as the guide for conducting the evaluation for the customer. The TEP should be detailed enough to address items such as scheduling, scan time, customer preparation, customer and evaluation team contacts, and a great deal of other items. The TEP identifies the expectations and the tempo for the evaluation process. It should cover all the pieces that go into an IEM-derived evaluation — from the work completed during the pre-evaluation all the way to the expectations for final report delivery. The TEP also incorporates information from the IAM that is directly relevant to the IEM process.

The TEP should be used to help document the overall evaluation and organize activities for the remaining phases. The TEP is really a map that has been approved by both sides of the evaluation in terms of actions that will be taken to evaluate the customer's INFOSEC status and the timing of each action, such as site visits, opening meetings, periodic updates, exit briefings, scanning windows, rules of engagement, and so on. If an action or task is planned for inclusion in the process, it should be included and detailed in the TEP for reference.

The document also acts as a record of the events to occur during the process. As the evaluation begins, the document is used for assisting coordination, managing customer expectations, and providing guidance. Then, as objectives are met and functions or information are documented, the TEP also begins functioning much like a checklist and validation tool. By the end of the evaluation, the TEP should show the process in a summarized format from beginning to end, including any changes in objectives, methods, plans, and so forth. In essence, you could consider the TEP a life-cycle report, documenting where the project began and with whom and leading all the way up to the completed findings. Figure 17.1 illustrates the road map to a successful IEM.

Figure 17.1 The TEP Road Map

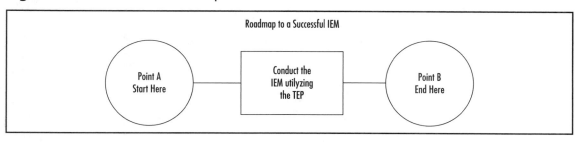

Building the Technical Evaluation Plan

By now, you should have most of the information you need to put together the TEP, since the TEP is completed at the end of the pre-evaluation phase of the IEM. The TEP is composed of 10 specific areas. They are:

- Points of contact
- Methodology overview
- Criticality information
- Detailed network information
- Customer concerns
- Customer constraints
- Rules of engagement
- Coordination agreements
- Letter of authorization
- Timeline of events

Source of the Technical Evaluation Plan Information

Throughout the pre-evaluation phase, we identified multiple activities that start to build the evaluation process for our specific customer. To effectively manage customer expectations, we must incorporate this knowledge into an easy-to-use plan of action for conducting the evaluation. This is our TEP. The information for the TEP comes from four primary sources: the IEM pre-evaluation process, the IAM pre-assessment process, the evaluation team, and the customer. Working in concert, these various sources of information can be combined to effectively address customer needs and manage customer expectations, which is the key to a successful implementation of the IEM. Figure 17.2 shows how multiple information sources feed into the TEP.

Figure 17.2 TEP Sources

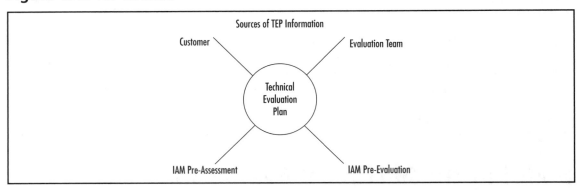

TEP Section I: Points of Contact

The first section of the TEP contains contact information for key players in both the customer and the evaluation team organizations. All means of communication should be documented here — phone numbers, e-mail addresses, site addresses, and so on. The requirements for number of contacts, roles of contacts, and so on are up to your team. At a minimum, the primary point of contact (POC) for both the customer and the evaluation team should be listed. Hopefully, most of the POC information was already gathered during the pre-evaluation and is located either in the IEM planning survey or the IEM checklist.

Contact information should come first in the TEP, since it often is the most needed type of information for customer staff who might not be working directly with the evaluation team. It will help the customer organization's executives understand a project they might be getting requests about, as well as giving them a starting point as to who can answer their questions. These types of questions are perfectly valid, especially coming from the involved parties who might not have been included in the beginning stages of planning for the IEM. You may also tend to get questions from people requesting a refresher on definitions relevant to any of the specific areas.

Evaluation Team Contacts

List all contacts for the planned evaluation team. Be sure to include roles and multiple ways to reach evaluation team personnel. The most important contact is obviously the team leader. In this section, it might be helpful to include a listing of individuals' expertise or a technology contact.

Customer Contacts

Remember, the organizational POC should be designated as someone who has the proper authority to make decisions in regard to this security evaluation. That person is likely being contacted by people within his or her own organization, whether to ask questions, voice concerns, or possibly to announce conflicts with scheduling. Keep in mind that in the IEM process, we are likely to have more than one customer representative. Probably we will have a single person handling the management side of things, but we will also have technical contacts to assist us in getting our technical needs addressed. List all contacts that have been identified so far in the IEM process.

TEP Section II: Methodology Overview

Section II of the TEP is specifically focused on describing how the IEM process will be conducted and the overall benefit to the organization. Since the TEP is a record of the agreed-on scope, having a detailed description of the IEM methodology and how it will be specifically applied to your customer will help with the overall understanding of the organization. Remember that some individuals who read the TEP will not have participated in any fashion with the IEM process to date. Therefore, it is important to clearly describe the entire IEM process.

Purpose of the IEM

This section should include discussion on why the IEM is being conducted for this specific customer.

Description of the IEM

The IEM description is key to continued understanding of the IEM process. It would be prudent to have the description entail key elements of the IEM training to include, at a minimum:

- Overall IEM description
- IEM as part of the NSA toolkit for conducting security reviews
- Ten IEM baseline activities (with descriptions)
- Benefits of doing the IEM activity
- IEM results

Here is a sample introduction to the IEM methodology. This is only a beginning. Check out the sample TEP provided in Appendix B for a more detailed example. Based on your knowledge of the customer and the industry they function within, you can customize the description to meet your needs:

> The INFOSEC Evaluation Methodology (IEM) is a hands-on methodology for conducting evaluations of customer networks utilizing common technical evaluation tools. The IEM covers the steps involved in a comprehensive evaluation of a customer's technical components, beginning with customer coordination and the definition of applicable scope for each project. Students will learn how the information defined during the IAM process will be used to create customized road maps for increased security posture.

Evaluation Tools to Be Used

The IEM uses the 10 baseline activities. Each of these activities requires some form of technical tool or manual technical process to address conducting these activities. In this section, list the tools that you plan to use to complete each of the baseline activities that you will conduct for the customer. Once again, remember that NSA *does not* recommend or endorse any specific technical tools for the IEM. This is where your technical expertise comes into play in defining your toolkit for the IEM process.

For purposes of the TEP and as a complete record of the scope agreed on by the customer and the evaluation team, it is helpful to include a listing of how the tools will be configured. Based on discussions with the customer to this point, the level of possible intrusiveness the customer is willing to accept should be clear. Some considerations that need to be included are:

- Settings of the tools for how extensive the scans will be. Include such factors as number of concurrent scans, how many threads in the scans, any automatic denial-of-service testing, or any automatic password checking by the tools.

- Handling of certain tools for host-based testing and password cracking. Will the customer install and operate, or will the evaluation team install and operate?

Any other configuration information related to the specific tools that are planned to be used will assist in greater understanding of is to occur during the testing process.

Tools & Traps…

Tool Misconfiguration

Correct configuration of the evaluation tools is important to avoid negative impact on the customer. If you run some evaluation tools in default mode — for example, denial-of-service tests and password cracking — you may be running scans on the customer that they have specifically requested not be run. If a customer is using account lockout after three unsuccessful logon attempts, an evaluation tool that runs a password cracker against all user accounts with a default of three attempts will lock out all user accounts and create issues for the customer. It's always good to have a custom configuration of the tools based on your expertise and what you feel provides the best value to the customer.

TEP Section III: Criticality Information

The majority of the information for this section comes from work done in the IAM pre-assessment process. This translates directly to the IEM process and the IEM TEP. The organizational criticality matrices and the system criticality matrices will map directly into the final report, creating a deliverable that is a trending and tracking mechanism the customer can use to help improve its INFOSEC posture.

Organizational Criticality Matrices

We looked at the organizational information criticality in the IAM process. Here we simply need to gather the already generated data and present it in a readily understood format. As we have tied the mission to INFOSEC goals and objectives, here we tie the goals and objectives to the actual information types present in the organization. As the evaluation progresses, documenting information and findings will map directly back to the TEP and information you have listed.

As discussed in an earlier chapter, if you haven't completed an IAM for the organization you are planning an evaluation for, you need to complete the IAM pre-assessment process to create the organizational and system criticality matrices and associated impact definitions. Based on the IAM process, information types are cataloged and their impacts based on the organization's mission, as follows:

- The first things that should be documented are the already categorized information types the customer defined. List each and every category the team defined, and give a brief description of each. If you rolled up subcategories into larger categories, go ahead and list them here as well. This will help further the definition of information types as well as give greater detail to people looking for information regarding a specific category.

- The next thing we need to define are the impact attributes (confidentiality, integrity, and availability). Because these terms can have different meanings to different people, it's a wise choice to explain them as they pertain to this assessment, to avoid any confusion.

- Next, list the impact definitions. Again, these are the High, Medium, and Low attributes that were discussed in prior chapters. Make sure they are clearly explained here as defined during the visit meetings. These descriptions can vary greatly in size and detail based on the customer organization and the number of impact attributes used in the process, but generally they should not exceed a page per definition.

- Last is the actual criticality matrix that was created involving the High, Medium, and Low impact attributes and all the organizational information types (as demonstrated in Table 17.1). A simple table here will do the trick. You can format or display the matrix and define and list information types any way you like. Just be sure that that information ends up here.

Table 17.1 Organizational Criticality Matrices Example for Company *X*

	Confidentiality	Integrity	Availability
Customer information	Medium	High	Low
Account information	High	High	Low
Employee information	High	Medium	Medium
Corporate finances	High	High	Medium
Research and development	Medium	Medium	Low

System Criticality Information

The System Information Criticality section of the TEP is very much like the Organizational Information Criticality section, though less detailed. The information attributes of High, Medium, and Low have already been defined and documented in the IAM pre-assessment process and should now be in the TEP; since the definitions must be the same at the organizational and system levels, they do not need to be listed again here. Information type definitions and rollups also need not be restated here, but the defined information types *do* need to be listed in regard to the system of which each may be a part.

For this section, document the system information criticality of each separately defined system. Although the system will be detailed in a later section of the TEP, a brief description of each system here will help readers understand what the criticality matrix of each system means in relation to their environment. All systems falling into the scope of the evaluation must be recognized here. Table 17.2 shows two system criticality matrices based on the Table 17.1 organizational criticality matrices.

Table 17.2 System Criticality Matrices Examples

System 1	Confidentiality	Integrity	Availability
Customer information	Medium	High	Low
Account information	High	High	Low
Employee information	High	Medium	Medium
System 2	**Confidentiality**	**Integrity**	**Availability**
Corporate finances	High	High	Medium
Research and development	Medium	Medium	Low

TEP Section IV: Detailed Network Information

The Detailed Network Information section is, obviously, expected to be very detailed. This section should be a technical and environmental description of all systems to be included in the IEM evaluation activities. If a system is not listed here, the final report should not include it in any capacity beyond an unreviewed or nonevaluated system — for example, an out-of-scope system connected to an in-scope system.

At a minimum, each system must be mapped to specific hardware, software, and connection configurations. It is understood that much of this information might not truly be available or known until after the evaluation is performed. That is acceptable, but every effort must be made to define each system in detail to eliminate any confusion in terms of system and scope boundaries. Just as you listed and detailed the information types comprising the organization's makeup, you should include in each system's description the relevant information types it contains. This is a very important characterization of the system, since this will be one of the main deciding factors when the time comes to determine which findings require priority in regard to mitigating resources.

Any available customer diagrams should be included here as well — the more detailed, the better. If none is available, it is highly recommended that you create one based on the verbal descriptions listed in this section. Many people are more adept at visual learning, and this process may be new to many of your customer contacts. Nontechnical individuals can more readily understand diagrams than text, so they will help minimize misunderstandings.

Include in this section any logical and physical boundaries that will impact the execution of the IEM process. We are still scooping the effort, and this information is critical to accomplishing this task.

> **TIP**
>
> Be sure that the customer and the evaluation team share a common definition of the terms *system* and *network*. Add those definitions in this section. A misunderstanding of these definitions can lead to serious issues in the IEM process. The National Center for Education Statistics (NCES) (nces.ed.gov/pubs98/tech/glossary.asp) defines a system as "a group of elements, components, or devices that are assembled to serve a common purpose. In a technological system, this refers to all hardware, software, networks, cables, peripheral equipment, information, data, personnel, and procedures (i.e., all technology resources) that comprise a computer environment." NCES (nces.ed.gov/pubs2003/secureweb/glossary.asp) defines a network as a "group of computers connected to each other to share computer software, data, communications, and peripheral devices. Commonly, the definition of a network includes the hardware and software needed to connect the computers together." So basically, a system does a specific task, and a network provides communications and interconnectivity.

TEP Section V: Customer Concerns

This section of the TEP addresses customer concerns — anything the customer mentions is an area of particular concern for them and they would specifically like more information about. For example, if a customer says they are concerned about their wireless networking implementation, then wireless networking should be listed as a customer concern. They haven't specifically limited the engagement to *only* the areas they are concerned about, but this section does identify areas of greater concentration for the IEM, or at least areas where more specific focus is required in the final report. Examples of customer concerns include (but obviously are not limited to):

- Is my wireless network secure?
- I'm not sure my staff is handling the antivirus tools correctly.
- My security manager says the network is 100 percent guaranteed secure. Is this correct?
- Is my configuration management process effective?
- I'm not sure I am meeting the regulatory requirements that are levied on me. Am I?
- Are there new regulations and legislation I need to be concerned about?
- I hear testing of system backups is important, and I want to assure we are doing it correctly.
- Are there new technologies that can cut my security management time?
- We seem to be getting hit a lot from the Internet. Is this normal?

Many of the concerns that were expressed during the IAM process can be carried over into the IEM process, since many concerns cross both the organizational security and technical security arenas. Addressing the customer concerns is an important part of managing customer expectations.

TEP Section VI: Customer Constraints

This section specifically addresses any identified customer constraints — any limitations placed on the customer or evaluation team that will affect the evaluation process. This is also a good place to identify necessary actions in emergency or crisis situations that could arise later in the evaluation process. Examples of customer constraints in the evaluation process include these:

- You are allowed to scan only during nonpeak processing hours.

- The evaluation cannot take place during a major system upgrade.

- The evaluation cannot occur during the last three business days of the month nor the first two business days of the month because of end-of-month processing.

- The customer does not have control of nor does it own the entire network IP range they are sitting on.

- Actual servers are located across the country, making it difficult to do a cost-effective host evaluation.

This list is just a few of the constraints you might see from the customer side. Transfer to this section any concerns that are applicable from the IAM process as well. Managing the IEM effort with an eye to the constraints goes a long way toward meeting the customer's expectations.

TEP Section VII: Rules of Engagement

The Rules of Engagement section addresses specific rules while the IEM is under way to ensure communication and minimize the impact on the customer's operations. You may have some crossover from the concerns and constraints sections here, but it is better to have the same information repeated more than once than to have it missed entirely.

Evaluation Team Requirements

The evaluation team members will need to understand their rules from both the internal and external side. Use this section to identify "do's and don'ts" for the evaluation process.

External Requirements

During the external portion of the IEM, the evaluation team needs to know, at a minimum, the following information:

- IP ranges (external) that are permitted to be scanned
- Timeframes during which scans can occur

- Immediate contact information within the customer organization for people who can be contacted in the event that servers, systems, or networks seem to react negatively to the IEM process

- Copy of the LOA in each evaluation team member's possession

Internal Requirements

During the internal portion of the IEM, the evaluation team needs to know, at a minimum, the following information:

- IP ranges (internal) that are permitted to be scanned

- Timeframes during which scans can occur

- Immediate contact information within the customer organization for people who can be contacted in the event that servers, systems, or networks seem to react negatively to the IEM process

- Physical access to the facility where the scanning will occur

- Copy of the LOA in each evaluation team member's possession

Customer Requirements

The customer must participate with the evaluation team in the overall rules of engagement. Certain information and actions are necessary to ensure a smooth evaluation:

- The evaluation team's scanning IP addresses (both internal and external addresses)

- Immediate contact information for the evaluation team

- Notification to any internal group, such as a Computer Incident Response Team (CIRT), that needs to know scans are occurring

- Information on the evaluation tools that will be used and any known exclusions to the toolset

TEP Section VIII: Coordination Agreements

Coordination agreements refer to items that need to be documented related to the understanding between the customer and the evaluation team. This section specifically addresses the level of detail of recommendations, deliverables, and any other agreements not otherwise documented in the TEP. Remember, the purpose the TEP is to *fully* document the scope of the effort.

Level of Detail of Recommendations

During the IEM pre-evaluation, you should have directly discussed with the customer the required level of detail of the final report's recommendations. This addresses the technical depth of the customer staff and identifies the level of effort necessary for the final report. According to NSA, we can break out the level of detail into three categories:

- Low level of detail or executive level (low detail)

- Moderate level of detail (normal)

- High level of detail (step by step)

For the main body of the final report, the normal acceptable level of detail for recommendations is the moderate level. This provides technical management and technical personnel enough detail to address the problem, without requiring a step-by-step procedure to accomplish the fix.

List of Agreed-On Deliverables

Including in the TEP a list of the agreed-on deliverables for the IEM process will assist you in meeting the customer needs and expectations. We have encountered situations where the customer needed an additional summary report for a client, vendor, bank, or insurance company, identifying the results of the evaluation in more detail than an executive summary but less detail than the full final report. Possible deliverables include:

- Weekly update reports (verbal presentation or written)

- Weekly financial expenditure reports

- Initial findings report

- Draft final report

- Final report

- Security road map/first-order prioritization of findings

The Coordination Agreements Section: A Catchall

The Coordination Agreements section of the TEP is the location in which you can put anything else that needs to be addressed to meet specific customer needs. As a "catchall," this section gives the TEP tremendous flexibility in meeting customer and evaluation team needs.

TEP Section IX: Letter of Authorization

Include the letter of authorization (LOA) in your TEP. Remember, the TEP is a *complete* record of the scope of your IEM effort.

TEP Section X: Timeline of Events

Here, in the last NSA IEM TEP required section, dates and events are recorded to ensure that both the customer and the evaluation team are in concert with regard to scheduling. The amount of detail you include regarding any activity or milestone is up to you and the customer, but make sure that each item can be readily understood without multiple phone calls for explanation. Minimum milestones to include are:

- Date of initial request

- Date of pre-evaluation site visit

- Date of onsite evaluation
- Date of final report delivery
- Dates of any major modifications

For some smaller evaluation engagements, this section can be an efficient tool for project management where the cost of a separate management effort may be unwarranted. On the other hand, large scenarios could require more detailed reporting and management effort, especially when multiple sites are involved. Here you might also want to define the method of delivery for products or the method of information gathering, whether you use online collaboration tools, conference calls, or even site visits.

TIP

Build a logical timeline that can the evaluation team can accomplish. Be sure the timeline includes time for the approval process on documents like the TEP and the final report.

Customizing and Modifying the Technical Evaluation Plan

Now we've outlined the main components of the IEM TEP, but to make the best use of this tool, it should be morphed into a document that's central to the way the customer and the evaluation team will operate together. NSA realizes that every situation is different and that some concessions may be required to perform an effective evaluation. It's understood that an independent firm may require particular aspects in their business practice or that some customer policies may require specific assurances or inclusions. In this regard the IEM is meant to be fluid, allowing for change; so too the TEP.

Modifying the Ten NSA-Defined Areas

One way to customize the TEP is through changes in the TEP's composition. By default, you may not remove sections and still be within the IEM guidelines. NSA considers the components discussed to be minimum requirements for any plan to be used in an evaluation. If a conflict arises and a section cannot be completed, the reasons or events leading to these issues need to be clearly documented. The section will remain, but the information detailed will relate to the lack of completion, not the actual topic itself. Adding sections is entirely up to the customer. Several items may be added as requested or as part of an overall independent business practice. Just a few items that can be used to add value to the document are these:

- **Executive summaries** Summaries can go a long way toward providing descriptions and instructions on how to read and understand the plan. They can also be used to summarize the methodology or provide background into the purpose or goal of this particular assessment.

- **Version history information**   This can be very useful for dealing with very fluid engagements where change is the standard. In the example in the appendices, you'll notice that a version control page was combined with approval authority to demonstrate acceptance and understanding of each change on one simple page.

Level of Detail

The level of detail is a very important aspect of the IEM TEP. Detail level can depend on many things, such as the level of involvement the customer organization wants to have with the evaluation process. A hands-on approach may dictate requirements for a very detailed plan as well as increase the chances for multiple revisions down the road. What exactly you include as detail should be based on your interactions with the customer. This should be worked out early in the pre-evaluation phase, and an introduction to a sample TEP during initial meetings would not be overboard. The amount of information recorded in each section is flexible, as long as all required aspects are included.

Format

The format of this document is almost entirely up to you. Certain basic rules should apply, such as the inclusion of a cover sheet and the original order of topics, but most of this is fair game for adjustment based on what is more effective in a given scenario. Some evaluations can be so large, with multiple evaluation teams in action, that an overall TEP is created as the main repository, with several detailed plans attached as appendices. Some systems may be in such revolving states and of sufficient size to warrant breaking out diagrams and detailed technical descriptions or inventories into subdocuments for ease of management.

Keep in mind that the TEP is a tool. Whatever helps improve the efficiency or usability of the tool should be considered appropriate, as long as you account for all required components and it can be used effectively by the customer and the evaluation team.

Getting the Signatures

No agreement is complete without signatures. The TEP is no different. Don't underestimate the importance of the signatures. The TEP is a document both parties will be held accountable for in the execution of the IEM process. It must be signed at the right time and at the right level within each organization. Spend time in the early stages of the pre-evaluation phase determining what the customer approval process will be for the TEP and any subsequent changes. As mentioned before, the TEP is a living document; therefore, the current approval process for the primary TEP must be understood, but expect that there will be changes to the TEP as the IEM moves forward. Address the engagement change process early.

Customer Approval

Sounds pretty simple, but the process of getting the customer to sign off on the TEP can be quite time consuming and tedious. Small to medium-sized organizations may only have one or two people who need to concur to get the signature on the TEP. Larger organizations may have a bureaucracy that will require multiple levels of approval before signature. You need to keep this in mind when determining a timeline for TEP approval. The other avenue most customer organizations will need to run the TEP through is the legal department. This is wise, especially considering the LOA that needs to be signed.

Evaluation Team Approval

With any luck, the evaluation team will be very familiar with the TEP format and content. Most likely the TEP will be written by the evaluation team, with the customer doing the approval process. Unless there are major additions or concerns about the scope or legality of some of the added items in the TEP, the signature would occur fairly easily by the evaluation team signature authority. If there are major changes or additions, the TEP may need to go through the evaluation team's approval process again. This includes team leader, senior management, and evaluation team legal counsel.

Summary

The TEP is a document that that is critical to the successful completion of the evaluation. The TEP is your IEM scope document. It lays out the critical details needed to successfully complete the evaluation process. It serves as your agreement between the evaluation team and your customer. Spend the necessary time putting together a good TEP and it will payoff in the end. The TEP is also your road map for completion of the IEM process for a specific customer.

To put together the TEP, you will use information from multiple sources: the customer, the evaluation team, the IAM pre-assessment process, and the IEM pre-evaluation process. If you haven't completed an IAM pre-assessment on the customer, you need to create the organizational and system criticality matrices to be able to complete the IEM process.

Understanding the background of the TEP or the goals behind it will aid you in putting together a plan that will efficiently manage IEM activities. Viewing the TEP is a working document should allow you to create a document that can be used and updated smoothly as the project rolls on. With the evaluation beginning under the added assurance of an approved and signed IEM TEP, both parties should have a better understanding of the level of effort and final products required to successfully complete the evaluation.

The 10 sections of the IEM TEP should encompass most of the information required to keep a good handle on the IEM activities. With the POC information, you know where to direct questions, and the remaining sections should supply everyone with information ranging from evaluation objectives to system configurations and diagrams. Detailed definitions and explanations further describe the story of this engagement. Boundaries have been set, and the likelihood of scope drift has been minimized with a signed agreement demonstrating the included systems.

With the amount of flexibility granted by the IEM, we can modify the TEP in many ways to fit the needs of our business practices as well as the customer's requirements. Understanding that the core 10 topics may not be removed, we can then add any pieces we deem necessary.

After this discussion centered around the IEM TEP, your understanding of NSA's expectations in terms of planning and assessment guidelines should be solid.

## Chapter 18

Starting Your Onsite Efforts

- **Preparing for the Onsite Evaluation Phase**

- **IAM vs. IEM**

- **IEM Baseline Activities**

- **The Role of CVE and CAN**

- **The In-Brief**

☑ **Summary**

Introduction

This chapter discusses the framework of the onsite evaluation phase, where the meat of the technical evaluations occurs. This also means that the majority of surprises are likely to occur during this phase, so flexibility is paramount. One of the objectives of the INFOSEC Evaluation Methodology (IEM) is to verify information regarding systems and controls documented during the INFOSEC Assessment Methodology (IAM). All technical controls are meant to support policy defined by the organization or any industry regulation or legislation.

The IEM has a set of 10 baseline activities that must be addressed to perform a comprehensive technical evaluation. These activities are designed to meet the need for evaluating the most common standard points of attack to a system and test the effectiveness of the security controls in place. Like the IAM, flexibility and the actual detailed execution of these activities is left up to the expertise of the evaluating team.

Part of the flexibility of the IEM also carries over into the requirement for the use of common vulnerabilities and exposures (CVE) identifiers in deliverable reports. CVE identifiers are one industry standard for identifying security weaknesses and are discussed in greater detail later in this chapter. Using these identifiers, we are able to maintain usefulness throughout the IEM process as well as into mitigation aspects, follow-up review, and research for the customer. Since the evaluation team is normally an outside entity, it is important for the customer to have the ability to interpret the deliverables, which may be needed a year or more down the road, after the evaluation team has finished its work.

To achieve a well-executed project, managing customer expectations is important. Through the use of the in-brief and TEP, we'll see how to set the tone for the evaluation by laying everything on the table before starting and achieving technical staff buy-in. The IAM and IEM methodologies present a "no surprises" attitude in that no critical security concerns should be a surprise to the customer in the final report. If issues are critical in nature, they should be brought to the organization's attention immediately. With the onsite evaluation phase, we take that same concept to heart: No activities should come as a surprise.

With an appropriately built and agreed-on schedule, we can keep to a minimum many of the potential surprises during the evaluation efforts. At this point, the only surprises that should arise (and they usually do) will be for the evaluation team, requiring not just the IEM but also the team and its schedule to be able to adapt on the fly.

Preparing for the Onsite Evaluation Phase

Preparations prior to beginning the IEM on-site evaluation phase are similar to those for the IAM Pre-Assessment Site Visit. Due to the often unexpected developments during on-site visits, a well developed plan of attack will facilitate a smooth process and ensure effective evaluation activities. On-site activities generally occur over a period of a few days to two weeks, depending on the scope and boundaries in place. A lot of work is covered in this timeframe, and a structured, organized approach is key to managing time constraints.

If the target system is of sufficient size and diversity or spread across multiple locations, consider what options you have for using multiple teams, but try to keep the timeline short. The sooner you can present findings, the sooner problems can be mitigated and the organization's security gap narrowed.

Scheduling

There is no predefined schedule or required plan of events to allow for IEM compliance during the onsite evaluation phase. The goal for creating a plan is simply to ensure that all 10 areas of the IEM baseline activities are addressed appropriately. This can be a fluid process, changing day by day, as long as all criteria are evaluated. The process for creating your schedule should be specific to your organization and is considered a business process by the National Security Agency.

A sample timeline with broad activities is outlined in the following sections. This sample obviously won't fit every environment, but it has been used successfully as a baseline schedule for multiple engagements. This schedule will need to be "fleshed out" with more specific and detailed events, but it serves well as a starting point in most situations. This timeline also hinges on the common practice of performing vulnerability testing during off-peak hours (such as evenings).

Day One Accomplishments

The first day is usually the least productive in terms of technical testing results, because you'll deal with the more routine tasks of getting set up in a working location, handling introductions, verify-testing windows and processes, and performing the in-brief. The main objectives are to complete the in-brief, begin ongoing automated testing, and initiate system mapping (discussed later in the chapter). Here are the typical accomplishments for Day 1:

- Conduct in-briefing
- Verify customer agreement with scope and schedule
- Site tour and working location setup
- Enumeration activities (system mapping)
- Off-hours vulnerability scanning configuration scheduling
- Begin password compliance testing procedures
- Begin network-sniffing procedures

Day Two Accomplishments

Day 2 is normally spent performing staff interviews, carrying out manual configuration checks, and reviewing the results of the previous evening's testing. Based on information gathered during the day, more detailed or system-specific scanning tools can be configured and scheduled for this evening's window. Day 2 accomplishments are typically these:

- Testing results review
- Staff interviews
- Manual configuration checks
- Continued off-hours vulnerability scanning configuration scheduling
- Continued password compliance testing procedures
- Continued network-sniffing procedures

Day Three Accomplishments

On Day 3, we continue reviewing the results of previous testing and staff interviews. We add the validation and analysis process for eliminating false positives. Normally, any scanning schedule for this evening is based on the need for secondary verification of findings between tools. Typical Day 3 accomplishments:

- Continued testing results review
- Continued staff interviews
- Manual configuration checks
- Validation and analysis
- Continued off-hours vulnerability scanning configuration scheduling
- Continued password compliance testing procedures
- Continued network-sniffing procedures

Day Four Accomplishments

The fourth day of the onsite evaluation is typically spent performing validation exercises and follow-up interviews as the validation process requires. At the same time, organization of the documented test results is started for reporting processes, as well as preparation of the out-brief materials. Typical Day 4 accomplishments are:

- Validation and analysis
- Follow-up interviews
- Documentation

Day Five Accomplishments

The last day is primarily dedicated to the out-brief. Depending on the size of the engagement and the number of findings, it can sometimes take most of the day to answer questions and detail specific recommended solutions, or debate the pros and cons of multiple solutions for a single finding. Often, the evaluation team provides hands-on assistance or guidance to help quickly mitigate more serious concerns. Typical Day 5 accomplishments:

- Out-briefing
- Mitigation assistance

In determining the schedule for more detailed technical testing of critical components (for example, Microsoft, Cisco, Solaris, and so on), the emphasis for time-intensive activities should be placed on priority systems as defined during the IAM process. Mapping this schedule into a basic timeline such as the one outlined here should give the plan a greater chance of success. On average, the technical evaluation team will usually consist of two or three members per customer site. This number will, of course, vary depending on specifics of each location, such as a data center vs. a remote user installation.

Flexibility and Adaptation

As a starting point, a completed IAM planning survey from previous efforts will help build our original schedule. Combined with configuration documentation, such as system inventories and network diagrams, there should be plenty of information to build a detailed picture of what to expect when you arrive onsite. Flexibility, however, is critical in many instances.

Depending on the amount of time that has elapsed between the IAM and the onsite evaluation of the IEM, changes are likely to have occurred. If the time period exceeds a month, it's a good idea to verify your understanding of the target system with the POC to try to avoid any surprises such as the installation of a new system or device your team has no experience with.

When you have a complete understanding of the *organization's* perception of the system, you can begin to evaluate whether that view really matches the actual implementation. Be prepared for surprises, such as systems being taken down for maintenance during your testing window or an IDS blocking your IP address. Even with properly planned schedules and communication, unplanned hindrances often occur. Be prepared to adjust the schedule as needed, and be careful not to set too aggressive a schedule.

Administrative Planning

Administrative planning sets the tone for project organization that allows your onsite efforts to focus on the technical evaluation and hopefully minimize any hiccups that may arise. Primarily, administrative planning is focused on the business needs of both the organization and the evaluating team:

- **Customer coordination**   We've said this before, but it needs to be emphasized: Communication between the team and the organization is integral to success. This includes scheduling of dates and times for meeting, testing windows, interviews, and the like. Similar to the IAM, data collection may occur throughout the process as new documents are created or updated by the organization.

- **Travel arrangements**   Often it's the mundane things that lead to problems with an evaluation, such as incorrectly booked travel arrangements (say, your plane landing an hour after the scheduled in-brief). Also consider making hotel accommodations. With technical testing, late hours and midnight trips to the organization's offices sometimes can occur. Because research is frequently an evening side product of the day's events, high-speed Internet access from a hotel room is often a "must have." In all planning, consider how a travel arrangement can help improve or hinder an evaluation team's efforts.

- **Checklists**   It's not a bad idea to create and use checklists based on each evaluation. This will help ensure the effectiveness of the evaluation team once it's onsite. Things you might include are security clearances (if needed), background checks, physical access to the organization (temporary badges), timeline of events, test plans, tool licensing, and organizational documentation (including IAM documents).

Technical Planning

Technical planning deals directly with the expected components for discovering vulnerabilities. The goal is to ensure that the evaluators don't have to do a last-minute scurry to put these together onsite:

- **Roles and responsibilities**   As part of building your evaluation team, you will want to base the functions on each evaluator's expertise. This process will, of course, be evaluation-specific based on the technologies in place at the organization. By splitting out the specific tasks and technologies, you can ensure that a networking specialist is reviewing scan results and configurations of Cisco routers and switches or conducting interviews with network operations.

- **Pre-visit technical review**   As part of the technical planning, documentation gathered during the IAM phases must be reviewed to assist in setting up timelines, schedules, experience required, and so on. More documentation may need to be requested depending on the length of time that has elapsed since the IAM. As well as planning and scheduling benefits, architecture and documentation reviews allow an evaluator to prioritize a focus area where, in his or her experience, vulnerabilities are more likely to occur.

- **Tool configuration**   Once you've reviewed available documentation and designated personnel with the required expertise, you can choose tools to perform the evaluation that map to the environment and experience of those involved. These tools and configurations should be tied directly back to the rules of engagement (ROE). Make sure that all tools to be used are approved by the customer for use on their systems. Many organizations have an approved security list for tools.

- **Support requirements**   Planning some of the basics up front will support your technical efforts. Make sure that you've made arrangements that assist rather than hinder your testing. For example, make sure you have required VLAN configurations or access to a data center, depending on what controls are in place between the location set aside for your use and the target system. If you'll be performing any dialup testing, ensure that analog lines are available for your use. In short, make sure all the supporting resources, such as enough network drops for your team, are taken care of in advance.

IAM vs. IEM

As mentioned previously, the IAM and the IEM are meant to be complementing endeavors. During the IAM, an organizational-level review of information systems and their respective security controls is conducted. Data types are evaluated and given impact priority rankings within the organization based on the three common security goals: confidentiality, integrity, and availability (CIA). Policies and procedures (P&P) are reviewed for effectiveness and appropriateness. Definitions for the impact of the failure of CIA are created on a High, Medium, and Low scale. Essentially, the planned and implemented security controls are assessed in conjunction with the value of the information as defined by the customer.

The IEM then steps in and takes the review deeper. The specific technical controls that have been mapped out are tested to ensure they are functioning as planned and expected. This task is performed with data gathered during the IAM process and incorporates both hands-on manual reviews and automated testing techniques. At minimum, the IAM pre-assessment site visit must be completed to perform an IEM. All the collected data and results tie directly back to the information documented in the IAM.

It is normal to have to perform additional documentation review during the onsite evaluation phase, especially if the IAM was performed months prior to the IEM. Documentation may have been updated or created in that timeframe, especially in regard to any IAM findings that were presented.

Vulnerability Definitions

The concept of vulnerabilities can sometimes be confusing because it has two similar yet separate meanings between the IAM and IEM. To understand the differences, we need to understand that there are two distinct sets of vulnerabilities — one for the IAM and one for the IEM. In essence, they are both weaknesses, yet they are categorized separately to show their impacts on each other.

IAM vulnerabilities are weaknesses within a process. They are usually discovered during documentation review or interviews during the IAM engagement. They relate directly to failures within an organization's P&P that can lead to the compromise of data security. One possible example is the lack of efficient contingency plan testing discovered when the organization admits that formal plans and test result documents are not created. In the event that a disaster occurs, confidence in the mitigating controls to continue or restore operations is at a low, which results in an IAM finding regarding contingency planning P&P.

IEM findings on the other hand, are weaknesses discovered during IEM testing of the system. These findings can be discovered through both manual and automated testing, but they deal specifically with the technical configuration and operation of the system or services. An example is the testing of DoS weaknesses in a router's operating system or configuration. Perhaps during that testing the device goes down, but the expected failover device does not step in and continue routing service. At this point, two IEM findings have been discovered: a weakness to DoS attacks and a failure in a technically based availability mitigation control.

We can easily see how the routing failover vulnerability the IEM discovered ties directly back to the IAM vulnerability discovered earlier in reference to contingency plan testing. For any security processes to be effective, the technical controls implemented must support the P&P enacted. We can likely tie the IEM DoS vulnerability back to an IAM patch management finding as well.

For now, we need to understand that the IAM and IEM vulnerabilities have distinct differences but are dependent on each other in much the same way a security manager may be dependent on a system administrator to implement appropriate controls that follow security guidelines. In the chapter discussing reporting, the methods used to correlate findings will be discussed in detail.

Onsite Evaluation Phase Objectives

The objectives for the onsite evaluation phase are rather simple: Verify that the technical implementation supports the organizational security model and hunt for weaknesses and information exposure. Of course, breaking it down into just these two elements may be oversimplifying things a bit, since the amount of work tends to be much more varied and diverse; however, all testing results lead directly back to these two concepts.

The easy portion is to identify technical weaknesses. These days, tools abound that can automate most of the technical testing you will need to perform a search for vulnerabilities. Even with detailed manual testing or the creation of specific security control test criteria, there is really only one focus: Find as many weaknesses as possible, and create solution recommendations to mitigate those weaknesses. Here it is easy to see a direct correlation between the security evaluation being performed and the overall goal of closing the security gap.

A difficulty often comes into play during the validation — that the technical controls support the organization's P&P. An evaluator needs to be able to focus directly on the technical vulnerabilities and their ramifications while keeping an eye on the bigger picture that may have led to the vulnerability. In this phase, a large group of activities are performed, but all with the same intentions.

Verification of "Known" and "Rogue" Components

Part of the process for ensuring that the technical implementation supports organizational P&P is to verify "known" components and discover any possible "rogue" components on the network. The system in question should be fully documented as part of any comprehensive security program. But remember, that documentation is only as helpful as it is accurate. To validate that the organizational processes for security are operating effectively, the devices and services available within the system need to match what is documented as being part of the functionality requirement for the system.

Undocumented devices, services, or rogue components constitute a threat to the system because they are not likely included in typical security testing boundaries nor taken into consideration in evaluating possible risks to a system. By identifying these components, the organization is given the opportunity to review, approve, and document any needed components while removing or disabling any unnecessary technology. Simply put, an unknown access point (either device or service) to the system is an unknown threat.

By the same token, components that have been removed from the system and not documented constitute a lack of consistency between the organization's understanding of the system and the actual technical implementation. This can lead to serious concerns that may need to be investigated, such as the theft of assets, loss of functionality, or diminishing effectiveness of controls. Of course, the seriousness will depend on the devices or services that are missing. It is not unheard of to discover that a failover router was removed and used elsewhere in an emergency situation while system owners continue to believe they have redundancy supporting their system.

TIP

Any findings of rogue or missing components also constitute a flaw in the organization's processes regarding configuration management and inventory management. In this case, we have used a technical evaluation activity to discover a process weakness in an organization security baseline area from the IAM.

Discovery of Technical Vulnerabilities

The discovery of technical vulnerabilities is performed by conducting the 10 IEM baseline activities. These are the areas that will be addresses in the process for finding technical weaknesses. One of the main objectives in the IAM is to bring to light weaknesses in an organization's security controls at an operational and management level. The IEM looks deeper into the technical level for ineffective security controls. Whereas all three types of control support each other directly, they require different skill sets and experience to manage.

The IEM baseline activities give a basic checklist of areas to test, based on common networking concerns and technologies, typical technical weaknesses, and the usual focus of malicious attackers. The IEM is not meant to simulate an attack or perform "red team" activities but to evaluate the current state of security controls and assist the organization in narrowing the security gap. The 10 baseline activities are discussed in greater detail later in this and subsequent chapters, but here is a quick list to help you familiarize yourself with them:

- Port scanning

- SNMP scanning

- Enumeration and banner grabbing

- Wireless enumeration

- Vulnerability scanning

- Host evaluation

- Network device analysis

- Password compliance testing

- Application-specific scanning

- Sniffing

One item that may help in this endeavor is the concept of *system mapping*. This begins with collecting the information about a system or its devices and building a map of known services, products, and configurations. System mapping is discussed in more detail in the next chapter. This is not an IEM process but a simple tool that has been used over the years to make sure that a detailed review of a system occurs.

Validation = Value Add?

No matter how a project is scoped or billed out, validation and analysis of technical data *must* be performed. This is not an option or a "value add," as might be seen in some instances, but mandatory. The organization must be given a specific set of vulnerabilities and recommendations that will improve their security posture. A list of "possible" vulnerabilities in a deliverable will, at best, slow the process for mitigating the actual nuggets of real weaknesses. At worst, it will lead to the dismissal of the findings as irrelevant, leaving possibly serious vulnerabilities unmitigated and open for exploitation.

Automated security-testing tools are great for increasing the efficiency of an evaluator, but they cannot replace that expertise. No tool will give 100-percent accurate results 100 percent of the time. An automated vulnerability scan of a 500-device network may produce thousands of possible vulnerabilities. Once these vulnerabilities are analyzed and validated by an experienced INFOSEC professional, that list of vulnerabilities may be slimmed down by 80 percent or more. Experienced evaluators are brought in for a reason. Their technical knowledge and understanding are required components of any successful evaluation.

Validation of findings can be performed in myriad ways. Manual system reviews, staff interviews, secondary tool testing, and, in some cases, exploitation can all be used to validate whether a vulnerability recognized by an automated tool is actually present. Exploitation may be out of scope in most instances, but a simple example is a Web-based directory-traversal vulnerability. The exploitation of this weakness by testing through a Web browser the ability to walk across unauthorized directories is not likely to cause any damage, whereas it will validate the finding and allow a screen capture for evidence.

Again, we must emphasize that to perform an IEM-compliant evaluation that provides an organization with quality deliverables, findings must be validated.

IEM Baseline Activities

The IEM sets forth a minimum baseline of 10 required activities, similar to the 18 required areas of review within the IAM baseline categories. Like the IAM baseline, these are the main categories of technical security controls where the required testing of control effectiveness must be completed.

Obviously, some specific tools are dedicated to performing evaluations within each of these areas, and some cover multiple areas. The only current NSA requirement is that at least one automated tool (or method) be used in evaluating the controls covered by each baseline activity. This does not mean a separate tool is required for each activity, but simply that each activity must be performed. For example, many vulnerability scanners in the market have incorporated additional functionality within the INFOSEC climate, such as password auditing, enumeration, or application-specific (normally Web related) auditing.

Nor does this mean that only one tool can be used per area when multiple tools may give a deeper technical review. In some instances, tools might overlap in areas, or different tools may be used against a separate resource in the system.

The evaluator is expected to bring knowledge of these automated tools into the process, with the capability to determine from the multiple tools available which ones fit the environment best. Each product has its own set strengths and weaknesses within the baseline activity it represents that may need to be addressed for each engagement. Here the IEM framework relies on evaluator expertise and experience to ensure the effective review process conducted by each activity.

WARNING

Many automated tools are discussed in this book; however, the NSA does *not* officially support or endorse *any* specific products. Discussions and examples using several different mainstream INFOSEC tools are used to help explain in greater detail the actions and expectations for the 10 IEM baseline activities.

The following IEM baseline activities are discussed in greater detail in the following chapters; we introduce them briefly here to tie together the expectations of onsite activities and give a broad overview of how they work together. They are as follows:

    I. Port scanning
    II. SNMP scanning
    III. Enumeration and banner grabbing
    IV. Wireless enumeration
    V. Vulnerability scanning
    VI. Host evaluation
    VII. Network device analysis
    VIII. Password compliance testing
    IX. Application-specific scanning
    X. Network sniffing

I. Port Scanning

Port scanning is a low-level review of the open ports on the target systems being tested. The main goal is to determine what TCP/IP ports are operating or "listening" on the systems being evaluated. After any organizational assessments and documentation review, this is normally the first activity performed. After the completion of this activity, a system mapping that lists all the open ports per host should be documented and available for further use in the remaining activities. This mapping can then be used to help streamline the remaining functions as well as assist in the first-step validation techniques, which are discussed later in this chapter.

The information gathered during this process can be used to investigate unauthorized or unknown services that have not been documented or do not provide a function of the organization. An example is to discover the multiple management services that tend to be installed by default on many operating systems but are either not used or have been replaced in functionality by other services, but not disabled. These undocumented services can often lead to providing system configuration information to anonymous remote attackers that can assist them in planning more detailed system attacks.

TIP

Within IP networking, various remote communication services are separated from interfering with each other by operating over a specific port. Combining an IP address with a specific port number creates what is commonly referred to as a *socket address* to define, separate, and manage network connections based on the service in use. HTTP, for example, normally connects over port 80, which allows us to define a target for communications with an IP address and port number.

Common services tend to run over generally accepted standard ports. These, referred to as the *well-known* ports, range between 0 and 1023. Although services may be assigned to a well-known port, it has become common practice to deviate from these standards for varying reasons. A system administrator might have multiple instances of the same service running on different ports or may have moved a sensitive service to a less common private port in an attempt to hide the service.

For more detailed information regarding port descriptions, please refer to the IANA port assignments at www.iana.org/assignments/port-numbers.

II. SNMP Scanning

Simple Network Management Protocol (SNMP) scanning is the search for a specific management service, supported by most operating systems and network devices. SNMP is a basic protocol used to support the management of network resources. Most SNMP implementations use UDP and TCP over port 161 and 162 for communications. This ties into port scanning as being an investigation into one of the most commonly used management services for gaining more information about the system target. The amount of information freely given away by a system with a default read community string can be staggering in many cases, reaching tens of thousands of lines of data. Obviously, this is not a service that should be easily available to those with less than honorable intentions.

In many cases, systems with SNMP enabled also support actual change capabilities through this service for remote users who know the actual write community string. This can include the functionality to change interface configurations, account settings, trust relationships, permissions, or other operational variables based on the system implementation. Some question whether this functionality within the SNMP implementation should be used at all due to some of the security concerns inherent to the service.

Some of the information garnered through the evaluation of SNMP services can be added to the system mapping to help further delineate the process for discovering weaknesses as we move forward through the baseline activities.

TIP

There is a lot of information on the Web regarding SNMP and its uses and security capabilities. Due in large part to SNMP's history of insecurities, you can find a multitude of articles on vulnerabilities and exploits. If any SNMP is located on a system, it's recommended that you research the vendor-specific implementations to better understand its functionalities. Because all SNMP products support differing functionality, understanding what that functionality is will help you determine the actual impact a vulnerability may have on the system.

III. Enumeration and Banner Grabbing

Enumeration and banner grabbing are the processes involved in gathering more information about the services running on the system. After completing a port scan, identified services should have been mapped for further review. With that information, the next step in discovering weaknesses is to discover what actual application or vendor product is providing that service.

Many vendors provide the same service capabilities with differing operations. Although they support the same functionality and often will be vulnerable to the same security risks, functionality implementation differences lead to vendor-specific weaknesses. With this in mind, we can perform testing on specific systems for known vulnerabilities that would actually affect that system. A common example is to prune the list of vulnerabilities you would test against a Microsoft Windows 2000 Server to exclude vulnerabilities that affect only devices running the Cisco IOS.

This activity or task is often referred to as *fingerprinting* the system. By identifying the vendors that have provided the service functionality, the underlying operating system can be determined, or at least narrowed down. For example, if you find Internet Information Server 6.0 through banner enumeration, you can combine that with other information in your system mapping, such as the Microsoft DS running on TCP port 445 for the same system to provide a fingerprint. At this point, the specific system will most likely be a Microsoft Windows product. With this information, you can begin tailoring your next level of testing as well as validate configuration documents and diagrams that have already been received.

IV. Wireless Enumeration

Wireless enumeration is a little bit different from the other enumeration activities due to the fact that you are trying to discover weakly controlled access points to the network and data exposure points.

The most common weaknesses in wireless networking are based within the protocol or due to configuration issues. Using automated tools, you can identify wireless devices and then investigate them for inappropriate configurations. Commonly, unknown wireless devices can lead to unprotected or unauthorized entry points within a network.

The goal with wireless enumeration is to identify the weaknesses that have become incredibly prolific in today's technology environments. Wireless technology provides such flexible data delivery possibilities at such a low price that it has widely infiltrated home, government, and corporate environments without full attention being paid to the security concerns it represents.

News reports on *war driving*, the hobby of searching and cataloging wireless networks while driving through a neighborhood or region, has helped raise the concerns about wireless network security. It has also introduced litigation regarding the act of recording wirelessly transmitted data and the unauthorized use of systems. Currently, many people see this act in a bad light, even when it is performed as a security evaluation function. For these reasons, the IEM determines that this activity is optional although highly recommended. As with all baseline activities, make sure the customer understands the activity. When you perform this function, be sure to take all proper care with any captured data, and be wary of wireless devices outside the scope of the evaluation.

NOTE

Generally, the information just presented refers to any network wireless network based in the IEEE 802.11 family, commonly referred to as WiFi. Though the standards have been around a while and have been adhered to pretty regularly, the base insecurities in the 802.11 family to date have led many vendors to incorporate their own proprietary security controls. Most of these have been shown to be just as insecure as WiFi, but research on the platforms in place will need to be conducted to determine if there are any weaknesses outside the standard WEP or configuration aspects.

V. Vulnerability Scanning

Vulnerability scanning is the next baseline activity, using, when appropriate, a system mapping from previous activities or at least incorporating the information already learned. Through vulnerability scanning, targets are tested for possible known vulnerabilities.

Each evaluation scenario is likely to have a separate defining requirement for specific tool configurations. There could be availability requirements that limit the amount of DoS testing that can be performed on the system, for instance. Perhaps a specific vulnerability test is known to restart services that require manual intervention. The specific aspects of how this baseline activity is performed are left up to the evaluators, who bring the technical background and expertise in using these tools.

WARNING

Remember that all security scanning tools can only look for "known" vulnerabilities. Not all weaknesses in every product have been identified; therefore, you can never guarantee that any system is 100-percent secure. No security scanning tool can test for 100 percent of all known vulnerabilities, either, so you cannot even guarantee a system is 100-percent secure from all known vulnerabilities.

Since most vulnerability-scanning tools use a different database, it has become common practice to use at least two different tools during this effort. With the availability of open source tools, this should not incur any additional licensing fees and will also help validate the findings process.

VI. Host Evaluation

Host evaluation is the process of evaluating a specific host for weaknesses in configuration or patch level. Configuration mistakes are a very common source of attacks and unauthorized accesses and must be reviewed carefully. This process can be done using custom automated scripts, commercial and open source products, or a good, old-fashioned manual review.

Whether this activity is performed using a common configuration standard such as NIST or NSA guidelines or using the organization's custom in-house requirements, it is a must for all evaluations due to the wide-ranging effects of configuration errors. Hopefully, the organization has in-house guidance that has already been reviewed against industry standards or best practices, allowing the evaluator to tie technical results directly back to an operational control. The IEM stipulates that all critical components must be tested, whereas other systems may only be a sampling. A typical stance is to evaluate all servers and sample a base of workstations.

VII. Network Device Analysis

Network device analysis uses many of the other IEM baseline activities to focus on the high-assurance security components of a system. These devices are normally perimeter units that make up that hard exterior in the description of many IT systems — a hard candy shell with a soft, chewy center. Since more is expected of these devices, it is only appropriate to focus on them when performing a security evaluation.

Along with performing a system mapping, vulnerability scan, and other compliance on these devices, you'll want to take a step back and review the overall architecture. Verify that clear-text protocols are not enabled for managing the devices, or that DMZ connections really provide a staging area to separate public access from internal access. The lack of an IDS system may not be a technical finding, but if warranted, it can be a technical recommendation. For this activity, we want to review with a top-down approach to make sure that expectations of the perimeter are being met.

Performing host evaluations on high-assurance devices is a must. Manual reviews of configurations are normally not intensive, time-consuming efforts, as they might be with operating systems, so it is recommended that you validate the configurations by hand, even if an automated tool is used to verify that these devices are properly configured to only pass or allow accepted traffic.

VIII. Password Compliance Testing

Password compliance testing is the validation of the organization's password policy. Most systems include the ability to define password requirements for users based on this policy. This testing is to ensure that technical controls support the policy and that they are not bypassed by system or individual accounts.

Remember that many organizational policies require (or at least they should require) that no passwords be transmitted or stored in clear text, so any Telnet or similarly unencrypted protocols, if used, should be considered a violation of this policy. Also, remember to appropriately schedule the timing of this activity because it normally will take longer than any other testing performed.

IX. Application-Specific Scanning

Application-specific scanning takes vulnerability scanning from a generalized system review to a more detailed, service-specific testing level. This activity is based on the organization's prioritization of the applications. Applications may include custom in-house systems, commercial databases, or clusters of single functioning resources such as Web sites and e-mail. This activity is very flexible based on environmental needs. Application-specific scanning can include limited testing as may be performed by general vulnerability scanners, custom application-specific vulnerability scanners, automated or manual configuration reviews, or any combination of these.

Code review may be an acceptable option as well, but considering the timeframe of an IEM, this would likely have to be done in a limited capacity or separated into another project. There are many ways to perform this activity, but employing an evaluator experienced in the application is important for obtaining a deeply detailed review.

X. Network Sniffing

Network sniffing is a way to see what is really traveling across the organization's infrastructure. Like password compliance testing, this activity can be time consuming and should be scheduled early in the onsite evaluation phase. It will also require a good bit of involvement from the local technical staff to mitigate the issues switched and routed networks place on sniffing in general. You need to remember to document your procedures for this activity in the ROE, to alleviate the concerns about data removal and privacy impact.

Due to the complex nature of this activity, the actual requirements are very flexible. The amount of data review required based on the environment may require it to be only a minimal activity to verify that routers or firewalls are only redirecting traffic as intended. One solution could be to place a sniffer behind a firewall being tested, to see what gets through. Another might be to validate the concerns of Telnet being used to manage a system by capturing a login session. These types of activities can be performed without the overhead of forwarding all traffic to a specific device, causing a large overhead on network devices and systems. Perform this activity as is appropriate for the environment.

Other Activities

The 10 IEM baseline activities set a standard minimum of activities and specific security controls for evaluating. Many other methods and concerns need to be evaluated on a case-by-case basis for the organization. Some of these methods or activities are not included as a part of the baseline due to their invasive nature. For example, DoS and war dialing are not standard requirements due to the amount of load they may place on a system as well as the opportunity for downtime they could represent. A detailed code review of an application will likely incur many more man hours than an IEM has scheduled and thus might be best served as a follow-on or additional project.

Penetration testing requires a very detailed level of expertise and often leaves the target system more vulnerable to exploit during and after the activity. Many exploits on a system include uploading root kits, backdoors, and loggers. One example is uploading the script *cmdasp.asp* to a vulnerable Microsoft Windows Internet Information Server (IIS). Although this exploit grants the attacker access to a shell prompt on the target, it also leaves that shell prompt available to anyone else with a Web browser.

These activities are not specific requirements, but an organization or environment may have an appropriate need for them. You can include these types of activities as needed to provide a valuable deliverable. An example is to perform war dialing on a dialup system or a separated range of phone numbers that the organization confirms will not interfere with daily operations.

The Role of CVE and CAN

The CVE project is meant to be a method for providing a standardized naming and information convention for discovered security vulnerabilities. Such a convention allows for cross-referencing a vulnerability across multiple vendor products and security tools. One need only look at the number of buffer overflow vulnerabilities that have been found for Sendmail over the years to realize that a method was needed to categorize and differentiate between distinct vulnerabilities that have similar exploits or impacts. For this reason, the CVE list is meant to be a dictionary of weaknesses, not a vulnerability database. Each weakness is treated like a word in a dictionary and details a specific criterion for information.

CVE identifiers (similar to serial numbers) are easy to recognize and understand. The identifier CVE-2001-0072 notes that this weakness is an approved CVE finding and was marked for review in 2001 with a unique number of 0072. On the CVE Web site, you can search on that name and discover its history, issue, and references. A weakness with CAN as the opening identifier — for example, CAN-2001-0073 — is considered to be a candidate for inclusion into the list. All the same information is available for candidates; they have simply not been officially approved and may be modified in the future.

The CVE list also takes into consideration that not all weaknesses are vulnerabilities and has set aside a classification for exposures. These are not inherent vulnerabilities but rather weaknesses that may have little to no impact on an organization's environment. An example is having null sessions anonymously available on a Microsoft Windows environment. Although this is not a true vulnerability, it can assist a user in gathering more information that can help discover vulnerabilities on a system. The IEM ties each weakness back to an information criticality, to give the organization a true understanding of the way it could impact the system.

For greater usability and reference, the IEM requires all available findings to be labeled with a CVE compliant identifier. Obviously not all findings will have a relevant CVE identifier, but label the ones that do. Doing so assists the organization with mitigation and priority concerns as well as incorporating a reusability feature so that the organization can review past evaluations and more easily research and understand findings and recommendations.

The CVE list is free, maintained by the MITRE Corporation and funded by the U.S. Department of Homeland Security. MITRE has granted the IEM course materials CVE-compatible compliance. Many security tools have also been granted compatibility and can assist in maintaining a CVE-compliant deliverable product for the customer organization. Although the methodology does not promote any tools at all, those that are CVE compatible make the evaluating team's job easier.

The In-Brief

The in-brief meeting occurs on the first day of the onsite evaluation phase and continues the process of customer communication and management buy-in begun during the IAM. All members of the evaluation team are present, as usually are the system owners, management staff, and the organization's technical staff. The IEM process requires no specific format other than the review of the TEP. At this point, the TEP has been completed and can help serve as a road map for much of the meeting.

As a business process, you might want to ensure that the TEP is signed and dated during the in-briefing, especially if any changes have occurred. Even if the TEP has already been signed, this provides another step of due diligence in that it is presented and approved onsite, where the scope of work should be stable, since you are now dealing with actual accountable time and resources. The focus of the meeting should be to review the evaluation plan that has been agreed to as well as several overall project aspects. The in-brief should:

- Reintroduce the goals and objectives for the evaluation
- Act as an introduction to the evaluation team
- Confirm schedules and plans
- Provide an overview of accomplishments to date (including IAM activities)
- Reiterate management buy-in
- Focus on technical staff buy-in
- Describe the evaluation methodology
- Review the tools and processes for evaluation

The culture within the organization will help to determine the formality of the briefing. This includes the actual process of the meeting, such as PowerPoint presentations, open discussions, Q&A sessions, or any other methods of conducting the meeting. Appropriate attire should match the organization's expectations for formality along with the other aspects of the meeting. After presenting the TEP, the evaluation team may also discover new political issues that may present a cultural concern for the evaluation, which should then be addressed before the close of the in-brief.

Presenting the TEP

Presenting the TEP is a must for the in-brief, and it is a great tool for providing a basic agenda. The TEP review will help to ensure that there are no misunderstandings or miscommunications regarding the process and the goals of the on-site evaluation phase. Make sure to cover each portion of the TEP, and to ensure agreement, it is sometimes easier to make this more of a discussion than a presentation.

- **Points of contact**   Make sure that all appropriate parties have the correct contact information for both the evaluation team members and the organization. Technical testing often leads to a schedule that is "off-peak" rather than normal business hours. If a system is inadvertently brought down, the organization should be notified immediately to rectify the situation, or the organization may need to contact an evaluator to stop a scheduled and unattended scan. Physical access to segments or after-hours access to facilities may be required on an ad hoc basis.

- **Methodology overview**   Here the process of the IEM needs to be described in an "executive summary" type of format. Explain the goals and the reasons for performing this evaluation. A discussion of the expectations and planned accomplishments will help solidify the process in the minds of those who may not have been involved with either the previously conducted IAM or the IEM to date. For the technical administrators present, a discussion of the tools that will be used and some of the basic configurations is appropriate. This helps involve the technical staff as well as offering a "last chance" opportunity for someone to speak up about known issues. For example, previous audits might have pointed out that a Nessus scan will disable the organization's 3COM routers. Rather than bring down the network, a finding can be documented at this point regarding those devices and minimize downtime for both the organization and the evaluation team as they await full network operations capabilities to continue testing.

- **Organization and system criticality**   Review the criticality matrices of the systems and the organization. Many times, the technical staff that is responsible for maintaining security controls on the systems might not have been involved with the part of the IAM process that maps out the business concerns and priorities. This will help them understand the value of the data and systems that are being evaluated. Combined with the definitions created by the organization for impact (high, medium, low), the technical staff that will be responsible for mitigating any findings will be able to understand and follow a prioritization list of technical findings that are tied directly to the value of the data or the system. At this point, review of the system description will help verify components for technical testing, especially if the plans call for deconstructed testing based on operating system, application, system, or the like.

- **Detailed network information**   This is the comprehensive description of the networks or systems to be evaluated. A review with the technical staff to confirm the evaluating team's understanding of the technical configurations of the system to be tested needs to occur. This review should include IP ranges, or subnets, specific target host IP addresses, and correct contact information for technical administrators for these networks or devices in case of an outage or error.

- **Customer concerns**   Reiterate the logic or reason that an IEM is being conducted. Why did the organization request an IEM? Make sure to cover all concerns that carry over from the IAM as well as any new technical concerns that have arisen for the IEM. Also include any concerns of the evaluation team regarding the technical testing based on the current understanding of the system.

- **Customer constraints**   Verify that everyone is in agreement in terms of any constraints being placed on the evaluation team. These constraints should include any applicable constraints identified in the IAM process and any specific technical constraints identified for the IEM. Include any constraints that the evaluating team may be placing on the testing as well, such as refusal to perform exploitation testing based on legal liability concerns.

- **Rules of engagement**   The ROE is a lengthy product, but there is a lot of information here. The TEP acts as a high-level overview of the process and objectives, whereas the ROE gets down and dirty with the details of exactly what you will be doing on the organization's systems. If technical staff members are getting involved for the first time, expect a lot of questions. This is your chance to really get buy-in from the technical members of the organization, who are likely feeling apprehensive about your visit and the actions you will be taking. Depending on how detailed your ROE is, you might also need to discuss several procedural items regarding what is expected not only of the evaluation team but the administrators as well. Exact procedures for password compliance testing and any other testing that may require the evaluators be granted elevated privileges should be documented and agreed on by the organization. When the organization's technical staff is comfortable with the process, or at least understands it, things will go much more smoothly when it's time to actually perform those tests.

- **Coordination agreements**   Any other concerns or details need to be reviewed with the onsite staff — even the basics of discussing the level of detail in which to describe findings and solutions. It's not unheard of to have an organization request greater detail on how a finding may affect a priority system, or to have a new administrator request more information about solutions than others. Some organizations are required to respond to all security evaluations and have the evaluation teams validate their planned approach for mitigation. Reviewing this type of arrangement will remind technical staff that they will be expected to respond in a timely manner.

- **Letter of authorization**   The LOA is the definitive document detailing the work to be completed. It should be reviewed with the technical staff, if for no other reason than to demonstrate the management level buy-in of the project.

- **Timeline of events**   No matter how well communicated and planned the evaluation, changes in the timeline of onsite activities are common. The more granular a schedule becomes with a large number of parties involved, the more likely times or dates are to slip. As discussed earlier, flexibility is a necessity for the onsite evaluation phase. Review the timeline carefully to ensure that all parties who are responsible for assisting with the efforts are going to be available as planned or have backups ready. Events may cause the timeline to be affected, but they can be addressed as they arise as long as everyone is in agreement with the latest schedule.

Remember that the TEP is a living document throughout the course of the engagement. The onsite evaluation phase is normally fast and furious, so expect changes that could require you to update the TEP. Be sure to get the appropriate sign-offs when this occurs and continue moving forward.

By following the TEP as an agenda of topics for the in-brief, you can review and discuss the major points of the engagement with the facilitators for the onsite evaluation phase.

Encourage questions throughout the meeting to ensure that everyone is on the same page before you begin. During the IEM, there is a constant need to set and maintain expectations; the in-brief is a great tool for taking care of this issue.

Notes from the Underground

Operational Security Teams

Don't forget to address operational security (OpSec) concerns when you're getting detailed technical contact information. Not only does the system administrator need to be aware of time windows and the source address of the system performing the testing, but so does the organization's OpSec team. Whatever name the organization's OpSec team goes by (CERT, IT Security Operations, Security Operations Center, or something else), whoever in the organization performs the duty of monitoring and responding to security threats and incidents needs to be made aware of the evaluation efforts.

If security monitoring and response are outsourced to a third party, be very careful and very specific to make sure that your activities will not result in a third-party response, such as dispatch of armed guards or police officers. This would be a perfect time to verify that you have a copy of your LOA as well!

If part of your evaluation involves testing the response capabilities, plan to put this early in your schedule so that you can get your introductions out of the way quickly! After that, you need to involve the OpSec teams so that they don't initiate response procedures based on your activities.

Cultural Sensitivity

One of the concerns to remember for the onsite evaluation phase is the cultural sensitivity required of the evaluation team. Systems administrators could take offense that outsiders are being brought in to perform a security evaluation, even if they perform their jobs admirably. Some may take it as an affront that management or their superiors don't trust them, or they could simply see it as a waste of time in their already overloaded schedules of maintaining systems. Others may worry about what the findings could mean for them.

In the in-brief, take the opportunity to help them understand the need for and logic behind unbiased security reviews. Reiterate the fact that the evaluation is intended to help the organization improve its security by using experienced INFOSEC professionals to review current configurations of the system, with a goal of providing mitigation recommendations before someone more unsavory exploits them.

Assure them that the IEM does not report *who* did what, why, or when. The IEM reports weaknesses based on what is currently present and does not make an effort to attribute those findings to any administrators. The concept of nonattribution is practiced in the IEM to help staff feel more comfortable with the activities that are taking place. The IEM's goal is to help reduce the security gap, not point out incompetent staff.

Another staff concern will be the elevated privileges that may be required for the "outsiders" to perform the evaluation. Any administrators should be concerned about this, because they have the same goal as you: to protect their system. Depending on the level of trust between the teams, such as internal organization reviewing department versus a third-party consultant, this concern can fluctuate widely. If there is deep concern, try to alleviate those fears through a set of procedures that don't compromise the results but may require additional time or input from the organization's technical staff. A good example is to decide who exports a copy of the SAM database off a Microsoft Windows server for password compliance testing and how that file is handled. It takes little effort on the part of the evaluation team to monitor the technical staff exporting this file to a disk and then be escorted to a physically controlled point where the testing occurs on an evaluator's system specifically set aside for this task. This prevents the evaluator from accessing the data without escort and ensures that the function occurs on an evaluator-controlled system.

If you make the technical staff a part of the process, their comfort level will increase, allowing them to be more open and helpful with the evaluation. We want to include the people who are responsible for maintaining these systems, and they in turn will hopefully want to include the tenets of security in their daily activities. The evaluation team is not just performing security work. They are acting in a "sales and marketing" capacity to constantly manage and maintain customer expectations. By realizing the issues the customer deals with, being sympathetic to those issues, and working around them without causing a major headache, the evaluator can perform his or her duties while helping the staff understand the value of the work being performed.

Summary

After reading this chapter, a basic understanding of the background behind the IEM baseline activities should be achieved, as well as the nontechnical factors for ensuring that those activities are a success. This chapter focused on many of those nontechnical factors, such as buy-in and expectations. Few things can ruin an evaluation more quickly than customer misunderstanding or dissatisfaction, and although these can easily be avoided through communication, it takes constant attention to maintain everyone's focus.

Detailed preparation and planning will help make an evaluation successful as well. You already laid much of the groundwork for this in the IAM process with the customer. By taking what was created in the IAM and successfully using the TEP and ROE, you can create a very detailed plan of attack to ensure the most effective use of time while onsite. Since this time is packed with activities, often leaving little time to breathe, that schedule will be paramount to creating a quality deliverable in the final report.

In keeping with the concept of getting the most possible use out of the product, compatibility with the CVE list is mandatory. This will make the final report usable to the customer long after the evaluation team has left the building. This works to your benefit as well in that if you're a consultant, you'll want your work to stand on its own so that customer follow-up calls are for assistance in mitigation or follow-on work, not for interpreting your documentation because details were not included or were difficult to research.

Remember that attention to detail also means attention to the customer. This includes acknowledging their concerns, constraints, and any sensitivity issues. The more your actions are perceived as helping, the more relevant and detailed your findings will be. Adapting to the environment and "working within the system" are attributes that will make this evaluation successful. The key best practices for accomplishing this goal that you should take away from this chapter are:

- Get technical staff buy-in.
- Pay attention to schedule and plan details.
- Be flexible in all aspects of the onsite evaluation phase.
- Incorporate CVE identifiers.
- Maintain a detailed technical focus through the 10 IEM baseline activities.
- Keep a big-picture focus to incorporate IAM criticalities and priorities.
- Validate all findings.
- Adhere to the TEP.
- Be aware of cultural sensitivities.
- Don't forget the little things.

## Chapter 19

Network Discovery Activities

Solutions in this chapter:

- **Goals and Objectives**

- **Tool Basics**

- **Port Scanning**

- **SNMP Scanning**

- **Enumeration and Banner Grabbing**

- **Wireless Enumeration**

☑ **Summary**

Introduction

In this chapter, we'll discuss the network discovery portion of the onsite evaluation phase. We'll also see some brief introductions to multiple tools available for use in each of the IEM baseline activities covered by the network discovery stage and some of their expected or common uses. Network discovery activities include the first four baseline activities: port scanning, SNMP scanning, enumeration and banner grabbing, and wireless enumeration.

For port scanning, we'll discuss some of the basics of how a port scanner works, why we are performing this activity, and what we're looking for in the results. We'll compare some utilities to see what options and features are out there, to help determine which tools might be better suited to each scenario.

In the second activity, we'll look very briefly at how SNMP operates and some of the things that make it an important service to evaluate for security purposes. We'll get a look at how some network management utilities can be used for security testing purposes, and we'll review other tools designed specifically for evaluating SNMP services, with security in mind.

The basic methods and reasons for performing enumeration are discussed, with the introduction of tools that include manual command-line interface (CLI) testing as well as automated graphical user interface (GUI) utilities. This activity builds off previous activities and takes things farther to discover more information about the target system.

The two most popular tools for performing wireless enumeration are discussed, as is the impact of exposed wireless services. Wireless enumeration has many aspects that must be considered before testing begins, and these should be documented and agreed to with the customer. The most common concerns are introduced, with recommendations on how to address them.

The onsite phase of the IEM relies very heavily on the evaluator's understanding of security concepts and technical issues. This chapter is meant to simply provide a framework for the activities that the IEM expects the evaluator to perform and to facilitate the use of discovered information. Documenting the results of these tests into a single system mapping for the organization's records and the evaluator's process management is covered for each activity. Our goal is to tie the activities together and provide a reference table of activities and results.

Goals and Objectives

The primary goal for the network discovery activities is to learn and document as much of the architecture and system configuration as possible. The two main tasks for mapping the evaluation system are discovery and enumeration. Through the use of automated tools, we want to discover all available resources and services and determine as much information about them as possible. This will help the evaluator to define further detailed testing into suspected exposure areas later in the onsite visit as well as verify that the organization's documentation matches its implementation.

For this methodology to work, the evaluator needs to be able to focus on the system as a whole, at the same time inspecting the smallest configuration details. The IEM requires a customized report, based on the organization's criticality measurements. Although the evaluator is performing each activity, he or she must constantly assess how each weakness may affect the security of the system as well as how a recommended solution may affect that system's operation and the organization's ability to implement it. The strength of the IEM lies in the evaluator performing the work, not any specific tool used to address each required activity.

Notes from the Underground…

System Terminology

One thing to remember while you're reading this chapter is the meaning of the term *system*. In the context of the IAM and IEM, a system is not limited to a single server or IP address but often refers to a collection of devices and data flow. For the purposes of this chapter, the term can be more closely related to the boundaries of the evaluation target.

For example, we might be evaluating two separate systems with hundreds of devices. The first system provides a certain business function and house-specific data sets. This system is limited across a few servers that provide front-end client services and back-end data management. These servers are clustered into a single major application (MA), and the boundary for the system crosses all the servers within. A second system might be the local area network (LAN) and all the client personal computers (PCs). This system can be classified as a general support system (GSS) and include routers, switches, etc.

When speaking about a specific device, we use more detailed terms such as *server, router,* or *resource*. The term *system* should be construed at the target evaluation boundaries.

The classifications GSS and MA are taken from the National Institute of Standards and Technology (NIST) documentation. You can find more information regarding NIST security guidance and standards at the NIST Computer Security Resource Center (CSRC), http://csrc.nist.gov/. The IAM and IEM map very well to NIST practices.

Results as Findings and Evaluation Task Attributes

During the network discovery, most concerns or findings are not usually true vulnerabilities. More often than not, those findings come from tools or manual investigations later in the onsite evaluation phase. The results or findings from the network discovery activities primarily fall into two categories, misconfigurations and differences in documentation, as well security exposures.

The IAM focuses mostly on the documentation of the system and the overriding organizational goals, whereas the IEM is meant to verify that those objectives are met and discover technical vulnerabilities. Part of the requirement for the IEM is to report all inconsistencies between the system mappings created from the network discovery activities and the organization's system documentation. This is where we either validate the organization's perception of the system or adjust that perception to match reality.

As discussed in a previous chapter, there is an important difference between a vulnerability and an exposure. During later IEM baseline activities, the focus of the evaluation shifts more to the discovery of weaknesses, whereas in the network discovery stage, the focus is predominantly on exposures. One of the things to keep in mind is that during the IAM processes, the evaluators should have learned detailed information regarding the purpose and function of the system. Discovered processes operating on the system that aren't required for operation are not technically vulnerabilities; they can, however, be considered exposures and should be reported as findings, with the recommendation of disabling those processes.

Services that are required for operation that present an exposure should also be reported, with a recommendation for an alternate solution. A common example would be the discovery of the telnet service running on a host. Considering that telnet transmits all data in clear text, including logins and passwords, the service inherently presents an exposure. The recommendation of migrating to SSH might be an acceptable solution to the customer, ensuring that all data is encrypted between the host and clients.

This is an area in the IEM baseline activities that requires a great amount of evaluator expertise. Unlike many vulnerability scanning tools that do the work for you, during the network discovery stage the evaluator must have a solid understanding of many common protocols and services. It is up to the evaluator to notice possible exposures and identify how they could affect the system.

System Mapping

A system mapping is not a required aspect of the NSA IEM; however, it is an excellent tool for documenting the work performed during the network discovery activities (see Table 19.1). By combining all the information gathered during these activities into a single document, you will create a mapping of a system's technical resources and services that most organizations do not have.

This document can then be used to verify much of the system configuration documentation that was reviewed during the IAM process. This allows you to trace back unknown or rogue services and resources that might be running against system policy. This helps the organization catch default services that often sneak past an administrator when he or she is hardening a server. It also helps provide a system baseline for the customer, which is often hard to find.

A system mapping can also assist the evaluator in determining where extra attention should be concentrated. From the completed document and even a partially completed mapping, it is usually easy to see where notoriously weak services are waiting for an attacker. This is the first step in identifying the "low-hanging fruit," or easily exploited vulnerabilities.

Table 19.1 IEM System Mapping

ABC123 IEM System Mapping					10/29/2004
XYZ Consulting			POC: Johnny Reboot		(555) 123.4567
Active Hosts:			Address Ranges:		192.168.1.0/24 172.16.2.0/24
IP Address / Device Name	Ports	Identified Services	Detected OS	Notes	
WiFi MAC Address	Type	Crypt	SSID	Discovered IP Address	Notes

Tool Basics

The variety of tools covered in this chapter range from incredibly simple and easy to the complex and advanced. Though most of the tools can be used with little experience, it is not recommended that an evaluator use these tools without experience and a solid knowledge of the tools, what they are trying to accomplish, and what the results mean. This chapter is meant to give a simple introduction to many of the more common available options, with the expectation that the reader has some knowledge of networking and TCP/IP.

It is highly recommended that readers download and review the tools that interest them, reading the included documentation and testing results to get a better understanding of how the tools operate and how they could affect an organization's systems. Obviously, not everyone runs the same base operating system for their security evaluation devices, so we're included tools for both the Microsoft Windows and UNIX platforms for all baseline activities. Most UNIX platform utilities also work on the new Mac OS X with minor adjusting, and, with just a little Internet searching you'll find guides for most tools. It is common practice, however, for many evaluators to use multiple platforms for their work so as not to limit themselves to a smaller set of options. The IEM does not make this a requirement, but as a business practice, Security Horizon requires all evaluators to be experienced in both the Windows and UNIX platforms, to maximize efficiency and customer results. In fact, Security Horizon standardizes on multiple toolkits per evaluator, to increase evaluator efficiency by allowing time-consuming evaluation tools to run on one unit. This allows the evaluator to perform checks, reporting, validation, and shorter testing from an available device.

The number of security tools available to perform these and other activities is much too large to include them all in this book. We chose tools based primarily on their prevalence in the industry. Some are rather new, and some are rather old, but the important thing is they get the job done.

Expected Usage and Requirements

The IEM expectations for the tools used are rather simple. At least one tool must be used within each of the baseline activities. Manual configuration checks can be considered a tool, depending on the evaluator and the organization's needs, although automated tools normally make things faster, with manual checks performed for more sensitive concerns.

Many activities justify the need to use more than one tool, either for different testing methods and test databases or to assist in validating the results reported each tool. Beyond the need to address each baseline activity, there are no other requirements. It is recommended that evaluators understand a wide variety of tools so that they can match the organization's needs to the tool that performs the best in that environment.

At the same time, one tool might cover multiple baseline activities. As discussed in this chapter, several port-scanning tools also have options that enable the evaluator to incorporate enumeration activities. This is an acceptable use of tools, as long as they are configured and run to support both activities.

Most tools offer differing levels of testing and reporting options. The evaluator's expertise is critical in determining the tools that fit the organization's environment. If an organization has banned the use of SNMP, there might not be a need for extensive SNMP evaluation; a quick scan to test for SNMP could be sufficient. At that point, any devices with SNMP enabled are automatically considered a finding because its mere presence is unacceptable to the organization. Conversely, if an organization is concerned about a new wireless networking implementation and security threats it could represent, a more detailed evaluation, including testing encryption strength, might be warranted. The IEM relies on the evaluator's knowledge and experience to make the call as to which tools best support each activity in any given scenario.

> **WARNING**
>
> Many automated tools are discussed in this book; however, the NSA does *not* officially support or endorse *any* specific products, brands, or platforms. Discussions and examples using several different mainstream INFOSEC tools are used here to help explain in greater detail the actions and expectations for the 10 IEM baseline activities.

Port Scanning

For port scanning, we use a variety of automated tools to discover the open ports responding on each of the resources in a system. In this, the first of the IEM baseline activities, what we are really trying to do is just determine "what's out there." By this point in the methodology, you should have already read several documents explaining the function of the system, the services it uses to perform those functions, the management services in place, or any number of configuration documents referring to the system's technical implementation. With port scanning, we start the network discovery portion of activities to see whether all those documents are accurate.

In a perfect world, the results of this activity should be exactly in line with the documentation. By not documenting the allowed and required services in the system, the organization could be leaving itself open to exposure. The administrative staff won't have instructions on what is acceptable. If the administrators are not informed that, for example, Telnet is not an acceptable system management tool, you could have logins and passwords floating in cleartext across the network, or even worse, on the Internet.

Port scanning is also a way to identify services that have inherent weaknesses, usually recognized only by experienced INFOSEC professionals. Through port scanning, these questionable services can be documented and marked for further research by either more detailed tools or manual configuration checks. An example is SSH; although SSH is a much better solution than Telnet for command-line management of a device, there are still security concerns with the configuration that a system administrator, whose primary goal is to make things work, might overlook. When this is recognized, the device can be scheduled for manual checks that might include verifying that protocol 1 is not allowed due to weak encryption. Root access login should also be disabled to minimize password attacks against the service as well as for auditing administrator actions. This activity requires experienced evaluators—not to operate the tools but to analyze the results.

Several of the more popular port-scanning utilities, with some of the more common uses and features, are introduced in brief in this section.

TIP

To understand the basics of TCP port scanning and some of the scanning options, it is important to understand the process that takes place in establishing a normal TCP connection. The client system initiates a connection by transmitting a synchronize (SYN) frame to the target; this frame includes connections parameters such as initial sequence numbers and the port to use for communication. The target machine responds with an acknowledgment (ACK) frame accepting the parameters from the SYN frame, as well as a SYN frame that includes its own required parameters (SYN/ACK). If everything is acceptable when the client machine receives the target's SYN, the client responds with an ACK frame of its own, and a full session is established. This process is often referred to as a *three-way handshake* (SYN, SYN/ACK, ACK).

Nmap

Nmap is likely the most popular scanning tool currently in use. Written by Fyodor, Nmap's source code has been released under the GNU General Public License (GPL) for free use. Currently at version 3.81, the Nmap tool supports most UNIX-based platforms, such as HP-UX, Linux, BSD, Mac OS X, and the Microsoft Windows platform.

Nmap's strength has always been the very quick port scan of specific targets or a range of targets. Added functionality has enabled Nmap to cross into multiple activities; however, in this section we concentrate on a brief review of the basic functionality of the port scan. The tool itself is capable of many varied tests and uses, but for the purposes of this book, we will review the most popular functions. (For a more detailed review of Nmap features and capabilities, review the man pages.)

Nmap utilizes a CLI. This allows for quick and easy use while making simple scripts easy to write o that you can manage specific tests or functions. The most basic use of Nmap from the CLI is *nmap <target>*. When run as a non-root user, this scan attempts to open a connection on every interesting port on the target machine (TCP Connect method) for scanning, also callable with the −*sT* option. This includes all ports from 1–1024 and any known service ports listed in the Nmap services file. Figure 19.1 is an example output from the command.

Figure 19.1 Nmap Output from the *nmap –st* Command

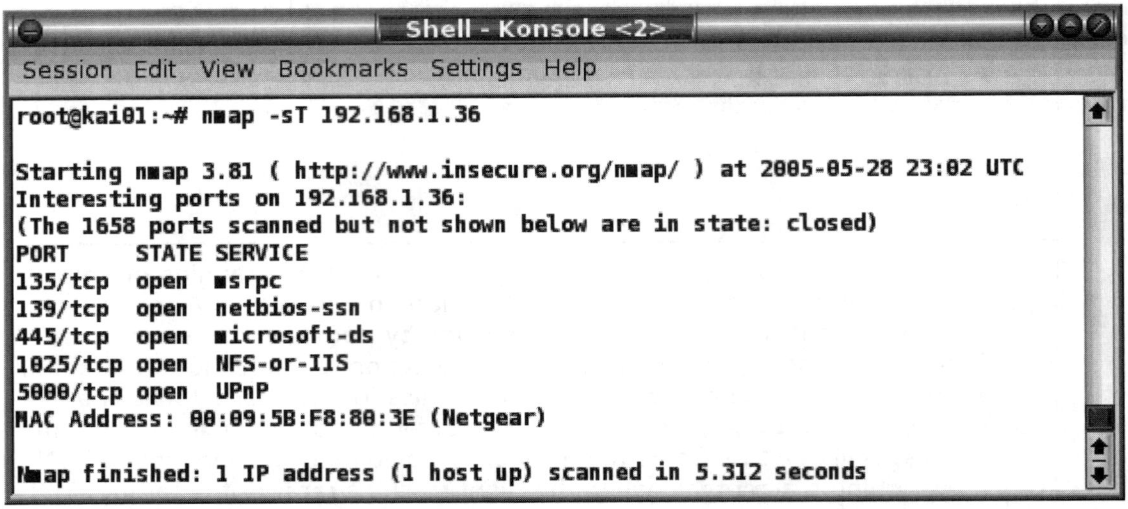

```
Shell - Konsole <2>

Session  Edit  View  Bookmarks  Settings  Help

root@kai01:~# nmap -sT 192.168.1.36

Starting nmap 3.81 ( http://www.insecure.org/nmap/ ) at 2005-05-28 23:02 UTC
Interesting ports on 192.168.1.36:
(The 1658 ports scanned but not shown below are in state: closed)
PORT      STATE SERVICE
135/tcp   open  msrpc
139/tcp   open  netbios-ssn
445/tcp   open  microsoft-ds
1025/tcp  open  NFS-or-IIS
5000/tcp  open  UPnP
MAC Address: 00:09:5B:F8:80:3E (Netgear)

Nmap finished: 1 IP address (1 host up) scanned in 5.312 seconds
```

As you can see, a total of 1703 ports were scanned on the target machine in just over 5 seconds, and five services were found listening. Those services are defined in the output using the nmap-services list, which is a basic list of "well-known" services and the ports they are associated with. At this point, no testing of the ports is attempted beyond verifying that they are listening.

Usually, it is easier to use the *–v* option when using Nmap, for a more verbose output, which you will see in future examples. By default, Nmap performs a ping scan (either an ICMP request or TCP ping to port 80) and scans only hosts that respond. Adjusting the ping scanning options is discussed in the following section.

NMAP Options

Nmap offers a wide variety of options and features for performing a scan besides the basic TCP Connect option. Not every option is relevant to each scenario (such as internal vs. external scans), and your configurations will be based on the environment to be evaluated and the other tools you use. For these reasons, we cover only a few of the basic, most commonly used functions here.

TCP SYN

Unlike the connect method described previously, a SYN scan does not complete a full TCP connection. A SYN frame is sent, and if a SYN/ACK response is received, the scan responds with a reset (RST) frame rather than actually establishing the connection. This is intended to be a more stealthy approach than performing a full connections scan, since it will not be logged by some resources; however, root privileges are commonly required to perform this scan. The option needed for running this type of scan is −sS. This is also the default scan option when run as root. The −sS scan is shown in Figure 19.2.

Figure 19.2 The −sS Scan

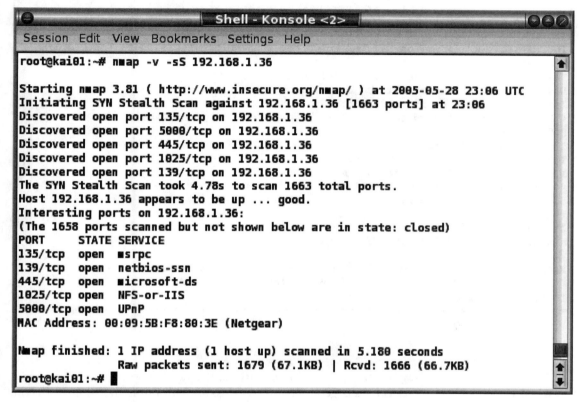

```
root@kai01:~# nmap -v -sS 192.168.1.36

Starting nmap 3.81 ( http://www.insecure.org/nmap/ ) at 2005-05-28 23:06 UTC
Initiating SYN Stealth Scan against 192.168.1.36 [1663 ports] at 23:06
Discovered open port 135/tcp on 192.168.1.36
Discovered open port 5000/tcp on 192.168.1.36
Discovered open port 445/tcp on 192.168.1.36
Discovered open port 1025/tcp on 192.168.1.36
Discovered open port 139/tcp on 192.168.1.36
The SYN Stealth Scan took 4.78s to scan 1663 total ports.
Host 192.168.1.36 appears to be up ... good.
Interesting ports on 192.168.1.36:
(The 1658 ports scanned but not shown below are in state: closed)
PORT      STATE SERVICE
135/tcp   open  msrpc
139/tcp   open  netbios-ssn
445/tcp   open  microsoft-ds
1025/tcp  open  NFS-or-IIS
5000/tcp  open  UPnP
MAC Address: 00:09:5B:F8:80:3E (Netgear)

Nmap finished: 1 IP address (1 host up) scanned in 5.180 seconds
               Raw packets sent: 1679 (67.1KB) | Rcvd: 1666 (66.7KB)
root@kai01:~#
```

UDP Scanning

Nmap separates the scanning of UDP and TCP ports into separate functions. To perform a UDP scan, you would use the −sU option. Due to the method for this scan, further validation will have to be performed to weed out any possible false positives. The application will send a 0-byte packet to each specified UDP and consider that port open unless an ICMP unreachable message is received. Hence, a firewall or access control list (ACL) blocking these response messages will cause Nmap to report these ports as being open, as shown in Figure 19.3. It can also be a very slow process. It is highly recommended that you consult the man pages before performing this scan so that you know what to expect.

Figure 19.3 Open Port Reports

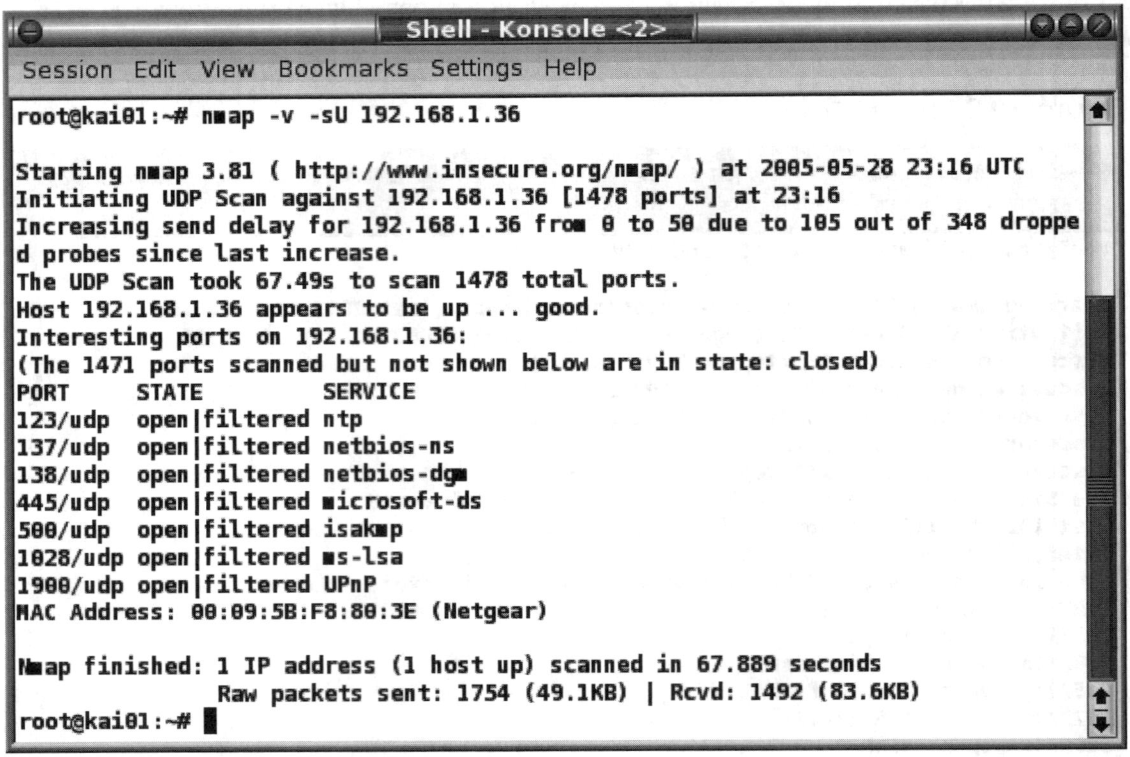
Shell - Konsole <2>
Session Edit View Bookmarks Settings Help
root@kai01:~# nmap -v -sU 192.168.1.36
Starting nmap 3.81 (http://www.insecure.org/nmap/) at 2005-05-28 23:16 UTC
Initiating UDP Scan against 192.168.1.36 [1478 ports] at 23:16
Increasing send delay for 192.168.1.36 from 0 to 50 due to 105 out of 348 droppe
d probes since last increase.
The UDP Scan took 67.49s to scan 1478 total ports.
Host 192.168.1.36 appears to be up ... good.
Interesting ports on 192.168.1.36:
(The 1471 ports scanned but not shown below are in state: closed)
PORT STATE SERVICE
123/udp open|filtered ntp
137/udp open|filtered netbios-ns
138/udp open|filtered netbios-dgm
445/udp open|filtered microsoft-ds
500/udp open|filtered isakmp
1028/udp open|filtered ms-lsa
1900/udp open|filtered UPnP
MAC Address: 00:09:5B:F8:80:3E (Netgear)
Nmap finished: 1 IP address (1 host up) scanned in 67.889 seconds
Raw packets sent: 1754 (49.1KB) | Rcvd: 1492 (83.6KB)
root@kai01:~#

As you can see, a UDP scan takes a great deal longer to run than a TCP port scan. Remember this when you're performing scans on a large number of systems. You will also notice the introduction of a new state, open|filtered. This means that Nmap did not receive a response and either the port is open or the response was filtered between the service and the scanning device.

Ping Scanning

Often you might simply want to run a quick "ping sweep" to determine what resources are up and responding to ICMP requests. This is likely one of the very first tests you would run once onsite. This type of test performs a ping sweep only and reports back live hosts without actually performing a port scan. The option to use for this type of scan is *–sP*. Note in Figure 19.4 that the entire 192.168.1.0 network was scanned, and four devices responded. You will also find the MAC address returned and the product vendor displayed, a newer feature of NMAP for all port scans.

Figure 19.4 Ping Scanning

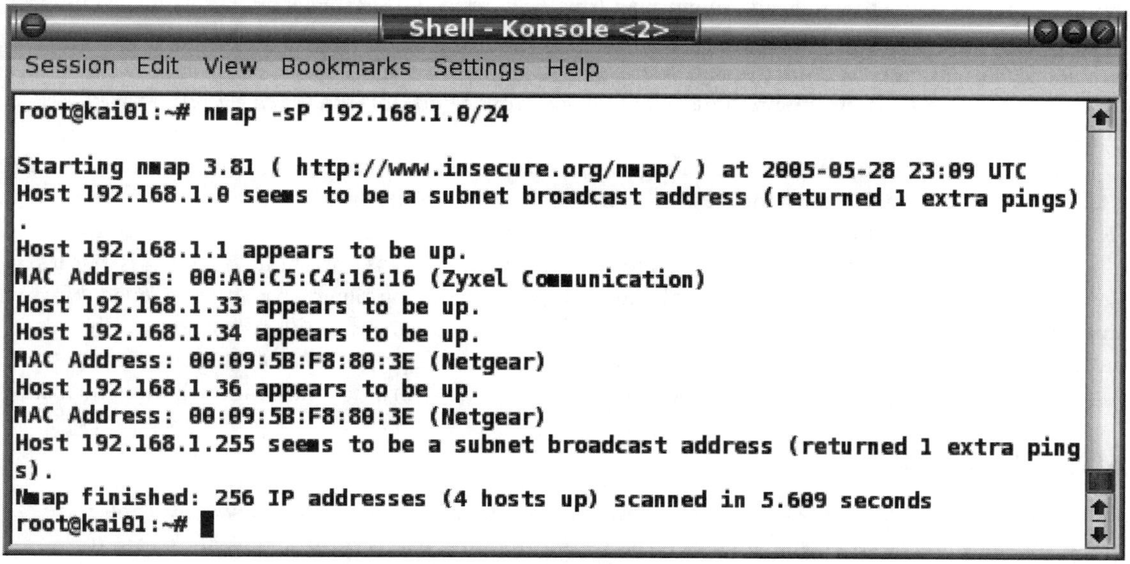

```
root@kai01:~# nmap -sP 192.168.1.0/24

Starting nmap 3.81 ( http://www.insecure.org/nmap/ ) at 2005-05-28 23:09 UTC
Host 192.168.1.0 seems to be a subnet broadcast address (returned 1 extra pings)
.
Host 192.168.1.1 appears to be up.
MAC Address: 00:A0:C5:C4:16:16 (Zyxel Communication)
Host 192.168.1.33 appears to be up.
Host 192.168.1.34 appears to be up.
MAC Address: 00:09:5B:F8:80:3E (Netgear)
Host 192.168.1.36 appears to be up.
MAC Address: 00:09:5B:F8:80:3E (Netgear)
Host 192.168.1.255 seems to be a subnet broadcast address (returned 1 extra ping
s).
Nmap finished: 256 IP addresses (4 hosts up) scanned in 5.609 seconds
root@kai01:~# ▊
```

Basic Nmap Options

Nmap has a large list of options beyond those already discussed. For more detailed and specific information, review the documentation provided with the program. These are just a few of the more common options and features that should be remembered when you're using Nmap.

There are several methods for relaying the evaluation target address to the program. As shown in previous examples, the two most common are passing a specific address or a Classless Inter Domain Routing (CIDR) block as an argument. An example is *nmap –v 192.168.3.0/24*. An option that fits well with this targeting is the *exclude* option, which allows you to specify certain addresses to avoid, such as yourself. Starting with the command used previously and specifying a couple of hosts to exclude would result in *nmap –v 192.168.3.0/24 --exclude 192.168.3.12, 192.168.3.65*.

Nmap is very versatile in allowing you to input target arguments in multiple fashion. As shown in the *exclude* function, you can separate targets in any argument using a comma. You can also input non-CIDR block groups using a hyphen. For example, *nmap –v 192.168.3.56-121* will target all IP addresses between 192.168.3.56 and 192.168.3.121. Nmap also supports the use of wildcards in target addressing. Another way to write the command to scan an entire class C CIDR block like the one listed previously is *nmap –v 192.168.3.**. This will effectively scan all addresses in the 192.168.3.0 class C network. The power for address arguments in Nmap is pretty interesting. The following command will work and provides great versatility for specifying targets and possibly sensitive resources to exclude as an example: *nmap –v 192.168.7-18.* --exclude 192.168.*.1-5, 192.168.*.254*.

The last, and more common, target input method is to use a list of hosts in a separate file. These can use all the same methods already mentioned (single addresses, CIDR block addresses, and groupings), separated by tabs, spaces, or new lines. The option for this is *−iL* and would look like *nmap −v −iL <targetfile>*. The *exclude* functionality can be incorporated using a specific host file as well, using the *--exclude* option. Using the previous example, we would end up with *nmap −v −iL <targetfile> --exclude <excludefile>*.

One way to speed up large address range scans is to use the *−n* option, which tells Nmap not to resolve the names of active IP addresses. Conversely, if name resolution is required, you can use the *−R* option, which tells Nmap to attempt to resolve the names of all IP addresses found active.

Sending Nmap output to the screen is pretty convenient for scans with limited addresses, but it's often easier to manage the output when it's directed to a separate log file for parsing as needed. Nmap supports three output formats: a single-line output for simplified parsing, a "human-readable" format, and an XML output. Respectively, those three output command options are *−oG <logfile>, -oN <logfile>, and −oX <logfile>*. A further option, *-oA <logfile>*, tells Nmap to output into all three formats.

SuperScan

SuperScan is a popular port-scanning tool with an easy-to-use Microsoft Windows GUI interface. The tool is developed and distributed by Foundstone, free of charge. Although a quick tool to use, it also allows for a decent amount of flexibility through simple configurations.

The tool also offers added benefits beyond the scope of this chapter that could assist you throughout your overall evaluation process. Although not required by the IEM, these tools may be an efficient solution for basic evaluation technical needs:

- Hostname Lookup (DNS Query)
- Ping and Traceroute ICMP Utilities
- DNS Zone Transfer Utilities
- Pre-Configured WHOIS Utilities
- HTTP Banner Grabbing

WARNING

The version of SuperScan discussed here is 4.0. This version supports only Microsoft Windows 2000 and XP and requires administrative privileges to operate. If you need to use the tool on an earlier Microsoft Windows platform or do not have administrative rights, the earlier version, SuperScan 3.0, is still available for download from the Foundstone site.

In the GUI, the second tab allows for the configuration of discovery options. Like Nmap, SuperScan performs a host discovery based on the evaluator's requirements prior to performing the scan using ICMP. ICMP messages are broken down into types. You might find that some types are blocked by a firewall, whereas others are not. The standard ICMP echo request (message type 8) is the default setting for SuperScan. This is the message sent when you perform a ping. Another option is an ICMP timestamp request (message type 13). The last two options are the ICMP address mask request (message type 17) and ICMP information request (message type 15). Many administrators block "pings" at the firewall, unaware that other ICMP message types are available.

On this same page, the evaluator can enable or disable UDP and TCP scanning as well define the specific ports to be checked. Ports can be assigned in ranges and can be read from an external text file. The UDP scan can be configured to require an ICMP destination unreachable (message type 3) to mark a port as closed or consider it open only if a data reply is collected. As with Nmap, be cautious about results when you're performing a UDP scan. The TCP scan can be configured using the same two major scanning approaches described with Nmap: a TCP Connect scan or a TCP SYN scan. All discovery services here can also be set with a user-defined timeout. The default should be satisfactory in most cases, although slower or distant networks (multiple hops) may require a longer timeout.

To bypass simple firewall rules or incorrectly configured devices, there is also an option to use a single source port for all scan attempts, rather than a dynamic port. A user-defined port can be entered for both UDP and TCP scanning. For internal testing purposes, you should rarely need to use this feature (see Figure 19.5).

Figure 19.5 Bypassing Simple Firewall Rules

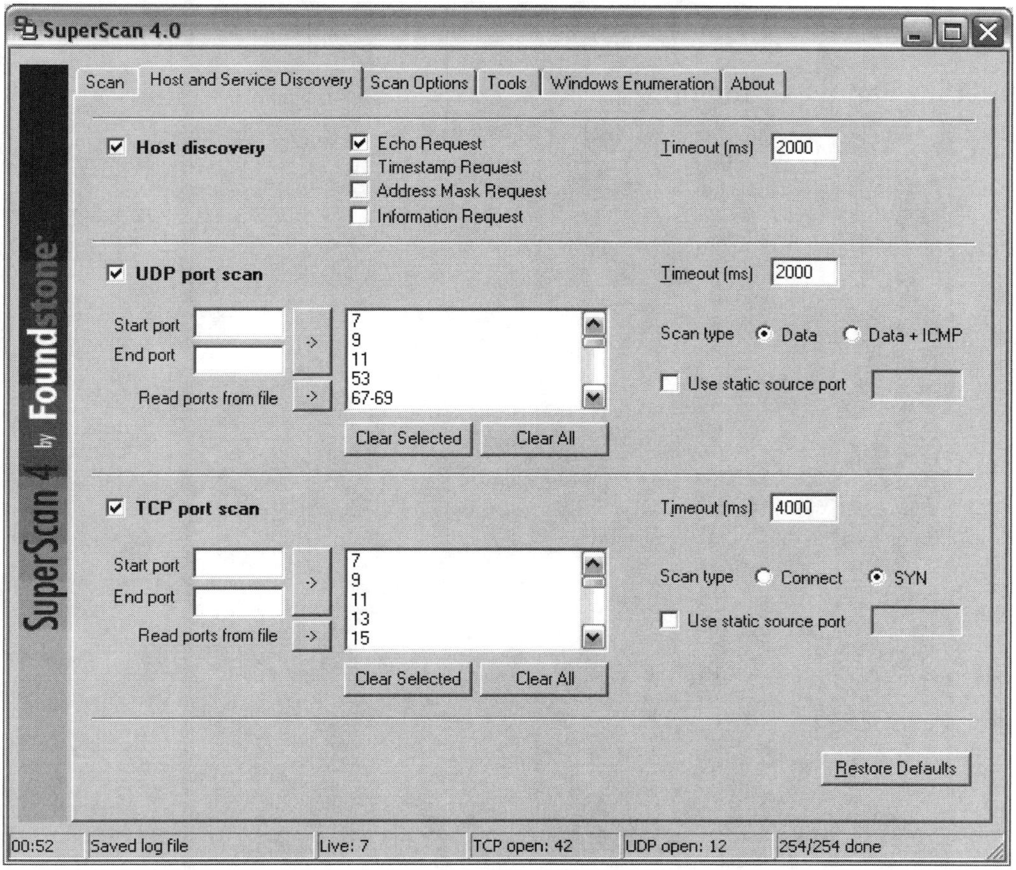

The third tab from the left, Scan Options, provides more options for configuring your scan. Here you can set the number of attempts for both host discovery and actual port scans against discovered hosts. One attempt is the default, and it is not likely that you'll need to increase this number, unless you are on a very slow connection such as dialup. Although running multiple passes across devices will greatly increase the elapsed time, you would probably be better off adjusting a combination of the timeouts from the previous settings page and the speed slider bar. This bar sets the amount of time the tool waits between sending out scan probes. The default setting, 10ms, should be adequate for most connections. If all target devices are on the same LAN (read: not running across 56k ISDN connections), setting the delay between 0ms and 5ms will probably be acceptable and will speed up the overall scan runtime.

You can also choose not to display hosts with no active ports. This is just a simple cleanup feature to remove inactive addresses from you report window, which can fill up very quickly when scanning multiple IP addresses or ranges. An added option is to randomize the order of the hosts scanned and the ports scanned. If you're scanning devices over multiple segments, this can be a beneficial tool for minimizing any bottlenecks that arise and cause slower traffic speeds for users. Some IDS devices are configured to look for successive scans along port ranges as well, which, although not a recommended or appropriate configuration rule, randomization can easily get past.

The last set of options concern banner grabbing (see Figure 19.6), which we address in the next section of this chapter. This is just another example of how some tools can cover multiple IEM baseline activity requirements.

Figure 19.6 Banner Grabbing

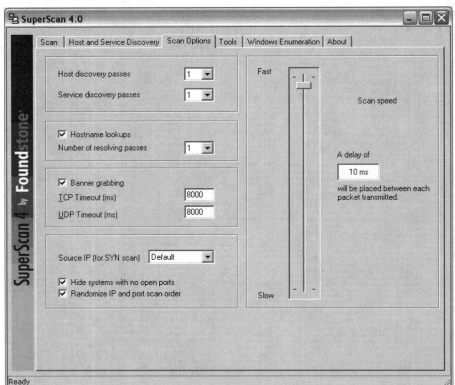

The first tab is the actual scan page. This page is broken down into three basic sections: a target address selection frame, a minimal results window, and a scan status window. In the following image, the scan status window is minimized to give a greater view of the results window.

In the target selection frame, you can enter target addresses one at a time or by range. These addresses are then displayed in the window to the right, allowing for multiple ranges or single address input for a single scan. You can also import addresses from a text file. SuperScan will recognize the same formats discussed earlier, including single IP addresses, CIDR block address ranges, and address groupings (for example, 192.168.6.24–68).

In the results window, the active ports of all discovered hosts, both TCP and UDP, are displayed. If DNS resolution was chosen and is operational, the hostname is displayed as well. After the scan is completed, a total number of hosts and TCP and UDP ports are displayed. In Figure 19.7 you can see the results for three out of seven live IP addresses discovered. For reporting purposes, you can view all the data collected by selecting the **View HTML Results** button at the bottom of the page. This outputs a clear and simple page for reviewing the data, without having to scroll through a small window. An example of this output is displayed in the next section, where the enumeration capabilities of SuperScan 4 are discussed.

Figure 19.7 Discovering Hosts with SuperScan 4.0

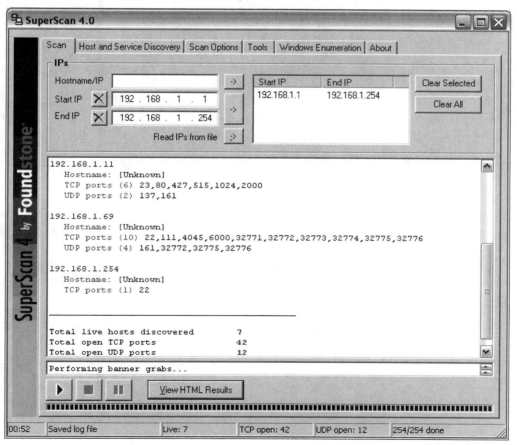

Overall, SuperScan 4 is a very simple-to-use Microsoft Windows-based port scanner that takes little time to understand and configure. The speed with which scans are completed, customizable for the scenario, is relatively fast.

ScanLine

ScanLine is another free tool from the security firm Foundstone. Formerly know as FScan, ScanLine is one of the most popular CLI-based port scanners for the Microsoft Windows platforms. In Figure 19.8 you can see the results of a basic port scan, run with the command *sl 192.168.1.5*.

Figure 19.8 Basic Port Scan Results

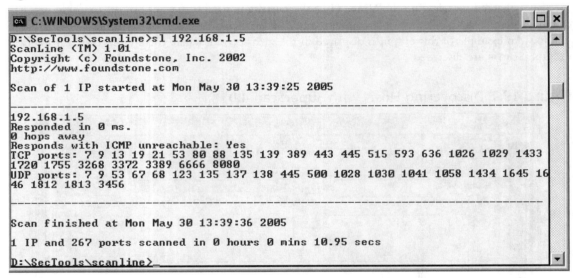

As you can see, by default ScanLine uses an internal list of ports to scan, if none is provided at the command line or in an optional external file. To declare a list of ports or ranges from the command line, the *–t* option can be used, and for UDP, the *–u* option. An example is *sl –t 21-25, 80, 443 –u 20-100 192.168.3.83*. For specifying ports using an external file, you would use the *–l <tcpportsfile>* option for TCP scanning and the *–L <udpportsfile>* option for UDP scanning. The *–v* option is also beneficial for viewing the tool status while running in verbose mode.

File output with ScanLine is very simple; you use the *–o <outputfile>* option to overwrite any data in the current output file or the *–O <outputfile>* option to append results to any data in the current output file. For people who predominantly use the Microsoft Windows environment, ScanLine is a great option for creating custom scripts using the argument and output options, as seen often with Nmap in the UNIX environment.

SolarWinds

SolarWinds is the first tool we will look at that was originally designed as, and is mostly still, a resource or network management tool. Over time, added security testing features have been incorporated to make this tool not just a multifunction management utility but also a multifunction security utility. The SolarWinds tools are a Microsoft Windows platform-based set of utilities.

The SolarWinds Network Management Toolset is currently available in version 8.1 and is a pay-for-use commercial product. There are four different pricing options based on the number of utilities in the suite, starting with the Standard Edition and adding more functionality all the way up to the Engineer's Edition. The utilities discussed in this chapter are not all available in the Standard Edition, so whichever tools interest you, make sure to verify that they are included in any edition you research.

The Port Scanner utility within SolarWinds can be configured under the **File | Settings** menu. From here, you can select or deselect specific ports to scan from a prepopulated list. You can also add custom ports not shown. Currently, the utility only supports a full TCP Connect scan, so some of the configuration options for stealth are not available. You can adjust timing configurations such as connection timeouts, maximum concurrent scan connections, and the time allotted between scans, or scan spacing. UDP scanning is not yet available as an option at the time of this writing. Also under the settings are a multitude of graphical display and output options for ease of use.

The main window for the utility is incredibly easy to use and understand. You only have a few options to set. Enter your starting and ending IP addresses, and decide whether you want to use the predefined ports discussed under the Settings menu or manually enter a range or multiple ranges of ports to scan. As you can see in Figure 19.9, the results are then displayed in a grid format in the main window.

Figure 19.9 Gridded Port Scanning

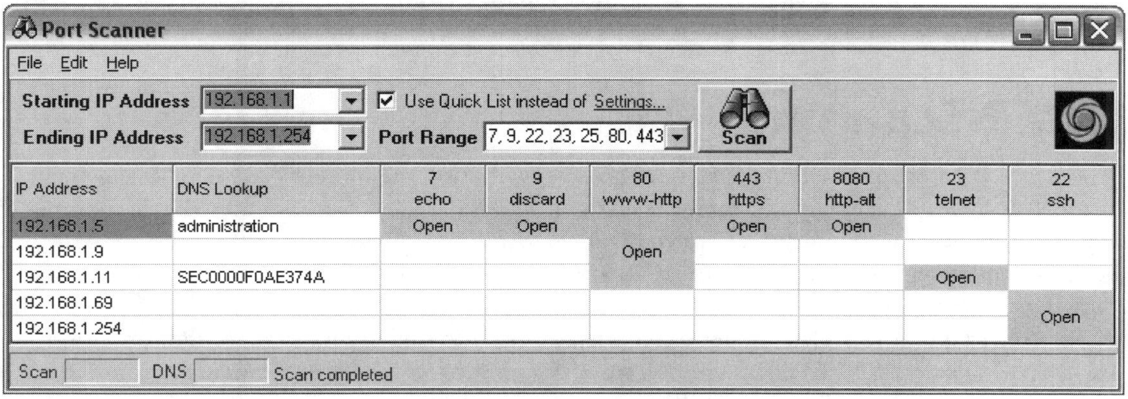

The output from the SolarWinds Port Scanner is in HTML format and for manual editing can easily be sent directly to several Microsoft applications, such as Word or Excel, under the **File | Send To** menu.

Port Scan System Mapping

At this point, after completing the port scanning of the system, the gathered information needs to be documented. This documentation is considered a business process, and not an NSA IEM process, so we will use the Security Horizon format for putting together a system mapping.

Taking the table displayed earlier in the chapter, we can now start cataloging the data on a detailed resource basis (see Table 19.2). The following table is an example of how our system mapping should look up to this point. This is obviously abbreviated, but should give a better understanding of what is being done. Several devices and ports were left off the list for brevity.

Table 19.2 IEM System Mapping

ABC123 IEM System Mapping					10/29/2004
XYZ Consulting			POC: Johnny Reboot		(555) 123.4567
Active Hosts:		4	Address Ranges:		192.168.1.0/24 172.16.2.0/24
IP Address / Device Name	Ports		Identified Services	Detected OS	Notes
192.168.1.36	TCP	135			
	TCP	5000			
192.168.1.69	TCP	22			
	TCP	898			
172.16.2.5 mohican	UDP	161			
172.16.2.6 navajo	UDP	161			
WiFi MAC Address	Type	Crypt	SSID	Discovered IP Address	Notes

SNMP Scanning

The second IEM baseline activity is scanning for devices using the Simple Network Management Protocol. SNMP has been around for years and continues to evolve but with the core goal of offering simple management services for networked resources. Obviously, since this service is all about management, it only stands to reason that there might be information or weaknesses in its configuration that could be exploited by an attacker.

To understand how SNMP relates to security, we need to understand some of the basics of how SNMP operates. SNMP is centered on three main functions: the agent, the manager, and the Management Information Base (MIB). The manager requests information or makes configuration changes to the target resource. The target resource runs an agent-based software application that responds to queries and commands. The MIB is often confused with a database of information on the device. In fact, it is simply a tree mapping that defines the types of information or objects available on that device. Most vendors adhere to a standard SNMP MIB, and then they simply add their own vendor-specific branches.

Each variable information type is a unique object identifier (OID), which is a sometimes-lengthy numerical tag. An example is the System Description variable, for which the OID is 1.3.6.1.2.1.1.1. This OID is from the standard MIB-II tree as defined in the Internet Engineering Task Force (IETF) request for comment (RFC) document 1213 (or simply RFC 1213) and usually contains text information about the device. Many OIDs are vendor specific, and the manager and agent both need to be aware of their existence. This is where the MIB comes into play because it stores the OIDs that are available, not the information variables that may be contained in them.

To actually relay information, SNMP uses five basic messages: *GET*, *GET-NEXT*, *GET-RESPONSE*, *SET*, and *TRAP*. The messages are fairly easy to understand, with *GET* and *GET-NEXT* being queries sent to an agent. The *GET-RESPONSE* message is the returned information requested by the manager device. The *SET* message allows a change in the configuration to be requested by the manager, with the agent responding using the *GET-RESPONSE* message to confirm the change or inform the manager of an error. The *TRAP* message allows the agent to act independently by sending information on an event-based timeframe. Messages to a remote logging device use the *TRAP* message.

SNMP is normally operated over TCP or UDP port 161, with SNMP traps communicating over TCP or UDP port 162. This is not always the case, however. Cisco, for example, uses TCP or UDP 1993. Remember this as you review your system mapping, which should now display port scan results, so that the SNMP scanning activity does not become limited to only the typical ports.

The tools discussed in this section are designed to act as an SNMP manager, requesting information and in some cases making changes on the target resources.

NOTE

SNMPv3 became an official standard in 2002 and incorporates many new security features in the protocol, such as user authentication and encryption. Unfortunately, implementation of these new features has been very limited, with most configurations not enabled. SNMPv3 features are an excellent recommendation for organizations that rely on SNMP for system management, to mitigate some of the inherent flaws with SNMPv2 (such as community strings being transmitted in cleartext).

SolarWinds

With its suite of network management tools, the SolarWinds Engineer's Edition offers a multitude of SNMP utilities. Since the background of SNMP is to manage network, it's no wonder that one of the premier network management tools has a strong showing in the IEM baseline activity of SNMP scanning. To be honest, the tasks that can be performed with SolarWinds and SNMP go way beyond the basic discussions of SNMP that are appropriate for this chapter. Here we briefly discuss three of the utilities, but we recommend testing the free demo version to see what other SNMP capabilities are available.

SNMPSweep

For a very quick pull, SNMPSweep (see Figure 19.10) is a very simple and fast utility for running a quick scan of SNMP-enabled hosts and pulling some basic information. It has only a few settings to configure, since it is meant for a quick, "down and dirty" sweep of the network as it looks for SNMP-enabled devices. Under the **File | Settings** menu are options for adjusting speed setting for ICMP queries (active host detection prior to scan) and SNMP traffic. The defaults should be fine in most instances. You can also configure DNS resolution of active hosts and enter multiple text strings to be transmitted as possible community strings to all devices.

Figure 19.10 Scanning SNMP-Enabled Hosts

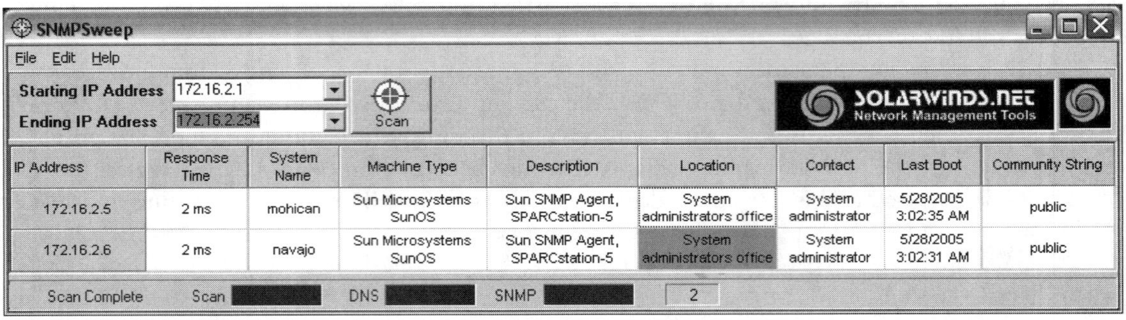

Once started, the scanner attempts to retrieve the information identified by the System branch of the MIB. As stated earlier, this is RFC 1223 OID of 1.3.6.1.2.1.1.1. This utility is excellent for ferreting out resources for more detailed scanning and testing.

MIB Walk

The MIB Walk utility is a great way to pull down all the SNMP-managed information about a device. It reads the device's MIB tree, then requests the information for every OID. This is extremely useful in determining the actual threat an exposed SNMP service presents. Some devices provide little information that's useful to an attacker; others "give away the farm".

The tool is very simple to use, requiring only the selection of the MIB tree to "walk" on the device, the community string configured for that MIB tree, and the IP address of the target. MIB Walk is further illustrated in Figure 19.11.

Figure 19.11 MIB Walk

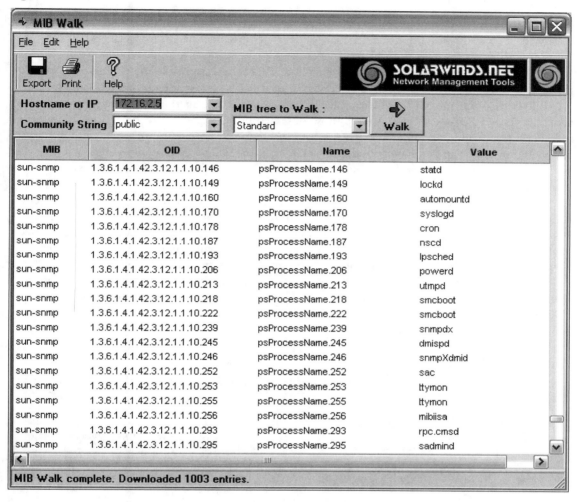

In the screen capture, we can see that the target device responded with 1003 entries. In the image, we have scrolled down to show some of the information available, such as processes currently running on the device. As an attacker, one might be pulled to notice that NFS is probably available on the box, considering that the *lockd* service is running and this is obviously a Solaris platform. One might also notice the combination of the *statd* and *sadmind* services, which have been subject to exploit in the past, with simple scripts available to test.

MIB Walk supports the export of data into myriad formats, including comma-separated values (CSVs), HTML, PDF, Word, and Excel. This makes the tool very useful for incorporating results into customer reports or any "body of evidence" documentation.

MIB Browser

For very detailed SNMP testing needs, the SolarWinds MIB Browser utility is a great resource. The MIB Browser boasts an internal database of over 1,000 standard and proprietary MIBs for interpreting the information from many devices in use.

Simple to configure, MIB Browser has two important settings available under **File | Settings**: the basic speed functions, which can be stepped up or down based on the current connection, and the OID fields. With the MIB Browser, you can configure the information type you want to see and how it is viewed. Some examples beyond those displayed in Figure 19.12 are Type, Raw Value (prior to being interpreted by the internal MIB database), Value (post interpretation), and Description. After configuration, it is a simple matter to identify a target and provide a community string.

Obviously, one important thing you'll notice in Figure 19.12 is the previously discussed interpretation of an OID's acceptable values and what they represent. The raw value for the OID 1.3.6.1.2.1.11.30 can be either a 1 or a 2. Unless you are already very familiar with each OID (both standard and vendor proprietary), many of these OIDs might mean very little to you. In this case, however, you'll notice that MIB Browser has interpreted the meaning of those values and presented them in human-readable fashion. By selecting the OID, more detailed information regarding its purpose is displayed in the lower-left corner, including read and read/write status.

Although out of scope for the purposes of the IEM, you might be interested to see the ease in which an OID setting can be changed on a host. Any value presented in blue can be configured via SNMP. Simply select the field and begin typing away or click the drop-down arrow and select the available option, as shown in Figure 19.12.

Figure 19.12 MIB Browser

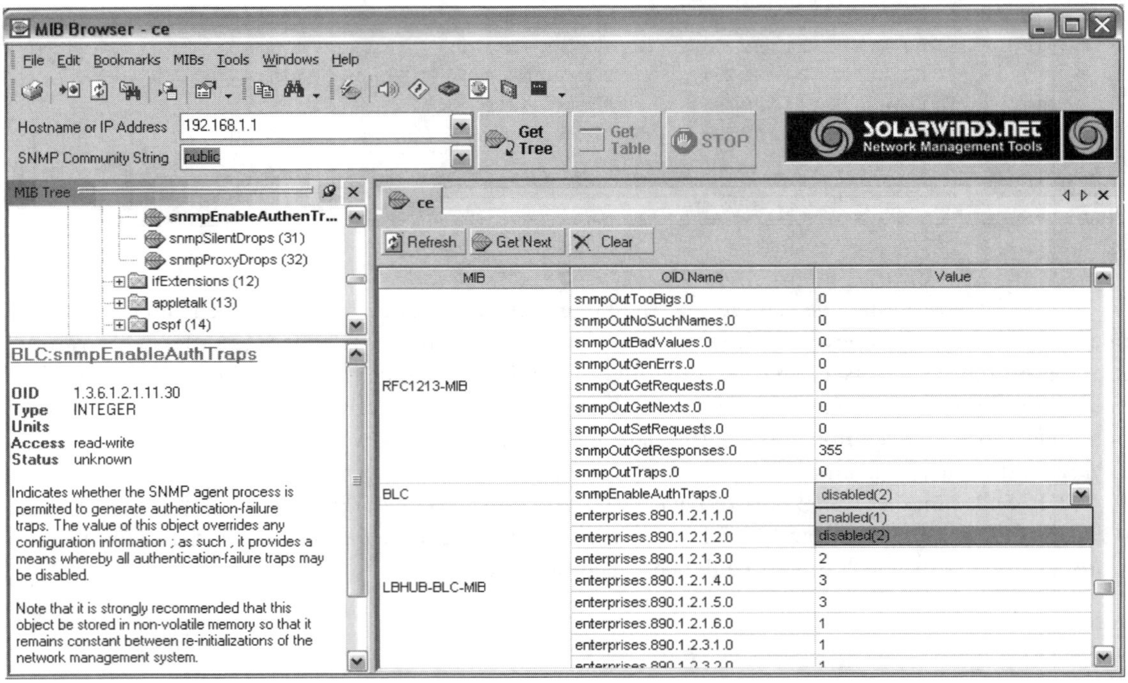

SNScan

Again from the team at Foundstone, SNScan is a free utility that can be used for the detection of SNMP devices. Many of the Foundstone tools are developed to assist administrators search new and serious exploits on their systems. SNScan was originally put out to identify Cisco devices with a potentially serious SNMP flaw. That original version is still available under the name CIScan; added functionality has been added to increase the usability of SNScan for performing basic SNMP detection.

To pop off a really quick scan of the system, simply define the target IP addresses or ranges, select from the predefined SNMP ports available, enter a community string, and go. You can adjust the timeout, but you should have little need to do so unless you encounter a very slow network. You can also use a text file to try multiple community strings, which is a great way to perform a quick dictionary attack against SNMP community strings.

The tool (see Figure 19.13) is great for taking a quick look, but it does not currently offer any data-exporting functionality. For personal use, we find this to be a great tool for discovering SNMP devices, then using the target address information in slower but more detailed utilities.

Figure 19.13 SNScan

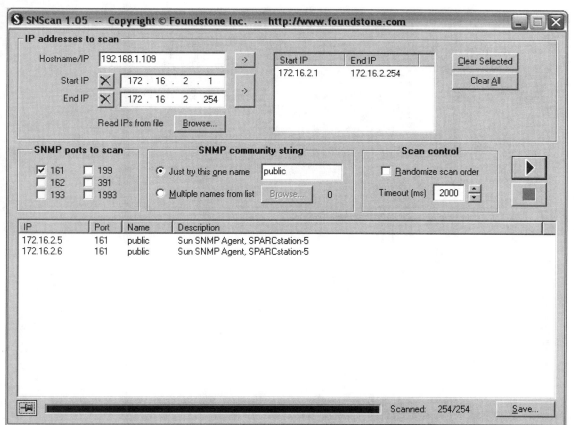

WS_Ping Pro-Pak

WS_Ping Pro-Pak is another set of tools designed originally for IT management purposes, but they have security functionality built in as well. Designed as an information-gathering tool for troubleshooting network problems, the suite also can be used for some network discovery requirements of security evaluations. WS_Ping Pro-Pak (see Figure 19.14) has been developed as a commercial product by Ipswitch.

The main window is very easy to navigate and the SNMP scanning functionality very simple to configure. From the main window, select the **SNMP** tab. You should be presented with the same window as in Figure 19.14. Simply enter the address of a target that you discovered during a port scan, define the community string, determine the OID (labeled **What** in the interface) you want to view, and click **Start**.

You also have the option to define your query. The radio buttons on the left act just as you would expect. By selecting **Get** and clicking **Start**, you will receive a *GET-RESPONSE* with the defined OID. Select *Get Next* and you will receive the next OID in the branch. Select *Get All Subitems*, and the application will return all OID information available under the selected branch of the MIB tree.

Figure 19.14 WS_Pin ProPack

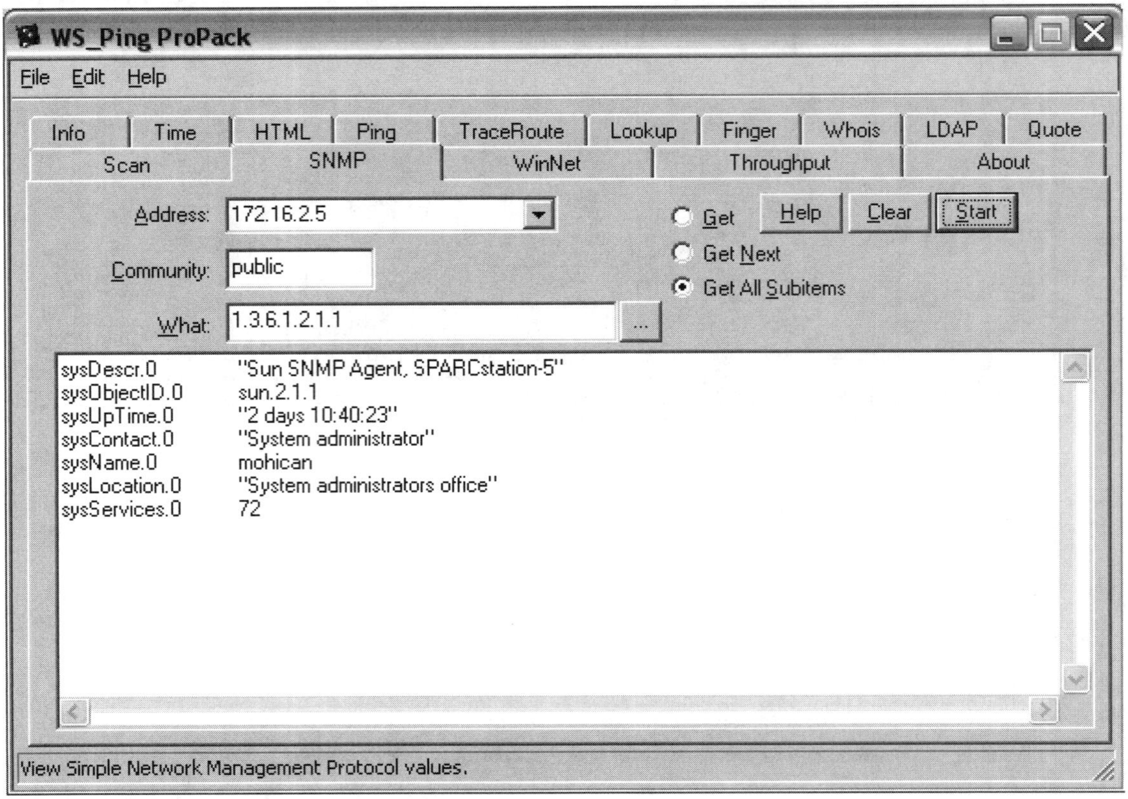

One drawback to the WS_Ping Pro-Pak SNMP utility is that you can query only one host at a time. This might be difficult for detecting SNMP-enabled hosts, but the strength of this utility is in its SNMP Object Selector. If you've detected SNMP devices via port-scanning techniques and you ant to do a fast review of selected hosts, this tool allows you to quickly and easily define the specific information you want.

By clicking the button marked ... just to the right of the **What** field, you can bring up the SNMP Object Selector, as shown in Figure 19.15. From here, you can easily drill down through the standard MIB tree and select only the specific OIDs you are interested in.

Figure 19.15 SNMP Object Selector

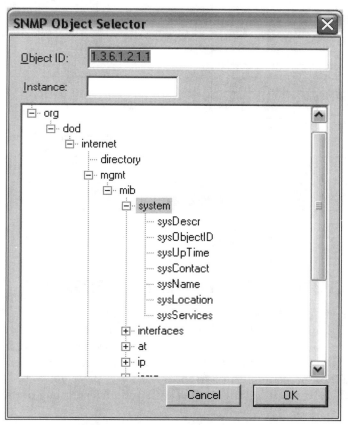

SNMP Scan System Mapping

Now that we have completed the second NSA IEM baseline activity, we can continue adding information to our system mapping. Here we want to add some of the more pertinent information discovered from SNMP scanning, such as discovered community strings, notes for further review, any enumerated information, and reference documentation.

Obviously, with the possibility of retrieving thousands of lines of data by performing a full MIB review, not all the SNMP information can be entered into a simple system mapping. As part of the Security Horizon business process, we deliver all information we collect (including handwritten notes) to the customer as part of a "body of evidence." We can reference SNMP data results by naming the document where that detailed information is stored (see Table 19.3).

Table 19.3 IEM System Mapping

ABC123 IEM System Mapping					10/29/2004
XYZ Consulting			POC: Johnny Reboot		(555) 123.4567
Active Hosts:		4	Address Ranges:		192.168.1.0/24 172.16.2.0/24
IP Address / Device Name	Ports		Identified Services	Detected OS	Notes
192.168.1.11	TCP	135			
	TCP	139			
	UDP	137			
192.168.1.36	TCP	135			
	TCP	139			
	UDP	137			
172.16.2.5 mohican	UDP	161	Sun SNMP SPARC-5	Sun OS	SNMP String: Public statd and sadmind running 172.16.2.5-SNMP.txt
172.16.2.6 navajo	UDP	161	Sun SNMP SPARC-5	Sun OS	SNMP String: Public 172.16.2.6-SNMP.txt
WiFi MAC Address	Type	Crypt	SSID	Discovered IP Address	Notes

Enumeration and Banner Grabbing

Enumeration and banner grabbing is the next activity in the NSA IEM baseline. This activity focuses on going deeper than your basic port scan to learn more about the actual applications listening on any ports discovered as well as learning more about the platform hosting those applications. The more we know about a device, the easier it is to discover possible weaknesses in either its networking applications or actual host processes. It is up to the evaluator to determine whether an information exposure is taking place, based on his or her experience and understanding of the criticality of the system.

Simply put, in this activity we try to identify target devices through advertisements by responding services about their vendor and, in some more technical methods, gauge how they respond. Many of the tools discussed here operate in different formats. Some are vendor specific, relying on basic platform operations used by different operating systems, such as NetBIOS. Others use basic protocol standard queries to view information advertised about a specific service. Many Internet services such as Web, e-mail, and FTP advertise their version information in responses. Other utilities have an inline description of response methods employed by different vendors and products. A host response can then be compared to these predefined formulas and weighted based on the known type that is more like the received response.

There is a huge variety of utilities and manual checks for this activity, too numerous to account for here. Instead we cover a few of the more commonly used items. The specific tools used to perform this activity, often referred to as *fingerprinting*, should be based on the evaluator's experience with each platform and the environment in which the IEM is being performed. The evaluator's experience with security weaknesses is invaluable at this stage, to recognize common components that have a history of weaknesses and target them for more detailed testing later in the evaluation.

Nmap

As described in an earlier section, by default Nmap uses a table list of services to describe each discovered port. This is a standard list of "well-known" services that run by default over specific ports. For example, any time TCP port 23 is detected, Nmap will display Telnet as the open service on the target, similarly corresponding SNMP with UDP port 161. If all services were locked into specific ports and administrators did not have the capability to change them, this would be a very accurate and fast solution. However, since the term "security through obscurity" has been bandied about, administrators have been moving services across different and varying ports. Running multiple instances of a single service also requires the use of multiple ports, often leading to the use of ports uncommon to that service.

Service detection takes more time than a typical Nmap port scan, yet it is still rather quick and efficient. To enable this option, simply add −s*V* to the arguments already in use. To include OS detection and service detection, which are discussed later in this section, simply add −*A* to the arguments passed to Nmap.

Nmap starts out performing the normal port scan, then dumps the results to the service-scanning component for review. The first simple check is a basic banner grab. Nmap opens a full connection and waits for any advertised information. As mentioned earlier, this is a very common practice for many Internet services. The results are compared to a list of service "signatures" within Nmap. This often ends up with the supplied vendor and version information, signaling the end of this test. If vendor information, but not version information, is received, this information is used in the next stage of detection to limit the probe testing performed.

If a full match was not obtained through the simple banner-grabbing technique, specific probes are sent to the host, based on probable matches. The probes begin with the most likely services that would be running on that specific port, such as HTTP signature probes to port 80 and 8080. Also included in this probability is any information gathered earlier, such as vendor information. The probes also include SSL detection, which will cause Nmap to open an SSL connection and then begin sending service detection probes. An example output is displayed in Figure 19.16, showing the services as detected.

Figure 19.16 Nmap Scan Output

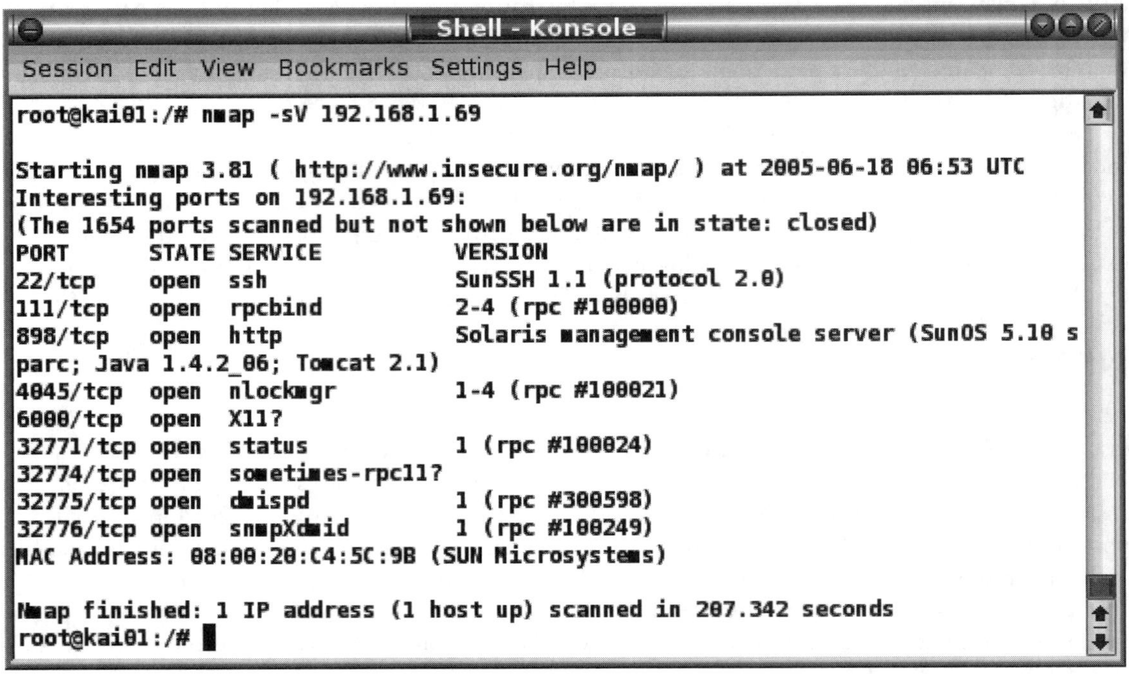
Shell - Konsole
Session Edit View Bookmarks Settings Help
root@kai01:/# nmap -sV 192.168.1.69
Starting nmap 3.81 (http://www.insecure.org/nmap/) at 2005-06-18 06:53 UTC
Interesting ports on 192.168.1.69:
(The 1654 ports scanned but not shown below are in state: closed)
PORT STATE SERVICE VERSION
22/tcp open ssh SunSSH 1.1 (protocol 2.0)
111/tcp open rpcbind 2-4 (rpc #100000)
898/tcp open http Solaris management console server (SunOS 5.10 sparc; Java 1.4.2_06; Tomcat 2.1)
4045/tcp open nlockmgr 1-4 (rpc #100021)
6000/tcp open X11?
32771/tcp open status 1 (rpc #100024)
32774/tcp open sometimes-rpc11?
32775/tcp open dmispd 1 (rpc #300598)
32776/tcp open snmpXdmid 1 (rpc #100249)
MAC Address: 08:00:20:C4:5C:9B (SUN Microsystems)
Nmap finished: 1 IP address (1 host up) scanned in 207.342 seconds
root@kai01:/#

You can see that, when available or identified, version information is included. These are often the exact responses advertised by the service. Although the expected results are similar, the method used for OS detection is different.

For OS detection, Nmap uses a fingerprinting technique that compares the TCP/IP stack implementation of the target to known deviations. Each vendor, and often product version, implements its networking structure differently. Whether it is the way it responds to ICMP requests, performs packet sequencing, generated timestamps, packet fragmentation bits, or myriad other items, each TCP/IP stack is different. The argument required to perform OS detection is *–O*, or, as stated earlier, to perform both OS and service detection, the argument *–A* can be used.

Obviously, generating the signatures for each test and platform required a large amount of testing by Fyodor and his volunteers to create a large list of known "anomalies." Figure 19.17 shows the successful detection of a Sun Solaris host and the normal port scan results. It also helps show the difference between normal port scan results and service detection on those results. Both the OS detection and service detection scans were performed on the same test system, yet only the service detection scan returns captured text from the service.

Figure 19.17 Service Detection Scan Return

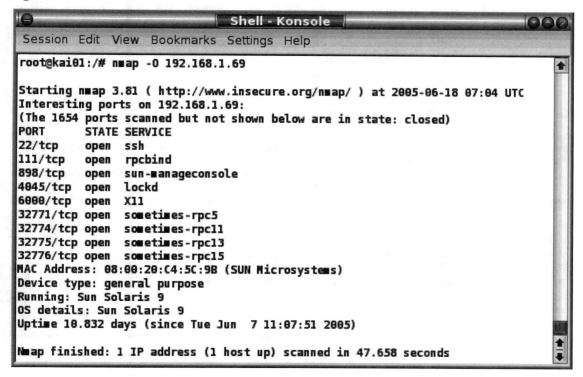

This discussion is meant as just a broad overview of the Nmap OS and service detection features. It does show how multiple techniques for enumeration operate, however.

THC-Amap

Amap is another tool for security testing and evaluations from the people at The Hacker's Choice (THC). Designed as an "application mapper" (hence the name Amap), it is another utility for the identification of services on a remote target. Amap is another free, command-line tool available with minimum license constraints.

Amap can be used independently with a simple command such as *amap 192.168.1.36 1-65535*. Amap then performs a signature-based test against the selected target and ports, attempting to resolve the host responses against a database of known packet responses. It can also be used in a more efficient method with an Nmap output file to input known targets and open ports to be tested with a command such as *amap −i nmapoutputfile*. This will significantly shorten the time it takes to test multiple targets and ports, due to the fact that Amap will then only test ports and targets already determined active.

In Figure 19.18 you can see a sample run of Amap against what is obviously a Windows device. The −*q* option removes all the extraneous probe information so that you don't have to see the incorrect match attempts. The −*b* option can also be beneficial because it reports the banner collected on that port as well. Some overlapping signatures may result in more than one match for each service. A perfect example is the SSH signature. This is a generic signature and is reported as a match, whereas other more specific signatures are also tested. An OpenSSH service will be matched twice—once for generic SSH and once for the more specific OpenSSH. If the more specific information is not as important and you are looking for fast results, the −1 option will result in Amap skipping all further testing on each port, once the first match is found.

Figure 19.18 Amap Run Against Windows

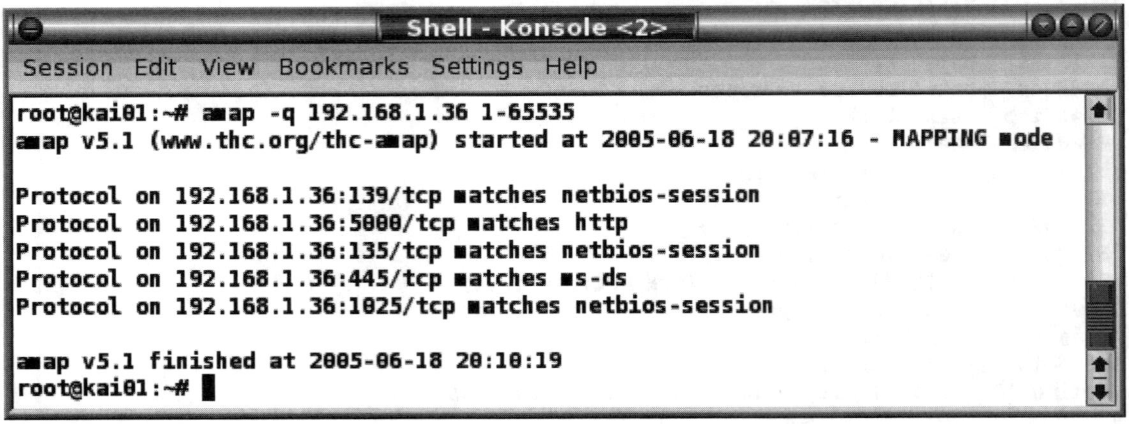

```
root@kai01:~# amap -q 192.168.1.36 1-65535
amap v5.1 (www.thc.org/thc-amap) started at 2005-06-18 20:07:16 - MAPPING mode

Protocol on 192.168.1.36:139/tcp matches netbios-session
Protocol on 192.168.1.36:5000/tcp matches http
Protocol on 192.168.1.36:135/tcp matches netbios-session
Protocol on 192.168.1.36:445/tcp matches ms-ds
Protocol on 192.168.1.36:1025/tcp matches netbios-session

amap v5.1 finished at 2005-06-18 20:10:19
root@kai01:~#
```

NBTScan

NBTScan is an open source scanner designed to query Microsoft Windows platform devices for NetBIOS name information. Available for multiple platforms, including Windows and Linux, it is a very easy-to-use tool specialized for Windows enumeration. It uses a NetBIOS status query over UDP port 137, which results in a very quick response with limited information from the host.

As you can see in Figure 19.19, in the basic run, NBTScan returns the NetBIOS name for the Windows device, the name of the currently logged-in user, and its server option. If the device has available file shares, whether an actual server product or a Windows desktop product with local file sharing enabled, it will display the result *<server>*.

Figure 19.19 NBTScan

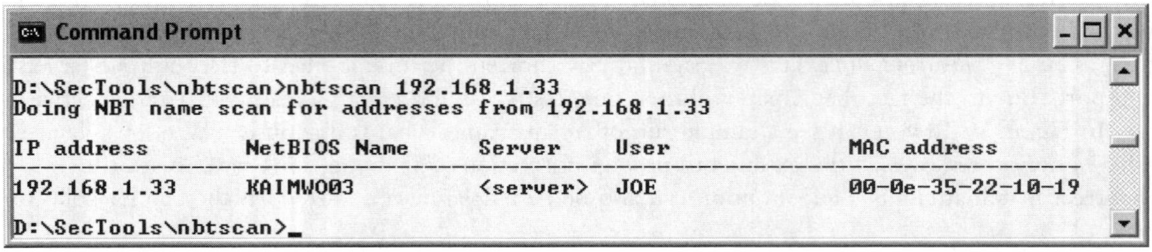

```
D:\SecTools\nbtscan>nbtscan 192.168.1.33
Doing NBT name scan for addresses from 192.168.1.33

IP address       NetBIOS Name     Server    User        MAC address
-----------------------------------------------------------------------
192.168.1.33     KAIMW003         <server>  JOE         00-0e-35-22-10-19

D:\SecTools\nbtscan>_
```

Another simple NetBIOS service enumeration operation is to use the *−v* option (see Figure 19.20). Combined this with the *−h* option, which formats the results in a more human readable result, and you are rewarded with information regarding the device and its Windows networking configuration. As you can see, the server ADMINISTRATION has multiple services operating in support of its local operations as well as in support of the Windows domain COLORADO.

Figure 19.20 The *−v* Option

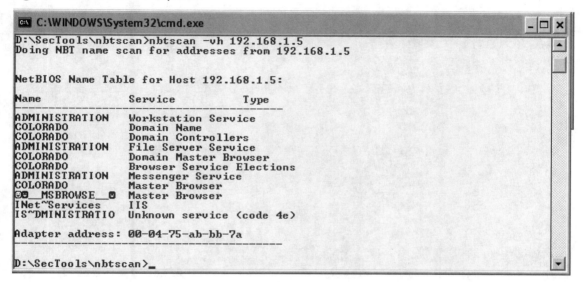

Although a very simple and basic tool to use, NBTScan can present good information specifically oriented around the Windows networking protocol.

SuperScan

By default, SuperScan records any banner information collected during a port scan. In its generated HTML reports, you can see the basic port scan information that the tool discovers at the top of the window. After that, it displays any received information from the target on a per-port basis.

In Figure 19.21, you can see that the IP address 192.168.1.69 has multiple services operating on both UDP and TCP ports. For the first port listed, TCP port 22, you can see the returned information under the **Banner** section. The banner itself has given the exact vendor and version for the service, Sun's SSH version 1.1. The response for the second port found, SunRPC, is also listed. This is just an example of the way one tool can be used to cover multiple IEM baseline activities.

Figure 19.21 A SuperScan Report

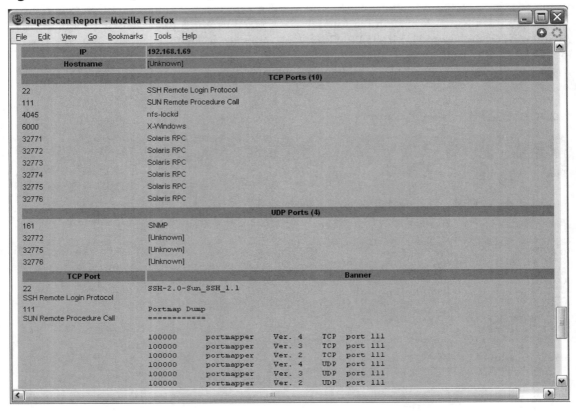

SuperScan also comes with a very easy-to-use Microsoft platform discovery utility. Under the tab **Windows Enumeration**, you will see a screen like the one shown in Figure 19.22. In the left window are optional types of enumeration scans. The very first one performs the same functionality as NBTScan, NetBIOS name retrieval, but in a GUI window. SuperScan automatically connects using a null session if you select that, or under **Options** you can set a specific user account and password to log in with.

> **WARNING**
>
> Be careful when you use an actual account to log in with. The password is not hidden by anonymous characters and is clearly visible even after the Options screen is closed and reopened. Leaving this utility running while away from your PC can expose this account information. The password is not stored anywhere after exit, however, so closing the program immediately after use should be standard procedure.

The amount of information gathered will, of course, depend on the level of privileges on the server, the server version, and whether it is a domain controller. With an inappropriately configured server, you can retrieve user account information, share information, permissions, running services, registry information, domain information and much more. The null session "feature" in Microsoft Windows has been considered a huge exposure, leaking serious amounts of information to unauthorized individuals.

Null sessions are a method of communication for Windows-based file and print services. They ease the administration of services, allowing anonymous queries from clients for resource information on a server. At the same time, they ease the enumeration of possible exposures for people with dishonorable intentions.

Figure 19.22 Null Session Feature

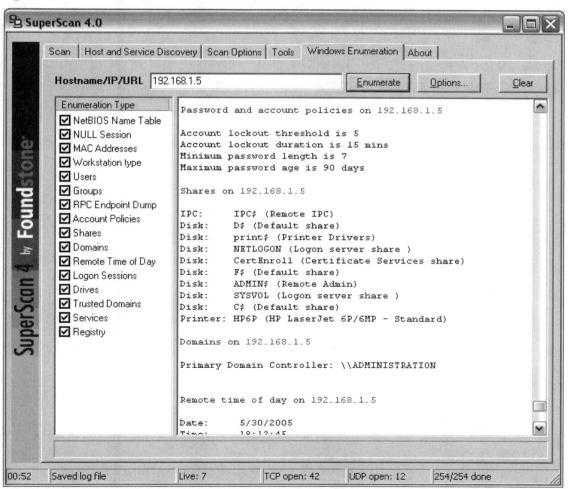

The example here displays only a small portion of what was reported, password policies, file and print shares, and domain information. The results also included users, groups, services, and more, all with only anonymous access.

WS_Ping Pro-Pak

Another utility in the WS_Ping Pro-Pak suite is the HTML tool. Again, the tool was designed from a management perspective to help administrators debug their HTML and discover problems. At the same time, it becomes a useful tool for performing security-based enumeration of a Web site.

The basic options for the HTML tool include a raw or formatted display of results, where the formatted option includes carriage returns. For faster testing, such as pure banner grabbing, you can set the tool to retrieve only the header information transmitted by the target (see Figure 19.23). If you deselect this option, the tool will retrieve the entire HTML document and present it in text form. Depending on the HTML, this may give more information such as literal paths or file information. This can also help identify the system and possible weaknesses, as well as exposures that could result from the HTML code itself.

Figure 19.23 WS_Pin ProPack

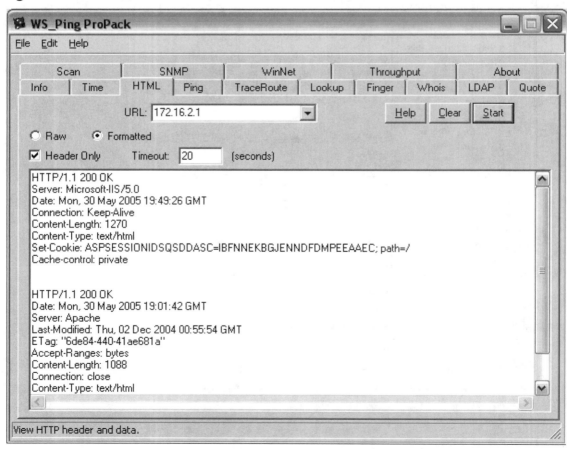

WS_Ping Pro-Pak also includes a GUI utility for performing finger queries as well as a Windows enumeration tool. Both operate similarly to other tools described in this chapter and are fairly simple to operate. One thing to remember about the WinNet Windows enumeration utility is that a null session must be manually created if the target and client are not trusted. This is simple enough to do—enter *net use \\target\IPC$ ""/user:""* from a command line. This will establish an anonymous null session to the target. To connect using a valid account, simply replace the first set of quotation marks with a password and the second set with the username.

UNIX Enumeration

Like Microsoft, UNIX products have enumeration services that enable us to learn more about their configuration. The three most common utilities are *finger, rpcinfo,* and *showmount.* With these three commands, we can collect process information, user accounts, and file mounts on UNIX devices with the services enabled.

In Figure 19.24, you can see the results of a query to a Solaris server with a specific finger vulnerability. When the argument *a b c d e f g h i* is added, the server responds with the entire user list. Normally the *finger* command will respond only with specified users, which makes it a great tool for verifying account information, such as e-mail names.

Figure 19.24 UNIX Enumeration Output

```
root@mercury:~# finger "a b c d e f g h i"@192.168.1.245
[192.168.1.245]
login        Name              TTY       Idle      When      Where
root         Super User        Console   <Jan  2, 2003>  :0
daemon       ???                         < .   .   . >
bin          ???                         < .   .   . >
sys          ???                         < .   .   . >
adm          Admin                       < .   .   . >
lp           Line prienter Admin         < .   .   . >
uucp         uucp admin                  < .   .   . >
nuucp        uucp Admin                  < .   .   . >
listen       Network Admin               < .   .   . >
nobody       Nobody                      < .   .   . >
noaccess     No Access User              < .   .   . >
nobody4      SunOS 4.X Nobody            < .   .   . >
russr        ???               pts/1     <Jun 16 13:29> 192.168.1.88
tdykstra     ???                         < .   .   . >
rcallow      ???                         < .   .   . >
tpham        ???                         < .   .   . >
sturner      ???                         < .   .   . >
gnotske      ???                         < .   .   . >
ffranks      ???                         < .   .   . >
dbuffo       ???                         < .   .   . >
nking        ???                         < .   .   . >
```

Telnet

Using Telnet or other command-line TCP connection applications such as Netcat is a perfect example of banner grabbing. The simplest way to define this concept is to connect to a host and review the service advertisement it generates, as returned to the client. We assume that this is a rather well-known method, so rather than go into much detail here, we'll just show examples of a few Telnet connections.

To retrieve the header information from a Web server, simply connect to the target using the command *telnet <target port>*, where *target* is the URL or IP address and *port* is the port the Web server is listening on. Once connected, type **HEAD / HTTP/1.0** to retrieve the site header information. An example output might be:

```
HTTP/1.1 200 OK
Content-Type: text/html
Date: Thu, 13 Sep 2007 11:41:03 GMT
Expires: Thu, 26 Oct 1995 00:00:00 GMT
Last-Modified: Thu, 13 Sep 2007 11:41:03 GMT
Pragma: no-cache
Server: RomPager/4.07 UPnP/1.0
```

An even simpler test is against an FTP server. Simply make the connection with the command *telnet <target> 21*, and you will be rewarded with a banner that normally includes both platform and FTP version information:

```
220 ce FTP version 1.0 ready at Sat Jun 18 11:57:47 2005
```

Similarly, we can gather information about e-mail services as well. Once you're connected via the command *telnet <target> 25*, a banner will be received that by default will display vendor and version information about the running e-mail application:

```
220 mail.testserver.com ESMTP Sendmail 8.12.11/8.12.10; Sun, 19 Jun 2005
07:39:34 -0600
```

Several commands within the simple message transfer mail protocol (SMTP) may help with enumeration as well. The *VRFY* command allows for the verification of e-mail accounts, which often include system accounts of the same name. If the system supports the *HELP* command, try that while connected to see what other tools might be available for enumeration testing. Here's an example response:

```
214-2.0.0    This is sendmail version 8.12.11
214-2.0.0    Topics:
214-2.0.0    HELO    EHLO    MAIL    RCPT    DATA
214-2.0.0    RSET    NOOP    QUIT    HELP    VRFY
214-2.0.0    EXPN    VERB    ETRN    DSN     AUTH
214-2.0.0    STARTTLS
```

```
214-2.0.0    For more info use "HELP <topic>".
214-2.0.0    To report bugs in the implementation send email to
214-2.0.0    sendmail-bugs@sendmail.org.
214-2.0.0    For local information send email to Postmaster at your site.
214 2.0.0    End of HELP info
```

Manual connections to services can be a great method for finding out what is running and discovering exposures that could lead to exploitation. This can be done from several applications such as Telnet or Netcat and often allows more investigation capabilities than an automated tool can provide.

DNS Queries

Domain Name System (DNS) enumeration is based on the Internet name to address mapping service. DNS is a rather important tool that supports the translation of named hosts to IP addresses, allowing for simpler network usage. Unfortunately, like any other service, it can be misconfigured to leak more information than is necessary, which assists in the reconnaissance activities of malicious attackers.

Device or service names are often created that match the function they provide, such as ftp. widgets.com or mail.widgets.com. These are required for basic use of e-mail and Web hosting can often include information that an entity really does not want the public to know. For example, any proxy-based firewalls that act as an intermediary to protect and hide the actual server should not be named firewall.widgets.com, although this happens frequently. This type of information can help an attacker determine where an organization's security controls and boundaries reside.

There are also concerns with public and private DNS data. An internal DNS tree often includes names such as hr.widgets.com, payroll.widgets.com, intranet.widgets.com, and many more. This can give an outsider far too much information about internal addressing schemes, as well as information for potential targets to play with if they crack the outer shell and get on the inside network. This information should only be available internally, but DNS hosts are often misconfigured to allow access to this information from the public network.

For basic user operations, DNS works as a basic query system. A client specifies the name of a host, and a DNS server responds with the IP address of the host in question. To replicate this information across multiple DNS servers, a zone transfer request is used. In this instance, a request for a domain is made, and the DNS server responds with all known information for that domain. Although this is not inherently a security violation, it can give too much information to a potential attacker much too easily. Zone transfers should be limited to known DNS peers only.

Multiple utilities already available, some already discussed in this chapter, have built-in functionality for performing DNS queries, including zone transfers. Many are simple Perl or batch scripts; others include a simple-to-navigate GUI. Figure 19.25 is an example of the tool *nslookup* that's available in the basic Windows platform (NT and above). The *ls* query requests basic information from a DNS server. As we can see, the single *-d* options represents a zone transfer, requesting all known information about a specific domain.

Figure 19.25 DNS Queries

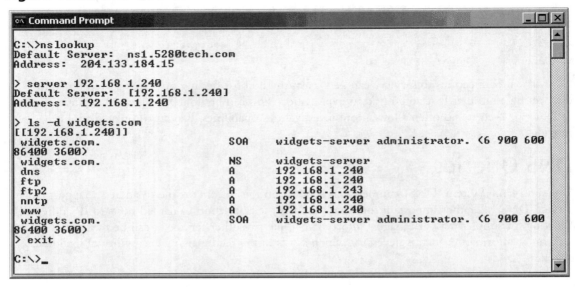

Enumeration and Banner-Grabbing System Mapping

Again, we continue to fill out our system mapping. With the completion of the third IEM baseline activity, we should have a pretty good understanding of most of the exposures to the system in terms of resources available to a remote client.

The system mapping can now be used to assist the fine-tuning of later activities, such as vulnerability detection (see Table 19.4). After the network discovery phase is completed, we can use this mapping to maximize efforts on what to test and how to test it, rather than just throwing everything at the system to see what sticks. The added effort you put in up front in creating the system mapping will pay off in the back end by assisting with validation efforts as well.

Table 19.4 IEM System Mapping

ABC123 IEM System Mapping					10/29/2004
XYZ Consulting			POC: Johnny Reboot		(555) 123.4567
Active Hosts:		4	Address Ranges:		192.168.1.0/24 172.16.2.0/24
IP Address / Device Name	Ports		Identified Services	Detected OS	Notes
192.168.1.36	TCP	135	NetBIOS	Microsoft Windows	Null Session open
	TCP	5000	HTTP		
192.168.1.69	TCP	22	OpenSSH Sun 1.1	Sun Solaris 9	Tomcat running, check for vulnerabilities
	TCP	898	Solaris Management Console Server		
172.16.2.5 mohican	UDP	161	Sun SNMP SPARC-5	Sun OS	SNMP String: Public statd and sadmind running 172.16.2.5-SNMP.txt
172.16.2.6 navajo	UDP	161	Sun SNMP SPARC-5	Sun OS	SNMP String: Public 172.16.2.6-SNMP.txt
WiFi MAC Address	Type	Crypt	SSID	Discovered IP Address	Notes

Wireless Enumeration

Wireless networking has seen a tremendous surge in the last five years. With the incredibly low cost of hardware and the amazing flexibility it allows in terms of network mobility, it's no wonder. Wireless client and gateway devices can be had for as little as $50. The most popular and cheaper devices are manufactured by vendors whose number-one market is the home network. These lean more to the "plug and play" type of solution rather than an appropriately configured secure solution. The price point of this solution also makes it difficult for many organizations to say no. In all honesty, security is really the only drawback to wireless networks in most environments and is often overlooked when reviewing wireless's benefits.

Wireless networks have been popping up in commercial and government arenas like crazy over the last few years. Unfortunately, there are inherent weaknesses in the 802.11 standards as well as client configurations. By default, most vendor products are currently configured without encryption enabled, and most users never bother to change these settings. Last year marked the fourth and final year of the World Wide War Drive (WWWD). The goal of the event's organizer, Chris Hurley, was to raise awareness of wireless security issues. To that effect, people across the globe took to the streets in an effort to discover and catalog as many wireless access points (AP) as possible. The results shown in Table 19.5 were published on the event's Web site:

Table 19.5 Wireless Access Points Tallied by the WWWD

Category	Total	Percent	Percent Change
Total AP Found	228537	100	N/A
WEP Enabled	87647	38.30	+6.04
No WEP Enabled	140890	61.6	-6.04
Default SSID	71805	31.4	+3.57
Default SSID and No WEP	62859	27.5	+2.74

Of over 225,000 APs, less than 40 percent were using encryption. And those aren't all home networks. Over 30 percent were using the default service set identifier (SSID) configured by the manufacturer. In all likelihood, most of those were simply dropped in place and used without any configuration by the user. Many industry insiders are referring to wireless as the new "modem" of IT security concerns because it can very easily leave the network wide open to a remote user. Instead of sitting at home, attackers can now sit in their cars.

Rather than drown this chapter in information regarding the state of wireless security and a discussion of the protocols, we'll cover the two most popular wireless enumeration tools and some of the more important aspects that need to be understood before we perform this activity. For a more detailed account of wireless networking pitfalls and solutions, we recommend you read an in-depth book published by Chris Hurley, Frank Thornton, and others: *War Driving Drive, Detect, Defend: A Guide to Wireless Security.*

Wireless Enumeration Obstacles

Prior to beginning any wireless enumeration, the evaluating team and the customer need to come to an agreement on the extent of that testing. The law regarding wireless network enumeration has been rather vague, although most experts agree that the cataloging of those networks is legal. The problem arises the instant you do anything other than simply discovering and cataloging.

The moment you connect to a wireless network, some experts believe, you break the law. At this point, you are using resources belonging to someone else without authorization and if you're discovered, it could lead to legal disputes. It's recommended that in the TEP, you document that wireless enumeration may include connection to discovered resources by the evaluation team. At the same time, unless there is a true need to connect, an evaluator may simply be better off documenting his or her findings and not connecting. Those discovered connecting might not belong to the target organization at all, but a neighboring entity. No agreement in place between the evaluation team and the customer will be of any use if you trespass on the network of an uninvolved organization.

There are also privacy concerns in regard to wireless enumeration. Any data captured as its transmitted over wireless network is the sole property of that organization, and recording this information can be considered a theft of information. Similar to the activity of network sniffing, this activity must be documented. If it is not required, it will likely be easier not to do it. The level of wireless network security evaluation is up to the customer, and any invasive procedures must be documented, including the return and destruction of private data.

As long as wireless enumeration is thoughtfully planned out and documented and due diligence used in performing the testing, the activity can be pretty straightforward.

Kismet

The first utility we'll cover is Kismet, an open source wireless detection utility designed for Linux. It uses a character-based GUI, ncurses, with the latest stable release being version 2005-04-R1 (the author has decided standardize his releases in dated versioning format). Started from a command line, Kismet's only real trick is getting the configuration operational.

Kismet relies on a passive listening mode, referred to as *rfmon,* to discover active networks. It does not send probes requesting beacon transmissions, and therefore it is completely nonintrusive to target systems. Unfortunately, *rfmon* capabilities are not supported by every vendor, because the client device must have firmware and driver support to use this function. The application documentation and the Web site have an excellent list of supported hardware and specific configurations within Kismet.

Kismet may be a time-consuming effort to get compiled, installed, and configured, but the supporting documentation is excellent and should answer most questions. Some of the added features beyond basic enumeration include wireless intrusion detection functions, logging compatibility with outside applications such as Ethereal and AirSnort, GPS mapping via *gpsmap*, and more. As you can see in Figure 19.26, the utility is fairly simple to use.

In the default display, the SSID of any discovered networks is listed under the name column. The column labeled **T** describes the type of device discovered; in this image all **A**s referring to APs. Client devices probing for available networks would be labeled with a **P**. The **W** column represents the use Wired Equivalent Privacy (WEP), which is an encryption method for 802.11 networks. The **CH** column represents the discovered frequency or channel the device is operating on. The number of packets received and the IP address range of the wireless network, if discovered, are also displayed. The **Flags** column shows current status information about the network. In the example, **U4** notifies us that the IP address range has been discovered up to 4 octets based on UDO traffic. **T3** tells us that the IP address range has been discovered up to 3 octets based on TCP traffic.

The window on the right in Figure 19.26 illustrates statistics regarding discoveries since the application began, such as the number of networks found, the number of cleartext and encrypted packets received, and more. In the bottom Status window you can see the latest information regarding Kismet's discoveries. Kismet definitely provides more functionality than simple wireless enumeration and is a great tool for more advanced security testing that is currently beyond the context of this chapter.

Figure 19.26 Kismet

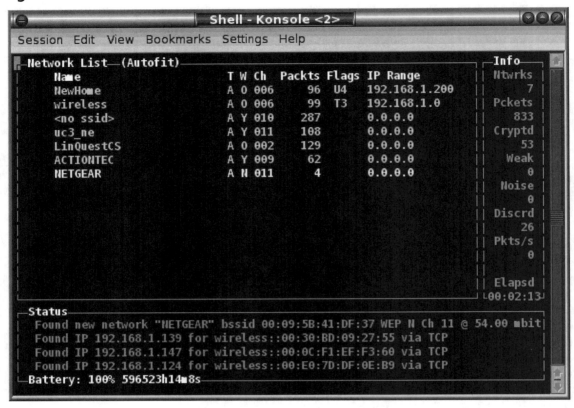

For logging, Kismet supports multiple output formats, including a raw data dump and filtered formats such as XML and CSV that show general discovered network information, a Cisco-specific dump of any Cisco Discovery Protocol (CDP) packets captured, and a dump of weak encryption packets for importing into AirSnort.

NetStumbler

Another widely popular wireless enumeration tool is NetStumbler. Built for the Microsoft Windows platform, NetStumbler is freely available product. The primary difference between Kismet and NetStumbler, besides the OS platform, is that NetStumbler performs active scanning. In this method, NetStumbler sends out beacon requests to determine information about wireless networks. In this mode, an AP configured to *cloak*, or not respond to beacon requests, will not be discovered by NetStumbler.

NetStumbler has an excellent GUI for quick and easy review of discovered networks. The tree view in the left window (see Figure 19.27) allows for basic device view display management, allowing you to group views by the channel they are operating on, their discovered SSID, and some preconfigured filters. For example, by selecting the appropriate filter on the left, the main view window will only display networks with encryption disabled or that are using the default vendor SSID.

Figure 19.27 NetStumbler

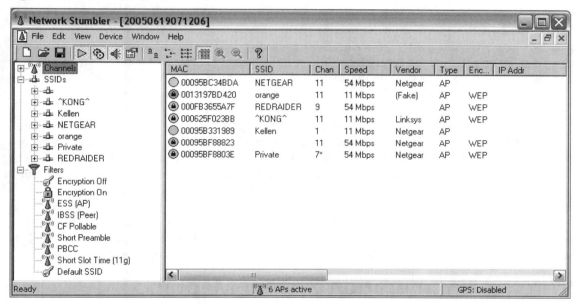

Each column or attribute in the display window is adjustable so that you can move the specific information into the main screen you want to see. NetStumbler reports far too much information per device to be viewed without scrolling. The most common information used for enumeration can easily fit into a single view, as shown. MAC address, SSIDs, channels, speed, vendor information, type of network, encryption, and IP addresses discovered are some of the most useful reporting features for enumeration. NetStumbler includes much more information regarding signal strength, signal-to-noise ratio (SNR), capability flags, and more that are beyond the scope of basic wireless enumeration.

NetStumbler supports a few common reporting formats that have been used in multiple staged projects such as the WWWD. The Wi-scan format has been used by multiple hobbyist competitions as well as groups trying to raise security awareness, because there are scripts available for combining multiple log files into a single aggregate. NetStumbler and Kismet are both GPS enabled, allowing for testing of signal range. This is a great added service for assisting the customer in determining their wireless exposure in terms of area availability. Often an organization will not be aware that its wireless networks are fully available in five levels of the parking garage across the street—an excellent place for the mischievous to hide while experimenting with the organization's network.

Added utilities for this function include gpsmap and GPSDrive, which work well with Kismet, and StumbVerter, which can create informational maps using NetStumbler data and Microsoft MapPoint.

Wireless Encryption Evaluation

Beyond the scope of the activity but perhaps a concern to the customer requiring additional testing is wireless encryption. The default WEP method has been shown to be vulnerable to key guessing, based on the collection of a certain number of packets. Simple utilities such as AirSnort and WEPCrack have been released that can determine the key in use when provided enough sample packets. Using a tool like Kismet to collect those packets and dump them for use is a trivial matter these days. Another utility call Aircrack has similar functionality but also includes a replay utility, aireplay, that can be used to increase the amount of encrypted traffic generated on the wireless network. This allows for a much faster collection of packets, cutting down the wait time on slower networks.

Vendors began incorporating their own proprietary security techniques, but the incompatibility between devices and vendors has made this a very slowly adopted security technique. Even some of those have already been proven weak, with utilities breaking their encryption. WiFI Protected Access (WPA) encryption technology has been released, but already weaknesses are being exposed, though it is still a much better solution than WEP. Adoption for WPA at this point seems rather slow, since it requires replacing an architecture with new equipment that may have already been put in place.

Again, this type of evaluation is beyond the normal scope of the IEM, but it can be included as added value for the customer if they have concerns in the area. Remember to document in detail any activity such as this in the TEP, so there are no misunderstandings about what will take place.

Wireless Enumeration System Mapping

Now that we have some information about the customer's wireless networking, we can add that to our system mapping. As a business process, the amount of information you document for the customer might vary, but a minimum should include the SSID of the network, encryptions status, and MAC address (see Table 19.6). In the case of rogue access points, provide as much information as possible that can help the customer identify the device.

Probing client devices should not be ignored, either. Many default PC configurations have the client automatically connect to any wireless network discovered. This means an attacker could host a fake access point, which the client will connect to. This gives the attacker a straight connection to the machine, often only a speed bump to the rest of the network. When you see the startled look on a laptop user's face in the airport, you can guess what just happened. Some networks send pop-up messages to clients, trying to entice them into using the WiFi service. This represents large exposure that can be easily exploited.

Table 19.6 IEM System Mapping

ABC123 IEM System Mapping					10/29/2004
XYZ Consulting			POC: Johnny Reboot		(555) 123.4567
Active Hosts:		9	Address Ranges:		192.168.1.0/24 172.16.2.0/24
IP Address / Device Name	Ports		Identified Services	Detected OS	Notes
192.168.1.36	TCP	135	NetBIOS	Microsoft Windows	Null Session open
	TCP	5000	HTTP		
192.168.1.69	TCP	22	OpenSSH Sun 1.1	Sun Solaris 9	Tomcat running, check for vulnerabilities
	TCP	898	Solaris Management Console Server		
172.16.2.5 mohican	UDP	161	Sun SNMP SPARC-5	Sun OS	SNMP String: Public statd and sadmind running 172.16.2.5-SNMP.txt
172.16.2.6 navajo	UDP	161	Sun SNMP SPARC-5	Sun OS	SNMP String: Public 172.16.2.6-SNMP.txt
WiFi MAC Address	Type	Crypt	SSID	Discovered IP Address	Notes
00:0F:66:03:43:EC	Infra	WPA	NewHome	192.168.1.200	
00:90:4B:37:26:9C	Infra	WPA	Wireless	192.168.1.0	

Summary

We've covered a wide array of available tools for performing the first four IEM baseline activities. There are obviously a lot of options for each IEM activity for both the UNIX and Windows platforms. After reading this chapter, the evaluator should understand the IEM's requirements for the operation of tools and the evaluation goals for each activity. Many of these tools work together very well to provide a flexible and efficient solution. Limited testing can be performed very quickly, allowing the evaluator to perform secondary testing in critical areas based on his or her understanding of the system and common security weaknesses.

Although this chapter focused primarily on the introduction of tools to achieve the goals of each activity, no utility can make up for the knowledge and experience of the evaluator. A successful IEM engagement hinges on the evaluator's ability to recognize potential weaknesses in context with the criticality of the system being evaluated. Getting the most out of each tool's capabilities relies on the strength of the evaluator, both with the tool and in understanding the baseline activity itself.

This chapter also introduced the concept of a system mapping. This is a rather common practice for many INFOSEC professionals and fits very well into the IEM. Although this remains a business process, the benefit it represents to the customer and the evaluation team is hard to ignore. The system mapping introduced here is simply an example and can be modified to fit evaluator and customer needs.

## Chapter 20

Collecting the Majority of Vulnerabilities

Solutions in this chapter:

- **Vulnerability and Attack Trends**
- **Conducting Vulnerability Scans**
- **Conducting Host Evaluations**
- **Validating Findings**
- **Mapping Findings to the IEM Process**

☑ **Summary**

Introduction

This chapter covers the vulnerability scanning and host evaluation portions of the IEM (see Figure 20.1). Vulnerability scanning is conducted from the network perspective, and host evaluations are conducted directly on the target components or systems. You will more than likely have a different view of the system when you're at the console than when you're evaluating the systems from the network.

Figure 20.1 Phases of the IEM

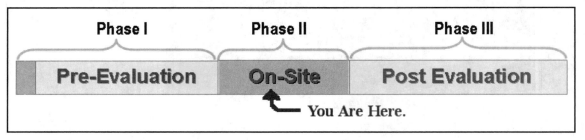

In this chapter we define vulnerability scanning and the goals of these scans in relation to the IEM. We also discuss current vulnerability and attack trends. Then we break out the vulnerability scanning tools (a.k.a. The Fun Part) and gather some findings! Of course, after gathering our findings from the vulnerability scans, we will need to validate and document them (a.k.a. The Not-So-Fun Part). As you can see from Figure 20.2, vulnerabilities play a key role in the management of risk and an organization's INFOSEC posture.

Figure 20.2 The Risk Triangle

The goal of this section of the evaluation is to identify vulnerabilities within the organization. Following the vulnerability-scanning portion of the chapter, we examine host evaluations and define their goals in relation to the IEM. We also discuss what to look for during host evaluations, go over the use of benchmark scripts, and map our host evaluation findings back to the IEM—*after* validating the findings, of course!

Vulnerability and Attack Trends

Computer Emergency Response Team (CERT) was created in November 1988, just after the Morris Worm hit, and has been tracking vulnerability notifications, security bulletins, and INFOSEC incidents ever since. Using the data it gathers, CERT has provided a fairly detailed group of statistics regarding INFOSEC incidents and vulnerability notifications that are released. Some astonishing trends have shown up in the past few years. In fact, the number of incidents reported grew so large that the metrics became essentially useless for meaningful incident tracking. The statistics for 2000–2003 are shown in Table 20.1; you can see the dramatic increase in reported incidents each year.

Table 20.1 Incident Tracking, 2000–2003

Year	2000	2001	2002	2003
Incidents	21,756	52,658	82,094	137,529
% Increase	221%	242%	156%	168%

(Note: According to CERT/CC Statistics 1988–2005 (www.cert.org/stats/cert_stats.html), 9,859 incidents were reported in 1999.)

In 2004, CERT ceased providing the number of reported INFOSEC incidents and is instead focusing on other projects, such as the E-Crime Watch Survey. What changed? Why are there so many incidents occurring each year? Here are some of the trends CERT is noticing:

- There is an increased threat to e-commerce sites.
- The time between vulnerability notification and exploit release (known as *time till exploit*, or TTE) is dramatically decreasing
- Web-enabled applications are increasing in popularity as an attack vector.
- There is an increase in High and Medium rated vulnerabilities, that are easy to exploit.
- There has been a massive increase in 'bot networks and 'bot network activity (a.k.a. botnets).
- Attackers are becoming more organized and well prepared.

Notes from the Underground

What Is a Botnet?

The term *botnet* is short for ro*bot net*work. A botnet consists of large numbers of systems that have been compromised (via virus, Trojan horse, and the like) and are commonly used for tasks such as conducting distributed denial of service (DDoS) attacks and sending spam. Hundreds, sometimes thousands, of computers will be part of a single botnet. Most of the time the end users are not even aware that their machine has been subverted and is being used for such dark purposes.

The most common method of compromise being used by botnet controllers and creators is via a Trojan program. The Trojan program is executed on the system, opens up an IRC channel specified by the 'bot creator, and waits for the person controlling the botnet to issue it commands. Many botnets are also for sale to the highest bidder. Lists of compromised computers are sold to spammers and other such unscrupulous people for use in their illicit activities.

CERT attributes the change in reporting to widespread use of attack tools that are becoming increasingly automated and easy to use. CERT also notes that it's become very commonplace for Internet-connected systems to be attacked. Automated attack tools and the short time from vulnerability announcement to exploit release are the two key factors that led CERT to revise its incident reporting. Only time will tell whether this new reporting mechanism will fill the needs of the INFOSEC community; providing better tracking and meaningful statistics.

It's a difficult task to track this information, since it's a fast-moving target. SANS releases a Top 20 list, a consensus list of critical vulnerabilities that require immediate remediation. Organizations use the SANS Top 20 list, shown in Table 20.2 (www.sans.org/top20/), to prioritize their efforts and resources so they can close the most dangerous security holes first. In actuality, the Top 20 list is really two Top 10 lists —the 10 most commonly exploited vulnerable services in Windows and the 10 most commonly exploited elements in UNIX and Linux are shown in Table 20.2.

Table 20.2 SANS Top 20 List for 1Q2005

Top Vulnerabilities to Windows Systems	Top Vulnerabilities to UNIX Systems
W1 – Web Servers & Services	U1 – BIND Domain Name System
W2 – Workstation Service	U2 – Web Server
W3 – Windows Remote Access Services	U3 – Authentication
W4 – Microsoft SQL Server (MSSQL)	U4 – Version Control Systems

Table 20.2 Continued

Top Vulnerabilities to Windows Systems	Top Vulnerabilities to UNIX Systems
W5 – Windows Authentication	U5 – Mail Transport Service
W6 – Web Browsers	U6 – Simple Network Mgmt Protocol (SNMP)
W7 – File-Sharing Applications	U7 – Open Secure Sockets Layer (SSL)
W8 – LSAS Exposures	U8 – Misconfiguration of Enterprise Services
W9 – Mail Client	U9 – Databases
W10 – Instant Messaging	U10 – Kernel

One interesting trend is that attackers are moving from OS-level attacks to application-level attacks. A favorite within the INFOSEC community seems to be Web-enabled applications, since they are more likely to be susceptible to buffer overflows, errors in boundary checking for variables, or SQL injection attack vectors. Usually these vulnerabilities are not trivial to exploit and require a deeper understanding of the application and its interactions with the underlying operating system. This is where today's more intelligent vulnerability assessment tools tend to shine.

But the security tools are only a portion of the overall INFOSEC evaluation effort. The person doing the evaluation (that would be you) contributes personal experience, knowledge, and the ability to reason. These skills are very important to the evaluation and are useful for weeding out false-positive findings as well as tailoring the evaluation to the organization's infrastructure. False positives are reported vulnerabilities that aren't real. An example of a false positive finding is if the vulnerability scanner notes an IIS-specific finding against an Apache server. The sidebar includes a few helpful URLs for locating INFOSEC mailing lists and tools that can help you keep up to date on vulnerabilities and their impacts.

Notes from the Underground

Useful Sites: INFOSEC Mailing Lists, Tools, and Information

Here are some rather useful sites for security tools and security mailing lists:

- Tools and mailing lists: www.securityfocus.com
- Tools: packetstormsecurity.nl
- Mailing list: lists.apple.com/mailman/listinfo/security-announce
- Mailing list archives: seclists.org
- Tools and security advisories: www.frsirt.com/english/index.php
- Tools and security advisories: www.microsoft.com/technet/security/

Vulnerability Scanning's Role in the IEM

As we have mentioned in previous chapters of this Part, the IEM process is an evaluation of an organization's INFOSEC posture. The vulnerability assessment portion of the IEM is a more detailed analysis of the components that comprise the organization's critical INFOSEC assets and infrastructure. By identifying potential vulnerabilities or configuration issues with the evaluated components, the organization then has the opportunity to mitigate these findings, based on your recommendations, to better their overall INFOSEC posture. This is an essential element to the security gap analysis, and gap reduction, processes.

Tools & Traps

Vulnerability Scanning Tools

It's important to know that not every tool or program is perfect. Each tool has a core area that it is better at than other areas. So it is best to conduct vulnerability scans using at least two different tools. Here are some of the more commonly used vulnerability-scanning tools:

- Nessus, www.nessus.org
- eEye Retina, www.eeye.com
- SAINT, www.saintcorporation.com
- GFi Network Security Scanner, www.gfi.com
- HFNetChk, www.shavlik.com
- ISS Internet Scanner, www.iss.net
- NeWT, www.tenablesecurity.com
- Firewalk, www.packetfactory.net/Projects/
- Benchmark scripts and RAT, www.cisecurity.org
- Microsoft Baseline Security Analyzer, www.microsoft.com/mbsa/

The vulnerability-scanning tools used during an IEM should be CVE and CAN compliant, meaning that they should list the appropriate CVE/CAN numbers for findings and give a High, Medium, or Low rating. CVE, or common vulnerabilities and exposures, is "a list of standardized names for vulnerabilities and other information security exposures. CVE aims to standardize the names for all publicly known vulnerabilities and security exposures." A list of CVE compatible products, services, and applications can be found at www.cve.mitre.org/compatible.

The Mitre Corporation maintains the CVE/CAN list, which is freely available to the public and is sponsored by US-CERT at the U.S. Department of Homeland Security. As of May 2005, over 10,000 unique information security issues were listed, with publicly known names. That's quite a few security issues! And more are discovered daily. You are not "required" to use the CVE/CAN list, but for the IEM process the NSA *highly* recommends that you use a CVE/CAN-compliant resource. What is required is that you use some form of vulnerability rating and identification system that is accessible by the customer. The standardized name and numbering scheme, as well as the mapping of the vulnerabilities to High, Medium, or Low criticality, are essential to the IEM and to correlating the findings to the organization's mission-critical INFOSEC resources. This helps to prioritize the findings so that the evaluation efforts are properly focused on what matters (to the organization). Figures 20.3 and 20.4 are actual CVE and CAN entries, respectively, provided here as an example.

Figure 20.3 A Sample CVE Entry

```
Name: CVE-2004-0121
Reference: IDEFENSE:20040309 Microsoft Outlook "mailto:" Parameter Passing Vulnerability
Reference: BUGTRAQ:20040310 Outlook mailto: URL argument injection vulnerability
Reference: MS:MS04-009
Reference: CERT-VN:VU#305206
Reference: BID:9827
Reference: XF:outlook-mailtourl-execute-code(15414)
Reference: OVAL:OVAL843


Argument injection vulnerability in Microsoft Outlook 2002 does not
sufficiently filter parameters of mailto: URLs when using them as
arguments when calling OUTLOOK.EXE, which allows remote attackers to
use script code in the Local Machine zone and execute arbitrary
programs.
```

Figure 20.4 A Sample CAN Entry

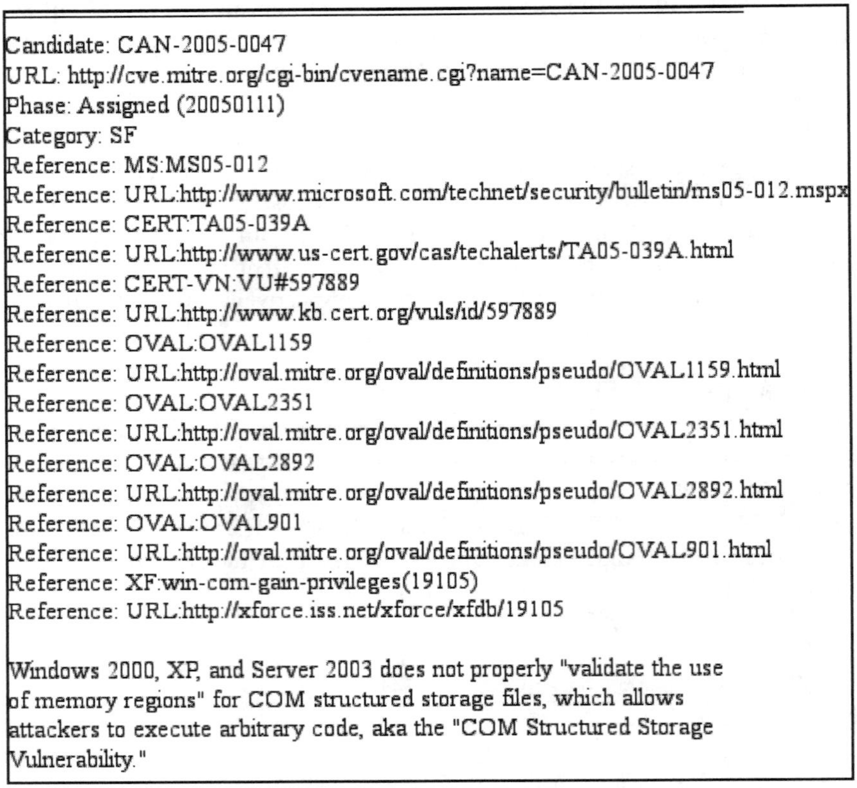

```
Candidate: CAN-2005-0047
URL: http://cve.mitre.org/cgi-bin/cvename.cgi?name=CAN-2005-0047
Phase: Assigned (20050111)
Category: SF
Reference: MS:MS05-012
Reference: URL:http://www.microsoft.com/technet/security/bulletin/ms05-012.mspx
Reference: CERT:TA05-039A
Reference: URL:http://www.us-cert.gov/cas/techalerts/TA05-039A.html
Reference: CERT-VN:VU#597889
Reference: URL:http://www.kb.cert.org/vuls/id/597889
Reference: OVAL:OVAL1159
Reference: URL:http://oval.mitre.org/oval/definitions/pseudo/OVAL1159.html
Reference: OVAL:OVAL2351
Reference: URL:http://oval.mitre.org/oval/definitions/pseudo/OVAL2351.html
Reference: OVAL:OVAL2892
Reference: URL:http://oval.mitre.org/oval/definitions/pseudo/OVAL2892.html
Reference: OVAL:OVAL901
Reference: URL:http://oval.mitre.org/oval/definitions/pseudo/OVAL901.html
Reference: XF:win-com-gain-privileges(19105)
Reference: URL:http://xforce.iss.net/xforce/xfdb/19105

Windows 2000, XP, and Server 2003 does not properly "validate the use
of memory regions" for COM structured storage files, which allows
attackers to execute arbitrary code, aka the "COM Structured Storage
Vulnerability."
```

Conducting Vulnerability Scans

By this time in the evaluation process, you should have a list of components (workstations, servers, network devices, and/or architecture-level devices) that make up the critical INFOSEC infrastructure for the organization. The critical INFOSEC infrastructure is made up of systems that handle the organization's critical information or that have a direct impact on mission operations.

As you may recall, the Technical Evaluation Plan (TEP) is the road map that guides the evaluation efforts and dictates which resources are necessary to properly conduct the evaluation. It also provides us with the "target list" for the evaluation. The list provided in the TEP is intended to include all components, networks, devices, and systems to be evaluated. But occasionally some essential components might not be on the list when they should be. If additional systems and components are discovered during the onsite phase of the evaluation, they should be added to the TEP's "target list" to ensure that they are accounted for, and evaluated, during this process.

NOTE

Vulnerability scanning is typically the portion of the evaluation with which the customer organization is most familiar. It's very important to ensure that the proper expectations are set for activities done during the evaluation and the deliverables.

For example, the customer may request an attack and penetration test (A&P) when what they are actually looking for is a comprehensive vulnerability assessment conducted by an independent third party to measure INFOSEC compliance with the Sarbanes-Oxley Act of 2002.

Breaking Out the Scanning Tools

Before you start scanning for vulnerabilities, let's look at a few points to keep in mind while conducting the scans:

- Depending on the type of scans being conducted and how the information is gathered, these tools can be intrusive and could cause adverse effects on the device being scanned.

- There is a potential for the vulnerability-scanning tools to present false positive findings. Both you, as the evaluator, and the customer should be aware of this. That is why it is so important to validate all findings.

- Some device issues cannot be checked for by a network vulnerability scan; thus we would depend on the information gathered from the device itself (to be obtained during host evaluations).

- In many cases, using the default configuration of these scanning tools will break something in the customer's networks. We'll want to ensure that we're using custom configurations based on our understanding of what the customer has installed and running on their networks.

There are a variety of vulnerability scanners out there, both commercial and freeware. Some work better at scanning Microsoft Windows networks; other scanning tools excel at scanning UNIX networks. That is why it is important to use more than one scanner — to fill the gaps in the evaluation results/findings left by other tools and to validate findings already discovered. NSA only requires that one tool, application, or activity be run to address each of the 10 baseline categories in the IEM, but past history has shown that it's prudent to run at least two different vulnerability scanners to address potential false positives and ensure comprehensive discovery of findings.

TIP

If you are planning to do UDP scanning during your assessments (which you should), be aware that it will significantly increase your scan times. If there is no service running on the UDP port that is being checked, the host will not respond. Since UDP is a connectionless protocol, your scanning tools have to wait for the specified UDP timeout to expire. When there is no service monitoring that UDP port, this will occur for each UDP port you scan.

Vulnerability Scanners: Commercial and Freeware

One of the more popular vulnerability scanners available commercially is Retina Network Security S canner (see Figure 20.5), developed by eEye Digital Security (www.eeye.com/html/products/retina/).

Figure 20.5 Retina Network Security Scanner

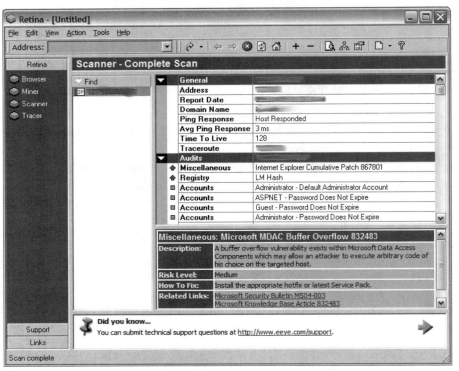

Retina Network Security Scanner has a very detailed vulnerability database that not only provides the vulnerability description, risk level, quick-fix information, and related links (to follow up for further information on the vulnerability) — it also provides the ability to fix many of the vulnerabilities it finds. It is important to note that this tool can only attempt to fix the vulnerabilities it finds on Microsoft Windows platforms, and it requires domain administrator privileges to do so.

Another commercial vulnerability scanner is SAINT, or the Security Administrators Integrated Network Tool (www.saintcorporation.com/saint/). This scanner (see Figures 20.6 and 20.7) runs on only UNIX, Linux, and Mac OS X. However, SAINT does have a remote mode that is available via two methods: add a *-r* on the command line when starting up SAINT or edit *saint.cf* in the SAINT config directory and set *$remote_mode* to *1*. This option allows you to run the SAINT scanner/server on a supported platform and permits you to interface with it via an Internet browser on an unsupported platform (such as Microsoft Windows). Note that the scans will still originate from the host running SAINT, not from the client.

Figure 20.6 SAINT Initial Screen

Figure 20.7 SAINT Data Collection

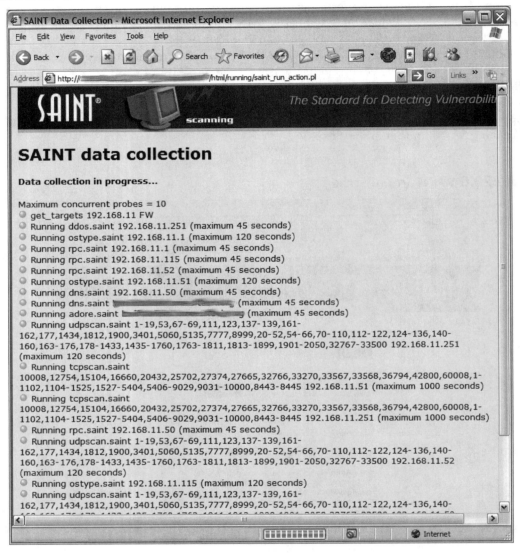

Next is a commercial version of the freeware tool Nessus, called Tenable NeWT (www. tenablesecurity.com). It's Nessus for the Microsoft Windows platform (see Figure 20.8). Normally, the Nessus server runs on only UNIX, Linux, Mac OS X, and other BSD variants; but it doesn't run natively on Microsoft Windows.

TIP

We were able to get Nessus, version 2.2.4 server and client, to compile and run within a Cygwin environment on Windows XP. It took some manual installation of certain libraries and header files, but it compiles and works! W00t!

There is a client for MS Windows, but not a Nessus server/scanner. This is where Tenable's NeWT comes in to fill the gap by providing a commercially supported, Nessus-based vulnerability scanner that runs on Microsoft Windows.

Figure 20.8 Tenable NeWT Scan in Progress

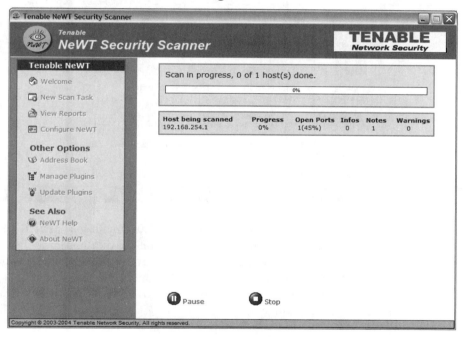

NeWT is somewhat lacking in reporting capabilities, as you can see by the report example in Figure 20.9. Furthermore, it was not able to banner-grab off the open ports to see what services are running on host 192.168.254.1. This resulted in NeWT reporting more false-positive findings than the other vulnerability scanners.

Figure 20.9 A Sample Tenable NeWT Security Report

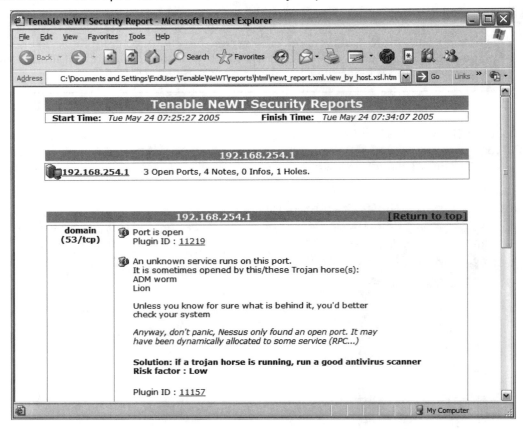

The next vulnerability scanner is also a patch management platform. Shavik HFNetChkPro (www.shavlik.com/hf.aspx) is a tool focused on assessing vulnerabilities on the Microsoft Windows platform and associated applications, which it does well (see Figure 20.10). There are four different versions, or feature sets, of HFNetChk: Basic Edition, Audit Edition, HFNetChkPro, and HFNetChkPro Plus. This tool is useful for discovering patches that are missing from workstations and servers in Microsoft Windows environments.

Figure 20.10 The HFNetChk Starting Screen

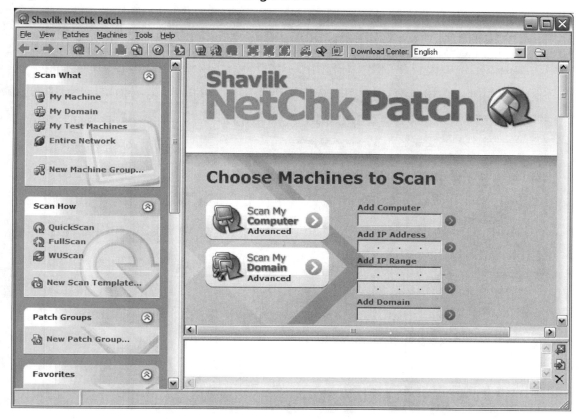

Figure 20.11 is a screen capture of an HFNetChk Pro report. It has a quick summary of the scan results, scan date/time, number of machines scanned, and the overall HFNetChk security assessment (summary) for the devices scanned. This information is very useful. If any critical issues come up on the report, it provides the evidence needed to get the issues resolved quickly.

Figure 20.11 A HFNetChk Report

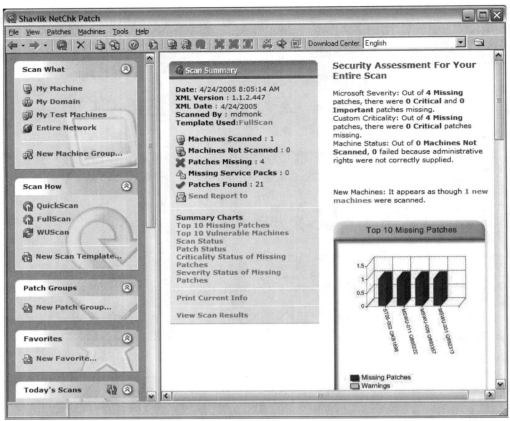

Another well-known vulnerability scanner is ISS Internet Scanner (www.iss.net), which has been a popular vulnerability scanner for several years and is the preferred scanning tool for many die-hard ISS fans. Like many vulnerability scanners, ISS Internet Scanner has a built-in discovery mode (ISS calls it "Asset Identification"). ISS states that Internet Scanner can identify more than 1,300 types of devices and uses a technology called Dynamic Check Assignment to tailor, in real time, the scanning rules and policies to the environment being scanned. This should help reduce false-positive and false-negative findings. One further note: The reporting functionality in Internet Scanner is fairly comprehensive. It has over 70 report templates by default and the ability to create custom report templates (see Figure 20.12).

Figure 20.12 ISS Internet Scanner Interface

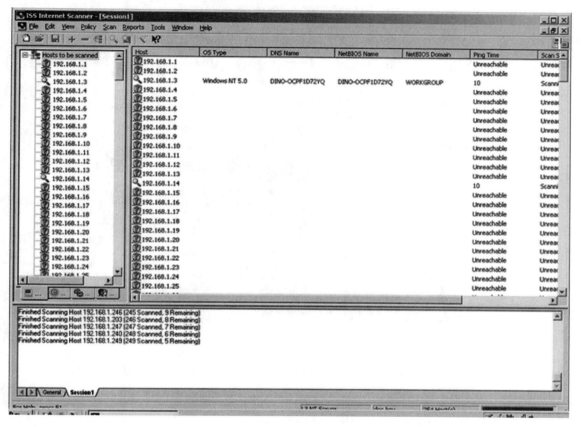

Now we get to nearly everyone's favorite freeware vulnerability scanner, Nessus (www.nessus.org). Nessus, probably the most popular freeware scanner, currently has a very large installed base of devoted followers. It is estimated that the Nessus scanner is being used by over 75,000 organizations worldwide (www.nessus.org/about/). That must mean Nessus is doing something right!

Nessus is highly configurable, able to run scans in multiple threads in parallel, and able to run detached scans and scheduled scans as well as interactive scan sessions. Figure 20.13 shows an example of Nessus running scans in parallel.

Figure 20.13 Nessus Running Scans in Parallel

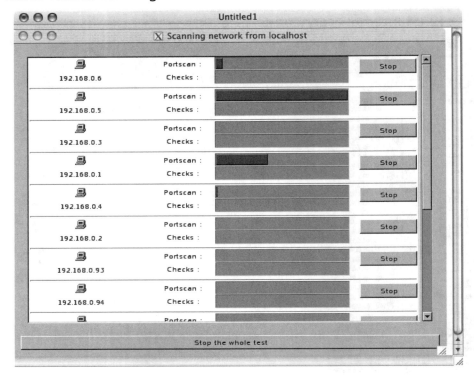

Figure 20.14 is an example of the Nessus reporting interface. Through this interface you can "drill down" into the details of the scan results. Do not forget to validate all findings and remove the false positives.

Figure 20.14 The Nessus Reporting Interface

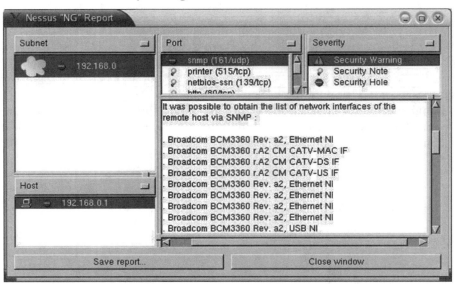

The next vulnerability assessment tool is GFi LANGuard Network Security Scanner (www.gfi.com/lannetscan/), or NSS, which is a Microsoft Windows–only scanner in that it runs on only Microsoft Windows and scans only Microsoft Windows platforms and associated applications or services. It's very selective in comparison to other popular vulnerability scanners. However, it should be noted that what NSS does scan, it scans well. When run locally on Microsoft Windows machines, this tool covers part of the host evaluation requirements for Microsoft Windows platforms (see Figure 20.15).

Figure 20.15 A GFi NSS Report Containing All Vulnerabilities

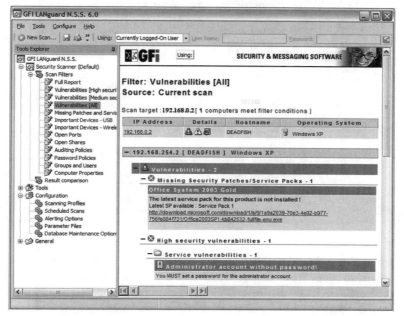

Notice how granular you can get with the reporting in LANGuard NSS. In addition to drilling down into the information gathered concerning the current scan target(s), GFi provides you with several scan filters to filter through the aggregate information that GFi maintains from each scan. This could provide you with a wealth of information over time. This tool is useful for trending analysis, metrics, and asset tracking/management (see Figure 20.16).

Figure 20.16 A GFi NSS High Vulnerability Finding Report

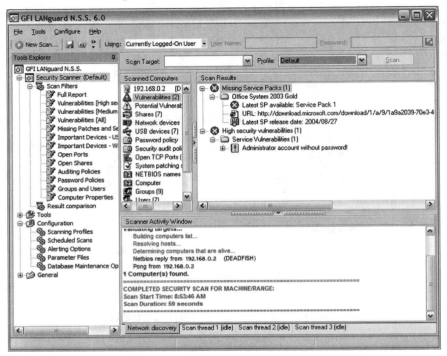

Using the vulnerability scanning tools is only part of the finding-gathering process. Vulnerability scans are conducted from a network perspective; the next part of our evaluation requires that we conduct host evaluations. Due to the host evaluations being conducted "at the console," so to speak, we hope to gain a more detailed view and analysis of the components, devices, servers, workstations, and so on we are evaluating.

Conducting Host Evaluations

Host-based evaluations, or console-level evaluations, are important to the evaluation process in that they provide us with a more detailed, more precise view of the components involved. Given that host evaluations are conducted on the device itself or via secure console communications to the device, we are able to access more detailed information about the device. The host-based evaluation is the third "perspective" we need for the IEM; the other two are the external and internal perspectives.

NOTE

According to the methodology, the NSA requires us to test 100 percent of critical systems. You are required to test 100 percent of the servers and critical workstations. But for noncritical workstations, a smaller "representative" subset is tested — approximately 10–15 percent of the workstations. By "representative" we mean that you should test workstations that are typical for the organization, such as the workstations that are similarly built via a common installation image.

Host Evaluation Example Tools and Scripts

Remember the three types of scans/perspectives: external, internal, and host based. Host based is the next perspective we need to cover in our evaluation. The problem with host evaluations is that the tasks can be time consuming, somewhat repetitive, and a bit tedious. Host evaluation tools and benchmark scripts are handy in that they help with the repetitive tasks involved in this type of evaluation.

Since the required checks generally necessitate local access, the bulk of host evaluation tasks are conducted manually, or in some cases via remote domain administrator access or SSH. The exceptions are routers, firewall, and switches where the device configuration is usually analyzed on a different host — for example, using the evaluator's system with RAT installed to check a Cisco router configuration. Firewall rulebases are generally checked manually by an evaluation team member.

Some tools cover more than one of the baseline activities, at least partially (in other words, provide data for vulnerability scanning and host evaluation activities). And some tools focus on certain operating systems or applications. Therefore, depending on the scope of the evaluation, your INFOSEC toolset may vary. No single INFOSEC tool will fulfill all assessment and evaluation needs or requirements. That's why it's recommended that all evaluation team members familiarize themselves with available tools. Since a large part of the host evaluation is more manual than tool oriented, we focus our discussion around the requirements rather than the supporting tools and scripts.

One example of a host evaluation tool that happens to be available for free from Microsoft is the Microsoft Baseline Security Analyzer (MSBA). The latest version of this tool as of this writing is v1.2.1 (see Figure 20.17). This tool is designed to evaluate the baseline security posture of Microsoft Windows platforms. It can scan the local machine as well as an IP network or Windows domain. Even though MSBA has network-scanning capabilities, we include it in this section due to the depth of its host-based evaluation functionality. MSBA provides more information to the host evaluation process than it does to the vulnerability scanning process.

Figure 20.17 Microsoft Baseline Security Analyzer Security Report

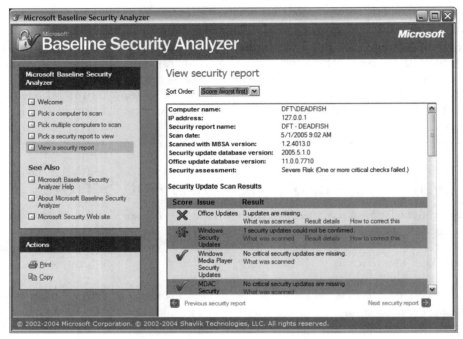

Benchmark Scripts and Custom Scripts

Conducting the host evaluations can be time consuming and tedious work. So what does any geek worth his (or her) salt do? They script it! A general rule of thumb is, "If you have to do it more than twice, script it." Thankfully, the Center for Internet Security (CIS) has put together sets of benchmark scripts and tools to measure a machine's security posture. According to information at www.cisecurity.org/bench.html, the machines are measured against "consensus best-practice security configurations for computers connected to the Internet." This provides you with the required baseline to measure the systems against. A quick note: The benchmark tools and scripts from CIS (see Figure 20.18 and www.cisecurity.org/benchmarks.html) are not free for commercial/consulting use, but they are free for individual users and government users. Commercial users are required to become CIS members to utilize the benchmark tools and scripts.

The following is a list of the operating systems, devices, and applications that CIS provides benchmarks and scripts for. First, the operating systems:

- Windows XP Pro

- Windows 2003 Server

- Windows 2000 Server, Pro

- Windows NT

- FreeBSD

- Solaris 2.5.1 through 10

- Linux
- HP-UX
- AIX
- OS X

The devices:

- Wireless Networks
- Cisco Router IOS
- Cisco PIX

The applications:

- Oracle Database
- Apache Web Server

Figure 20.18 The CIS Benchmarks and Tools Listing

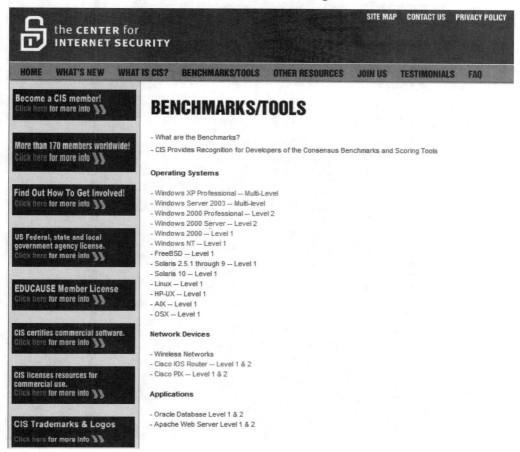

The CIS benchmarks for Windows have a GUI interface, and the benchmarks for the supported UNIX/Linux platforms are accessed via a command-line interface. Figure 20.19 is an example of the CIS benchmark scoring tool being run on Microsoft Windows. The Windows 2000 Professional security template is shown as selected. The security template contains the "best-practices benchmarks" that the system is to be measured against. The Microsoft Windows templates are stored in *.inf format.

Figure 20.19 The CIS Benchmark Tool Using the Windows 2000 Pro Security Template

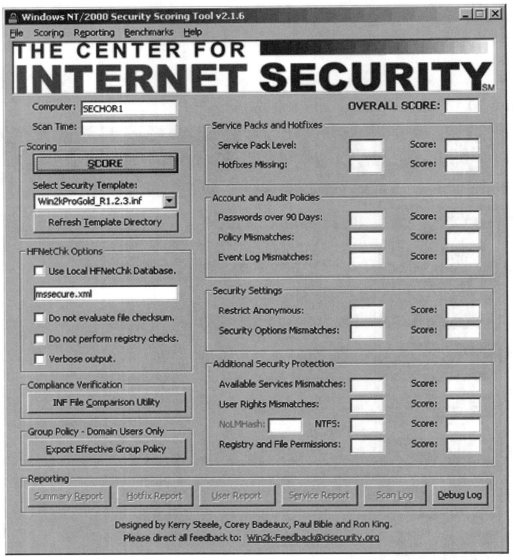

Figure 20.20 is a screen capture of the Solaris CIS benchmark tool being run. As you can tell, it has a command-line interface rather than a GUI interface. Execution of the CIS tool is done via the UNIX shell. Due to what is being checked and where the files are that are being checked, root access is required to run the CIS benchmarks on UNIX.

Figure 20.20 The CIS Benchmark Tool for the Solaris Platform

```
* Lead Developer                                : Jay Beale         *
* Benchmark Coordinator and Gadfly              : Hal Pomeranz      *
*                                                                   *
* Copright 2001 - 2003 The Center for Internet Security  www.cisecurity.org *
*                                                                   *
* Please send feedback to sol-scan@cisecurity.org.                 *
*********************************************************************

            Investigating system...this will take a few minutes...

                        ******

Now a final check for non-standard world-writable files, Set-UID and Set-GID
programs -- this can take a whole lot of time if you have a large filesystem.
Your score if there are no extra world-writable files or SUID/SGID programs
found will be 3.56 / 10.00 .  If there are extra SUID/SGID programs or
world-writable files, your score could be as low as 3.29 / 10.00 .

        You can hit CTRL-C at any time to stop at this remaining step.

The preliminary log can be found at: ./cis-most-recent-log

                        ******
```

Host Evaluations: What to Look For

Now that we are here at the host, what do we look for? We're glad you asked, since that is what we are going to discuss next. The host evaluation can be broken down into several areas: auditing, file/directory permissions, OS and application services, user rights assignments, and patch management.

Auditing

Auditing is basically security logging, or logging events that are important in terms of security. For example, a Windows domain group policy object (GPO) may require the logging of all accesses of system-critical files. Or every time the registry is modified, a log entry is created. You can imagine how quickly these log files would grow, and it usually turns out that quite a few unimportant events are being logged as well. This serves to make the monitoring of audit logs more difficult, but it's not a task the organization can afford to let slide.

By default, Microsoft Windows does not audit (log) many activities that could be considered detrimental to a system or its data. UNIX systems are better about logging events, but critical systems require more stringent auditing be enabled to be really effective. The organization should enable (better) auditing on these devices so that critical components can be monitored more effectively. It is part of the evaluation to verify that auditing is enabled and that events are being monitored. It's very easy to ignore the audit logs when they start to overflow with logged events; some events are important, though for our evaluation purposes, most are not.

All log events on Microsoft Windows platforms are entered into one of three main logs:

- Application log
- System log
- Security log

On UNIX (or Linux) systems, most logs are stored in /var/log or /var/adm. Some important log files to check are:

- syslog
- messages
- secure
- maillog

Keep in mind that this list is not all-inclusive! There may be additional log files to check, depending on the organization. They may have a "home-brew" application that is doing its own thing logging-wise. It is up to the evaluator (you again) to validate that auditing is enabled and working according to the organization's policies and procedures. Ensure that auditing is being monitored and tracked. You should check to see if critical log events are being tracked and acted on. For example, a syslog entry shows a problem with a drive on one of the Solaris servers. Does the organization create a trouble ticket (or something similar) for the event to track it to resolution? Is the event ignored until data is lost? These are the kinds of things you will be looking for.

> **NOTE**
>
> Something to keep in mind is that even though systems have auditing turned on, it does not necessarily follow that anyone is paying attention to what is logged. Not only should the organization be auditing events (logging), they should be monitoring the logs and acting on events that require attention. The INFOSEC Assessment Methodology (IAM) process examines this piece.

File/Directory Permissions

Certain files and directories should be protected a bit more stringently than the default permissions that are set by the OS/application installation. These files and directories should be restricted to the proper owner and group and should have the proper permissions set.

For example, the following code shows the proper ownership and permissions on the file /etc/passwd:

```
[mdmonk@dotcomd ~]$ ls -lsa /etc/passwd
4 -rw-r--r--  1 root root   2308 May 22 21:03 /etc/passwd
```

Notice that the file is owned by user root and group root. Permissions are set to *-rw-r--r--*. This means that the owner has read/write access, the group has read access, and world (everyone on the system) has read access. The initial dash signifies that no sticky bit has been set on the file, and the SUID and/or SGID bits have not been set. The sidebar includes an explanation of the terms *sticky bit*, *SUID* and *SGID bits* as well as *inode*. These permissions are set properly, since some services/applications need to access the /etc/passwd file to verify that a user is valid for that system but doesn't need to modify the file — read-only access versus read/write access.

Notes from the Underground

Sticky Bit? SUID? SGID? What Are You Talking About?

When someone mentions those terms, they are talking about permission flags for files and directories in a UNIX file system. Actually, the permission flags are part of the inode and not the file/directory, but it's easier for a person to associate the information with an actual filename, so we'll treat *inode* and *filename* as interchangeable terms (even though they aren't). The inode is a data structure that holds information about the file it references. There is an inode for each file, and this is used to uniquely identify each file by using these two items of information: the file system it resides on and the file's inode number on that system.

An inode contains the following information: device (where the inode is stored), file-locking information, mode of the file, type of file, number of links (*man ln*) to the file, the file owner's user ID and group ID, file size in bytes, file access time, file modification time, inode modification time, and the file's physical location on the system (file system addresses for the file's blocks on disk).

Back to the bits and permission flags: There are 12 bits representing inode/file permissions: set UID; set GID; sticky; read, write, and execute for owner; read, write, and execute for group; and read, write, and execute for world/other. As you can see, they add up to 12.

The Set UID (SUID) bit (the twelfth bit) is set for any application where it has to run as a different user than the one who started the application. For example, /usr/bin/passwd has permissions of *-r-s--x--x*. The *s* represents the SUID bit, meaning that when /usr/bin/passwd is executed, it is executed as though user *root* had executed it, with *root's* privileges.

The set GID (SGID) bit (the eleventh bit) is the same as SUID only it applies to the file's group rather than the file owner.

The sticky bit is the tenth bit. If the sticky bit is set, that tells UNIX systems that once the application is executed, they should keep it in memory. This was used in earlier days to help reduce application start times — back in the days before fast disk access and faster/larger banks of memory were available.

Depending on the UNIX or Linux distribution you are evaluating, key files and directories are in different locations (for example, SSL certificates are stored in /usr/share/ssl rather than /usr/lib/ssl). That's why it's important to have an evaluation team member who is familiar with the UNIX/Linux versions being evaluated. However, scripted solutions can help. With scripted solutions, each distribution's default locations for the various essential files and directories can be stored in a configuration file or separate script. The knowledge of the default locations and basic checks can be scripted to assist the evaluation efforts.

Microsoft Windows key files and directories are generally stored in the C:&backslash;Windows or C:&backslash;WINNT directories, depending on the version of Windows that's running. Probably the most important directories in C:&backslash;Windows and C:&backslash;WINNT are the System, System32, Security, and Repair directories. At a minimum, those directories should be secured.

The following list is a sample of essential system files on Microsoft Windows:

- Ntoskrnl.exe
- Ntkrnlpa.exe
- Hal.dll
- Win32k.sys
- Ntdll.dll
- Kernel32.dll
- Advapi32.dll
- User32.dll
- Cdi32.dll
- Ntldr
- Boot.ini

The files listed are important to Microsoft Windows functionality. If they are compromised, the server is potentially compromised.

OS and Application Services

Not every application or service should be installed and running. We know it sounds like fun, but having SMTP, SNMP, HTTP, HTTPS, IMAP, POP3, FTP, SMB, LDAP, and the like all running on a machine not assigned those roles is just asking for trouble. A server (or workstation) should be running only the services and applications necessary to fulfill its operational role(s). The more services running, the more avenues of attack available to a malicious user.

The evaluator should check the list of installed services and applications against the server's assigned role(s). If the server is serving only Web pages (HTTP or HTTPS), it's unlikely that an SMTP service is required to be installed. If a service or application is necessary to fulfill the server's role(s), it should be documented, either in the build documentation or where the organization tracks exceptions to policy.

User Rights Assignments

User rights assignments can be a difficult topic to address, because political issues could be involved — for example, additional rights granted to "a buddy" in a different department or admin rights granted to the HR database administrator so that the system administrator doesn't have to be bothered all the time. User rights should be granted based on roles in the organization, not based on individual users. It is much easier for the organization to manage user rights via roles than per individual.

The evaluator should check to ensure that user rights assignments are being granted based on organizational roles. For example, an accountant probably doesn't need domain administrator rights. And the database administrator probably shouldn't have the root password on the Solaris server (that's what *sudo* is for, as we'll see in a moment).

The concept of least privilege is a fundamental tool in managing user rights, whether the rights are assigned or inherited. Briefly, the concept of least privilege is this: Grant the user access to the resources they need, not access to the resources they want. The two usually differ. Let's take the case of a database server in a large organization. Quite often, due to separation of roles and/or duties, the system administrator and database administrator are two different people or teams. The database administrator may require root-level privileges to run certain commands on the server, but giving him or her the root password is normally a breach of security policy (at least one would hope!) — and that person having access to the root password is *way* more privileges than he or she needs.

So a method or facility for providing limited access to privileged commands would come in handy here. On UNIX/Linux/*BSD systems, the command *sudo* is the recommended method for granting limited access to privileged areas and commands on the system. Sudo (*superuser do*) allows a system administrator to grant certain users or user groups the ability to run some or all commands as another user (commonly as root) and log all executed commands and command arguments.

Patch Management

In patch management, we check to see whether the organization has any patch or configuration management in place. Many organizations install a server or workstation and don't follow up with related security or application patches. This leaves the organization very vulnerable to attacks as new vulnerabilities are discovered. An organization cannot safely exist on today's Internet without some form of patch management being used. It's simply not safe.

Something you should keep in mind is that an organization might not be able to apply certain patches or service packs. A very common example is that Service Pack 2 for Windows XP cannot be applied to some systems, because essential applications running on the systems have not been ported to work on XP SP2. If SP2 for XP is installed, those applications cease working. If essential business applications are running on the system (that was upgraded to SP2) and the applications no longer function or are inaccessible due to the upgrade, the organization might get a *bit* irritated. Most organizations tend to frown on downtime. So, if a patch cannot be applied due to restrictions (technical, organizational, or otherwise), note it in the evaluation documentation and look for ways to mitigate or reduce the risk associated with not applying that patch. Looking for additional vulnerability mitigation methods is something you should already be doing so that you can provide more than one recommendation per finding.

Mapping the Findings to the IEM Process

It's all well and good to come up with findings, but are the findings valid? Are they even important to the organization's mission or to the evaluation? These are questions you have to ask during the next step of the vulnerability scanning and host evaluation portion of the IEM. Correlating the data/findings, validating the findings, and mapping the findings to the IEM are the tasks ahead of us next.

We need to briefly mention a subject (which will be discussed in more depth later in this text): first-order prioritization of findings. This is a general ranking process used to help focus our efforts on the most important findings that affect critical portions of the organization's INFOSEC infrastructure.

Vulnerability Scans and Host Evaluations: Correlating the Data

In the previous sections, our goal in showing the various vulnerability scanning and host evaluation tools was to introduce you to some of the more familiar and popular tools you could end up using during your own evaluations. Keep in mind that there are more scanning and evaluating tools out there than we have covered here.

Now we will correlate the scan and evaluation data sets, filter out false-positive findings, and map the findings back to the IEM process. To save time, we have summarized some of the findings from the scans conducted for this text. The screen captures are from the actual tools that were used to scan these devices.

Table 20.3 contains a summary of the devices we are evaluating. We prefer to keep a spreadsheet updated with this information so that key information is more readily available for the evaluators. You'll find that this helps identify some findings as false positives right off the bat. For example, if a server is Windows 2000 running an IIS Web server and the finding is only relevant to Apache servers, it's a fairly safe bet that the finding is a false positive.

Table 20.3 A Sample Evaluation Components List

Hostname	IP Address	OS	Component/Device Roles
intgw.evalnet	192.168.0.1	Linux-kernel 2.4, iptables	Firewall
imsohackable.evalnet	192.168.0.2	Windows XP	Developer workstation running various services
ownable.evalnet	192.168.0.3	Windows 2000	File and print sharing
opensun.evalnet server	192.168.0.4	Solaris 10	Web, SMTP, SNMP, and database
securemac.evalnet	192.168.0.5	Apple OS X 10.3	Workstation
lj5.evalnet	192.168.0.50	HP JetDirect	Print server
shnas.evalnet	192.168.0.51	SnapOS	Network attached storage (NAS)

Tables 20.4 and 20.5 show findings and affected IP addresses. The left columns of Tables 20.4 and 20.5 contain the assigned finding number, which we assign for tracking purposes. It isn't a number that will exist outside of our evaluation working documents, but it helps in tracking findings through the evaluation process. A more formal organization of the findings will occur during the post-evaluation phase. By "showing our work," our due diligence is shown, with the discovery of the finding and subsequent analysis of the finding, whether it is valid or a false positive. Documenting your evaluation efforts is key!

Table 20.4 A Sample Findings List

Finding #	Finding	Severity	Exploit Vector	Affected IP Address
F1	OpenSSH may be vulnerable. Multiple issues with OpenSSH ver 3.7.1 and below.	High	Remote	192.168.0.1, 192.168.0.4, 192.168.0.5
F2	SMTP may be a mail relay.	High	Remote	192.168.0.4
F3	Buffer overflow in the ISAPI DLL filter for Macromedia JRun 3.1.	High	Remote	192.168.0.2
F4	Oracle 9i 9.0.x database server allows local users to access restricted data.	High	Local	192.168.0.4
F5	admin.php in PHPGEDVIEW allows remote attackers to obtain sensitive information via *phpinfo* command.	Low	Remote	192.168.0.2
F6	Buffer overflow in Apple iTunes before ver 4.8 allows remote attackers to execute arbitrary code.	High	Remote	192.168.0.5

Continued

Table 20.4 Continued

Finding #	Finding	Severity	Exploit Vector	Affected IP Address
F7	Vulnerabilities in Microsoft Windows Terminal Server and Remote Desktop could allow a remote attacker to execute arbitrary code or crash the server.	Medium	Remote	192.168.0.2,192.168.0.3

Table 20.5 Another Sample Findings List

Finding #	Affected OS/App	CVE	CVE/Scanning Tool Recommendation
F1	OpenSSH	CAN-2003-0682, CAN-2003-0786, CAN-2003-0787	Upgrade to the latest version of OpenSSH.
F2	Sendmail 8.9 and below	CAN-1999-0512	Upgrade to the latest version of Sendmail 8.9.x.
F3	Jrun 3.1 and below	CVE 2002-0801	Apply latest patches for JRun, 3.x or upgrade to JRun 4.x.
F4	Oracle 9i 9.0.1 and below	CVE 2002-0571	Apply latest patches for Oracle 9i 9.0.x.
F5	PHPGedView 2.6.1 and below	CVE 2004-0033	Upgrade admin.php and/or PHPGEDVIEW to latest revision.
F6	iTunes 4.8 and below, on Apple and Microsoft Windows	CAN 2005-1248	Upgrade to iTunes
F7	Microsoft Windows 2000 and XP	CVE 2002-0864, CAN 2002-0863	Apply appropriate patch for operating system.

Summarize and Validate Findings

We've said it before, but we'll say it again: All findings must be validated! This is an extremely important point. You do not want to turn in to a client a final report containing false-positive findings or findings that don't even matter to the customer. Take the time to verify that cross-site scripting vulnerability or to verify the SNMP community strings discovered.

Summary

In this chapter we discussed vulnerability scanning and host evaluations in relation to the INFOSEC Evaluation Methodology. As you can now see, this section of the evaluation requires much more thought than perhaps was initially considered. It's not as simple as "Turn on *insert tool name*\> vulnerability scanning tool, have it crank through the subnets, and churn out findings." Modern INFOSEC tools do simplify the task of gathering the suspected vulnerabilities, but the tools do not replace the evaluator's intellect, ability to reason, knowledge, and experience. The evaluator brings his or her skills, technical and nontechnical experience, and appropriate knowledge base to the evaluation efforts. The vulnerability scanning tools provide a tidy list of suspected vulnerabilities, but they are not human and they do not have the ability to reason.

The chapter started with a reminder of which phase of the IEM that vulnerability scanning takes place in. Then we continued on to the subject of vulnerability scanning itself. The risk triangle was introduced to show where vulnerabilities impact an organization's INFOSEC posture and risk profile. Do you recall what the other two sides to the risk triangle were? That's right — threats and asset value. After that we talked about vulnerability and attack trends so that we can be more aware of what we are "up against" when conducting the vulnerability scans. CERT provided us with some eye-opening numbers of incidents reported, but it was a reality check that we needed. The statistics are a subtle reminder that it is not safe "out there" on the Internet.

Then we got to the "Why are we here?" section. We discussed various reasons for conducting an IEM, and we talked about the role vulnerability scans play in your INFOSEC evaluations. Next came the tools section, which listed several vulnerability scanning tools, provided screen captures to familiarize you with the various interfaces to the tools, and briefly noted items of interest regarding each tool.

The vulnerability scanning tools provided us with network-based vulnerabilities, but that isn't the whole picture, is it? We also have to conduct host evaluations to provide a more complete picture of the INFOSEC posture of the organization. Host evaluations are used to gather findings directly from the workstations, servers, network devices, security devices, and the like. You might have different findings based on your perspective to the host/device/component; whether the finding is from an external scan, an internal scan, or a host-based evaluation. These are three different perspectives you can get information from.

Once we gather all our findings, we have to validate them, remove false-positive findings, and map the findings back to the organization's critical INFOSEC systems. By providing multiple recommendations (three per finding is highly suggested) for the mitigation of the critical findings, we hope to present the customer with a viable road map toward the reduction of their organization's security gap and the strengthening of their security posture.

## Chapter 21

Fine-Tuning the Evaluation

Solutions in this chapter:

- **Network Device Analysis**
- **Password-Compliance Testing**
- **Application-Specific Scanning**
- **Network Protocol Analysis**
- **Finalizing Your Findings List**
- **Mapping Findings Back to the IEM Process**

☑ **Summary**

Introduction

This chapter covers the remainder of the scanning, or hands-on, portion of the IEM. As mentioned in the previous chapter, you will more than likely have a different view of the system when you're at the console than when you're evaluating the system from the network. The same can be said of the remaining tasks, in regard to the organization's INFOSEC posture. By conducting network device analysis, password-compliance testing (more commonly known as *password cracking*, but we aren't supposed to call it that anymore), application-specific scanning, and network protocol analysis, we should finally have "the big picture" when it comes to the organization and the status of its INFOSEC resources. It sounds like there is still a lot left to do. And there is; but the tasks go quickly, so don't worry too much.

In this chapter we fine-tune the evaluation. Our goals are to evaluate network devices (routers, firewalls, intrusion detection systems [IDSs], and the like), conduct password-compliance testing, perform application-specific scanning (on Web servers, databases, and e-mail servers), and do a bit of network protocol analysis. All these tasks "flesh out" the evaluation team's understanding of the organization's environment. And unless the evaluation team needs to conduct retesting, these tasks represent the last of the hands-on testing part of the IEM process (see Figure 21.1).

Figure 21.1 Phases of the IEM

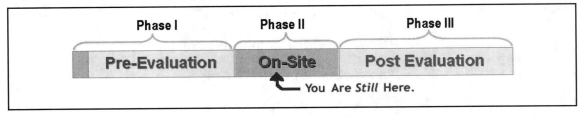

Let's get to work.

Network Device Analysis

The part we refer to as *network device analysis* or *evaluation* is where you examine the border devices or high-assurance devices. When we refer to border devices, think of devices such as routers, firewalls, IDSs, VPN/gateway devices, proxy devices, and the like.

Approaches Used in Network Device Analysis

For the IEM, we use two approaches in our network device analysis/evaluations. The *design approach* is an evaluation of the design of the perimeter and defenses for the organization. The *technical approach* is a technical evaluation of the various perimeter device configurations and settings. The output of these two approaches combine to provide the evaluation team a comprehensive view of the perimeter and perimeter defenses and contribute to a more complete picture of the organization's overall INFOSEC posture.

Evaluating the Perimeter Design and Defenses

When you are evaluating the organization's perimeter and perimeter defenses, the evaluator's experience and knowledge come into play in a big way. For example, let's say that the organization we are evaluating has a firewall in place and a proper ruleset applied and requires all Web traffic to go through a proxy—all good security practices. *But* there is a machine that is dual-homed, with a network interface connected to the outside network (Internet) and a network interface connected to the internal network. That one machine is a hole into the organization's infrastructure; bypassing an otherwise decent security perimeter. That is why the evaluator's experience and knowledge are so important; not everyone could recognize an improperly configured machine or locate holes in perimeter defenses.

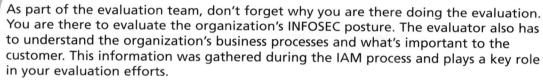

TIP

As part of the evaluation team, don't forget why you are there doing the evaluation. You are there to evaluate the organization's INFOSEC posture. The evaluator also has to understand the organization's business processes and what's important to the customer. This information was gathered during the IAM process and plays a key role in your evaluation efforts.

For example, a perceived misconfiguration could in actuality be a requirement for a customer's business-to-business (B2B) connectivity. This is not something you (as part of the evaluation team) would be aware of unless you have the organizational criticality matrix and system criticality matrix(es) as a guide for your efforts. These documentation items are included in the technical evaluation plan (TEP).

We like to use the M&M candy analogy, equating an organization's infrastructure to an M&M—you know, hard candy shell and soft chocolate center. The hard candy shell is the perimeter and perimeter defenses; the soft chocolate center represents the organization's internal infrastructure. When a hole is punched in the hard outer shell (the perimeter), the soft chocolate center (the organizational infrastructure) is vulnerable. It takes only one misconfigured machine to negate the risk mitigation effects a security perimeter provides.

To evaluate the perimeter, you'll initially look for devices that increase the security of the infrastructure—firewalls, routers, IDSs, and the like. The organization should have provided this information to you in the diagrams and documentation you requested earlier in the IEM process. If you have a diagram or documentation of the perimeter and perimeter defenses, you next need to validate those resources. Do they exist? Are they in use (for example, in the rack, but not plugged in)?

Basically, you are examining the design of your customer's perimeter and associated perimeter defenses. We'll talk about examining the security configuration and settings later in this chapter. Questions you might want to answer with the results of this part of the evaluation are:

- Is the perimeter design sound?
- Is the perimeter being circumvented at all (for example, by dual-hosted machines)?

- Is there a Web or e-mail proxy in place? Both?

- Is there an IDS in place? Are the logs being monitored and acted on?

- Is there auditing in place for the perimeter network devices?

- Is there a central syslog server to collect audit logs?

- If so, has that server been hardened and access restricted?

The bulk of the tasks for network device analysis are part of the "evaluating the configuration of network devices" approach, which just happens to be our next topic. Look at the design approach as the way we get our working list of perimeter devices to evaluate the security configuration.

Evaluating Network Device Configurations

To evaluate the perimeter devices and perimeter defenses, a little bit of information goes a long way toward helping our efforts. The following is a list of some useful information or documentation to have regarding the organization for this portion of the evaluation:

- Diagram of the perimeter, including border devices, DMZ hosted machines, and any third-party connectivity coming into the infrastructure

- Documentation of the security device configurations and supporting policies/procedures

- Any contracts for outsourced INFOSEC infrastructure or roles

- Evaluation team members with experience on the device platforms and applications to be evaluated

WARNING

Take special care with the organization's sensitive security device configurations, such as firewall rule sets and router configurations. Considering the sensitivity of the information, some organizations may require the evaluation team to leave such documentation onsite.

If sensitive information or documentation needs to be transferred and it has to leave physical control of either the organization or the evaluation team, the data should be encrypted. If you have to receive the documents via e-mail or some other electronic delivery method, the information should be encrypted with the agreed-on encryption methods. (Issues such as this should be addressed in the TEP.)

What are you looking for when you do this part of the network device analysis? It depends. Though the process is the same for all network devices, you will look for different issues depending on the type of device and/or the vendor of the device being analyzed. Firewalls require you to look at the ruleset or rulebase—to consider whether it is it just a gateway device or whether it handles VPNs too (or even other applications!), whether the underlying OS has been hardened, and so on.

Routers require the analysis of the router configuration, a verification of the running IOS version, and other considerations. Considering the number of vendors of security devices and differing versions of devices in use today, this part of the evaluation really requires a specific knowledge base to properly assess them. The knowledge and experience required may differ depending on the technologies in use. This is a subtle reminder to know the environment and tailor the evaluation team to the environment being evaluated.

Table 21.1 lists some of the items that should be checked for each device. They are broken into two broad categories: firewalls and routers/switches. We purposely did not include the other devices in this category, since they will be covered later in this chapter when we get to application-specific scanning. These are devices such as proxies, SMTP gateways, and Web and e-mail servers.

The lists in Table 21.1 are not all-inclusive; they are simply valid examples to get you started.

Table 21.1 Network Device Evaluation Checks

Firewalls:	Routers and Switches:
Check rulesets/rulebases	Check for open ports (check using port scanner)
Any proxy servers configured (as part of the firewall)	Evaluate router/switch configuration
Check for default settings	Check for cleartext protocols in use
Check underlying OS: Has it been hardened? What services are available?	Run vulnerability scanner against device
Patches and firmware updates: Any missing?	Check ACLs
Check for known issues listed on manufacturer's site	Check OS version and patch level (IOS, CatOS, JunOS, etc.)
Check for known or recently discovered issues listed on security portal sites	

Firewalls can be tricky beasts, and some have been known to "flatline" due to improper handling of aggressive vulnerability scans. Keep this in mind when you are checking the perimeter devices and Internet-accessible devices. Not every firewall is made the same. Ensure that you have the proper firewall expertise on your evaluation team. A Cisco PIX admin, might not be well versed in administrating CheckPoint firewalls or vice versa. Also, ensure that you have the administrators of the equipment being evaluated handy to assist if any of the devices stop responding. It's always best to have the organization's administrators on hand or on call when you are conducting your evaluation tasks. If the administrator is able to correct the issue in a timely manner, the end users might not even know there was a problem—it could be fixed quicker than they could say, "Hey! Who broke the Internet!"

On the subject of tools, there are few INFOSEC tools out there to help you with these particular tasks. The tasks are mostly manual processes. But do not despair—a couple of security tools can help you with some of your evaluation tasks.

To assist with the router configuration checks, the Center for Internet Security (CIS) has a tool called Router Audit Tool, or RAT, which is available at www.cisecurity.org/bench_cisco.html. RAT analyzes the router configuration, compares it to its baseline (modifiable by you), and produces a report for the device. The report has a listing of the rules RAT checked and a pass/fail score, the raw score for the device, and the weighted score for the device (on a scale of 1–10). RAT also provides, whenever possible, the IOS/PIX commands necessary to correct the issues it identified.

Another tool that can be very handy in evaluating network devices is SolarWinds (available at www.solarwinds.net/). You probably remember it from the SNMP portion of the evaluation. That's why we bring it in at this point as well. SolarWind's SNMP scanning functionality is pretty nice and will help with the router/switch analysis. It can provide TFTP server functionality as well to assist in the collecting of router/switch configurations.

Password-Compliance Testing

Password-compliance testing, also known as password cracking—it is highly recommended that we refer to the activity by the former term rather than the latter, but we all know what we're talking about: cracking passwords. It's about testing to see how many users are complying with the organization's password policies. Or is it more about the number of passwords that can be cracked in under a minute? Either way, this part of our evaluation tests the organization's compliance with its published password policies and procedures.

Password-Compliance Testing Methods

There are three types of password-checking methods or attacks:

- Brute-force attacks
- Dictionary attacks
- Hybrid attacks (combining dictionary and brute-force methods)

A *brute-force attack* is one in which the password-cracking tool cycles through a specified grouping of characters such as a–z, A–Z, 0–9, or !@#$%^&*()-=+ for a specified password length—say, five to seven characters, encrypting every combination of the characters in the character sets and trying each against the password hash stored in the password file until a collision occurs. A *collision* happens when the string that will be accepted as the password is obtained or guessed. For example, if you tell the password-compliance testing tool to perform a check using passwords between five and seven characters long and using the lower- and uppercase alpha characters and numbers (a–z, A–Z, and 0–9). The tool will cycle through every combination starting with *aaaaa*, then *aaaab*, then … well, you get the idea. Obviously, a brute-force password-cracking attempt will take much longer than a dictionary attack. But a brute-force attack could be your only chance to obtain complex passwords. A dictionary attack might not crack the more complex passwords.

For the bulk of user passwords, a dictionary attack is a useful, and quicker, method of password-compliance testing. A *dictionary attack* is one in which the password-cracking tool will go through and encrypt each word in a dictionary and check the encrypted hash against the encrypted hash entries in the password file. Basically, if the hashes are a match, the password has been found. Once again, you have to consider the organization and environment you are evaluating. Passwords come in all shapes and sizes. If you are evaluating a trucking company, you might want to include in your password-cracking attempts a dictionary file containing trucking industry-specific terminology. Or if you are in an area where English isn't the primary language—for instance, Peru—you might want to consider adding to the efforts a dictionary file containing words in the local language or dialect. If you walk by the Windows administrators' cubes and hear Backstreet Boys or similar music playing, you know you should add the boy-band dictionary to your password-compliance tests. Additional dictionary files exist for many languages and a variety of topics, genres, and industries. Tailor your password-compliance testing efforts to the organization. You could find your password-compliance testing will go a bit easier if you do.

The last testing method is called the *hybrid attack method*. Just as you might guess, this is a combination of the brute-force attack and the dictionary attack. This method of password testing is better at getting passwords that are a concatenation of letters and numerics, such as *security01, secretpassword69, imnumber1*, and so on. The dictionary attack gets the dictionary word portion of the password, and the hybrid attack then tries to brute-force the rest of the password. Take the password *security01*, for example—the dictionary attack would catch the word *security*, and then the password-cracking tool would try to brute-force guess the rest of the password by tacking numbers on. This method doesn't always work, but no method will get 100 percent of the passwords in a realistically limited amount of time. But remember that no password is entirely secure.

NOTE

Given the limitations of passwords, one trend in the security industry has been to recommend moving from passwords to *passphrases*. More complexity is involved with passphrases, and they're longer (and so much more difficult to crack) than passwords.

Methods of Obtaining the Password File

Without physical security, there can be no security. How is that important here, in the password-compliance testing world? For one thing, there are more offline password-cracking tools than there are online password-cracking tools. Online password-cracking tools don't work in offline mode, where the password file is given to the tool and it doesn't have to obtain it off the "wire" (the network). So if the organization has a system or component that needs to be protected, restricting physical access to the device is an essential first line of defense. If you can get physical access to a system, it is a trivial task to obtain access to the files you need by popping in a bootable CD and rebooting the system, especially if auditing is not turned on. If auditing is not enabled and it's a Microsoft Windows machine, the fact that the machine was even rebooted, let alone that the password file (a critical file) was copied, will probably go unnoticed.

Notes from the Underground

Password Paranoia

Some organizations won't want you, an external third party, to have access to their password file(s). There's nothing wrong with that, but since they don't want to grant you access to their password files, the organization will have to conduct the password-compliance evaluation activity and provide you with the general results from the testing.

They don't have to tell you whose password was weak, or anything that detailed. But they *do* have to provide you with enough information to fulfill your evaluation requirements.

How do you get that pesky password file, anyway? We need it for our password evaluation efforts. How you get the password file and what the file name is depend on the operating systems involved. Windows 95/98 differs from Windows NT, which is different from Windows 2000/XP/2003, which in turn is different from *any* UNIX or Linux system. With UNIX, Linux, and BSD systems, it's a bit easier since the password file and shadowed (inaccessible by nonroot users) password file are normally stored in a uniform place (/etc/).

To obtain the password file from a Windows machine, which on Windows is called the Security Accounts Manager (SAM) file, administrator access is required. You should also know whether it is an Active Directory (AD) server, or a workstation, or whatever the role of the system is. Access to the password file, and access to an accurate password file, depends on this information. If the machine is not an AD server, access to the password file is much easier. If it *is* an AD server, you have to run the password-gathering tool as a domain administrator (not only a local administrator account) from the console of the server using a tool such as pwdump3 (pwdump and pwdump2 will not work in that situation). Normally, the SAM file is stored in %SYSTEMROOT%\System32\Config\SAM, and a backup is maintained in %SYSTEMROOT%\ Repair\sam.

Access to the password file(s) in UNIX, Linux, or BSD (we'll refer to all OSs in this category as *UNIX*) systems is more uniform, at least in terms of the location of the relevant files. The files needed from a UNIX system are /etc/passwd and /etc/shadow. Example output is shown here. This is from a Solaris 10 system:

```
-bash-3.00$ uname -a
SunOS monstersun 5.10 Generic sun4u sparc SUNW,Ultra-4
-bash-3.00$ ls -lsa /etc/passwd /etc/shadow
   1 -rw-r--r--  1 root       680 May 12 12:25 /etc/passwd
   1 -r--------  1 root       375 May 12 12:26 /etc/shadow
```

Notice that everyone on the system has access to at least read the /etc/passwd file, and read access is granted only to root for the /etc/shadow file. These file permissions are important to note. Nonprivileged processes might need to do a user lookup in /etc/passwd, but all that is stored in the /etc/shadow file are the usernames and passwords. So it's safe to limit access to the /etc/shadow file to root only, which is what the login process runs as. So permissions are set safely and properly on these files. That's why you require administrator or root-level access to conduct some of the evaluation tasks.

Next we get into the password-compliance testing tools in the following section.

Password-Compliance Testing Tools

There are several password-compliance testing tools. Some are commercial, and some are open source. Additionally, some of the tools do more than just crack passwords; some gather the passwords from the local system for you, some get the passwords from the network, and some tools require you to provide the password file. In fact, some password-cracking tools will do all these things.

Let's look at some examples of password-compliance testing tools, but we won't go into the gory details of each tool, since they all basically do the same thing. Some tools are better than others, and some just cost more.

One of best-known "password auditing and recovery applications" (another term for password-cracking utility) is LC5, the latest version of L0phtCrack by @stake (recently acquired by Symantec; www.atstake.com). LC5 is a fast password-cracking tool, with support for scheduled password audits, cracking Windows and UNIX passwords, remote password auditing, international character support, and password quality scoring (see Figure 21.2).

Figure 21.2 An LC5 Screen Capture

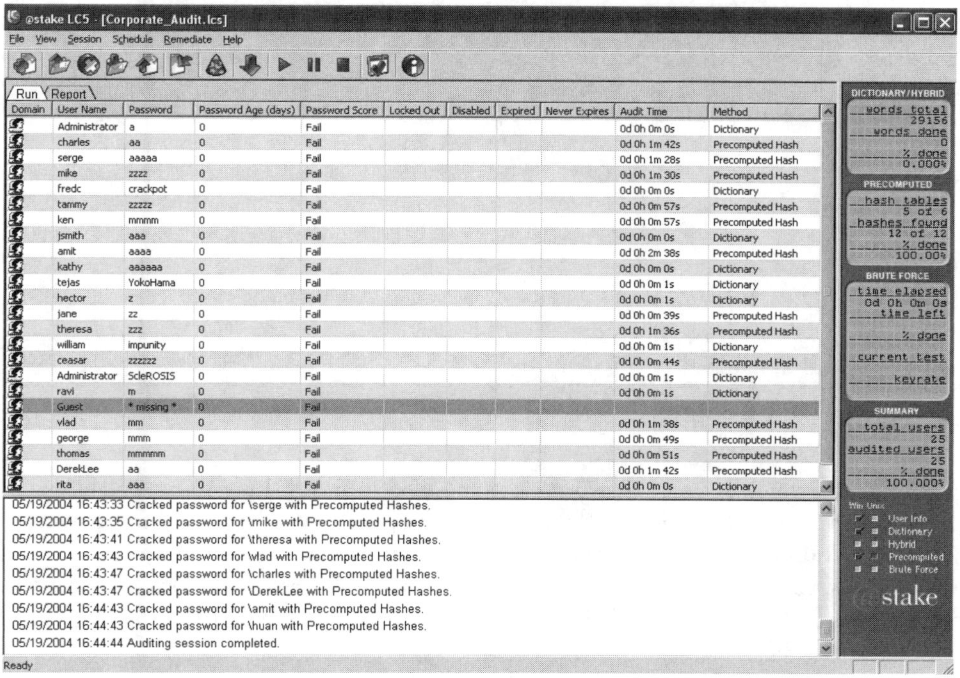

Next is an open source project called ophcrack 2.0 (see Figure 21.3). You can find this project at http://ophcrack.sourceforge.net. It's called the *time-memory tradeoff cracker* because it relies on the precomputed hash tables already being in memory. So, by sacrificing memory, the password–cracking time is drastically decreased. The ophcrack Web site offers the option to submit a Windows password or Windows password hash to be cracked. The speed at which this tool works is pretty awesome. Here are some statistics from the ophcrack Web site:

- Average running time for the demo using table set SSTIC04-2.7k (1.1 GB)

- Alphanumeric passwords: 1.67 seconds

- Passwords with one nonalphanumeric half: 26.14 seconds

- Passwords with two nonalphanumeric halves (not cracked): 42.14 seconds

Figure 21.3 An ophcrack Screen Capture

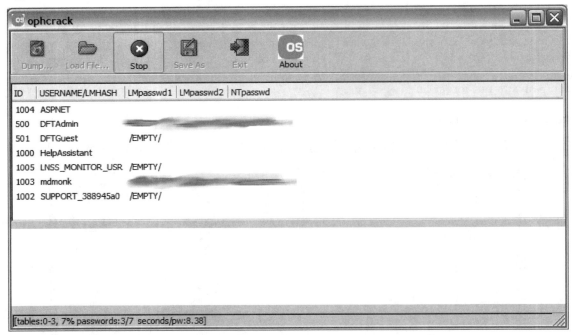

Another popular open source password cracker called John the Ripper is available at www.openwall.com/john/ (see Figure 21.4). John the Ripper is a command-line password cracker that runs on several different architectures. Its primary purpose, according to the John Web site, is to detect weak UNIX passwords. Not only does John the Ripper handle password files from UNIX, it can crack Kerberos AFS passwords and Windows NT/2000/XP/2003 LM hashes. OpenWall also has word lists (dictionary files) available on its site.

Figure 21.4 A John the Ripper Screen Capture

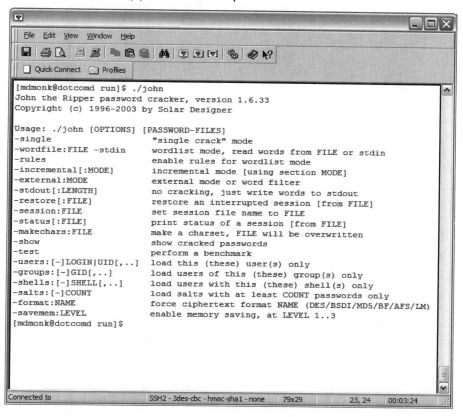

```
[mdmonk@dotcomd run]$ ./john
John the Ripper password cracker, version 1.6.33
Copyright (c) 1996-2003 by Solar Designer

Usage: ./john [OPTIONS] [PASSWORD-FILES]
-single                    "single crack" mode
-wordfile:FILE -stdin      wordlist mode, read words from FILE or stdin
-rules                     enable rules for wordlist mode
-incremental[:MODE]        incremental mode [using section MODE]
-external:MODE             external mode or word filter
-stdout[:LENGTH]           no cracking, just write words to stdout
-restore[:FILE]            restore an interrupted session [from FILE]
-session:FILE              set session file name to FILE
-status[:FILE]             print status of a session [from FILE]
-makechars:FILE            make a charset, FILE will be overwritten
-show                      show cracked passwords
-test                      perform a benchmark
-users:[-]LOGIN|UID[,..]   load this (these) user(s) only
-groups:[-]GID[,..]        load users of this (these) group(s) only
-shells:[-]SHELL[,..]      load users with this (these) shell(s) only
-salts:[-]COUNT            load salts with at least COUNT passwords only
-format:NAME               force ciphertext format NAME (DES/BSDI/MD5/BF/AFS/LM)
-savemem:LEVEL             enable memory saving, at LEVEL 1..3
[mdmonk@dotcomd run]$
```

Even though some of the vulnerability scanners on the market will also do password gathering and cracking for you, this is still an activity an evaluation team member should conduct with a dedicated password-cracking tool. You might encounter an organization that doesn't want password cracking conducted, and that is their right to refuse that portion of the evaluation, as long as the reasons are documented and signed off on. But I offer this as a (hopefully) convincing argument if the organization doesn't want you to conduct password-compliance testing: I was part of a team performing an evaluation at an organization in which password-compliance testing was a required task. Of 585 Active Directory accounts, I was able to obtain the password for 174 of the accounts in the first 60 seconds. This isn't an exceptional number, either; it's a fairly accurate representation of end-user password strength (or lack thereof) in most organizations.

Application-Specific Scanning

Application-specific scanning is where we get to more closely analyze some of the network-available applications. Each app scanner is designed to evaluate certain applications, and it usually does that application very well. Unfortunately, no single app scanner will fill all scanning needs.

Remember to tailor your INFOSEC tool set to the evaluation requirements. For example, if there are no Oracle instances to be evaluated, you probably wouldn't need to bring in your Oracle database guru.

The DMZ

Previously I mentioned DMZ devices. When I say "DMZ-hosted devices," I am referring to devices or servers that are specifically hosted in the organization's DMZ. Examples of these types of devices are Web servers, e-mail servers, and SMTP gateways. *DMZ* stands for *demilitarized zone* and refers to the area where Internet-facing, trusted servers are hosted. Note that having a DMZ is optional; an organization might not have one. We mention DMZs specifically because there is overlap with these devices. They will be scanned during the vulnerability scanning phase and checked during the host analysis phase, so we should have a very good idea of what these servers are made up of. To complete the picture, we have to run specific checks and scans against the applications themselves—hence the term *application-specific scanning.*

Types of Applications to Be Scanned

Since quite a bit of the work has already been completed (or at least started) during other activities of the IEM, all that's left for the server-side evaluations is to finish with the application checks. During this part of the evaluation, we check out the database instances, e-mail server/services, Web server/ services, and any proprietary applications the organization is using. We're looking for vulnerabilities and configuration errors with the applications and services themselves.

The categories of application to be scanned are databases, Web servers, e-mail servers, and proprietary applications. Many of the vulnerability scanners and host evaluation activities have already taken care of most of the required checks, and all that's left are the checks specific to the type of application.

For databases, we check the access and authorization mechanisms, privilege assignments, the access control methods, and the auditing that is enabled. We check database versions and patch levels to ensure that everything is properly patched and up to date. We also verify that default accounts do not have the default passwords still in place. With databases, disasters quickly follow when password management and access controls are lacking. The most used attack vector with databases is SQL injection.

Notes from the Underground

SQL Injection Defined

SQL injection is a hacking technique for exploiting Web-enabled applications that use client-supplied data as input in SQL queries, without doing any taint checking of the input and stripping out potentially harmful characters prior to executing the SQL query.

For e-mail servers, as with most Internet-facing servers, the most common attack vector is buffer overflow attacks. Additionally, with e-mail servers, one of our essential evaluation tasks is to ensure that the e-mail server isn't acting as an open relay. Usually an e-mail server would act as an open relay due to a server misconfiguration. By open relay, we mean an e-mail server that will send e-mail for a client, even if the client isn't authorized to send e-mail via that server. We'll check application versions and patch levels to ensure that the application is properly patched and up to date.

Web servers are probably the most commonly attacked servers; they require us to pay special attention to these devices. Approximately 75 percent of all security incidents are targeted at Web applications. They can be a weak link in the organization's infrastructure and are quite often used by malicious hackers as "jumping-off points" into the organization and to launch network attacks. Web servers are usually attacked using buffer overflow attack, or cross-site scripting attacks, so these are the primary issues we check when evaluating Web servers.

Now let's briefly look at a few of the application-specific scanning tools. The tools are fairly straightforward and generally provide excellent output for your evaluation reports and evidence gathering.

WebInspect, by SPI-Dynamics (www.spidynamics.com/products/webinspect/), is a Web application-scanning tool. It simulates many Web-based application attacks such as cross-site scripting attacks, parameter manipulation, brute-force attacks, and many others (see Figure 21.5). It's a pricey product, but it is *very* good at what it does.

Figure 21.5 A SPI Dynamics WebInspect Screen Capture

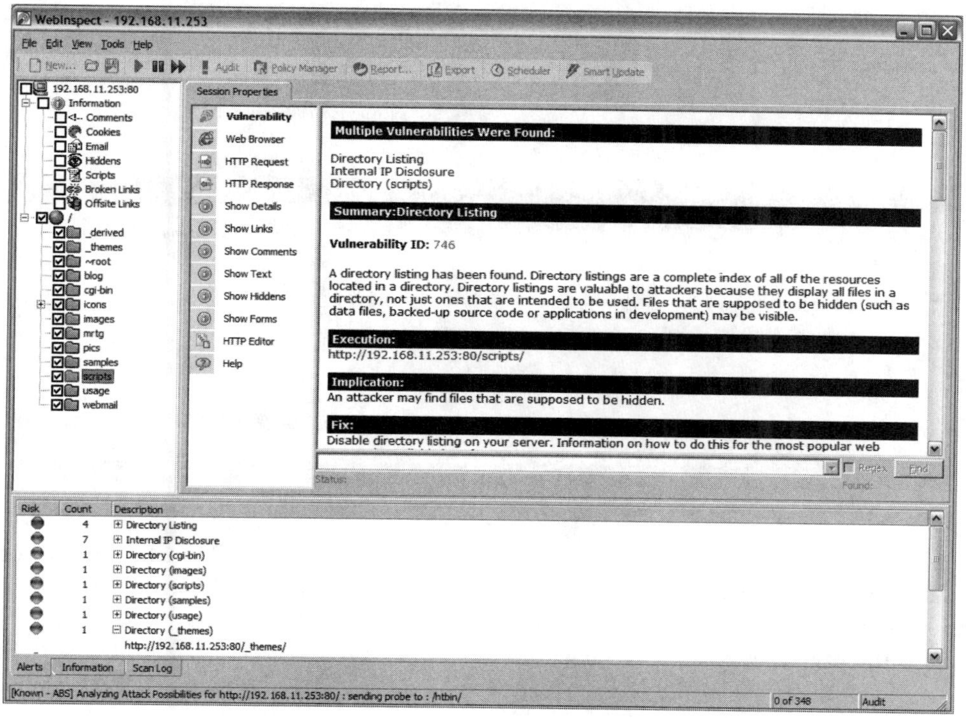

Next up is an open source app called Wikto, which is an extended version of Nikto, written for the .NET environment (see Figure 21.6). Wikto/Nikto can do something other application scanners cannot do: It comes with the Google Hacking Database (GHDB). This allows you to check Google for information it might have concerning the servers you are scanning. This is a very cool, and very useful, feature.

Figure 21.6 Wikto in Action

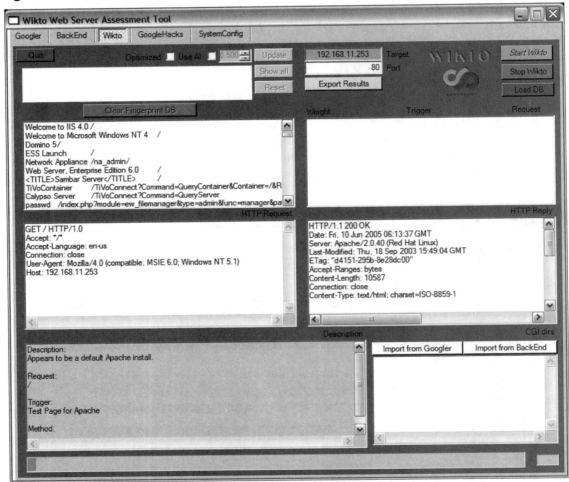

There are many other application-specific scanners, but we're limited on the amount of space we can dedicate to this area. We have given you a brief introduction to the application-scanning tool genre. To ensure that your application-specific scanning needs are met, you'll need to do some research into these various tools yourself.

Network Protocol Analysis

Network protocol analysis is an activity that might not always be conducted during the IEM process due to the privacy issues involved. When you are analyzing network traffic at the protocol level, you are seeing everything (unless it's encrypted). All the cleartext protocols are captured and decoded for you to view. This bothers some organizations. It is something to keep in mind when you're conducting the evaluation. If the organization permits network protocol analysis, you need to ensure that all data you gather and information you see is considered proprietary and subject to your nondisclosure agreement. If you have questions about anything you see during network scanning, consult your team lead. The NSA IEM urges organizations to consider conducting the network analysis during an evaluation, and for that reason it is considered one of the 10 baseline activities.

Why Perform Network Protocol Analysis?

As an evaluation activity, network analysis is important for validation of previously gathered results, for locating potential "hot spots" in the organization's network, and for detecting cleartext protocols in use (such as Telnet, FTP, IMAP, and POP3). "Hot spots" are areas of a network that are highly congested or under a heavy network traffic load. Network "hot spots" are issues that an organization should be aware of but might not be. The help desk could get calls from end users saying "E-mail is slow" or "The Internet is slow," and other signs of network congestion may pop up. But without looking at the network traffic and mapping the traffic patterns, it would be very difficult for an organization to diagnose the network problems. They would appear as somewhat random network outages/events. A network protocol analyzer can provide evidence needed to resolve network issues. Therefore, that can be a good selling point when you encounter organizations that are being difficult about having network-level protocol analysis done as part of the IEM.

Introducing Network Protocol Analyzers

Prior to starting up your network traffic analyzer, check to see if it is a switched environment. What we mean by "switched environment" is one in which network switches are used rather than network hubs. A switched network is more efficient, but it also foils our network analysis activities. You will have to get the network administrator to set up a "spanned port" for you. This will permit your network analyzer to see all the network traffic crossing that switch.

Note

Ensure that the port configuration is returned to normal (not spanned) or disabled after you are finished with the network protocol capture and analysis. Usually it's a good idea to notify the customer POC and team lead when you are finished.

We mention only a few of the available network protocol analyzers here, since most accomplish the same activities and tasks in similar fashions. We briefly introduce you to some of the popular protocol analyzers (you'll thank us later for not going over them all).

The first network analyzer we'll mention is Ethereal (http://ethereal.com/). This is a very popular open source network protocol analysis tool. Even though it's free, Ethereal has all the standard features you would see in a commercial-grade protocol analyzer (see Figure 21.7), and some features you won't find in the commercial ones. Personally, we use Ethereal quite often. It's a reliable network analysis tool and very feature-rich—and arguably the best open source protocol analyzers available today.

Figure 21.7 The Ethereal Packet Decode Window

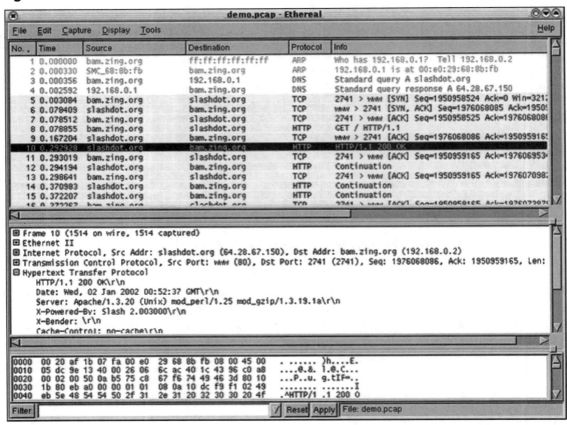

Another protocol analyzer is EtherPeek NX from WildPackets (www.wildpackets.com/products/etherpeek_nx). EtherPeek NX claims to be the first protocol analyzer to offer both frame decoding and expert analysis in real time during packet capture. Figure 21.8 is a screen capture showing EtherPeek NX during a packet capture; Figure 21.9 shows EtherPeek NX offering its expert analysis.

Figure 21.8 An EtherPeek NX Sample Packet Capture

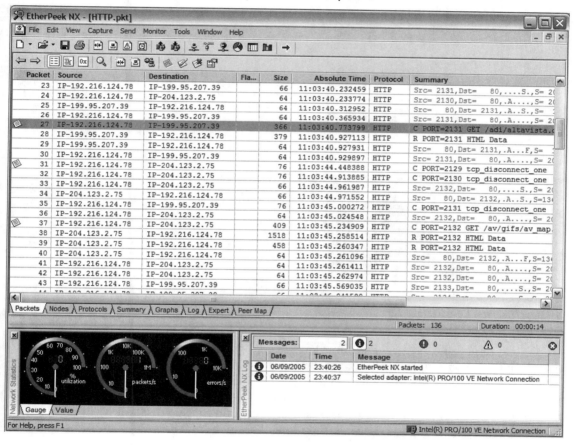

Figure 21.9 EtherPeek NX Expert Analysis and Problem Detection

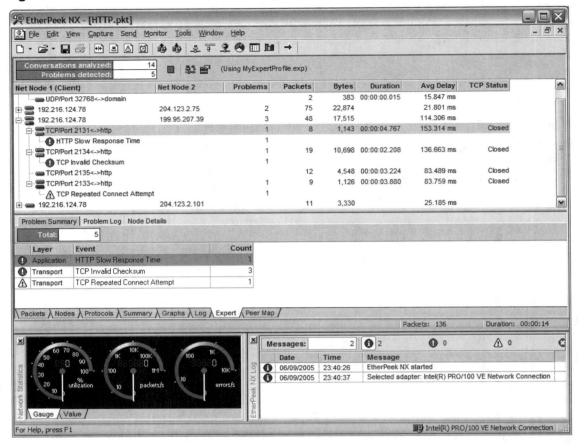

As you can probably see just from these few screen captures, protocol analyzers share a fairly common interface or look and have a common feature set. Protocol analysis has been around for quite a while and isn't a very lively technology area; it's seen no really new innovations in recent times. Nearly any protocol analyzer should fit your needs as long as it provides the standard protocol analyzer functionality. Oh yeah, and it has to have cool colorful gauges, too. (Not really.)

Summary

In this chapter we completed the technical portion of the INFOSEC Evaluation Methodology. We did an evaluation/analysis of all network devices, including firewalls, routers, and IDSs. We conducted password-compliance testing, also known as password cracking. We discussed application-specific scanning and how it supplements the results from our vulnerability scans and host evaluations. Finally we examined network protocol analysis and its role in the IEM. We covered quite a bit of material and concepts, but it was a fun ride.

It's important for you to remember that all these tasks are in support of the IEM process. Nothing is standalone; all tasks have a purpose. As mentioned in the previous chapter, this section requires more thought and interaction than you perhaps initially thought. It can be an eye-opener once you see the amount of manual work ahead of you during an evaluation.

## Chapter 22

The Onsite Closing Meeting

Solutions in this chapter:

- **Organizing the Meeting**

- **TEP Overview**

- **Setting Timelines**

- **Overview of Critical Findings**

- **Points of Immediate Resolution**

- **What Do You Do with the Information That You Have Collected?**

☑ **Summary**

Introduction

You have been working side by side with many individuals from your customer organization and performing multiple technical tests. Now it's time to close out the onsite phase of the IEM. These individuals are curious and possibly nervous about what the evaluation team has been doing and the types of things being discovered. In this chapter we discuss the *out-brief meeting* that you'll hold with the customer. The purpose of the out-brief is to present an overview of critical findings that you identified during the onsite activity, provide immediate resolution for the findings, address any customer concerns, and communicate the timelines and status to the customer. You will gain some valuable insight into ways to successfully organize and conduct the out-brief meeting and demonstrate the IEM's business value to the customer.

Organizing the Meeting

"Begin with the end in mind" is a truism that captures the essence of the planning process for the customer out-brief meeting. It is important that you look at the TEP to check the onsite schedule and start preparing for the out-brief meeting ahead of time. Planning ahead for the meeting is essential to having a successful out-brief. Take the time to determine when the meeting will be held, where it will be held, who will attend, what information will be presented, and how the meeting will be conducted.

TIP

To allow you and your team enough time to prepare a successful out-brief meeting, we recommend that you start preparing three to five days ahead of the scheduled meeting.

Time and Location

You will find that it can be a challenge to set the final time and location for the out-brief meeting. The size and scope of the evaluation tends to determine the number of people who need to be involved in the out-brief. In bringing a group of people together, you must take many factors into account. Work closely with the organization POC to help select a day and time that will accommodate all attendees' work schedules. Most of the time, the in-brief meeting attendees will also be involved with the out-brief meeting and should be forewarned. Depending on the number of findings, the meeting typically is one to two hours in length. Having breaks and refreshments during the meeting can help create a successful and comfortable meeting.

The meeting location should be central and convenient for the most important attendees. Most organizations require that conference rooms be reserved ahead of time. The room should be able to accommodate all attendees as well as provide conferencing capabilities for remote attendees. Try to visit the scheduled room several days before the meeting to see its layout and identify any equipment and special needs for the meeting.

Warning

During the out-brief meeting, you will be discussing critical security findings that should be considered sensitive and be protected. We once had a customer who scheduled the out-brief in their company lunchroom during lunch hour! Not only was the noise level unbearable, it was difficult to be discreet about our findings from the evaluation.

Evaluation Team and Customer Involvement

During the evaluation, you will work with many different individuals from the customer organization. Work closely with your POC to identify the individuals who need to be invited to the out-brief meeting and the ones it might be best to avoid inviting. Not only is the out-brief the time to share the evaluation findings and recommendations—it is also the time to close any remaining items or issues that were brought up during the onsite activities. Each company that offers the IEM will go about managing engagement in its own way. The following sections highlight the individuals who should attend the meeting.

The Customer

You might not have input into who should be involved with the out-brief, but it is important to try to get as many people from the customer side, to ensure that there are no surprises at the end of the evaluation. Sometimes final evaluation outcomes are not presented to the people who need them the most to make the necessary security improvements. The out-brief can provide a great forum for knowledge transfer of valuable security information from the evaluation team to the customer team. You will want the following people at the meeting:

- The **POC** is the person who represents the organization and who interfaces with the evaluation team from start to completion of the IEM evaluation.

- **Upper management** representatives can help gauge company risk tolerances on presented critical findings and can provide management guidance on following the evaluation recommendations to the rest of the organization. Having at least one upper-management representative involved in your out-brief ensures that all disputes will be resolved and all recommendations approved and managed by a business owner.

- Key **security management and staff** will need to know the outcome of the evaluation and be able to continue to support other organization staff members in resolving the evaluation findings.

- Key **network management and engineers** for all network-related findings need to attend.

- Key **system management and administrators** for all platforms and systems targeted during the evaluation need to attend.

- **Contract personnel** ensure that all deliverables up to this point have been met.

The Evaluation Team

Although it's not required, it is recommended that you never have more people from your organization than the customer has present. You don't want to intimidate and/or overwhelm the customer. You will want the following people from your company at the meeting:

- The **evaluation team** that performed the evaluation. If not all members are available, we recommend that you have the evaluation team lead there to represent the team.

- The **sales contact** who routinely interfaces with the customer and was the one who sold them the evaluation. By having this person involved, you can provide additional training for future sales opportunities as well as provide a "check and balance" to keep the sales process clean and honest. We're not saying that salespeople are dishonest, but we have seen instances where more was promised initially than was or could be delivered. The involvement of the salesperson helps build trust and furthers the relationship with the customer by providing a level of comfort that the evaluation was performed and controlled as expected.

Presentation Needs

How your message is received relies on he way it is delivered. Studies have shown that people remember 50 percent of what they see and hear. To successfully get your message across in your meeting, you should use several visual tools:

- **PowerPoint**   This is a great visual aid for enhancing a presentation, but it can negatively impact the message you are trying to convey if it's not used correctly. Be sure to create a backup copy of your presentation on a CD, disk, or Flash drive!

- **Whiteboard or flip chart**   These are great tools for highlighting and illustrating key points of your presentation, especially for drawing recommended network architectural changes. Be sure in advance that all markers work and that you have an eraser for the whiteboard.

- **Handouts**   These are ideal for allowing people to follow along with your presentation. Print your PowerPoint slides using the Handout format with three slides per page. This will allow enough room on the right side of each slide for note taking, and it condenses the amount of paper needed for copies.

If you plan to use a PowerPoint presentation, you might need to provide one or more of the following types of equipment:

- **Laptop**   For running the presentation. A fully charged battery should be able to get you through most meetings.

- **Overhead projector**   Might be provided by the customer. As you plan for the out-brief meeting, check with the organization POC, if one will be available. You might have to provide the projector yourself. Additionally, check that the scheduled room has a projection screen or, at a minimum, a blank wall.

- **Laptop wireless remote**   This is not required but is recommended. We have been in rooms where the presentation laptop was in the back of the room while the presenter was at the front of the room. Additionally, some remotes have a laser pointer that can be used to highlight key points in the slides.

TIP

Use the following presentation tips to "professionalize" and visually enhance your presentation. Be careful not to include too many types of visuals in your presentation. You want your message, not the visuals, to be the focus of your presentation:

1. Be consistent from slide to slide by using the same font size and format.

2. Make each slide easy to read. The title of the page should summarize your message with a maximum of bulleted key items.

3. Use color to emphasize facts and ideas.

4. Choose the right font size. We've attended too many presentations that could not be seen by the majority of the audience.

5. Avoid using too many animations and graphics in your presentation. They should be used to help convey and emphasize your message, not distract the audience from it.

The Agenda

Preparing an agenda for the out-brief is no different from doing so for any other business meeting. The out-brief cannot be everything to everyone, but you should know who will be attending the meeting, since that information will be helpful in preparing your agenda. Having a clear agenda provides an outline for the meeting and can be used as a checklist to make sure that all areas of the TEP are covered. Key things to focus on in creating the agenda are assigning a time limit for each discussion item (and sticking to it), the types of topics you plan to cover, and start and stop times for the meeting. Once the agenda is complete, have the organization POC distribute copies to all attendees at least a day in advance. The agenda items will include:

- Reviewing the TEP and how the overall evaluation was accomplished
- Reviewing critical findings and immediate resolutions
- Reviewing timelines and expectations for the rest of the evaluation process
- Question and answer session

TEP Overview

You began the onsite activities with an in-brief meeting, where the Technical Evaluation Plan (TEP) was reviewed with the organization's staff and the evaluation team. The TEP is a living document that is used as a key management tool for the entire evaluation process. It contains the objectives and goals of the evaluation, boundaries of testing, and customer concerns and constraints that should be addressed during the evaluation. Reviewing the TEP during the out-brief meeting can ensure that the evaluation team addressed all fundamental areas of the TEP and will help communicate the overall comprehensiveness of the evaluation process.

The Evaluation Process

The IEM is a structured, flexible, yet repeatable process for performing technical evaluations for any organization. Many of the attendees of the out-brief have probably never been exposed to a technical evaluation. If they have been involved with a security audit or vulnerability assessment, it is more than likely that they have not been involved with the IEM process. It is important that you spend enough time educating your audience about the process that they come away with an understanding of the way information was collected and analyzed.

How Was Information Collected?

It is important to cover the 10 baseline activities of the IEM for collecting technical information and discuss what each activity is trying to accomplish. Some customers will ask for additional activities outside the 10 baseline IEM activities; be sure to cover those as well. This is also a good time to discuss any technical testing constraints that occurred during the evaluation as well as established network and system boundaries defined in the TEP.

The Tools

For various reasons, some people think it is taboo to discuss the tools that were used during technical testing. Let's face it—this is not rocket science! Many Internet sites and reference books explain how to use the majority of testing tools. The out-brief provides a great opportunity to demonstrate your expertise with these tools to your customer. Give a brief explanation of each tool used, in what phase of the process the tool was used, and how the tool was used.

While we are on this topic, it is imperative that you know how each tool works. That does not mean that you have to understand each switch that can be passed to the tool, though that's important; we mean that you should understand how the tool elicits and evaluates responses from systems and applications. Does the tool make assumptions? Are there any technical limitations that can cause unreliable results for the tool? When no switches are used for the tool, what default settings are used? Will the tool work on a subnet or just a single host? Rely on your experience as a tester; don't always rely on the output of your tools. They can sometimes mislead you in how they interpret responses from systems. How do you know whether the host that you are testing remotely is responding? Maybe it is a router or a firewall response.

Customer Documentation

All customer documentation that was collected during the evaluation should be briefly discussed in terms of the way the information was used during the onsite activities and how it will be used during the post-evaluation phase. In some situations, the evaluation team could receive new or supporting documents as late as this meeting. This is the case when an individual has forgotten to provide documentation to the evaluation team in support of a finding that is presented during the meeting. It is recommended that you have all customer documentation present during the meeting, in case it needs to be used as a reference or if the customer needs to verify version information. We have received older versions of customer documentation in organizations that lack version control. The types of documentation that you might have collected could include, but is not limited to:

- INFOSEC policies, procedures, and standards for implementing security at the organization
- Customer inventory sheets to help identify rogue systems and critical components
- Architectural diagrams illustrating firewall, IDS, router, switch, wireless, and DMZ layouts for identification of physical and logical boundaries, critical paths, and architectural weaknesses
- System configurations for networking equipment (router, switch, wireless, etc.)
- Firewall rules (host and network), proxy rules, router ACLs
- Password files for password-compliance testing
- Application-specific configuration files (Web server, DNS, SMTP, etc.)
- Organizational and system criticality documentation, if the customer has been through an IAM

Customer Concerns

Managing customer expectations and concerns is critical during the out-brief meeting. Have the customer concerns been met, or will the evaluation results conflict with the organization's goals, expectations, and concerns? The TEP will provide initial concerns and expectations from the customer perspective as well as the evaluation team's. Keep notes on additional concerns that arise during the evaluation activities and during the out-brief meeting. They should be addressed during the meeting and in your final report.

What Is Driving the Evaluation?

It is imperative that the entire evaluation team understand the reason the customer wants the evaluation. Don't assume that organizations in the same industry have identical concerns. Each organization is unique, with different strategies, tactics, and risk tolerances. The following are some concerns that we have seen in past evaluation experiences:

- Regulation and standards compliance (Sarbanes-Oxley [SOX], HIPAA, GLBA, FISMA)
- The organization had a recent security incident
- A competitor had a recent security incident
- Meeting security objectives
- Insurance requirements
- Partner requirements
- The organization is starting to build a security practice and will use the evaluation findings as a road map

Customer Constraints

For a number of reasons, the evaluation team will not be allowed to perform various types of testing, or testing may be limited to specific dates and times that have limited impact on the customer mission.

This can make it difficult to gather the information required to perform a comprehensive evaluation. Not all participants in the meeting will be aware of the constraints. It is recommended that in the out-brief meeting, the presenter cover these constraints as well as the impact of those restrictions on the evaluation. One example is when the evaluation team is able to identify a finding but not validate it because of constraints that the customer has placed on the evaluation.

Protecting Testing Data

Customer information gathered during the IEM process should be protected at all times. The last thing you and the customer want is to have information about their vulnerabilities leaked into the public forum because you didn't protect the information. Not only does it expose the customer to potential malicious activity, it could bring a lawsuit against you and the company you work for. The following recommendations provide guidance on how to ensure protection of your customer's sensitive and proprietary data:

- Encrypt all communications between your firm and the customer that could contain sensitive information regarding the evaluation activities.

- Keep all communications about the client internal to the evaluation team and your customer POC.

- Use encryption on all systems to protect customer data that is collected during the evaluation.

- Keep all paper documents locked in a secure location.

Setting Timelines

As with any engagement, we need to identify timelines and keep track of milestones during the evaluation. Keeping the customer updated on your progress during the evaluation can help you manage customer expectations and adds a level of professionalism to the evaluation team efforts. During the out-brief meeting, you want to present an outline of the timelines that have been established for the evaluation. Cover all major milestones that have been accomplished, as well as ones that you've failed to meet, and what the customer should expect during the post-evaluation phase.

Important Events During Testing

Covering important events that occurred during testing allows you to communicate the comprehensiveness of the IEM process to the customer without "tooting your own horn." The customer wants to know that work was performed and what they are paying for. Services are less tangible than products and are based on status reports and the final deliverable. Communicating details about the process ensures that the organization appreciates the value of the evaluation service. The larger the evaluation, the more events you will have. Some key events that should be covered are:

- When the onsite phase began and ended

- Onsite visits, if multiple sites are being evaluated

- When key interviews were performed
- When each of the 10 baseline activities began and ended
- When specific goals and concerns were met—for example, incident response to scanning activities

Final Report Delivery

The out-brief meeting is used wrap up the onsite activities and to communicate critical findings discovered during this phase. It is important to discuss the timelines for the post-evaluation process and the point at which the customer should expect delivery of the final report. In most cases, the customer can expect to receive the report within two to six weeks after the out-brief meeting. This delivery date varies based on the size of the evaluation that is being performed and the amount of information that needs to be analyzed.

Briefly outline the document structure of the final report. Most organizations expect to see an executive summary that will not contain a lot of technical detail as well as a technical section that can be used by the organization's technical staff members. Find out how detailed should the report be. When making recommendations, can you summarize, or does it have to be a step by step? How will the customer expect to receive raw tool output? Will there be a CD? Will the customer want to know which tool was used to identify the finding for validation after the recommended fix has been implemented?

Overview of Critical Findings

Up to this point in the out-brief, you have provided a brief summary of the IEM process, discussed customer concerns and expectations, and covered important events that happened during the onsite evaluation. Now it is time to specifically discuss the critical findings discovered during the evaluation. Show the customer what you have found and discuss why each finding is considered a critical finding for the organization. For each finding, offer multiple recommendations to either mitigate or minimize the impact of the vulnerability on the organization. The majority of the time allocated for the out-brief meeting should be spent discussing the findings and recommendations.

You might be asking, "What is a critical finding?" In the following chapters, you will find detailed information on organizing and analyzing all the data you collected as well as creating the system vulnerability criticality matrix (SVCM) and the overall vulnerability criticality matrix (OVCM). The SVCM and OVCM will be used to provide a detailed analysis of the information security posture of each system based on the technical rating of each vulnerability and the organizational and system criticality rankings defined during the IAM process.

In the out-brief, you will not offer this type of detailed analysis. Each vulnerability will be given a risk rating, with a High, Medium, or Low label, using industry standards for technical vulnerabilities. You will find that most vulnerability scanners have in their signature databases predefined ratings for every vulnerability. Make sure you understand how the vendor of each tool has decided on these ratings. It is recommended that you use multiple vulnerability scanners. You will sometimes find that each scanner has a different rating for the same vulnerability. This is where your expertise as a security professional comes into play to offer a final technical rating. Some things to consider when you have to perform a rating analysis are discussed in the following sections.

How Does the Vulnerability Impact the System?

Vulnerability impacts more than just the system itself — it is about how a vulnerability can affect the way the system supports the organization's mission and objectives. The initial impact of a vulnerability will affect the system or the data on the system in one of three ways:

- Loss of confidentiality
- Loss of integrity
- Loss of availability

What Is the Likelihood That a Threat Will Exploit the Vulnerability?

What type of skill would a threat need to have to take advantage of the vulnerability? Has exploit or proof-of-concept code been published for the vulnerability? Are any worms or viruses in existence that use the vulnerability as an attack vector? Is the system Internet facing? Does the vulnerability exist on an operational system that could directly impact the customer mission? These key questions can help provide insight into the characteristics associated with each threat and the threat's likelihood of success in exploiting the vulnerability.

Mapping to Business Mission and Objectives

Many companies today follow the old principle of "consulting by the pound," whereby the more information they can throw at the customer, the more value the customer will receive. We have worked with customers for which evaluations were performed in this manner. The organization POC gets a call from the receptionist to pick up a package from her because it will not fit into his mailbox. He stops by the receptionist to find a three- to five-inch-thick report. He starts to review the report, starting at page one and slowly going through each page. As he reaches about page 10 or 15, he starts to speed up. By the time he ends at the last page, he can't recall what he just read because the majority of the report was tool output. Overwhelmed by the report, the POC ends up stashing it on a shelf to be used as a bookend, never to be used for its intended purpose. Sound familiar?

After gaining some experience by performing multiple IEM evaluations, you will find common vulnerabilities across many organizations and multiple systems in each organization. Yet each finding will have varying influences on the security posture and risk to the organization. The IEM takes into account the mission function of each system and the way the loss of confidentiality, integrity, or availability of the system would affect the organization's mission. This is one of the main factors differentiating the IEM from other technical methodologies and is the real business value-add of the IEM. To say to a customer, "We discovered 10 High vulnerabilities in your environment" is not as practical as saying "We discovered 10 High vulnerabilities, and eight of those were identified on eight mission-critical systems." We recommend that you present each finding in this manner because it provides a much stronger frame of reference for the customer.

Positive vs. Negative Findings

To this point, we have been discussing findings that have a negative impact on the organization. Be wary of merely presenting negative findings in the out-brief. You could get someone in the meeting asking, "Geez, are we doing anything positive?!" You also don't want to make individuals look bad. This can cause tension and hostility in the meeting, and if you're invited back, you will not receive any cooperation from these individuals. You are there to help the organization, and presenting positive findings, in addition to the negative findings, will help convey the nonattribution characteristics of the IEM.

Points of Immediate Resolution

For every finding you present, you should provide multiple recommendations to help minimize the impact of or mitigate the finding. These recommendations should be based on the organization's security policy, industry best practices, industry standards, and any regulations that the organization must comply with. Providing multiple remediation solutions to the organization will assist them in determining the best way to deal with the risk of the finding. Take into account any customer constraints, such as cost, that will impact the types of solutions you will introduce. Presenting recommendations that fly in the face of known constraints provides no value to the customer.

Short Term vs. Long Term

When a report is generated by a vulnerability scanner, you will find the recommended fixes are geared toward "quick-fix" solutions: "Implement patch from vendor"; "Change this registry setting"; "Limit access to this port." We all know what happens when we apply "Band-Aid" fixes to problems—you might stop the bleeding but not fix the symptom!

Identifying the same technical finding across multiple systems in an environment can be indicative of a weakness in a policy or procedure or that someone failed to follow a process. For example, installing a patch across multiple systems is a great short-term fix, but a long-term fix is to review the organization's patch management process (if they have one) to look for any weaknesses. Maybe you are seeing the same configuration management issue across multiple systems. Tie your solutions into the organization's information security policy. By doing so, you will assist the organization in dealing with each findings immediately as well as identify long-term solutions that will ultimately assist the organization in reducing risk. Remember, many of these organizational types of findings will be discovered during the IAM process, allowing the IEM process to verify whether the system really works as documented or intended.

What Do You Do With the Information That You Have Collected?

Your out-brief meeting was successful, and it is time for you to go back to the office to start the post-evaluation process. Be sure that you have all the documentation you need from the organization and that you have all the technical raw output from each tool that was used during the evaluation. The next step is to protect all the customer information before you leave the site. Encrypt all data on testing systems and removable media. All customer documentation that is considered sensitive should be stored in a lockbox. Make backups of encrypted data. The last thing that you would want is that you show up at the office to find that your testing system will not boot!

Summary

We have covered a lot of topics in this chapter. Please remember that the out-brief is usually only one to two hours long, depending on the size of the assessment. The out-brief provides the evaluation team with a way to communicate what has been done up to this point in the evaluation, the types of critical findings identified, the way each finding impacts the customer, the type of solutions that can be implemented to minimize the impact or mitigate each finding, and when to expect the final report from the evaluation. You don't want to leave the customer site with unanswered questions or surprises.

Chapter 23

Post-Evaluation Analysis

Solutions in this chapter:

- **Getting Organized**

- **Categorization, Consolidation, Correlation, and Consultation**

- **Conducting Additional Research**

- **Analyzing Customer Documentation**

- **Developing Practical Recommendations**

☑ **Summary**

Introduction

If you have been involved in conducting any type of technical assessment or evaluation in the past, you know that such processes can often produce a large amount of data that can take a significant amount of time to organize, analyze, and correlate. You must be able to analyze the data in an efficient amount of time but still be able to provide an accurate and high-quality final report to the customer. Organizing the data collected during the evaluation is a critical component of the post-evaluation phase of the IEM.

The variety of tools used during the evaluation produce raw data in diverse formats. You must be able to organize the evaluation data in ways that make sense to you or are meaningful to the person who will analyze the data so that it can be turned into usable information. The final deliverable is dependent on how you break down the complex raw data collected during the onsite activities into its most basic elements and relationships, then how you are able analyze the data, through the process of categorizing, consolidating, correlating, and consulting, to develop practical and effective solutions for the customer. This chapter walks you through this process.

Getting Organized

At this point, we need to discuss what to do with the data that has been collected. Throughout the onsite evaluation process, the evaluation team identified and verified potential vulnerabilities and weaknesses of the customer's systems. Organizing the raw data that has been collected can be either simple or complicated, depending on the number of people involved in collecting data during the evaluation. The way you organize your data will be up to you or the person who will be performing the final analysis. Each person has different tools and techniques for correlating, analyzing, and understanding the associations between the various evaluation tool results and the evaluation goals. To better understand the various approaches to data organization, let's first look at the types of analysis and reporting needs you have.

Analysis Needs

The first and foremost analysis need is knowledge. Knowledge is not about how much training or how many certifications a person has. Knowledge is individualistic. It is inherent to individuals and is acquired through the natural process of experience and learning. The competence, often referred to as *expertise*, of each evaluation team member is essential to successfully analyze captured data and apply critical problem-solving techniques to guide the customer in making important decisions concerning their information security.

The logical approach to analyzing data depends on a systematic way of organizing the raw results produced by your security tools. The security tools that are most commonly used for evaluations generate a log or report of their findings, typically to a flat file of some format type such as ASCII, PDF, HTML, XML, binary, or RTF. This can be problematic during the analysis process, since these files are frequently viewed and searched. The first step is to organize these data files into a practical structure that will allow you to discern where different types of IEM evaluation data can be found. Once you've amassed all the evaluation raw data, you might consider categorizing the data and utilizing a tree structure for organization, as shown in Figure 23.1.

Figure 23.1 A Tree File Structure for Two Baseline Activities

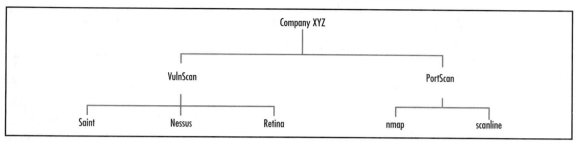

As illustrated, the parent directory is named after the organization for which the evaluation was conducted. Under the parent directory are subdirectories that are mapped to the 10 baseline activities of the IEM. Each baseline directory includes subdirectories that contain the results of each tool employed for that activity during the evaluation. It is recommended that you follow a naming standard for your raw data files for easier identification of their contents. For example, the nmap security tool offers a number of port-scanning types and features. You might name the results file of an nmap TCP SYN scan against a single network something like *SYN_Scan* using the *−oA* nmap switch. When multiple networks are scanned, such as 192.168.1.0/24, 192.168.2.0/24, and 192.168.3.0/24, you might use the following naming standard: *SYN_Scan_Net_1*, *SYN_Scan_Net_2*, *SYN_Scan_Net_3* for each respective scan result. The nomenclature for your raw data files may include perspective and/or boundary information, which we cover later in this chapter.

TIP

To keep from having to change filenames during the analysis process, we advise establishing a naming standard prior to the evaluation so that all members on the evaluation team are utilizing the same standard. It is best to follow the same standard for each evaluation that you perform, to limit any confusion for yourself or any of your team members.

Once your data is organized, you need a way to correlate data among your evaluation tools. Unfortunately, there are no known "point and click" solutions for this task. You will be spending a considerable amount of time reviewing the evaluation raw data and need a means of documenting your findings. Evaluation teams have used the following three approaches to achieve this goal:

■ **Spreadsheet approach**   Using spreadsheets for data organization, correlation, and tracking is the most common approach used not only by evaluation teams but by companies in general. We have seen Internet service providers (ISPs) use spreadsheets like a database to document and track thousands of pieces of critical customer network connectivity information. Why not? Spreadsheets are easy to use and have minimal training requirements for users. If used properly, they can be used not only to track multiple types of data but also when quantification of data and the creation of graphs are needed. In the following chapters, you will create a system vulnerability criticality matrix (SVCM) and the overall vulnerability criticality matrix (OVCM), which have the appearance and layout of a spreadsheet. It may be only natural to utilize the spreadsheet approach for your data analysis needs. Most spreadsheet packages, like Microsoft Excel, provide a tabular worksheet design, which you can use to document and correlate findings identified for each IP address. It is recommended that you devise a spreadsheet template that will be used to document common evaluation information. A person who has mastered the full features offered by most spreadsheets will be able to create a full template workbook that will be able to calculate all your IEM quantification needs. Using a centralized spreadsheet could cause problems when multiple team members need to access and modify data in the workbook.

- **Database approach**   Databases are powerful in this respect: Once you get data into them, you can manipulate the data in multiple ways. The problem you will have is finding a commercial product that will fulfill your IEM analysis needs. The key to a good database is its design. If you are to design your own database, you must understand the types of records and fields that are needed and understand the relationships between them. How will the database be accessed? Is there a requirement to offer this database to the customer? How will the data in the database be protected? You have to evaluate the true ROI of creating such a database.

- **Document approach**   This approach uses templates to correlate and document findings for each IP address. This approach is similar to the spreadsheet approach uses of a word-processing package such as Microsoft Word.

Most evaluation teams are composed of several individuals. The team lead should coordinate the collection and consolidation of information during the analysis phase. The team lead will set and manage timelines to increase team productivity and keep the effort on track. This responsibility includes organizing team meetings and assigning individual responsibilities for the successful execution of the project. Responsibilities include:

- Technical writing assignments
- Host evaluation analysis
- Network evaluation analysis
- Application-specific analysis

An initial team kickoff meeting should be conducted to start the analysis process. Ongoing meetings will be conducted to manage the progress of each member and for review of findings from the evaluation, discussing impact of the findings to the customer, and brainstorming recommendations that will be presented to the customer.

Reporting Needs

The team lead will delegate and track writing assignments. It is critical that the technical findings be translated into information that will be easily understood by and usable to the customer. Some key responsibilities have been identified in providing a quality final deliverable to the customer:

- **Team lead**   The lead delegates and manages all analysis and reporting responsibilities and needs and interfaces with the customer when needed.

- **Technical writer**   Technical writers are a great asset that can aid in the process of turning the technical information into common language that is understandable to nontechnical people.

- **Quality assurance**   It always helps to have a third set of eyes to review the document and make sure that all expectations have been met.

Categorization, Consolidation, Correlation, and Consultation

Now that you have a general idea of your analysis and reporting needs, it is time to begin taking action. It is the moment to begin making sense of all the evaluation data using the "4 Cs": categorization, consolidation, correlation, and consultation. If you have never done this before, it might seem like a daunting task. Relax! Don't let yourself be inundated by the process or the details that some tools create. You have been provided with some ways to consolidate and categorize the data. First, there are several points worth keeping in mind while you're analyzing the raw data.

False Positives and False Negatives

In the previous chapter, we talked about knowing how your evaluation tools elicit responses and how they interpret responses from systems and applications. During the analysis process, you will consolidate and compare data to eliminate two common issues that are known to most security tools: false positives and false negatives.

When a security tool reports the existence of a finding that does not actually exist, the reading is known as a *false positive*. This occurs because security vulnerability scanners use a signature database that contains logic for the identification of known vulnerabilities. Sometimes the vulnerability check relies on the banner information that the service provides. This can be troublesome when vendors do not change the application banner during upgrades or when the organization that is using the application purposely changes the banner to throw off "script kiddies" and malicious mobile code. The Apache Web server is a good example of an application that is known to generate false positives for this reason.

Often, vulnerability checks expect specific types of responses and will make assumptions when the criteria have not been met. For example, Nessus ID 11875 checks for the existence of the OpenSSL ASN.1 Parsing vulnerability by sending an invalid client SSL certificate, which can lead to a denial of service if exploited by an attacker. We have seen this reported on many evaluations against systems that are running the latest version of OpenSSL. Reviewing the Nessus plug-in that performs this check, we find that the plug-in is expecting an error code (0x0A or 0x2a) from the application to determine whether the vulnerability exists. If the service replies with any other response, such as a TCP RST or a TCP FIN, the author of the plug-in concludes that this is not the expected response from the application and reports the existence of the vulnerability.

Another type of false positive occurs when a vulnerability is reported for a specific application, but the application is not running on the system. This is caused by the vulnerability check being created for a specific application but being found in multiple applications. So, the vulnerability may exist on the system, but it is not being reported for the correct application.

By now, you probably have guessed what a *false negative* is. It is a security vulnerability that affects the OS or application but that has not been identified. This can be caused by a security tool not having the appropriate checks, the person running the tool configuring the tool with specific checks disabled, or some type of filtering device denying some part of the vulnerability check communication.

We can reduce the number of false positives and negatives by comparing the output from multiple tools and relying on not only your security expertise but your network and system administration expertise. Later, we will discuss what to do when you do not have the experience or knowledge to effectively evaluate a finding.

> **NOTE**
>
> One of the values of following a comprehensive technical evaluation methodology is reducing the number of false positives and false negatives. This is a point that should be communicated to the customer during the sales process and during the out-brief meeting. But remember, the IEM is not the panacea for false positives or false negatives. You must rely on your evaluation experience, too.

Evaluation Perspectives

The approach that was used for the evaluation data collection activities must be kept in mind during the analysis process. The evaluation might involve more than one type of perspective in the scope of work. When we speak of *perspective*, we base it on the location of the person performing the evaluation when the vulnerability was identified. This is usually based on physical location, but it can be a logical location. For example, say that the customer wants an external evaluation but wants the evaluation team to be physically at the customer office. This is accomplished by connecting the testing systems "outside" of the customer internal network via a logical segmentation or through a network port on an external networking device. Although the evaluation team is physically onsite, the testing is performed from an external perspective, and all findings will be presented in that light. In the IEM, you can use three approaches during the evaluation: external exposures, ,internal exposures, and system boundaries.

External Exposures

External exposures are findings that were identified from outside the organization, typically from an Internet perspective. The 2004 Computer Crime and Security Survey, conducted by the Computer Security Institute (CSI), illustrates that the most likely source of an attack is an external threat source. The mainstream of Internet threats are not targeting specific companies but are searching the Internet for known vulnerabilities to gain unauthorized access to systems and information. Most organizations, particularly those that have never had an evaluation performed, do not know where they are at risk from external threats and usually want to start the evaluation from this perspective.

Internal Exposures

"Eggshell" security is a term used to describe the security posture of most organizations across all industries. This is a product of the way people have viewed and implemented security throughout history. Think of castles surrounded by high and impenetrable stone walls and a drawbridge to allow trusted travelers to cross over crocodile-infested moats. In the epic movie *Lord of the Rings: The Two Towers*, the people of Rohan take refuge in the great fortress of Helm's Deep, consisting of several layers of stone walls and caverns behind to protect its occupants from external threats. We have always been concerned with external threats and tend to be less attentive to protecting ourselves from internal threats. Yet internal security incidents have been shown to have a greater negative impact on organizations.

Insiders know more than outsiders about where your "keys to the kingdom" are and the inherent weaknesses of the security mechanisms and controls that protect them. Organizations tend to have fewer security controls internally and a propensity to monitor less for unauthorized access on mission-critical systems. When performing technical testing, it is important to keep detailed information on where inside the company you were performing the technical evaluation when you identified the internal exposures. This information, which typically consists of IP address and segment information, can aid in identifying not only host vulnerabilities but weaknesses in network access controls as well.

NOTE

When an external threat breaches an organization's perimeter security controls, it has the same visibility and access to internal exposures as an internal threat and should be considered an internal threat.

System Boundaries

Here it is important to revisit the definition of a system. A *system* is something that transmits, stores, or processes critical information within a customer organization. We defined system boundaries during the scoping phase of the IEM and documented them in the TEP. When we refer to system boundaries, we are alluding to one of the following attributes: the *physical* boundary of the system or the *logical* path the information traverses from one entrusted entity to another.

It is fairly simple to get a mental grasp on physical boundaries, because they are tangible. We deal with physical boundaries every day. When it comes to understanding logical boundaries, however, it is best to have an up-to-date architectural diagram that illustrates where each logical "zone" exists.

Conducting Additional Research

During your analysis, you will come across findings that will inevitably need additional research, for one of several reasons. The reported findings from a tool might not contain sufficient detail for you to perform an accurate analysis. Maybe you do not have enough experience or have limited or no knowledge on the product about which the finding is reported. You cannot be an expert at everything (regardless of what your sales guy is saying). What you can be, though, is resourceful. When you don't understand a finding or you need an answer to something that you cannot answer yourself, it is essential that you know where to find the answer. It is said that "Information is power," and we live in the Information Age. If you want to know something, go find it. The Internet has made information and people accessible at our fingertips. This openness does not come without caveats. Let's review some additional research resources that you may need to rely on during your analysis.

Resources

A multitude of Internet resources can provide information you need for your research on findings discovered during your evaluations. Not all the resources at your disposal will provide accurate or reliable information. You may be looking for technical information about a finding to match customer expectations on finding deliverables. Maybe you are looking for threat information to understand the likelihood and probability of the finding being abused. Or you could be looking for version information of a potentially affected product for which a finding is being reported. Here is a brief list of some resources that you can use for your research:

- **Search engines**   Although Google has a large following, you might prefer another search engine. It is advised to learn some of the advanced search capabilities of the search engine of your choosing. As with a vulnerability scanner, it is recommended that you use several search engines due to their various capabilities. Search engines such as Dogpile (www.dogpile.com) provide the ability to perform searches by simultaneously using multiple search engines.

- **Security Web sites**   At several trusted security Web sites you can find information on vulnerabilities and exploits:

    - Packet Storm, http://packetstormsecurity.com

    - Securiteam, www.securiteam.com

    - Linux Security, www.linuxsecurity.com

    - INFOSYSSEC, www.infosyssec.com

    - Security Focus, www.securityfocus.com

- **Mailing lists**   Multiple security mailing lists provide information pertaining to vulnerabilities, threats, and practices. Since you are performing an evaluation, you might be more focused on vulnerability disclosure and research lists. But beware. The information posted on lists frequently provides vague vulnerability information and every now and then is erroneous because the information could be theoretical and untested. You will sometimes find a "bug finder" who does not fully understand the technical issues of a vulnerability and posts inaccurate information. In cases such as this, some lists provide an obfuscated e-mail address of the poster, which can be useful in putting you in contact with the bug finder. It is recommended that you use a list archive site such as Neohapsis (http://archives.neohapsis.com), which provides a search feature for current and archives security list postings.

- **Vulnerability databases**   A *vulnerability database* is a centralized database of information on security vulnerabilities. This information can include vulnerability description, impact of vulnerability, references on vulnerability, solutions and workarounds, and exploit information.

We say "can provide" because not all databases are built the same way. Lack of standards, attempts to stay updated, and providing accurate, dependable, and complete information plague users of current vulnerability databases. Are we saying not to use them? Not at all. Just as you should not fully rely on the output of your tools, you need to understand the weaknesses of vulnerability databases and work with them. Here is a list of the major vulnerability databases that exist on the Internet today:

- OSVDB, www.osvdb.org/
- BID, www.securityfocus.com/bid/
- ISS X-Force, http://xforce.iss.net/
- Secunia, www.secunia.com/
- Security Tracker, www.securitytracker.com/
- ICAT, http://icat.nist.gov/icat.cfm
- CVE, http://cve.mitre.org/

- **Vulnerability notification services**   Vulnerability notification services disseminate technical security information, warnings, and advice to the Internet community. They are commonly known as Computer Emergency Response Team (CERT); most organizations are familiar with the US-CERT at Carnegie Mellon University. Other countries have their own versions of the US-CERT. The Computer Incident Advisory Capability (CIAC) is another vulnerability notification service that releases technical security vulnerability bulletins to the general public.

- **Vendor Web sites**   Most vendors are starting to jump on the security wagon by providing security information and fixes for their products. In some instances, a vendor denied a vulnerability existed in its product, even though a proof-of-concept exploit exists for the vulnerability. We have also seen cases in which a vendor acknowledges a vulnerability but gives it a lower security risk rating than it perhaps should have.

Consulting Subject Matter Experts

It's not what you know but who you know. This truism pertains to many aspects of our lives, including evaluations. Having access to subject matter experts (SME) will prove valuable when you're researching abstract security findings. At times during your research, you will have a difficult time finding the details needed to complete a full impact analysis on a finding. It could be that the vulnerability is new and the original security advisory was released with unclear information or the finding is an older vulnerability that has not been kept up to date in the vulnerability databases. Perhaps you are searching for a tailored and practical solution to mitigate a finding. Unless you have the resources and expertise to deploy a vulnerable test system on which to perform your own analysis, you will have to resort to consulting a trusted SME.

Other Team Members

The first place to look for trusted SMEs should be within your evaluation team and then within your organization. Security people have a wide range of IT experience that was acquired in previous "lives," before they entered the dark side of the security world. Arguably, what sets a security professional apart from other IT personnel is mindset. When you can't find an SME on the evaluation team, look within your organization's IT department. Usually, every company has a team of network and system administrators who are responsible for the mission-critical systems of that company. Many times, these individuals are a wealth of knowledge and have experience that surpasses the skills needed for their specific job functions. Where they don't have the knowledge, they usually have a friend or two who does.

External Resources

Networking with other security professionals is where you will glean the biggest value for attending security conferences and events. You will find that most security specialists are open to sharing their knowledge in areas in which they are known to have expertise. You must take care when dealing with external resources, however. You must maintain the confidentiality of your customer and not leak detailed information about where the security finding was discovered. All that you need to tell an external resource is an adequate amount of technical information about the finding to help you get the information that you need for your research. Consulting external resources can also involve reading previous posts or posting a general question to specific mailing lists. Chances are that you have a question that some other researcher is investigating!

NOTE

Check all your contractual agreements between the evaluation team and the customer to verify that you are permitted to contact external resources for research purposes. We have had customers who want to know up front the individuals who will be involved with the entire evaluation and might want background investigations performed on them.

Analyzing Customer Documentation

Throughout the evaluation process, the evaluation team accumulates different types of documentation that support the way the customer organization's security is designed, implemented, and maintained. This information can range from INFOSEC policy and procedures, security technical implementation guides (STIGs), network architectural diagrams, access controls, and host configurations to past security assessment results. During the analysis process, you will use these types of documents as references in understanding the customer's security paradigm and mapping findings and solutions to their security culture. At times you will have to ask the customer POC for documentation that was either overlooked or never delivered to the evaluation team.

INFOSEC Policies and Proceures

Security policies are the foundation of a successful information security program within an organization. Policies provide a framework for defining a desired posture that the organization is working toward attaining through best operational security practices and will be used when formulating your recommendations. You will find purpose and strategy of the information security program, guidelines for everyday operational security practices, regulatory and industry compliance standards, appropriate ways to respond to security incidents, and references to additional complementary security documents.

During your analysis, among all the findings you could find a common theme that points to a weakness with a security practice. Maybe the company needs a patch management process or already has one that needs to be updated. Perhaps the company policy is not being implemented and individuals need to be educated on the information security policy. If it is found that the information security policy needs to be updated or added to, we recommend you follow industry best practices and standards to keep your recommendations subjective.

Knowing up front how the organization implements technical security controls on hosts is important when you're performing host evaluations. Most companies are still maturing their information security program and have not implemented standard host configurations, commonly referred to as a STIG. Sometimes you will find that STIGs have been documented but were put together by an individual who had no security background. It is also common to find that OS STIGs exist within an organization, but STIGs for mission-critical applications do not. Where STIGs are not found, it is recommended to go along with one of the following known standards:

- Center for Internet Security (CIS), www.cis.org
- National Institute of Standards and Technology (NIST), http://csrc.nist.gov
- National Security Agency (NSA), www.nsa.gov/snac/
- Defense Information Systems Agency (DISA) STIGs, http://csrc.nist.gov/pcig/cig.html

WARNING

Be careful when you're following or recommending a STIG standard, especially on operational systems. If the standard is fully implemented, your customer could end up with a system that might not operate properly or functions but nothing else can be done on it. We have seen situations in which customers started to apply STIG configurations and crashed the system. If you're not familiar with a STIG setting and the way it could impact the system, refer to the additional research section of this chapter.

Previous Evaluations/VA/Penetration-Testing Results

The evaluation team may or may not get access to the results of any prior testing that has been performed against the organization. It's helpful for the evaluation team to know what findings were previously identified and how the organization dealt with the risk of the findings. Were the findings accepted, fixed, or not addressed? You do not want to create noise in your final deliverable with findings that have been acknowledged and accepted by the organization. This is not to say that these findings should not be revisited. The risk from a vulnerability can change over time.

If you discover issues that were assumed to be fixed, it's possible that either the finding is a false positive or the issue was not resolved properly. You must carry out further investigation with the customer to accurately report the finding to them. You should never make an assumption about identified findings.

Be prepared to answer the question as to why previous tests did not identify findings that the IEM process has uncovered. This could occur due to the type of security test that was performed, the lack of a comprehensive methodology being utilized, or maybe the finding was discovered but not properly analyzed. This is not the time to bash your competitor; instead, educate the customer on the value of the IEM and why it can be more effective than conventional approaches in discovering security issues.

Developing Practical Recommendations

Up to this point we have been discussing analysis issues and the process of evaluating and correlating the evaluation raw data. You have trudged your way through volumes of raw data and are on the verge of losing your sanity. The data has been categorized, consolidated, and correlated. So now what? You have uncovered problems that have varying degrees of impact on the organization's mission-critical systems, and you now need to document practical and effective solutions. It is recommended that you provide multiple solutions per finding to give the customer some flexibility in selecting the best solution for them. Take into account that an identified recommendation may address a single finding or multiple findings, and there could be multiple solutions that mitigate one finding. The recommendations that you present will entail operational, managerial, and/or technical improvements to the organization's information security way of life.

So, you might be asking, "What is a practical recommendation?" This is best determined by understanding the appropriate level of security for the organization to accomplish its mission objectives and to do it securely. What is the organization's risk tolerance? How will the finding impact the organization? Will new risks be introduced into the customer's environment if they follow the evaluation recommendations? What types of threats are likely to exploit the identified findings? Will there be sacrifices that the customer will have to accept to be protected from the identified risks? The answers to these questions will start the process of guiding you toward completing the IEM analysis process and improving your customers' overall security posture.

Level of Detail

In the Coordination Agreements section of the TEP, you will find particulars about the level of detail the customer expects with reference to the recommendations in the final report. As an evaluator, you want to make sure that you understand these requirements before you start your analysis and research. They will help determine the level of effort required to collect details about each finding. What follows are recommended details that you will want to document for each finding that will be useful during the formation of your final recommendations. It is advised to create a template that you'll use during your evaluation research—something like the one shown in Table 23.1 and described in the following subsections.

Table 23.1 An Example of a Finding Research Template

Finding	Description	References	Threat Likelihood	Business Impact Criticality Rating	Recommendations

Finding

Use a short yet descriptive title for the finding—usually only one sentence in length and containing enough detail to communicate the finding. For example, let's say that a host is found to be vulnerable to a format sting attack against the *ssl_log* function in the Apache *mod_ssl* module. A title could be written as follows: "Apache *mod_ssl-2.8.18 - 1.3.31 mod_ssl ssl_log* function format string." In this example, the finding is seen to include the product name, affected version information, and a brief description of the vulnerability.

Description

The description section is a technical description of the finding and usually a short paragraph in length. An example description of the previously mentioned Apache finding may be written as follows: "The *mod_ssl ssl_log* function in Apache contains a flaw that may allow an attacker to execute arbitrary messages. The issue is triggered due to a *ssl_log()* format string error within the *mod_proxy* hook functions."

References

It is recommended that you use reputable references when presenting a finding. The IEM is partial to using CVE identifiers as a reference. You may think about documenting additional references that provide detailed information about the finding. Usually, we find it valuable to document three references. You might not use all of this information in the final report, but it's worth having in case you need to provide additional sources.

Criticality Rating

Depending on the scope and complexity of the organization's environment, the criticality rating of the vulnerability in relation to risk can be challenging. This is likely due to the subjective nature of deciding on the criticality rating of a finding. The ultimate goal of the criticality rating is to provide a description of the vulnerability in terms of how it relates to the customer's environment, which will eventually be linked to asset criticality for prioritization of short- and long-term remediation efforts.

Criticality ratings are categorized as High, Medium, or Low to convey the overall risk impact on the system the vulnerability signifies to the organization. The rating will consider such factors as the exposure perspective of the finding, business impact of the vulnerability (loss of confidentiality, integrity, or availability), threat likelihood analysis, and remediation effort. As you can see, you will have to rely not only on the information uncovered during your research but also on your experiences as a security professional. It is recommended that you articulate the definitions of your criticality ratings so that your customer is aware of the risk impact of the vulnerability. Here we provide an example definition for each rating:

- **High** A High risk finding is usually assigned to vulnerabilities that will have a high threat or impact potential and allow unauthorized privileged access, allow execution of code, or grant the ability to alter the system in some way. It's recommended that you correct these types of findings immediately.

- **Medium** A Medium risk finding is representative of a vulnerability that poses a medium level of risk to the organization and will allow a threat immediate access to the system with unprivileged access. The risk gives a threat the opportunity to continue to attempt gaining privileged access on the system.

- **Low** A Low risk finding is defined as one that provides sensitive information that could lead to further attempts to impact the confidentiality, integrity, or availability of the system.

Business Impact

It is common information security language to express impact in terms of the loss of confidentiality, integrity, or availability. Eventually, a vulnerability could pilot the way to the loss of all three impact attributes. It is advised to report on the initial impact of the finding against a system. Briefly describe the type of attack and how it can be carried out by a threat. For those of you who are new to information security, we provide brief definitions for each impact attribute:

- **Loss of confidentiality** This is the result of the information being read or copied by an unauthorized individual.

- **Loss of integrity** This is the result of the unauthorized or unintentional alteration of data.

- **Loss of availability** This is the inaccessibility of information or services to authorized persons.

Here is an example business impact statement for the Apache *mod_ssl* finding we discussed earlier: "It is possible that the flaw may allow a remote attacker to execute arbitrary messages via format string specifiers in certain log messages for HTTPS, resulting in a loss of integrity."

Threat Likelihood

Standard mainstream security assessments offered by "run-of-the-mill" companies focus only on vulnerabilities. By now, you should understand that not all vulnerabilities are created equal. A vulnerability that exists internally may be ranked with a lower risk rating than if it were exposed to external threats.

To fully understand the risk of a finding, you must consider the value of the asset to the organization, the threat likelihood, and the business impact and rating of the vulnerability. You should already understand the nature of the vulnerability through your research efforts and have been provided the business value of the asset through the system criticality matrix developed during the IAM process.

It is important to fully comprehend threat sources, motivations, and capabilities that could abuse the identified finding. Vulnerabilities may be the focal point for multiple threats, and threats may appear from the existence of multiple vulnerabilities. Are there any known threats exploiting the vulnerability? What type of skill level is required to exploit the finding? Is there publicly available exploit code? What is the visibility of the finding to the identified threats?

Threat likelihood can increase the overall criticality rating of a finding. Every day, the changing "threatscape" of the Internet can increase or decrease an organization's external risk exposure. The types of Internet threats that you identify for your customer could include:

- Organized crime
- Governments
- Terrorists
- Competitors
- Insiders
- Professional hackers
- Script kiddies
- Worms, viruses, and malware

Recommendations

Providing the customer with multiple recommendations to deal with a negative finding allows them to make an informed decision on the level of protection that is acceptable to the organization. Each problem will almost always have multiple solutions. Many organizations look to the IEM to gain better insight into their security posture. On the other hand, the results of the IEM will trigger the start of establishing a comprehensive security program.

One of the greatest challenges you will face as an evaluator is translating all the findings into practical solutions to reduce the organization's security exposures. Depending on the evaluation testing perspectives and your understanding of the customer's environment, you might not consider security mechanisms in the context of the entire environment. Effective security solutions should be built on layered security strategies and include both preventative and detection security measures. In time, preventative measures will fail, and organizations need the ability detect malicious activity for prompt response.

The recommendations must be cost-effective for the customer so that they are not spending thousands of dollars to protect resources that do not support the organization's mission. The likelihood of the evaluation team knowing the customer's budgetary capabilities and limits is slim to none. Your recommendations should include a best-of-breed solution, a midlevel solution, and a low-level solution. This flexibility provides options for the customer that will empower them to choose a customized solution that matches all their monetary, operational, technical, and human resources. Vulnerability remediation should not be based solely on the ease or low cost of implementing the recommended solution. Furthermore, it should not be assumed that the most complex vulnerabilities should be addressed immediately or with long-term solutions. The next chapter addresses the way the IEM approach in defining a prioritized road map will guide the customer in focusing their remediation efforts.

Keep in mind the entire life-cycle costs for all solutions that you recommend. We have seen companies that focused only on the initial purchase costs of a security solution and did not properly plan for ongoing maintenance and training expenses. The cost of fixing a finding can have a significant influence on how it is rectified.

Customer expectations, scope of findings, and constraints may have an impact on scheduling a selected recommendation in a customer environment. For example, you might have discovered a finding that involves implementing a vendor patch for the mitigation of a security hole across 50 servers. What OS is involved? Does the customer have an automated method to deploy the patch? How much time is needed to test the patch before deployment? How often are change control requests reviewed and scheduled in the customer environment? Will personnel be available to perform the recommendation? Are there physical or logical limitations? Does the customer have an automated way of validating the patch application?

Tying in Regulations, Legislation, Organizational Policies, and Industry Best Practices

Due to the flexibility and comprehensiveness of the IEM, you may be performing an evaluation to fulfill regulatory or legislative requirements. As an evaluator, you must be conscious of any regulations and/or legislative responsibilities that are applicable to your customer. This could be a challenge for the evaluation team when the customer organization crosses regional and national boundaries. You will usually find the details of these requirements in the TEP document. Be aware, though, that some customers are not aware of their compliance responsibilities or are not fully aware of the compliance requirements.

Summary

The IEM process is a culmination of many activities resulting in the identification of security findings and recommendations that reflect the overall business mission, desired security posture, and the risk to the company. The chapter discussed strategic approaches for the organization and analysis of the raw data that was collected during the onsite evaluation process. We discussed how to determine risk through fully understanding the impact of a finding by not only looking at the security vulnerability but providing real business value to the IEM process, combining the threat likelihood, the value of the asset, and the criticality of the finding. You learned how to conduct additional research to formulate remedial recommendations that provide the customer with practical immediate and long-term recommendations to eliminate identified risks and meet business goals. In the next few chapters, we discuss how to use this information to provide a prioritized road map of the evaluation findings and create the final evaluation report.

## Chapter 24

Creating Measurements and Trending Results

Solutions in this chapter:

- **The Purpose and Goal of the Matrixes**
- **Information Types**
- **Common Vulnerabilities and Exposures**
- **NIST ICAT**
- **Developing System Vulnerability Criticality Matrixes**
- **Developing Overall Vulnerability Criticality Matrixes**
- **Using the OVCM and SVCM**

☑ **Summary**

Introduction

Now that you have the findings and you know why they are an issue for your customer, it is time to present them to the customer management. The biggest issue that we have seen in our years of doing evaluations is the standardization of reporting formats. In this chapter we cover the sources of findings information and how this information can be put into a single chart that the customer can use as a road map to improving their security posture.

We all know that the findings or results of your evaluation are important information to the customer; the problem we run into is how to present the information in an understandable manner. The findings are usually reported in three levels of understanding: executive, management, and technical. This chapter focuses on the executive and management portions, along with developing a simple graphic table that will provide prioritization of the findings at a glance for senior management. This table will allow senior management to readily track the work being accomplished and how that work directly impacts the security posture of the organization.

Keep in mind as you read this chapter, and again as you develop these matrixes for the first time, that they are meant to provide a detailed picture of findings and the organization's security posture for the executive and senior levels of management. With each successive evaluation, management can compare the findings to see how the security posture has been improved. This becomes a repeatable process that can be used over and over again. Another secondary benefit is the ability to see repeat findings that may have been reported as closed and now are reopened or simply have not been addressed.

The Purpose and Goal of the Matrixes

As mentioned in the previous chapter, you should have no expectation that all the findings will be closed when you and your team do follow-on evaluations. In the theoretical world, it is easy to see that all findings should be closed, but reality sets in when you realize that's not the case. Some findings are not worth the effort or cost to close. This topic could lead into a full-blown discussion of risk management, but at this point we will leave it in this simple state. You should have mitigated all findings from previous evaluations through risk management by doing one of three things:

- Close the exposure (elimination)
- Insure or budget for the exposure loss (mitigation)
- Take the risk (acceptance).

Notes from the Underground

Risk Management

Every organization has a job or mission. Because organizations use automated IT systems to process their information to support their missions, risk management is critical to protecting information assets from IT-related risk. The principal goal of a risk management process is to protect the organization and its ability to perform its mission, not just its IT assets. Although the IEM is not a risk management methodology, it is a tool that can be used to gather the information needed to perform risk management. You can obtain a good foundation for understanding risk management by reading and understanding NIST SP 800-30, "Risk Management Guide for Information Technology Systems," a publication that can be found at http://csrc.nist.gov/publications/nistpubs/800-30/sp800-30.pdf.

The matrixes do not provide any finding details or recommendations for the technicians and administrators, although these individuals can still use the matrixes as a road map. The primary targets for the matrixes are the organization's management and executives. The matrixes are a snapshot of the posture and prioritization of the findings based on the technical and management weighting. Before we go into the development of the matrixes, let's look at the information that you will need to put this all together.

Simply put, the three things you need are the information types impacted, industry standard ratings, and evaluation team expertise. As we begin this process, keep in mind that it is built on the work we did in the organizational assessment, which was a top-down approach. We will use some of that top-down approach and then go bottom-up to build the final product, the overall vulnerability criticality matrix.

Information Types

The impacted information types are pulled directly from the organizational information criticality matrix (OICM) or system information criticality matrix (SICM) that we developed during the pre-assessment phase of the organizational assessment (the IAM). If the assessment and the evaluation are accomplished concurrently (at the same time), you will still have the IAM as it is developed by your team. If you are trying to do the evaluation without having accomplished the organizational assessment, then stop right here, because you will not be able to create these final reporting matrixes. The IEM final products are directly dependent on input from the organizational pre-assessment. Failure to use or draw the information from the organizational assessment will mean that the evaluation is not IEM compliant.

If you attended the NSA Information Security (INFOSEC) Assessment Methodology (IAM) and NSA INFOSEC Evaluation Methodology (IEM) classes, you will remember the matrix shown in Table 24.1. It was the first criticality matrix we developed during the IAM. Table 24.1 shows how there are four critical information topics for the organization called COPS. Each information topic is a rollup of probably several subelements each. For the purposes of this book, we won't go into the development of this matrix; instead we'll consider it one of the input variables from the organizational assessment that is unique to each and every organization.

Table 24.1 The COPS OICM

COPS OICM	Confidentiality	Integrity	Availability
Criminal Records	M	H	M
Informants	H	M	M
Investigations	M	M	M
Warrants	L	H	H

What we want to consider here is that there is some prioritization by impact value, not by information topic. Each of the information topics is a rollup of multiple subtopics. The information topics reflect the "50,000-foot view" of what management considers the important information. All of these were determined to be of equal value when the OICM was developed. To prioritize the impact values, let's first assign a number to each of the rows (see Table 24.2). Assigning the number will help ensure that we can properly track the rows later on as they are broken down into the system criticality matrixes.

Table 24.2 The Numbered OICM for COPS

COPS OICM	Confidentiality	Integrity	Availability
Criminal Records (1)	M	H	M
Informants (2)	H	M	M
Investigations (3)	M	M	M
Warrants (4)	L	H	H

Once the numbers are assigned, we can pass the numbering down to the system criticality matrixes. Again we will use matrixes that were used in the IAM class for the examples. Table 24.3 shows that three of the critical information topics—criminal records, investigations, and warrants—are used (in other words, the process transmitted or stored) on the Federal Agents Comprehensive Tracking System (FACTS).

Table 24.3 The FACTS SICM

FACTS	Confidentiality	Integrity	Availability
Criminal Records (1)	M	H	M
Investigations (3)	M	M	M
Warrants (4)	L	H	H

In Table 24.4 you can see that two critical information topics, informants and warrants, are used on the Secret Network of Operational Programs (SNOOP) system. The main reason we number the information topics is to ensure that we transfer the rows correctly as we develop the system vulnerability matrixes and that we have the ability to map backward to the OICM. This will be important as you develop multiple vulnerability criticality matrixes.

Table 24.4 The SNOOP SICM

SNOOP	Confidentiality	Integrity	Availability
Informants (2)	H	M	M
Warrants (4)	L	H	H

With this part completed, we can now transfer the information from the information criticality matrixes to the vulnerability criticality matrixes. A vulnerability criticality matrix is a simple chart or table that shows the importance of the customer findings in a format that is easy to understand. The most significant finding is always at the top left of the matrix; the least important finding is always at the bottom right, as depicted in Table 24.5.

Table 24.5 An Example of an Early SVCM

		HIGH			Medium			Low	
		IC1	IC2	IC3	IC4	IC5	IC6	IC7	IC8
High	V1								
	V2								
	V3								
Medium	V4								
	V5								
	V6								
Low	V7								
	V8								

The top row of this chart shows information categories (IC) in order of severity, beginning with the highs and then the mediums and then the lows. The left column of the chart is the findings (V) in order of the highest to lowest. If you were to start with the FACTS SICM and transfer the information categories, it would look like Table 24.6.

Table 24.6 The Top Row of the FACTS Vulnerability Criticality Matrix

FACTS Vulnerability Criticality Matrix	Finding Number	Severity	High			Medium					Low
			Criminal Records Integrity	Warrants Integrity	Warrants Availability	Criminal Records Confidentiality	Criminal Records Availability	Investigations Confidentiality	Investigations Integrity	Investigations Availability	Warrants Confidentiality

As you can see, the method of transferring the critical information topics is to start with the top row of the SICM. Scan across each row, from left to right, and as you find a high-impact attribute, put that impact attribute in the row. There is no prioritization of these impact attributes at this point. They are placed in the order found. Continue this process for all the highs, and then start over doing the same thing for each of the medium-impact attributes and then the low-impact attributes. Once you have all the impact attributes accounted for, you can arrange the High values in any order you feel is appropriate based on your expertise. Do the same thing with your Medium values and then your Low values.

Once this process is complete, we'll need to look at the findings themselves. Since you already completed the order of precedence identification in the last chapter, we will only look at the impact rating and a possibly very good source for them.

Common Vulnerabilities and Exposures

To quote the Mitre Web page defining the Common Vulnerabilities and Exposures (CVE), it is "A list of standardized names for vulnerabilities and other information security exposures—CVE aims to standardize the names for all publicly known vulnerabilities and security exposures." Further defined, "the CVE is a dictionary, *not* a database. The goal of CVE is to make it easier to share data across separate vulnerability databases and security tools. While CVE may make it easier to search for information in other databases, CVE should not be considered as a vulnerability database on its own merit."

We strongly encourage you to utilize CVE-compliant tools. They are continuously updated to ensure that the findings identified during an evaluation are traceable through the use of different tools. The benefit of using CVE tools is that the customer will have a common identification that can be used for research and tracking. Also, your team and other security consultants will be able to track and correlate previous findings.

Currently, once a finding or vulnerability is submitted to Mitre for inclusion in the dictionary listing, it goes through a stringent process of review. Initially, each submitted finding is listed as a "candidate" (CAN). CVE candidates are those vulnerabilities or exposures under consideration for acceptance into CVE. Candidates are assigned special numbers to distinguish them from CVE entries. Each candidate has three primary items associated with it:

- Number (also referred to as a *name*)
- Description
- References

The number, also referred to as a *name*, is an encoding of the year that the candidate number was assigned and a unique number N for the Nth candidate assigned that year—for example, CAN-1999-0067.

Established practices are followed when a candidate is created. If the Editorial Board accepts the candidate, an official CVE entry is created that includes the description and references. The candidate number is converted into a CVE name by replacing the *CAN* with *CVE*. For example, when the Editorial Board accepted the candidate CAN-1999-0067, the candidate number was converted to CVE-1999-0067, and the resulting new entry was added to CVE.

Starting October 19, 2005, CAN entries will no longer be created or maintained. All the current CAN entries will be migrated to a CVE number. There should be no significant effect for end users of the CVE system. If you enter an old CAN number, the system will still retrieve the information and show you the new CVE number. The big difference will be the addition of a "status" line to the CVE information. That status line will be the only indication of whether or not a CVE is Candidate, Entry, or Deprecated.

The issue that we have seen is that the CVE process does not assist in identifying the impact value to an organization. Though that was never the intended function of the CVE, having an initial or recommended impact value would be nice. That is where the National Institute of Standards and Technology stepped in to help the community. You can find more information about the CVE at www.cve.mitre.org/.

NIST ICAT

The National Institute of Standards and Technology (NIST) developed ICAT. (The ICAT name does not officially stand for anything today; initially the ICAT project was intended as a database of Internet attacks used by malicious hackers, and ICAT was its acronym. As the project changed its focus to a searchable database of all system findings, what ICAT stood for became obsolete but the name ICAT was kept.) Today ICAT is a searchable index of information on computer vulnerabilities. It provides search capability at a fine granularity and links users to vulnerability and patch information.

One of the nice things about using the ICAT search capabilities is the simple process of inputting the CVE or CAN number and getting more information than is available in the CVE dictionary. ICAT allows you to search by vendor, product, version, keyword, or severity. The ICAT database, as shown in Figure 24.1, is a filterable search engine that allows you to quickly locate findings in the database and identify their initial or recommend severity level.

Figure 24.1 A NIST ICAT Screen

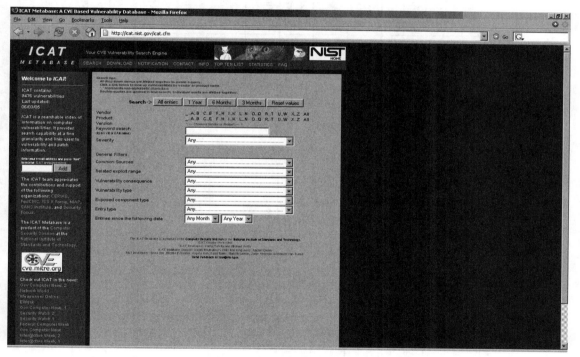

As with any input tool used in developing and implementing the reporting portion, the ICAT is not meant as the last or only word in the severity level. ICAT is a starting point for which you, with your expertise and the input of the customer, will determine the final severity level. You can find more information on the ICAT at http://icat.nist.gov/icat.cfm.

Developing System Vulnerability Criticality Matrixes

Starting with FACTS system that we use in the COPS example during the NSA courses, let's look at how the system vulnerability criticality matrix (SVCM) is developed. Now we have the impact attributes and the findings transferred to the chart, as depicted in Tables 24.7 and 24.8.

Table 24.7 The Initial FACTS SVCM Chart

FACTS Vulnerability Criticality Matrix	Finding Number	Severity	High			Medium					Low
			Criminal Records Integrity	Warrants Integrity	Warrants Availability	Criminal Records Confidentiality	Criminal Records Availability	Investigations Confidentiality	Investigations Integrity	Investigations Availability	Warrants Confidentiality
CVE 2001-0013	2	H									
Organizational	3	H									
CVE 2002-0571	4	H									
Organizational	5	M									
CVE 2002-1024	7	M									
Operational	8	L									
CVE 2002-1025	9	L									

Table 24.8 The Initial SNOOP SVCM

SNOOP Vulnerability Criticality Matrix	Finding Number	Severity	High			Medium					Low
			Criminal Records Integrity	Warrants Integrity	Warrants Availability	Criminal Records Confidentiality	Criminal Records Availability	Investigations Confidentiality	Investigations Integrity	Investigations Availability	Warrants Confidentiality
CVE 2002-0801	1	H									
Organizational	3	H									
CVE 2002-0571	4	H									
Organizational	5	M									
CVE 2002-1060	6	M									
Operational	8	L									
CVE 2004-0033	10	L									

Take a good look at these charts. You should notice some things right off the bat. No finding number 1, 6, or 10 is showing in the FACTS matrix, and numbers 2, 7, and 9 are missing from the SNOOP matrix. There are also three findings that do not have a CVE number. But don't panic. First, the missing findings are findings that do not apply to this system. Not every finding applies to all systems. As for the findings that don't have CVE numbers, as we said before, a lot of findings are organizational or common end-user configuration issues and so they will not have a CVE number.

You can actually see now why we number the findings and the critical information topics. When you went from the OICM, you had to map each information criticality topic to the appropriate system. Not all information topics will apply to all systems, nor will all the findings discovered during the evaluation apply to every system. Initially you might think that you should just list all of them and then put a "Not Applicable" (N/A) for the findings, but that would create a rather large and unwieldy chart for each system. To enable the customer to use these charts, we strongly recommend that you put only the findings that are applicable to each system on the appropriate chart.

As for the non–CVE findings, let's face it—some findings are so new that they might not have gone through the CVE process yet. Some findings you will come across will affect a system but will not be technical in nature. Consider the finding "weak passwords." You *could* search the ICAT for the keywords *weak passwords* and severity *high*, and you would get 12 matching findings. But none of those CVE findings would cover the fact that there is no enforcement of strong passwords. So, the result is that you have ended up identifying an organizational or operational finding that has no related CVE number, even though this is a common finding in many organizations. The CVE system does not address configuration issues or administrator error.

Don't skip, hide, or ignore nontechnical findings identified during the evaluation. There is a place for them in the chart, and they are just as valuable to the customer. Also, this is the place where you would incorporate the organizational findings that were identified during the IAM assessment portion.

The next portion becomes a little more difficult for junior security analysts. This is where you identify the applicability of a finding to the impact attributes. You say, "Huh?" Well, think about the differences in what various findings do when exploited. Some findings affect the confidentiality of information; others affect availability or integrity. Some findings can and will affect all the impact attributes.

Again, a good starting point if you have not done this before is to use the ICAT database. When you input a CVE in the keyword search, you can use the output as your starting reference. For example, if you were to use finding number 2 from FACTS, CVE 2001–0013, you would get the information shown in Table 24.9.

Table 24.9 ICAT CVE-2001-0013 Output

Vulnerability Name:	CVE-2001-0013
Published Before:	2/12/2001
Summary:	Format string vulnerability in nslookupComplain function in BIND 4 allows remote attackers to gain root privileges.
Severity:	High
Vulnerability type	Input Validation Error
Exploitable Range:	Remote
Loss type:	Security Protection (Gain super user access)
Reference 1:	Source: CERT
	Type: General and Patch
	Name: CA-2001-02
	www.cert.org/advisories/CA-2001-02.html#http://www.cert.org/advisories/CA-2001-02.html
Reference 2:	Source: PGP Security
	Type: General and Patch
	Name: Vulnerabilities in BIND 4 and 8
	www.pgp.com/research/covert/advisories/047.asp#http://www.pgp.com/research/covert/advisories/047.asp
Vulnerable software and versions:	ISC, BIND, 4.9.3
	ISC, BIND, 4.9.5-P1

From reading this table you should be able to determine that this finding would affect all the impact attributes due to the fact that as a superuser, the attacker can view, modify, change, and delete anything they want on that box. But this is not necessarily the same for all findings. If you take a look at FACTS finding number 4, CVE 2002-0571, you would see that the output from ICAT, listed in Table 24.10, is not the same.

Table 24.10 ICAT CVE-2002-0571 Output

Vulnerability Name:	CVE-2002-0571
Published before:	7/3/2002
Summary:	Oracle Oracle9i database server 9.0.1.x allows local users to access restricted data via a SQL query using ANSI outer join syntax.
Severity:	High
Vulnerability type:	Design Error
Exploitable range:	Remote
Loss type:	Security Protection (Gain other access) Confidentiality
Reference 1:	Source: Neohapsis Type: General Name: ansi outer join syntax in Oracle allows access to any data archives.neohapsis.com/archives/bugtraq/2002-04/0175.html
Reference 2:	Source: Ciac Type: General Name: Oracle9i User Privileges Vulnerability www.ciac.org/ciac/bulletins/m-071.shtml
Reference 3:	Source: ISS X-Force Type: General and Patch Name: oracle-ansi-sql-bypass-acl(8855) www.iss.net/security_center/static/8855.php
Reference 4:	Source: Security Focus Type: General and Patch Name: bid 4523 www.securityfocus.com/bid/4523
Vulnerable software and versions:	Oracle, Oracle9i, 9.0 Oracle, Oracle9i, 9.0.1

From this output in ICAT we see that the impact to the organization is still significant, High, but the affected impact attribute is confidentiality and not integrity or availability. There have been many discussions and heated debates about how a finding affects impact attributes, but we are not going to go into that area here. This book is meant to give you the basic information to do this work yourself. Your expertise and experience will determine whether you add more impact attributes to a particular finding. For the examples we are using, we decided to use the default output from ICAT for the identification of affected impact attributes.

Once you have done your analysis and identified the affected impact attributes for each finding, you need to show which ones are *not* affected. For this we will use the simple N/A for each block that is not an affected impact attribute, as shown in Tables 24.11 and 24.12.

Table 24.11 The FACTS SVCM with Some Attributes Marked "Not Applicable"

FACTS Vulnerability Criticality Matrix	Finding Number	Severity	High			Medium					Low
			Criminal Records Integrity	Warrants Integrity	Warrants Availability	Criminal Records Confidentiality	Criminal Records Availability	Investigations Confidentiality	Investigations Integrity	Investigations Availability	Warrants Confidentiality
CVE 2001-0013	2	H									
Organizational	3	H									
CVE 2002-0571	4	H	N/A	N/A	N/A		N/A		N/A	N/A	
Organizational	5	M									
CVE 2002-1024	7	M	N/A	N/A		N/A		N/A	N/A		N/A
Operational	8	L									
CVE 2002-1025	9	L	N/A	N/A	N/A		N/A		N/A	N/A	

Table 24.12 The SNOOP SVCM with Some Attributes Marked "Not Applicable"

SNOOP Vulnerability Criticality Matrix	Finding Number	Severity	High			Medium					Low
			Criminal Records Integrity	Warrants Integrity	Warrants Availability	Criminal Records Confidentiality	Criminal Records Availability	Investigations Confidentiality	Investigations Integrity	Investigations Availability	Warrants Confidentiality
CVE 2002-0801	1	H									
Organizational	3	H									
CVE 2002-0571	4	H	N/A	N/A	N/A		N/A		N/A	N/A	
Organizational	5	M									
CVE 2002-1060	6	M		N/A	N/A	N/A	N/A	N/A		N/A	N/A
Operational	8	L									
CVE 2004-0033	10	L	N/A	N/A	N/A		N/A		N/A	N/A	

NOTE

We want to emphasize that although the information displayed here is based on the output of ICAT, you should use your personal expertise to determine the appropriate applicability. What we really don't want to see is analysts simply using the defaults from any tools. This would result in as poor a quality as though you were merely cutting and pasting the findings from a default tool output—or worse, just printing it and handing it to your customer as the deliverable.

Now the hard part is done. Let's look at the easy part: calculating the value of the findings. The first part of this task can be negotiated with your customer. When determining the value for each block in the matrix, you want to ensure that you use some standardization. For this task we decided to use the information shown in Table 24.13, which is based on the most common impact attribute weights: High, Medium, and Low.

Table 24.13 Finding Weights

Technical Finding	High	Moderate	Low
Information Criticality Impact	3	2	1
Vulnerability Severity	6	4	2
Organizational Finding	**High**	**Moderate**	**Low**
Information Criticality Impact	4.5	3	1.5
Vulnerability Severity	4.5	3	1.5

The calculation is simple and based on the idea that a finding of High = 9, Medium = 6, Low = 3. These values are the same without regard to the source of the finding being organizational or CVE. The difference is use of the initial value weights. For technical findings, we have given two-thirds of the weight to the vulnerability severity value and one-third of the weight to the information criticality impact value. For the organizational findings we have split the weights 50-50.

After a few years of debating the numerical value of various formulas used to do this calculation, we decided that we needed something that is easy for customer comprehension and yet provides a mapping to the IAM. You'll recall that in the IAM the values that are most consistently used by customers are High, Medium, and Low. Most organizational findings will probably come from the organizational assessment that was, or is, concurrently being done. For the weighting we looked at various methods and formulas being used and decided that we needed to put the weight on the factor that the INFOSEC industry has recognized—vulnerability severity. Let's face it, information criticality impact values change with each customer and even with each time the process is repeated, even with the same customer.

Now that you understand that technical finding weights are based on an industry standard impact value and that information criticality weights are based on customer opinions, you should see why we give two-thirds of the weight to industry standards and one-third to customer opinions. This, if you think about it, is the same logic that was used with the organizational findings. Because there are no industry standards for organizational findings, we have to agree that the end result is that both are opinions.

The customer's opinion is important; do not fool yourself into thinking that your opinion is more important. Yes, you might have the expertise and background to say to yourself that more weight should be given to your opinion since that is what the customer is paying for. Consider that you will be trying to justify how your opinion is more important than what the customer has already documented in the OICM definitions. We do not recommend getting into that discussion or debate with your customer, and we strongly recommend that you give the customer's opinion equal value to your own opinion.

Does this mean that you are limited to using three impact levels? No. Does this mean that you cannot use a different weighting? No. Does this mean that you are limited to using the values of 9, 6, and 3? No. This is still *your* evaluation of the customer. You can use as many impact levels as fit the customer.

We have occasionally seen four levels, but that is a rarity. What is important for you to understand is that you should start simple using the model we have just shown you and then expand and tailor it to fit to your customer. At the same time, keep in mind that to be most effective for the customer, you need to ensure that the process is repeatable—not just the activities but in the reporting phase—to allow the customer to compare the reports from different evaluations.

Notes from the Underground

FIPS Pub 199

Yes, some industries do provide a starting block for organizations to work with. These are not intended to be the ultimate answer, just the minimum standards by which you can work. One of the better standards to work with if you have never worked with a customer to develop any yourself is from the NIST Federal Information Processing Standards (FIPS) Publication 199 (FIPS Pub 199), "Standards for Security Categorization of Federal Information and Information Systems." FIPS Pub 199 defines three levels of potential organizational impact, should your customer incur a loss of confidentiality, integrity, or availability:

- The potential impact is Low if the loss of CIA could be expected to have a limited adverse effect on organizational operations, organizational assets, or individuals. A limited adverse effect means that, for example, the loss of CIA might (1) cause a degradation in mission capability to an extent and duration that the organization is able to perform its primary functions but the effectiveness of the functions is noticeably reduced; (2) result in minor damage to organizational assets; (3) result in minor financial loss; or (4) result in minor harm to individuals.

- The potential impact is Moderate if the loss of CIA could be expected to have a serious adverse effect on organizational operations, organizational assets, or individuals. A serious adverse effect means that, for example, the loss of CIA might (1) cause a significant degradation in mission capability to an extent and duration that the organization is able to perform its primary functions but the effectiveness of the functions is significantly reduced; (2) result in significant damage to organizational assets; (3) result in significant financial loss; or (4) result in significant harm to individuals that does not involve loss of life or serious life-threatening injuries. Adverse effects on individuals may include, but are not limited to, loss of the privacy to which individuals are entitled under law.

Continued

> ■ The potential impact is High if the loss of CIA could be expected to have a severe or catastrophic adverse effect on organizational operations, organizational assets, or individuals. A severe or catastrophic adverse effect means that, for example, the loss of CIA might (1) cause a severe degradation in or loss of mission capability to an extent and duration that the organization is not able to perform one or more of its primary functions; (2) result in major damage to organizational assets; (3) result in major financial loss; or (4) result in severe or catastrophic harm to individuals involving loss of life or serious life-threatening injuries.
>
> So you are probably wondering why we quoted these definitions from NIST FIPS Pub 199 instead of just referencing them. There are two reasons: (1) to show you how even definitions like these tend to be so generalized that they provide a lot of latitude for customer interpretation, and (2) to ensure that all of you reading this book have a good foundation to start with when working with customer definitions.

Now that you have defined values to input into the charts that we have been developing, it is a simple process to add the values together where they intersect. Once you have done this for all blocks that are not N/A, your charts should look something like Tables 24.14 and 24.15.

Table 24.14 FACTS with Values Added

FACTS Vulnerability Criticality Matrix	Finding Number	Severity	High			Medium					Low
			Criminal Records Integrity	Warrants Integrity	Warrants Availability	Criminal Records Confidentiality	Criminal Records Availability	Investigations Confidentiality	Investigations Integrity	Investigations Availability	Warrants Confidentiality
CVE 2001-0013	2	H	9	9	9	8	8	8	8	8	7
Organizational	3	H	9	9	9	7.5	7.5	7.5	7.5	7.5	6
CVE 2002-0571	4	H	N/A	N/A	N/A	8	N/A	8	N/A	N/A	7
Organizational	5	M	7.5	7.5	7.5	6	6	6	6	6	4.5
CVE 2002-1024	7	M	N/A	N/A	7	N/A	6	N/A	N/A	6	N/A
Operational	8	L	6	6	6	4.5	4.5	4.5	4.5	4.5	3
CVE 2002-1025	9	L	N/A	N/A	N/A	4	N/A	4	N/A	N/A	3

Table 24.15 SNOOP with Values Added

SNOOP Vulnerability Criticality Matrix	Finding Number	Severity	High			Medium					Low
			Criminal Records Integrity	Warrants Integrity	Warrants Availability	Criminal Records Confidentiality	Criminal Records Availability	Investigations Confidentiality	Investigations Integrity	Investigations Availability	Warrants Confidentiality
CVE 2002-0801	1	H	9	9	9	8	8	8	8	8	7
Organizational	3	H	9	9	9	7.5	7.5	7.5	7.5	7.5	6
CVE 2002-0571	4	H	N/A	N/A	N/A	8	N/A	8	N/A	N/A	7
Organizational	5	M	7.5	7.5	7.5	6	6	6	6	6	4.5
CVE 2002-1060	6	M	7	7	N/A	N/A	N/A	N/A	6	N/A	N/A
Operational	8	L	6	6	6	4.5	4.5	4.5	4.5	4.5	3
CVE 2004-0033	10	L	N/A	N/A	N/A	4	N/A	4	N/A	N/A	3

There is one last step in developing these system vulnerability criticality matrixes: adding color to the charts. To do this we need to decide which vulnerability criticality weight values in the chart define what is high, medium, or low. Right now as you read this you are saying, "That's easy, right?" Well, yes. We use a scale from 3 to 9. Then we add color based on what value in the block. Table 24.16 shows the scale that we have used.

Table 24.16 Vulnerability Criticality Weight

HIGH = 8 – 9
MEDIUM = 5 – 7.5
LOW = 3 – 4.5

In the NSA IEM classes it is taught that the weights used are Low (covering 3.0 to 4.5), Medium covering 5.0 to 7.5), and High (covering 8.0 to 9.0). This, combined with the coloring of Red for high, Yellow for medium, and Green for low, does add to the goal of showing that the more critical a finding to an organization, the higher in the chart it should be.

We would show you what the colorized version of the charts would be at this point but as you might have noticed, all our diagrams are in black and white for printing purposes. So you will have to make your own charts and add color to see how this part works and what it looks like.

Notes from the Underground

Changing Impact Attributes

On occasions, the customer has wanted to change the impact attributes at this point. We strongly encourage you to dissuade the customer from changing them. Changing any impact attributes, even adding new ones, would mean starting over with the OICM. This would require stepping back and redoing several days' worth of work. Changing the values or adding a new value can cause the impact definitions to change, possibly resulting in greater cost for the customer and a feeling of wasted time for your team members.

Developing Overall Vulnerability Criticality Matrixes

Once you have all the system vulnerability criticality matrixes completed, it is time to move on to the overall vulnerability criticality matrix (OVCM). Keep in mind that every system that was included in the scope of the evaluation will require a separate SVCM. At this point, it's also a good practice to compare each of the SVCMs for consistency. By this we mean that you should ensure that the critical information topics that you have mapped directly from the OICM did not get mixed up when you mapped them to each individual system.

Now comes what is probably the easiest part of the process: merging the SVCMs into the OVCM. Again, we want to emphasize that there are multiple SVCMs for each system, but only one OVCM. The first step is to add a new column to the chart to allow for tracking of the findings to the applicable system, as shown in Table 24.17.

Table 24.17 COPS OVCM Header

COPS Overall Vulnerability Criticality Matrix	Finding Number	Systems Affected	Severity	High			Medium					Low
				Criminal Records Integrity	Warrants Integrity	Warrants Availability	Criminal Records Confidentiality	Criminal Records Availability	Investigations Confidentiality	Investigations Integrity	Investigations Availability	Warrants Confidentiality

As you look at this chart header, keep in mind that you will need to decide on a simple but effective method to identify which systems are which. In the example we've been using in this chapter, it is fairly easy to identify each system. We can identify the FACTS system by *F* and the

SNOOP system by *S*. As a result, all we need to add to the Systems Affected column is an *F* or *S* to allow the customer to see if a finding affects more than one system. Table 24.18 shows the entire OVCM for the COPS organization with the Systems Affected column filled in.

Table 24.18 The COPS OVCM with Systems Affected

COPS Overall Vulnerability Criticality Matrix	Finding Number	Systems Affected	Severity	High			Medium					Low
				Criminal Records Integrity	Warrants Integrity	Warrants Availability	Criminal Records Confidentiality	Criminal Records Availability	Investigations Confidentiality	Investigations Integrity	Investigations Availability	Warrants Confidentiality
CVE 2002-0801	1	S	H	9	9	9	8	8	8	8	8	7
CVE 2001-0013	2	F	H	9	9	9	8	8	8	8	8	7
Organizational	3	F,S	H	9	9	9	7.5	7.5	7.5	7.5	7.5	6
CVE 2002-0571	4	F,S	H	N/A	N/A	N/A	8	N/A	8	N/A	N/A	7
Organizational	5	F,S	M	7.5	7.5	7.5	6	6	6	6	6	4.5
CVE 2002-1060	6	S	M	7	7	N/A	N/A	N/A	N/A	6	N/A	N/A
CVE 2002-1024	7	F	M	N/A	N/A	7	N/A	6	N/A	N/A	6	N/A
Operational	8	F,S	L	6	6	6	4.5	4.5	4.5	4.5	4.5	3
CVE 2002-1025	9	F	L	N/A	N/A	N/A	4	N/A	4	N/A	N/A	3
CVE 2004-0033	10	S	L	N/A	N/A	N/A	4	N/A	4	N/A	N/A	3

One of the benefits of merging the charts is that the customer can quickly see how many systems a particular finding affects. It is very common that a single finding will affect multiple systems, and this greatly reduces the repetition in the chart. Consider from the chart in Table 24.18 that finding number 4, CVE-2002-0571, is applicable to both the FACTS system and the SNOOP system. This finding is a design error in the Oracle 9.0.1.x database server that is mitigated by installing a patch, but this should not be shown in the OVCM as two findings. Putting the finding as one and showing that it is applicable to both systems allows management to easily see that there is one finding that needs to be addressed.

Keep in mind that this chapter has used a fairly simple organization that has only two systems. The total OVCM had only 10 findings, four critical information topics, and a total of nine impact attributes. This makes for a fairly small chart. Imagine if you had a much larger organization. It is not uncommon for organizations to have as many as 10 or 15 critical information topics.

Add to that the fact that the customer might want to use more impact attributes beyond the CIA. If they added nonrepudiation and accountability, you would have 15 impact attributes. And we all know that there are usually more than 10 findings. Consider if there were 45 findings—that would make for a very large OVCM.

Using the OVCM and SVCM

So now you have created the SVCMs and the OVCM. What are you going to do with them? As with any output related to the evaluation, you should have a purpose and a user group that the charts are intended for. Each chart has a use and an intended target audience. None of the charts is intended for use by the system administrators.

The SVCMs are system specific. Each of these charts should be intended for the system mangers of that particular system. Each chart contains the specific findings for that particular system. Consider the political atmosphere of many organizations. The system managers do not want to have their peers knowing the findings related to their systems. The system managers don't need to know the findings for systems that they have no responsibility for or management of. Keeping the SVCM system specific also makes for a usable size chart for each manager to track the work that needs to be done.

The OVCM is intended for senior or executive management; it contains the rollup of all the findings. This chart is intended to give the senior or executive management the "big picture" of the findings that need to be addressed.

Summary

In this chapter, you learned how to present the evaluation findings in a standardized reporting format. This report format is not intended as a working tool for the system administrators but rather as a single chart that the customer can use as a road map to improving their security posture.

The intended audience for the SVCMs is the system managers. The intended audience for the OVCM is the senior or executive-level management. The development of the matrixes is a bottom–up approach versus the top–down approach that was used during the assessment. Beginning with the SICMs, you map the each of the impact attributes by order of severity. Each finding's severity is based on two factors: the common vulnerability and exposures (CVE) value and the impact attribute value. If a finding does not have a CVE value, the weighted value that is used is 50/50. An excellent source for the finding weights is the NIST ICAT if the finding is technical in nature and has been entered into the CVE process.

Not all findings will normally be found on all systems, and not all findings will affect every impact attribute. You will need to use your expertise to decide which impact attributes are affected. Once you have added the values used for each weighting, you will be able to add color to the charts for ease of identification.

When all of the SVCMs, are completed you will be able to create an OVCM. This chart is a rollup or merger of all the SVCMs into one chart.

## Chapter 25

Trending Metrics

Solutions in this chapter:

- **Metrics and Their Usefulness**
- **The INFOSEC Posture Profile**
- **The INFOSEC Posture Rating**
- **Value-Added Trending**

☑ **Summary**

Introduction

You now know how to build the executive and senior management charts for tracking the vulnerabilities that have been identified. This is good, but does it answer the customer's question, "How are we doing?" No, it doesn't. Although the charts provide a means for seeing what work needs to be done, they do not provide a description of the overall security posture of the organization. For that we need some kind of metrics that will readily identify the current security posture.

Metrics and Their Usefulness

Why do we want metrics? The answer to that question is really in two responses. First, executive management wants to know whether their expenditures on security have met their expectations for security protection. Second, executive and senior management want to know at a glance just what their security status is. You have probably heard the question, "So what is the bottom line; how are we doing?" or "So how do we compare to our competitors?" To answer these questions, you need to understand why managers ask them.

Return on Investment

Security has been and will continue to be an overhead expense for all organizations, much like payroll and other administrative tasks that are required to keep an organization running. The question that seems to pop up every few months in the security industry is, What is the value of all the security work that takes place in an organization? Organizations want to see what the return on investment (ROI) for the security budget is now and what it's expected to be in the future. Making such an estimate is a very difficult task. After all, if the security team is doing its job, the organization will likely not see a measurable impact from security problems.

When we're talking about IT security, ROI has historically focused on returning actual organizational payback where implementing tools, devices, or training should reduce operating costs. This is almost never the case. Since security acts as a version of insurance for your data or information, any return provided by required security should focus on this aspect.

Over the years there have been many attempts to define the ROI for security. There is by no means only one way to determine ROI for security. Currently, several projects are under way that are still working to determine this magic formula. More information on this topic can be found by doing a simple search on the Internet for *security ROI*.

For our purposes, we use a simplified formula that is based on the annual loss expectancy. Simply put, how much do you expect to lose from a single security incident each year? The annual loss expectancy of a single security breach that costs $1 million and has a 35 percent probability of occurring would be reflected as:

Incident Cost × Probability = Annual Loss Expectancy

$1,000,000 × 0.35 = $350,000

This is good, but it does not take into account the factor of mitigation, so we add this factor by multiplying the probability by the mitigation factor. Consider the impact that computer worms have had over the past few years or even the various Sober virus variants. If you have installed up-to-date antivirus software, you could expect to have mitigated about 50 percent of the probability. Or if you implemented strong user awareness training, you could mitigate about 80 percent of the probability of occurrence. (Can anybody say customer choices?) This makes the formula slightly different, as follows:

Incident Cost × (Probability × Mitigation) = Annual Loss Expectancy

$1,000,000 × (0.35 × 0.5) = $1,000,000 × 0.175 = $175,000 (Antivirus
Software Mitigation)

$1,000,000 × (0.35 × 0.2) = $1,000,000 × 0.07 = $70,000 (User Awareness
Training Mitigation)

If the cost of implementation is known — antivirus $75,000, user awareness program $10,000 — you can show a simple ROI by demonstrating that the cost of mitigation is less than the cost of loss. Now, this does not take many factors into account and is not meant as an introduction or tutorial on determining ROI.

How Do We Compare?

If you can't prove ROI on security, how do you know you are making any progress? This can be shown to the customer as a simple numeric value. We'll show you how to calculate two numeric values. The first one is the INFOSEC Posture Profile (IPP); the second is the INFOSEC Posture Rating (IPR). They are designed to be flexible enough that you can utilize either one for your customers.

Each numeric value will show the customer their security posture. This is especially useful when you have a parent/child relationship in an organization. Consider the situation of a large university, where all the colleges within the university might not be able to conduct the evaluation at the same time. The standards to which they are held do not change from college to college. Conducting the evaluation and creating the IPP or IPR for each college allows the university to see how the colleges' security postures compare.

The concept used here is to provide the customer the ability to do trend analysis of vulnerabilities and mitigations over a period of time, to show the progress toward improving their security posture. Each of these numeric values, IPP and IPR, is designed to bring together both the IAM and IEM findings, to give an overall snapshot of an organization's security posture. Whether you use the IPP or the IPR, you should understand that it is generated for a specific customer at a specific time and thus cannot be legitimately compared among organizations. That said, continuous use of the IEM and this metric at the same organization can provide the ability to trend the organization's security posture and show improvements or declines in security posture.

The INFOSEC Posture Profile

The INFOSEC Posture Profile (IPP) was developed by the NSA and is focused on the DoD. The IPP is based on the DoD concept of Computer Network Defense (CND). CND is the application of security and operations to support the concept of defense in depth (DiD), first developed by the DoD and published in a white paper you can download from http://nsa1.www.conxion.com/support/guides/sd-1.pdf.

Defense in Depth

To understand how to use the IPP, you need to understand how CND is applied to meet the goals of the DiD strategy. This chapter is not meant as a tutorial in DiD or CND, but it is important we review the high points. DiD is a layered security strategy designed to provide protection for the information data.

The concept is that you and your customer can use a practical strategy for achieving information assurance in your computing environments. The concepts of DiD are based on the utilization of "best practices" to fit the computing environment. Good DiD requires a strategy that relies on the intelligent application of techniques and technologies that exist today. These techniques and technologies will change as advances are made. The bottom line here is that no single solution will work for every organization, so you must provide the best mixture of techniques and technologies that fits your customer's environment based on their underlying requirements for security.

CND and DiD both recommend a balance among your customer's protection capability, cost, performance, and operational considerations. Implementation of the DiD strategy is based on focusing on the four areas of CND: *Defend* the network and infrastructure, *Protect* the local and wide area communications networks, *Provide* protection for data transmitted over these networks, and *Defend* the enclave boundaries. As you look at each of these areas you need to consider the technologies and techniques that will best fit your customer's environment, and consider the following factors and how they apply to the decisions that you make.

Adversaries or Threats

Every organization has adversaries or threats. Therefore, each organization needs to identify, in advance, who or what is the threat, what is their reason for attacking (motivation), and the possible ways that they can attack. Adversaries can be anything from a script kiddie who wants to make a name for him- or herself in the underground up to and including nation-states that want to weaken another country or economy. In between these significantly different threats are things like corporate espionage and criminals who attack to make a profit at your customer's expense. These are malicious adversaries that receive the most publicity in the news, but don't forget the nonmalicious threats such as fire, water, power failures, and the most common threat, user error.

Once you have identified the appropriate threats, you can look at the current protection schema by considering confidentiality, integrity, and availability. Think of these as protection services that you are providing for your organization or customer. These services are always included in the CND concepts of Protect, Detect, Respond, and Sustain. Organizations should expect attacks; they would not be in business if they did not have something important that needs protection. Organizations should employ tools and procedures that allow them to react to and recover from attacks.

Protect

Protect is based on the hardening or securing of the system and components. In the commonly used CND, this is proper system configuration management and remediation management. If you don't know what you have and how it is "supposed" to be used, how can you protect the system? If you don't have a defined approach to fixing problems that pop up, how will you fix those problems? Unfortunately, in many organizations this is an ad hoc process and is the reason that *Protect* is difficult to implement and maintain.

Detect

Detect is based on the ability to identify anomalous activity. Simply put, this is the implementation of an audit. If you don't monitor the activities that are occurring on the network, how will you know if something unusual is happening? This means that you will have to identify normal activity to be able to identify abnormal activity.

Respond

Respond is the ability to report and react to anomalous activity. This definitely builds on *Detect*. Once you have identified an abnormal activity, you must determine whether it is malicious or nonmalicious. Then what do you do? How will the activity be reported, and to whom? Are there defined processes for reacting to the abnormal activity?

Sustain

Sustain is the ability to maintain the proper level of security through a mature process. This can be the normal day-to-day activity known as network management. Network management can be a nightmare for some organizations because they have not implemented *Protect, Detect,* or *Respond*. This creates an organization that is continuously in "fire-fighting mode," dealing with issues over and over again based on what is going wrong today.

As we are all aware, to implement these principles and create a sound DiD strategy, you must have three elements: people, technology, and operations. These must be balanced to provide the best coverage for the price. Relying too much on one element will result in exposure to attacks.

People

People represent the beginning of a complete information security package, starting with senior management. The senior management must have a commitment to protecting the information based on a clear understanding of the threats. Senior management provides the policy and procedures needed for effective information security. Senior management must provide the resources needed to implement the policies and procedures, with clear understanding of roles and responsibilities and personal accountability. Training must be included in this resource assignment for all personnel, especially critical personnel. Having the senior management commitment includes the establishment of both physical and personnel security, allowing the organization to monitor and control access to facilities, information, and critical elements of the IT environment.

Technology

Technology is available in a variety of components and services. Technology can be used to detect attacks, malicious activity, or even nonmalicious activity. But what technology should be used? Every organization should employ its defined policies and processes for technology acquisition. These are normally based on the information security architecture and standards found in the security policy. The organization should have defined criteria for selecting and procuring products. These products should be implemented with defined and standardized configuration guidance. Prior to implementation there should be a process to assess the risk that could be introduced to the system by implementing the technology. When you implement technology in the DiD strategy, you should look at the following information security principles: defense in multiple places, layered defenses, security robustness, robust key management, and event correlation.

Defense in Multiple Places

Adversaries can and will attack from multiple angles. Your organization or customer must employ protection mechanisms at different locations to be resistant to all classes of attack. Defensive locations, called *focus areas*, include networks and infrastructure, enclave boundaries, and computing environment:

- Defending the network and infrastructure provides protection of the LAN and WAN by ensuring confidentiality and integrity of the data transmitted.

- Defending the enclave boundaries provides resistance to active network attacks.

- Defending the computing environment provides access controls on hosts and servers to resist insider or distributed attacks.

Layered Defenses

No single product or service is a cure-all for the inherent weaknesses of a network. Given enough time and resources, an adversary will find an exploitable vulnerability. The best method to mitigate this threat is through the use of multiple countermeasures that present different obstacles to the adversary. These countermeasures should include both protection and detection measures. This strategy will increase the adversary's risk of detection and reduce his or her chance of success. A common example in large networks is perimeter firewalls in conjunction with intrusion detection and implementation of more granular firewalls and controls on the internal network.

Specify the Security Robustness

Specifying the security robustness involves understanding the value of what you are protecting and placing appropriate technical controls in the appropriate place. One example is the deployment of strong perimeter defenses and implementation of security templates for workstations and servers. This makes sense because it is usually operationally effective and suitable to deploy stronger mechanisms at the network boundary than at the user desktop.

Robust Key Management

Infrastructures are lucrative targets. Deploying robust key management and public key infrastructures, such as PKI or PGP, that support all the information assurance technology that is deployed will ensure that your systems are resistant to attack.

Event Correlation

Deployed infrastructures should be able to detect intrusions, analyze them, and correlate the results to provide enough information to react accordingly. This will allow the operations staff to answer the following questions: Am I under attack? Who is the source? What is the target? Who else is under attack? What are my options?

Operations

Operations focus on all the activities required in maintaining and sustaining the organization or customer's security posture on a daily basis. Operations will always include:

- Maintaining the security policy and ensuring that all personnel are aware of and following the policy.

- Certifying and accrediting systems to ensure that good risk management decisions can be made.

- Managing the security posture by keeping patches and virus definitions and access control lists updated.

- Providing key management services.

- Performing security readiness reviews, commonly called *assessments,* to ensure that the controls are functioning correctly.

- Monitoring and reacting to threats or attacks as they occur.

- Recovery and resumption of operations from attacks or nonmalicious events such as fire or flood.

DiD is simply a means of using multiple controls to implement a more complete security posture based on perceived threats or adversaries. We know that we cannot achieve a 100 percent secure stance, because that would leave us with 0 percent usability. For example, we could deny all inbound or outbound connections to the Internet, but in today's computing environment the network usability would suffer greatly. We want to avoid weak links through the balance of people, technology, and operations. Each of these elements is used to maintain the organization or customer's ability to *Protect, Detect, Respond,* and *Sustain* their information assurance.

Developing the INFOSEC Posture Profile

As we stated earlier in this chapter, the greatest value of using these metrics is the ability to utilize all the organizational and technology findings to create a value-added numeric value. To bring these findings together, you first need to understand the mappings of the findings to the areas of *Protect, Detect, Respond,* and *Sustain.* First let's look at the categories of information from the IAM:

- Management
    1. INFOSEC Documentation
    2. INFOSEC Roles and Responsibilities
    3. Contingency Planning
- Technical
    4. Identification and Authentication
    5. Account Management

6. Session Controls

7. Auditing

8. Malicious Code Protection

9. Maintenance

10. System Assurance

11. Networking/Connectivity

12. Communications Security

- Operational

13. Media Controls

14. Labeling

15. Physical Environment

16. Personnel Security

17. Education Training and Awareness

Each of these baseline INFOSEC categories is mapped to one of the four pillars of DiD: *Protect, Detect, Respond,* and *Sustain,* as shown in Table 25.1.

Table 25.1 IAM Mapping for IPP

Protect	Detect
• Identification and Authentication	• Auditing
• Session Controls	**Respond**
• System Assurance	• Contingency Planning
• Networking / Connectivity	**Sustain**
• Malicious Code Protection	• INFOSEC Documentation
• Communications Security	• INFOSEC Roles and Responsibilities
• Media Controls	• Configuration Management
• Labeling	• Account Management
• Physical Environment	• Maintenance
• Personnel Security	• Education Training and Awareness

Then we need to look at the 10 baseline activities from the IEM and the way they map to the four pillars of CND (see Table 25.2).

Table 25.2 The IEM Baseline Activities

Port Scanning	Host Evaluation
SNMP Scanning	Network Device Analysis
Enumeration & Banner Grabbing	Password Compliance Testing
Wireless Enumeration	Application Specific Scanning
Vulnerability Scanning	Network Sniffing

Now as you look at these you should be thinking that it is not that easy to map the activities. The IEM was much simpler because it uses topics, not activities. So we need to determine exactly what information is being derived from the IEM activities. The easy answer is findings. But that is not very useful information if we do not know what that information applies to. So, what is the purpose and defined information output of each of the activities? To recap the information previously covered in other chapters, the goal of each activity is as follows:

- Port scanning
  - Identify enabled network services on systems
  - Look for unauthorized or unnecessary services
  - Look for back doors
- SNMP scanners
  - Enumerate systems on the network
  - Identify community strings
- Wireless enumeration tools
  - Identify access points and potential exposures
- Enumeration and banner grabbing
  - Verification of operating system
- Vulnerability Scanners
  - Identify well-known vulnerabilities on systems
- Network device analysis
  - Analyze security architecture for well-known vulnerabilities and insecure configurations
- Host evaluation
  - Analyze configuration, discretionary access control, and policies against accepted standards (NSA, DISA, NIST, etc.)
- Password-compliance testing
  - Evaluate adherence to password policy and determine whether password filters are being effectively implemented

- Application-specific scanning
  - Evaluate security configuration of critical applications
- Network sniffing
  - Identifies sensitive information traversing the network (login, passwords, server configurations via Telnet, etc.)

Each of these activities provides valuable output, and if we look at the output we can see that basic information types can be mapped as shown in Table 25.3.

Table 25.3 IEM Mapping for IPP

```
                                  Detect
                                   • Auditing Implementation
      Protect                          • IDS
       • Remediation Managment          • Firewalls
           • Patches                    • Host Based
           • Hotfixes                Respond
           • Virus Signature Updates  • Reactive Measures
       • System Configuration            • Incident Response
           • Permissions                 • Incident Alerting
           • ACL                      Sustain
           • Privileges               • Network Management
           • Passwords                    • Patch Management Processes
           • System Services              • Group Policy Administration
                                          • Role-based Policies
                                          • Mandatory Access Control
```

Now that we know the mapping, the next step is to determine the applicability of each finding to each of the CND areas: *Protect, Detect, Respond*, and *Sustain*. Each finding affects one area only. Though you could argue that some findings could directly affect more than one topic, such as INFOSEC documentation, each finding maps to only one pillar of the CND. Evaluator expertise is needed here to determine which area or aspect of the CND each finding applies to (see Table 25.4).

Table 25.4 The COPS OVCM

COPS Overall Vulnerability Criticality Matrix	Finding Number	Systems Affected	Computer Network Defense	Severity	High			Medium					Low
					Criminal Records Integrity	Warrants Integrity	Warrants Availability	Criminal Records Confidentiality	Criminal Records Availability	Investigations Confidentiality	Investigations Integrity	Investigations Availability	Warrants Confidentiality
CVE 2002-0801	1	S	D	H	9	9	9	8	8	8	8	8	7
CVE 2001-0013	2	F	P	H	9	9	9	8	8	8	8	8	7
Organizational	3	F,S	S	H	9	9	9	7.5	7.5	7.5	7.5	7.5	6
CVE 2002-0571	4	F,S	R	H	N/A	N/A	N/A	8	N/A	8	N/A	N/A	7
Organizational	5	F,S	S	M	7.5	7.5	7.5	6	6	6	6	6	4.5
CVE 2002-1060	6	S	P	M	7	7	N/A	N/A	N/A	N/A	6	N/A	N/A
CVE 2002-1024	7	F	P	M	N/A	N/A	7	N/A	6	N/A	N/A	6	N/A
Operational	8	F,S	S	L	6	6	6	4.5	4.5	4.5	4.5	4.5	3
CVE 2002-1025	9	F	P	L	N/A	N/A	N/A	4	N/A	4	N/A	N/A	3
CVE 2004-0033	10	S	R	L	N/A	N/A	N/A	4	N/A	4	N/A	N/A	3

Going back to the COPS overall vulnerability criticality matrix (OVCM), we now can see that we need to add another column to the chart, to apply the mapping of the CND pillars. We have labeled the column *Computer Network Defense* and used *P* for *Protect*, *D* for *Detect*, *R* for *Respond*, and *S* for *Sustain*. Now we need to calculate the IPP for this customer. First we will determine the number of High, Medium, and Low findings for each of the CND aspects. This is done by adding up each severity independently for each aspect (see Table 25.5).

Table 25.5 Computer Network Defense Summary by Severity

Protect	Respond
High = 1	High = 1
Medium = 2	Medium = 0
Low = 1	Low = 1
Detect	Sustain
High = 1	High = 1
Medium = 0	Medium = 1
Low = 0	Low = 1

Once you have added the number of findings by severity and CND aspect, you can calculate the value of each area. To do this we use the model that we have used throughout this book: High is worth 3, Medium is worth 2, and Low is worth 1. Now let's multiply the total findings for each severity by the assigned value. When you have all the values for each severity, sum each CND aspect for the rating value (see Table 25.6).

Table 25.6 INFOSEC Posture Profile Calculation

```
Protect                          Respond
High:     1 x 3 = 3              High:     1 x 3 = 3
Medium:   2 x 2 = 4              Medium:   0 x 2 = 0
Low       1 x 1 = 1              Low       1 x 1 = 1
          Total = 8                        Total = 4

Detect                           Sustain
High:     1 x 3 = 3              High:     1 x 3 = 3
Medium:   0 x 2 = 0              Medium:   1 x 2 = 2
Low       0 x 1 = 0              Low       1 x 1 = 1
          Total = 3                        Total = 6
```

With these totals or rating values, we can insert the values into the COPS OVCM and easily show the customer their current IPP (see Table 25.7). Once again we want to point out that we have used a very simple organization with only a few findings spanning two systems. The results for a large organization with multiple systems and many findings will significantly increase the values for each aspect.

Table 25.7 The COPS OVCM with IPP

COPS Overall Vulnerability Criticality Matrix / INFOSEC Posture Protect = 8 Detect = 3 Respond = 4 Sustain = 6	Finding Number	Systems Affected	Computer Network Defense	Severity	High			Medium					Low
					Criminal Records Integrity	Warrants Integrity	Warrants Availability	Criminal Records Confidentiality	Criminal Records Availability	Investigations Confidentiality	Investigations Integrity	Investigations Availability	Warrants Confidentiality
CVE 2002-0801	1	S	D	H	9	9	9	8	8	8	8	8	7
CVE 2001-0013	2	F	P	H	9	9	9	8	8	8	8	8	7
Organizational	3	F,S	S	H	9	9	9	7.5	7.5	7.5	7.5	7.5	6
CVE 2002-0571	4	F,S	R	H	N/A	N/A	N/A	8	N/A	8	N/A	N/A	7
Organizational	5	F,S	S	M	7.5	7.5	7.5	6	6	6	6	6	4.5
CVE 2002-1060	6	S	P	M	7	7	N/A	N/A	N/A	N/A	6	N/A	N/A
CVE 2002-1024	7	F	P	M	N/A	N/A	7	N/A	6	N/A	N/A	6	N/A
Operational	8	F,S	S	L	6	6	6	4.5	4.5	4.5	4.5	4.5	3
CVE 2002-1025	9	F	P	L	N/A	N/A	N/A	4	N/A	4	N/A	N/A	3
CVE 2004-0033	10	S	R	L	N/A	N/A	N/A	4	N/A	4	N/A	N/A	3

So now you have the rating profile for COPS. Is this a good profile or a bad profile? Only time will tell. This value is applicable to this organization at this time and provides the baseline of where the organization stands as far as its current security posture. The profile tells the organization which of the four aspects of the CND is the weakest by the highest number, but it does not provide any comparison to any other organization. The main reason that there is no way to compare the DoD organizations that utilize the IPP is that there is insufficient empirical data to define what a good rating profile should be. At this time we recommend that you utilize the profile and develop a trend analysis for the security posture. With each successive evaluation, the customer can compare the profiles obtained and determine whether they are meeting their security requirements.

The INFOSEC Posture Rating

The INFOSEC Posture Rating (IPR) was developed for organizations that do not utilize or might not even understand the DiD and CND concepts. This is not to say that these organizations are less informed. Each has a different objective and usually much different requirements to meet, as discussed in previous chapters.

The IPR works well for commercial and federal organizations that do not have a DoD requirement to meet. This numeric rating is intended to provide a number value of the current security posture of a specific organization. The IPR is customized for each customer for which you utilize it and should not be used to compare organizations. The value to the customer is that the continuous use of the metric at the same organization will provide the customer the ability to do trend analysis of the organizational security posture.

The concept behind using the IRP is that it is based on the average of all findings, with weighting applied based on the severity of the findings. Using the OVCM that we developed in the last chapter, we can see how the weighting has already been applied (see Table 25.8).

Table 25.8 The COPS OVCM

COPS Overall Vulnerability Criticality Matrix	Finding Number	Systems Affected	Computer Network Defense	Severity	High			Medium					Low
					Criminal Records Integrity	Warrants Integrity	Warrants Availability	Criminal Records Confidentiality	Criminal Records Availability	Investigations Confidentiality	Investigations Integrity	Investigations Availability	Warrants Confidentiality
CVE 2002-0801	1	S	D	H	9	9	9	8	8	8	8	8	7
CVE 2001-0013	2	F	P	H	9	9	9	8	8	8	8	8	7
Organizational	3	F,S	S	H	9	9	9	7.5	7.5	7.5	7.5	7.5	6
CVE 2002-0571	4	F,S	R	H	N/A	N/A	N/A	8	N/A	8	N/A	N/A	7
Organizational	5	F,S	S	M	7.5	7.5	7.5	6	6	6	6	6	4.5
CVE 2002-1060	6	S	P	M	7	7	N/A	N/A	N/A	N/A	6	N/A	N/A
CVE 2002-1024	7	F	P	M	N/A	N/A	7	N/A	6	N/A	N/A	6	N/A
Operational	8	F,S	S	L	6	6	6	4.5	4.5	4.5	4.5	4.5	3
CVE 2002-1025	9	F	P	L	N/A	N/A	N/A	4	N/A	4	N/A	N/A	3
CVE 2004-0033	10	S	R	L	N/A	N/A	N/A	4	N/A	4	N/A	N/A	3

Now to determine the IPR, we add all the severity values and divide that total by the number of values that were added together:

(Sum All Values Not "N/A") / (Number of Values Added Together) = INFOSEC Posture Rating

In this case, this would be:

403 / 60 = 6.72

The IPR is susceptible to skewing by excessive low findings, but we believe that it is probably 95 percent accurate. You can validate this accuracy by repeating the process with the same customer and trending the change in their security posture. There is a bonus in using this simple method: It is simple enough for any customer to quickly understand the mathematics behind the number without a lot of discussion on how it was developed.

Now that you have a numeric value, what does that mean? Recall from earlier chapters that we have already set a scale for the customer to identify the severity of the numeric value calculated for each finding (see Table 25.9). We can use that value already defined for the customer and now tell them their security posture.

Table 25.9 The IPR Scale

High = 8.0 to 9.0
Medium = 5.0 to 7.5
Low = 3.0 to 4.5

Using this scale, we can say that the customer has a Medium overall security posture, because their IRP is 6.72. This could even be used in a briefing graphic to allow for better visualization of a customer's status. One point of consideration in making the graphic is the addition of color. Due to the black-and-white printing of this book, the graphic shown in Figure 25.1 is not as dramatic as it could be.

Figure 25.1 An IPR Graphic

Value-Added Trending

What does trending do for each level of an organization? That is a good question that is probably drawing a few groans from some of the readers of this book. But in fact, value-added trending (VAT) of the security posture has benefits for every level of the organization.

Executive management is always looking for some standard or measurement of how their security posture is meeting requirements. Many would call this *due diligence,* and they would not be wrong.

Executive-level management needs the "warm and fuzzy" feeling that they have done all that is required and possibly be able to show that they have exceeded the requirements. VAT also allows the executive level to see the effectiveness of the security program and budget.

Middle to senior management needs a tracking mechanism that allows them to see what progress is being made. This progress is usable for budget justifications and prioritization of work assignments. Without any tracking and a viable picture of the security posture, middle management is unable to focus on long-term goals and objectives. Instead, middle management will stay in the "fire-fighting mode" of operation.

Administrators and technicians can use trending to see what progress has been made. Though when rolled up, the numbers usually don't mean much to this level, it is easy to give them a numeric value based on their systems only. This allows them to see what significant improvements can be made easily and which mitigations will take time and probably out-year budgeting to accomplish.

Summary

In this chapter you have seem the "why and how" of building an effective metric for your customer that allows for trending of the security posture. This metric allows the senior or executive level to answer the questions "How are we doing?" and "Was it worth the cost?" Although there are many projects under way that are trying to determine the return on investment (ROI) for security, there is no industry standard for answering that question.

What *can* be answered is the "How are we doing?" question. To answer this question, you need a simple but effective method to calculate a numeric value. We showed you how to build two different versions of a security metric: the INFOSEC posture profile (IPP) and the INFOSEC posture rating (IPR). Each is designed to be flexible enough to be used in any industry. The factor that will normally drive the choice of metric is the customer. From experience we have seen that the IPP is a DoD preference or requirement, whereas the IPR is for all other customers. This quite possibly won't be the case all the time, but we believe that there is more usability and flexibility in the IPR.

The IPP is based on the implementation of CND to meet the DiD strategy. DiD requires that you use a layered strategy to provide protection for data. To implement the CND, you need to intelligently implement the techniques and technologies that are current and that fit your customer organization. The implementation of the CND is based on four aspects: *Protect, Detect, Respond*, and *Sustain*. Each of these aspects provides for a layered defense aimed at four areas: defend the network and infrastructure, protect the local and wide area communications networks, provide protection for the data transmitted over these networks, and defend the enclave boundaries. Development of the IPP requires you to map the 18 IAM information topics and the 10 IEM activities to the four aspects of the CND. Though there is a viable argument that some topics could directly affect more than one topic, such as INFOSEC documentation, each finding maps to only one pillar of the CND. Once all the findings are mapped, you will be able to do some simple math and give your customer a snapshot in time of their security posture. This is not something that could be used to compare different organizations, but it is very effective when doing the trend analysis of the security posture of one organization.

The IPR was developed for organizations that do not utilize or might not even understand the DiD and CND concepts. The IPR works well for commercial and federal organizations that do not have a DoD requirement. This numeric rating is intended to provide a number value of the current security posture of a specific organization. The IPR is customized for each customer and should not be used to compare organizations. The value to the customer is that the continuous use of the metric at the same organization will provide the customer the ability to do trend analysis of the organizational security posture. The IPR is developed by determining the average of all the findings, including organizational and technical, with weighting applied based on the severity of the findings. There is a mathematical susceptibility to skewing of the value by having an excessively large number of low findings, we have found that counting duplicate findings only once will reduce any possibility of skewing. One of the nice benefits of using the IPR is that it is a numeric value that lends itself to a briefing graphic that is easily understood by executive management.

Administrators and technicians are not the prime target for developing any trending metrics, but there is benefit to be gained at all levels of an organization by trending the security posture. Executive-level management can see their status and how much improvement has been made. Middle management can look at the trends to prioritize and justify budgets to improve the security posture. Both of the metrics, the IPP and the IPR, can be drilled down to show administrators or technicians the posture of the systems they are responsible for. This will help them understand the organizational security goals and what they can do to meet those goals.

## Chapter 26

Final Reporting

Solutions in this chapter:

- Pulling All the Information Together
- Making Recommendations
- Creating the Final Report
- Presenting the Final Report

☑ Summary

Introduction

Your team has completed the onsite technical evaluation of your client, and now it's time to review all the information you gathered, create the final report in a clear, understandable format, and present it to the customer. The final report will contain many things and provide your customer with more than just recommendations and options. The final report should ensure that not only does it bring added value but that it will help the organization create a plan, or road map, to a better, more secure information security posture.

Part of the value-add for the customer is the followup after you present all the documentation and the evaluation is complete. You've probably seen or heard of that information security company that simply runs a tool and hands in a report. You want to show the organization that you honestly want to improve the company's security posture. You want to relay to the organization that you will be there while they are incorporating your recommendations and will be there in the future, not only for the next evaluation but for information and ideas on how to apply the recommendations to the findings you and your team have uncovered. You should be a partner in the process with your customer, as much as you can.

Regarding the information security company that simply runs a tool and hands in a report: Do you think this company will be asked back to do another evaluation? Will the organization receiving this report recommend that company to another organization? The answer to both questions should be obvious: *No!* Of course you must make money, but a better way to increase you client base is to become known as an information security company that cares about its customers' information security and will be there when a customer needs help.

The other thing you'll want to cover here is the fact that, because this information is so sensitive, you will only store it for a certain period of time (30–45 days is typical). For that reason, you'll want to perform the followup during that window of time, ensuring that the customer has all questions answered. After all, a final report that the customer can't use is worthless. After the 30–45 days, you will typically destroy the information because you're probably not set up to act as a secure storage facility. This clause is usually mentioned in the contract with the customer before the engagement begins.

Pulling All the Information Together

You and your team have spent a great deal of time and effort evaluating the information security posture of your customer organization. In the process of doing the evaluation, you have collected information that now needs not only further review but to be organized in a way that is beneficial to your client. Before you are able to collect all the data and coalesce it into a useful document for the customer, the following tasks should be conducted:

- A team meeting
- Research
- SVCM and OVCM
- Review

The Team Meeting

Many things that go into having a successful meeting: reserving a room of the right size, supplying pens and pencils, deciding who will facilitate. The purpose of the team meeting is to get everyone refocused. Many of us are working on multiple projects, and we need to set aside time to bring all the material together in an organized manner. This would be the time to:

- **Set up the agenda**   Discuss the objectives, who has done what, and what needs to be done to complete the evaluation and turn in the final report on time.

- **Bring up questions about your findings**   In the initial meetings following the onsite evaluation, a lot of the time is used to discuss your findings, how they could affect your client, and what would be the best solution for the organization.

- **Assign work**   Review where everyone is with their responsibilities and assign any work that needs to be completed.

- **Create an action plan and deadlines**   The action plan should contain a list of tasks that need to be done, with names attached and deadlines.

- **Consult any additional expertise that might be needed**   With so many advancements in technology and the different ways organizations do business, it could be possible that you will need to bring in additional expertise to complete the evaluation.

- **Any other applicable information**   Make sure everyone is on the same page, and utilize good communication to ensure a quality product.

NOTE

Writing the final report does not have to be the responsibility of one person. In many cases, multiple team members will contribute to the actual writing of the final report. Assign the writing responsibility according to the abilities of individual team members.

Research

Further research will probably be necessary to confirm or refute many of the vulnerabilities that you and your team uncovered during your evaluation. During this phase, you and your team should do research into the vulnerabilities that you have found and discover the latest fix or patch for each vulnerability, taking into consideration the effect your recommendation could have on the applications your client is running. This is another great place to add value to your evaluation by helping your customer understand how these vulnerabilities can impact their organization. Remember, during your research your goal is to analyze your data, keeping in mind your customer's information security so you can make the appropriate recommendations that will advance the organization's information security posture.

Research has been underrated in the information security field. This activity should be something that an information security professional does on a regular basis.

The SVCM and OVCM

You create two matrixes during the IEM to help your customer understand their vulnerabilities and the risks they represent to the organization. The system vulnerability criticality matrix (SVCM) and the overall vulnerability criticality matrix (OVCM) are created using the information criticality matrixes that were developed in the IAM; these are used during the IEM to aid the customer. This type of information is created during the IAM, but with the IEM we start at the system level and move to the organizational level. The purpose of the SVCM is to provide a detailed snapshot of the customer's security posture at a very high level. We call this a *first-order prioritization* of the customer's findings.

To create these matrixes, you must base them not only on your findings and knowledge of information security, but also on the customer's input. Customer input refers to the information provided by the customer that gives you and your team insight as to how a particular vulnerability could directly impact your client. This step is normally performed in the NSA IAM pre-assessment phase. This snapshot not only assists the customer in prioritizing their vulnerabilities but also assists you in tracking vulnerabilities through successive evaluations.

Review

In pulling your information together after the onsite evaluation phase, with the amount of information that you and your team have collected it is important to continue to work together to make sure that your information is accurate and that you take the time to determine the vulnerabilities that are present within the organization. During this review process, it is important to review not only your notes and findings, but those of your evaluation team. We cannot emphasize enough how vital it is for you and your team to work together during this review process. Remember to share not only the information from your scans, but any interviews or conversations you had with members of the organization and any notes you took, no matter how insignificant you thought they were at the time. At this point in the review, your team should have a conversation on all the information you have gathered, including the findings, good and bad, as well as best practices that could help the organization.

> **NOTE**
>
> Examples of good and bad findings:
>
> - **Good findings**   Findings that you and your team come across during your evaluation that reveal good security practices.
> - **Bad findings**   Findings that reveal poor configurations (of firewall, default passwords, or the like) or other technical security issues.

Making Recommendations

The Recommendations section of your final report is critical when it comes to adding value to your evaluation. Now you have finished your technical evaluation of your client, reviewed the information that you have collected, used your own expertise and possibly brought in other experts who might be able to add insight on specific platforms and/or business models, you need to review your data. It is time to organize a list of your findings from high to low criticality or however the client requested the information. Findings should be discussed in direct relation to their impact on the customer organization, based on three things: customer input, industry ratings (CVE/CAN/ICAT), and your professional experience.

> **TIP**
>
> The information security professional who works for the organization that you are evaluating might already feel angry, disturbed, or anxious that you and your team are in his or her network poking around. They probably think, no matter what your team has explained in the in-brief, that you are there to point out what they are doing wrong. You need to assure these professionals that you are not there to show their managers what hasn't been done or who didn't secure what, but instead to show the organization the gaps that currently exist in their organization.
>
> One way to improve this situation is to remember, when discussing findings and vulnerabilities in your final report, that the individuals who maintain the systems security will be directly affected by not only your findings but your recommendations. Chances are that you will find critical security concerns during your evaluation. It is a good idea to add positive findings and comments in your final report so it doesn't seem as though you're attacking the individuals concerned. Without these positive findings, the individuals within the organization could take your report as a personal insult, which in turn could make it difficult for them to accept and implement your recommendations.
>
> These positive findings could also give the organization as well as the individual(s) an idea of what they are doing well and what security practices they can build on. An example of a positive comment is something like, "Our evaluation determined that the organization's network and IT systems were configured with security in mind."
>
> Other examples of good or positive findings could look something like these:
>
> During the INFOSEC evaluation, many good findings were documented, indicating that your security team included security within the development life cycle. The good findings included:
>
> - Enforcement of strong password policies
> - Evidence that the IDS team reviews logs on a regular basis
> - Disabling of finger service

Findings

Findings are security concerns that you uncovered during your evaluation. This section of the report should be broken into three sections: High, Medium, and Low. You should have developed the definitions for the criticality findings with the customer, through interviews and conversations. Use these definitions to assign the risk impact levels to each of the vulnerabilities. Examples of what these definitions might look like are:

- **High criticality findings**   Loss could result in the unauthorized release of information that could have a significant impact on the organization's mission or financial assets or result in loss of life.

- **Medium criticality findings**   Loss could result in the unauthorized release of information that could have an impact on the organization's mission or financial assets or result in harm to an individual.

- **Low criticality findings**   Loss could result in the unauthorized release of information that could have some degree of impact on the organization's mission or financial assets or result in harm to an individual.

Defining what is a High, Medium, or Low criticality finding depends on the impact to the customer. There are many ways to determine factors at each level of criticality, but the bottom line is how the finding impacts the organization. These definitions are not something the evaluation team can come up with on their own, and normally we prefer that the customer create them completely on their own while the evaluation team acts in the role of facilitator to the process. Again, this is a task that should have been conducted in the NSA IAM process and migrated over to the evaluation. For technical findings, we see that most standard definitions for High, Medium, and Low have been developed already by various organizations and will require only minor modifications by the evaluation team.

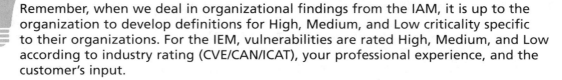

TIP

Remember, when we deal in organizational findings from the IAM, it is up to the organization to develop definitions for High, Medium, and Low criticality specific to their organizations. For the IEM, vulnerabilities are rated High, Medium, and Low according to industry rating (CVE/CAN/ICAT), your professional experience, and the customer's input.

When listing the findings in your report, discuss the most critical findings first, medium second, and if appropriate, list the low findings last. Write your findings so that first you categorize them in relation to whether they represent external exposures, internal exposures, or systems boundary issues. Clearly explain each vulnerability using language your client will understand, but try to limit your definition to about two to three sentences.

Your report should also list finding name, the corresponding common vulnerabilities and exposures (CVE/CAN) number where applicable at a level of detail that is appropriate to your audience, severity rating, and recommendations. When possible, use the Cadillac, Chevy, and Yugo model.

Notes from the Underground

Cadillac, Chevy, and Yugo

If you have been working in the security arena and/or mitigating vulnerabilities, you might be familiar with the Cadillac, Chevy, and Yugo model. This is simply a way of providing recommendations to your customer that allows them to have options. After all, if we only provide the customer with the best possible solution, what are the chances that they will be capable of implementing it across the entire organization? Financial and resource constraints will limit their abilities to do that. By providing multiple levels of recommendation, where available, you give the customer options and allow them to have a greater positive impact on their security posture.

Here are the three parts of the model:

- **Cadillac** This is not always the best solution for the organization, but it is, for sure, the top of the line. This solution is probably the most expensive and time consuming, but it offers the highest level of protection.

- **Chevy** This is the middle-of-the-road solution for your client. This solution offers to reduce the risk to the organization, but not as much as the Cadillac. Of course, this solution will cost less than the Cadillac and require fewer resources to implement.

- **Yugo** As you have already realized, this solution is the cheapest for your client. It provides some elimination of risk immediately, with very little cost to the organization. This can be a great temporary patch until your client has the resources to implement the Cadillac or Chevy.

NOTE

If you or your organization do not use the CVE, it is strongly suggested that you use something similar that will provide your client with the definitions and information needed to fully understand a vulnerability. The use of this type of standard allows you and the customer to cross-reference specific vulnerabilities and weaknesses across different platforms, databases, and tools. The CVE provides users free services and databases that can strengthen an organization's information security.

The importance of using the CVE standard is that you and your team can determine a standard rating for each of the vulnerabilities that you discovered. This process will gain value as your team completes annual evaluations and can use the CVE scores to compare the current security posture of the organization to past evaluations.

Recommendations

Knowing the security issues is only half the battle. Providing your customer recommendations in the form of options for your findings is critical. As we mentioned earlier in this section, it is very important to create or provide your client with a specific way to resolve a finding. Your recommendations should be specific to your client while taking into consideration any concerns or constraints the client has. Following the results from the SVCM and the OVCM will assist you in determining the findings you uncovered that are critical and will help you prioritize them in the report.

When considering recommendations, you should use what we call the *multiple-solution path*. This path consists of offering multiple solutions such as patches, upgrades, filters, and enhancements. Your recommendations should talks about how your findings are important to your client, the risk (see Figure 26.1), and how might they affect the mission of the organization. Unfortunately, it is not always easy to know the concerns and constraints relating to politics and finances. Sometimes the most common solution will not always work for your client. Some of the concerns and constraints you could come across when dealing with customers are:

- Time
- Finances
- Personnel
- Government requirements/restrictions

Knowing your customer's concerns and constraints will allow you to make the appropriate recommendations that are exclusive to your customer.

Each component of the risk triangle — threat, asset value, and vulnerability — must be present for there to be risk (see Figure 26.1). Removing one of the components eliminates the risk to the organization. In most cases, if you are able to minimize the vulnerability, which may be the easiest of the components, you will minimize the risk.

Figure 26.1 The Risk Triangle

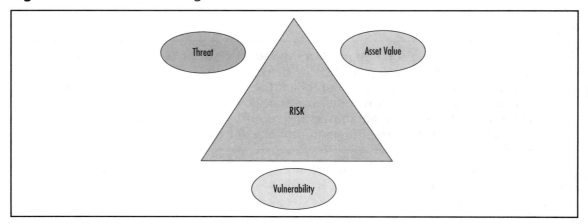

Creating the Final Report

This section presents a collection of proven and established strategies that are effective in preparing a final report. It will take more than following these simple practices to create a great report, but use these as a guide in helping you produce a quality final report that will add value and assist your customer in developing a stronger security posture.

Organizing the Data

Begin the process of organizing and discussing the data you have collected as soon as possible after the onsite evaluation.

- Utilize all your team's notes because you could have missed something important.
- Set goals and assign responsibilities to ensure a high-quality report that's delivered on time.

Discussion of Findings

Review the definitions for High, Medium, and Low criticalities that you and your team developed from the discussions and interviews with the client.

- Provide more than one solution for the customer, to allow them to have some control over the remediation process.
- Determining the appropriate discussion of a finding should be done individually, as well as including all the notes taken by the team.
- Determine the risk to your customer while developing discussion of the findings.

Final Report Delivery Date

Depending on the size of the organization, the vulnerabilities found, and the required detail, the final report is usually delivered to the customer two to eight weeks after the onsite evaluations. It is customary to provide your client with a draft of the final report for review before delivery of the final product. If any new high-criticality findings are discovered during this phase, you should notify your client before you complete the report.

The Cover Letter

The cover letter should include who you are, your business process, and the appropriate contact information for a responsible person at your organization. This person will be responsible for providing answers to customer questions and performing followup with the customer. The cover letter should also give a very brief summary of what the customer can expect to find in the final report.

The Executive Summary

The executive summary is a brief description and high-level overview of what is in the final report. When writing the executive summary, keep in mind that your goal is to summarize what you and your team have done and what you've found during the evaluation. Your audience is the customer organization's management team, so now is not the time to get overly technical. Save the technical language for the final report.

Some of the items you should cover in the executive summary are:

- **Organization synopsis**   This includes a description of the customer organization and what they do. Are they part of a larger organization? Include the organization mission, vision, focus, location, size, and organizational structure.

- **Purpose for the evaluation**   This should include why you and your team were asked to do the evaluation and by whom. What benefit is the organization hoping to gain from your efforts?

- **System description**   Describe the system or systems within the customer organization and which, if not all, systems were part of the evaluation. Include specific servers, high-assurance devices such as routers, switches, and firewalls, and IP-address ranges.

- **Summary of evaluation**   Briefly describe what was done during the evaluation process and include a timeline of important events. Also include a brief description of the IEM, what it consists of, and where it came from.

- **Major findings and recommendations**   List the most critical vulnerabilities to the organization that you and your team discovered and how they were uncovered in your evaluation. Following the vulnerabilities should be at least two options or recommendations to resolve your findings. Remember, not all findings in the executive summary need to be negative in nature. (Refer to the Cadillac, Chevy, and Yugo definitions of recommendations.)

- **System vulnerability criticality matrix**   The SVCM is included here so the management can have a snapshot of vulnerabilities in their organization as well as a picture of their organization's security posture. Include one SVCM for each system.

- **Overall vulnerability criticality matrix**   The OVCM gives an overall security posture of the organization and is often too large to include in this section. If that is the case, include just the upper-left portion of the matrix.

The INFOSEC Profile

This section of the report identifies the organization's vulnerabilities and allows the organization to assess its security posture. As discussed earlier, you can report vulnerabilities using the NIST SP 800-53, which identifies the 17 baseline information security classes, or simply organize the vulnerabilities from High to Low according to the ways they might affect the organization.

The Introduction

The information in the introduction is similar to the executive summary but with a greater amount of detail. You want your audience to have a complete understanding of who you are and what you and your team have done as well as information about the process and methodology that you used. This section should include information about your organization and where you are located as well as your mission statement. Explain why your organization was asked to do the evaluation, when the evaluation was conducted, why your team uses the IEM, and what background and expertise your team brings to the evaluation. Reiterate that what you and your team are doing is an evaluation and not an audit, inspection, certification, or risk analysis. Explain what you and your team expect to accomplish during the evaluation. In the introduction you should include the background information.

The background information should include the name and address of the organization that you are evaluating as well as the scope of the evaluation, including when the work was done as well as dates and locations of the evaluation. A table of IP addresses that were provided and used in the evaluation could also be included here.

You should also discuss why the evaluation was done, and reiterate the fact that you and your team did an information security evaluation and not any type of certification or accreditation.

Within the Background Information section, address the following points:

- **Organization's mission** By stating or elaborating on the organization's mission, this section helps the reader understand why the evaluation was done and why the organization's information is critical.

- **Purpose of the evaluation** Why was the evaluation done? What was the driving force behind having someone do an information security evaluation? How is the organization going to use the results of your evaluation?

- **Organization's information criticality**

- **System criticality (from the IAM pre-assessment)**

- **The technical evaluation plan (TEP)**

  - Concerns

  - Constraints

Also include:

- The system vulnerability criticality matrix (SVCM)

- The overall vulnerability criticality matrix (OVCM)

- Technical data (CD)

- Rules of engagement (ROI) as predetermined by your team and the customer

INFOSEC Analysis

The purpose of the INFOSEC Analysis section of the final report is to give clarity to your customer's information security posture. To accomplish this clarity, identify the vulnerabilities and specifically outline how these vulnerabilities could affect the organization. At this point in the evaluation, you should know how your client would like you to present the vulnerabilities you found during your evaluation.

The following are some sample outlines for presenting your analysis.

TIP

The most common way to present your findings is to list them according to the client's predefined High, Medium, and Low criticality levels.

Technical Areas

- External Exposures
- Internal Exposures
- System Boundaries

High-Criticality Findings

- **Finding:** SNMP set public community
  - **Finding ID #:** 1
  - **CVE/CAN:** CAN-1999-0517
  - **Category:** Identification and Authentication
  - **Location:** *xxx.xxx.xxx, xxx.xxx.xxx*
  - **Severity:** High
  - **Discussion:** The SNMP default public community name is specified, allowing anyone the ability to change the computer's system information if they use this default value. An attacker can use SNMP to obtain valuable information about the system, such as information on network devices and current open connections. In this case, the ability exists to actually change information, because the SNMP Set password is set to Public.
  - **Recommendations:**
  - Option 1: If the SNMP Service is not necessary, disable or remove the it.
  - Option 2: If your organization requires the use of the SNMP Service, you should take steps to secure the SNMP community names and the community strings.
- **Finding:** Telnet default account accessible
  - **Finding ID #:** 2
  - **CVE/CAN:** No common corresponding vulnerability
  - **Category:** Technical Finding

- **Location:** *xxx.xxx.xxx, xxx.xxx.xxx, xxx.xxx.xxx*
- **Severity:** High
- **Discussion:** An accessible default account was detected through Telnet. Default accounts through Telnet allow attackers easy access to remote systems by providing a network-accessible service on the server or printer.
- **Recommendations:**
  - Option 1: Disable the Telnet account/service on each network.
  - Option 2: Change the password for the account to something difficult to guess.

Medium-Criticality Findings

- **Finding:** Access Validation Error
- **Finding ID #:** 3
- **CVE/CAN:** (CVE-2000-0475)
- **Category:** Technical Finding
- **Location:** *xxx.xxx.xxx, xxx.xxx.xxx, xxx.xxx.xxx*
- **Severity:** Medium
- **Discussion:** A local user or attacker could gain access and/or additional privileges to another user's desktop. Microsoft Windows 2000 could allow an attacker to gain increased privileges on the local system. The Windows 2000 security architecture restricts processes through a system of sessions, Windows stations, and desktops. A local attacker could create a process that runs in a higher-privilege context ("desktop") than the local user. This would give the attacker access to certain input devices available to the higher-privilege desktop, for instance, allowing the user to monitor local logins to record usernames and passwords.
- **Recommendation:**
  - Install the appropriate Microsoft patch for your systems. Reference: ww.microsoft.com/technet/security/bulletin/fq00-020.mspx.
- **Finding:** IisVirtualUncShare: IIS virtual UNC share source read
- **Finding ID #:** 4
- **CVE/CAN:** (CVE-2000-0246)
- **Category:** Technical Finding
- **Location:** *xxx.xxx.xxx, xxx.xxx.xxx, xxx.xxx.xxx*
- **Severity:** Medium

- **Discussion:** Microsoft Internet Information Server (IIS) could reveal the source code of files that reside on a UNC network share. A remote attacker could request a file from the Web server that resides on a network share and append specific characters to the end of the URL to cause the Web server to return the text source of the file to the browser. An attacker could send your source code to him- or herself, thus stealing your source code.

- **Recommendation:**
  - Install the appropriate Microsoft patch for your system. Reference: http://support. microsoft.com/support/contact/default.asp.

Low-Criticality Findings

- **Finding:** Design Error
  - **Finding ID #:** 5
  - **CVE/CAN:** (CVE-2003-0007)
  - **Category:** Technical Finding
  - **Location:** *xxx.xxx.xxx, xxx.xxx.xxx, xxx.xxx.xxx*
  - **Severity:** Low
  - **Discussion:** Microsoft Outlook 2002 does not properly handle requests to encrypt e-mail messages with V1 Exchange Server Security certificates, which causes Outlook to send the e-mail in plaintext, aka "Flaw in how Outlook 2002 handles V1 Exchange Server Security Certificates could lead to Information Disclosure."
  - **Recommendation:**
    - Install the appropriate Microsoft patch for your system. Reference: http:// microsoft.com/technet/security/bulletin/ms03-003.mspx.

- **Finding:** Access Validation Error
  - **Finding ID #:** 6
  - **CVE/CAN:** (CVE-2002-1186)
  - **Category:** Technical Finding
  - **Location:** *xxx.xxx.xxx, xxx.xxx.xxx, xxx.xxx.xxx*
  - **Severity:** Low
  - **Discussion:** Internet Explorer 5.01 through 6.0 does not properly perform security checks on certain encoded characters within a URL, which allows a remote attacker to steal potentially sensitive information from a user by redirecting the user to another site that has that information, aka "Encoded Characters Information Disclosure."
  - **Recommendation:**
    - Install the appropriate Microsoft patch for your system. Reference: http://microsoft. com/technet/security/bulletin/ms02-066.mspx.

TIP

Do not use a default finding write-up from a commercial tool. You and your customer want your discussions to be original.

The Conclusion

In the same way that we open with an introduction section that introduces the final report, we close with a conclusion section that concludes it. The conclusion basically summarizes your report, bringing all the main ideas together and stressing anything that might be important to your customer.

Impress on your client a sense urgency and that they should give the vulnerabilities you and your team have discovered immediate attention. Follow up with a brief statement discussing the majority of the findings and an idea of how your client can get started on the remediation.

Talk about what good INFOSEC security is and how it can benefit the organization. Include a short paragraph on good policies, training, and implementation. Reiterate that the recommendations in the final report are not requirements but simply guidance that will help your client reduce risk and improve their INFOSEC security posture.

Include positive statements about the organization and its people and a willingness to work with the organization in the future. Finally, include your contact information and the contact information of a responsible party in your organization.

TIP

It is always nice to point out or reiterate a good or positive finding in the conclusion.

Three other areas that should be mentioned are posture description, posture profile, and security practices.

Posture Description

Now that you are familiar with the organization and have the data and information from your evaluation, you are in a position to make an educated statement about the customer's security posture. You are also in a position to stress to the customer the changes the customer needs to make to better their security posture.

Posture Profile

The overall INFOSEC Posture Profile (IPP) is fairly brief and to the point while showing the organization a score that directly relates to the vulnerabilities that you and your team found during the evaluation. The IPP is based on the four aspects of the DOD Computer Network Defense (CND):

- **Protect**   Systems configuration and remediation management
- **Detect**   Audit implementation
- **Respond**   Reactive measures
- **Sustain**   Network management

After calculating each of these areas based on the average of all your findings, you can determine the IPP. The IPP can then be used to provide your team the ability to trend vulnerabilities and develop countermeasures over time. This will allow the organization to track progress and improve their security posture. The higher the IPP score, the greater the risk to the organization.

NOTE

The IPP has limited value if it is only used once and should not be used to compare various organizations.

Security Practices

In addition to the findings and recommendation that you have provided to the client, it is also a good idea to provide your client with some good security practices. These security practices should be those practices that are generally accepted in the information security field. They could be suggestions or guidelines for the organization you are evaluating that will help them improve their security posture. Some security practices that you can recommend might be more in-depth, such as these:

- **Performing annual evaluations and penetration tests**   IT systems in organizations are constantly changing and new vulnerabilities are being discovered at a very rapid rate. Annual evaluations and penetration tests allow an organization to assess its security posture and the state of its IT security.

- **Include IT security within the life cycle of all your systems and applications**   Too often, organizations develop applications and systems and then think about their security. Security should be considered in all phases of the development life cycle, from design and development to implementation and maintenance.

- **Configuration management process**   This is an important part of controlling and maintaining a secure environment through tracking and documenting the mechanisms used on your systems.

You can also include some good security practices that are brief and to the point, such as:

- Remove default passwords
- Reevaluate the configuration of your security tools
- Develop an IT security policy

Presenting the Final Report

The final report is what you leave with the customer; in the end it will be all that is left to represent you when you have left the customer's site. The first thing you need to remember when you present the final report is the deadline. Don't be late with it! An organized, well-written final report that is delivered on time or ahead of schedule will leave a lasting positive impression of your organization. A final report that is thrown together and does not take into consideration the customer's expectations will not only make you and your team look bad but could give the organization an impression that the work you did was poor and unprofessional. Before you present the customer with any information, make sure you are clear on their expectations.

Summary

You and your team have just completed an INFOSEC evaluation of an organization. You are almost done, but you know you need to analyze the information and organize it in a way that is useful to your client. To do this, you need to put together a final report that talks about and defines the vulnerabilities that could impact your client. Included in you report should be recommendations specific to your client so that they can begin to start the required implementation.

Pulling everything together in the form of team meetings will help your team focus on what needs to be done to deliver a quality final report. During this time you will bring up any questions about the evaluation and findings, assign work to the team members, create action plans, and discuss deadlines.

The most important part of pulling your information together will be your findings and how you organize them in a way that is valuable to your customer. During this time you will discuss in detail the findings and how they could impact your client and create recommendation so your client can develop a road map to secure their information.

As you and your team discuss the findings, continue to keep in mind how they affect your customer and the customer's risk from the vulnerability.

In the end you are leaving your client a final report that will be the lasting impression of the work you and your team performed.

## Chapter 27

Summing Up the INFOSEC Evaluation Methodology

Solutions in this chapter:

- **Examples of INFOSEC Tools by Baseline Activity**

- **Technical Evaluation Plan Outline and Sample**

Introduction

Throughout this part of the book, you've learned about a methodology that is attempting to lay out a standard baseline for technical evaluations. If you've been in the business a while, it's likely that none of the information was truly new to you. If you're just getting into this type of work, you'll want to keep in mind that all we've done is give you a new tool for your toolbox. Once the majority of information security consultants are beginning from the same square on the playing board, it will be easier for customers to understand what to expect when they request this type of work. All we're doing here is building a common starting point for technical evaluations.

One thing we'd like to reiterate is that there is simply no replacement for valid experience in this arena. Unlike the occupations of old, such as blacksmiths, there is no apprentice program. Any individual who is enterprising enough can walk out to the sidewalk and hang up their shingle, proclaiming themselves *security consultants*. In all likelihood, this is normally done from a desire to capitalize on the increasing information security marketplace, but it can have a detrimental effect on customer organizations that are trying to legitimately secure their information assets.

Nearly everyone has read the stories of the young man who becomes an apprentice to the local blacksmith. He spends years learning the trade and how to do the work professionally and correctly. After an investment of 10–15 years, the now older man is considered a professional. But that's not the end of our scenario. This same young man is enrolled in a guild, which acts as a governing body for the education of new blacksmiths. The guild ensures that each man in the program has achieved a level of knowledge deemed appropriate before allowing him to call himself a blacksmith. The key is that the community accepts the guild's word as to who is reliable and knowledgeable. The public directs requests for service to only those individuals who were certified or deemed appropriate.

We don't have any of that in the current world of information security. There are no strict guidelines about who can be considered a reliable practitioner of the "black art" of INFOSEC. Attempts to create something like a guild system have been either centralized around a specific industry or have been watered down by loopholes in the founding organizations.

One example is the ISC(2) Certified Information System Security Professional, or CISSP, program. Although a valiant effort has been made to control the quality of individuals receiving the certification, it's often impossible to verify this type of thing. Let's face it—people can easily lie on their certification applications. And a test, no matter how extensive, can always be studied for rather than passed based on actual experience. The beginning of every successful control mechanism has been to develop a set of acceptable performance criteria that can be followed by professionals within the industry. As the industry grows and matures, new people come into that profession and are introduced to these basics.

The INFOSEC Evaluation Methodology (IEM) is an example of that. The NSA has recognized a need in the marketplace to standardize our practices. In the NSA's opinion, the IEM is strictly the minimum baseline of activities that must take place if one is to conduct a truly valuable and comprehensive technical evaluation. With that in mind, remember that you're not locked into doing *only* these things. Nor are you stuck with the report formats, tool selections, or metrics we've shown you in this book. These are simply tools for your toolbox. You can expand and extend the IEM to fit the needs of both your own organization and your customers.

The Pre-Evaluation Phase

The pre-evaluation phase can be said to start as soon as you have initial contact with the customer. This is the point at which you can guide the customer and provide advice on what may be needed to help improve their security posture. For instance, if you get a call from someone requiring a *penetration test*, it's easy enough to agree because the work sounds like fun. But is it what the customer needs? Will it honestly improve their security posture, or will it leave them with a false sense of security?

We're also setting the scope and the rules of engagement and laying out the evaluation plan that we'll follow during the evaluation. Customers need to understand what will happen during the evaluation, that their concerns have been taken into account, and that they can track everything that is occurring.

Many of the requests for evaluations we receive have been based primarily on compliance. What regulations is the organization liable for adhering to? Is it a financial institution concerned with meeting Gramm-Leach-Bliley guidelines? Is it a university or college that needs to comply with the Family Education Rights and Privacy Act (FERPA)? Some organizations need to comply with multiple regulations. You'll need the knowledge of these documents and understanding of specific ways they can impact the customer.

As opposed to the NSA IAM, where we only had a single point of contact, the IEM requires multiple points of contact, both administrative and technical. Whereas the administrative contacts will be primarily concerned with setting up our meetings with important personnel, assigning us appropriate workspace, and maintaining a schedule for the evaluation; the technical points of contact will provide us with more detailed information. This could include anything from concerns about existing systems we will be evaluating and windows of opportunity for the evaluation activities to network connections or addresses from which to conduct our activities.

Rules of engagement (ROE) are developed in concert with the customer. This is the customer's evaluation and we want to ensure that it is done according to their specifications. Items of interest include the activities that are allowed, when they are allowed, and on what systems they are allowed. ROE also lists the opposite for each of these things. What systems are considered out of scope? When are we *not* allowed to conduct evaluation activities? What activities should be excluded from the evaluation due to appropriate customer concerns?

Never forget that legal representation during the entire evaluation process is recommended as a protective measure. Although honest security professionals never go into these types of arrangements with malicious intent, misunderstandings and accidents do occur. We want to ensure that the customer has given us full license to conduct the agreed-on activities. And in most cases, utilizing legal counsel as a conduit for this line of business can provide client/attorney privilege that protects the sensitive findings in court cases.

All this information is placed into the technical evaluation plan (TEP) that will serve as a guide for all activities related to this evaluation. The information in the TEP should never be a surprise to the customer. We often ensure customer approval by requesting their signature and date on the TEP itself, prior to beginning any of the onsite evaluation activities. The signature helps reinforce management buy-in of this process and serves as documentation that the customer agrees with our understanding of the evaluation activities.

The Onsite Evaluation

In the onsite evaluation phase, the proverbial rubber meets the road. Here we address the 10 baseline activities that NSA requires for a comprehensive evaluation. As you saw in earlier chapters, we've tried to establish a repeatable and simple process that will provide value to the customer organization. Assuming that the customer is serious about information security, you provide experience-driven recommendations that are viable solutions for the customer, and they implement some or many of your recommendations; the security posture of the customer organization is thus improved.

The first thing we do in the IEM is conduct the opening meeting, called an *in-brief*. This is where we reinforce the management buy-in and let all associated customer employees know how the evaluation will be conducted. In the in-brief, we'll explain the IEM, where it came from, and what areas we'll be looking at while we evaluate their systems. We really want the customer to walk away from this meeting with a clear and comfortable understanding of the evaluation team and the evaluation process.

As we begin the evaluation activities, it's important to understand the difference between an organizational finding and a technical finding. Whereas the organizational finding is normally discovered during the IAM and revolves around policies, process, or procedures, the IEM findings are more technical and are based on the technical implementation or configuration of technical systems. Both of these findings are used later in the final road map that we deliver to the customer organization.

The first general area of activities in the IEM centers around information gathering. We're looking to enumerate all the systems, machines, devices, services, and more that are used in or using the customer network. This activity includes running port scans to locate and identify all the hosts, services, and devices on the network. We're also looking to gain information about those items. For example, the banner-grabbing activity of the IEM tries to identify specifically what service or application is running on a certain port. All the information we gain from these activities will help us narrow our search for findings within the customer organization.

The next set of activities—the automated vulnerability scans and the host evaluations that are conducted on critical servers and workstations—often creates the bulk of technical findings. Each of these activities generates a number of important findings. Your experience comes into play when you need to determine which findings are real and which ones are false positives. This can be a time-intensive activity, but if it's handled and interpreted correctly, the customer will gain tremendous value from this piece of the IEM.

In the final set of activities, we bring the evaluation down to a point where we are gaining greater detail about the security posture of the customer's technical systems. For example, we can gauge the effectiveness of the customer's password policy by performing password-compliance testing. The configuration of high-assurance devices such as firewalls, routers, and switches will provide clues to the ways that network traffic is allowed to move in and out of the customer network and points at which there could be issues.

The last activity performed during the onsite evaluation phase is the out-brief. If there were critical findings, we want to ensure that the customer understands what they are. We're not out to impress the customer by giving them a final report full of surprises and critical findings. In fact, if we locate critical findings during the onsite phase, we want to notify our contacts immediately. The out-brief is your chance to show the customer how the work has been progressing, what you've found thus far, and when they can expect further information.

The Post-Evaluation Phase

The post-evaluation phase of any evaluation tends to be the most tedious. It conjures images of techies sitting at their desks rummaging through tons of data collected during the onsite phase, looking for problem areas. In fact, this is often the case. A big problem with many security companies is their tendency to run a piece of software, dump out the default report, and send it to their customer with the logo replaced with their own. The true value in any evaluation comes down to the quality analysis performed by the security experts. Without proper analysis, the results have very little value to your customer.

But even if you conduct the best analysis possible, you still need a means by which to communicate those findings to the customer. What does it all mean to them? What is the *real* impact to the customer?

To help answer these questions and aid you in communicating the big picture back to the customer, NSA created a set of matrixes. These matrixes provide a clear picture of findings that have the biggest impact to the organization, based on information gained during the IAM and the IEM processes.

Along with the matrixes comes the introduction of two metrics that can be used to trend security posture over time. Depending on your requirements, the customer might choose to use one or the other of the two metrics. One was intended specifically for Department of Defense systems; the other one has more commercial value. That's not to say that are not interchangeable; they are. Again, use what works for your customer.

Finally, we arrive at the point at which we create the final report and deliver it to the customer. Your final report should reflect the attitude and personality of the customer organization while still conveying the important facts. And don't think your work is through once the customer has the report in hand. You still have a responsibility to follow up with your customer and ensure that they understand the findings your team located and the recommendations you made to eliminate or mitigate those findings. The actual format of the final report depends heavily on your own business processes, but we've made suggestions on what areas are important to include.

As a final reminder, remember that it's important for every security professional to have a plethora of tools in their toolkits. The NSA INFOSEC Evaluation Methodology should be one of those tools. When the information security industry begins to standardize on those things that professionals consider acceptable, we can not only begin controlling the quality of the individuals who are performing this type of work, but the customers themselves will benefit. Imagine a world where a customer calls you up asking for a security evaluation and they have a pretty good idea of what they should expect.

Examples of INFOSEC Tools by Baseline Activity

Here are some of the tools we discussed in Part 2.

Port Scanning

Tool Name: Nmap (v.3.81)

Developer: Fyodor (Insecure.org)

Platform/OS: UNIX, Linux, FreeBSD, NetBSD, OpenBSD, Solaris, OS X, Microsoft Windows, HP-UX, AIX, DigUX, Cray UNICOS

Commercial or Freeware?   Freeware (GPL)

URL: www.insecure.org/nmap/

NOTE

Microsoft Windows XP SP2 disabled the ability to use RAW sockets, it throttled the number of permitted outbound TCP connections, and disabled the ability to send spoofed UDP packets. This is "fixed" in Nmap version 3.55 and newer.

Nmap is a tool that fits into more than one baseline activity. It can provide a wealth of information.

Tool Name: ScanLine (v.1.01)

Developer: McAfee (formerly FoundStone)

Platform/OS: Microsoft Windows

Commercial or Freeware?   Freeware

URL: www.foundstone.com/resources/proddesc/scanline.htm

NOTE

ScanLine is the replacement for Fscan. This is a command-line scanner for the MS Windows platform; it can handle scanning in a highly parallel fashion and provides more scanning capabilities than Fscan did.

Tool Name: Scanrand (part of paketto v.2.0p3)

Developer: Dan Kaminsky

Platform/OS: Compiles on Linux (RedHat, Mandrake, and Debian), FreeBSD, MinGW (on MS Windows)

Commercial or Freeware?   Freeware

URL: www.doxpara.com

NOTE

Libnet (v1.0.2) and libpcap are *required*.

> **Tool Name:**   SuperScan (v.4.0)
>
> **Developer:**   McAfee (formerly FoundStone)
>
> **Platform/OS:**   Microsoft Windows
>
> **Commercial or Freeware?**   Freeware
>
> **URL:**   www.foundstone.com/resources/proddesc/superscan4.htm

NOTE

SuperScan v3.0 and v4.0 are available from this site. Version 4.0 provides more functionality but doesn't seem as fast as version 3.0.

> **Tool Name:**   MingSweeper (v.1.0alpha5, build 130)
>
> **Developer:**   HooBie
>
> **Platform/OS:**   Microsoft Windows NT/2000/XP
>
> **Commercial or Freeware?**   Freeware
>
> **URL:**   www.hoobie.net/mingsweeper/index.html

NOTE

MingSweeper is a network reconnaissance tool. It is designed for scanning large address spaces and for high-speed node discovery and identification. It is capable of doing ping sweeps, reverse DNS sweeps, TCP scans, and UDP scans as well as OS and application identification.

SNMP Scanning

> **Tool Name:**   SolarWinds Network Management Toolset
>
> **Developer:**   SolarWinds.net Network Management

Platform/OS: Microsoft Windows

Commercial or Freeware?   Commercial

URL: www.solarwinds.net/Toolsets.htm

NOTE

SolarWinds toolset is much more than a simple SNMP scanner. Considering how much functionality this application suite provides, it could be considered a one-stop shop when it comes to network management and troubleshooting.

Tool Name: Snscan (v.1.05)

Developer: McAfee (formerly FoundStone)

Platform/OS: Microsoft Windows

Commercial or Freeware?   Freeware

URL: www.foundstone.com/resources/proddesc/snscan.htm

NOTE

Snscan is a decent SNMP scanning tool but limited in its capabilities and information it provides.

Tool Name: GetIF (v.2.3.1)

Developer: Philippe Simonet

Platform/OS: Microsoft Windows

Commercial or Freeware?   Freeware

URL: www.wtcs.org/snmp4tpc/getif.htm

NOTE

This is an excellent freeware SNMP tool for MS Windows. Very handy and easy to use.

Tool Name: Braa (v.0.8)

Developer: Mateusz "mteg" Golicz

Platform/OS: Linux, FreeBSD, OpenBSD

Commercial or Freeware?   Freeware

URL: http://s-tech.elsat.net.pl/braa/

NOTE

Braa is a mass SNMP scanner. What separates this tool from the rest is the way it handles multiple queries simultaneously. According to the author of this tool, it is able to scan dozens or even hundreds of hosts simultaneously, in a single process.

Braa implements its own SNMP stack and requires a system that implements BSD sockets and supports POSIX syscalls.

Enumeration and Banner Grabbing

Tool Name: Winfingerprint (v.0.6.2)

Developer: Vacuum

Platform/OS: Microsoft Windows

Commercial or Freeware?   Freeware

URL: http://winfingerprint.sourceforge.net

NOTE

Winfingerprint is a host/network enumeration and scanning tool. It is capable of the following scan types: TCP, UDP, ICMP, RPC, SMB, and SNMP. If you ant to do TCP SYN scans, you must have WinPcap installed as well. Otherwise the scans will be nonblocking connect() based.

Tool Name: NBTScan (v.1.5.1)

Developer: Alla Bezroutchko (Inetcat.org)

Platform/OS: Microsoft Windows NT/2000/XP, OS X, Linux, Solaris, FreeBSD, OpenBSD, HP-UX, AIX

Commercial or Freeware?   Freeware

URL: www.inetcat.org/software/nbtscan.html

This is an easy-to-use NetBIOS scanner. It is used for enumerating resources available via NetBIOS on the network.

Tool Name: Xprobe2 (v.0.2.2)

Developer: Fyodor Yarochkin and Ofir Arkin

Platform/OS: Linux, Solaris, FreeBSD, OpenBSD, NetBSD

Commercial or Freeware? Freeware

URL: http://sys-security.com/index.php?page=xprobe

Xprobe2 is a remote active OS fingerprinting tool. It does its OS fingerprinting a bit differently than other tools. Xprobe2 relies on fuzzy fingerprint matching, guesswork (based on probabilities), simultaneous multiple matches, and a signature database.

Tool Name: hping2 (v.2.0.0–rc3)

Developer: Lead Maintainer: Salvatore Sanfilippo (see www.hping.org/authors.html for additional contributors)

Platform/OS: Linux, OS X, Solaris, FreeBSD, OpenBSD, NetBSD

Commercial or Freeware? Freeware

URL: www.hping.org

hping2 is a command-line-oriented TCP/IP packet assembler and analyzer. Hping2 supports the following protocols: ICMP, TCP, UDP, and RAW-IP. Additionally, it has a *traceroute* mode. Hping2 has so many features, it would take up too much space to list them all. Note: hping3 is in development.

Tool Name: Netcat (*NIX: v1.10, Windows: v1.11)

Developer: Hobbit

Platform/OS: Linux, Solaris, SunOS, OS X, AIX, HP-UX, Irix, Ultrix, BSDi, FreeBSD, NetBSD, OpenBSD, UnixWare, NeXT, Microsoft Windows

Commercial or Freeware?   Freeware

URL: www.vulnwatch.org/netcat/

NOTE

Netcat is *essential* for every INFOSEC toolbox. There's a reason people call it the "Swiss army knife of TCP/IP"—it can do so much. Read up on this tool and you will see how useful it is. Simply put, Netcat is a UNIX utility for reading and writing data across network connections, using TCP or UDP for its protocol. Netcat can act as a client *or* a server and can be used directly or accessed via programs or scripts. Flexibility is the best word to describe Netcat.

Wireless Enumeration*

Tool Name: Kismet

Developer: Kismetwireless.net

Platform/OS: Linux (preferred), OS X, FreeBSD, OpenBSD, NetBSD, and limited support on Microsoft Windows

Commercial or Freeware?   Freeware

URL: www.kismetwireless.net/

NOTE

Kismet is a passive wireless network detector, protocol analyzer, and intrusion detection system. Kismet works with any wireless card that supports raw monitoring mode (rfmon). Kismet can capture and analyze 802.11a, 802.11b, and 802.11g traffic. Kismet on Windows works only with remote captures, since there are no public rfmon drivers for Windows (win32). Furthermore, Kismet on Windows requires Cygwin to provide the necessary POSIX layer.

Tool Name: Netstumbler

Developer: Marius Milner

Platform/OS: Microsoft Windows 2000/XP/2003, PocketPC 2002, 2003

Commercial or Freeware?   Freeware (not open source)

URL: www.stumbler.net (Netstumbler forums: http://www.netstumbler.net)

NOTE

Netstumbler is a Microsoft Windows-only wireless network detector. It is free but not open source. It's a very popular freeware wireless network detector and does its job pretty well. But unlike Kismet, Netstumbler isn't passive. It uses active probing to detect wireless networks.

Tool Name: Airsnort

Developer: Snax

Platform/OS: Linux, Microsoft Windows

Commercial or Freeware?   Freeware

URL: http://airsnort.shmoo.com/

NOTE

Airsnort is a wireless network tool designed to recover wireless encryption keys. Airsnort passively monitors for wireless transmissions, and when it has enough packets gathered, it computes the encryption key (in less than a second!). Airsnort requires approximately 5–10 million encrypted packets to guess the encryption key.

Tool Name: AiroPeek NX

Developer: WildPackets

Platform/OS: Microsoft Windows XP (SP1), 2000 (SP3)

Commercial or Freeware?   Commercial

URL: www.wildpackets.com/products/airopeek/airopeek_nx/overview

NOTE

AiroPeek NX is an expert wireless network analyzer that provides expert diagnostic tools for troubleshooting and managing your wireless infrastructure. AiroPeek can do site surveys, wireless LAN analysis, wireless LAN monitoring, and application layer protocol analysis.

Vulnerability Scanning

Tool Name: Nessus (v.2.2.4)

Developer: Renaud Deraison

Platform/OS:

Commercial or Freeware? Freeware

URL: www.nessus.org

NOTE

Nessus is probably the most popular open source vulnerability scanner in use today. It is used for remote vulnerability scanning and can be used for local host scanning too. It has an up-to-date CVS/CAN-compliant vulnerability database and built-in scripting capabilities (via NASL), and each security test is written as a plug-in in NASL, so you are able to view the code being executed and modify it to fit your needs or the needs of the organization you are evaluating. There are over 6000 plug-ins (vulnerability checks) available with the default install of Nessus.

Tool Name: NeWT (v.2.1)

Developer: Tenable

Platform/OS: Microsoft Windows

Commercial or Freeware? Commercial

URL: www.tenablesecurity.com

NOTE

NeWT stands for *Nessus Windows Technology*. As the name states, this is a version of Nessus built to run on Microsoft Windows platforms. It has the same capabilities and checks as Nessus.

Tool Name: Retina (v5.2.12)

Developer: eEye

Platform/OS: Microsoft Windows

Commercial or Freeware? Commercial

URL: www.eeye.com/html/products/retina/

NOTE

Retina is a really good vulnerability scanner, but it is commercial and somewhat pricey. It has an excellent vulnerability database, and the reporting capabilities are much more flexible than in previous versions.

Tool Name: SAINT (v.5.8.4)

Developer: Saint Corporation

Platform/OS: UNIX, Linux, OS X, FreeBSD, Solaris, HP-UX 11

Commercial or Freeware?   Commercial

URL: www.saintcorporation.com/saint/

NOTE

SAINT stands for *Security Administrators Integrated Network Tool*. SAINT is a vulnerability assessment tool that is also CVE/CAN compliant (as well as IAVA). This tool is excellent for measuring compliance (for example, for GLBA, SOX, and HIPAA), and the reporting capabilities are quite good.

Tool Name: VLAD the Scanner (v.0.9.2)

Developer: BindView

Platform/OS: Linux, OpenBSD, FreeBSD, OS X

Commercial or Freeware?   Freeware

URL: www.bindview.com/Services/RAZOR/Utilities/Unix_Linux/vlad.cfm

NOTE

VLAD is an open source vulnerability scanner that tests for the SANS Top 10 vulnerabilities (http://www.sans.org/top20/top10.php). VLAD requires several Perl modules: LWP::UserAgent, HTTP::Request, HTTP::Response, Net::DNS::Resolver, IO::Socket, IO::Pty, IO::Stty, Socket, Net::SNMP, Net::Telnet, Expect, File::Spec, and Time::HiRes.

Tool Name: LANGuard Network Security Scanner (v6.0).

Developer: GFi

Platform/OS: Microsoft Windows

Commercial or Freeware?   Commercial

URL: www.gfi.com/lannetscan/

NOTE

LANGuard NSS is primarily a Microsoft Windows vulnerability scanner, but GFi recently added some Linux checks/scans to the product. LANGuard NSS is an excellent vulnerability scanner and enumeration tool for Microsoft Windows platforms. Not only does it do vulnerability scanning and enumeration activities, but it can handle patch management as well.

Tool Name: Typhoon III

Developer: NGS Software

Platform/OS: Microsoft Windows NT/2000/XP

Commercial or Freeware?   Commercial

URL: www.nextgenss.com/typhon.htm

NOTE

Typhoon is another vulnerability scanner that provides much of the same information as other scanners, but it goes about it differently; using NGS's spidering technique. Typhoon is a high-speed scanner and can do application-level checks as well (such as cross-site scripting attack checks and SQL injection checks).

Host Evaluation

Tool Name: CIS Benchmark Tools/Scripts

Developer: Center for Internet Security (CIS)

Platform/OS: Microsoft Windows NT, 2000, 2000 Pro, 2000 Server, 2003 Server, and XP Pro; OS X, FreeBSD, Solaris 2.5.1–10, Linux, HP-UX, AIX, wireless networks, Cisco IOS Router, Cisco PIX, Oracle Database 8a, 9a, and 10g, and Apache Web Server

Commercial or Freeware?   Free for noncommercial use

URL: www.cisecurity.org/benchmarks/

NOTE

The CIS Benchmark Tools measure the assessed system or application against widely accepted security benchmarks and best-practice security configuration for computers connected to the Internet.

Tool Name: Microsoft Security Baseline Analyzer (v.1.2.1)

Developer: Microsoft

Platform/OS: Microsoft Windows 2000, XP and 2003

Commercial or Freeware? Freeware

URL: www.microsoft.com/technet/security/tools/mbsahome.mspx

NOTE

The Microsoft Baseline Security Analyzer (MSBA) is an easy-to-use tool that helps determine the security state of the evaluated machine, in accordance with Microsoft security recommendations, and offers remediation guidance.

Tool Name: HFNetChk / HFNetChkPro (v.5.0)

Developer: Shavlik

Platform/OS: Microsoft Windows 2000, XP and 2003

Commercial or Freeware? Commercial (demo available)

URL: www.shavlik.com/hf.aspx

NOTE

Though HFNetChkPro is listed as a patch management solution, it is also very good at checking for vulnerabilities and missing patches and security updates and provides a method for mitigating many issues remotely. That's why we listed this tool in the Host Analysis section—it covers more baseline activities in this section.

Network Device Analysis

Tool Name: Firewalk (v5.0)

Developer: Mike Schiffman

Platform/OS:

Commercial or Freeware?   Freeware

URL: www.packetfactory.net/firewalk/

NOTE

Firewalk is an active reconnaissance network security tool that attempts to determine what layer 4 protocols an IP forwarding device will allow to pass through. Firewalk is designed for testing firewalls and other IP forwarding devices. Building Firewalk requires libnet 1.1.x, libpcap, and libdnet.

Tool Name: RAT (Router Audit Tool)

Developer: CIS (Center for Internet Security)

Platform/OS: Microsoft Windows, UNIX, Linux

Commercial or Freeware?   Free for noncommercial use

URL: www.cisecurity.org/rat/

NOTE

The Router Audit Tool from CIS can download the configuration from the device to be evaluated (router, PIX firewall) and check the configuration against the settings defined in the provided benchmarks. RAT provides a list of all the rules to be checked, along with a pass/fail score for each, the raw overall score, the weighted score (scale of 1–10), and a list of IOS/PIX commands that will correct the issues identified.

Password-Compliance Testing

Tool Name: Brutus (v.AET2)

Developer: HooBie

Platform/OS: Microsoft Windows

Commercial or Freeware?   Freeware

URL: www.hoobie.net/brutus/

NOTE

Unsure whether this application is still in development. It's a remote password cracker.

Tool Name: L0phtCrack (v.5.0)

Developer: Symantec (formerly @Stake)

Platform/OS: Microsoft Windows

Commercial or Freeware?   Commercial

URL: www.atstake.com/lc/

NOTE

LophtCrack (LC5) has been around for quite some time and is very well known. LC5 can test the password strength of Windows and UNIX passwords. Now LC5 comes with tables of precomputed password hashes, which makes the password-testing phase go quicker.

Tool Name: OPHCrack (v.2.0)

Developer: Philippe Oechslin

Platform/OS: Microsoft Windows, Linux

Commercial or Freeware?   Freeware

URL: http://ophcrack.sourceforge.net/

NOTE

OPHCrack is also referred to as the "time-memory tradeoff cracker." It uses precomputed hash tables loaded into memory to dramatically speed the password-cracking process. OPHCrack can obtain the password hash in any one of three ways: through the encrypted SAM file, through the local SAM file, and through the remote SAM file.

Tool Name: John the Ripper (v.1.6)

Developer: Openwall Project

Platform/OS: UNIX (11 flavors), Microsoft Windows, OS X, Linux, BeOS, FreeBSD, OpenBSD, NetBSD

Commercial or Freeware?   Freeware

URL: www.openwall.com/john/

NOTE

John the Ripper is a fast password cracker that was developed for the task of detecting weak UNIX passwords. Since then, John the Ripper has expanded to test not only UNIX passwords (several of the most common crypt() password hash types) but Kerberos AFS and Microsoft Windows NT/2000/XP/2003 LM hashes as well. Contributors to the project have submitted patches to test the password strength of several applications and services.

Application-Specific Scanning

Tool Name: WebInspect

Developer: SPI   Dynamics

Platform/OS: Microsoft Windows 2000/XP/2003

Commercial or Freeware?   Commercial

URL: www.spidynamics.com/products/webinspect/

NOTE

WebInspect is an application security assessment tool. It identifies vulnerabilities at the Web application layer. WebInspect is great for measuring compliance, making Web application vulnerability assessments, or checking the configuration of a Web application. SPI Dynamics provides the industry's largest Web application vulnerability database with WebInspect.

Tool Name: AppDetective

Developer: Application Security Inc.

Platform/OS: Microsoft Windows 2000/XP/2003

Commercial or Freeware?   Commercial

URL: www.appsecinc.com/products/appdetective/

NOTE

AppDetective is a network-based vulnerability scanner for database applications. It supports the scanning of MySQL, Oracle, Sybase, IBM DB2, MSSQL, Oracle Application Server, and Lotus Notes/Domino. AppDetective allows you to assess the three primary application tiers: Web front-end, application/middleware, and back-end database. AppDetective locates, examines, reports, and fixes security holes and configuration issues.

Tool Name: Wikto (v.1.6)

Developer: SensePost

Platform/OS: Microsoft Windows

Commercial or Freeware?   Freeware

URL: www.sensepost.com/research/wikto/

NOTE

Wikto is a port to Microsoft Windows of the tool Nikto (www.cirt.net/code/nikto.shtml). Wikto has three main sections of functionality: back-end miner, Nikto-like functionality, and Googler. It is a Web server scanner that performs comprehensive tests against Web servers for multiple issues. Including over 3,200 potentially dangerous files/CGI/scripts, it obtains the versions on over 625 servers and version-specific problems on over 230 servers.

Something to keep in mind: Neither Nikto or Wikto are stealthy at all.

Tool Name: Achilles

Developer: Robert Cardona of Systegra

Platform/OS: Microsoft Windows

Commercial or Freeware?   Freeware

URL: www.mavensecurity.com/achilles

NOTE

Achilles is a general-purpose Web application security assessment tool. Achilles acts as a HTTP/HTTPS proxy that permits the user to intercept, log, and modify Web traffic on the fly.

Tool Name: IKE-Scan (v.1.7)

Developer: NTA Monitor Limited

Platform/OS: Linux, FreeBSD, OpenBSD, NetBSD, Solaris, OS X, HP-UX, Microsoft Windows (via Cygwin)

Commercial or Freeware?   Freeware

URL: www.nta-monitor.com/ike-scan/

NOTE

The IKE-scan tool scans IP addresses for VPN servers by sending a specially crafted IKE packet to each host within a network. Most hosts running IKE will respond, identifying their presence. The tool then remains silent and monitors retransmission packets. These retransmission responses are recorded, displayed, and matched against a known set of VPN product fingerprints.

Tool Name: kold (v.1.9)

Developer: FX

Platform/OS: Requires the OpenLDAP libraries

Commercial or Freeware?   Freeware

URL: www.phenoelit.de/kold/

NOTE

kold, or Knocking on LDAP's Door, is a dictionary attack against an LDAP server. It queries the LDAP server, dumps all users from a given DN, and tries to find the password for each user account. The newest version includes Windows 2000 AD attacks and a list of default DNs to attack.

Tool Name: SPIKE Proxy (v.1.4.8)

Developer: Immunity

Platform/OS: Linux, Microsoft Windows

Commercial or Freeware?   Freeware

URL: www.immunitysec.com/resources–freesoftware.shtml

NOTE

SPIKE Proxy is a tool for looking at application-level vulnerabilities in Web applications. It covers such things as SQL injection and cross-site-scripting attacks, but it's written in a completely open Python infrastructure, so it's customizable for Web applications that other tools break on.

Network Protocol Analysis[1]

Tool Name: Ethereal (v.0.10.11)

Developer: Gerald Combs and the Ethereal dev community

Platform/OS: Microsoft Windows 98/ME/2000/XP/2003, Linux, Solaris, OS X, BeOS, FreeBSD, OpenBSD, NetBSD, AIX, HP-UX

Commercial or Freeware?   Freeware

URL: http://ethereal.com/

NOTE

Ethereal is probably the most popular open source network protocol analyzer. It can dissect over 680 protocols and has a very comprehensive feature-set. Ethereal is the network protocol analyzer of choice for many folks.

Tool Name: Ettercap (v.NG-0.7.3)

Developer: Alberto Ornaghi and Marco Valleri

Platform/OS: Linux, OS X, Solaris, FreeBSD, OpenBSD, NetBSD, Microsoft Windows 2000/XP/2003

---

[1] Network sniffing has privacy issues in that all cleartext protocols are visible. The organization might not want you to see their data "up close and personal."

Commercial or Freeware?   Freeware

URL: http://ettercap.sourceforge.net/

> **NOTE**
>
> Ettercap is a suite for conducting man-in-the-middle attacks on local area networks (LANs). Ettercap provides for the capture of live connections, content filtering on the fly, and several other interesting features. It supports active and passive protocol dissection and has many features that contribute to the network and host analysis portions of evaluation efforts.

Tool Name: Sniffer (v.4.7.5)

Developer: Network General

Platform/OS: Microsoft Windows NT, 2000, XP

Commercial or Freeware?   Commercial

URL: www.networkgeneral.com

> **NOTE**
>
> Network General's Sniffer is one of the more well-known commercial network protocol analyzers. This product has been around for a long time and provides excellent expert decodes and analysis. The Network General Sniffer product line consists of Sniffer Distributed, Sniffer Portable, Sniffer Mobile, Sniffer Voice, and Sniffer Wireless.

Tool Name: EtherPeek NX (v.3.0.1)

Developer: WildPackets

Platform/OS: Microsoft Windows 2000, XP

Commercial or Freeware?   Commercial

URL: www.wildpackets.com/products/etherpeek/etherpeek_nx/overview

> **NOTE**
>
> EtherPeek NX claims to be the first network protocol analyzer to offer both expert diagnostics and frame decoding in real time during packet capture. It is fast and accurate, and the interface is easy to navigate. WildPackets offers four different protocol analyzers: EtherPeek NX, EtherPeek SE, EtherPeek VX, and EtherPeek for Mac.

Tool Name: Snoop

Developer: Sun Microsystems

Platform/OS: SunOS, Solaris

Commercial or Freeware?   Freeware (comes with the OS)

URL: N/A

NOTE

Snoop is a network analysis tool that comes with the Solaris operating system. Snoop captures packets from the network and displays their contents. If you are working on a Solaris machine, Snoop is essential.

Tool Name: Tcpdump (v.3.8.3)

Developer: Originally Lawrence Berkeley National Lab (LBNL); now maintained at Tcpdump.org

Platform/OS: UNIX, Linux, *BSD, OS X, Microsoft Windows

Commercial or Freeware?   Freeware

URL: www.tcpdump.org

NOTE

Tcpdump, simply put, dumps traffic from the network. It prints out the packet headers on the monitored network interface. You can also match on Boolean expressions or pipe the output to "grep." It is a very flexible and easy-to-use network troubleshooting tool.

Technical Evaluation Plan Outline and Sample

The Technical Evaluation Plan (TEP) plays a critical role in meeting a customer's needs and expectations. The TEP should be organized as a logical document to provide the greatest value to the customer.

The following outline introduces the TEP format and is intended to provide a guide for the development of a flexible evaluation plan. It can be tailored and formatted to meet your or your customer's needs.

I. **Important Evaluation Points of Contact**   POC name, phone number, and e-mail address.

II. **Methodology Overview**   Describe the methodology to be used to conduct the evaluation, and identify the specific evaluation tools to be used during the evaluation process.

III. **Organizational and System Criticality Information**   A representation of the information criticality for each organizational system, determined by discussion with the customer. Utilize information from the IAM where applicable. Include organizational criticality matrix, system criticality matrix, impact value definitions, and system descriptions.

IV. **Detailed Network Information**   Include physical boundaries, identified subnets and IP ranges, detailed network diagrams, and contact information for system owners and administrators.

V. **Customer Concerns**   Include applicable customer concerns from the IAM and additional technical customer concerns.

VI. **Customer Constraints**   Include applicable customer constraints from the IAM and additional technical customer constraints.

VII. **Rules of Engagement**   This section provides the agreed-on approach and limitations related to the execution of the evaluation.

VIII. **Internal and External Customer Requirements**   Evaluation team's scanning IP addresses, immediate contact information for assessment team, notification of personnel on assessment activities, CIRT coordination for test purposes.

IX. **Coordination Agreements**   This is a catchall area. How detailed does the customer want the recommendations to be? Will the standard low level for the executive summary and the midlevel for technical staff be acceptable, or will more detail be required? What are the deliverables? Discuss other agreements not yet addressed.

X. **Letter of Authorization**   Include the approved letter of authorization.

XI. **Timeline of Events**   This is a sequence of important events and their associated dates, such as the date of the receipt of the request letter, date of proposal or contract, customer coordination dates, planned internal and external dates, and report delivery date.

NOTE

The document included in this appendix is only a *sample* and should not be considered a complete or comprehensive template.

Sample Technical Evaluation Plan

Technical Evaluation Plan (TEP)

Prepared for

Organized Union for Critical Healthcare

June 4, 2008 (V3.2)

Prepared by:

Security Rocks

Anywhere USA

I. Evaluation Points of Contact

The individuals in Table 27.1 are the primary points of contact for the evaluation effort with OUCH.

Table 27.1 Points of Contact

Name	Position	Phone	E-Mail Address	Organization
Ima Hungry	Team Leader	555-1111 × 6543	ima.hungry@ srocks.com	Security Rocks
Bob Smith	Team Member	555-1111 × 6511	bob.smith@ srocks.com	Security Rocks
Wilma Flintstone	Team Member	555-1111 × 6522	stoneages@ srocks.com	Security Rocks
Bean Counter	CIO	555-1212 × 1234	dstove@ouch. com	OUCH
Penny Frugal	MIS Manager	555-1212 × 1412	pfrugal@ouch. com	OUCH
Shirley Secure	Risk/Security Specialist	555-1212 × 1321	sbutto@ouch. com	OUCH
Mia Trusta	ISP Contact	555-3456	trustmia@ 3rdparty.com	Third party

II. Methodology Overview

The methodology used to conduct this evaluation is the National Security Agency's INFOSEC Evaluation Methodology (IEM). The IEM is an internationally recognized methodology for which the application is not dependent on a specific industry or type of client. This methodology incorporates a customer's requirements and needs along with regulatory requirements for the specific client. The IEM is technically focused and provides 10 IEM baseline activities that should be included as part of any evaluation. Ultimately, after completion of the 10 baseline activities, the customer is provided with an understandable and usable set of recommendations that, when implemented, will improve the overall security of the organization. The technical tools that are used to collect INFOSEC information will be a combination of commercial, freeware, and shareware tools. These tools will assist in gaining a larger cross-section of the system/network status and provide a means to identify and eliminate false positives throughout the evaluation process. The 10 IEM baseline activities used to collect the information about the organization's current technical security posture are:

- Port scanning
- SNMP scanning
- Enumeration and banner grabbing
- Wireless enumeration
- Vulnerability scanning
- Host evaluation
- Network device analysis
- Password compliance testing
- Application-specific training
- Network sniffing

III. Organizational and System Criticality Information

The organizational and system criticality information is gained from either a previously conducted INFOSEC assessment utilizing the IAM or during the pre-evaluation phase of the IEM. In our case, this information came from an IAM conducted in June 2004. The information was reviewed with the OUCH staff to ensure its currency.

The OUCH Mission

The Organized Union for Critical Healthcare (OUCH) has been contracted by Our Lady of Perpetual Pain Memorial Hospital to handle their information processing. The facility can house up to

5000 patients at a time. The day-to-day operations require automated information systems support for tracking and controlling information that includes admitting/releasing patients, administering medications, scheduling surgeries, feeding patients, tracking traffic to and from the hospital morgue, and various other information for doctors, nurses, and staff. OUCH has developed a single networked system that allows all the functions to be performed from terminals throughout the facility. The connectivity includes all databases and applications so that the information is readily available no matter where in the facility it is needed.

OUCH Impact Definitions

The following are OUCH's definitions for the impact to their organization should they lose confidentiality, integrity, and/or availability (CIA) of their critical information:

- **High**   Loss of public trust, preventable significant patient injury or death or loss of patient for greater than 30 minutes, or regulatory takeover and fines in excess of $10,000 per day.

- **Medium**   Loss of some public confidence, preventable minor patient injury or loss of patient for greater than 10 minutes but less than 30 minutes, or regulatory fines in excess of $5,000 but less than $10,000 per day.

- **Low**   Minor bad press, loss of patient for less than 10 minutes, or regulatory fines less than $5,000 per day.

NOTE

These impact definitions are overly simplified for the purpose of providing an example and should not be used as serious definitions. Real-world examples encompass much greater detail than these and focus on setting levels and thresholds for occasions when certain criteria are met to move to the next higher or lower level of impact.

OUCH Organizational Criticality

OUCH has identified four primary areas of critical information the organization is concerned about in terms of protecting and safeguarding their customers, employees, and the OUCH business. These four areas of critical information are scheduling, monitoring, patient information, and corporate information. Based on meetings with OUCH key staff, Security Rocks developed the OUCH organizational information criticality matrix (OICM) shown in Table 27.2, which was approved by OUCH staff. This matrix takes into account the OUCH impact definitions mapped against the critical information in relationship to CIA.

Table 27.2 The OUCH OICM

Critical Information Area	Confidentiality	Integrity	Availability
Scheduling	Medium	High	Medium
Monitoring	High	High	High
Patient Information	High	High	Medium
Corporate Information	High	High	Medium
Overall	**Confidentiality**	**Integrity**	**Availability**
OUCH Information Criticality	High	High	High

System Information Criticality

OUCH identified only one system that processes, transmits, or stores the critical information identified during this process. OUCH has developed a single networked system that allows all the functions to be performed from terminals throughout the facility. The connectivity includes all databases and applications so that the information is readily available no matter where in the facility it is accessed. The system information criticality matrix (SICM) in this case will exactly match the OICM (see Table 27.3). If another system were to be identified that processes any one or more pieces of critical information, another SICM would be created to reflect this situation.

Table 27.3 The OUCH SICM

Critical Information Area	Confidentiality	Integrity	Availability
Scheduling	Medium	High	Medium
Monitoring	High	High	High
Patient Information	High	High	Medium
Corporate Information	High	High	Medium

IV. Detailed Network Information

The OUCH day-to-day operations require automated information systems support for tracking and controlling information that includes admitting/releasing patients, administering medications, scheduling surgeries, feeding patients, tracking traffic to and from the hospital morgue, and various other information for doctors, nurses, and staff. The network diagram in Figure 27.1 provides the logical layout of the existing network at OUCH. This information has been confirmed with OUCH as being current.

Figure 27.1

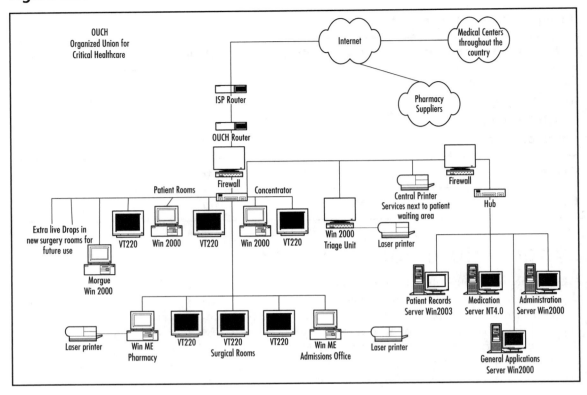

V. Customer Concerns

OUCH has expressed the following concerns related to the organization's security operations:

- Being compliant with new regulatory requirements such as the Health Information Portability and Accountability Act (HIPAA)
- Contract renewal with Our Lady of Perpetual Pain is 12 months away
- Avoid bad publicity related to security incidents
- Wireless networking security (just installed the system)
- Management of user accounts
- Training of medical staff on need for security (they say it's inconvenient)

VI. Customer Constraints

OUCH has identified the following constraints related to the evaluation:

- Hardware and network owned by Our Lady of Perpetual Pain; OUCH only provides the management
- Hardware located across three buildings but on one campus
- OUCH needs 24/7 operations, cannot lose connectivity while the evaluation is under way

VII. Rules of Engagement

This section provides the agreed-on approach and limitations related to the execution of the evaluation.

- OUCH will provide Security Rocks with a cubicle, phone access, fax access, printer access, and network access for the internal portion of the evaluation.

- OUCH will provide Security Rocks with internal static IP addresses for the duration of the internal evaluation.

- Security Rocks will do external scanning from the following IP addresses: 10.10.10.10 and 10.10.10.100.

- OUCH documentation is allowed to leave the OUCH site as long as it remains under reasonable protection.

- Security Rocks may only scan during nonpeak operating hours, which have been identified as Monday through Friday from 6:00 P.M. to 6:00 A.M. and on weekends.

- OUCH will notify the OUCH Computer Incident Response Team (CIRT) of the testing schedule to avoid issues with false identification of malicious activity. (This is not a penetration test; prior notice to CIRT will occur.)

- The team lead (Ima Hungry) will be Security Rocks' primary point of contact at all times. Her cell phone number is 555-1234. This contact should be used if there is an emergency or if questions arise.

- Shirley Security will be OUCH's primary emergency point of contact (cell 555-1212) for any issues while the testing is under way.

- OUCH has approved the following tools for use in the evaluation: SAINT, Nessus, Whisker, SPIDynamics WebInspect, Ethereal, and LC5. Configurations will disable all denial-of-service testing and shall limit active strings to no more than five on any given IP to avoid system impact. OUCH has not excluded any specific tools from the scanning process but has asked to be notified prior to running a tool not on the approved list.

VIII. Internal and External Customer Requirements

Evaluation team's scanning IP addresses, immediate contact information for assessment team, notification of personnel on assessment activities, CIRT coordination for test purposes. This section describes network connections and IP addresses, facilities, scan windows, relevant IP addresses or subnets to access, and immediate administrator contact information for the customer.

IX. Coordination Agreements

This section provides additional detail not previously covered by any other TEP section.

Level of Detail of Recommendations

OUCH has a competent technical staff that can implement recommendations without a step-by-step "how to" provided in the final report. Therefore, the standard medium level of detail will be used in the recommendations.

Deliverables

OUCH and Security Rocks have agreed to the following deliverables:

- Technical Evaluation Plan Draft
- Technical Evaluation Plan Final
- Weekly Status Report
- Preliminary Findings Presentation (PowerPoint)
- Final Report Draft
- Final Report Final

Other Agreements

No other evaluation agreements have been requested or implied.

X. Letter of Authorization

Attached is the OUCH signed letter of authorization. A copy of this document will be in the possession of all Security Rocks staff while the evaluation is being conducted.

XI. Timeline of Evaluation Events

OUCH and Security Rocks have identified the following timeframes for completion of the evaluation effort:

- **Initial Engagement Agreement**   May 15, 2005 – Complete
- **Pre-Evaluation Begins**   May 24, 2005 – Complete
- **TEP Prepared and Approved**   June 4, 2005 – Complete, this document
- **Onsite Evaluation**   June 15, 2005–June 30, 2005
- **Post-Evaluation**   July 1, 2005–July 23, 2005
- **Final Report Draft Delivered**   July 24, 2005
- **OUCH Comment on Final Report Draft**   Due NLT July 31, 2005
- **Final Report Delivered**   August 7, 2005

## Part 3

Business Continuity & Disaster Recovery

## Chapter 28

Business Continuity and Disaster Recovery Overview

Solutions in this chapter:

- **Business Continuity and Disaster Recovery Defined**

- **Components of Business**

- **Cost of Planning versus Cost of Failure**

- **Types of Disasters to Consider**

- **Business Continuity and Disaster Recovery Planning Basics**

☑ **Summary**

Introduction

Powerful Earthquake Triggers Tsunami in Pacific. Hurricane Katrina Makes Landfall in the Gulf Coast. Avalanche Buries Highway in Denver. Tornado Touches Down in Georgia. These headlines not only have caught the attention of people around the world, they have had a significant effect on IT professionals as well. As technology continues to become more integral to corporate operations at every level of the organization, the job of IT has expanded to become almost all-encompassing. These days, it's difficult to find corners of a company that technology does not touch. As a result, the need to plan for potential disruptions to technology services has increased exponentially. Business continuity and disaster recovery (BC/DR) plans were certainly put to the test by many financial firms after the terrorist attacks in the United States on September 11, 2001; but even six years later, there are many firms that still do not have any type of business continuity or disaster recovery plan in place. It seems insane not to have such a plan in place, but statistics show that many companies don't even have solid data backup plans in place. Given the enormous cost of failure, why are many companies behind the curve? The answers are surprisingly simple. Lack of time and resources. Lack of a sense of urgency. Lack of a process for developing and maintaining a plan. This part, the following nine chapters, will help you overcome some of those challenges.

A study released by Harris Interactive, Inc. in September 2006 indicated that 39% of CIOs who participated in the survey lacked confidence in their disaster readiness. There's good news and bad news here. The bad news, clearly, is the fairly high lack of confidence in disaster plans in firms with revenues of $500M or more annually. The good news is that only 24% of CIOs in 2004 felt their disaster plans were inadequate. Although the *increase* in lack of confidence may appear to be a negative, it also highlights the increasing awareness of the need for comprehensive disaster readiness and a more complete understanding of what that entails. Back in 2000, some companies might have thought a "good" disaster readiness plan was having off-site backups. After the terror attacks, bombings, anthrax incidents, hurricanes, and floods that hit the United States (and other major incidents worldwide) since that time, most IT professionals now understand that off-site backups is just a small part of an overall strategy for disaster recovery.

In today's environment, no company can afford to ignore the need for BC/DR planning, regardless of the company size, revenues, or number of staff. The statistics on the failure rate of companies after a disaster are alarming (discussed later in this chapter) and alone should serve as a wake up call for IT professionals and corporate executives. Granted, the cost of planning must be proportionate to the cost of failure, which we'll address throughout Part 3 of this book.

Let's face it—very few of us want to spend the day thinking about all the horrible things that can happen in the world and to our company. It's not a cheery subject, one that most of us would rather avoid—which also helps explain the glaring lack of BC/DR plans in many small and medium companies (and a share of large companies as well). Stockholders of publicly held companies are increasingly demanding well thought-out BC/DR plans internally as well as from key vendors, but in the absence of this pressure, many companies expend their time and resources elsewhere. Business continuity and disaster recovery planning projects have to compete with other urgent projects for IT dollars. Unless you can create a clear, coherent, and compelling business case for BC/DR, you may find strong executive resistance at worst or disinterested apathy at best.

You may wonder why you should have to champion this cause and push for some sort of budget or authorization to create such a plan. The truth is that you shouldn't, but since a disaster will probably have a disproportionately high impact on the IT department, it's very much in your own self-interest to try to get the OK to move forward with a planning project.

In this chapter, we'll look at some of the impediments to BC/DR planning as well as some of the compelling reasons why spending time, money, and staff hours on this is well worth the expenditure. We'll provide you with specific, actionable data you can use to convince your company's executive or management team to allocate time and resources to this project. We'll also look at the different types of disasters that need to be addressed—they're not all obvious at first glance. Finally, we'll provide a framework for your BC/DR planning.

Business Continuity and Disaster Recovery Defined

Before we go too far, let's take a moment to define *business continuity* and *disaster recovery*. These two labels often are used interchangeably, and though there are overlapping elements, they are not one and the same. *Business continuity planning* (BCP) is a methodology used to create and validate a plan for maintaining continuous business operations before, during, and after disasters and disruptive events. In the late 1990s, BCP came to the forefront as businesses tried to assess the likelihood of business systems failure on or after January 1, 2000 (the now infamous "Y2K" issue). BCP has to do with managing the operational elements that allow a business to function normally in order to generate revenues. It is often a concept that is used in evaluating various technology strategies. For example, some companies cannot tolerate any downtime. These include financial institutions, credit card processing companies and perhaps some high volume online retailers. They may decide that the cost for fully redundant systems is a worthwhile investment because the cost of downtime for even five or ten minutes could cost millions of dollars. These companies require their businesses run continuously, and their overall operational plans reflect this priority. Business continuity has to do with keeping the company running, regardless of the potential risk, threat, or cause of an outage.

Continuous availability is a subset of business continuity. It's also known as a zero-downtime requirement, and is extremely expensive to plan and implement. For some companies, it may be well worth the investment because the cost of downtime outweighs the cost of implementing continuous availability measures. Other companies have a greater tolerance for business disruption. A brick-and-mortar retailer, for example, doesn't necessary care if the systems are down overnight or during nonbusiness hours. Although it may be an inconvenience, a retailer might also be able to tolerate critical system outages during business hours. Granted, every business that relies on technology wants to avoid having to conduct business without that technology. Every business that relies on technology will be inconvenienced and disrupted to some degree to have to conduct business without that technology. The key driver for business continuity planning is how much of a disruption to your business is tolerable and what are you able and willing to spend to avoid disruption? If money were no issue, every business using technology would probably elect to implement fully redundant, zero-downtime systems. But money *is* an issue. A small retailer or even a small online company can ill afford to spend a million dollars on fully redundant systems when their revenue stream for the year is $5 to $10 million. The cost of a business disruption for a company of that size might be $25,000 or even $100,000 and would not justify a million dollar investment. On the other hand, a million dollar investment in fully redundant systems for a company doing $5 billion annually might be worth it, especially if the cost of a single disruption would cost more than $1 million. As previously mentioned, your BC/DR plan must be appropriate to your organization's size, budget, and other constraints. In later chapters, we'll look at how to assess the cost of disruption to your operations so you can determine the optimal mitigation strategies.

Disaster recovery is part of business continuity, and deals with the immediate impact of an event. Recovering from a server outage, security breach, or hurricane all fall into this category. Disaster recovery usually has several discreet steps in the planning stages, though those steps blur quickly during implementation because the situation during a crisis is almost never exactly to plan. Disaster recovery involves stopping the effects of the disaster as quickly as possible and addressing the immediate aftermath. This might include shutting down systems that have been breached, evaluating which systems are impacted by a flood or earthquake, and determining the best way to proceed. At some point during disaster recovery, business continuity activities begin to overlap, as shown in Figure 28.1. Where to set up temporary systems, how to procure replacement systems or parts, how to set up security in a new location—all are questions that relate both to disaster recovery and business continuity, but which are primarily focused on continuing business operations. Figure 28.1 shows the cycle of planning, implementation, and assessment that is part of the ongoing BC/DR maintenance cycle. We'll discuss this in more detail later, but it's important to understand how the various elements fit together at the outset.

Figure 28.1 Business Continuity and Disaster Recovery Planning, Implementation, and Revision Cycle

Components of Business

There are many ways to break down the elements of business, but for the purposes of BC/DR planning, we'll use three simple categories: people, process, and technology. As an IT professional, you understand the importance of the interplay among these three elements. Technology is implemented by people using specific processes. The better defined the processes are, the more reliable the results (typically). Technology is only as good as the people who designed and implemented it and the processes developed to utilize it. As we discuss BC/DR planning, we'll come back to these three elements repeatedly. When planning for BC/DR, then, we have to look at the people, processes, and technology of the BC/DR planning itself as well as the people, processes, and technology of the plan's implementation (responding to an emergency or disaster). Let's look at each of the three elements in this light. Figure 28.2 depicts the relative relationship of people, process, and technology in most companies.

Figure 28.2 How People, Process, and Technology Interact

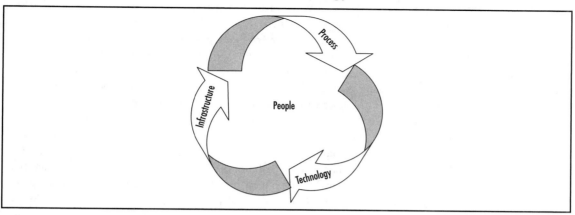

People in BC/DR Planning

Clearly, people are the ones who do the actual planning and implementation of a business continuity and disaster plan, but there are many aspects to the people element that often are overlooked during the planning process. In this section, we'll look at a few of the commonly missed elements. However, as you read through this, keep your own organization in mind. Every company is different and therefore every BC/DR planning process will have to be different. A small retail outlet's IT planning for BC/DR will be very different from a call center or a manufacturing facility. There is no "one size fits all" approach, so although we can point out the major elements, you'll need to fill in the specifics for your company.

Let's begin with one very interesting fact. According to a recent IBM white paper, 80% of all data losses are human-caused. That's the *people* part of the equation. People are responsible for designing, implementing, and monitoring processes intended to safeguard data. However, people make mistakes every single day. As one National Transportation Safety Board official put it when interviewed about a plane crash, there are multiple layers of systems in place to ensure the plane doesn't crash, but sometimes a series of bad choices or errors leads to a critical event. The same is true with your IT infrastructure. Hopefully, there are multiple layers of processes, procedures, and cross-checks in place to prevent human-caused disasters, but sometimes these fail. If 80% of data loss is attributable to human error, that leaves 20% of data loss attributable to other causes such as equipment malfunction, natural disasters, and terrorism (which is in the same general category of "human-caused" but at a different level altogether).

We'll discuss the specific steps needed to form your BC/DR plan later in this chapter and in subsequent chapters. Now, though, let's look at some general guidelines. Your BC/DR plan requires people from across your organization in order to be effective. As an IT professional, you may know who has which laptop and how applications are secured across the network, but you very likely have no idea how things run, on a day-to-day basis, in other parts of the company. You may not know what data, what processes, what parts of the technology puzzle are critical to various departments. You certainly will not know critical dates, key milestones, or other information that people in other departments know. To create a plan without input from across the company almost guarantees the plan will fail—if not during the planning stage then certainly in the implementation stage. Getting key people in the company to participate in the planning helps you develop a more robust plan and, just as important, helps you identify the key people needed to implement the plan, should that become necessary.

Another key aspect to people in BC/DR planning is that it's critical to remember that if a disaster hits your company, people will have a wide variety of responses. Some people, especially those with emergency preparedness training, will rise to the occasion and start taking effective action through leadership roles. Others will be completely overwhelmed and unable to act effectively (or at all). Understanding this is important when creating your BC/DR plan because it will not be "business as usual" when an emergency hits. Emotional and physical stress may reduce effectiveness of even the most prepared individuals, so working with this assumption will help ensure a successful plan and more importantly, a successful outcome when the plan needs to be implemented.

As an IT professional, it may be that you do not have primary responsibility for your company's BC/DR planning. That said, you may be the only person in the company that recognizes the need for this type of planning. Therefore, you may have to champion the cause and rally resources to get the planning going. If you're a senior manager in a small or medium-sized firm, you may, in fact, be the go-to resource for both the planning and implementation of a BC/DR plan. Regardless of your role, we will discuss the broader implications of BC/DR throughout so that you can either include them yourself or ensure that others in the organization are including them. Our objective is to help you create an effective BC/DR plan for IT, but that cannot be accomplished in a vacuum. It will need to be integrated across the organization in order to be effective when it counts—when things go wrong.

Process in BC/DR Planning

Process in BC/DR planning also has two phases: the planning phase and the implementation phase. The processes your company uses to run the day-to-day business are key to the long-term success of the business. These processes were developed (and hopefully documented) in order to manage the recurring business tasks. Things outside the normal recurring tasks typically are handled as exceptions until they recur often enough to create a new process, and the cycle continues. If your business is suddenly hit by a disaster—fire, flood, earthquake, chemical spill, and such—your processes are immediately interrupted. How quickly you recover from this and either reimplement or reengineer your processes to get the business up and running again relies on the processes delineated in your BC/DR plan. By developing a process for handling various types of emergencies and disasters, you can rely on these when people are stressed out and business is interrupted. Trying to develop effective processes in the face of an emergency is usually not at all successful. Having simple, well-tested processes to rely on when disaster strikes is often the difference between eventual recovery and business failure.

As you'll see later, the processes used by the company in day-to-day operations need to be evaluated and prioritized. What processes are critical to the ability of the company to conduct operations? What processes can be put on hold during an emergency? Circumstances surrounding the emergency certainly come into play—time of year, where you are in various business cycles, and so on. When looking at your payroll process during an emergency, for example, you'll also need to understand the normal timing of these processes within the company. A power outage right *after* payroll is processed may be far less critical than a power outage just before payroll is processed. As we look at processes within the company, we'll keep these kinds of timing issues in mind. However, this is another justification for having a wide array of interests represented during the BC/DR planning phases, so you can evaluate these aspects and factor them in appropriately. Let's look at an example from the Human Resources department. In Figure 28.3, you can see a portion of a simple flowchart that HR could construct to assist both IT and HR in the aftermath of a disaster.

Figure 28.3 Sample Human Resources Process Flowchart

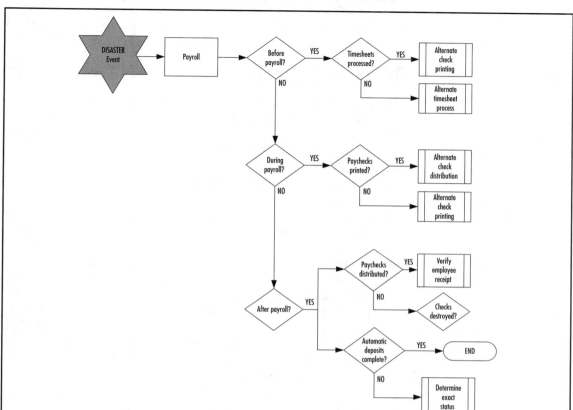

As you can see in Figure 28.3, there are defined steps in your company's payroll process. These steps become the framework for a decision flowchart to help HR staff determine what steps need to be taken in the aftermath of a significant event with regard to payroll processing. The first step is to determine the exact status of payroll—did the disaster hit before, during, or after payroll? Then, depending on the status, what would be the appropriate steps to take and how can these steps be taken if key systems are down? Although you might think that payroll should be the least of your company's concerns in the immediate aftermath of a disaster, your company's employees will think otherwise. They may need to seek alternate accommodations such as staying in a nearby hotel or they may need to purchase food, medical supplies, or transportation. They may be relying on that very paycheck in order to provide them adequate funds to pay rent or eat that week. Without addressing payroll needs, your company will be unnecessarily increasing the stress levels for all employees, even those who may not be dependent on receiving those funds immediately. Perhaps more importantly, this issue might not matter on the first day or two after an event, but what happens if your company's building was destroyed in a fire and it will be weeks before you resume normal operations?

This process clearly helps HR understand the current process they use and what processes may be needed in the event of a minor, major, or catastrophic event. It might also help them see ways to improve processes in their current day-to-day operations since few of us ever take the time to map out key processes. You don't need to use flowcharts, though they do provide a good visual, but you do need to find some standardized method of evaluating processes and creating contingency plans. We'll discuss this later in more detail.

Technology in BC/DR Planning

Technology is clearly the piece of the puzzle that you, as an IT professional, will be most familiar with. As you participate in your company's BC/DR planning (or head it up, as previously mentioned), you will be in the best position to understand what happens with various technology components during various types of disasters. Part of the reason for BC/DR planning is to look at your use of technology and understand which elements are vulnerable to which types of disasters. A power outage, for example, impacts all the technology in a building. Suppose you have battery backup or generators for lights and certain computers but no power for air conditioning in Miami in July? Timing and circumstance come into play and working closely with your facilities person, for example, will help you look at the plan in a more holistic (and realistic) manner than you might on your own.

As we look at BC/DR planning, we'll also look at various vulnerabilities of different technologies and discuss, in broad strokes, strategies, tools, and techniques that might be helpful to mitigate or avoid some of these risks. We won't delve into specific technology solutions as those are ever-evolving, but we will look at common methods used today and what needs to be considered as you look at your unique circumstances. In some cases, your BC/DR planning may yield information you can use to make the business case for why the firm should authorize the purchase of a particular technology or service. For example, if you've been trying to get funding approved for colocation services to speed up user access to critical business data across a wide geographic area, you can use the results of your BC/DR planning to add to the business case. Clearly, colocation can be part of a solid business operations management strategy and can also be an integral part of a business continuity and disaster recovery plan. When you can add strength to your business case, you're more likely to find executive support for funding.

As an IT professional, you will need to work closely with members of other departments to understand the technology needs in an emergency—not only what technology is needed to get the business back up and running (business continuity) but also what is needed to manage the crisis. These are two distinct (but probably overlapping) concerns that should be assessed and addressed by your plan.

Looking Ahead...

Business Continuity and Disaster Recovery Planning Resources

There are numerous organizations, worldwide, that focus on business continuity planning and/or disaster recovery planning. Many of these organizations provide training, methodologies, and certification tracks. For anyone interested in becoming a focused specialist in one of these areas, you would do well to investigate these various organizations. If you're involved with business continuity or disaster recovery planning and want to stay current on the latest trends from the field, be sure to bookmark a few of these sites. We've listed just a few here, but a quick Internet search will yield more resources.

The Business Continuity Institute (UK): http://www.thebci.org/

DRI International (US): http://www.drii.org/DRII/index.htm

GlobalContinuity.com (South Africa): http://www.globalcontinuity.com/

Department of Homeland Security Business Readiness (US): http://www.ready.gov/business/index.html

Disaster Recovery Journal (US): http://www.drj.com/

The Cost of Planning versus the Cost of Failure

Companies typically look at their "top" line and their "bottom" line. Top line is revenue, and many publicly held companies chase after top-line growth, meaning they want to aggressively increase revenues. This often means they are grabbing a larger share of the market or are pushing the market to expand. It does not, however, account for the cost of doing so. If you pick up another $100 worth of business but it costs you $125 to do so, you may have top-line growth, but your bottom line (profitability) will suffer. In some cases, this makes sense in the short term—you can capture market share that becomes profitable at some later point in time. Other companies look just for bottom-line growth—revenues minus expenses (and other things) equals profit—so if a company's revenues minus expenses is greater than last year's, it means that the company has generated a larger profit (generally speaking). However, if your company is losing market share and lays off three-quarters of the workforce and closes four locations, things are not going well, even if you end up with short-term bottom line growth. Therefore, most companies look for a balance between top and bottom line growth.

You might be wondering what all this has to do with BC/DR planning, so let's connect the dots. The cost of planning might be significant in terms of staff time, resources, and the like, and might impact your bottom line (depending on many factors). If your company is concerned only with top line growth, they may not be overly concerned with the cost of a BC/DR project plan. You may also find that key customers desire or demand that your company have such a plan, so you might argue that creating this plan could contribute to top-line growth. If you're able to capture a new customer because you have a BC/DR plan, that's clearly going to help your case. On the other hand, if you work for a company strictly concerned with bottom-line growth, you may have a much bigger challenge. You can certainly see if having such a plan would improve operational efficiencies or land you a new client. Short of that, you might have to point out the potential hit to the bottom line if you experienced a disaster without a BC/DR plan in place. However, you can be sure that failure to mitigate the impact of a disaster will absolutely impact both your top and bottom lines, and will likely put your company's very existence at peril. Therefore, when you compare the cost of planning to the cost of failure, there is only one approach that makes business sense—and that is to plan to the extent it makes financial sense to do so.

Disasters can result in enormous losses—financial, investor confidence, and corporate image. It can also lead to serious legal issues, especially when more and more private data is being captured, stored, and transmitted across the very public Internet. These losses and legal challenges can have a small, short-term impact but more often than not, they have a significant, long-term impact, and in some cases imperil the very existence of the company.

In companies that do have some sort of disaster plan in place, it more than likely resides in or originates from the IT department. IT staff have long understood the business implications of the outage of even one server (phones ringing off the hook is one measure of the importance of even a single server or business application). However, it's also clear that IT equipment—routers, servers, switches, hubs, firewalls, and more—are just part of the overall business equation. Certainly, without these technology components in place, business as usual will be limited at best. However, without also considering the way in which your company earns income and the way in which it conducts its business, all the IT planning in the world won't protect a company if a disaster strikes. A holistic approach to the business is needed in order for any business continuity and disaster recovery planning to be realistic and effective. This involves every key area of your business and the various stakeholders that represent those business units. It won't help if you can keep your Web site's e-commerce functions up and running if your warehouse operations have come to a screeching halt.

Most IT departments have some minor disaster recovery procedures in place. If your firm performs backups of critical data on servers, you have basic disaster recovery capabilities, assuming those backups are taken off-site or are stored (or performed) remotely. Though you might think this is quite obvious, you would probably be surprised to know how many companies (and IT professionals themselves) either fail to make backups or fail to store them in a safe location. However, most small, medium, and certainly most large companies at least have a reasonable data backup solution in place. This, in and of itself, is a good start but does not constitute a BC/DR plan. For example, if your area was flooded and you were unable to enter your building, could the company continue operations? If this is one location out of many, perhaps. If this is your only location, perhaps not. It depends, of course, on the nature of your business. If you have a warehouse full of product that is also underwater, you might have contracted with your suppliers to direct ship to customers in the event of a disaster. Did you also develop a plan for how customers would place orders or how you would track and invoice those orders? Clearly, the technological component is a critical link in the chain, but it's not the only link. Throughout the remainder of this part, we'll look not only at the IT components but the other non-IT elements that need to be in place as you develop your BC/DR plan so that you don't overlook any crucial aspects of the business.

Disaster planning is about recovering after an event, but business continuity planning is not just about recovering from outages of key technical components, it is a way of looking at and managing business. BC planning is about looking ahead and seeing what could potentially disrupt your company's operations and then finding ways to mitigate or avoid those events. It really is a coordinated and integrated approach that spans the entire company and all its operations. As in any other area of life, one or two poor decisions can usually be corrected or overcome, but when things get stressful it's highly likely that a string of poor decisions could literally spell disaster for your company. The point of BC/DR planning is to help avoid those pitfalls that can be avoided and to provide a sane, rational, well thought-out approach to managing the disaster when an event does occur. If the number of poor decisions can be held to a minimum, there is a stronger likelihood that you will avoid compounding the problem and perhaps even be able to come out of it quickly and in relatively good shape.

Human nature is a funny thing. When we're young, we think nothing bad can ever happen to us. When we're older, we may we think we can play the odds. As trite as it may sound, failing to plan is planning to fail. In an *Entrepreneur* magazine article in 2003, author Dan Tynan included a quote that sums up the situation with small businesses. "Small companies often spend more time planning their company picnics than for an event that could put them out of business," explains Katherine Heaviside, principal of Epoch 5, a Huntington, New York, public relations firm that specializes in crisis communications (http://www.entrepreneur.com/magazine/entrepreneur/2003/april/60242.html).

In a study of companies that experienced a major data loss without having a solid BC/DR plan in place, 43% never reopen, 51% will close within two years, and only 6% will survive long-term. (Cummings, Haag & McCubbrey, 2005.). Let's repeat that: only 6% will survive long-term. That's a 94% mortality rate for companies that experience a major data loss. In August 2002, the American Management Association released a study indicating that more than half of the surveyed companies had no disaster recovery or crisis management plan in place. Another report from Gartner, Inc. indicated that less than 10% of small and medium businesses had disaster plans, and that 40% of companies that experience a disaster without a disaster recovery plan will go out of business within five years. Looking specifically at fires, the most common disasters businesses experience, it is estimated that 44% of companies whose premises experience a significant fire do not recover at all, primarily because they have no BC/DR plans in place. The World Trade Center bombing in Manhattan in 1993 resulted in 150 out of the 350 businesses located in the center going out of business—that's about a 42% failure rate. Contrast that with many of the financial firms who had well-developed and tested BC/DR plans that were located in the Twin Towers on September 11, 2001—a majority of them were back up and running within days.

An October 2005 survey by the Advertising Council found that 92% of businesses say it is important to plan for emergencies; 88% agreed having some sort of emergency plan would make sense; 39% said they actually had a plan. What's interesting is that 12% of companies did not think having an emergency plan would make sense. Although the question was not posed to these companies, it would certainly be interesting to understand why these companies feel a plan is not needed. Studies point to the broadly-held but incorrect notion that the time and expense of creating a plan will far outweigh any upside return. However, as you've learned, that's just not true. Many BC/DR planning activities can be accomplished relatively quickly and with little or no funding. If the 12% of companies that feel no need to plan for emergency understood there was an almost even chance the company would go out of business if it did experience an emergency, their thinking might shift.

Small businesses, those most likely to avoid, delay, or short-cut business continuity planning and disaster recovery planning are most susceptible to the long-term impact of emergencies and disasters. Yet, these same small companies are the economic engine of many economies around the world. In the United States, small businesses account for 99% of all employers (that's right, large companies employ 1%), 75% of all new jobs, and 97% of all U.S. exporters. It can therefore be argued that BC/DR planning is extremely important for companies of all sizes, even small companies.

Regardless of the size of your company, the odds are high that if your company experiences any sort of disaster—natural or man-made—it has between a 40 and 50% chance of going out of business as a result. Certainly, the strength of the company, the industry, and other factors come into play when looking at long-term survival of companies hit by disasters, but it's clear that if your company doesn't have a business continuity and disaster recovery plan, it is essentially taking a 50% chance on failing. Without a well-conceived business continuity and disaster recovery plan, that's an enormous gamble to take. It impacts not just the corporate entity itself, but the lives of all the employees and suppliers as well. The ripple effect can be massive and it will impact you, your staff, their families, and the rest of the community.

There are many people who will counter with the argument that a company could spent a lot of money on planning and *never* have to deal with a disastrous event. True. Many people drive their entire lives and never have a single auto accident, but they probably all have auto insurance. Clearly, the question is one of balance. If your company does $50M in annual revenue, a cost of $1M for BC/DR planning is very little to pay for that type of insurance. If your company does $1.25M annually, you probably don't need to (and can't) spend $1M on BC/DR planning. Clearly, the cost of planning must be balanced with the cost of doing nothing and the risk of going out of business. Like auto insurance, you certainly hope you'll never need to use it, but you don't want to get caught without it either. Ultimately, it's less expensive to expend an appropriate and proportionate amount of time and resources to create and maintain the plan than to face even one disaster without a plan. For example, if your company is in the Gulf States region of the United States, you need to have an emergency plan in place in the event a hurricane hits the area, as has happened repeatedly in the past few years. On the other hand, if your firm is located in the desert Southwest of the United States, you don't need to plan for hurricanes but you will have to plan for power outages and lightning strikes. Even though this is obvious, it bears repeating because you don't need to overengineer your BC/DR plan. You will need to evaluate the potential impact to your company of various types of events and then create a plan for just those events most likely to occur and most likely to have a critical impact on operations. When you do this, you use your planning time effectively, and the cost of planning will certainly be far lower than creating an all-encompassing plan or the cost of facing a disaster empty-handed.

While we're on this topic, let's take a moment to look at how the cost of planning (investment) and the cost of failure (loss) impact the people, processes, and technology of a company. The impact, though not immediately apparent, is significant and worth exploring briefly.

WARNING

A bad plan or incomplete plan is often worse than no plan at all. An ill-conceived or incomplete plan may lead people to mistakenly assume that emergency and contingency plans are in place when, in fact, they are not. A false sense of security can lead to an even bigger problem than the disaster event itself precipitates. Remember, if a disaster strikes your area, emergency personnel will be going to hospitals, nursing homes, day care centers, and schools to help. Your business will be pretty low on the list of priorities, so you need to be prepared to take matters into your own hands. If employees falsely believe the company is prepared for disaster, you're facing a whole host of problems. A poorly conceived plan may also lead to significant financial penalties and legal liabilities since it might be argued you had the opportunity to plan and failed to do so. We'll explore some of the potential legal issues later.

People

Spending time and resources to plan for emergency responses, from an organizational perspective, is an excellent investment for many reasons. One that might not be immediately evident is that when employees understand that the company has contingency plans in place, they tend to feel that the company is organized, positioned for success, and concerned for their safety. It provides an opportunity for the company to demonstrate its commitment to its employees' well-being, which can help retain key employees. Companies that run in a perpetual ad hoc manner are often more at risk of losing key employees for this same reason. Will a solid BC/DR plan keep employees happy? Of course not, but it does contribute to an overall environment that fosters respect and concern for employee well-being.

In addition, a crisis that is well-managed by the company is less likely to cause key employees to seek employment elsewhere. A well-managed event also keeps employees calm and focused so business can get back to usual as quickly as possible. A well-managed crisis can also enhance a company's reputation, leaving it stronger than it was before the incident. One example of excellent crisis management (not IT-related) was when the Extra Strength Tylenol pain product was contaminated with cyanide in 1982. The company quickly asked retailers to pull *all* of its products from store shelves until it could understand the nature and extent of the "attack." The year prior to the incident, Tylenol had about 35% of the billion dollar analgesic market, or about $350 million in annual sales. Immediately afterward, its market share was 0%. However, within four years, the company has regained almost all its former market share (98% of precontamination sales revenues). Although this example is outside the domain of IT professionals, it points to the opportunity a company has to manage an emergency. It gets one shot to get it right and its future reputation rides on the decisions made during the crisis. Today, the "Tylenol incident" as it is sometimes referred to, is held up as an excellent example of how a company can and should respond to a crisis.

The effect of stress on people during an emergency cannot be overemphasized. Having a well-thought-out and well-rehearsed BC/DR plan will reduce that stress considerably. In turn, people will be able to function again and return to their jobs more quickly. Thus, the very act of planning how to take care of the people in your organization during an emergency can quickly impact the company's ability to return to normal operations—and revenue generation. BC/DR planning, then, directly impacts the top and bottom line and the cost of planning will quickly offset the cost of an unmanaged event.

Process

BC/DR planning can provide an opportunity for a company to evaluate and improve its business processes. As your project team (we'll discuss the team later in the section) evaluates business processes as it relates to BC/DR, it might discover new ways to streamline operations. For example, in planning for a major disruption due to a natural disaster, your team might uncover new methods while determining "bare minimum" requirements. If a process takes 20 steps and four departments now, you might find that the pared down approach discussed in a post-disaster scenario would actually work well all the time. When you're forced to look at everything from the ground up (which is what happens when you're dealing with a disaster), you discover that you don't need all the bells and whistles. This can sometimes translate into streamlined processes that can be incorporated into the day-to-day operations.

In addition, documenting critical business processes can truly mean the difference between life and death for the corporate entity. If you are unable to resume some sort of operations in a reasonable time frame after a disaster, your company is not likely to survive. The cost, then, may be the ultimate corporate cost—failure to exist. This is not only unfortunate for the corporate shareholders (whether publicly or privately held), but it impacts the lives of all the company's employees and their families and takes a toll on the community as well. The ripple effect is enormous and should not be quickly discounted.

Technology

Scrambling to deal with technology issues once a disaster has hit is guaranteed to cost your firm more than if you have a solid plan in place. For example, if you need temporary computing facilities, it's less costly to have a contingency contract in place beforehand than to desperately call various facilities looking for assistance while the smoke clears. Not only will you be in a better frame of mind emotionally in the planning phase (vs. the reaction phase after a disaster), you'll be in a much stronger position to negotiate the details of a contingency contract.

In addition, if the disaster impacts other companies, it might also create a competitive situation that drives the price for technology components up. Again, being able to calmly negotiate and procure commitments for emergency services beforehand almost always generates lower costs when those contracts are activated by an emergency. Finally, it is customary for most companies to provide service to contract holders before they provide service to noncontract holders. If you're currently a customer, you're going to get service before the person who just called in today looking for assistance. So, prenegotiating anticipated emergency services can generate lower costs and a higher ROI on your BC/DR planning process.

Common Challenges...

Dealing with Optimists and Pessimists

When developing your BC/DR plan, you have to find some balance between the optimists and the pessimists. The optimists will dismiss many potential risks and dangers and will often minimize the potential impact of events. On the other hand, pessimists believe every possible danger is likely to occur and to have a much larger impact than it likely would should it occur. Part of your job is to try to remain balanced and realistic, especially when it comes to developing mitigation strategies. Additionally, many BC/DR planners place a disproportionate amount of time and attention on major catastrophes. As you'll see throughout this section, we first look at the most common scenarios and then turn our attention to major events. The thinking is this: If you spend time to prepare for the common, smaller events, you can then perform a second round of planning for major catastrophes, or create two different planning teams. If you're ready for the next Category 5 hurricane but you fail to have a solid plan in place for a workplace fire (the most common business emergency), you'll be doing yourself, your employees, your company, and your community a disservice. So, in the end, you will need to balance the need for disaster planning with the financial and organizational constraints of your company and focus on the smaller, more likely events first. This can best be accomplished by listening to both the optimists and the pessimists and finding acceptable middle ground.

Types of Disasters

So far, we've spent time talking about *why* it's important to plan for disasters. Now, let's turn our attention to the types of disasters that might occur. The reason for this is that there may be a few you don't think of immediately (or at all) that might potentially impact your company. Although this list is extensive, it is certainly not exhaustive. Throughout this section, we'll continually give examples of a variety of disasters because we want to make sure you cover all your bases and think through all potential threats to your company. You and your BC/DR planning team should be sure to look at your company's specific location(s), your industry, and your operations to determine exactly what types of disasters and events could have a significant impact on you. This list should be a good starting point and might also spark ideas about other elements that could be essential to include in your company-specific plan. Not only is it important to review the entire list and be sure you've covered your bases, you also have to start with the more likely events and move outward from there. As mentioned, fire is the most common business emergency companies face. So, if you don't have an established fire plan, you're really a sitting duck. As you'll see in Chapter 30, risk assessment should be holistic and broad in scope, but it should also then narrow down your focus to those risks that are most likely to occur and that will have the biggest impact on your company's operations.

As an IT professional, your job may be limited to dealing with just the technology aspects of the BC/DR plan, but you need to be aware of all the various threats because your company will be relying on you to understand and address the potential impact of threats on the company's technological operations. Technology is so pervasive in most organizations these days that IT will be one of the key drivers in both the planning phase and the implementation/recovery phase. Therefore, it's critical that you and your IT team be well-versed in all aspects of BC/DR planning.

Threats or hazards come in three basic categories:

- Natural hazards
- Human-caused hazards
- Accidents and technological hazards

Clearly, natural hazards are ones that can sometimes be anticipated and the effects mitigated; other times, they come without warning and must be responded to. Human-caused hazards also can sometimes be anticipated and other times come as a surprise. Finally, accidents can happen and accidents span the range from minor to major to catastrophic. Included in this category are what often are termed "technological threats" because they involve the failure of buildings or infrastructure technology. Let's look at these categories in more detail.

Natural Hazards

Natural hazards are the types of disaster events that usually come immediately to mind when we mention business continuity and disaster recovery planning. In the past several years, the news has been full of headlines about natural disasters. Clearly, the tsunami that hit Indonesia the day after Christmas in 2005 was a catastrophic event. The hurricanes that hit the Gulf Coast of the United States, most notably Hurricane Katrina, also caused catastrophic failures. Keep in mind that natural hazards can be minor, major, or catastrophic in nature, so your planning should account for these three potential threat levels. In addition, natural hazards can be anticipated or unanticipated.

The tsunami that hit Indonesia was anticipated to the degree that scientists around the world measured the power of the undersea earthquake. It was unanticipated in that few knew that a massive wall of water would hit various shorelines from Thailand to Kenya within a matter of hours. Hurricane Katrina was, for all intents and purposes, anticipated, but grossly underestimated by the public and private sector. Regardless, the impact in both cases was total devastation. There are numerous cases of companies and organizations that had disaster plans that went into limited effect because, prior to these events, no one could realistically imagine that level of devastation. In the United States, the Federal Emergency Management Agency (FEMA) was widely criticized for failing to effectively implement and manage a disaster plan in New Orleans in the aftermath of Hurricane Katrina. The news was rife with heart-rending stories of human suffering and death due to massive confusion and disorganization. Individual companies were fairly powerless in this situation, but companies that had plans in place for evaluation, remote data backup, storage, and such undoubtedly got back up on their feet faster and more effectively than those that did not have such plans in place.

Cold Weather Related Hazards

- Avalanche
- Severe snow
- Ice storm, hail storm
- Severe or prolonged wind

Warm Weather Related Hazards

- Severe or prolonged rain
- Heavy rain and/or flooding
- Floods
    - Flash flood
    - River flood
    - Urban flood
- Drought (can impact urban, rural, and agricultural areas)
- Fire
    - Forest fire
    - Wild fire—urban, rural, agricultural
    - Urban fire
- Tropical storms
- Hurricanes, cyclones, typhoons (name depends on location of event)
- Tornado
- Wind storm

Geological Hazards

- Earthquake
- Tsunami
- Volcanic eruption
    - Volcanic ash
    - Lava flow
    - Mudflow (called a *lahar*)
- Landslide (often caused by severe or prolonged rain)
- Land shifting (*subsidence* and *uplift*) caused by changes to the water table, man-made elements (tunnels, underground building), geological faulting, extraction of natural gas, and so on

Although this list does not contain every possible variation, it should give you a good starting point for determining which hazards are applicable to your geographic locations. Remember that BC/DR planning should involve people across your organization and that includes various locations. If you have offices in London, Mumbai, Perth, and New York, each location should be represented in order to effectively review potential hazards based on the geography of the area, the key business functions at each location, and other factors we'll discuss in subsequent chapters.

Human-Caused Hazards

Human-caused hazards, also known as *anthropogenic* hazards, are a bit more diverse in their nature. Some of the items on the list may surprise you. Since most are intentional, we will just list them without categorization.

- Terrorism
    - Bombs
    - Armed attacks
    - Hazardous material release (biohazard, radioactive)
    - Cyber attack
    - Biological attack (air, water, food)
    - Transportation attack (airports, water ports, railways)
    - Infrastructure attack (airports, government buildings, military bases, utilities, water supply)
    - Kidnapping (nonterrorist)
- Bomb
    - Bomb threat
    - Explosive device found
    - Bomb explosion

- Explosion
- Fire
    - Arson
    - Accidental
- Cyber attack
    - Threat or boasting
    - Minor intrusion
    - Major intrusion
    - Total outage
    - Broader network infrastructure impaired (Internet, backbone, etc.)
- Civil disorder, rioting, unrest
- Protests
    - Broad political protests
    - Targeted protests (specifically targeting your company, for example)
- Product tampering
- Radioactive contamination
- Embezzlement, larceny, theft
- Kidnapping
- Extortion
- Subsidence (shifting of land due to natural or man-made changes causing building or infrastructure failure)

Accidents and Technological Hazards

Accidents and technological hazards often are related to man-made hazards but differ only in that they are usually unintentional. If intentional, they fall under the category of man-made hazards. Regardless of the category in which we place them, they are issues that can be overlooked in the planning process.

- Transportation accidents and failures
    - Highway collapse or major accident
    - Airport collapse, air collision, or accident

- Rail collapse or accident
- Water accident, port closure
- Pipeline collapse or accident
- Infrastructure accidents and failures
    - Electricity—power outage, brown-outs, rolling outages, failure of infrastructure
    - Gas—outage, explosion, evacuation, collapse of system
    - Water—outage, contamination, shortage, collapse of system
    - Sewer—stoppage, backflow, contamination, collapse of system
- Information system infrastructure
    - Internet infrastructure outage
    - Communication infrastructure outage (undersea cables, satellites, etc.)
    - Major service provider outage (Internet, communications, etc.)
    - Systems failures
- Power grid or substation failure
- Nuclear power facility incident
- Dam failure
- Hazardous material incident
    - Local, stationary source
    - Nonlocal or in-transit source (e.g., truck hauling radioactive or chemical waste crashes)
- Building collapse (various causes)

The list of disasters here is enough to make you want to hide your head under a pillow for a while and wait for the images to fade. Unfortunately, these are all incidents that can and have occurred, and the best way to deal with these kinds of unimaginable uncertainties is to imagine them and develop a methodical plan for handling them. To be sure, if one of these more major events occurs and you have to deal with it, it's unlikely you'll follow your plan to the letter. It's impossible to imagine everything you'll be experiencing and have to deal with until you're in the middle of it. Having a solid plan in place that's been tested and practiced will reduce the stress of the situation and increase the likelihood that you've anticipated the major issues you'll need to address. In dire circumstances, that can mean the difference between surviving or not, between recovering or not.

Common Challenges...

Corporatewide Participation

Although your specific role in the company may not bear responsibility for business continuity and disaster planning, you may need to lead the charge. As an IT professional, you understand the immediate implications of a power outage or a cyber attack or even a building evacuation on your business. If you're leading the BC/DR planning, you'll need to educate yourself to the larger business issues for two reasons. First, you'll need to understand the broader business issues involved with business continuity and disaster recovery, not just the IT issues. Second and perhaps more important, you'll need to gain executive support for your BC/DR planning initiative. Executive support is key to success for any type of project and this is no exception. If the folks "upstairs" don't support the project, you'll have a hard time gaining the authority, funding, staffing, or resources needed to create a successful BC/DR plan. Going through the motions without creating a workable plan is almost worse than having no plan at all—it may provide a false sense of security to your organization. If or when disaster strikes, your plan has to work, it can't just be words in a document. Gaining executive support, a topic we'll discuss in the next chapter, is key to success, as is participation across the organization.

Electronic Data Threats

Although this area falls under human threats and accidents, we're going to take a moment to delineate in more details some of the threats facing electronic data. Some of these areas are well known to you and some might serve simply as reminders of elements to include in your company-specific BC/DR plan. Attacks to computer systems, networks, and electronic data occur every single day. The question is not if, but when a network will be attacked—internally or externally, intentionally or accidentally. Recall the IBM study mentioned earlier, in which it was estimated that 80% of all data loss is human-caused.

Personal Privacy

Personal privacy is an area that increasingly has been in the spotlight, and with good reason. More and more personal data is stored in electronic format on servers and hard drives around the world. From students' financial aid records to employees' social security numbers, to patients' private health data, to consumers' credit card numbers, the electronic world is afloat with very private data. Clearly, when this data falls into the wrong hands, either intentionally or inadvertently, bad things can and do happen.

Companies in recent years that have failed to safeguard this type of data have faced sometimes daunting charges, including financial ruin, huge and expensive lawsuits, and in some cases, increased regulation from governmental or regulatory agencies. This, in turn, increases the cost of doing business and makes the company that much less competitive in the marketplace. It can throw a company into a death spiral—personal data is compromised, the company receives negative publicity, customers stop doing business with them, legal (or other recovery) expenses skyrocket, and so on until the firm has no choice but to cease operations. Granted, this is the most dire situation but it's also not outside the realm of real possibility for companies that routinely deal with sensitive data. As you develop your BC/DR plan, you'll need to pay special attention to the types of data your company deals with and how those types of data need to be managed, particularly in avoiding or recovering from an incident.

Privacy Standards and Legislation

Privacy standards are constantly evolving, so any very specific information provided here will be dated before long. However, it's worth spending just a bit of time reviewing some of the major privacy standards and legislation in the United States, if for no other reason than to remind you to take a look around your firm and determine what data might need special or additional protection and handling in the event of a disaster or security incident. This list is not exhaustive, but should serve as a good starting point to get you thinking along these lines.

Gramm-Leach-Bliley Act (GLBA)

The Gramm-Leach-Bliley Act (GLBA) was enacted in late 1999 and was intended to enhance competition in the financial services industry. Among other provisions, the GLBA requires financial institutions (and others that operate in the financial services industry) to create and implement policies to protect private information from foreseeable threats in both security and data integrity. GLBA also has provisions requiring financial institutions to develop written security plans detailing how the company plans to protect clients' nonpublic personal information. The plan must include, at minimum, four elements:

- At least one employee assigned to manage the safeguards
- A thorough risk management plan for each department that handles nonpublic information
- A plan to develop, implement, test, manage, and monitor data security
- A process for updating and changing the plan as methods of collecting, storing, transmitting, and managing data change

There are many provisions of the GLBA that you must comply with if you work within the financial industry, and chances are good that if these regulations apply to you, you're already well aware of them. However, if for any reason you believe these regulations may apply to your firm, you should consult with appropriate legal and financial counsel to determine your responsibilities. For additional (general) information on GLBA, you can check out Wikipedia at http://en.wikipedia.org/wiki/Gramm-Leach-Bliley_Act#Privacy; you can also get more formal information on the U.S. government Web site at http://www.ftc.gov/privacy/privacyinitiatives/glbact.html.

Health Insurance Portability and Accountability Act (HIPAA)

Anyone working in the health care industry in the United States is well aware of the Health Insurance Portability and Accountability Act (HIPAA). This regulation creates requirements for health care providers (and others in the health care industry) to protect personal data, especially health care information. It requires companies to create policies and procedures to ensure this data is kept confidential and is shared only with authorized parties. In its original form, it was intended to establish national standards for electronic health care transactions and to ensure the security and privacy of health data. For general information on HIPAA, you can visit Wikipedia at http://en.wikipedia.org/wiki/HIPAA or visit the U.S. government's Health and Human Services (HHS) Web site at this URL: http://www.hhs.gov/ocr/hipaa/.

Common Challenges...

If Disaster Strikes, Will You Still Be Compliant?

It was a major effort for many organizations to become (and remain) compliant when privacy and security regulations went into effect, but can these same companies maintain compliance in the face of disaster? HIPAA and other regulations require that companies plan for foreseeable threats, but it's important to think this all the way through to the practical, day-to-day operations. If, for example, your company is forced to resume operations from alternate locations or with employees working from home, how will your privacy and security plans hold up? Even though you may not be able to address every potential pitfall, you must address privacy and security through your BC/DR plan to the same extent you plan alternative operations. If patient information will be taken by phone and written on paper while computer systems are being reconfigured and communications are being reestablished, for example, how will you protect privacy? Remember that HIPAA and other regulations require you maintain appropriate levels of security at *all times*, not just when everything is humming along just fine.

Although you and your organization may be well-versed in the requirements of regulations that apply to your industry or business sector, also be sure that you include these topic headers in your BC/DR plan so you can remain as compliant as possible in the event of a security incident or natural disaster. At the end of the day, you need to be sure you're addressing the threats most reasonable people could foresee. As an IT professional, you've probably become very well-versed with the requirements that apply to your company and your industry, so be sure to bring this expertise to the table when creating your BC/DR plan and consult with outside experts as needed. The fines and regulatory issues that can result from noncompliance could, in themselves, be a disaster for your firm.

Social Engineering

You're well aware of the potential for social engineering when it comes to protecting network data and maintaining security. However, social engineering takes on a whole new meaning when disaster strikes. The unfortunate truth of the matter is that people don't always "rise to the occasion" when a disaster hits. After Hurricane Katrina, it was widely reported that many people who had no legitimate claim were collecting government payments of various kinds. The information systems and methods of validating legitimate "clients" were clearly impaired. If disaster strikes your firm, what kind of data would someone want to get their hands on and what ruses could they use to gather that information? Remember, during any type of incident—whether a major snow storm, a massive earthquake, or anything in between—people are more emotional and vulnerable. Your employees are only human and may be far more vulnerable to social engineering techniques than they might otherwise be. Your BC/DR plan should certainly take this into account in order to help mitigate the impact on security and data integrity as well as on your company's confidential data and operations as a whole. During your planning phase, focus on the kinds of data that might be of value to outsiders, then focus on the most common or likely social engineering scenarios. If you attempt to build in these safeguards at a time when everyone is relatively sane and rational, there's a much better chance that employees will be able to resist social engineering tactics during a disaster.

Fraud and Theft

It's well known within IT circles that most corporate fraud and theft is committed by company insiders. This means that your first priority during a disaster will be to mitigate opportunities for internal fraud and theft, then look for ways to safeguard against potential external sources. There are numerous types of fraud and theft related to computer and IT technology and unfortunately they are constantly evolving. Whatever threats are delineated in this book will undoubtedly be surpassed by new variations and new schemes within days or weeks. No company can remain completely immune to these threats, but every company can put safeguards in place to prevent the most blatant acts. Next, we've listed a few categories of fraud and theft that you can use as a jumping off point in your planning to assess your company's specific and unique vulnerabilities.

General Business Fraud

This is the catch-all category, and is included first because it is the most common area. Each company has a unique risk profile in this area. It would be well worth your time to look into this for both emergency and nonemergency situations. Unfortunately, without monitoring, any area of business is vulnerable to fraud or theft and there are usually signals along the way that are missed or disregarded for a variety of reasons. Managers become busy and miss signs; analysts make incorrect assumptions or ask the very perpetrators of fraud for additional information. The list goes on. Now, take this and multiply it by a factor of 100, which represents the chaos and stress of an emergency or disaster event. People, processes, and technology are all in disarray during and after an event. Often, people are focusing on short-term safety and survival. Only emergency processes are implemented and normal safeguards may be suspended or simply not viable. Technology is rudimentary, if available at all. This leaves the company wide open to potential fraud and theft during an emergency.

Since every business is unique, there is no one failsafe method of preventing, spotting, or stopping internal fraud or theft. However, there are some general guidelines you can use for both normal and emergency operations.

1. If it seems odd, it is.

2. Evaluate your assumptions.

3. If it can't be tracked, monitored, and accounted for, evaluate the activity.

4. If it falls outside standard operating procedures, scrutinize it.

5. Spot inspections and random detailed reviews on normal activities can reveal problems.

Most of the time, a manager or colleagues can tell when someone is behaving in an odd manner. Even during times of stress and emergency, people typically behave with some consistency. If someone is behaving in an odd manner, investigate it. If a transaction or activity seems odd, investigate it. Turning your back on potential problems can lead to much bigger problems down the road, including legal problems and termination of business operations.

Sometimes an odd activity or behavior, especially during a stressful event or disaster, is written off as being caused by the emergency—and sometimes that's the case. However, rather than assume that is the case, look for evidence that supports or contradicts your assumptions. For example, don't assume someone has authority to remove files, equipment, or assets from the building—look at your disaster recovery plan and determine who actually *is* authorized for these activities. An unauthorized employee could be trying to capitalize on a bad situation, or an outsider could spot an opportunity to turn a quick profit.

Whether in normal operations or in an emergency, your goal should be to ensure that there are processes in place to monitor and track the movement of people, technology, and business assets to the greatest extent possible (within a reasonable limit). Creating a lot of bureaucratic processes causes people to circumvent the system, so be sure that whatever safeguards you have in place are lean and streamlined to the greatest extent possible. If someone is attempting to circumvent operational processes, it should raise a flag. In an emergency or disaster, there may well be exceptions that must be made quickly to ensure the safety of the people and assets of the business. However, if you have emergency processes delineated in your BC/DR plan and you have tested and rehearsed these, the exceptions should be fewer and more reasonable. This can help you and other employees spot unusual activities or behavior, even during a disaster. Often, when a potential thief is directly questioned about an activity, it will cease. Though this is not always the case, it can help thwart these crimes of convenience.

Spot inspections and random data reviews can also be helpful, both during normal operations and emergencies. Smart thieves are good at flying "below the radar" and will work hard to keep up normal appearances; you won't always be alerted to problems by seeing dramatic anomalies. Therefore, it can be helpful to do spot inspections and data reviews. Though you may be limited in your role as an IT member (and not a corporate executive), you can certainly keep an eye out for these issues within your department. For example, perhaps you have an inventory of low-cost spare parts and you see these are being used with a very slight increase in frequency, despite the fact that your company hasn't added any new equipment. At first, you might assume that as the equipment ages, it's very likely to need replacement parts. You could easily dismiss this. However, you could also ask the people who are signing out these parts where the trouble ticket is or where the report is, or which desktop computer this was installed in. Talk with the user whose desktop computer was allegedly worked on—was a technician working on his or her computer? If so, did he or she request it? What was the reported problem? Even though you may have all this data in a trouble ticket, randomly verifying some of these tickets might help you spot a problem. You might discover the parts that were allegedly used are easy to slip into someone's pocket for resale online. Spot checks and random analysis can help prevent this type of fraud and theft. During an emergency, it might be less obvious, but simply keeping your eyes open and asking questions can help. Having easy-to-use processes in place for emergencies can help limit the movement of people, data, and company assets to legitimate purposes.

Remember, your company's data may be of particular interest to employees or competitors, and during times of crisis, standard safeguards may fall by the wayside. What can you do, within the confines of the IT department, to ensure data safety and integrity during an emergency? How can you prevent theft and fraud? What are the likely scenarios to arise and what processes can you use to mitigate or avoid these issues?

Looking Ahead...

IT, Security, Disasters, ...and the Law

One of the emerging trends in IT and IT security is the increased demand that companies secure private data such as social security numbers, credit card numbers, home addresses and phone numbers, financial data, medical data, and more. As the amount of electronic data collected and stored increases, so too does the risk to individuals. Recent headlines are rife with examples of personal data being lost, stolen, hacked, or modified. Companies can no longer say "we did our best" without proving that their best was at least up to current industry standards. Looking ahead, companies can expect three major trends to impact how they manage IT security. These standards will apply during normal business operations and emergencies—companies won't be able to easily blame breaches and theft on emergencies that were foreseeable and manageable, as is the case with many of the disaster events listed earlier in this chapter. These three key trends, which you should monitor for your IT organization, are:

- The continuing expansion of the requirement to provide IT (and data) security
- The emergence of a standard definition of "reasonable security"
- The imposition of the duty to warn

Consumers and regulators alike are raising their expectations regarding IT security, and companies are both legally and ethically bound to make serious, effective efforts to safeguard private data. Emergency and disaster conditions may soften those requirements just a bit, but don't assume your company will be able to hide behind a disaster or event if data is lost, stolen, mishandled, or inappropriately disclosed. If your firm deals with data that is sensitive, confidential, or private in nature, consult with your firm's legal counsel to understand fully the legal and regulatory requirements your firm will be subject to during a crisis, emergency, or disaster. As you've noticed, we've continually emphasized the legal aspects of BC/DR because of the increasing regulation of electronic data.

Managing Access

It doesn't get more basic than this: Managing access to data is the first and most important element of managing data security and integrity. It also has to be an integral part of your BC/DR plan. In the aftermath of a major event, it sometimes becomes a "free for all," with everyone (and no one) in charge. Who should have access to data and systems in an emergency? If you allow only one person that access, what if that one person is on vacation halfway across the world when disaster strikes, or worse, injured during the event and unable to perform his or her duties? Clearly, access that is too restrictive could significantly delay the ability of the company to get back up and running after a disaster or event. The opposite is also a danger—giving half the company the authority to make changes, request access, or manage data could also put the company at risk by creating lack of accountability and certainly a tangled trail to unwind should something go wrong.

In a disaster or emergency, physical access is often one of the areas most likely to be impacted. How can you manage physical access to a building that has one whole side blown off or a building that is structurally unsound? You may not be able to do anything about it when faced with the situation, but if you try to imagine how you would manage it and include that in your BC/DR plan, you may have a chance to reduce or avoid this issue later on.

Beyond physical access are the electronic methods of access control that are well known to IT professionals. Again, you need to take a look at your access control methods in light of various disaster/event scenarios. What are the critical systems, who should have access to them in an emergency, and what (if any) failsafe systems can you put in place so that the right people have access to the data when needed? As you'll see in our BC/DR planning later in this book, one of the most effective methods of planning for these kinds of situations is to develop likely scenarios and work your way through all aspects to ensure your plan is thorough. A good plan provides a solid framework without being either too restrictive or too vague. It's a delicate balance to achieve but it can be done using a logical, consistent project management framework, which we'll discuss in the next chapter and throughout the remainder of this book.

Business Continuity and Disaster Recovery Planning Basics

Your role as an IT professional is unique in BC/DR because on one hand, you are not necessarily responsible for the company's comprehensive BC/DR planning; but on the other hand, technology is so integral to most corporate operations, IT can't be completely separated out as a stand-alone issue. As a result, we will continually address BC/DR in a holistic manner and allow you to determine the most appropriate role for your IT group within your company.

The elements that should be included in your plan will extend beyond the walls of the IT department, so you'll need to form a project team with expertise in several areas. Figure 28.4 shows some of the areas that might be included, depending on the type of products and services your company creates.

Figure 28.4 Elements of a Business Continuity and Disaster Recovery Plan

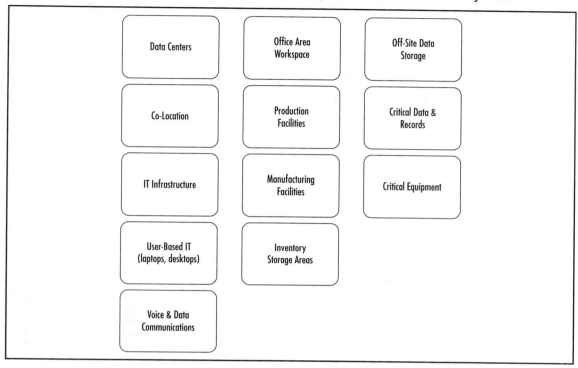

You're no doubt familiar with the concept of *reliable system design* and *single point of failure* when it comes to designing, implementing, managing, and repairing the IT infrastructure for your company. Briefly, these concepts relate to building in redundancies and safeguards so that if one key component fails, the entire company doesn't come to a screeching halt. You probably also understand that having two servers or routers in the same rack leaves your network vulnerable—the single point of failure could be as simple as someone tripping and spilling a large cup of coffee on the rack itself. You might conscientiously make backups, verify the backups and store them securely, but leave them on-site. The single point of failure could be as minor as something falling on the rack holding your tape backups or as major as a serious fire in the server room or building. The reason for discussing this concept at this juncture is that as you look at your business continuity and disaster recovery options, you need to assess your risks with regard to reliable systems and single points of failure. For example, you may want to evaluate your availability solutions as part of an overall business strategy to reduce operational risks, minimize the occurrence and cost of downtime, and maximize data and IT service availability. These availability solutions will also likely impact your compliance with a variety of regulations by providing protection and reliability of information resources as well. Additionally, these solutions will impact your BC/DR risk assessment and planning. If these solutions are not currently in place, this BC/DR planning process may help you build the business case for implementing some of these technologies. If they are currently in place, you can look at them with a fresh perspective to determine how they contribute to an overall business continuity strategy. We'll discuss this in more detail in Chapter 30.

With that, let's look at contingency planning basics: the basic steps to be taken to create a solid BC/DR plan for your company. The basic steps in any BC/DR plan, shown in Figure 28.5, include:

- Project Initiation

- Risk Assessment

- Business Impact Analysis

- Mitigation Strategy Development

- Plan Development

- Training, Testing, Auditing

- Plan Maintenance

Figure 28.5 Business Continuity and Disaster Planning Steps

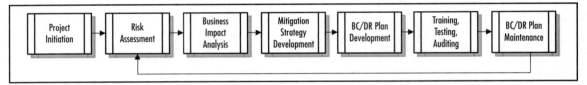

Those of you familiar with project management methodologies will notice the similarity in the BC/DR planning process to PM processes, and with good reason. Creating a BC/DR plan can (and should) be approached as a discrete project that has a defined start, middle, and end. As with many other IT projects, once the BC/DR plan is completed, it must be maintained so that it stays current with changes in the company, its technology, and the broader business landscape. We'll discuss each of the sections here briefly to provide an overview, and we'll delve more deeply into each of these areas in subsequent chapters.

Project Initiation

Project initiation is one of the most important elements in BC/DR planning, because without full organizational support, the plan will be incomplete. As an IT professional, there may be limits to what you can do to create an organizationwide functional BC/DR plan. For example, you may know how to set permissions for a particular business application, but do you really know how users interact with it and what would be required to get the business back up and running with regard to that particular business function? If the application server is destroyed and you have data backups, do you also have a backup server? Do you have a way to allow users to connect to the application securely? Where are users located? How will business resume? Can it resume without that application in the near-term or not? You will not likely be able to answer these questions. It requires the input and assessment from subject matter experts in other departments and divisions. Therefore, getting executive and companywide support for the BC/DR planning process is absolutely key to its success. We'll discuss this in more detail in the next chapter.

Risk Assessment

Risk assessment is the process of sitting down with key members of your company and looking at the potential risks your company faces. These risks run from ordinary to extraordinary—from a fire or minor flood in a server room to a catastrophic loss such as an earthquake or major hurricane and everything in between. Again, as an IT professional, you can certainly lend your expertise to this process by helping define the likely impact to technology components in various types of disasters or events, but you can't do it alone. For example, it's likely that your transportation manager understands the potential business impact of bad weather around the country, not just in your local area. Your marketing manager might best understand the potential business risk of a contaminated product or a Web site breach. Some of these areas may fall into pure business continuity planning and may be more suitable for others in your organization. However, in almost all companies, IT expertise must be included in the business continuity and disaster recovery risk assessment process. In Chapter 30, we'll discuss risk assessment in depth.

Business Impact Analysis

In a sense, this is where "the rubber hits the road." Once you've delineated your risks, you need to turn your attention to the potential impact of these various risks. This is one area that, as an IT professional, you clearly need input from your company's experts. As mentioned earlier, you might understand the technical aspects of an application server going down, but what is the actual business impact, and can that be tolerated? For example, you might determine that your ERP application cannot be down. Period. E-mail and your Web server, however, can go down, even though both events would be disruptive. Once you understand these parameters, you can develop an IT-based strategy to meet the requirements that result from this analysis. We'll look at business impact analysis and how IT interacts with this process in Chapter 31.

Mitigation Strategy Development

If you're part of a small company, your mitigation strategy might be quite simple. Keep several copies of backups off-site and keep several copies of key information such as employee list, phone numbers, emergency service phone numbers, key suppliers, and customers in a binder off-site in a secure but accessible location. That might be the extent to which you choose to mitigate your risks. However, for most companies, the process is a bit more complex. For each identified risk that has a significant business impact, you need to look at your options. How can the risk and impact be tolerated, reduced, avoided, or transferred? We'll discuss mitigation strategies in Chapter 32.

Plan Development

After you've gone through the analysis steps, you'll be ready to develop your plan. As with other types of IT project plans, you'll want to outline the methodology you're going to follow so that you improve your chance of success and reduce your chances for errors and gaps. This includes standard processes like developing business and technical requirements, defining scope, budget, timeline, and quality metrics, and so forth. We'll discuss these elements in Chapter 33 and we'll use standard IT PM methodologies to help you create a solid plan, regardless of the size of your company.

Training, Testing, Auditing

Once the plan has been developed, people need to be trained on how to implement it. In many cases, scenario-based case studies can be a good first step (though this may be part of the plan development stage as well). Running through appropriate drills, exercises and simulations can be of great help, especially for disasters or events that rank high on the list of "likely to occur." In Chapter 34, we'll discuss emergency preparations. Then, in Chapter 35, we'll look at some of the ways you can train, test, and audit your plan so that you can develop a process that closely tracks with your company and the way it operates.

Plan Maintenance

Finally, plan maintenance is the last step in the BC/DR planning process, and in many companies, it is "last and least." Without a plan to maintain your plan, it will become just another project document on a file server or sitting in a binder on a shelf. If it doesn't get maintained, updated, and revalidated from time to time, you'll find that the plan may be rendered useless if a disaster does strike. Maintenance doesn't have to be an enormous task, but it is one that must be done. Most importantly, there must be an organizational commitment to do so and someone within the company to own it. We'll look at this in Chapter 36.

Summary

Business continuity and its subset, disaster recovery, are not new concepts to business, but the act of consciously assessing and planning for potential problems certainly has been underscored by disastrous events in the past decade including earthquakes, tsunamis, hurricanes, typhoons, and terrorist attacks. Companies need to plan for potential disasters that will impact their ability to continue operations and earn income. Without a plan to recover from any disaster or event, no matter how large or small, many companies fail. The statistics speak for themselves. The odds are between 40% and 50% that a company will fail after a fire or significant data loss, and that only 6% of companies survive long-term after a major incident.

When developing a business continuity and disaster recovery plan, you need to look at the three core components of business: people, process, and technology. When you take a holistic view of the company and its operations through the lens of these three elements, you're more likely to understand the best approach to your own unique BC/DR planning process. People, process, and technology must be considered in an integrated and holistic manner since they are closely tied together.

Through your BC/DR planning process, you may find additional information you can use to support the purchase or implementation of a particular technology or service. If that technology or service will not only help day-to-day operations but will also fit nicely into a BC/DR strategy, you have effectively doubled the usefulness of the technology and reduced the perceived cost. Building the business case can help tilt the budget decisions in your favor. In addition, through reviewing business processes for your BC/DR plan, you may discover new or improved ways to run daily operations, which will add to the perceived value (or reduce the perceived cost) of your BC/DR activities.

In some companies, even a little downtime can be devastating, but in the majority of companies, some downtime can be tolerated, though it will still be disruptive. You and your planning team will need to thoroughly assess the company's tolerance for downtime and disruption in order to develop an effective plan. We'll discuss this in later chapters in more detail. It's important to keep the business failure statistics in mind as you make your plans. Fire is the most common business emergency, and 40% to 50% of businesses fail after a major fire. Without a well-defined BC/DR plan, your company is putting the welfare of its employees, stakeholders (or shareholders), suppliers, vendors, and the community in which it operates at risk. Many BC/DR planning activities and remedies cost little or nothing to implement, so doing nothing is not an acceptable "no cost" option. It is simply imprudent and irresponsible for companies of all sizes to fail to plan.

Disasters impact different types of companies in assorted ways. A flooded retail location has a different set of challenges than a flooded nursing home. The impact of a biohazard incident is far different if it occurs at or near a day care center than near a remote manufacturing facility. As an IT professional, you and your team should fully understand the potential risks to your company in your location(s). As we move through this book, you'll learn how to prioritize and address a variety of risks and threats your company might face.

Also as we move through this section, we'll rely upon standard project management tools to help develop the BC/DR plan. For those of you with formal PM training and skills, these steps will be familiar. For those of you less familiar with these methods (or for those of you who hate a lot of "process"), don't panic. We'll review the necessary steps and provide plenty of guidance along the way. We'll avoid getting bogged down with the very fine, detailed aspects of project management. Instead, we'll simply use it as our framework to help guide us through the process of risk assessment; business impact analysis; mitigation strategy development; plan development; training, testing and auditing; and plan maintenance.

## Chapter 29

Project Initiation

Solutions in this chapter:

- **Elements of Project Success**
- **Project Plan Components**
- **Key Contributors and Responsibilities**
- **Project Definition**
- **Business Continuity and Disaster Recovery Plan**

☑ **Summary**

Introduction

In Chapter 28, we discussed the relationship of disaster recovery and business continuity activities. You learned that disaster recovery plans are implemented in the immediate aftermath of a business disruption. Business continuity activities usually begin after the immediate impact of the disruption, event, or disaster has been addressed. It should be clear, then, that business continuity and disaster recovery (BC/DR) are two distinct plans that intersect. Each can be planned as a separate project using standard project management (PM) methodologies, or they can be planned as one larger, integrated plan. The steps needed to deal with the immediate aftermath of a disaster and the steps needed to ensure the business stays up and running may be one and the same for some companies. Only you and your project team will be able to make that distinction. However, regardless of the approach you take, you'll need to design your BC/DR projects as formal IT projects in order to avoid costly mistakes such as erroneous assumptions or gaping holes in your plan.

A project is defined as a set of tasks having a defined start and end point and specific objectives, requirements, and goals. Clearly, both business continuity and disaster recovery planning qualify as projects under this definition. The BC/DR planning process can, and should, be constructed as a project plan and each component (BC, DR) can then be implemented as projects. There is good reason for mentioning this. One of the reasons many companies fail to develop effective plans is that they do not approach BC/DR planning as a *project*. They see it as an all-encompassing, all-consuming, never-ending task; it becomes overwhelming or vaguely defined. No one can get in gear or stay motivated to complete a never-ending task. This also adds to the erroneous belief that BC/DR planning is just for large companies with deep pockets.

In this chapter, we're going to look at the process of creating a project plan for your BC/DR activities. If you're already familiar with IT project management, these steps will be familiar and should serve as a good reminder. If you're not familiar with IT project management, this chapter will help you become better acquainted with IT PM best practices and guide you through the process. You won't find an overly technical or detailed plan here; what you will find is a framework you can customize to the unique needs of your organization. If you're a certified Project Manager, you will find that these steps follow general guidelines, but may not adhere to the PM methodology of your choosing.

As with any IT project, there are numerous elements that tend to contribute to the likelihood of success. In this chapter, we'll begin by discussing those factors and how they relate, specifically, to your BC/DR planning efforts. We'll continue by looking at the elements you should include, how you might want to organize the project and your team(s), and how to develop success criteria so that you can mark your progress and recognize success.

Whatever you do, don't skip this chapter. It creates the framework for the rest of the book, and it will be relatively painless to get through this chapter without having nightmares or falling asleep. Throughout the remaining chapters, we'll refer to our progress diagram to help you keep a visual image of where we are in the overall process. Figure 29.1 shows we're in the first step, project initiation.

Figure 29.1 Business Continuity and Disaster Recover Project Plan Progress

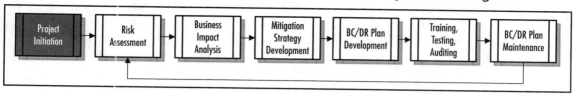

Elements of Project Success

Numerous studies through the years show there are a set of factors that, when present, tend to make projects more successful. The Standish Group International began researching project success and failure back in the 1990s. They've published a report called the CHAOS Report every two years. Each time the list is updated, the order of success factors changes slightly, but the same factors consistently show up in the top eight positions. These factors are:

- Executive Support
- User Involvement
- Experienced Project Manager
- Clearly Defined Project Objectives
- Clearly Defined Project Requirements
- Clearly Defined Scope
- Shorter Schedule, Multiple Milestones
- Clearly Defined Project Management Process

In this section, we'll discuss each of these factors as it relates to your BC/DR project.

Executive Support

Executive support for any IT project is typically the number one success factor. It makes sense that support from the top of the organization for an IT project tips the odds of success in your favor since executives have the ability to provide funding, resources, staffing, and political cover. If they are convinced there is a clear business need, they will go to bat for you and help ensure you get what you need to succeed.

How does that translate to BC/DR planning? As we discovered in Chapter 28, BC/DR planning has to be a comprehensive plan that covers every critical aspect of your business. In order for your plan to be successful, you *must* work with people from all key areas of your company. In order to do so, you clearly need the authority and reach that executive support can provide. You'll need to pull people away from other projects and tasks to participate on this project, and their managers are certainly going to be asking questions like——Who authorized this? How will this impact my other projects? Who is responsible for making this decision? If the senior managers or executives of your organization are behind you 100%, your authority to move forward on this project will be supported and others within the organization will typically fall in line. Granted, they may not be happy to shift their priorities to make room for this project, but they will if their boss and their boss's boss say so. Related to this, if you and your project run into resistance that you cannot overcome, you can escalate the issue through the proper channels and expect to find support as it reaches the executive ranks (assuming you're in the right).

Common Challenges

Gaining Executive Support

Some people in IT find it difficult to garner executive support for projects, and there are three common reasons and some fairly straightforward solutions to these challenges.

1. In many cases, IT staff get too wrapped up in the technology and fail to acknowledge and highlight the business need for the solution. In the case of BC618/DR planning, you can cite the statistics provided in Chapter 28 as primary reasons for requiring a BC/DR plan. Throughout this book, you'll read about cases and examples of the business case for BC/DR planning that you can use in your discussions with executives.

2. Another common reason for failing to get support for BC/DR planning is a simple failure to communicate clearly, concisely, and convincingly. You don't need a huge presentation with graphics and Flash animation to make your point. You need to figure out who your audience is, what you want them to understand when you're finished, and how you should present the information. Some audiences want a PowerPoint presentation with bullet points; some audiences want a one-page written summary; still other audiences want a five-minute verbal presentation with a one-paragraph written summary. There is no one single correct way to present the information other than this: *Determine the preferred format for your intended audience and create a short, concise presentation using nontechnical language.* Most executives have heard of VoIP, NAS, SANs, and TCP/IP, but don't understand the underlying implications of these terms. Therefore, keep it nontechnical and clear. Keep your objectives in mind and lay out your information in a logical progression.

3. Finally, a third common reason for failure to get executive support for IT projects is that IT projects sometimes appear (to executives) as bottomless pits into which time, money, and resources fall. You'll need to provide executives with a ballpark estimate for how long you believe the project will take and roughly how much it will cost (time and money) to complete. Here's the danger——until you've completed the initial project work, you probably won't know the answers to these questions. It becomes a circular problem because you can't give an estimate until you do some planning and you can't do the planning until you've provided executives with an estimate.

One way to short-circuit that problem is to tell executives you don't know how long it will take or what it will cost, but that it is critical that you be given the OK to find out. If you view your project as a two-part process where the first part is to create a rough estimate for time and cost so you can get approval for the larger planning project, you might gain support early. Alternately, you may be able to work with a few key people in the organization such as your financial person, one or more of your key ops people, and your facilities person to come up with a ballpark estimate you're all comfortable with. Building this coalition early on may also help solidify your project team and could provide critical mass within the organization for the planning project.

Executives understand business and finance—they don't necessarily understand technology. Many are comfortable using technology and a vast majority understand the need to utilize technology effectively within an organization; few understand the terminology and the underpinnings of technology. Therefore, you have to speak business with them. Rather than saying "we need to investigate availability solutions for WAN and LAN support," you need to break it down and say "we need to investigate our options for providing data access across the entire company, both here in the building and across the globe." Both say roughly the same thing, but the second statement is business-centric, the first statement is techno-speak. If writing (or nontechnical writing) is not your strong suit, write up what you want to say and ask someone in a nontechnical department to work on it with you. For example, go to your Human Resources or Marketing department and ask someone to assist you. It would be better to get feedback from someone outside the decision-making loop than to submit your technical document to a decision-maker who doesn't understand it and won't take the time to ask you to explain it. Executives are typically very busy and they like when things are boiled down to their essence in plain language. It helps them quickly understand the situation and make a rational decision. You want to help them do just that.

From the Trenches…

When the Answer Is "No!"

The ideal scenario rarely matches reality. In today's IT world, budgets and capabilities are stretched to the breaking point and highly charged issues such as security and regulatory compliance garner the most visibility. You may very well find that your company is reluctant (at best) or unwilling (at worst) to devote time or money to developing a business continuity or disaster recovery planning project. Even though this is a suboptimal long-term business decision, the demands on a company's resources can sometimes be such that BC/DR planning is just not valued or appreciated. If you're an IT professional pushing for BC/DR planning in your company and you find you're hitting a brick wall, there are things you can do to help facilitate this process. Although you may not be able to set aside time (or money) to create a fully separate project for BC/DR, you can incorporate BC/DR concepts in all your other IT project plans. For example, if you're evaluating the implementation of a new server, new application, or new technology, include an assessment of the BC/DR concepts and include elements that will help you mitigate risk and plan for outages as you would within the scope of a formal BC/DR plan. The most basic BC/DR plan is to have redundancy and backups and most IT staff work to develop these attributes in the normal course of IT operations. There is a fair amount of coverage you can get if you begin adding BC/DR elements to your basic IT planning, projects, and operations. It won't ever substitute for a full BC/DR plan, but at least it will begin to move your IT operations in that direction without putting undue pressure on your time or your budget. So, if your company won't move beyond "no" when you discuss BC/DR plans, use the information throughout the remainder of this book in your IT operations.

User Involvement

You've probably been involved with projects that were going to dramatically impact end users, and yet no one talked with end users for months, if ever. These projects are almost always doomed to fail. User involvement consistently shows up in one of the top three spots on the list of success factors for IT projects. Many technology projects have failed because users were not involved and key decisions were made that were directly counter to user needs and wishes. Clearly, you can create any solution you want but you can't force users to use it. You can't force users to understand and accept convoluted processes for doing their once-simple tasks, to flex *around* awkward requirements of the technology. Although there can be compelling business drivers that force users to change their processes and methods, these should be created with user input and collaboration, not in the dark recesses of the IT department.

So, who are the users in a BC/DR planning project? There are essentially two sets of users. The first set includes those who will be involved in planning the BC/DR project itself. These folks may or may not be the same ones who will implement these plans should disaster strike. Therefore, you would do well to have both sets of users involved in this project. For example, you might want to have one team that focuses on defining the critical business processes that need to be addressed in the plan. A second (or subsequent) phase of the project plan could include a second project team that includes those people from around the company that would be responsible for implementing a BC/DR plan and would therefore define the implementation phase. If you work in a small company, this might be the same group of people. In larger companies, it might be two overlapping or two separate teams.

Whatever your approach, be sure to include the key people in the project from start to finish. Later in this chapter, we'll discuss who should be involved. For now, keep in mind that if you and your team create a great plan without input from those who will be the "boots on the ground" in an emergency, your plan is highly likely to fail under the stress of a disaster.

Experienced Project Manager

Experienced project managers bring a wealth of knowledge and skill to the table. They often have had some formal project management training or education and they may have achieved a standardized certification in one or more methodologies. Most importantly, though, they have been in the trenches managing projects, and have realistic understanding of what it takes to get the job done.

When we're looking at BC/DR specifically, an experienced project manager is likely to be more effective at working across organizational boundaries and in bringing together a diverse group of people and interests. Working effectively with people at all levels of the organization and in all areas of the company is critical to the success of a BC/DR plan. An experienced project manager is more likely to understand how to navigate the political waters as well as the organizational red tape that inevitably crops up during the development and implementation of cross-departmental projects.

In addition, an experienced project manager will utilize a defined set of steps, a methodology, to deliver consistent results. Most experienced project managers have developed a system of defining and managing projects that delivers positive results. They have spent years, for the most part, honing their methods to generate an optimal outcome. Most adhere, in general terms, to standardized methodologies but each experienced and successful project manager undoubtedly will have customized those methodologies to suit their specific needs. This is key to delivering a successful BC/DR project plan. With the actual survival of your company at risk, it's imperative to have the most successful outcome possible. An experienced PM will increase your odds of such an outcome, though no single (or multiple) success factors guarantee success.

Clearly Defined Project Objectives

Clearly defined project objectives might sound incredibly obvious, but you might be surprised at how often projects are launched without clearly defined objectives. Clearly defined objectives are quite important because your BC/DR plan must be scaled to your organization's unique needs. Without defining the objectives, you and your team might spend a disproportionate amount of time planning and implementing a part of the plan that is less important, or you might short-change a very important area.

One way the task of defining objectives can contribute to BC/DR success is to develop a high-level list of functional areas of your company and invite key people from those areas to help define the objectives. This accomplishes two critical project objectives: it ensures that all functional areas are included and it brings together the people most able to develop appropriate objectives. As an IT professional, you are not in a position to develop objectives for BC/DR planning for, say, the Human Resources or Marketing department. You understand the technology but not the business or operational objectives, in most cases. In addition, you need to get these stakeholders together to agree on objectives because you will have to prioritize. During an emergency or disaster, many business operations, tasks, and objectives become secondary to the survival of people and the survival of the company. Determining these needs helps determine the project's objectives and this will help focus you and your team on the critical aspects of the business.

Clearly Defined Project Requirements

Related to objectives are requirements. Developing clear and complete requirements can also make the difference between success and failure, especially for an IT-related project. The requirements are those capabilities, attributes, and qualities that must be part of the final project deliverable. Defining these early in the project development cycle is important because going back to add them in later (called *rework*) is both inefficient, costly, and fraught with both errors and additional project risk.

Requirements are not the same as project objectives. The objectives should drive the requirements. Objectives are what you want to accomplish, requirements are how you will accomplish those objectives. For example, if an *objective* for your BC/DR plan is continuous availability of three key business applications and related data, your *requirements* would have to delineate this objective. Requirements may have to be refined or developed later in the project definition process as details about the project become clear. However, clear requirements before project work begins is absolutely critical to project success. Unclear requirements cause confusion, duplication of effort, rework, and wasted work. If your objective is continuity availability but you never specify which applications, which data, which users, which business functions, which locations, which customers (etc.) fall under that objective, you will undoubtedly find your project wandering off on its own.

Requirements typically fall into three categories:—business, functional, and technical requirements. *Business requirements* help you determine what the business needs to survive a disruption. This helps you understand the major building blocks of your company, how they work together, and what key areas should be prioritized. *Functional requirements* detail things such as which processes, methods, and resources need to be available during and after a business disruption. *Technical requirements* delineate things such as servers, network infrastructure, and business application requirements. The more specific your requirements, the more likely you are to have a successful outcome——a BC/DR plan that works when implemented. You can think of it this way. If you get in your car with a destination in mind but no particular route, you are more likely to take longer to get there than if you mapped out your route before you left the house. For those of you who immediately think "Yes, but I'd use my GPS navigation system," remember, there is no GPS equivalent in a project. To define your requirements during project work (the rough equivalent of using a GPS system) is to guarantee that you'll end up miles off course at the other end of the project. Though you may need to make several passes through your requirements definition phase to add detail and clarity as you *define* and *organize* your project, you should not begin the actual work deliverables (*Work Breakdown Structure* tasks) until you have clearly defined requirements.

Clearly Defined Scope

Related to clearly defined project objectives is a clearly defined project scope. *Scope* is defined as the total amount of work to be accomplished. Scope typically is defined through the project's objectives. Making sure payroll can be run during a disaster may be one objective; making sure your company can still take, fulfill, and invoice customer orders is another objective. If these are the only two objectives for your BC/DR plan, you can fairly easily determine the project's scope. Therefore, clearly defined objectives lead to a clearly defined project scope.

Scope creep happens to many projects, and BC/DR is a project type that is perhaps more susceptible to scope creep than many other types of projects. For example, it's not hard to imagine that you decide that being able to process payroll during a crisis will be critical to the well-being of your firm's employees, so you include a high-level objective to that effect. However, as the project planning stages progress, someone mentions that the Human Resources director also wants the ability to easily set up direct deposit for people during a crisis in the event they cannot come to their work location to pick up a check. Your scope has just experienced creep——as you may know or suspect, it's one thing to ensure that payroll can be processed per usual, but another thing entirely to suddenly add the ability to go to direct deposit in an emergency. Clearly, additional steps must be included in the project plan to enable this capability, especially if it does not currently exist or if it will need to exist in a different way. For example, it is likely that people who want to use direct deposit currently have to submit a form with a voided check from their bank account and it must go through one or two payroll cycles before it is effective. During a disaster, employees will not have access to the form, they may not have access to their checkbooks, and they won't know how to accomplish that without talking with someone from HR. Additionally, it might be unacceptable for it to take two payroll cycles for this to occur during an emergency. Therefore, your team will need to develop possible solutions or alternatives for this new requirement and address it in your plan. So, although the HR director may have wanted this to be accomplished, he or she may not realize what it will take to accomplish this. Be sure to have clearly defined objectives, make sure that each objective is necessary during an emergency, and have the people (in this case, HR) responsible for that business function develop the potential solutions to the objective. This helps reduce scope creep and helps manage clearly defined objectives and clearly defined scope.

Shorter Schedule, Multiple Milestones

Studies have repeatedly shown that shorter schedules with more milestones generate more successful results. How does this apply to BC/DR planning? In most cases, BC/DR planning is a comprehensive look at the business and its processes to determine critical functions and emergency procedures for those critical functions. You may choose to break your BC/DR planning project down into smaller projects—for example, one project plan for each functional area and one master plan that ties these all together. You may choose to perform your planning in an iterative mode so that during the first pass, you develop just the most basic, mission-critical solutions and each iteration after that builds on the one prior. Only you and your project planning team can determine the best approach to this, but keep in mind that long schedules typically just get longer. People lose focus, enthusiasm, and interest. Resources start being pulled away from the project the further out in time you go.

Milestones are, by definition, project markers that help you gauge progress. Milestones are checkpoints that can help you stay on budget, on schedule, and on scope as your project progresses.

The more milestones (within reason) your project has, the more likely it is to be successful because you are consistently comparing where you stated you wanted to be with where you actually are. This regular course correction can certainly keep your project on target far better than an occasional checkpoint that may leave you wondering how you got so far off course.

Your company may be reluctant to undertake a full BC/DR project because executives might fear that it will go on forever and never produce a result or might cost far more than the company can afford in terms of staff time and money. If you run into massive resistance, you might want to parse your plan out into well-defined stages and get executives to sign off on the phased approach. Then, when you can show success with the first phase, you may more easily gain support for subsequent phases.

TIP

If you take a phased approach to your planning, be careful to clearly delineate what is and *is not* part of each phase. You want to avoid executives believing that Phase One will cover something in another phase. You also want to be sure that Phase One delivers a meaningful barebones BC/DR plan at the very least. The phased approach is most often useful when executives are uncertain about the potential costs and benefits, and success in the first phase can engender support for subsequent phases, but it can also lead to a false sense of security. You'll have to find the appropriate balance for your organization.

Clearly Defined Project Management Process

A clearly defined project management process typically goes hand-in-hand with an experienced project manager. As mentioned, an experienced PM is likely to have a set of methods, procedures, and associated documents that he or she has used successfully in the past. Most experienced PMs will hone those processes and procedures over time so that they become almost second nature. If you're an inexperienced project manager, you can increase your odds of success by using a well-defined project management process. Throughout the remainder of this book, we'll use standard PM processes that will help you develop a more successful BC/DR project plan. If you have a methodology that you've used successfully in the past, feel free to utilize that in conjunction with the material presented in this book. You'll find that the presentation of PM processes in this book follows a fairly standard format and should be compatible with any standardized process you choose to use. The key is to select a process and use it from start to finish so there are no gaps in the process, which inevitably lead to gaps in the plan.

As you can see from the success factors listed, achieving project success is not rocket science, but it does require a consistent approach and attention to detail. As business continuity and disaster recovery continue to show up in the news headlines, executives are becoming more aware of the need to invest in BC/DR plans. Clearly, regulatory pressure, shareholder requirements, and vendor initiatives also have pushed this to the forefront of many executive's awareness. Some companies' executives, however, are still a bit behind the curve, usually because they do not have regulators or shareholders pounding on their door asking for their BC/DR plans. If you work in one of these companies, you may still face a bit of an uphill battle, but by reviewing the project success factors and developing a strategy for approaching this planning, you are likely to find a solution that fits your company's needs.

From the Trenches...

Even Small Companies Need a Plan

If you're an IT service firm, you may be able to provide a great service to your customers by talking with them about their business continuity plans. There are millions of small companies out there, from sole proprietors to partnerships to small companies of five or ten employees. At a very basic level, they should have a solid data backup plan. If an author is working on a manuscript while traveling, what happens if the laptop is lost, stolen, or broken? Though this may sound very basic to you, be assured that millions of people don't give this much thought until they have an unfortunate incident that costs them thousands of hours, dollars, or headaches. Whether you work in a small company or in a service firm for small companies, you should keep BC/DR plans in mind when looking at how they work and how they should be protected. Most companies (including individuals) are thankful when you bring a solution to the table that helps them prevent a catastrophe. For the author, it might be as simple as backing up to a CD, USB drive, or online backup location to prevent a serious, costly data loss. Remember, keep it simple, especially for small companies and individuals. Find the minimum they'll need to stay in business and make sure that is what's protected. Everything else after that is just icing on the cake.

Project Plan Components

Now that we've reviewed the success factors, let's look at standard project management plan components. If you have a methodology you use, this should track (generally) with yours. If you don't have a methodology you use and you're not familiar with project management, this will give you a basic overview. Our goal is not to delve into the details of project management—for that, you can pick up a copy of *IT Project Management* from Syngress.

The basic steps in a project are:

- Project Definition
- Forming the Project Team
- Project Organization
- Project Planning
- Project Implementation

- Project Tracking
- Project Close Out

Let's look at each of these briefly, and as they relate to BC/DR planning. Keep in mind that project planning and project management are both linear and iterative processes. This means that there is a logical flow that defines the order in which steps are taken; at the same time, many steps are revisited over time to add additional detail that helps more clearly define the project. For example, some elements cannot be known at the beginning of a project, so an estimate is used until enough detail is developed to go back and refine the original estimate. Although this sounds like it could lead to interminable planning (and it could), the goal is to continually move forward and to refine and hone details as they become known. This approach actually prevents "analysis paralysis," in which planners feel they cannot move forward because they do not have enough information or detail yet. Instead, this approach allows you to use estimates or placeholders so you can move forward and develop the additional detail as quickly as possible. A good example of this conundrum is the budget for a project. In many cases it's difficult, if not impossible, to give a useful estimate for the cost of a project until you've defined the project's scope, objectives, and requirements. At the same time, it can be all but impossible to get the go-ahead for a project until executives have some idea of what it will cost. In some companies, this becomes a circular problem that causes projects to just spin in a loop, going nowhere fast. To overcome this, you may have to do some initial project definition work to develop a ballpark estimate to get the OK for the project to develop additional detail to give a more refined estimate of the cost. It may sound like a lot of rework, but it's actually refining instead of redoing, and this typically leads to forward progress.

TIP

If you're having trouble getting a budget approved for your BC/DR project plan because you don't yet know what it will cost or how long it will take to accomplish it, you may have to do some savvy negotiating with decision-makers. For example, in some companies it might be effective to ask for a specific budget to investigate the cost of a BC/DR planning project. If you can get some staff time and a small budget allocated to investigate this, you may be able to come up with a fairly realistic ballpark estimate for the actual BC/DR planning project. In other companies, it might be more effective to look at annual revenues and talk to one of the financial people in the company to estimate the cost, in terms of lost revenue, lost market share, and lost customers, if a disaster were to hit. Using some estimate from a financial analyst within the company will lend credibility to your estimate and should at least help you get a budget for the first phase or for an investigation into the potential cost of developing a full BC/DR plan. In still other companies, the only real constraint might be money, so you might get a go-ahead to use staff time and corporate resources as long as you don't spend any cash outside the company. This might be acceptable in the near-term and help you get your planning project underway with executive support.

You'll have to be creative and persistent, in some cases, but the importance of creating a BC/DR plan cannot be overemphasized. Finding the right approach within your organization is probably the most important first step.

Project Definition

Project definition is the first phase of any project. In some companies, it's easier to get approval for a subproject plan whose only deliverable is a clear idea of what the project will be. The definition phase can include a variety of elements; we're going to look at this from both a BC/DR planning perspective and an IT perspective.

First, let's talk about project origins. In some cases, you may be approached by the CIO or another executive in the company about creating a BC/DR plan. In other cases, you may be pushing your organization to create a plan. If the former is the case, it's quite common that someone has given you marching orders to which you're expected to conform. The problem is that without doing the requisite research and planning activities, a directive to create "a BC/DR plan with x, y, and z" in it will likely be off-target. It will have gaps or will include things that are not needed. So, how should you proceed if this project is dropped in your lap? The first step is to talk with the person who handed you the project. He or she is most likely the project sponsor. Get a clear understanding of expectations and what the project should entail. Typically, you can extrapolate key elements that should be included in the plan and from there, you can check back with the project sponsor. This step should never be skipped, and unless your company is run as a dictatorship, you should always make sure you come back with questions, suggestions, and revisions. Rarely will a project be handed to you that is so well-defined that you can just put together a plan to accomplish the objectives and off you go. Remember that executive objectives are usually quite different than the objectives needed for a solid BC/DR plan. For example, an executive may need to show compliance with a particular regulatory requirement. Your job would be to develop project requirements that would, when implemented, result in regulatory compliance. Although closely related, you can see that the executive's objectives and the project's objectives are not always one and the same.

Problem and Mission Statement

Often the most effective starting point is a problem statement. In the case of BC/DR, it might be as simple as "Our company operates in two geographic locations and generates $25M in annual sales. We do not currently have a disaster plan for either location and the company is at risk as a result." Remember, you don't have to overengineer this, but a clear problem statement helps keep you focused as you move forward so you work on solving the *right* problem. A brilliant project that solves the *wrong* problem is useless.

Next, you should create a mission statement. This, too, can be a fairly simple statement (and should not require a three day off-site to accomplish it) such as "To create a business continuity and disaster recovery plan for both of our company's locations that will address the major risks to our company and that will provide a path to recovery of the basic, mission-critical systems including a, b, and c." When you define a problem and then define what the desired outcome (mission statement) looks like, you have created your start and end points. This helps you define the scope of the project and gives you a clear end in sight so you can begin planning a finite project.

Potential Solutions

Once you've defined your start and end point, you can develop a list of potential solutions. This is an important and often-skipped step in project planning. One potential solution to be evaluated in all projects is "do nothing." Although it's often not a viable option, it keeps things real and helps you evaluate all potential solutions against the do-nothing option. Even though it's highly unlikely that a do-nothing solution would be appropriate for BC/DR planning, it should nonetheless be included. You can then measure other options against the cost of doing nothing and use it as a reality check both with your project team and with your executive team.

Looking at all potential solutions will help ensure you don't pigeon-hole your project early on. The creative process of getting the project team together to brainstorm potential solutions may yield surprising results. For example, you might find that there is a vendor that sells solutions that will address all your BC/DR needs. You may find that you already have implemented many of the needed systems, and emergency procedures are all that are needed to create a solid BC/DR plan. Until you brainstorm all potential solutions based on the start and end point you've defined, you won't know what your options are.

That said, we're assuming that the solution will be to develop some sort of BC/DR plan. Though standard project management steps make sense throughout, the specific subject does need to be considered. After you've completed the risk assessment phase, which is part of the actual project work, you'll be in a much better position to determine the potential solutions. Then, you can select the one that meets project and organizational constraints and requirements.

Requirements and Constraints

Another important element is to understand project requirements and constraints early on. Every project will have a stated or implied budget, timeline, and expected deliverables. You *will* have to revisit these once you select a solution, but you often can't select a solution until you have some basic requirements in mind. If the project was handed to you, you should go back to the person for clarification about these expectations. If you're initiating the project, you should try to develop some realistic expectations that you can bring to your boss or the decision-maker for feedback. If you're way out of the ballpark, this is a great time to find out. If expectations are significantly misaligned, this is the best place to find that out and correct it. It only will get worse from here. For example, is your budget likely to be $10,000 or $10,000,000? The budget will have a huge impact on the solutions you may choose to consider. Is your timeline four weeks or four months or four quarters? Again, your project will need to meet time requirements. What about technical requirements? Does your company have multiple locations? Are there employees who travel or work in the field? Do your customers purchase your products online? Do they place orders online? Understanding some of the high level technical requirements will also be needed before you can select the optimal project solution.

Once you've developed your initial list of requirements and constraints, you should be able to identify which solution(s) best meet your project's problem statement and mission statement (problem and desired outcome). If more than one solution appears to be feasible and desirable, you may have to look at other factors to find the most optimal solution. What factors? Sometimes they're political—perhaps your CIO is partial to a particular vendor because they deliver the best customized solutions; perhaps your timeline would be better met by one solution; perhaps your budget constraint is really the most important aspect and one solution fits your budget better. The first major objective in a BC/DR plan is a risk assessment, which will drive many of your requirements. This is an excellent example of the iterative process needed in IT project management. You may have some requirements and constraints that are known at the outset of project planning; others may have to be developed later when more data has been collected.

Success Criteria

Another element often skipped in project planning are success criteria. How will you know your project is a success? If you know this, you have a better chance of creating a successful project plan. If you develop the criteria by which you'll judge or evaluate success, you're less likely to find yourself chasing after ever-changing definitions of success. It doesn't mean they won't change or that you won't have to work hard to maintain these success criteria once the project is underway, but it gives you a known starting point. If you're not familiar with success criteria, here's a rather mundane example that should help. Let's say you need to clean up your office because it's a mess. Your success criteria might be these: 1) all loose papers are filed in marked file folders, thrown out, recycled or shredded, as appropriate; 2) all books are stored in a bookshelf or stored in the company library in Conference Room A; 3) all writing utensils are stored in a pencil holder or in a desk drawer; 4) desk top is free of extraneous equipment not currently in use; 5) all computer hardware and software (other than desktop or laptop computer and associated devices) are restocked in the lab or an appropriate location (not your office or your desk). Even though this might seem obvious, it essentially tells you what your office will look like once you finish cleaning it up. Most of us don't need a list of success criteria to know if we've successfully cleaned our office, but you can probably see how this could be extremely useful in project planning.

Project Proposal

Once you select your optimal project solution, you'll need to put together a brief project proposal. Essentially, the project proposal should include all the elements we've just delineated. It should be submitted to the project sponsor (we'll discuss the project sponsor in a moment) or to your boss. If your organization has a process for submitting project proposals, use that format. If not, include the elements listed here (you can modify to meet your specific needs):

- Business case (can include the problem and mission statements)
- Financial analysis (if appropriate)
- High level scope, timeline, budget, and quality metrics
- Requirements, constraints, assumptions, exclusions
- High-level resource needs
- Phase schedule (if a phased approach will be used)
- Success criteria
- Risks, mitigation, and alternatives (risks to the project, not BC/DR risks)
- Recommendations

The project proposal can serve several purposes simultaneously. First, it can be used to convince executives that a business continuity and disaster recovery plan is needed and that you've given serious thought to the subject. It can be used to rally others in the organization around the need for a BC/DR plan and begin the process of gathering support and critical mass for such as project. Finally, it documents the beginning of the project so that you don't have to needlessly and repeatedly revisit these decisions and this data in the future. This can help the project move forward instead of sideways and help momentum build instead of just spinning in circles.

Estimates

Although it's outside the scope of this book to discuss estimating in detail, it is worth talking briefly about estimates. First, estimates are dangerous. More often than not, they become targets. The vice president catches you in the hallway and asks how much this BC/DR plan will cost. Without thinking too hard about it, you reply that you think it shouldn't really take more than a month and about $5,000. Congratulations, you've just committed yourself to two targets! Though you may preface your response with "well, it's really early but I'm guessing…" you may still have a problem. The VP may simply remember one month and $5K. She's a busy person, after all, and she remembers just the facts. So, use extreme caution when tossing around estimates, especially ones that are just wild guesses.

Estimates can be generated based on past experience of similar projects, and these estimates, called *parametric estimates*, tend to be fairly accurate. When you can say "the ABC Project was very similar in scope and requirements and it took six months and cost about $50,000" you're in much better shape because the odds are good, if the projects really *are* similar, that estimates should be close. If you don't have a similar project you can use for comparison, you have to develop an estimate from scratch. These can be created top-down or bottom-up. The *top-down* approach is the fastest but least accurate method. The bottom-up is the slowest but most accurate method. A top-down estimate would start with an estimated budget, let's say, $100,000. From past project experience (this is where the "experienced project managers" as a success factor comes into play), you might know that designing the requirements is usually about 10% of the budget, so you could estimate that designing requirements will cost $10,000. You might also know that planning the project is typically 18% of the project budget, so planning should cost about $18,000, and so forth. If you don't have a lot of project experience or a lot of experience at this company, you generally cannot create realistic top-down estimates. *Bottom-up estimates* typically are developed after you've created your detailed Work Breakdown Structure, after you know what your tasks and deliverables are. Once that is known, it's a simple matter of adding up the cost of each task and developing a total. The biggest problem with bottom-up estimating is that you won't end up with an estimate early in the planning cycle. If you're trying to get project approval based on an estimate, a bottom-up approach won't work because it will require you do a fair amount of planning before you ever develop an estimate. In fact, the result of bottom-up estimating is usually close to a real number you can use as a target or commitment (as opposed to an estimate that will need additional refinement).

We've covered the basics of project definition very briefly. If there are elements you're accustomed to using or elements required by your company, certainly use them. If you're not familiar with these or other project definition elements, there are plenty of great resources on IT project management you can use, including one by this author mentioned earlier.

Project Sponsor

A project sponsor often is the person that hands the project to you and assigns you as project manager. In other cases, especially situations in which you are initiating the project on your own, you'll need to identify a project sponsor. A project sponsor is someone in the organization who has the authority—both organizational and political—to help you accomplish your project goals. He or she should have enough knowledge about the company and the project to help you make sound decisions, create a budget and timeline (or approve them), help remove obstacles, rally resources, and support and evaluate choices and decisions all along the way. If you haven't yet identified your project sponsor, you should do so early. Finding the right project sponsor can make all the difference to you and your project's success. If your project was handed to you, don't assume that person is also the project sponsor. Ask. The question that usually gets to the bottom of the issue is "are you the person who will approve the budget and schedule?" If no, you haven't found your project sponsor. He or she should be authorized to approve project documents, budget expenditures, and schedules. Some companies may operate differently, but the project sponsor normally has the authority and responsibility to approve expenditures, assign resources to your project, and remove obstacles to your success.

Keep in mind that your project sponsor for a BC/DR plan may be different than a typical IT project sponsor. The sponsor might be an executive vice president responsible for regulatory compliance, the project sponsor might be someone who oversees facilities. It's hard to say who your project sponsor will be for a BC/DR project, but it should be someone who 1) understands the importance of a BC/DR project and 2) who has the organizational and political power to help a BC/DR project get off the ground.

Common Challenges

Project Sponsor MIA

Some project sponsors go MIA (missing in action) and become impossible to contact. If you're in search of a project sponsor, be sure to select someone you're confident will be available to you on a regular basis. You shouldn't have to run to the project sponsor for approval of every single item, but you should meet with your project sponsor regularly (via phone, net meeting, or in person) to discuss project progress. Should your project sponsor be someone who is not good at returning e-mail or voice mail or regularly travels and is unavailable, your project will likely run into significant delays. Find a sponsor who will be available and then make sure you use your time with the sponsor productively. Be prepared, have an agenda, and get on with it. Some project sponsors go MIA if they find their time is not being used productively. Don't expect to chit chat over a double tall nonfat half caf vanilla latte with your project sponsor—stay focused and your project sponsor may actually look forward to your meetings. Waste their time, and they'll dread (and then avoid) your meetings.

Forming the Project Team

You should form a project team pretty early in the project cycle for numerous reasons. You're unlikely to have all the knowledge you need to develop a sound plan by yourself and you will eventually need the input from various subject matter experts during the course of the project. Studies repeatedly show that those who help plan a project are more likely to contribute positively to the project because they feel a sense of control and ownership. Therefore, you would be ill-advised to create the plan on your own and unveil it to your project team. Instead, decide who should be on the project team, form the team, and create the plan.

There are times when it's not initially clear who should be on the project team. This may well be the case with a BC/DR project because it crosses so many organizational boundaries. One approach is to create a preliminary project team whose sole job it is to create the basic project definition and then determine who the right team members should be. In some cases, the original team might be suitable; in other cases, the team may require a few new members or the removal of a few existing members whose long-term participation just doesn't make sense. For example, it might be that the initial planning meeting(s) include area directors or vice presidents—especially if this project has high visibility, is related to ongoing regulatory compliance, or has been assigned by an executive. Once the high level definitions are created, directors or VPs may then select members of their teams to join the project team and they, themselves, may bow out. This is entirely appropriate. The key is to develop your project team with an eye toward covering all your organizational bases. You don't want neither a team that's too narrow in focus nor a team that is so large as to be difficult to manage and coordinate. You can choose to look at your company in many different ways. One is to include the basic functions, which typically are operations, human resources, finance, facilities and security, logistics/ purchasing, public relations and, of course, IT. Another way to look at it is by reviewing various categories. When forming your team, you could also consider these elements, which we'll touch on briefly next.

- Organizational
- Technical
- Logistical
- Political

Organizational

The first place to look is at your company's organizational chart. This will help you identify geographic locations, functional departments, or divisions of the company. These should all be included in your BC/DR planning process. Clearly, there will be some overlap that can help you pare down team members. For example, you may have an HR manager or director at each of 10 worldwide locations. You may need all of them to work as a subteam on HR needs during a crisis or you may select two of the most experienced to represent HR on our BC/DR team. If there are significant differences among your various worldwide locations, you'll need to look at the best way to approach HR needs, especially IT needs. For example, how is payroll processed in the Netherlands compared to how it's processed in Brazil or Australia? If it's all done through a single payroll processing company, you have different options than if each country processes its own payroll. There is no single right approach, so your best bet may be to form a preliminary team with the understanding that it probably has too many representatives and should be pared down once roles and responsibilities are known and understood.

WARNING

Things can get very political very fast when discussions of mission-critical areas of the business begin. Everyone wants to think of their part of the business as being critical to the company (i.e., if it's not mission-critical, why does it exist at all?). Many people become quite concerned when their area of business is not tagged as "essential to operations." Therefore, be on the lookout for power plays and bruised egos here. It's a delicate balance. You may need to resort to scenario-based questions to help people understand what BC/DR planning *is* and *is not*. For example, you might ask, "If this building caught on fire, what's the bare minimum we would need to get back up and running again?" This can help focus people on the project's objectives rather than on worries that their department or job function isn't included. Also, it often helps to indicate that *work* will be required of team members—that usually rids the team of the people who want to feel important but do not want to be held accountable for deliverables.

Technical

Which different technical specialties should be included? You may be unable to answer this question until you understand which areas of your business are mission-critical. The technologies used in areas of the business not considered mission-critical may not be represented in your planning. Alternately, they may be included in business continuity planning but not in disaster recovery planning since these technologies may not be needed immediately but will be needed in the long-term recovery of the business. Remember that technical issues involve not just the IT department but the facilities functions as well. How the building is heated, cooled, powered, maintained, and more impacts the IT function. If you have power but no heating or cooling, you may not be able to get systems up and running again. With the integration of the various technical components of your business, whether that's desktop computers, large server clusters, manufacturing systems, healthcare devices, and others, there are numerous technological factors to be considered in addition to IT-specific systems. Understanding how these work together and what elements truly are mission-critical in the aftermath of a disaster is an important area to explore in your project planning work. Understanding how you'll transition from disaster recovery to business continuity also requires a close integration of IT and non-IT technology management.

Logistical

There are two logistical components—one related to disaster recovery and one related to business continuity. In the immediate aftermath of an emergency or disaster, the most important tasks are related to stopping the impact of the event. If there's flooding, one disaster recovery task might be to move servers or computers to higher ground or to contact your company's other locations and let them know they will need to pick up the slack. These steps "stop" the effect of the flood. After those tasks are underway, business continuity activities typically begin. How can the business get up and running again? To continue with the flood example, it might be locating a temporary office building or arranging with a contractor to come in and begin pumping water out and start repairs. These all involve logistics of various kinds. Those in your company responsible for logistics and/or purchasing should certainly be included in the BC/DR planning activities.

As mentioned, it's often quite helpful to contract for emergency services before an emergency. You can lock in better rates before demand spikes the cost. You can calmly and rationally order what you need rather than ordering whatever comes to mind during the emergency. You can develop and maintain a relationship with a variety of firms to provide those services; as an existing customer, you're likely to get preferential or priority service during an emergency. Your logistics staff need to be involved with negotiating contracts for these mission-critical needs before disaster strikes.

Political

One element often overlooked are the political aspects of managing a crisis. Your company may need to communicate publicly after a crisis to assure stockholders and key customers that the company is intact and prepared to maintain or resume operations. This was the case with many of the financial institutions in the days following the September 11th attacks on the World Trade Center in downtown Manhattan. In addition, there may be internal political ramifications related to managing a crisis or emergency in your firm that should be addressed as part of your BC/DR plan. As an IT professional, you may not be aware of these political needs, so you should include people on your team who will be up to date on internal and external political requirements for your plan.

Project Organization

The project organization includes how you will organize and run your project. It begins with identifying the right project sponsor. Assuming you have a project sponsor, one of your first organizational tasks will be to define the elements that must go to the project sponsor for approval. Typically, the project sponsor approves the project scope, budget, and schedule, and any significant changes therein. Avoid having to get sponsor approval for every single expenditure and every single change or you'll forever be chasing your project sponsor trying to get requisite approval rather than getting project work done. Other organizational elements are discussed briefly next. Again, it's not an exhaustive or comprehensive list but just a reminder of the top level items and how they relate to BC/DR planning. In most cases, these are developed with your project team.

Project Objectives

You've developed the problem statement, the mission statement, high level requirements, constraint, and an optimal solution through the project definition stage. Now, you need to develop project objectives. The objectives for a BC/DR plan can be very narrow or very wide, depending on your company's specific situation. In this section, we'll list some of the types of BC/DR plans companies create. From there, you can develop specific objectives suitable to your company.

Business Continuity Plan

Focuses on sustaining the company's business activities, particularly those related to revenue generation and management of corporate obligations (employee payroll and health care insurance are two notable examples). A business continuity plan can be written for a specific business process or for all key business processes. As mentioned earlier, projects with smaller scope and more milestones tend to be more successful, so it might make sense for you to break your BC plan into smaller subplans, each addressing a specific set of mission-critical business processes. In most cases, a BC plan addresses the long-term recovery processes needed for the company to resume normal operations. Clearly, almost every company's BC plan will have an IT component since almost every company operating today (in the United States) utilizes IT to some extent.

Continuity of Operations Plan

This plan focuses on restoring mission-critical operations at an alternate location and performing these functions for an extended period of time. This type of plan addresses a wide variety of companywide concerns and typically is developed independent from a BC/DR plan, but clearly there are overlapping components that may need to be coordinated across the projects. A continuity of operations plan might be developed as the overarching project and the BC and DR plans may be considered subplans. IT operations and alternate IT arrangements clearly are an important part of any continuity of operations plan.

Disaster Recovery Plan

This plan focuses on restoration of key business processes immediately following an emergency or disaster. Unlike a BC plan, the DR plan typically does not include processes and procedures for ensuring the continuing and ongoing operations of the company long-term. Within the DR plan, there should be an IT section devoted to the technological needs of the company during an emergency and a section on the initial steps needed to restore all affected IT systems including business applications, servers, network infrastructure, and computer facilities to normal operations. It will also include the identification and specifications for an alternate operations site following an emergency. In some companies, noncomputer technologies such as communications equipment (cell phones, walkie-talkies, Blackberries) fall under the purview of the facilities manager rather than the IT department. As an IT professional, you are in an excellent position to understand how all corporate technology can be effectively deployed and utilized during an emergency, so your input on this topic, even if it's ultimately managed by some other department, can be extremely helpful.

Crisis Communication Plan

A crisis communication plan should be developed, either as part of your BC/DR plan overall, or as a separate but related project. Communicating effectively during a crisis can make a difference in determining whether the company ultimately succeeds or fails. It also can help employees maintain a sense of calm and order by giving them important information they might not have access to otherwise. During normal operations, employees gather information about the company from a variety of informal sources—instant messaging, chat, e-mail, and hallway conversations with coworkers. During a crisis, employees often are cut off from one another or unable to use normal communications channels. Planning for this and providing consistent and clear communications for employees and external parties helps organize recovery efforts and helps reduce some of the anxiety employees face when a disaster hits their company. Questions such as "was anyone injured?", "will I still get paid this Friday?", and "where should I report to work on Monday?" can be answered through the processes developed in advance.

In addition, you may have a large enough community or market presence that the media is swarming. Even if you're a small company and you experience a large fire, the local media may show up asking questions about how and when the company will resume operations. Without a clearly articulated crisis communication plan that kicks into gear when a disaster hits, you could end up with an uninformed employee talking inappropriately with the media, sharing unflattering information rather than having an official company spokesperson answering questions in an intelligent and thoughtful manner.

Cyber Incident Response Plan (CIRP)

This is certainly a plan that should be developed within the IT department and is most likely separate from the BC/DR plan. Although we typically think of disasters as large, physical events such as earthquake, fire, or flood, a security breach into a corporate network's critical areas can be a huge disaster on a number of levels. Therefore, your firm will need a CIRP as part of the DR portion of the BC/DR. The CIRP establishes procedures to immediately address cyber attacks against the organization. Procedures to identify the nature and extent of the attack, the ability to mitigate and stop the damage, and to recover from and resume IT operations should all be included. Clearly, cyber threats are ever-evolving and your CIRP will need to continue to evolve and be updated on a regular basis. Incidents such as unauthorized access, denial of service, data theft, data alteration, and unauthorized system reconfiguration are all examples of problems to be addressed by a CIRP. Like the BC and DR plans, the CIRP plan requires a specialized team that is trained and at the ready. A Cyber Incident Response Team (CIRT) should be formed and trained to quickly and effectively take action immediately upon discovery of a cyber incident. Typically, the faster and more decisive the action taken, the less damage done to the company's computer assets.

Occupant Emergency Plan

This type of plan is related specifically to the building's occupants. It includes how to safely exit the building in the event of a fire; where to gather outside the building or where to congregate inside a building if the best option is to *shelter-in-place*. It also details procedures for contacting emergency personnel including fire, police, and medical assistance. This plan is typically part of the Facilities department, but in the absence of such a department, you should include these types of plans in your BC/DR plan, either as part of the overarching BC/DR plan or as a subplan that ties in. Clearly, if the building experiences structural damage as part of the effects of an earthquake or bomb, it will impact other aspects of the company's operations and a BC/DR plan will be implemented. Developing fire drills and evacuation procedures (for example) may or may not be considered part of your company's BC/DR plan, though these details should be managed by someone at your company. In the absence of a Facilities department or manager, these functions often are handled by the Human Resources department.

We've run through six different types of plans that are all related, in one way or another, to business continuity and disaster recovery planning. Clearly, they all overlap to some extent. It's important that you evaluate your company's emergency and disaster readiness and determine which of these types of plans will most suit your company's needs. Some of these plans may be developed independently from the BC/DR plan. In other cases, you may form a steering committee or designate a Program Manager to oversee the development of a number of related subplans.

Project Stakeholders

Broadly defined, the stakeholders for a BC/DR plan can include the government, various regulatory agencies, financial markets, public shareholders, private shareholders, employees, vendors, suppliers, contractors, and the community at large. That's a large list and clearly, it's not appropriate to invite them all to your planning sessions. However, it is important that your project team consider the broadest scope possible so that you can ensure that various stakeholder interests are considered and included when appropriate. For example, if your firm is subject to financial, legal, or environmental regulations, these must be considered as part of your overall BC/DR plan. If your firm is subject to these regulations, you will most likely require input and assistance from specific subject matter experts such as your financial or legal counsel. If you have in-house experts responsible for maintaining compliance to various regulations, these folks can be invaluable resources as part of your planning team.

However, let's narrow the scope for a moment. *Stakeholders* are, by definition, those who have a stake or interest in the outcome, results, or activities of the project. This is important because we're not only talking about the *results* of the project but the *activities* of the project. That means that if you need to pull people from other departments or off of other projects, those department or project managers are stakeholders in your project—they have a stake in the outcome of your project. Their interest may be limited to when they can get their personnel back in the department or project. As you develop your BC/DR planning project, keep in mind all potential stakeholders. If your project is going to pull resources from other departments, for example, be sure to include those department managers in high-level project progress reports (if appropriate) so they are aware of the project's progress and have a contact person they can go to for status update or timelines. In small companies, this probably won't make much sense, but in larger companies or companies that are geographically dispersed, it can make the difference between gaining support for your project and irritating a bunch of people who have the distinct ability of making your life as project manager difficult.

The usual suspects should also be included in the list. Executives are stakeholders since they have a vested interest in the outcome (and effectiveness) of the project. They may have legal obligations as well, so they may be very closely tied into the project's objectives and outcomes. Even if there are no legal obligations, the executives or senior managers of the company should certainly care about the project's outcomes and objectives since the very survival of the company may depend on how well you define, create, implement, and maintain your BC/DR plan. Other stakeholders include facilities management, Human Resources (representing both HR functions and employees as a whole), operations management, marketing/sales/PR management, financial/legal management, and of course, IT management. If there are other departments in your company not represented by the preceding categories, include them if appropriate.

At this point, you may have a long list of project stakeholders. That's OK. At this point, you need to be *inclusive* rather than *exclusive*. As you move through your project planning process, you will develop communications plans to address the various categories of stakeholders so that you don't have a list of a thousand people to whom you have to report every day. Stakeholders' interests and concerns must be addressed, but it doesn't mean they need to participate in the project itself.

Project Requirements

Poorly defined project requirements can cause project failure, so what can you do to develop better project requirements? It begins with project definition, which we discussed earlier. What problem are you trying to solve? What is your mission statement or big-picture outcome? When you know what problem you're solving and what you're trying to achieve, you have defined the boundaries of your requirements.

Another activity that adds to the success of project requirements development is involving the right people early. If you wait until your plan is 50% complete to bring the Facilities Manager into the loop, you're likely to have missed something important or you have to rework much of your plan. Failing to bring the Facilities Manager into the loop at all would be even worse. It's not inconceivable that a plan would be created by the IT folks and completely omit facilities issues such as heating, cooling, drainage, and other issues. IT folks are smart but, like any other specialists, can become myopic and miss things that are obvious to others. So, word to the wise. Bring in the right experts early, and have them help develop the project requirements. It's easier to pare down requirements later than to try to add to them when you discover an omission or gap later on.

Let's look at some examples of project requirements for a BC/DR plan. Clearly, you'll need to create your own list and modify it as you move through your project in order to address the specific needs of your company, but this should give you a running start. You should start by delineating requirements known at the outset of the project, but accept that project management is an iterative process and you will have to revisit your requirements as more information becomes known and details become clearer. So, let's look at some samples.

- E-commerce functionality (define which functionality this includes) must remain up 99% of the time, enabling customers to place and manage orders and to receive order status. Functionality includes product presentation, price and product information presentation, search, shopping cart, payment, order processing, credit card processing, customer order notification, warehouse order notification, warehouse pick tickets, shipper notification, customer shipment tracking notification, and inventory management.

- E-commerce customer service must remain available 85% of the time, enabling customers to interact with company representatives to answer questions and resolve problems.

- Customer order fulfillment must remain in place, regardless of company warehouse status.

- Employees must be paid on a regular basis or on the normal schedule during an emergency.

Notice that the first requirement describes functional and technical requirements. Sometimes they're closely intertwined, other times you can list technical requirements and functional requirements separately. In this case, the e-commerce functions are required and the technical requirements of that functionality are described. Don't get caught up in whether something is a functional or technical requirement at first, just be sure to capture the requirements. You can always move them around later once you've capture the requirements.

This example shows a company that does 100% of its business via a Web site (or Web sites). Clearly, Web site uptime is critical and will be the primary focus of BC/DR planning efforts.

However, there are a lot of backend functions required to ensure that the Web site does more than electronically keep track of orders. Product must be in stock in inventory somewhere, someone must pick it, pack it, and ship it, and notify the customer it's been shipped. The on-hand inventory must be updated, credit cards have to be charged, income accounts must be updated, and so forth.

Well-defined project requirements will help you ensure that your project works once it's implemented. Although people rarely feel there is adequate time to plan (including creating project requirements), they will be forced to find the time to deal with the aftermath of a disaster. Thus, the choice is to take time to plan now to reduce the time to recover later, or extend the time to recover later with the high likelihood that recovery will fail and the business will close its doors.

Project Parameters

Project parameters are scope, budget, schedule, and quality. The scope of a project typically is defined by the objectives and resulting technical and functional requirements. However, you can also create scope statements. One method that is particularly helpful is to state what *is* and *is not* included in the project. Often by creating paired statements, you generate a clear picture of what the project work will entail. Although it may seem redundant to state what is not included, it helps avoid making incorrect assumptions. We all know that 100 people can read a statement and come away with 100 different interpretations of that statement. When you include both IS and IS NOT statements, you help narrow down the interpretations so that you are more confident that everyone is literally and figuratively on the same page. Scope is defined as the total amount of work to be accomplished; budget is the total cost; timeline is the schedule or total duration of the project; and quality is the number of defects you're willing to accept. In this case, defects might be total hours of downtime per incident.

The budget and schedule for the project will certainly require multiple refinements. However, you may be handed a deadline or a specific budget amount to which you must manage the project. In most companies, there is neither unlimited time nor unlimited money, so you will be required to limit one or more parameters. Just as a quick review, Figure 29.2 shows the relationship of scope, budget, schedule, and quality.

Figure 29.2 The Relationship among Project Parameters

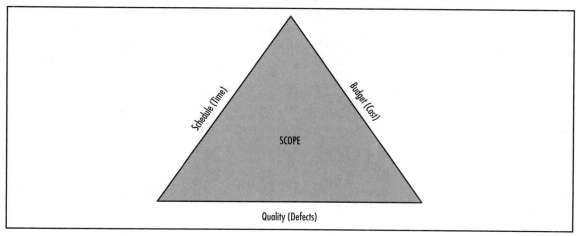

The project's scope should be defined at the outset by the amount of time and money you can devote to the project and also by the level of quality you require. Any change to the project's schedule, budget, or quality requires a change to the scope or to another parameter. For example, in Figure 29.3, you can see that if you reduce the budget and keep the schedule the same, the scope is reduced by a corresponding amount.

Figure 29.3 Reducing Budget Reduces Scope

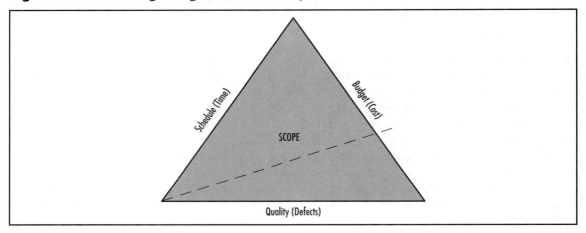

Another alternative to reducing scope is to increase another parameter. If you have to reduce your budget by 30%, you may be able to increase your schedule by some amount to offset the reduction in budget. If you have to reduce your schedule (meet a tight deadline), you really have only four choices: increase your budget, reduce your quality, reduce your scope, or cancel the project. In the case of a BC/DR project, cancelling the project is not a viable option (though often done), but in many other types of IT projects, it may actually be a viable alternative to consider. Figure 29.4 shows the impact on other project parameters of reducing the schedule to meet a deadline. In this case, the option is to cut the scope significantly. In other cases, you might choose to keep the scope the same but reduce quality or keep the scope the same and increase the budget. The bottom line is that you cannot reduce the schedule without impacting one or more of the other parameters.

Figure 29.4 Reducing Schedule to Meet a Deadline

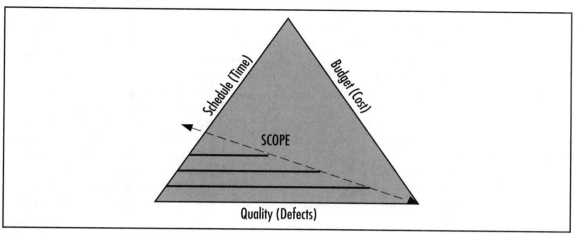

If you decrease the schedule and don't want to reduce the scope, you typically have to increase the budget. Sometimes you can reduce the quality, but that gets tricky. Quality usually is defined as the number of defects. In a BC/DR plan, it might mean the difference between requiring 90% critical systems availability and 75% critical systems availability. Although 75% might be considered a lower quality metric, it doesn't mean you're actually accepting a "poor" quality project deliverable. There are various areas in your BC/DR plan where you may say that a certain number or percentage is acceptable. This typically is done to address the interplay between planning for business continuity and working within known constraints.

If you have a specific budget or timeline, you'll have to compromise throughout your project planning process. Although it's best to start with the most optimal solution and scale it back from there, you may also start out knowing that you have significant constraints within which you have to work, and you begin your planning process there. Remember, it's unlikely that any realistic plan you devise will be perfect. The goal is to create a plan that is workable and that ultimately will keep you in business after you experience a business disruption such as a natural disaster or a security breach. In many cases, the cost of the project will be predetermined—an executive might say, "We understand this is important but our funds are stretched. We can devote $5,000 to this project over the next three months and not a nickel more." Therefore, your budget will be your *least flexible* parameter. This means that everything else will have to flex around your budget. Often this forces you to take longer to complete a project or to accomplish less work than desired. Regardless of whether or not you feel the parameters are optimal, you will have to manage your project to them.

Project parameters need to be ranked from least flexible to most flexible. The least flexible item is usually the one to which you must manage the entire project. In this case, we're assuming that the least flexible parameter will be your budget. Another parameter must be designated as most flexible in order to provide your team with the flexibility it needs to develop and implement the project successfully. The most flexible parameter is the one that will change when things go wrong (and they will go wrong). The other two project parameters may flex or not, depending on your company's constraints and the project's needs. As you develop these parameters, you will have to come back and make modifications once more detail is known. This typically occurs during or after the development of the Work Breakdown Structure (discussed later in this chapter). Once you know what tasks are involved in your project, you'll be able to create a better timeline, a tighter budget, and a more realistic view of the total project scope. Parameters can then be marked as less flexible, most flexible, or not labeled. By default, any project parameter not labeled as most or least flexible will flex only if needed.

Keep in mind that the project parameters are all interrelated. You can't change one without impacting the others. It's a certainty that something will go wrong in your project—the project management adage says "Things are more likely to go wrong than likely to go right" sums up how projects tend to run. Therefore, one of the project parameters must be able to flex. In a BC/DR project plan, this could be the scope, the timeline, or the quality. If your budget is least flexible and your scope is most flexible, you would do less project work if you find yourself straining your budget. If your timelines is most flexible, you would push your schedule out into the future to accommodate a tight budget. This might mean that you avoid overtime or that you schedule this project work around other higher priority projects. Finally, your quality might be the most flexible item and you might decide that your organization can put up with longer outages than originally identified. Sometimes a company will look at the cost of a BC/DR plan and determine that if the cost of creating the plan is X, then it is willing to put up with an outage of 0.25X at any given time. Some people think that designating a parameter as the one that will flex is a crafty way of saying you don't have to make a solid commitment and hit real targets. No so. The reality is that you will find that as the project moves forward, unanticipated things happen to which you must respond. When you have your project parameters labeled as most to least flexible, you know how to make appropriate decisions. If you go into your project saying that you will hit all four project parameters on the nose, you have very little chance of success. It doesn't mean that you won't give your absolute best effort to meeting the metrics to which you've committed, but it does give you (and your project sponsor) a solid framework in which you can make decisions when things change or go wrong. Also keep in mind that as you move through your project definition and project planning stages, your project parameters will become better defined. You may have to settle for estimates in the early stages and redefine these parameters as detail becomes known. Once you have a project plan in place, you will have to commit to those parameters as targets, but you'll still need to understand the interplay of these parameters to make appropriate adjustments as project work progresses.

Project Infrastructure

Project infrastructure refers to the tools and resources you'll need to have at your disposal as you develop your BC/DR project. This might include computers, software applications, testing labs, communications equipment, and more. For example, if you're working with a team located in several countries around the world, your project infrastructure might include some sort of collaboration software, net meeting capabilities, along with e-mail and instant messaging. Since you'll likely be working at different hours, depending on the time zones involved, you'll need tools that allow you to manage a cohesive team while working within the local constraints. Your infrastructure needs for your team should also be viewed with an eye toward your BC/DR planning. Which of these tools might be useful if one location were to experience a natural disaster or business disruption? Which of these tools would be completely useless or inappropriate? Whenever possible, you should look at the technology and infrastructure tools you use in your planning process to determine whether it would also be a good tool during a disaster or event.

The infrastructure for a BC/DR planning project may be as simple as e-mail, instant messaging, and a shared folder on a network drive. It might be quite a bit more complex, especially if you work in a large, geographically dispersed organization with multiple sites or many different business units. Clearly, the infrastructure for a 10-person software development company or a 50-person nonprofit social agency is very different than the infrastructure needed for a 10,000-person, 40-worldwide-location, 10-business-unit type of company.

Defining the infrastructure you'll use to plan and implement your project is important at the outset so that you know what you will have access to, what you can use, and what's off limits. Defining your infrastructure needs may impact your budget if you don't have the infrastructure in place, but in most cases, it's a matter of simply defining what infrastructure you'll need, how you'll acquire it, and how you'll utilize it to accomplish project objectives.

Remember that geographically dispersed teams may have varying levels of access to infrastructure such as conference calling, video conferencing, net meetings, e-mail, instant messaging, shared team intranet web sites or portals, and so on. For example, some members of the team may have access to wireless Internet access, others may have to be at a corporate location to connect. Some members of the team may be able to make international phone calls, others may not. Some members of the team may have reliable communications lines, others may not. Keep these considerations in mind as you plan your project's infrastructure.

Project Processes

Processes needed for developing and running a BC/DR plan are similar, if not identical, to running any other sort of IT project. If you're an experienced project manager, you probably have notes on processes and procedures you've used in the past, which you can pull out, dust off, and review. In most cases, these processes and procedures can be reused, though usually with slight modification. If you're not an experienced project manager, you might be wondering what sorts of processes you'll need. There are numerous resources you can reference; we've included a few of the basics here to give you a jump start.

Clearly, you'll need to adjust existing processes to address the unique needs of your BC/DR team. In many cases, an experienced PM has a set of documents he or she uses for every project, modifying the processes slightly each time to fit the circumstance. If you're not an experienced project manager, you will need to define all the project processes you plan on using. Some may argue against documenting these processes, stating they are a waste of time to document. It may not be useful to document every process, but it is well worth your while to define and document (and later archive) these processes for two primary reasons. First, it will reduce problems later if you have a set process for handling common project tasks or processes. Consistency in project work typically yields higher quality results, so defining processes that can be reused during the project (such as the process for generating progress reports or the process for running team meetings) will help save time and lead to better results. For example, if you're stumbling around during each team meeting because you don't have or aren't following a set process for running team meetings, you're wasting everyone's time. You'll find that people begin to skip team meetings because they view them as a waste of time. This leads to other problems that ripple through the project. A second compelling reason for creating these processes and documenting them is that at the end of your project, you can review these processes, make adjustments, and file them away. When your next project comes along, you simply have to pull out the files, review them for appropriateness, make minor modifications, and move along in your project work. Using processes that have been used and tested over time usually leads to higher productivity and lower stress for you and your team. You should take advantage of any opportunity to save yourself time and aggravation.

Team Meetings

Project processes in a BC/DR planning project are basically the same as those used in any other type of IT project plan, with one exception. BC/DR plans typically span across organizational and functional boundaries. Many IT projects do not. You'll need to determine how the team works together and how information will be shared, stored, and archived. You'll also need to address the logistical aspects such as determining how, when, and where the team will meet. Letting team members know how meetings will be set, at what interval, how they'll be notified or reminded, how agendas are determined, and how meetings will be run is all part of defining the team meeting process.

Reporting

You'll need to develop a two-tiered reporting process. One level of reporting will be you, as IT Project Manager, reporting to your project sponsor regarding the overall status of the project and any challenges or roadblocks you encounter that impact the project or with which you need sponsor assistance. The other level of reporting will be reporting from your project team to you, as IT Project Manager. You'll need to develop reporting methods using processes and procedures familiar to those in your company. Whenever possible, you want to avoid reinventing processes and procedures for two reasons. First, developing new procedures often leads to resistance because team members are unfamiliar with them. Second, new procedures can cause unintended effects that can ripple through the team or the department's productivity. Whenever possible, keep reporting requirements focused. Avoid dragging a wide net gathering every last detail. There may be an appropriate place to create a repository, such as creating a project-related *wiki* into which team members can dump all their collective knowledge. Keep formal reporting to the elements that actually impact the project's progress and ultimate success. Your teammates will appreciate your lean operating style and you won't have to pour through reams of documents to find pertinent details.

Escalation

How will problems within the project or external problems that impact the project be escalated? It's important to define this process before it's needed. You'll need to know which problems require sponsor notification or sponsor approval versus problems that require escalation through a different channel than the project sponsor. If you have a problem with a team member that cannot be resolved, how will that be handled? By you? Your boss? The team member's boss? If you have a major problem getting payment for an approved expenditure to a vendor, how should that be escalated? If you run into a serious project roadblock and all work has to come to a stop until it's resolved, how is that escalated? Your basic escalation procedures may include a division of internal and external. Problems that are internal to the team will be treated in one manner, problems external to the team (i.e., within the company at large) will likely be treated in a different manner. Similarly, problems internal to the company will be addressed in one way, problems external to the company (i.e., with vendors or regulators) will most likely be handled in a different manner.

The escalation procedures for each category should include *boundaries*—which issues qualify for escalation? If possible, create specific and quantifiable metrics for deciding which issues are escalated. In most cases, these escalation procedures should be provided to the team so they understand how issues will be resolved. There may be a subset of the escalation procedures you choose not to share with the team, but in general the more the team knows about how things will work, the more effective they can be in making project-related decisions.

Escalation procedures should also indicate the chain of command for various types of problems so that you know which is the appropriate resource to utilize should a problem arise. Which types of issues should be brought to your manager, to your sponsor, to someone else's manager, to the executive team?

Finally, delineate how escalated issues will be tracked and closed. Some project managers like to dispatch issues as Closed–Resolved, Closed–Unresolved, Open, and Deferred. Whatever categories you choose, define how they'll be used and use them consistently.

Project Progress

How will the progress of project work be tracked? You might choose to have task and project progress tracked through team reporting, through an interactive team web site, or through other tools you may have used in the past or have available to you for this project. Again, as with reporting, keep it simple. It's human nature to fudge reports and progress notes if the requirement for producing such documentation is overly burdensome. In plain English, encourage your team to give you the real data you need with as little effort as possible. Think about how you'll need to report project progress to the executive team and to your project sponsor, then determine the bare minimum you need to know from your team. Start from there and add to the tracking requirements only as needed. Also, just because certain data may be available to you or your team, it doesn't mean that data helps you monitor project progress or help move the project forward any better. Keep it streamlined and simple whenever possible and be sure that you're asking for data that actually is useful in monitoring or managing the project.

Change Control

Most projects encounter the need for some sort of change along the way. In a BC/DR project, one of the most likely sources of change is that a new technology is being implemented. For example, if your firm decides to implement a customer relationship management (CRM) solution, you'll need to add that to the scope of your BC/DR plan so that you can address the specific needs related to this application. The business will not stand still while you're planning your BC/DR project, so there's a good likelihood some sort of change will be required as you move forward. What process will you use to control change?

Though it's outside the scope of this chapter to discuss change control in detail, a few reminders will probably help. First, though it may sound clichéd, it's still true: Control change or change will control your project. Define a change request process so that needed changes must be formally requested. This provides you and your team the opportunity to evaluate the requested change. In too many companies, someone (usually an executive) with clout will demand a change to the project and everyone on the project team will scurry around trying to incorporate that change. Without a formal process for managing it, change will be introduced into your project in a random fashion. Once you have a defined process for requesting change, you should develop a defined process for evaluating change. The evaluation should include the risks involved with making the change, the risks involved with not making the change, and the impact to the scope, schedule, budget, and quality of the project if the change is implemented. Finally, you should have a change tracking process that indicates that a change was requested, reviewed, accepted, and incorporated.

Quality Control

Quality control is a topic that can fill volumes on its own, so we'll limit our discussion to quality control as it relates to BC/DR projects. Clearly, one error in the project plan could mean the difference between getting a critical system back up and running in one hour versus one month. However, it's unrealistic to expect that you will have zero defects in your project plan and implementation. How much quality is enough? It's always an interplay between how much time and money you have and how critical the systems are. For example, you might decide to spend a disproportionately greater amount of time testing your CRM or ERP BC/DR functions and a disproportionately lesser amount of time testing some other part of your plan. If your CRM or ERP application is the most critical application from a corporate perspective, you may choose to devote the most planning, implementation and testing to this area to ensure as close to 100% quality as possible. Although specific quality metrics for BC/DR plans may be difficult to develop or measure, you can use qualitative methods to determine what level of quality is required for each element of your plan.

There are many other project processes that you'll no doubt develop or use, but these are some of the basics to get you started thinking along these lines. If it's something you do repeatedly, you should consider developing a process for it so that you can perform more consistently and not have to think about (or reinvent) the process over and over again.

Project Communication Plan

Technically speaking, the communications plan may be considered part of the project processes. However, communications are so vital to the success of any project that it's listed as a separate entity because it has a unique level of importance and awareness. With a BC/DR plan, your need to communicate across departmental, positional, and geographic boundaries may be greater than in any other IT project plan you've worked on. That can be a tall order for even the most seasoned project manager. How can you be sure you're communicating to the right people with the right language in the right frequency and the right medium? One of the best ways is to check with your subject matter experts, who are typically the founding members of the team. If you're going to be working with technology plans that touch the entire organization, you will probably need to communication with all corners of the organization. Those people on the team who represent the various areas of the company are probably in the best position to provide input as to how, when, and in what format to communicate with their constituents. It will ultimately depend on where your BC/DR plan falls in the overall list of priorities. If your plan is low on the list of priorities, timely and positive communication might help boost its rating. On the other hand, there are times when you might want to communicate only as needed in order to keep your project flying below the radar (to avoid it being canceled or reduced in scope, for example). Typically, communicating project progress is good for the project and a bit of positive PR can go a long way. However, in BC/DR projects that may not be too popular to begin with, you may decide your best move is to keep your team and your project sponsor fully informed but avoid more expansive communications. A discussion with your manager or project sponsor on this topic will help you develop an effective communication plan that fits in with the overall political climate of your organization.

Common Challenges

Communicating Results of a Low Priority Project

We can emphasize the importance of business continuity and disaster recovery planning until the cows come home, but the truth of the matter is that some companies just don't care. You might find IT professionals creating BC/DR plans almost on the sly or as part of another IT initiative so they don't have to formally announce a project that will get stonewalled from the start. Depending on how your company runs, it may be possible that you're working on a BC/DR plan without a formal charter—without formal recognition or approval from existing corporate authorities. As we've mentioned several times, some basic BC/DR planning can be incorporated in other IT activities. Though this is not an optimal situation, it is better than doing no BC/DR planning at all. So, how do you communicate to the organization if you have no formal BC/DR plan or if you know that your BC/DR activities might be thwarted if they came to light? Your communication plan, in that case, may be limited to those individuals who will be impacted by your plan. You may choose not to use the terms *business continuity* or *disaster recovery*. Instead, you may ask, "What would happen if this system went down?" This is clearly something that must be addressed in any organization, so if using the phrase BC/DR planning will get you off-track, don't use that language.

For those of you who might think this is a bit underhanded, remember that IT staff have to deal with the reality of system outages every day, whether a server fan goes out and the unit overheats or whether a vital cable is disconnected from a router. The point is that business disruptions will occur, regardless of whether you plan for them or not and regardless of what you call them. So, you might as well build in some BC/DR planning to your IT activities and avoid an all out communications blitz if that's what it takes to protect your company, your employees, and your job. Granted, if you don't have executive level authorization or support for your BC/DR project, you will not be able to count on wildly successful results, but that doesn't mean you can't still make a positive impact... quietly.

Project Planning

Planning the BC/DR project involves all the typical steps you'd undertake in any IT project planning process. However, there are two key elements in the project planning process worth discussing here. Developing the Work Breakdown Structure for your BC/DR plan essentially defines the scope of the project. By definition, the Work Breakdown Structure (WBS) is the list of outcomes that must be accomplished in order to successfully complete the project; it describes 100% of the required work. Therefore, a well-developed WBS helps you deliver a successful project. The *critical path* is, by definition, all tasks in the project that if delayed will delay the completion of the project. Why is this important? If you are trying to meet a deadline for completing your BC/DR plan, you'll need to understand which tasks in the WBS are on the critical path and which are not. Those that are on the critical path can delay project completion, those not on the critical path cannot delay project completion. As a result, tasks not on the critical path are more flexible as to when they can be scheduled. Let's look at WBS and critical path in more detail as they relate to creating your BC/DR plan.

Work Breakdown Structure

The top level of your WBS in your BC/DR plan will most likely follow the structure of this book: Risk Assessment, Business Impact Analysis, Risk Mitigation Strategy Development, Plan Development, Emergency Preparation, Training, Testing, Auditing, Maintenance. As we move through the remaining chapters of this section, you can compare your WBS structure to the material in this book. You may have additional elements for your WBS that are specific to your company's BC/DR needs; feel free to include those.

Remember, the completed WBS should describe the total amount of work to be accomplished. If there is a mismatch at this point, you need to reassess your WBS or your project's scope. These two items should be aligned so that the scope is fully described in the WBS (or that the WBS fully describes the desired scope). The elements of your WBS may vary from those outlined in this book, but the overall elements should match fairly closely. If there are any discrepancies, be sure they were by intent and not by accident.

Critical Path

The critical path in your BC/DR plan will describe exactly how long the project will take and which tasks will delay the project if you run into problems on those tasks. Remember, tasks not on the critical path are the tasks that provide you and the project team with a bit of flexibility. As you probably know, tasks not on the critical path, by definition, have some float. *Float* is (essentially) the time flexibility of a task—it can be completed this week or next week without impacting the overall timing of the project. Tasks can move on or off the critical path. A noncritical path task that is delayed long enough may end up on the critical path. A critical path task may, for some reason, move off the critical path if you discover there is some flexibility in the timing of the task. The key is to understand the tasks that are on the critical path and make sure you keep a close eye on these tasks if you are working on a tight timeline. If your schedule is your least flexible element (as discussed earlier), then you will have to manage to your critical path more than to your budget. You might face this situation if you are required by a customer to provide a BC/DR plan by a certain date in order to close a large deal. You may also be required by certain regulatory or governmental agencies to complete and submit a BC/DR plan by a certain deadline in order to meet compliance requirements or to avoid heavy financial or legal penalties. In these cases, your critical path will define your project's timeline and will be the key to successfully managing to a required schedule.

Looking Ahead...

Strategically Planning Your Project Schedule

In planning your business continuity and disaster recovery activities, you're likely to find that the risk assessment and business impact analysis are the most tangible aspects to the process and are therefore the phases that move along smoothly. Conversely, when you get into the actual risk mitigation and emergency response strategies, you may find the project getting bogged down. It's easier for most people to sit around and discuss theoretical issues (what happens if the building catches fire, how would that impact the business) than to devise practical solutions within given constraints. In scheduling your project, you may want to account for this and move the early phases along more quickly and allow more time for strategy development rather than giving equal time to each phase or section of the planning process.

Project Implementation

Since we're focusing on the IT aspects of a business continuity and disaster recovery plan, we need to state the obvious: IT is a moving target. Unlike an area such as facilities, which is usually a fairly stable and static area, IT is always changing. From reconfigurations to new security threats to moving a data center, there's no shortage of change in the IT department. How does this impact your BC/DR project implementation? It means that you will need to build in a process for monitoring change in the IT department and assessing what should be incorporated into your BC/DR plan. Here's an example. A nonprofit agency decides it needs an IT BC/DR plan. The IT director, with her staff of four, creates a plan. In the meantime, they have funds that must be spent before the end of the fiscal year that are earmarked for a case management application. The application must be implemented and it requires the use of Windows Server 2003 and SQL Server 2005. These should certainly be included in the plan so BC/DR issues can be addressed. If the agency's location has a major fire, how will the server hardware be affected? Is it on-site? What about backups? What arrangements should be made to have alternative server hardware available? What arrangements should be made for off-site backup and data recovery? How will this be shaped by the implementation of the new application? These are the kinds of questions that may come up throughout the lifecycle of your BC/DR planning process because other IT projects are in various stages of planning, design, implementation, and testing. Each of these must be assessed for their impact on your BC/DR planning and each must be assessed for the BC/DR impact on these projects. The interaction between your BC/DR planning activities and all your other IT projects is a two-way street—each ultimately impacts the other.

Ideally, you should strive to add BC/DR types of assessments and considerations into your standard IT processes. Over time, you'll discover this makes keeping your BC/DR plan up-to-date a bit less onerous. You might also discover ways to save time and money or streamline processes along the way.

Managing Progress

Managing project progress is often a matter of organizational and project manager traits. As unique as each company and each project is, there are a few things that you should keep in mind for your BC/DR planning project. As mentioned previously, you should have some method of ensuring that current IT changes and initiatives are evaluated in your BC/DR planning. It would make no sense to develop a risk mitigation strategy for a technology that is being phased out or to purchase some solution that is easily rolled into a current or planned initiative. As simple as this sounds, it's often complex in practice. It's easy to suggest that various technologies be evaluated as part of your BC/DR plan; it's another matter entirely to make sure that happens. Your project processes (described earlier in this chapter) should include some method of keeping an eye on what's going on in the IT department across the enterprise. You should develop a method of evaluating and incorporating technological components. We'll look at risk assessment in detail in the next chapter and that will provide you with some of the tools to evaluate the risk to various technologies. Once you understand the risk and the potential strategies to reduce that risk, you will have a better sense of which IT initiatives underway in your organization will likely come into play. It might be at that point that you talk with the entire IT team to see how their work impacts your project and how your project might impact their work.

In addition to keeping an eye on changing technology, you'll need to make sure you use a consistent method to monitor and measure project progress including standard tools such as reporting, dashboards, and whatever tools you are accustomed to. Since this type of project spans beyond the scope (and authority) of the IT department, you'll also need to use your best people skills to keep the project moving forward since it's likely you won't have the authority to require that project work be accomplished. This is true of many types of IT projects, and it's especially true of BC/DR projects that definitely cross all organizational boundaries and that often have a low priority in the day-to-day scheme of things.

Managing Change

Any experienced IT project manager will tell you that managing a project is managing change. Despite our best efforts, our plans are always subject to change in the dynamic world of business. Although there must be certain areas that are nonnegotiable (these are typically the least flexible project parameters), there must be some room for change in a project in order for it to have any chance for success. Earlier we discussed the importance of preventing 40 people to request/demand changes to your project. Without requiring the consistent use of your defined change management process, you'll end up with a project scope that is all over the map and four times larger than originally defined. As an IT project manager, you're probably familiar with managing change, but perhaps not across corporate boundaries. Let's review a few pointers for managing change effectively:

1. Define a simple, easy-to-use change management process.

2. Require that all requested changes go through the change management process.

3. Evaluate each requested change as to how it will impact the current project plan.

4. Evaluate the risk to each requested change and determine if it increases or decreases risk in the plan.

5. Incorporate the requested change into the plan and update all parts of the plan impacted by the change.

6. When possible, incorporate one change at a time so each can be properly evaluated.

7. Do not allow random or informal change requests to become incorporated into the plan.

8. Communicate with those requesting change as to the status of their request.

9. Communicate the rationale for rejecting a change request and be willing to listen. It may be possible you overlooked a critical factor or misunderstood key data.

10. Keep track of all requested changes and how they are ultimately handled (accepted, rejected, postponed) and why.

Project Tracking

The metrics used to track projects vary with each company and with each IT PM's systems of project tracking, so there is no single, universal method for tracking a project. One of the keys to a successful project is to create multiple milestones so that you can easily see where you are versus where you said you would be. At minimum, you should create milestones for each phase of work. Using our framework as an example, you should have a milestone at risk assessment, business impact analysis, and other phases. However, if these phases or sections are going to span months, you should create interim milestones. If you have a small company and your risk assessment activities will span a week or two, one major milestone is probably sufficient. Milestones will keep you on track but you shouldn't create so many that you drive yourself and everyone around you nuts.

As an experienced IT PM, you also know that tracking involves monitoring the budget, keeping an eye on the scope and quality, and making sure change is being properly handled. Depending on how your company operates and what tools are available, you can use any one of a number of programs to track project progress, schedules, expenditures, and such. With BC/DR planning, you'll need to make sure that whatever you ask of team members to enable you to track the project is available to them. Remember that the Facilities Manager may not have access to the same tools you do or that they may not be as comfortable with project tracking tools as you are.

There are more detailed ways to evaluate and track project progress including Earned Value Analysis, Schedule Performance Index, Cost Performance Index, and Estimate At Completion, to name several of the more commonly used tools. Discussion of these tools is outside the scope of this book but you can certainly learn more about these methods through a variety of sources.

Project Close Out

In most IT projects, project close out involves a hand-off to some other organization. It might be that the new wireless infrastructure is now managed by a different subset of IT staff or that the new application is now maintained through normal application maintenance procedures. The same holds true for your BC/DR plan. Once you have completed the plan, it must be kept up to date through some sort of maintenance procedures. In many organizations, this is as simple as an annual review of the plan and a paper walk-through of the business continuity and disaster recovery steps delineated in the plan. In other companies, it might involve actually testing out some of the BC/DR procedures and even testing some of the defined recovery processes. Maintenance of the plan is important if for no other reason than the plan took a lot of time and effort to create and it takes far less effort to keep it current. As we've mentioned, an outdated plan can be worse than no plan at all because incorrect assumptions might be made. For instance, if a legacy system was slated as a fail-safe backup technology and that legacy system has since been decommissioned, your fail-safe backup is gone. If a disaster strikes now, the assumption that there is a bottom line fail-safe option is incorrect and could spell the difference between the company surviving the incident or not. Be sure your project close out activities include handing off the BC/DR plan in such as way as it will be maintained. It can be helpful to schedule the annual check up at the close of the project so that it will be on the calendar, though it's also likely that in 12 months, that calendar will change and your review plans may be impacted.

Also as part of best practices in project management, it's a great idea to have a post-project review session to review what worked, what went wrong, and how project processes could be improved in the future. Taking away lessons learned and best practices from each project you participate in (or lead) can help improve organizational results and your personal effectiveness as an IT project manager. It will also save you time and money in the future to avoid the obvious mistakes. The goal is not to stop making mistakes—mistakes will always happen—but to avoid making the same mistake twice. Capturing best practices and lessons learned from across the organization might help you fine-tune other IT projects in progress and might also help streamline your BC/DR project review process.

Key Contributors and Responsibilities

Thus far, we've talked in fairly general terms about the business continuity and disaster recovery planning process. In this section, we'll discuss key contributors to your BC/DR plan and what the roles and responsibilities should be in an ideal scenario. While we outline the ideal scenario, you'll need to take a look at your company specifically and make modifications as needed. For example, your company may be so small there is no Facilities manager and that task falls to the Human Resources director or the IT director. Your company may be so large that there are multiple levels of Facilities management up to and including a vice president. You'll need to scale the information in this section to your company's size and needs, but this will give you a good overview to use as your starting point.

First, let's list the roles and contributors and then delve into the details of each:

- Information Technology
- Human Resources
- Facilities/Security
- Finance/Legal
- Warehouse/Inventory/Manufacturing/Research
- Purchasing/Logistics

- Marketing and Sales
- Public Relations

Information Technology

Since we're focusing on information technology in this BC/DR planning process, you clearly need representatives from the IT group on this project. Which members of the team should participate? Well, that largely depends on the size and scope of your IT department. If it's a three-person IT department, all three of you probably have to participate. If you have a team of 40, you will need to select those people best suited to this project. Some of the factors you can consider in making your decision can be:

- Experience working on a cross-departmental team
- Ability to communicate effectively
- Ability to work well with a wide variety of people
- Experience with critical business and technology systems
- IT project management leadership

Experience Working on a Cross-Departmental Team

Having IT people on your BC/DR team that have successfully worked on a cross-departmental project can help facilitate the success of your BC/DR project. They may have established positive working relationships with key people in other departments that you can draw upon for your BC/DR project. They may have learned how to navigate some of the tricky political waters in your organization or they may simply have developed a broader organizational perspective that can help as you work across departmental boundaries to develop a successful plan.

Conversely, you want to try to exclude those who have developed a reputation for being difficult and not working well with others (especially in other departments). Though you don't always have a choice as to who's on your team and who's not, avoid troublemakers from the start. If you need their expertise on the project, try to contain them and restrict their interaction with others to a bare minimum. For example, if you have someone on the team that is the subject matter expert for a critical business application, try to have that person work with as small a subset of the project team as possible. It's better to annoy three people than 30.

Ability to Communicate Effectively

The business continuity and disaster recovery project planning process is all about being able to discuss risks, alternatives, and strategies that work for a variety of stakeholders. Without the ability to communicate effectively with all kinds of people—technical, nontechnical, executive, management, and front-line—your team and your project will suffer. It's not uncommon to find some of the best technical people are the most challenged in terms of interpersonal communication skills. If that's the case in your IT department, you may want to include a few generalists who understand the technology and can also communicate effectively with a variety of people. These folks can act as translators, taking very technical or detailed information and paraphrasing it for other non-IT members of the team. If you don't have at least one person on the team who is an excellent communicator with regard to IT, you may well find that you have some serious miscommunications that occur through the course of the project.

Ability to Work Well with a Wide Variety of People

The ability to work well with a wide variety of people often accompanies the ability to communicate effectively. IT members on the BC/DR team will have to interact with end-users, facilities people, financial people, and many others during the course of the project.. The last thing you need is someone from the IT department representing the BC/DR project in a way that alienates the rest of the company. An example that probably jumps to mind for many of you might be the stereotypical "know it all" IT person who talks down to those who don't understand the intricate details of the technology. These people tend to simply make enemies where none existed and you don't need the added problems this type of person brings to a cross-functional team project.

Here's one more tip: Because your team may need to communicate with corporate vice presidents, department heads, or front-line staff, make sure that you, as project manager, or someone on your team is comfortable talking candidly and appropriately with people in all positions. Some people get nervous talking with those who are much higher up in the corporate hierarchy and are unable or unwilling to speak candidly. Others don't understand what constitutes "appropriate" communication and they tend to drone on or disclose inconsequential or embarrassing information. Make sure you or someone on your team is comfortable with and capable of interacting at all levels of the organization into which this BC/DR project may take you.

Experience with Critical Business and Technology Systems

Having people from the IT department with experience in critical business and technology systems almost goes without saying, but we'll say it anyway so it's not overlooked. Clearly, the critical business systems from IT's perspective may not be the same critical business systems from the CEO's perspective or from the financial analyst's perspective. You'll have time to test out your assumptions as you move through your project. If you're a small IT shop, this is probably a moot point. In larger IT departments, you'll need to look at your staffing needs and determine who should participate. This almost always runs into problems because your IT staff have many other roles, responsibilities, day-to-day tasks, and project tasks they need to address. Often you are forced to choose between the person who is your first choice and the person who has the time or bandwidth to deal with your project. Unfortunately, the person who gets things done and delivers the best results is probably the person with the least time and bandwidth available.

In addition, you'll need to balance the needs of your project with the needs of the IT department's ongoing activities. If you're in the middle of a roll out of a new technology, it's going to be tough to find the time and resources to also participate in BC/DR planning. This may impact your overall BC/DR schedule or it might force you to work creatively with those subject matter experts. One potential work around is to flag the technologies you think are critical but wait until you've confirmed this information with the rest of the organization. Once you've identified critical systems from an organizational perspective, you can then tap necessary resources. This small work around might provide a bit of flexibility so that you can still utilize the subject matter experts you need without reworking your schedule or theirs.

IT Project Management Leadership

We're assuming you're the IT project manager and you're heading up this project. However, whenever you can tap others with leadership ability, you'll get that much more mileage from your project. Clearly, you want people with leadership abilities who can also work effectively as part of a team. You don't need four or five people all trying to manage the project. Good leaders usually know how to follow and to head up smaller groups or initiatives within a project team. Tap into these resources to take some of the burden off your shoulders as long as these folks won't be the cause of messy political maneuvers and power plays. Remember, a good project manager willingly delegates to others on the team and spends more of his or her time monitoring project progress. When you have competent people on the team who will take leadership roles, your job of delegating and monitoring will be that much easier.

Human Resources

Depending on how your company is organized, you may find that Human Resources (HR) encompasses many of the other functions listed in this section. In small companies, HR ends up being the catch-all for all the miscellaneous functions that have no home. In large companies, the miscellaneous functions typically are large enough to require a distinct department such as facilities, security, or public relations. We'll stay focused on traditional HR functions in this section, but as you read through subsequent sections, keep in mind they may be housed in HR. Regardless of how or where the function is managed, they all need to be represented in the BC/DR planning process.

Human Resources typically is responsible for helping to recruit new employees; managing the legal issues around hiring, firing, and performance management; and managing the payroll process including periodic paychecks, contributions to retirement accounts or saving accounts, increases due to promotions or raises, and managing other required paperwork such as verifying citizenship or the right to work in the country.

How will these functions be impacted by a fire in the building or a flood or earthquake in the area? The best person to answer that question is someone (or several people) from the HR department. What computer systems do they use to process payroll and other HR functions? What applications do they use? What forms are required by law? What forms are required by the company? These are questions your HR specialists will have to answer when you get into the BC/DR planning process. For now, think of who in your company is responsible for these functions and add them to the list of team members.

Facilities/Security

As mentioned, the function of facilities and security may be handled by your HR staff if you're in a small company, or these functions may be handled by someone in operations. Regardless of where these two functions are housed, they are a critical part of the BC/DR planning process and should be represented by subject matter experts. Facilities typically handles the management of the office, warehouse, manufacturing, or storage spaces including cleaning, maintenance, set up, build outs, and remodels. They deal with occupancy and tenant issues as well as other legal or licensing requirements related to business operations in the facility. The department (or function) also usually handles the installation, management, and monitoring of key utilities such as electricity, gas, water and, in some companies, communications equipment (Internet connections, telephones, cell phones, mobile radios, mobile devices, walkie talkies, etc.).

Security includes controlling and monitoring access to the building, facilities, and grounds, dealing with imminent dangers such as structural, mechanical, or electrical failures, and sometimes dealing with employees who have been terminated or who are behaving in a manner contrary to acceptable and safe means. Security provided by most companies is to secure the assets of the company, not to provide policing services. Therefore, you can't assume that your security staff deals with all aspects of security. Nevertheless, both facilities and security functions should be well-represented in your BC/DR planning project. You'll need to answer questions such as these: What is our fire drill policy? How is the building evacuated in the event of a fire or other internal disaster? What plans are in place for protecting staff from external dangers such as nearby chemical spills, noxious fumes, or railroad derailment? If something happens to the building, how will access to and from the building be controlled? What tools, supplies, and equipment will be needed by the company's emergency staff to communicate with each other and manage the initial impact of a business disruption such as a fire, explosion or earthquake? Again, these questions should not be answered at this juncture, but these are the types of questions that will be asked and answered later, within the scope of your BC/DR project plan.

Finance/Legal

In some companies, it is the finance department, not Human Resources, that handles the payroll processing function. Finance also handles the tracking and managing of accounts payable (money owed to others) and accounts receivable (money owed to the company). Clearly, the company's very survival depends on being able to keep track of what is owed and what is due. Without the ability to manage the income and outflow of funds, the company cannot survive for very long. Certainly, the bank with which your company does business has records of recent transactions, so the cash in the bank is relatively secure. The problem clearly is with the receivables and payables. No company can survive the loss of information related to these types of transactions, so understanding what systems track that data as well as where and how that data is stored, backed up, and archived will be critical to your BC/DR plan.

The legal aspects of data security in the event of a disaster is a topic too broad to discuss at length in this book. However, there are important legal considerations when looking at your company's responsibilities for data security and integrity in the normal course of business as well as in the face of a major or minor business interruption. AThere are definite legal requirements to be dealt with. Although the legal aspects may not be your responsibility to address, as IT project manager your job is to ensure the project meets all requirements, and some of those requirements may be legal. You should contact your company's legal counsel and discuss your BC/DR plans with them. You can then follow their recommendations as to how to ensure your BC/DR plans meet minimum legal requirements.

As with other corporate functions, you'll need to be sure the financial and legal requirements are met within the scope of the BC/DR plan. This may include compliance with financial or legal requirements related to data security and integrity; it may include simply being able to process payroll after a significant business disruption or understanding how you'll recreate your accounts payable and accounts receivable files so you can resume the task of collecting money due and paying money owed.

Warehouse/Inventory/ Manufacturing/Research

If your company maintains warehouses or facilities with inventory, manufacturing, research, or other similar activities, you'll need representatives from these areas to answer specific questions related to the BC/DR process. Certainly some of these areas are covered by facilities and security such as access to secure areas or repair of broken or ruptured pipes, for example. However, facilities staff will not be able to tell you which equipment is mission critical, which research is vital to the ongoing success of the company, or which inventory is most important to the company. These are questions that can be answered only by experts in those areas. Because this may well be the heart of corporate operations, you may need to use a phased approach to BC/DR planning with this group. For example, what would it take to get back up and running in a minimal manner? Next, determine what it would take to get back up and running in a normal manner. These are often two distinct phases that must be planned out. We'll address this in more detail later in the book.

Common Challenges

Using the "What If"...

Remember, it's likely that just about everyone in every corner of your company will view their work as vital to the ongoing success and operations of the company. In reality, there are critical functions and important support functions, but not everything that goes on is actually mission critical. Unfortunately, you'll be caught in the middle of the stream. As IT project manager for this BC/DR project, you won't necessarily have the expertise to say which are and are not critical functions, so you'll be dependent upon subject matter experts to make that determination. At the same time, they are the very ones with the vested interest in their areas or activities being labeled "critical" or "vital" to ongoing operations. One method to sort this out is to ask specific questions rather than vague, values-based questions. Instead of asking, "What's the most important function here?", you may need to ask, "What if this system went down? What would you do?" or "What if this room caught on fire and charred everything to bits, what would you do?" Asking specific scenario-based questions can help you move past egos and agendas to the underlying issues. If you're extremely lucky, you might actually get a team of people who are willing to clearly identify mission-critical, important, and support activities with the proper perspective.

Purchasing/Logistics

Purchasing and logistics may be two distinct functions within your company or they may be handled by one group. They may go through finance or HR or they may be tied to other departments such as warehouse or research. These functions may even be much more informal than that, such as departmental managers having the authority to purchase supplies as needed. Regardless of how this is handled in your company, you'll need to ensure that these functions are addressed in your BC/DR plan.

Purchasing and logistics are involved in three distinct ways. First, if your company regularly purchases things like equipment, inventory, and supplies used in the normal course of business, you have to deal with the potential disruption of this function. Second, you may need to arrange for the purchase of services and supplies related to disaster readiness. For example, you may need to contract with a remote data center for backup computing services in the event of a disruption at your primary place of business. In this case, the purchasing folks may get involved in terms of preparing or reviewing contracts, developing requests for information (RFI), or requests for quotes (RFQ) or requests for proposals (RFP). Emergency services provided by third-party vendors are typically less expensive and more reliable when contracted for outside the scope of a business disruption and your purchasing or logistics folks may be involved. In addition, there may be other emergency supplies your company chooses to keep on-site or available such as emergency medical supplies, food, water, office supplies, tents, clothing, whatever is appropriate to your company and its unique needs. Third, you'll need to incorporate emergency methods for purchasing and logistics in the event of a disaster. If you urgently need to purchase three new servers, how will this purchase be authorized and completed if your company is temporarily running out of the CEO's garage?

Marketing and Sales

Marketing and sales activities rely heavily on customer information. Marketing staff typically mine corporate customer data or target market data to determine the best approach for marketing, advertising, and related activities to generate sales for the company. Sales data, whether generated online, by phone, or in a brick-and-mortar setting, is used to determine inventory levels, purchasing requirements, manufacturing lead times, and a whole host of other corporate decisions. What would happen if your CRM system went down or the building in which the server hosting the CRM application caught fire? What would happen if your marketing and sales staff did not have access to key customer data, sales history, or order history? Marketing and sales are the engines that drive the revenues that make everything else in the company possible, so these deserve a special place in your BC/DR planning. These are the activities that get revenue coming in the door to help your company resume or continue operations after a business disruption. So, while IT systems and physical facilities rank high on the list of priorities in a BC/DR plan, pay special attention to what the marketing and sales folks have to say and be sure you include them in your planning sessions.

Public Relations

You may ask "What does public relations have to do with your BC/DR plan?" In February 2007 JetBlue (NASD: JBLU), a low-cost airline, experienced systemwide problems due to bad weather across much of the United States. In some cases passengers were held on planes away from the gate for up to eight or ten hours. Although this was not an IT failure, it was a serious business disruption caused by bad weather. This is exactly the type of scenario a BC/DR plan for an airline should account for. "What would happen if bad weather forced us to cancel or delay flights across the United States?" is the question the airline should have asked and answered prior to a weather event (and they may well have done so). However, they failed to address one of the most basic concerns. Many trapped passengers could not understand why the plane did not just taxi back to a gate and allow passengers to get off, or why portable stairs were not rolled up to the plane on the tarmac to allow passengers to disembark onto buses or other vehicles to take them back to the terminal. This was not done. News channels on TV and radio were quick to broadcast the news of these delays and passengers or those waiting for them alerted the media to these issues and the media frenzy began. When it was all said and done, all JetBlue could do was mop up the damage through its marketing and PR departments. In this case, they announced they were instituting a passenger's bill of rights and would compensate passengers who were delayed or rerouted. Was it too little, too late? It's too soon to tell what the long-term impact will be but the stock tumbled from a high of $16.62 per share on January 16, 2007 to a low of $12.56 on February 20, 2007, a drop of almost 25%. Can the company recover from the loss in its market capitalization (price per share × number of outstanding shares)? Can the company recover from the loss in consumer confidence? Time will tell, but remember the not-too-cheery statistics on recovering from a major failure. Even though this may not qualify as a major or catastrophic failure, it was a significant event that had an immediate impact on market capitalization and revenues—that's "major" in most people's minds.

Public relations can go a long way in smoothing over the public image of the company and soothing bruised and battered customers. There are numerous examples of companies owning up to a problem immediately, taking steps to stop or resolve a serious problem, and recovering consumer confidence over time. PR can be extremely helpful to your company should you experience a major disaster or outage. Suppose you are an e-commerce company and there is a breach of your Web site and customer names and other personal data are stolen? How will you deal with this? Certainly from an IT perspective, you'll lock the virtual doors and investigate. From a corporate perspective, however, you may need to engage in some serious PR to help manage the company's image.

If you're in a small company, this function may be handled by the owner, the general manager, or the HR staff. However, don't discount the need for these kinds of activities in the face of a business disruption. Even if you don't have a dedicated department or even a dedicated staff member for marketing and PR, you can identify a firm that specialized in PR and perhaps develop a relationship with them prior to a business disruption. At the very least, you may want to identify two or three firms in your area (both in and outside your immediate geographic area) that could be resources for you in the event of a business disruption. Perception impacts how your shareholders, stakeholders, vendors, suppliers, customers, employees, and community view your company. There is an opportunity to shape perception in the immediate aftermath of an event, even if it is to calm frayed nerves or reassure the public that immediate and decisive action is being taken. Don't miss this opportunity because you dismissed the value of PR in a BC/DR plan.

From the Trenches...

Marketing, PR, Spin—What's the Difference?

Many IT people are focused so intently on staying up to date with technology that they are not familiar with the difference between marketing, public relations, and spin. Let's take a brief detour to discuss these. Marketing includes the activities a company undertakes to make consumers aware of the products and services it offers or to create demand for those products and services. For example, Coca Cola airs commercials on television to make consumers aware of the attributes of the beverages it offers for sale in order to increase consumer awareness of the Coca Cola products as well as (hopefully) to increase demand for the products. That's marketing. Public relations or PR is done to announce pertinent corporate news and information to the public, typically through news outlets. For example, a press release may be issued when a company hires a new CEO or when it executes a new union contract or decides to implement a new enterprise software application. Any time the company wants to disseminate information about the company (and not specifically about a product or service), it may engage in PR activities. Clearly, there is some cross-over. If a company discovers a new process that is used in a new product or service it is offering, there is a mix between marketing and PR activities. "Spin" is a term often used in conjunction with PR, and it has negative connotations. It typically means that the company is putting a positive or company-biased slant on the information. PR activities may attempt to put the most positive face possible on a situation, whereas spin often implies disingenuous or dishonest motives. Unfortunately, some companies that experience a problem attempt to put spin on the situation rather than address it in an honest and forthright manner. To use an analogy, PR would say, "The glass is half full" rather than half empty. The statement is true, but it points the listener to the positive aspects of the situation. Spin, on the other hand, would say "It's dangerous to fill the glass more than half way full, it could overflow and hurt someone." It's not true and they're trying to make you think anything other than "half full" is bad simply because they can't provide more than "half full." Keep this in mind if you're in charge of developing your crisis communication plan. It's fine to put your best foot forward—just make sure that foot doesn't end up in your mouth.

We've delineated the more common functions found in small, medium, and large companies alike, but we know this list is not exhaustive. Take inventory of your company—look at your company's Web site, intranet, or phone directory to make sure you have all the subject matter expertise from all the departments represented. Also keep in mind that during your project, you may interview these folks but they may not be a formal part of the project team. In some cases you might find it more productive to create a list of interview questions to ask each subject matter expert or departmental representative. You can then compile that information and rank system and information criticality based on your own assessment or (more ideally) the assessment of a small subset of subject matter experts. For example, you may gather and collate all this information and bring it to three corporate vice presidents or to the senior management team for discussion. You may want to avoid trying to be the referee among competing interests and you may not be in the best position to make some of those calls. You *are* in the best position to ensure you gather the relevant data from the subject matter experts and present it to those who can and should make those decisions. If it is left to you and your project team to cull through the data and make those decisions, be sure to present your conclusions and decisions to your project sponsor for formal, written approval before moving forward. This will cover you in the event of a turf war and will hopefully help you avoid any organizational or political gaffes as well.

Project Definition

OK, let's take a moment to regroup. So far in this chapter, we've reviewed the basic process of creating an IT project plan with an eye toward the specifics of business continuity and disaster recovery. We've looked at the key resources and stakeholders you'll need to consider including in your project planning process. While we were looking at those key resources, we also discussed the various business functions and what kinds of questions you might ask to ascertain the criticality of those functions. So, we understand what the project plan should look like and who should be involved.

Now let's turn our attention to the project definition. As we discussed earlier in this chapter, first you'll need to define or understand what the basic project parameters are—the scope, budget, schedule, and quality for this project. In most companies, one or more of these parameters are assigned to you, but not in all cases. Next, you'll need to define the business, functional, and technical requirements. These need to be determined before you can begin your risk assessment, which is the first "work" phase within the BC/DR project plan and which is discussed in the following chapter. The business requirements define the scope of the project. Will you be addressing the top three critical systems, all critical systems, or all business systems? The functional requirements tell you what the plan must do or accomplish to meet the business requirements. Do these critical systems need to have full redundancy or do they need to be available within 72 hours of any serious business disruption? The technical requirements tell you how these business and functional requirements will be met. Will you use a backup data center or will you rely on another location of your own company to provide the backup services or redundancy you need? What are the requirements to set up your critical applications in another location? How exactly will your data be backed up, verified, and archived? As you can see, by starting with your business requirements, you can then develop functional and then technical requirements.

As IT professionals, the temptation is strong to begin with the technical requirements, but you clearly could miss some critical data with that "bottom up" approach. That said, you no doubt already have some technical solutions in place, and these should be incorporated into your planning. For example, if you already have a solution in place for backing up and archiving data in a secure manner (i.e., data is secure while being backed up and backup itself is off-site in a secure location), then this should be rolled into your BC/DR plan. So, if you have the backup scenario figured out, you can then look at your business requirements and ensure your backup plan adequately addresses backing up the four critical business applications defined in the business requirements. You can also look at your backup process in light of your functional requirements to determine whether your backups meet those specifications. For example, perhaps you realize through developing functional requirements that the period between backups is too long. Perhaps trying to recover from an outage that occurs the day before a scheduled weekly backup would be too difficult or time consuming, or even impossible if it was due to a severe business disruption. You might conclude that it would be better to do a twice per week backup to not only meet your current business needs but to provide the kind of business continuity and disaster recovery capability called out in your business and functional requirements. As mentioned earlier, you may choose to have different subsets of your project team for different phases of the project. You may want to get all the major business units together to develop the business requirements. You may want to have subject matter experts from each of the business areas help develop the functional requirements, and you may then have just IT staff work on the technical requirements.

One last note here before we look at the details of business, functional, and technical requirements. You may find that it makes more sense for you to put together your BC/DR planning team and perform the first major task, the risk assessment. The risk assessment phase, discussed in the next chapter, will help you look at the potential risks to your systems and to your business. You might choose to create several deliverables from your risk assessment phase that help you develop or refine your project requirements. You may decide that it makes sense to create general business and functional requirements so you can ensure your project falls within required parameters. That is, you might choose to create high level business and functional requirements that fit into your budget, your timeline, or your overall objective for the scope of the project. You might then go into the risk assessment phase and come back to your requirements with more specific information. If you do this method, it is more likely that your business and functional requirements will define a project scope (budget and schedule) that meet the goals or objectives you've been handed. From there, you can continue to refine. If you go into the risk assessment phase without a general understanding of the business and functional requirements, there's a good chance your scope is going to balloon quickly. So, keep in mind that both methods (define requirements then assess risk or assess risk to define requirements) have their own set of benefits, risks, and limitations. Be aware of these as you make your decisions and remember that the key is to use a process that works best for your business.

Business Requirements

Business requirements are the first step in developing BC/DR project requirements because you must first understand the critical areas of your business. What questions should you ask to ascertain which are the critical business functions? As you know, if you ask users what the most important systems are, they'll give you a list a mile long. Rather than ask that type of question, many experts advise using scenario-based questions to help focus attention and elicit useful information. This may take a bit longer in the short-term but will save you time and headaches later. Keep in mind, too, that the first major deliverable for your BC/DR plan is likely to be the risk assessment, which may lead you back to modifying your business, functional, and/or technical requirements. Each iteration should move more quickly and inject less change into the prior iterations. So, if you create your business requirements, then do your risk assessment, you may find the priorities for the business requirements change or that a critical system was omitted during the first go-round. This is a normal part of project planning. However, if you find that each iteration is injecting more change and more uncertainty or more confusion to the process, you need to step back and assess what's happening. It might be that the project is beginning to manage you (rather than you managing the project), or it could be some key assumptions were incorrect or that your organization is in the midst of a significant change. Be aware that a project plan that feels like shifting sand beneath your feet is in danger of getting out of control and failing. Let's look at some questions you can use to elicit the type of business information you need to create a useable BC/DR plan, understanding that some of the answers to these questions may change slightly over time. You can tailor these questions to the specifics of your organization but this should give you a good start.

- What would happen if the server room caught on fire and the sprinkler system went off?

- What would happen if there was a fire in the building and we had to evacuate the building immediately? What would happen if we were not able to reenter the building for three weeks or a month?

- What would happen if a security breach was discovered in our customer database?

- What would happen if we discovered that our Web server had been hacked?

- What would happen if an earthquake (hurricane, tornado, flood) destroyed this building and many of our employees' homes in this area?

- What would happen if a major snow storm made it impossible for employees to get to work for a week or two?

- What would happen if a chemical spill from a nearby plant or railroad forced us to evacuate this building for a week? A month? Six months?

- What would happen if electricity to this site were cut or unavailable for half a day, one day, one week, one month?

- What would happen if our high-speed connection to the Internet were to go out for half a day, one day, one week, one month?

- What would happen if a bomb went off in this building and we could not get back into it, ever?

- What would we do if major transportation routes (air, rail, road, sea) were shut down or disrupted?

- What would we do if key people were killed, injured, or missing?

As you can see, these questions elicit information because they create "what if" scenarios to which team planners have to respond. It gets people thinking in very concrete terms and you, as project manager, can help step them through this process. Again, since there may be aspects to the BC/DR planning process that do not fall under your direction or management, you may not be responsible for managing this process. However, whether you're heading this up or simply participating as part of the team, you can bring your skills and expertise to the team process and help step people through this process. By envisioning "what would happen if," you can help craft a realistic view of what the next steps would be. Immediately, people will begin thinking about what they would do without a server or without an application or without the resources at their desks—and this helps you begin to determine what the technological priorities and needs are for your BC/DR plan.

Functional Requirements

Once the business requirements are developed, you can begin to craft the functional requirements. Functional requirements state what is needed, not necessarily the technology that will fulfill that need. For example, the sales department might say "We'll need a way to contact our customers. If the Internet connection and e-mail are down, will we have phones? If we have phones, we can call customers but how will we get their phone numbers?" The functional requirement might be to always have access to the most current customer contact information. For example, some small businesses might keep a printed copy of their customer list at their attorney's office, which has branches in four cities other than the one in which you're located. Although this might seem extremely low-tech, the only requirement is that the solution meet the needs of the organization. This can include the need to have low-tech, low-cost solutions available to the most common business disruption scenarios. Only you and your company can determine what's most appropriate. The functional requirements describe what functions or features must be available. When you delve into the technical requirements, you can define the technological counterparts to the functional requirements.

When asking and answering the questions listed earlier in the business requirements section, listen carefully. Chances are good the functional requirements will start forming there. Your planning team will say, for example, "If our servers are down, we'd need a way to contact our customers." This is a business and a functional requirement. The business requirement is that customer contact is a vital aspect of the business; the functional requirement is that there needs to be some method for accessing current customer contact information in the event of a server outage. If the team ponders the question, "What if our entire server room caught on fire and was destroyed? What would you do without the tools you currently use to do your job?", you're likely to begin to understand that they might be able to get by without the billing system as long as they had a printout of the current status of accounts payable and accounts receivable, but they would not be able to continue business operations in the near-term at all without the Web server being up. That's good information. You now know that the Web server functions are critical, the billing system functions are important but not critical.

As you work through these scenarios, you may want to create a system of ranking these requirements so that you can gain agreement with the team of subject matter experts as to the relative importance of these requirements. You'll have to listen carefully if you're in charge of this process because people may describe one priority and then assert another. Using the billing system example, when you ask about what they would do in a particular situation, they may indicate that they could get by without the billing system because if they had current data, they could keep track manually; even though that might be a major task, it would be doable. However, if you then move to a ranking system and indicate the Web server function would be mission-critical but the billing system would not be, you might get some disagreement. You may need to manage the situation by helping people understand the point of the ranking system—which is to determine what you'd need within hours of a disruption versus what you'd need within days or weeks of a disruption. Table 29.1 provides a few suggestions for ranking systems that you might find helpful, but feel free to create whatever works best for your organization that will lead to clarity and agreement.

Table 29.1 Sample Ranking Systems

Sample One	Sample Two	Sample Three	Sample Four	Sample Five
Mission-Critical	Very High	Red	One	Revenue
Critical	High	Orange	Two	Support
Important	Normal	Yellow	Three	Maintenance
Support	Low	Green	Four	Other

The Sample One ranking system is fairly self-explanatory. The ranking is related to how critical a system is to the ongoing company operations. The Sample Two system uses commonly used word to describe priorities. Sample Three uses the color system, similar to the threat level system the U.S. Department of Homeland Security uses. Sample Four is obviously a simple priority ranking system using numbers. Sample Five is an example of a customized list you might create to indicate that anything related to revenue generation is the most important priority; anything related to supporting business operations and revenue is second. Tasks that maintain business operations come in third and the "Other" category is the catch-all. You can create any ranking system that is appropriate for your organization, but spend some time defining the categories you choose to use so that you will know where the boundaries are for each category. This will help everyone have a shared understanding of the categories and will help everyone to consistently rate and rank priorities as a team.

Technical Requirements

The technical requirement will define how the business and functional requirements will be met. As the IT professional on the team, you will have the unique vantage point of understanding how these current business and functional requirements are being met with technology. As stated earlier, it's entirely possible that some or many of your business and functional requirements for BC/DR planning are being met with current technology strategies. As you review the business and functional requirements, you can begin assessing how close or far your technology is from the desired state. In most cases what you'll find is that your technology solutions in place meet some but not all of your BC/DR requirements. This is essentially a gap analysis that tells you where your technology meets business and technology requirements for BC/DR and where it partially or completely misses the mark.

Technical requirements are important for reasons stated earlier, but they are also important because these will form the foundation of specific tasks related to defining the required technological solutions so you can go out to bid for these products or services; so you know what would need to be replaced; so you know what resources you'll need at a remote/off-site data center, and so on. When it's all said and done, you should have a complete list at the end that defines server types, server capabilities (number of processors, speed, RAM, disk space, network connections, etc.), applications, application requirements, application configuration needs, user configuration needs, and more. If this is currently part of your standard IT operations, then you may have all the configuration and technical needs documented already. If this is the case, you'll need to make sure everything is up to date and accounts for any new or changed technology implementations (current or upcoming). Most importantly, you'll have to determine where and in what format this data should be stored so that it is available to you in the event the server room, building, or location is destroyed or inaccessible.

As you can see, your BC/DR planning process ideally will help you make better use of existing technological solutions and help you implement new ones to meet your needs. You may discover through this process that one or more of your existing solutions is a perfect fit for your BC/DR needs. You may discover that some existing solutions are only being partially utilized or that they can be utilized in new and different ways. Finally, you may discover large gaps in your BC/DR technology readiness and this should give you the information (and ideally, the organizational support) you need to implement the right solutions for your company.

As you can see, developing the business, functional and technical requirements are all inter-related and none happens in a vacuum. As you develop your BC/DR plans, you should continually assess your current practices, processes and capabilities. In some cases, you'll find that what's already in place will work perfectly with your "best case" BC/DR plans. In other cases, you'll find that you want to modify existing processes and methods slightly to address your optimal BC/DR requirements. In still other cases, you'll find areas of the business (and technology) that is critical to ongoing operations that are completely exposed. This is the good news—the BC/DR planning process should help you assess these areas from the top down (business, functional, technical) and from the bottom up (technical) and determine the status of your current business operations as it related to BC/DR. From a known state, you can make intelligent choices about how much work you need to do to provide the level of readiness required for your business.

Business Continuity and Disaster Recovery Project Plan

Those of you familiar with project planning know that the project plan itself will be comprised of several major elements. The first element includes the various project definitions, which we've covered at length in this chapter. The project parameters (scope, budget, schedule, quality) should be defined, the project requirements must be delineated so they fall within the project's parameters. Once the project definition stage is complete, you create your Work Breakdown Structure (WBS). As you know, the WBS defines all the major and minor tasks of the project that, when taken as a whole, describe the total amount of work in the project, or the project scope. The WBS we're using as the framework for this book and for our BC/DR plan is as follows:

1. Project Definition
2. Risk Assessment
3. Business Impact Analysis
4. Risk Mitigation Strategies
5. Plan Development
6. Emergency Preparation

7. Training, Testing, Auditing

8. Plan Maintenance

Project Definition, Risk Assessment

We've discussed project definition at length in this chapter and we've also linked it to the risk assessment to be discussed in detail in Chapter 30. The risk assessment is the phase in which all potential risks to the business are listed and then evaluated both for likelihood of occurrence and impact in the event of an occurrence. As a company and as a project team, you'll need to create a cut-off point so that risks that fall below the line are not addressed. This is one way the scope (and as a result, the budget and schedule) of the project are managed. We'll look at how to perform this phase of project work in the next chapter.

Business Impact Analysis

Business impact analysis, covered in detail in Chapter 31, looks at how the business would be impacted if the major risks were to occur. In order to make this process productive, it occurs after the risk assessment so that only the risks that fall above the cutoff point, or above the risk line, are addressed. This, too, contributes to your ability to manage the scope, budget, and schedule of the project.

Risk Mitigation Strategies

Tying the risks with the business impact analysis together yields your BC/DR priorities. Clearly, you want to address only risks that have a high likelihood of occurrence and a medium to high impact should they occur. If a risk has a low risk of occurrence and it would have a low impact on your business, you may choose to not plan for that particular risk. Every company has to make that call individually—there is no single right answer, though there are real world limitations to the value of planning too far down the risk/impact ladder. It probably isn't of any benefit to spend two weeks and 300 staff hours planning for something that probably won't happen, and if it did happen, would impact only six of your company's 148 employees and none of your company's top 100 clients. In Chapter 32, we'll look at how to develop strategies to manage the risk including ideas on how to reduce, avoid, and transfer risk.

Plan Development

Once you've assessed your risk and the impact of those risks, and developed strategies for mitigating those risks, you'll need to start working on putting those strategies into action. That means developing a set of tasks that will deliver the required results. Plan development will include creating the project plan's WBS tasks related to actual BC/DR activities (as opposed to plan activities) as well as all owners, deliverables, and success criteria. We'll look at this in Chapter 33 in detail.

Emergency Preparation

Part of every BC/DR project plan should be the actual emergency preparations that a company should undertake, and we'll look at this in detail in Chapter 34. If your job is limited to IT-related functions, you might find that your role here is limited. Emergency preparations include the specific steps to take in the immediate aftermath of a disaster and the definition of when business continuity activities should begin. Though this might be outside the scope of your responsibilities or authority, we'll cover the basics so you can be a knowledgeable contributor to the overall BC/DR planning process. If your job as the project manager for this BC/DR project includes all aspects of BC/DR planning, then this section will help you rally the resources you need to create an effective emergency response plan.

Training, Testing, Auditing

Chapter 35 covers the tasks you'll need to include in your BC/DR project plan related to training staff for emergency response and for implementing the BC/DR plan should that be necessary. Testing is something all IT professionals are familiar with and this takes on significance when you look at testing from the BC/DR perspective. Finally, you'll need to audit and assess strategies after you've trained staff and tested the plan. This is part of the iterative process you'll use throughout the project management process. It is here where you discover key gaps or broken processes; it is here you have the opportunity to fix these gaps, errors, and omissions so that your BC/DR plan is as solid as possible within the given constraints of the organization.

Plan Maintenance

As we've discussed, an out-of-date plan is sometimes worse than no plan at all because it allows staff across the organization to make assumptions about BC/DR readiness that may simply be wrong. If your plan was crafted several years ago, there's a high likelihood it is no longer current. If you have a plan that you believe may be relatively current, you can short-track some of your planning processes by reviewing the plan against the steps delineated throughout this book. For example, you may choose to perform the risk assessment and business impact analysis with fresh eyes then compare the results to the plan you have. If there are significant gaps or disconnects, you may choose to scrap the old plan altogether or modify, update, and test the existing plan. The choice is yours. Whichever path you choose, whether you have an existing plan or are creating one for the first time, you should build in tasks that allow the plan to be periodically reviewed and updated. In Chapter 36, we'll discuss some of the methods companies use to do this so that you can create a maintenance plan for your BC/DR plan that makes sense for the way you do business today and in the future.

From the Trenches...

Perfect World versus Reality

Throughout this section, we'll discuss perfect-world scenarios as well as real-world realities. Project planning rarely follows the prescribed methods, timelines, and order we've discussed. It's useful to understand best practices and preferred methods so that you can strive to mirror those in your work. However, it's highly likely that there are one or more mitigating factors that come into play with your project planning process. To assume that things will follow the defined order and work out perfectly is to set yourself up for disappointment and failure. The goal should be to strive to follow the predefined processes and steps to the greatest degree possible and to diverge from those only with intent and conscious choice. Anytime you find yourself diverging from best practices, make sure you ask yourself if this is by accident, by choice, or by necessity. That should help keep your project on track while still giving you the flexibility to deal with the specifics of your organization. As long as you're aware that you're taking a side road or alternate path, you can still arrive at the same destination. It's when you close your eyes and hit the gas pedal that you're likely to get yourself (and your project) into trouble.

Summary

Planning your BC/DR project is similar to other IT projects you've defined, developed, and managed in the past with the possible exception of the reach of the project. A BC/DR plan reaches into every corner of your organization and tests your assumptions about what you do, how you do it, and how important those things are to the viability of the company in the short- and long-term.

We looked at the elements that drive success in any IT project and looked at the specific factors that you'll need in order for your BC/DR project to be a success. Clearly, having executive support means that those further down the organizational ladder will be compelled or required to participate and to give this project the appropriate priority in the corporate scheme. Other success factors discussed include involving the right people early in the process, having an experienced project manager, clearly defining project objectives, requirements, and scope, as well as setting a shorter schedule with multiple milestones and using a well-defined project management process.

The project plan components are standard IT project plan components that should be incorporated into your planning process. We looked at the elements including project definition, forming the project team, organizing the project, planning the project, implementing the project, tracking project progress, and closing out the project. Although there should have been no surprises here, we did cover some of the more important elements in each of these categories related specifically to BC/DR project plans.

A business continuity and disaster recovery project plan requires that key contributors throughout the organization participate with you to identify the bottom-line needs of the organization. As an IT professional, there's simply no way you can know all you need to know about how business operates on a day-to-day basis to create an effective BC/DR plan without key contributors from your various business units or functional groups. Including people from facilities, accounting, legal, human resources, engineering, and others will be crucial to success, and with the information discussed in this chapter, you should now have a better idea of who needs to participate and what you can expect them to contribute.

Another important aspect of the BC/DR project plan is the definition of the project including the business, functional, and technical requirements. As you learned, this is likely to be an area that requires additional detail or refinement. Most companies find that it makes the most sense to create initial high-level definitions and then come back after the risk assessment and business impact analysis are complete to refine those definitions. The business requirements define what is needed to operate the business in the aftermath of a disaster (disaster recovery) and in the longer-term (business continuity). The functional requirements delineate what is needed by way of functionality so that the business can get up and running as quickly as possible should a business disruption occur. Finally, the technical requirements, with which you may be best acquainted, determine exactly what the technical specifications are that will meet the requisite functional and business requirements.

Lastly, the BC/DR project plan elements are the elements specific to the BC/DR activities. We looked at the framework that will be used throughout this section as an example of one potential approach to the Work Breakdown Structure for the project. This includes risk assessment; business impact analysis; risk mitigation strategy development; plan development; emergency preparedness; training, testing, and auditing; and plan maintenance. Each area will be discussed at length in the upcoming chapters.

## Chapter 30

Risk Assessment

Solutions in this chapter:

- **Risk Management Basics**
- **Risk Assessment Components**
- **Threat Assessment Methodology**
- **Vulnerability Assessment**

☑ **Summary**

Introduction

In this chapter, we're going to discuss the concept and practical application of risk management. We'll look at the broad business perspective, the practical business continuity and disaster recovery planning perspective, and the IT-centric perspective. We'll look at risk management to understand the overall process, then delve into the risk assessment process. This is where the first phase of project work begins.

To help you keep track of where we are in our overall planning process, you'll see an image similar to that shown in Figure 30.1 at the outset of each chapter. As you can see in Figure 30.1, we've completed the basic project initiation steps (see Chapter 29) and we're moving into risk management. Clearly, we can't create a viable BC/DR plan until we know which specific threats the company faces. Every company faces numerous common threats such as the potential for a server failure or power outage; but each company also faces numerous threats that are either unique to the organization or unique in their potential impact. Throughout this chapter, we'll discuss risk management from a BC/DR perspective, but there may be risks your business faces that are not mentioned. In Chapter 28, we provided a fairly extensive list of potential threats to be addressed, but the list is not exhaustive and you'll need to look at your own business with other knowledgeable members of your company to determine what risks you'll need to assess. We'll cover many of those threats in more detail in this chapter and the information provided may be new or surprising to you. At the very least, it should serve to prompt you to think about these events in light of business continuity and disaster recovery planning processes.

Figure 30.1 Business Continuity and Disaster Recovery Project Plan Progress

One of the common objections to BC/DR planning is that there are just too many things that could go wrong to plan for them all. That's partially correct—there are thousands of things that *can* go wrong, but fewer things that actually are *likely* to go wrong. Just because something may not happen doesn't mean that it shouldn't be planned for. Let's use driving to work as an example. There are hundreds, if not thousands, of threats to you as you drive to work each day, but you still took some basic precautions to reduce, remove, or avoid certain risks. First, you probably took a driver's education class when you were learning to drive so you could learn the basic rules of the road. That's risk reduction. Second, you probably obey traffic controls and signals such as stop signs and signal lights. That's another risk reduction strategy. Third, you probably have car insurance so that if something does go wrong, you won't face exorbitant costs related to repairing the car. That's a risk transference strategy. Still, it doesn't prevent someone from plowing through a red light or losing control of their car going 75 miles per hour on the highway. So, you've done what you can to reduce your risks and you also realize there are risks that you can do nothing about. The only way to take your risk profile to zero would be never to go in a motorized vehicle anywhere and never to go near roadways containing motorized vehicles. Not very practical, but effective. It may be effective but it is neither feasible (for most) nor desirable as a risk mitigation strategy. Just because you can't manage all the risks involved with driving a car, it doesn't stop you from getting in your car and driving to and from work five days a week. You can't control all the risks but most people will still do what they can, within reason, to limit their risks—like take a driver's education course, follow traffic laws, and buy insurance. So, it makes sense to try to address the risks we can in business, recognizing there will be risks we do not or cannot address. We'll also discuss risk concepts including avoidance, reduction, acceptance, and transference of risk. These are four general methods that can be used to manage risk and we'll discuss how these apply to your BC/DR planning process. We'll look at the risks to your company and to your IT operations to help you determine which are acceptable, which must be mitigated (reduced or avoided), and which can be transferred, all within the constraints unique to your company. Risk management must fit within the financial and time constraints of the company to be viable; in other words, they must be reasonable. When you finish reading and absorbing this chapter, you'll have information you can use to go back to your executive team to gain support for your BC/DR project if you've been unable to gain that thus far.

Risk Management Basics

Risk management is a general topic that looks at how all risks are managed across the enterprise. The number and type of risks companies face in today's world are many and varied. For example, companies face risks to the value of their company through gyrations in the stock market, they face shareholder lawsuits for mismanagement of the company, and they also face risks based on currency fluctuations in an international trading environment. These are just three risks companies face with regard to the value of the company. The value of the company impacts its ability to raise additional capital, the interest rates it receives on loans, and the rating of any bonds the company may try to issue (or has issued). This is just one type of risk management focused on financial risks to publicly traded companies. Let's look at some other types of risks. There are risks associated with union contracts, labor agreements, or outsourcing agreements. There are risks associated with products such as product tampering, product malfunction, product contamination, or product failure. These are risks companies face related specifically to the products they make or sell. We're not going to delineate every possible risk a company could face, nor are we going to have an in-depth discussion of risk management here. However, it should be clear to you that risk management is a large undertaking at any company and there are risks beyond business continuity and disaster recovery that your company has probably already addressed or is aware of.

Let's begin with looking at the risk management process visually. Figure 30.2 contains a flowchart that indicates the four basic steps in risk management:

- Threat assessment
- Vulnerability assessment
- Impact assessment
- Risk mitigation strategy development

Figure 30.2 Risk Management Process Overview

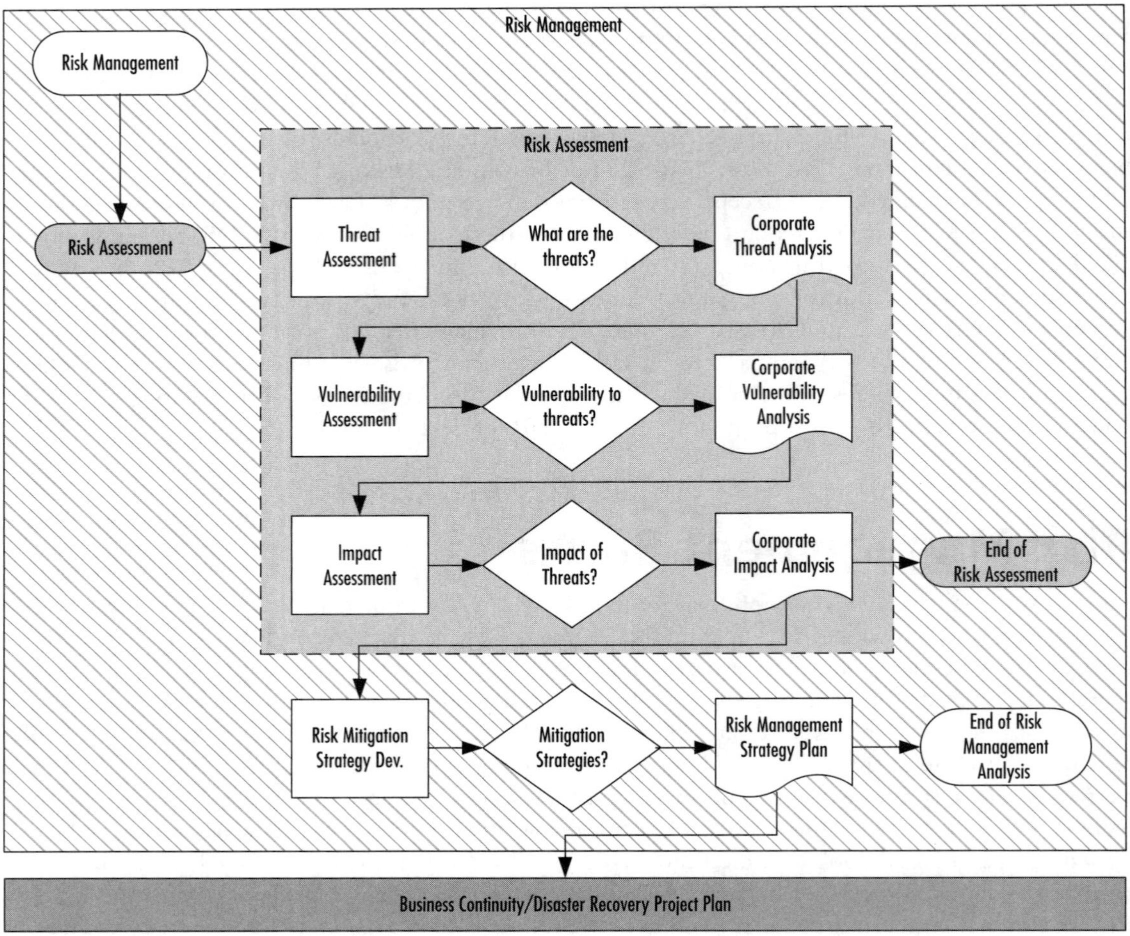

We're going to focus on threat and vulnerability assessment later in this chapter. In the next chapter, we'll discuss the impact assessment process in more detail, though we will mention it throughout this chapter as appropriate. In Chapter 32, we'll discuss risk mitigation strategy development in detail, but again, we'll also touch upon it as we discuss threat and vulnerability assessments in this chapter. As you can tell, these four areas are intertwined and it's difficult to discuss one aspect without also touching upon the others. However, we'll save our in-depth discussions of impact assessment and mitigation strategies for later chapters.

We've used shading in Figure 30.2 to indicate the general boundaries of risk assessment versus risk management. However, we're far less concerned with the boundaries than the actual work products. In each of the phases, there is an assessment and an analysis that should result in a report or written document. This helps you move from one phase to the next in an orderly and coherent manner. You can also use these phases as part of your Work Breakdown Structure to delineate tasks, deliverables, timelines, and deadlines. Let's begin with a brief look at each of these four areas just to be clear about definitions and boundaries.

From the Trenches...

Risk Management Certification

There are numerous organizations that offer risk management courses and certification programs. If this is an area of interest to you, a quick Web search will yield a variety of resources. There are also numerous links found in the risk management section on Wikipedia at http://en.wikipedia.org/wiki/Risk_management. At the bottom of the listing, you'll find links on certifications, degree programs, organizations, institutes, and training. Some of the certifications and programs listed are industry specific, notably insurance and finance. However, there are numerous general-purpose certifications and courses you may find of interest as well.

Risk Management Process

The process of managing risk includes assessing potential and also analyzing the trade–offs, or opportunity cost. Imagine a company that says we need to make sure our systems never go down. The potential for systems to go down occasionally is very high; most systems go down for one reason or another from time to time. The cost of those system outages varies, usually in direct correlation to the time the system is down. If the system is down for 10 minutes while it's rebooted due to an emergency patch installation, the cost may be negligible. If the system goes down for days because the database is corrupted by a hacker and restoring back to the previously validated database data experiences a few problems, the cost is much higher. Now, let's offset that with the opportunity costs. If we spend $5,000 on various systems to keep that server up and running, that's $5,000 we *couldn't* spend on something else, such as marketing materials, advertising, or employee wages. In addition, there's the cost of the downtime versus the cost of the solution. What does one hour of downtime for that server cost your company in lost sales, lost productivity, lost reputation, or lost consumer confidence? That's the opportunity cost of downtime.

The point is not to get into a detailed financial discussion regarding business costs but to understand that for every activity that occurs, some other activity cannot occur. For every dollar spent doing something, that dollar cannot be spent doing something else. Clearly, if you have $50 left at the end of the week, you can only spend that $50 once. If you choose to spend that $50 on dinner and the movies, you cannot also spend that $50 on the latest electronic toy. Every choice made excludes other choices not selected. Understanding opportunity costs within the risk management process is important because you can't manage every risk to zero. In some cases, it simply can't be brought that low; in other cases, the opportunity cost of doing so is disproportionate to the benefit. These assessments require some level of qualitative assessment (an assessment made without hard data, a value judgment). Understanding all aspects of the decision-making process will help you and your team make better decisions based on the unique requirements and constraints of your company.

Two other useful concepts in this process are *magnitude* and *frequency*. For example, an earthquake's impact to business operations would have a high magnitude, meaning the impact would be extreme. However, in many places, even those prone to earthquakes, the frequency is relatively low. California does experience fairly regular earthquakes, but the frequency of large earthquakes that impact business operations is relatively low.

Finally, each threat and potential mitigation strategy has a cost and a benefit. As we discuss various threats later in this chapter, we'll look at costs—in dollar figures and in the cost to human life and business operations. There's also the benefit of the mitigation, which ideally should more than offset the cost of the event. Let's look at a concrete example. The cost of installing fire suppression systems in a building may be $15,000. Typically, fire suppression systems cost about $5.00 per square foot; specialty fire suppression systems may run as high as $10.00 per square foot. Compare the total cost of installation with the cost of a major fire in terms of 1) building damage, 2) equipment damage (desks, computers, carpet, decorations, files, records, inventory), 3) IT equipment damage, and 4) human injury and death. $15,000 looks like an excellent investment because the cost of installing the system is far lower than the benefit it provides by way of risk reduction. These are the kinds of assessments you'll need to complete for your BC/DR plan. Let's look at each of the phases briefly so you understand the framework for the entire risk assessment process.

Threat Assessment

We've used the words "risk" and "threat" several times, almost interchangeably. Although this is correct in a general context, it's not quite accurate in a specific risk management context. *Business risk* is defined as:

> The total process of identifying, controlling, and eliminating or minimizing uncertain events that may affect businesses. It includes risk analysis, cost benefit analysis, selection, implementation, and testing of selected strategies, and maintenance of those strategies over time.

The key words here are "identifying, controlling, eliminating, or minimizing uncertain events." Risk management is about trying to manage uncertainty. We can't ever completely remove all risk all the time, but we can find ways to reduce or eliminate many risks to some degree. The process of risk management is the process of determining which risks should be addressed and how they should be addressed.

A more IT-centric view of risk management was defined by Joan S. Hash in the Computer Security Division of the Information Technology Laboratory at the National Institute of Standards and Technology (http://csrc.nist.gov/publications/nistbul/itl02-2002.txt):

> "Risk is the net negative impact of the exercise of a vulnerability, considering both the probability and the impact of occurrence. Risk management is the process of identifying risk, assessing risk, and taking steps to reduce risk to an acceptable level. The objective of performing risk management is to enable the organization to accomplish its mission(s) (1) by better securing the IT systems that store, process, or transmit organizational information; (2) by enabling management to make well-informed risk management decisions to justify the

expenditures that are part of an IT budget; and (3) by assisting management in authorizing (or accrediting) their IT systems on the basis of the supporting documentation resulting from the performance of risk management. Risk management encompasses three processes: risk assessment, risk mitigation, and evaluation and assessment."

Both business risk and IT-specific risk must be addressed using the same methodology; only the details will differ. We can use the following equation to define risk as well:

$$\text{Risk} = \text{Threat} + (\text{Likelihood} + \text{Vulnerability}) + \text{Impact}$$

Thus, risk could be viewed as the combination of the threat itself, the likelihood of that threat occurring, the vulnerability of the organization or system to that threat, and the relative or absolute impact of that threat on the organization or system. Likelihood and vulnerability are shown in parentheses simply to indicate that some people prefer to assess these in one pass or as one value. For example, vulnerability could be construed to include likelihood; others may want to specifically break out the likelihood from the vulnerability. Either method is acceptable as long as you account for both factors in your equation. Although this might seem like splitting hairs, it's important to define these various elements so that we can discuss them at the level of detail needed to perform a thorough and meaningful risk assessment. We'll discuss *threats* and *threat sources* in depth later in this chapter.

Vulnerability Assessment

The *vulnerability assessment* analyzes how vulnerable, susceptible, and exposed a business or system is to a particular threat. It should include an assessment of how *vulnerable* a particular system is to a threat as well as the *likelihood* of that threat occurring. The likelihood portion of the assessment can be part of the vulnerability assessment, though you could also break it out as a separate process if desired. As long as your risk assessment includes vulnerability and likelihood assessments, you should be in good shape. Clearly, it is useful to know that a system is *vulnerable* to a threat that has a 90% *chance* of occurring, a 50% *chance* of occurring, or a 1% *chance* of occurring. The vulnerability and the likelihood of the event are closely related and the results are used as inputs to the impact assessment. Clearly, a server that is outside the firewall is far more vulnerable to external attacks than a server inside the firewall. This is an example of relative vulnerability since both servers are vulnerable but one more so than the other. How likely is it that either server will be attacked? Probably 100% for the server outside the firewall and perhaps 90% for the server inside the firewall in today's attack-laden environment. As you can see, creating relative assessments for vulnerability and likelihood result in different risk profiles for the two servers. We'll look at this in greater detail a bit later in this chapter.

Impact Assessment

The impact assessment analyzes how great or small the impact of a threat occurrence will be on the business or system. An earthquake has an enormous impact on a business that is in or near the epicenter of the quake; it has a lesser impact on businesses further from the epicenter; it may have a slight impact on other companies around the country if infrastructure fails or if key suppliers or vendors are located in the region impacted by the earthquake. Therefore, impact varies based on numerous factors. Clearly, a fire contained to the lunchroom has a much lower impact than a fire that engulfs the entire building. We'll look at the impact of various threats in detail in Chapter 31 but also in conjunction with our discussion of the risk assessment process throughout the remainder of this chapter.

Risk Mitigation Strategy Development

We mentioned four distinct strategy types of risk mitigation earlier in this chapter. You can reduce, avoid, accept, or transfer risks. Each strategy comes with an associated cost. For example, it's far more expensive in many cases to completely avoid a risk than it is to reduce the impact of the risk. Most businesses are more likely to build in state-of-the art fire suppression systems rather than construct a building with absolutely no flammable materials. The cost of building a completely fireproof building is far higher than installing a high-quality fire system. However, each company has to make that assessment. There are certainly situations in which building a fireproof facility is not only cost effective, it may be the only viable option for a particular type of company.

Some risks are worth accepting. As we discussed in the introduction to this chapter, we all accept risks in our everyday lives. We drive cars, we cross a busy intersection on foot, we eat unhealthy food, we buy high-risk stocks. These are all risk-laden activities but we accept these risks. We may find ways to reduce our risk such as obeying traffic signals when driving and crossing streets; we may limit our intake of junk food to some extent; or we may put 25% of our investment funds in a savings account. These are all attempts to reduce risk but there is also an element of acceptance. It's like saying, "I'll accept 35% of this risk," meaning I'll obey traffic signals but I'll still drive my car. You've accepted that even if you obey traffic laws, there's still a chance, albeit a smaller one, that you could end up in an accident.

Risk mitigation strategy development is the process of deciding which risks you should address and in what manner. The inputs to this are the risk assessment analysis or reports, which delineate which threats exist, how vulnerable your systems are, and how likely the threat is to occur as well as the impact of these occurrences on your business. The compilation of this data will help drive sound business decisions because you'll be able to look at your entire risk profile and decide how to proceed. Since there are rarely perfect solutions in business, your job during this phase is to make intelligent decisions and trade-offs in light of the data collected. For now, let's turn our attention to the risk assessment components.

People, Process, Technology, and Infrastructure in Risk Management

Earlier in the book we introduced the framework of "people, process, and technology, a framework that works well for IT projects. However, for business continuity and disaster recovery planning, a fourth category needs to be included: *infrastructure*. As IT professionals, it's relatively easy to look at technology and assess the various risks. It's a bit more difficult to assess the risks to people and the processes they use to run the businesses, but it's part of normal IT project planning in most cases. Assessing the infrastructure, however, is a bit out of the ordinary for IT planning, which is why we expanded our model to specifically include it. In BC/DR planning, the infrastructure, which includes the building and facilities of the company, the utilities to the building, and the external infrastructure such as transportation and utilities, must also be assessed. Let's look at these four components using the earlier power outage example.

People

If the power goes out in the building, how likely is it that people will be able to get anything done? Many offices have no windows, so they'd be working with emergency lights that illuminate only exits and major hallways, for example. People will be distracted, they'll be gathering around people's desks discussing the outage, not focused on work. If the outage is from a storm outside, they may be concerned about getting home safely from work that day or the status of power at their own homes. People respond in a variety of ways to small and large events. How the people in your company respond will be based on numerous factors including the kinds of work they perform, the types of people your company hires, and more. For example, if your company hires former medical personnel, they may respond well to emergencies. Looking at the employee population and understanding how they are likely to respond to small and large business disruptions will help in your planning.

Process

What about the processes? Let's assume the power to the building is out. It doesn't matter if the server room has emergency power or not, does it? Users' desktop computers aren't available and the software they use to get their jobs done is unavailable. If the company has any processes still done by people without technology, those processes can proceed but sooner or later, those processes will require computer data as input or output. In many cases, then, continuing with those few processes that are not dependent upon technology (or electricity in general) will cause systems to get out of sync. If materials are off-loaded from an incoming delivery truck and placed in inventory and paper inventory sheets keep track of materials, quantities, and locations, that may help the delivery truck get back on the road, but it causes a problem on the other end. Now, there is inventory in stock that is not included in the last computer inventory count. Will that paperwork ever end up being input or will it take a cycle count in three months to discover the problem? This is a small example of how all business processes are impacted by this single threat, a power outage, even if the process isn't directly impacted by the threat.

Technology

Clearly, technology is the heart of operations in many companies today, especially those located in industrialized nations. Without technology, most things just come to a grinding halt. It's almost hard to understand the impact of technology on our lives until you're forced to do without. If the power's ever gone out in your home, even for a few hours, you suddenly realize you can't get on the Internet to get news, you can't update your stock portfolio online or on your desktop, you can't watch TV, you can't make a pot of coffee, you can't tell what time it is, you can't recharge your cell phone, and on and on. Yes, you can fire up your laptop for as long as the battery lasts, but if you don't have a wireless Internet card, you still can't get out to the Internet. Most people find their normal lives just come to a halt. We're at a loss because we've become so accustomed to having uninterrupted power $24 \times 7 \times 365$. Clearly, people living in areas where electrical service is less reliable are more aware of the impact, but they also have developed risk mitigation strategies—they may have generators or solar power to their homes in order to offset that risk for example, or they have simply designed their operations around these facts.

The important concept here is that technology is needed so that the *people* in the company can use the *processes* defined to conduct business. Technology, by itself, is a pervasive business tool, but it is most often useless without the context of people and process. As we continue our discussion of risk assessment, keep that fact foremost in mind. It will help as you look at risks to remember that there are four elements to be addressed with every risk: people, process, technology, and infrastructure. By incorporating this four-pronged view of risk, you can help reduce the chance that your plan will have any significant gaps.

Infrastructure

Infrastructure is sometimes included in the technology segment of "people, process, and technology" but it's useful in BC/DR planning to address it as a discrete category. Most IT professionals understand the term infrastructure from an IT standpoint, but from an organizational standpoint, it refers to things such as the building and facilities, the utilities coming into the building, and the external infrastructure such as public transportation, public utilities, communication services, and any other local, state, or national resources pertinent to your business. Corporate infrastructure typically is managed by the facilities manager or by someone assigned those duties, whether in finance, operations, or Human Resources. External infrastructure typically is managed, owned, controlled, or regulated by the local, state, or federal government. Within a BC/DR risk assessment, the risk to the company's infrastructure from various threat sources must be evaluated and assessed. Risks to the external infrastructure must also be understood, though mitigation strategies will clearly differ for resources you control or own versus those you do not. In a natural disaster or serious external event, there are usually disruptions to external infrastructure components that have far-reaching effects, which are often underestimated in the planning stages. It's difficult to realistically assess what will happen if a major freeway collapses or a nearby chemical plant explodes. Your business will have to rely upon local officials, including fire, police, and emergency medical staff, to address the external events. Your business will also need contingency plans with regard to your business operations in such an event.

IT-Specific Risk Management

Risk management across the business enterprise is a wide and varied topic, as you've seen. IT-specific risk management is a subset of overall business risk management. That said, there are some very unique risks in IT that exist nowhere else in the enterprise.

The Computer Security Division of the Information Technology Laboratory (ITL) of the National Institute of Standards and Technology issued a document outlining the steps in IT risk management, NIST Special Publication 800-30 (July 2002). Per the ITL: "ITL develops technical, physical, administrative, and management standards and guidelines for the cost-effective security and privacy of sensitive unclassified information in federal computer systems. The Special Publication 800-series reports on ITL's research, guidance, and outreach efforts in computer security, and its collaborative activities with industry, government, and academic organizations." (Source: NIST Special Publication 800-30, http://csrc.nist.gov/publications/nistpubs/800-30/sp800-30.pdf).

IT Risk Management Objectives

The ITL document provides an excellent framework for IT risk management, a complete discussion of which is outside the scope of this book. The ITL document outlines what have become industry best practices with regard to IT risk management. Clearly, the greatest risk to IT is the data stored on and traveling across IT equipment. There are three needs with regard to electronic data: *confidentiality*, *integrity*, and *availability* (we discuss these three concepts in greater detail later in this chapter).

The objectives of IT risk management are to enable the company to achieve its strategic objectives by:

- Securing IT systems more fully

- Enabling management to make well-informed decisions with regard to the purchasing and implementation of IT systems

- Enabling management to authorize (accredit) the IT systems on the basis of supporting documentation that results from the IT risk management activities

The System Development Lifecycle Model

From these three objectives, you can see that IT risk management is a subset of overall risk management because the IT systems must enable the company to achieve its objectives in a secure and cost-effective manner. IT risk management ideally is incorporated completely into a company's system development lifecycle (SDLC) activities, which have five phases (the names for the steps may vary slightly depending on whether you're focused on the lifecycle of software development or hardware and application implementation):

1. Analysis/Requirements

2. Design/Acquisition

3. Development/Implementation

4. Integration and Testing/Operations or Maintenance

5. Disposal

In some cases, a system may be in several stages simultaneously. Regardless of the phase (or the terminology), the methodology for risk management is the same. As with project management, risk management is an iterative process. As you can see from the data in Table 30.1, the phases and phase characteristics track closely with overall risk management and BC/DR planning activities. For example, phase one is an assessment of risks and the development of requirements. Phase 2 is the development or acquisition.

Table 30.1 SDLC Phases

SDLC Phases	Phase Characteristics	Support from Risk Management Activities
Phase 1—Initiation	The need for an IT system is expressed and the purpose and scope of the IT system is documented.	Identified risks are used to support the development of the system requirements, including security requirements, and a security concept of operations (strategy).

Continued

Table 30.1 Continued

SDLC Phases	Phase Characteristics	Support from Risk Management Activities
Phase 2—Development or Acquisition	The IT system is designed, purchased, programmed, developed, or otherwise constructed.	The risks identified during this phase can be used to support the security analyses of the IT system that may lead to architecture and design tradeoffs during system development.
Phase 3—Implementation	The system security features should be configured, enabled, tested, and verified.	The risk management process supports the assessment of the system implementation against its requirements and within its modeled operational environment. Decisions regarding risks identified must be made prior to system operation.
Phase 4—Operation or Maintenance	The system performs its functions. Typically the system is being modified on an ongoing basis through the addition of hardware and software and by changes to organizational processes, policies, and procedures.	Risk management activities are performed for periodic system reauthorization (or reaccreditation) or whenever major changes are made to an IT system in its operational, production environment (e.g., new system interfaces).
Phase 5—Disposal	This phase may involve the disposition of information, hardware, and software. Activities may include moving, archiving, discarding, or destroying information and sanitizing the hardware and software.	Risk management activities are performed for system components that will be disposed of or replaced to ensure that the hardware and software are properly disposed of, that residual data is appropriately handled, and that system migration is conducted in a secure and systematic manner.

Source: Stoneburner, Gary; Goguen, Alice; Feringa, Alexis, NIST Special Publication 800-30, "Risk Management Guide for Information Technology Systems." Recommendations of the National Institute of Standards and Technology, July 2002, p. 5. http://csrc.nist.gov/publications/nistpubs/800-30/sp800-30.pdf.

There are many excellent resources on IT risk management, and rather than go into more detail on the subject here, we'll direct you to these resources:

1. The US National Institute of Standards and Technology publications are available on the Internet at http://csrc.nist.gov, including Special Publication 800-26, "Security Self-Assessment Guide for Information Technology Systems," and Special Publication 800-30, "Risk Management Guide for Information Technology Systems."

2. Operationally Critical Threat, Asset, and Vulnerability Evaluation (OCTAVE). OCTAVE provides best practices for evaluating IT security. It was developed by the Computer Emergency Response Team at Carnegie Mellon University. http://www.cert.org/octave.

3. Control Objectives for Information Technology (COBIT) was developed by IT auditors and provides a framework for assessing IT security, developing performance metrics, and monitoring performance over time. http://www.isaca.org/cobit.htm.

4. Common Criteria (International Standards Organization (ISO)) 17799. These criteria represent the international standard for testing IT security systems. Information about the criteria can be found at http://www.commoncriteria.org and a copy of the criteria can be purchased from ISO at http://www.iso.org.

Other helpful Web sites include:

- Computer Security Institute: http://www.gosci.com
- SANS Institute: http://www.sans.org
- Center for Internet Security (CIS): http://www.cisecurity.org
- Computer Emergency Response Team (CERT): http://www.cert.org
- Critical Infrastructure Assurance Organization (CIA): http://www.ciao.gov
- National Institute of Standards and Technology (NIST): http://www.nist.gov
- Computer Security Resource Center: http://csrc.nist.gov

The IT risk assessment process intersects with our business continuity and disaster recovery planning risk assessment in that we need to assess the various risks (including, but not limited to, security) to the company and the IT systems in the larger risk arena. However, the goals are the same: to enable businesses to meet their strategic objectives. Clearly, being in business after a disaster or major business disruption is an objective of every organization.

Identifying risk for IT systems includes two major components: systems and operating environment. The systems data includes, but is not limited to:

- Hardware
- Software (OS and applications)
- System interfaces (internal, external connection points)
- People who support the IT systems
- Users who use the IT systems

- Data, information, and records

- Processes performed by the IT systems

- System's value or importance to the organization (system criticality)

- System and data sensitivity (confidential, trade secret, medical data, etc.)

The operating environment data can include:

- The functional requirements of the IT system

- The technical requirements of the system

- Users of the system

- Security policies (company policies, industry, regulatory, governmental requirements)

- Security architecture (to assess vulnerability to cyber threats)

- Level of protection needed for confidentiality, integrity, and availability (CIA)

- Current network topology, network diagrams

- System interfaces, information flow diagrams

- Data storage protection

- Technical controls (added security products, identification requirements, access requirements, audits, encryption methods, etc.)

- Physical controls (access control, monitoring, etc.)

- Organizational controls (policies and procedures defining acceptable methods and behaviors)

- Operational controls (backup policies and procedures, personnel security, system maintenance, off-site storage or computing capabilities, etc.)

- Environmental controls (power, temperature, humidity)

These items are included to give you additional insights into the areas you'll need to investigate throughout your risk assessment phase. Some items may not be relevant to you and you can delete them from your list. You and your team may have other items not listed that you want to include. It's better to be inclusive at this juncture. You can always pare down your list later, but if you trim it down too early in the process you may miss critical threats, threat sources, and vulnerabilities.

Risk Assessment Components

The risk assessment is shown in the shaded area in Figure 30.2 earlier. There are three distinct steps defined in the preceding section. So, let's begin with a discussion of *threats* and *threat sources*. If you look up the definition of threat and threat source, you'll see pretty much the same or very similar definitions. In this book, we're likely to use the two terms interchangeably as well. However, it is worth noting the distinction just to help clarify the risk assessment process.

A power outage threatens just about every business. The threat, then, is a power outage. However, the threat source is where the power outage comes from. For example, power outages can occur when ice storms break power lines, when transformers are struck by lightning or when substations or the power grid itself experience some major failure of the power infrastructure. These are all *threat sources*—where the threat actually comes from. Does this matter? Well, in general discussions of threats, it's often not very useful to discuss a threat source separate from the threat. Most of the time, we simply discuss a power outage. However, in BC/DR planning, understanding the *threats* and *threat sources* can help you uncover potential risks to your company or IT systems about which you were previously unaware. If we discuss a power outage in a general manner, you might think about power going out to the server room or even power going out to the building. If you fail to consider the possibility of power going out because a train derails and wipes out a nearby substation, have you adequately addressed all the threats? That's a judgment call in many cases. The likelihood of a train derailing and wiping out a nearby substation has got to be pretty low on the likelihood meter, unless, of course, there are 90 trains per day and the substation is adjacent to the tracks.

As you can see from this one example, there is no one set of threats that will fit every company. In the following sections, we're going to discuss threats and threat sources, but it is almost certain not to be a comprehensive list. We'll get you started in this assessment and you'll need to add details unique to your company and your geographic location(s).

Figure 30.3 shows the steps in the risk assessment segment. This is a subsection of Figure 30.1 shown earlier.

Figure 30.3 Risk Assessment Subprocess

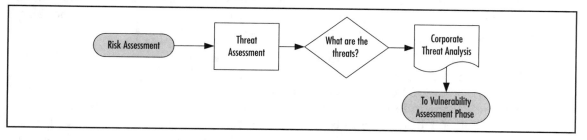

The risk assessment begins with the assessment of all potential threats and an analysis of those threats. The output from this phase is the input to the vulnerability assessment phase. Some companies may choose to look thoroughly at each threat and create a full assessment of each threat (such as threat, vulnerability and impact for power outage or flood). However, it's advisable to create a detailed threat assessment first. If you get caught up in the details of looking at a specific threat before all threats have been delineated, you may waste time and resources planning for the wrong things. You may only be able to see the relative risk of various threats once the entire list has been created. Be sure to keep this in mind and focus on generating a comprehensive threat assessment before moving into the vulnerability assessment phase. Otherwise, you risk rework, errors, and gaps in your final BC/DR plan.

Information Gathering Methods

There are numerous methods you can use to gather data about your company's risks. Some of the methods are described briefly in this section. If you have preferred methods or a process unique to your company, feel free to use those as well.

1. **Questionnaires**.   Standardized questionnaires can elicit data from specific groups or individuals. Questionnaires can help limit input and feedback to those areas most useful.

2. **Interviews**.   Interviews with subject matter experts can be extremely helpful in uncovering needed information. This process is particularly helpful when you have subject matter experts who cannot or should not participate on the BC/DR team but whose input is vital. Interviews can be conducted using the questionnaire instrument to help direct and focus the interview. However, sometimes a more freeform interview can yield more information. Questionnaires often contain unintentional biases and allowing an interviewee to discuss the topic without the constraints of a questionnaire can often yield data that might otherwise have been missed.

3. **Document Reviews**.   Reviewing corporate and organizational documents can help identify threats, threat sources, and vulnerabilities. These documents may also be extremely helpful in understanding the company's current critical processes and functions so that systems can be properly prioritized later in the process.

4. **Research**.   Internal and external research can be extremely helpful and often is needed to round out the data collected. Your team can gather reams of data on the frequency and likelihood of storms, earthquakes, or other natural events from a variety of governmental resources (many of which are referenced throughout this chapter). Your team can also gather data from local fire departments, police departments, and other local organizations. Finally, there may be a lot of data about past business disruptions or events archived within the company that may be helpful in understanding threats, threat sources, and vulnerabilities to things such as break-ins, thefts, or cyber crimes to name just a few.

These four methods should yield the data that you need to use as input to your assessment. However, it should be clear that these four methods could also yield reams of data, some (or much) of which might be useless or off-target. Before launching into your threat assessment, you should decide how to limit your data gathering efforts so that relevant data is most likely to be gathered. Review your questionnaires and interview questions to be sure they are focused and targeted on risk assessment for business continuity and disaster recovery planning. Limit your review of documents and research to those items specifically related to BC/DR. Although this might sound obvious, it is sometimes overlooked in the desire to avoid gaps or omissions in the planning process. Information overload happens quickly, so be sure to clearly define what data you're collecting so you don't end up sifting through reams of irrelevant information.

Natural and Environmental Threats

We've chosen to divide threats into natural threats—those caused by natural phenomenon and found in the environment—and human threats—those caused by humans either intentionally (including terrorism) or accidentally. Natural or environmental threats occur everywhere, but there are certain geological boundaries that determine whether you're more likely to experience a tornado or a hurricane, an electrical storm or an ice storm. We'll review some of the major threats and discuss business considerations. We'll also point you to a few resources that might be of interest or assistance to you and your team as you perform your risk assessment. You might be tempted to skip over this section or just skim the headers thinking you're already well aware of natural disasters, but resist that temptation. The information contained in the following sections is intended to expand your understanding of these threats as well as to spark thoughts on how these events may relate to your business operations.

Before we delve into the details of various natural and environmental threats, let's remember that these threats impact *people*, *process*, *technology*, and *infrastructure*. Though you'll undoubtedly take a very IT-centric view of these threats, you should also ask how these threats will impact the people, processes, technologies, and infrastructure of your business.

Fire

We've listed fire first because it is the most common disaster businesses have to deal with. Each year in the United States, fire causes thousands of deaths and injuries and costs billions of dollars in property damage. Fires are caused by a wide range of events, some of which are intentional, some accidental, and some environmental. Intentional fires come under the banner of arson and we'll discuss arson a bit later (and arson, itself, can be classified as "intentional" or "terrorism" depending on other factors).

Fires cause injury and death to people, but fires also cause damage to buildings, systems, and corporate records. If your firm does not already have a fire response plan in place, you should start your fire threat assessment by setting up a meeting with your local fire department representatives. It is important to understand what can and cannot be expected from the fire department in terms of fire and emergency response in your area. It's also helpful to have the fire department do a walk-through to help you identify and remove (or reduce) fire risks. In many cases, this type of walk-through is required by law before a business can occupy a commercial building. However, in some cases, it may not be required or things within the facility may have changed significantly since the inspection. Be prepared for the fire inspection to yield negative results. This may impact business operations in the near term. For example, if there is a serious and imminent fire danger in your building due to improperly stored chemicals, the fire department may require the building be evacuated and locked until proper fire protections and practices are in place. If you suspect there are significant fire hazards in your facility, you should speak to senior management about it to get the situation resolved as quickly as possible. However, if you feel the danger is that serious, scheduling a meeting with a fire inspector could force the issue to be resolved before human life is lost.

Clearly, most companies do not have conflagrations waiting to happen, so you will usually get solid recommendations from your fire inspector or perhaps a few minor violations to correct. You'll learn a lot about how fires start and how they should be contained by talking with your local fire crew. You can also find out how to develop fire drills and safe fire evacuation procedures, if those are not already in place.

You may also wish to contact your insurance carrier to learn about fire prevention and protection measures that make sense for the type of business you're operating. They clearly have a vested interest in preventing fires since the fewer fires you have, the more money they make. Insurance companies will typically provide information resources and, sometimes, free training to assist you in fire prevention and containment.

Most companies develop and practice fire drills and clearly post evacuation routes throughout the building. These practices *may* reduce the company's potential liability in the event of a fire with injury or death, but more importantly, they *will* reduce the likelihood of injury or death. Evacuation maps should be posted clearly and everyone should know the shortest route outside and the closest exits. Larger facilities may also assign crew leaders responsible for making sure their area is evacuated and taking a head count once outside. If you have fire equipment such as automatic fire doors, sprinkler systems, or fire extinguishers, make sure managers and supervisors are familiar with these systems and their use. You may choose to conduct training on emergency equipment such as fire extinguishers so that people have hands-on experience prior to a real emergency. If the first time someone attempts to use a fire extinguisher is during an actual fire, they may be unable to read or process step-by-step instructions. If they've run through it a few times in nonemergency situations, they have a better chance of using the fire extinguisher effectively during the emergency. Talk with your insurance company and local fire department to learn how to prevent, contain, and manage fires in the workplace.

With regard to IT systems, you should certainly see about having chemical fire suppression systems installed in your server rooms, though most current building codes will address this issue adequately. Servers that are sprayed with water from overhead sprinklers may have a higher risk of water damage than fire damage. Those of you occupying older buildings should consult with your facilities manager or fire inspector about what type(s) of fire suppression (if any) exists in your building and more specifically, in your server room(s).

TIP

The cause of fires can be internal or external to the company. Several natural hazards can spark fires. Electrical storms, tornados, earthquakes, and drought can all cause fires to flare, so when you begin looking at fire as a potential threat to your company, also be sure to look at all potential threat sources. If you plan for an electrical fire in the building but neglect to address the potential for wildfires sparked by lightning storms or drought, you will have an incomplete risk assessment and leave your company vulnerable to those threat sources.

Floods

Floods are characterized by relatively high water flow that spills over the natural or artificial banks of a stream or waterway or that submerges land not normally below water level. External floods, like fires, can be caused by a variety of factors. Just to reinforce definitions used earlier, floods can be considered a threat, but the threat sources are many. Floods can be caused by:

- Heavy winter or summer rains
- Melting snow
- Swollen rivers (from rain, snow melt, broken dams, etc.)
- Broken levies or dams
- Tsunamis (which can cause flooding of large areas after the initial wave hits)
- Extremely high tides (typically caused by tsunamis, hurricanes, and powerful storms)
- Broken water mains

Depending on your location, you may be able to identify additional flood threat sources. Floods are the most common of all natural disasters, so there's a good chance your company will have to deal with flooding at some point in time. Floods can impact the building, the equipment (desks, chairs, file cabinets, computers), records (paper and electronic documents of all kinds), and people (drowning, injury, shock, etc.). Floods can also cause power outages and destabilization of the infrastructure. For example, a flood can cause landslides or the ground beneath the building to shift or sink, causing a serious failure of the building structure (or serious risk of failure). Landslides of surrounding areas can occur when the ground becomes too saturated. Landslides and other ground shifts (called *subsidence*) can not only impact your building but can disrupt the transportation infrastructure, including airports, railroads, and roadways. Flooding can also cause buildings to become uninhabitable. Doors, walls, floors, and ceilings can warp or split. Dangerous and noxious mold of various types can proliferate in the right conditions.

In the United States, the federal and state governments have various agencies that provide information about the nature, severity, and frequency of natural disasters in various geographic locations along with information on preventing (when possible) or mitigating the impact of these events. They often provide excellent emergency management resources and in some cases, free or low-cost training.

In many instances, buildings located in flood plains were built before modern flood plains were defined. In other cases, buildings are built and areas later become flood plains. Regardless, it's important to understand where the flood plains are in your area (if any) and how they might impact your business. This is most important for small and medium companies that may have moved into a leased facility. If you are not the owner of the building, you may not be fully aware of the flood risks in the area. Unfortunately, not all landlords are honest and you might have inadvertently placed your business in harm's way. You might not discover it until your insurance carrier contacts you about flood insurance requirements or until you experience a loss and discover you have no flood insurance or that your flood insurance was voided due to your location in a flood plain.

As with fires, it's a good idea to understand the best routes out from the building and away from the area in the event of a flood. If you're going to shut down early due to heavy storms in the area, it's also useful to let employees know in advance which roads, bridges, under- or overpasses are closed and which routes out are best.

If you are subject to flooding, you can look at standards set by the National Flood Insurance Program, part of the Federal Emergency Management Agency (FEMA), at http://www.fema.gov/business/nfip/.

The risk of flooding to your IT components follows the general flooding risks. Desktops, laptops, routers, switches, hubs, printers, and cabling are all subject to failure if exposed to water, whether the power on those devices is on or off at the time. In some cases, you might evaluate whether it makes sense to flood-proof your server room, though in most cases, the answer is likely to be no. If the rest of the building is underwater, paying to seal a server room may not be a good investment, but only you and your team can make that assessment. We'll look at business impact analysis and risk mitigation strategies (and associated costs) in upcoming chapters.

Emergency lighting systems are useful in many types of emergencies—from fire to flood to power outages, so we'll list them once here as an item "strongly suggested" for a variety of emergencies. Does emergency lighting reduce your risk of these various threats? No, but it does reduce the overall risk of injury and death of your employees. The cost of installing these systems is relatively small and if they prevent one serious injury or one death, it will have been an excellent investment. This is an example of the cost/benefit being extremely favorable—small cost, large benefit.

Severe Winter Storms

Much of the midwestern and northern states in the United States experienced severe winter storms in early 2007, and the southern and southeastern states had devastating tornadoes (discussed in a later section).

Severe weather is a fact of life and if scientists are correct, it appears the globe is in for more severe weather in the coming decades. Severe winter storms include significant snow fall, strong winds, freezing rain, ice, and often freezing or subzero temperatures.

During heavy storms, people often can't get to or from work or they get stuck en route. Once at work, they may worry about their homes and families and be less productive. Driveways, sidewalks, and entries may become blocked or slippery and pose a hazard to people and vehicles. Technology can be affected by winter weather in the event that technology is exposed to the elements such as outdoor pumps, electronics, or mechanical devices that freeze and do not function.

Severe winter weather can disrupt a business by preventing it from opening for days at a time because no one can physically get to the building, employees and customers alike. In some cases, employees may be able to work from home if systems in the building are still functioning. Unlike loss of power or loss of cooling, even if the heat in the building goes out, the servers and other IT equipment will continue to function normally and may enable some portion of the business to continue. For example, if you have web servers, they may keep serving up web pages, taking online orders and tracking online orders, even if no product is leaving the warehouse.

In addition, extremely cold temperatures can cause pipes to burst, which can cause a variety of problems. The pipes that burst are typically those carrying water, but other pipes can burst potentially causing an environmental hazard (though this is more rare). Freezing pipes can cause flooding, so the threat may be flooding but the threat source is a winter storm, something you might not immediately think about.

Heavy snow and/or ice can build up on roofs and walls, causing structural damage and collapse. In cases of very heavy snow, people may be unable to remove the snow (steep roofs or large areas such as warehouses) or there may simply be nowhere to shovel the snow, as was the case in upstate New York in February 2007 when parts of the area were dealing with over 12 feet of snow.

If your company is located in a place where there is snow, ice, and cold temperatures, you may want to consider keeping supplies in the building in the event employees are unable to leave. This should include food, water, blankets, emergency medical supplies, batteries, radios, and possibly battery-powered televisions. Depending on the nature of your business, the location, and the climate, emergency power generators and portable heaters might be warranted. You should also arrange for snow and ice removal from driveways, parking lots, and sidewalks. Remember to clear snow and ice from emergency areas such as doorways, electrical boxes (main circuit panels, for example), and fire hydrants.

Common Challenges

Winter Weather Warnings
On March 3, 2007, the St. Cloud Times (Minnesota) reported that a warehouse roof had collapsed after heavy snow, the second such collapse in that storm. It also reported 911 vehicles off the road, 411 car crashes in a 12-hour period (6:30 P.M. to 6:30 A.M.), and 99 spin outs. Airline flights in and out of the area were delayed or cancelled. And here's

something you might not think about—the fire department was asking people to dig out hydrants in case of fire. When it's 20 degrees below zero, fire is usually a welcomed thought, but if your house or company is on fire, you hope the fire department can find the hydrant before the building is consumed in flames. This is a great example of a risk that you might not think about beforehand, but is obvious once it's pointed out. (http://www.sctimes.com/apps/pbcs.dll/article?AID=/20070303/NEWS01/103030016/1009)

One final word on winter storms—don't assume that just because you're located in a warm climate that you don't need to plan for winter storms. If you use suppliers, vendors, or contractors located in cold climates, they could be impacted by winter weather and that, in turn, could affect your business operations. Winter storms do sometimes impact warm climates, as well. In January 2007, a winter storm dropped four to six inches of snow on parts of southern Arizona, an area that gets measurable snowfall about once every 10 years. Roads and bridges were frozen; schools and some businesses were closed for the day because there is no snow removal equipment in those parts. Did anyone have to implement a disaster recovery plan as a result? Doubtful, but it does pay to avoid assumptions and look at all possibilities before dismissing them.

Electrical Storms

Electrical storms can occur any time of the year and in any climate, though they're most likely to be found during hot, humid summer months in the United States. There are an estimated 25 million lightning flashes in the United States each year. About 300 people are injured and an average of 66 people are killed each year in the United States due to lightning strikes. Lightning kills more people per year than tornados, on average, though they occur one or two at a time and are therefore less visible to the public than the death of, say, 60 people in a single tornado. Lightning can cause power outages, fires, damage to buildings, falling debris (trees, poles, etc.), and injury or death to people (and animals). High winds sometimes accompany electrical storms, and these can contribute to flying or falling debris, power outages (lines blown down or struck by falling debris), and structural damage to buildings as well.

From the Trenches...

The Positive and Negative Sides to Electrical Storms

According to the National Oceanic & Atmospheric Administration (NOAA), a department within the U.S. Department of Commerce, lightning originates in certain types of clouds in the region of snow crystals, snow, and ice pellets. The motion of the storm causes the

Continued

snow crystals to become positively charged and the snow and ice pellets to become negatively charged. The positively charged particles rise within the storm while the negatively charged particles remain in the middle to lower portion of the storm. This difference of electrical potential can cause cloud-to-cloud lightning. In some cases, the negatively charged particles toward the bottom of the cloud create positive charges to form on the ground and in the immediate vicinity of the cloud. This increases the likelihood of cloud-to-ground lightning strikes. Not all lightning originates from the bottom of the cloud, however. When it originates from the top of cirrus anvil clouds, the lightning is called positive lightning.

For more on lightning, electrical storms, and other weather phenomena, visit the NOAA's Web site at http://www.noaa.gov/index.html.

Electrical storms can cause power outages, but they also can cause power spikes, surges, and dips. Power that is too high or too low can damage a wide range of electrical equipment, including all IT equipment. During electrical storms, power to buildings may fluctuate. We're all aware of the damage a power surge can do to electrical equipment, but extended low power (brownout) can also damage electrical equipment. Many companies invest in uninterrupted power supplies (UPS) to provide either battery backup to equipment, which typically just allows for an orderly shutdown of equipment. Batteries must be tested regularly and replaced and a process for doing so should be part of your BC/DR plan, if you have battery backup. UPS systems can also provide failover power, which provides ongoing power for some extended period of time when equipment loses power. Usually these systems rely on backup power generators that run on diesel or other fuel, so be sure that fuel is checked for backup power systems on a periodic basis. Checking the readiness of UPS systems should be part of normal IT operations processes and a process for ensuring disaster readiness should also be incorporated.

Many UPS systems provide power conditioning as well. This serves to keep the power from surging too high or dropping too low. If you have these systems in place, you are already familiar with them. If you do not have them in place, a bit of research will help you determine the best solutions for your firm based on the variety of unique conditions and constraints. Clearly, you can spend a little or you can spend a lot—the benefits typically do track with the costs, but you'll have to make some intelligent trade-offs based on your company's needs.

TIP

Contrary to popular belief, lightning protection systems do not prevent the building from being hit by lightning. Instead, they work on the assumption your building *will* be struck. They mitigate the damage by giving the lightning a preferred pathway into the ground, directing the lightning through the system. Also contrary to popular belief, if you're caught outside during a thunderstorm and cannot seek shelter, you should assume the "lightning crouch," going up on the balls of your feet and covering your ears in a crouched position. The old belief was that lying on the ground was best, but this actually can increase your chance of being struck. For more on lightning safety, visit the NOAA Web site's online weather school at http://www.srh.noaa.gov/srh/jetstream/index.htm.

Drought

You might not think drought has anything to do with you or your company, but you might be surprised by some of the statistics. For instance, drought has a greater impact than any other natural hazard and its costs in the United States alone are estimated to be between $6 billion and $8 billion annually.

According to the National Drought Mitigation Center at the University of Nebraska in Lincoln (UNL):

> "Drought produces a complex web of impacts that spans many sectors of the economy and reaches well beyond the area experiencing physical drought. This complexity exists because water is integral to our ability to produce goods and provide services. Impacts are commonly referred to as direct or indirect. Reduced crop, rangeland, and forest productivity; increased fire hazard; reduced water levels; increased livestock and wildlife mortality rates; and damage to wildlife and fish habitat are a few examples of direct impacts." *Source*: http://drought.unl.edu/risk/impacts.htm.

The impacts are environmental, social, and economic, and can be widespread. Droughts impact businesses in a variety of ways but many are long-term effects hard to predict or quantify. For example, areas experiencing prolonged drought may find populations shifting out of the area in search of employment or new opportunities. Natural population shifts (those not driven by drought or other natural hazards) can also impact water availability. The shift in the U.S. population toward the western and southwestern states including southern California, Nevada, Colorado, Arizona, and New Mexico, among them, has put enormous stress on water resources in those areas. So, while there may or may not be drought conditions in some areas, there are water resource problems in many areas that can have the same long-term impact as drought.

Clearly, if your company's business activities involve the use of or reliance on water as a resource, you need to look at local, state, and national plans for drought mitigation. Some of the indirect impacts of drought can affect a wider range of businesses beyond those that rely on forests, streams, and lakes, according to the Drought Mitigation Center at UNL:

> "Many economic impacts occur in agriculture and related sectors, including forestry and fisheries, because of the reliance of these sectors on surface and subsurface water supplies. In addition to obvious losses in yields in both crop and livestock production, drought is associated with increases in insect infestations, plant disease, and wind erosion. Droughts also bring increased problems with insects and diseases to forests and reduce growth. The incidence of forest and range fires increases substantially during extended droughts, which in turn places both human and wildlife populations at higher levels of risk."

TIP

Drought obviously increases the risk of wildfires, so if your company is located in an area that could be vulnerable to wildfires, you'll need to take drought into account in your planning. Wildfires sparked by electrical storms and drought are common in many areas of the United States and your BC/DR planning should address these various threat sources.

Earthquake

The U.S. Geological Survey defines earthquakes in this way: "Ground shaking caused by the sudden release of accumulated strain by an abrupt shift of rock along a fracture in the Earth or by volcanic or magmatic activity, or other sudden stress changes in the Earth." *Source*: http://www.usgs.gov/hazards/.

Most people who live in earthquake-prone regions are well aware of that fact. They feel tremors from time to time and either have lived through minor or major earthquakes or have heard stories from those who have. However, you might be surprised to know how often small earthquakes occur. Figure 30.4 shows an earthquake map from the U.S. Geological Survey Web site taken March 6, 2007. The key indicates quakes that were within the last hour, the last day, and the last week. Though the color coding is not shown (shades of gray may not adequately convey the data), it should be clear from the abundance of boxes on the map that many small earthquakes occur every day throughout the California and Nevada region.

Figure 30.4 Earthquake Map for California and Nevada

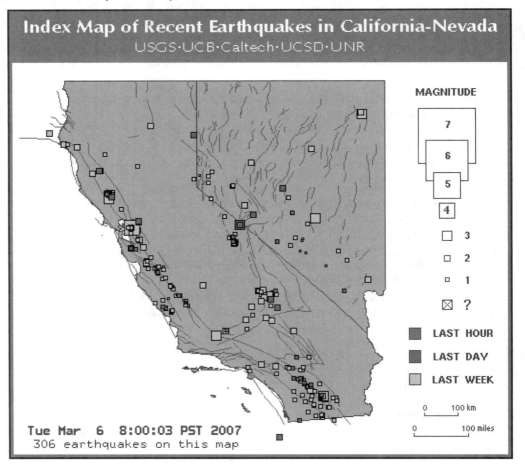

Source: http://quake.usgs.gov/recenteqs/.

Most of these quakes are below a 3.0 in magnitude, but the map certainly gives a good indication of the number of earthquakes in a given timeframe and the severity of each. Most are so small that most people won't feel them and they certainly won't cause any structure damage. However, we're all aware of the large quakes that have hit and the severe damage they caused. Damage from a single earthquake can cause in the hundreds of millions of dollars, though clearly the large earthquakes have a lower frequency of occurrence than the smaller ones that cause little or no damage. That said, scientists estimate there is a 62% chance of an earthquake with a magnitude of 6.7 or higher occurring in the San Francisco Bay Area of California between now and 2032 (*Source*: http://pubs.usgs.gov/gip/2005/15/).

Earthquakes can cause damage and have an indirect impact far from the epicenter of the quake. As witnessed in late 2005, undersea earthquakes can trigger tsunamis (though that is not the only source of tsunamis), which have a devastating effect for thousands of miles.

Although you may have earthquake preparedness plans in place if you live in an earthquake prone region, you should review your preparedness in light of the most current data available for your area. There may be new regulations regarding building safety, hazardous material handling, and others that may impact your business. Though you may be aware of many of these, a quick review of the latest information and regulations related to your area and your firm can help reduce your legal risks even if they can't change your earthquake risks. If your company is not located in an earthquake region, you should still assess the potential for a large earthquake in your area and determine whether creating a preparedness plan for such an event would make sense. Also keep in mind that your business operations can be severely impacted by an earthquake that occurs elsewhere. Key Internet infrastructure and communication sites could be disrupted, causing Internet traffic to slow or stop. Communications and power infrastructure can fail, causing disruptions far beyond the immediate impact area. Supply lines, shipping routes, roadways, manufacturers, importers/exporters, suppliers, and vendors may all be impacted by an earthquake so your preparedness needs to extend past the walls of your building and include an assessment of the risk your key business relationships face. We'll discuss this in more detail in the next chapter, but it's good to keep this in mind as you review these various threats. You'll continually need to "scan the horizon" to see how any of these threat sources might directly or indirectly impact your business operations.

TIP

Earthquakes are a good example of the need to balance the potential for a disaster with the frequency and impact of that disaster. An earthquake could be classified as a *threat*, the *threat sources* could be defined as shifting ground (subsidence), fire, gas leaks, explosions, infrastructure damage, building damage, structural failure (collapsing buildings, roadways, bridges), human injury and death, to name the most common of them. There are residual or longer-term threat sources from earthquake including disease outbreak, water shortages, water contamination, food shortages, food contamination, and even civil unrest. For more on earthquake maps, occurrence patterns and more, visit the U.S. Geological Survey's Web site at http://quake.usgs.gov/. There is an abundance of information on earthquake data from around the United

States and around the world. There are useful articles on earthquake preparedness that might be useful to those of you in earthquake prone areas. Even if you've lived in an earthquake zone all your life, you will probably still learn a few helpful facts from a visit to the site.

Tornados

A tornado is a revolving column of dry air that occurs over land (unlike hurricanes, which originate over water, and can spawn tornados). Tornados have been observed on every continent on earth except for Antarctica, though the most tornados occur in the United States. Tornados are found most often in the central part of the United States, though hurricanes can cause tornados in southern and eastern states as well. Wind speeds typically do not exceed 110 mph, though some tornados have been observed with wind speeds in excess of 300 mph, were more than one mile across, and traveled over a dozen miles on the ground.

Tornado damage usually is limited to the direct path of the storm, but the path of the storm is often extremely unpredictable. Like those that live in earthquake regions, most people know if they live in a tornado-prone area and have taken standard precautions. Tornados can disrupt businesses through physical damage to the facility, but it often has an even greater impact on the employees of a business whose homes may be destroyed or severely damaged by a storm that did not hit the business location. Employees will be worried about friends, neighbors, and family; they may lose their home or they may see their neighbor's home destroyed, causing severe emotional stress and trauma. People may be injured or killed and emergency services may not be able to reach the victims in a timely manner or at all. Tornados can also destroy needed infrastructure including telephone poles, power poles, power stations, roadways, and even emergency services (the fire house or hospital could be in the direct path of a tornado, for example). Tornados, like earthquakes, hurricanes, and many other natural disasters, can damage the infrastructure to the degree that emergency service providers are unable to reach your location for hours, days, or weeks.

Emergency preparedness information is widely available and you should be sure the information you have on how to prepare for and respond to a tornado is up to date. Again, keep an eye on the horizon and determine if any of your key business partners, suppliers, vendors, or customers are located in areas subject to tornados.

Hurricanes/Typhoons/Cyclones

Hurricanes are defined as "severe cyclones, or revolving storms, originating over the equatorial regions of the Earth, accompanied by torrential rain, lightning, and winds with a speed greater than 74 miles per hour" (*Source*: http://www.usgs.gov/hazards/). Of course, a revolving storm with winds of 65 miles per hour will also be devastating, even if it is not officially classified as a hurricane. In the United States, we've grown accustomed to hearing about Category 3 storms or Category 4 storms. Hurricane Katrina was alternately classified as a Category 4 and Category 5 storm because the wind speed changed over time. Regardless of the category or wind speed, hurricanes and tropical storms pose a significant threat to people and businesses (and more). Hurricanes bring destructive winds, torrential rain and flooding, storm surges of ocean water, and tornados. Hurricanes originate over warm ocean water but can travel across land and cause significant damage over coastal and inland areas.

This was the case in several of the recent storms including Hurricanes Katrina, Rita, and Wilma in 2005. More than half of the U.S. population lives within 50 miles of a coast and this number is increasing every year. Many of these areas, especially the Atlantic and Gulf coast regions, are in the direct path of hurricanes.

TIP

Cyclones, typhoons, and hurricanes are all the same weather phenomenon; the name changes with the geographic location. The term cyclone is used for many types of tropical storms but most typically is used for storms that originate in the southwestern Indian Ocean. Typhoons originate in the northwestern Pacific Ocean (Pacific Rim area), and hurricanes originate in the northeast Pacific or Atlantic Oceans. However, storms can cross various boundaries, so the actual terminology used is somewhat arbitrary. A tropical storm by any other name is just as devastating.

As with many other natural hazards, there is very little you can do to avoid the risk short of relocating to an area that is not subject to those kinds of risks. Unlike tornados that can be spawned without warning, most hurricanes are tracked long before they hit land. Therefore, people often have the option of evacuating before the storm hits. As we saw with Hurricane Katrina, there were numerous problems with evacuation, including an underestimation of the strength of the storm, the inability of people to evacuate (gas shortages, traffic jams, etc.), or even the financial inability of people to make alternate arrangements (among other reasons). There is, of course, the problem with false alarms. The cost of evacuating, for individuals and businesses, is significant. Businesses have learned that they don't need to shut down for every hurricane that threatens their area, but that's a dangerous risk to take. If the speed, path, or strength of the storm is underestimated, lives can be lost. Therefore, your business leaders will need to assess the appropriate actions to take based on your company's type of business, location, and risk of hurricanes.

The cost to IT can be significant. Hurricanes bring high winds and rain, so power outages, flooding, and structural damage are the norm. If your building is destroyed by a hurricane, your IT resources are gone. How will you recover your operations in the face of total devastation? If you have a data center located elsewhere, you might recover far more quickly. If your backups were in a bank vault two miles away and the bank has been flattened, you might be out of luck. We'll look at the potential business impact of hurricanes in the next chapter.

Tsunamis

Tsunamis are defined as large destructive sea waves generated by earthquakes, volcanic eruptions, or large landslides. The tsunami that occurred in the Indian Ocean in December 2004 killed 200,000 people in 11 countries. It was a horrific example of the devastation a tsunami can cause. Though early warning systems do exist, they were not helpful in notifying people in the affected areas. Tsunamis have struck North America and the areas especially vulnerable are the five Pacific States—Hawaii, Alaska, Washington, Oregon, and California—and the U.S. Caribbean islands.

The United States has redoubled its efforts to improve early warning systems, and with the numerous communication channels now available to most people in the United States including TV, radio, the Internet, e-mail, instant messaging, land and cell phones, the likelihood of early warning is better than it was two decades ago. However, because 50% of the U.S. population lives within 50 miles of a coastline, there is also a good chance that evacuation routes would quickly become clogged if a metropolitan area such as Seattle or San Francisco needed to evacuate in advance of a tsunami warning. Therefore, it's vital for businesses in these areas to understand the potential risk and the mitigation strategies available to them. For more information on tsunamis, you can visit the U.S. Geological Survey Web site dedicated to tsunami information at http://www.usgs.gov/hazards/tsunamis/.

Volcanoes

Volcanoes are vents in the surface of the Earth through which magma and associated gases erupt. The shape of the volcano is formed by the erupted material and typically forms a cone shape. Those living in volcano regions are well aware of the risks. Volcanoes, like other natural hazards, can occur with or without warning. However, unlike hurricanes or tornados, volcanoes don't change locations. Though some inactive volcanoes may be forgotten or disregarded, they are known points in the Earth from which magma and gas can erupt. Planning for a volcanic eruption typically includes evacuation because the lava flow is unpredictable in its path and moves more quickly than most people realize. It is sometimes impossible to get out of the path of lava flow; sometimes it creeps slowly forward for days and residents (and businesses) have time to collect their belongings and evacuate before watching the hot lava devour their house.

Businesses in volcanic areas should prepare evacuation plans and certainly be prepared for the possibility the building will be burned or covered by lava or that the ash that often accompanies an eruption could make the air and water hazardous. Ash particles are typically very fine and quickly clog filtration systems for water and air.

Avian Flu/Pandemics

Let's start with some definitions. An *epidemic* is an outbreak of a contagious disease that spreads rapidly to a local population. A *pandemic* is defined as an epidemic that covers a very wide geographical area including entire regions, countries, or continents. According to the U.S. Centers for Disease Control (CDC), the Avian Flu does not *currently* pose a threat as either a potential epidemic or pandemic. However, the propensity of viruses to mutate creates some future risk of epidemic or pandemic outbreaks.

The Avian Flu (also called bird flu) has gotten a lot of press in recent years. The flu naturally occurs in bird populations but in recent years has been seen in humans. Many wild birds carry the virus in their intestines but do not get sick from it. However, it is highly contagious and domesticated birds are at high risk of contracting the virus, getting sick, and dying from it if they are exposed. There are numerous variations of the virus and therefore it is difficult to assess the risk to humans. Some strains have a low chance of infecting humans, others a much higher likelihood.

The media is responsible for much of the hype and hysteria surrounding bird flu. According to the CDC,

> "Most cases have occurred in previously healthy children and young adults and have resulted from direct or close contact with H5N1-infected poultry or H5N1-contaminated surfaces. In general, H5N1 remains a very rare

disease in people. The H5N1 virus does not infect humans easily, and if a person is infected, it is very difficult for the virus to spread to another person. While there has been some human-to-human spread of H5N1, it has been limited, inefficient and unsustained. For example, in 2004 in Thailand, probable human-to-human spread in a family resulting from prolonged and very close contact between an ill child and her mother was reported."

The virus is contracted through close contact with infected birds or surfaces and human–to–human spread is caused by close contact with the carrier(s). However, the danger is that all influenza viruses have the ability to change and there is a possibility a strain could occur that spreads easily among the human population. Because this virus does not naturally occur in humans, we have no natural antibodies to fight off these viruses.

The issue your company should address is not how it will handle the bird flu itself, but how it might be impacted by a pandemic flu of any sort (avian flu and pandemic flu are not one and the same). According to the CDC:

- A pandemic may come and go in waves, each of which can last from six to eight weeks.

- An especially severe influenza pandemic could lead to high levels of illness, death, social disruption, and economic loss. Everyday life would be disrupted because so many people in so many places become seriously ill at the same time. Impacts can range from school and business closings to the interruption of basic services such as public transportation and food delivery.

- A substantial percentage of the world's population will require some form of medical care. Health care facilities can be overwhelmed, creating a shortage of hospital staff, beds, ventilators, and other supplies. Surge capacity at nontraditional sites such as schools may need to be created to cope with demand.

- The need for vaccine is likely to outstrip supply and the supply of antiviral drugs is also likely to be inadequate early in a pandemic. Difficult decisions will need to be made regarding who gets antiviral drugs and vaccines.

- Death rates are determined by four factors: the number of people who become infected, the virulence of the virus, the underlying characteristics and vulnerability of affected populations and the availability and effectiveness of preventive measures.

Source: http://www.pandemicflu.gov/general/index.html#impact.

Not a pretty picture, but as with all disaster planning, it's better to go in well–armed with current and accurate information.

You might be arguing that if a pandemic hits, you'll have no control over the situation. Even though that may be true, you still have to provide some sort of contingency plans. Let's look at a possible scenario. Your company sells an enterprise-level software product. It's used at major corporations throughout the world. It seamlessly integrates into their messaging and communications applications and they rely heavily on this application. Your largest client, a Fortune 100 company, comes to you and asks, "What plans do you have to support this product in the event of an Avian Flu outbreak?" Here's a variation on the theme. Your company's vice president of Global Sales comes to you saying she is trying to close a deal with a Fortune 500 client that would mean tens of millions of dollars in revenue for the company. However, in order to close the deal, she needs the IT group's "Avian Flu Readiness Plan" to allay concerns by the potential client about your company's ability to respond to global service and support needs in the event of an outbreak or other pandemic.

So, you might think that if the avian flu hit, you'd shut your doors until it blew over, but you may not be able to hide your head in the sand for long. The difficulty, of course, is that IT systems are not impacted by the flu—people and processes are. So, as the IT professional in the group, you have to figure out how you can provide the services required of you in the event that tens, hundreds, or even thousands of your staff are out sick, quarantined, or unable to report to work. In pandemics, there is a fairly high mortality rate, though it usually impacts the young, old, and infirm the hardest. Still, what if key staff die or are too ill to work for an extended period of time?

It seems callous to be worried about business in the face of death and serious illness, but businesses provide important services that are needed all the time. Shutting the doors may seem like the best option and for some companies, it might be, but you can't make that determination off the top of your head. In the business impact analysis, we'll revisit this topic. As a threat, the avian flu or pandemic flu are just abstract concepts, but they are worth looking at in terms of your company's vulnerability to these events and the impact they might have on your company, your employees, your customers, your supply chain, and your community.

TIP

For more information on pandemics, you can visit the CDC Web site at http://www.pandemicflu.gov or the CDC's main Web site at http://www.cdc.gov/index.htm.

This section on natural and environmental hazards is not exhaustive, but it should give you a solid start in investigating the threats and threat sources your company might face. As you read through the various hazards, you may have thought of other threats not listed or you may have learned about threats you didn't think applied to your business. For example, not everyone would think about the risk of fire or flooding from an earthquake. If your company is located in a low-lying area and there is a dam or water containment system uphill, an earthquake can break the containment and send water downhill, flooding your building, street, or neighborhood. These kinds of examples point to the importance on doing research and being familiar with the surrounding area. You won't know that you need to plan for flooding if you don't know the reservoir is located just three miles away uphill from you or that you need to plan for wildfires because just over the crest of the hill is an open grassland. In the next section, we'll look at human-caused hazards and here too, you'll need to be aware of your surroundings. What does the company across the street or around the corner do? Do they work with hazardous materials or noxious chemicals? Could there be a biohazard or chemical spill in the area? Is there a railway that runs near your building or a major freeway? Is there a nuclear power plant in the region, is nuclear waste transported on roads near your building? These are the kinds of things to consider as you read through the remainder of this chapter, as you develop your threat list and research potential hazards in your area.

Human Threats

Human threats, like environmental or natural hazards, come in all sizes and shapes. Although we might like to distinguish between intentional and unintentional acts, that goes only to motive and intent, not impact and outcome. So, we'll look at these threats without regard to whether or not they're intentional except in a few cases. Terrorism is, by definition, intentional as is war, theft, and sabotage, to name a few. Other threats such as fire, chemical spills, or electronic data loss can be caused by intentional acts or human error. Remember the statistic from IBM cited earlier in the book—that 80% of data loss is human caused? They don't specify whether that's intentional or accidental. So, regardless of the intent, the effect is the same. Let's go through some of these human-caused hazards in some detail. You may learn new facts that help you plan better or you may simply become aware of one or more threats you didn't previously know about.

Fire

Human-caused fires can be located inside or outside as in the case of improper wiring or unattended campfires. Fires are the most common business disaster, so regardless of what other planning you do, you should certainly ensure you have a solid fire recovery plan and you practice fire drills and fire procedures regularly.

Most commercials buildings have fire suppression systems; some buildings have fire doors to prevent fire from running uncontrolled through a building. Fire extinguishers, alarms, smoke detectors, and other fire equipment should be located at strategic places throughout the building, should be well marked, and should be tested regularly to ensure proper functioning.

Arson is an intentionally set fire. The local fire department may investigate any fires in your building to determine the cause. Some insurance companies may prohibit payment of insurance claims in some circumstances so be sure to have someone from finance or legal review your company's insurance policy, especially with regard to fire.

Theft, Sabotage, Vandalism

Theft, sabotage, and vandalism are all intentional acts carried out by employees, building employees (not associated with your company), former employees, and strangers. Many of these types of problems can be effectively thwarted by having security procedures in place. These include controlling access to the grounds, the buildings, and certainly to the inner offices, labs, server rooms, and other areas within the building that contain expensive, sensitive, or strategic materials. Most IT professionals understand that security begins with controlling and monitoring physical access and the same is true for your business as it is for IT equipment.

Theft can come in many different forms, some of which might not immediately come to mind, such as:

- Software piracy (are employees stealing software from the company or installing illegal software?)

- Counterfeiting (of currency or any other commodity of value, including company checks, ID badges, software, etc.)

- Theft of proprietary information (intellectual property, trade secrets, confidential data, etc.)

- Equipment theft (from office supplies to servers and everything in between)

You might think of some of these elements, but when you view them in light of BC/DR planning, you might find you need to take a few additional steps to address these. For example, you might have a plan for how you'd get your business back up and running after a fire, but what if someone came in and stole two critical servers? First, is the data safe? Second, how would you recover? Those are the kinds of considerations to include when you think about what could be stolen or damaged within the walls of your company. Keep in mind, too, that as with most computer fraud or theft, most company fraud or theft is perpetrated by those *inside* the company, not by mysterious outsiders.

If your facility is small, be sure to have a process in place for monitoring visitors or those entering the building such as strategically locating a receptionist or someone's office near the entry way. In some companies, this falls to the HR staff to manage. In larger facilities, you may need to have a more formal method of monitoring and controlling access such as visitor sign in, presentation of identification, and the issuance of a visitor badge. Many companies require cell phones and other digital devices to be left with the front desk so that photos or recordings cannot be made while in the building. This prevents someone from stealing trade secrets or casing the property to determine the best way to burglarize the building during off-hours.

Any of these acts is intentional, and prevention is typically the best solution. However, should your business be vulnerable to theft, sabotage, or vandalism due to the location, the nature of the work you do, or the likelihood of having disgruntled employees or vendors, you should review your plans for preventing and recovering from these threats. However, since we're focusing on IT, we're going to cover theft, sabotage, and vandalism in the IT realm in just a bit.

Labor Disputes

If your company includes union workers or your company interacts with another company that includes unions and union workers, there is a risk that labor disputes will disrupt business. Remember that you have to look at your company as well as at your key suppliers, vendors, contractors, outsourcers, and even customers. A major disruption in any of those areas could temporarily or permanently disrupt your business. For example, if you're a supplier to a large manufacturing company and that company represents 75% of your sales, what happens if they shut down for six to eight months during a labor dispute? How will your company survive? Clearly, it's not desirable to have such a large portion of your revenue stream from a single source, but that's sometimes a business reality. Your executives may realize this puts your company at risk but the upside profit potential may be compelling. Therefore, as the BC/DR planning team, you need to assess this risk both internally and externally and determine both the likelihood and the impact a potential labor dispute would have on your business. Keep in mind, too, that there are various ways labor disputes can play out—from work slow downs to strikes to sabotage. Each of these scenarios may have a slightly different impact on your company and your operations, and each should be assessed as a separate threat source.

Workplace Violence

The unfortunate reality is that there is violence in the workplace. Whether from disgruntled former employees or unhappy current employees, violence can occur without warning. According to the U.S. Department of Labor's Occupational Health and Safety Administration (OSHA), homicide is the fourth leading cause of occupational injury in the United States. In 2004, the latest year for which data is currently available, there were 551 homicides out of 5,735 fatal workplace injuries.

Before you start looking suspiciously at your coworkers, keep these facts in mind: 71% of workplace homicides are robbery related and only 9% are committed by coworkers. Although any person or company could experience workplace violence, the likelihood of violence increases with these factors:

- High interaction or exposure to the public

- Exchange of money or funds

- Working very late or very early, especially alone

- Guarding valuable assets or money

- Regularly dealing with volatile situations or violent people

Cab drivers, liquor store staff, late night convenience store staff, and safety officers (police and security guards) are occupations at the top of the risk list (*Source*: http://www.cdc.gov/niosh/violfs. html). If you believe your company's premises, location, or type of business may be at risk of workplace violence, you should certainly take preventive measures if you have not already. There are numerous resources available, from government Web sites to on-site training programs that can train your staff to prevent and address workplace violence effectively.

If we look at workplace violence from a business disruption point of view, a serious injury or death could result in the premises being sealed off as a crime scene for some period of time. Equipment such as computers or other needed items could be seized as part of the investigation. Employees will be impacted and productivity will suffer; good employees may choose to find employment elsewhere, and your reputation in the community, in your industry, or in the eyes of potential employees may suffer.

TIP

If you're interested in learning more about preventing workplace violence, visit the OSHA Web site focused on that topic at http://www.osha.gov/SLTC/workplaceviolence/evaluation.html.

The U.S. Department of Health and Human Services Centers for Disease Control and Prevention (CDC)'s National Institute for Occupational Safety and Health (NIOSH) has additional resources related to workplace safety, and you can download videos on preventing workplace violence by visiting this link: http://www.cdc.gov/niosh/docs/video/violence.html.

Terrorism

The very nature of terrorism is that it cannot be planned for and sometimes cannot be prevented. Therefore, your assessment should include not the threat of terrorism but the threat sources that stem from it. This goes back to many of the issues we've already discussed—what if your power goes out or there's a chemical spill or an anthrax release (we'll cover biohazards in an upcoming section)? How will you address the results of terrorism? When you look at it this way, it seems to become a slightly more manageable topic. Ultimately, each company has to assess its vulnerability based on geographic location, the nature of its business, its international business connections, its political involvement, and more. If your company is vulnerable to terrorism, there's a good chance you have a strong team in place that has already addressed this. Nuclear power plants, power stations, airports, and others have developed contingency plans because of federal or state mandates to do so. If you believe your company should have a stronger plan to prevent or address a terrorist threat, you should involve high level executives or managers in your company and discuss next steps. There may be resources at the U.S. Department of Homeland Security that can be helpful to you or you may wish to consult with a private firm that specializes in this area to address the specific threat of a direct attack on your company.

However, most companies are not the target for such an attack, but may be in the area of an attack or may experience the result of an attack. Addressing the likely threat sources in your area that potentially could be targets for terrorists will help you devise a plan that will help address the aftermath of an attack, even if you don't know whether the incident was intentional or accidental.

TIP

If you're interested in learning more about preventing workplace violence, visit the OSHA Web site focused on that topic at http://www.osha.gov/SLTC/workplaceviolence/evaluation.html.
    The U.S. Department of Homeland Security has a wide variety of resources, including information on terrorism, on their Web site at http://www.dhs.gov/index.shtm.

Chemical or Biological Hazards

Chemical hazards are present in a variety of manufacturing environments, whether the chemicals are the *result* of the manufacturing process or are used *within* the manufacturing process. A biological hazard, often called a *biohazard*, is defined as a danger to humans or the environment resulting from biological agents or conditions. Both chemical and biological hazards can occur as the result of an accident, sabotage, or terrorism.

If your company is not involved with chemical or biological agents, you may still face risks in this regard. You need to look in your local area and determine what other types of companies exist. If a chemical plant is located four miles away, what is the risk to your operations? What if it's next door? Fifteen miles away? Your local and state agencies may regulate these types of companies, so there may be information that's easily available to you. Some research on local companies should also reveal the nature of work that your commercial and industrial neighbors do. If you run into trouble locating this information, you might be able to contact a friendly commercial leasing (real estate) agent. Commercial leasing agents often have their fingers on the pulse of the community and can tell you who your neighbors are and what type of work they do. Your local Chamber of Commerce may also be able to provide useful information. Keep in mind that you're more likely to encounter these kinds of hazards in a heavily industrialized area, so you can look at your location and determine where the industrial areas are in relation to your operations. Areas that are heavily residential with a bit of commercial building space are less likely to pose a threat of chemical or biological hazards.

If your company is involved with chemical or biological research or manufacturing, you no doubt have safety procedures in place with regard to these agents. However, you and your team might review your safety procedures with an eye toward BC/DR planning. What types of containment procedures are in place? What sort of evacuation procedures are practiced? What are the countermeasures or remedial activities that should occur should a spill, leak, or release occur? In some cases, your company's activities (or the chemicals and biohazards) may be closely regulated by government or industry and the procedures and requirements address these questions. However, you may need to take this information as input to your business continuity and disaster recovery planning by asking how operations would be impacted by a chemical or biological hazard. Would you have to set up operations elsewhere? How long would it take to reoccupy the building, or would you have to permanently move? If the servers and other IT equipment were inaccessible due to contamination, what would you do? How would you resume operations? These are the kinds of questions you'll ask and answer as part of this process. For now, the key is to determine what, if any, risk you have to internal chemical or biological hazards.

We haven't addressed the risk of the release of these agents as part of sabotage or terrorism, but the result would be the same. If a chemical plant in the area were to be the victim of sabotage or a terror attack or just an accident by a careless employee, the net result to your firm is the same.

If a chemical or biological agent were to be released in your area as part of a terror attack, you would have to address the same types of issues such as whether the best course of action is to evacuate the building or to shelter-in-place. If you believe your company may be vulnerable to these types of threat sources, you may want to contact your local police and fire department for guidance on how to handle these types of incidents. The bottom line, however, is what data you need to develop a sound BC/DR plan that addresses the impact of this type of threat.

War

This type of threat clearly exists for many companies around the world. For U.S.-based companies, the risk is greatest for divisions of the company that may be located in areas of political or economic instability. Plans for shifting operations from areas experiencing war, civil war, or civil unrest should be made in areas that are vulnerable. BC/DR plans should examine which areas of the company may be vulnerable and how they can be protected. Remember that not only would local operations in a war zone be disrupted but vital knowledge, equipment, or assets could be stolen from the company. Therefore, the BC/DR plan must look holistically at the people, process, technology, and infrastructure of the organization in areas vulnerable to war or civil unrest and assess the vulnerability to these various threats.

Cyber Threats

We placed cyber threats last because it is a large and ever-changing topic. We'll cover some of the common threats in this section, but we recognize that they will shift and change quickly. The good news is that many, if not most, of these threat sources are ones that you and your IT team are very familiar with and as such, your BC/DR plan should be fairly easy to construct in this area. Most of these threat sources have to be assessed and addressed through normal IT operations and security assessments (and certifications), so you may already have all the data you need to include in your BC/DR plan.

The bottom line in IT is data security. Sure, a stolen server is a hassle to replace, a hacked Web site is a pain to repair, but ultimately all these threats result in compromising one (or more) of three basic areas: confidentiality, integrity, and availability (CIA).

Confidentiality refers to the protection of data from unauthorized disclosure. Unauthorized, unintended, or unanticipated disclosure can result in legal action, financial loss, loss of public confidence, or embarrassment. For example, personal medical information is protected by law and any unauthorized disclosure of such information, regardless of whether it was intentional or not, is illegal. Companies dealing with personal health information including hospitals, health clinics, doctors offices, optometrists, and prosthetics companies, to name just a few, are all subject to these kinds of regulations. However, confidentiality also can include keeping trade secrets confidential from competitors or keeping embarrassing information from spreading through unintended or unanticipated channels.

Integrity has to do with the information being protected from unauthorized or unintended modification. Hackers often have as one of their goals the modification of data—whether that data includes user permissions, network access, or business data modification such as pricing on a Web site or pay rates for employees. Integrity issues can stem from intentional acts such as wayward employees or external hackers, but it can also result from accidents and errors. Someone might make accidental changes, enter erroneous data, or corrupt a database just with a few incorrect clicks of the mouse. Inaccurate data may be from an error, it might stem from intentional fraud (such as changing payroll data or pricing on a Web site), or just bad decisions. Regardless of the intent behind it, these losses can also add up. In some cases, your company may face legal liabilities. There are almost always financial consequences including lost productivity, downtime, lost or lower sales, or untraceable losses, to name a few.

Availability pertains to critical business data being available when needed. If a database is corrupted, it is not available for use. If a Web site is hacked, it is not available for use. If a Web site is flooded with connection requests (a Denial of Service attack), it is not available for use. These kinds of availability problems can also be intentional or accidental. Lack of availability impacts productivity for the IT department (busy fixing availability issues) and for end users (unable to retrieve needed information in a timely manner).

Anyone working in IT for any length of time knows about CIA and about the various methods used to attack these three areas of data security. You are also probably painfully aware of how unintentional errors or poor decisions can impact CIA as well. One wrong setting, one incorrect click of the mouse, and users can be granted incorrect access, data can be changed or deleted, data can be exposed to unauthorized access.

Most likely as you've worked in your IT operations, you've identified the critical data for your organization and ensured it was protected against loss of CIA. These are basic operational areas that most IT departments do as part of defined security procedures. Basic steps such as creating and reviewing security logs, analyzing network traffic patterns, and other types of standard IT security operations typically are built into your everyday activities.

For your BC/DR planning, you'll need to review all your IT operations in light of the potential for these security threats occurring. For example, you might have a computer incident response team (CIRT) in place to address a breach in network security. Have you also taken it a step further and looked at what the impact on business operations would be if, say, a client database was attacked? How would your business recover from that? The answer is likely that it depends on the nature of the attack. You'd first probably need to understand whether the data was looked at, modified, or stolen and how the attack was carried out. This would dictate your next steps and would also tell you the potential impact of the incident on short- and long-term operations. So, even though you may have plans in place to prevent and address potential data security issues, you may not have business continuity and disaster recovery plans in place related to these specific threat sources.

As a starting point, you can review your IT security processes and procedures and determine whether they need to be updated or expanded to address new and evolving threats. Then, take those procedures and include the security threat sources in this BC/DR risk assessment. From there, you can treat these threat sources as you would any other threat source except that you're probably already ahead of the curve with much of this data. Look across the enterprise to see how these incidents could disrupt not just IT activities, which you probably have already determined at length, but corporate operations as well.

Looking Ahead...

Business Impact Analysis

Business impact analysis (BIA) is the next step in the risk management process and it's covered in depth in the next chapter. However, let's take a moment to define BIA so you can begin formulating ideas and thoughts about BIA while you're in the risk assessment phase. *Business impact analysis* is the process of identifying all potential impacts to your business from all identified threat sources that could disrupt the business. Later in this chapter, we'll analyze threat sources based on the company's vulnerability to these threats and you'll rank these in order of importance. You'll probably decide to limit your business impact analysis to those threat sources that are most likely to occur and your company's vulnerability to those threats. After you've identified and analyzed the business impact of each selected threat source, you will use that data as the input for developing mitigation strategies. It's helpful to keep the overall process in mind as you move through each phase of the assessment so that information, ideas, or suggestions relevant to upcoming phases can be captured during the process.

Cyber Crime

Cyber crime is an evolving field of study and unfortunately, there is no dearth of people interested in perpetrating cyber crimes. In the United States, there are numerous federal and state agencies that may deal with cyber crimes, depending on factors such as the suspected originating location of the crime, the scope or span of the crime, and the nature of the crime. For example, financial crimes and those related to personal identity theft for the purpose of financial gain are often handled by the U.S. Secret Service, a division of the U.S. Treasury. Other crimes are handled by the U.S. Department of Justice, and still others are handled by the FBI.

TIP

For more on these national resources, visit these links:

- U.S. Secret Service Electronic Crimes Task Force: http://www.secretservice.gov/ectf.shtml

- U.S. Secret Service Criminal Division: http://www.secretservice.gov/criminal.shtml

- U.S. Department of Justice Computer Crime and Intellectual Property Section: http://www.cybercrime.gov/ (*Note*: The use of the acronym IP on this Web site indicates "intellectual property" and not "Internet Protocol.")

- FBI's Cyber Investigations: http://www.fbi.gov/cyberinvest/cyberhome.htm

- Federal Trade Commission: http://www.ftc.gov/

- Securities and Exchange Commission (SEC): http://www.sec.gov/

For more information on state and local resources, contact your local law enforcement agency or your state's Attorney General's office.

As an added note, you can help your company's employees avoid becoming the victims of cyber crimes by providing training and education on topics such as how to avoid falling victim to phishing schemes, how to report suspicious behavior, how to avoid auction and lottery scams, and so on. This education not only helps employees avoid these problems at home, but it helps keep corporate resources safer as well.

Unfortunately, the types of crimes committed are limited only by the twisted imaginations of people intent on wreaking havoc. Following is a brief list of the headlines that appeared in mid–March 2007 on the U.S. Department of Justice's CyberCrime.gov Web site, which gives a good indication of the breadth and depth of cyber crime:

- Romanian Hacker Broadcasts eBay Customer Accounts (March 12, 2007)

- Los Angeles-Area Man Charged with Uploading Academy Award 'Screener' onto Internet (February 22, 2007)

- Software Piracy Ringleader Extradited from Australia (February 20, 2007)

- Duracell Employee Pleads Guilty to Stealing Trade Secrets (February 2, 2007)

- Man Pleads Guilty to Stealing Morgan Stanley Trade Secrets Relating to Hedge Funds (February 1, 2007)

- Former Antelope Man Sentenced to 20 Months in Prison for Fraudulently Obtaining Microsoft Software: Defendant Cracked Code Needed to Activate Software Causing More than $500,000 in Losses (January 25, 2007)

- First Conviction in Hewlett Packard Pretexting Investigation (January 12, 2007)

- Anderson Man Charged with Criminal Copyright Infringement (December 28, 2006)

- Defendant Sentenced in Online Piracy Crackdown (December 19, 2006)

- Two Michigan Residents Plead Guilty to Criminal Copyright Infringement (December 15, 2006)

As you can see from a scan of these headlines, the crimes are rather diverse—software piracy, trade secrets, copyright infringement, pretexting, online piracy—the list goes on. As an IT professional, you know how difficult it is to keep up on all the latest cyber crime methods, but you also know that if you or someone in your organization is not up-to-date, you may well fall victim to cyber crime. Rather than go into a long list of potential threats, let's just create a general list of items as a start. Remember, cyber crime is committed for three basic purposes—to make money, to earn bragging rights, or to disrupt business. Money usually is made by stealing electronic data and selling it or making unauthorized use of it. Clearly, this fits into the "confidentiality" element of the CIA model. Bragging rights often are sought by hackers, and those types of crimes often span the entire CIA framework. Finally, disruption of business often entails the integrity or availability of data, though breaching confidentiality can also create a disruption in some cases.

The common categories of cyber crimes include:

- Identity theft (through a variety of means)

- Corporate identity theft (through a variety of means)

- Hacking corporate network or intranet (to breach confidentiality, integrity, availability)

- Hacking corporate Web site or extranet (to breach confidentiality, integrity, availability)

- Creating backdoors for unauthorized access (to breach confidentiality, integrity, availability)

- Stealing/selling confidential data (trade secrets, drawings, plans, intellectual property)

Loss of Records or Data—Theft, Sabotage, Vandalism

Although loss of records or data falls under a variety of cyber crime categories, it's worth listing as a separate category anyway. An error or an intentional act can create data loss. Even in the case of unintentional loss (error), the perpetrator is unlikely to come forward voluntarily. In some cases of error, the person may not even know they have caused a data loss. This can happen when ill-trained staff are given tasks to perform outside their skill levels. In other cases, a careless error is made and the person making it is unaware of the error or the resulting data loss. Even if asked, he or she might not understand or realize that their actions may have caused the problem. However, in most cases, the person causing the problem is aware or becomes aware of it. If your company has the type of culture that will severely punish someone making that type of error, you won't likely get people volunteering the truth. It makes it difficult, then, to ascertain whether someone intentionally or inadvertently caused the problem. If it was intentional, you have sabotage going on and you need to find the source and remove access to systems. If it was an error, it may be an one-time event or you have a training issue on your hands. In that case, you may want to restrict access to those systems until the person can demonstrate reasonable competence.

IT System Failure—Theft, Sabotage, Vandalism

IT system failure is similar to loss of data—it can be intentional or unintentional. Intentional acts that bring systems or networks down are sabotage and should be addressed as crimes. Vandalism occurs when systems have been physically broken or destroyed. Unauthorized modification of a Web site is also considered vandalism, especially if it is modified in a way to visually indicate it has been breached such as changing the text or links on a page or inserting a banner, picture, or other data in the Web site. When we talk about IT system failure and theft, we're primarily concerned with the physical theft of equipment including servers, routers, firewalls, test equipment, software, cabling, and any other IT-related asset. The theft of these items disables one or more IT systems, thus falling in the category of IT system failure.

Infrastructure Threats

Infrastructure threats are large, external environmental issues that you rarely have any control over preventing, addressing, or resolving. These issues include:

- Building-specific failures (structural damage, systems failures)
- Public transportation disruption (roads, railways, airports, seaports, waterways)
- Loss of utilities (power grid failure, gas supply failure, water supply failure)
- Petroleum or oil shortage
- Food or water contamination
- Regulatory or legal changes

Building Specific Failures

Buildings are designed and built by humans, so there's always a chance that the architect or builder could make an error that results in the part of the building becoming unstable or failing. Buildings can fail because of human error in the design and construction of the building. The materials themselves can fail as has been the case where inferior concrete was used. Buildings not built to code or that are not properly inspected can be at risk of structural failure.

Other building-specific failures include non-IT system or equipment failures (IT system failures are covered in a later section), communications equipment failures (telephone lines, communications lines, Internet connections), safety systems (fire and alarm systems), internal power failure (circuit breakers, wiring issues, circuit capacity, etc.), heating/cooling failure, and manufacturing line (production) failure. These types of systems typically are managed by the facilities manager. In smaller companies, some or all of these systems may be managed by the building's management company or directly by the building owner/landlord. If you are occupying a building you do not own or manage, you may want to set up an appointment with the manager to go over the building's systems so you understand things like how old the equipment is, the likelihood of it breaking, the estimated duration of critical repairs, and so on. For example, if you're occupying an older building and you learn that the heating system is 45 years old and that parts would be next to impossible to get, you should probably come up with a Plan B related to loss of heat. Statements like "Yeah, the next time it breaks, we're just going to replace the system" should give you a clear indication that a heat failure could take days or weeks to repair.

Public Transportation Disruption

Disruption of public transportation can have a local impact such as the inability of employees to get to work in a timely manner (if at all) or the inability of employees to evacuate due to an impending storm. On a larger scale, your suppliers, vendors, and contractors can all be impacted by transportation disruptions, so your entire supply chain should be evaluated for vulnerabilities to the same threat sources you're looking at for your company.

Loss of Utilities

Loss of utilities usually is localized to a specific region and can be caused by an number of things including weather events, sabotage, error, technology failure (a switch or transformer fails, for instance), or terrorism. In some cases, power loss can cover an entire geographic region, such as when power fails on an entire section of the U.S. power grid.

NOTE

An article in the Washington Post by Justin Blum points to the vulnerability of the U.S. power grid to terrorist attacks. The article, entitled, "Hackers Target U.S. Power Grid: Government Quietly Warns Utilities To Beef Up Their Computer Security" (March 11, 2005. http://www.washingtonpost.com/wp-dyn/articles/A25738-2005Mar10. html) states, " 'A sophisticated hacker, which is probably a group of hackers...could probably get into each of the three U.S. North American power [networks] and could probably bring sections of it down if they knew how to do it,' said Richard A. Clarke, a former counterterrorism chief in the Clinton and Bush administrations." A rather unsettling thought. For more on the U.S. power grid and how it works, you can read up on it on Wikipedia at http://en.wikipedia.org/wiki/Electric_power_transmission.

Disruption to Oil or Petroleum Supplies

There has been a lot of discussion of late with regard to global oil supplies (especially as it relates to global warming issues). Regardless of your opinions on the topic, oil supplies are finite and are managed by large groups—countries or cartels—and the availability and cost of oil and petroleum products is controlled by those few. Oil and petroleum supplies can be disrupted by war, civil unrest, sabotage, weather, or political will. If supplies are disrupted, how will your business fare? Employees may not be able to get to work (long gas lines or no gas, as was evidenced in the late 1970s in the United States); suppliers may not be able to manufacture or deliver their products to you (oil is used in manufacturing and for fuel); products needed for your manufacturing may be unavailable or significantly more expensive; timelines may be pushed out due to delays in getting materials and supplies; costs may skyrocket due to limited supplies, and the list goes on. If your company is dependent upon oil or petroleum production or supply, you clearly need to evaluate the threats and threat sources so you can create effective mitigation strategies. These tasks may fall outside your purview as an IT professional, but as with other business risks, it's important that you be as well-informed as possible so you can participate fully in developing the best BC/DR plan possible.

Geophysicist M. King Hubbert predicted in 1956 that U.S. oil production would reach its highest level in the early 1970s. Though severely criticized by oil experts and economists, Hubbert's prediction came true in 1970. The term "Hubbert's Peak" is used to indicate the peaking of oil production in a particular area. Oil companies routinely use Hubbert's calculations to help them determine the yield of a particular oil field, so clearly Hubbert's data has been found to be accurate over the years. Kenneth Deffeyes, a geologist who worked for Shell Oil Company and later became a professor at Princeton, built on Hubbert's work and found that worldwide oil production will peak in this decade. Regardless of which side of this debate you fall on, you might find some interesting information by using the search term "Hubbert's Peak" on your favorite search engine.

Food or Water Contamination

Contamination of the food or water supply is disruptive to all life forms. Contamination can be accidental as in the case of an oil or chemical spill or it can be an intentional act of sabotage or terrorism. The impact of these events can be local, regional, or national though they usually are contained to a specific geographic region. Chances are good that if food or water is in short supply in your area, your employees will not be concerned with coming to work but with finding food or water. Your company's operations will be secondary to everyone in that event and you may not need to plan for this other than to assume you will suspend operations until the issue is resolved. Food or water contamination or shortages in other areas could impact your supply chain, so looking at your business as well as that of your business partners may turn up some risks you hadn't seen that might be worth addressing in your mitigation plan.

Regulatory or Legal Changes

Changes to regulations or legal rulings setting precedents could impact your business, but the place they're most likely to impact you is after a disaster. For example, there may be health and safety regulations that impact your ability to resume operations, especially if something has happened to your facility. Opening your doors without adhering to these regulations could result in having operations shut down or having stiff legal and/or financial penalties imposed. Changes in any of the legal areas, such as data security, could also impact your firm in the aftermath of a disaster. If a server inadvertently ends up in the wrong hands and data was not encrypted or due diligence was not used to secure the data or the computer, you may have another disaster on your hands.

The best way to address this is to have someone on your team review the current regulatory and legal requirements for your firm and do a bit of research to find proposed or impending changes. Then, determine how your company would be impacted by these changes during normal business and in the aftermath of a disaster. This is especially true for data security requirements within the IT arena. You can begin to build in or modify processes to address these changes so that they are part of your everyday operations, if appropriate. Often it's easier and less costly to scan the horizon and build in your safeguards in this manner than to try to retroactively address these kinds of issues in the aftermath of a disaster.

Looking Back

We've looked at a wide variety of threats and threat sources, and continually tied them back to corporate operations and, where applicable, IT. As we've mentioned, it's not exhaustive and in some cases, we did not go into tremendous detail because of changing threats or changing laws and regulations. However, this section should have given you a good idea of how to look at potential threats and threat sources as well as how to think through the potential threat and impact to your business.

Threat Checklist

The list, shown in Table 30.2, is provided for your convenience. It is a reiteration of all the threats listed in the previous sections. You may want to use this list as a starting point in your threat assessment. You can add any threats not included in the list and remove those you're confident will not impact your business. Again, be sure to avoid removing threats before you look at your company's total environment—internal, external, and extended (key suppliers, vendors, outsourcers, partners, and customers).

Examine how these threats and threat sources impact the *people*, *processes*, and *technologies* your company needs to operate as well as the *infrastructure*. In the next chapter, we'll look specifically at how these threats and threat sources can impact your immediate operations as well as how they might impact your key customers, suppliers, vendors, contractors, outsourcers, or partners. However, if you have any thoughts on impact as you move through this portion of the risk assessment, be sure to jot them down for later use.

Table 30.2 Threat Checklist

Natural/Environmental Threats
Fire (can be human-caused)
Flood
Severe winter storm
Electrical storm
Drought
Earthquake
Tornado
Hurricane/Typhoon/Cyclone
Tsunami
Volcano
Avian Flu/Pandemics

Continued

www.syngress.com

Table 30.2 Continued

Human-Caused Threats

Fire, Arson
Theft, Sabotage, Vandalism
Labor disputes
Workplace violence
Terrorism
Chemical and biological hazards
War, Civil unrest

Infrastructure Threats

Building-specific failures
Non-IT equipment, System failures
Heating/Cooling, Power failures
Public transportation disruption
Oil, petroleum supply disruption
Food, water contamination
Regulatory, legal changes

IT-Specific Threats

Cyber threats (CIA)
Equipment or system failure
Production line equipment failure
Loss of data or records

For your convenience, in Table 30.3 we've also included a slightly different view of some of the IT specific threats you might want to consider in your planning. It's not intended to be comprehensive, but it should help get you started.

Table 30.3 IT-Specific Threats

Threat To...	Specific Threats
Hardware	Equipment failure (intentional, unintentional damage)
	Power outage
	Equipment reconfiguration (authorized, nonauthorized)
	Equipment sabotage
	Equipment theft
Software	Bugs, glitches
	Data corruption
	Data security breach (deleted, stolen, modified)
	System configuration changes (errors or sabotage)
Infrastructure	Internet connection(s)—failure, tampering, destruction
	Wireless networks—failure, tampering, destruction
	Network backbone—failure, tampering, destruction
	Cabling—failure, tampering, destruction
	Routers, infrastructure hardware—failure, tampering, destruction

Figure 30.5 shows the output from this phase of the risk assessment, which is a document listing all potential threats and threat sources you have looked at for your company. Although you may be able to skip over a few that clearly don't apply, your list should be inclusive rather than exclusive at this junction. This document will be used as the input for the vulnerability assessment phase, discussed later in this chapter. At the end of the entire risk assessment phase, you'll have a more streamlined list of threats that you'll use in your business impact analysis, discussed in Chapter 31.

Figure 30.5 Deliverable from Threat Source Assessment

Table 30.4 provides a sample of how you could organize your threat data so that you're ready to move into subsequent phases. Regardless of how you organize your data, be sure you capture it in a consistent and logical manner.

Table 30.4 Risk Assessment Table

Item No.	Threat Name	Threat Source	Vulnerability Rating	Likelihood Rating	Existing Controls	Impact Rating	Overall Risk Rating
001	Fire	Internal					
002		External					
003	Flood	Internal					

This matrix shows Fire as a threat and then delineates the threat source as *Internal* or *External*. If there is a fire in the building, you may evacuate. If there is a fire in the area making leaving the area difficult or dangerous, your best solution might be to shelter-in-place. This is an example of how a single threat (fire) has two different sources and how the vulnerability, likelihood, impact, and mitigation strategies might differ for each. Therefore, to list "fire" without listing the threat sources, you might miss something in your assessments. You may choose to create additional columns or include additional details. For example, an internal source of fire could be limited to the server room or could be elsewhere in the building. Is it useful for you to make that distinction? If so, add that detail. If not, don't add unnecessary detail. Also in this table, we've included a column labeled Existing Controls, which can be used to list controls or measures that are already in place. For example, if your server room has a state-of-the-art fire suppression system, you can list that as a control. If your building has a fire suppression system and you practice fire evacuation drills, you can list that as a control. These are things that are already in place that are mitigating your risk. In some cases, these controls may be sufficient; in other cases, you'll need to add layers of control to bring the risk down to an acceptable level. By listing controls already in place, you can spend less time on risks that are already addressed and more time on those that are not addressed in an effective manner. As you go through this assessment, it can be helpful to list these kinds of items or to add/delete columns as needed. Creating the right data fields now will make your work easier later on because this matrix will help you capture information as it comes up. The goal is to find a balance between too much and too little detail.

If you have a preferred method for approaching this that will account for your threats and threat sources adequately, feel free to use it. The end result is to have a comprehensive assessment from which you can build a plan without getting bogged down in useless detail. One final word: You may start out with more detail than you need and pare down as you see how your planning is progressing. Sometimes when you have a bit of perspective on the topic, you can see more clearly what *is* and *is not* needed. Err initially on the side of inclusion, pare down later.

Threat Assessment Methodology

Before we head into the vulnerability assessment phase, we're going to discuss threat assessment methodologies that might be useful to you in evaluating various threats. In essence, there are two ways you can approach this. The first is to use a *quantitative* approach, in which you attempt to use hard numbers to represent threats, vulnerabilities, and impacts. In some companies, this may be the norm or it may be required for some reason. The second method is a *qualitative* approach, where you attempt to define the relative threats, vulnerabilities, and impacts. You use qualitative, or value-based language such as "high," "medium," and "low." We'll look at both methods and provide a few samples so you can determine which approach would be best for your BC/DR team. Keep in mind that you should pick one approach and stick with it; mixing and matching can result in unclear or meaningless data. Once you've read through this section, you should have a good idea of which approach fits best with the culture and requirements of your company.

The reason we're discussing these two different approaches is because if you're fighting an uphill battle in your company with regard to the cost or benefit of this BC/DR plan, you may need to come up with quantitative assessments to sway decision-makers. They may not be convinced by statements like "more" or "extremely high"; they might be convinced by "20% chance" or "$250,000 loss." If you have support for your BC/DR plan, you may opt for the qualitative approach, which is less precise but faster and easier to derive.

Quantitative Threat Assessment

A quantitative assessment can be defined as observations that involve measurements and numbers. They are specific and measurable. If you say, "The server costs $850 more than the desktop system," you are making a quantitative statement. In contrast, if you say, "The server is more expensive than the desktop system," you are making a qualitative assessment since "more" is not specific and measurable.

Let's start with the threat of a power outage. We can look at the possible threat sources—what could cause a power outage? As you learned in the previous sections, there are numerous potential sources of a power outage. Let's begin with an electrical storm with lightning that causes a localized power outage. If your building is susceptible to power outages in storms and those outages do not affect neighboring buildings, you may start with a power outage that impacts just your building. Again, this is where a thorough threat assessment is helpful. You can gather actual data from the National Weather Service or other reliable sources on the number of storms per year in your area, on average. If you want to know more about local weather conditions and history, you might be able to get some valuable information from your local news station's meteorologist. Sometimes they are more than willing to share information with you and they might be able to point you to resources you'd otherwise miss. You can also gather data from the power company on the number of times power has gone out in your building or your area over the past five years or on average. Once you have that data, you have very specific, quantifiable information. When looking for quantitative data on any of your threats and threat sources, you may need to be creative.

From the Trenches…

Finding Your Data Weasels

In every company, there are always a few people (sometimes more) who relish the challenge of a good data search. At one company, there was a young man whom people had affectionately nicknamed "the data weasel" because he could "ferret" out just about anything—there was not a piece of information he could not eventually retrieve (though his typical turnaround time was less than 30 minutes). There may be people in your company who participate in "Google races" to see who can find a specific piece of information the fastest (think of the TV show *Who Wants to Be a Millionaire?*—who in your company would make a great "Phone-A-Friend"?). If you need data on the number of storms in your area that have dumped more than 10 inches of snow in the past 10 years, or number, frequency, and duration of local power outages, turn to your company's data weasels. Give them specific data to search for and a deadline for completion and leave them to it. Be sure to ask them to capture the source of their data so you can be sure it's credible before relying upon it. By leveraging the natural skills and interests of people in your company or on your team, you can effectively delegate tasks to others who will enjoy the challenge and will produce great results.

What if you can't easily find that data? You can gather anecdotal evidence, though this by its very nature is much more qualitative than quantitative. You can probably talk to your facilities person or staff who have worked at the company for several years and get their input. Will they know exactly how many storms with lightning have come through the area? No. Will they have an idea of how many times power has gone out in the building or the area? Probably. They may not have an exact number but you may well get a response like, "It seems to happen every year or two" or "I can't remember the last time that happened and I've been here five years."

To create a quantitative assessment, we need to make sure we're comparing "apples to apples," so all numbers will be converted to annual numbers. For example, if you have a power outage every other year, the annual power outage would be 0.5 chance of an outage. If an outage occurs once every four years, you have a 25% or 0.25 chance per year because the risk is only 1 in 4 that you'll have a power outage in any given year. The numbers should all be annualized so that comparisons are accurate.

Let's look at a risk diagram, shown in Figure 30.6. Remember that we'll quantify some of these other numbers through our assessments later in this chapter and in upcoming chapters. We'll quantify these in this section so you can see how the process works and then you can develop the remainder of the needed input values later as you develop the data. In other words, you can do your likelihood assessment later and input the values later but we'll review the entire model here so you can see the road ahead.

Figure 30.6 Risk Assessment Methodology—Quantitative

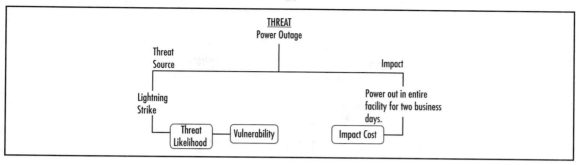

On the left side of the diagram, you can see one threat source listed. Ideally, each threat source for a power outage should be addressed in this manner. In this case, the threat source we're looking at is a lightning strike. First, we assess the likelihood of occurrence. If your data indicates this happens once every four years, then you would enter the value of 0.25 under the threat likelihood since we want to know the likelihood in any given year. Next, you would assess your vulnerability. In this case, let's say that every time there's a serious lightning strike (once every four years), your power goes out. That means that when lightning strikes, your power will go out. That's a 1:1 ratio, or 100%, so we'll insert the number 1. Now, on the threat source of this equation, we have:

$$0.25 \times 1 = 0.25$$

This is sometimes referred to as the *risk value*. We're keeping the example simple so we can walk through the logic of it. In English, this equation says that although there's only a 25% chance the threat will occur, there's a 100% chance it will affect us when it occurs.

Next, we move to the other side of the diagram and look at the impact. In this example, we're assuming that when the power goes out, it's out in the entire facility and it's out for two days. (Of course, if your building loses power every four years for two days, you should be having a chat with your power company.) What is the cost of not being able to work for two days? Your servers are down, your employees cannot access desktops, printers, or IT resources, there are no lights, no heating/cooling—no productivity. How many sales do you lose? What impact does this have on your customers? Your inventory? Your order backlog? This is where having your team comes into play as members from different organizations can help you make these assessments. This is some of what we'll cover in the next chapter, but for now, let's assume the following:

- Lost sales per day: $18,000, total cost $36,000 for the outage
- Fixed costs per day: $4,200, total cost $8,400 for the outage
- Damage to reputation: unspecified, arbitrary value set at $2,000, total cost: $4,000

Note that you may decide to set a value for damage to reputation at a daily rate just to give you some measurement that can be used consistently. If you have a method for calculating this to a more exact figure, feel free to use it. Otherwise, a daily rate for these unspecified costs may help by providing an "order of magnitude" estimate. In this case, we're using $2,000 per day and this amount will be used for any "damage to reputation" suffered from any threat source. Therefore, we'll be able to understand the impact of a one-day event versus a month-long event. Though there is a multiplier effect that occurs with an extended period of downtime or outage and you may choose to address this, we're using a single value. We also recognize that the use of an arbitrarily set value, such as $2,000 per day for "damage to reputation," is qualitative in nature. Still, assigning a dollar value to it and using it consistently across all threats will mitigate that to some extent. Now, let's calculate our impact costs:

$$\$36,000 + \$8,400 + \$4,000 = \$48,400$$

So now we know that if this threat occurs, it will cost the company $48,400. Now, let's input that into our earlier equation as shown here and reflected in Figure 30.7.

$$0.25\% \times \$48,400 = \$12,100$$

Figure 30.7 Total Risk Cost per Year of Power Outage from Lighting Strike

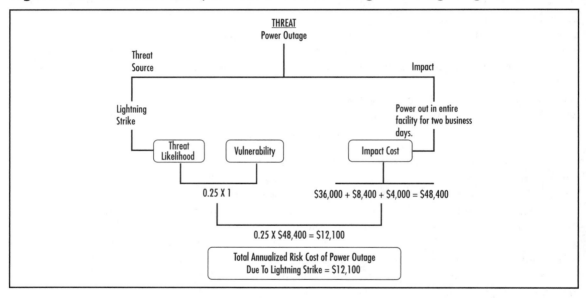

If you know that your annualized risk cost is $12,100 for a power outage from a lightning strike, it's much easier to determine whether a $10,000 backup power generator makes sense. You may also decide that it's worth investing $5,000 to have the power company install equipment that will make your power system less likely to fail. These are your risk mitigation strategies that we'll develop in Chapter 32. You can see that having an annualized value can certainly help you and your team come up with a number of reasonable risk mitigation strategies. Clearly, a solution that costs $100,000 is probably not a good investment because it would take you about eight years to recoup your investment ($100,000/$12,100 = 8.26). How cost effective is additional equipment for $5,000 to make the problem go away? Probably very effective and as such, an excellent investment. We use terms like "probably" in this case because there may be mitigating circumstances we don't know about. For example, suppose that $5,000 solution costs $1,000 annually to maintain. Is it still a good deal? What if it lasts for only four years? Is it still a good solution? Without knowing all the details, it's hard to make a solid assessment. This is part of what's covered later in Chapter 32. For now, we'll use straight numbers and assume that a $5,000 solution is just that—and as such, it would make a lot of sense.

The second thing to consider when looking at potential mitigation strategies is that there may be additional *benefits* to a particular solution. If, for example, the $100,000 solution would also extend the serviceable life of all computers in the building by 1.37 years, it might be a better solution. You'd need to calculate the value of extending all computers' serviceable life by 1.37 years and comparing that to the cost of the solution. Another possibility is that the $100,000 solution meets industry requirements that will be enforced starting in three years; the $5,000 solution does not meet requirements. Now what's your best option? This is certainly a place where getting your finance folks into the loop will help; they can develop what-if scenarios for your different options and you, as the IT expert, can help everyone understand the additional benefits (or risks) that come with various solutions. Some solutions you'll consider may inject a new risk into the mix; some solutions will mitigate risks in areas you hadn't expected. Keeping your eyes open for possibilities will help you maximize your results.

Will calculating your values be this easy? Probably not. You most likely have far more factors to consider when calculating the cost of an outage, for example. However, you can also decide as a team what degree of accuracy you require in order to create an effective plan. If exact numbers are not required, you can use a qualitative model.

Qualitative Threat Assessment

Qualitative assessments use words or relative values to express risk, cost, and impact. The first step in using a qualitative system is to define the scale you want to use and then use it consistently. You can use systems like those shown in Table 30.5 or Table 30.6, or you can develop a customized scale to fit your needs.

Table 30.5 Qualitative Scale Examples

Numeric	Frequency	Impact
6	Constant	Extremely high
5	Very frequently	Very high
4	Frequently	High
3	Infrequently	Low
2	Very infrequently	Very low
1	Never	Extremely low

One suggestion is that you use a scale with an even number of variables; the one we used has six. This forces a choice between two options, "frequently" or "infrequently" or "high" or "low," and can prevent someone from selecting the middle value (present when there are an odd number of choices) to be safe. Whatever scale you use or whatever number of variables you opt for, be sure to define these elements to everyone's satisfaction. It's important to have a shared understanding of what these values mean so that when you're using them for the risk assessment, you're all using them in the same manner.

When assessing likelihood, you can define a scale that works for your organization. Table 30.6 shows the likelihood matrix developed by the National Institute of Standards and Technology. This matrix is specific to security risk vulnerabilities but provides a good example of how to define these types of qualitative assessments.

Table 30.6 NIST Likelihood Matrix

Likelihood Level	Description
High	The threat-source is highly motivated and sufficiently capable, and controls to prevent the vulnerability from being exercised are ineffective.
Medium	The threat-source is motivated and capable, but controls are in place that may impede successful exercise of the vulnerability.
Low	The threat-source lacks motivation or capability, or controls are in place to prevent, or at least significantly impede, the vulnerability from being exercised.

Source: National Institute of Standards and Technology, "Risk Management Guide for Information Technology Systems," Special Publication 800-30, July 2002, p. 21.

Now, let's look at the same example we looked at previously only this time, let's use the qualitative method. First, we map out the threat, as shown in Figure 30.6 earlier and repeated here in Figure 30.8 for your convenience.

Figure 30.8 Power Outage Threat Assessment—Qualitative

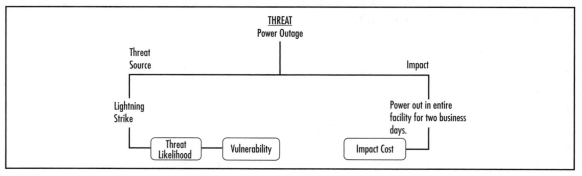

Now let's assign values. Let's say we know that these outages happen once every four years. We might determine that deserves a rating of "infrequently" and we can assign it the value of 3. Using the same system, we can say that the vulnerability when the storm hits is 100% (per our quantitative assessment), which would place it on the scale as "extremely high" and give it a rating of 6. So, the left side of our equation = 2, 6.

On the right side, we want to assess the impact cost, but we're not using exact dollar amounts. We could say, well the cost of being down two days would be about average because we can catch up later without too much trouble and our fixed costs aren't through the roof. Therefore, you might assess your impact cost as being "low" or a level 3. If you take the average of these, you have $2 + 6 + 3 = 11/3 = 3.66$. This puts it on the scale at "high" if we round up (any number above 3.5 would be 4, any number 3.5 and below would be 3). This is depicted in Figure 30.9.

Figure 30.9 Total Risk Value per Year of Power Outage from Lighting Strike

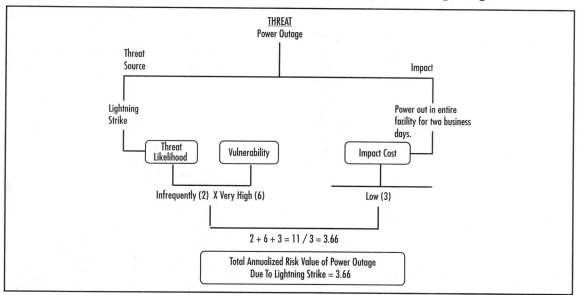

You might decide you don't like converting these assessments to numbers—that's fine. You might also decide you want a scale with a few more options, say a 10 item scale—that's fine, too. The point here is that you can make assessments without hard dollar figures and still come up with a meaningful assessment. In the case of the power outage, you might argue that the value of 6 for "very high" under vulnerability skews this data in a way you don't like because it's not weighted, for example. However, when you do this assessment using this scale for a number of threat sources, you may find that your data shakes out as expected. For example, you might perform this same assessment on a power outage from an internal failure and decide its total risk value is 3.5. You can then look at these two sources and ask, "Do we really have a slightly greater risk value if we experience a two-day power outage every four years versus our internal power failure that could take us down for a week but only happens once every eight years?" If the answer is no, you may want to go back and better define your scale or reassess the values you used in one or the other assessment. However, in most cases what you'll find is that after a few of these, you get the feel for the scale and you begin to see that your data tracks with the reality of the situation. Once you're confident your scale is working, you can tackle the more difficult or more intangible threat sources.

Another rating scale could range from 1 to 100 to give you a bit more fine-tuned result. An example of this is shown in Figure 30.10. If you really want to keep it simple, you can use a five-element, single-rating system and come up with something similar to that shown in Figure 30.11. In Figure 30.10 and Figure 30.11, the costs are delineated in terms of the relative impact cost of 1) loss of revenue, 2) damage to servers, 3) damage to the database, and 4) damage to user computers. These two examples assume that the servers were able to shut down without incident but that there was damage to a database as a result of the sudden loss of power. This is just an example to show you how you might assess your IT components. You might also choose to delineate things like firewalls, routers, and cabling in your list, if it's helpful in making a qualitative assessment.

Figure 30.10 More Refined Qualitative Scale

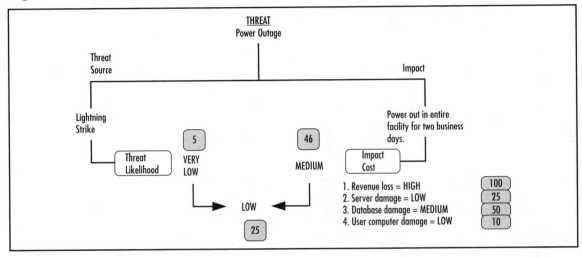

Figure 30.11 Simple Qualitative Scale

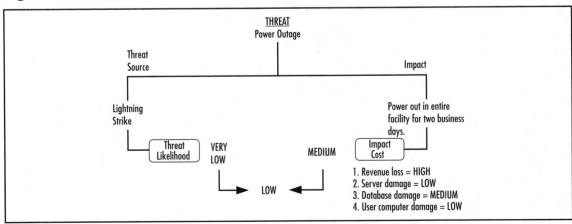

Whether you choose to use a quantitative system or a qualitative system, be sure everything is clearly defined and that you apply these ratings consistently. What you'll end up with at the end of your risk assessment phase is a chart, table, or document delineating each threat, the likelihood of that threat, the vulnerability to that threat, and the impact should that threat occur. From there, you'll develop your risk mitigation strategies because you'll be able to see the big picture and create optimal solutions for your firm.

Vulnerability Assessment

A *vulnerability* is defined as the weakness, susceptibility, or exposure to hazards or threats. A vulnerability in a software program, for example, is a weakness that poses a problem if discovered and exploited. Vulnerabilities in the case of business continuity and disaster recovery are the various areas of the business and IT systems that are exposed or susceptible to the threats defined in the previous assessment phase. Vulnerabilities can be exploited intentionally or triggered unintentionally. As you know, a change to a security setting in one area of the operating system can create a vulnerability elsewhere in the system without the IT administrator even being aware of it. The analysis of vulnerabilities in BC/DR planning must include IT systems, but it should not be limited to IT systems. Clearly, people, processes, technology, and infrastructure are vulnerable to the threats delineated earlier. Therefore, while our focus will continue to be IT-related data, we have to cast a wider net so that the BC/DR plan is complete.

The result of the threat assessment becomes the input to the vulnerability assessment, as shown in Figure 30.12, which is the second section of the larger image presented at the beginning of the chapter in Figure 30.2.

Figure 30.12 Vulnerability Assessment Phase of Overall Risk Assessment

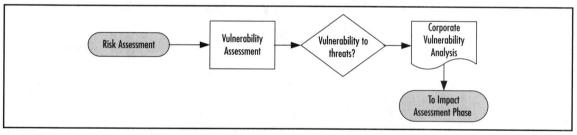

Some people like to break out this assessment into likelihood of occurrence and vulnerability to the threat based on the likelihood. Others prefer to keep it simple and use a straightforward vulnerability assessment. The value in breaking it out, as shown in the previous section, is that the likelihood of something occurring may be high but the vulnerability to that threat source may be low. Conversely, you could say something is unlikely to occur but if it does, you are very vulnerable, as would be the case with a major earthquake or hurricane. Thus, the value in breaking it out into likelihood and vulnerability might be that you can address those issues unlikely to occur but to which you're very vulnerable as a separate element of your BC/DR planning. Another approach is to simply look at the vulnerability as the likelihood of occurrence and then assess the potential impact through the business impact analysis.

Once you have your threat sources listed in detail, you may choose to subdivide your list and assign segments to appropriate subject matter experts. For example, you could give the entire list to four subteams, each specializing in a particular area such as IT, facilities, finance, HR, and/or operations. You could also create subteams to look at each threat source from the people, process, technology, and infrastructure framework. You could divide your team in two and have half address the internal threat sources and the other half address the external threat sources. However you subdivide the work, you should hold a final full team review to ensure there are no gaps. If time and resources allow, you could have each group's deliverable be handed to another subgroup so that each group's work is reviewed by another group (i.e., Group A's results are reviewed by Group B; Group B's results are reviewed by Group C; Group C's results are reviewed by Group A). The point is not to chastise another group for errors or omissions, but simply to make sure every angle has been considered and reviewed appropriately.

NOTE

The Business Continuity Institute (www.thebci.org) provides certification in business continuity planning. In conjunction with the Disaster Recovery Institute (www.drii. org), they have developed and published a set of guidelines that describe best practices. You can download the PDF file using this link: http://www.thebci.org/ 10Standards.pdf.

People, Process, Technology, and Infrastructure

We've continually pointed out that BC/DR planning activities require research into the impact on people, processes, and technology. In the case of BC/DR plans, infrastructure might be a fourth category that could be included (some might include it in technology). Infrastructure in this case includes the building itself, heating/cooling systems, power to the building, among others. When you're assessing your business risks, these four areas come into play. When you begin your vulnerability assessment, these four areas should also be considered. If you've done a thorough job in your threat assessment, these areas will be covered, but a quick reminder to look at your plan from this perspective at this point will help ensure there are no gaps.

People

When performing a vulnerability assessment, you need to ask and answer the question: How vulnerable are our staff and the people in our community to these threats? Some threats may not impact people beyond their ability to be productive at work (a one-hour power outage, for example). Other threats may not only impact your staff but the surrounding community, as is the case in major natural disasters. If you look at how vulnerable people are to the various threats, you can determine your overall risk with each threat source. For example, people are particularly vulnerable to phishing and social engineering. This is not a systems vulnerability—there is little a system can do to stop a person from deciding to respond to a phishing or social engineering ruse. So, if someone willingly hands over a "power user" account name and password, the system is vulnerable, but only because a person was vulnerable first. Looking at threats and vulnerabilities in this light will help not only in determining the overall risk value of each threat source but in developing effective mitigation strategies later.

Process

How vulnerable are your business and IT processes to these various threat sources? In some cases, your processes may not be very vulnerable at all, as might be the case in a brief power or server outage. You already have processes in place for normal IT operations and minor outages and equipment failures are probably covered in your standard operating procedures. Other processes might be very vulnerable, such as is the case when a natural disaster occurs. In those cases, it's typical that all business and IT processes are vulnerable because there is nothing about a disaster that is "business as usual." For example, how would you handle, process, and fulfill customer orders after a disaster that made your building uninhabitable for weeks? What could you do to get back up and running? How would your processes have to flex or change? As you review the vulnerability of each of your critical business processes to the various threat sources, you'll begin to see which processes need to be reviewed, revised, or reinvented for use in an emergency. We'll discuss this in the business impact analysis as well as in the mitigation strategy development chapters.

Technology

Clearly, technology is vulnerable to numerous threat sources and as an IT professional, you're aware of most (if not all) of them. How vulnerable is your server to an internal or external attack? How vulnerable is your web server? These are questions you've probably already addressed through standard IT security assessments and operating procedures. As you go through this particular risk assessment process, you also need to broaden your outlook a bit and ask how vulnerable your systems are to the disaster threat sources such as floods, hurricanes, and fires. Since your perspective is an IT-centric perspective, you probably have the most detailed information available on this subject. As you go through the vulnerability assessment, this data should be captured. Don't assume that your standard operating procedures have addressed the vulnerabilities and don't assume that your current "emergency plans" will be adequate for all threat sources. Approach this topic with fresh eyes to see what else you can add to the process.

Infrastructure

Clearly, infrastructure is vulnerable to some threat sources and not to others. A building is vulnerable to flooding if it's in a low lying area or in a location that could flood. If the building is at the top of a hill overlooking the town, there's a good chance it is not vulnerable to external flooding, but any building could potentially be vulnerable to internal flooding (broken plumbing within the facility). As you review your threat sources, your facilities expert will likely be in the best position to understand the vulnerability of the company's infrastructure to threat sources. As a team, you may all want to think about the vulnerability of external infrastructure in your area to threat sources since these will clearly impact your business. For example, is there a seaport, power plant, airport, or dam nearby that could be vulnerable to the threat sources? If so, what impact would these have on your business?

Vulnerability Assessment

A vulnerability assessment can be qualitative or quantitative, but in many cases a qualitative assessment is used. It's difficult to put a hard number on a vulnerability, so using a rating scale such as those shown in Table 30.5 is usually most effective. The key is to get an accurate picture of the vulnerability to each threat source. When viewed in total, you'll be able to make any needed adjustments to individual vulnerability ratings. For example, you might use a scale of 1 to 100, with 100 being most vulnerable and 1 being least vulnerable. When you view your final list of threat sources and vulnerabilities, you might see that some of the vulnerability ratings are out of sync with the rest—those can be modified so that your overall vulnerability picture is accurate. As with other rating systems, be sure that you define it and then use it consistently. Also, because you may choose to subdivide the work, it's vital that everyone have the same understanding of the ratings and apply them in the same manner.

A vulnerability assessment typically uses various data sources as input. These include prior risk assessments, security requirements, security test results, regulatory requirements (HIPAA, GLBA, etc.), and prior problems. According to the National Institute of Standards and Technology's "Risk Assessment Guide for Information Technology Systems," the types of vulnerabilities that exist and the methodologies needed to determine vulnerabilities will vary depending on the nature of the system and in particular, the phase of the SDLC it is in. Accordingly,

- If the system has not been designed yet, the vulnerabilities assessment should focus on the organization's security policies, planned security procedures, and system requirements definitions, and vendor's (or developer's) security product analyses (white papers, etc.).

- If the system is in the process of being implemented, the vulnerabilities assessment should focus on more specific information such as the planned security features, security and design documentation, and the results of system certification, testing, staging, and evaluation.

- If the system has been implemented and is operational, the vulnerabilities assessment should include the analysis of the system's security features, security controls (technical, operational, and environmental), and standard IT operating procedures.

However, we are looking beyond just IT systems to the larger organization, so we need to expand our view of vulnerabilities just a bit. Even though these other areas may fall outside your direct line of authority, you should be familiar with them so you can participate fully on the BC/DR planning team or head it up effectively, whichever the case. You may choose to use a three-item scale (high, medium, low), or you may choose to use a wider numeric scale such as 1 through 10 or 1 through 100.

The vulnerability assessment can be accomplished using the same methods described earlier in the threat assessment: questionnaires, interviews, document reviews, and research. In addition, you can develop scenario questions based on the identified threat sources to help you assess vulnerability. For example, you might ask your subject matter experts to respond to a set of questions similar to those shown in Table 30.7.

Table 30.7 Vulnerability Assessment Questions

Statement	High	Medium	Low
1. If the plumbing pipes in the building were to burst, what is the vulnerability of our IT systems to water damage?			
2. If the building were to catch on fire, what is the vulnerability of our IT systems to water damage from fire suppression systems?			
3. If the building were to become flooded by heavy rains, what is the vulnerability of our IT systems to water damage?			

As you can see from these sample statements, we've identified three threat sources for water damage/flooding: internal flooding, water damage from fire suppression systems (which might not be in the server room but adjacent to or above the server room), and external flooding. We have also not asked (here) what the likelihood is of these threats occurring. We are simply assessing how vulnerable we believe these systems would be should these events take place.

Once the vulnerability assessment is complete, you can develop a risk value for each of the threat sources. This risk value can be derived numerically if you've used either a quantitative system or a qualitative system that uses numbers for the scale. Once the vulnerability assessment is complete, you should analyze the data. This analysis should include a thorough review of all the threat sources, likelihood, and vulnerabilities ratings. A final assessment of the data should allow you to adjust ratings that seem out of balance with other data, which is sometimes the case with qualitative assessments. The interim "risk value" for each threat source should be reviewed and verified. The value is considered interim at this point because we have not yet conducted the impact analysis. Therefore, you will have a "risk value subtotal" in a sense, which can be reviewed at this juncture. If you recall, the risk equation can be stated as:

Risk = Threat + (Likelihood + Vulnerability) + Impact

Rather than repeat the material presented in the previous section, we'll leave it to you to go back through your threat source list and perform the vulnerability assessment. The result of this phase is a document that lists, at minimum:

1. All potential threat sources (except those purposely excluded).
2. The likelihood of each threat source occurring.
3. The vulnerability of your company and IT systems to those threat sources.
4. Interim risk value for each threat source.

The deliverable from this phase is the vulnerability assessment and analysis, as shown in Figure 30.13. This data is used as the input to business impact analysis phase, covered in detail in the next chapter. You might have a team meeting to review the final data and present a report to your project sponsor and your corporate executives at this juncture. This can help bring visibility to your efforts and should underscore the need for the BC/DR planning project itself. The document can also be provided to various subject matter experts within the firm for one final review to ensure there are no gaps or errors at this point in the process. If you have a formal sign-off procedure in place, you may want to obtain formal approval for this document before moving onto the next phase of your project plan.

Figure 30.13 Deliverable from Vulnerability Assessment

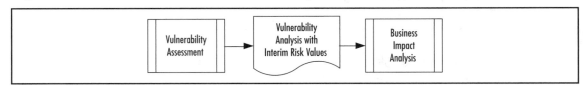

Looking Ahead...

Business Impact Analysis

The next step in the risk assessment is to perform the business impact analysis (BIA). It is in this phase that you will look at the company's business processes (including those associated with IT functions) and develop a rating or assessment of the criticality of those systems. Then, you can determine which business functions must be restored and in what order. Clearly, in the aftermath of a disaster or business disruption, functionality must be restored in a methodical and logical manner and the BIA will provide that roadmap. The input to the BIA is the output from this phase of the assessment, so don't launch your BIA until you've completed this phase to your satisfaction.

Summary

Business continuity and disaster recovery planning begins with a thorough risk assessment. Risk assessment is part of a larger risk management process found in most businesses. The four major components of the BC/DR risk assessment are threat assessment, vulnerability assessment, impact assessment, and risk mitigation strategy development. In this chapter, we focused on threat and vulnerability assessment. In order to perform a thorough threat assessment, you need to look at threats and threat sources both internal and external to the company. It is often helpful to assess risk based on the potential risks to people, process, technology, and infrastructure. People are not only the company's employees but its vendors, partners, customers, and the larger community in which it operates. Processes are all the business and IT processes used in the business. Processes are used to generate revenue, track expenses, and manage operations from facilities management to human resources and beyond.

From an IT-centric viewpoint, the key components to address in the risk assessment include hardware, software (OS and applications), system interfaces (internal, external connection points), people who support the IT systems, users who use the IT systems, data, information and records, processes performed by the IT systems, system's value or importance to the organization (system criticality), and system and data sensitivity (confidential, trade secret, medical data, etc.). The operating environment in which the IT systems function include a wide variety of elements. Among them are the functional and technical requirements of the systems; security policies, procedures, and controls; network topology and information flow diagrams, data storage protection policies, procedures, and controls; encryption, physical, and environmental controls.

The methods used to gather data for any of the assessment phases typically includes questionnaires, interviews, document reviews, and research. Questionnaires can be helpful in structuring desired input but also can have the downside of containing built-in biases, often unintentionally. Interviews can be conducted with subject matter experts and yield more useful information than questionnaires but may also generate a lot of tangential or unneeded data. Reviewing documents and performing research can supplement the questionnaire and interview process.

Once you've defined the methods you'll use to gather the necessary data, you can begin your review of various threats. We discussed many different types of threats that fall into three primary categories: natural and environmental threats, human-caused threats, and infrastructure threats. Infrastructure threats are caused either by natural or human causes, and it's important to delineate these because they involve people, processes, and technologies outside of the company and the company's control. As such, they sometimes can be overlooked in BC/DR planning. Natural threats include those we might commonly think of such as fire, flood, or earthquake, but we also discussed other less obvious threats including volcanoes, droughts, and pandemics. Human-caused threats can be intentional as in the case of terrorism, labor disputes, or workplace violence, or they can be unintentional as can be the case with fire, flood, or a security breach. Infrastructure threats include those to the building as well as external to the building and the company. Public transportation including roads, rails, seaports, and airports are all external infrastructure elements that need to be assessed. Other external elements include threats to water and food supplies, biological and chemical hazards, and public utilities such as the power grid, petroleum and fuel supplies, or telecommunications.

The threat assessment methodology begins with a list of all potential threats and threat sources. Each threat source is then evaluated. Some people like to assess likelihood of occurrence and vulnerability to the threat; others prefer to include both likelihood and vulnerability in a single assessment. Regardless of whether you choose to break them into two distinct ratings or one rating, the likelihood of occurrence and vulnerability rating(s) should be assessed for each threat source. The argument for making two separate assessments is that a threat may have a high likelihood of occurring but your company and its people, processes, technology, and infrastructure may not be vulnerable to those threat sources. Others would argue that if there is a low vulnerability, the likelihood of occurrence doesn't come into play and should therefore not be assessed separately. Either method is acceptable as long as you make a conscious decision as to how to proceed and use the same process throughout your risk assessment cycle.

You can perform a quantitative assessment in which actual values such as dollars or frequency are known. The benefit to this type of assessment is that you can generate hard data that can be used in a standard cost/benefit analysis. The downside is that not all values are easy (or possible) to derive and an unacceptable amount of time or money may be required to generate that data. You can also perform a qualitative assessment in which values are relative. These types of assessments use labels such as high, medium, and low or an arbitrary numbering system such as 1 to 100 where 1 = no chance or extremely low, 50 = medium chance or about average, and 100 = will occur or extremely high chance. These kinds of systems are much easier to implement but typically generate less specific data that is unsuitable for a standard cost/benefit analysis. In analyzing threat data, qualitative measurements are often sufficient to generate a clear picture of the threats facing the organization.

The vulnerability assessment may include the likelihood of occurrence or it may be a separate rating. However, the same processes can be used to evaluate vulnerability as were used to assess threats. Questionnaires, interviews, document reviews, and research can help in generating data needed to assess the actual or relative vulnerability to a threat. This rating is compiled with the threat assessment data and is used as the input to the business impact analysis phase, discussed in the next chapter.

The bottom line is that your risk assessment activities will end up generating a list of threats and threat sources that you'll be able to evaluate. You can sort the list and decide which risks you need to address, which can be accepted, and which should be transferred. You'll have the data to make this decision once you complete the business impact analysis, the third major step in the risk assessment process.

## Chapter 31

Business Impact Analysis

Solutions in this chapter:

- **Business Impact Analysis Overview**

- **Understanding Impact Criticality**

- **Identifying Business Functions and Processes**

- **Gathering Data for the Business Impact Analysis**

- **Determining the Impact**

- **Business Impact Analysis Data Points**

- **Preparing the Business Impact Analysis Report**

☑ **Summary**

Introduction

In Chapter 30, you learned about risk management and the process for assessing risks. In this chapter, we turn our attention to the process of business impact analysis. Risk assessment looks at the various threats your company faces; business impact analysis looks at the critical business functions and the impact of not having those functions available to the firm. These two assessments look at the company from two different angles. The risk assessment starts from the threat side, and the business impact analysis starts from the business process side. When you're managing general business risk, you might actually start with the business impact analysis. However, in planning for business continuity as an outgrowth of disaster recovery, it makes more sense to understand the full picture regarding risks and threats and then look at business impact. However, if you have a methodology you use that starts with business impact analysis, that's fine. Both outputs—from the risk assessment and the business impact analysis phases—are used as input to the mitigation strategy development. As long as you have those ready before you start the mitigation phase you should be all set. Figure 31.1 depicts where we are in the planning process thus far.

Figure 31.1 Business Continuity and Disaster Recovery Planning Process

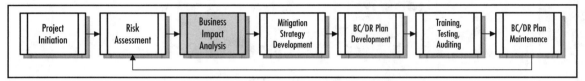

You can see, in Figure 31.2, that we'll be focusing on the third and final segment of the risk assessment phase introduced in Chapter 30 (refer to Figure 30.2 in Chapter 30 for the full diagram). In this chapter, we're going to concentrate on the impact of various business functions on your operations. We'll begin with discussing the general framework of performing a business impact analysis and conclude with the specifics of performing an impact analysis for your business continuity and disaster recovery (BC/DR) plan.

Figure 31.2 Impact Assessment Process

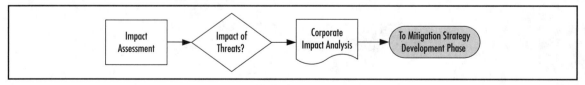

Business Impact Analysis Overview

The fundamental task in business impact analysis (BIA) is understanding which processes in your business are vital to your ongoing operations and to understand the impact the disruption of these processes would have on your business. From an IT perspective, as the National Institute of Standards and Technology (NIST) views it: "The BIA purpose is to correlate specific system components with the critical services that they provide, and based on that information, to characterize the consequences of a disruption to the system components" (*Source*: NIST "Contingency Planning Guide for Information Technology Systems, NIST Special Publication 800-34, p. 16). So, there are two parts to the BIA: the first is to understand mission-critical business processes and the second is to correlate those to IT systems.

As an IT professional, you certainly understand the importance of various IT systems, but you may not be fully aware of the critical business functions performed in your company. Even if your role in this project is limited to managing the IT elements in this BC/DR plan, you should still pay close attention to the material in this chapter for two main reasons. First, understanding the critical business functions is important in terms of understanding how to recover IT systems in the event of a significant business disruption. You might think that System A is most critical, based on a number of assumptions you're making. However, through this process, you might find that System B or C is really what keeps the company up and running on a day-to-day basis or that without System D, System A doesn't really matter. Second, if you have any aspirations at all of moving up the corporate ladder toward that CIO job, your understanding of the overall business will certainly help you achieve those goals. Today's CIO needs to have a solid background in technology *and* business, so understanding the critical business functions in your company will pay off in many ways for you.

According to the Business Continuity Institute (www.thebci.org), a recognized leader in business continuity management and certification, there are four primary purposes of the business impact analysis:

- Obtain an understanding of the organization's most critical objectives, the priority of each, and the timeframe for resumption of these following an unscheduled interruption.

- Inform a management decision on Maximum Tolerable Outage (MTO) for each function.

- Provide the resource information from which an appropriate recovery strategy can be determined/recommended.

- Outline dependencies that exist both internally and externally to achieve critical objectives.

Source: The Business Continuity Institute, Good Practices Guidelines, 2005, p. 21.

Business impact analysis is the process of figuring out which processes are critical to the company's ongoing success, and understanding the impact of a disruption to those processes. Various criteria are used including customer service, internal operations, legal or regulatory, and financial. From an IT perspective, the goal is to understand the critical business functions and tie those to the various IT systems. As part of this assessment, the interdependencies need to be fully understood. Understanding these interdependencies is critical to both disaster recovery and business continuity, especially from an IT perspective. Would it make sense for your IT staff to spend three days trying to recover System D if System A is still out of commission? Until you perform the BIA, there may be no real way to know.

Business impact analysis includes the steps listed earlier, but we can break them out into a few more discrete activities or steps:

1. Identify key business processes and functions.

2. Establish requirements for business recovery.

3. Determine resource interdependencies.

4. Determine impact on operations.

5. Develop priorities and classification of business processes and functions.

6. Develop recovery time requirements.

7. Determine financial, operational, and legal impact of disruption.

The result of performing these seven steps is a formal business impact analysis, which is used in conjunction with the risk assessment analysis to develop mitigation strategies (discussed in Chapter 32).

The two primary impact points of any business disruption are the operational impact and the financial impact. The operational impact addresses the nonmonetary impact including how people, processes, and technology are impacted by a business disruption and how best to address that impact. The financial impact addresses the monetary impacts and how a business disruption will impact the company's revenues.

Upstream and Downstream Losses

In addition to the direct impact of a business disruption such as an earthquake or flood, there are also indirect impacts you should consider. These can be viewed as upstream and downstream losses. *Upstream losses* are those you will suffer if one of your key suppliers is affected by a disaster. If your company relies on regular deliveries of products or services by another company, you could experience upstream losses if that company cannot deliver. If you run a manufacturing company that relies on raw materials arriving on a set or regular schedule, any disruption to that schedule will impact your company's ability to make and sell its products. This is how a disaster elsewhere can impact you, even if your company is unharmed. *Downstream losses* occur when key customers or the lives in your community are affected. If your business supplies parts to a major manufacturer that is shut down due to a hurricane or earthquake, your sales will certainly suffer. Similarly, if your company provides any type of noncritical service to your community and there is a flood or landslide, your sales could take a hit while residents of the community deal with the disaster. If you operate a chain of restaurants or movie theaters or golf courses, residents will be more focused on dealing with the disaster than on entertainment and leisure pursuits. These are considered downstream losses even if your business, itself, has not taken the direct impact of a disaster.

Keep in mind, too, that people, businesses, and communities are interrelated; very few (if any) companies exist in isolation. A natural disaster or serious disruption can create a chain reaction that ripples through the business community and impacts the local or regional economy.

From the Trenches...

Protecting Your Assets

Business continuity and disaster recovery planning can certainly help you mitigate some of your risks. In Chapter 32, we'll develop specific strategies for doing so. However, keep in mind that various types of insurance can help as well. This is considered *risk transference* and is a well-accepted business practice. Consider looking into business income interruption and extra expense insurance. If a business disruption occurs, you could have both an immediate and long-term impact to your company's revenues. Not only will it not be business-as-usual, you'll have the added expenses of lost productivity, lost customers, and higher costs. Some of your out-of-pocket expenses might ultimately be covered by insurance, such as the loss of equipment from a storm or building collapse. Other expenses, however, won't be covered. When revenues decrease and expenses increase, it can create a devastating financial picture for your company. Some basic business insurance policies cover expenses and loss of net business income, but it may not cover business interruptions that occur away from your business, such as to your key supplier, vendor, customer, or even your utility company. This type of insurance can typically be purchased as additional coverage to an existing policy. We're not suggesting you purchase additional insurance (and we have no connections to the insurance industry), but we do suggest you look at your financial exposure and your current insurance policy and decide if you're properly protected. Of course, insurance alone will not protect your business from failing in the face of a serious disruption or event—that's where a solid BC/DR plan comes in.

Understanding the Human Impact

Although this chapter is focused on recovering business systems, it's clear that people are a major factor in business continuity efforts—not only from a planning and implementation perspective but from the impact perspective as well. If a natural disaster strikes, it's possible that some or all of your company's employees will be impacted. It's possible that some may die or be seriously injured. Although no one likes to think about these possibilities, they cannot be ignored in a BC/DR plan. As you assess business functions and business processes, you'll also need to identify key positions, key knowledge, and key skills needed for business continuity. In some sense, this begins to cross over into what is traditionally called *succession planning*. In publicly traded companies or high profile start ups, the company often purchases what's called *key man insurance*. This insurance covers the cost of losing a high ranking executive in the company, the assumption being that if someone at that level were suddenly unavailable to carry out that function, the business would suffer financial losses.

Key Positions

Succession planning in companies covers many areas, but typically it's discussed in terms of replacing key employees as well as how to transfer the reins of the company from one leader to the next. Succession planning can include training employees to move up the corporate ladder and assume leadership positions. From a risk management perspective, it can also address who will replace key employees in the event of a planned or unplanned departure. For example, if a company was started by a couple of business partners, at some point before their retirement, they should spend time identifying their successors—whether family members or trusted employees—and identifying the path to hand over the leadership of the company. When done in a thoughtful and predetermined manner, this can help smooth the transition. In terms of BC/DR, this plan can help identify who should step up should something happen to the company's founders or executives.

Beyond key man succession and insurance, the BC/DR plan needs to look at key positions within the company and understand the role of each in the business continuity realm. For example, if you have complex database applications, you may identify a database administrator (DBA) as a key role in the business recovery process. Ideally, your existing database administrator would take care of this, but what if she was unable to respond to the business disruption because she was injured or unable to get to the site (or worse)? Rather than identifying specific people, you should identify roles, responsibilities, skills, and knowledge needed. Even though you'd prefer your own DBA to recover the system, if she was unavailable for any reason, you would know that you need a DBA to recover your systems and you could go to external sources to locate a temporary or permanent DBA replacement.

Human Needs

Beyond replacing needed skills and positions, it's important to keep the human impact in mind throughout your planning. As mentioned earlier in this section, everyone responds to disasters differently. If a portion of the building catches on fire and burns, it's likely that those employees in the area at the time the fire breaks out will experience the event in a variety of ways. Some people will evacuate and stand in the parking lot laughing about the close call, even as the fire engines pull in. Others probably will be frightened by the experience and may become shaky, disoriented, or panicky. Still others might seem fine immediately afterward but days or weeks later, they begin to display odd behavior that might be the result of a delayed onset of stress from the event. Clearly, the bigger the event (earthquake, tornado, hurricane), the bigger the human toll in terms of death, injury, and emotional distress.

A good business continuity plan will address the human factors for two reasons. First, addressing employee needs is simply the right thing to do. Although there are companies that may demand that employees report to work following a serious business disruption or face termination, most companies understand that everyone will have different needs. Some may report back to work, some may need to deal with family problems, some may be physically or emotionally unable to return to work immediately. The company's policies with regard to employee needs and requirements in the aftermath of a business disruption or natural disaster should be developed by your Human Resources department; however your BC/DR plan must take these varied responses into consideration. If your IT systems recovery effort hinges on two experienced network administrators, you need to address these as risks in your plan and develop mitigation strategies along with them.

The second reason for addressing employee needs in your BC/DR plan is because it makes good business sense. The ideal scenario might be that everyone is fine and shows up to work, but reality is often far different from that. You can demand that people show up all you want, but if faced with a choice between work and family, between work and health, people will usually choose family and health first. In some cases, insisting people return to work before they are ready can make things worse—they may not be able to concentrate and therefore may make recovery efforts worse instead of better. Incorporating this reality into your plan will mean that you and your team come up with appropriate alternatives that can address the lack of key staff in the aftermath of a business disruption. This helps the employees who may be unable to come back immediately and also helps the company recover in the fastest, most efficient manner possible.

We won't dwell on the human element in this chapter, but we will mention it again in key places to keep it foremost in your mind so that as you determine the impact of various risks, you can also keep the human factor in mind.

Understanding Impact Criticality

As you're thinking about your company and its critical functions, which we'll review following this section, you should keep a rating scale in mind. Later, after you've compiled your list, you can assign a "criticality rating" to each business function. It's important to have an idea of your rating system in mind before you review your business functions so you can spend the appropriate amount of time and energy on mission-critical functions and less time on minor functions. For example, when you sit down with the finance group, you want to keep them focused on defining the mission-critical business functions while listing all business functions that would be needed for business continuation.

Criticality Categories

You can develop any category system that works for you but as with all rating systems, be sure the categories are clearly defined and that there is a shared understanding of the proper use and scope of each. Here is one commonly used rating system for assessing criticality:

- Category 1: Critical Functions–Mission-Critical
- Category 2: Essential Functions–Vital
- Category 3: Necessary Functions–Important
- Category 4: Desirable Functions–Minor

Obviously, your business continuity plan will focus the most time and resources on analyzing the critical functions first, essential functions second. It's possible you will delay dealing with necessary and desirable functions until later stages of your business recovery. Many companies identify these four areas and set timelines for when each of these categories will be functional following a business disruption. Let's look at each category in more detail. You can use these category descriptions as-is or you can tweak them to meet your company's unique needs.

Mission-Critical

Mission-critical business processes and functions are those that have the greatest impact on your company's operations and potential for recovery. Almost everyone working in a company has an innate understanding of the mission-critical operations within their department. The key is to gather all that data and develop a comprehensive look at your mission-critical processes and functions from an organizational perspective. What are the processes that must be present for your company to do business? These are the mission-critical functions. One way to get people to focus on the mission-critical functions is to ask (whether through questionnaire, interview, or workshops) what the first three to five things people would do in their department following a business disruption once the emergency or imminent threat of a business disruption subsides. This often gives you the clearest view of the mission-critical business functions in each department.

From an IT perspective, the network, system, or application outage that is mission-critical would cause extreme disruption to the business. Such an outage often has serious legal and financial ramifications. This type of outage may threaten the health, well-being, and safety of individuals (hospital systems come to mind). These systems may require significant efforts to restore and these efforts are almost always disruptive to the rest of the business (in the case that any other parts of the business are actually able to function during such an outage). The tolerance for such an outage, whether from the IT system or the function/process it provides, is very low and the recovery time requirement is often described in terms of hours, not days.

Vital

Some business functions may fall somewhere between mission-critical and important, so you may choose to use a middle category that we've labeled "vital" or "essential." How can you distinguish between mission-critical and vital? If you can't, you may not need to use this category. However, you might decide that certain functions are absolutely mission-critical and others are extremely important but should be addressed immediately after the mission-critical functions. Vital functions might include things like payroll, which on the face of it might not be mission-critical in terms of being able to get the business back up and running immediately but which can be vital to the company's ability to function beyond the disaster recovery stage.

From an IT perspective, vital systems might include those that interface with mission-critical systems. Again, this distinction may not be helpful for you. If not, don't try to force your systems into this framework; simply don't use this category. You'll end up with just three categories—mission-critical, important, and minor. If that works for you, that's fine. If you use this category, your recovery time requirement might be measured in terms of hours or a day or two.

Important

Important business functions and processes won't stop the business from operating in the near-term but they usually have a longer-term impact if they're missing or disabled. When missing, these kinds of functions and processes cause some disruption to the business. They may have some legal or financial ramifications and they may also be related to access across functional units and across business systems.

From an IT perspective, these systems may include e-mail, Internet access, databases, and other business tools that are used in a support function, whether to support business functions or IT functions. If disabled, these systems take a moderate amount of time and effort (as compared to mission-critical) to restore to a fully functioning state. The recovery time requirement for important business processes often is measured in days or weeks.

Minor

Minor business processes are often those that have been developed over time to deal with small, recurring issues or functions. They will not be missed in the near-term and certainly not while business operations are being recovered. They will need to be recovered over the longer-term. Some minor business processes may be lost after a significant disruption and in some cases, that's just fine. Many companies develop numerous processes that should at some point be reviewed, revised, and often discarded, but that rarely occurs during normal business operations due to more demanding work. In some sense, a business disruption can be good for those small business functions and processes as they may be reworked or revised or simply pared down after a disruption. You may use the process of performing your BIA to recommend paring down these minor business functions as well, though your time is better spent focusing on the mission-critical and vital elements. You may make notes about which functions and processes could be pared down outside of the BC/DR planning process and hand this off to the appropriate SMEs for later action.

From an IT perspective, these types of system outages cause minor disruptions to the business and they can be easily restored. The recovery time requirement for these types of processes often is measured in weeks or perhaps even months.

Tip

Be sure to prompt participants to think about all business processes throughout the year. Some functions and processes occur only during certain times of the year, such as tax season, year end, holidays, and such, and these might be missed during the process. If they're important enough processes, there's a good chance they'll be included, but project management best practices don't rely on luck—they rely on process. Be sure you to ask about any special processes that occur throughout the calendar year that might not immediately come to mind for participants.

Recovery Time Requirements

Related to impact criticality are recovery time requirements. Let's define a few terms here that will make it easier throughout the rest of the analysis to talk in terms of recovery times. As you read through these definitions, you can refer to Figure 31.3 for a representation of the relationship of these elements.

Maximum Tolerable Downtime (MTD).   This is just as it sounds—the maximum time a business can tolerate the absence or unavailability of a particular business function. (*Note*: The BCI in the UK uses the phrase Maximum Tolerable Outage (MTO) instead.) Different business functions will have different MTDs. If a business function is categorized as mission-critical, or Category 1, it will likely have the shortest MTD. There is a correlation between the criticality of a business function and its maximum downtime. The higher the criticality, the shorter the maximum tolerable downtime is likely to be. Downtime consists of two elements, the *systems recovery time* and the *work recovery time*. Therefore, MTD = RTO + WRT.

Recovery Time Objective (RTO).   The time available to recover disrupted systems and resources. It is typically one segment of the MTD. For example, if a critical business process has a three-day MTD, the RTO might be one day (Day 1). This is the time you will have to get systems back up and running. The remaining two days will be used for work recovery (see Work Recovery Time).

Work Recovery Time (WRT).   The second segment that comprises the maximum tolerable downtime (MTD). If your MTD is three days, Day 1 might be your RTO and Days 2 to 3 might be your WRT. It takes time to get critical business functions back up and running once the systems (hardware, software, and configuration) are restored. This is an area that some planners overlook, especially from IT. If the systems are back up and running, they're all set from an IT perspective. From a business function perspective, there are additional steps that must be undertaken before it's back to business. These are critical steps and that time must be built into the MTD. Otherwise, you'll miss your MTD requirements and potentially put your entire business at risk.

Recovery Point Objective (RPO).   The amount or extent of data loss that can be tolerated by your critical business systems. For example, some companies perform real-time data backup, some perform hourly or daily backups, some perform weekly backups. If you perform weekly backups, someone made a decision that your company could tolerate the loss of a week's worth of data. If backups are performed on Saturday evenings and a system fails on Saturday afternoon, you've lost the entire week's worth of data. This is the recovery point objective. In this case, the RPO is one week. If this is not acceptable, your current backup processes must be reviewed and revised. The RPO is based both on current operating procedures and your estimates of what might happen in the event of a business disruption. For example, if a tornado touches down in your town and your data center is without power, you may implement your BC/DR plan. If you have an alternate computing location, you may transfer operations to that location. Your next step would be to determine the status of the data. Are you attempting to update systems using backups or were these alternate locations kept up to date? When was the last data backup performed relative to business operations? What do you need to bring systems up to date? These are the questions you'd need to answer after a business disruption. Therefore, it's important to define your RPO beforehand and ensure your recovery processes address these timelines.

Let's look at how these elements interact. Figure 31.3 graphically depicts the interplay between MTD, RTO, WRT, and RPO. If your company has mission-critical and vital business processes that do not interact with computer systems of any kind, you still need to perform a business impact analysis in order to understand how these manual systems may be impacted by a business disruption, especially natural disasters. At the end of this chapter, we'll walk through an example to help illustrate these concepts. Most companies use technology and computer systems to some extent and the graphic in Figure 31.3 shows how the recovery time is impacted by a business disruption.

Figure 31.3 Critical Recovery Timeframes

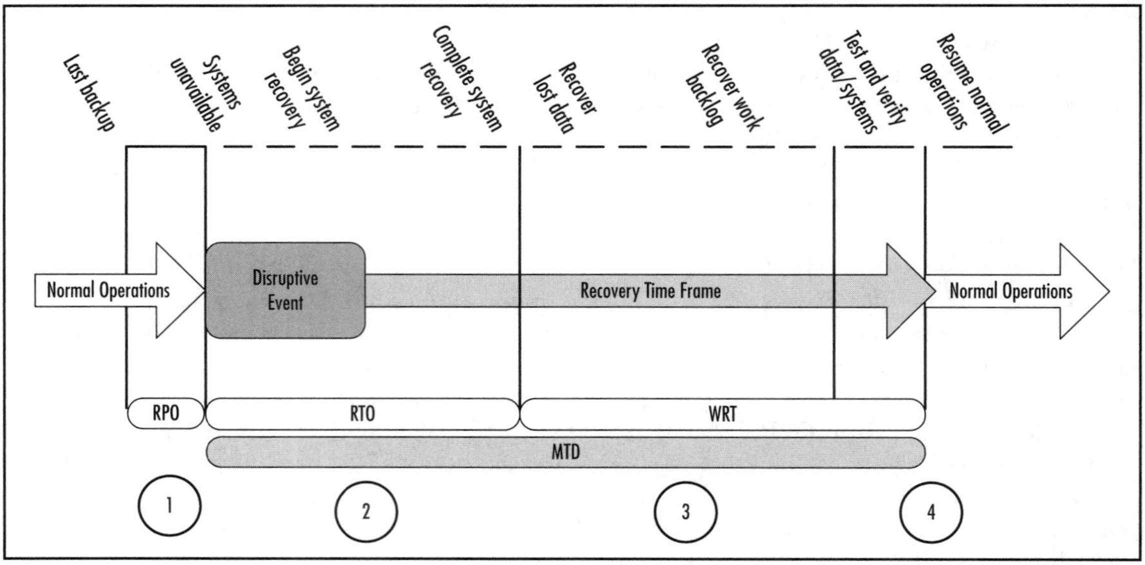

- **Point 1:**   Recovery Point Objective—The maximum sustainable data loss based on backup schedules and data needs

- **Point 2:**   Recovery Time Objective—The duration of time required to bring critical systems back online

- **Point 3**: Work Recovery Time—The duration of time needed to recover lost data (based on RPO) and to enter data resulting from work backlogs (manual data generated during system outage that must be entered)

- **Points 2 and 3**: Maximum Tolerable Downtime—The duration of the RTO plus the WRT.

- **Point 4**: Test, verify, and resume normal operations

During normal operations, there is usually some gap between the last backup performed and the current state of the data. In some operations, this may be minutes or hours; in most organizations it is hours or days. This timeframe is the recovery point objective. In most organizations, this is the same as the period of time between backups. We see at circle 1 that there is a gap showing the point of the last backup and the state of current data, just before the disruption occurs. That's the point at which one or more critical systems becomes unavailable and business continuity and disaster recovery planning activities are initiated. The first phase of the Maximum Tolerable Downtime (MTD) is the recovery time objective. This is the timeframe during which systems are assessed, repaired, replaced, and reconfigured. The RTO ends when systems are back online and data is recovered to the last good backup. The second phase of the MTD then begins.

This is the phase when data is recovered through automated and manual data collection processes. There are two elements of work recovery time. The first is the manual collection and entry of data lost, typically because systems went down between backups. The second phase addresses the backlog of work that may have built up while systems were down. Most companies try to recover the data up to the disruptive event to bring the systems current and then address the backlog, but your business processes may dictate a different recovery order. The key is to understand that there is a delay between the time the systems are back online and the time when normal operations can resume. During the periods indicated by circles 2 and 3, emergency workarounds and manual processes are being used. These are processes that will be developed later in your BC/DR planning process. For example, if a CRM system is down, what processes will your sales, marketing, and customer sales service teams use to interface with and manage customer service delivery? You'll define that in the planning process. Circle 4 indicates the transition from business continuity and disaster recovery back to normal operations. There may be some overlap as manual processes are turned back over to automated processes and you may choose to do it in a rolling fashion—perhaps by department or geographic region.

As you collect your impact data, you'll also need to begin determining the recovery time objectives. You may choose to create a rating system so you can quickly determine recovery time objectives. For example, you might determine that mission-critical business systems or functions should have recovery windows as follows:

- **Category 1**: Mission-Critical—0–12 hours

- **Category 2**: Vital—13–24 hours

- **Category 3**: Important—1–3 days

- **Category 4**: Minor—more than 3 days

You and your team, with input from the subject matter experts, can determine the appropriate maximum tolerable downtime (MTD) requirements. For some companies, a mission-critical business function could have an MTD of a week. For others, it might be 0 to 2 hours. There is an inverse correlation between the amount of time you can tolerate an outage and the cost of setting up systems that allow you to recover in that time frame. If you can't afford much downtime, you'll clearly have to invest more in preventing downtime and in having systems in place that allow fast recovery times. If you're a small company and can afford a longer MTD, you can spend less on preventing or recovering from outages.

Let's look at an example. In a small company, you may very well be able to do without even mission-critical systems for a couple of days or a week if you really had to. It's possible that you contract with an outside IT service provider to maintain, troubleshoot, and repair your computer systems. If you want a guaranteed two-hour response time, your monthly maintenance costs will be significantly higher than if you sign up for a guaranteed next business day response. So, if you really can't afford to be without that mission-critical business function for more than about eight hours (two-hour response time, six-hour repair time), you'll have to pay more to your service company and you'll probably also have to purchase additional computer equipment to provide some redundancy to prevent extended downtime. These costs add up and the less disruption your business can afford, the more it will cost you to prevent or mitigate those risks. We'll discuss this in more detail in the following chapter, but it's within the business impact analysis segment where you have to begin making these kinds of assessments.

It's important to note during your impact analysis and subsequent mitigation planning phases that there is an optimal recovery point. Figure 31.4 shows the inverse relationship between the cost of disruption and the cost of recovery. Earlier in this section, we discussed the fact that any business continuity and disaster recovery plan had to be tailored to the unique needs and constraints of the organization. This is particularly true when it comes to the financial costs involved with disruption and recovery.

Figure 31.4 Optimal Balance between Cost of Disruption and Cost of Recovery

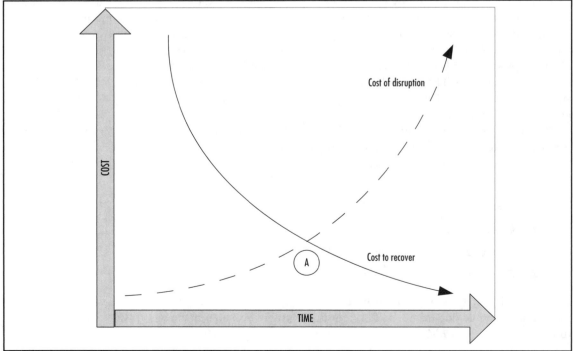

You can see that the longer you allow a disruption to go on, the more expensive it becomes to the business. Conversely, the longer you have to recover, the less expensive recovery itself becomes. This makes sense when you understand that the longer a business disruption goes on, the more lost revenues, lost sales, and lost customers you accumulate. At the same time, if you need to recover your systems immediately, it's going to cost more to implement things such as zero downtime solutions and hot sites. If you can afford to take a bit more time to recover you have more options, and these options are typically less expensive. If you start plotting these points, you will find an optimal point between these two costs, shown in Figure 31.4 by point A. Each company's intersecting points (point A) will be different based on your company's financial constraints and operating requirements.

Looking Ahead…

Making the Business Case Makes Your Life Easier

During the assessment and implementation of IT systems over the course of the past few years, you may already have addressed (and invested in) some of the elements needed to reduce the time to recover or to reduce the cost of a disruption. If so, be sure to make note of these systems or investments and be sure to include them in your planning. One way to help make the business case for continued investment is to show how the systems already implemented have made an impact or have contributed to your BC/DR plan. For example, suppose you implemented a mirrored site to allow users to gain access to key data more quickly. That mirrored site also serves as a backup and reduces the cost of disruption to a single site. It also reduces the amount of time it takes to recover, thereby pulling your point A down and to the left (toward lower cost, less time). This investment, then, has contributed to optimizing your balance between cost of disruption and cost to recover while also improving user productivity. Being able to establish and articulate these kinds of IT benefits within your organization may not only win support for your BC/DR plan, it might also help you move up the corporate ladder.

Next, let's look at what the entire analysis process looks like, as shown in Figure 31.5. After we explore this, we'll take a look at the specific data required for inputs and outputs to this process.

Figure 31.5 BIA Inputs and Outputs

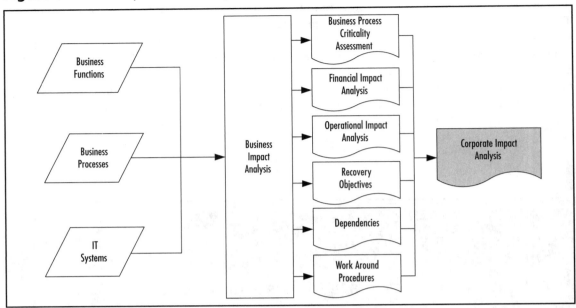

In this segment of BC/DR planning, we're looking at business functions, processes, and IT systems to determine criticality. Business functions can be defined as activities such as sales, marketing, or manufacturing. Business processes can be defined as how those activities occur. Are your sales conducted via a Web site, via telephone, via sales calls? How are orders processed? How are employees hired? These are business processes, they describe how the functions get done. By first identifying business functions, you can focus on the key processes in each function to develop a comprehensive view of your company. The third input area, shown in Figure 31.5, is IT systems. In most companies, the business processes are carried out in part through computer systems, applications, and other automated systems. Identifying mission-critical business functions and processes and how they intersect with IT systems will help you map out your business continuity and disaster recovery strategies.

Once you have compiled that data, you'll perform the analysis to generate the needed outputs, including the criticality assessment, the impact assessments (financial and operational), required recovery objectives, dependencies, and work-around procedures. The work-around procedures will enable you to get critical business functions back up and running as quickly as possible. These work-around procedures may be used during the RTO and WRT periods discussed earlier and shown in Figure 31.3. As you can see, the output is a comprehensive corporate impact analysis. This is the same output shown in Figure 31.2 and is the end of the larger risk assessment phase in our overall BC/DR planning process. The impact analysis will be used as input to the risk mitigation planning segment of the BC/DR project and we'll discuss that in Chapter 32.

Identifying Business Functions

In this section, we're going to walk through some of the more common business functions found in business today. It's not a comprehensive list but it's intended to do two things. First, you can include these in your BIA and you'll know you've got the major items covered. Second, you can use this to spur your thinking to include other areas that might be related to the items listed. You should begin by listing all the business functions that come to mind unless it's clear they should *not* be included. As with your risk assessment, it's best to begin by scanning the wide horizon and narrowing your focus later on. It's always easier to cut than to try to find gaps later.

When possible, it's advisable to create a list of all the functional areas of the business and gather SMEs from each area to discuss the critical business functions. Although it's more time consuming to get everyone in a room together, you will more quickly discover interdependencies in this manner. If SMEs sit quietly by themselves and come up with the critical business functions alone, they might miss the elements that are vital to other areas. An alternate method of gathering this data is to have the SMEs generate a list of questions to ask others in their area and compile the results. When the compiled results are ready, the subject matter experts from all areas of the company can meet to go over the results with the specific mission of finding interdependencies. How you manage this aspect of the project will have everything to do with how your company runs on a day-to-day basis.

The common business functions include those shown here. They're listed in alphabetical order, not necessarily in the order in which you would review these areas. The order in which these are reviewed will be dictated by the project management processes you've defined, the data gathering methods you choose, and the structure of your company. Following this section, we'll discuss the specific data points you need to gather from each of these areas.

1. Facilities and Security
2. Finance
3. Human Resources
4. Information Technology
5. Legal/Compliance
6. Manufacturing (Assembly)
7. Marketing and Sales
8. Operations
9. Research and Development
10. Warehouse (Inventory, Order Fulfillment, Shipping, Receiving)

As we look at these business functions, keep your business in mind and think about the key processes that occur in each functional area. After you've documented your key business processes, you will assign a criticality rating to them similar to the ones discussed earlier. As a reminder, you may also want to document key positions, skills, and knowledge in these functional areas. For example, what would the impact be if your head of facilities was injured in a building collapse and your company needed to operate from an alternate location? Who would head that up? What skills or knowledge would be needed in order to temporarily (or permanently) replace your facilities manager in the aftermath of a business disruption? These human factors should be assessed in conjunction with the major business functions.

Facilities and Security

Your company may be located in a single office in a small office building or it may span several continents. Regardless of how many physical locations your company operates, you need to understand the critical processes performed by facilities and security management with regard to your business operations. If a business disruption were to occur, what processes and procedures would be needed in order to get your business back up and running? For example, if the building is damaged or destroyed, physical security of the building will be disrupted. Employees won't be able to just swipe their badge at the front door. Is this a critical business function or not? It depends. If the building is destroyed, it doesn't matter that they can't get into the building. You don't just need an alternate process, you need an alternate location. Once an alternate location is established, you need facilities support. So, the critical business function, in this example, is having a place of business ("facilities"). Security and access are secondary. Notice how it helped to think of a specific scenario—it focused our thinking so we could see the key areas. Is having a place of business a critical business function? Not in the formal definition of a business *process*, but it's certainly important. Security usually involves a process—adding employees to access lists, providing employees with badges, IDs, or other identification, and granting them appropriate access to company resources. This might be highly important during normal business functioning, but does it impact the company's mission-critical operations? It depends on your business. If you work in a secure research environment, facilities and security may be mission-critical. If you work in a software development firm where employees could check code out of an online library and work from home, facilities and security may not be mission-critical at all. Facilities and security, though, may have some critical business functions beyond these macro-level functions just mentioned. For example, is facilities involved with the receiving or shipping of products, inventory, or other tangible goods? If so, these may be critical business functions to be included.

Finance

By definition, the financial workings of the company are critical business functions, but not all financial functions are mission-critical functions. For example, tracking receivables and payables are critical business functions because without the ability to keep track of what others owe you and what you owe others, you have no idea about the financial status of the company. Employee payroll is another critical business function (which is a financial transaction that might fall under the purview of the Human Resources department). If employees are not paid, if appropriate withholding and other taxes and deductions are not taken, your company faces serious problems, with employees and with state and federal authorities.

If your company has legal obligations to pay back a loan from a bank or make payments or reports to investors, these also might be critical business functions to be included in your analysis. In some cases, you may have some leeway with regard to repayment if you experience a natural disaster, but don't count on it. Your financiers don't care, they just want payments on time and in full. Therefore, keeping track of these kinds of financial and legal obligations may be considered critical business functions, depending on the nature of your company and its financing structure.

Accounting, finance, and reporting functions within finance should be reviewed and analyzed. There are many interdependencies in financial functions that cross over into HR, marketing, sales, IT, and operations. If key IT systems were to go down, which business processes would be impacted? Which processes and functions would have to get back up and running first in order to keep the business going?

Human Resources

If your firm experiences some sort of natural disaster, your Human Resources staff will be busy trying to fulfill a number of roles. Employees will usually contact HR for information on the status of the building, the status of the company, whether they should report to work, where they should report to work, and so on. Employees may also use HR as a clearing house for information about the well-being of other employees or information on the broader community. Finally, employees will be looking to HR for information on how, when, and where they'll get paid. In fact, this will likely be the first question many employees ask, especially if the business disruption happens just prior to or on payday. The staff in HR will be in the best position to provide guidance on the kinds of issues for which employees come to them. From there, you can compile a list of critical business functions. Remember, create a list of all business functions, then prioritize them later. If IT systems were to go down, which HR functions and processes are mission-critical? How would they be accomplished in the absence of IT systems? How would this impact other areas of the company?

IT

Critical business functions for IT? It seems like almost all of them are critical most of the time, especially if you judge by the phone calls, hallways pleas, and e-mails begging for assistance when one of the applications, servers, or hardware goes down. However, ultimately, the hardware and software should support the critical business functions, so the IT functions, in large part, will be driven by all the other departments. HR might say "we have to have our payroll application"; marketing might say "without our CRM system, we can't sell any products"; manufacturing might say "without our automated inventory management system, we can't even begin to make anything." Therefore, the IT department's critical business functions are driven externally, to a large degree. However, there are also business functions that occur within the IT department critical to the company's ability to recover and continue doing business after a disaster. For example, the IT department needs to create backups of all data that changes after a disaster. If a disaster happens on a Tuesday and you're able to get some systems back up and running by the following Monday, backups need to start on Monday, as soon as data begins being generated, saved, or changed. Therefore, backup processes can be viewed as critical business functions from the IT view.

Legal/Compliance

There are numerous mission-critical business functions related to legal and compliance areas of your company. If your firm is subject to legal or regulatory statutes and requirements, you're already well aware of these constraints. You need to view these constraints and requirements in light of a potential business outage to determine which of these are mission-critical, which are vital or important, and which are minor in nature. For example, if your firm deals with private or confidential personal data, it must be protected at all times, even if you move to a manual system for the duration of a system outage. Which systems, then, should be recovered first? Which business processes are mission-critical? Those related to remaining in compliance, both in terms of business process and business data, should be ranked very high on your list.

Manufacturing (Assembly)

If your company is involved with the manufacturing, assembly, or production of tangible products, you obviously need to scour this area for mission-critical functions since your ability to produce your products is the engine that drives your company. There may be some systems that can come online later, but there are likely to be certain systems that must be up and running in order for any manufacturing, assembly, or production to occur. Identify these business processes and systems by understanding what would happen if the production equipment were to be damaged or destroyed. Next, understand what would happen if the production equipment was left in tact but upstream or downstream events impacted your customers or vendors. The impact analysis needs to include both internal and external elements. What business processes should you put in place to deal with the potential loss of a key supplier? For now, you should be identifying the potential impact of various business disruptions to your manufacturing operations, keeping both internal and external (upstream/downstream) disruptions in mind.

It's also important to understand the interaction between any manufacturing/assembly automation equipment and IT systems. If IT systems go down, how are automation systems impacted? If automation systems go down, how are IT systems impacted? What manual processes can be implemented in the absence of either automation systems or associated IT systems?

Marketing and Sales

Marketing activities help create demand for the company's products and services by establishing or expanding knowledge of the company and its products/services. Sales activities are those actions that actually create a sales transaction and bring revenue into the company. Some companies may determine that marketing activities in the aftermath of a business disruption can be put on hold while sales activities should be a top priority. Other companies may see marketing activities as mission-critical in the aftermath of a business disruption because they are businesses that need to stay in touch with customers, keep their products/services in front of customers, and cannot afford to let rumors and erroneous information about the company's status float around, especially in today's world of instant, on-demand news. How you approach marketing and sales functions in your firm from a business continuity and disaster recovery standpoint will depend largely on the size of your company, its market visibility and other internal factors. Clearly activities that support the company's ability to perform sales transactions will most often be considered either vital or mission-critical activities and systems.

Operations

If your company doesn't manufacture, assemble, or produce tangible products, it probably develops and sells intangible products such as service, software development, research, analysis, and others. Whatever it is your company does, it sells something in order to generate revenue. Therefore, your operations are what end up generating those goods and services that are sold to customers. As with manufacturing and assembly, operations are what generate sales and therefore are almost always part of the most urgent mission-critical business functions. Although "operations" is a rather broad and vague term, each company knows exactly what its operations are and how these operations contribute to revenue generation. It is within that scope of knowledge that these activities should be assessed for criticality.

Research and Development

Some companies or organizations are funded through investors, through grants, or operate as nonprofits. They may be dedicated solely to research and development and may not generate revenue in the traditional sense of the word. However, every organization needs funding and that funding almost always comes with some sort of expectations and requirements about what is to be achieved with that funding. Therefore, you can view activities that bring in funding as your sales activities and can assess their criticality in that light. For example, if your organization does biochemical research and you're funded by federal or state programs, you still have business functions related to deliverables to consider. Is the next round of funding predicated upon the successful delivery of the results of current development or testing? If so, you have several mission-critical systems to consider along with assessing the impact of a business disruption to your research. Do you have live cultures growing in a lab that need to be tested and assessed? If so, what would happen if the research building was destroyed by fire or by an earthquake or tornado? How would your research be impacted and how would you recover? Though these are a bit different from traditional business functions and are not related directly to IT systems, these are questions that should be asked and answered if you're in this business.

Warehouse (Inventory, Order Fulfillment, Shipping, Receiving)

If your company deals in tangible goods of any kind, you have processes for handling inventory, order fulfillment, returns, shipping, and receiving. In some companies, these functions are handled by outside firms. For example, you may manufacture or assemble a product that is sent out daily on trucks to some other company that handles the remaining inventory processes. Nonetheless, your company has to keep track of what it makes and what it ships out at minimum. So, there are two elements here, the actual manufacturing or assembly (covered earlier) and the tracking, storing, and moving of these products. These two functional areas are closely tied together and the interdependencies in these areas should be given special attention. If IT systems go down, how are these activities impacted? If the building is ravaged by fire or flood, how are these activities impacted?

Other Areas

There may be other functional areas not listed here that exist in your company. If so, be sure to explore each functional area and determine the various business processes used in each area along with their relationship to the business's IT systems.

Looking Ahead...

Flaws Exposed

It's important to understand that a business impact analysis is a thorough business assessment that involves an unbiased study of the entire organization. When you start looking at the workings of the company in a very close and detailed manner, things may start to look less than stellar, like when you shine a very bright light on something and you suddenly see all its flaws quite clearly. Your corporate executives might take one of two positions. In the best case, they will appreciate the opportunity to closely examine the company's operations and find ways to improve it along the way. In the worst case,

Continued

they will hesitate, stonewall, or misdirect you in order to prevent you from uncovering business processes that are broken, inefficient, or worse, illegal. So, be prepared for a variety of reactions from the top to the bottom of your organization. Also, if you're so inclined, you might begin preparing your organization for this level of scrutiny, being sure to communicate the positive aspects of this process.

Ideally, you can double your mileage from this project by using it as an opportunity to perform your BIA and to streamline business operations. Just be prepared for a few bumps in this road, especially if you suspect that the business processes are not too pretty in some areas of the company. Remember, too, that a well-executed BIA can help you garner *more* support for your BC/DR planning project as people in the organization begin to understand the undesirable effects a disaster or disruption would have on the business. Sometimes seeing the flaws is motivation enough to fix them.

Gathering Data for the Business Impact Analysis

As we discussed in Chapter 30, there are four primary ways of gathering information: questionnaires, interviews, documents, and research. This holds true for the BIA as well. Before you can develop questionnaires or interviews, however, you have to know what you're looking for. You may choose to gather subject matter experts who then create questionnaires or interview questions. As a project team, you may create a number of very specific questions or scenarios to be presented to subject matter experts (SME) in the form of questionnaires or interviews. The additional information will come from either the project team or SMEs reviewing documents or performing targeted research.

Where to start this sometimes daunting process? One of the best places to start is with your company's organizational chart. Lacking that, try the company's phone directory—electronic or paper. In many cases, the functional areas of the company are clearly spelled out. This can be a good place to determine sources for subject matter experts as well. You can begin by creating a list of each functional area such as each division or each major work area such as manufacturing, warehouse, operations, development, among others. List subdepartments or subdivisions under each of the major headings, as appropriate. Now, you should have a comprehensive list of the major and minor departments, which are often the functional areas, in your company. Check for duplication and remove any areas that are repeated or that clearly should not be included. The key at this juncture is to generate a comprehensive list of business functions that can later be prioritized. Also remember there may be internal or external dependencies that raise the criticality of particular business functions.

As previously discussed, asking questions and providing scenarios to consider can help people focus on specific business issues and generate better responses. Some questions you might ask of your subject matter experts to help them focus on the key aspects of the impact analysis include these:

1. How would the department function if desktops, laptops, servers, e-mail, and Internet access were not available?

2. What single points of failure exist? What, if any, risk controls or risk management systems are currently in place?

3. What are the critical outsourced relationships and dependencies? What are the upstream and downstream risks to your business function?

4. If a business disruption occurred, what workarounds would you use for your key business processes?

5. What is the minimum number of staff you would need and what functions would they need to carry out?

6. What are the key skills, knowledge, or expertise needed to recover? What are the key roles that must be present for the business to operate?

7. What critical security or operational controls are needed if systems are down?

8. How would this business function in a backup recovery site? What would be needed in terms of staff, equipment, supplies, communications, processes, and procedures? (This crosses into the disaster recovery element, which we'll discuss more in a later chapter.)

Data Collection Methodologies

For the business impact analysis, it is advisable to collect data through questionnaires, interviews, or workshops, which are in many ways group interviews. Additional data can be gathered using documents and research, but this data should be gathered only to support or supplement data gathered through direct contact with business subject matter experts. The reason for this is fairly obvious. Only those who actually perform various business functions can assess the criticality of those business functions. You could sit down and read documents all day long and never get a clear picture of what's really mission-critical and what's just important. Therefore, you should rely primarily on questionnaires, interviews, and workshops for this segment of your data gathering. Let's look at methodologies you can use for these three data gathering methods.

Questionnaires

Questionnaires can be used to gather data from subject matter experts (SME) in a fairly efficient manner. Though it takes time to develop a highly useful questionnaire, SME's responses will be consistent, focused, and concise. They can fill out the questionnaires regarding their business units, business functions, and business processes at a time that is convenient for them (within a specified timeframe), thereby increasing the likelihood of participation. On the downside, questionnaires that are sent out may be ignored, pushed aside, or forgotten. In order to generate a timely and meaningful response to your team's questionnaire, you can create a methodology that will increase your response rate.

First, it's important to appropriately design the questionnaire. If it's full of useless questions, if it's visually confusing or overwhelming, you'll decrease your response rate. The questionnaire should be clear, concise, easy to understand, and fast to fill out. If you want to use a Web-based questionnaire that records data in a database, so much the better. You can send out reminders with a link to the questionnaire as frequently as needed. With a paper-based questionnaire, there's a lot of moving of paper and the increased likelihood that the paper will be misplaced, lost in a pile, or simply thrown out.

It's also important to explain the purpose of the questionnaire to the participants in a manner that helps them buy into the process. Focus on what's in it for them, not for you. They probably don't care that *you* need this data, but they will care that this data could help prevent some problem in *their* jobs. Ideally, you should hold a kick off meeting where the questionnaire is introduced and explained, the purpose of it is clearly articulated, and the process for completing the questionnaire is explained. For example, you might let people know that the questionnaire is available at a particular location, that it takes a total of three hours to complete per department, but that it can be completed in segments and the questionnaire-in-progress can be saved for later completion. You should let people know who the contact person is if they run into problems and when the questionnaire must be completed.

If your company is the type of company that likes to have a bit of fun in these kinds of meetings, you can also announce small prizes that will be awarded to departments or individuals who complete theirs correctly first, who are most thorough, and so forth. Be careful, though, you don't want to leave the impression that this is a race to the finish (where important details can be lost) or that "cute" answers are appropriate. You can, however, announce that for any SME that submits a complete and thorough questionnaire by the deadline will be entered into a hat for the chance to win some prize such as a portable music player, a new cell phone, dinner for two at a nice restaurant, among others. Sometimes small incentives to do the right thing can go a long way in getting people to participate in the manner expected and needed. Considering how vital this particular data is to your entire BC/DR plan, it's usually worth a small investment to get people to participate appropriately, if this type of activity fits in with your corporate culture. Be sure to provide information on how respondents can get assistance with the questionnaire—either from a technical standpoint (if it's an electronic or Web-based questionnaire) or an administrative standpoint. If they don't understand exactly what a question means, who should they contact? How should they contact them? What is the contact person's e-mail, location, phone number, and work hours? Be sure to provide this information so you don't inadvertently create roadblocks for yourself.

Finally, let the team know how they'll learn about the results of the questionnaire. Most people dislike spending time filling out a form only to never hear about it again. If they are willing to take the time needed to provide this data, there should be some reciprocity. For example, if this data is all pumped into a database, a report on each respondent's data could be provided back to them for verification. Once the data is reviewed by your team, there may be additional questions. Respondents should be told, in advance, about the process for following up with them regarding their responses to the questionnaire.

Once questionnaires are completed, you and your team should review them to ensure they are complete. In some cases, you may choose to create a process whereby certain questionnaires are followed up by an interview. This might be in the case of the most critical business functions or where questionnaire data indicates there may be confusion, conflict, or incomplete data. Any follow-up interviews should follow a specific format as well so that targeted data can be collected.

Interviews

If your team has decided that data will be gathered through interviews, you'll still need to create a questionnaire type of document that will provide the interviewers with a set of questions to which they gather responses. Free form or informal interviews will yield inconsistent data across the organization and you'll have a wide array of meaningless data. Develop a questionnaire and use it as the basis of the interview process. Each interview should follow a predefined format and the questions asked of each respondent should be the same. Develop a questionnaire, interview, or question sheet from which the interviewer will work and also develop a corresponding data sheet onto which the interviewer can record responses. Look to find methods to speed up the interview process. For example, don't use a rating system of ten elements that use 1 as NEVER and 10 as ALWAYS with eight other word/number combinations. This will be cumbersome for the interviewer to describe and will be almost impossible for the interviewee to remember. If you choose, you might say, "On a scale of 1 to 10 with 1 being never and 10 being always, how often would you say you access the CRM database on a telephone sales call?" This sort of sliding scale can be used because the respondent does not have to remember 10 different descriptions—what does three mean again? However, the danger is that each respondent is going to give you a different sliding scale number if the range is 10. Instead, you might use a three-element scale without numbers. "How often do you use this system during a telephone sales call? Never, sometimes, or always?" That's much easier for the respondent to remember and evaluate and it's also more likely to generate a more consistent response across all respondents.

Our goal is not to go into the pros and cons of various data gathering methods, but to point out that there are unintentional problems you can build into a questionnaire or survey that can skew your results. If your organization has a group that develops market surveys or questionnaires, you may ask them to review your questionnaire before rolling it out. They might spot something you missed and help you gather better data. We all know the output is only as good as the input, so making sure your data gathering methods are clean will help on the other side of this assessment process.

Once an interview is conducted, the data needs to be reviewed and verified by the interviewee. Due to the nature of an interview, it's possible one of the people (interviewer, interviewee) misunderstood the question or response. Therefore, once the data is prepared, it should be reviewed by the interviewee before being finalized. You want to avoid having the interviewee rehash their previous responses, but you do want to provide an opportunity for additional insights and information that clarify previous responses. Follow-up interviews, if needed for clarification, should be scheduled as quickly after the initial interview as possible so that the data, response, and topic are still fresh in the interviewee's mind.

Workshops

Data collection workshops can be an effective method of gathering needed data. If you choose this method of gathering data, you might still choose to create a questionnaire so that you can be sure you cover all the required data points. Identify the appropriate level of participating personnel and gain agreement as to participants. Choose an appropriate time and place for the workshop, ensure the appropriate amenities will be available (white boards, refreshments, etc.). Develop a clear agenda for the meeting and distribute this, in advance, to meeting participants. Identify the workshop facilitator and clearly define his or her role in the process. Identify workshop completion criteria so the facilitator and participants are clear about what is expected, what the required outcomes are, and how the workshop will conclude. The facilitator's job is to ensure the workshop objectives are met, so these objectives must be clearly articulated prior to the start of the workshop. Develop or utilize an appropriate process for dealing with issues during the workshop so that participants stay on topic and focused on the key objectives. Some companies use the concept of a "parking lot," where issues are written up on note cards and collected or written on sticky notes and posted on a white board or an empty wall. Use an issue tracking methodology that allows you to stay on topic but make note of issues. Also identify the method you'll use for addressing those issues that cannot be (or should not be) resolved during the course of the workshop. Finally, ensure that the results of the workshop are written and well documented and that participants have the opportunity to review the results for errors and omissions before they are finalized.

TIP

Select the format for data gathering that is least intrusive on people's time and that is most aligned with how you normally work. Business continuity and disaster recovery planning are often very low on people's priorities and anything you can do to reduce the effort it takes to provide the data you need will pay off.

Determining the Impact

We've delineated some of the more common business functions. Now, let's turn our attention to some of the specific impacts to a business. As with other lists, this one is extensive but not necessarily exhaustive. Be sure to review this list and remove any items that do not pertain to your business and add any elements that are not included that do relate to your business. Remember, too, that a business disruption can run that gamut from a hard drive failure to an earthquake that levels your building to a pandemic that impacts an entire region or nation. Once you've looked at all the potential impact points, we'll discuss specific data points to collect and analyze as well as how to put those together with your risk assessment data. The impact of any business disruption may include:

1. **Financial.** Loss of revenues, higher costs, potential legal liabilities with financial penalties.

2. **Customers and suppliers.** You may lose customers and suppliers due to your company's problems or you may lose customers or suppliers if they experience a business disruption or disaster.

3. **Employees and staff.** You may lose staff from death, injury, stress, or a decision to leave the firm in the aftermath of a significant business disruption or natural disaster. What are the key roles, positions, knowledge, skills, and expertise needed?

4. **Public relations and credibility.** Companies that experience business disruptions due to IT systems failures (lost or stolen data, modified data, inability to operate due to missing or corrupt data, etc.) have a serious public relations challenge in front of them. These kinds of failures require a well-thought-out PR plan to help support business credibility. What impact would system outages or data losses have on your public image?

5. **Legal.** Regulations regarding worker health and safety, data privacy and security, and other legal constraints need to be assessed.

6. **Regulatory requirements.** You may be unable to meet minimum regulatory requirements in the event of certain business disruptions. You need to fully understand these regulations and their requirements related to business disruptions, both natural and man-made.

7. **Environmental.** Some companies may face environmental challenges if they experience failures of certain systems. Understanding the environmental impact of system and business failures is part of the business impact analysis phase.

8. **Operational.** Clearly operations are impacted by any business disruptions. These must be identified and ranked in terms of criticality.

9. **Human Resources**.   How will staff be impacted by minor and major business disruptions? What is the impact of personnel responses to business operations? What are the qualitative issues to be addressed (morale, confidence, etc.)?

10. **Loss Exposure**.   What types of losses will your company face? These include property loss, revenue loss, fines, cash flow, accounts receivable, accounts payable.

11. **Social and corporate image**   (strongly tied to public relations). How will employees, customers, suppliers, partners, and the community view your company? How will its image be altered by a minor or major business disruption?

12. **Financial community credibility**.   How will banks, investors, or other creditors respond to a minor or major business disruption? If the cause is a natural disaster, the challenges are different than if the cause is man-made. If the company failed to secure or protect data or resources, there are additional consequences both to the corporate image and to the company's credibility in the marketplace.

(Adapted from the Disaster Recovery Institute)

After you've compiled a list of your business functions and processes, you should assign a criticality rating to them. Payroll, accounts payable, and accounts receivable usually qualify as mission–critical business processes. Furniture requisitions for new employees usually fall to the bottom of the list as minor. Rate all your identified business processes and sort them in order of criticality. You might end up with a table or matrix that looks something like that shown in Table 31.1.

Table 31.1 Business Function and Criticality Matrix

Business Function	Business Process	Criticality
Human Resources	Payroll	Mission-critical
	Employee background checks	Important
Finance	Debt payments/loan servicing	Vital
	Accounts receivable	Mission-critical
	Accounts payable	Mission-critical
	Quarterly tax filings	Mission-critical
Marketing and Sales	Customer sales calls	Mission-critical
	Customer purchase history analysis	Vital

Business Impact Analysis Data Points

The number and type of data points you collect in your business impact analysis is largely a function of the size and type of company in which you work. Smaller companies will have fewer data points, larger companies will have more. However, you can also inundate yourself with too many data points if you don't take a focused approach. Some companies are extremely slow moving, analytical types of companies in which all data must be collected and assessed. Other companies move at the speed of light (typical in start ups) and want to grab just the high points and move on. The plan you devise needs to find a balance between information overload and superficial data. Be sure to include enough detail so that you can actually develop strategies that will help your company survive a serious business disruption, but don't allow the information floodgates to open and overwhelm you with minutiae.

Table 31.2 shows various data points you can consider collecting along with a brief description of the purpose or focus of that data point. Feel free to modify this to suit your unique needs.

Table 31.2 Business Impact Analysis Data Points

Data Point	Description	IT Dependencies
Business function or process	Short description of the business function or process (we'll use "function" from here on).	Describe primary IT systems. used for this business function.
Dependencies	Description of the dependencies to this function. What are the input and out put points to this function? What has to happen or be available in order for this function to occur? What input is received, either from internal or external sources, that is required to perform this business function? How would the disruption of this business function impact other parts of the business? How and when would this disruption to other functions occur?	Describe IT systems that impact or are impacted by this business function. Are there any internal or external IT dependencies?
Resource dependencies	Is this business function de-pendent upon any key job functions? If so, which and to what extent? Is this business function dependent upon any unique resources? If so, what and to what extent (contractors, special equipment, etc.)?	Describe secondary/support computer/IT systems required for this business function to occur.
Personnel dependencies	Is this function dependent on specialized skill, knowledge or expertise? What are the key positions or roles associated with this function? What would happen if people in these role were unavailable?	Describe key roles, positions, knowledge, expertise, experience, certification needed to work with this particular IT system or IT/ business function.

Table 31.2 Continued

Data Point	Description	IT Dependencies
Impact profile	When does this function occur? Is it hourly, daily, quarterly, seasonally? Is there a specific time of day/week/ year that this function is more at risk? If there a specific time at which the business is more at risk if this function does not occur (tax time, payroll periods, year end inventory, etc.)?	Describe the critical timeline related to this function/ process and related IT systems, if any.
Operational	If this function did not occur, when and how would it impact the business? Would the impact be on time or recurring? Describe the operational impact of this function does not occuring.	Describe the impact on IT if this business function does not occur. Describe the impact on IT if this business function does not occur.
Financial	If this function did not occur, what would be the financial impact to the business? When would the financial impact be felt or noticed? Would it be one time or recurring? Describe the financial impact of this function not occurring.	
Backlog	At what point would work become backlogged?	Describe how a backlog. would impact IT systems and other related or support systems.
Recovery	What types of resources would be needed to support the function? How many resources would be needed and in what timeframe (phones, desks, computers, printers, etc.)?	What resources, skills, and knowledge would be required to recover IT systems related to this business function?
Time to recover	What is the minimum time needed to recover this business function if disrupted? What is the maximum time this business function could be unavailable?	How long would it take to recover, restore, replace, or reconfigure IT systems related to this business function?

Continued

Table 31.2 Continued

Data Point	Description	IT Dependencies
Service Level Agreements	Are there any service level agreements in place related to this business function? What are the requirements and metrics associated with these SLAs? How will SLAs be impacted by the disruption of this business function?	How would IT service levels be impacted by the disruption or lack of availability of this business function? How do external SLAs impact IT systems?
Technology	What hardware, software, applications, or other technological components are needed to support this function? What would happen if some of these components were not available? What would be the impact? How severely would the business function be impacted?	What IT assets are required to support/maintain this business function
Desktops, laptops, workstations	Does this business function require the use of "user" computer equipment?	What is the configuration data for required computer equipment?
Servers, networks, Internet	Does this business function require the use of back-end computer equipment? Does it require connection to the network? Does it require access to or use of the Internet or other communications?	What is the configuration data for required servers and infrastructure equipment?
Work-arounds	Are there any manual work-around procedures that have been developed and tested? Would these enable the business function to be performed in the event of IT or systems failures? How long could these functions operate in manual or work-around mode? If no procedures have been developed, does it seem feasible to develop such procedures?	Are there any IT-related work-arounds related to this business function? If so, what are they and how could they be implemented?

Table 31.2 Continued

Data Point	Description	IT Dependencies
Remote work	Can this business function be performed remotely, either from another business location or by employees working from home or other off-site locations?	Can this business function be performed remotely from an IT perspective? If so, what would it take to enable remote access or the ability to remotely perform this business function?
Workload shifting	Is it possible to shift this business function to another business unit that might not be impacted by the disruption? If so, what processes and procedures are in place or are needed to enable that function?	Are there other IT systems or resources that could pick up the load should a serious disruption occur?
Business/data records	Where are the business records related to this function stored or archived? Are they currently backed up? If so, how, with what frequency, where?	How and where are backups stored? Based on data provided, is the current backup strategy optimal based on the risks and impact?
Reporting	Are there legal or regulatory reporting requirements of this business function? If so, what is the impact of a disruption of this business function to reporting requirements? Are there reporting work-arounds in place or could they be developed and implemented?	Are there other ways reporting data could be generated, stored, or reported if key business functions or systems were disabled?
Business disruption experience	Has this business function ever been disrupted before? If so, what was the disruption and what was the outcome? What was learned from this event that can be incorporated into this planning effort?	Has IT ever experienced the disruption of this business function in the past? If so, what was the nature and duration of the disruption? How was it addressed and what was learned from the event?
Competitive impact	What, if any, is the compe-titive impact to the company if this business function is disrupted? What would the impact be, when would the impact occur, when would	

Continued

Table 31.2 Continued

Data Point	Description	IT Dependencies
	the potential loss of customers or suppliers occur?	
Other issues	What other issues might be relevant when discussing this particular business function?	Are there other IT issues related to this specific business function that should be included or discussed?

Once you've collected all these data points for all your business functions and processes, you have a comprehensive understanding of your business, its key functions, and what would happen if those functions were disrupted. In the next chapter, we'll discuss how to develop risk mitigation strategies based both on the various risks your company faces and on the criticality of the various business functions as defined in this phase of the assessment.

Common Challenges

Data Overload

The difficulty with the business impact analysis is that it can generate huge volumes of data that need to be sorted, assessed, and analyzed. There is no shortcut to getting this done, but it might help to keep the outcome in mind. The result you're looking for is an analysis of the critical functions and processes used in your company to conduct your company's business. Using the scenario approach can really help you focus in on the end result. If servers go down, if power goes out, if fire rages, if tornados strike, what are the most important things your company needs to accomplish to get business going again? We'll address the disaster recovery elements in an upcoming chapter—the things you need to do to stop the impact of the disruption or emergency before business can resume. For now, you need to understand what is absolutely essential to keep your business running. If you can keep this in mind as you go through this process, you're likely to be able to tune out the irrelevant and extraneous data more effectively.

Understanding IT Impact

As you can see from Table 31.2, the IT functions can be correlated to the business functions and processes at each step. As you gather this data, you will need to continually correlate the business functions/processes with the IT systems used to carry out or facilitate those functions in order to avoid gaps in your planning. In most cases, the subject matter experts and participants in this analysis will discuss the relationship of the IT systems to these functions. However, it's important to continually look at the intersection of IT systems to these business functions since the SMEs and departmental representatives may not fully understand the interdependencies of data or systems across the enterprise. For example, an SME might understand that use of the CRM system is vital to her job, but she may not have a clue that the CRM system resides on a server on the fourth floor and requires data updates from three other sources. From an IT perspective, you'll see this vital CRM function as a series of servers, applications, and data flows. As you work with the BC/DR team to map out the business functions and processes, you'll need to develop a parallel map of how that information intersects with IT equipment and functions.

In addition, you'll need to develop an understanding of how long it would take to replace or repair IT equipment based on the assessment of criticality. When you move into the risk mitigation phase, you might decide that the most optimal solution is to implement a fully redundant system for three key functions because the replacement or repair time for these systems exceeds the maximum tolerable downtime. The analysis of the data gathered in this phase must include IT-specific data so that you can optimize your risk mitigation strategies (coming up in Chapter 32).

The impact of IT on business functions (and the impact of business functions on IT) is usually already pretty well understood by the IT department through normal IT activities. However, the information gathered in this business impact analysis phase will bring to light new priorities, new gaps, and new challenges to be addressed through the IT department. Understanding how this data impacts IT and how IT impacts this data is key to developing a solid BIA and a comprehensive BC/DR plan.

TIP

You may want to encourage your subject matter experts to include their assessment of the impact on IT systems and the impact of IT systems on their critical business processes. By having them include this data, you can see IT from their perspective. You might learn something new about how they use IT systems or what you can do to mitigate risk to key business processes using IT technologies. At the very least, it will help flesh out your IT impact analysis.

Example of Business Impact Analysis For Small Business

Let's look at an example to help make this entire process a bit more tangible. A company of about 125 employees works out of a single location. They're situated in a light industrial area surrounded by warehouses and wholesalers. They sell a variety of specialty building hardware such as hard-to-find latches, fasteners, locks, and more. They purchase products from a variety of manufacturers and distributors and sell to a niche market in their region. These customers call in orders periodically. They also run a Web site that has seen sales grow significantly in the past three years, so that Web sales are now equal to non-Web sales.

The company, which we'll call ABC Hardware, does about $20 million a year in sales, about half of that online. Their facility is a large space comprised mostly of warehouse space with some office space. They ship and receive packages daily for Web operations and they ship weekly for their non–Web customer orders.

This company's risks include:

- Risk of fire in the building
- Risk of flooding in the area
- Risk of chemical spill in the area
- Risk of upstream/downstream losses by suppliers, vendors, customers

Let's focus on the risk of a fire in the building. If a fire struck the building, the damage might be contained to one of the areas, either warehouse or office. If the warehouse experienced a fire, inventory would be damaged and the ability to process inventory (receive, pick, pack, ship) would be impaired. If the office area were to have a significant fire, computer systems, including the inventory management system, would be damaged or destroyed.

So, what are the critical business functions impacted by a fire in the warehouse? First, we have the sales function because inventory would be damaged. Second, we have the inventory function because physical systems for managing inventory would be damaged.

What are the processes impacted by a fire in the warehouse? The company has processes in place for the following:

1. Picking orders.
2. Packing orders.
3. Staging orders for shipment.
4.` Tracking shipments.
5. Receiving new inventory.
6. Stocking new inventory.
7. Updating inventory systems with shipping and receiving data.
8. Managing damaged or missing inventory.
9. Processing returns of damaged or wrong items.
10. Inputting inventory data into inventory system.
11. Replenishing packing materials.
12. Repairing warehouse equipment.
13. Cleaning warehouse areas.

You can see from the list that items 11 through 13 are not critical processes. Other items on the list may not be mission-critical either, but we started with a full list of what goes on in the warehouse. If a fire engulfed the warehouse area, it's possible the building would be off-limits due to safety concerns, the offices might be filled with smoke and unusable, and the inventory might be smoke and water damaged by the fire suppression systems or by the water the fire department would hose in to put the fire out. Therefore, let's assume that a fire would impact all these processes listed. The company has no inventory it can ship to customers. What are the most important processes that have to get back up and running in order for the company to generate revenue and continue operations?

Remember, there are probably 14 other companies out there that are waiting for ABC Hardware to falter so they can swoop in and steal ABC's customers. ABC cannot afford to wait around for the water to dry and the smoke to clear before getting back into business. So, let's look at these first 10 items, along with criticality and comments, shown in Table 31.3.

Table 31.3 Example of Business Process and Criticality for Small Business

Business Process	Criticality	Comment
Picking orders	Mission-critical	Orders cannot be picked if inventory is damaged.
Packing orders	Mission-critical	Orders cannot be packed if they are not picked.
Staging orders for shipment	Mission-critical	Orders cannot be shipped if not picked and packed.
Tracking shipments	Mission-critical	Orders cannot be shipped if not picked and packed.
Receiving new inventory	Important	New inventory can be added to inventory system.
Stocking new inventory	Minor	New inventory cannot be stocked until damaged inventory is addressed.
Updating inventory systems with ship/rec data	Mission-critical	No shipments going out but. incoming inventory should be added so the company knows how much good inventory they have. Damaged inventory should be removed from stock as quickly as possible.
Managing damaged/ missing inventory	Mission-critical	Normally, managing damage. inventory is a minor process. In the aftermath of a fire, damaged inventory should be processed as quickly as possible to enable the company to dispose of it as quickly as possible.
Processing returns of damaged/wrong items from customers	Minor	Normally, processing damaged and returned items from customers would be a high priority. In the aftermath of a fire, this falls to a lower priority.

Continued

Table 31.3 Continued

Business Process	Criticality	Comment
Inputting inventory data into inventory system	Mission-critical	In order for the company to sell its products, it needs to know, very quickly, what inventory it has that is sellable and what inventory it has that is damaged and must be discarded.

As you can see from this example, what normally might be high-priority processes shift to lower priorities in the aftermath of a fire. The key to recovery for this company is to sort out its inventory quickly so it knows what it can and cannot sell to customers. The IT systems are not damaged (though a few warehouse computers might need to be replaced) and order processing can still occur. This includes taking phone and online orders, processing orders, comparing orders to inventory levels, charging customer accounts or credit cards, and recording customer data (address, phone, etc.). Thus, the sales function for the company is relatively unharmed but the ability of the company to process and fulfill those sales is impacted.

The business impact analysis for this company now has identified the critical functions in the warehouse with regard to sales, inventory management, and shipping/receiving. The list is not exhaustive. For example, it does not include shipping supply replenishment. In the immediate aftermath of the fire, shipments cannot go out so this isn't a problem. However, it's likely that shipping supplies have been destroyed either by fire, smoke, or water, and need to be replaced before any shipments can go out. If the entire warehouse is impacted, there may be no saleable inventory and shipments will have to wait. In other cases, there may still be saleable inventory and the lack of shipping supplies would actually become a major problem. Therefore, replenishing shipping supplies as a process in the aftermath of a disruption might be mission-critical. This is how walking through scenarios helps you see the mission-critical processes more clearly.

What is the maximum tolerable downtime for these critical business functions and processes? Some of this company's customers are custom homebuilders who are working on tight timelines. They will not wait for a delayed order from ABC Hardware and will look elsewhere for these products. Therefore, ABC believes that with most of their orders, they have one week to recover operations before they begin losing serious revenue. In the risk mitigation phase of their assessment, this company's staff can devise a number of strategies to deal with this scenario either to prevent a fire from occurring or to create alternate fulfillment strategies in the event a fire does occur.

You can continue to expand this example to include other data. For example, you can include the expected financial impact, as shown in Table 31.4. The example is not complete but just shows the beginning of this process as a sample of how you might capture financial impact data. The first function, the sales function, in this example, is not immediately impacted by the fire in the warehouse. Sales are still generated through the Web site and sales people may still be able to access CRM systems and other sales tools to generate sales. The problem is not on the sales generation side but the order fulfillment side. At some point, the company's inability to process inventory and orders will affect sales. Customers whose orders are delayed may cancel, rumors may cause other customers to order from your competitors. If you can't receive new inventory or ship out existing orders, these will eventually impact sales, but not immediately. If you can forecast the delayed financial impact, that's great, but if you can't, just make a note that there is one down the line. We've also included an increased cost for customer service. If you have a fire and word gets out, customers may call about their orders, call to change or cancel their orders, or call to get assurance their order is in process. This may generate more work for customer service, which may need to bring in temporary help to staff the phones or work overtime to handle the increased volume.

Table 31.4 Financial Impact Example

Business Function	Business Process	Financial Impact
Sales	Generating new orders	Delayed impact
Warehouse	Picking orders	$2,000 per day
	Packing orders	$2,000 per day
	Shipping orders	$10,000 per day
	Receiving inventory	$4,500 per day
Customer service	Handle customer problems	$3,000

So far, we've seen little or no IT impact. The damage was contained to the warehouse and other than three computers used at the shipping and receiving stations, there was no other impact to IT. However, there are other IT tie-ins. For example, how will the company know the exact status of the inventory? When was the last inventory count performed? What is the status of the orders that were picked and packed—were they shipped or not? Which customer orders went out and which were on the dock awaiting shipment? Which returns were on the dock when the fire started and which were already processed? As you recall from our discussion in this chapter, there is usually a lag between the last backup or the last known good state and the time of the business disruption. In this case, the company needs to quickly figure out the current status of its inventory as well as the status of customer sales and returns. It needs to know exactly what the status of everything is so that it can figure out what to do and in what order. IT may need to run special reports, print out inventory, shipment, or order lists in order to help warehouse functions get up and running again. These are disaster recovery tasks that the warehouse and IT staff will have to work together on to determine what might be needed.

You can extend this scenario and ask, what if the IT systems were located next to the warehouse and they were destroyed by fire? What if the fire started in the server room and spread to the warehouse? Now the scenario has changed significantly because not only do you have damaged inventory and uncertain status of shipments but you don't have IT system data immediately available to help sort things out. Sales data, inventory status, payables, receivables are all unavailable. The server room is charred, all systems are unusable. Now what?

Let's extend this just a bit so you can get the bigger picture. Table 31.5 shows some of the other operational impacts that might occur as a result of a warehouse fire. The impact on operations shows, for example, that customer perception is not impacted in the sales function. Customers may or may not know about the warehouse fire and if they can still place their order via the phone or Web, there is no immediate impact to customer perception. The same holds true for the customer perception of picking and packing orders. Customers usually don't know how their order shows up at their door (nor do they usually care), they care that the right products show up on time. Therefore, we begin to see a customer perception impact in the processes of "ship orders" and "receive inventory." If inventory can't be shipped, customers don't receive their orders as promised and this impacts customer perception. If inventory can't be received, it isn't available for sale and the customer sees that products are out of stock. We won't go through every cell in the grid, but you can use this to understand how various operations are impacted by a warehouse fire. The employee impact, in this case, is focused on warehouse staff, who are highly impacted by the warehouse fire. Though we did not do it in this example, you could also document the key knowledge and expertise needed to carry out these functions. For example, the key skills needed in this case are people who know how to manage inventory so that orders are properly filled and inventory levels are properly tracked. This data can be added, as appropriate. The same can be done for the IT side of the process. If IT systems were down, which processes would be impacted and how would other operations be impacted? What skills and expertise would be needed for workarounds and recovery?

Table 31.5 Operational Impact of Warehouse Fire

Business Function	Business Process	Cash Flow	Investor/ Market Confidence	Market Share	Competitive Position	Customer Perception	Employee Impact
Sales	Generate new orders	Medium	Medium	Medium	High	N/A	Low
Ware house	Pick orders	High	Medium	Medium	High	N/A	High
	Pack orders	High	Medium	Medium	High	N/A	High
	Ship orders	High	Medium	High	High	High	High
	Receive inventory	Medium	N/A	N/A	N/A	High	High
Customer service	Handle customer problems	Low	Low	Low	Medium		

As you can see, this scenario focused just on the warehouse department. The warehouse manager or someone designated by the manager should participate in this business continuity planning process. Only someone working in the warehouse is going to be familiar enough with the various day-to-day processes to generate a realistic view of the impact of various business disruptions. Once they have walked through all the risk scenarios (we mentioned fire, flood, chemical spill, and upstream/downstream impacts earlier), they can assign the criticality, the maximum tolerable downtime, the operational impact, financial impact, and the employee impact.

You may also choose to include additional columns in your impact table (or in your analysis if you choose not to use a tabular format) such as the financial impact and the legal impact. In this scenario, we also could have included the dependencies. Sales are impacted by the availability of inventory data (you can't sell inventory you don't have on hand or on order). Receivables are impacted by the ability to pick, pack, and ship inventory. Payables are impacted by the ability to receive inventory and manage missing/damaged inventory. Payroll is impacted by having to work additional hours to manage inventory damage from the fire as well as to perform work outside the normal scope of warehouse operations. Expenses go up because additional supplies must be purchased to replace the supplies lost in the fire. Sales are down because shipments cannot go out until inventory is adjusted and some customers have purchased elsewhere. The building has to be cleaned by a professional company that specializes in recovering from fire damage and that impacts operations and increases the company's expenses with an unplanned expenditure.

What you'll discover from this process is that as you walk through these scenarios, you'll begin getting ideas about how to mitigate the impact of these disruptions. When we discuss mitigation strategies, you'll find that one mitigation strategy might be helpful for three or four different risk scenarios. Thus, what would reduce your risk in the event of a fire might also be an excellent strategy for mitigating the risk of flooding or a chemical spill in the area. These economies are found only by thoroughly assessing risks and impacts so you can see the big picture and develop optimal mitigation strategies.

Now that you have identified the critical business processes for the warehouse department, you can also look at the impact a flood would have. For example, if employees cannot get to work, if trucks cannot come in to deliver inventory, if trucks cannot pick up shipments, many of these activities are impacted. If the warehouse area is flooded, you have a similar problem as you did with a fire. If the area surrounding the building is flooded but your inventory and IT systems remain in tact, you have a different set of challenges.

By identifying the critical business functions and processes, you can clearly see the impact various risk sources would have on the business. You can assign criticality and maximum tolerable downtime in preparation for developing effective strategies for addressing these risks.

If you were to continue with this example, you would define specific recovery objectives based on criticality, you would identify organizational and system dependencies, and you would define work-around procedures that could be used. This would comprise the impact analysis for the warehouse department for the risk of fire. If you expand it to include the same assessments for each threat source identified in your risk assessment, you would have a comprehensive impact analysis for your warehouse department. Each department in the company would complete this process and you'd have the risk assessment and impact analysis for the entire company. As you can see from just this small example, it's a large undertaking and may well take more time than any other part of your project. Allow enough time to get this completed but don't let it get long and drawn out. Most of this can be completed by departments in a reasonable amount of time, though the more complex the business systems, the longer it will take to perform this assessment.

Preparing the Business Impact Analysis Report

There is no standardized format for a business impact analysis report and, as with many other processes, this document will likely follow your company's standard format. At minimum, the report should include the business functions, the criticality and impact assessments (see the list is Table 31.2) and the maximum tolerable downtime (MTD) assessment for each. Dependencies, both internal and external, should be noted and the correlation to IT systems should be delineated.

This report should be prepared in draft format with initial impact findings and issues to be resolved. The participating managers, SMEs, and BC/DR team members should review the findings. Revise the report based on participant's feedback to the draft document. If needed, you can schedule a draft review meeting to discuss the finding in the draft. Often this is helpful (and needed) to resolve conflicts with regard to the criticality and maximum tolerable downtime ratings, since there is a correlation between these ratings and the cost of mitigating the risks and reducing downtime. Once the feedback has been gathered, revise the draft and finalize the document. This document, depicted at the outset of this chapter in Figure 3.2, is used along with the risk assessment as an input to the risk mitigation process. To assist you in preparing your final report, we've recapped the elements you may choose to include.

- Key processes and functions
- Process and resource interdependence
- IT dependencies
- Criticality and impact on operations
- Backlog information
- Key roles, positions, skills, knowledge, expertise needed
- Recovery time requirements
- Recovery resources
- Service level agreements
- Technology (IT and non-IT technology)
- Financial, legal, operations, market, staff impacts
- Work-around procedures
- Remote work, workload shifting
- Business data, key records
- Reporting
- Competitive impact
- Investor/market impact
- Customer perception impact
- Other (business-specific data not already included)

Summary

Performing the business impact analysis requires you to look at your entire organization from top to bottom. You can begin by gathering subject matter experts, whether division heads, departmental managers, or designated staff, from various parts of your company. These people should be those in the company best able to answer the questions related to critical business activities. This relates to how your company generates revenues, tracks customers and sales, and other key business processes.

Data can be gathered using questionnaires, interview, workshops, documents, and research. There are pros and cons to each approach, so be sure to select the method most appropriate to your organization. Since each company is unique, there is no "one size fits all" template you can use to delineate all critical business processes for all companies. However, throughout this chapter, we discussed a wide variety of business functions, processes, and approaches that can help you develop a comprehensive list of your company's critical processes as well as the key roles, expertise, and knowledge needed to carry out those critical processes.

Once this data is collected, each process must be assessed for criticality. In the big picture, how critical is each business process to your company's ability to continue operating? Using a three- or four-point rating system will help you look across the depth and breadth of your organization to understand which processes and functions are mission-critical, which are vital or essential, which are important, and which are minor. Your risk mitigation planning efforts will focus first on mission-critical processes and then to vital or essential processes.

You'll also need to develop your recovery time objectives (RTO) for each critical function. In some cases, you might choose to associate a recovery time with criticality ratings. For example, mission-critical functions might need to be recovered within 24 hours whereas vital or essential functions might need to be recovered within 72 hours. Alternately, you can assign criticality and then assign recovery time objectives to each process individually. This might make more sense in companies where there are numerous mission-critical processes that cannot be simultaneously addressed. Again, this is a decision you and your team have to make regarding recovery objectives. Input from division or departmental experts is key to understanding required recovery timeframes as well as key interdependencies that exist among departments, processes, and systems.

There is a relationship between the cost of recovery and the cost of downtime. Each company has to assess these costs and make decisions regarding the optimal point of intersection. The longer the company goes without a key process, the more expensive it becomes due to loss of sales and increase in costs associated with the outage. However, recovery costs go down the longer you have to recover. If you need to recover within hours, your costs to provide this type of recovery capability will be significantly higher than if you need to recover within days. The point at which downtime costs and recovery costs intersect is the optimal point for planning, though in the real world, it can be difficult to determine the exact point of intersection. Keeping this concept in mind, however, will help you find the best solutions for your company.

The business impact analysis uses business functions, business processes, and IT systems as the input points. The analysis is performed so that each process is identified and analyzed. The output for each process and function includes criticality assessment, financial impact analysis, operational impact analysis, recovery objectives, dependencies, and work-around procedures. When this is documented for each business function and key business process, you have a comprehensive look at your company and a solid business impact analysis.

## Chapter 32

Mitigation Strategy Development

Solutions in this chapter:

- **Types of Risk Mitigation Strategies**
- **Risk Mitigation Process**
- **IT Risk Mitigation**
- **Backup and Recovery Considerations**

☑ **Summary**

Introduction

Risk mitigation is defined as *taking steps to reduce adverse effects*. Risk mitigation is a commonly used process within traditional business risk management, but as you'll see in this chapter, there are unique aspects to risk mitigation related to business continuity and disaster recovery.

Your data gathering phase has concluded and now it's time to put all this data to work. The mitigation strategy development phase of the business continuity and disaster recovery project plan, shown in Figure 32.1, is where you develop strategies to accept, avoid, reduce, or transfer risks related to potential business disruptions.

Figure 32.1 Business Continuity and Disaster Recovery Project Plan Progress

Developing the risk mitigation strategies is the last phase of risk management activities, which was shown in Figure 30.2 in Chapter 30. This last segment, depicted here in Figure 32.2, includes the inputs of the risk assessment and business impact analysis data. This information, along with risk mitigation data, is used to develop strategies for managing risks in a manner that is appropriate for your company. Once you have the risk management section completed, you can begin to draft your business continuity and disaster recovery plan.

Figure 32.2 Risk Mitigation Strategy Development Phase

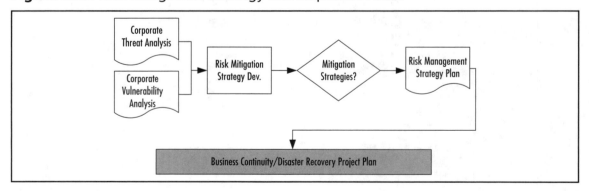

As we've mentioned before, it's important to develop risk mitigation strategies that match your company's profile. If your company is very risk averse and wants to avoid risk at almost any cost, your strategies will be appropriate for that objective. On the other hand, if your company doesn't mind taking on a bit of risk, your BC/DR strategies will be different than a more conservative, risk-averse company's approach. There is no one-size-fits-all answer in the risk mitigation phase—you'll have to create a strategy that meets your company's financial, operational, and risk management goals.

Types of Risk Mitigation Strategies

Let's begin with a quick review of standard risk mitigation strategies. These will be useful as you develop your strategies, and a clear understanding of your options at the outset will help you and your team make better decisions. The four standard choices are acceptance, avoidance, limitation, and transference. As you read through these four options, refer to Figure 32.3, which shows the relationship between time and cost for each option and the relative cost of each option to the others over time.

Figure 32.3 Cost vs. Time for Risk Mitigation Strategies

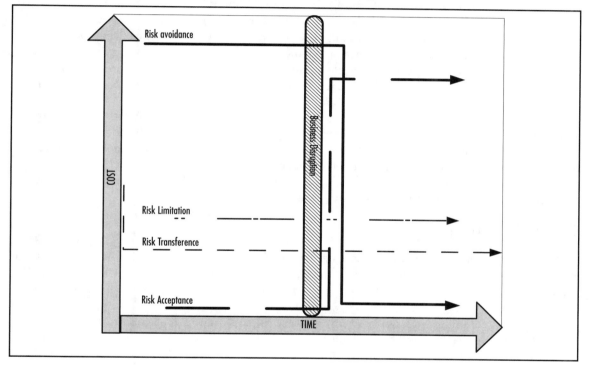

Risk Acceptance

Risk acceptance is not really a mitigation strategy because accepting a risk does not *reduce* its effect. However, risk acceptance is part of risk management. There are various reasons why companies may choose risk acceptance in certain situations. The most common reason is that the cost of other risk management options, such as avoidance or limitation, may outweigh the cost of the risk itself. Insurance companies are notorious for risk acceptance in the sense that they will allow a damaged tree limb to fall on your car and then pay for the repair of the car rather than pay to avoid the car repair expense and cut the limb down before it causes damage. In their case, they know that the limb may not fall down or that your car may not be present when the limb falls. They're taking their chances because if they paid to cut down every damaged tree limb reported to them by their customers, they'd spend a lot of money avoiding risks that were not actually going to occur. These companies spend millions of dollars each year analyzing the odds and are therefore able to make highly sophisticated risk management decisions.

Your company, on the other hand, is probably not in the odds-making business, especially when it comes to business continuity and disaster recovery planning. As you develop your strategies, you should consider the implications of "doing nothing." This can be a way of ensuring that you're taking appropriate actions because if you consider the implications of accepting the risk, you can see the potential consequences and weight them out against other options.

As you can see in Figure 32.3, the cost of risk acceptance is very low at the beginning (it may even be zero), but after a business disruption, the cost can be significantly higher than other risk management strategies. The company may be willing to save money today knowing that it will have a disproportionately large expenditure later if a business disruption occurs. That's key—you have to understand that you're betting that the business disruption will not occur or if it does, it will be far enough in the distant future that you're willing to take the financial risk.

A word of caution here: Small businesses often take the stance that they cannot afford to avoid, limit, or transfer risk and therefore, they accept risk by default. This is a mistaken and limited view and should not be the default position going into this planning. Risk acceptance should be evaluated along with the other options to determine the implications, appropriate actions, and costs of various mitigation strategies. Risk acceptance is the least expensive option in the near-term and the most expensive option in the long-term should an event occur.

Risk Avoidance

Risk avoidance is the opposite of risk acceptance because it's an all-or-nothing kind of stance. To continue with the insurance example, cutting down the tree limb would be risk avoidance. The insurance company would be avoiding the risk that the tree limb would fall on your car, on the house, or on a passerby.

In business continuity and disaster recovery plans, risk avoidance is the action that avoids any exposure to the risk whatsoever. If you want to avoid data loss, you have fully redundant data systems or you manually shut down systems and move them in advance of an oncoming hurricane. Risk avoidance is usually the most expensive of all risk mitigation strategies, but it has the result of reducing the cost of downtime and recovery significantly. Figure 32.3 shows this relationship—the cost is very high early on but the cost after a business disruption is lower than other strategies. Shutting down systems is costly in advance of a hurricane, but if they are packed and shipped to another location and fired up, the cost to recover from the business disruption is minimal. This option is not feasible for many types of risks or for many types of companies. However, it is a viable option to consider as you develop your risk mitigation strategies.

Risk Limitation

Risk limitation is the most common risk management strategy employed by businesses. You choose to limit your exposure through taking some action. For example, performing daily backups of critical business data is a risk limitation strategy. It doesn't stop a disk drive from crashing, it doesn't ignore the potential for disk failure, it accepts that drives fail and when they do, having backups helps you recover in a timely manner. In Figure 32.3, you can see that risk limitation strategies fall between acceptance and avoidance both in terms of early costs and costs after the business disruption. In a sense, it's an average of the two. Risk limitations include installing firewalls to keep networks safe, creating backups to keep data safe, practicing fire drills to keep employees safe, and more. We'll discuss various risk limitations you can take with regard to your key business processes throughout the remainder of this chapter because this is, by far, the manner in which most businesses choose to deal with their risks.

Risk Transference

Risk transference involves handing the risk off to a willing third party. Many companies outsource certain operations such as customer service, order fulfillment, or payroll services. They do this in many cases so they can focus on their core competencies, but they can also do this as part of risk management. For example, if you outsource your payroll services, you may choose to select a processing company that is not located in the same geographical region as your firm. If you're in the southeastern United States, you may choose a company in the Midwest or that has multiple processing sites around the United States so that it can process payroll regardless of weather events.

Another example of risk transference is purchasing insurance or other insurance types of services. In order to transfer risk, you usually have to pay some other company some amount of money to assume that risk, whether it's an IT shop that will manage your security or databases for you, or an insurance company that will pay for losses in the event of a business disruption. Figure 32.3 shows that, relative to other choices, your risk transference will usually cost more as some sort of up-front or ongoing fee, but that the overall cost will be somewhere in the same area as risk limitation. One important point to note, however, is that risk limitation usually has an end-point cost where risk transference can be ongoing. For example, you make insurance premium payments every month or quarter, regardless of whether or not you experience an event that requires your insurance company to step in. With risk limitation, you typically put some system in place, such as a firewall or redundant system. The cost of that implementation is finite and known and usually ends at some point in time. Thus, while the near-term costs of risk limitation and risk transference may appear to be similar, it's important to understand the *duration* of the cost with regard to these strategies.

Common Challenges

Under the Radar

Some companies don't like to discuss risk either because they don't want to acknowledge it or because they are cavalier about the risks they face. This latter stance is most commonly found in small, entrepreneurial start-ups that have their hands full just getting the

Continued

business off the ground. Often the larger a company gets, the more it is willing to discuss, plan for, and mitigate various kinds of risks. This may be, in part, due to outside pressures of financial markets or investors. If you're working in a small company that doesn't want to address risk, you may run into challenges even getting a BC/DR plan off the ground. As we discussed earlier in the section, you may be able to implement many of the BC/DR plan elements without making a big, formal process out of it. If this is the only way you can do BC/DR planning, it may be worth working in stealth mode. For example, when you look at data backup methods, you may choose to select and implement technologies and processes that not only meet your backup needs but provide an adequate level of BC/DR capabilities as well. You should certainly follow the rules, regulations, and procedures in your company, but you may find that you have a bit of leeway when it comes to implementing technology solutions that will meet the broader needs of the company, even if the company doesn't want to know about it.

The Risk Mitigation Process

In order to develop a risk mitigation strategy, you first have to know your options. In previous chapters, we looked at the various risks, threats, threat sources, vulnerabilities, and impacts. Next, we need to look at the recovery profile including the recovery requirements, options, timeframe of options (compared with maximum tolerable downtime or MTD), and cost versus the capability of options. From there, we can select appropriate options. Once these elements are known, acomprehensive strategy can be devised. The strategy will ultimately also include identifying off-site requirements and alternate facilities, and developing business unit strategies. In the following sections, we'll look at the recovery steps specifically.

Recovery Requirements

Recovery requirements typically are broken down by functional areas including facilities and work areas, IT systems and infrastructure, manufacturing and production (operations), and critical data/vital records. Your company may have other recovery requirements. If so, they should be included in this section. The recovery requirements are developed for the critical business processes identified in the business impact analysis. They help identify the resources that should be the focus of the recovery strategy since there is a cost involved with developing and implementing a mitigation or recovery strategy. If a process is not mission critical (or essential), it is likely not a good candidate for the expenditure of time and effort to develop mitigation strategies. Recovery requirements can be categorized even within the functional areas. For example, a recovery requirement category for facilities is alternate office space. Another category might be a crisis management center or a communications command center. Once you identify the recovery requirements, you can begin to review recovery options.

Recovery Options

For each critical business function or process, you have identified the impact on the organization; the dependencies to other functions; the IT dependencies, the key positions, skills, and knowledge needed; and the time requirement for recovery (among other things). Based on this data and on the recovery requirements, you can develop a variety of recovery options. Typically these options will come with varying timelines of their own as well as varying costs and capabilities. At this juncture, your primary concern is to develop a list of viable options based on the business impact analysis data you have. For example, if you have a requirement for an alternate computing facility, you have numerous options available including borrowing computer space from a local firm to setting up a colocation center outside your own geographic area and many other options in between. These options, unless absolutely outside the realm of possibility, should be listed so they can be included in the subsequent evaluation steps.

There are three basic recovery options you can consider. Each of these can also be considered part of a mitigation strategy, as you'll see. You can acquire the option *as needed*, you can *prearrange* for an option, or you can *preestablish* an option. Figure 32.4 shows the relative cost relationship of these three options.

Figure 32.4 Cost Relationship of Recovery Options

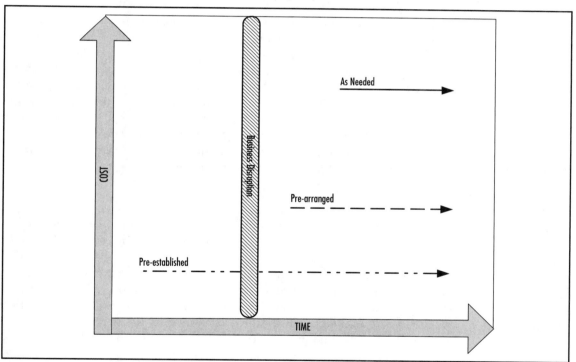

Notice that *as needed* options often take longer to implement after a business disruption and typically cost more. However, the cumulative cost may still end up being lower than *prearranged* or *preestablished* options, especially if one-time setup fees or recurring maintenance fees are required for those other options. *Prearranged* options are typically less expensive than *as needed* solutions, and they often can be implemented in a more timely manner since availability should be guaranteed in the arrangement. Finally, *preestablished* solutions can be implemented almost immediately, but they often have a recurring cost or a sunk cost in advance of the disruption. This can make their total cost more than other options. Clearly, *time* is one of the major factors in each of these options. Let's look at each of these options in more detail.

As Needed

Acquiring resources as needed at existing market rates and within existing market availability following the business disruption is one recovery approach. If the disruption is isolated to your company, as would be the case in a fire or building collapse, market rates and availability might be acceptable. If the disruption is broader in scope, such as an earthquake or volcano eruption, market rates may skyrocket while availability may plunge. In some cases, availability may go to zero, regardless of the price you're willing and able to pay.

Prearranged

Prearranged options involve making arrangements in advance for the quick shipment or delivery of materials, supplies, and capabilities later. These types of arrangements typically involve a contractual agreement with a vendor to supply required systems, products, or services within an agreed upon time frame following a business disruption. There is often a cost to creating these arrangements or a charge above existing market rates built into the contract. For example, if delivering new IT systems is prearranged with a computer maker, there may be an up-charge over the existing market cost of the systems for fast turnaround, expedited or custom system configurations, testing, shipping, delivery, and setup. However, these would all be specified in the contract so that costs would be contained and would be known in advance. In addition, availability requirements are included in the contractual agreement so your firm is not subject to the vagaries of the open market in the aftermath of a major event.

Preestablished

Preestablished recovery options are those that are purchased, configured, and implemented prior to a disruptive event and are used only for recovering from a disruptive event. A company-owned alternate computing site that is activated only in the aftermath of a business disruption would be considered a preestablished recovery option. Often the cost of this type of solution is lower on a per-unit basis because the expenditures can be timed and managed. However, the cost over time may be higher, depending on the cost of these preestablished options. For instance, if you purchase IT systems in the exact configuration of existing systems and have them stored at an alternate location in the event of an emergency, those systems sit idle until (and unless) there is a business disruption. Unlike working systems, these are sitting idly and are therefore nothing but nonproductive expenses. Certainly, if your company experiences a disruption, the cost of these preconfigured, preinstalled machines is suddenly a good investment. If your company never experiences a disruption, the systems become outdated and useless. Never having been in production, they must nonetheless be upgraded or replaced periodically, leading to additional costs.

TIP

For IT systems, preestablished and prearranged solutions are often best. Trying to get IT systems acquired, shipped, set up, configured, and online in the aftermath of a business disruption is a major undertaking. Anything you can do in advance, within the constraints of your organization, will be well worth it if your company faces a disruption. You'll have to balance the cost of preparing against the cost of dealing with the aftermath. In some companies, this cost can't be justified. In larger companies, it almost always makes financial and organizational sense to make arrangements in advance.

Recovery Time of Options

Once you've developed your list of recovery requirements and options, you can look at the recovery time of each option. For example, borrowing space for your computers from another local company might be prearranged and therefore it could be implemented within a matter of hours. A colocation facility, if preestablished, potentially could be online within minutes of a business disruption. Buying new computers and setting them up in a temporary work location such as a local hotel conference room or mobile office unit is another option but it typically would take days to get that set up. Having defined the maximum tolerable downtime for your critical business processes, you must now compare that data to the recovery time of the options you're considering. Any option that does not meet MTD requirements should be removed from further consideration at this juncture. In this way, only options the meet MTD requirements will be assessed in terms of cost and capability.

Cost versus Capability of Recovery Options

You should have a pared down list of recovery options based on those that meet MTD *and* recovery requirements. Next, you'll assess the cost of each of the remaining options and list the capabilities included in that cost. Some options may have various levels of cost/capability. In most cases, the higher the capability, the higher the cost. Since all mitigation strategies will ultimately have to meet the company's financial constraints, this data is critical to making the right decisions for your company. There are additional attributes that can and should be included in the cost/capability assessment. These are:

- Cost—the cost of the mitigation or recovery option.
- Capability—the capabilities of the option.
- Effort—the amount of effort it will take to implement and manage the option.
- Quality—the quality of the product, service, or data associated with the option.
- Control—the amount of control the company will retain over the critical business process.

- Safety—in cases where physical safety is a concern, this attribute rates the safety of the solution. If setting up a few braces on a faltering ceiling over the data center is among your recovery options, its safety attribute would be about zero compared to other options.

- Security—the estimates of physical and virtual (information and network access) security the option provides.

- Desirability—the assessment of the overall desirability of an option. In many cases this is a qualitative judgment based on quantitative data. If so, the quantitative data should be included. The reasons for rating desirability as high, neutral, or low should be delineated.

You can create a matrix to review these attributes and help you make sound decisions. Table 32.1 shows a grid related to various options related to acquiring critical IT systems; Table 32.2 shows options related to establishing alternate computing facilities. These are two different approaches to mitigating risk and as you assess these attributes, you can make decisions as to your best options.

Table 32.1 Example: Options for Acquiring Critical IT Systems

Option	Cost	Capability	Effort	Quality	Control	Safety	Security	Desirability
As needed	High	Unknown	High	Low	Low	N/A	N/A	Low
Pre-arranged	Medium	Meets require-ments	Medium	Medium	Medium	N/A	N/A	Medium
Pre-established	Low	Meets require-ments	Low	High	High	N/A	N/A	Medium

Table 32.2 Example: Options for Establishing Alternate IT Facilities

Option	Cost	Capability	Effort	Quality	Control	Safety	Security	Desirability
Company cold site	Medium	Meets require-ments	Medium	Low	High	Medium	Medium	Medium
Out-sourced hot site	High	Meets require-ments	Low	High	Low	High	High	Medium

Remember that these options are being considered only because they met the recovery requirements including time to recover. Therefore, they're all viable options at first glance. However, additional analysis is required to understand the particular needs of your company and the viability of these various options.

Recovery Service Level Agreements

Any agreement you enter into for recovery services should include specific metrics such as time, cost, availability, response time, throughput, bandwidth, and so on. These metrics all fall under the category of service level agreements (SLA) and can include a number of different elements including:

- Response time to initial request for services
- Technical capacities—computer equipment specifications, storage space, voice and data capacities, speeds, bandwidth availability, test equipment, among others
- Access to recovery facility and equipment
- Access to adequate work area and access for staff
- Security procedures and guarantees
- Processing controls
- Access to technical and functional support (time, response time, etc.)

Another important aspect to reviewing recovery service level agreements is to look at any existing SLAs you may have with external parties such as your clients or customers. If you have contractual agreements to process data or ship orders within a specific period of time, you will need to review your recovery options in light of those contractual agreements. Although these SLAs should have been identified in your business impact analysis as critical business functions, it's good to take the opportunity here to ensure your risk mitigation strategies address your contractual obligations and in particular, any SLAs that are currently in place.

Review Existing Controls

In some cases, you may already have all or part of these controls in place. For example, you might have a very robust data backup solution in place and by adding an additional service or two, you can meet these recovery requirements fairly easily. The reason for reviewing these controls after you've reviewed your recovery requirements is because you want to be able to look at existing solutions with fresh eyes. If you were to begin by examining existing solutions and try to fit them into your recovery options, you might have a built-in bias toward existing solutions. This is especially true if you were the one who championed or implemented the solution or if you happen to know that it was a very expensive, high-end solution. To avoid these natural biases, it's best to review your recovery options first then compare the optimal solutions to existing solutions. In some cases, you'll find that existing solutions meet requirements. In other cases, solutions might actually exceed requirements. Finally, you will undoubtedly find areas where existing solutions do not meet requirements and you'll need to address these areas.

If you find that you have solutions in place that address various recovery requirements, be sure to include these in your risk mitigation strategy document. As stated previously, this might be an opportunity to show the value of a previous investment or at least to show how an existing investment is serving dual purposes. In addition, you want to include these existing solutions in your risk mitigation strategy so that you keep these systems in mind as your systems and BC/DR plans change over time. For example, if you have a solid backup solution that is part of your risk mitigation strategy, that should be noted so that if you decide in the future to modify your backup strategy, you can evaluate the impact on your BC/DR plan. You may have a checklist (on paper or just in your mind) of things you consider when you look at technology investments—speed, compatibility, cost, security. Be sure to add BC/DR to your list so that any future investments can be evaluated in light of BC/DR requirements as well.

> **TIP**
>
> Leverage existing assets, processes, and procedures to the greatest extent possible, but don't be afraid to rip a solution out by the roots if it doesn't meet your immediate and long-term needs. Don't continue to support a failing (or failed) solution just because no one wants to be the one to terminate it. This BC/DR planning process can help you identify areas for improvement. It may also provide you with the financial and organizational support you need to update legacy systems that have outlived their usefulness.

Developing Your Risk Mitigation Strategy

The steps in developing your risk mitigation strategy are these:

1. Gather your recovery data.
2. Compare cost, capability, and service levels of options in each category.
3. Determine if the options remaining are risk acceptance, avoidance, limitation, or transference and which, if any, are more desirable.
4. Select the option or options that best meet your company's needs.

Now that you've gathered this data on various recovery options, you can review them in relation to cost and capabilities and service levels.

This data can now be compiled into a document in whatever format is suitable for your needs. Some people like to use a grid or matrix, others prefer an outline format. The key is to create a highly usable document that delineates the choices you've made. Let's look at a two examples. In our first sample, we look at a small segment of data that might be included with regard to backups. This uses a grid or matrix style and it should give you an idea about what data to include and how you might approach it. In our second sample, we'll use text without a grid so you can compare which method might work better for you.

Sample 1: Section from Mitigation Strategy for Critical Data

Category	Option	Cost, Capability, SLAs	Risk Mitigation Selection
Data backup—frequency	Continuous	Expensive, zero downtime, exceeds MTD	Potential solution, depending on cost to implement.
	Daily	Moderate, up to 8 hours of potential lost data, 3 hours to restore, meets MTD	Implement daily backup. process to reduce likelihood of significant data loss and to reduce recovery time to meet MTD
	Weekly	Moderate, up to five days of potential lost data, 12 hours to restore, may meet MTD	
	Monthly	Low, does not meet MTD	
Data backup—type	Full	Longest backup time, shortest recovery time, meets MTD	
	Incremental	Medium backup time, longest recovery time, exceeds MTD	
	Differential	Medium backup time, medium recovery time, meets MTD	Differential backup meets. MTDs at the lowest cost
Data backup—method	Tape backups	Longest recovery time, least expensive, may not meet MTD	
	Electronic vaulting	Long recovery time, somewhat expensive, may not meet MTD	
	Data replication	Medium recovery time, medium expense, may meet MTD	
	Disk shadowing	Fast recovery time, medium expense, may meet MTD	Based on cost constraints, this option may meet MTD. This and disk mirroring will be explored in terms of cost, time, and feasibility.

Continued

Sample 1 Continued

Category	Option	Cost, Capability, SLAs	Risk Mitigation Selection
	Disk mirroring	Fast recovery time, medium expense, may meet MTD	Based on cost constraints, this option may meet MTD. This and disk mirroring will be explored in terms of cost, time, and feasibility.
	Storage virtualization	Fast recovery time, high expense, removes localized failure risk, meets MTD	
	Storage area network	Fast recovery time, higher expense, removed single point of failure, may remove localized failure risk, meets MTD	
	Wide area high availability clustering	Fast recovery time, higher expense, removes single point of failure, may remove localized failure risk, meets MTD	
	Remote mirroring	Continuous availability, zero recovery time, highest expense, removes single point of failure and localized failure risk, exceeds MTD	

Sample 2: Section from Mitigation Strategy for Critical Data

Critical Data Recovery Options *(selected choice is <u>underlined</u>)*

1. Data backup frequency

   A. Continuous—expensive, zero downtime, exceeds MTD. Not suitable due to cost.

   B. <u>Daily—moderate, up to eight hours potential lost data, 3 hour recovery time, meets MTD. Best choice based on cost and time factors.</u>

   C. Weekly—moderate, up to five days lost data, 12 hours to restore, may meet MTD. Although cost is acceptable, the recovery time for this option just barely meets MTD and does not provide any leeway. Therefore, this option is not as suitable as daily.

   D. Monthly—low cost, does not meet MTD. Not suitable due to time.

2. Data backup type

    A. Full—uses the fewest tapes, takes the most time to back up, least time to recover, exceeds MTD. Not suitable due to time to back up.

    B. Incremental—uses moderate number of tapes, takes less time to back up than full, moderate time to recover. Just barely meets MTD. Not suitable due to time to recover.

    C. Differential—uses moderate number of tapes, takes less time to back up than full, takes less time to recover than incremental. Meets MTD. Suitable due to time and cost.

3. Data backup method

    A. Tape backup—longest recovery time, least expensive, does not meet MTD.

    B. Electronic vaulting—longer recovery time, somewhat expensive, may not meet MTD.

    C. Data replication—medium recovery time, medium expense, may meet MTD.

    D. Disk shadowing—fast recovery time, medium expense, may meet MTD.

    E. Disk mirroring—fast recovery time, medium expense, may meet MTD.

    F. Storage virtualization—fast recovery time, high expense, removes localized failure risk, meets MTD.

    G. Storage area network—fast recovery time, higher expense, removed single point of failure, may remove localized failure risk, meets MTD.

    H. Wide area high availability clustering—fast recovery time, higher expense, removes single point of failure, may remove localized failure risk, meets MTD.

    I. Remove mirroring—continuous availability, zero recovery time, highest expense, removes single point of failure and localized failure risk, exceeds MTD.

As you can see from both examples, you may need to do additional research before deciding on the right backup method for critical data. It's clear that a weekly backup scheme might work, but the problems inherent in a local backup process might not be acceptable. You can also see from the data that while a weekly differential backup strategy might be acceptable, disk mirroring is also an option. In some cases, these two backup objectives might be at odds, might be redundant, or might not make sense for your organization. Once you've looked at this data, you can determine the best risk mitigation strategy for that business function and ultimately, for your entire business.

Your final strategy might be to set up disk mirroring and perform weekly backups of data that are sent to a remote data storage vault. This reduces your recovery time if something happens to a disk (mirroring) and also protects you if you have a fire in the building that destroys all disks. You should include a section to your Critical Data Recovery Options called "Selected Strategy" and delineate the exact strategy you select. When you move into writing your business continuity and disaster recovery plan, you'll have the information you need in order to begin implementing these strategies. Avoid having to review this material at length by including enough information so that the rationale behind the selected strategy is clear.

Remember, too, that when you're selecting your strategy, you should consider risk controls already in place and attempt to build on, rather that replace or circumvent, those solutions. There may be some cases where you want to completely revamp your approach, and this is the place to make those decisions. In other cases, you may simply confirm that you're covered in these areas. For example, you may already have disk mirroring and remote data backups in place. If so, you've looked at your

MTD, cost, and capability requirements and determined that these solutions are acceptable. Make a note of that finding. Later, when you're looking at your BC/DR plan, you don't want to have to go back through all these steps to determine if you used due diligence in making this decision. If something goes wrong down the line, you will also have documentation to show that you used a logical and accepted methodology for making these decisions.

For each critical business process, you need to identify an associated risk mitigation strategy. Some strategies will cover more than one critical business process, so you should not end up with as many strategies as you have critical business functions and processes. For example, your data management strategies will cover many of your critical business processes. By assessing this data with the big picture in mind, you can find areas where risk mitigation choices can cover more than one critical area. If you were to look at these strategies area by area only, you might miss opportunities to generate some *economies of scale*, which come from being able to apply one solution to many problems. These solutions become less expensive when they have more than one use. As mentioned earlier, any time you can use a solution across multiple business functions, you have a stronger business case for the expenditure. If you implement a remote data storage solution that meets data availability requirements for normal day-to-day business and it also meets your business continuity and disaster recovery needs, you're going to find more support for the cost and implementation of such a solution. At the very least, you'll be able to make a stronger business case for the investment.

People, Buildings, and Infrastructure

We're including this as a separate section because depending on the nature of your business, you may not yet have addressed the elements. In looking at the business impact, for instance, you may have deal with critical business functions, but you may not have addressed the impact to people, to buildings, or to other infrastructure.

If there is a business disruption, your company may have very specific needs related to people—staff, contractors, vendors, or the community. Some of these may already be addressed in your plan. For example, in the aftermath of a natural disaster, people need ready cash so they can buy food, medical supplies, and other immediate needs. If your company is located in a rural area where access to banks and ATMs is limited, you may want to ensure that your recovery plan includes being able to cash paychecks for employees or advance them cash against future paychecks. That may already be covered in your critical business functions under payroll, but it's a good idea to think through this again to ensure you have covered all your bases. However, there may be other areas that should be addressed in risk mitigation related to people. For example, fire drills are risk mitigation strategies that are useful not only for fires but for other types of emergencies that require people to evacuate the building in a safe and orderly manner. Keep this in mind as you devise your risk mitigation strategies.

What other risks can be mitigated for people, buildings, and infrastructure? You might have a landscaping company come out and remove all trees, bushes, and grasses that are within 50 feet of the building if you are situated in a place prone to wildfires. That would be a risk mitigation strategy related to the building and infrastructure that might not show up because it's not a critical business function.

You might go back through your risk assessment and see if there are any elements related to people, buildings, and infrastructure that have not yet been addressed in terms of impact or mitigation. Add these to your assessment process here. Remember, too, that sometimes doing nothing (risk acceptance) is an acceptable solution as long as it is an active decision based on research and consideration and not just a passive default position.

IT Risk Mitigation

We've discussed business impact and risk mitigation extensively. Now, let's turn our attention to the specifics of IT risk mitigation. Although the technology you use in your company will change over time and may not be the same as that discussed here, this section should give you a good feel for how to develop a risk mitigation strategy for your IT systems.

Risks to your data include not only the natural disasters we went over earlier in this section, but data disruptions and outages due to data center outages (fire, power, etc.); hardware or software failures; network security breaches; data security breaches that can include lost, stolen, modified, or copied critical data; and disruption due to critical data not being available to legitimate users (Denial of Service attacks, etc.). Your risk and impact assessments should have covered these areas and this is a good time to check to ensure all your data risks are addressed.

Critical Data and Records

Through looking at your maximum tolerable downtime and the cost of disruptions (lost productivity, lost revenues, etc.), you have a solid understanding of the impact a loss of various critical data would have on the organization. If you don't yet have this understanding, you should go back through the risk, vulnerability, and impact assessments with an eye toward critical data and records to determine where you critical data is stored, who generates it, what they do with it, and what they would do without it.

In addition, you should assess legal and regulatory requirements related to critical data, whether this is personal medical data, personal financial data, or other data impacted by regulations, statutes, and laws. If you've been addressing this type of data for some time in your IT department, you may have the solutions in place to meet existing regulation. However, it would also be wise to consult with your legal counsel to determine if there are new or upcoming regulations likely to impact your organization in the future. These should be included in your assessment, if possible, so that you can develop a comprehensive data management plan within the scope of your BC/DR plan. Finally, you should review all existing controls as well as your proposed solutions in light of disaster recovery and business continuity. In some cases, your risk mitigation strategies might appear to be acceptable, but when you begin running through possible disaster or disruption scenarios, you discover that your strategies have a few holes in them. If you find you are covered, then you can be confident your BC/DR plan will meet your data needs. If you do discover some gaps, you can be relieved that at least you found them now and not in the aftermath of a disaster. At this juncture, you can look at potential solutions to address any gaps you discover between your existing data protection/data recovery solutions and those needed for BC/DR needs.

Critical Systems and Infrastructure

Once you understand your data management and data protection needs within the scope of the BC/DR planning process, you can begin to evaluate hardware and software solutions, vendors, and costs. There is no magic solution that will cover all your needs and if you've been working in IT for any length of time, you already know that painfully well. However, if your analysis reveals gaps in your coverage, you'll need to look at various methods of addressing those gaps from rip-out-and-replace to patching existing systems.

If you can identify hardware, software, and vendors that can meet your needs for the next three to five years, you'll be doing well on the planning horizon. Don't try to build a solution that will last for ten years, you'll waste time and money looking for the perfect solution. Instead, look for a solid solution that meets your data management, data security, and data recovery requirements now and into the next few years. Then evaluate the cost to acquire, implement, and manage the solution. You'll have to make a few compromises, as you know, but if you have your data constraints and budget as known variables, you can devise an acceptable (or even optimal) solution that fits within those parameters.

Reviewing Critical System Priorities

Through your business impact analysis, you should have developed an assessment of critical IT systems that includes a prioritization of assets. For example, you might have found through your assessment of critical business functions that these IT assets have the following priorities:

- LAN Server (user authentication, etc.)—High

- Internet access—Low

- E-mail access—Low

- CRM application server—High

- Inventory management system server—Medium

- Financial systems—Medium

Based on these assessments, you should review your risk mitigation strategies to ensure that they meet or exceed your requirements for recovery based on these priorities. Dependencies between systems, especially those deemed as high priority or mission critical, should be reviewed. There might be a preferred or required order for restoration of systems after a disruption that should be addressed in the risk mitigation strategy. For example, if it's critical to restore the LAN server before the CRM server because the CRM server requires authentication data from the LAN server, this should be part of the risk mitigation strategy. Later this will be included in your specific data recovery plans but it is in this segment (and perhaps in the business impact analysis) where these dependencies are identified.

Backup and Recovery Considerations

We're assuming that as an IT professional, you're well aware of various backup and recovery options, both those your firm has implemented and those you've learned about in the marketplace. In this section, we're going to cover some of common backup and recovery options so that you can review your risk mitigation strategies in light of these options. This may help you see options you had overlooked or forgotten about; it might bring to light new options you had not considered. We won't go into a lot of detail about these options, but we will provide a quick look at them to help ensure you have the best risk mitigation strategy possible given your current technology, organizational constraints, and budget.

Alternate Business Processes

Your risk management data should already contain your key business processes and alternate methods (workarounds) for handling these processes during a business disruption, whether that disruption is to the IT systems, the building or the surrounding area. We've covered a lot of this material, so this section is just a quick reminder in case you have overlooked any of these areas that may be relevant to your business operations.

Customer Service.   During a disruption or emergency, it's vital to most companies to still have the capability to provide support or customer services. Depending on the nature of the work your company does, this may be one of your most critical business functions. IT should clearly understand which technologies are required to deliver acceptable levels of customer service during a business disruption.

Administration and Operations.   We've focused on these activities in Chapter 31 in great detail, so we won't cover them again here. You should have detailed documentation on the key business administration and operations processes for your business. These details should be at the heart of your risk mitigation strategy development.

Key Business Information and Documents.   Most businesses rely heavily upon electronic data of all kinds—e-mail, text documents, presentations, among others. Data essential to ongoing operations should be identified so that IT mitigation strategies can be developed. In addition, strategies for dealing with less critical data in the absence of key IT systems should be developed. You might decide, for instance, that certain data must always be available so a continuous availability solution will be implemented. Other data is essential but not mission-critical. For that data, you may develop a fast-track recovery solution.

Essential Equipment.   Other equipment essential to ongoing operations should be looked at in terms of how disruption of IT and non-IT systems may impact the availability of equipment. In some companies, IT systems run manufacturing, order fulfillment, or other operations-oriented equipment. How will the disruption of business impact these systems? How will the disruption of critical IT systems impact these operational systems? What can be done to reduce the risk to these systems?

Premises.   We've discussed fire drills as a way to reduce the risk of injury or death to staff in the event of a fire or other building disaster. In addition to fire drills, there may be other ways to reduce risks to the premises. Insurance is certainly part of the equation, but fire inspections, emergency lighting, and other emergency systems can be put in place to protect the premises and employees.

IT Recovery Systems

You're undoubtedly familiar with many IT recovery systems, but as part of your risk mitigation strategy development, you should scan the technological horizon to see what's available in today's market. Sometimes IT departments develop risk management strategies based on current technology and never update those strategies. Systems put in place five years ago that are not reviewed and updated can inject additional risk into your organization, and puts your BC/DR plan at risk. Clearly what was innovative five years ago may be close to being a legacy system now. What was extremely expensive three years ago has probably dropped in price significantly. Revisit your technology solutions with an eye on what's available in the marketplace today. You might decide to upgrade, replace, or supplement existing solutions. The list included in this section is not exhaustive but should spark thoughts about solutions to consider. Be sure to do some independent research to supplement this data so that you have a comprehensive and current look at your IT recovery options before developing your mitigation strategies.

Alternate Sites

The largest decision you'll need to make is whether or not to develop alternate sites. You can have a dedicated site wholly owned by your company, you can create a reciprocal agreement with another division or company, or you can go to an external vendor for a commercially leased facility. Let's look at the most common options.

Fully Mirrored Site

Mirrored sites are fully redundant sites that mirror everything going on in the live site. This is by far the most expensive and extensive IT risk mitigation strategy. For some companies, this solution might make sense. Mirrored sites provide the highest degree of availability (and therefore risk mitigation) because every transaction that happens on the live site is also processed on the mirrored site simultaneously. Sometimes a solution implemented for load balancing purposes may also serve as a risk mitigation solution. For example, if you have two mirrored sites so that users can access data quickly, it might be that this same configuration works well in the event that one or the other site goes down. Certainly user access to data will slow considerably if one of the sites goes down, but the transactions can still occur while the initial site is being repaired. Mirrored sites typically are owned and managed by the company, which can reduce the cost of implementation.

Hot Site

A hot site is usually a site leased by a commercial vendor to your company for emergency purposes. The vendor will guarantee an identical technical configuration with communications that allow you to switch your IT operations to that commercial site within a specified time frame, usually within one to four hours. These sites typically provide enough space for hardware, supporting infrastructure (racks, cables, phones, printers), and support personnel. This is sometimes less costly than a fully mirrored site, but that depends on your technology and response time needs.

Warm Site

Warm sites are partially equipped premises with some or all of the required equipment. Warm sites are often sites used during normal operations for less critical functions that are taken over for critical IT functions during a business disruption. For example, you might have a site located in your primary location and a second site in a remote office or satellite building. You might keep a server at the remote site configured with your critical business applications with Internet access to backup data. In the event of a business disruption or disaster to the primary site, the secondary site could fire up the server, restore from the most recent backup, and resume critical operations within a matter of hours.

Mobile Site

Mobile sites are self-contained units that can be transported to establish an alternate computing (or working) site. These often are contained within a mobile trailer that is delivered by truck to a specified location. Commercial vendors lease these types of units. Due to the time and expense of configuring a mobile site, these arrangements should be preestablished far in advance of anticipated demand.

Cold Site

A cold site is started up "cold" in the aftermath of a disruption. These kinds of sites are the least expensive in advance of an emergency but take the longest to bring online after a disruption. If your recovery needs are three or four days out, this might be the most cost-effective solution for you. However, your BC/DR plan should include plans for how and where you could establish a cold site should you select this option. Trying to come up with these arrangements in the aftermath of a disaster or serious disruption will be far less effective than planning in advance. That might mean identifying facilities in your area that could host a cold site, understanding how your communications needs would be met, and how you'd furnish and staff this site.

Reciprocal Site

You may be able to make arrangements with another company or another division of your company for use in the event of a significant business disruption. For example, you might make arrangements with another company in your area for reciprocal assistance in the event that one of your businesses is disrupted. However, if a natural disaster hits the area, it's possible both companies will be impacted, so you need to assess the risks of such an arrangement. If you can create an arrangement with a firm outside your geographic area, you'll reduce the localized risk. Remember, however, to create solid agreements with plenty of detail delineating how, when, where, and at what cost these reciprocal arrangements will be implemented. You don't want another company disrupting your business for minor problems, and the use of these arrangements should be very clearly defined. That said, this type of arrangement might make sense for small businesses that can't afford to contract with commercial vendors for alternate sites.

Disk Systems

Disk systems solutions continue to evolve in terms of capabilities. They also tend to become less expensive over time as well. We'll take a quick look at some of the solutions available to you today.

RAID

Redundant arrays of inexpensive disks (RAID) come in several forms. The ability to hot-swap disks from a RAID array can be an important attribute of your disk recovery strategy. We won't run through all the permutations of RAID but you should be aware that there are newer implementations of RAID including RAID10 and RAID50, among others. Also keep in mind that you can implement hardware-based or software-based RAID systems; each has pros and cons associated with them.

Remote Journaling

Remote journaling is a method in which every write and update operation is written to another device. This can be an effective *part* of a data recovery solution, but not a standalone solution. It can be helpful in cases of network intrusion or data corruption. Journaling done in real time creates a mirrored copy. This journal data can be transmitted over a communications link to another site enabling extremely fast recovery in the event of a security breach, data corruption, or other failure.

Replication

Disk replication involves copying data on to a primary and secondary server. *Shadowing* and *clustering* are two methods of accomplishing replication. *Shadowing* happens asynchronously—changes are collected and applied to the secondary server periodically. Shadowing can be part of a risk mitigation strategy, but keep in mind that any corruption or error on the primary server will be replicated to the secondary server. *Clustering* is a higher-end solution than shadowing and it provides high availability. Server clustering works in a manner similar to RAID for disk drives. With clustering, several servers are tied together and periodically synchronize with one another. If a server goes down, the workload shifts to the remaining servers. This process is transparent to users who connect to the application and have no idea which server is providing data. As you probably know, clusters provide load balancing for users and this same functionality provides a level of risk mitigation as well.

Electronic Vaulting

Electronic vaulting is the process that transmits backup data of your systems to a remote location. Backups don't need to be transported and stored off-site and in the event of a business disruption; they may be easier to access than tapes locked in a bank vault or other secure off-site location. Electronic vaulting can dramatically reduce recovery time, especially if used in conjunction with remote journaling.

Standby Operating Systems

As you well know, the operating system with associated patches and upgrades is a critical aspect to being able to get applications back online. Having standby drives with preconfigured operating systems available can reduce risks and recovery times. Every time you upgrade your production systems, you can upgrade your standby systems so that the OS is ready to go in the event of a failure, breach, or disruption.

Network-Attached Storage (NAS)

Storage with a network interface can be attached to the network in any location that provides network connectivity. Thus, a storage unit could be contained in a vault, a server room, or in the middle of a work area. These types of storage devices are easy to install and maintain.

Storage Area Network (SAN)

A storage area network is a dedicated high-speed network for data storage. Storage is independent from servers and is stored across the storage network. In most organizations, much of the LAN traffic is dedicated to backup, mirroring, "heartbeats," and disaster-recovery activities. With a SAN, these activities are restricted to the storage network and bandwidth on the LAN is freed up for more user-centric data needs.

Desktop Solutions

Your organization should already have some process in place for backing up user data. In the Microsoft Windows operating system, most users save data to the My Documents folder or to a designated network location. For enterprise applications, user data may be stored more centrally. Regardless of your configuration, it's important that critical user data be backed up periodically. Ideally, this process should be automated so it does not rely on user compliance with established backup processes. Backups of user data should also be stored securely off-site. In your business impact analysis, you may have determined that there were certain job functions that required special attention. These computers should be flagged as critical and risk mitigation strategies for key user's computers should be developed.

Creating standardized file management processes will also assist in any recovery efforts (and therefore mitigate risk). For example, requiring users to store all important documents in their named folder on a network share can help reduce the likelihood of data loss, corruption, or breach. If users travel with laptops, be sure to establish backup and security procedures for mobile users.

From the Trenches...

Lost and Stolen Laptops—It's Not Always about the Hardware

Laptops are lost and stolen everyday. Sometimes a tired traveler leaves a laptop behind, sometimes a thief wants the hardware. Other times, the thief is targeting the information on the laptop. Lost and stolen laptops have been in the headlines recently because the data on them was sensitive and unencrypted. If you have users working with sensitive data, whether that's the company's strategic direction, corporate finances, or private customer data, be sure that all data is encrypted and that the operating system requires user authentication. Even though there are ways around user access restrictions on stolen laptops, it's tough to overcome strong encryption. Although laptops will always be lost or stolen, the data on them doesn't have to fall into the wrong hands. Implement strong encryption on all laptops that deal with sensitive data and be sure users understand the importance of encryption. Ideally, the encryption system will work seamlessly in the background so the user doesn't have to take any special action to protect data. Anytime security measures can be automated, you'll end up with stronger security than if left to users to remember and employ.

In addition to implementing backup and encryption policies and procedures, risk can be reduced through standardizing hardware, software, and peripheral equipment. Reducing the number of variables not only helps in day-to-day IT activities, it can significantly reduce recovery time after a significant event. Documenting hardware, software, and configuration data along with vendor contact information can reduce the risk of serious disruption should user systems be impacted.

Software and Licensing

Software and license data must be backed up and stored in a secure off-site location along with data. It doesn't do much good to store the database information if the licensing data is lost. The licensing for each operating system, application, user, and desktop system should be captured and stored in a secure manner in the event of a partial or total disruption of business.

Web Sites

There are often two risks related to corporate Web sites. The first is the security risk due to the nature of external (public) Web sites. As you know, Web sites are like large neon signs saying to hackers "Enter Here." Risk mitigation strategies for Web sites include implementing strong security measures along with auditing and monitoring activity on the server. Documentation on the security and configuration settings for the Web site are important in the event the web servers go down or in the event of a security breach. In addition, many corporate Web sites are used to conduct e-commerce transaction and the disruption of these transactions can have a significant impact on revenue streams and on customer perception of the company. Some companies use load balancing strategies to ensure Web sites have high availability, and these same strategies also act as excellent risk mitigation strategies. However, if a Web site is breached or data is corrupted, it's possible these problems will be replicated to all virtual sites, so additional risk mitigation strategies may be needed.

Summary

In this chapter, you learned about a process you can use to develop risk mitigation strategies for critical business and IT functions. The inputs to this process are the risk assessment data and the business impact analysis. The key steps in this process are developing recovery requirements, understanding the recovery time of the options under consideration, comparison of these times to maximum tolerable downtime requirements, a review of the cost and capabilities of each option, the service level agreements related to each option, and finally, the selection of the option to be implemented. This process is done for all critical business processes identified. An additional review should consider dependencies between processes, functions, and IT systems. As is often the case, one solution may address several key requirements. Your review of options should attempt to find the simplest, most comprehensive, and cost-effective solution that meets your company's critical business needs now and into the near future.

## Chapter 33

Business Continuity/ Disaster Recovery Plan Development

Solutions in this chapter:

- **Phases of Business Continuity and Disaster Recovery**

- **Defining BC/DR Teams and Key Personnel**

- **Defining Tasks, Assigning Resources**

- **Communications Plans**

- **Event Logs, Change Control, and Appendices**

☑ **Summary**

Introduction

The bulk of your work in developing your business continuity and disaster recovery plan is complete when you get to this point. Granted, you may be reading this section through from start to finish before developing your plan (recommended) and therefore you will have none of the actual work completed. However, things move quickly in the business world and there are some of you who are doing the work as you read each chapter. Either way, this is where everything comes together.

The risk analysis you performed led you into your vulnerability assessment. That data helped you develop an assessment of the impact various risks would have on your business. Finally, you took all your data and identified mitigation strategies—actions you could take to avoid, reduce, transfer, or accept the various risks you found. With that, you now have to develop a plan that takes your mitigation strategies and identifies both methods for implementing those strategies, and people, resources, and tasks needed to complete these activities.

In Chapter 34, we'll go over emergency activities including disaster response and business recovery, so we'll refer only briefly to those elements in this chapter where appropriate. In Chapter 35, we'll discuss training and testing and in Chapter 36, we'll discuss maintaining the plan. All of these are elements that should be included in your BC/DR plan as well.

The plan basically needs to state the risks, the vulnerabilities, and the potential impact to each of the mission-critical business functions. For each of these, there should be associated mitigation strategies. In some cases, there will be multiple mitigation strategies; in other cases, you may have elected to simply accept the risk. However, all of this should be clearly laid out in your documentation thus far. Next, you need to determine how and when those strategies are implemented and by whom.

Your work breakdown structure will look something like this:

1. Identify risks *(complete)*.

2. Assess vulnerability to risks *(complete)*.

3. Determine potential impact on business *(complete)*.

4. Identify mission-critical business functions *(complete)*.

5. Develop mitigation strategies for mission-critical functions *(complete)*.

6. Develop teams.

7. Implement mitigation strategies.

8. Develop plan activation guidelines.

9. Develop plan transition guidelines.

10. Develop plan training, testing, auditing procedures.

11. Develop plan maintenance procedures.

As you can see from this simplified list, you should already have items one through five completed. We'll discuss developing teams in this chapter as it relates to carrying out the BC/DR plan, not the planning team that you should already have in place (and who hopefully have helped you accomplish tasks one through five). We'll cover developing plan activation and transition guidelines in this chapter before heading into Chapter 34. At the end of this chapter, you'll have items one through nine complete (or will understand how to complete them when you begin project work).

As with previous chapters, we'll begin with a review of where we are in this process (see Figure 33.1). Creating the BC/DR plan entails putting together the information you've developed so far and adding a bit more detail. We'll create the BC/DR plan document in this chapter, but keep in mind we'll have to circle back later to add detail that we develop in upcoming chapters.

Figure 33.1 Project Progress

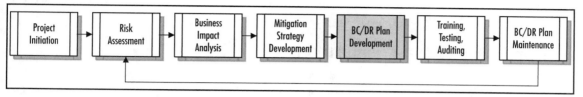

Phases of the Business Continuity and Disaster Recovery

Hopefully you'll never need to put your BC/DR plan into action, despite all the hard work you put into it. If you do need to use your plan, however, you'll need to have clear and specific guidelines for how and when to implement it. Let's begin with a quick look at the phases of the plan: activation, disaster recovery, business resumption or business continuity, and transition to normal operations.

Figure 33.2 Phases of Business Continuity and Disaster Recovery

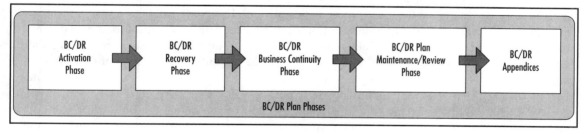

Activation Phase

The activation phase of your BC/DR plan addresses the time during and immediately after a business disruption. In this section of your plan, you need to define when your BC/DR plan will be activated and in what manner. You don't want to activate your plan for every little glitch your business runs into, so you'll need to develop a clear set of parameters that you can use to determine if or when to activate your BC/DR plan. In addition, you will need to define how your plan is activated, including who has the authority to activate it and what steps that person (or persons) will take to initiate BC/DR activities.

Activation includes initial response and notification, problem assessment and escalation, disaster declaration, and plan implementation. After you have begun implementing the plan, you proceed into the recovery phase, as shown in Figure 33.2.

It is in this activation phase that you should define various disaster or disruption levels so that you know when, if, and how to implement your plan. For example, if you experience a network security breach, you'll have to activate different phases of your plan than if the server room is flooded. Therefore, defining various disaster types and levels is important in understanding what should trigger the implementation of BC/DR plans. You may choose to use a three-level rating system, as described here. However, make sure that whatever system you devise, it's tailored to your specific business configuration and that it gives you the guidance you'd need to make these crucial decisions based on predetermined and agreed-upon criteria.

Major Disaster or Disruption

The possibility or likelihood of this type of disaster occurring is low but the business impact is extremely high. This event disrupts all or most of the normal business operations of the company and all or most of its critical business processes. The disruptions occur because all or a majority of systems and equipment have failed or are inaccessible. This includes destruction to the entire facility; a major portion of the facility; or entire networks, subnets, or sections of the business. Once you've defined what this level of disaster or disruption entails, you should define the process for determining which parts of your BC/DR plan should be activated and which team members should be called upon. We'll discuss triggers more in a moment; for now you should attempt to define the business systems, mission-critical functions, and major operations that when affected would cause a major disruption. This will help you develop appropriate triggers to determine when and how to activate your BC/DR plan.

Intermediate Disaster or Disruption

An intermediate disaster is likely to occur more frequently than a major disaster, but less frequently than a minor disaster (hence the "intermediate" designation). Its impact will be less than a major and more than a minor event. This type of disruption or disaster interrupts or impacts one or more mission-critical functions or business units, but not all of them. Operations will experience significant disruption, entire systems or multiple systems may fail or be unavailable, but not all of them. An intermediate event could include a fire or flood in the building that impacts IT systems and equipment, structural damage to part of the building where critical operations occur or where vital equipment is located. As with the other two levels of disruption, it's important to define not only what each tier consists of but which parts of the BC/DR plan should be activated and which team members should begin implementing BC/DR activities. As with a major disruption, clearly delineate which systems, functions, and operations would be impacted to earn an intermediate designation so you can define triggers that will address these types of situations.

Minor Disaster or Disruption

Minor disruptions occur every day in the business world and rarely, if ever, are BC/DR plans called into action. The likelihood of a minor event occurring is high, the associated disruption is low. The effects typically are isolated to one component, one system, one business function, or just one segment of a critical business function. Normal operations can often continue, almost uninterrupted, in the face of a minor disruption. Critical business functions still occur for some period of time after this type of disruption. The failure of a single system or service can typically be addressed during the normal course of business. For example, the failure of a single server, system disk, or phone system is problematic but usually does not require the activation of a BC/DR plan. There may be examples, however, where minor disruptions should be addressed by the activation of part of a BC/DR plan. If that is the case, be sure to clearly identify those disruptions along with which sections of the BC/DR plan should be implemented when and by whom.

Activating BC/DR Teams

Clearly, the BC/DR plan cannot activate itself, someone or a team of people need to make appropriate assessments of the situation and make a determination as to whether or not to activate the plan or portions thereof. Therefore, it's also important to create and maintain various BC/DR teams that handle the response to the business disruption by implementing appropriate sections of the BC/DR plan. We'll discuss the makeup of these teams later in this chapter, but for now we'll list some of the BC/DR teams you may want to define and populate as you continue in this planning process.

- Crisis management team
- Damage assessment team
- Notification team
- Emergency response team
- Business continuity coordinator or lead
- Crisis communication team
- Resource and logistics team
- Risk assessment manager

Depending on the size and nature of your company, you may or may not need some of these functions. It's also possible that one person may fill one or more roles if you're working in a small company. We'll discuss these roles in more detail in a section coming up later in this chapter.

Developing Triggers

If you're familiar with project management, you're probably familiar with triggers. Typically, risks and triggers are identified so that if a project risk occurs, a trigger defines when an alternate plan or method should be implemented. The same is true here. If you are going to implement your plan, you'll need to define how and when that should occur—those are your triggers. For example, if you use the three categories of major, intermediate, and minor, you'll need to define what actions are taken in each case. Each level of disruption should have clearly defined triggers. Let's look at a hypothetical example. You're the IT manager of a small firm and the head of the BC/DR team. You're at home one evening just sitting down to dinner when one of the data processing operators who works until 9 P.M. calls you. She reports that there was a fire in the building, it's been evacuated, and the fire department is on the scene. You ask her a series of questions and ascertain that the fire seems to have been contained relatively quickly but that some of the networking gear may have been damaged either by the fire or by the fire containment efforts. She believes the server room is in tact but she's not sure. If you have clearly defined triggers in place, you may determine that this appears to be either a minor or an intermediate disruption and that you should most likely activate a portion of your BC/DR plan. The trigger might be defined as a series of steps such as:

1. Business disruption event has occurred.

2. Disruption to business operations has occurred.

3. Initial assessment by employees on the scene indicates intermediate level damage, including the following:

   ■ A portion of the network is or may be out of service.

   ■ One or more critical servers is or may be out of service.

   ■ A portion of the physical facility has been impacted by the disruption.

   ■ It is likely employees will not be able to resume normal operations within two hours.

This is an example of a trigger you could define for intermediate types of events. As you've done previously, using scenarios helps you define these elements more clearly. By defining three statements and four attributes, you have a good understanding of whether or not to activate the BC/DR plan for intermediate outages. You also have a defined timeline—if normal business operations cannot resume within two hours. This should be tied to your overall maximum tolerable downtime (MTD) and other recovery metrics developed earlier. If your MTD is 24 hours, an intermediate disruption might be something that will disrupt normal operations for two to six hours. You and your team will need to define these various windows, but be sure to tie your triggers to your recovery metrics.

Your intermediate activation steps are related to the trigger. Once you know you should activate your plan, you should define the immediate steps to be taken. This helps remove any uncertainty about next steps and helps begin a focused response effort. An example of the first steps for an intermediate disruption are shown here.

1. If a disruption appears to be **intermediate** on initial assessment, within two hours:

   ■ Attempt to gather information from the emergency responders, if appropriate.

   ■ Activate the damage assessment team.

   ■ Notify the crisis management team to be on standby notice.

2. After two hours from event notification, gather initial evaluation from damage assessment team.

3. After three hours, notify crisis management team of next steps (stand down, fully activate).

4. Within three hours of event notification, BC/DR plan should be implemented if assessment indicates intermediate or major disruption.

Notice, though, that our description of the actual disruption levels includes trigger information. How many systems are impacted? How extensive is the damage? The more clearly you can define these details, the more precise your triggers will be, and this will help you determine if and when to activate your plan. Spend time clearly defining the circumstances that will warrant plan activation at the various levels you've defined and also spend time defining initial steps to be taken in each phase so that you have checklists of next steps.

Transition Trigger—Activation to Recovery

Another trigger to define is when to move from one phase to another. In this case, that means when to move from the activation phase to the recovery phase. This transition is one that typically occurs fairly naturally, so you don't need to over-engineer this. However, you may want to define the transition trigger like this:

1. The damage assessment team's initial evaluation indicates an intermediate disruption.
2. The crisis management team has been called in and is on scene.
3. The immediate cause of the event has stopped or been contained.
4. The intermediate section of the BC/DR plan has been activated.

You may wish to define other triggers for your transition, from activation to recovery, suitable to your organization. When defining your triggers throughout, keep your maximum tolerable downtime (MTD) and other defined metrics in mind so that you can work within those constraints. For example, if your MTD is very short, your time between activation and recovery also should be very short. In this case, you may have to err on the side of timeliness and take action with incomplete or preliminary data. You'll have to balance your need to collect information with your need to get the business back up and running as quickly as possible (and within your MTD constraints). Rarely, if ever, is there perfect data in an emergency (or any other time). Defining these triggers and constraints clearly in your plan can help you make better decisions in the stressful aftermath of a business disruption or disaster. Help the team make the best decisions possible by spending time now to define these triggers as clearly and unambiguously as possible.

Recovery Phase

The recovery phase is the first phase of work in the immediate aftermath of the disruption or disaster. This phase usually assumes that the cause of the disruption has subsided, stopped, or been contained, but not always. For example, in the case of flooding, you may decide that if it's external flooding, you will wait until waters subside to begin recovery efforts. This may be required by local officials who restrict access to flooded areas. However, in other cases, you may be able to or choose to initiate recovery efforts while flooding is still occurring. This might include placing sandbags around the entryways to the building or removing equipment that is not yet under water. As you can tell, may of your actions will be dictated by the specifics of the situation, so there's no simple rule to follow here. However, we can say that recovery efforts have to do with recovering from the immediate aftermath of the event, whether or not the event is still occurring. This phase may also include evacuating the facility, removing equipment that can be salvaged quickly, assessing the situation or damage, and determining which recovery steps are needed to get operations up and going again. The recovery phase is discussed in detail in Chapter 34.

Transition Trigger—Recovery to Continuity

You'll learn more about recovery activities in Chapter 34, so you'll need to circle back and define these triggers after you understand the information covered in that chapter. At this juncture, you can make a note that you need to develop triggers that help you know when to transition from recovery efforts to business continuity efforts. Typically, these triggers will have to do with determining that the effects of the disruption have been addressed and are not getting any worse. For example, if you experience a fire in the building, the fire is out, the assessment has been done, any equipment or supplies that can be salvaged have been, and alternate computing facilities have been activated. Those are activities that take place in the recovery phase and when these are all complete, it's time to move into the business continuity phase, which typically includes starting up systems so that business operations can resume. Defining these points should include specific events that have occurred, milestones that have been met, or time that has elapsed. Also keep your MTD in mind as you define triggers for this transition.

Business Continuity Phase

The business continuity phase kicks in after the recovery phase and defines the steps needed to get back to "business as usual." For example, if you have a fire in the building, the recovery phase might include salvaging undamaged equipment, ordering two new servers from a hardware vendor, and loading up the applications and backup data on the servers at a temporary location so that you can begin to recover your data and your business operations. The business continuity phase would address how you actually begin to resume operations from that temporary location, what work-arounds need to be implemented, what manual methods will be used in this interim period, and so forth. The final steps in the business continuity phase will address how you move from that temporary location to your repaired facility, how you reintegrate or synchronize your data, and how you transition back to your normal operations. This detail is discussed in Chapter 34. You'll also need to define triggers here that define when you end business continuity activities and when you resume normal operations. Again, as with the other triggers, you should strive to be as clear and concise as possible. You'll have enough to deal with later if you do end up activating and implementing your plan, so spend time here to save yourself a headache later on.

Although it might seem intuitive that you'll resume normal operations when everything is back to normal, things sometimes do not return to normal after a business disruption of any magnitude. Certainly, business operations will resume, but some things may change permanently as a consequence of this disruption. For example, your company may decide as a result of a major fire or flood that it wants to move to a new location and it's going to do that while operating from the alternate site. That would complicate things because it would mean moving from the alternate site to a new site, with all the concomitant challenges inherent in both resuming normal operations and moving to a new facility. Though this example may seem outside the bounds of normal business decision-making, be assured that disruptions can change the way companies see their businesses and the way they approach operations. Another example is developing a work-around that's used in the recovery phase that works so well that someone decides to use it full time. When do you transition back to normal operations if you incorporate BC/DR work-arounds? When do you officially transition back to normal operations if you decide that the new server role or network configuration actually works better than the original? It might be a simple matter of formally evaluating the change, agreeing to make it permanent, and declaring you're now running under normal operating conditions. You and your team can define these triggers in advance and you may need to modify them later but at least you won't be working with a blank slate.

Maintenance/Review Phase

The maintenance phase has to occur whether or not you ever activate your BC/DR plan. On a periodic basis, you need to review your BC/DR plan to ensure that it is still current and relevant. As operations and technology components change, as you add or change facilities or locations, you'll need to make sure that your plan is still up to date. One common problem in BC/DR planning is that companies may expend time to develop a plan but they often do not want to (or will not) expend the time and resources necessary to keep the plan current. Old plans are dangerous because they provide a false sense of security and may lead to significant gaps in coverage. If a plan is not maintained, then all the time and money invested in creating the plan is wasted as well. In addition, if you end up activating your BC/DR plan at some point, you'll want to assess the effectiveness of the plan afterward, when things settle down. You should do this relatively close to the end of the recovery and business continuity cycles so that lessons learned can be captured and applied to your BC/DR plan before memories fade and people go back to their daily routines. Reviewing the plan in the immediate aftermath of a disruption will give you valuable insights into what did and did not work. Incorporating this knowledge into your plan will help you continue to hone the plan to meet your evolving business needs. This is discussed further in Chapter 36.

Defining BC/DR Teams and Key Personnel

There are numerous people in positions that are critical to the activation, implementation, and maintenance of your BC/DR plan. Although these may not all be relevant to your organization, this will serve as a good checkpoint to determine who should be included in your various phases. You'll also need to form teams to fulfill various needs before, during, and after a business disruption or disaster. Where possible, you should specify a particular position or role that meets the need rather than specifying individuals. If your Facilities Manager should participate in the Damage Assessment Team, for example, you should specify the Facilities Manager and not Phil, who happens to be the Facilities Manager now. That will allow your plan to remain relevant whether Phil wins the lottery and leaves the company, gets hit by a bus and is out for an extended period of time, or is promoted to vice president.

Though we briefly define types of teams and their roles in the BC/DR effort, you should take time to clearly define the roles and responsibilities of each team. Having clear boundaries will help ensure that teams are not working at cross-purposes and that all aspects of the plan are covered. Gaps and omissions occur when these kinds of definitions are ill-formed. If helpful, you can create team descriptions that read like job descriptions and you can task members of your HR department on the BC/DR team to assist with or lead this activity. A good team description will identify the following attributes:

- Positions or job functions included on the team (Facilities Manager, HR Director, etc.)
- Team leader and contact information
- Team mission statement or set of objectives
- Scope of responsibilities (define what *is* and *is not* part of this team's mission)
- Delineation of responsibilities in each phase of BC/DR (i.e., when will the team be activated and deactivated?)

- Escalation path and criteria
- Other data, as needed

Crisis Management Team

In most companies, the composition of crisis management team will mirror the organizational chart. It should have representatives from across the organization and should bring together members of the company who have the expertise and authority to deal with the after-effects of a major business disruption. The crisis management team (CMT) will decide upon the immediate course of action in most cases and when necessary, they can contact senior management. They will direct the distribution and use of resources (including personnel) and will monitor the effectiveness of recovery activities. They can adjust the course of action, as needed. They should be in charge of activating, implementing, managing, and monitoring the business continuity and disaster recovery plan and should delegate tasks as appropriate.

Management

Each company has a management team or structure that oversees the business and its operations. You'll need to determine which positions from your management team should be included in your plan. Remember to review all the phases. For example, you might decide that only a member of the management team can cause the BC/DR plan to be activated. Management might be required to decide when to transition from disaster recovery to business continuity activities or they might be the one(s) to decide how and when the BC/DR plan should be tested. Identify the positions that should participate as well as define how they should participate in each phase.

Damage Assessment Team

A damage assessment team should be comprised of people from several key areas of the company, including Facilities, IT, HR, and Operations. Your company's damage assessment team may contain other members, depending on how the company is structured and what type of business you're in. If you work in a small software development firm, you may just need the CEO, the IT manager, and the office manager to operate as the damage assessment team. In larger companies with multiple locations, you'll need to have several damage assessment teams or you may choose to create a mobile team that can fly to any site and assess damage within 24 hours of an incident. You may choose to have both a local and a mobile corporate team so that the right team can be called in. If the building floods, you may not need the mobile team to come in. However, if you have a large fire, earthquake, or other major event, you may need the support services of a mobile damage assessment team.

Operations Assessment Team

You may choose to have a separate operations assessment team comprised of individuals who can assess the immediate impact on operations. A damage assessment team may be tasked with this job, but in some types of companies, you may need a separate operations team that can assess what's going on with operations and how to proceed. The operations assessment team can also be tasked with beginning recovery phase activities, monitoring and triggering the transition from activation to recovery, recovery to business continuity, and BC to normal operations.

IT Team

Clearly, you need an IT team that can not only assess the damage to systems, but can begin the disaster recovery and business continuity tasks once the plan is activated. This IT team will work closely with the damage assessment team and/or the operations assessment team to determine the nature and extent of damage, especially to IT systems and the IT infrastructure. You may not need some of the technical specialties listed here, but this should be a good starter list for you to work from to determine exactly what expertise you'll need on your team.

- Operating system administration
- Systems software
- Server recovery (client server, Web server, application server, etc.)
- LAN/WAN recovery
- Database recovery
- Network operations recovery
- Application recovery
- Telecommunications
- Hardware salvage
- Alternate site recovery coordination
- Original site restoration/salvage coordination
- Test Team

Administrative Support Team

During a business disruption, there are a wide variety of administrative tasks that must be handled. Creating an administrative support team that can respond to the unique needs of the situation as well as provide administrative support for the company during the disruptions is important. This might include ordering emergency supplies, working with vendors arranging deliveries, tracking shipments, fielding phone calls from the media or investors, organizing paper documents used for stopgap measures, and more.

Transportation and Relocation Team

Depending on the specifics of your BC/DR plan and the type of company you work in, you may need to make transportation arrangements for critical business documents, records, or equipment. You may need to move equipment in advance of an event (like a hurricane or flood) or you may need to move equipment after the event to prevent further damage or vandalism. Relocating the company and its assets before or after a disruption requires a concerted effort by people who understand the company, its relocation needs, and transportation constraints.

Media Relations Team

You may recall that in Chapter 28, we mentioned the need to create a crisis communication plan because you will need to provide information about the business disruption/disaster to employees, vendors, the community, the media, and investors. One key area that should be well-prepped is media relations. Unlike other stakeholders mentioned, the media makes its living selling interesting stories. Since a disruption at your business may qualify as news, you might as well craft the message rather than leaving it to outsiders. Creating a team that knows how to handle the media in a positive manner and that understands the policies and procedures related to talking with the media is vital to help ensure your company's image and reputation are maintained to the greatest extent possible. Certainly, if your company is at fault, you will have to deal with a different set of questions than if your company experiences a natural disaster. Still, you'll need to manage the story either way.

Human Resources Team

The aftermath of a crisis is an incredibly stressful time for all employees. Having an HR team in place to begin handling employee issues is crucial to the well-being of the employees and the long-term health of the company. Retaining key employees, adequately addressing employee concerns, facilitating insurance and medical coverage, and addressing pay and payroll issues are part of this team's mission. This team may also be responsible for activating parts of the BC/DR team as it relates to hiring contract labor, temporary workers, or staff at alternate locations.

Legal Affairs Team

Whether your legal experts are internal or external to your company, you should identify who needs to address legal concerns in the aftermath of a business disruption or emergency. If you hire outside counsel to assist you with legal matters, you should still assign an internal resource as the liaison so that legal matters will be properly routed through the company. If you operate in a heavily regulated industry such as banking, finance, or health care, you should be well aware of the constraints you face, but having a legal affairs team can assist in making decisions that keep your company's operations within the bounds of laws and regulations. Even if you're not in a heavily regulated industry, you may need advice and assistance in understanding laws and regulations in your recovery efforts.

Physical/Personnel Security Team

In the aftermath of a serious business disruption, you will need a team of people who address the physical safety of people and the building. These might be designated Human Resource representatives, people from your facilities group, or both. If you work in a large company or in a large facility, you may have a separate security department or function that manages the physical and personnel security for the building. If this is the case, designated members of their team should be assigned to be part of the BC/DR team. If you don't have a formal security staff, be sure that the members of this ad hoc team receive training. Someone from HR or facilities might be willing to take on the role of security in the aftermath of a disaster, but they need to be trained as to the safest, most effective method of managing the situation. Training for part-time or ad hoc security teams is crucial because if a natural disaster strikes, emergency personnel such as your fire or police department will focus on helping schools, day care centers, nursing homes, and hospitals first. Your company may fall very low on the list of priorities, so having trained staff that can fill the gap in an emergency may literally mean the difference between life and death. We'll discuss training later in the book, but keep this in mind as you develop your teams.

Procurement Team (Equipment and Supplies)

Every company has some process in place for procuring equipment and supplies. In small companies, this might fall to the office manager or operations manager. In larger companies, there's usually a purchasing department that handles this function. Regardless of how your company is organized, you need to determine, in advance, how equipment and supplies will be purchased, tracked, and managed after a localized disaster such as a fire or in the aftermath of a widespread disaster such as a hurricane or earthquake. This includes who has the authority to make purchases and from whom, what dollar limit the authority carries, and how that person (or persons) can get authority to make larger purchases. For example, a company might specify that three people have the authority to purchase equipment and supplies up to $2,000 per order and up to $20,000 total. Beyond that, they have to have the president or vice president sign off on purchases. This predetermined purchasing information can also be communicated to key vendors so they know the three people who are authorized and what the authorization limits are. In this way, if disaster strikes, the company can turn to trusted vendors who, in turn, know the rules. This can expedite the recovery process.

Keep in mind that this team needs to be large enough that there is no "single point of failure." If you authorize only one person and something happens to that one person, you'll be scrambling to obtain emergency authorization for other individuals. Instead, authorize enough people to provide flexibility but not so many as to create chaos. Also, be sure your limits are appropriate to the type of business you run. If you may need to replace computers at $1500 a piece, make sure the limits reflect that. If a purchaser has a $1,000 limit per item, that will preclude him or her from making a simple purchase needed to get the company running again.

General Team Guidelines

Though we recommend populating teams first with needed skills based on *roles* and *positions* within the company, we also recognize that ultimately *people* are assigned to the team. People should be chosen to be on teams based on their skills, knowledge, and expertise, not because someone wants to be on a team or because someone's boss placed them on a team. In a perfect world, you could choose team members solely on competence, but we all know that in the real world, that's not always the case. Occasionally, you get the people who have the most time on their hands, who sometimes are the junior members of the team, or the least competent people in the department. You have to work within your organization's constraints and culture, but also strive to populate your teams with the right people with the right skills. Ideally, these are the same people who perform these functions under normal conditions. It doesn't make sense to have the database administrator take on media relations duties during an emergency, just as you don't want the marketing VP managing the restoration of the CRM database, if possible. Certainly, in small companies many people are called upon to perform a variety of tasks and if that's the case, the same will be true if the BC/DR plan has to be activated. The teams also should be large enough that if one or more members of the team are unable to perform their duties, the team can still function. If you have other personnel or other parts of the organization that can wholly take up the BC/DR activities, so much the better. If not, you may also choose to designate key contractors or vendors to assist as alternates in the event of a catastrophic event. These personnel should be coordinated and trained as alternates along with internal staff.

Looking Ahead

Specialty Vendors Help BC/DR Plans

There are numerous specialty vendors that can provide tremendous assistance to your firm in the event of a business disruption such as a fire or chemical spill. Although the numbers and types of firms in your area will vary, you should consider your specific needs in advance of any disruption and search for a firm that will meet your needs, even if that firm is located across the country. These firms provide a wide and unusual assortment of services, some of which are listed here:

- Chemical oxidation
- CO_2 blasting
- Condensation drying
- Contact cleaning
- Corrosion removal
- Damp blasting
- Degreasing
- Deodorizing
- Fogging for odor removal or disinfection
- Manual hand wiping
- High pressure and ultra-high pressure jetting
- High temperature steam jetting
- Hot air drying
- Low pressure jetting
- Microwave drying
- Ozone technology
- Sanitation

- Steam blasting
- Vacuum drying
- Water displacement

As you can see, this is quite a list and it's not exhaustive. Be sure to think through the various scenarios that apply to your firm and determine which specialty services might best be outsourced to a qualified third party. You'll save yourself time and money in the long run and you'll likely get up and running much more quickly with targeted, competent help than if you try to do everything on your own.

BC/DR Contact Information

After you've developed the requirements for your teams in terms of the specific skills, knowledge, and expertise needed, you'll identify the specific people to fill those roles. Part of plan maintenance, discussed later in this book, involves ensuring that the key positions are still in the BC/DR loop and that key personnel are still aware of their BC/DR responsibilities.

Another mundane but crucial task in your planning work is to compile key contact information. Since computer systems often are impacted by various types of business disruptions—from network security breaches to floods and fires—you'll need to have contact information stored and available in electronic and hard copy. It should be readily available at alternate locations and copies should be stored in off-site locations that can be accessed if the building is not accessible. However, since this list contains contact information, it should also be treated as confidential or sensitive information and should be handled and secured as such. This information should include contact information for key personnel from the executives of the company (who will need to be notified of a business disruption) to BC/DR team members to key suppliers, contractors, and customers, among others.

Develop a list of the types of contact information you need, including:

- Management
- Key operations staff
- BC/DR team members
- Key suppliers, vendors, contractors (especially those with whom you have BC/DR contracts)
- Key customers
- Emergency numbers (fire, police, etc.)
- Media representatives or PR firm (if appropriate)
- Other

After you've identified the contact information you want to include, you'll need to determine where and how this information currently is maintained. In most companies, this information is stored in a multitude of locations and is not easily compiled with a few clicks of the mouse. You may need to develop a process for maintaining an up-to-date list, both electronically and on paper, of these key contacts. For example, many of your key contacts may be in a contact management application made available to everyone in the company. However, information such as executives' cell phone numbers and home phone numbers may not be included in this companywide contact database, for obvious reasons (especially if you work in a medium to large company). Therefore, you'll need to have a copy of the contact information plus information not included there. Developing a process for gathering and maintaining that data is an important part of BC/DR readiness. If a serious business disruption occurs in the middle of the night—for example, the building catches on fire—who will you contact? How will you know who to contact? Where will you find the key phone numbers you need if you can't get back into the building and you can't access computer systems? Since notification is one of the first steps in activating your BC/DR plan, you'll need to have key phone numbers available (*you* meaning the person(s) responsible for activating the plan). Develop a process for this during your BC/DR planning project and make sure that your maintenance plan includes regularly updating this information.

In addition to developing and maintaining a contact list, you should also define a contact tree. This defines who is responsible for contacting other teams, members of the company, or the management team. That way, each team member is tasked with specific calls to specific people and the notification process is streamlined.

Common Challenges

Maintaining Up-to-Date Contacts

Maintaining up-to-date contact information can be a challenge, especially since that information seems to change so frequently. If you work in a small company, you may task your office manager or other administrative support staff with maintaining this list and preparing an updated list once per month or once per quarter, storing it in designated locations and distributing it to key personnel. In larger companies, this task becomes a bit more difficult as contact information typically becomes fragmented—the contacts needed by the marketing group are not the same contacts needed by the IT group. Therefore, you may choose to have departmental responsibility for maintaining key contacts relevant to that business function. If you choose that route, be sure you still have someone with high-level BC/DR responsibility who oversees the maintenance of BC/DR contact information, which in this example would include the departmental representatives who have the contact information for their units. The master BC/DR contact list should be maintained by someone on the BC/DR team and should include, at minimum, contact information for key executives, department heads, regional managers (other locations), and key BC/DR vendors, contractors, and suppliers. Regardless of the method you choose for managing your contact information, be sure that it includes a process for regularly updating it. Also update the contact tree once the contact list is revised.

Defining Tasks, Assigning Resources

The tasks and resources that need to be assigned have to do both with implementing the mitigation strategies you've defined as well as fleshing out the rest of the plan. First, you have to ensure your risk mitigation strategies will be properly implemented. This may mean creating project plans to address any new initiatives you need to undertake in order to meet your risk mitigation requirements. We'll assume you've got that covered as part of your risk mitigation strategy. If not, now's the time to develop your work breakdown structure, tasks, resources, and timelines for completing any risk mitigation strategies that need to be completed in advance of a disruption. This might include purchasing and installing new uninterruptible power supplies for key servers, updating your fire suppression systems, or implementing a data vaulting solution. Other mitigation strategies such as arranging for an alternate site need to be completed in advance, but activating it requires a different set of tasks that occur later. Finally, strategies that include accepting risk mean there probably are no additional tasks at this time.

Other tasks have to do with defining your BC/DR teams, roles, and responsibilities; defining plan phase transition triggers; and gathering additional data. Let's start with tasks related to some major activities including alternate sites and contracting for outside BC/DR services. Clearly, there are other tasks and resources you'll need, but this should get you started in developing your own list of tasks, budgets, timelines, dependencies, and constraints for the remaining BC/DR activities in your plan.

As you develop these tasks, keep in mind standard project management processes:

1. Identify high-level tasks, use verb/noun format when possible (i.e., "test security settings" rather than "security settings").
2. Break large tasks into smaller tasks until the work unit is manageable.
3. Define duration or deadlines.
4. Identify milestones.
5. Assign task owners.
6. Define task resources and other task requirements.
7. Identify technical and functional requirements for task, if any.
8. Define completion criteria for each task.
9. Identify internal and external dependencies.

We're not going to go through all that detail for these next two high-level tasks, but you should include this level of detail in your plan.

Alternate Site

Although this should be part of your BC/DR plan, it's worth calling it out separately due to its importance and the need for advance work. If part of your risk mitigation strategy is to develop an alternative site or off-site storage solution, you should develop a number of details before moving forward. These should be tasks (or subtasks) within the WBS just discussed, so let's look at some of the details you might include. Also keep in mind that you need to develop a trigger that helps you determine if or when you fire up the alternate site. You probably don't want to activate the alternate site if you have a minor or even an intermediate disruption, so how do you define when you should? When all systems are down or when some percentage of systems are down? You have to take your MTD into consideration along with other factors such as the cost of firing up the alternate site and the cost of downtime. If your downtime is estimated to be 12 days and that cost is $500,000 but the cost of firing up the alternate site is three days and $250,000, is it worth it to activate the alternate or should you just hobble along until you can restore systems at the current location? There's no right or wrong answer, it's going to depend on your company's MTD, potential revenue losses, cost of starting up the alternate site, and so on. Have the financial folks on your BC/DR team prepare some analyses to determine metrics you can use to help determine your trigger point. As you're going through the activities listed in this section, keep these factors in mind.

Selection Criteria

Selection criteria are the factors you develop to help you determine how to select the best alternate site solution for your company. This includes cost, technical and functional requirements, timelines, quality, availability, location, and more. Be sure to consider connectivity and communications requirements in this section along with your recovery requirements such as maximum tolerable downtime.

Contractual Terms

Determine what contractual arrangements are appropriate for your company. Many vendors have predetermined service offerings and contracts are fairly standard. Other companies can accommodate a wider range of options and will work with you to develop appropriate contractual language. In either case, be sure to run these contracts past your financial staff and your legal counsel to make sure you are fully aware of the financial and legal consequences of these contracts in advance of signing them. If you're not clear what they mean operationally, be sure to talk with the vendor and add clarifying language to the contract. Do not simply take the vendor's word that a particular paragraph or section means something. Verbal agreements are always superseded by written contracts, so make sure the contract spells it out clearly. You don't want to rely on verbal commitments made by employees no longer with the company when it comes to implementing your BC/DR solutions, so be sure to put everything in writing in advance.

Comparison Process

Be sure to specify what process you'll use to select the vendor. This might include a list of technical requirements the vendor must meet, but it might also include an assessment of the vendor's geographical location, financial history, and stability and industry expertise, among other things. Selecting the right vendor for an alternate site or off-site storage is a very important aspect to your BC/DR success and should be undertaken with the same rigor as your other planning activities.

Acquisition and Testing

Once you've selected your alternate site or off-site storage vendor and completed the contract, you will need to make whatever additional arrangements are needed for developing this solution so that it is fully ready in the timeframe you've designated. This might include purchasing additional hardware and software, setting up communications channels, and testing all solutions implemented. Create a thorough acquisition and testing plan for this phase so you can transition to it as seamlessly as possible in the event of a business disruption. During your testing phase of the BC/DR plan, you should test the process for firing up this solution on a periodic basis.

Contracts for BC/DR Services

Although we highly recommend you involve your purchasing, finance, and/or legal professionals in executing your BC/DR contracts, you should also have a general understanding of some of the elements to consider. As with alternate site considerations, keep your MTD, your costs, and potential losses in mind. Have your financial folks help you with performing financial analyses to determine what makes financial and business sense for your company. If a firm wants to charge you $50,000 for some sort of contract but your downtime estimate with associated revenue and collateral loss is only $40,000, the contract might not be worth entering. Additionally, determine your triggers for calling upon these contractual arrangements so you don't prematurely fire up these contracts or avoid using them during times when they should be activated.

Develop Clear Functional and Technical Requirements

You know from project management fundamentals that developing functional and technical requirements is often what defines the difference between success and failure. The same is true here. If you have not clearly and fully defined your functional and technical requirements, you'll get all kinds of vendor responses. The more specific you are, the more fully a vendor can address your needs. In addition, if you leave too many elements open to discussion, you'll endlessly discuss possibilities without being able to identify appropriate solutions. Have these discussions in advance, then come to a firm agreement about the requirements. If some requirements appear to be optional or "nice to have," then list them as options and not as requirements. Pare down your requirements to the elements you absolutely must have. Remember, the more options you include, the higher the cost is likely to be. Therefore, if cost is an issue (and it almost always is an issue), be sure to list what you require and what you desire as separate items. When this information has been finalized, write up formal requirements documents that you can provide to potential vendors. Also, be sure that your requirements documents are reviewed by subject matter experts, including IT experts and those in your company who understand regulatory, legal, and compliance issues. Your requirements should meet all these needs before going out to the vendors.

Determine Required Service Levels

Service levels are typically part of technical requirements, but we've listed them separately because they are vitally important when developing Requests for Proposal (RFP) or Requests for Quote (RFQ) from vendors. You may have contractual obligations to provide certain levels of service to your customers, so you may need to specify requirements for your vendors that meet or exceed these metrics. Even if you have no externally facing service level agreements (SLA), you should still specify SLAs in your contracts with vendors. If you're contracting for Internet connectivity, you should specify bandwidth, minimum upload and download speeds, and maximum downtime per specified period, for example. These may sound like technical requirements, but let's look at how this can play out in a contract. You write up your requirements, which include bandwidth, minimum upload/download speeds, and maximum downtime. Three vendors respond to your RFQ to provide backup Internet connectivity to your company in the event of an outage from your main vendor or in the event that your company's facilities are damaged. All three companies give you quotes that indicate they can meet or exceed those three requirements (bandwidth, speed, availability). However, those are not contractual terms, those are the company saying they *can* meet or exceed those metrics. If it's not in the contract, it's just a statement of capabilities, not a commitment. A service level agreement will specify minimum bandwidth availability during a 24-hour period, 7 days a week. It would state that you will have access to [insert bandwidth metric] 24 hours a day, seven days a week until [insert termination metric or trigger]. This way, the vendor can't provide you the bandwidth you requested only from 11 P.M. to 6 A.M. on Saturdays and Sundays and short you the rest of the time. Granted, most vendors are on the level and want to provide the services to you they've agreed upon, but that's why contracts exist—to clearly define who does what, when, and at what cost. This keeps the guess work (and the finger pointing) to a minimum.

Compare Vendor Proposal/Response to Requirements

Once you receive vendor responses to your proposals, you should evaluate how closely each vendor comes to meeting the requirements of your plan. Any vendor that does not meet the requirements should not be considered further. There may be two exceptions to this. First, if your requirements are unique enough that no single vendor can meet your needs, you may have to circle back and find two or more vendors who can work together to meet your unique requirements. Second, you may discover from vendor responses that your requirements were too broad, inclusive, or vague, and that none of the vendors' responses meet your requirements exactly. In that case you may have to refine your requirements and go back out for bid. Assuming your requirements are well written, your next step is to eliminate vendors that cannot meet your needs and focus only on those vendors who addressed your requirements fully in their responses.

Identify Requirements Not Met by Vendor Proposal

If there are one or more requirements not met by any vendor, you may need to find two or more vendors to work together to provide the full range of services you need. If none of the vendors met a particular requirement, you may also choose to review that requirement and reassess it in light of vendor responses. Remember, you contract with vendors in order to leverage their specific expertise. If none of them meet a particular requirement, you may wish to talk with several of your short-list selections to find out why they did not address that aspect. It might be redundant or otherwise unneeded. In that case, you should revise your requirements to reflect this new information.

Identify Vendor Options Not Specified in Requirements

Vendors also may offer additional options not specified in your requirements. Again, based on the vendor's expertise, they may offer additional choices that can round out your requirements or plan.

Utilizing their expertise can be a good way of ensuring you have the best solution in place. For example, the vendor might say (in essence), "Everyone who's asked for A, B, and C also has found that D was an extremely important option they'd overlooked. Perhaps you'd like to add D to your plan as well." They may be sharing industry expertise and best practices with you, or they may simply be trying to up-sell you. You'll have to look carefully at these options and perhaps do some independent research to determine whether these options are "must have," "nice to have," or "useless add-ons." If you have an established relationship with these vendors, they'll more than likely offer you additional options but won't put pressure on you to upgrade unless they feel it's vital to your success. However, we all know there are sales people that will try to sell you every option they can think of just to make a bigger sale, so you have to be an active participant in the transaction. Know your options, know what makes sense, do some additional research, and determine if any of the additional options would enhance your plan or fill in gaps you didn't realize existed. Don't be forced into upgrades and options you don't really need just because you have a very persuasive sales person in front of you.

From the Trenches...

Managing the Sales Process

Sometimes your purchasing department manages the purchase of goods and services, but when you're talking about the purchase of backup, storage, or alternate site services for your BC/DR plan, there's a good chance you will be directly involved. If you haven't been involved with the sales process in the past, you might find yourself being swayed by excellent sales people—the ones who can convince you that you need something you really don't. Most sales people are honest and are trying to balance their need to sell with your need for the product or service they're selling. They also realize that loyal customers are borne out of an honest sales experience, not out of strong-arming someone into purchasing more than they need. In order to be successful in the process, take time to be clear about *your* objectives *before* a sales meeting. If you intend on making a purchasing decision at that time, write down the terms or parameters you will accept. Keep these to yourself but know that this is your bottom line. If the sales person cannot or will not meet your bottom line objectives, there is no deal to be struck.

The same holds true in any negotiation—know what your bottom line is and work toward meeting (or exceeding) that bottom line. If you have developed clear requirements and you know your bottom line, you should be able to successfully navigate the sometimes tricky sales process. Negotiation skills can help you in all aspects of life and they'll certainly help you in the business world. If you're interested in learning more about the art of negotiation, there are thousands of helpful books, courses, and seminars you can turn to for more information.

Communications Plans

Earlier in this section, we discussed the need for various communications plans. In this section, we'll define various communications plans you should develop and identify some of the common elements in such a plan. If you already have communications plans in place, you can use this section as a checkpoint to ensure you've got all your bases covered. For each plan, you should define specific steps just as you would for any other process in your BC/DR plan. You should define the following:

- Name of communication team, members of team, team lead, or chain of command
- Responsibilities and deliverables for this team
- The boundaries of responsibilities (what they *should* and *should not* do)
- Timing and coordination of communication messages (dependencies, triggers)
- Escalation path
- Other information, as appropriate

Communications plans can be assigned to other, existing teams. A good example of this is that the employee communication plan may be the responsibility of the HR team. There's no need to create additional teams to execute communications plans if these activities fall within the scope of defined teams. However, in some companies, it might make sense to have most of the communications come from one dedicated communications team in order to maintain control over communications and to ensure that a single, consistent message is delivered to all stakeholders. The decision is yours and usually is based on how large the company is and how it currently operates.

Internal

The internal communication plan is really part of the BC/DR activation and implementation plan. If a business disruption occurs, you need to have a process in place for notifying BC/DR team members. This is done as part of BC/DR plan activation and is a critical aspect that should be clearly delineated. How will team members be notified and updated? What processes, tools, and technology are needed? Are these included in your plan yet? If not, add them to your WBS or in a section called Additional Resources so they are captured and addressed in advance of a business disruption.

Employee

Employee communication is also internal communication but differs because it is any communication that goes out to employees who are not part of the BC/DR implementation. If a business disruption occurs, you'll need to know how to notify all employees. You'll also need to let them know answers to the most basic questions including what happened, what is being done to address the problem, and who they should go to for more information. For example, if the building burns down overnight, employees may show up for work in the morning as scheduled. The BC/DR team may already be in action but the general employee population needs information. How this information is communicated and by whom should be identified. It often makes sense to develop an information tree so that key communicators know to whom they should go for updates and official information. For example, in a small company, you may designate the HR manager as the person who will communicate with employees on all BC/DR matters. The HR manager should know who to go to for information on the status of the BC/DR activities. This might be the Facilities manager or the BC/DR team leaders (who should be identified in the activation plans, discussed earlier in this chapter).

Customers and Vendors

Customers and vendors typically require different types of communications but the information is often similar. They may need to be notified of the business disruption, the basic steps being take to rectify the problem, the estimated time to recovery and any work-arounds needed in the meantime. If you are developing crisis communications plans for the first time, be sure to read the case study that follows this chapter, entitled "Crisis Communications 101," for more information on how to communicate in a crisis.

Shareholders

If you have shareholders of any kind (debt or equity investors, shareholders, etc.) you must communicate the nature and extent of the disruption. In most cases, they are concerned with the ongoing viability of the company and possibly the short-term financial impact of the disruption on the company. Therefore, communication with this group requires that specific issues be addressed. As you can tell, these issues are very different than, say, employee issues, so someone well-versed in investor relations should be charged with this communication. In most companies, this task falls to the CEO or a high-ranking corporate officer who can specifically address the concerns of those who have a financial stake in the company.

The Community and the Public

In addition to communicating with all the other stakeholders we've mentioned, you also will need to communicate with the general public. Local newspapers, TV, and radio stations will certainly take an interest in a localized business disaster such as a fire or flood. National and international media may also take interest if the event is unique in some way or is part of a widespread disaster. Members of the local community may also have more than just vicarious interest—they may need to understand the impact your business disruption may have on them. Businesses in communities don't exist in isolation, and what happens to one business may have a ripple effect on other businesses even if those other businesses are not customers or suppliers.

Communicating with the media is a tricky proposition and many executives at large firms go through extensive media training sessions in order to learn how to deal with the media. Although an extensive discussion of this topic is outside the scope of this book, you will learn the basics by reading the case study that follows this chapter. Additional media relations training resources are readily available online and there are hundreds of excellent books on the topic as well. As the leader of the BC/DR project plan, you may or may not be called upon to communicate with the media, but being prepared is always a good idea.

This plan should be well thought-out and you may wish to seek legal counsel with regard to what must be disclosed, to whom, and in what time frame. As you learned in the case study presented earlier in this book ("Legal Obligations Regarding Data Security" by Deanna Conn), there are numerous legal requirements regarding notification and remediation that must be met in certain circumstances. To ensure you comply with regulations and laws in your industry, be sure to seek appropriate input from subject matter experts as you craft your shareholder communication plan.

TIP

Many public relations firms specialize in crisis communications. You can work with this type of firm in advance to develop appropriate communications plans. You can also contract with these kinds of firms to assist with communications in the aftermath of a major event. In most cases, they can advise you on the best course of action, potential communications pitfalls, and provide guidance regarding certain legal issues. You may also need to get a legal opinion in certain matters, especially if death or injury occurred on your company's premises or as a result of company action. The PR firm you work with can help you understand how to communicate effectively and when to seek additional input before, during, and after your business disruption.

Event Logs, Change Control, and Appendices

In traditional IT, event logs track a variety of system and network activities. In a broader sense, you may choose to create a BC/DR event log for tracking various events and milestones. For example, your decision to activate your BC/DR plan may be based on two or three event types occurring, either simultaneously, in quick succession, or within a specified time period. These events may trigger the activation of the BC/DR plan itself, or they may signal the point in time when it's appropriate to move to the next stage in your plan. Having a chronological log of events can help clarify circumstances so appropriate decisions can be made in a timely manner.

Event Logs

As an IT professional, you're probably well versed in reviewing event logs as they pertain to systems and security events. However, in BC/DR, event logs are not necessarily logged by a computer system. In many cases, event logs are hard copies developed sequentially over time by making notes on what happens when. Event logs help you track events, in order, over time, and can help in identifying appropriate triggers for key activities.

Keep in mind that these logs establish who knew what and when, so they may become legal documents at some point in the future. You have to balance the need for timely information with the potential for litigation As unfortunate as it may be, sometimes too much documentation leaves the company open to lawsuits, even when the company has acted as best it could given the circumstances. We don't suggest you do anything illegal or unethical—quite the opposite—but you may want to talk with your legal counsel to understand what can and cannot become evidence in the event there is a lawsuit that stems from some sort of business disruption. If something can become a legal document or be used as evidence in some manner, you should be aware of that going in. Your legal counsel may have recommendations about how to record data to minimize the possibility of litigation while maintaining accurate, useful logs.

In the absence of specific legal advice on how to develop logs, the best general advice is to record only the relevant information and stick to the actual facts, not conjecture. Instead of "Barnett seemed confused by the request to review the equipment," you might simply say, "Barnett was contacted regarding reviewing the equipment at 11 P.M., 2/22/07" or "Barnett had numerous questions regarding the request to review equipment. Issue escalated to Barnett's boss, Martina." All these statements are true but the first statement contains conjecture—was Barnett confused or did you just assume he was because of the look on his face? If you state in your log that Barnett was confused, this might be the basis of a lawsuit claiming that appropriate action was not taken in a timely manner. Stating only the facts keeps everything moving forward and does not unnecessarily open the door to legal problems down the road.

On the other side of the legal coin, there may be legal or regulatory requirements to log certain events or make notifications within a certain timeline. Event logs can help you operate within these legal requirements as well. If you operate under these constraints, be sure to include these requirements in your BC/DR plan, perhaps with hard copy templates of the event logs, so that your team knows clearly what the logging or notification requirements are in the stressful aftermath of a business disruption.

Change Control

Change control is a necessary element in any project and BC/DR planning is no exception. There are two types of change control you'll need to develop. First, you need to devise a method of updating your BC/DR plan when change occurs in the organization that impacts your plan. Second, you need a method of monitoring changes to the BC/DR plan to ensure they don't inject additional uncertainty or risk into your plan. Let's look at both of these scenarios briefly.

As companies grow and expand, numerous changes occur to the organization's infrastructure. This can include departmental reorganization, the creation of new departments, the expansion to additional facilities, and more. It also comes with changes to the IT infrastructure including the location and duties of servers, the implementation of new applications and technologies, and the reorganization of existing infrastructure components. All these kinds of changes impact the existing BC/DR plan. These elements should be addressed in the plan maintenance activities. You can't control the change that occurs in the organization, but you can put in place a system for assessing change and how it impacts your BC/DR plan. In most cases, this occurs during the periodic review of the plan.

A subset of change control is version control. Be sure to include a process for managing revision history for your BC/DR plan. Many people choose to simply put a small table at the beginning of the document outlining the changes in chronological order. Table 33.1 shows an example of a revision history table that might be used in your BC/DR plan.

Table 33.1 Revision History Table

Revision Number	Revision Date	Detail
1.0	02.22.07	Finalize first version of BC/DR plan
1.1	03.20.07	Modify network diagrams in Section 4.2
2.0	06.05.07	Revise plan to include acquisition of ABC Co.
2.1	11.05.07	Include new specifications and contract for alternate site.

You can define what constitutes a major and minor revision. Typically, going from 1.0 or 1.1 to 2.0 is considered a major revision (when the number to the left of the decimal point increases); going from 1.0 to 1.1 or 2.11 to 2.2 is considered a minor revision (when the number(s) to the right of the decimal point increase). Clearly, the numbering scheme is not quite as important as keeping track of revisions, unless you work in a company that has a very formal system for revision control in place. A quick note in the Detail section can help clue you in to the changes in the revision. Some people also like to document more extensive information about the changes and this can be done in the beginning of the document. For example, you could create paragraphs labeled, "Changes in Revision 1.1," and note the key changes made to the document. This helps you see at a glance how the plan has changed without reading the entire document. There are numerous systems for managing revisions and you should select one that is consistent with the way your company operates. Don't make it into a huge production or it may be circumvented, but do use some system for tracking changes so you don't have to compare two documents side by side to figure out what changed between revisions.

Distribution

Although the plan is not yet complete, you should devise a strategy here for distributing and storing the final BC/DR plan. The revision history will help you and the team with version control, but you will still need a method of distributing the latest revision or notifying the team that a new version exists. In some cases, the plan may be stored in a software program that performs version control and revision notification. In that case, you're pretty well set other than adding team members to the notification list. If you're not using such a program, you can still maintain the plan on a shared, secured network location and provide team members or team leads with access to the folder. Keep in mind that this document is a very sensitive document and all precautions should be taken to ensure it does not fall into the wrong hands, is not leaked to competitors or to the media, or otherwise compromised. Use standard security and encryption where this document is concerned. Distribute the document in soft copy via e-mail only as needed. If possible, simply e-mail a notification that a new version is available while maintaining the document in the secure location. Remind people that the document is sensitive and should not be copied, distributed, or otherwise handed out. The document should only be distributed to those who have a defined need to know.

Finally, be sure you create a process or method for *printing* the updated plan so you have a hard copy version available if systems go down. The BC/DR team lead or leads should all have a paper copy in a secure location, both on-site and off-site. When new versions are available, old versions should be shredded or destroyed in a secure manner.

Appendices

Any information relevant to your plan that does not belong in the body of the plan should be attached or referenced as an appendix. There are no strict rules about what should or should not be included in the appendices, but it's usually detail required for successful implementation of the plan that may pertain to only one group or subset of BC/DR teams. For example, you might include the technical specifications of mission critical servers in an appendix. As servers are moved, updated, or decommissioned, you can easily update the related appendix without modifying the plan itself.

Contracts with external vendors should be kept as appendix items so that they are located in one central place for reference. Your finance and/or legal departments may want to retain originals of these contracts, which is fine, but be sure to include copies in your BC/DR plan. If you have to activate your plan, you don't want to have to run around looking for someone from finance or legal to determine how and when you can activate your external contracts.

Templates for event logs, communications, and other predefined processes can be included. In event log templates, be sure to include time, date, event, notification requirements, legal, or compliance issues and other requirements so they're easily accessible in the event of a business disruption or disaster.

Key contact information should be included in the plan, but you may choose to include it as an appendix, especially if it changes frequently. If you choose to do this, you should include key contacts within the body of the plan and use the appendix for additional contact information, as appropriate. The reason for including the key contact information within the body of the plan is twofold. First, key contacts are integral to the successful activation and implementation of the plan. As such, that information should be incorporated into the body of the plan. Second, if that information changes, it should trigger a BC/DR plan revision. Key personnel need to be trained, they need to understand their roles individually and as part of the BC/DR team, and they need to be given the tools, resources, contacts, and information needed to do so successfully. If a key member of the BC/DR team leaves, for any reason, the person replacing them needs to be brought up to speed. This should trigger a quick review of the plan. If the successor has been assigned by virtue of position (the Facilities manager resigns and a replacement is hired), the replacement needs to be trained in all aspects of their duties with regard to the BC/DR plan. If the successor is not assigned and needs to be found, looking through the roles and responsibilities of this position can help you select the right person to fill the gap.

Any other information that is related to the plan that needs to be updated, maintained, and correlated to the BC/DR plan itself should be included as an appendix. Don't throw everything you can think of into an appendix and think you're covered. More is not necessarily better in this case, but do be sure to include key information you'd want to have quick access to in the event of a natural disaster or other significant business disruption. To give you a few ideas about what else might be attached to your plan in an appendix, we've provided the following list. Not all of these elements are needed by every company, but you can pick and choose based on your unique situation.

- Critical work space equipment and resource information and related vendor data
- Critical IT hardware, software, equipment and configuration information, and related vendor data

- Critical manufacturing, production and warehousing information and related vendor data

- Critical data and vital records information, including storage and retrieval information

- Alternate IT or work site information

- Crisis management center resources and information

- Insurance information including all relevant policies, policy numbers, and insurance contact information

- Service level agreements (that you must provide to customers or that vendors must provide to you)

- Standards, guidelines, policies, and procedures

- Contracts related to BC/DR

- Forms

- BC/DR Plan distribution list

- Glossary

Every company and every BC/DR plan is different, so there is no hard-and-fast rule about where information belongs, as long as critical data is included in a logical manner. If writing a plan or organizing data is not your strong suit, be sure to recruit assistance to draft a plan that makes sense. It should follow a logical progression and match the way your company does business to the greatest extent possible.

Additional Resources

What other resources do you need to successfully implement and maintain your plan? In the next chapter, we'll discuss emergency and business recovery plans, so some of this may come up in that context. However, if there are communication tools, equipment, or resources you think of as you develop your plan, they should be noted in a section called Additional Resources (or other similar heading) and they should be added to your WBS to ensure someone takes ownership of gathering these needed resources.

What's Next

When you complete the work in this chapter, you should have a fairly robust BC/DR plan in the works. It will have gaps related to specific emergency and disaster recovery efforts (see Chapter 34), and in training, testing, auditing, and maintaining the plan (see Chapters 35 and 36), but other than that it should be well on its way to completion. If not, step back and review your data, your plan, and your company to determine what is missing and how you can address those gaps.

Summary

Putting your business continuity and disaster recovery plan together requires pulling together the data previously developed and adding a bit more detail. Understanding the phases of the BC/DR plan helps you develop strategies for managing activities if you have to implement your plan. The typical phases are activation, disaster recovery, business continuity, and resumption of normal activities. The plan must also be tested and maintained, regardless of whether it's ever implemented.

Potential disruptions need to be categorized and we discussed three levels: major, intermediate, and minor. By clearly defining these for your organization, you can ensure you understand what recovery steps should be implemented. This will define how and when you activate your BC/DR plan. After the plan is activated, a trigger should define when disaster recovery tasks begin. These recovery tasks should be well defined in your BC/DR plan and we'll cover these in detail in the next chapter. The transition from disaster recovery to business continuity should also be well defined so that you can begin to resume business activities, though things will not be back to business as usual at this juncture. This is also discussed in detail in the next chapter.

Developing your BC/DR teams is a vital part of your planning. There are numerous roles and responsibilities in each phase of your BC/DR work and defining these and populating your teams in advance is crucial to your success if the plan is ever activated. In addition, these teams will need to be trained in implementing the BC/DR activities.

After you've created your teams, you can further develop your planning tasks and assign resources, timelines, and budgets. You can identify task dependencies, develop milestones, and create completion criteria for key tasks. Since each company's set of tasks will vary widely, we presented only a sampling of high-level tasks related to acquiring an alternate computing site and contracting with vendors.

Communications plans are part of the BC/DR process because if a business disruption occurs, many different groups of people will need status updates and information. This includes employees, management, shareholders, vendors, customers, and the community, among others. You'll need to decide who needs to know what and when they'll need to know it. Then, you'll need to develop distribution methods appropriate to those groups (and to the circumstances of the disruption).

Event logs can help you manage the business disruption from start to finish, but remember that these may become legal documents later on. You may wish to consult with your legal counsel regarding what should and should not be included in the event logs. For example, it's generally considered fine to include facts but not conjecture or opinion. Sticking to the facts helps keep the log clear and concise and can avoid misinterpretation of data. In addition, there may be legal or regulatory requirements for event logging or notification, so be sure to include this in your process and make a note of it in any log files you develop (whether soft or hard copy).

Keeping track of document revisions is a bit of a "housekeeping" task but an important one when it comes to your BC/DR plan. Use a simple, concise method of ensuring that the plan is updated and that everyone has the latest plan. Develop a method for distribution and storage of the plan so that it's accessible to key personnel in the event of a disruption. Finally, include additional data such as technical requirements, service level agreements, and vendor contracts as appendices to the main BC/DR plan. Keeping all relevant data with the plan can make plan implementation and maintenance much easier.

## Chapter 34

Emergency Response and Recovery

Solutions in this chapter:

- **Emergency Management Overview**
- **Emergency Response Plans**
- **Crisis Management Team**
- **Disaster Recovery**
- **IT Recovery Tasks**
- **Business Continuity**

☑ **Summary**

Introduction

The most basic rule about planning for emergencies is this: Keep it simple. The more complicated your emergency response plans are, the less likely they will be effective in a real emergency. It's sometimes easy to overengineer a plan in the relative calm of everyday business activities. When an emergency strikes, people are not likely to remember a lot of rules, procedures, and details. As you read in the preceding case study, "Crisis Communications 101," there are three basic rules to remember. It's pretty easy to remember three rules. So, when you create your emergency response and disaster recovery activities, you should strive to keep things simple. Once the emergency has subsided, you can begin to put more complex plans into place to begin restoring business operations.

We're not going to go into tremendous detail on emergency response, but we will provide a few pointers. If you want to create a detailed emergency response plan, you can work with local emergency responders who will be best able to provide details relevant to your community, its resources, and its geography. We'll also discuss computer incident response, disaster response, IT recovery, and business continuity.

In addition, we've provided several detailed checklists for emergency and disaster response and recovery in the final chapters of this section that you can use to develop your own detailed checklists.

Emergency Management Overview

Regardless of how your company is organized, managed, and run, your emergency management process should follow a very simple rule: assign clear roles. If no one knows who's in charge or who has the authority to make decisions, nothing gets done. On the other hand, if everyone believes they have the authority to make decisions, chaos will reign. The aftermath of Hurricane Katrina is testament to this problem—everyone assumed some other organization was in charge, no one knew to whom to turn for solutions. The Federal Emergency Management Agency (FEMA) was assumed to be in charge but was clearly late in gaining control of the situation. As a result, thousands of people were without food, water, ice, and shelter for an extended period of time. The lesson from this catastrophe that companies can learn is this: someone has to be clearly in charge and take immediate and effective action.

Throughout earlier chapters in this section, we've referred to the fact that emergency responders may not be able to get to your company for an extended period of time because they will prioritize your business lower than hospitals, schools, or nursing homes, to name a few. Therefore, your BC/DR plan should include some sort of internal emergency response capability in the event emergency responders are not available.

NOTE

Whenever possible, use your community's emergency responders to assist you in an emergency. Dial 911 or contact emergency services in your area as quickly as possible after a disaster or emergency occurs. At the same time, have your emergency response team respond to the incident. In many cases, first responders can help save lives by providing early care until trained professionals arrive. Administering CPR, for example, can help keep someone alive until paramedics arrive. Whenever possible, be sure to contact your emergency responders for assistance since most company's employees lack the training and experience to provide the same level of emergency support.

Emergency Response Plans

Emergency response plans stem from the risks you've identified for your company. Remember, though, the emergency response is the *immediate* response to the incident. If fire breaks out, the emergency response is evacuating the building and calling the fire department while perhaps having trained employees use fire extinguishers to try to control the blaze. These are the basics of a fire emergency response. However, there are other kinds of risks your company faces and these also require emergency response plans. Rather than creating a separate plan for every type of event that could occur, it's often advisable to create a basic emergency response checklist that can be used regardless of the emergency. The basics don't change—contact appropriate emergency personnel, get people out of harm's way, determine if there have been fatalities or injuries, determine if anyone is missing or unaccounted for, determine the source of the emergency, take measures to contain or halt the source of the problem if possible, and so on.

Develop an emergency response plan that meets the needs of your company without getting too complicated. A simple response plan that covers a variety of similar emergencies will help ensure things run more smoothly if an emergency does occur. For example, there might be several different reasons you would choose to evacuate your building—a fire, internal flooding (burst pipes, etc.), or a bomb scare. The threat sources are different, but the action is the same. Therefore, look through your risks and identify which emergency actions would be needed. Then, group them together so you can develop just three or four emergency responses, if possible.

The basic set of emergency response tasks are these:

- Protect personnel
- Contain incident
- Implement command and control (Emergency Response Team, Crisis Management Team step in)
- Emergency response and triage (medical, evacuation, search and rescue)
- Assess impact and effect
- Notification
- Next steps

The response procedures include protection of people first, containment of the emergency second, and assessment of the situation third. Regardless of the type of plan you create, these should be your priorities. Although it seems intuitive that you'd address the health and safety of people first, it's not always the first thing that comes to mind when an emergency strikes, so having a well-rehearsed set of procedures for emergency response that focuses on getting people to safety first then addressing the emergency will help form an appropriate response if something does occur.

Each plan should include:

- Roles and responsibilities

- Tools and equipment

- Resources

- Actions and procedures

Roles and responsibilities identify who's on the team and what they should do in an emergency. Tools and equipment for those emergency roles should be identified. This might include fire extinguishers, first aid kits, hard hats, haz-mat suits, walkie-talkies, shovels, and more. Any tools identified by the ERT should be purchased and stored in a suitable location. A list of these supplies should be maintained and someone on the ERT should be responsible for periodic inventory as well as testing and replenishing of supplies. For example, first aid kits have various medicines such as antibiotic creams and aspirin that expire and should be replaced periodically. Other resources the ERT might need should be acquired or identified. If specialized equipment such as a fire truck with an extension ladder would be needed to reach top stories of the building, that should be noted. The local fire department should be contacted to determine whether they have appropriate resources (such as a truck with an extension ladder). If equipment is not available, alternate plans should be created that address the specific needs. The company should also develop numerous evacuation scenarios and procedures that address the possibility of a fire in the upper floors of the building. Finally, actions and procedures should be developed that the ERT will initiate in the event of an emergency.

We've provided a detailed emergency response checklist for you and you can see that there is extensive detail in the list. It provides a generic step-by-step process that you can tailor to your company's specific situation so that you have a solid emergency response plan in place. The plan must be executed by people, so let's take a moment to discuss the role of the emergency response team.

From the Trenches...

Powering Up after Katrina

Hurricane Katrina has become an icon for many people. The enormity of the storm and its impact took most disaster planners off-guard and few organizations responded effectively in the aftermath of the storm. For many, the most immediate need was for electrical power. Imagine trying to restore power in an area where power poles were torn down, transmission lines were shredded, employees' homes were destroyed, roads were blocked, and communications were nonexistent. That's the situation faced by Mississippi Power's CIO Aline Ward. For a fascinating recount of what Aline Ward did to restore power to the area, visit this link: http://media.techtarget.com/digitalguide/images/Misc/AwardMississippi.pdf. It's a real world view of the aftermath of a natural disaster of massive proportions and how one person managed to bring order from the chaos to get power back to the area in record time.

Emergency Response Teams

Your company should have an emergency response team with defined roles and responsibilities for team members. Each person should clearly know the bounds of their authority and to whom they should turn for help or for escalation of issues. In previous chapters, we've referred to a Crisis Management Team (CMT), which may or may not be the same as an Emergency Response Team (ERT). If you're in a small company, it may be the same set of people, but in many cases these are not the same people because the skills required are different.

The ERT leader is responsible for activating and coordinating the emergency response and for notifying civil authorities such as the police or fire department, contacting hospitals or paramedics, and so on. The ERT leader also should be a member of the Crisis Management Team and should coordinate closely with the CMT to ensure that the appropriate level of BC/DR activation occurs in a timely manner. Emergency response and disaster recovery activities can occur in parallel. Typically, only trained members of the ERT can address the actual emergency. Members of the CMT can begin assessing damage, evaluating options, and implementing the BC/DR plan as soon as possible.

The ERT is also responsible for ensuring proper communication equipment is available prior to an event, for activating and distributing that communication equipment in an event, and for communicating appropriately throughout the event.

Emergency response team members should receive training on the aspects of the job they'll be expected to perform in an emergency. If team members are expected to fight small fires by using fire extinguishers, they should be trained not only on the use of the fire extinguishers but on how to fight fires. This includes safety procedures for fire fighting as well as methods for fighting different types of fires. Training is critical to ensure team members' safety and effectiveness in an emergency.

Emergency response training may include:

- Relocation and evacuation safety and techniques
- Fire fighting equipment, safety, and techniques
- Search and rescue safety and techniques
- Hazardous material handling
- Chemical spills or leaks (liquid, airborne, etc.)
- CPR, first aid, and emergency medical skills
- Water safety, water rescue
- Cold weather survival

- Emergency shut off/shutdown procedures
- Damage assessment and control

Obviously, the type of training required depends largely on your company, the nature of its business, and its geographical location. Identify the types of emergency response training that would be helpful for your staff to have and develop training plans to ensure training occurs periodically. Skills should be tested, rehearsed, and refreshed from time to time. Also, develop some method for responding to the loss of ERT members through retirement, attrition, or transfer. Finally, be sure several people on the ERT have similar skills and training so your team does not have a single point of failure. If only one person knows how to shut off the main electrical breaker and he or she is injured in an explosion, you have a problem (well, several major problems, actually).

It's also helpful to assign ERT members roles and responsibilities outside of emergency situations related to continued preparedness. For example, the ERT might be responsible for staging emergency training sessions or simulations on an annual basis that the entire company participates in. It might also be tasked with periodically checking fire extinguishers (e.g., are they where they should be, are they well-marked, are they functional, have they been tested, have they expired?) or checking emergency lighting from time to time. This keeps the team in tact and functional during nonemergencies, which can help them work together as an effective team during an emergency. It also helps maintain safety measures for the company, which is another risk mitigation strategy. If no one is responsible for checking fire extinguishers, there's a good chance you'll run into a problem if a fire actually does flare up. Define roles and responsibilities for ERT members that help reduce your company's risks and liabilities.

Crisis Management Team

There are hundreds, if not thousands, of books on crisis management available and if this is an area of interest, you should do additional research to delve into the details of this topic. As you know from watching the news or reading blogs, there are all kinds of crises that companies have to manage, not all of them related to BC/DR. In this section, we'll cover the basics of crisis management with an eye specifically toward BC/DR activities.

When you declare an emergency, disaster, or crisis event that must be managed, you begin implementing your BC/DR plan. The crisis management team (CMT) is the team responsible for making the high-level decisions; for coordinating efforts of internal and external staff, vendors, and contractors; and for determining the most appropriate responses to situations as they occur. They should be well versed with the BC/DR plan and the various team leaders for BC/DR activities either should be part of the crisis management team or should report to them.

Emergency Response and Disaster Recovery

The CMT oversees the emergency response team and the disaster recovery team(s). Once an emergency occurs, the emergency response team leader should take charge of managing the emergency itself, and the leader of the crisis management team should begin coordinating efforts between ERT, civil emergency responders (if appropriate), and other initial activities related to the BC/DR plan. The ERT leader should be a member of the CMT and should report to the team periodically throughout the emergency response. The ERT should be quickly released back to emergency duties while someone from the CMT documents the information provided by the ERT. This is part of the event log that should be initiated and maintained throughout the event. In addition to coordinating the emergency response, the crisis management team also coordinates activities related to initiating the disaster recovery efforts. Once the ERT leader has notified the CMT that the actual emergency has ceased and that disaster recovery can begin, the CMT takes over coordinating all activities. Typically, once the disaster recovery efforts conclude and business continuity efforts begin, the crisis management team winds down and operations may resume through normal management channels. This is a decision each company must make based on its unique structure, but in general, the CMT leader should manage the situation until it makes sense to hand over control to the operations team.

One very important note. You should clearly define the point at which the CMT stands down and normal operations take over. If you fail to clearly identify this line of demarcation, you risk having turf wars, power struggles, and people working at cross-purposes. Create a clear set of criteria for when the CMT hands over operations so that there is no question in anyone's mind about how the transition should occur. This is usually not a major issue in companies where the members of the CMT are members of the senior management team. In some companies, however, there may be confusion over roles, responsibilities, and authority, so be sure to clearly delineate these in advance.

Alternate Facilities Review and Management

The CMT is responsible for overseeing the activities related to disaster recovery and business continuity at alternate sites. They should review the activities leading up to activating the alternate site and should be the ones with final authority over decisions that need to be made related to the alternate site, such as bringing in additional services, equipment or vendors if original arrangements do not meet current needs. They are responsible for resolving problems and issues that arise and should be the final decision makers for escalated issues.

Communications

Crisis communications covers a lot of territory and may involve numerous teams working in a coordinated fashion, but the messages being communicated should originate from or be approved by the CMT. In an emergency situation, you should avoid having multiple sources of communications going out since it can cause confusion, error, frustration, and worse. Though you don't want to create a bottleneck in your communication stream, in the early stages after a business disruption or emergency, strive to have the CMT clear any messages going out. This not only will ensure that the message is correct and consistent, it will keep the CMT in the loop as well. This establishes a two-way communication channel between the CMT and the teams working on disaster recovery activities and helps in the coordination of activities and teams. This is critical for disasters or disruptions that also disrupt communication lines.

Human Resources

Representatives from Human Resources should be included on the CMT so that they can specifically address the needs of employees and maintain a communication channel with employees through preplanned methods. They should track employees who may be injured from the event or not available for work due to leaves of absence, vacations, and so on. They should provide support for injured employees and their families including facilitating access to emergency or ongoing medical or psychological services. They can also assist employees with financial, legal, and insurance issues related to the injury or death of an employee or family member. They should prepare and update an employee head count to determine who is available for recovery operations and who may be available later for business continuity activities. If temporary staff or contractors are needed, they can help select, manage, oversee, and monitor temporary staff as well as manage timecards and other payments for such staff. Last but perhaps most important, they can determine the status of payroll and ensure employees get paid in a timely manner. This is one of the biggest concerns employees will have in the aftermath of disaster, and having someone actively manage and monitor this process can alleviate some of the stress of the situation. Pro-actively addressing these concerns will also reduce the number of calls, e-mails, and contacts related to questions about payroll, freeing up time to address other HR-related concerns.

Legal

Depending on the nature of the disaster or disruption, you may need to have the CMT contact legal counsel. The firm's lawyers or legal representatives may need to review or approve emergency contracts; review language in agreements with vendors, suppliers, or contractors; review documents related to injury, death, or property damage; or address regulatory and compliance issues. As soon as the CMT is activated, it should be someone's specific responsibility to contact legal counsel and notify them of the event so they can provide appropriate information, feedback, and guidance throughout the remainder of the event and during its aftermath.

Insurance

As we've discussed, insurance is a risk transference method and one used by many, if not all, businesses today. In some cases, your firm may be required to hold certain types of insurance; in other cases, it may be voluntary. Your BC/DR plan should have contact information for your insurance company representatives and they should be notified upon activation of the CMT. The CMT may also perform an initial damage assessment and document it for the insurance company. This might include taking photographs or video images as well as making detailed notes. Members of the CMT team should also begin gathering documents related to insurance claims and submit loss estimates to the insurance company. Finally, someone on the CMT should review the insurance documents to determine exclusions, limitations (financial, time, location, cause, etc.), or maximums on various policies. Any issues with insurance should be escalated to management and/or legal counsel for review and resolution.

Finance

The CMT should also have representatives from the financial department available to assess the status of the company. This might include assessing the cash availability of the company, the viability (or advisability) of processing employee payroll early, or to provide advances to employees. Financial representatives also need to assess the status of the accounts payable and receivable to ensure bills and invoices are issued in a relatively timely manner and that revenue and payments are received in a timely manner as well. A process for managing, tracking, and monitoring expenditures during the disaster or disruption should be implemented and managed by the financial representative(s) on the CMT. Estimates for repairs and other expenditures should be submitted to this team for review and approval.

Upon resumption of business operations, the financial team should assess the status of the company's finances and report to executives or senior management.

Disaster Recovery

We discussed the different phases of business continuity and disaster recovery in Chapter 33, including activation, disaster recovery, business continuity recovery, and maintenance/review. In this section, we're going to discuss the disaster recovery activities in a bit more detail. This detail belongs in your BC/DR plan, but breaking it out into sections in this manner will help you process and manage the massive amount of detail required to address these activities properly. Once you've developed your emergency response, disaster recovery, and business continuity responses, you can (and should) include that information in your BC/DR plan. We've included various checklists that you can use as the basis for creating your own checklists or project plans. These can be included in the body of your BC/DR plan or as appendices at the end of your document for ease of use.

Activation Checklists

You may find it helpful to develop a variety of checklists, which can be extremely useful in making quick decisions for moving forward. Since you and your team may not have time to rehearse these plans frequently, checklists can help remind you of critical steps to take, regardless of the situation. Activation checklists should delineate all the activities and triggers that should take place prior to and during plan activation. This begins with some sort of disruptive event occurring, someone notifying the BC/DR team, and someone determining that the BC/DR plan should be activated as a result of the disruptive event. Remember, there may be some minor events that do not trigger the activation of the BC/DR plan, so deciding what criteria will be used to activate the plan in whole or in part should be part of the process.

Recovery Checklists

The recovery phase also has specific tasks that should be undertaken. The specific steps to be taken should be defined in your BC/DR plan. If you've looked at the various risks and potential impacts of these risks, you should have numerous scenarios that require planning. By developing plans for various scenarios, you will have the steps you need in almost any type of disaster because even though the details of the disaster may vary, the steps you need to take will be the same in a major disaster or a minor disaster. As with the activation phase, there is a long list of items you can use for this stage of work. Remember, all these lists are intended solely to get you thinking about how you will manage your company's BC/DR efforts, so you will need to modify them accordingly.

IT Recovery Tasks

The tasks needed to recover IT systems are probably quite familiar to you, but they should be delineated within your BC/DR plan. Each subteam should have a clear set of guidelines and procedures for how and when they will perform their work. Be sure to note dependencies within the checklist so that teams don't work at cross-purposes. You can add items to the checklist as checkpoints for these purposes, much like milestones are used in project plans.

Part of IT recovery involves responding to, stopping, and repairing problems caused by system failures, security breaches, or intentional data corruption or destruction. Depending on the nature or severity of the attack or incident, you may need to activate a computer incident response team (CIRT). Let's take a moment to discuss computer incident response and the team that performs these tasks.

From the Trenches...

Training Is Not Optional

When disaster strikes, most people resort to what they know best; they fall back on their training. The same is true of IT professionals. In the face of a major system outage or security breach, IT staff will do what they've been trained to do. Training is not an option for emergency preparedness, it is a *requirement*. Emergencies by their very nature are incredibly stressful and chaotic. People, by their very nature, feel most comfortable in any situation when they know what to expect and what to do. In an emergency, they won't necessarily know what to expect, but they will know what to do if they've been trained. Training is also important for CIRT teams because security incidents can be devastating to a company. CIRT members should know what to look for and exactly what actions to take in order to address a potential security breach or other serious incident. It doesn't help to shut down a server if the firewall has been breached; it doesn't help to shut down e-mail if the virus has infected a server. In addition to general IT skills, CIRT members should represent the various areas of expertise required in your IT department including servers, infrastructure, security, database administration, and applications, to name a few. CIRT members also should have checklists or step-by-step instructions to follow for standard incident types such as security breach, firewall breach, virus outbreak, and so on. This helps reduce stress and ensures everyone follows standard procedures to halt the immediate impact of any computer-related incident.

Computer Incident Response

Most IT departments have some process in place for addressing and managing a computer incident. An incident is defined as any activity outside normal operations, whether intentional or not; whether man-made or not. For example, the theft in the middle of the night of a corporate server is an incident. A Web site hack or a network security breach is also an incident. A database corruption issue or a failed hard drive is also an incident, but for the purposes of this discussion, we're going to stick with the emergency kinds of incidents and leave the more routine incident handling to your existing IT operations procedures. For example, we'll assume you can handle a bad hard drive or a failed router through standard operating procedures and we won't cover that here. What we will cover are the incidents that require a swift and decisive action to stop the incident from continuing. This includes events such as a network security breach or a denial of service attack and events such as a fire in the server room or a flood in the building.

The first step in this process is to form a computer incident response team. You may already have a team in place that addresses computer incidents such as security breaches. If that's the case you have the foundation of a computer incident response team (CIRT) that can be used in the event of a more widespread disruption such as a fire, earthquake or flood. The members of the team, like the ERT, should have defined roles and responsibilities. As with the ERT, team members should also be trained in their roles. For example, if you have staff responsible for monitoring network security and they notice a potential breach through a particular port, they should also know how to shut down that port and have the network permissions that enable them to do so. If all they know how to do is monitor the log file or traffic, for example, and have no idea how to shut down a port or stop the problem, it could be hours before the problem is addressed. Therefore, members of your CIRT should have training and appropriate network permissions to address these problems.

CIRT Responsibilities

In order for the CIRT to be effective, its duties must be well defined. There are five major areas of responsibility for the CIRT team. These are:

- Monitor
- Alert and Mobilize
- Assess and Stabilize
- Resolve
- Review

Monitor

Every network must be monitored for a variety of events. Some of these are failure events that indicate a problem has occurred such as a hardware failure or the failure of a particular software service to start or stop appropriately. Other events are tracked in log files for later review or auditing. These might include failed login attempts or notification of a change to security settings, for example. Other incidents may include unusual increases in certain types of network traffic or excessive attempts to login to secure areas of the network. Whether the event stems from intentional or unintentional acts, the network needs to be monitored. The CIRT should be involved with helping to determine what should be monitored as well as assisting in monitoring the network. Not all events have significance and sometimes it's only through seeing recurring events that a pattern can be discerned. Therefore, having experienced team members monitor the network will help reduce the lag time between an unwanted event and a response.

While a serious security breach might not cause you to activate all or part of your BC/DR plan, suppose you had some very strange activity on four of your corporate servers and the CIRT member couldn't determine the source of the anomalies. Is this a disaster or not? If it's caused by fire in the server room, yes. If it's caused by an errant software update that was just applied, maybe not. The point is that your CIRT team should monitor the network activity and take appropriate action regardless of the source of the problem. In some cases, this will involve activation of the BC/DR plan, in other cases it won't.

Alert and Mobilize

Once an unusual, unwanted, or suspicious event has occurred, the CIRT member should alert appropriate team members and mobilize for action. This may involve shutting down servers, firewalls, e-mail, or other services. As part of a BC/DR plan, this can also include being alerted that the event or disaster disrupted network services, such as a data center fire or theft of a corporate server after a fire in another part of the building. Alerting and mobilizing should have the effect of stopping the immediate impact of the event.

Assess and Stabilize

After the immediate threat has been halted, the CIRT team assesses the situation and attempts to stabilize it. For example, if data has been stolen or databases have been corrupted, the nature and extent of the event must be assessed and steps must be taken to stabilize the situation. In many cases, this phase takes the longest because determining exactly what happened can be challenging. If you have members of your team that have been trained in computer forensics, they would head up this segment of work. If you do not have members of your team trained in this area, you should decide whether it would be advisable to provide this training to staff or hire an outside computer forensics expert. Outside consultants can be helpful in this case for the simple fact that they work in this arena day in and day out and are most likely more up-to-date and experienced in this area than staff that occasionally goes to training and rarely (if ever) puts that training to use. The decision is yours based on the skills, expertise, and budget of your company. Having in-house expertise can be a good first step and you can always hire an outside expert on an as-needed basis.

Keep in mind that you have defined maximum tolerable downtime and other recovery metrics. A review of these should be included as part of the assess and stabilize procedures so that plans and actions can accommodate these requirements.

Resolve

After determining the nature and extent of the incident, the CIRT can determine the best resolution and implement it. Resolution may involve restoring from backups, updating operating systems or applications, modifying permissions, or changing settings on servers, firewalls, or routers.

Review

Once the event has been resolved, the CIRT should convene a meeting to determine how the incident occurred, what lessons were learned, and what could be done to avoid such a problem in the future. Within the scope of a BC/DR plan, this might involve understanding how the recovery process worked and what could be done differently in the future to decrease downtime, decrease impact, and improve time to resolution.

From the Trenches...

Computer Emergency Response Team (CERT)

There are numerous terms and acronyms floating around regarding computer emergencies, computer incidents, and computer security. The grandfather of them all, however, is the concept of computer emergency response developed by the Software Engineering Institute (SEI) at Carnegie Mellon University. We mentioned this resource earlier in the section and thought this would be a good time to mention it again. The Web site has a vast array of information and resources you can access. When developing your BC/DR plan for the IT portion of your business, read up on the latest trends and knowledge on the Web site at www.cert.org. Head to this URL for details on creating a CERT team: http://www.cert.org/csirts/action_list.html. It's a great resource for IT professionals even outside the scope of BC/DR planning as well.

Computer incident response is an activity that spans disaster recovery, business continuity, and normal operations. It is likely the CIRT team will have day-to-day responsibilities as part of standard IT operations or that CIRT activities will be building into IT standard operating procedures. However, if an earthquake hits the area or a flood shuts down operations, the CIRT's expertise can be put into play immediately as part of the BC/DR response. Be sure to integrate CIRT responsibilities into your BC/DR plans.

The skills of CIRT members should be kept up to date so they are aware of and can respond to the latest threats, vulnerabilities, and issues on the IT realm. Although training is important for IT staff in general, CIRT members need to be aware of the constantly evolving threats and vulnerabilities. They need to have the tools and skills necessary to recognize and resolve problems in a timely and effective manner. This is accomplished in part through training. CIRT members must also take responsibility for staying up to date on the latest trends by reading technical journals, newsletters, Web sites, blogs, and other related materials.

Business Continuity

Business continuity begins when disaster recovery ends. As we've discussed, it's not a sharp cutover from one phase to the next. Though we've discussed this to some extent throughout the preceding chapters, we haven't really looked at what it takes to move from the disaster recovery phase to the business continuity phase specifically.

The disaster recovery efforts include stopping the effect of the disaster and getting basic operations set up. For example, if your building was destroyed, disaster recovery would include salvaging anything from the building you could, activating an alternate work site, activating an alternate computing site (may be the same or different than the alternate work site), and setting up and restoring network components, servers, and systems. Now that disaster recovery, from an IT perspective, is complete, business continuity kicks in. These steps include managing business processes in work-around mode, if needed, and assessing the status of operations and beginning to normalize operations. For example, it's possible that some systems can be restored almost immediately, whereas other systems may take several days or a week to restore. The work-arounds in place may allow some operations to resume but others to remain dormant. Backlogs in some areas are created, data gets out of sync, and the state of the business is perhaps more chaotic now than it was during the disaster when it was clear that no business operations would take place. Therefore, having a plan for business continuity steps is critical to your eventual success.

Part of the challenge of the business continuity phase is determining what should be restored, what should be salvaged, and what should be replaced. There is certainly a time consideration that needs to be factored in along with the obvious financial considerations. Repairing and replacing have their own sets of challenges and the options should be reviewed prior to making decisions to move forward. In order to process all the information needed, the various teams should work together to identify optimal solutions. Some of the factors to be considered include:

- Executive/administrative
- Business operations
- IT operations—infrastructure
- IT operations—end users
- Communications
- Facilities, security, and safety

As with the other emergency and disaster response activities listed in this chapter, we've also developed a business continuity checklist you can use as the basis for your business continuity planning activities. Since every business is different, the checklist you find in the final chapters of this section is fairly generic. It lists major level activities you should consider including. Not all activities on the list will be appropriate for your organization. There may be areas *missing* from the checklist that you'll need to resume operations at your firm. However, if you start with these lists, there's a better chance you'll include what you need to successfully resume business at your company.

As you'll see in the checklist, the last two activities are reviewing what happened during the disruption or disaster and adding that knowledge to your BC/DR plan. Once your firm gets back to business as usual, no one will have the time to capture this data. It's vital that you capture lessons learned from the incident and build them into your BC/DR plan so that the mistakes made aren't repeated and the innovations or positive lessons learned can be incorporated. This is part of plan maintenance, but it also should be part of your BC/DR activities as well.

Summary

In this chapter, you learned about emergency plans and emergency responses that should be included in your BC/DR plan. Emergency response is the initial response to a disaster or disruption. The first response should be to get people out of harm's way and to determine if there are fatalities or injuries. Secondary efforts should be to stop the source of the problem whether that's through calling civil emergency responders (fire, bomb squad, police) or through attempting to address the problem with an emergency response team (fighting a fire, turning off gas or electric sources, containing hazardous spills, etc.). Emergency responders should be trained in appropriate skills such as safe building evacuation methods, CPR and first aid, fire fighting, hazardous material containment, and others. Emergency plans should be well conceived and well rehearsed because people will fall back on their training in an emergency.

The crisis management team may activate the emergency response or the emergency responders may notify the crisis management team of an event. In any case, the crisis management team coordinates emergency efforts and activates the BC/DR plan based on the specifics of the situation. The CMT is also responsible for coordinating recovery efforts and should manage these activities through the business continuity stage. Roles and responsibilities should be well defined to avoid confusion or working at cross-purposes. Activities the CMT typically manages can include the emergency and disaster response, activating alternate work sites and facilities, managing corporate communications, interfacing with insurance and legal representatives, and working with the finance department. You can define other appropriate activities for your CMT to reflect the specifics of your business.

Because disasters are by their very nature chaotic events, it helps to have checklists you and your team can use to manage activities in the aftermath of a major disaster or disruption. Activation includes all activities related to assessing a situation and determining what recovery plans should be implemented as well as taking initial steps toward that end.

Within disaster recovery, there are specific IT recovery tasks that should be performed as well. Separate IT recovery checklists should be created so that you have a clear plan about how to recover from various events. These checklists should include information regarding the maximum tolerable downtime (MTD) and other recovery metrics that have been established. The lists also should include timelines, milestones, and dependencies that need to be addressed. Some companies form computer incident response teams (CIRTS) or computer emergency response teams (CERTS) to respond quickly and effectively to computer-based incidents. The activities of the CIRT occur in the day-to-day operations of the company (outside the BC/DR domain) and are also part of BC/DR activities. Defining how the CIRT should operate and interact with your BC/DR plan is vital to ensure an effective response.

Business continuity activities begin after recovery efforts have concluded, though there is usually some overlap. Business continuity activities include the limited resumption of business operations, typically in manual or work-around mode. These activities pose a unique set of challenges from an IT and operations perspective because data must be managed differently until IT systems are fully back online and normal operations can resume. The business continuity checklist should include steps needed to resume limited operations, it should identify requirements and dependencies, and it should include timelines, milestones, and checkpoints. The resumption of normal business operations typically occurs when the company either reoccupies its original facility and all equipment is back up and running, or when the company decides on a permanent business location (which may be the alternate site or newly acquired site). Criteria for determining the cutover to "normal operations" should be developed and the CMT should hand over operations to the management team toward the end of the business continuity phase. Clearly defining this cutover as well as roles and responsibilities will help prevent confusion during this last phase of activity.

## Chapter 35

Training, Testing, and Auditing

Solutions in this chapter:

- **Training for Emergency Response, Disaster Recovery, and Business Continuity**

- **Testing Your Business Continuity and Disaster Recovery Plan**

- **Performing Security Audits**

☑ **Summary**

Introduction

At this point, you have your BC/DR plan pretty well defined and ready to go. The next step in the process, as shown in Figure 35.1, is training, testing, and auditing. Training includes training staff on their roles and responsibilities related to the BC/DR plan as well as training them in the specific skills they'll need to carry out their roles effectively. Testing is the process of testing the plan, and there are various methods for doing so that we'll discuss in this chapter. Finally, there is the process of auditing the IT systems that form the foundation of most BC/DR plans.

Figure 35.1 Business Continuity and Disaster Recovery Project Plan Progress

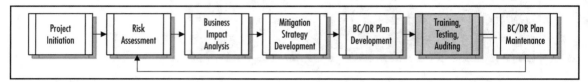

There's an interrelationship between testing, training, and auditing as shown in Figure 35.2. Performing one impacts the other two—when you test the plan, you're training and auditing to some extent.

Figure 35.2 Training, Testing, and Auditing Activities

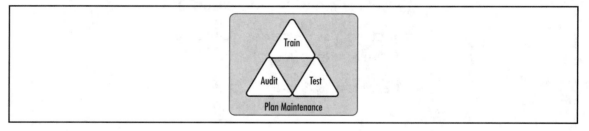

Training, testing, and plan maintenance are all bound together. Testing the plan trains staff and maintains the plan. Training staff tests and maintains the plan. As you train staff and test your plan, you will likely find areas that require modification. These modifications are made through the change management process defined as part of the plan maintenance phase. The information you glean from training and testing can be extremely useful in honing your plan in advance of a disruptive event. Testing and training go hand in hand, so let's begin by discussing training. We'll discuss plan maintenance in Chapter 36.

Training for Disaster Recovery and Business Continuity

There are two distinct parts of disaster recovery and business continuity training. The first is the actual physical response to the disruption or emergency. That might involve evacuating a building if there's a fire, grabbing a fire extinguisher to douse a fire in the server room, or finding the water main if there's flooding inside the building. These actions all require some basic training so responders know what to do and how to do it safely. There's little point in a responder grabbing a fire extinguisher and subsequently being burned by the fire because he or she did not know how to properly use the equipment or properly extinguish a fire. That's one aspect of training. The second aspect of training has to do with ensuring that the various response teams know how to implement the BC/DR plan and that they have the skills needed to do so. For example, you might want to provide periodic training for your IT staff so they can stay up to date on the latest threats and security measures or training for alternate BC/DR staff on performing a system restoreand verification routine.

Emergency Response

Your BC/DR team should have an emergency response team (ERT) identified and these team members should be trained in appropriate emergency response activities. Each company should identify the likely emergency responses needed and provide training in these activities. If your firm is located in an area prone to flooding, earthquakes, hurricanes, or tornados, you should provide training in emergency response related to these events. In addition, basic first aid and CPR training should be part of all emergency responders' training, and some companies find it useful to provide this training to all employees.

The specialized skills for the ERT might include fire fighting techniques or building evacuation procedures, for example. These specialized skills require training in order to protect the safety of the responders and to enable the responders to be effective. As mentioned in Chapter 34, your local fire or police department may provide this type of training or may be able to recommend firms that provide this type of training.

Your BC/DR plan should include the designation of an ERT as well as a list of required training/ skills, certification requirements (if any), as well as periodic refresher courses. The ERT leader should be responsible for managing this. He or she should ensure team members have the training and/or certifications required and should arrange for the periodic testing and refreshing of these skills.

We discussed training needs for emergency responders in Chapter 34, so we mentioned it here briefly, primarily as a reminder to you to address and include emergency training in your plan. Let's focus now on disaster recovery and business continuity training.

Disaster Recovery and Business Continuity Training Overview

Disaster recovery is a crucial step that can mean the difference between the company's eventual recovery or failure. Training can help improve the chances for eventual success. Disaster recovery and business continuity training includes defining the scope and objectives for the training, performing a needs assessment (gap analysis), developing training, scheduling and delivering training, and monitoring/ measuring training. In this section, we'll discuss disaster recovery and business continuity training as one since they are so closely related. However, as you develop your training plans, you may find it helpful to separate these two phases out so you can pinpoint distinct training needs. Remember, too, that you may choose to perform training while testing your plan. It depends largely on how you approach your testing. We'll discuss testing in detail later in this chapter, so you may revise your thinking on this once you're read through the entire chapter.

Training Scope, Objectives, Timelines, and Requirements

Ideally, you should develop a training project plan that ties in with the BC/DR project plan. The training plan should include a statement of scope (what *is* and *is not* included) as well as a list of high-level objectives. These objectives might be parsed out to include objectives for each of the implementer groups (emergency responders, crisis management team, damage assessment team, disaster recovery team, etc.). In addition, the timelines for training various teams should be developed. Keep in mind that some people may be members of more than one team, so training and training subjects should take that into consideration. Then, develop requirements for training. One of the easiest ways to make sure training meets its stated objectives is to clearly define the objectives, then list the requirements to meet those objectives. For example, suppose you want to provide training for your computer incident response team (CIRT). For simplicity's sake, we'll use a very limited set of objectives, but it will give you a good idea of how to approach this section of the project. The data is organized in Table 35.1 for your reference.

Table 35.1 Sample CIRT Training Outline

Topic	Details
Scope	Train all net admins on monitoring network traffic for security-related issues. Does not include training net admins on how to set up auditing or enabling log files for security monitoring.
Objectives	1. Develop awareness of current security threats. 2. Develop understanding of log files to monitor. 3. Understand what to look for in log files. 4. Understand how to investigate suspicious log file entries, data, or trends. 5. Understand how to respond to suspicious network activity.
Timeline	Initial training will be developed and delivered within 30 days. Training is a two-hour session. Refresher courses will be held quarterly for 30 minutes. Attendance by all net admins is required.
Requirements	1. Locate latest threat data and trend information. 2. Location of [specified] log files. 3. Ability to read and understand log entries. 4. Ability to understand and spot trends. 5. Ability to take [specified] action to address suspicious or malicious network activity.

This example is simply to demonstrate that you should develop scope, objective statement, a timeline, and a set of requirements for your training. It also shows you that you can do this relatively quickly and that it doesn't have to become a massive project itself. As you test your project plan, you'll also find areas that should be addressed by training, so you will likely need to revise these plans once or twice as you go through the training and testing phases.

Performing Training Needs Assessment

The needs assessment phase is essentially a gap analysis. You should review current skill sets against required expertise to carry out various functions and determine what sort of training would best fill the gap. In many cases, training needs become evident during the testing of the plan. Later in this chapter, we'll discuss specific steps you can take to test your plan. As you test your plan, you'll see areas where specialized or updated skills and knowledge will be required to successfully execute the plan. You can make note of these potential skill gaps during your plan testing and circle back to include these in your training plans. Remember, a training needs assessment should be performed on the same periodic basis as your plan testing schedule or on some other periodic basis. People leave the company, are promoted, or change jobs. You need to ensure that at any given moment, your organization has the skills it needs to implement your BC/DR plan successfully. In many cases, a company's routine training plans will cover many (if not all) of the essential skills, but any skills that would not normally be covered through routine training should be flagged for special consideration.

TIP

If you work in a small company, you may need to cross-train people to perform mission-critical functions if your BC/DR teams are not large enough to reduce the risk of small companies. Also, teams should be familiar with other teams' tasks, objectives, and requirements so that teams can cooperate in a seamless fashion in the chaotic aftermath of a serious disruption.

Developing Training

Many companies have limited time or funds available for training, much less for BC/DR training. However, many studies support the thought that companies that train their employees benefit not only from improved productivity but greater loyalty as well. Targeted training to maintain or improve skills, especially those related to mission-critical business functions, can be accomplished relatively quickly and often at a reasonable cost. As with other risk factors in BC/DR planning, the risk of having untrained personnel can easily be mitigated through training, and it may also help drive productivity within the organization. (*Hint:* That's the business case you use to get your BC/DR-specific training budget approved.)

Common Challenges

The ROI of Training

Many companies have little time or money for training, especially if the company is under tight financial constraints. Many top-level managers look at the line items with an eye toward the bottom line and training is one of the items that gets slashed early in the budget-tightening process. However, experts agree that might not be the best long-term move.

"There is evidence that suggests that training can have productivity payoffs," says Robert D. Atkinson, vice president of the Progressive Policy Institute (PPI) and director of the Technology & New Economy Project. "Training can have positive ROI (return on investment) because it can lead to productivity improvement.

"There's also a lot of evidence that when…companies introduce new technology…, the benefits of that technology are significantly enhanced if companies concurrently train their workers."

(*Source:*http://www.ppionline.org/ppi_ci.cfm?knlgAreaID=107&subsecID=175& contentID=253143)

Granted, training costs have to be aligned with organizational and financial constraints, but most companies can find creative ways to develop and deliver cost-effective training. The proliferation of online training courses along with local resources makes finding affordable training easier than ever.

When developing training, create clear, specific, measurable outcomes. A measurable outcome means that it either *was* or *was not* accomplished. Either Jill can restore the database from backups using the written procedures or she can't. Either Tony can safely shut power off to the manufacturing floor or he can't. Also keep in mind that not all training for your BC/DR plan will be extensive training. Some may be as simple as showing Tony where the power shut off is and how to perform a power shutdown for the manufacturing floor. Other training, such as how to restore various IT systems that are closely integrated or interconnected, may require training in several knowledge areas as well as hands-on experience (ideally in a similarly configured lab environment) performing the activities in the requisite order. When appropriate, problems should be designed into the training so students can also learn how to troubleshoot and think creatively when things don't go according to plan.

Training should provide some sort of materials (printed, soft copy, web-based, etc.) that capture and reinforce the skills and knowledge presented. The training should also be designed to use several elements such as written, classroom lecture, hands-on (lab), and field (exercises). The more ways you use to deliver training, the more likely it is students will absorb it. Finally, use a final quiz or exam to ensure students have grasped the key concepts and can apply them appropriately. The final test or exam should reflect the training outcomes identified.

In the next section of this chapter, we'll talk about training staff on the BC/DR plan. The outcomes and other deliverables for BC/DR training should be developed as with any other type of training.

Scheduling and Delivering Training

Scheduling and delivering training is a secondary challenge after getting the training budget approved. These days, you can often find various training programs online that people can attend on their own schedule. If you use a flexible online learning system (either your own or an external one), be sure to set timelines and test for knowledge along the way. For example, if you decide that some of your network admins should attend an online course provided by a third-party training provider, you should develop some method of assessing whether or not the net admins learned what they should have. Some online courses are better than others, some test knowledge better than others. Be sure to verify the quality of the training in advance and find ways to verify that students learned the required materials.

If training is developed and delivered in-house in a classroom or lab setting, it may be a bit more difficult to manage. If you develop training that moves quickly, is interesting, engaging, and relevant to the students, it's much more likely you'll be able to get students to attend your training sessions. If necessary, you may need to call upon the organizational clout of your project sponsor to help you get the training scheduled and delivered in a reasonable timeframe.

TIP

Since some of the training will be specific to BC/DR, you may find people saying, in essence, "it can wait, there's no rush." You'll have to find creative ways to counter that, but one way that might work is to say, "If you knew that the building would burn to the ground next week, would you want this training to have already happened?" In most cases, the answer is yes. Since fires are the most common business disaster and can occur completely without warning, you might be able to gain consensus on a reasonable training timetable. If you can tie your BC/DR training into other business objectives, you may have an even greater chance of success.

Monitoring and Measuring Training

The first step in monitoring and measuring training is the development of clear objectives and outcomes for the training. If you don't know what should be accomplished in training, you won't be able to determine if the training was effective.

Exams and hands-on demonstrations of skills can be extremely effective in testing and verifying knowledge. For physical skills such as using a fire extinguisher or performing CPR, both a test of knowledge and a demonstration of skills is best. The same is true for some types of "logical" skills such as restoring a server or verifying user permissions. In some cases, the best you'll be able to do is verify that the training occurred and that several basic concepts were retained by students. An example of this might be restoring an enterprise resource planning (ERP) system that cannot be easily recreated in a lab setting.

Monitoring also involves ensuring key personnel have actually attended required training and have not somehow accidentally fallen through the cracks. If staff leave or move into different positions, their replacements need to be trained, so you need to develop some method of periodically checking your key BC/DR staff positions and ensure they are still in place and ready to perform their assigned BC/DR duties. These vary widely from one company to the next. You may be able to work with your HR group if they have an established system for tracking employee training and certification in place.

Training and Testing for Your Business Continuity and Disaster Recovery Plan

There are four basic ways to train staff regarding the BC/DR plan, and these also simultaneously test the plan. These are paper walk-throughs (or tabletop exercises), functional exercises, field exercises, and full interruptions. Regardless of how you implement it, you need to cover specific elements in your training. Team leaders, in particular, need to know how and when to activate the plan as well as how to notify, assemble, and manage their teams. Specifically, they need to know how to:

- Use the plan effectively.

- Understand their individual and team roles and responsibilities.

- Notify, assemble, and manage their team members.

- Operate as a cross-functional team member.

- Communicate effectively across organizational boundaries in a stressful situation, often without the aid of common communication tools such as phones, e-mail, or other devices.

The most basic part of the training is understanding the plan and how to utilize it. That includes understanding how and when to activate it and how to implement the steps defined. If your BC/DR plan ends up being 50 pages long, you can be sure that no one will take time to read it if the building is on fire. The role of training is both to familiarize people with the plan elements and processes and to reinforce the basic knowledge of the plan. In an ideal scenario, the plan document is accessible immediately upon notification of a disruptive event and someone starts managing the plan. However, in the real world, there's a small probability that things will progress in an ideal manner. Therefore, having a team well versed in the initial steps of the plan will provide an effective, early response. Be sure that your training objectives reflect the specific knowledge you need students to gain such as how to use the plan, what the boundaries of their assigned roles are, and so on. Clear, specific, and measurable outcomes for BC/DR plan training are as important as for any other type of training.

Everyone involved with the BC/DR implementation needs to understand their specific roles and responsibilities once a plan is activated. Training should address both the BC/DR process itself as well as the specific skills needed by team members to be effective in their designated roles. For example, a database administrator may be part of the IT damage assessment team. She may be an outstanding DBA but may not have the specific skills to know how to approach the IT damage assessment process. She should be trained in the process of performing the IT damage assessment as well as in the overall BC/DR process. That way, she will understand how and when the IT damage assessment is performed, how it impacts other BC/DR activities, and how to perform the duties of that role.

Another example is an administrative assistant who is also tasked with being the crisis team coordinator. He might have the skills to manage multiple tasks at once, communicate and update people effectively, and so on, but he needs to understand the specific roles and responsibilities of the coordinator role. If there are tasks within that role he doesn't understand or know how to do, appropriate training needs to be provided. He may not know, for example, how to use emergency communication equipment such as walkie talkies. A simple thing to learn, perhaps, but not something you want to take time to teach him in the midst of a serious emergency.

Team leaders head up their individual teams (be sure to assign alternates or backups for key roles) and they must also be able to work effectively as part of the ERT or CMT. That means there has to be a leader assigned or selected for the crisis management team. Without such a designation, it's likely there will be confusion or perhaps a bit of jockeying for position. Leaders like to lead. Leaders can be extremely effective members of a team if they are confident the team has a competent leader. Otherwise, they'll naturally try to step in to fill the gap. That's fine if only one person steps up, but it's a problem if four or five (or more) people step up. Therefore, understanding roles and responsibilities is a key part of the initial training.

Many companies will implement a crisis management team comprised of leaders of other teams. This structure means that departments that have little interaction during normal business operations may have to work closely together during an emergency. It may even mean that someone higher in the organizational hierarchy is reporting to someone lower in the hierarchy during the emergency. Think of this scenario. Perhaps you have an area director on your CMT because she understands operations. Suppose the person designated to head up the CMT is the Facilities manager because he has experience in CMT as well as several related certifications. In the early stages of a disruptive event, the Facilities manager, as head of the CMT, is directing all activities, including those of the director of operations. This may be an appropriate situation but clearly, everyone has to be comfortable with this structure. The director has to be comfortable taking orders, temporarily, from the Facilities manager. There are numerous scenarios you can construct in which various levels of the organization have to work together seamlessly without anyone pulling rank inappropriately. Your training should address these cross-functional needs, define lines of authority and decision-making, and ensure that all team members are comfortable with the decision-making structure of the BC/DR process.

Finally, training should address the communication needs across the organization. As we've discussed previously, there are numerous communication needs throughout the lifecycle of a disaster and the team should understand this. The training should address the various communication groups (groups to whom the CMT should communicate), the appropriate frequency and content of the communication, and the appropriate distribution mechanism. Remember that during a disruption, your teams may not have access to standard communications equipment so communications plans and training should address various contingencies.

Now that we've looked at basic training elements, let's look at four commonly used methods of training, to which we referred earlier. These are the paper walk-through, the functional and field exercises, and full interruption. Figure 35.3 depicts the relative accuracy and organizational disruption each type of test generates. The least disruptive type of test is the paper walk-through, and it's the one most organizations do. The results from a paper walk-through are obviously going to be less accurate than functional or field tests. However, paper walk-throughs, if done well, can still yield extremely helpful results that can be incorporated into the plan to incrementally improve it.

Figure 35.3 Relative Disruption and Accuracy of BC/DR Plan Test Methods

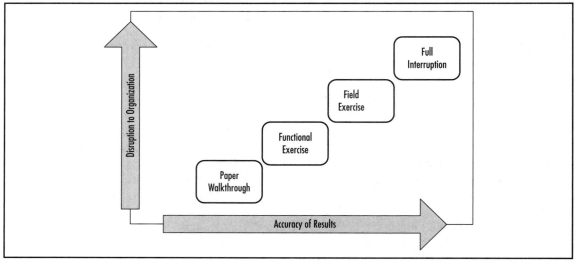

Paper Walk-through

In most companies, if you can manage to schedule a paper walk-through of your BC/DR plan once a year, you've scored a major victory. As gloomy a prediction as that is, it reflects the reality in today's organizations. However, if you've managed to get approval to put together your BC/DR plan, you can make a pretty strong case that without a walk-through, you'll never know if it works or not. It's like carrying a spare tire that's flat—it's of absolutely no consequence until you need it. You want to know if your BC/DR plan will work if needed, and the only way to determine that is to test it out. A paper walk-through will take time to step through but it's time well spent. There are eight discrete steps you can take to run an effective paper walk-through. These steps also apply to the other types of training (functional, field, etc.).

Develop Realistic Scenarios

The first step is to develop realistic scenarios for your walk-through. You should develop scenarios based on those risks determined by your assessment to be the highest risk, highest likelihood, and highest impact. Although it may be interesting or fun to walk through some oddball scenario (space aliens land and their magnetic field erases only the zeros on all disk drives), it's not particularly useful. Focus on the things most likely to occur. Start with a fire in the building, since statistically speaking, that's the disaster most likely to strike businesses. Also create scenarios that involve your highest risk/impacts. Remember, you will likely need to perform several walk-throughs based on various threats. However, it is possible after you've run through several scenarios that your team is familiar enough with the process that future walk-throughs can use a single scenario that covers the all the bases. Ideally, you'll perform a paper walk-through for each of your major risks. Given the time and budget constraints most of you are facing, that's probably not realistic, but it at least can be held as the ideal.

Develop Evaluation Criteria

The key to any successful test of your plan, whether it's a paper walk-through or a full interruption, is to have criteria by which you'll evaluate the success of that training. We'll discuss test criteria in a bit more detail later in the chapter as well. For your paper walk-through, you might develop criteria that include:

- How well participants were able to follow and utilize the plan
- How well participants were able to communicate across team lines
- How well the checklists or defined steps worked to achieve the stated objectives
- How confident participants felt with their implementation of the plan
- How confident participants feel about implementing the plan in the future

Provide Copies of the Plan

Members of the crisis management team should be given the latest copies of the plan in advance of the walk-through. The hope (but usually not the reality) is that they'll look through the plan prior to the walk-through. However, the likelihood is they will not, so your training and testing need to work on the assumption that prior reading or familiarization will not occur (despite what people might claim). In addition, individual team members that might be participating, such as members of a damage assessment team or an emergency response team should be provided their section of the plan. If helpful, you may want to create a flowchart of your plan's processes in order to help individual team members visually see and understand how things should proceed. This often helps individuals understand their roles within the larger plan and operate more effectively as part of the larger team. Figure 35.4 shows a portion of a sample flowchart. The adage "A picture's worth a thousand words" is very true in this case. Checklists and simple flowcharts can be helpful in an emergency if staff are familiar with how they work and how to utilize them.

Figure 35.4 Sample Flowchart of BC/DR Plan (Partial)

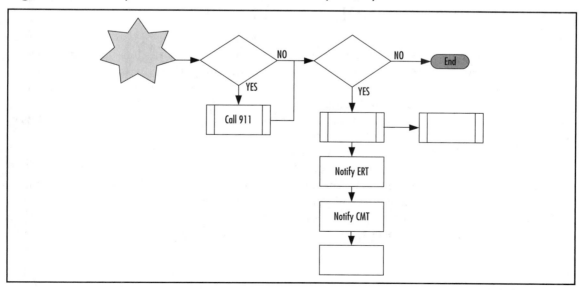

Divide Participants by Team

If your walk-through includes members of different teams, having them sit together can help the flow of the walk-through. If they need to confer or make notes among themselves, they can do so more effectively by being in close proximity to one another. It also helps reduce cross-talk and interruptions. Be sure to have alternates attend the training and work alongside their counterparts. If you have vendors you've designated as team members, they should also be included in the training.

Use Checklists

If you have checklists for your key processes be sure to provide copies of these checklists and ensure the team uses these checklists. If they find steps that are out of order, missing, or redundant, they can correct the checklists quickly. Like flowcharts, using checklists will also help maintain direction and forward progress during the walk-through.

Take Notes

Someone should be tasked with keeping notes about the process, major issues that arise, and the like. If you run the walk-through with various teams, each team should be responsible for keeping notes on their process and their section of the plan as well.

Identify Training Needs

As you train staff in the use and implementation of the plan, you should specifically keep an eye open for additional training needs. Be sure to ask training participants to make a note of any skills they believe they need in order to effectively carry out the BC/DR plan. Those closest to the job are in the best position to identify skills gaps and you can develop a list of training needs from these run-throughs. Of course, you might end up with a long wish-list, so you'll have to prioritize and sort through the training requests to determine what is a high priority and what can wait (or is not needed).

Develop Summary and Lessons Learned

After the walk-through, you should compile and summarize the notes collected. You should summarize the lessons learned from the exercise and schedule a follow up meeting. This follow-up meeting should be held a day or two after the walk-through (i.e., not immediately following the walk-through, but not four weeks later) so that participants have a chance to think about the walk-through and bring their thoughts, suggestions, and feedback to the follow-up meeting. You can use the data collected from this process to modify future walkthrough sessions and to modify the BC/DR plan as needed.

An annual walkthrough of the plan is often used as a combination of plan familiarization, training, and testing. In some cases, that may be adequate, but this type of exercise is really the bare minimum. Also, be sure to flag your team members in some manner so that if someone leaves or is promoted, for example, you can either notify the alternate or designate and train a replacement. One of the biggest risks you face to your plan is people not being familiar enough with it to implement it properly when needed. This happens for a variety of reasons and a regular training schedule can help reduce that risk.

Functional Exercises

Functional exercises are used to actually test some of the plan's functionality. In most cases, if you want to test all the functionality, you'll plan field or full-scale interruptions, discussed in the next sections. However, it's often helpful and adequate to perform a paper walk-through along with functional exercises. Functional exercises train staff in critical procedures or functions needed to respond to and address the disruption.

Typically, functional exercises make use of scenario-based scripts and run for two to three hours. The team is divided into two groups Alternates make an excellent second group for training purposes. A script starts off the sequence of events, which typically takes about 15 to 20 minutes. The ERT and CMT teams have to respond to the scripted events using their training and BC/DR plan. The second group, we'll call them the alternates here, act as nonteam members. For example, if the scenario includes evacuating the building, alternates may behave as employees might—panicking, not following instructions, and so on. If the scenario involves assessing injuries, alternates can have scripted injuries the ERT team has to deal with. The alternates use a menu of responses or events based on the specific scripted scenario to prompt the team members. The goal of this type of functional training is to get members to work as a team, to help members understand their roles and responsibilities, and to communicate effectively under stressful conditions.

Tip

If confusion crops up during the functional exercises, be sure to stop the exercise and clarify. Although it may break from the realistic scenario you've created, the primary purpose is training and testing the plan. If gaps or errors become obvious or there massive confusion during the exercise, stop and address it immediately. It might mean spending a couple of minutes clarifying roles and expectations or making notes about areas of the plan that need modification. The few minutes you spend clarifying can make all the difference in the confidence and competence of staff if they are ever called upon to put their training to the test. The same holds true for field exercises, discussed later.

As with any other type of training, you should have clear objectives and outcomes identified for functional exercises. For example, if you're going to teach staff how to restore a database from three weeks' worth of incremental backup tapes pulled across the Internet from a remote data vault, you should list the key knowledge you expect staff to gain. This might include:

- How to determine that the database needs to be restored (i.e., is the local copy destroyed, corrupted, offline, etc.)

- How to access the data vault backups (location, login credentials, accessing data, etc.)

- How to restore the data (what order, what locations, what settings, etc.)

- How to verify the restore (verification of file names, sizes, locations; sample test scripts, etc.)

A functional test of the BC/DR plan follows the same path. If you want to test some of the functions of your plan, develop step-by-step instructions and have participants use those steps to test the function. As we've mentioned, testing the plan is a great training tool and functional exercises go a long way toward both ends.

Field Exercises

Field exercises involve fairly realistic exercises based on likely scenarios. You've undoubtedly seen stories on these kinds of exercises on your local news stations. From time to time, local emergency responders exercise their skills by practicing scenarios. If you would like to practice your emergency and disaster recovery response using full-scale field exercises, you may be able to coordinate such exercises with your local emergency responders. They may welcome the opportunity to test their skills and to help train your staff in the process. If so, you have an excellent resource at your disposal that will not only test and hone your skills but provide valuable input into your disaster planning.

Most companies barely have the time or resources to do an annual paper walk-through of their plan, so it's not likely you'll be able to run through a real-world scenario. That said, if your company works in a dangerous industry (hazardous chemicals, explosives, power, etc.), you may want (or be required by law) to perform field exercises to assess and improve readiness. It's not until a situation is unfolding, even in a simulated manner, that some problems with a plan come to light. As useful as paper walk-throughs and functional exercises can be, they may still leave knowledge gaps or plan problems that you just won't know about until a real situation presents itself. Field exercises can reduce the risk of plan gaps but at a much greater expense of time and resources. For some companies, this investment makes sense.

Full Interruption Test

Like a field exercise, a full interruption test can be for the organization or just for specific systems within the organization. It activates all components of the plan and interrupts all mission-critical functions. The full interruption test will also activate the alternate work sites or facilities and off-site storage facilities, and the plan is actually implemented in whole. This type of full interruption test can be announced or unannounced. Clearly, an unannounced test simulates a real disruption or disaster more accurately than an announced test, but is also more disruptive.

Most companies are unlikely to be willing to disrupt their operations long enough to perform a full interruption test. However, there may be instances when a full disruption of a single business unit (rather than the whole company) is an acceptable trade-off for the knowledge and readiness that can be achieved through this type of realistic simulation.

Training Plan Implementers

If you have specific personnel designated as plan implementers, you may want to develop a specific training session for these staff. They should understand exactly what their roles are and how to implement the plan, should it be necessary. Because the situation in the aftermath of a serious disruption or disaster is extremely stressful and chaotic, plan implementers should rehearse implementing the initial steps of the plan frequently enough that they're very comfortable with it. They should know by rote what to do, who to contact, and what steps they need to take in several likely scenarios. This memorization and practice of key first steps will help them if they are called upon to implement the plan. As we mentioned earlier, people fall back on their training in an emergency, so the plan implementers should be extremely comfortable with their responsibilities in this regard to prevent a total breakdown of the plan in the aftermath of a serious event.

Testing the BC/DR Plan

There are numerous reasons for testing the plan. The obvious reason is to make sure that the plan will work in the event of a real disruption or disaster. However, the underlying reasons that testing helps the plan work more effectively is that testing serves these purposes:

- Checks for understanding of processes, procedures, and steps by those who must implement the plan

- Validates the integration of tasks across the various business units and management functions

- Confirms the steps developed for each phase of the plan's implementation

- Determines whether the right resources have been identified

- Familiarizes all involved parties with the overall process and flow of information

- Identifies gaps or weaknesses in the plan

- Determines cost and feasibility

As you read through the training section of this chapter, it probably became clear to you that training and testing a BC/DR plan are closely integrated. One way of training staff on the implementation of the BC/DR plan is to test the plan (and training will test the plan). If you choose to test your plan through BC/DR training, be sure to include the items listed here as objectives or deliverables for your training.

TIP

If you have designated an alternate site, off-site data storage, or backups, these should be tested for failover capabilities periodically. Don't wait for disaster to strike to test these important capabilities.

Understanding of Processes

The processes, procedures, and steps taken by the various team members once the plan is activated (including how and when to activate the plan) should be the primary outcome of the testing phase. This phase should uncover any missing processes. It should also identify and verify processes and their interdependencies. Mission-critical functions should be restored first and the plan processes should address these priorities effectively.

In addition, the linear progression of the plan itself (first do this, then this) should be understood by participants. By walking through these processes, participants both learn the processes, and can verify that they make sense. Often, a BC/DR plan is created by a specialized team of subject matter experts, but it's not until the people who may be called upon to implement that plan (who may not be the same SMEs) that flaws are found. Any problems found with the plan through this phase should be noted and the change management process should be used to modify the plan appropriately.

Understanding the processes also includes understanding the work-arounds and manual processes that should be implemented during BC/DR activities. If you've identified moving to manual systems or work-arounds if certain systems fail, these processes and procedures should be identified, tested, and verified. In addition, they should be looked at from the perspective of how manual processes might interact with automated systems. In some scenarios, you might have one or two key systems down and other systems still up and running. How will the manual and automated systems interact, how will manual processes be tracked and managed, how will work-arounds impact systems still running? These are the kinds of questions that must be addressed when examining the processes of the BC/DR plan. All work-arounds, manual processes, and associate forms and paperwork should be included in this test phase.

Validation of Task Integration

Any walk-through or test of the plan should involve key personnel from mission-critical business functions as well as members of the BC/DR team. During the validation of task integration, these business subject matter experts will be best able to identify if the tasks are listed in the right order, with the right dependencies, with the right requirements, or resources, and such. The integration of tasks is often where plans fail in implementation due to the complexity of most businesses today. This is particularly true when looking at IT systems, which are at the heart of most recovery efforts. If tasks are not properly identified and sequenced, it can take hours, days, or weeks to uncover the source of the problem. The time and place to do this is in the plan testing phase, not during an emergency.

Confirm Steps

In addition to testing the tasks and their integration, the testing should confirm each of the steps delineated in the plan. This confirms that all necessary steps are listed and in the correct order. It's often when you're walking through the plan step-by-step that you discover errors or omissions. If you're fortunate enough to have captured the correct data the first time around, this step will confirm that your plan is as complete as possible.

Confirm Resources

At each step during the testing, you should ask and answer, "What resources are required to perform this step?" When you're thinking through scenarios, it's easier to identify needed resources. These might include people, skills, equipment, and supplies. It doesn't do much good to teach employees how to administer first aid if there are no first aid kits in the building. This step of the testing should look at needed resources for each step. For example, you need to be sure that the resources are not simultaneously required by two different teams or in two different places, just as you would in any other type of project resource management plan. If you do not have those resources at the time of the test, you should flag these steps as incomplete or in need of resources and create an action item to obtain these resources as soon as possible.

Familiarize with Information Flow

Communications are extremely important during a business disruption or disaster and are very difficult to maintain in those circumstances. This section of the test identifies who needs to know what and when. It identifies where information must flow and how it will flow. It identifies information needs for the mission-critical business functions as well as for the ERT and the CMT groups. As staff become familiar with the flow of information through the BC/DR plan, they are more likely to have a heightened awareness of this flow during an actual event. Some communications will inevitably break down during a disaster, but the training you provide here by testing the information flow of the plan will help reduce the likelihood of a serious communication and information flow breakdown. In addition, the heightened awareness of information flow here helps build awareness of information flow through the organization on a normal day-to-day basis. This can help bridge communication gaps that currently are impacting operations and productivity.

The other type of information flow you need to address is the flow of data through IT systems and the organization. As you test your plan, you can identify how data flows through systems and determine whether your disaster recovery and business continuity plans addresses this appropriately. In large companies, there are numerous data and IT systems interdependencies that have to be identified. Testing your plan can help you look at data flow in light of BC/DR activities and make necessary adjustments.

Identify Gaps or Weaknesses

As you test the plan using checklists, paper walk-throughs, and simulations, the plan's gaps and weaknesses, if any, should become evident. It's usually not until we put something into a realistic scenario that we can see whether or not there are any problems. If you identify gaps or weaknesses, these can be addressed through modifications to the BC/DR plan. Omissions are often spotted as well—What *is* the number to call to replace your servers? Who *is* the contact person to report injured staff who can't report to work? Other details can be missed during the creation of the plan, such as where licensing information is stored or whether a particular backup will run on a new server or CPU type. The technology issues can be massive and overwhelming and though you probably can't test every scenario, you can test the most likely ones.

Determines Cost and Feasibility

It's difficult to completely understand potential costs of implementing the plan when you're creating it. You can create realistic scenarios and estimate potential costs, but as you test the plan, you're likely to understand more fully the potential costs for implementing, managing, and maintaining the plan. This information can be helpful in finalizing your plan or in revising your plan to meet your company's budgetary constraints. In addition, the overall feasibility of the plan will be tested. Again, it's relatively easy to think that someone could perform steps in a particular order or achieve certain milestones in a particular time frame when you're developing the plan. When people actually put parts of the plan to the test, it's likely that some aspects are simply impossible to implement or manage as expected. The feasibility of the various steps, processes, and work-arounds is tested and can be revised to reflect the reality of the situation rather than the perfection of the situation on paper.

By testing the plan through training and through looking at these specific issues, you will have the best possible plan in place short of actually putting it to the test. Of course, the irony of the situation is that despite your best efforts on the BC/DR plan, you hope you never need to find out how good that plan is. Having trained and tested using the methods described in this chapter, along with any training and testing methods appropriate for the unique needs of your organization, you increase your odds of successfully pulling your company through a major (or minor) disruption or disaster. We all know that few things in life mirror the perfect world of planning. The following conversation with a seasoned BC/DR executive sheds light on the difficulties of implementing and managing BC/DR planning in the real world.

From the Trenches...

How It Works in the Real World

Debbie Earnest, an experienced IT professional, has a background in manufacturing, infrastructure, and software. She managed a DR group for about 18 months, so she's been on the front lines of BC/DR planning. She's currently working for a major B2B software services company based in the United States. She was kind enough to take time out of her busy schedule to sit down and talk with us about her experience with business continuity and disaster recovery planning and implementation.

What are the significant challenges in BC/DR planning?

Many companies are in a bit of denial. Everyone says they need an ERP system with data flowing seamlessly through the company. That's great on paper, but how do you create that? Any hiccup upstream affects multiple systems downstream. The complexity of systems integration and interoperability is difficult in normal day-to-day operations, never mind in the midst of a crisis.

This complexity becomes a significant challenge in BC/DR planning that can quickly become overwhelming. When you begin looking just at mission-critical functions, there are so many interdependencies and so many points of failure that it becomes difficult to figure out where to start or how to cover them all. You can spend X dollars on disaster recovery planning and systems and you may still not be able to recover. That expenditure is then seen as a waste of money and, of course, that comes with its own set of problems. Even though your plan may not have addressed just one of a thousand failure points, if the one you missed is the one that comes into play, your plan may fail despite your best efforts.

BC/DR should really not be driven by IT, but in reality, it is. Companies cannot function without IT systems and IT staff are used to thinking about what could go wrong and how they should plan to avoid it. They are pretty good about risk management because they know that even a corrupt database can cause an outage for a period of time, or a fire in the UPS in the data center can cause a disruption. Many companies are so large or so complex, you just can't do business on paper anymore. Even trying to set up viable work-arounds or manual methods is next to impossible.

Another significant impediment to BC/DR planning is corporate mergers. It's difficult enough to develop a sound BC/DR plan for one company, but when you have the day-to-day IT tasks coupled with the tasks of integrating two disparate technology systems, BC/DR planning is almost impossible. There's no real clear solution to this problem other than to continue to build BC/DR systems into your plans as you move forward.

Perhaps the biggest problem is the budget. Unfortunately, when companies are looking for places to tighten their belts, they usually start cutting the BC/DR staff and activities. I worked for a company that was doing about $1B annually and when things got tight, they began eyeing the dedicated BC/DR jobs for elimination. Those people saw the writing on the wall and all eventually left the organization. This exemplifies the problem. Companies may think BC/DR is a great idea, but when it comes to including it in the budget and defending it at budget meetings, it doesn't happen.

What advice to you have for those trying to develop BC/DR plans?

Companies must figure out what is absolutely critical. Business leaders often can't identify critical components—to them every system they work with is critical. Therefore, the best approach is to say, "OK, this system goes down. What happens on Day 1? What happens on Day 2? Day 3?" By asking them these kinds of scenario-based questions, you can discern the relative priorities of the various systems. In some cases, the best you can do is develop a BC/DR plan that addresses the top three business functions and even then, it still may not be adequate. Again, it goes back to the number of failure points that exist in the organization. In some companies, it's manageable. In large corporations, it's pretty much impossible to cover everything.

The goal, from my perspective, is to never get into a disaster situation—build in safety valves along the way. The first line of coverage is to build it into your systems. IT people are used to thinking about downtime and outages and have developed almost an instinct for providing the first line of DR defense—primarily stemming from the rigorous availability demands from companies today.

In BC/DR planning, you can try dividing it into two basic levels: Level 1 = Data Loss, Level 2 = Building Loss. Since IT staff are pretty good about figuring out how to avoid data loss, the Level 1 defense can be the best line of protection. If you have sound methods in place for avoiding data loss, you are reducing your risk significantly. Identify what the Level 1 systems are and how they provide protection.

You also have to look at alternate sites in advance, if that's going to be part of your Level 2 plan. To try to get an alternate site after a disaster will take you twice as long and cost twice as much, so planning in advance is definitely the preferred approach.

Finally, you have to test and practice the plan. In some companies I've worked in, we simply did a paper walk-through of the plan once per year and revised it accordingly. Although that may not be ideal, it's about as much as you can squeeze out of some organizations for BC/DR purposes.

From your perspective, what's the bottom line?

The real issue is time and money—there's never enough of either. There is no perfect BC/DR plan, but having one is better than not having one. You have to ask, based on your company, what is the bare minimum? At the very least, plan for that. Then set expectations so no one is looking for perfection, it just doesn't exist.

Test Evaluation Criteria

Before embarking on the testing phase, you should develop clear evaluation criteria for your tests. In many cases, the easiest way to create test criteria is to go through the various checklists or steps in your BC/DR plan and create corresponding questions. Let's look at an example involving the notification step in the activation of the plan.

1. Was the primary team member able to begin the notification process successfully?
2. How many team members were contacted?
3. How long did it take to notify team members?
4. Were there any missing or incorrect phone numbers?
5. How many team members were contacted via their primary methods vs. alternate methods?
6. How many team members were not on the notification list?
7. Were there any names on the notification list that should not have been?
8. Would this have worked if phone systems were out?

You can create a set of questions for each phase of the plan and use these to evaluate the test results. You can then measure the performance against the ability to complete each step, the thoroughness of each step, the effectiveness of each step and the accuracy and validity of each step.

Recommendations

Based on test results, you should develop recommendations. These recommendations may result in modifications to the BC/DR plan, but they may result in modifications to other areas as well. For example, you might find areas in which staff need additional training. You might find through these tests that there are areas of the business not included in the plan that should be or that there are operational changes that are recommended based on the test results. Recommendations for each team as well as for each phase of the plan should be developed. Be sure to include a process for incorporating recommendations so they are actually utilized and not overlooked.

Performing IT Systems and Security Audits

By definition, an audit is the systematic examination against defined criteria. If your company is required to comply with laws or regulations, you have no doubt been through rigorous audits. The audits you perform to conform to these regulations may help in your BC/DR planning and may need to be included in your plan. For example, if you must comply with HIPAA (Health Insurance Portability and Accountability Act) standards, your BC/DR plans must address these issues and your audit of the plan has to include these parameters as well. Your audit should include both business continuity and systems audits.

IT Systems and Security Audits

Auditing IT systems involves a set of tasks that help reduce the risk of an intrusion or attack. Audits are concerned primarily with ensuring the company maintains data confidentiality, integrity, and availability, because these are the areas that typically come under attack. In some cases, this can disable a company's critical business functions; in more extreme cases, it disables the company's entire operations and creates a significant legal or financial liability for the firm as well.

An IT systems audit typically focuses on conducting a systematic evaluation of the security of various IT systems by measuring how well it conforms to established criteria or requirements. It includes an assessment or review of the network and systems' physical configuration and environment, the configuration of the software, the handling (storage, transport, access, etc.) of data, sensitive data in particular, and user access. Security audits are often performed in conjunction with compliance efforts, though even companies not subject to compliance regulations should undertake periodic IT audits.

Hardening systems is a risk mitigation strategy that is employed by virtually every company using IT systems today. Hardening systems, as you're probably aware, consists of taking actions to minimize the attack footprint of a system or network. This includes actions such as removing network protocols not in use, disabling ports or services not being used, removing unused user accounts, reducing permissions to the least possible, and automating the updating of anti-virus and anti-spyware data files, to name just a few examples.

With respect to BC/DR planning, systems auditing should include several key elements. These include:

- Ensuring IT risk mitigation strategies are in place and properly implemented/configured.

- Ensuring systems identified by the BC/DR plan are still in place and functioning.

- Identifying areas where new technology has been implemented and may not be incorporated into the BC/DR plan.

- Identifying areas where technology has been retired or modified, resulting in the need to revise the BC/DR plan.

- Reviewing the processes identified in the BC/DR plan with respect to IT systems to ensure the steps and processes are still correct, complete, and relevant.

- Verifying that the IT incident response team (CIRT, CERT or whatever term you use) is in tact and has a clear understanding of roles, responsibilities and how to implement the IT-specific segments of the BC/DR plan.

- Reviewing data regarding various systems to ensure they are still compliant with the BC/DR plans. These systems include operating systems, networking and telecommunications equipment, database and applications, systems backups, security controls, integration, and testing. Any of these areas is subject to frequent change. An audit can help assure the BC/DR plan will still work if implemented.

This is not an exhaustive list, but it provides examples of what types of data an IT audit within the scope of a BC/DR plan might include. The key is to identify how IT systems have changed (or remained the same) and assess how and where that impacts the BC/DR plan. Most IT systems are not static and even gradual changes over time can end up creating a significant change to the way a BC/DR plan must be implemented. Referring to the interview with IT professional Debbie Earnest earlier in the chapter, you can see that with the complexity of systems, the proliferation of corporate mergers and acquisitions, and the ever-changing technological landscape, your best bet for keeping your BC/DR plan up to date will be through the IT audit process. Periodic auditing is an excellent operational practice for IT and it doesn't take too much more effort to include a check of key elements from the BC/DR plan during these audits. We'll discuss maintaining the BC/DR plan in more detail in the next chapter, but keep in mind that IT audits are the easiest way to maintain the BC/DR plan from an IT perspective primarily because they involve a periodic review that is likely already part of your standard operating procedures. Adding a few extra steps to your audit plan is easier than trying to perform a fully separate BC/DR audit every quarter or every year. It's also easier to address gradual changes as they occur than to try to assess how much change has occurred since the prior year's review of the plan.

Summary

Training and testing your BC/DR plan are tightly integrated activities. Training staff for the specific roles, responsibilities, and actions they take during the implementation of the BC/DR plan also tests the plan. On the flip side, testing the plan trains staff in the implementation and management of the plan. Therefore, these two activities should be viewed as a whole and plans for training and testing should be complementary rather than redundant.

Training activities should be defined for emergency responders. These skills often are taught by community organizations such as the local fire department or other local organizations. Skills include building evacuation, fire fighting, and first aid. Training should include safety procedures as well as instruction on the use of specialized equipment. These skills should be reviewed and refreshed periodically through exercise, drills and simulations, if possible.

Training for business continuity and disaster recovery is a slightly more difficult undertaking. Training can take any of several forms and the training activities are also plan testing activities, so there's a great deal of overlap. Training for BC/DR should include training team members on their specific roles and responsibilities during the implementation of the BC/DR plan. It should also include training on specific skills needed to effectively implement and manage the plan. Cross-functional teamwork and communications should also be part of the BC/DR training.

In order for the training to be effective, you should develop clear, specific, and measurable outcomes for your training. This should include scope of training, requirements for training, and learning outcomes expected. You may need to perform a training needs assessment before developing the training requirements. As you test the plan, you'll also identify areas that may require additional staff training, and these can be added to your training requirements. Developing the training can be done in conjunction with developing the testing plan for your BC/DR plan in order to achieve some efficiencies in your efforts. Finding time to schedule and deliver training is a challenge in most organizations, so if you can find a way to tie these efforts or outcomes into larger business objectives, you might have greater success. The results of training activities should be monitored and measured to ensure the training achieved its objectives and that revisions to the training based on input and feedback can be incorporated in the next iteration.

Testing the plan helps train team members on the use of the plan, on their specific roles and responsibilities, and on communicating across the organization. Testing the plan will also help you identify processes, procedures, steps, or checklists that are incorrect, have gaps, or require revision for some reason.

There are four primary ways plans are trained and tested, though there are an infinite number of variations. A paper walk-through is the easiest and least disruptive way to test your plan, but it yields the least accurate results as compared to other methods. However, because it is least disruptive, it *is* the easiest for most organizations to implement and the results can help improve the quality of the BC/DR plan significantly. Functional exercises test subsections of the plan and the functionality of various components. An example of a functional exercise is having IT test the steps in the BC/DR plan related to restoring a server from remote backups. These types of tests can help uncover problems that would otherwise go unnoticed, but they take more time and resources to perform than paper tests. Field exercises and full interruptions certainly provide the most realistic simulations, but most companies will be reluctant to plan and pay for this type of training. In some types of industries, this type of exercise is a requirement either for health and safety reasons or due to legal or regulatory requirements. Regardless of which type of training and testing you undertake, you should pay special attention to the skills and training needs of the plan implementers. They should be well versed in how to activate and implement the plan so that they can do so relatively easily if a disruption or disaster occurs.

Testing the plan checks for understanding of the processes, procedures, and steps defined. It validates the integration and dependencies of tasks across various business and functional units. It also helps determine if the right resources have been identified for the various steps. Ultimately, it familiarizes the implementers with the entire process and uncovers potential gaps, errors, or omissions. Finally, the cost and feasibility of implementing a plan can be better assessed through testing.

IT systems and security audits are typically part of company's standard IT operating procedures and they may be required by law or regulation (HIPAA, etc.). In addition, BC/DR-specific IT audit tasks can be included in standard auditing procedures to reduce the amount of additional work that might be required to test the BC/DR plan. Some of the elements you might choose to audit in this manner include ensuring the IT risk mitigation strategies have been implemented per the BC/DR plan, ensuring the processes and procedures for IT work-arounds are feasible and meet requirements and identifying changes to technology that impact (or are impacted by) the BC/DR plan.

## Chapter 36

BC/DR Plan Maintenance

Solutions in this chapter:

- BC/DR Change Management
- Strategies for Managing Change
- BC/DR Plan Audit
- Plan Maintenance Activities
- Project Close Out

☑ Summary

Introduction

Maintaining the plan you've developed may end up being the biggest challenge you face in the entire business continuity and disaster recovery plan process. If you found lack of enthusiasm or outright resistance to the BC/DR process, you may find that support for maintaining the plan simply vanishes. However, there is some good news amidst this gloomy outlook. First, you actually *have* a plan to maintain. People within the organization have participated in evaluating the business, developing mitigation strategies, and perhaps even testing the plan. The other good news is that, as we've discussed throughout this section of the book, there are many areas in which you can incorporate BC/DR strategies and activities in your standard operating procedures. For example, many of the IT strategies implemented to provide continuous (or very high) availability are strategies that are also BC/DR risk mitigation strategies. We've pointed out that it's extremely helpful to incorporate BC/DR strategies in your operational plans whenever possible to reduce the outright resistance you may face to BC/DR planning.

In this chapter, we'll discuss various considerations for maintaining your BC/DR plan, especially in the face of indifference or resistance. As you can see from Figure 36.1, we're in the last phase of our BC/DR planning project.

Figure 36.1 Business Continuity and Disaster Recovery Project Plan Progress

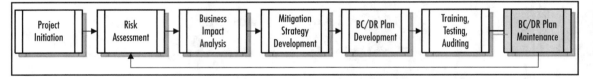

BC/DR Plan Change Management

Change is constant in organizations—change in operations, change in technology, change in personnel, change in regulations—the list goes on. You might be wondering how you can possibly reflect these changes in your BC/DR plan without having a full-time dedicated BC/DR team. It is challenging, but there are a few strategies you can use to reduce the complexity and enormity of the task. Change management has several discrete steps, as depicted in Figure 36.2. As you can see, the first step is to monitor changes. There are numerous sources of change that we'll discuss shortly. The next step is to decide how the changes impact your BC/DR plan. Not all changes have an impact on your plan, but you need to assess change before you can make that determination. If a change impacts your plan, the next step is to determine how to address the change in your plan. This typically involves cycling back and performing a modified version of your risk assessment, business impact analysis, and mitigation strategy development. This iterative process can be accomplished relatively quickly in many cases, but your assessments will have to specifically look at the suggested change and the impact on the entire plan.

Figure 36.2 Change Management Process

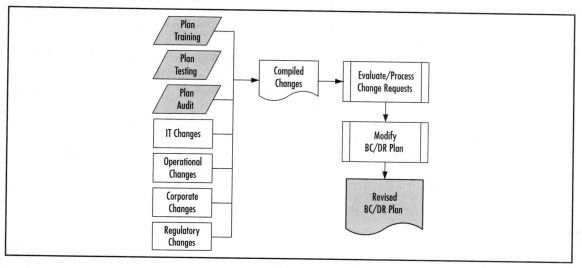

We've discussed plan training, testing, and auditing in Chapter 8, so let's continue now by looking at how these inject change into the BC/DR plan and then we'll examine other sources of change that impact a BC/DR plan.

Training, Testing, and Auditing

In Chapter 8, we discussed the activities related to developing, delivering, and evaluating training. You learned that training often involves testing the plan, and that testing the plan trains staff on how to implement the plan and carry out the tasks assigned. Changes will naturally come out of these processes, and that's part of the purpose of training and testing. It's difficult, if not impossible, to develop a perfect plan the first time through. It's not until you try putting the plan to work that you discover steps out of order, errors, omissions, or redundancies. As you deliver your training and perform your testing, you should capture a list of changes that need to be made to the BC/DR plan. These changes should be submitted for review. Not all requested changes should be made for a variety of reasons. We'll discuss the change review process in the section entitled "Strategies for Managing Change" later in this chapter.

Changes in Information Technologies

The IT audit discussed in Chapter 8 is one of the ways you can keep track of changes to IT, but clearly this area is the one most subject to change and risk. You and your IT team are more than likely extremely familiar with reviewing and assessing change—from the location and duties of various servers to the implementation of new applications to the reorganization of existing infrastructure. As you know, even the most innocuous changes can suddenly inject all kinds of problems into your network systems. As you continue to manage your day-to-day IT operations, you should consider including an additional step in some of your processes that remind you to assess the process against BC/DR. For example, you likely have a process for evaluating the implementation of new technology. Consider adding one step in the process that says, "Assess impact of this new technology on BC/DR plans." It is a deceptively simple step and admittedly, it can open up a whole set of problems or questions you'd like to avoid. The flip side is that if two or more technologies are being considered, there may be one that contributes to BC/DR more than the others. In that case, you might be able to build in additional BC/DR capabilities with little effort.

As systems are upgraded, swapped out, modified, or retired, be sure to include a line item task to consider the impact on BC/DR plans. In some cases, this will be simply an item to be checked off. In other cases, you might discover that changing a system will have a large impact on your BC/DR plans. In those cases, you'll have to balance the potential change (for better or worse) against other alternatives. Regardless of your final decision, be sure to flag these changes so the BC/DR plan can be updated as a result.

From the Trenches…

Incorporating IT Changes

IT systems are at the heart of most BC/DR plans. As a result, changes to IT systems often have the biggest impact on the BC/DR plan. For most organizations, the easiest way to make sure IT changes are reflected in the BC/DR plan is to keep a list of IT changes and a brief assessment of the impact on the BC/DR plan. As the periodic review or audit of the BC/DR plan occurs, this list of IT changes can be incorporated. It might be as simple as keeping the list of changes in a spreadsheet or document in the same folder as the BC/DR plan. Since IT changes so frequently, the first questions to be asked should be, "How will this change enhance or degrade our ability to recover from a significant outage?" If the change will enhance it, you're set (though you still need to take an integrated or holistic look at the change and how it impacts other parts of the organization and the BC/DR plan). If the change will degrade your ability to recover from a significant outage, you need to assess whether this is a wise move or whether there are other options available that will meet your needs and be neutral or positive as it applies to BC/DR.

Changes in Operations

During your risk assessment, you determined the mission-critical business functions that needed to be addressed in your BC/DR plan. Clearly, operations are not static and changes over time to operations may impact the BC/DR plan. Reorganization, expansion, new departments, new facilities, and new management structures can all impact operations in a variety of ways. In some cases, changes in operation happen slowly over time and these changes may go unnoticed as it relates to the BC/DR plan. The BC/DR plan audit (discussed later in this chapter) can be an effective method of reviewing operations against the BC/DR plan. If the business's mission-critical operations have changed over time or if the processes used to accomplish these functions have changed, the BC/DR plan is at significant risk of failure and should be revised. For example, if your company has slowly moved from bricks-and-mortar retail to e-commerce, many key processes may have changed. If the mix has shifted slowly over time, you might not notice it until you test the plan or perform a BC/DR audit. Obviously, the key is to be sure your BC/DR plan addresses your mission-critical business functions and if those shift over time, you plan needs to be updated. Changes to operational processes should be implemented as needed, but it would help if your operations staff understood that any changes to their key processes should be flagged so the BC/DR team can review the impact of those changes on the plan and revise as needed.

Corporate Changes

Corporate mergers, acquisitions, spin-offs, restructuring, and other types of corporate changes can have a major impact on the BC/DR plan. As these changes are considered and discussed, the BC/DR team should assess the potential impact to the plan. Of course, in many cases, these activities are not publicly announced until the deal is sealed, so your team may be caught off guard. As you read in the interview with Debbie Earnest (see Chapter 8), these kinds of changes are among the most challenging to deal with from a BC/DR perspective. IT staff will have a big enough challenge figuring out how to incorporate the required IT changes for daily operations much less trying to figure out how all this impacts BC/DR activities. Per Earnest's suggestion, the best you can do most of the time is to continually look to incorporate BC/DR activities into your normal operations and planning activities and to continually look to protecting data first. Sometimes, the BC/DR elements can be addressed through standard IT planning processes with an additional line item task. Assessing how the plans impact BC/DR may help the team choose from among several viable alternatives or it might point out a path that optimizes immediate and BC/DR capabilities.

Legal, Regulatory, or Compliance Changes

Changes to the legal, regulatory, or compliance landscape will certainly trigger required changes to your BC/DR plan. For example, if laws change regarding data security, you will have to review your BC/DR plan to determine whether your existing plan meets these new requirements or whether you'll need to implement additional tools, technologies, or processes. As with other changes, it's sometimes as simple as looking at the current BC/DR plan and determining that no change is needed. Other times, a major change may require you to cycle through all phases of the BC/DR project planning stages and create a plan for implementing required changes. In most cases, changes in this arena will impact operations or IT and the impact to the BC/DR plan will be addressed through those channels.

Strategies for Managing Change

Two key strategies for managing change are having a process for monitoring and a process for evaluating change requests. It's usually easier to monitor change and respond to it as needed over time rather than sitting down once a year and trying to remember (or determine) what's changed since your last review of the plan. The easiest way to monitor change throughout the organization, as it relates to BC/DR plans, is to include an additional step or two in standard operating procedures. These steps can be as simple as "Determine impact, if any, on BC/DR plan. If impact exists, submit BC/DR change request to [insert position responsible for managing BC/DR change requests]."

Common Challenges

Removing Roadblocks

Most IT professionals are accustomed to dealing with change requests. In the BC/DR process, there are really two separate and distinct activities: change notifications and change requests. *Change notifications* are those changes that are being made, regardless of impact to the BC/DR plan. These include changes to the organization, personnel, operations, or the larger regulatory environment. These changes need to be addressed by the BC/DR plan. *Change requests* are elements that trigger changes to the BC/DR plan. In some cases, a change notification triggers a change request. Other times, a change notification does not trigger a change request. You may choose to take these two functions out and ask your operations staff to incorporate a *change notification* process. In this way, they can notify the BC/DR team of change. The BC/DR team can then evaluate that change and generate a change request for the BC/DR plan, if appropriate. The rationale behind dividing this process in two in this manner is that operations staff might resist the use of a "change request" because, from their perspective, the change is not being requested, it is being implemented. Therefore, the use of the term change notification may help reduce resistance within the organization to the process of keeping the BC/DR team up to date. A simple change of terminology may melt resistance to the process of keeping your team up to speed on organizational changes that may impact the BC/DR plan.

Monitor Change

Implementing processes for monitoring change can make your job of maintaining the BC/DR plan much easier. Develop processes that can be incorporated into everyday processes so that as changes occur, they can quickly be assessed for their potential impact on the BC/DR plan. If the change has no impact, it can be ignored (from a BC/DR perspective). If the change will have an impact, a change request should be submitted to the BC/DR team. (*Note:* We'll use the term *change request* to keep it simple, but it will refer to either a change request or notification.) Remember, a change request may be a simple matter of noting that the leader of the Emergency Response Team has changed. This change request should trigger the appropriate revision to the BC/DR plan including contact names, phone numbers, and team rosters. The same is true of other types of changes. If the IT group is implementing a new server, there may be a change request generated to note the new technical specs of the server in the event of an outage, or it may trigger a quick review of the specs for servers at the alternate computing site to ensure the alternate site still meets BC/DR needs.

People

People leave organizations, they get promoted, or they move into different jobs. A periodic review of changes to the organization can help you determine if there have been personnel changes that impact your plan. This can be part of the BC/DR plan audit, discussed later in this chapter.

Process

Changes to processes should be monitored as well. Subject matter experts or members of the BC/DR team can be tasked with monitoring changes to key processes and flagging changes for BC/DR review. Many corporate processes remain fairly unchanged over time; however, some companies that are in high growth mode or that are streamlining operations, for example, might have significant changes to their daily operations. Changes to mission-critical functions should be reviewed with the highest priority since these changes could potentially cause the BC/DR plan to fail if implemented without these changes.

Technology

Changes to IT have been discussed, but some technology may fall outside the scope of IT management. If your company works with scientific equipment, manufacturing equipment, or other specialized technology, changes in this arena should be monitored and assessed to determine whether the BC/DR plan requires modification. Often changes in technology create changes in processes, so the trigger for review and modification may come from either area. However, a process for triggering a review should be included in your technology implementation plans to make BC/DR plan maintenance as low maintenance as possible.

Evaluate and Incorporate Change

The change review process should be a well-defined process for your BC/DR plan and someone should be responsible for processing change requests. In some cases, this is the BC/DR project manager, in other cases, it may be a role assigned to a team member or it may be managed through some other existing process.

Most project managers use a change management process for managing their projects and the same types of processes are useful here. As you know, not all changes requested can or should be implemented into a plan. Additionally, even if a change should be made to a plan, there are numerous considerations before incorporating the change into the plan. If you have a standardized change management process that you've worked with successfully in the past, you may want to use it here. Be sure to review your process to ensure it's appropriate to change management in the BC/DR process.

Not all changes should be incorporated, and reviewing changes individually and then as a group will help you and the team determine which changes should or must be implemented. Any changes that are required by law, regulation, or compliance clearly must be made, though there may be several different approaches to incorporating the change that will meet the requirements. In that case, further analysis may be required. Ultimately, for each change you consider, you need to determine the impact on the other elements of the BC/DR plan. For example, if your company moves to a new location, you need to assess the threats again. There may be a chemical processing plant in the new neighborhood that you have to consider. It might be that your business moved in order to get away from that chemical processing plant and to reduce certain risks. Some changes increase your risks, other changes reduce your risks. Some changes may have a strong effect on the business impact analysis outcomes, others may have no effect at all. For each change, you'll need to cycle briefly through all your assessment steps to see how a potential change impacts (and is impacted by) each area. After the assessment, if you and the team decide the change should be incorporated, it can be implemented and the BC/DR plan can be revised accordingly. This also means that the change should be incorporated in the training, testing, and auditing processes and procedures.

Here are some points to consider:

1. Compile all change requests and prioritize based on potential risk, vulnerability, impact (if applicable).

2. Determine if any change requests are required for legal, regulatory, or compliance reasons. If so, flag these as required changes.

3. Review compiled change requests, review for redundancy, relevancy, etc. Revise compiled list as appropriate.

4. Prioritize compiled list. For each item, determine how the change impacts (or is impacted by):

   a. Selected risks and threats

   b. Threat vulnerability

   c. Business impact analysis

   d. Risk mitigation strategies

5. Assess potential cost, risk profile (does it inject or reduce risk?), desirability, feasibility, and interaction with other elements of the plan.

6. Determine if change request should be incorporated, delayed, rejected, or closed.

7. For each change request incorporated, document impact to BC/DR plan in detail. Advise change requestor of change acceptance, if appropriate.

8. For each change *incorporated*, determine need for additional training or testing activities. Trigger notification for training, testing, or auditing if appropriate.

9. For each change *delayed*, document reason for delay and how change will be processed later. Communicate decision to change requestor, if appropriate.

10. For each change *rejected or closed*, document reason for denying change. Communicate with change requestor, if appropriate.

11. For all approved changes, make revisions to BC/DR plan, note change in plan, and notify plan stakeholders of plan revision, if appropriate.

BC/DR Plan Audit

You might wonder why you would audit your BC/DR plan if you're also performing training and testing. The plan audit is a process in which you review the BC/DR plan against specific requirements. For example, you may review it against the organization's business practices, objectives, strategies, or changing financial situation. You may also review the plan against external constraints such as legal or regulatory requirements.

The audit does not test the plan. From an audit perspective, there is no assurance that the steps and processes included in the plan will work. The audit does not train people in the use of the plan or in the skills needed to implement and execute the plan. The audit is a more impartial review of the plan to assess whether it meets the company's overall needs. An audit should be performed as a standard project and an audit plan should be created. This plan should include, at minimum:

- Audit scope, timeline, requirements, and constraints

- Review of corporate risks and risk management strategies including BC/DR

- Review of business impact

- Review of BC/DR plan development activities

- Review of BC/DR plan test plans and activities

- Review of BC/DR plan training plans and activities

- Review of BC/DR change management and plan maintenance processes

This assists in maintaining the plan because gaps or weaknesses in any of these processes or activities can be spotted and addressed. Reviewing these elements may result in the generation of change requests that should be processed by the BC/DR team.

Plan Maintenance Activities

There are a number of activities beyond change management that can help you keep your plan up to date and ready to go. We've listed a number of these activities here and of course, if you think of others that will help your team, be sure to add them to the list.

1. If the plan is revised, the BC/DR team members (or those who should have the latest copy of the plan) should be notified in a timely manner.

2. The plan should use a revision numbering system so team members know whether they have the latest version of the plan.

3. Review, update, and revise key contact information regularly. This includes staff, vendors, contractors, key customers, alternate sites and facilities, among others.

4. Create a BC/DR plan distribution list that is limited to authorized personnel but that includes all relevant parties. This distribution list should include off-site and remote facilities that may be used in the event of BC/DR plan activation.

5. Be sure there are up-to-date copies of the BC/DR plan off-site in the event the building is inaccessible.

6. Be sure there are up-to-date paper copies of the BC/DR plan on-site in the event IT systems go down.

7. Implement a process whereby all old versions of the plan are destroyed or archived and new versions replace them. This helps avoid a scenario where team members are working from different versions of the plan.

8. Always check soft copy and remote storage copies of your plan when changes are made to the plan. If you store copies off-site or at your alternate work site, these versions should be updated any time the plan is modified.

9. Whenever significant changes are requested or implemented, test the plan. This will ensure there are no new areas of concern and will help train staff on the changes.

10. Integrate BC/DR considerations into operational processes to reduce plan maintenance efforts in the future.

11. Assign responsibility for managing BC/DR change notification and requests to someone on the BC/DR team. The project management adage that a task without an owner won't get done is especially true here.

12. Document plan maintenance procedures and follow these procedures to avoid introducing additional risk into the project.

13. Incorporate training into the change process so changes to people, process, technology that are incorporated into the BC/DR plan also trigger changes to training plans.

14. Be sure to include BC/DR plan testing, training, auditing, and maintenance activities in your IT or corporate budget for future activities related to BC/DR.

Project Close Out

At this juncture, you should be ready to close out your BC/DR project. If you've been working through each step as you've read through these chapters, you should have a fairly comprehensive and rigorous BC/DR project plan in place. If you decided to read the material, create the project plan, and then initiate project work, you now have a clear roadmap for how to proceed. In either case, the result should be a clear, comprehensive, and reasonable business continuity and disaster recovery plan that should address the major threats to your company and mitigate risks to the most critical business functions. You should have developed procedures related to monitoring change, implementing change, and maintaining the BC/DR plan that can be folded into standard corporate operations to reduce the BC/DR effort going forward.

Now that you've completed work on your plan, you may be ready to launch into a training or testing activity or you may be ready to put the whole project away until the next review period. Regardless of what you decide your next steps are, you should take time to do several project close-out activities.

1. Be sure all documentation is complete and finalized.

2. Be sure the BC/DR plan is distributed to appropriate personnel.

3. Announce plan completion to project sponsor and other project stakeholders.

4. Announce plan completion to company to increase awareness and celebrate success.

5. Announce training or testing plans, if appropriate.

6. Hold a project review session to discuss lessons learned and incorporate into process. This should not be held at the same time as a project close out or celebration. This should be a working meeting to capture best practices and lessons learned.

7. Hold project close out meeting to celebrate completion and recognize individual efforts, as appropriate.

8. Complete any staff reviews related to project work.

9. Submit summary or close-out report to project sponsor, executive team, or other stakeholders, as appropriate.

10. Update legal or compliance documentation to reflect BC/DR readiness, as appropriate.

11. Set date for next BC/DR audit, review, testing, or training.

Your BC/DR plan will never be perfect and there may be times when it seems it is never complete. However, if you have taken the time and expended the effort to work through the suggestions throughout this section, you should have a solid BC/DR plan that provides a clear roadmap for staff so they know how to keep your business running even when disaster strikes. Along the way, you and your team may have learned a lot more about your company, how it operates, and what contributes to its success. It is our hope that you will never need to find out just how good your plan is and that your efforts will help improve your business operations outside of the realm of disaster readiness.

Summary

Once your BC/DR plan is developed, you need to implement methods for managing change. This includes monitoring changes to the organization that may impact, or be impacted by, the BC/DR plan. Change to the BC/DR plan comes from a variety of sources, including the training, testing, and auditing activities discussed in Chapter 35. Change in IT infrastructure, systems, and processes is the most common organizational change and one that potentially has the biggest impact on the BC/DR plan. Changes in operations can also dramatically impact BC/DR plans. Some operational changes happen slowly over time and may go unnoticed until an audit or plan test. Other changes may be more obvious. In either case, changes to operations should trigger change notifications or change requests. Corporate mergers, acquisitions, spin-offs, and restructuring activities can also have a significant impact on BC/DR plans. In many cases, these changes cannot be anticipated and the BC/DR team may simply have to respond to changes as they occur. Changes in the legal, regulatory, or compliance arenas may trigger mandatory changes to the organization or to the BC/DR plan. These changes should be flagged as required and their impact on the BC/DR plan should be assessed.

Since organizations are always changing, you may find you have more cooperation through creating a change notification process. Since operations staff will implement changes to their processes as they see fit, you may be able to get them to notify the BC/DR team of changes so the team can assess the impact and generate a change request to the BC/DR plan, if appropriate. Another strategy for monitoring change can be to include an additional step in standard operating procedures that includes a quick assessment of the potential impact of activities on the BC/DR plan. People, processes, and technology are ever-changing in organizations and developing easy-to-use processes for monitoring change and the potential impact on the BC/DR plan can assist in plan maintenance.

When change requests are generated, the BC/DR team should have a clear, consistent methodology for evaluating and incorporating change. Not all change requests should be implemented for a variety of reasons. Using established criteria to evaluate change requests will help reduce the risk that changing the plan injects into the process. Factors such as cost, feasibility, desirability, interaction with existing processes, and risk impact should be assessed before changes are accepted. If a change is accepted, it should be incorporated into the plan, the plan should be revised, and plan stakeholders should be notified the plan has been revised. Updated copies of the plan should be distributed appropriately and old versions should be destroyed or archived. If requested changes are delayed or declined, the change requestor should be notified of the decision and the rationale for the decision.

The BC/DR plan should be audited periodically to review it from a business perspective. This audit typically does not evaluate the process, as does a test nor does it necessarily help in training. Its purpose is to review whether the plan meets a stated set of criteria such as business practices, legal, or compliance requirements. Along with testing and training, auditing the plan helps maintain the plan by identifying areas the plan is diverging from business practices or requirements. Should problems be found, change requests should be generated, evaluated, and incorporated as appropriate.

There are numerous plan maintenance activities that can be incorporated into standard operating procedures throughout the organization. In addition, there are various steps you can include in your process to help keep the plan up to date. These include triggers for updating staff rosters, contact information, and vendor lists. Creating a method for notifying the team regarding the availability of a revised plan and processes for updating plans at remote sites, off-site storage locations, among others will help ensure that your most recent version of the plan is available in hard and soft copy, both on- and off-site, to the people who are responsible for implementing the plan, if needed.

Finally, the project should be closed out as you would close out any other project. This might include providing a summary document to your project sponsor and to corporate executives, performing staff evaluations and reviews, notifying the company as a whole that the project was successfully completed, holding a project review session to gather lessons learned, holding a project celebration to recognize individual and team efforts, and most importantly, setting a date for the next BC/DR update, review, audit, or test.

After all your hard work and diligent effort, the best scenario will be that your plan is never implemented. Even though you may not see your plan in action, you may find that the process of creating this plan has improved your knowledge and understanding of your company and perhaps improved some of your company's business processes along the way.

## Chapter 37

BC/DR Checklists

Solutions in this chapter:

- Risk Assessment

- Crisis Communications Checklist

- Emergency and Recovery Response Checklist

- Business Continuity Checklist

- IT Recovery Checklists

- Training, Testing, and Auditing Checklists

- BC/DR Plan Maintenance Checklist

Risk Assessment

Risk management includes the three elements of the risk assessment: threat assessment, vulnerability assessment, and impact analysis. This information is the input to the risk mitigation phase that concludes the risk assessment portion of the business continuity and disaster recovery project work.

The first step in business continuity and disaster recovery planning is the risk assessment. Included here are top-level items that should be included. You can modify this list to suit your specific needs. Refer to the specific chapters for detailed information on these topics.

Threat and Vulnerability Assessment

1. Identify all natural threats.
2. Identify all man-made threats.
3. Identify all IT and technology-based threats.
4. Identify all environmental/infrastructure threats.
5. For each threat, identify threat sources.
6. For each threat source, identify the likelihood of occurrence.
7. Based on likelihood of occurrence, assess company's vulnerability to each threat source.
8. Based on likelihood and vulnerability, prioritize list of threats to company.

Business Impact Analysis

1. Based on prioritized list of threats, assess impact of each threat on business operations.
2. Based on threats, perform upstream and downstream loss analysis.
3. Prioritize business functions into mission-critical, important, minor (you can customize categories to suit your needs).
4. For each mission-critical business function, assess the impact of the loss of this function.
5. For each mission-critical business function, assess the impact of various threats to this function.
6. Develop a prioritized list of mission-critical business functions with the highest business impact.
7. For the highest priority functions, identify the recovery time requirements including maximum tolerable downtime (MTD).
8. For business systems, business functions, and IT systems, identify the following: business process criticality, financial impact, operational impact, recovery objectives, dependencies, and work-arounds.

Mitigation Strategies

Risk mitigation strategies are developed after the risk assessment phase is complete. Strategies should be developed based on the mission-critical business functions and the risks to the company. Cost, capability, and recovery times are among the aspects to be considered. IT systems can be included in the risk mitigation strategies or can be addressed as a separate set of strategies.

1. For each mission-critical function, identify risk mitigation strategies for consideration including risk acceptance, avoidance, transference, and limitation.

2. For each mission-critical function, identify the recovery requirements and potential recovery options.

3. For each recovery option considered, identify the time, cost/capability, feasibility, service level requirements, and existing controls in place.

4. For each mission-critical option, select the optimal risk mitigation strategy.

5. For IT systems, identify mission-critical IT systems, equipment, and data.

6. For each mission-critical IT component, identify risk mitigation strategies.

7. For each risk mitigation strategy selected, develop implementation plan.

Crisis Communications Checklist

It's likely you'll need more than one type of communication plan. This checklist provides the generic elements to consider and you can modify, as appropriate, for each type of communication plan you need to develop. Therefore, this list refers to a single communication plan but should be used for all communications plans you need to develop.

Remember the three rules of crisis communication:

1. Don't lie.

2. Appoint a single spokesperson.

3. Provide who, what, when, where, why, and how.

Communication Checklist

1. Define communications needs.

2. Develop communication plan objectives based on target audience (employee, customer, media, etc.).

3. Identify and detail triggers for activating the communications plan.

4. Delineate all assumptions related to the need, objectives, and triggers for the plan.

5. Develop distribution list and methodology based on likely communications scenarios (i.e., if e-mail or phones are down, how will information be communicated?). Develop list of distribution alternatives.

6. Develop list of all contacts needed for distribution of this plan.

7. List all legal or regulatory constraints that may impact message or timing of message.

8. Develop communication template to assist in crisis communication situations.

9. Develop message content (see next).

10. Identify message and distribution authorization or escalation channels.

11. Establish distribution channels.

12. Identify frequency of communication.

13. Keep communication log.

Message Content

The template for the message can include specific information that *should* always be conveyed such as corporate commitments, policies, or other data related to the incident. The template also should include areas in which caution is recommended. This might mean not disclosing employee names or home addresses, not releasing names of victims or casualty counts, and so on. Include specific language that can be used as well as a reminder to provide the who, what, when, where, why, and how of the situation.

1. Disaster declaration statement to be communicated to BC/DR team, employees, investors, shareholders, customers, vendors, contractors, as well as community and media contacts.

2. General disaster information including:

   a. Notification and clarification of event

   b. Impact of event

   c. Current status and condition of people, facilities, and equipment

   d. Frequency of updates, estimated time of next update

3. Specific information and instructions for various stakeholders and groups including:

   a. Employees

   b. Vendors, suppliers, contractors

   c. Customers

   d. Business partners

   e. Community and media

   f. Legal and regulatory notification requirements

4. Contact information for additional information (corporate spokesperson or communication team leads, as appropriate).

Business Continuity and Disaster Recovery Response Checklist

This is a basic checklist you can use to identify the primary steps in your response to any serious business disruption or disaster. Modify this checklist to include details pertinent to your company's BC/DR plan. This checklist can be used as a high-level response list and can be used as the basis for developing an action flowchart for response activities. You may choose to refer to additional checklists here to point the teams to more detailed lists in each of the response areas.

Disruptive or disaster event occurs.

1. Initial response.
2. Notification.
3. Problem assessment.
4. Escalation.
5. Disaster declaration.
6. Plan activation.
7. Plan implementation activities and logistics.
8. Disaster recovery phase implementation.
9. Business continuity phase implementation.
10. Resumption and normalization of business activities.
11. Review of event, revision of BC/DR plan based on lessons learned.

Emergency and Recovery Response Checklist

We discussed the different phases of business continuity and disaster recovery, including activation, disaster recovery, business continuity recovery, and maintenance/review. In this chapter, we've provided numerous checklists to help you sort through the details. You can use these checklists to help develop your plan and also as appendices to your own BC/DR plan to provide people with step-by-step roadmaps for emergency and recovery responses.

This detail belongs in your BC/DR plan, but breaking it out into sections in this manner will help you process and manage the massive amount of detail required to address these activities properly. Once you've developed your emergency response and business continuity response data, you can (and should) include it in your BC/DR plan.

Activation Checklists

You may find it helpful to develop a variety of checklists, which can be extremely useful in making quick decisions for moving forward. Since you and your team may not have time to rehearse these plans frequently, checklists can help remind you of critical steps to take, regardless of the situation. We've included three short checklists in this section; you can expand upon them as desired.

Initial Response

1. Receive initial notification of possible, impending, or in-progress disruption or disaster.
2. Alert appropriate emergency response organizations (fire, police, etc.), if needed.
3. Access BC/DR plan.
4. Notify and mobilize damage assessment team and the crisis management team.
5. Assess damage, determine appropriate BC/DR activation steps.
6. Notify appropriate BC/DR team members.
7. Prepare preliminary event report or log. Communicate with appropriate parties.

Damage and Situation Assessment

1. Receive initial notification of possible, impending, or in-progress disruption or disaster.
2. Review preliminary event report or log.
3. Assess structural damage, health and safety impact and risks.
4. Determine extent and severity of disruption to operations.
5. Assess potential financial loss.
6. Determine severity based on predefined categories (see categories described earlier in this section).
7. If impact is minor, take no further action and continue to monitor situation.
8. Prepare final assessment and report, notify BC/DR teams of findings.
9. If impact is intermediate or major, declare disaster and update event report or log, communicate with appropriate parties.

Disaster Declaration and Notification

1. Review disaster level assessment, impacts, and other data gathered during initial response phases.
2. Activate BC/DR teams if they have not already been activated.
3. Review recovery options based on disaster assessment.
4. Select best recovery options for the situation, begin plan to implement recovery options (see next phase).
5. Notify management and crisis communications teams.
6. Prepare a disaster declaration statement that can be communicated to employees, BC/DR team and community contacts.
7. Monitor progress.
8. Document results in event log, communicate with appropriate parties.

Emergency Response Checklists

There are numerous emergency responses required in the aftermath of an event. This list is not meant to be comprehensive nor should you assume items that may not be on the list are unimportant. In developing your emergency response plans, be sure to utilize local experts including fire, police, and search and rescue teams to provide input on what measures you and your company's employees can reasonably take and which measures should be left to trained experts.

Emergency Checklist One—General Emergency Response

1. Determine the nature and extent of the emergency.
2. Identify whether anyone has been killed or injured.
3. If injuries have occurred, dial 911 to report the emergency or dispatch emergency medical personnel, as appropriate.
4. Determine if any danger still exists. If so, take appropriate precautions or measures to prevent further death, injury, or damage.
5. Notify crisis management team.
6. Dispatch appropriate trained medical personnel to assist with triage or to manage the situation until emergency responders arrive.
7. Notify civil authorities regarding the nature and extent of the emergency.
   - Police
   - Fire
   - Search and rescue
   - Hazardous Materials Team
8. Notify corporate executives.

Emergency Checklist Two—Evacuation or Shelter-in-Place Response

1. Install, identify, and/or test alarms and emergency signals.
2. Identify parameters that would trigger building or facility evacuation procedures.
3. Identify parameters that would trigger shelter-in-place procedures.
4. Identify evacuation/shelter leaders.
5. Identify evacuation routes and assembly points.
6. Identify building search-and-rescue procedures.
7. Identify procedures for securing and shutting down facility.

8. Identify shelter-in-place procedures and internal assembly points (safe areas).

9. Identify method of ascertaining if anyone is missing or unaccounted for.

10. Identify communication methods and frequency following an evacuation or shelter-in-place.

11. Identify provisions needed for shelter-in-place (food, medical supplies, communications equipment, etc.).

Emergency Checklist Three—Specific Emergency Responses

Develop specific step-by-step emergency response checklists for highest risk threats. These will utilize many of the same steps as other responses but should be tailored to these events to provide consistent and fast response procedures for staff.

1. Fire—internal or external.

2. Flood.

3. Earthquake.

4. Hazardous materials spill control.

Emergency Checklist Four—Emergency Response Contact List, Maps, Floor Plans

1. External emergency contact numbers:
   - Police, sheriff
   - Fire
   - Hospital
   - Ambulance
   - Other

2. Emergency response team contact numbers:
   - Emergency response team leader
   - Medical staff
   - Evacuation or shelter-in-place leaders
   - Search and rescue staff
   - Crisis team manager and/or corporate executive contact

3. Maps:
   - Evacuation routes and assembly areas
   - Shelter-in-place assembly areas

- Escape routes from site—primary and secondary (may need several options depending on disaster scenario)
- Floor plans
- Location of fire doors, fire extinguishers
- Location of utility closets, circuit breaker panels, power lines
- Location of gas, electric, water lines
- Location and nature of hazardous materials

Emergency Checklist Five—Emergency Supplies and Equipment

Depending on the size of your company, the location of the facilities, and the nature of the business, you may need other supplies than those listed. Be sure to develop a list of supplies and equipment needed, a schedule for testing needed equipment on a periodic basis, a procedure for performing periodic maintenance on equipment, and a process for performing a periodic inventory count of supplies.

1. First aid supplies (portable kits, additional supplies).
2. CPR training and equipment.
3. Fire suppression equipment (fire extinguishers, etc.).
4. Hazardous materials safety equipment.
5. Hazardous materials containment and clean up equipment/supplies.
6. Water, water purification tablets, shelf-stable food supplies (for shelter-in-place).
7. Clothing, blankets, and other materials (injuries, cold climates, shelter-in-place).
8. Emergency communications equipment (walkie talkies, batteries, etc.).

Recovery Checklists

The recovery checklists are broken out into numerous separate lists. Modify these lists to suit your organization's individualized needs.

Recovery Checklist One—General

1. Perform a quick assessment to determine which members of the BC/DR team are available to assist with recovery activities.
2. Identify any travel needs for BC/DR team members (if some are coming from other sites or locations). Be sure to consider the need for local transportation and lodging as well.
3. Identify who will be working at the original site and who will be working at the alternate site (if applicable).

4. Identify resources required including computer equipment, communication links (Internet, dial up, etc.), communications equipment (walkie talkies, cell phones, land lines, etc.), office equipment, office supplies, BC/DR plans, contact lists, and inventory lists.

5. If needed, arrange for access to site or alternate site for vendors, contractors, or employees traveling in from other locations.

6. Notify and activate alternate work site and/or crisis communication command center. Distribute contact information including location, personnel, and phone numbers to key personnel including management, BC/DR team, crisis management team, and HR as appropriate.

7. Provide local contact information and chain of command information (who should people contact for various recovery needs?).

8. Order replacement computer hardware, software, data and voice communications equipment.

9. Locate configuration information and most current backups.

10. Order faxes, printers, routers, cabling, copiers, tapes, tape backups, disk drives.

11. Order forms used in normal course of business. Develop forms needed for recovery operations if they do not already exist.

12. Ship key documents to alternate site.

13. Order stationery, business cards, other business-specific printed matter, if applicable.

14. Prepare process for receiving, tracking, and dispensing equipment and supplies.

15. Prepare process for receiving and tracking data backups and critical records.

16. Finalize preparations for restoring site or activating alternate site.

17. Document results in event log, communicate with appropriate parties.

Recovery Checklist Two—Inspection, Assessment, and Salvage

1. Provide damage assessment team with inventory or list of critical resources at damaged site.

2. Ensure all team members have proper safety equipment and have been trained in or reminded of their proper use.

3. Ensure all team members are aware of proper safety procedures and guidelines.

4. Provide team members with forms or process for assessing and reporting damage.

5. Inspect building, utilities (gas, electric, water).

6. Inspect for hazardous materials, chemicals, or hazardous conditions.

7. Inspect resources and vital records for damage including water, fire, water, dust, ice, or physical damage (crushed, tipped over, etc.).

8. Determine potential for further damage or hazard.

9. Determine potential for salvage and restoration.

10. Determine any timelines that may be relevant (equipment sitting in water, operating in extreme heat or cold, etc.) to the salvage operation and to prevent further damage and deterioration.

11. Record assessments in event log.

12. Acquire salvage and restoration equipment, as needed.

13. Remove hazardous materials, as appropriate.

14. Relocate equipment, records, and other salvaged resources, as appropriate.

15. Perform restoration, as appropriate.

16. Document results in event log, communicate with appropriate parties.

WARNING

Any items on the list may be performed by outside contractors, including those specially trained and certified in handling hazardous materials, chemical spills, and so on. Listing these items here does not imply that your team should perform these tasks, simply that they should be performed by appropriately trained personnel.

Business Continuity Checklist

The business continuity phase follows the disaster recovery phase and is focused on resuming business operations. Operations are not normalized or fully restored during this phase but initial business operations, including those deemed mission-critical, are initiated during this phase. At the end of the business continuity phase, normal business operations should resume, which signals the transition out of the BC/DR plan and back into normal operations.

Resuming Work

Work may be resumed on a limited basis in the original building or work location if it can be occupied after the disruption or disaster. If not, an alternate work site (AWS) should have been set up during the disaster recovery phase if this is part of your BC/DR plan. Once set up, the AWS should be brought online so that employees can begin work. Work activities typically resume on a limited basis. The restoration of the original facilities or a decision to permanently use alternate facilities will trigger the move to normalization of operations.

Resuming Work

1. Receive notification that work site is fully set up (disaster recovery phase end point).

2. Ensure all employees are aware of work location (original site or alternate site).

3. Ensure all employees have equipment, tools, supplies, and resources needed to begin limited resumption of work.

4. Check that computer networks, user computers, and other IT resources are installed, configured, tested, and ready for users.

5. Test communications equipment including phone, Internet access, wireless connectivity, and the like.

6. Provide employees with appropriate site access.

7. Review BC/DR plan to understand which mission-critical functions should begin, in what order tasks should be started, and what dependencies exist.

8. Review BC/DR plan to review maximum tolerable downtime (MTD) and other key recovery metrics.

9. Develop plan for resuming operations based on outcome of review.

10. Identify areas where manual or work-around methods will be implemented.

11. Identify methods for tracking and managing all manual or work-around procedures that are not part of the standard operating procedures.

12. Identify backlogs that may be created as a result of partial resumption of services. Determine if these backlogs are acceptable and if so, how they will be managed once normalization begins.

13. If backlogs are not acceptable, determine what other systems, processes, or procedures must be put into place to avoid backlogs.

14. Determine the status of elements required to avoid backlog, develop plan to put needed elements in place before resuming activities.

15. Resume limited operations.

16. Monitor results.

17. Begin backup procedures to protect new data or new work product(s).

18. Develop status report for crisis management team.

Human Resources

1. Ensure Human Resources (HR) has accounted for all employees. Appropriate actions should be underway if any employees were killed or injured in the event.

2. Take appropriate measures to ensure HR data is available and has been updated.

3. Begin reviewing personnel issues to resolve problems that stem from the disaster or disruptive event including medical or counseling services, insurance issues, and financial issues.

4. Work with department heads to determine if positions need to be filled.

5. Work with department heads to determine if contractors or temporary workers are needed to assist in the restoration or resumption of work activities.

6.   Review and implement payroll process. Distribute updated payroll information to all employees.

7.   Develop status report for crisis management team.

Insurance and Legal

1.   Review insurance and notify insurance carrier.

2.   Conduct internal assessment of damage and potential insurance coverage.

3.   Identify potential insurance gaps or language that may limit claim.

4.   If necessary, contact legal counsel for advice and guidance regarding the disaster event (insurance, other liability, regulatory issues, etc.).

5.   Provide copies of event logs, damage assessments, and other pertinent documentation to insurance carrier.

6.   Submit appropriate paperwork regarding loss.

7.   Prepare appropriate documentation for legal review or regulatory compliance.

8.   Develop status report for crisis management team.

Manufacturing, Warehouse, Production, and Operations

Whether or not you move into an alternate work site, you will need to address issues with manufacturing, warehouse, production, or other operations that normally took place at your original site. If you've made arrangements for alternate sites for these functions, you should modify the list presented earlier ("Resuming Work") to reflect the specific needs of your manufacturing, warehouse, production, or operations in addition to the tasks listed here.

1.   Inspect work site (original or alternate) to determine suitability for resuming operations on a limited basis.

2.   Review equipment inventory list to ensure all needed equipment is present and operational.

3.   Review materials inventory list to ensure all needed materials are available in sufficient quantities to resume operations on a limited basis.

4.   Review manual or work-around methods for managing and tracking inventory, production output, and other data if needed IT systems are not back online.

5.   Determine the method of tracking and managing all manual or work-around methods until systems come back online. Determine how backlog of data will be addressed once systems come back online.

6.   Obtain backup data to determine status of previous, pending, and new orders in the system. Review inventory and shipping data to determine the status of all orders.

7. For all open orders, determine priority and status of each. Develop prioritized order list to determine manufacturing, production, or operational priorities with the understanding that work will resume on a limited basis.

8. Set up and test operations on a trial basis to determine if quality, quantity, and specifications for production are acceptable. If not, take corrective action.

9. If trial run is successful, notify key customers or clients of updated status and timeline for delivery.

10. If trial run is successful, begin operations on a gradually increasing basis. Create checkpoints at all critical areas to ensure production meets requirements at each step. Take corrective action as needed.

11. Identify transportation and shipping options at original or alternate site.

12. Begin shipping, receiving, and managing inventory as appropriate.

13. Develop status report for crisis management team.

Resuming Normal Operations

1. Review assessment from HR regarding status of all employees.

2. Review assessments from damage assessment team, crisis management team, and other teams related to the current status of the facility.

3. Review assessments from CIRT or IT team regarding current status of IT systems.

4. Review assessments from manufacturing, warehouse, production, and operations regarding current status.

5. Review building damage assessment reports, determine feasibility and desirability of returning to original facility.

6. If returning to facility, develop project plan for repairing damage. Develop scope, budget, and timeline for return.

7. If not returning to facility, determine options to locate and occupy new facility. Develop costs and alternatives.

Existing Facility

1. If staying in existing facility, get bids for repairs from contractors.

2. Select contractor, initiate and supervise repairs.

3. Obtain appropriate permits for occupancy.

4. Notify insurance company regarding facility. Update policy, as appropriate.

5. Develop list of equipment, supplies, furniture, and other resources needed for resumption of business in original facility.

6. Purchase and obtain necessary equipment, supplies, furniture.

7. Install IT infrastructure components including LAN cables, servers, routers, firewalls, and such.

8. Install communications equipment (phone lines, Internet access).

9. Install furniture.

10. Install and test computers, workstations, printers, faxes, copiers, and other office equipment.

11. Install and test building access and security measures.

12. Distribute necessary supplies (paper, pens, business cards, etc.).

New Facility

1. If staying in alternate facility, review existing contracts for suitability, contact appropriate representatives to negotiate new contract/arrangement for permanent occupancy.

2. Contact legal representative to review any new, modified, or updated contracts.

3. Obtain appropriate permits for occupancy.

4. If locating new facility, work with real estate professional (if desired) to locate suitable facility.

5. Negotiate for facility including tenant improvements and other improvements or modifications, as needed. Sign lease or contract after appropriate legal review.

6. Notify insurance company regarding facility. Update policy, as appropriate.

7. Develop list of equipment, supplies, furniture, and other resources needed for resumption of business in facility if such resources are not already in place and available.

8. Purchase and obtain necessary equipment, supplies, furniture.

9. Install any needed IT infrastructure components including LAN cables, servers, routers, firewalls, and such that are not already in place at AWS.

10. Install any additional communications equipment (phone lines, Internet access), as needed.

11. Install furniture as needed.

12. Install and test any additional computers, workstations, printers, faxes, copiers, and other office equipment, as needed.

13. Modify and test building access and security measures, as needed.

14. Distribute necessary supplies (paper, pens, business cards, etc.), as needed.

Transition to Normalized Activities

1. Determine appropriate timeline to transition to normalized activities.

2. Notify all BC/DR team members of schedule and tasks for transition.

3. Notify all department heads of timeline for transition.

4. Identify all operational concerns or constraints regarding transition.

5. Freeze production environment at alternate locations.

6. Perform full data backups of all critical data and vital records.

7. Ship all backups and critical records to original or new location ("location" from hereon).

8. Transfer all needed personnel, equipment, machinery, equipment, and supplies to location.

9. Restore and test systems at location.

10. Verify all business systems including IT, manufacturing, production, communications, and such are installed and functional at location.

11. Redirect network traffic, communications traffic (phone lines, voicemail) to location.

12. Provide appropriate physical (building) and logical (IT, network) access to employees.

13. Resume normal activities.

14. Initiate normal data and vital records backup routines.

15. Clean up and close down alternate sites according to contractual agreements.

16. Perform post-disaster review to compile and discuss lessons learned, mistakes made, and improvements found during the event.

17. Modify BC/DR plan based on outcome of post-disaster review.

IT Recovery Checklists

The tasks needed to recover IT systems are probably quite familiar to you, but they should be delineated within your BC/DR plan. Each subteam should have a clear set of guidelines and procedures for how and when they will perform their work. Be sure to note dependencies within the checklist so that teams don't work at cross-purposes. You can add items to the checklist as checkpoints for these purposes, much like milestones are used in project plans.

We've included items related to recovering office work space and business operations in this section because they are intertwined with IT recovery efforts. You can reorganize these checklists to suit your approach to BC/DR.

IT Recovery Checklist One—Infrastructure

1. Review BC/DR team member assignments, ensure all team members are present or accounted for.

2. Convene brief planning meeting to ensure all team members understand the situation, the recovery options selected, the requirements and other constraints.

3. Provide all team members with updated contact information (if appropriate) and chain of command for problem notification and escalation.

4. Ensure all team members have inventory lists, equipment purchase order or shipment information, and that they understand recovery procedures moving forward.

5. Review equipment at alternate site (if used) or at main facility (if used). Ensure all equipment needed for selected recovery option is appropriate and meets requirements.

6. Review procedures for receiving, tracking, and testing IT equipment.

7. Receive backups from storage facility or confirm online availability of backups.

8. Inspect and test backup media, if appropriate.

9. Review or develop floor plans for replacement equipment including IT systems, communications equipment, and infrastructure components.

10. Review network diagram to verify location and connectivity of infrastructure components such as routers, switches, hubs, and gateways.

11. Review network addressing scheme, system configuration data, and security configuration data.

12. Connect all IT components to network.

13. Run procedures to configure infrastructure components.

14. Configure or restore security settings and security devices including firewalls, gateways, and routers.

15. Restore network servers and other critical equipment via backups.

16. Redirect data and voice traffic to alternate location, if appropriate. If you are restoring at the original site, ensure data and voice traffic are properly routed and working.

17. Provide network access to designated employees at alternate site.

18. Test and verify all network connectivity and security settings.

19. Document results in event log, communicate with appropriate parties.

Recovery Checklist Two—Applications

1. Review recovery procedures for critical applications. Verify needed servers are restored and online, as appropriate.

2. Review mission-critical data to determine which applications should be restored first.

3. Review internal and external data or application dependencies. Take action, as appropriate, to ensure all dependencies are addressed in the correct order and timing.

4. Review security settings—acquire passwords or reset passwords, as needed.

5. Restore, configure, and verify operating systems if not already performed.

6. Restore, configure, and verify applications.

7. Restore application data from backups, as appropriate. Ensure data is the most current available.

8. Verify integrity of data and functionality of applications.

9. Notify key users of application availability. Inform users of procedures to address data backlogs, if appropriate.

10. Document results in event log, communicate with appropriate parties.

Recovery Checklist Three—Office Area and End-User Recovery

1. Review teams and check to ensure team members are present or accounted for.

2. Review MTD and other constraints to ensure compliance with recovery requirements.

3. Verify that team members have necessary alternate work space inventory lists.

4. Review equipment at alternate location, determine if it meets recovery requirements. Note any discrepancies or gaps.

5. Review or revise material receiving, inventory management, and distribution procedures so when new equipment and supplies arrive, they can be properly managed.

6. Review floor layout for alternate work space, determine location of office furniture and equipment including copiers, file cabinets, bookcases, and printer stands.

7. Review network diagram and connectivity. Ensure office layout accommodates existing network, communication, and power connection points. Modify as needed.

8. Receive and set up office furniture per plan. Assign work areas to team members.

9. Receive and set up computers, workstations, printers, and other IT-related user equipment.

10. Set up copiers, faxes, network printers, and telephones at designated locations.

11. Provide office supplies to team members as needed.

12. Provide documents, manuals, and other materials that may have been stored at and retrieved from an off-site storage facility.

13. Reroute voice and data communications to alternate work location. Notify key personnel of current location, contact information, and status.

14. Ensure connectivity to key servers, applications, and data.

15. Set up help desk or customer service function at alternate location.

16. Document results in event log, communicate with appropriate parties.

Recovery Checklist Four—Business Process Recovery

1. Verify user workstations, desktop, and laptop computers are restored and have access to necessary network resources.

2. Ensure all key personnel or designated users have usernames and passwords for alternate site access.

3. Complete workstation, desktop, or laptop restoration, as needed.

4. Retrieve critical records and forms from storage, if applicable.

5. Receive and process new transactions manually until transactions can be handled electronically.

6. Verify integrity of data on restored systems. When tests are completed satisfactorily, transition to processing transactions electronically.

7. Identify work backlog and implement processes to address backlog to enter data into systems.

8. Begin using restored systems for new transactions.

9. Begin data backup procedures to protect new data being entered into recovered systems.

10. Document results in event log, communicate with appropriate parties.

Recovery Checklist Five—Manufacturing, Production, and Operations Recovery

1. Review maximum downtime and other constraints.

2. Assemble manufacturing, production, or operations recovery team (called "operations" from hereon).

3. Tour alternate operational areas to assess status or tour original operational areas to assess current damage and status. Review safety requirements against current status.

4. Review environmental conditions including heating/cooling, humidity, or dust levels, air filtration status (dust, odors, airborne contaminants, etc.). Determine if current condition and status meet operating requirements.

5. Inspect any stored hazardous materials or chemicals for safety.

6. Inspect and test, as appropriate, all safety devices including fire extinguishers, smoke detectors/ alarms, emergency lighting, among others.

7. Verify sufficient electrical (or other power) exists to run machinery and equipment.

8. Verify teams have alternate facility operating procedures and inventory lists.

9. Review equipment against inventory lists and operating requirements. Address any gaps or discrepancies.

10. Review and revise, as needed, equipment receiving, inventory management, and equipment distribution procedures. Ensure that equipment and inventory arriving at the alternate (or damaged original) location is tracked and monitored.

11. Receive any critical equipment, parts, supplies, or materials from off-site storage, vendor shipment, or salvage from original location.

12. Receive and inspect any salvageable or existing inventory. Assess status, dispatch inventory as appropriate (destroy, store, repackage, reuse, etc.).

13. Review floor layout for manufacturing, production, or operational activities. Ensure proper connections including power, data, or network exist in the proper locations.

14. Place equipment in locations and install, connect, and test.

15. Install and test auxiliary equipment including printers, copiers, telephones, walkie talkies, radios, and other equipment needed for operations.

16. Provide operational and configuration documentation to team leaders or equipment operators, as appropriate.

17. Install and configure any IT-related equipment including interfaces, workstations, desktops, and such.

18. Set up connectivity between operations and IT systems at alternate locations, as needed.

19. Test equipment, machinery, and configurations.

20. Test output of operations for quality, quantity, and other required attributes.

21. Test voice and data network to ensure connectivity.

22. Ensure operators have information needed to begin production including logins, passwords, keys, or other necessary tools.

23. Review and implement any manual work-arounds for production or inventory management needed.

24. Review and implement any electronic production or inventory management procedures, as needed.

25. Begin manufacturing, production, or operations on limited basis.

26. Test and verify output. Expand or increase production as warranted.

27. Document results in event log, communicate with appropriate parties.

Training, Testing, and Auditing Checklists

Business continuity and disaster recovery training can be accomplished through testing the plan. Testing the plan results in training participants, therefore they are referred to as one activity here.

Training and Testing

1. Identify scope, timeline, and requirements for training.

2. Determine training needs for each participant group (ERT, CMT, damage assessment, IT, etc.).

3. Develop training approach (may use testing methods for training, see item 6).

4. Develop training objectives.

5. Develop training or testing duration and cost estimates.

6. Develop training or test scenarios.

7. Develop training or testing method (paper walk-through, functional, or field exercises, full interruption).

8. Develop training or testing evaluation criteria.

9. Identify training or testing participants.

10. Identify training or testing resources needed.

11. Deliver training or conduct testing.

12. Evaluate training or testing based on evaluation criteria.

13. Collect and analyze lessons learned.

14. Revise training, testing, or BC/DR plan, as appropriate.

IT Auditing

1. Identify IT risk mitigation strategies selected.

2. Audit IT risk mitigation strategies to ensure they have been properly implemented and configured.

3. Audit IT systems to ensure systems identified in BC/DR plan are still in place and functioning.

4. Identify new technology implementations (planned or in progress) and assess against BC/DR objectives. Recommend revisions to technology plans or BC/DR plans as appropriate.

5. Identify technology to be replaced or decommissioned (planned or in progress) to assess the impact on BC/DR plans. Recommend revisions to technology plans or BC/DR plans as appropriate.

6. Audit all processes in BC/DR plan related to IT systems to ensure steps, processes, requirements, tools, supplies, and resources identified are still accurate, current, relevant, and complete.

7. Audit IT response team to ensure team is intact, ready to respond, has clear understanding of roles/responsibilities, has tools/resources to implement plan.

8. Audit existing systems to ensure compliance with current BC/DR plans including:

   - Operating systems
   - Networking and telecommunications equipment
   - Database and applications
   - Systems backups
   - Security controls
   - Integration and testing
   - Other (define)

BC/DR Plan Maintenance Checklist

Training, testing, and auditing are three activities that generate useful information about the BC/DR plan and therefore contribute to plan maintenance. Change management and BC/DR plan audits also contribute to keeping the plan up to date. Modify the following list to meet the requirements of your organization.

Change Management

1. Review contact list. Update and revise as needed.

2. Review vendor list. Update and revise as needed.

3. Review vendor contracts. Update, extend, revise as needed.

4. Review team membership (ERT, CMT, CIRT, etc.). Update and revise as needed.

5. Review team membership changes. Assess training needs.

6. Develop, document, and implement formal BC/DR plan change management processes:

   a. Monitoring changes that impact or are impacted by BC/DR plan.

   b. Evaluating change notifications and requests.

    c.   Implementing appropriate changes to BC/DR plan.

    d.   Testing, training and auditing revised plan.

    e.   Notifying stakeholders of changes incorporated, delayed, or denied.

    f.   Revising BC/DR plan appropriately.

    g.   Distributing updated copies of the BC/DR plan to appropriate parties.

7. Review lessons learned from training, testing, and auditing. Assess impact to BC/DR plan, revise plan as needed.

8. Review changes to IT systems and processes. Assess impact to BC/DR plan. Make changes as needed.

9. Review changes to operations, including mission-critical business processes and functions. Assess impact to BC/DR plan, revise plan as needed.

10. Review changes to corporation including mergers, acquisitions, spin-offs, downsizing, and so on. Assess impact to BC/DR plan, revise plan as needed.

11. Review and revise risk assessment. Perform subsequent planning steps (impact analysis, risk mitigation, training, testing) to update BC/DR plan.

12. Update flowcharts and checklists, as needed.

13. Distribute revised plans to distribution list. Notify appropriate parties that a revised plan as well as how to obtain it and how to dispose of the outdated copies of the plan.

14. Destroy or archive old copies of the plan including hard and soft copies, on- and off-site copies, and copies that may be stored with trusted vendors, partners, or at alternate work sites or facilities.

15. Perform periodic audit BC/DR plan, incorporate recommendations and changes.

16. Perform periodic test of BC/DR plan, incorporate recommendations and changes.

17. Perform periodic training of BC/DR plan, incorporate recommendations and changes.

Index